AF662990

Bhaumik

The Railways Act 1989

Kolkata

Eastern Law House Private Ltd.
54 Ganesh Chunder Avenue
Kolkata (Calcutta) 700 013

New Delhi

Eastern Law House Private Ltd.
36 Netaji Subhash Marg, Daryaganj
New Delhi 110 002

Bhaumik
The Railways Act 1989

— Containing —

ALLIED STATUTES, RULES, REGULATIONS, SCHEMES, ETC.

Tenth Edition

by

H.K. Saharay

MA (Triple), MCom, LLB, PhD (Lond), Barrister

Kolkata New Delhi

EASTERN LAW HOUSE

Published and processed by
EASTERN LAW HOUSE PRIVATE LTD.
54 Ganesh Chunder Avenue
Kolkata (Calcutta) 700 013
Tel: (033) 2215-1989
Email: mail@elh.co.in
www.elh.co.in

First Edition 1950
Second Edition 1957
Third Edition 1964
Fourth Edition 1972
Fifth Edition 1978
Sixth Edition 1981
Seventh Edition 1989
Eighth Edition 2003
Ninth Edition 2010
Tenth Edition 2017

©
The Estate of K.N. Bhaumik and
Eastern Law House Private Ltd.
2017

Whilst all reasonable care has been taken to ensure accuracy of the contents of this book, no person associated with the creation or publishing of this book shall have responsibility for any loss or damages that may be caused to any person due to errors or omissions which may have crept in inadvertently in this publication. Disputes, if any, are subject to Kolkata jurisdiction.

ISBN 978-81-7177-314-5

Printed at
Dey's Offset, Kolkata

Preface to the Tenth Edition

The goodwill of earlier editions of Bhaumik on the Railways Act, 1989 has already been established. The present edition is revised to maintain that standard. This edition has been thoroughly revised with the primary object to ensure the usefulness of this book to its readers. The up to date case-laws of the Supreme Court in particular, and of the High Courts of India in general have been incorporated in this edition. This edition is made more compact and comprehensive in all respects.

I sincerely record my acknowledgment of the constant co-operation I have received from the publishers and the members of the staff for bringing out this edition.

Bar Library Club
Calcutta High Court
2nd January 2017

H.K. Saharay

Preface to the First Edition

The Indian Railways Act (IX of 1890) has undergone material legislative changes since the 15th of August, 1947, when the *British* India being divided into two Dominions, India and Pakistan attained the Dominion Status by the Indian Independence Act, 1947. Some changes were effected by the Adaptation of Laws Order of 1947 and 1948, and lastly by that of the 26th January, 1950, from when India has become the Sovereign Democratic Republic of India. Many changes have been effected by several Acts passed from time to time by the Dominion Legislature, the most important of them being Act No. LVI of 1949, by which s. 30 and sub-s. (2) of s. 72 have been omitted, new sections for s. 32, s. 41, s. 73, s. 76 and s. 114 have been substituted, new ss. 72A, 74A to 74E and 82A to 82J and the First Schedule have been inserted, and ss. 31, 47, 75 and 106 have been amended.

It has been my endeavour in the following pages to supply to practitioners and the public a work upon the Railways Act which will not only give what now the provisions thereof are, but will also give a clear exposition of the case law bearing upon them. The annotations have been concise but not at the sacrifice of substance. At the suggestion of Mr. B.L. Rajgarhia, F.R.S.A., Merchant, Calcutta, for which I should thank him, I have added a Chapter on General Information which, I hope, will be highly informative to the public. Rules, Forms, Allied Laws etc., have been incorporated in the book, which will enhance the utility of the book. The (Pakistan) Adaptation of Laws Order, 1949, Act No. VII of 1948 and Act No. II of 1949 (Pakistan), have been inserted in App. D of the book.

I must thank Mr. M.G. Poddar, Solicitor, as in compiling the book I had the privilege of availing myself of his very big library, but for which it would have been difficult for me to find out the amendments, in the absence of a Government publication of the Act, and to incorporate the recent cases in the book.

My thanks are also due to Mr. Manik Lal Bardhan of Public Relations and Publicity (Railways) Calcutta, Mr. Nandlal Banka and Mr. J.C. De, M.A., B.L., Advocate, for the keen interest they have taken in the publication of the book. Though last, not least, are my thanks due to the Manager, Sree Gouranga Press, for having the printing of the book completed within a very short time and so admirably.

10 June, 1950 K.N.B.

Contents

SECTION PAGE

Chapter XIII

Liability of Railway Administration for Death and Injury to Passengers due to Accidents

Chapter XIV

Regulation of Hours of Work and Period of Rest

Chapter XV

Penalties and Offences

Chapter XVI

Miscellaneous

Table of Cases

The
Railways Act, 1989

(Act No. 24 of 1989)

[3rd June 1989

An Act to consolidate and amend the law relating to Railways.

BE it enacted by Parliament in the Fortieth Year of the Republic of India as follows:

CHAPTER I
Preliminary

1. Short title and commencement. (1) This Act may be called the Railways Act, 1989.

(2) It shall come into force on such date[1] as the Central Government may, by notification in the Official Gazette, appoint:

Provided that different dates may be appointed for different provisions of this Act, and any reference in any such provision to the commencement of this Act shall be construed as a reference to the coming into force of that provision.

1 **Statement of objects and reasons of the Bill for the Railways Act 1989** The Indian Railways Act 1890 was enacted at a time when the railways in India were mostly managed by private companies. The Government of India primarily played the role of a coordinating and regulating authority in various matters, such as inter-railway movement of traffic, fixation of rates, sharing of revenue earnings, apportionment of claims, liability amongst the railways, providing reasonable facilities to passenger and goods traffic, etc. This role was accordingly reflected in the Act. But now, except for a very small portion of the railways, the entire railway system has become part of the Government of India. To give effect to the changes in the railway system from time to time, the Act had also been amended

1 1st July 1990, *vide* S.O. 475(E), dated 12th June 1990, Gazette of India, Extra, Pt. II., s. 3(*ii*), dated 12th June 1990.

a number of times since its enactment in 1890. In addition, as some of the original provisions enacted in 1890 had continued without any change, a need for their replacement by new provisions, more responsive to the needs of the present day was felt. Besides, some other provisions have become redundant. There has also been a demand, both within and outside Parliament, for the re-enactment of the Act so as to reflect the large number of changes that have occurred in the railways. It has, therefore, become necessary to consolidate and amend the law relating to railways by a new Railways Act.

The Bill, while giving effect to the changes that are necessary due to the change of circumstances, provides, among other things, for the following matters:

(*i*) The constitution of railway zones, abolition of existing zones and appointment of General Managers as heads of these railway administrations.

(*ii*) Power has been given to the Central Government to fix the rates for the carriage of passengers and goods by railways.

(*iii*) Statutory recognition of the railway receipt as a negotiable instrument.

(*iv*) Specifically provides for limiting the monetary liability of railway administration in respect of payment of compensation for loss, damage, etc., of goods.

(*v*) The offences included in the Act have been rationalised and a few offences have also been included in the Act.

The Bill seeks to achieve the aforesaid objects.

2 Passage of the 1989 Bill This bill was presented to the Lok Sabha on 25th April 1986 and then it was referred to the Joint Select Committee for Report which was submitted on 5th November 1986. The bill was discussed and passed in the Lok Sabha on 3rd May 1989 and in the Rajya Sabha on 10th May 1989. The bill was assented to by the President on 3rd June 1989.

3 Commencement of the 1989 Act This Act has come into force on and from 1st day of July 1990.[2]

4 Amendment to the Railways Act 1989 This Act was amended by the Railways (Amendment) Act 1994 (Act 28 of 1994).[3] The amending Act of 1994 amended ss. 123, 125, 126 and 128 of the 1989 Act and inserted into it s. 124A. The said amending Act of 1994 also amended ss. 2, 13, 15, 16, 17 and 24 of the Railway Claims Tribunal Act 1987. The Railways Act 1989 was further amended by the Railways (Amendment) Act 2003,

2 *See* Gazette of India, Extra, dated 12.6.1990, Part. II, s. 3(*ii*), p. 2 (No. 321).

3 It received the assent of the President on 26th April 1994. It was published in the Gazette of India, dated 26.4.1994, Part. II, s. 1, Ext. p. 1 (No. 19).

the Railways (Second Amendment) Act 2003, the Railways (Amendment) Act 2005, and the Railways (Amendment) Act 2008. The Amending Act of 2008 has inserted cl. (7A), cl. (37A) and IVA under the heading "Land Acquisition for A Special Railway Project."

5 Corresponding provisions in the old Act 1890 Section 1 of the Railways Act 1989 (Act 24 of 1989) corresponds to s. 1 of the Indian Railways Act 1890.

6 No power of local Legislature to enact provisions relating to railways The Railways Act of 1989 is a Central Act and the local Legislature has no authority to enact provisions relating to railways which are inconsistent with those of the Central Act. Hence criminal proceedings against a State Railway as the Governor-General in Council cannot be legally prosecuted under s. 14, Bengal Licensed Warehouse and Fire Brigade Act 1893, for using unlicensed warehouses even if these warehouses were being used for the purpose of storing customers' goods in connection with the ordinary course of railway's business. The licence fee prescribed by Bengal (Act 1 of 1893) is a tax in aid of the funds of local authority and hence railway administration is not liable unless notification has been issued by the Central Government declaring the railway administration liable to pay the licence fee in respect of their warehouses situated in any of the municipalities to which the provisions of Bengal (Act 1 of 1893) apply.[4] [Now, the Bengal Act of 1893 has been repealed by the West Bengal Fire Services Act 1950.]

7 Carriers Act (1865) and Railways Act Railways are not common carriers.[5] The liability of a railway as a carrier was not the liability known to English common law as the liability of a common carrier, but was the liability of a bailee as defined in ss. 152 and 161 of the Indian Contract Act 1872. But the extensive provisions have been made to relieve the railway administration of its basic liability as a common carrier.[6]

The Carriers Act 1865 has been repealed by s. 22 of the Carriage of Road Act 2007 with effect from 1st day of March 2011.

8 Rules of construction

A. *Two rules of construction.* There are two well established rules of construction, namely, (1) where the words of a statute are in themselves precise and unambiguous, no more is necessary than to expound those words in their natural and ordinary sense, and (2) where alternative constructions are equally open, that alternative is to be chosen which will be consistent with the smooth working of the system which the statute purports to be regulating, and that alternative is to be rejected which

4 *R.E. Marriott* v *Municipality of Howrah* AIR 1941 Cal 319; ILR (1941)1 Cal 345.
5 *Rallia Ram Dingra* v *G.G. in Council* ILR (1944)2 Cal 487; AIR 1946 Cal 249.
6 *Chhogalal* v *Secretary of State* AIR 1933 Nag 261; 29 NLR 333.

will introduce uncertainty, friction or confusion into the working of the system.[7]

B. *Construction of Railways Acts.* Railways Acts are to be construed strictly against the company and liberally in favour of the public.[8] Where under Acts of Parliament railways are made not only, and not even principally, for the private benefit of shareholders, but for the public benefit as furnishing lines of traffic which from the time the railway is made, the public have the right to use, it is the duty of the court to consider that in any provisions such as those, the public interest and the private interest are impartially and justly regarded upon the one side and upon the other; and if upon words or expressions at all ambiguous it would seem that the balance of hardships or inconvenience would lie strongly against the public on the one construction or strongly against a private person on another construction, it is consistent with all sound principles to pay regard to the balance of inconvenience in determining such a doubtful question of construction.[9]

9 Railway Board Circulars The circulars issued by the Railway Board ordering reservation of selection posts in the railway service in favour of the members of the Scheduled Castes and Scheduled Tribes do not fall outside Art. 16(4) of the Constitution of India and are not *ultra vires* on that ground.[10]

10 Railway Manual abandonment of service Rule 2505 of the Railway Manual provides that if a railway employee remains absent unauthorisedly for a period of more than 3 days his services can be terminated. Unauthorised absence from duty by a railway servant for about one year and a half would amount to abandonment of service.[11]

11 Indian Railway Establishment Manual (IREM) Vol. 1, erroneous promotions and inter se seniority Para 228 of the Indian Railway Establishment Manual, Vol. 1 deals with erroneous promotions. Broadly speaking, loss of seniority of an employee, a railway servant may happen due to the administration errors in two types of cases (*i*) Where a person has not been promoted at all because of administrative error. (*ii*) Where a person has been promoted but not on the date from which he would have been promoted but for the administrative error. Each such case should be dealt with on its merits.[12]

7 *Collector of Customs, Baroda* v *Digviyaysinghji Spinning and Weaving Mills Ltd. Jamnagar* AIR 1961 SC 1549.
8 *Parkar* v *G.W. Rly.* 7 Scott (NR) 835; 7 Man & G 253.
9 *Dixon* v *Caledonian and Glasgow and South-Western Railway Co.* [1880]5 App Cas 820.
10 *General Manager, Southern Railway* v *Rangachasi* AIR 1962 SC 36.
11 *Chief Engineer (Construction)* v *Keshava Rao* (2005)11 SCC 229.
12 *Union of India* v *Tarsern Lal* (2006)10 SCC 145.

The policy decision taken by Railway Authorities to regularise services of Material Checking Clerks (MCCs) appointed on *ad hoc* basis was a one-time measure. It was not to be followed as a precedent and therefore it was not necessary to follow it subsequently. *Inter se* seniority of direct recruits and promotees is regulated by r. 302 of the Indian Railway Establishment Manual. An employee appointed to a post according to rules is entitled to seniority from the date of his appointment and not from the date of his confirmation. But where initial appointment is *ad hoc* and not according to rules and the appointment is made as a stopgap arrangement, period of officiation does not court for seniority. When *ad hoc* appointment is made, it should be done according to rules. If mandatory provisions of the rules are not complied with, the period does not court for seniority.[13]

If a Scheduled Caste/Scheduled Tribe candidate is promoted earlier by virtue of rule of reservation/roaster than his senior general candidate and the senior general candidate is promoted later to the said higher grade, the general candidate regains his seniority as such earlier promoted Scheduled Caste/Scheduled Tribe candidate. The earlier promotion of the Scheduled Caste/Scheduled Tribe candidate in such a situation does not confer upon him seniority over the general candidate even though the general candidate is promoted later to that category.[14]

12 Indian Railway Establishment Manual—statutory canteen The difference between the non-statutory recognised and non-statutory non-recognised canteen is that these canteens are not started with approval of the Railway Board as required under paragraph 2831 of the Railway Establishment Manual. Where canteen is situated in the premises of the Division of Northern Railway, then it shall *ipso facto* correspond to statutory canteen.[15]

13 Railway Establishment Code, r. 2544(g) Pension Inclusion of "resuming allowance" to arrive at average emoluments is made for "running staff" of railways. So, far as pre 1986 retires are concerned, there was recomputations of pension to give benefits of the 5th Pay Commission as on 1st January 1986. Running allowance that has been considered at the time of retirement is not to be considered again while fixing national pay.[16]

14 Appointment of Inquiry Officer Charges were framed against the delinquent in consequence of raid by vigilence department. In such case the Chief Vigilence Officer cannot be appointed as Inquiry Officer. Besides, if the delinquent makes application to summon witness, that prayer ought

13 *Union of India* v *Dharan Pal* (2009)4 SCC 170.
14 *Union of India* v *Virpal Singh Chauhan* AIR 1996 SC 448.
15 *Mohan Singh* v *Chairman, Railway Board* AIR 2015 SC 3027.
16 *Union of India* v *S.R. Dhingra* AIR 2008 SC 856.

to be considered by the Inquiry Officer. Refusal of the Inquiry Officer to consider the prayer would amount to unfair proceeding of the enquiry.[17]

15 Instructions in Indian Railways Vigilance Manual 1996 The finding that non-adherence of the mandatory instructions and guidelines contained in paras 704 and 705 of the Vigilance Manual has vitiated the departmental proceedings initiated against the respondents by the railway authority cannot be accepted. Such finding and reasoning is wholly unjustified and cannot be sustained. Paras 704 and 705 of the Manual cover the procedures and guidelines to be followed by the investigating officers in trap cases against the railway officials. Such instructions contained in paras 704 and 705 of the Vigilance Manual 1996 are procedural in character and not of substantive nature. Any violation of such instructions would not *ipso facto* vitiate the departmental proceedings initiated against the respondents on the basis of the complaints submitted by the investigating officers to the railway authorities.[18]

16 Appointments and promotions under Railway Establishment Code Railway employees were appointed on permanent basis and were promoted as per circular of the Railway Board and/or in accordance with the Rules. Incorporation of Rule 328(2) by the Railway Board wiping out not only the promotions granted to employees but also length of service of employees for about nine years is arbitrary and cannot be allowed to be operative to the detriment of employees.[19]

The status, promotion, scales or pay, increments, etc. of the officers, employees of Railway Co-operative Stores/Societies cannot be treated at per with railway servants. Their service conditions are not regulated by Railway Administration but are governed by bye-laws of societies subject to control and sanction by Registrar under State Act. Thus, Railway Establishment Code is not applicable to them.[20]

17 Ad hoc appointment and fixation of seniority Where appointments are made without going through process of selection, such appointments are to be treated as having made under the Rules. *Ad hoc* period which is continuous can be taken into consideration for the purpose of fixation of seniority.[1]

18 Promotion challenged after lapse of long time The appellant though junior to the respondent was empanelled and promoted. The promotion of the

17 *Union of India* v *Prakash Kumar Tandan* 2009 Lab IC 991 (SC).

18 *Chief Commercial Manager, South Central Railway* v *G. Ratnam* (2007)8 SCC 212.

19 *Haribans Misra* v *Railway Board* AIR 1989 SC 696; (1989)2 SCC 84.

20 *Union of India (Railway Board)* v *J.V. Subhaiah* AIR 1996 SC 2890; (1996)2 SCC 258.

1 *Raj Kishore Vishwakarma* v *Union of India* (1997)11 SCC 619.

appellant was challenged after lapse of four years. The Supreme Court dismissed the appeal on the ground of belated challenge.[2]

19 Ad hoc promotion Para 216 of Railway Establishment Manual indicates that *ad hoc* promotion is permissible pending regular selection. When the appellants were issued separate appointment letters in which it was clearly mentioned that their seniority was subject to the finalisation of the selection for promotion to the post of First Fireman which was in progress. Thus, the appellants in this situation cannot claim seniority over the respondents who had already been appointed to the posts of First Fireman on *ad hoc* basis and were after due selection regularised on those posts.[3]

20 Regularisation of casual Mates When the petitioners were directly appointed as Mate though on casual basis and having continued as such Mates for more than 22 to 25 years, it will be wholly inequitable to require them to be regularised against the lower posts of Gangman in Class IV.[4]

21 Allotment of Railway bungalows with out-houses Railway bungalows including their out-houses were allotted to officers of railway by the railway administration. Other employees of railway were permitted to stay in those out-houses. Their occupation therein were only permissive. They would not be entitled to allotment of those out-houses as a matter of right.[5]

22 Breach of administrative rules The administrative rules, regulations and instructions which have no statutory force, do not generally give rise to any legal right in favour of the aggrieved party and cannot be enforced in a court of law against the administration. The executive orders appropriately so called do not confer any legally enforceable rights on any persons and impose no legal obligation on the subordinate authorities for whose guidance they are issued.

Their breach may expose the subordinate authorities to disciplinary or other appropriate action, but they cannot be said to be in the nature of statutory rules having the force of law, subject to the jurisdiction of *certiorari*. It is well settled that the Central Government or the State Government can give administrative instructions to its servants how to act in certain circumstances, but that will not make such instructions statutory rules which are justiciable in certain circumstances.[6]

23 International carriage of goods by rail International carriage of goods by rail is governed by the Convention Concerning International Carriage by Rail (or COTIF) 1999. The COTIF incorporates the CIM Uniform Rules.

2 *A.J. Fernandis* v *The Divisional Manager, South Central Railway* 2000(8) Scale 61.
3 *T. Vijayan* v *Divisional Railway Manager* AIR 2000 SC 1766.
4 *Union of India* v *Moti Lal* AIR 1996 SC 3306; (1996)7 SCC 481.
5 *Union of India* v *Surajdeo Podar* AIR 1999 SC 2308; (1998)6 SCC 339.
6 *Chief Commercial Manager, South Central Rly.* v *G. Ratnam* (2007)8 SCC 212.

The CIM Uniform Rules apply subject to certain exceptions "to all consignments of goods for carriage under a thorough consignment note made out for a route over the territories of atleast two States" and particularly over times or services included in the list provided for in Arts. 3 and 10 of the COTIF. The CIM Uniform Rules "may also be applied to international carriage through traffic using in addition to services on railway lines, land and sea services and inland waterways."[7] When there is "rail-sea transport" each State is required to make out a suitable note[8] which would indicate that the carrier would be entitled certain additional exemptions from liability, if it is proved that loss, damage or delay occurred in the course of sea transit between the time when the goods were loaded on board the ship and the time when they were discharged from the ship.[9]

The effect of the additional exemptions is to put "the carrier" into a position with regard to liability broadly similar to that of a carrier of goods by sea under contract governed by the "Hague or Hague Visby Rules."

24 Consignment note Under the CIM Uniform Rules, the consignor presents to the railway a "consignment note"[10] which contains certain particulars specified in the Rules for loading and unloading of goods.[11] The contract of carriage of goods is concluded as soon as the railway "has accepted the goods for carriage together with the consignment note."[12] The railway must also certify receipt of the goods and the date of their acceptance for carriage by affixing a date stamp to a duplicate of the consignment note.[13] The duplicate consignment note remains in the custody of the consignor who exercises his right under the CIM Uniform Rules. The consignor's right to modify contract is extinguished even if he is in possession of the duplicate of the consignment note in four cases. They are: (*i*) when the consignee has taken possession of the consignment note; (*ii*) when the consignee has accepted the goods; (*iii*) when the consignee has exercised his right to require the railway to hand over the consignment note and deliver the goods; and (*iv*) when the consignee is entitled to give orders modifying the contract of carriage.[14]

25 Brief history of railway[15] Railway is a kind of land transportation in which freight and passenger carrying vehicles with flanged wheels move

7 COTIF, Art. 24.
8 CIM Uniform Rules, Art. 38(1).
9 *Ibid* Art. 38(2).
10 *Ibid* Art. 12(1).
11 *Ibid* Art. 13.
12 *Ibid* Art. 11(1).
13 *Ibid* Art. 11(2) or Art. 6.
14 *Ibid* Art. 18(2).
15 Jame's World Railways; A.W. Bruce; The Steam Locomotive in America; Concise Encyclopedia of World Railway Locomotives (1959); Bulletin of the International Railway Congress; Japanese National Railways at a Glance.

over two parallel steel rails. The track gauge varies from country to country. The development of railways is one of the important landmarks in the progress of human civilization. In the early nineteenth century introduction of railways played important role in surging Industrial Revolution. Owing to self-guiding characteristic and the low rolling friction, a locomotive of relatively modest horsepower can pull a long train of cases.

The railway originated in England, but the use of wheeled vehicles on rail lines was found long before the advert of mechanical traction. There was a railway in Europe as early as 1550. Before the end of the sixteenth century running railways were introduced in Britain. In the eighteenth century horse-drawn railways were in use not only in England but also in Wales and Scotland. In 1797 Richard Trevithick made three models, one of which represented a self-propelled steam engine or locomotive. In 1808 Trevithick exhibited a locomotive and carriage on a circular track in London. In 1812 the first practical and successful locomotive was built. In 1813 William Hedley built "Puffing Billy". It was for handling coal trucks between Wylam Colliesy and the Wharves at Lesnington-on-Tyne. In 1823 Stephenson was invited by Edward Pease to built a railway from Stockton to Dastington. It was completed and ceremonially opened on 27th September 1825. In 1836 the opening of the London and Greenwich Railway introduced the first public passenger service to London.

In 1838 London and Birmingham railway was opened and in 1840 the line from London to Southampton was completed. Parliament of Britain authorised the construction of over 400 railways between 1844 and 1846. After the First World War the Railways Act 1921 was passed. Separate railway companies were amalgamated into four main groups on 1st January 1923, namely, London, Midland and Scottish Railway, London and North Eastern Railway, Great Western Railway and Southern Railway. At the outbreak of the Second World War the railways were placed under the control of the Government. At the end of the war the state of railways deteriorated considerably. In 1946 a bill was introduced in Parliament for nationalisation of railways in Britain and it was passed as the Transport Act and became the law on 6th August 1947. On 1st January 1948 the British Railways were completely nationalised. A transport bill in 1953 intended to decentralise British Railways was passed with effect from 6th May 1953. On 24th January 1955 the British Transport Commission (BTC) announced an extensive and ambitious modernisation British railway system. In 1968 steam locomotives were completely withdrawn.

26 India The East India Company in 1849 gave the first contract to the East Indian Railway Company for construction of railway line from Calcutta to Mirzapur. The second contract was made in the same year between the East India Company and the Great Indian Peninsula Company for construction of railway line from Bombay to Kalyan. Though the second contract was made later than the first contract, yet it was completed earlier than the first contract. The railway line of about 32 Kms between Bombay and Thane was opened on 16th April 1853 and the railway line of about 35 Kms from Howrah to Hooghly was opened on 22nd August 1854. Since then continuous steps were being taken to construct more railway lines particularly at the initiative and encouragement of Lord Dalhouse, the then Governor-General to develop communication system and to connect important cities and ports of India. At the end of 1868 it was found that the railway line had spread over to 6043 Kms approximately. Initially the contracts for construction of railway line was awarded to private agencies, but the Government of India changed this policy from March 1869 and decided to construct the railway line by itself with from objectives. One was to step up the speedy construction of railway lines in different posts of India, and the other was to carry on business for more profits from railways. The Great Famine of 1878 impeded the progress of construction of railway lines due to paucity of fund, but the Government realised the necessity and importance of development of communication for supply of food grains to famine-stricken places. Thus, the Government of India also encouraged the Indian Provincial states to construct railways within their own territories. It is estimated that there were about 37,130 Kms of railway lines in 1900 which were increased to 51,990 Kms in or around 1914. On the basis of the recommendation of the Railway Enquiry Committee of 1921 the Government of India took over the management of Railways in India except a few branch lines which were managed by some private concerns.

27 The Indian Railways Act 1890 The Indian Railways Act 1890 was passed by the Government of India with a view of coordinating and regulating the powers vested in private companies which were managing different railways in different parts of India. The network of Indian railway system is the second largest in the world after the railway system of the USSR. The Government of India earns the highest revenue from the Indian railways. The Railway Board under the (Indian) Railway Board Act 1905 is vested with the power of administration and management of railways under the overall supervision of the Minister for railways.

28 Railway zones There are fifteen railway zones, namely (*i*) Central, (*ii*) Eastern, (*iii*) Northern, (*iv*) North-Eastern, (*v*) North-East Frontier, (*vi*) Southern, (*vii*) South-Eastern, (*viii*) Western, (*ix*) Southern Central (*x*) North Central, (*xi*) South Western, (*xii*) East Central, (*xiii*) East Coast, (*xiv*) West Central and (*xv*) North Western. Each zone has separate head-quarter and is under the control of a General Manager who remains responsible for its operation, maintenance and financial affairs.

29 Metro railway The Mechanical Electrified Transportation Railway Operation (METRO) was introduced first in Kolkata as underground metro-railway in India. The entire stretch of the project became operational on 27th September 1995. The most modern metro in India was inaugurated on 24th December 2002 from Kashmir Gate to Seelampur in Delhi.

2. Definitions. In this Act, unless the context otherwise requires,—

(1) "authorised" means authorised by a railway administration;

[16][(1A) "Authority" means the Rail Land Development Authority constituted under section 4A;]

(2) "carriage" means the carriage of passengers or goods by a railway administration;

(3) "Claims Tribunal" means the Railway Claims Tribunal established under section 3 of the Railway Claims Tribunal Act, 1987 (54 of 1987);

(4) "classification" means the classification of commodities made under section 31 for the purpose of determining the rates to be charged for carriage of such commodities;

(5) "class rates" means the rate fixed for a class of commodity in the classification;

(6) "Commissioner" means the Chief Commissioner of Railway Safety or the Commissioner of Railway Safety appointed under section 5;

(7) "commodity" means a specific item of goods;

[17][(7A) "competent authority" means any person authorised by the Central Government, by notification, to perform the functions of the competent authority for such area as may be specified in the notification;]

(8) "consignee" means the person named as consignee in a railway receipt;

(9) "consignment" means goods entrusted to a railway administration for carriage;

(10) "consignor" means the person, named in a railway receipt as consignor, by whom or on whose behalf goods covered by the railway receipt are entrusted to a railway administration for carriage;

(11) "demurrage" means the charge levied for the detention of any rolling stock after the expiry of free time, if any, allowed for such detention;

(12) "endorsee" means the person in whose favour an endorsement is made, and in the case of successive endorsements, the person in whose favour the last endorsement is made;

(13) "endorsement" means the signing by the consignee or the endorsee after adding a direction on a railway receipt to pass the property in the goods mentioned in such receipt to a specified person;

(14) "fare" means the charge levied for the carriage of passengers;

(15) "ferry" includes a bridge of boats, pontoons or rafts, a swing bridge, a fly-bridge and a temporary bridge and the approaches to, and landing places of, a ferry;

16 *Inserted* by the Railways (Amendment) Act 2005 (w.e.f. 30.8.2006).
17 *Inserted* by the Railways (Amendment) Act 2008 (w.r.e.f. 31.1.2008).

(16) "forwarding note" means the document executed under section 64;

(17) "freight" means the charge levied for the carriage of goods including transhipment charges, if any;

(18) "General Manager" means the General Manager of a Zonal Railway appointed under section 4;

(19) "goods" includes—

(*i*) containers, pallets or similar articles of transport used to consolidate goods; and

(*ii*) animals;

(20) "Government railway" means a railway owned by the Central Government;

(21) "in transit", in relation to the carriage of goods by railway, means the period between the commencement and the termination of transit of such goods, and unless otherwise previously determined—

(*a*) transit commences as soon as the railway receipt is issued or the consignment is loaded, whichever is earlier;

(*b*) transit terminates on the expiry of the free time allowed for unloading of consignment from any rolling stock and where such unloading has been completed within such free time, transit terminates on the expiry of the free time allowed, for the removal of the goods from the railway premises;

(22) "level crossing" means an inter-section of a road with lines of rails at the same level;

(23) "luggage" means the goods of a passenger either carried by him in his charge or entrusted to a railway administration for carriage;

(24) "lump sum rate" means the rate mutually agreed upon between a railway administration and a consignor for the carriage of goods and for any service in relation to such carriage;

(25) "non-Government railway" means a railway other than a Government railway;

(26) "notification" means a notification published in the Official Gazette;

[18][(26A) "officer authorised" means an officer authorised by the Central Government under sub-section (2) of section 179;]

(27) "parcel" means goods entrusted to a railway administration for carriage by a passenger or a parcel train;

(28) "pass" means an authority given by the Central Government or a railway administration to a person allowing him to travel as a passenger, but does not include a ticket;

(29) "passenger" means a person travelling with a valid pass or ticket;

18 *Inserted* by the Railways (Second Amendment) Act 2003 (w.e.f. 1.7.2004).

[19][(29A) "person interested" includes,—

(*i*) all persons claiming an interest in compensation to be made on account of the acquisition of land under this Act;

(*ii*) tribals and other traditional forest dwellers, who have lost any traditional rights recognized under the Scheduled Tribes and Other Traditional Forest Dwellers (Recognition of Forest Rights) Act, 2006 (2 of 2007).

(*iii*) a person interested in an easement affecting the land; and

(*iv*) persons having tenancy rights under the relevant State laws;]

(30) "prescribed" means prescribed by rules made under this Act;

(31) "railway" means a railway, or any portion of a railway, for the public carriage of passengers or goods, and includes—

(*a*) all lands within the fences or other boundary marks indicating the limits of the land appurtenant to a railway;

(*b*) all lines of rails, sidings, or yards, or branches used for the purposes of, or in connection with, a railway;

(*c*) all electric traction equipments, power supply and distribution installations used for the purposes of, or in connection with, a railway;

(*d*) all rolling stock, stations, offices, warehouses, wharves, workshops, manufactories, fixed plant and machinery, roads and streets, running rooms, rest houses, institutes, hospitals, water works and water supply installations staff dwellings and any other works constructed for the purpose of, or in connection with, railway;

(*e*) all vehicles which are used on any road for the purposes of traffic of a railway and owned, hired or worked by a railway; and

(*f*) all ferries, ships, boats and rafts which are used on any canal, river, lake or other navigable inland waters for the purposes of the traffic of a railway and owned, hired or worked by a railway administration,

but does not include—

(*i*) a tramway wholly within a municipal area; and

(*ii*) lines of rails built in any exhibition ground, fair, park or any other place solely for the purpose of recreation;

(32) "railway administration", in relation to—

(*a*) a Government railway, means the General Manager of a Zonal Railway; and

(*b*) a non-Government railway, means the person who is the owner or lessee of the railway or the person working the railway under an agreement;

19 *Inserted* by the Railways (Amendment) Act 2008 (w.r.e.f. 31.1.2008).

[20][(32A) "railway land" means any land in which a Government railway has any right, title or interest;]

(33) "railway receipt" means the receipt issued under section 65;

(34) "railway servant" means any person employed by the Central Government or by a railway administration in connection with the service of a railway; [21][including member of the Railway Protection Force appointed under clause (*c*) of sub-section (1) of section 2 of the Railway Protection Force Act, 1957 (23 of 1957);]

(35) "rate" includes any fare, freight or any other charge for the carriage of any passenger or goods;

(36) "regulations" means the regulations made by the Railway Rates Tribunal under this Act;

(37) "rolling stock" includes locomotives, lenders, carriages, wagons, rail-cars, containers, trucks, trolleys and vehicles of all kinds moving on rails;

[22][(37A) "special railway project" means a project, notified as such by the Central Government from time to time, for providing national infrastructure for a public purpose in a specified time-frame, covering one or more States or the Union territories;]

(38) "station to station rate" means a special reduced rate applicable to a specific commodity booked between specified stations;

(39) "traffic" includes rolling stock of every description, as well as passengers and goods;

(40) "Tribunal" means the Railway Rates Tribunal constituted under section 33;

(41) "wharfage" means the charge levied on goods for not removing them from the railway after the expiry of the free time for such removal;

(42) "Zonal Railway" means a Zonal Railway constituted under section 3.

1 Corresponding provisions in the old Act of 1890 Sub-sections (4), (5), (7), (11), (27), (38) and (41) of s. 2 of the Railways Act 1989 correspond to cls. (*a*), (*b*), (*c*), (*d*), (*e*), (*g*) and (*h*) of s. 46C of the old Act of 1890 respectively and sub-secs. (15), (19), (28), (31), (32), (34), (35), (37) and (39) of s. 2 of the new Act correspond to sub-secs. (2), (9), (15), (4), (6), (7), (13), (10) and (11) of s. 3 of the old Act and sub-sec. (30) of s. 2 of the new Act corresponds to cl. (*d*) of s. 56B of the old Act.

2 Definitions

Authorised. This word is defined in s. 2(1) of the Railways Act 1989 (hereinafter it is called as the Act) to mean authorised by a railway

20 *Inserted* by the Railways (Amendment) Act 2005 (w.e.f. 30.8.2006).
21 *Inserted* by the Railways (Second Amendment) Act 2003 (w.e.f. 1.7.2004).
22 *Inserted* by the Railways (Amendment) Act 2008 (w.e.f. 31.1.2008).

administration. The expression "railway administration" is again defined in s. 2(32) of the Act in exhaustive way. There is no corresponding definition of the word "authorised" in the old Act.

Authority. The term "authority" has been defined in s. 2(1A) of the Railways Act 1989 as inserted by the Railways (Amendment) Act 2005 with effect from 30th August 2006. It means the Rail Land Development Authority constituted under s. 4A of this Act.

Carriage. This word is defined in s. 2(2) of the Act to mean the carriage of passengers or goods by a "railway administration" as defined in s. 2(32) of the Act. There is no corresponding definition in the old Act. The carriage of goods may be for hire or reward.[1]

Claims Tribunal. It is defined in s. 2(3) of the Act as the Railway Claims Tribunal which was established under s. 3 of the Railway Claims Tribunal Act 1987, that is prior to the commencement of the new Act. The main object of the Railway Claims Tribunal Act 1987 is to enquire into and determine claims against a railway administration for loss, destruction, damage, deterioration or non-delivery of goods or animals entrusted to it to be carried by railway or for the refund of fares or freight or for compensation for death or injury to passengers occurring as a result of railway accidents or untoward incidents or for matters connected therewith or incidental thereto.[2]

Classification. Section 2(4) of the Act defines classification. It means classification of commodities made under s. 31 of the Act. Thus, s. 2(4) is to be read with s. 31 for the purpose of determining the rates to be charged for carriage of such commodities. The corresponding provision of s. 2(4) of the Railways Act 1989 is to be found in s. 46C(*a*) of the old Act.[3]

Class rate. This expression is defined in s. 2(5) of the Act as the rate fixed for a class of commodity in the "classification" within the meaning of s. 2(4) of the Act. The corresponding provision of s. 2(5) of the Act is to be found in s. 46C(*b*) of the old Act.

Commissioner. According to s. 2(6) of the Act it means the Chief Commissioner of Railway Safety or the Commissioner of Railway Safety appointed under s. 5 of the Act. There is no corresponding provision in the old Act.

Commodity. Section 2(7) of the Act defines this term as a specific item of goods. The corresponding provision of s. 2(7) is to be found in s. 46C(*c*) of the old Act.

1 *Wurzel* v *Honghton Main Home Delivery Service* [1937]1 KB 380.
2 Preamble to the Railway Claims Tribunal Act 1987.
3 *Western Railway, Bombay* v *R.R. Tribunal* AIR 1955 Mad 513; ILR (1956) Mad 67.

Competent authority. The expression "competent authority" as defined in s. 2(7A) of the Railways Act 1989 means any person authorised by the Central Government, by notification, to perform the functions of the competent authority for such area as may be specified in the notification. This expression has been inserted in the Act by the Railways (Amendment) Act 2008 with effect from 29th February 2008.

Consignee. According to s. 2(8) of the Act, consignee is a person who is named as consignee in a railway receipt. There is no corresponding provision in the old Act for this term. Ordinarily, consignee means a person to whom a consignment is made.

Consignment. Section 2(9) of the Act defines consignment as goods entrusted to a railway administration for carriage. There is no corresponding provision for this term in the old Act. Consignment is an act or process of consigning goods.

Consignor. According to s. 2(10) of the Act consignor means the person named in the railway receipt as a consignor by whom or on whose behalf goods covered by railway receipt are entrusted to railway administration for carriage. There is no corresponding provision for this term in the old Act.

Demurrage. It is defined in s. 2(11) of the Act as the charge levied for the detention of any rolling stock after the expiry of free time, if any, allowed for such detention. Section 46C(*d*) of the old Act has also defined the term "demurrage". Demurrage is not a service to be performed by a Board and is on any view, a charge leviable on goods.[4]

Endorsee. It is defined in s. 2(12) of the Act as the person in whose favour an endorsement is made, and in the case of successive endorsements, the person in whose favour the last endorsement is made. There is no corresponding provision in the old Act.

Endorsement. It has been defined by s. 2(13) of the Act as the signing by the consignee or the endorsee after adding a direction on a railway receipt to pass the property in the goods mentioned in the receipt to a specified person. There is no corresponding provision in the old Act of this term.

Fare. "Fare" is defined by s. 2(14) as the charge levied for the carriage of passengers. Payment for extra comfort in a reserved carriage is also a part of the fare.[5] Inclusion of catering charges for travel being legally levied by the Railway Administration is part of the fare.[6] There is no corresponding definition of fare in the old Act.

Ferry. The definition of "ferry" given in s. 2(15) of the Act is extensive. It includes a bridge of boats, pontoons or rafts, a swing-bridge, a fly-bridge

4 *Trustees of the Port of Madras* v *Arunchand Pyarelal* (1976)3 SCC 167.

5 *A.G.* v *Furness Railway* [1899]2 QB 267.

6 *Apakshaben V. Shah* v *Union of India* 1996(2) Civ LJ 631 (Guj).

and a temporary bridge and the approaches to, and landing places of, a ferry. Section 3(2) of the old Act has also defined ferry in the identical terms.

To constitute a ferry two points on two sides of a river for conveying persons and property are necessary. A ferry is in the nature of a highway and is the exclusive right to carry passengers across a river, or steam or arm of the sea. It is *publici juris* and when a ferry is erected, another cannot be erected without a *ad quod* damnum.[7]

Forwarding note. Section 2(16) of the Act defines "forwarding note" as a document executed under s. 64 of the Act. Thus, forwarding note is to be construed in the context of s. 64 of the Act. There is no corresponding provision in the old Act.

Freight. Freight is defined in s. 2(17) of the Act as the charge levied for the carriage of goods including transhipment charges. There is no corresponding provision in the old Act. It is the compensation paid to a carrier for transporting goods.[8]

Freight is different from fare in the sense that the former is a levy charged for carriage of goods, whereas the latter is a levy charged for carriage of passengers. Nothing is freight unless there is involved in it a contract to carry goods; for freight is a sum payable in respect of a contract to carry, and if there is no contract to carry, then the sum paid as freight is not freight in point of law.[9]

General Manager. A General Manager of a Zonal Railway according to s. 2(18) is appointed under s. 4 of the Act. There is no corresponding provision in the old Act.

Goods. The definition of goods given in s. 2(19) of the Act is extensive and includes (*i*) containers, pallets or similar articles of transport used to consolidate goods; and (*ii*) animals. Section 3(9) of the old Act defines "goods" to include inanimate things of every kind.

Government railway. This expression is defined in s. 2(20) of the Act to mean a railway owned by the Central Government. There is no corresponding definition of this expression in the old Act. By this definition it means that the railway is fully owned and controlled by the Central Government.

In transit. The term "in transit" is defined in s. 2(21) of the Act in relation to the carriage of goods by railway which means the period between the commencement and the termination of transit of such goods. Unless the transit is previously determined (*i*) it commences as soon as the railway

7 *Purnendu Bikash Maity* v *Chairman, District Board* AIR 1963 Cal 74.
8 Black's *Law Dictionary,* 10th Ed., 2014.
9 *Keith* v *Burrows* [1876]1 CPD 722; [1877]2 App Cas 636 (HL); see *Shillito* v *Biggart* [1903]1 KB 683 (Com Ct).

receipt is issued or consignment is loaded, whichever is earlier, and (*ii*) it terminates on the expiry of the free time allowed for unloading of consignment from any rolling stock and where such unloading is completed within such free time, transit terminates on the expiry of the free time allowed for removal of the goods from the railway premises. In this context it is necessary to take into consideration the definition of "rolling stock" as given in s. 2(37) of the Act and also that of "wharfage" in s. 2(41) of the said Act.

Level crossing. The expression "level crossing" means, according to s. 2(22) of the Act, an inter-section of a road with lines of rails at the same level. It has no corresponding definition in the old Act. But under the old Act legal duties were imposed on the railway administration to ensure the safety of a member of the public in level crossing.[10]

Luggage. The word "luggage" as defined in s. 2(23) of the Act means the goods of passenger either carried by him in his charge or entrusted to a railway administration for carriage. There is no corresponding definition of the word "luggage" in the old Act.

There is a distinction between luggage and personal luggage. The personal luggage includes whatever a passenger takes with him for his personal use or convenience according to the habits of the particular class to which he belongs either with reference to the immediate necessities or ultimate purpose of the journey.

Lump sum rate. According to s. 2(24) of the Act lump sum rate means the rate mutually agreed upon between a railway administration and a consignor for the carriage of goods and for any service in relation, to such carriage. This term "lump sum rate" has no corresponding definition in the old Act.

Non-Government railway. Section 2(25) of the Act defines non-Government railway as a contrast of the definition of "Government railway" in s. 2(20) of the said Act. A non-Government railway means a railway other than a Government railway. In a non-Governmental railway, the Government at the Centre or at a State does not have any share or right of ownership. There is no corresponding definition of such term in the old Act.

Notification. A notification is defined in s. 2(26) of the Act to mean a notification published in the Official Gazette. Though "Official Gazette" has not been defined in the said Act, yet this term can be defined in the context of s. 3(39) of the General Clauses Act 1897, whereby it shall mean the Gazette or the Official Gazette of a State. There is no corresponding definition or the word "notification" in the old Act.

Officer authorised. The term "officer authorised" has been defined in s. 26A of the Railways Act 1989 as inserted by the Railways (Amendment)

10 *Union of India* v *Lalman Badri Prasad* AIR 1954 VP 17.

Act 2003 with effect from 1st July 2004. It means an officer authorised by the Central Government under s. 179(2) of this Act.

Parcel. The word "parcel" is defined in s. 2(27) of the Act as goods entrusted to a railway administration for carriage by a passenger or a parcel train. The corresponding definition of "parcel" is to be found in s. 46C(*e*) of the old Act.

Pass. The word "pass" is defined in s. 2(28) of the Act to mean an authority given either by the Central Government or by a railway administration to a person allowing him to travel as a passenger. But it excludes a ticket. Section 3(15) of the old Act also defines the word "pass".

There is a difference between "pass" and "duty pass". A duty pass is issued by the railway under the Rules and it can be used only for journeys on duty and a railway servant is not entitled to travel with the duty pass while he is not on duty.[11]

Passenger. It has been defined in s. 2(29) of the Act to mean a person travelling with a valid pass or ticket. It has no corresponding definition in the old Act. The passenger may also include a class of passenger or possible passengers.[12]

GRP Constable on Duty. A GRP Constable in discharge of official duty was crushed under a train. The deceased is covered by the definition of s. 2(29) of the 1989 Act and his dependents are entitled to compensation on account of untoward incident.[13]

Bona Fide Passenger. *Explanation* to s. 124A of the Railways Act 1989 does not give room to take view that in order to be considered as coming within the definition of "passenger" both in s. 124A and s. 2(29) of the said Act, the person concerned must hold a valid ticket to travel as a passenger in a particular train. The use of the expression, in *Explanation* "by a train carrying passengers" would imply that person holding a valid ticket can travel in any train which takes him to his destination and use of indefinite article "a" and not the definite article "the", therefore, would imply that the framers of the Act or legislation had in view, the possibility of a person holding a valid ticket to travel by any train that takes him to his destination. In a case where deceased holding a valid ticket for train No. 582 boarded train No. 581, he cannot be said that he was not a *bona fide* passenger. So long as the deceased satisfies the definition of a "passenger" occurring in s. 2(29) and in *Explanation* to s. 124A therein, railway administration cannot escape its liability if the case falls outside the purview or exceptions

11 *Mariayayi* v *Union of India* AIR 1971 Mad 488; 84 Mad LW 461.
12 *Aschendrenner* v *US Fidelity & G. Co.* 292 US 80.
13 *Minn Mai Devi* v *Union of India* 2001(1) Civ LJ 586.

(*a*) to (*e*) to s. 124A of the said Act. Thus, the deceased is deemed to be passenger and the claimant is entitled to compensation.[14]

Person interested. This expression "person interested" is defined in s. 2(29A) of the Railways Act 1989 as inserted by the Railways (Amendment) Act 2008 with effect from 31st January 2008. This expression includes— (*i*) all persons claiming an interest in compensation to be made on account of the acquisition of land under this Act; (*ii*) tribals and other traditional forest dwellers, who have lost any traditional rights recognised under the Scheduled Tribes and Other Traditional Forest Dwellers (Recognition of Forest Rights) Act 2006; (*iii*) a person interested in an easement affecting the land; and (*iv*) persons having tenancy rights under the relevant State laws.

Prescribed. The word "prescribed" as defined in s. 2(30) of the Act means those rules which are prescribed or made under the said Act. The corresponding definition of "prescribed" is to be found in s. 56B(*d*) of the old Act.

In ordinary sense, the word "prescribed" is used for the purpose of conferring power to make rules.[15] The word "prescribed" as defined under s. 2(16) of the Code of Civil Procedure means prescribed by rules.[16]

Railway. The word "railway" as defined in s. 2(31) of the Act is not extensive but also exclusionary in some matters. It means and includes broadly many matters which are dealt with under six heads. But it excludes from its purview two subject-matters, such as (*i*) a tramway wholly within a municipal area, and (*ii*) lines of rails built in any exhibition ground, fair, park or any other place solely for the purpose of recreation. The corresponding definition of "railway" is to be found in s. 3(4) of the old Act of 1890.

CITY BOOKING OFFICE. For a City Booking office to fall within the ambit of "Railway", it should either be an office or a warehouse of a railway. An office or warehouse of another person though licensed or permitted by the railway would not fall within the ambit of the expression "Railway".[17] Similarly, staff quarters or any building of a residential character cannot be deemed to be part of a railway.[18]

It is found that the city booking agencies do not fall within the expression "Railway", no further question would arise and the transport, if any of

14 *Vinodamma* v *Union of India* AIR 2010 Kar 174.

15 *Guruviash* v *State of Madras* AIR 1958 Mad 249.

16 *Tarinikamal* v *Prafulla Kumar* AIR 1979 SC 1165; (1979)3 SCC 280; (1979)3 SCR 340.

17 1994 AIR SCW 4762; JT 1994(7) SC 583.

18 *Lodaior Lodi* v *Emperor* AIR 1927 All 646; 26 CrLJ 648.

goods/consignment from the railway station/godown to the city booking agencies would not be entitled to the exemption provided by sub-sec. (8) of s. 28A of the Uttar Pradesh Sales Tax Act 1948. If however, it is found that the city booking agencies fall within the ambit of the expression "Railway" as defined in the Railways Act 1989, such transport of goods/ consignment from the railway station/godown to the city booking agency would be covered by the said sub-sec. (8). Even so, it does not follow that the sales tax authorities of the State have no power to check the transport goods/consignment from the railway station/godown to the city booking agencies to satisfy themselves that it is indeed a transport to the city booking agency. If they find it not to be so, it shall be open to them to adopt such proceedings in that behalf as are open to them in law.[19]

CLEARING OF CITY'S REFUSE. Railway employed in clearing city's refuse does not fall within the definition of "Railway".[20]

MEANING OF RAILWAY. "Railway" includes steamer. Jetty is a ferry but a jetty uncoupled with steamer cannot be regarded as a part of steamer. Thus, where a deceased person standing on a jetty to inboard a steamer was not a passenger of a steamer within the meaning of s. 82A of the old Act.[21]

The definition of "railway" is very wide under both the new Act and the old Act. Any land within the limits of the boundary marks of a railway and any office or other work constructed for the purpose of or in connection with the railway is also included in the definition.[1]

TRAMWAY. In view of the definition of "railway" given in s. 311(2) of the Government of India Act 1935 corresponding to Art. 366(20) of the Constitution of India, a system, though a tramway, which is not wholly within a municipal area, is a railway. The tramway between Shahadara in Delhi and Saharanpur in UP and passing through four districts and run by a company registered under the Indian Tramways Act 1886 was held to be a railway.[2]

APPLICABILITY OF PAYMENT OF WAGES ACT 1936. The Payment of Wages Act 1936 is applicable not only to employees of railway administration engaged specifically upon railway track but also to other employees of the administration.[3]

19 *S.T.O.* v *Union of India* 1995 Supp (1) SCC 410.
20 *Sahari Rajwarni* v *Calcutta Corpn.* AIR 1955 Cal 307.
21 *Mohammad Khaliluddin* v *Union of India* AIR 1962 Pat 109; (1962) BLJR 354.
1 *Samuel Tippee* v *State* AIR 1963 Ori 20; 28 Cut LT 508.
2 *S.S.L. Rly. Co.* v *Saharanpur Municipal Board* AIR 1967 SC 1747.
3 *Union of India* v *M.S. Chaudhri* 1970 Lab IC 165.

RAILWAY—DEFINITION IN CONSTITUTION. It may be recalled that the power to legislate in respect of railway lies only in the Union Government. Thus railway occurs at item No. 22 of the Union list in the Seventh Schedule of the Constitution. This necessitated a definition of railway to be given in the Constitution of India and Art. 366(20), Constitution of India seeks to answer the need. But the definition of railway in Art. 366(20), Constitution of India is a negative one. It stands as follows: "Railway does not include—

(*a*) a tramway wholly within a municipal area, or

(*b*) any other line of communication wholly situated in one State and declared by Parliament by Law not to be a railway".

Going by the definition of the expression "railway" as contained in Art. 366(20) of the Constitution of India the appellant in *Shahdara (Delhi) Saharanpur Light Rly. Co. Ltd.* v *Municipal Board*[4] is a railway. All the provisions of the Railways Act 1890 have been extended to the appellant excepting s. 135 of the said Act. If the appellant is a "railway", otherwise the mere fact that the provisions of s. 135 of the Railways Act 1890, have not been applied, is of no consequence.

STAFF QUARTERS OR BUILDING OF RESIDENTIAL CHARACTER. Staff quarters or any building of a residential character cannot be deemed to be part of a railway, and the fact that the place happens to be between two lines makes no difference if the lines by themselves are so quite apart that there can be even private lands between the line.[5]

NAVIGATION COMPANY. Navigation company which undertakes to carry goods despatched by Railway to other places was held to be "Railway".[6]

GENERAL CONTRACT BETWEEN RAILWAY COMPANY AND ANOTHER COMPANY. Where there is a general contract between a Railway Company and another company that the latter company has to take the goods delivered at the out-agencies of the Railway Company, carry the goods by their boats and hand them over to the railway stations of the Railway Company and in return for this service to get a certain percentage of the charges, such an agreement does not make the company working the boats a Railway Company and it does not cease to be a common carrier of goods.[7]

Railway administration. Section 2(32) of the Railways Act 1989 defines "railway administration" from two aspects, one from the aspect of a

4 AIR 1967 SC 1747.

5 *Emperor* v *Lodai* AIR 1927 All 646; 50 All 34; 25 All LJ 710; 28 CrLJ 648; *Margam Aiyar* v *S.J. Mercer* AIR 1914 Mad 196; (1914)23 IC 177; 15 CrLJ 225; (1914) MWN 124.

6 1912 Punj LR 233.

7 *Madura Co. Ltd.* v *P.C. Xavier* AIR 1931 Mad 115.

Government railway and the other from the aspect of a non-Government railway. So far as a Government railway is concerned railway administration means the General Manager of a Zonal Railway. And so far as a non-Government railway is concerned railway administration means the person who is the owner or lessee of the railway or the person working the railway under an agreement. The corresponding definition of the expression "railway administration" is also to be found in s. 3(6) of the old Act.

RAILWAY ADMINISTRATION AND GOVERNMENT ADMINISTRATION. The definition of "railway administration" is so wide that it includes the Government administering the railways.[8] The manager of the railway is equated to the Government under the definition of the old Act.[9] Station Master or Chief Transportation Superintendent of Railway does not fall within the definition of railway administration under s. 76B of the old Act.[10]

Since the definition of "railway administration" includes Government, and as such railways owned by Government can sufficiently be represented by the Union of India. Where the railway administration to which the goods were consigned and the railway administration on which the loss occurred, the suit may be brought against the Union of India.[11] All the major railways are one entity owned and run by the Union of India. Thus, railway administration owned and managed by the Central Government are not separate entitles for the purpose of a suit.[12]

REPRESENTATION OF RAILWAY ADMINISTRATION. The definition of "railway administration" under s. 3(6) of the old Act would mean the manager of the railway but that does not warrant the inference that a suit against the railway administration can be brought against the manager of that railway. The said definition does not make the railway administration or its general manager a legal entity or a corporate body or a judicial person to represent the railway administration as such in suits.[13] But the prosecution of a manager of the railway in a representative capacity for any offence under s. 14 of the Bengal Licensed Warehouse and Fire Brigade Act 1893 cannot be said to be misconceived by reason merely in the form of complaint. Section 197 of the old CrPC (corresponding to s. 233 of the CrPC 1973) and s. 270 of the Government of India Act 1935 have no application to such a case.[14]

8 *Natwar Lal* v *Union of India* AIR 1957 MP 157; see *Kerala State* v *G.M.S. Rly., Madras* AIR 1965 Ker 277 (FB).
9 *Baijnath Singh* v *Oudh Tirhat Rly.* AIR 1960 All 362.
10 *State of Assam* v *Union of India* AIR 1975 Gau 74.
11 *Chandra Mohan Saha* v *Union of India* AIR 1953 Assam 193 (FB).
12 *State of Kerala* v *G.M.S. Rly., Madras* AIR 1965 Ker 277 (FB).
13 *State of Kerala* v *G.M.S. Rly.* AIR 1976 SC 2538; (1977)1 SCR 419; (1976)4 SCC 265; (1977)1 Mad LJ 60 (SC).
14 *Marriott* v *Municipality of Howrah* AIR 1941 Cal 319; 42 Civ LJ 855.

MANAGER—GENERAL MANAGER OF A RAILWAY. In view of definition of "railway administration" in (old) s. 3(6) Manager was equated to the Government. Manager satisfies the definition of Managing Agent given in s. 2(*f*) of the Workmen's Compensation Act 1923.[15] The definition of "railway administration" given in (old) s. 3(6) of the Act does not make the railway administration, or its General Manager a legal entity or a corporate body or a juridical person to represent the railway administration as such.[16] Where a railway designated one of its officers as the "General Manager", then he is the "Manager" within the meaning of s. 3(6) and s. 77 of the Railways Act 1890.[17]

In a case where the railway is administered by a Government or State, a suit of claim under s. 80 can be brought against the Government or the State concerned. It is not necessary that the railway administration, as such through the Manager or anybody else, should be impleaded as a party defendant in the suit.[18] Summons or notice of suit may be served either on the Manager or Government administering the railway.[19]

Railway land. The words "railway land" are defined in s. 32A of the Act. This expression has been inserted in the Act by the Railways (Amendment) Act 2005 which has come into force on 30.8.2006. This expression means "any land in which a Government railway has any right, title or interest".

Railway receipt. The term "railway receipt" as defined in s. 2(33) of the Act means the receipt issued under s. 65 of the said Act. Thus, the term "railway receipt" in s. 2(33) of the Act is to be read along with s. 65 of the Act. Section 2(33) has no corresponding provision in the old Act.

A railway receipt is a document of title of goods, and, for all purposes, represents the goods. When the railway receipt is handed over to the consignee on payment, the property in the goods is transferred.[20]

Railway servant. According to the definition as given in s. 2(34) of the Act, a railway servant means any person employed by the Central Government or by a railway administration in connection with the service of a railway and member of the Railway Protection Force appointed under cl. (*c*) of sub-sec. (1) of s. 2 of the Railway Protection Force Act 1957.

15 *Baijnath Singh* v *Oudh Tirhut Railway* AIR 1960 All 362.
16 *State of Kerala* v *General Manager, S. Railway* AIR 1965 SC 277; (1965)1 CrLJ 256.
17 *Radhamadhab Kundu* v *Union of India* 61 CWN 433.
18 *Chandra Mohon* v *Union of India* AIR 1953 Assam 193; see also *Natwarlal* v *Union of India* AIR 1957 MP 157; *State of Kerala* v *General Manager, Southern Railway* AIR 1965 SC 277; (1965)1 CrLJ 256.
19 *Union of India* v *Abdul Razak* AIR 1956 Pat 511.
20 *CIT* v *Bhopal Textiles Ltd.* AIR 1961 SC 426.

Section 2(34) of the Railways Act 1989 defines "railway servant" where persons are appointed by railways on part-time basis and not appointed pursuant to any rules of recruitment or orders issued by Railways, they cannot be held to be railway employees or railway servants. Thus, the Central Administrative Tribunal has no jurisdiction to entertain their applications for regularisation of their services.[21]

RAILWAY PORTERS AND KHALASI—STATUS. As to licensed railway porters, providing facilities for handling or carrying luggage of passengers who travel in trains is an obligation cast on the railway administration. The system of licensing porters is adopted in discharge of that obligation. Though they are licensees, the terms and conditions for the issue of licence clearly indicate that the railway administration supervises over the work of the licensed porters and time of work is fixed by the administration. They are to receive payment for the work from the railway administration or as the case may be, from the passengers at rates fixed by the railway administration. They are to wear uniforms and badges supplied by the railway administration during the period of work. They are afforded medical facilities so long as they remain licensed porters. The railway administration has disciplinary control over them. The terms of the contract of licence and the overall control vested in the administration are sufficient indicia for holding that the licensed porters are "railway servants" employed by the railway administration in connection with the service of a railway, as mentioned in s. 3(7) of the (old) Railways Act, and therefore, "workmen" under s. 2(1)(*n*) of the Workmen's Compensation Act 1923.[1]

A railway *khalasi* in the railway carriage section is allowed to deal with the preparation and issuance of railway passes in the office of the works manager, he in fact is performing public duties and discharging public functions, auxiliary to those of the works manager and his office. Such a *khalasi* is a railway servant.[2]

SOME ILLUSTRATIVE CASES. Under s. 2(34) of the Railways Act 1989 [corresponding to s. 3(7) of the old Act] the following persons were considered whether they fall within the meaning of railway servant:

(*i*) A cabin man was a railway servant.[3]

(*ii*) A person engaged by a railway to pass steepers paid partly by the railway and partly by contractor was a railway servant.[4]

21 *Phool Badan Tiwari* v *Union of India* (2003)9 SCC 304.
1 *K. Narayanan* v *Divisional Supdt., Southern Railway* 1980 Lab IC 776; 1979 Ker LT 851.
2 *Bajranglal* v *State of Rajasthan* AIR 1976 SC 1008 (1011); (1976)2 SCC 217 (221).
3 *Motiram Chandiram* v *Emperor* AIR 1941 Sind 117; 195 IC 833.
4 *A.V. Joseph* v *J.L. Lammond* AIR 1924 Rang 373.

(*iii*) A contractor engaged for performing services to the railway is railway servant.[5]

(*iv*) Petitioner working as a clerk in the office of the security officer, Eastern Railway would clearly fall within the ambit of the definition of railway servant.[6]

(*v*) The officers and members of the Railway Protection Force which is an armed force of the Union are deemed to be railway servants only for the limited purpose of exercising powers conferred on the railway servants by or under the old Act.[7]

(*vi*) A catering contractor employed by the railway administration and subject to considerable supervision and control by the administration in the manner of execution of the contract is a railway servant.[8]

"*Rate*". "Rate" merely means scale of amount of any other charges. Definition of "rate" under s. 3(13) of old Act cannot be applied to s. 29(2) of the old Act.[9] Rate is an amount paid or charged for a good or service.[10]

The word "rate" as defined in s. 2(35) of the Railways Act 1989 was defined similarly in s. 3(13) of the old Act. It includes (*i*) any fare, (*ii*) freight, or (*iii*) any charge for carriage of (*a*) any passenger, or (*b*) goods. The definition of "rate" as defined in the old Act could not be applied to the expression "rates of any other charges" in s. 29(2) of the old Act which empowered the Central Government to fix the rate of any other charges for the whole or any part of a railway. Under s. 3(13) of the old Act the word "rate" would merely mean the scale of amount of any other charges.[11] Under the old s. 3(13) "rate" would include other payments that could be levied by way of penalty under r. 161 of the Indian Railways Conference Association Rules.[12]

Regulation. Section 2(36) of the Railways Act 1989 defines the word "regulations" as those made by the Railway Rates Tribunal under this Act. There is no corresponding definition of this word in the old Act.

Rolling stock. This term as defined in s. 2(37) of the Railways Act 1989 includes (*i*) locomotives, (*ii*) lenders, (*iii*) carriages, (*iv*) wagons, (*v*) rail-

5 *Union of India* v *B.N. Prasad* AIR 1978 SC 411; (1978)2 SCC 462; (1978)2 SCR 397.
6 *H.K. Bose* v *Union of India* 89 CWN 1167.
7 *Shiv Kumar* v *Union of India* 1987 Lab IC 746.
8 *Divl. R.M. Eastern Rly.* v *Satyajit Majumdar* 1991 Lab IC 1062.
9 *Union of India* v *M.P. Sugar Mills* AIR 1969 SC 630; (1969)1 SCC 320; (1969)3 SCR 75.
10 Black's *Law Dictionary*, 10th Ed., 2014.
11 *Union of India* v *M.P. Sugar Mills* AIR 1969 SC 630; (1969)1 SCC 320; (1969)3 SCR 75.
12 *J.C. Textile Mills* v *Chief Commercial Superintendent, N.R.* 1998 AIR SCW 1804; AIR 1998 SC 1959.

cars, (*vi*) containers, (*vii*) trucks, (*viii*) trolleys, and (*ix*) vehicles of all kinds moving on rails. This definition is more extensive than the definition of this term given in s. 3(10) of the old Act. Rolling stock means the movable property, such as locomotives and rail-cars, owned by a railroad.[13]

Station to station rate. The term "station to station rate" is defined in s. 2(38) of the Railways Act 1989 to mean a special reduced rate applicable to a specific commodity booked between specified stations. The corresponding definition of this term is to be found in s. 46C(*g*) of the old Act.

Traffic. The definition of "traffic" in s. 2(39) of the Railways Act 1989 corresponds to s. 3(11) of the old Act and includes rolling stock of every description as well as passengers and goods. Traffic does not include a person going to railway station to see off a friend for travelling by a train. Under the old Act "traffic" included "rolling stock" as well as passengers, animals and goods.[14]

Tribunal. Section 2(40) of the Railways Act 1989 defines tribunal as the Railway Rates Tribunal constituted under s. 33 of the said Act.

Wharfage. The word "wharfage" as defined in s. 2(41) of the Railways Act 1989 means the charge levied on goods for not removing them from the railway after the expiry of free time for such removal. The corresponding definition of this word is to be found in s. 46C(*h*) of the old Act. It is the fee paid for landing, loading, or unloading goods on a wharf. It is also the accommodation for loading or unloading goods on a wharf.[15]

SCOPE. Wharfage is a charge levied by railway not in its capacity as a carrier but as involuntary warehouseman of a trader who has failed to take delivery of his goods within the prescribed time. Under the charge for haulage or terminals it is not a charge which every trader is compelled to pay, it can be avoided by removing his goods within permissible free time which is invariably a reasonable one and dictated by existing or local condition.[16] The rate of wharfage depends on factors which must necessarily differ from station to station, e.g. the density of traffic, the amount of warehousing space available, the habits of local traders etc. A classification made on taking these factors into consideration would be a reasonable one.[17] The liability to pay wharfage under s. 46C(*h*) of the old Act was an absolute liability. The wharfage comes into operation from the point when free time terminates. A free time is available to consignee for unloading and clearance of goods after the wagon is placed at the railway siding or at any place where the unloading can be possible.[18]

13 Black's *Law Dictionary,* 10th Ed., 2014.
14 *Komarain* v *Emperor* 1922 MWN 34.
15 Black's *Law Dictionary,* 10th Ed., 2014.
16 *Puttu Lal* v *N.E. Railway* AIR 1960 All 438.
17 *Ibid.*
18 *D.R. Rly. Co.* v *C.G. Colliery Co.* AIR 1965 Pat 49.

REASON FOR CHARGING WHARFAGE. The main reason for charging wharfage is that if no wharfage were to be charged or its rate kept very low, there would be no incentive on the part of the trader to take early delivery of goods thereby cluttering up station premises with unnecessary goods at the cost of more legitimate goods traffic. Thus, even a charge on a telescopic rate was held to be justified.[19]

DEMURRAGE AND WHARFAGE. Both demurrage and wharfage would fall within the head "station terminals" because they are charges levied for the use either of the wagon or of the platform or goods shed after the transit or conveyance is complete and is not incidental to the conveyance as such.[20]

Special railway project. This term has been defined in s. 2(37A) of the 1989 Act as inserted by the Railways (Amendment) Act 2008 with effect from 31.1.2008. It means a project, notified as such by the Central Government from time to time, for providing national infrastructure for a public purpose in a specified time-frame, covering one or more States or the Union territories.

Zonal Railway. The term "Zonal Railway" as defined in s. 2(42) of the Railways Act 1989 means Zonal Railway constituted under s. 3 of the said Act. There is no corresponding definition of this term in the old Act. Section 2(42) of the Railways Act 1989 is, therefore, to be read with s. 3 of the said Act for the purport and scope of the term "Zonal Railway".

"Terminals". Terminals are the charge levied for services incidental to the business of the railway. The operation of the terminals ends with the expiry of the authorized time, while wharfage comes into operation from the point free time terminates.[21]

SUBBA RAO, J. (as he then was), speaking on behalf of the Supreme Court in *Raichand* v *Union of India*,[22] considered the question whether demurrage and wharfage charges were "terminal charges" and analysing the nature of these charges, pointed out (at page 71 of the Report)—

> "Terminal charges are of two categories: (1) charges for services, and (2) charges for accommodation and appliances which facilitates business. The 'service terminals' comprise of remuneration for the handling of goods at the terminal station, i.e. where the railway employees are engaged in weighing, loading, unloading, etc. As distinguished from this 'service terminals' there are 'station terminals' which are charges for providing accommodation incidental to the business of a carrier, such as 'working

19 *Puttu Lal* v *N.E. Railway* AIR 1960 All 438.

20 *Raichand Amulakh* v *Union of India* (1964)5 SCR 148; AIR 1964 SC 1268; 66 Bom LR 315.

21 *Pattu Lal* v *G.M., N.E. Rly.* AIR 1960 All 438.

22 AIR 1964 SC 1268; (1964)5 SCR 148.

charges, repairs, renewals, insurance of station buildings, hydraulic power, fixed appliances, etc'. Both demurrage and wharfage would fall within the head 'station terminals' because they are charges levied for the use either of the wagon or of the platform or goods shed after the transit or conveyance is complete and is not incidental to the conveyance as such. As the wharfage and demurrage are charges in respect of goods unloaded from wagons and kept at the station and also in respect of goods kept on platforms of the station, the said charges could certainly be described as charges in respect of the station."

3 Railways Act 1989 and Fatal Accidents Act 1855 for compensation Under the Railways Act the legal representatives have not been specifically made eligible to apply for compensation. Since there is no corresponding provision in the Railways Act in respect of compensation for loss of estate and person entitled to claim compensation, would be entitled to be governed by provisions of the Fatal Accidents Act 1855. Therefore, loss of estate falling within s. 2 of the Fatal Accidents Act 1855 could be claimed by legal representatives of the deceased. The Railways Act 1989 will only supersede the provisions of s. 1A of the Fatal Accidents Act 1855 whereas loss to the estate of the deceased computable under s. 2 of the Fatal Accidents Act can be claimed by legal representatives but from a forum created under the Railway Claims Tribunal Act 1987 in view of the bar of jurisdiction of civil court.[23]

4 Services of railways hospital and jurisdiction of consumer forum A particular hospital was set up for the purpose of granting medical treatment to railway employees and their dependants. Apart from the nominal charges other hospital facilities are rendered to railway servants as part of their service conditions. Medical services of such hospital fall within the ambit of "service" under s. 2(1)(*o*) of the Consumer Protection Act 1986 and the railway employees or their dependants are consumers under s. 2(1)(*d*) of the said Act. Thus, an aggrieved person can have recourse to consumer forum under the Consumer Protection Act 1986.[24]

5 Pay scale reduction is arbitrary Railway Tower Wagon Drivers (TWDs) and Goods Train Driver (GTD) were paid same pay as per finding by the Central Administration Tribunal (CAT) for the last 40 years. Reduction of pay scale to TWDs on ground that they were granted higher pay scale by mistake. No cogent reasons or materials were placed before the CAT for the same. Plea by Railways that duties of both posts were different and recruitment criteria were also different. This plea was raised by the Railway for the first time before the Supreme Court without any supporting data. Thus, such vague averments could not persuade the Supreme Court to

23 *Dhyan Singh* v *Union of India* AIR 2009 P&H 56.

24 *Laxman Thamappa Kotgiri* v *G.M., Central Railway* (2007)4 SCC 596.

disturb the concurrent findings. Order of reduction of pay scale of TWDs held to be arbitrary.[25]

6 Pensionary benefits Persons who retire from service after 31st March 1960 form a class by themselves irrespective of their entry in service. Further classification or differentiation among them was never intended by r. 2423-A of Railway Establishment Code as amended from time to time read with r. 2301 of the Railway Pension Rules. Rule 2423-A/R-II of Code as amended in 1976 providing that benefit of addition of years to qualifying service would be granted only if recruitment Rules confers such benefit when a person is appointed. Amendment cannot be retrospective in effect in respect of person already in service but would be prospective, it would be applicable only to those candidates appointed after the date of the amendment introducing the proviso.[26]

7 Grant of sanction for recognition of canteen requisites The following requisites for recognition of railway canteen as per Railway Establishment Manual, r. 2831 are—(*i*) Railway Board must be approached prior to starting of canteen; (*ii*) sanction must indicate financial implications involved, which would thereafter have to be vetted duly by Financial Advisor and General Accounts Officer of Railway Board; and (*iii*) it must provide details, number of staff to be employed in canteen as well as recurring and non-recurring expenditure to be regulated by Railways.[27]

CHAPTER II
Railway Administrations

3. Zonal Railways. (1) The Central Government may, for the purpose of the efficient administration of the Government railways, by notification, constitute such railways into as many Zonal Railways as it may deem fit and specify in such notification the names and headquarters of such Zonal Railways and the areas in respect of which they shall exercise jurisdiction.

(2) The Zonal Railway existing immediately before the commencement of this Act shall be deemed to be Zonal Railways constituted under sub-section (1).

(3) The Central Government may, by notification, declare any unit of the railways engaged in research, development, designing, construction or production of rolling stock, its parts or other equipment used on a railway, to be a Zonal Railway.

(4) The Central Government may, by notification, abolish any Zonal Railway or constitute any new Zonal Railway out of any existing Zonal Railway or Zonal Railways, change the name or headquarters of any Zonal Railway or determine the areas in respect of which a Zonal Railway shall exercise jurisdiction.

25 *Union of India* v *Jagdish Pandey* AIR 2010 SC 3019.
26 *Union of India* v *V.D. Dubey* AIR 2010 SC 425.
27 *Shri Krishan* v *Union of India* (2014)10 SCC 415.

1 Scope Section 3 of the Railways Act 1989, which has no corresponding provision in the old Act, confers power on the Central Government to constitute zonal railways for efficient functioning of administration by a notification in the Official Gazette.[1] The zonal railways which were constituted under the old Act would function as such until there is any change or abolition thereof under the Railways Act 1989.[2] Any change or abolition of any zonal railway may be made by the Central Government under a notification in the Official Gazette.[3]

2 Meaning of words

(a) *"Central Government."* The term "Central Government" appearing s. 3 of the Act has not been defined in s. 2 of the Act. Thus, this term is to be construed in the context of s. 2(8) of the General Clauses Act 1897 and judicial decisions.[4]

(b) *"Existing."* The word "existing" used in s. 3(2) and s. 3(4) of the Act means something in present force, activity or effect at a given time.[5]

3 Formation of new railway zone The matter of reorganisation of the railway zone was under consideration of the Government of India since 1981. Thereafter a study group was formed to examine the matters and make recommendations. In 1996 a decision was taken by the Government for a zone at Hazipur. If benefit of a Zonal Headquarters in a particular place is more suited than any other place in the zone, it would not effect the ultimate efficient functioning of the Railway Administration. Section 3 of the Railways Act 1989 mentions about the constitution of railway zones for the purpose of efficient administration. The concept of "efficiency" should not be approached in a doctrinaire or pedantic manner. Thus, formation of zones in backward areas for providing proper facilities and services will improve the efficiency and not retard it.[6]

4 Judicial review—scope of—interest of zonal railway only Railways administration is a specialized field. It has to cater to the needs of the entire country. It has limited resources and limited number of railway engines and railway coaches, particularly AC coaches, more particularly AC-1 class coaches. Railway will have to distribute and utilise the available resources and the available rolling stock equitably, uniformly and appropriately to serve all the sections of the country. It is for the railway

1 Section 3(1) of Railways Act 1989.
2 Section 3(2), *ibid.*
3 Section 3(4), *ibid.*
4 *State of VP* v *Moula Bux* AIR 1962 SC 145; (1962)2 SCR 848; (1961)2 SCJ 549; *Uttam Bala* v *Asstt. Collector of Customs and Central Excise* AIR 1970 SC 1765; (1970)2 SCC 396; (1971)1 SCR 714.
5 See Black's *Law Dictionary.*
6 *Federation of Railway Officers Association* v *Union of India* (2003)4 SCC 289.

administration to decide where, how and when trains or coaches should be added or the timings should be changed. The courts do not have data inputs, specialised knowledge or the technical skills required for running the railways. The High Court cannot, therefore, interfere in regard to only one sector without having any material or information about the requirements of other sectors available, existing demands and constraints, safety requirements etc. Nor can the High Court direct introduction of trains or additional coaches of a particular category or direct change in timings of a train. Changing the timings of a train is not a simple process, but requires coordinated efforts, as it would affect the timings of other trains. Courts, bureaucracy and political leaders should give up the tendency to compel and pressurize the railway administration to cater to only parts of the country particularly to the State or area to which they belong. Any attempt to promote only regional interests would affect the national interest. The railways should have the freedom and independence to grow, develop, improve and serve the nation.[7]

4. Appointment of General Manager. (1) The Central Government shall, by notification, appoint a person to be the General Manager of a Zonal Railway.

(2) The general superintendence and control of a Zonal Railway shall vest in the General Manager.

1 Scope The Central Government is empowered to appoint a person as the General Manager of a Zonal Railway by notification in the Official Gazette. The General Manager is vested with the power of superintendence and control of a Zonal Railway. There is no corresponding provision of s. 4 of the Act to the old Act.

2 Meaning of terms

(a) *Notification.* See the definition in s. 2(26) of the Act.

(b) *Zonal railway*. See the definition of s. 2(42) of the Act.

(c) *Superintendence.* It connotes the act of superintending, care and oversight for the purpose of direction and with authority to direct. It implies administrative control enabling the authority enjoying such power to give directions to the subordinate to discharge its administrative duties and function in the manner indicated in an order.[8]

(d) *Control.* The word "control" is synonymous with superintendence, management or authority to direct, restrict or regulate. Control is exercised by a superior authority in exercise of its supervisory power.[9]

7 *Union of India* v *J.D. Suryavanshi* AIR 2011 SC 3605.

8 *State of Bihar* v *J.A.C. Saldanha* (1980)1 SCC 554; AIR 1980 SC 326; (1980)2 SCR 16.

9 *Shamrao Vithal Co-op. Bank Ltd.* v *Kasargode P. Maliya* AIR 1972 SC 1248; (1972)4 SCC 600; (1972)2 SCR 162.

(e) *Vest.* The word "vest" clothes varied colours from the context and situation in which it is used in a statute of rule.[10] It means to confer ownership (of property) on a person or to give a person an immediate, fixed right of present or future enjoyment.[11]

[12][CHAPTER IIA

Rail Land Development Authority

4A. Establishment of Railway Land Development Authority. The Central Government may, by notification, establish an authority to be called the Rail Land Development Authority to exercise the powers and discharge the functions conferred on it by or under this Act.

4B. Composition of Authority. (1) The authority shall consist of a Chairman, Vice-Chairman and not more than four other members.

(2) The Member Engineering, Railway Board shall be the Chairman, *ex-officio* of the Authority.

(3) The Vice-Chairman and three other members shall be appointed by the Central Government from amongst persons who are or have been working in the Civil Engineering, Finance and Traffic disciplines of any railway administration and having adequate experience in the relevant discipline as the Central Government may consider necessary.

(4) The Central Government shall also appoint a member who shall be a person from outside the railway administration and having adequate experience in such field as it may consider necessary.

4C. Terms and conditions of appointment of Vice-Chairman and other Members. The terms and conditions of appointment of the Vice-Chairman and the other Members of the Authority, other than the Chairman, and the manner of filling casual vacancies among them shall be such as may be prescribed.

4D. Functions of Authority. (1) The Authority shall discharge such functions and exercise such powers of the Central Government in relation to the development of railway land and as are specifically assigned to it by the Central Government.

(2) In particular, and without prejudice to the generality of the foregoing power, the Central Government may assign to the Authority all or any of the following functions, namely:

(*i*) to prepare scheme or schemes for use of railway land in conformity with the provisions of this Act;

(*ii*) to develop railway land for commercial use as may be entrusted by the Central Government for the purpose of generating revenue by non-tariff measures;

10 *Vatticherukuru Village Panchayat* v *Nori V. Deekshithulu* (1991)2 SCR 531; 1991 Supp (2) SCC 228; JT 1991(5) SC 140.

11 Black's *Law Dictionary*, 10th Ed., 2014.

12 *Inserted* by the Railways (Amendment) Act 2005 (w.e.f. 30.8.2006).

(*iii*) to develop and provide consultancy, construction or management services and undertake operation in India in relation to the development of land and property;

(*iv*) to carry out any other work or function as may be entrusted to it by the Central Government, by order in writing.

4E. Powers of Authority to enter into agreements and execute contracts. Subject to such directions as may be given to it by the Central Government, the Authority shall be empowered to enter into agreements on behalf of the Central Government and execute contracts.

4F. Procedure of transaction of business of Authority. The Authority shall have power to regulate, by means of regulations made by it, its own procedure (including quorum at its meetings) and the conduct of all business to be transacted by it, the constitution of Committees and Sub-Committees of Members and the delegation to them any of the powers (excluding the power to make regulations under this Chapter) and to perform duties of the Authority.

4G. Appointment of officers and other employees of Authority. (1) For the purpose of enabling it efficiently to discharge its functions under this Act, the Central Government shall provide the Authority with such officers and other employees, and the Authority shall, subject to the rules as may be made by the Central Government in this behalf, appoint, whether on deputation or otherwise, such number of officers and other employees as it may deem necessary.

(2) The salaries and allowances payable to, and the other terms and conditions of service of, the officers and other employees appointed for the purpose of the Authority, shall be such as may be prescribed.

4H. Salaries, allowances, etc. to be defrayed out of Consolidated Fund of India. The salaries and allowances payable to the Vice-Chairman and other Members of the Authority and the administrative expenses including the salaries, allowances and pension payable to the officers and other employees of the Authority shall be defrayed out of the Consolidated Fund of India.

4-I. Power of Authority to make regulations. (1) The Authority may, with the previous approval of the Central Government, make regulations, consistent with this Act and the rules made thereunder for carrying out the provisions of this Chapter.

(2) Every regulation made by the Authority under this Chapter shall be laid, as soon as may be after it is made, before each House of Parliament, while it is in session for a total period of thirty days which may be comprised in one session or in two or more successive sessions, and if before the expiry of the session immediately following the session or the successive sessions aforesaid, both Houses agree in making any modification in the regulation or both Houses agree that the regulation should not be made, the regulation shall thereafter have effect only in such modified form or be of no effect, as the case may be; so, however, that any such modification or annulment shall be without prejudice to the validity of anything previously done under that regulation.]

Scope This Chapter IIA has been inserted in the Railways Act 1989 by the Railways (Amendment) Act 2005 with effect from 30.8.2006. This Chapter relates to rail land development authority. To attain the main objective certain new provisions have been included in this Chapter. Sections 4A to 4-I of the Act now specifically deal with—(*i*) the establishment of railway land development authority; (*ii*) composition of that authority; (*iii*) terms and conditions of appointment of vice-chairman and other members, the chairman of the authority to be the member of engineering railway board, *ex officio*; (*iv*) functions of the authority; (*v*) powers of the authority to enter into agreements and execute contracts; (*vi*) procedure of transaction of business of authority; (*vii*) appointment of officers and other employees of authority; (*viii*) salaries, allowances etc. to be defrayed out of consolidated fund of India; and (*ix*) power of authority to make regulations.

CHAPTER III
Commissioners of Railway Safety

5. Appointment of Chief Commissioner of Railway Safety and Commissioners of Railway Safety. The Central Government may appoint a person to be the Chief Commissioner of Railway Safety and such other persons as it may consider necessary to be the Commissioners of Railway Safety.

1 Scope This section provided for appointment of the Chief Commissioner of Railway Safety and such other persons as Commissioners of Railway Safety by the Central Government. There is no corresponding provision of s. 5 in the old Act.

2 Meaning of word—Commissioner This word is defined in s. 2(6) of the Railways Act 1989 to mean the Chief Commissioner of Railway Safety or the Commissioner of Railway Safety.

6. Duties of Commissioner. The Commissioner shall—

(*a*) inspect any railway with a view to determine whether it is fit to be opened for the public carriage of passengers and report thereon to the Central Government as required by or under this Act;

(*b*) make such periodical or other inspections of any railway or of any rolling stock used thereon as the Central Government may direct;

(*c*) make an inquiry under this Act into the cause of any accident on a railway; and

(*d*) discharge such other duties as are conferred on him by or under this Act.

Duties of Commissioner Section 6 of the Act lays down the duties of the Commissioner which are as follows:

(*a*) He shall inspect any railway with a view to determine whether it is fit to be opened for the public carriage of passengers and report thereon under s. 22 of the Act.

(*b*) He shall make periodical or other inspection of any railway or of any rolling stock as defined in s. 2(37) of the Act.

(*c*) He shall make an enquiry under s. 114 of the Act into causes of any accident on a railway.

(*d*) He shall discharge some other duties as are conferred on him by or under the Act.

Section 6 of the Act has no corresponding provision in the old Act.

7. Powers of Commissioner. Subject to the control of the Central Government, the Commissioner, whenever it is necessary so to do for any of the purposes of this Act, may—

(*a*) enter upon and inspect any railway or any rolling stock used thereon;

(*b*) by order in writing addressed to a railway administration, require the attendance before him of any railway servant and to require answers or returns to such inquiries as he thinks fit to make from such railway servant or from the railway administration; and

(*c*) require the production of any book, document or material object belonging to or in the possession or control of any railway administration which appears to him to be necessary to inspect.

Scope Section 7 of the Act empowers the Commissioner to exercise the following powers subject to the ultimate control of the Central Government:

(1) He may enter upon and inspect any railway or any rolling stock used thereon. The words "railway" and "rolling stock" have been defined in s. 2(31) and s. 2(37) of the Act respectively.

(2) He may, by an order in writing addressed to a railway administration, require the attendance before him of any railway servant and to answer to such queries as he may think fit. This power is to be construed in the context of the definitions of the terms "railway administration" in s. 2(32), "railway servant" in s. 2(34) of the Act.

(3) He may require the production of any book, document or material objects belonging to or in the possession or control of any railway administration which appears to be necessary to inspect in determining any issue.

This section has no corresponding provision in the old Act.

8. Commissioner to be public servant. The Commissioner shall be deemed to be a public servant within the meaning of section 21 of the Indian Penal Code (45 of 1860).

1 Scope The Commissioner shall be deemed to be a public servant within the meaning of s. 21 of the Indian Penal Code 1860 for the purpose of invoking penal provision against a person.

2 "Public servant" The term "public servant" is defined in s. 21 of the Indian Penal Code to denote certain persons as public servants. A public servant is an authority by Government or a semi-Government body.[1] Under the old Act as it stood before the amendment in 1955, every railway servant was deemed to be a public servant only for the purposes of Chapter IX of the Indian Penal Code which deals with offences by or relating to public servants. But subsequent to that amendment all railway servants have become public servants not only for the limited purposes but also generally. They are also public servants under the Prevention of Corruption Act 1947 (now repealed by the Prevention of Corruption Act 1988).[2] Persons employed by a Railway owned and managed by the Government of India are public servants.[3]

> **9. Facilities to be afforded to Commissioners.** A railway administration shall afford to the Commissioner all reasonable facilities for the discharge of the duties or for the exercise of the powers imposed or conferred on him by or under this Act.

Scope A railway administration as defined in s. 2(32) of the Act shall afford all reasonable facilities to the Commissioner for the purpose of discharging his duties under s. 6 of the Act or for the exercise of powers under s. 7 of the Act. There is no corresponding provision of s. 9 in the old Act.

> **10. Annual report of Commissioners.** The Chief Commissioner of Railway Safety shall prepare in each financial year an annual report giving a full account of the activities of the Commissioners during the financial year immediately preceding the financial year in which such report is prepared and forward, before such date as may be specified by the Central Government, copies thereof to the Central Government, and that Government shall cause that report to be laid, as soon as may be, after its receipt before each House of Parliament.

Scope The Chief Commissioner of Railway Safety shall prepare an annual report giving a full account of the activities of the Commissioner during the financial year immediately preceding the financial year in which such report is prepared for laying before each House of Parliament with copies to the Central Government within the time specified by it. This section has also no corresponding provision in the old Act.

1 *Ramesh* v *State of Maharashtra* AIR 1985 SC 1655; (1985)3 SCC 606.
2 *Ram Krishan* v *State of Delhi* AIR 1956 SC 476; 1956 CrLJ 837; 1956 SCR 182; 1956 SCJ 432. See *Bajrang Lal* v *State of Rajasthan* (1976)2 SCC 217; AIR 1976 SC 1008; (1976)3 SCR 497.
3 *R.R. Chowdhury* v *S. Ganguly* AIR 1959 SC 1310.

CHAPTER IV
Construction and Maintenance of Works

11. Power of Railway Administrations to execute all necessary works. Notwithstanding anything contained in any other law for the time being in force, but subject to the provisions of this Act and the provisions of any law for the acquisition of land for a public purpose or for companies, and subject also, in the case of a non-Government railway, to the provisions of any contract between the non-Government railway and the Central Government, a railway administration may, for the purposes of constructing or maintaining a railway—

(*a*) make or construct in or upon, across, under or over any lands, or any streets, hills, valleys, roads, railway, tramways, or any rivers, canals, brooks, streams or other waters, or any drains, water-pipes, gas-pipes, oil-pipes, sewers, electric supply lines, or telegraph lines, such temporary or permanent inclined-planes, bridges, tunnels, culverts, embankments, aquaducts, roads, lines of railways, passages, conduits, drains, piers, cuttings and fences, in-take wells, tube wells, dams, river training and protection works as it thinks proper;

(*b*) alter the course of any rivers, brooks, streams or other water courses, for the purpose of constructing and maintaining tunnels, bridges, passages or other works over or under them and divert or alter either temporarily or permanently, the course of any rivers, brooks, streams or other water courses or any roads, streets or ways, or raise or sink the level thereof, in order to carry them more conveniently over or under or by the side of the railway;

(*c*) make drains or conduits into, through or under any lands adjoining the railway for the purpose of conveying water from or to the railway;

(*d*) erect and construct such houses, warehouses, offices and other buildings, and such yards, stations, wharves, engines, machinery apparatus and other works and conveniences as the railway administration thinks proper;

[1][(*da*) developing any railway land for commercial use;]

(*e*) alter, repair or discontinue such buildings, works and conveniences as aforesaid or any of them and substitute others in their stead;

(*f*) erect, operate, maintain or repair any telegraph and telephone lines in connection with the working of the railway;

(*g*) erect, operate, maintain or repair any electric traction equipment, power supply and distribution installation in connection with the working of the railway; and

(*h*) do all other acts necessary for making, maintaining, altering or repairing and using the railway.

1 *Inserted* by the Railways (Amendment) Act 2005 (w.e.f. 30.8.2006).

1 Corresponding provision This section corresponds to s. 7 of the old Act.

2 Scope Section 11 of the Act lays down power of railway administration as defined in s. 2(32) of the Act to execute all necessary works as specified in cls. (*a*) to (*h*) of the said s. 11.

3 Power of railway administrations A railway administration has unfettered power to execute all works necessary for construction and maintenance of a railway. But such works must be reasonably necessary for the authorised purpose.[2] A Railway Company under s. 7 of the old Act had power to lay lines without consent of a Municipality across a public street vested in that Municipality.[3] Where a warehouse was used for the purpose of storing customers' goods in the ordinary course of railway business, no prosecution would be for not obtaining licence under the Bengal Licensed Warehouse and Fire Brigade Act 1893.[4] [The said Act has been repealed by the West Bengal Fire Services Act 1950.]

4 Legal duties of railway administration

(a) *Level crossing.* Level crossing is a public crossing and therefore it is the legal duty of the railway administration to assure reasonable safety. The most obvious way of doing it is to provide gates or chain barriers and to post a watchman who should close them shortly before the train passes. Failure to do so by itself an act of negligence provided the railway administration had taken other steps, such as fixing caution board on either side, sufficient in the circumstances to caution effectively a passer-by of average alertness and prudence.[5] Though it is not a statutory duty to give warning of approaching train a railway line crossing which is used a thorough fare, yet it is implied and inherent function to be discharged by the railway administration. Failure to do so would amount to negligence on its part.[6]

Writing on a sign board requiring a vehicle to stop and also requiring a conductor of a vehicle to get down for checking as contemplated in Rules were not visible in a case. In absence of sign board there is no statutory duty of a driver or a conductor of a vehicle. But there is a common law duty of a driver or a conductor to stop, see and hear the coming of any railway carriage. Where the driver did not stop the vehicle at the level crossing, he was held to be guilty of negligence even though there was no curve or obstruction at the point. Since there was no caution board nor

2 *B.B.L. Rly.* v *Nrisinghacharan* AIR 1943 Cal 128; ILR (1943)1 Cal 172. See also *Subhas Dutta* v *Union of India* (2001)1 CLJ 653; Cal LT 2001(3) HC 36.

3 *Bombay Municipality* v *G.I.P. Rly.* AIR 1916 PC 3.

4 *Marriott* v *Municipality of Howrah* AIR 1941 Cal 319; ILR (1941)1 Cal 345.

5 *Union of India* v *Lalman Badri Prosad* AIR 1954 VP 17.

6 *Swarnalata Barua* v *Union of India* AIR 1963 Assam 117.

was there any other indication to show that the road was cutting across railway line or gate, handrail to alert passer-by, the railway was deemed to be negligent.[7]

(b) *Toilets at railway station.* Where the railway demolish toilets at the railway station, on the ground that they were being used by trespassers, the action amounted to cessation of essential facilities. Thus, the railway was directed to provide the toilet facilities at the station by pay and use system.[8]

(c) *Construction of canal.* Construction of canal causing loss to the plaintiff due to diminished flow of water from the river was not authorised by s. 11(*h*) of the Railways Act 1989 which corresponds to s. 7(*f*) of the old Act.

5 Upgradation of railway halt to railway station Upgradation of railway halt to railway station is an administrative decision. Thus such decision cannot be interfered with by a writ court even if one is aggrieved by such upgradation.[9]

6 Exercise of powers A Railway Company is bound to exercise the power given to it in derogation of individual rights with moderation and discretion and not negligently.[10] Where a Railway Company, in the course of making a cutting through rock, at a short distance from a private dwelling-house, conducted its operations by blasting, and pieces of stone were hurled on to the buildings and into the garden, injunction was granted by court.[11] Where the Legislature has authorised a railway to be made, by means of a tunnel or otherwise, through a town or close to houses or buildings, the Railway Company is bound, not only to make compensation for any damage which the making of the railway may occasion to adjacent erections, but also, where there may be two modes of constructing their works, to adopt that course which would do the least amount of injury to the neighbouring property.[12] When an injury is caused by the improper construction or maintenance of a railway, resulting in the fall of an embankment, the Railway Company is liable for such improper construction or maintenance of the railway.[13]

7 *Union of India* v *United India Insurance Co. Ltd.* AIR 1998 SC 640; (1997)8 SCC 683; JT 1997(8) SC 653.
8 *Ramanathsekhar* v *Pandho Padhaya* AIR 1987 Bom 98; 1986 Mah LR 812; (1986)2 Bom CR 60.
9 *Ram Ashray Prasad Sinha* v *Union of India* AIR 2000 Pat 160.
10 *Biscoe* v *G.E. Rly.* LR 16 Eq 636; 21 WR 902.
11 *Arnold* v *Furness Rly.* 22 WR 613.
12 *Freehold General Land Investment Co.* v *Metropolitan District Rly.* 14 LT 96.
13 *G.W. Rly. of Canada* v *Braid* 8 LT 31; 11 WR 444.

It cannot be said that a Railway Company has exceeded its powers when owing to the exigencies of the railway it closes a level crossing at a certain point and fulfils all the requirements which the law imposes upon it by providing another level crossing at another point lower down the line.[14] The power conferred by s. 7 of the old Act on a Railway Company to carry a line of railway across the street subject to the control thereof by the Governor-General is not cut down by the Land Acquisition Act 1894.[15]

7 Acquisition of land by railways Acquisition of land by railways is not necessary for erection of transmission towers. Railway electrification is in public interest. Thus the railway is not bound to acquire land under the Land Acquisition Act 1894.[16]

8 Power to execute works for transmission lines It is true that in terms of s. 27D of the Indian Electricity Act 1910 and ss. 12 and 14 of the Electricity Act 2003, no person other than those authorized or otherwise exempted by an Appropriate Government or the Appropriate Commission shall be entitled to engage in the activities of transmission or distribution of electricity. In the case of railways, the transmission of electricity is governed by the provisions of the Railways Act 1989 and not by the enactments governing electricity. Section 11(*a*) and (*g*) of the Railways Act 1989 clearly authorize the railways to construct necessary transmission lines, dedicated for their own purpose. It is not possible to read this section in a restricted manner in which it was sought to be conveyed. This is because the principal part of s. 11 authorizes the Railway Administration to execute all necessary works for the purpose of constructing or maintaining railways. Sub-section (sic) (*a*) of the section authorizes Railways to make or construct in or upon, across, under or over any lands electric supply lines. Under sub-sec. (sic) (*g*) thereof, the railways are authorized to erect, operate, maintain or repair any electric traction, equipment, power supply and distribution installation in connection with working of the railways. This will certainly include construction of transmission lines. That being so there is no substance in the submission made by the Uttar Pradesh State Electricity Board. Thus railways having entered into power purchase agreement with the National Thermal Power Corporation Ltd. with the permission of the Government was perfectly legal.[17]

14 *Harilal* v *B.B. & C.I. Railway* 44 Bom 705; AIR 1920 Bom 155.
15 *Taylor* v *Collector of Purnea* 14 Cal 423; *Municipal Corporation of Bombay* v *G.I.P. Railway* 41 Bom 291 (PC); 21 CWN 447; 25 CLJ 209; *Gangaram* v *Secretary of State* 30 Cal 576.
16 *Md. Waris* v *Union of India* AIR 2006 Jhar 116.
17 *Union of India* v *Chairman, UP State Electricity Board* AIR 2012 SC 960.

12. Power to alter the position of pipe, electric supply line, drain or sewer, etc. (1) A railway administration may, for the purpose of exercising the powers conferred on it by this Act, alter the position of any pipe for the supply of gas, water, oil or compressed air, or the position of any electric supply line, drain or sewer:

Provided that before altering the position of any such pipe, electric supply line, drain or sewer, the railway administration shall give a notice indicating the time at which the work of such alteration shall commence, to the local authority or other person having control over the pipe, electric supply line, drain or sewer.

(2) The railway administration shall execute the work referred to in sub-section (1) to the reasonable satisfaction of the local authority or the person receiving the notice under the proviso to sub-section (1).

1 Corresponding provision This section corresponds to s. 8 of the Indian Railways Act 1890.

2 Scope This section empowers a railway administration to alter the position of any pipe, electric supply line, drain or sewer for the purpose of exercising power vested upon it under this Act. But it is incumbent on the railway administration to give notice indicating the time at which the work of such alteration shall commence to the local authority or other affected persons.

3 Meaning of local authority The expression "local authority" used in proviso to s. 12(1) of the Act is to be construed in the context of s. 3(31) of the General Clauses Act 1897.[18] Local authority is an administrative unit of a local government or a group of people responsible for the government of a particular area, town or city.[19]

13. Protection for Government property. Nothing in sections 11 and 12 shall authorise—

(*a*) a railway administration of the Government railway to do anything on or to any works, lands or buildings vested in, or in the possession of, a State Government without the consent of that Government; and

(*b*) a railway administration of a non-Government railway to do anything on or to any works, lands or buildings vested in, or in the possession of, the Central Government or a State Government, without the consent of the Government concerned.

1 Corresponding provision This section corresponds to s. 8A of the Indian Railways Act 1890.

2 Scope Section 13 has two parts: (*a*) A railway administration of the Government railway shall not do anything with regard to the property of the State Government without its consent. (*b*) A railway administration

18 *Surya Kant Roy* v *Imamul Hak* (1975)1 SCC 531; AIR 1975 SC 1053; (1975)3 SCR 909; *Union of India* v *R.C. Jain* AIR 1981 SC 951; (1981)2 SCC 308; (1981)2 SCR 854.

19 Black's *Law Dictionary,* 10th Ed., 2014.

of a non-Government railway shall not do anything with regard to property of the Central Government or State Government without the consent of the Government concerned. The terms "Government railway" and "non-Government railway" are to be construed in the light of the definitions in s. 2(20) and s. 2(25) of the Railways Act 1989 respectively.

14. Temporary entry upon land to remove obstruction, to repair or to prevent accident. (1) Where in the opinion of a railway administration—

(*a*) there is imminent danger that any tree, post or structure may fall on the railway so as to obstruct the movement of rolling stock; or

(*b*) any tree, post, structure or light obstructs the view of any signal provided for movement of rolling stock; or

(*c*) any tree, post or structure obstructs any telephone or telegraph line maintained by it,

it may take such steps as may be necessary to avert such danger or remove such obstruction and submit a report thereof to the Central Government in such manner and within such time as may be prescribed.

(2) Where in the opinion of a railway administration—

(*a*) a slip or accident has occurred; or

(*b*) there is apprehension of any slip or accident to any cutting, embankment or other work on a railway,

it may enter upon any lands adjoining the railway and do all such works as may be necessary for the purpose of repairing or preventing such slip or accident and submit a report thereof to the Central Government in such manner and within such time as may be prescribed.

(3) The Central Government may, after considering the report under sub-section (1) or sub-section (2), in the interest of public safety, by order, direct the railway administration that further action under sub-section (1) or sub-section (2) shall be stopped or the same shall be subject to such conditions as may be specified in that order.

1 Corresponding provision Section 14(1) corresponds to s. 15 of the old Act and s. 14(2) corresponds to s. 9 of the old Act.

2 Scope Section 14 of the Act deals with the authority of a railway administration to enter temporarily upon land to remove obstruction, to repair or to prevent imminent danger. The Central Government may also on the basis of a report submitted to it direct that in the interest of public safety further action shall be stopped or the same shall be subject to such conditions as may be specified in the order.

3 Powers to construct works Powers to construct works are to be exercised with ordinary care and skill and with some regard to the property and rights of others. They are granted on the condition sometimes expressed as in the Indian Railways Act 1890 and sometimes under where not so expressed that the undertakers "shall do as little damages as possible" in the exercise of the statutory powers. Therefore, if a person or body of persons having statutory authority for construction of works exceeds or abuses the powers conferred by the legislature the remedy of a person injured is by action or suit and not by a proceeding for compensation under the statute which has been so transgressed.[20]

15. Payment of amount for damage or loss. (1) No suit shall lie against a railway administration to recover any amount for any damage or loss caused in the exercise of the powers conferred by any of the foregoing provisions of this Chapter.

(2) A railway administration shall pay or tender payment for any damage or loss caused in the exercise of the powers conferred by any of the foregoing provisions of this Chapter, and in case of a dispute as to the sufficiency of any amount so paid or tendered or as to the persons entitled to receive the amount, it shall immediately refer the dispute for the decision of the District Judge of the district and his decision thereon shall be final:

Provided that where the railway administration fails to make a reference within sixty days from the date of commencement of the dispute, the District Judge may, on an application made to him by the person concerned, direct the railway administration to refer the dispute for his decision.

(3) The reference under sub-section (2) shall be treated as an appeal under section 96 of the Code of Civil Procedure, 1908 (5 of 1908), and shall be disposed of accordingly.

(4) Where any amount has been paid as required by sub-section (2), the railway administration shall, notwithstanding anything in any other law for the time being in force, be discharged from all liabilities to any person whatsoever in respect of any amount so paid.

1 Corresponding law This section corresponds to s. 10 of the old Act which deals with payment of compensation for damage caused by lawful exercise of power under Chapter III of the Act.

2 Scope This section provides for certain pre-conditions for filing a suit against a railway administration to recover any amount for loss or damage caused to an aggrieved party in exercise of powers by the railway administration under ss. 11, 12, 13 and 14 of the Act. The first condition is that if a railway administration pays or tenders payment for damages or loss to the aggrieved party, no suit will lie. But if any dispute is raised as to the sufficiency of the amount so paid or tendered, the railway administration shall immediately refer the dispute to the District Judge within whose jurisdiction the subject matter of the dispute falls for his decision. The second condition is that if the railway administration fails to make any reference of dispute to the District Judge within 60 days from

20 *H.H. The Gaekwad of Baroda* v *Gandhi Kasturchand* 27 Bom 344; 30 IA 69.

the date of commencement of the dispute, the aggrieved party may make an application to the District Judge who will then direct the railway administration to refer the dispute for his decision. When such reference is made on the direction of the District Judge, the reference will be treated as an appeal under s. 96 of the Code of Civil Procedure 1908. The District Judge will then dispose of the appeal in accordance with law. If the railway administration makes payment in pursuance with the order of the District Judge in the appeal under s. 96, Code of Civil Procedure. The railway administration will be discharged from all liabilities to any person whatsoever in respect of any amount under the order of the appeal court so paid.

3 Remedy of person injured If a person or body of persons having statutory authority for construction of works exceeds or abuses the powers conferred by the legislature, the remedy of a person injured is by action or suit and not by a proceeding for compensation under the statute which has been so transgressed.[21] Where a Collector refuses to adjudicate upon a claim for damages under the (old) Act, s. 10, cl. (2), does not debar a claimant from seeking his remedy in a civil court.[1]

16. Accommodation works. (1) A railway administration shall make and maintain the following works for the accommodation of the owners and occupiers of lands adjoining the railway, namely:

(*a*) such crossings, bridges, culverts and passages over, under or by the sides of, or leading to or from, the railway as may, in the opinion of the State Government, be necessary for the purpose of making good any interruptions caused by the railway to the use of the lands through which the railway is made; and

(*b*) all necessary bridges, tunnels, culverts, drains, water sources or other passages, over, under or by the sides of the railway, of such dimensions as will, in the opinion of the State Government, be sufficient at all times to convey water as freely from or to the lands lying near or affected by the railway as it was before the making of the railway or as nearly as possible.

(2) Subject to the other provisions of this Act, the works specified in sub-section (1) shall be made at the cost of the railway administration during or immediately after the laying out or formation of the railway over the lands traversed and in such a manner as to cause as little damage or inconvenience as possible to persons interested in the lands or affected by the works:

Provided that—

(*a*) a railway administration shall not be required to make any accommodation works in such a manner as would prevent or obstruct the working or using of the railway, or to make any accommodation

21 30 IA 69; 27 Bom 344 (supra).
1 *Rameswar* v *State of West Bengal* 34 Cal 470.

works with respect to which the owners or occupiers of the lands have been paid compensation in consideration of their not requiring the said works to be made;

(*b*) save as hereinafter, in this Chapter, provided, no railway administration shall be liable to execute any further or additional accommodation works for the use of the owners or occupiers of the lands after the expiration of ten years from the date on which the railway passing through the lands was first opened for public traffic;

(*c*) where a railway administration has provided suitable accommodation work for the crossing of a road or stream and the road or stream is afterwards diverted by the act or neglect of the person having the control thereof, the railway administration shall not be compelled to provide any other accommodation work for the crossing of such road or stream.

(3) The State Government may specify a date for the commencement of any work to be executed under sub-section (1) and, if within three months next after that date, the railway administration fails to commence the work or having commenced it, fails to proceed diligently to execute it, the Central Government shall, on such failure being brought to its notice by the State Government, issue such directions to the railway administration as it thinks fit.

Explanation. For the purposes of this section, the expression "lands" shall include public roads.

1 Corresponding provision This section corresponds to s. 11 of the Indian Railways Act 1890. The purport and object of both the sections are similar.

2 Scope In *Governor-General-in-Council* v *Municipal Council, Madura*[2] LORD SIMONDS, interpreting the provisions of ss. 11 and 12 of the (old) Indian Railways Act (corresponding to ss. 16 and 17 of the Railways Act 1989) observed as follows: "The provisions which for the purpose of this case appear to demand particular examination are in s. 11(1)(*b*), s. 11(3)(*b*) and s. 12. But it is important to observe upon the general structure of s. 11 that sub-sec. (3) of s. 11 contains nothing more than provisos on the two preceding sub-sections, and in this connection the well-established rule of construction must be borne in mind which was thus stated by LORD WATSON in *West Derby Union* v *Metropolitan Life Assurance Society*.[3] "I am perfectly clear that, if the language of the enacting part of the statute does not contain the provisions which are said to occur in it, you cannot derive these provisions by implication from a proviso." What then do sub-secs. (1) and (2) of (old) s. 11, upon which sub-sec. (3) contains provisos, enact? They appear to be unambiguous. The obligation imposed upon the Railway, so far as relevant for the present

2 AIR 1949 PC 39.

3 [1897] AC 647 at p. 652; 66 LJ Ch 726.

purpose, is to make and maintain a culvert which will in the opinion of the Provincial Government be sufficient at all times to convey water as freely from or to the lands lying near or affected by the railway as before the making of the railway or as nearly so as may be. It is clear that the obligation under (old) sub-sec. (1) is to be measured by the conditions existing at the time of the making of the railway. The words "as freely, etc." set the standard and define the obligation. The adjoining owner is not to be injuriously affected by the construction of the railway: the *status quo* is to be preserved. The nature of the works having been prescribed by (old) sub-sec. (1), the time within which they are to be carried out is laid down by (old) sub-sec. (2). Then come the provisos in (old) sub-sec. (3). The proviso in (*a*) is a qualification upon the statutory obligation for the benefit of the railway. So also is the proviso in (*c*). It is the proviso in (*b*) that is immediately relevant and it must first be observed that it is in form negative. It does not purport to vest any new rights in any person or to impose any new duty upon the railway. Whence then arises the obligation of the railway, for which the respondent contends to make accommodation works, the standard of which is determined not by the conditions existing at the making of the railway but by those which come into existence at a later date? It must be conceded that it can only arise, if at all, from an affirmative which is to be implied from the negative. And this affirmative must amount to no less than a new obligation upon the railway, at the instance of the adjoining owner within ten years or of the Provincial Government for all time, at its own cost to make accommodation works rendered necessary or convenient by a change of conditions which has taken place after the railway has been constructed. Their Lordships cannot accept such an implication as a fair interpretation of the proviso, unless it is otherwise meaningless. But it is by no means impossible to give meaning and effect to the proviso without doing violence to its language and to the canon of construction to which reference has been made. For the "further or additional accommodation works" mentioned in the sub-section may be required not because those originally constructed have become insufficient owing to a change of conditions, but because the adjoining landowner has miscalculated what the conditions originally existing would demand for the commodious use of his land, and is given an opportunity within a limited time of making a fresh demand. Nor would it be unreasonable in the circumstances which prevail in large parts of India that an unlimited time should be given to the Government to require that the same standard should be established and maintained.

But it further appears to them that some assistance is given to this view by the language of (old) s. 12. The section is clearly intended to cover works which the railway is not bound to construct under (old) s. 11. For they are works which are to be erected at the expense of the adjoining owner or the Government. It is difficult to see what scope the section can have, if under (old) s. 11(3)(*b*) the Government can for all time requisition such further or additional accommodation works as the commodious use of adjoining land may from time to time with altering conditions require. There is, however, a clear reconciliation between the sections if the former relates only to such works as the physical conditions and use of the land at the time of construction of the railway required.

3 Closing of level crossing Railway company can close the level crossing at a certain point and open a new line at any point lower down the line and thus fulfil all the requirements which the law imposes upon it.[4] When a railway crosses a public carriage road, the authorities owning the railway are under obligation to erect and maintain good and sufficient gates across the road and must employ proper persons to maintain the same, so as to keep it open for the traffic and the vehicles to pass when no train is likely to pass and to shut the same when a train is approaching. S.R. 229/3(*b*) seems to have been made under the Railways Act and, as such, has the force of law.[5]

4 Warehouse The railway administration has power to erect and use such warehouses as may be necessary to it in connection with the construction of the railway and it has this power irrespective of any provisions to the contrary which may be contained in any other enactment.[6]

5 Central Government to control construction and maintenance of all railways The scheme of the Indian Railways Act is that all railways administered by the Government should work under the immediate and general administrative control of the Central Government. As it is the Central Government which has been given authority under s. 7(2) of the (old) Indian Railways Act (corresponding to s. 11 of the Railways Act 1989) to control all matters relating to the construction and maintenance of railways, so it would clearly be inconsistent with the general scheme of the Act which the Act contemplates should be shared between the Central Government and some local authority as the exercise of any controlling power by a local authority might lead in certain cases to the frustration of the object with which a railway had been constructed.[7]

6 Construction of new line Where a new broad gauge line was sought to be laid, clearance from the Environment Act 1986 was not required even though, the line passes over rivers, etc. in view of s. 11 of the old Act (corresponding to s. 16 of the Railways Act 1989) under which the Environment Act cannot stop the construction and maintenance of railways.[8]

4 *Harilal* v *B.B. & C.I. Railway* AIR 1920 Bom 155; 44 Bom 705.
5 *Union of India* v *Hindustan Lever Ltd.* AIR 1975 P&H 259.
6 *Mariott* v *Municipality of Howrah* AIR 1941 Cal 319; ILR (1941)1 Cal 345.
7 *Mariott* v *Municipality of Howrah* AIR 1941 Cal 319; ILR (1941)1 Cal 345.
8 *Goa Foundation* v *Konkan Rly. Corpn.* AIR 1992 Bom 471.

7 Accommodation work The objection under s. 11 of the old Act was measured by the conditions existing at time of the making of the railway.[9] Where petitioners were allotted plots of railway siding for unloading and accommodating consignments carried by railways for which they were required to pay licence fees as per agreement, the railway authority could not demand more licence fees beyond that stipulated in the agreement.[10]

8 Meaning of word—"land" The word "land" in restricted sense means soil, but in its legal acceptation it is a generic term, comprehending every species of ground, soil, or earth whatsoever, as meadows, pastures, woods, moors, waters, marshes, furze and heath. It also includes houses, mills, castles and other buildings. Besides, an indefinite extent upwards, it extends downwards to the globe centre, hence the maxim, *cujus est solum ejus est usque ad caelum et ad inferos*, or more curtly expressed *cujus est solum ejus est altum* (whoever owns the soil everything up to the sky and down to the depths). The word "land" would be variously understood by different persons. In a legal sense it is a comprehensive expression.[11] Land is an immovable and indestructible three-dimensional area consisting of a portion of the earth's surface, the space above and below the surface, and everything growing on or permanently affixed to it.[12] In s. 16 the word "land" has been used to include public roads as well.[13]

17. Power of owner, occupier, State Government or local authority to cause additional accommodation works to be made. (1) If an owner or occupier of any land affected by a railway considers the works made under section 16 to be insufficient for the use of the land, or if the State Government or a local authority desires to construct a public road or other work across, under or over a railway, such owner or occupier, or, as the case may be, the State Government or the local authority, may, at any time, require the railway administration to make at the expense of the owner or occupier or of the State Government or the local authority, as the case may be, such further accommodation works as are considered necessary and are agreed to by the railway administration.

(2) The accommodation works made under sub-section (1) shall be maintained at the cost of the owner or occupier of the land, the State Government or the local authority, at whose request the works were made.

(3) In the case of any difference of opinion between the railway administration and the owner or occupier, the State Government or the local authority, as the case may be, in relation to—

(*i*) the necessity of such further accommodation works; or

(*ii*) the expenses to be incurred on the construction of such further accommodation works; or

9 *Governor-General-in-Council* v *Municipal Council, Madura* AIR 1949 PC 39.
10 *Biswa Ranjan Bose* v *G.M., Eastern Rly.* Cal LT 1991(2) HC 53.
11 *P. Rami Reddy* v *State of AP* (1988)3 SCC 433; AIR 1988 SC 1626; JT 1988(3) SC 47.
12 Black's *Law Dictionary,* 10th Ed., 2014.
13 *Explanation* to s. 16, Railways Act 1989.

(*iii*) the quantum of expenses on the maintenance of such further accommodation works,

it shall be referred to the Central Government whose decision thereon shall be final.

1 **Corresponding provision** This section corresponds to s. 12 of the old Act.

2 **Applicability of the section** Section 17 of the Railways Act 1989 has no application where the further accommodation work is carried on in pursuance of Government orders.[14]

3 **Right of municipal corporation** Right of the Municipal Corporation of Bombay to enter upon railway premises and lay pipes between their mains after giving the Railway Company reasonable notice is not taken away by s. 12 of the old Act (corresponding to s. 17 of the Railways Act 1989).[15] Section 12 of the old Act was intended to cover works which the railway was bound to construct.[16]

18. Fences, gates and bars. The Central Government may, within such time as may be specified by it or within such further time, as it may grant, require that—

(*a*) boundary marks or fences be provided or renewed by a railway administration for a railway or any part thereof and for roads constructed in connection therewith;

(*b*) suitable gates, chains, bars, stiles or hand-rails be erected or renewed by a railway administration at level crossings;

(*c*) persons be employed by a railway administration to open and shut gates, chains or bars.

1 **Corresponding provision** This section corresponds to s. 13 of the old Act.

2 **Scope** This section empowers the Central Government to require within specified time, fences, gates and bars to be provided by a railway administration for protection and safety of the public.

There would be a breach of statutory duty under s. 18 of the Act (corresponding to s. 13 of the old Act) only if a demand has been made by the Central Government. When there was no notification under s. 13(*c*) of the old Act requiring a suitable gate for erection by the railway administration at places where a railway crosses a public road on the level, there was no legal obligation on the part of the railway to erect a gate and post a gateman at a level crossing arose.[17] The degree of care

14 *S.I. Railway Co.* v *Municipal Council, Madura* AIR 1945 Mad 427; ILR (1946) Mad 333.

15 *G.I.P. Rly.* v *The Municipality Council, Madras* (1899)23 Bom 358.

16 *Governor-General-in-Council* v *Municipal Council, Madura* AIR 1949 PC 39.

17 *Divisional Railway Manager* v *K.S.R.T.C.* (1997)2 Civ LJ 495.

required where there is no statutory duty cast upon the railway administration to erect a gate or to post a gateman at the level crossing would certainly be more at a public level-crossing than that required at accommodation crossing. The question of erection of gate would depend on the situation of the crossing, visibility of the rail track from the road, any sharp turns or curves and the extent of the road traffic etc.[18]

There is a duty to close gates of level crossing when trains pass. Negligence to close the gate is a statutory negligence.[19] At railway level crossing where red lights and gongs are provided, these warn and alter the public sufficiently in advance not to proceed further. The closing of the gate is an additional step taken by the railway as provided in s. 13 of the old Act and Rules 227 to 235 of the General Rules framed under s. 47 of the old Act.[20]

3 Negligence and neighbourhood principle Where railways are involved in dangerous or perilous operations, they are, at common law, to take reasonable and necessary care, on the "neighbourhood" principle, even if the provisions of s. 18 of the Railways Act 1989 (corresponding to s. 13(*c*) and (*d*) of the old Act) is not attracted. The claim for compensation before the Motor Accidents Claims Tribunal for collusion between railway and bus at unmanned railway level crossing for breach of statutory duty on part of the railway was held to be maintainable.[1]

4 Safeguards against accidents at level crossing Section 18 of the Railways Act 1989 (corresponds to s. 13 of the old Act) empowers the Central Government to require the railway administration to provide *inter alia* gates at level crossings on railway-track. As regards the level crossing over a public carriage road, the railway administration must employ persons to open and shut such gates etc. and such gates must be kept constantly closed against the roads on both sides of the railway, except when horses, cattle or vehicles are crossing and must be closed again as soon as such traffic has passed. The persons employed by the railway administration to open and shut the gates are, before opening them, bound to see that the railway is safe for the purpose of crossing, and if they open the gate when

18 *Shankerrao Laxman Rao* v *Union of India* AIR 1959 MP 128; 1959 Jab LJ 112.

19 *Union of India* v *Hindustan Lever Ltd.* AIR 1975 Punj 259.

20 *V. Krishnappa Naidu* v *Union of India* AIR 1976 Mad 95; (1976)2 Mad LJ 353; 88 Mad LW 704.

1 *Union of India* v *United India Insurance Co. Ltd.* AIR 1998 SC 640; (1997)8 SCC 683; JT 1998(8) SC 653.

it is unsafe to cross, they do so at the railway administration's peril.[2] In the case of *Union of India* v *Lalman Badri Prosad,*[3] KRISHNAN, CJ. observed as follows:

> "A level crossing is on the one hand a danger spot in view of the possible movement of trains, and on the other is an invitation to the passerby. This is a public crossing and not merely one by private accommodation. Therefore it is the legal duty of the railway to assure reasonable safety. The most obvious way of doing it is to provide gates or chain barriers and to post a watchman who should close them shortly before the train passes. But failure to do so is not by itself an act of negligence provided that the railway had taken other steps sufficient in those circumstances to caution effectively a passerby of average alertness and prudence. At a reasonable distance on either side, prominently written boards can be affixed, asking the road-users to beware of trains. If the track on either side is visible from near the caution board or within a short distance from the crossing, this would be sufficient because a diligent road-user could look round and see the train. On the other hand, if there is a bend in the track or there are trees or bush in between, or the road on either side of the crossing is very far below the level of the railway track, or for any other similar reasons the track is not visible beyond a short distance, then even the caution boards are useless. In that case, gates are indicated. Similarly board may be affixed along the railway, say, half to three-fourths of a mile in either direction calling upon the engine driver to whistle. A whistle by driver can supplement, but cannot replace gates or caution boards as a device to protect the users of a crossing. All these aspects of maintaining a level crossing have been considered by the railway authorities in accordance with s. 7, Indian Railways Act and guiding principles have been laid down."

The statutory duty of the railway administration mentioned in s. 18 of the Railways Act 1989 (corresponding to s. 13 of the old Act) does not arise till the Central Government requires it to do so.[4] Where there is no such statutory duty, the question of erecting a gate would depend on the situation of the crossing, visibility of the rail track from the road, any sharp turns or curves and the extent of the road traffic, etc.[5] Even though (old) s. 13(*c*) of the Indian Railways Act provides that the Central Government may

2 *Yatayat Nigam* v *Union of India* AIR 1983 Raj 17; 1982 Raj LR 673; ILR (1982)32 Raj 724; 1982 Raj LW 391; 1982 WLN 258.

3 AIR 1954 VP 17.

4 *Harak Chand* v *Union of India* AIR 1958 MP 93; 1957 MPLJ 617. Also see *Mokshada Sundari Ghosh* v *Union of India* AIR 1971 Cal 480; 75 CWN 964.

5 *Shankerrao Laxman Rao* v *Union of India* AIR 1959 MP 128; 1959 Jab LJ 112.

require a railway administration to erect suitable gates, chains, bars, stiles or hand-rails at places where a railway crosses a public road on the level, the statutory duty of the railway administration does not arise, till the Central Government requires it to do so. In the absence of any such requisition, there is no such liability on the railway administration to do any of the things mentioned in the section. Mere absence of the gate or the gateman or the sign boards for whistling or railway track indication would not amount to an actionable negligence of the railway administration as it could not be said that the railway administration has not used its discretion reasonably and that it was liable for actionable negligence inasmuch as the road traffic did not justify putting up the gate and the gateman at the railway crossing.[6] But the railway's duty to give warning at level crossing of approaching train need not be necessarily a statutory one and that duty is implied and inherent in the function of running railways and failure to give warning at level crossing amounts to negligence on railway's part.[7]

The observations in *Swarnalata Barua's* case to the effect that where a railway line crosses a busy road at such a point that the incoming trains are not visible due to houses and bridges until the passer is on the railway track there is no question of contributory negligence inasmuch as the first duty in such case is cast upon the railway authorities to arrange for the safety of the passers and it is the obvious duty of the railway administration to take adequate steps to warn the public of the approaching train, was quoted with approval in a Patna case. The road passing along the level crossing without any gate or even without a fencing raised by two poles with iron chain fixed at both sides of the road on the poles, was claimed to be a private road. Even if the road was a private road but the public in general were allowed to pass even as licensees, that should hardly make any difference.[8]

Mere knowledge or a reasonable belief about the approaching of any train or engine is a sufficient warning to the public not to cross the level crossing.[9] In a manned level crossing one of the gates was open. A truck entered through the unclosed gate when the engine hit the truck killing one and injuring others it was a case of negligence.[10]

6 *Pravin Chandra Mulji* v *Union of India* (1969)6 Guj LT 75.

7 *Swarnalata Barua* v *Union of India* AIR 1963 Assam 117.

8 *Ramesh* v *Union of India* AIR 1965 Pat 167.

9 *V. Krishnappa Naidu* v *Union of India* AIR 1976 Mad 95; (1976)2 Mad LJ 353; 88 Mad LW 704.

10 *Mata Prasad* v *Union of India* 1978 ACJ 155 (All).

5 Accident at level crossing and contributory negligence A defence based on contributory negligence proceeds on the assumption that the person raising the defence was himself negligent and that negligence would not afford a cause of action to the plaintiff, either because of its remoteness to the accident or because the plaintiff who had the last opportunity to avoid the accident, did not do so, or that he did not act with reasonable care and prudence. This negligence of the claimant was the direct cause of the accident but for which the accident would not have taken place. The principle of contributory negligence is that the plaintiff's negligence has contributed in part to his own harm and, thus reduces the damages payable to him and as such it affects the measure of damages.[11]

The question of contributory negligence came up for consideration. Where a railway line crosses a busy road at such a point that the incoming train is not visible until the passer is on the railway track, there is no question of the contributory negligence, in case of accident inasmuch as the first duty in such a case is cast on the railway authorities to arrange for the safety of the passers and that it would be the obvious duty of the railway administration, whether as invitors or licensors, to take adequate steps either to fix there a gate or a chain or at least to post a man to warn the drivers of the vehicles of an approaching train. The high heaps of construction materials for the road were stacked on both flanks of the road. The first appellate court held that in view of the stack obstructing driver's visibility, he ought to have been vigilant before crossing the railway track. Patna Division Bench in appeal differing from this view, held in such a situation there is no scope for application of the principle *volenti non fit injuria* or the doctrine of contributory negligence.[12] *Ramesh's* case was followed in *Union of India* v *S. Ghosh,*[13] which held that if it is an invitation to cross; person going across meeting with accident is not guilty of contributory negligence and is entitled to compensation.

6 Railway's liability against trespasser and liability for error of judgment It is a maxim based on elementary principle that no man can take advantage of his own wrong (*Nallus Commodum Caper Potest De Injuria Sua Propria*). As stated in Maxwell: a man may not take advantage of his own wrong, nor can he plead in his interest, a self-created necessity.[14] On this principle a trespasser sustaining injury cannot recover damages if he had himself courted the accident, though the accident may have been partly due to the negligence of the owner of the land or his servants and agents. In a case

11 *Yatayat Nigam* v *Union of India* AIR 1983 Raj 17; 1982 Raj LR 673; ILR (1982)32 Raj 724; 1982 Raj LW 391; 1982 WLN 258.

12 *Ramesh* v *Union of India* AIR 1965 Pat 167.

13 AIR 1973 Pat 129.

14 Maxwell on *Interpretation of Statutes*, 12th Ed., p. 212.

there was no requisition by the Central Government for raising gate at a place where railway track crossed a road. The accident occurred. The person, who met the accident was held as a trespasser. Further, although the driver was wrong in anticipating that the victim would check himself, it was merely an error of judgment. On facts in that case it was held no action would lie for such error of judgment.[15]

7 Fencing Section 18(*a*) of the Railways Act 1989 (corresponding to s. 13(*a*) of the old Act) gives power to the Central Government to require the railway, among other matters, to provide fences and to maintain the same. In the absence of such requirement, there is no statutory obligation on the railway to fence the railway track on both sides when the railway track runs between residential houses and quarters on both sides. Therefore where one trespasses on the railway line which is not secured by fencing and is injured, the railway cannot be held liable.[16]

8 Enumeration of precautions—not exhaustive The enumeration of precautions mentioned in s. 18 of the Railways Act 1989 (corresponding to s. 13 of the old Act) is not exhaustives. When the defects in contrivance of an engine are not mentioned, it cannot be on the authorities urged that such defect would not make a railway company liable. It is not possible to give a complete catalogue of all sorts of precaution which must be taken by a railway company to ensure that no damage is done to owners of neighbouring lands. Each case must depend upon its own circumstances and the court has to decide whether there was negligence to such an extent as to make the company liable.[17]

9 Duty on railway administration There is obviously no statutory duty on a railway administration to cut all grass from the railway track and to see that at no place any grass grows or that any dry grass is allowed to remain there. At the same time this may be a reasonable precaution which a railway administration should take. Where the dry grass is allowed to remain on the railway track so close to the rails and so high in stature it may amount to negligence on the part of railway administration. The railway administration are bound not only to use due care as to the construction and use of their engines, but also to use due care in keeping the line of railway and the land belonging to them on each side of it in a proper state. The method of maintaining a fire line of 10 ft. clear of grass as required by the standing orders is no doubt a reasonable precaution.

15 *Mokshada Sundari Ghosh* v *Union of India* AIR 1971 Cal 480; 75 CWN 964.
16 *Vijay Shanker* v *Union of India* AIR 1958 Punj 246; 60 Punj LR 221.
17 *B.B. & C.I. Rly.* v *Dwarka Nath* AIR 1936 All 771; 58 All 771.

But the company is bound to see that the order is carried out. If it has allowed the rules to become ineffective and allows dry fodder to be placed on the fire line, the railway company is guilty of actionable negligence.[18]

10 Nuisance to public and remedy The term 'nuisance' as used in law is not capable of exact definition. It has been used with meaning varying in extent by the old writers, and even at the present day there is no entire agreement whether certain acts or omissions shall be classed as nuisances or whether they do not fall under other divisions of the law of tort.

Nuisance is that activity which arises from unreasonable, unwarranted or unlawful use by a person of his own property, working obstruction or injury to right of another, or to the public, and producing such material annoyance, inconvenience and discomfort that law will presume resulting damage.[19] And public nuisance is an unreasonable interference with a right common to the general public, such as a condition dangerous to health, offensive to community moral standards, or unlawfully obstructing the public in the free use of public property.[20]

Where there is no restriction imposed on the railway company as regards their right to use locomotive only at scheduled times or at a particular speed, whatever nuisance or inconvenience may be caused to the public in general it cannot be regarded as a violation of any duty which the company owe to them or as amounting to any negligence which may form a ground of action so far as they are concerned.[21] If a railway company makes the railway so as to intercept a public highway in a manner not authorised by any Act, by putting up gates at the point of intersection, so as to constitute a nuisance in blocking up the way, a passenger along the highway is not justified in prostrating those gates to make his way good across the line of railway, but should seek his remedy by *mandamus* or other legal proceeding against the company.[22]

Unless the engine using smoke-emitting fuel is so defectively constructed as to be incapable of consuming its own smoke, though used with proper care no penalty is incurred by the company. Consequently no penalty attaches where the engine, though properly constructed on the principle of consuming its own smoke, is so carelessly used on a railway as to emit

18 *B.B. & C.I. Rly.* v *Dwarka Nath* AIR 1936 All 771; 58 All 771.
19 Mitra's *Legal and Commercial Dictionary*, 6th Ed, 2006.
20 Black's *Law Dictionary,* 10th Ed., 2014.
21 *B.N. Railway Co.* v *Tara Prosad* AIR 1928 Cal 504; 48 CLJ 45.
22 *Ellis* v *L. & S.W. Rly.* 26 LJ Ex 349; 5 WR 682.

instead of consuming its smoke.[23] A railway company has not, by reason of the powers in its special Act enabling it to work the line in the way most convenient to itself, any power to commit an act which, if committed by a private person, would constitute a nuisance, and be restrainable by injunction accordingly.[24]

11 Demolition of unmanned level crossing In absence of any requirement mandated by the Central Government, no duty is cast on the railway administration to make provision for the fence/gate/bar as contemplated in s. 18 of the Railways Act 1989. The railway administration foreseeing possibility of accidents and to prevent illegal activities of clandestine siphoning of forest produce and mining minerals has decided to close/demolish the unmanned level crossing involved. In doing so, the availability of alternative route to obviate public inconvenience has also been taken note of. In view of such a conscious decision taken by all the Authorities concerned, no intervention by the High Court in exercise of extra-ordinary writ jurisdiction in matter of PIL under Art. 226 of the Constitution is warranted.[25]

12 Installation of check gate at level crossing Railway administration has statutory obligation to provide sufficient safeguards to level crossing by putting railway check gate and keeping it closed at time when trains are due to pass at level crossing area. Putting up such safeguards could avoid accident. Railway administration failed to discharge their statutory duty by not posting guard or installing check gate. Non-compliance of statutory obligations would amount to negligence.[26]

> **19. Overbridges and underbridges.** (1) Where a railway administration has constructed lines of rails across a public road at the same level, the State Government or the local authority maintaining the road, may, at any time, in the interest of public safety, require the railway administration to take the road either under or over the railway by means of a bridge or arch with convenient ascents and descents and other convenient approaches, instead of crossing the road on the level, or to execute such other works as may, in the circumstances of the case, appear to the State Government or the local authority maintaining the road to be best adapted for removing or diminishing the danger arising from the level crossing.

23 *Manchester, Sheffield & Lincolnshire Rly.* v *Wood* 29 LJ MC 29; 8 WR 24.

24 *Smith* v *Midland Rly.* 37 LT 224; 25 WR 861.

25 *Damodar Mishra* v *East Coast Rail* AIR 2015 Ori 62.

26 *Shyam Naik* v *General Manager, East Coast Railways, Rail Vihar, Bhubaneswar* AIR 2012 Ori 38 relying on *N.K.V. Bros. (P) Ltd.* v *M. Karumai Ammal* AIR 1980 SC 1354.

(2) The railway administration may require the State Government or the local authority, as the case may be, as a condition of executing any work under sub-section (1), to undertake to pay the whole of the cost of the work and the expense of maintaining the work, to the railway administration or such proportion of the cost and expenses as the Central Government considers just and reasonable.

(3) In the case of any difference of opinion between the railway administration and the State Government or the local authority, as the case may be, over any of the matters mentioned in sub-section (1), it shall be referred to the Central Government, whose decision thereon shall be final.

1 Corresponding provision This section corresponds s. 14 of the old Act.

2 Scope Section 19 of the Act provides that a railway administration shall require the State Government or local authority to consent to the construction of overbridges and underbridges across a public road in the interest of public safety. The railway administration shall also require the State Government or local authority to share the cost of such work and expenses of maintenance thereof. In case of any difference of opinion between the railway administration on the one hand and the State Government or local authority on the other hand, it shall be referred to the Central Government which decision shall be final. Sub-section (3) of s. 19 provides for a statutory arbitration machinery for determination of a dispute between the railway administration and the State Government or local authority as the case may be.

20. Power of Central Government to give directions for safety. Notwithstanding anything contained in any other law, the Central Government may, if it is of the opinion that any work undertaken or may be undertaken, is likely to alter or impede the natural course of water flow or cause an increase in the volume of such flow endangering any cutting, embankment or other work on a railway, issue directions in writing to any person, officer or authority responsible for such work to close, regulate or prohibit that work.

Scope Section 20 empowers the Central Government to give direction to any person or authority for safety.

There is no corresponding provision of s. 20 in the old Act.

[1][CHAPTER IV-A
Land Acquisition for a Special Railway Project

20A. Power to acquire land etc. (1) Where the Central Government is satisfied that for a public purpose any land is required for execution of a special railway project, it may, by notification, declare its intention to acquire such land.

1 *Inserted* by Railways (Amendment) Act 2008 (w.r.e.f. 31.01.2008).

(2) Every notification under sub-section (1), shall give a brief description of the land and of the special railway project for which the land is intended to be acquired.

(3) The State Government or the Union territory, as the case may be, shall for the purposes of this section, provide the details of the land records to the competent authority, whenever required.

(4) The competent authority shall cause the substance of the notification to be published in two local newspapers, one of which shall be in a vernacular language.

20B. Power to enter for survey, etc. On the issue of a notification under sub-section (1) of section 20A, it shall be lawful for any person, authorised by the competent authority in this behalf, to—

(*a*) make any inspection, survey, measurement, valuation or enquiry;

(*b*) take levels;

(*c*) dig or bore into sub-soil;

(*d*) set out boundaries and intended lines of work;

(*e*) mark such levels, boundaries and lines placing marks and cutting trenches; or

(*f*) do such other acts or things as may be considered necessary by the competent authority.

20C. Evaluation of damages during survey, measurement, etc. The damages caused while carrying out works on land such as survey, digging or boring sub-soil, marking boundaries or cutting trenches or clearing away any standing crop, fence or forest or doing such other acts or things which may cause damages while acting under section 20B particularly relating to land which is excluded from acquisition proceeding shall be evaluated and compensation shall be paid to the persons having interest in that land, within six months from the completion of the said works.

20D. Hearing of objections, etc. (1) Any person interested in the land may, within a period of thirty days from the date of publication of the notification under sub-section (1) of section 20A, object to the acquisition of land for the purpose mentioned in that sub-section.

(2) Every objection under sub-section (1), shall be made to the competent authority in writing, and shall set out the grounds thereof and the competent authority shall give the objector an opportunity of being heard, either in person or by a legal practitioner, and may, after hearing all such objections and after making such further enquiry, if any, as the competent authority thinks necessary, by order, either allow or disallow the objections.

Explanation.—For the purposes of this sub-section, "legal practitioner" has the same meaning as in clause (*i*) of sub-section (1) of section 2 of the Advocates Act, 1961 (25 of 1961).

(3) Any order made by the competent authority under sub-section (2) shall be final.

20E. Declaration of acquisition. (1) Where no objection under sub-section (1) of section 20D has been made to the competent authority within the period specified therein or where the competent authority has disallowed the objections under sub-section (2) of that section, the competent authority shall, as soon as may be, submit a report accordingly to the Central Government and on receipt of such report, the Central Government shall declare, by notification, that the land should be acquired for the purpose mentioned in sub-section (1) of section 20A.

(2) On the publication of the declaration under sub-section (1), the land shall vest absolutely in the Central Government free from all encumbrances.

(3) Where in respect of any land, a notification has been published under sub-section (1) of section 20A for its acquisition, but no declaration under sub-section (1) of this section has been published within a period of one year from the date of publication of that notification, the said notification shall cease to have any effect:

Provided that in computing the said period of one year, the period during which any action or proceedings to be taken in pursuance of the notification issued under sub-section (1) of section 20A is stayed by an order of a court shall be excluded.

(4) A declaration made by the Central Government under sub-section (1) shall not be called in question in any court or by any other authority.

20F. Determination of amount payable as compensation. (1) Where any land is acquired under this Act, there shall be paid an amount which shall be determined by an order of the competent authority.

(2) The competent authority shall make an award under this section within a period of one year from the date of the publication of the declaration and if no award is made within that period, the entire proceedings for the acquisition of the land shall lapse:

Provided that the competent authority may, after the expiry of the period of limitation, if he is satisfied that the delay has been caused due to unavoidable circumstances, and for the reasons to be recorded in writing, he may make the award within an extended period of six months:

Provided further that where an award is made within the extended period, the entitled person shall, in the interest of justice, be paid an additional compensation for the delay in making of the award, every month for the period so extended, at the rate of not less than five per cent of the value of the award, for each month of such delay.

(3) Where the right of user or any right in the nature of an easement on, any land is acquired under this Act, there shall be paid an amount to the owner and

any other person whose right of enjoyment in that land has been affected in any manner whatsoever by reason of such acquisition, an amount calculated at ten per cent of the amount determined under sub-section (1), for that land.

(4) Before proceeding to determine the amount under sub-section (1) or sub-section (3), as the case may be, the competent authority shall give a public notice published in two local newspapers, one of which shall be in a vernacular language inviting claims from all persons interested in the land to be acquired.

(5) Such notice shall state the particulars of the land and shall require all persons interested in such land to appear in person or by an agent or by a legal practitioner referred to in sub-section (2) of section 20D, before the competent authority, at a time and place and to state the nature of their respective interest in such land.

(6) If the amount determined by the competent authority under sub-section (1) or as the case may be sub-section (3) is not acceptable to either of the parties, the amount shall, on an application by either of the parties, be determined by the arbitrator to be appointed by the Central Government in such manner as may be prescribed.

(7) Subject to the provisions of this Act, the provisions of the Arbitration and Conciliation Act, 1996 (26 of 1996) shall apply to every arbitration under this Act.

(8) The competent authority or the arbitrator while determining the amount of compensation under sub-section (1) or sub-section (6), as the case may be, shall take into consideration—

(*a*) the market value of the land on the date of publication of the notification under section 20A;

(*b*) the damage, if any sustained by the person interested at the time of taking possession of the land, by reason of the severing of such land from other land;

(*c*) the damage, if any, sustained by the person interested at the time of taking possession of the land, by reason of the acquisition injuriously affecting his other immovable property in any manner, or his earnings;

(*d*) if, in consequences of the acquisition of the land, the person interested is compelled to change his residence or place of business, the reasonable expenses, if any, incidental to such change.

(9) In addition to the market-value of the land as above provided, the competent authority or the arbitrator, as the case may be, shall in every case award a sum of sixty per centum on such market-value, in consideration of the compulsory nature of the acquisition.

20G. Criterion for determination of market value of land. (1) The competent authority shall adopt the following criteria in assessing and determining the market value of the land,—

(*i*) the minimum land value, if any, specified in the Indian Stamp Act, 1899 (2 of 1899) for the registration of sale deeds in the area, where the land is situated; or

(*ii*) the average of the sale price for similar type of land situated in the village or vicinity, ascertained from not less than fifty per cent of the sale deeds registered during the preceding three years, where higher price has been paid;

whichever is higher.

(2) Where the provisions of sub-section (1) are not applicable for the reason that:

(*i*) the land is situated in such area where the transactions in land are restricted by or under any other law for the time being in force in that area; or

(*ii*) the registered sale deeds for similar land as mentioned in clause (*i*) of sub-section (1) are not available for the preceding three years; or

(*iii*) the minimum land value has not been specified under the Indian Stamp Act, 1899 (2 of 1899) by the appropriate authority,

the concerned State Government shall specify the floor price per unit area of the said land based on the average higher prices paid for similar type of land situated in the adjoining areas or vicinity, ascertained from not less than fifty per cent of the sale deeds registered during the preceding three years where higher price has been paid, and the competent authority may calculate the value of the land accordingly.

(3) The competent authority shall, before assessing and determining the market value of the land being acquired under this Act,—

(*a*) ascertain the intended land use category of such land; and

(*b*) take into account the value of the land of the intended category in the adjoining areas or vicinity,

for the purpose of determination of the market value of the land being acquired.

(4) In determining the market value of the building and other immovable property or assets attached to the land or building which are to be acquired, the competent authority may use the services of a competent engineer or any other specialist in the relevant field, as may be considered necessary by the competent authority.

(5) The competent authority may, for the purpose of determining the value of trees and plants, use the services of experienced persons in the field of agriculture, forestry, horticulture, sericulture, or any other field, as may be considered necessary by him.

(6) For the purpose of assessing the value of the standing crops damaged during the process of land acquisition proceedings, the competent authority may utilise the services of experienced persons in the field of agriculture as he considers necessary.

20H. Deposit and payment of amount. (1) The amount determined under section 20F shall be deposited by the Central Government, in such manner as may be prescribed by that Government, with the competent authority before taking possession of the land.

(2) As soon as may be after the amount has been deposited under sub-section (1), the competent authority shall on behalf of the Central Government pay the amount to the person or persons entitled thereto.

(3) Where several persons claim to be interested in the amount deposited under sub-section (1), the competent authority shall determine the persons who in its opinion are entitled to receive the amount payable to each of them.

(4) If any dispute arises as to the apportionment of the amount or any part thereof or to any person to whom the same or any part thereof is payable, the competent authority shall refer the dispute to the decision of the principal civil court of original jurisdiction within the limits of whose jurisdiction the land is situated.

(5) Where the amount determined under section 20F by the arbitrator is in excess of the amount determined by the competent authority, the arbitrator may award interest at nine per cent. per annum on such excess amount from the date of taking possession under section 20-I till the date of actual deposit thereof.

(6) Where the amount determined by the arbitrator is in excess of the amount determined by the competent authority, the excess amount together with interest, if any, awarded under sub-section (5) shall be deposited by the Central Government, in such manner as may be prescribed by that Government, with the competent authority and the provisions of sub-sections (2) to (4) shall apply to such deposit.

20-I. Power to take possession. (1) Where any land has vested in the Central Government under sub-section (2) of section 20E, and the amount determined by the competent authority under section 20F with respect to such land has been deposited under sub-section (1) of section 20H with the competent authority by the Central Government, the competent authority may, by notice in writing, direct the owner as well as any other person who may be in possession of such land to surrender or deliver possession thereof to the competent authority or any person duly authorized by it in this behalf within a period of sixty days of the service of the notice.

(2) If any person refuses or fails to comply with any direction made under sub-section (1), the competent authority shall apply—

(*a*) in case of any land situated in any area falling within the metropolitan area, to the Commissioner of Police;

(*b*) in case of any land situated in any area other than the area referred to in clause (*a*), to the Collector of a district,

and such Commissioner or Collector, as the case may be, shall enforce the surrender of the land, to the competent authority or to the person duly authorized by it.

20J. Right to enter into land where land has vested in Central Government. Where the land has vested in the Central Government under section 20E, it shall be lawful for any person authorized by the Central Government in this behalf, to enter and do other act necessary upon the land for carrying out the building, maintenance, management or operation of the special railway project or part thereof or any other work connected therewith.

20K. Competent authority to have certain powers of civil court. The competent authority shall have, for the purposes of this Act, all the powers of a civil court while trying a suit under the Code of Civil Procedure, 1908 (5 of 1908) in respect of the following matters, namely:

(*a*) summoning and enforcing the attendance of any person and examining him on oath;

(*b*) requiring the discovery and production of any document;

(*c*) reception of evidence on affidavits;

(*d*) requisitioning any public record from any court or office;

(*e*) issuing commission for examination of witnesses.

20L. Utilization of land for the purpose it is acquired. (1) The land acquired under this Act shall not be transferred to any other purpose except for a public purpose, and after obtaining the prior approval of the Central Government.

(2) When any land or part thereof, acquired under this Act remains unutilized for a period of five years from the date of taking over the possession, the same shall return to the Central Government by reversion.

20M. Sharing with landowners the difference in price of a land when transferred for a higher consideration. Whenever any land acquired under this Act is transferred to any person for a consideration, eighty per cent of the difference in the acquisition cost and the consideration received, which in no case shall be less than the acquisition cost, shall be shared amongst the persons from whom the lands were acquired or their heirs, in proportion to the value at which the lands were acquired, and for the purpose, a separate fund may be maintained which shall be administered by the competent authority in such manner as may be prescribed by the Central Government.

20N. Land Acquisition Act 1 of 1894 not to apply. Nothing in the Land Acquisition Act, 1894 shall apply to an acquisition under this Act.

20-O. Application of the National Rehabilitation and Resettlement Policy, 2007 to persons affected due to land acquisition. The provisions of the National Rehabilitation and Resettlement Policy, 2007 for project affected families, notified by the Government of India in the Ministry of Rural Development *vide* number F. 26011/4/2007-LRD, dated the 31st October, 2007, shall apply in respect of acquisition of land by the Central Government under this Act.

20P. Power to make rules in respect of matters in this chapter. (1) The Central Government may, by notification, make rules to carry out the purposes of this chapter.

(2) In particular, and without prejudice to the generality of the foregoing power, such rules may provide for all or any of the following matters, namely:

(*a*) the manner of appointment of arbitrator under sub-section (6) of section 20F;

(*b*) the manner in which the amount shall be deposited with the competent authority under sub-sections (1) and (6) of section 20H;

(*c*) the manner of maintenance and administration of separate fund for the purposes of section 20M.]

1 **Objections to acquisition of land** Period of 30 days for filing objections would commence from the date of publication of the substance of notification

Note. Chapter IV-A has been *inserted* by the Railways (Amendment) Act 2008 with effect from 31.01.2008. Section 4 of the said Amending Act of 2008 has repealed the Railways (Amendment) Ordinance 2008. This new Chapter IV-A relates to land acquisition for a special railway project.

in newspapers and not from date of publication of notification in the Official Gazette.[2]

2 Acquisition of lands by railways—notification Lands covered by the notification consisted of a residential colony. In the said notification brief description of the land and purpose for which the land is intended to be acquired has been mentioned. Requirements in law under sub-sec. (2) of s. 20A of the Railways Act 1989 as amended in 2008 appear to be satisfied as the notification was issued in public interest and for special railway project. Petitioners who are land losers are required to be compensated adequately. The objections made in the representation of the petitioners have not been properly considered and decided by the respondent authorities. Therefore, fair evolution should be made by the authorities concerned keeping in mind the principle of minimum damage while achieving public purpose.[3]

3 Publication of notification in newspaper Requirement under the law of "publishing notification in a newspaper" is not an empty formality. It is definitly with "a purpose" and that "purpose" is that public at large takes "note" of the same and "acts" on the same. In matter of publication of notification under s. 20E(3) of the Railways Act 1989 as amended in 2008, the period of one year is to be reckoned from the date of publication of the notification in a "newspaper" and not in a "Official Gazette."[4]

CHAPTER V
Opening of Railways

21. Sanction of the Central Government to the opening of railway. No railway shall be opened for the public carriage of passengers until the Central Government has, by order, sanctioned the opening thereof for that purpose.

Scope The Central Government is only authorised to sanction the opening of railway for the public carriage of passenger by an order. This section corresponds to s. 18 of the old Act.

22. Formalities to be complied with before giving sanction to the opening of a railway. (1) The Central Government shall, before giving its sanction to the opening of a railway under section 21, obtain a report from the Commissioner that—

(*a*) he has made a careful inspection of the railway and the rolling stock that may be used thereon;

2 *Tukman Sinngh* v *Union of India* AIR 2011 All 51.
3 *Brajesh Kumar* v *Union of India* AIR 2013 Jhar 92 relying on *Competent Authority* v *Bangalore Jute Factory* (2005)13 SCC 477.
4 *Reghjibhai Kanjibhai Kharsan* v *Union of India* AIR 2011 Guj 67.

(*b*) the moving and fixed dimensions as laid down by the Central Government have not been infringed;

(*c*) the structure of lines of rails, strength of bridges, general structural character of the works and the size of, and maximum gross load upon, the axles of any rolling stock, comply with the requirements laid down by the Central Government; and

(*d*) in his opinion, the railway can be opened for the public carriage of passengers without any danger to the public using it.

(2) If the Commissioner is of the opinion that the railway cannot be opened without any danger to the public using it, he shall, in his report, state the grounds therefor, as also the requirements which, in his opinion, are to be complied with before sanction is given by the Central Government.

(3) The Central Government, after considering the report of the Commissioner, may sanction the opening of a railway under section 21 as such or subject to such conditions as may be considered necessary by it for the safety of the public.

1 Scope Section 22 of the Railways Act 1989 which corresponds to s. 19 of the old Act provides for certain formalities to be complied with before giving sanction by the Central Government to the opening of a railway under s. 21 of the said Act. There formalities are stated in cls. (*a*) to (*d*) of sub-sec. (1) of s. 22 of the Act. The compliance of the formalities are furnished in a report by the Commissioner appointed by the Central Government under s. 5 which is to be read with s. 2(6) of the Act. If the Commissioner is of the view that the railway cannot be opened without any danger to the public, he must stated the grounds thereof in his report. He is also required to state in the report what other requirements are to be complied with before giving the sanction by the Central Government. The Central Government may grant sanction of the opening of railway after consideration of the report of the Commissioner subject to such conditions as it may consider necessary for the safety of the public.

2 Public safety While constructing a flyover, a subway under the track is provided with walls on both side to prevent the flow of traffic over the railway line and to obviate the need of level crossing gate and to avail railway employees on duty for 24 hours at level crossing, interference in the construction of the wall was not permissible. There steps are necessary in order to facilitate "public safety".[1]

23. Sections 21 and 22 to apply to the opening of certain works. The provisions of sections 21 and 22 shall apply to the opening of the following works if they form part of, or are directly connected with, a railway used for the public

1 *Nishatganj Vyapar Mandal* v *State of UP* AIR 1994 All 84. (No compensation was awarded for affecting business prospect).

carriage of passengers and have been constructed subsequent to the giving of a report by the Commissioner under section 22, namely:

(*a*) opening of additional lines of railway and deviation lines;

(*b*) opening of stations, junctions and level crossings;

(*c*) re-modelling of yards and re-building of bridges;

(*d*) introduction of electric traction; and

(*e*) any alteration or reconstruction materially affecting the structural character of any work to which the provisions of sections 21 and 22 apply or are extended by this section.

Scope Provisions of ss. 21 and 22 apply to the opening of certain works as specified in cls. (*a*) to (*e*) of s. 23 of the Act which corresponds to s. 20 of the old Act.

24. Temporary suspension of traffic. When an accident has occurred on a railway resulting in a temporary suspension of traffic, and either the original lines of rails and works have been restored to their original standard or a temporary diversion has been laid for the purpose of restoring communication, the original lines of rails and works so restored, or the temporary diversion, as the case may be, may, without prior inspection by the Commissioner, be opened for the public carriage of passengers, subject to the following conditions, namely:

(*a*) the railway servant incharge of the works undertaken by reason of the accident has certified in writing that the opening of the restored lines of rails and works, or of the temporary diversion will not in his opinion be attended with danger to the public; and

(*b*) a notice of the opening of the lines of rails and works or the diversion shall be sent immediately to the Commissioner.

Scope Temporary suspension of traffic is permissible when an accident occurs on a railway for the purpose of restoring communication without prior inspection by the Commissioner under the following circumstances: (1) The railway servant in-charge of the work has certified in writing that owing to the accident the opening of the restored lines of rails and works or of the temporary diversion will not be attended with danger to the public; and (2) a notice of the opening of the lines of rails and works or diversion shall be sent immediately to the Commissioner. Section 24 of the Act corresponds to s. 21 of the old Act.

25. Power to close railway opened for the public carriage of passengers. Where, after the inspection of any railway opened and used for the public carriage of passengers or any rolling stock used thereon, the Commissioner is of the opinion that the use of the railway or of any rolling stock will be attended with danger to the public using it, the Commissioner shall send a report to the Central Government who may thereupon direct that—

(*i*) the railway be closed for the public carriage of passengers; or (*ii*) the use of the rolling stock be discontinued; or

(*iii*) the railway or the rolling stock may be used for the public carriage of passengers subject to such conditions as it may consider necessary for the safety of the public.

1 Scope The Commissioner appointed under s. 5 read with s. 2(6) of the Act is also empowered under s. 25 of the Act to recommend to close a railway in view of impending danger to the public for using it to the Central Government. The report of the Commissioner may contain any of the following suggestions: (1) that the railway be closed for the public carriage of passengers; or (2) that the use of the rolling stock as defined in s. 2(37) be discontinued; or (3) the railway or the rolling stock may be used for the public carriage of passengers subject to certain conditions. Such power of the Commissioner is embodied in s. 25 of the Act which corresponds to s. 23 of the old Act.

2 Base guidelines to be followed When a Committee is set up laying down various principles and guidelines for allotment of rates, the Committee should follow the base guidelines in the event of conflicting orders of the court.[2]

26. Reopening of closed railway. When the Central Government has, under section 25, directed the closure of a railway or the discontinuance of the use of any rolling stock—

(*a*) the railway shall not be reopened for the public carriage of passengers until it has been inspected by the Commissioner and its reopening is sanctioned in accordance with the provisions of this Chapter; and

(*b*) the rolling stock shall not be used until it has been inspected by the Commissioner and its reuse is sanctioned in accordance with the provisions of this Chapter.

1 Corresponding law This section corresponds to s. 24 of the old Act.

2 Scope Section 26 deals with reopening of a closed railway. A closed railway under s. 25 of the Act cannot be reopened under s. 26 of the Act without fulfilling two conditions: (1) It has been inspected by the Commissioner and its reopening for public carriage of passengers has been sanctioned in accordance with the provisions of Chapter V of the Act. (2) The rolling-stock shall not be used until it has been inspected by the Commissioner and its use is sanctioned in accordance with the provision of Chapter V of the Act.

2 *Arjun Kumar Samanta* v *Shree Ram Trading & Supply Co.* AIR 1994 Cal 156; 98 CWN 934.

27. Use of rolling stock. A railway administration may use such rolling stock as it may consider necessary for the construction, operation and working of a railway:

Provided that before using any rolling stock of a design or type different from that already running on any section of the railway, the previous sanction of the Central Government shall be obtained for such use:

Provided further that before giving any such sanction, the Central Government shall obtain a report from the Commissioner that he has made a careful inspection of the rolling stock and, in his opinion, such rolling stock can be used.

1 Corresponding provision This section corresponds to s. 24(2) and (3) of the old Act.

2 Scope Section 27 provides that a railway administration may use such rolling stock as it may consider necessary for the construction, operation and working of a railway subject to two conditions. First, where the rolling stock or design or type different from the earlier one is proposed to be used on any section of the railway, the previous sanction of the Central Government is required to be obtained. Secondly, before giving any such sanction, the Central Government shall obtain a report from the Commissioner in this regard.

3 Negligence in use of rolling stock If a railway administration performs statutory permitted acts negligently, then the railway administration will be responsible.[3] A truck loaded with waste cotton caught fire by the sparks of fire emitting from an old locomotive engine, the train running at a narrow gap from a truck parallelly to the truck. The railway was found negligent and saddled with the responsibility for damage to the goods.

28. Delegation of powers. The Central Government may, by notification, direct that any of its powers or functions under this Chapter, except section 29, or the rules made thereunder shall, in relation to such matters and subject to such conditions, if any, as may be specified in the notification, be exercised or discharged also by a Commissioner.

1 Corresponding provision This section corresponds to s. 25 of the old Act.

2 Scope Section 28 confers power on the Central Government to make rules under Chapter V except s. 29 of the Act by notification in the Official Gazette.

29. Power to make rules in respect of matters in this Chapter. (1) The Central Government may, by notification, make rules to carry out the purposes of this Chapter.

3 *Jugaldas* v *Harilal* AIR 1986 Guj 88; (1986)2 ACC 276; 1986 ACJ 743.

(2) In particular, and without prejudice to the generality of the foregoing power, such rules may provide for all or any of the following matters, namely:

(*a*) the duties of a railway administration and the Commissioner in regard to the opening of a railway for the public carriage of passengers;

(*b*) the arrangements to be made for and the formalities to be complied with before opening a railway for the public carriage of passengers;

(*c*) for regulating the mode in which, and the speed at which rolling stock used on railways is to be moved or propelled; and

(*d*) the cases in which and the extent to which the procedure provided in this Chapter may be dispensed with.

1 Corresponding provision This section corresponds to s. 22 of the old Act.

2 Scope Section 29 empowers the Central Government to make rules by a notification in the Official Gazette to carry out the purposes under Chapter V of the Act.

CHAPTER VI
Fixation of Rates

30. Power to fix rates. (1) The Central Government may, from time to time, by general or special order fix, for the carriage of passengers and goods, rates for the whole or any part of the railway and different rates may be fixed for different classes of goods and specify in such order the conditions subject to which such rates shall apply.

(2) The Central Government may, by a like order, fix the rates of any other charges incidental to or connected with such carriage including demurrage and wharfage for the whole or any part of the railway and specify in the order the conditions subject to which such rates shall apply.

1 Corresponding law This section corresponds to s. 29 of the old Act.

2 Scope Section 30 of the Act deals with power of the Central Government to fix rates for the carriage of passengers and goods from time to time by general or special order either for the whole or any part of the railway.

3 "Rates of any other charges"—meaning Definition of the word "rate" as in (old) s. 3(13) (corresponding to s. 2(35) of the Railways Act 1989) cannot be applied to the expression "rates of any other charges" occurring in (old) s. 29(2) (corresponding to s. 30(2) of the Railways Act 1989).[1]

4 Constitutional validity The provisions of (old) ss. 29 and 42 are not invalid on the ground that absolute power has been given to the Central Government to fix the rates of freight etc. for all railways including the

1 *Union of India* v *M.P. Sugar* AIR 1969 SC 630; (1969)1 SCC 320; (1969)3 SCR 75.

non-Government railways. It is also difficult to hold that the legislature has delegated its authority in the matter of regulation of rates for all railways including the non-Government railways. The power in the case of non-Government railways has to be exercised in conformity with the principles of natural justice.[2]

5 Charging at a higher rate Where the railway administration charged at a higher rate for the actual mileage covered by the passenger, there was a contravention of the provisions of (old) s. 29(1) of the Indian Railways Act.[3]

6 Promise to levy concessional tariff-rate and promissory estoppel Earlier the doctrine of executive necessity was regarded as sufficient justification for the Government to repudiate even its contractual obligation. But there occurred a radical change of outlook first in *Anglo Afgan Agencies'* case.[4] In this case with a view to give incentive to exporters of woollen goods the Textile Commissioner on behalf of the Government represented through Export Promotion Scheme that the exporters would be granted entitlement certificate of "value equal to 100 per cent of the f.o.b. value". But later the Textile Commissioner without affording to the exporter any hearing reduced the import entitlement and thereby refused to grant entitlement certificate of the full f.o.b. value. It was held by reason of the doctrine of promissory estoppel the Government is bound to issue entitlement certificate of full f.o.b. value. The Supreme Court observed the crown cannot escape by saying that estoppels do not bind the crown, for that doctrine has long been exploded. Nor can the crown escape by saying in aid the doctrine of executive necessity, that is the doctrine that the crown cannot bind itself so as to fetter its future executive action. Under Indian Jurisprudence the Government is not exempt from liability to carry out the representation made by it as to its future conduct and it cannot on some undefined and undisclosed ground of necessity or expediency fail to carry out the promise solemnly made by it, nor claim to be the Judge of its own obligation to the citizen on an *ex parte* appraisement of the circumstances in which the obligation has arisen. As stated by LORD DENNING a promise intended to be binding, intended to be acted upon, and in fact acted upon is binding.[5]

A company set up a Fertilizer Factory for manufacture of urea the main raw material of which was Naptha required to be carried by railway.

2 *Dehri Rohtas Light Railway Co. Ltd.* v *Union of India* AIR 1970 Pat 109; ILR 48 Pat 399.

3 *Dhirendra Nath* v *Dominion of India* 60 CWN 776.

4 *Union of India* v *Anglo Afgan Agencies* AIR 1968 SC 718; (1968)2 SCR 366; (1968)2 SCA 31; (1968)1 SCWR 553.

5 *London Properties Ltd.* v *High Trees House* [1947] KB 130.

The company was assured to be given a concessional tariff rate *subject to review when the traffic starts moving,* when the company just came to the position requiring Naptha to be transported to their factory, the railway administration declined to give the concession. The Railway Rates Tribunal did not accede to the plea that by reason of promissory estoppel, the railway is debarred from withdrawing the concession because the company suffered no loss. The Supreme Court overruling this approach observed: It is true in the formative period it was generally said that the doctrine of promissory estoppel cannot be invoked by the promise unless he has suffered "detriment" or "prejudice". It was often said simply, that the party asserting the estoppel must have been induced to act to his detriment. But what is now required is that the party asserting the estoppel must acted upon the assurance given to him. Must have relied upon the representation made to him. It means, the party has changed or altered the position by relying on the assurance or the representation. The alteration of position by the party is the only indispensable requirement of the doctrine. It is not necessary to prove further any damage, detriment or prejudice to the party asserting the estoppel. The Supreme Court refused to grant to the company any relief because the representation was not clear and unqualified.[6]

7 Penal demurrage charges Power of the Central Government for fixation of rate is vested with the Railway Board under the Railway Board Act 1905. The said Railway Board Act 1905 is still in force by virtue of Art. 372 of the Constitution of India. Only due to enactment of the Railways Act 1989 the Railway Board is not denuded to exercise the power of the Central Government. Therefore, the rate circular No. 74 of 2005 dated 19th December 2005 fixing rate of demurrage charges issued is to be treated as the circular issued by the Central Government and cannot be held to be beyond the purview of s. 30 of the Railways Act 1989. Paragraph 3.3 of the rate circular is not sub-delegation of legislative power by the Central Government for fixing demurrage charges. Chief Commercial Manager (CCM), Chief Operations Managers (COM) and Divisional Railway Manager (DRM) exercise statutory power by virtue of paragraph 3.3 to implement rate circular in progressive manner. Statute does not prescribe mode or manner of publication of the circular. Circular published in Railway Website, railway offices, all relevant railway establishments and terminal stations is sufficient and as such non-publication of the rate circular in Gazette would not make the said circular unenforceable. More so, penal demurrage can be implemented only after giving wide publicity and due notice of 48 hours. Lack of amenities for

6 *Delhi Cloth & General Mills* v *Union of India* AIR 1987 SC 2414; (1988)1 SCR 383; (1988)1 SCC 86; JT 1987(4) SC 35; (1987)3 SCJ 328.

loading and unloading workers in various Railway Goods Sheds cannot be ground to challenge rate circular.[7]

8 **Power to fix penal demurrage rates** Prescription of penal rates for demurrage and wharfage in Railway Board Circular is within the competence of the Railway Board under the Railways Act 1989. The said prescription is neither arbitrary nor violative of Art. 14 of the Constitution.[8]

31. Power to classify commodities or alter rates. The Central Government shall have power to—

(*a*) classify or reclassify any commodity for the purpose of determining the rates to be charged for the carriage of such commodities; and

(*b*) increase or reduce the class rates and other charges.

1 **Corresponding provision** This section corresponds to s. 42 of the old Act.

2 **Scope** Section 31 empowers the Central Government (1) to classify or reclassify the commodity, and (2) to increase or reduce the class rates and other charges.

3 **Jurisdiction of Railway Rates Tribunal** Declaration to the effect that rates between two stations are unreasonable falls within the jurisdiction of the Railway Rates Tribunal.[9]

4 **Quasi-judicial order** Although there is no provision to give reason for an order passed by the Central Government for classifying commodities or altering rates for carriage of goods by railway, yet the order is of quasi-judicial nature and as such duty is cast upon the Central Government to act judicially in such matters.[10]

5 **Charge of demurrage** When the demurrage is levied on the rates and not wagons, the same is not beyond the power of the Board or the provisions of the Act. The rules are not arbitrary or discriminatory on the ground that different basis is applied for steel plants having distinguishing features.[11]

6 **No special service by railway** When the railway authority was only taking the wagon to the adjacent siding which was part of railway station and was not created for special service and the opposite party carried goods from the point of factory premises to the wagon on their own line using

7 *Ultra Tech Cement Ltd., Chennai* v *Union of India* AIR 2015 NOC 218 (Ker).

8 *Nbk Trade Linker Pvt. Ltd.* v *Railway Board, Ministry of Railways* AIR 2013 NOC 412 (All).

9 *Union of India* v *West Coast Paper Mills Ltd.* AIR 1971 SC 349; (1970)3 SCC 606; (1971)2 SCR 594.

10 *Dehri Rohtas Light Rly. Co. Ltd.* v *Union of India* AIR 1970 Pat 109; ILR 48 Pat 399.

11 *Uttar Pradesh State Electricity Board* v *Union of India* AIR 1992 All 135.

their own engine, the railway authority could not be said to be rendering any special services to the opposite party for which they could be held liable to pay any charge beyond the normal freight charge.[12]

7 Indian Railways Conference Association Rules Rule 161A of the Indian Railways Conference Association Rules providing for recovery of penal charges for overloading from consignee is not violative of Art. 14 of the Constitution on the ground that it punishes consignee instead of delinquent consignor because the extra rate is a higher rate, that is something like a surcharge for the excess load, to meet the said expense principle of "delinquency" is not ingrained in this levy.[13]

8 Enhancement of freight charge with retrospective effect When freight charge is enhanced and claim is made with retrospective effect, a suit for injunction against railway is maintainable.[14]

> **32. Power of railway administration to charge certain rates.** Notwithstanding anything contained in this Chapter, a railway administration may, in respect of the carriage of any commodity and subject to such conditions as may be specified,—
>
> (*a*) quote a station to station rate;
>
> (*b*) increase or reduce or cancel, after due notice in the manner determined by the Central Government, a station to station rate, not being a station to station rate introduced in compliance with an order made by the Tribunal;
>
> (*c*) withdraw, alter or amend the conditions attached to a station to station rate other than conditions introduced in compliance with an order made by the Tribunal; and
>
> (*d*) charge any lump sum rate.

1 Corresponding provision This section corresponds to s. 46 of the old Act.

2 Scope Notwithstanding anything contained in Chapter VI of the Act a railway administration is empowered to (*a*) quote station to station rate, (*b*) increase, reduce or cancel after due notice station to station rate, (*c*) withdraw, alter or amend the conditions attached to a station to station rate, (*d*) charge any lump sum rate, in respect of any commodity.

3 Railway Tribunal decision and Supreme Court's jurisdiction The provision of s. 46 of the old Act (corresponding to s. 32 of the Railways Act 1989) about

12 *Union of India* v *Railway Rates Tribunal* AIR 1992 Ori 15.

13 *J.C. Textile Mills* v *Chief Commercial Superintendent, NR* 1998 AIR SCW 1804; AIR 1998 SC 1959; (1998)5 SCC 126; JT 1998(3) SC 297.

14 *Union of India* v *Modi Industries* AIR 1973 SC 1281; (1973)1 SCC 781; (1973)3 SCR 835.

the finality of the Railway Tribunal's decision would not affect the jurisdiction of the Supreme Court under Art. 136 of the Constitution.[15]

4 Demand of under charges Goods were booked and transported on payment of freight charges at class 140 by Railways themselves knowing fully well that the station was open for half rake and not full rake. Merely because forwarding station has not been notified as open for handling train load tariff, benefit of train load classification cannot be denied to consignment which otherwise fulfils all conditions prescribed for application of train load. After goods were booked and payment made for transportation of goods to destination, Railway Authorities at destination cannot charge higher amount by bringing in different classification. Demand made by Railway Authorities for payment of ₹72,736 as under charges for release of retained bags was held to be without any justification.[16]

5 Claim for refund of excess of freight charged The claimants booked bamboo cuts for transportation by Railways from New Bongaigaon to Amlai-Railways charged freight taking distance between two stations as 1769 km. via MLDT/DKAE which was longer route. But goods were transported through shorter route covering distance of 1510 km. only. Freight was charged under provision of "station to station route". As per rules, Railway Administration was obliged to carry goods by shortest route at charges by cheapest route. No material was produced contrary to the provision of the Goods Tariff Rules 1992. Railways are not to make undue profits by charging freight on basis of longer route in name of "station to station rate" and then carrying goods by shorter route. Thus, the claimants are entitled to refund to excess freight charged.[17]

CHAPTER VII
Railway Rates Tribunal

33. Constitution of the Railway Rates Tribunal. (1) There shall be a Tribunal, to be called the Railway Rates Tribunal, for the purpose of discharging the functions specified in this Chapter.

(2) The Tribunal shall consist of a Chairman and two other members to be appointed by the Central Government.

(3) A person shall not be qualified for appointment as the Chairman of the Tribunal unless he is, or has been, a Judge of the Supreme Court or of a High Court and of the other two members, one shall be a person, who, in the opinion of the Central Government, has special knowledge of the commercial, industrial or economic conditions of the country, and the other shall be a person, who, in the opinion of the Central Government, has special knowledge and experience of the commercial working of the railways.

15 *Raigarh Jute Mills Ltd.* v *Eastern Rly.* AIR 1958 SC 525; 1958 SCJ 720; 1959 SCR 236.

16 *Arihant International Ltd., Guwahati* v *Union of India* AIR 2013 NOC 160 (Gau).

17 *Kalpataru Agro Forest Enterprise* v *Union of India* AIR 2013 Gau 30.

(4) The Chairman and the other members of the Tribunal shall hold office for such period, not exceeding five years, as may be prescribed.

(5) In case the Chairman or any other member is, by infirmity or otherwise, rendered incapable of carrying out his duties or is absent on leave or otherwise in circumstances not involving the vacation of his office, the Central Government may appoint another person to act in his place during his absence.

(6) A person who holds office as the Chairman or other member of the Tribunal shall, on the expiration of the term of his office (not being an office to fill a casual vacancy), be ineligible for re-appointment to that office.

(7) Subject to the provisions of sub-sections (5) and (6), the Chairman and other members of the Tribunal shall hold office on such terms and conditions as may be prescribed.

(8) No act or proceeding of the Tribunal shall be invalidated merely by reason of—

(*a*) any vacancy in, or any defect in the constitution of, the Tribunal; or

(*b*) any defect in the appointment of a person acting as a Chairman or other member of the Tribunal.

1 Corresponding provision This section corresponds to s. 34 of the old Act.

2 Scope Section 33 of the Act provides for constitution of the Railway Rates Tribunal for the purpose of discharging certain functions as specified in Chapter VII of the Act. This special Tribunal is vested with power to follow a procedure which is appropriate and adequate for deciding a dispute whether concession granted by the railway authority in the matter of freight rates to certain mills is discriminatory. The High Court will decline to decide this dispute in a writ-petition.[1] The Tribunal can decide reasonableness of charges other than standardised terminal charges. But it cannot decide vires of the rules empowering railway to collect such amount.[2]

3 Railway Claims Tribunal—not a civil court The Railway Claims Tribunal is not a civil court being the creature of a statute.[3]

34. Staff of the Tribunal. (1) The Tribunal may, with the previous approval of the Central Government, appoint such officers and employees as it considers necessary for the efficient discharge of its functions under this Chapter.

(2) The terms and conditions of service of the officers and employees of the Tribunal shall be such as may be determined by regulations.

Corresponding law This section corresponds to s. 36 of the old Act.

1 *Ranbir Singh* v *Chief Commercial Supdt.* AIR 1961 Punj 263.
2 *Raichand* v *Union of India* AIR 1964 SC 1268; (1964)5 SCR 148.
3 *Birla Cement Works* v *G.M., Western Rly.* AIR 1995 SC 1111; (1995)2 SCC 493; JT 1995(2) SC 59.

35. Sittings of the Tribunal. **The Tribunal may sit at such place or places as it may find convenient for the transaction of its business.**

Corresponding provision This section corresponds to s. 38 of the old Act.

36. Complaints against a railway administration. **Any complaint that a railway administration—**

(*a*) is contravening the provisions of section 70; or

(*b*) is charging for the carriage of any commodity between two stations at a rate which is unreasonable; or

(*c*) is levying any other charge which is unreasonable,

may be made to the Tribunal, and the Tribunal shall hear and decide any such complaint in accordance with the provisions of this Chapter.

1 **Corresponding provision** This section corresponds to s. 41(1) of the old Act.

2 **Applicability of the section** A complaint under s. 41(1)(*b*) of the old Act (corresponding to s. 36(*b*) of the Railways Act 1989) relates to charges mentioned in s. 29(1) of the old Act (corresponding to s. 30(1) of the Railways Act 1989) while s. 41(1)(*c*) of the old Act (corresponding to s. 36(*c*) of the Railways Act 1989) relates to a complaint in respect of any other charge referred to in s. 29(2) of the old Act (corresponding to s. 30(2) of the Railways Act 1989). Clause (*c*) of s. 41(1) of the old Act therefore, includes within it a charge for carriage of any goods between places other than two stations.[4]

3 **Rate** The word "rate" means scale or amount of charges. It includes, hauling charges. Therefore a complaint against hauling charges is maintainable under s. 41(1)(*c*) of the old Act (corresponding to s. 36(*c*) of the Railways Act 1989).[5]

4 **Terminal charges** See *Raichand* v *Union of India*[6] for the nature of such charges.

5 **Wagon load rates** The expression "wagon load rate" has to be understood in the context where it occurs in conjunction with "station-to-station rate" which is the third type of rate as specified on r. 63. In the threefold classification of rates both "station-to-station rates" as well as "wagon load rates" are concessional rates, that is, they would be less than the schedule class rates. The expression "station-to-station rate" cannot be understood

4 *Union of India* v *Indian Sugar Mills Association* AIR 1968 SC 22; (1968)2 SCA 397; (1968)1 SCJ 591; (1967)3 SCR 219.

5 *Union of India* v *Motilal Padampat Sugar Mills* AIR 1969 SC 630; (1969)1 SCR 320; (1969)3 SCR 75.

6 AIR 1964 SC 1268; (1964)5 SCR 148.

as meaning merely a rate which prevails between two stations so also the expression "wagon load rate" cannot be understood to mean merely the rate applicable to a wagon load.[7]

6 Jurisdiction of the Tribunal The Tribunal has no jurisdiction to entertain or try complaints as regards the reasonableness or otherwise of rates and charges made prior to the making of the complaint. It can fix a reasonable rate for the future. It has also no power to order refund of such charges.[8] The Railway Rates Tribunal has power to fix a rate or charge with effect from the date of filing of complaint.[9] It has no power to make a direction to refund. In view of the law laid down by the Supreme Court, the Railway Rates Tribunal could not have given any relief in respect of a complaint with regard to the unreasonableness or otherwise of the rates and charges which had already become due and payable.[10]

7 Unreasonable rate The burden of proving unreasonable rates or charges under sub-sec. (1), cl. (*b*) or (*c*) of s. 41 of the old Act (corresponding to cl. (*b*) or (*c*) of s. 36 of the Railways Act 1989) rests on the complaint. In such cases it is relevant to consider mainly the working costs of the railway administration and other material circumstances. The special or concession rates charged in one zone cannot be regarded as the sole basis for charges in other zones.[11]

Fixation of differential freight rates by railway is not necessarily discriminatory and violative of Art. 14 of the Constitution of India.[12] Where the Railway Rates Tribunal declares that the charge made by the Railway Board levying tariff at the standard rates but on the footing that for each kilometre the goods are transported the charge will be levied at three times the standard rate is reasonable and discriminatory, the Tribunal does not exceed its jurisdiction.[13] Sections 27, 28 and 41 of the (old) Act (corresponding to ss. 70, 36 of the Railways Act 1989) do not estop the Central Government from imposing restriction or from interfering with traffic facilities or from practising discrimination.[14]

7 *Western Railway, Bombay* v *R.R. Tribunal* AIR 1955 Mad 513; ILR (1956) Mad 67; (1956)1 MLJ 417.
8 *Upper Doab Sugar Mills Ltd.* v *Shahdara (Delhi) Saharanpur Light Railway Co. Ltd.* AIR 1963 SC 217; (1963)2 SCR 333; 1963 SCD 303.
9 *Union of India* v *Railway Rates Tribunal* AIR 1975 Mad 28; (1975)1 Mad LJ 96; 88 Mad LW 204.
10 *Union of India* v *Indian Sugar Mills Association* AIR 1968 SC 22; (1967)3 SCR 219; (1968)1 SCJ 591; (1968)2 SCA 397.
11 *Raigarh Jute Mills* v *Eastern Railway* AIR 1958 SC 525; 1958 SCJ 720.
12 *Ranvir Singh* v *Chief Commercial Superintendent* AIR 1961 Punj 263.
13 *Union of India* v *West Coast Paper Mills Ltd.* AIR 1971 SC 349; (1971)2 SCR 594; (1970)3 SCC 606.
14 *Hiralal Sutwala* v *The State* AIR 1953 Nag 58; ILR (1952) Nag 770; 1953 CrLJ 48.

8 Appeal to Supreme Court Where finding of the Tribunal proceeds upon appreciation of evidence which has been examined in great detail, the finding of the Tribunal cannot be challenged in appeal with special leave under Art. 136 of the Constitution of India.[15] When the principles adopted by the Railway Rates Tribunal in deciding complaint are not in any way incorrect or do not suffer from any such error as would justify in examining the whole evidence considered by the Tribunal, it is not necessary for the Supreme Court to discuss in detail in the case and go into the question as regular court of fact.[16]

9 Siding and maintenance charges Siding and maintenance charges are fixed by the Railway Rates Tribunal not only on the basis of All India Cost incurred by railways but also on the zonal basis. Thus, the question of closing the siding in 1996 was not tenable.[17]

10 Complaint—jurisdiction of Tribunal—writ jurisdiction Complaint questioning reasonableness of punitive charges levied under ss. 73 and 82 of the Railways Act 1989 can be filed before Railway Claim Tribunal functioning on the date when demand was made. Rates at which wharfage charges will be payable are to be fixed by the Central Government according to the provision of s. 30 of the said Act. Validity or reasonableness of rates fixed by the Central Government in exercise of power conferred by s. 30 of the said Act cannot be questioned before the Railway Claim Tribunal. Bar of jurisdiction of courts mentioned in s. 43 of the said Act does not apply to writ jurisdiction. Railway administration is entitled to weigh or reweigh goods meant for carriage between two stations, but such act cannot be done behind the back of a person who would be prejudiced by reason of s. 79 of the said Act. Since there are disputed questions of fact involved in the writ petition, these cannot be decided by the Writ Court and as such the appropriate forum for such purpose is the Railway Claim Tribunal.[18]

37. Matters not within the jurisdiction of the Tribunal. Nothing in this Chapter shall confer jurisdiction on the Tribunal in respect of—

(*a*) classification or re-classification of any commodity;

(*b*) fixation of wharfage and demurrage charges (including conditions attached to such charges);

15 *Union of India* v *West Coast Paper Mills Ltd.* AIR 1971 SC 349; (1971)3 SCC 606; (1971)2 SCR 594; see *Union of India* v *Motilal Padampat Sugar Mills* AIR 1969 SC 630; (1969)1 SCC 320; (1969)3 SCR 75.

16 *Union of India* v *India Sugar Mills Assocn.* AIR 1968 SC 22; (1967)3 SCR 219.

17 *Union of India* v *Lord Krishna Sugar Mills* AIR 1999 SC 2188; (1999)4 SCC 195; JT 1999(3) SC 236.

18 *Bhagaban Dey* v *Union of India* AIR 2010 Cal 13.

(*c*) fixation of fares levied for the carriage of passengers and freight levied for the carriage of luggage, parcels, railway material and military traffic; and

(*d*) fixation of lump sum rates.

1 Corresponding provision This section corresponds to s. 39 of the old Act.

2 Matters outside jurisdiction of Railway Rates Tribunal The following matters have been excluded from the jurisdiction of the Railway Rates Tribunal:

(*a*) classification or reclassification of any commodity;

(*b*) fixation of wharfage and demurrage charges;

(*c*) fixation of lump sum rates;

Section 39 of the old Act (corresponding to s. 37 of the Railways Act 1989) does not confer jurisdiction but only provides for means for exercise by the Tribunal of the jurisdiction which it has otherwise got under other sections.[19] The Railway Rates Tribunal has no jurisdiction to pass a decree in favour of the complainants for the refund of excess charges or freight collected from them.[20] Interference by a writ of *certiorari* with the opinion of the Tribunal or omission to decide an issue as it was unnecessary is not warranted.[21]

3 Power of Tribunal The Tribunal can decide only reasonableness of charges. It cannot decide vires of the rules empowering railways to collect such amount.[1]

4 Jurisdiction Section 39 of the old Act (corresponding to s. 37 of the Railways Act 1989) does not confer any jurisdiction on the Tribunal. It only provides means for exercise by the Tribunal of the jurisdiction which has been conferred by other sections of the Act.[2] The Tribunal has no jurisdiction to give effect to its order prior to the date of the institution of the complaint.[3] The Tribunal has no jurisdiction to make an order for payment of compensation or damages or for refund to over-charges. The Tribunal has no jurisdiction in the matter of refund of the amount claimed,

19 *Upper Doab Sugar Mills Ltd.* v *Shahdara (Delhi) Saharanpur Light Rly.* AIR 1963 SC 217; (1963)2 SCR 333.

20 *Hindustan Materials* v *R.R. Tribunal* AIR 1958 Mad 471.

21 *Shree Bajrang Jute Mills*, in re AIR 1962 Mad 218.

1 *Raichand Amulakh* v *Union of India* AIR 1964 SC 1268; (1964)5 SCR 148.

2 *Upper Doab Sugar Mills Ltd.* v *Shahdara (Delhi) Saharanpur Light Rly. Co. Ltd.* AIR 1963 SC 217; (1963)2 SCR 333; 1963 SCD 303.

3 *Southern Railway* v *The Railway Rates Tribunal* AIR 1955 Mad 476; 68 Mad LW 341.

and, therefore, the provisions of s. 26 of the (old) Act do not appear to stand in the way in bringing the suit for refund of charges levied in excess of reasonable charges since such a suit would not be for anything done or omissions made by the railway administration in violation or contravention of the provisions of Chapter V of the (old) Act. If the railway administration has received payment of unreasonable charges, that is not "anything done or omission made" in violation or contravention of Chapter V of the (old) Act. Section 26 of the (old) Act is no bar to the jurisdiction of a civil court.[4]

38. Powers of the Tribunal. (1) The Tribunal shall have the powers of a civil court under the Code of Civil Procedure, 1908 (5 of 1908) for the purposes of taking evidence on oath, enforcing the attendance of witnesses, compelling the discovery and production of documents, issuing commissions for the examination of witnesses and of review and shall be deemed to be a civil court for all the purposes of section 195 and Chapter XXXV of the Code of Criminal Procedure, 1973 (2 of 1974) and any reference in such section or Chapter to the presiding officer of a court shall be deemed to include a reference to the Chairman of the Tribunal.

(2) The Tribunal shall also have power to pass such interim and final orders as the circumstances may require, including orders for the payment of costs.

1 Corresponding provision This section corresponds to s. 40 of the old Act.

2 Powers of the Railway Rates Tribunal The Railway Rates Tribunal is vested the discretionary power to grant such relief as it considers necessary. Where the Tribunal had exercised its discretion and limited the relief from the date of the judgment, it could not be termed as illegal or arbitrary.[5]

39. Reference to the Tribunal. Notwithstanding anything contained in section 37, the Central Government may make a reference to the Tribunal in respect of any of the matter specified in that section and where any such reference is made in respect of any such matter, the Tribunal shall make an inquiry into that matter and submit its report thereon to the Central Government.

Reference by Central Government to Tribunal The Central Government may make reference to the Railway Rates Tribunal any of the matters specified in s. 37 of the Act. It means that s. 39 operates as an exception to s. 37 of the Act. Where any such reference is made to the Tribunal by the Central Government, the Tribunal shall make an inquiry into such matter and submit its report thereon to the Central Government.

4 *Bharat Pvt. Ltd.* v *Union of India* (1971)12 Guj LR 378.
5 *Hindalco Industries Ltd.* v *Union of India* (1994)2 SCC 594.

40. Assistance by the Central Government. (1) The Central Government shall give to the Tribunal such assistance as it may require and shall also place at its disposal any information in the possession of the Central Government which that Government may think relevant to any matter before the Tribunal.

(2) Any person duly authorised in this behalf by the Central Government shall be entitled to appear and be heard in any proceedings before the Tribunal.

Assistance to the Railway Rates Tribunal by the Central Government The Central Government is required to assist the Railway Rates Tribunal with all information in its possession which are relevant to any matter before the Tribunal. The Central Government shall also authorise a person to appear before the Tribunal on behalf of the Central Government.

41. Burden of proof, etc. In the case of any complaint under clause (*a*) of section 36—

(*a*) whenever it is shown that a railway administration charges one trader or class of traders or the traders in any local area, lower rates for the same or similar goods or lower charges for the same or similar services than it charges to other traders in any other local area, the burden of providing that such lower rate or charge does not amount to an undue preference, shall lie on the railway administration;

(*b*) in deciding whether a lower rate or charge does not amount to an undue preference, the Tribunal may, in addition to any other considerations affecting the case, take into consideration whether such lower rate or charge is necessary in the interests of the public.

Burden of proof Section 41 deals with the burden of proof for a complaint made under s. 36(*a*) of the Act against a railway administration.

42. Decision, etc., of the Tribunal. The decisions or orders of the Tribunal shall be by a majority of the members sitting and shall be final.

1 **Corresponding provision** This section corresponds to s. 46A of the old Act.

2 **Finality** The provision as to finality of the Tribunal's decision does not affect the Supreme Court's jurisdiction under Art. 136 of the Constitution.[6]

3 **Judgment of tribunal** Section 46A of the Indian Railways Act 1890 which corresponds to s. 42 of the Railways Act 1989 provides that the judgment of the Tribunal was final, but by reason thereof the jurisdiction of the Supreme Court to exercise its power under Art. 136 of the Constitution of India was not excluded. The starting point of limitation for filing a suit to recover the excess amount of freight paid was the date of the Supreme Court's order and not the date of the Tribunal's judgment.[7]

6 *Raigarh Jute Mills Ltd.* v *Eastern Railway* AIR 1958 SC 525; 1958 SCJ 720.
7 *Union of India* v *West Coast Papers Mills Ltd.* (2004)2 SCC 747.

43. Bar of jurisdiction of courts. **No suit shall be instituted or proceeding taken in respect of any matter which the Tribunal is empowered to deal with, or decide, under this Chapter.**

1 **Corresponding provision** This section corresponds to s. 45 of the old Act.

2 **Bar to jurisdiction of civil court** Where a suit was filed by a company against railway for charging excess amount of charge for loaded wagons and additional charges for empty wagon, the Tribunal had exclusive jurisdiction under s. 41 of the old Act (corresponding to s. 36 of the Railways Act 1989), consequently the suit was not maintainable before the civil court.[8] But the civil court has jurisdiction to entertain a suit for refund of charges realised by a railway, because the Tribunal cannot grant the relief in this regard.

Transshipment charges are terminals and not tolls for using a ferry and therefore a civil court has no jurisdiction to entertain a claim relating to such charges.[9]

In view of s. 9, Code of Civil Procedure all suits of civil nature is cognizable by a civil court except when their cognizance is either expressly or impliedly barred. This section of the Railway Act is an example of express bar. No suit is tenable in civil court for anything done or any omission made by railway administration in violation or in contravention of any provision of this chapter except in so far as contrary has been provide in the Act. Section 36 of the Act provides a remedy by way of complaint in particular cases before the Railways Rates Tribunal. In this connection it is apposite to mention that when statute provides that particular remedy can be sought in a particular forum in a particular way it must be sought in that forum and in that particular manner, and all other forums and modes of seeking it are excluded.[10] The jurisdiction conferred upon the Tribunal by s. 41 of the (old) Railways Act (corresponding to s. 36 of the Railways Act 1989) and relating to matters set out in cls. (*a*) to (*c*) thereof is restricted by the terms of s. 29(3) and s. 42 of the old Act (corresponding to s. 30 and s. 31 of the Railways Act 1989).[11]

8 *Gwalior Sugar Co. Ltd.* v *Union of India* AIR 1996 MP 219.

9 *Pannalal* v *B.N. Railway* AIR 1932 Nag 53.

10 *Premier Automobiles* v *K.S. Wadke* AIR 1975 SC 2238; (1976)1 SCC 496; 1976 SCWR 9; 1975 Lab IC 1651; 48 FJR 252; (1976)2 Serv LR 168; 1976 SCC (Lab) 70; ILR (1976) Kant 18; (1976)1 SCR 427; (1975)2 Lab LJ 445; *Munshi Ram* v *Chheharta Municipality* AIR 1979 SC 1250; (1979)3 SCC 83; 1979 SCC (Tax) 205.

11 *Union of India* v *West Coast Paper Mills* AIR 1971 SC 349; (1971)2 SCJ 522; 1970 SCD 1125.

This section has to be strictly construed. It does not bar a civil suit for refund of the amount realised by the railway administration by way of wharfage or demurrage charges filed on the ground that the rules authorising the administration to do so are *ultra vires* or that the amounts so collected are in excess of the rule.[12]

This section does not bar a suit or application before Claims Tribunal in cases of contract, e.g. where wagons were supplied in the plaintiff's railway siding under a contract and freight charges were revised and claimed from the plaintiff. Suit for injunction against the railway administration against retrospective claim at enhanced freight charges for supply of wagons is maintainable and the court can give proper relief; also it was within the jurisdiction of the court to decide whether a clause in the contract was valid or not and whether proper notice for enhancement was given in accordance with the terms of agreement.[13] Section 26 of the old Act (corresponding to s. 43 of the Railways Act 1989) did bar a suit when the plaintiff's claim in substance was that the railway administration had acted in a discriminatory manner and had denied the plaintiff's equality of treatment in the matter of freight rates for transport of raw materials to the plaintiff's mill by giving all other paper mills the benefits of concessional freight rates while denying concessional freight rate to the plaintiff's paper mills.[14] This section, however, does not bar a suit or application before Claims Tribunal for refund of charges made in excess of reasonable charges.[15] The Calcutta High Court held that a suit for refund of excess passenger fare is barred under this section.[16] A suit in the civil court or an application before Claims Tribunal for refund of unreasonable charges recovered from the plaintiff is not barred by (old) s. 26 (corresponding to s. 43 of the Railways Act 1989).[17]

3 Defence A person accused of an offence under the (old) Indian Railways Act, e.g. s. 109(1) (corresponding to s. 155 of the Railways Act 1989) can allege a contravention of the provisions of (old) Chapter V by the railway

12 *Raichand Amulakh* v *Union of India* AIR 1964 SC 1268; (1964)1 SCWR 248; 66 Bom LR 315; (1964)5 SCR 148.

13 *Union of India* v *Modi Industries Ltd.* AIR 1973 SC 1281; (1973)1 SCC 781; (1973)3 SCR 835.

14 *Union of India* v *Straw Products* AIR 1984 Cal 291.

15 *Upper Doab Sugar Mills Ltd.* v *Shahdara (Delhi) Saharanpur Light Railway Co. Ltd.* AIR 1963 SC 217; (1963)2 SCR 333; (1963) SCD 303; *Bharat Private Ltd.* v *Union of India* (1971)12 Guj LR 378.

16 *Dhirendra* v *Dominion of India* 60 CWN 776.

17 AIR 1963 SC 217; AIR 1973 SC 1281 relied on *Union of India* v *Mansukhlal Jethalal* AIR 1975 Guj 116.

administration in his defence since he cannot be said to have taken proceedings thereby.[18]

44. Reliefs which the Tribunal may grant. In the case of any complaint made under clause (*b*) or clause (*c*) of section 36, the Tribunal may—

(*i*) fix such rate or charge as it considers reasonable from any date as it may deem proper, not being a date earlier to the date of the filing of the complaint;

(*ii*) direct a refund of amount, if any, as being the excess of the rate or charge fixed by the Tribunal under clause (*i*).

1 Corresponding provision This section corresponds to s. 41(3) of the old Act.

2 Reliefs to be granted by Tribunal under s. 36(b) or (c) Section 44 confers power on the Tribunal in respect of complaints against railway administration under s. 36(*b*) or s. 36(*c*) to grant any of the following reliefs: (*i*) Fixing rate or charge as it considers reasonable with effect from a date not earlier than the date of filing of the complaint, (*ii*) direction for a refund of amount being the excess of the rate or charge. The Tribunal is given the discretion to mould the ancillary relief. But the direction is to be exercised with circumspection consistent with justice equity and good conscience keeping in review always the given fact and circumstances of the case.[19]

45. Revision of decisions given by the Tribunal. Where a Railway Administration considers that since the date of decision by the Tribunal, there has been a material change in the circumstances on which it was based, it may, after the expiry of one year from such date, make an application to the Tribunal and the Tribunal may, after making such inquiry as it considers necessary, vary or revoke the decision.

1 Corresponding provision This section corresponds to s. 41A of the old Act.

2 Revision of decision of the Tribunal Section 45 empowers the Railway Rates Tribunal to revise its decision on the basis of an application made by the railway administration after the expiry of one year from the date of its decision on the ground of material changes in the circumstances of the case. A company filed a complaint before the Railway Rates Tribunal against the railway administration. The Tribunal reduced the charges but on revision revoked its earlier order. On appeal to the Supreme Court it was held that in the circumstances of the case the order of revocation of

18 *Emperor* v *Narayan* AIR 1923 Bom 1; 47 Bom 465.
19 *Hindalco Industries Ltd.* v *Union of India* (1994)2 SCC 594.

previous orders was the only choice left to the Tribunal. Thus, the order of the Tribunal was proper and it was not necessary to remand the matter back to the Tribunal.[20]

46. Execution of decisions or orders of the Tribunal. The Tribunal may transmit any decision or order made by it to a civil court having local jurisdiction and such civil court shall execute the decision or order as if it were a decree made by that court.

1 Corresponding provision This section corresponds to s. 46B of the old Act.

2 Execution of order of Tribunal The decision or order of the Tribunal can be executed only through civil court treating the same as if it were a decree made by that court. An order for payment of costs made by the Tribunal could under s. 46B of the old Act (corresponding to s. 46 of the Railways Act 1989) be transmitted to a civil court having local jurisdiction over the subject matter and executed by that court as if it were a decree.[21]

47. Report of the Central Government. The Tribunal shall present annually a report to the Central Government of all its proceedings under this Chapter.

48. Power of the Tribunal to make regulations. (1) The Tribunal may, with the previous approval of the Central Government, make regulations consistent with this Act and rules generally to regulate its procedure for the effective discharge of its functions under this Chapter.

(2) In particular, and without prejudice to the generality of the foregoing power, such regulations may provide for all or any of the following matters, namely:—

(*a*) the terms and conditions of service of the officers and employees of the Tribunal;

(*b*) the award of costs by the Tribunal in any proceedings before it;

(*c*) the reference of any question to a member or to an officer of the Tribunal or any other person appointed by the Tribunal, for report after holding a local inquiry;

(*d*) the right of audience before the Tribunal, provided that any party shall be entitled to be heard in person, or by a representative duly authorised in writing, or by a legal practitioner;

(*e*) the disposal by the Tribunal of any proceedings before it, notwithstanding that in the course thereof there has been a change in the persons sitting as members of the Tribunal;

(*f*) a scale of fees for and in connection with the proceedings before the Tribunal.

20 *Jaipur Udyog* v *Union of India* AIR 1975 SC 1056; (1975)1 SCC 682.

21 *Upper Doab Sugar Mills Ltd.* v *Shahdara (Delhi) Saharanpur Light Rly. Co. Ltd.* AIR 1963 SC 217; (1963)2 SCR 333.

Corresponding provision This section corresponds to s. 44 of the old Act.

CHAPTER VIII
Carriage of Passengers

1 Facilities In *The Queen* v *Railway Commissioners,*[1] HUDDLESTON, B. in expressing the word 'facilities', observed: "It is clear that the word has no reference to excessive charges at all, but is used with reference to the convenience to be afforded in receiving and forwarding and delivering traffic, and so on, and the return of carriages." COTTON, LJ. observed: "What I think comes within those words 'afford all reasonable facilities', is the providing proper accommodation in the stations and in the carriages for the receiving and forwarding passengers, and for getting them in and out of their carriages and the like. The mere fact that the charge is beyond that which Parliament has sanctioned is not, in my opinion, a refusal to afford reasonable facilities."[2] The railway company is bound, according to their powers, to afford reasonable facilities for the carriage of all goods, as traffic, but there is no obligation on the company to carry any particular class of goods at railway risk if they do not think fit to do so. A railway company is not bound to find reasonable accommodation for the public further than it is in the interests of railway traffic that it should be found.[3] It is a facility or convenience so plainly necessary for the proper and convenient use of the railway by the public.[4] In *John Watson* v *Caledonian Railway*[5] LORD DUNEDIN observed: "If a trader is entitled to have a wagon of his own put on the line as a matter of right, whether that matter of right depends on a statutory provision or whether it depends upon the common law applicable to common carriers and the like, that is a thing he can have declared in the Courts of the country, and that is a thing he is entitled to have quite irrespective of whether his demand is for a reasonable facility or is not. In one sense, the right to reasonable facilities is a statutory right, because it is the only statute that gives the person the right to have a reasonable facility, but the moment that person confesses that he has no other right, the precise determination of what, in the concrete, is or is not reasonable facility is a matter that has been committed by the legislature to the jurisdiction not of the Courts, but of the Railway Commissioners." In the case of facilities in respect of length of platforms, waiting rooms, booking offices and the like, it is not enough to show that such facilities would be conducive to the convenience of the public; it is

1 22 QBD 642.
2 *G.W. Rly Co.* v *Railway Commissioners* [1881]7 QBD 182.
3 *Holyhead Local Board* v *L.N.W. Railway* (1880)4 Railway & Can Tr Cas 37.
4 *Nottingham Corporation* v *Midland Railway Co.* (1922)17 Railway & Can Tr Cas 72.
5 14 Railway & Can Tr Cas 185.

necessary also to show that they are facilities which can be reasonably required of the railway company, after making due allowance for the degree in which the company have made provision for the accommodation of the goods traffic of the place, taken as a whole, and, further, that they must be such facilities as it is within the power of the company to grant.[6]

2 Duty of Railway Company to passengers and public A Railway Company is bound so to fence station that the public may not be misled, by seeing a place unfenced, into injuring themselves by passing that way, being the shortest, to the station.[7] Defendants, a Railway Company, constructed a bridge in place of a public footway crossing their line, and also over a roadway adjoining. The bridge was fenced with wooden hoardings, where it crossed the rails and with open ornamental work, with triangular openings, where it crossed the road. Plaintiff, a child, about four years of age, went upon the bridge, in company with another child, for the purpose of crossing over, and instead of walking straight forwards, he placed his back against the hoardings and slid along until he came to the ornamental iron-work when he fell through backwards on to the road, and was injured. There was evidence of negligence to go to the jury, and it was defendants' duty to keep the bridge in such a state as not to be dangerous to anyone using it in a lawful manner and there was no negligence on the part of plaintiff contributory to the accident.[8]

A Railway Company is bound to find at every station reasonable means for passengers to alight. A railway train drew up at a small station with the engine and part of one of the carriages beyond the platform. A passenger in the carriage, having parcels in her hands, opened the door and waited on the iron step some time for assistance; but no one coming to assist, she, fearing that the train would move on, tried to alight by getting on to the footboard, and in so doing fell and injured herself for which injury she brought an action against the Railway Company. It was the duty of the Railway Company to provide suitable means for alighting of passengers.[9]

A Railway Company must take reasonable precautions and provide sufficient staffs to control the crowds at the station and if anybody is injured by reason of failure to take proper precautions the company will be liable.[10] But a Railway Company is not required by law to have a force

6 *Newry Navigation Co.* v *G.N. Railway* (1889)7 Railway & Can Tr Cas 176.

7 *Burgess* v *G.W. Railway Co.* [1858]32 LTOS 76.

8 *Lay* v *Midland Railway Co.* [1875]34 LT 30; also see *Cliff* v *Midland Railway Co.* [1870]5 QB 258 (264, 265).

9 *Robson* v *N.E. Railway Co.* [1876]2 QBD 85; 35 LT 525; *Smith* v *Victorian Railway Comr.* [1902]28 VLR 44.

10 *Hogan* v *S.E. Railway Co.* [1873]28 LT 271; *Fraser* v *Caledonian Railway Co.* [1902]5 F 41.

capable of resisting and overcoming whatever violence a drunken or riotous mob may choose to exhibit.[11]

A carrier is liable to damages in respect of any injury caused to a passenger as a natural result of the overcrowding. What constitutes overcrowding is a question of fact. But a proof of mere overcrowding is not sufficient to fix the company with liability; it must further be established that the injury is the result of the overcrowding.[12] In other words, "unless the overcrowding in fact conduces to the damage complained of, no cause of action arises."[13]

Where there is a statutory obligation to fix the maximum number of passengers for a compartment of a railway carriage and the railway administration fixed the said number, any overcrowding in breach of such statutory obligation may be taken as *prima facie* evidence of negligence, but even in such a case to fix the railway administration with liability for the injury it must be established that the injury sustained resulted from that negligence.

"A company does violate and contravene the Act if having sufficient powers, it keeps its platforms, booking offices and other structures at any station in such a condition, as to space and other arrangements, as to cause dangerous or obstructive confusion, delay or other impediment to the proper reception, transmission or delivery of the ordinary traffic of that station, whether consisting of passengers or goods."[14]

49. Exhibition of certain timings and tables of fares at stations. (1) Every railway administration shall cause to be pasted in a conspicuous and accessible place at every station in Hindi and English and also in the regional language commonly in use in the area where the station is situated,—

(*i*) a table of times of arrival and departure of trains which carry passengers and stop at that station, and

(*ii*) list of fares from such station to such other stations as it may consider necessary.

(2) At every station where tickets are issued to passengers, a copy of the time-table in force shall be kept in the office of the station master.

Corresponding provision This section corresponds to s. 65 of the old Act.

50. Supply of tickets on payment of fare. (1) Any person desirous of travelling on a railway shall, upon payment of the fare, be supplied with a ticket by a

11 *Cannon* v *M.G. Railway* [1876]6 LR Ir 199.

12 *Met Railway Co.* v *Jackson* [1877]3 App Cas 193; 47 LJCP 303.

13 *Cobb* v *G.W. Railway Co.* [1894] AC 419.

14 *S.E. Railway Co.* v *Railway Commissioners of Hastings* (1879-81)3 Railway Can Tr Cas 464 (508).

railway servant or an agent authorised in this behalf and such ticket shall contain the following particulars, namely:—

(*i*) the date of issue;

(*ii*) the class of carriage;

(*iii*) the place from and the place to which it is issued; and

(*iv*) the amount of the fare.

(2) Every railway administration shall display the hours during which booking windows at a station shall be kept open for the issue of tickets to passengers.

(3) The particulars required to be specified on a ticket under clauses (*ii*) and (*iii*) of sub-section (1) shall,—

(*a*) if it is for the lowest class of carriage, be set forth in Hindi, English and the regional language commonly in use at the place of issue of the ticket; and

(*b*) if it is for any other class of carriage, be set forth in Hindi and English:

Provided that where it is not feasible to specify such particulars in any such language due to mechanisation or any other reason, the Central Government may exempt such particulars being specified in that language.

1 Corresponding provision This section corresponds to s. 66 of the old Act.

2 Scope of section Section 50 provides for supply of tickets on payment of fare stating the specified particulars on the ticket. Section 66 read with s. 68 of the old Act (corresponding to ss. 50 and 55 of the Railways Act 1989 respectively) indicate that a person cannot be passenger so as to travel on a railway unless he has obtained a proper pass, ticket or permission from a railway servant. Thus a person who travels on a train without a proper pass, ticket or permission is a trespasser and cannot be called a passenger within the meaning of s. 82A of the old Act (corresponding to s. 124 of the Railways Act 1989).[15] When a passenger purchases a ticket from railway, there comes into existence a contract between railway administration and passenger for carriage of the latter's person. If a "half ticket" is obtained railway administration for carriage of an adult person, then the contract is caused by misrepresentation to financial prejudice of railway administration. That does not make the contract void from its inception, but it becomes voidable at the option of railway administration under s. 19 of the Contract Act 1872. Moreover, s. 113 of the (old) Railways Act (corresponding to s. 138 of the Railways Act 1989) provides for realisation of excess charge from a passenger travelling with an improper ticket and thereby validating the improper ticket.[16]

15 *Ramchandra Prasad Sinha* v *Union of India* AIR 1959 Pat 316. See *Sundri* v *Union of India* AIR 1984 All 277; 1984 All WC 438; 1984 All CJ 383 (FB). (Only the dependants of a *bona fide* passenger are entitled to get compensation in the event of death occurring in an accident).

16 *Union of India* v *Benode Kumar* AIR 1962 Cal 48; 65 CWN 727E.

51. Provision for case in which ticket is issued for class or train not having accommodation for additional passengers. (1) A ticket shall be deemed to have been issued subject to the condition of availability of accommodation in the class of carriage and the train for which the ticket is issued.

(2) If no accommodation is available in the class of carriage for which a ticket is issued, and the holder thereof travels in a carriage of a lower class, he shall, on returning such ticket, be entitled to a refund of the difference between the fare paid by him and the fare payable for the class of carriage in which he travels.

1 **Corresponding provision** This section corresponds to s. 67 of the old Act.

2 **Refund of difference** Section 67 of the old Act (corresponding to s. 51 of the Railways Act 1989) operates not only in the case where there are compartments of particular class available, but there is no room in those compartments, but also in a case where there is no compartment of that class at all.[17] The remedy of a passenger with a third class ticket carried in a goods wagon who refuses to travel may apply for refund of fare and not to sue for breach of contract.[18]

Though a ticket has been defined in the old Act to include a season ticket as well, still what is contemplated in s. 67(3) of the old Act cannot be said to apply to season ticket-holder. Where a season ticket holder was obliged to travel by lower class only on account of the exercise of the railway administration of right under the rule to vary or alter the train, the season ticket-holder could not question the right of the railway administration to alter or vary the trains and he could not make the railway administration liable for any loss or damage.[19] It is the obligation of the railway administration to provide berths and seats to a passenger who has obtained reservation well in advance and if such a passenger encounters much inconvenience and discomfort during the journey due to negligence of railway administration, the railway cannot escape its liability of payment of compensation.

52. Cancellation of ticket and refund. If a ticket is returned for cancellation, the railway administration shall cancel the same and refund such amount as may be prescribed.

1 **Corresponding provision** This section corresponds to s. 67(2) of the old Act.

2 **Refund on cancellation of ticket** A person is entitled to refund an amount as prescribed by railway administration on return of his ticket for cancellation.

17 *Manendrd Chandra* v *E.I. Rly Co.* AIR 1927 Pat 352; 8 Pat LT 676.

18 *Shankar Narayan* v *Bansi Light Rly Co. Ltd.* AIR 1947 Bom 390; ILR (1947) Bom 172; 49 Bom LR 178.

19 *A. Krishniyya* v *Dominion of India* AIR 1955 Mad 619; (1955)2 MLJ 159.

53. Prohibition against transfer of certain tickets. A ticket issued in the name of a person shall be used only by that person:

Provided that nothing contained in this section shall prevent mutual transfer of a seat or berth by passengers travelling by the same train:

Provided further that a railway servant authorised in this behalf may permit change of name of a passenger having reserved a seat or berth subject to such circumstances as may be prescribed.

1 **Corresponding provision** This section corresponds to s. 70 of the old Act.

2 **Object and scope** The object of this section is to stop the evil practice prevalent in some big cities of purchase of railway tickets and reservation of seats by person other than *bona fide* travellers and transfer by them. Accordingly this prohibits transfer of tickets against which reservation of a seat or berth has been made. An exception has been for mutual transfer of seats or berths by passengers travelling in the same train.

3 **Penalty** If an accused is found using railway season ticket issued in the name of different person by pretending to be that person, he can be charged under s. 419, Indian Penal Code. Even if the old Act did not specifically provide for the abuse of season ticket, the accused could not escape his criminal liability.[20]

4 **No unreasonableness** Rule 39(*b*) of Railway Administrative Rules which required the holder of a season ticket to sign his name and mention his age on the ticket was held to be reasonable rule in order to prohibit the transfer of certain tickets.[1]

54. Exhibition and surrender of passes and tickets. Every passenger shall, on demand by any railway servant authorised in this behalf, present his pass or ticket to such railway servant for examination during the journey or at the end of the journey and surrender such ticket—

(*a*) at the end of the journey, or

(*b*) if such ticket is issued for a specified period, on the expiration of such period.

1 **Corresponding provision** This section corresponds to s. 69 of the old Act.

2 **Exhibition and surrender of passes and tickets** A passenger who had obtained a monthly ticket is liable to produce the same at the time of his journey and if he fails to produce it he is liable to pay the fare for the journey between the stations for which his ticket was issued. A passenger cannot be said to be travelling without a ticket merely because he does not

20 In re, *Malameswara Rao* AIR 1957 AP 4.
1 *Pallonji N. Metha* v *State* AIR 1952 Bom 421.

happen to have the ticket with him and therefore cannot produce it when called upon to do so.[2]

Under the present Act, s. 54 provides for exhibition of the ticket or pass on requisition by a railway servant. If a passenger fails or refuses to present for examination a pass or ticket, he shall be dealt with under ss. 138, 139 and 140 of the present Act. If a person fraudulently travels or attempts to travel without a proper pass or ticket, he shall be dealt with according to the provisions of s. 137 of the present Act.

The guard of a train may demand to see the tickets of passengers on the ground that he suspects a person of travelling without any valid ticket or pass.

55. Prohibition against travelling without pass or ticket. (1) No person shall enter or remain in any carriage on a railway for the purpose of travelling therein as a passenger unless he has with him a proper pass or ticket or obtained permission of a railway servant authorised in this behalf for such travel.

(2) A person obtaining permission under sub-section (1) shall ordinarily get a certificate from the railway servant referred to in that sub-section that he has been permitted to travel in such carriage on condition that he subsequently pays the fare payable for the distance to be travelled.

1 Corresponding provision This section corresponds to s. 69 of the old Act.

2 Scope A person cannot be a passenger so as to travel on a railway unless he has obtained a proper pass, ticket or permission of a railway servant. Thus, if a person does so, in contravention of the provision of the Act, he cannot be called as passenger.[3] Section 55 prohibits a person from entering into or travelling by train without valid pass or ticket.[4]

3 Meaning of term The term "a proper pass or ticket" used in s. 68 of the old Act (corresponding to s. 55 of the Railways Act 1989) must be construed to mean a pass or ticket by which the person would be authorised to enter a carriage for the purpose of travelling therein as a passenger.[5]

56. Power to refuse to carry persons suffering from infectious or contagious diseases. (1) A person suffering from such infectious or contagious disease, as may be prescribed, shall not enter or remain in any carriage on a railway or travel in a train without the permission of a railway servant authorised in this behalf.

(2) The railway servant giving permission under sub-section (1), shall arrange for the separation of the person suffering from such disease from other persons

2 *Hari* v *Ruskin* 44 Cal 279; 25 CLJ 610.

3 *Ramchandra Pr. Sinha* v *Union of India* AIR 1959 Pat 316; see also *Sundri* v *Union of India* AIR 1984 All 277; 1984 All WC 438; 1984 All CJ 383.

4 *Ram Dayal* v *Emperor* AIR 1925 Oudh 479.

5 *B.N. Rly. Co.* v *Devi Dutt* 9 CPLR 1.

in the train and such person shall be carried in the train subject to such other conditions as may be prescribed.

(3) Any person who enters or remains in any carriage or travels in a train without permission as required under sub-section (1) or in contravention of any condition prescribed under sub-section (2), such person and a person accompanying him shall be liable to the forfeiture of their passes or tickets and removal from railway by any railway servant.

1 Corresponding provision This section corresponds to s. 71 of the old Act.

2 Scope Section 56 empowers the railway administration to refuse entry or remain in a railway carriage if he suffers from any infectious or contagious diseases without permission of a railway servant. Even if permission is given to such a person, the railway servant shall arrange for separation of such person from other persons in the train. If such person enters or remains in a train without permission of the railway servant, such person and any person accompanying him shall be liable to forfeiture of their passes or tickets and removal from railway by any railway servant.

57. Maximum number of passengers for each compartment. Subject to the approval of the Central Government, every railway administration shall fix the maximum number of passengers which may be carried in each compartment of every description of carriage, and shall exhibit the number so fixed in a conspicuous manner inside or outside each compartment in Hindi, English and also in one or more of the regional languages commonly in use in the areas served by the railway.

1 Corresponding provision This section corresponds to s. 63 of the old Act.

2 Overcrowding Assuming that overcrowding amounts to actionable negligence, the plaintiff in order to claim damages must prove that the negligence has resulted in some damages or injury to him. Proof of mere inconvenience is not sufficient.[6]

3 Object of the section In order to prevent any danger to the health and life of passengers, this section provides limit of passengers to occupy a compartment. The capacity of the compartment must be exhibited in some conspicuous place inside or outside the compartment.[7]

4 Meaning of word "compartment" The word "compartment"is not used in the same meaning throughout the old Act. Somewhere it appears to mean partial partition and in somewhere as complete separation.[8]

6 *Union of India* v *Shri Nivas Mal* AIR 1955 Pat 282; 33 Pat 249.
7 *Ishwar Das* v *King Emperor* AIR 1922 Pat 8; 23 CrLJ 257.
8 *Dadabhoy* v *Khanderao* (1900)24 Bom 293; 1 Bom LR 688.

58. Earmarking of compartment, etc., for ladies. Every railway administration shall, in every train carrying passengers, earmark for the exclusive use of females, one compartment or such number of berths or seats, as the railway administration may think fit.

1 **Corresponding provision** This section corresponds to s. 64 of the old Act.

2 **Female compartment** A compartment earmarked for journey by females is required to be allotted at least for second class passengers. This may be read along with s. 162 of this Act which provides for penalty of a male person travelling in a railway compartment earmarked for female passengers.

59. Communications between passengers and railway servant in charge of train. A railway administration shall provide and maintain in every train carrying passengers, such efficient means of communication between the passengers and the railway servant in charge of the train as may be approved by the Central Government:

Provided that where the railway administration is satisfied that the means of communication provided in a train are being misused, it may cause such means to be disconnected in that train for such period as it thinks fit:

Provided further that the Central Government may specify the circumstances under which a railway administration may be exempted from providing such means of communication in any train.

1 **Corresponding provision** This section corresponds to s. 62 of the old Act.

2 **Duty to exercise reasonable care** The duty of a Railway Company is to exercise due care and skill in carrying passengers, or as BLACKBURN, J. has said in *Gee* v *Metropolitan Railway Co.,*[9] that a Railway Company is not bound to carry passengers safely and securely, at all events, but to take all reasonable cares that in the management of their trains the passengers are not exposed to undue danger. A carrier of passenger is not an insurer, but he is under a duty to use a very high decree of care with regard to his carriage. But, there is no obligation on the part of a railway company to exercise extraordinary care with reference to the exceptional or extraordinary circumstances affecting a particular individual. All that is obligatory on a Railway Company is to exercise all reasonable cares in the management of their trains so that the passenger is not exposed to undue danger. In the case of *Christie* v *Griggs,*[10] Sir James Mansfield has said: "There is a difference between a contract to carry goods and a contract to carry passengers. For the goods the carrier was liable at all events, but he did not warrant the safety of the passengers. His undertaking as to them

9 [1873] LR 8 QB 161.
10 (1809)2 Camp 79; (1809)170 Eng Rep 1088 (PC).

went no further than this, that as far as human care and foresight could go he would provide for their safe conveyance."

60. Power to make rules in respect of matters in this Chapter. (1) The Central Government may, by notification, make rules to carry out the purposes of this Chapter.

(2) In particular, and without prejudice to the generality of the foregoing power, such rules may provide for all or any of the following matters, namely:

(*a*) the convenience and accommodation (including the reservation of seats or berths in trains) to passengers;

(*b*) the amount of refund for the cancellation of a ticket;

(*c*) the circumstances under which change of names of passengers, having reserved seats or berths, may be permitted;

(*d*) the carriage of luggage and the conditions subject to which luggage may be kept in the cloak rooms at the stations;

(*e*) diseases which are infectious or contagious;

(*f*) the conditions subject to which a railway administration may carry passengers suffering from infectious or contagious diseases and the manner in which carriages used by such passengers may be disinfected;

(*g*) generally, for regulating the travelling upon, and the use, working and management of the railways.

(3) Any rule made under this section may provide that a contravention thereof shall be punishable with fine which shall not exceed five hundred rupees.

(4) Every railway administration shall keep at every station on its railway a copy of all the rules made under this section and shall also allow any person to inspect it free of charge.

1 Corresponding provision This section corresponds to s. 47 of the old Act.

2 Scope Section 60 empowers the Central Government to make rules for carrying out the purposes of Chapter VIII of the Act by a notification published in the Official Gazette. These rules may relate to (*i*) convenience and accommodation in train for passengers; (*ii*) amount of refund for cancellation of ticket; (*iii*) change of names of passengers having reserved seats or berths, (*iv*) carriage of luggage and keeping luggage in the cloak room, (*v*) diseases which are infectious or contagious, (*vi*) conditions for carrying passengers suffering from infectious and contagious disease, (*vii*) regulating travelling, working and management of railway. Contravention of any such rule shall result in punishment with fine for a sum not exceeding five hundred rupees.

3 Rules under the old Act The general rules framed under s. 47(1) of the old Act and rules found in standing orders are not merely for guidance of railway employees. They are clearly intended for safety of passengers and to guard against accident. A breach of those rules is *prima facie* a tort for which an action for damages will lie.[11] When a railway administration issues season tickets, it can also frame rules in this regard. Such rules cannot be said to be *ultra vires*.[12] The railway authority can frame rule to exclude any person from railway premises if that person is not a *bona fide* passenger. Rule framed by E.I.R. Co. Under heading "Travelling by alternative routes" does not permit a passenger to travel beyond the place which he has to reach.[13] Bye law or rule providing for special accommodation or convenience of a particular class of individuals is legal.[14] Where railway company makes rules that the interval between the issue of a return ticket and midnight of the same day shall be counted as one day is not *ultra vires*.[15]

It is not open to a railway company to enact any such rule which is inconsistent with the provisions of the Indian Railways Act. In *Firm Sohanpal Munna Lal* v *E.I. Railway,*[16] a consignment of goods was handed over by the plaintiff to the railway officials at Agra station and was accepted by them for despatch to Amroha. After the package had been taken over by the goods clerk and duly marked, the plaintiff was told to come later for the railway receipt. No receipt was, however, taken by him. It appeared that the package was actually despatched from Agra but was mis-sent to a wrong destination and was consequently lost. In a suit for damages against the railway the defendant pleaded a rule, framed under the provisions of s. 47(1)(*f*) of the old Indian Railways Act, which said—'Goods will in all cases be at the owner's risk until taken over by the railway administration for despatch and a receipt in the prescribed form has been granted duly signed by an authorised railway servant." PIGOTT, J. (WALSH and GAKUL PRASAD, JJ. concurring) observed in the judgment as follows: "As however, the case has been referred to a Full Bench for an expression of opinion on the general questions of law involved, and those questions have been argued before us, I think it advisable to add a few words. It seems to me that, if a rule like that relied upon by the railway company in the present case, (a rule supposed to have been made in virtue of the powers conferred by s. 47 of Act No. IX of 1890) is put forward as limiting the statutory liability imposed upon the railway company by s. 72

11 *Governor General-in-Council* v *Sushil Kumar Mukherji* ILR (1950)2 Cal 372.
12 *A. Krishniyya* v *Dominion of India* AIR 1955 Mad 619. See *Nanhulal* v *Gaya Lodging H. Committee* AIR 1964 Pat 98.
13 *Secy. of State* v *B. Murli Monohar* AIR 1928 All 670.
14 *Birjbasi* v *Emperor* AIR 1920 All 106.
15 *Karachi Municipality* v *Khatanmal* AIR 1914 Sind 149.
16 44 All 218 (FB).

of the old Act (corresponding to s. 64 of the Railways Act 1989) then that rule is consistent with the provisions of the old Act and is of no effect. I do not think it is open to the railway company to enact, by means of a rule, that although as a matter of fact goods have been delivered to a duly authorised servant of the administration to be carried by the railway, nevertheless the court shall not deem them to have been so delivered unless and until the railway servant in question has performed a particular act. To this extent I agree with the decision of the Bombay High Court in *Ramchandra Natha's* case.[17]

In *Jalim Singh* v *Secretary of State,*[18] STEPHEN, J. observed as follows: The real question depends upon the construction that is to be placed upon ss. 47 and 54, Indian Railways Act. For the present purposes these two sections need not be distinguished. By s. 47 railway company may make general rules for regulating the terms on which it will warehouse or retain goods at any station. By s. 54, railway company may impose conditions for receiving goods. For the present purposes, these two things are the same. In both cases these rules and conditions have to be consistent with this Act. Now, what does that mean? The railway company has cast upon it the duties of an ordinary bailee. As I read the Act, it cannot wholly divest itself of those duties but it may determine the conditions under which that duty may vest and in particular it may specify the point of time at which it shall vest. The general common law embodied in s. 72 is by those sections liable to be cut down to a certain extent by those rules under ss. 47 and 54. The question is to what extent. And the answer is: as far as is reasonable, which really means the same thing as being consistent with the Act."

In *Ramchandra Natha* v *G.I. Railway Co.,*[19] HEATON, J., made the following observation: "This (s. 47) gives no express power to make rules regarding the liability of the railway and that liability it seems to me remains precisely as defined by s. 72. To hold otherwise would be to assume that the legislature conferred, not expressly but indirectly or by implication, a power to modify by rule the natural meaning of a section of the Act. I think this cannot be so, firstly because it is a manner of making laws that I cannot attribute to a responsible legislature; and secondly because I think it is directly against the provision that the rules must be consistent with the Act."

A railway company cannot escape a statutory liability by framing rules inconsistent with the provisions of the Act.[1] Rule 2 framed under s. 47(1)(*f*)

17 (1915) ILR 39 Bom 485.
18 31 Cal 951; 8 CWN 725.
19 (1915) ILR 39 Bom 485; 17 Bom LR 496.
1 *State* v *Sheo Bhagwan* 58 All 576; AIR 1936 All 69.

of the old Act which provides that goods will, in all cases, be at owner's risk until taken over by the railway administration for despatch and a receipt in the prescribed form has been granted duly signed by an authorised railway servant is inconsistent with the provisions of s. 72 of the old Act (corresponding to s. 64 of the Railways Act 1989) and is *ultra vires.*[2]

The condition requiring that goods shall be removed from the railway premises within a certain period after which demurrage and wharfage will be charged may be a valid condition relating to the delivery but the further condition laid down in r. 28(2) of the Goods Tariff, Part-IA, provides that the railway is not liable in respect of any loss, destruction, deterioration or damage to such goods arising from whatever causes if the goods are not removed within the time allowed free of demurrage and wharfage is not a condition affecting delivery. Such a condition exempting the railway from its liability for loss cannot be held to be valid because it not only exceeds the rule-making power of the railway but is also inconsistent with the liability imposed on the railway under s. 72 of the (old) Indian Railways Act.[3] Until the free time expires, there will be no charge leviable for demurrage or wharfage against the consignee. Whether wharfage had become due or not depends upon the time when the railway wagon was placed at the siding where unloading could be possible and when unloading took place.[4]

Rules 19 and 27 of Railways General Classification of Goods and General Rules do not absolve liability of railway in respect of goods in the custody of a railway company.[5] Where a rule was framed that persons who tendered as luggage articles not classifiable as such would do so at their risk, that rule was held inconsistent with the provisions of the Act and that the railway company was not absolved from its liability to compensate loss.[6] A railway company can also frame rules, otherwise than under s. 47 of the old Act in the exercise of the general powers of administration. But such a rule cannot provide for a penalty.[7] Such a rule (gratuity rule of E.I. Railway Co.) conferring a discretion on the railway cannot be sought to be enforced.[8] Rules in G.I.P. Railway time table Part II, though not made under s. 47, have been held to be valid as there is no inconsistency between them and the Indian Railways Act of the General Rules made

2 *Union of India* v *Hamirmull* AIR 1959 Cal 400.
3 *Governor-General-in-Council* v *Jagannath* AIR 1943 Lah 244.
4 *Dehri Rohtas Light Railway Co. Ltd.* v *General Godhar Colliery Co.* AIR 1965 Pat 49.
5 *Secretary of State* v *Sheo Bhagwan* 58 All 576; AIR 1936 All 69.
6 *Velayat Hossein* v *B.N.W. Railway* 36 Cal 919.
7 *State* v *Pallonji N. Mehta* ILR (1953) Bom 36; AIR 1952 Bom 421.
8 *Secretary of State* v *Bhola Nath* 60 Cal 909; AIR 1933 Cal 409.

under it (11 CrLJ 568). Rules 31(2), Goods Tariff No. 28 of Indian Railway Conference Association falls within the scope of s. 47(1)(*f*) of the old Act and is not *ultra vires.*[9] Clause 6 of the forwarding note which authorised the Railway Administration to re-measure, re-weigh, re-classify and re-calculate rates and charges and collect any amount that may have been under-charged, is valid.[10]

Where a railway entered into a contract at the place of despatch to charge freight on two chairs by weight, it is not justified in charging freight by measurement at the place of destination, notwithstanding r. 127 of the Guide and Coaching Tariff which provides that parcels "will be charged by weight or by measurement, whichever gives the greater charge," and r. 23 which reserves the right to the railway to correct any charges provided that the "Railway have the right of re-measurement, re-weighment, re-classification and re-calculation of rates, etc." Once having entered into a contract to charge by weight it cannot subsequently claim to charge by measurement. It is not a claim to measure for the first time and to calculate in accordance with such measurement and that cannot be permitted.[11] Where in respect of a consignment of firewood, the railway receipt was given charging the goods at the despatching station at maund rates, the railway is not entitled to charge subsequently at wagon rates, even though larger wagons may have been used for the purpose.[12]

4 Unconstitutional The rules made by the Central Government must be consistent with the provisions of the fundamental rights guaranteed by the Constitution of India. A rule restricting sale of platform tickets for a particular period in the interest of pilgrims visiting the place does not violate Art. 19(1)(*d*) of the Constitution of India.[13] Rule 7(*e*) as to disposal of offensive goods is not *ultra vires.*[14]

Appointment of Railway Tourist Agent Rules 1980 is not violative of Art. 14, Constitution of India, because the conditions or criteria prescribed by the Rules for recognition of a person as an authorised Railway Tourist Agent are reasonable and conducive to the object sought to be achieved.[15]

9 *Union of India* v *Radhikaran* AIR 1959 AP 17.
10 *Dominion of India* v *Virjee Doyal* ILR (1953)1 Cal 45; AIR 1952 Cal 70; 55 CWN 758.
11 29 NLR 306.
12 1933 ALJ 1180.
13 *Nanhu Lal* v *Gaya Lodging House Committee* AIR 1964 Pat 98.
14 *Mahamed* v *Union of India* AIR 1966 Ker 97; ILR (1966)1 Ker 404; 1965 Ker LJ 1085; 1966 Ker LT 80.
15 *Inder Mal Jain* v *Union of India* AIR 1984 SC 415; 1984 UJ (SC) 855; (1984)1 SCC 361.

5 Rules must be published in India Gazette The rules imposed on all railways by Government by a notification do not become the rules of a particular Railway Co., till they are published in the Gazette of India in the manner provided by s. 47 of the old Act.[16] In the restricted sense that delivery had not been taken, the goods may be said to have been unclaimed, but where ownership in the goods had been asserted and directions given as to their retention, it cannot be said that the goods have been unclaimed in the general sense of the word. The power given to the railways by the rules must be strictly construed. But it is not necessary to publish change in freight rates in order to bind the public by that change.[17]

6 Grant of lifetime free pass to travel by First Class A.C. Coach Grant of unlimited free travel by First Class A.C. Coach throughout the life for serving and retiring as member of Railway Board with his family members is arbitrary and violative of Art. 14 of the Constitution.[18]

CHAPTER IX
Carriage of Goods

61. Maintenance of rate-books, etc., for carriage of goods. Every railway administration shall maintain, at each station and at such other places where goods are received for carriage, the rate-books or other documents which shall contain the rate authorised for the carriage of goods from one station to another and make them available for the reference of any person during all reasonable hours without payment of any fee.

1 Corresponding provision This section corresponds to s. 60 of the old Act.

2 Scope Section 61 provides that every railway administration shall maintain at each railway station rate-books or other documents for carriage of goods from one station to another.

62. Conditions for receiving, etc., of goods. (1) A railway administration may impose conditions, not inconsistent with this Act or any rules made thereunder, with respect to the receiving, forwarding, carrying or delivering of any goods.

(2) A railway administration shall maintain, at each station and at such other places where goods are received for carriage, a copy of the conditions for the time being in force under sub-section (1) and make them available for the reference of any person during all reasonable hours without payment of any fee.

1 Corresponding provision This section corresponds to s. 54 of the old Act.

16 *Hari Lal* v *B.N. Railway Co.* 15 CWN 195; 9 IC 331; 13 CLJ 150.
17 *Secretary of State* v *Thakurdas* AIR 1927 All 316; 100 IC 260.
18 *Rekha Bhasin* v *Union of India* AIR 1998 Del 314.

2 Duties as bailee Section 54 of the old Act (corresponding to s. 62 of the Railways Act 1989) does not provide anything to do with the responsibility of a railway company as a bailee.[1] A railway company or administration is not empowered to make rules for exemption from liability for any loss, deterioration or destruction of, or damage to goods.[2] A railway company cannot divert itself wholly of duties as bailee in respect of goods consigned, but it may determine conditions under which its duty may vest and in particulars it may specify the point of time at which it shall vest.[3]

3 Power to impose conditions This section does not authorise fixation of warehousing rates.[4]

Section 54 of the old Act (corresponding to s. 62 of the Railways Act 1989) gives the railway administration a power to impose conditions not inconsistent with the old Act or with any general rules thereunder with respect to the receiving, forwarding or delivering of any animals or goods. Section 55 of the old Act (corresponding to s. 83 of the Railways Act 1989) gives it a lien on the goods for any rate, terminals or other charges due to it so as to entitle it to detain the whole or any of the goods for enforcing such payments and even to sell the same for their recovery. The obligation or liability to refund an overcharge, and power to levy undercharge, by necessary implication involves the necessary liability or right to re-weigh the goods for the due performance of the principal obligation or right as between the parties to any contract of consignment. In short the railway company is entitled to re-weigh the consignment and collect the excess charge for the excess weight at the destination and to detain and sell the goods, if the undercharge is not paid, and credit the sale proceeds towards the undercharge and demurrage if then due by defaulter. As a necessary counterpart of such right of the railway company is the right of the consignor or consignee to claim a refund of any overcharge recovered from him, as expressly provided for in s. 77 of the (old) Act (corresponding to s. 99 of the Railways Act 1989). As in the case of determining and collecting an undercharge, so in the case of refunding an overcharge, a right to re-measurement, re-weighment and re-calculation must necessarily be implied. If a right to re-weigh goods is an accessory to the substantive right of the company to calculate an undercharge, same is the case with the right of a party entitled to a refund of an overcharge. If a consignee has *prima facie* good reasons to think, before he is actually called upon to surrender his railway receipt and to pay the overcharge, that an incorrect weight has been entered in the consignment, he has the right to ascertain to the knowledge of the company.[5] In this case the

1 *Sohanlal Munnalal* v *E.I. Rly* AIR 1922 All 9 (FB).
2 *Union of India* v *Shantilal N. Jain* AIR 1957 MP 192.
3 *Jalim* v *Secy. of State* (1904)31 Cal 951.
4 *G.I.P. Railway* v *Kiran Devi* AIR 1960 All 371; 1960 ALJ 16.
5 *Harakchand* v *G.I.P. Railway Co.* AIR 1927 Nag 77.

learned Judge held the previous cases in *Janki Das* v *B.N. Railway Co.*[6] and *Ramjas* v *I.G.N. & Railway Co.*[7] as incorrectly decided and followed *Rohilkhand & Kumaon Railway* v *Ismail.*[8]

No general rule as to whether a railway company has authority to charge excess freight at the place of destination can be laid down. In *Chuni Lal* v *Nizam's Guaranteed State Railway Co.*[9] the railway company had charged for the carriage of certain goods the freight at the wagon rate, but at destination it was re-calculated at maundage rate. It was not a case of "re-measurement, re-weighment, re-classification and re-calculation of rates." In *Chhotey Lal Panna Lal* v *R.K. Railway,*[10] the railway company was not entitled to charge freight in excess of what had been paid on consignment. In *Secretary of State* v *Harbans Prasad,*[11] it was held that condition No. 6 noted on the back of the railway receipt was applicable and the railway company had authority to charge excess freight.

In *Firm Ram Lal* v *Secretary of State,*[12] a railway company charged at a lesser rate than the actual rate on a certain consignment of goods through the mistake of its clerk who thought that the goods were home materials. On reaching its destination the railway company charged on it an excess by calculating the freight at a higher rate. The consignor therefore filed a suit for recovery of the excess paid by him. The railway company was within its rights to charge freight at the higher rate at the place of destination, in view of condition No. 6 printed on the back of the railway receipt. The same view was adopted in the case of *Firm Ganga Prasad* v *Secretary of State.*[13] A rule reserving the railway company's right of re-measurement, re-weighment, re-calculation and re-classification of rates, terminal and other charges at the place of destination does not give the railway company power to alter the contract between the parties. Where a railway company originally agreed to carry plaintiff's goods according to the maund rate, it was not open to the company to alter that contract and charge according to the wagon rate.[14]

A railway administration cannot impose any condition absolving it from responsibility as a carrier. It cannot avoid or unduly restrict its liability by framing its own rules and if any such rules are found to be

6 16 CWN 356.
7 22 CWN 310.
8 13 ALJ 417.
9 29 All 228.
10 54 All 557.
11 52 All 81.
12 AIR 1937All 400.
13 AIR 1937 All 642.
14 *Bombay, Baroda & C.I. Railway Co.* v *Firm Budh Sen Pusp Chand* 21 CLJ 830; *Allauddin* v *G.I.P. Railway Co.* 14 ALJ 494; *Chuni Lal* v *Nizam's Guaranteed State Railway Co. Ltd* 29 All 228.

unreasonable or inconsistent with the Act, they will be declared *ultra vires.*[15] A railway circular imposing restriction on booking of coal in "smalls" was held to be inconsistent among others with the provisions of s. 54 of the old Act (corresponding to s. 62 of the Railways Act 1989).[16] Section 54(1) of the old Act permits a railway administration to impose conditions with respect to receiving, forwarding or delivering of any animal or goods, but such conditions must not be inconsistent with the provisions of the old Act or with any general rules framed under the old Act. Thus, if the Central Government or railway administration in exercise of rule making powers conferred on them by the provision of the Act make any rule in consonance with the provision of the Act, such rule cannot be declared *ultra vires.*[17] A railway company can impose conditions by making rules under s. 54(1) of the old Act as regards form of packing as a condition precedent to acceptance of goods by it for being carried at railway risk.[18]

4 Suit for value of goods Suit for recovery of value of goods on ground that sale of goods by railway without notice before sale was unlawful. Thus, no written claim by consignor was necessary.[19]

5 Re-booking of goods Where consignor who was also consignee had given authority to another person to take delivery, railway administration has no power to re-book goods upon their reaching destination on application of the person who was only authorised to take delivery of the goods. Under the relevant rules whenever re-booking is done an application is taken from consignor or consignee, as the case may be, for that purpose, and after re-booking of goods railway receipts are sent to him under registered cover.[20]

6 Goods Tariff Rules Goods described as "Kalanji" seeds in railway receipt at the place of consignment were classified at the destination as "Kalajira" subject to higher tariff and undercharge on that basis was collected. There was no evidence on record to show that the two terms described were identical article. Thus, the railway was entitled under r. 15 of the Goods Tariff Rules No. 28 to correct charges at destination and recover undercharge.[1]

7 Minimum carrying capacity of wagon Whereafter taking all the relevant factors into consideration the minimum carrying capacity of the wagon is determined, it cannot be said that the fixation of the minimum carrying

15 *Hardayal* v *B. & N. W. Rly Co.* AIR 1929 Pat 296; 8 Pat 808.
16 *Satyanarayan Musarka* v *Union of India* AIR 1975 Cal 316; 78 CWN 884.
17 *Shakti Narayan* v *Union of India* 1981(2) CHN 212; (1981)2 CLJ 312.
18 *Secretary of State* v *Vasant Ram Chopra* AIR 1927 All 400.
19 *Union of India* v *M.M. Mudaliar* AIR 1972 Mad 140; 84 Mad LW 869.
20 *Mohd. Ekram* v *Union of India* AIR 1959 Pat 337; ILR 37 Pat 1355.
1 *Union of India* v *Firm Keshari Chand* AIR 1962 Ori 49.

capacity is done arbitrarily and fact that these were certain imperfection or some alternative method was available could be of no consequence.[2]

8 Indian Railway Conference Association Rules Rule 161A of the Indian Railway Conference Association Rules provides for penalty for overloading of coal. This rule also contains a *non-obstante* clause which would in any event override rr. 6 and 29 of the Eastern Railway Coal Tariff Part-I.[3] Rule 161A further provides for recovery from the consignor penalty for overloading both under the old Act and the new Act.[4]

63. Provision of risk rates. (1) Where any goods are entrusted to a railway administration for carriage, such carriage shall, except where owner's risk rate is applicable in respect of such goods, be at railway risk rate.

(2) Any goods, for which owner's risk rate and railway risk rate are in force, may be entrusted for carriage at either of the rates and if no rate is opted, the goods shall be deemed to have been entrusted at owner's risk rate.

1 Corresponding provision This section corresponds to s. 74(1) and (2) of the old Act.

2 Scope A railway administration may be entrusted for carriage of goods either at railway risk rate or owner's risk rate. It is generally expressly stated at initial stage of booking for carriage of goods. When the consignor has not opted either of the rates, the goods are deemed to be entrusted at owner's risk.

64. Forwarding note. (1) Every person entrusting any goods to a railway administration for carriage shall execute a forwarding note in such form as may be specified by the Central Government:

Provided that no forwarding note shall be executed in the case of such goods as may be prescribed.

(2) The consignor shall be responsible for the correctness of the particulars furnished by him in the forwarding note.

(3) The consignor shall indemnify the railway administration against any damage suffered by it by reason of the incorrectness or incompleteness of the particulars in the forwarding note.

1 Corresponding provision This section corresponds to s. 72 of the old Act.

2 Loss of goods in transit A consignor of goods is required to execute a forwarding note while entrusting goods to a railway administration for

2 *Ahmadabad Electricity Co. Ltd.* v *Union of India* AIR 1988 Guj 169; (1988)29 Guj LR 133.

3 *J.C. Textile Mills* v *Chief Coml. Supldt., N.R.* 1998 AIR SCW 1804; 1998 All LJ 1314; AIR 1998 SC 1959; (1998)5 SCC 126; JT 1998(3) SC 297.

4 *Ibid.*

carriage unless it is required under any rule as prescribed under s. 64 of the Act. A person claims for damages for loss of goods in transit in absence of affidavit of the loading clerk. Presumption was drawn as to correctness of entries made in the forwarding note.[5]

3 Liability of railway administration A railway receipt is issued on the basis of information furnished in the forwarding note for the purpose of intimating the railway charges and no admission is conveyed thereunder either about the weight or description of goods stated therein. The liability of a railway ought not to be fastened on the basis of railway receipt. The word "delivered" occurring in s. 72 of the old Act (corresponding to s. 64 of the Railways Act 1989) refers merely to a physical event and is devoid of any legal significance and restriction of liability created by s. 72 of the old Act.[6] A railway company cannot escape liability by providing in a rule that in respect of any loss, destruction, deterioration or damage to goods which arises from whatever causes if the goods are not removed within the time allowed free of demurrage and wharfage exceeding an amount.[7] But the railway cannot be held liable for non-delivery of tank wagon to the consignor if it is seized and destroyed by the Calcutta Corporation for the oil being adulterated.[8]

4 Meaning of forwarding note Definition of "forwarding note" as defined in s. 2(16) is to be read with s. 64 of the Act. Forwarding note contains particulars of goods furnished in a prescribed form supplied by the railway administration to a person who entrusts any goods to the railway for carriage.

5 Label delivery of goods To facilitate quick delivery as well as to avoid demurrage charges label delivery facility is in vogue. But if the consignor refuses to make payment of freight for excess weight carried, the railway administration is competent to discontinue the facility of label delivery.[9]

65. Railway receipt. (1) A railway administration shall,—

(*a*) in a case where the goods are to be loaded by a person entrusting such goods, on the completion of such loading; or

(*b*) in any other case, on the acceptance of the goods by it, issue a railway receipt in such form as may be specified by the Central Government.

(2) A railway receipt shall be *prima facie* evidence of the weight and the number of packages stated therein:

Provided that in the case of a consignment in wagon-load or train-load and the weight or the number of package is not checked by a railway servant authorised in this behalf, and a statement to that effect is recorded in such railway receipt

5 *Union of India* v *Roop Narayan* AIR 1997 Raj 123; (1997)3 Raj LW 1697.
6 *Union of India* v *Hamirmull Champalal* AIR 1959 Cal 400.
7 *Governor General in Council* v *Jagan Nath* AIR 1943 Lah 244.
8 *Juggilal Kamlapat Oil Mills* v *Union of India* AIR 1976 SC 227; (1976)1 SCC 893.
9 *Parshottamdas Revandas & Sons* v *Union of India* AIR 1999 Guj 26.

by him, the burden of proving the weight or, as the case may be, the number of packages stated therein, shall lie on the consignor, the consignee or the endorsee.

1 Railway receipt and liability of railway administration "Railway receipt" as defined in s. 2(33) of the Act is to be read in the context of s. 65 of the Act. It is a document issued by a railway administration to a person who entrusts the railway with carriage of goods which are to be loaded or on acceptance of such goods. The form of railway receipt is prescribed by the Central Government. A railway receipt is a *prima facie* evidence of the weight and number of package entrusted to a railway administration for carriage. But where a railway receipt contains a statement of a railway servant that the weight or number of packages has not been checked by him, the burden of proving the particulars of goods consigned lies on the consignor, the consignee or the endorsee. When a railway receipt contains a remark, the same does not amount to admission, on the past of a railway administration that number of articles mentioned therein had in fact been loaded. However, if any package is found to be missing at the destination, the responsibility is required to be fixed. For that purpose examination of outward tally book and "forwarding note" are necessary.[10]

2 Railway receipt and effect on weighment Railway receipt did not contain any endorsement by railway servant that goods have not been weighed or packages have not been counted. Railway receipt shall be taken to be *prima facie* evidence of weight of consignment. Disputes regarding the weighment and number of packages should be resolved before delivery of goods. No notice of hearing nor any inquiry was made before issuing demand notice. Every step was taken behind the back of the petitioner. Such an action has civil and evil consequences. The demand notice was liable to be quashed.[11]

66. Power to require statement relating to the description of goods. **(1) The owner or a person having charge of any goods which are brought upon a railway for the purposes of carriage by railway, and the consignee or the endorsee of any consignment shall, on the request of any railway servant authorised in this behalf, deliver to such railway servant a statement in writing signed by such owner or person or by such consignee or endorsee, as the case may be, containing such description of the goods as would enable the railway servant to determine the rate for such carriage.**

(2) If such owner or person refuses or neglects to give the statement as required under sub-section (1) and refuses to open the package containing the goods, if so required by the railway servant, it shall be open to the railway administration to refuse to accept such goods for carriage unless such owner or person pays for such carriage the highest rate for any class of goods.

10 *Union of India* v *Roop Narayan* AIR 1997 Raj 123; (1997)3 Raj LW 1697.
11 *Mahaver Traders* v *Divisional Railways Manager* AIR 2010 MP 59.

(3) If the consignee or endorsee refuses or neglects to give the statement as required under sub-section (1) and refuses to open the package containing the goods, if so required by the railway servant, it shall be open to the railway administration to charge in respect of the carriage of the goods the highest rate for any class of goods.

(4) If the statement delivered under sub-section (1) is materially false with respect to the description of any goods to which it purports to relate, the railway administration may charge in respect of the carriage of such goods such rate, not exceeding double the highest rate for any class of goods as may be specified by the Central Government.

(5) If any difference arises between a railway servant and such owner or person, the consignee or the endorsee, as the case may be, in respect of the description of the goods for which a statement has been delivered under sub-section (1), the railway servant may detain and examine the goods.

(6) Where any goods have been detained under sub-section (5) for examination and upon such examination it is found that the description of the goods is different from that given in the statement delivered under sub-section (1), the cost of such detention and examination shall be borne by such owner or person, the consignee or the endorsee, as the case may be, and the railway administration shall not be liable for any loss, damage or deterioration which may be caused by such detention or examination.

1 Corresponding provision This section corresponds to s. 58 of the old Act.

2 Object The object of the section is to forbid the giving of a false description of goods carried by the railway and so protect the railway company from being created into carrying goods at less than the due rate. In *Mousell Bros.* v *L. & N. S.W. Railway*[12] the object of the statute was very clearly stated as follows: "It is the duty of every person sending goods by a carrier to make use of no fraud or artifice to deceive him, whereby his risk is increased, or his care and diligence may be lessened."

3 Scope Section 66 requires the consignor if so requested by an authorised railway servant to deliver "an account in writing" containing such a description of the goods as may be sufficient to determine the rate which the railway administration is entitled to charge. If the account is materially false the provisions of s. 100 of the Act will become applicable. In *Sorabji Dadabhai* v *B.N. Railway Co.,*[13] while dealing with s. 58 of the old Act (corresponding to s. 66 of the Railways Act 1989) and s. 75 of the old Act (corresponding to s. 100 of the Railways Act 1989) ROWLAND, J. observed as follows: The language used in the two sections is not identical but speaking for myself in my opinion the "declaration" is not a separate thing from the "account" and "description" referred to in s. 58; it appears to me

12 [1917]2 KB 836.
13 AIR 1936 Pat 393; 15 Pat 394; 163 IC 685.

that these provisions in s. 58 are of general application but that in the special circumstances described in s. 75 the account and description to be given under s. 58 must include a declaration as to value. In taking this view I observe that s. 75, cl. (1) contemplates payment of or engagement to pay a percentage on the value declared by way of compensation for increased risk; while s. 58 speaks of such a description of the goods as may be sufficient to determine the rate which the railway administration is entitled to charge. It is clear that had the full value been declared the railway would have been entitled to charge more. Section 78 though not divided into sub-sections contains two distinct provisions relating to responsibility for the loss, destruction or deterioration of goods with respect to the description of which an account, materially false, has been declared under s. 58. First, it is enacted that if the loss, destruction or deterioration is in any way brought about by the false account the railway administration shall not be responsible at all. This covers cases where the nature of dangerous goods has been fraudulently concealed and damage resulted. Secondly, that in any case the administration shall not be responsible "for an amount exceeding the value of the goods if such value were calculated in accordance with the description contained in the false account." The agent without any fraudulent intention described the contents of the 12 bags of sugar candy as alum. During the transit, a fire broke out in the train and a large portion of sugar candy was destroyed. In a suit for damage against the railway company for non-delivery, the railway was liable to the plaintiff in respect of the lost bags for the value of the contents as declared, and not for the actual contents, in spite of the misdescription that had been made innocently and without fraudulent intent.[14]

All that s. 58 of the old Act (corresponding to s. 66 of the Railways Act 1989) contemplates is a description of such a general nature as may be sufficient to determine the correct freight chargeable. There is no statutory obligation on a consignee of a box containing miscellaneous stationery articles to hand in a precise invoice describing separately every article in it. Where the box actually contained the following articles, namely, (1) two gross red-blue pencils, (2) five gross black lead pencils, (3) 20 gross swadeshi brass nibs, (4) 700 dozens sewing machine English needles, and (5) three dozen playing cards, and the contents of the box were described as 'stationery pencil', it was held that they cannot be said to have been described with material falsity.[15]

4 Liability of consignor Where goods are detained for no fault of the consignor but due to act of third parties, the consignor cannot be liable to pay demurrage charge. When goods are booked by the consignor and the

14 *Ishwardas* v *G.I.P. Railway* 3 Bom 120.

15 *Chunilal* v *Governor-General-in-Council* AIR 1949 Mad 754.

information given by the consignor is accepted as correct for the purpose of freight, there is no admission on the past of the railway that the description of goods as furnished by the consignee to correct. In the absence of independent evidence regarding quality of goods as shown in the railway receipt it cannot be said that the quality deteriorated in transit. Where penalty for loading wagons in excess of permissible capacity, there is no inconsistency between the rule and provision of the old Act.[16] When the reweightment of the consignment is done in route in the absence of the consignor, by the railway, the same should be informed to him to avoid confusion about the actual weight and over-weight.[17]

67. Carriage of dangerous or offensive goods. (1) No person shall take with him on a railway, or require a railway administration to carry such dangerous or offensive goods, as may be prescribed, except in accordance with the provisions of this section.

(2) No person shall take with him on a railway the goods referred to in sub-section (1) unless he gives a notice in writing of their dangerous or offensive nature to the railway servant authorised in this behalf.

(3) No person shall entrust the goods referred to in sub-section (1) to a railway servant authorised in this behalf for carriage unless he distinctly marks on the outside of the package containing such goods their dangerous or offensive nature and gives a notice in writing of their dangerous or offensive nature to such railway servant.

(4) If any railway servant has reason to believe that goods contained in a package are dangerous or offensive and notice as required under sub-section (2) or sub-section (3), as the case may be, in respect of such goods is not given, he may cause such package to be opened for the purpose of ascertaining its contents.

(5) Notwithstanding anything contained in this section, any railway servant may refuse to accept any dangerous or offensive goods for carriage or stop, in transit, such goods or cause the same to be removed, as the case may be, if he has reason to believe that the provisions of this section for such carriage are not complied with.

(6) Nothing in this section shall be construed to derogate from the provisions of the Indian Explosives Act, 1884 (4 of 1884), or any rule or order made under that Act, and nothing in sub-sections (4) and (5) shall be construed to apply to any goods entrusted for carriage by order or on behalf of the Government or to any goods which a soldier, sailor, airman or any other officer of the armed forces of the Union or a police officer or a member of the Territorial Army or of the National Cadet Corps may take with him on a railway in the course of his employment or duty as such.

16 *Straw Products Ltd* v *Union of India* AIR 1995 Raj 193.
17 *Darshan Kumar* v *Station Master* AIR 1986 J&K 74.

1 Corresponding provision This section corresponds to s. 59 of the old Act.

2 Scope Section 67 of the Act prohibits a person taking with him or consigning on a railway dangerous or offensive goods without distinctive mark on the outside of the package. A railway servant has authority to deal with such goods. A person sending a dangerous article by railway without notifying its characters to railway servant is liable for any accident resulting from his negligence in combination with other causes which he did not contemplate.[18] Fire-works are dangerous goods within the meaning of s. 59 of the old Act.[19]

68. Carriage of animals suffering from infectious or contagious diseases. **A railway administration shall not be bound to carry any animal suffering from such infectious or contagious disease as may be prescribed.**

Corresponding provision This section corresponds to s. 54(3) of the old Act.

69. Deviation of route. **Where due to any cause beyond the control of a railway administration or due to congestion in the yard or any other operational reasons, goods are carried over a route other than the route by which such goods are booked, the railway administration shall not be deemed to have committed a breach of the contract of carriage by reason only of the deviation of the route.**

1 Corresponding provision This section corresponds to s. 76A of the old Act.

2 Deviation of route The railway is to carry the goods to the place of destination without deviation from the usual route. If it deviates from the usual route and the goods are lost for any reason whatsoever, the railway is liable and the provisions in the Risk Note cannot relieve the railway from the liability.[20] Where the goods were damaged during transit due to deviation of route and transfer of wagon, the railway administration was held liable.[21] Where the railway deviates from the ordinary route by which it carries goods and the deviation is not imperative, the railway administration forfeits the protection given to them.[1] The present section has been enacted to relieve the railway from liability for deviation of route in certain cases. Deviation of route is now made permissible and would not be regarded as a breach of the contract of carriage if the railway administration is able to prove that such deviation was due to some cause beyond the control of railway administration (e.g. flood) or due to congestion in the yard or other operational reasons.

18 *Lyell* v *Ganga Devi* (1877)1 All 60 (FB).
19 *E.I. Rly* v *Kalidas Mukherjee* (1899)26 Cal 465.
20 *Mahesh Glass Works* v *Governor-General-in-Council* AIR 1950 All 543; 1950 ALJ 625.
21 *Union of India* v *Endupudi Narsimham & Sons* AIR 1964 Ori 34; 29 CLJ 647.
1 *Prabhulal Thakur* v *Union of India* AIR 1964 Ori 82; ILR (1963) Cut 459.

3 Protection of railway In case of deviation from contracted route the railway for the purpose of protecting itself from liability should strictly prove the reasons which compelled them to make the traffic on a route other than the one over which goods were booked and for which freight had been recovered. Mere repetition of the expression "congestion in the yard or other operational reason and the like" in the written statement is not sufficient.[2]

70. Prohibition of undue preference. A railway administration shall not make or give any undue or unreasonable preference or advantage to, or in favour of, any particular person or any particular description of traffic in the carriage of goods.

1 Corresponding provision This section corresponds to s. 28 of the old Act.

2 Scope Section 70 of the Act aims at putting an embargo on giving undue preference in favour of any particular person. It is based on the principle that the power derived from the monopoly of railway carriage must be used in a fair and just manner in respect of all persons and all descriptions of traffic passing over the railway area. In other words, equal charges should normally be levied against persons or goods of the same or similar kinds passing over the same or similar area of the railway lines and under the same or similar circumstance; but this rule does not mean that, if the railway administration charges unequal rates in respect of the same or similar class of goods travelling over the same or similar areas, the inequality of rates necessarily attracts the provisions of (old) s. 28 (corresponding to s. 70 of the Railways Act 1989). All cases of unequal rates cannot necessarily be treated as cases of preference because the very concept of preference postulates competition between the person of traffic receiving preference and the person or traffic suffering prejudice in consequence. It is only as between competitors in the same trade that a complaint of preference can be made by one in reference to the other.[3]

3 Undue preference The expression 'undue preference' has not been defined in the Indian Railways Act. The definition of the term is to be found in the English Act known as the Railway and Canal Traffic Act 1888, on which the Indian Act is modelled. Section 55 of that Act says: "The term 'undue preference' includes an undue preference or an undue or unreasonable prejudice or disadvantage, in any respect, in favour of or against any person or particular class of persons or any particular description of traffic."

2 *Union of India* v *Steel Authority of India Ltd.* AIR 1997 Ori 77.

3 *Rajgarh Jute Mills* v *Eastern Railway* AIR 1958 SC 525 (528-529); 1959 SCR 236; 1958 SCJ 720; *Delhi Cloth & General Mills* v *Union of India* AIR 1987 SC 2414; (1987)3 SCJ 328; (1987)3 Cur Civ Cas 983. See *Virlad Coal Merchant, Patiala* v *Union of India* AIR 1984 SC 95; (1984)1 SCC 619; (1984)1 SCR 657.

The act of the company in reserving a railway compartment for any particular class of passengers may amount to undue preference provided other circumstances exist and are proved to render such act unreasonable and disadvantageous to other passengers, for instance, if it is proved that the train by which the petitioner wanted to travel was full and no room was available for him except in the reserved compartment. The departmental rule enabling the Company to reserve a compartment for a class of ordinary passengers may be a violation of the term of s. 42(2) of the old Act in certain circumstances but the Company has a general power to regulate its traffic and arrange for the accommodation and convenience of its passengers so long as it does not bring itself within that section. A railway company has an absolute right to regulate its own traffic in its own way, its own interest being the best security that its strict legal right to do so will not be abused so long as it does not contravene any express provision of the law.[4]

The term 'undue preference' includes almost every form of undue preference, prejudice or advantage or disadvantage as between different traders, different localities or different classes of traffic. A railway company shall hold out equal opportunities and equal facilities to all persons using the railway. But the legitimate interests of competition with rival lines are not to be lost sight of. When a firm undertakes to send regular and complete loads, producing a certain adequate increase of economy and profits to the company that may be a sufficient consideration for a differential charge.[5] To justify interference by the commissioners it was not sufficient merely that a distinction in the fares of different lines, even of the same company, existed, unless it created an undue preference or prejudice.[6]

Differences in treatment may not amount to undue preference or prejudice for special reasons attached to particular cases, for instance—

(*a*) where goods are delivered in a more convenient form for handling.[7]

(*b*) inequality in the rate of charge in cases where unequal distances are traversed.[8]

(*c*) where the cost of working a section of the railway line justifies higher charge.[9]

4 *Emperor* v *Narayana Krishna* AIR 1923 Bom 1; *Bhupendra* v *King-Emperor* AIR 1924 Cal 687.

5 *Nicholson* v *G.N. Railway Co.* 5 CBNS 366; *Evershed* v *L. & N.W. Railway Co.* 2 QBD 254.

6 *Innes* v *L.B. & S.C. Railway* [1875]3 Ry & Can Tr Cas 155.

7 *L.& N.W. Railway Co.* v *Evershed* [1873]3 App Cas 1029.

8 *Denaby* v *M.S. & L. Railway Co.* [1885]11 App Cas 97.

9 *Nitshill & L.C. Co.* v *Caledonian Railway* [1874]2 Ry. & Can Tr Cas 39.

But if it can be shown that charges were made, either as regards a particular train or as regards a particular station so much an amount as to be calculated to prevent the use of those trains or the traffic to those stations, it would be refusing reasonable facilities for receiving and forwarding passengers by those trains, and if it was stated and proved that it was done with the object of preventing the use of the accommodation that might also give the railway commissioners power to entertain the question of the quantum, if it was shown either from the excess that it was calculated to have that effect or that it was done for the purpose of having that result.[10]

A railway company increased their rate for traffic in carrying coals from collieries in their district to places beyond it in 1913. In 1916 they entered into an agreement with certain coal-owners in the district to carry their coal for a certain period at a rate less than the increased rate imposed in 1913. A colliery agent in the district, for whom the railway company had carried coal during the period mentioned in the agreement, to which he was not a party, declined to pay carriage charged at the increased rate, and paid only at the old rate. The railway company brought an action to recover the difference between the two rates. As the owners who were parties to the agreement were charged at a lower rate, the increased rate was not "charged equally to all persons" as required by s. 90 of the Railway Clauses Consolidation Act 1845, and was invalid.[11]

All cases of unequal rates cannot necessarily be treated as cases of undue preference. The application of s. 28 arises where the competition between two persons or classes of goods is either admitted or proved. The initial burden to prove preference is on the person making the complaint. When such burden is discharged by the proof of unequal rates as between the complainant and his competitor, it is for the railway administration to prove that the preference is not undue. In considering the question of undue preference, the Tribunal is entitled to consider whether the lower charge levied by the administration in respect of the competing class of goods was necessary in the interest of the public.[12]

4 Undue or unreasonable prejudice or disadvantage A Circular dated 2.4.73 purported to have been issued by the G.M., Eastern Railway under s. 54 of the (old) Indian Railways Act (corresponding to s. 62 of the Railways Act 1989) read with paragraph 201 of the Goods Tariff No. 33, Part I, which restricted the booking of coals in 'smalls' to 5 quintals per day from any station on the Railway is inconsistent with the last part of (old) s. 28 and r. 201 of Goods Tariff No. 33, Part I and *ultra vires* of (old) s. 28.

10 *G.W. Railway* v *Railway Comms.*, in re 50 LJQB 483.
11 *North Staffordshire Railway* v *Edge* 89 LJ KB 78; 36 TLR 115 HL (E).
12 *Raigarh Jute Mills* v *Eastern Railway* AIR 1958 SC 525; 1958 SCJ 720; 1959 SCR 236.

The impugned Circular also offends the petitioner's fundamental right under Art. 19(1)(*g*) as the conditions are not reasonable restriction in the interest of general public within the meaning of cl. (6) of Art. 19 of the Constitution of India.[13] Declaration that rates between two stations are unreasonable is within the jurisdiction of Tribunal.[14]

The principle of equal treatment envisaged in this section is the same as embodied in Art. 14 of the Constitution of India and the only difference is that Art. 14 is general in terms while (old) s. 28 is specific in its application.[15]

If the Central Government differentiates between the Government Railways and the non-Government Railways in the matter of fixation of rates or freight, etc., there is no violation of Art. 14 of the Constitution of India since the Government Railways are a class by themselves.[16]

5 Out of turn release of wagon—prejudice to indentor of wagon Where prior to the registration of petitioner's indent for supply of wagons for loading lime, indents for two wagons for loading charcoal and fourteen wagons for loading timber were already registered and the charcoal timber and lime all fell under item No. (1) in priority 'E' of the schedule to the General Order issued by the Central Government the sudden release of wagons out of turn to the petitioner would be in contravention of r. 201(10) which read as follows:

> "201(10). *Allotment / loading orders.* Each item of wagon registration is given a serial number in the order of registration. Allotment/Loading Orders are issued in accordance with the priority of registration and also having regard to preferential schedules prescribed by the Railway Board quotas and restrictions in force and other operating considerations."

The out of turn allotment may be prejudicial to the trader concerned, for, on perusal of the wagon demand/priority Register he may arrange for the goods. And when wagon is allotted before the anticipated time, he may not be in a position to load requiring cancellation of registration. Thus, writ petition alleging such prejudice for out of turn allotment succeeded and out of turn allotment was cancelled.[17]

6 Railway Commissioners to give remedy In *Emperor* v *Narayan Krishna Gogte*[18] MARTEN, J., in his separate judgment, observed as follows: "In conclusion I will again quote from *Perth General Station Committee* v

13 *Satyanarayan Murarka* v *Union of India* 78 CWN 884; AIR 1975 Cal 316.
14 *Union of India* v *W.C. Paper Mills* AIR 1971 SC 349; (1970)3 SCC 606; (1971)2 SCR 594.
15 *Ranvir Singh* v *Chief Commercial Superintendent* AIR 1961 Punj 263.
16 *Dehri Rohtas Light Railway Co. Ltd* v *Union of India* AIR 1970 Pat 109; ILR (1970) Pat 399.
17 *K.P. Sons* v *Union of India* AIR 1982 MP 81; 1982 MPLJ 126; 1982 Jab LJ 227.
18 AIR 1923 Bom 1.

Ross[19] and this time I will cite what LORD WATSON, another great judge, said in that case at p. 479: "But the legislature has not committed to the ordinary tribunals of the country the duty of determining whether the implied obligation of giving accommodation to the public has been duly fulfilled. When a member of the public having the right to use a railway or a station has reason, or without reason thinks fit to complain that some facility which he ought to have has been withheld from him, and that an undue preference had been shown to others in the same position, a Court of Law can give him no remedy. He must resort to the tribunal which the legislature has constituted for that purpose, the Railway Commissioner, and until they have decided in his favour, he is not in a position, and no Court would be justified in holding, that he stands possessed of the right which he asserts."

7 Lease of parcel space—when permissible Statute does not prescribe any particular manner in which wagons are to be leased. There is a policy decision of contract of lease of Front Second Class Luggage Rake (FSLR) and Ventilated Parcel Van (VP). Lease given after auction process is not violative of statutory provisions. Auction of luggage space in train for particular period is permissible provided auction contractor adheres to prescribed tariff.[20]

71. Power to give direction in regard to carriage of certain goods. (1) The Central Government may, if it is of the opinion that it is necessary in the public interest so to do, by general or special order, direct any railway administration—

(*a*) to give special facilities for, or preference to, the carriage of such goods or class of goods consigned by or to the Central Government or the Government of any State or of such other goods or class of goods;

(*b*) to carry any goods or class of goods by such route or routes and at such rates;

(*c*) to restrict or refuse acceptance of such goods or class of goods at or to such station for carriage,

as may be specified in the order.

(2) Any order made under sub-section (1) shall cease to have effect after the expiration of a period of one year from the date of such order, but may, by a like order, be renewed from time to time for such period not exceeding one year at a time as may be specified in the order.

(3) Notwithstanding anything contained in this Act, every railway administration shall be bound to comply with any order given under sub-section (1) and any action taken by a railway administration in pursuance of any such order shall not be deemed to be a contravention of section 70.

19 [1897] AC 479.
20 *S.K.L. Co.* v *Chief Commercial Officer* AIR 2016 SC 193.

1 Corresponding provision This section corresponds to s. 27A of the old Act.

2 Scope Undue preference by railway administration is statutorily prohibited but preferential treatment in respect of goods or class of goods can be accorded if the Central Government by a special or general order in public interest so directs.[21]

Under the Railways Act, traffic in regard to sponsored coal is assigned higher priority 'C' in the Preferential Traffic Schedule, but mere sponsoring at the State level by the Director of Industries does not guarantee sanction or allotment of a particular number of coal wagons for any particular year much less for the subsequent years or in perpetuity. The sponsoring by the Directorate is mere recommendation within ceiling limits. The Director, Movement (Railway) proceeds to sanction, keeping in view the likely availability of coal and coal wagons and in anticipation of things likely to take shape. This is inherently variable and open to fluctuation. Allotment/supply of wagons is regulated according to operational exigencies from time to time and *inter se* seniority of class of consumers who remain alterable from time to time. The Director, Movement (Railways) is expressly given the power under the Schedule to cancel or reduce the allotment/supplies of wagons. He can lay down the period of validity of programme/sanction from time to time. The validity of programme/sanction carries no guarantee of allotment/supply of wagons. In order to be eligible for obtaining allotment of wagon under priority C, it is necessary for the person indenting the wagon to satisfy the various conditions specified therein. They are: (*i*) that the coal is to be loaded from the collieries; (*ii*) that the coal to be loaded is in conformity with the commodity quotas laid down from time to time for certain types of coal and/or in accordance with the programmes and movements sponsored or recommended by the Coal Controller and/or any committee appointed by him; (*iii*) or it is sponsored or recommended by the State Government and/or other recommending authorities and accepted by the railway administration; (*iv*) or it is sponsored or recommended by Director, Movement (Railways); (*v*) and it must be in accordance with the Zonal Scheme applicable to each field and the principles of transport rationalisation in force time to time. Where the allottee of coal wagon filed a suit to restrain the railway administration from in any manner suspending, obstructing, interfering with or withholding the supply of coal wagons to the plaintiff-allottee, the trial court decreed the suit *ex parte*, directing that 9 coal wagons a month be continued to be allotted to the plaintiff in the infinite future, irrespective of all other varying

21 *Vikilad Coal Merchants* v *Union of India* AIR 1984 SC 95 (102-103); (1984)1 SCC 619 (631-632).

conditions. The trial court assumed to itself the jurisdiction which vested in Director, Movement (Railways) and granted a decree for fixed number of coal wagons to continue to be allotted to the plaintiff in the infinite future irrespective of all other varying conditions. The direction of the civil court, therefore, ran clearly in derogation of the provisions contained in ss. 27, 27A, 28 of the Railways Act (old) read with the Preferential Traffic Schedule.[1]

3 Preferential Traffic Schedule—vires In exercise of power under s. 27A of the (old) Railway Act, the Central Government issued Preferential Traffic Schedule directing that all railway administration shall give special facilities for or preference to the transport of goods or class of goods specified in the Schedule. A list of sponsoring authorities authorised to sponsor coal movements under Priority C (*iii*) is set out in Annexure B to Schedule. There is a further provision under Item (*iii*) that besides the sponsoring authority mentioned in Annexure B, movement of coal may be sponsored by "any other authority who may be appointed by the Government from time to time".

By an order dated 1st April 1972, the Government of India, Ministry of Railways added Entry 'GX' to the Indian Railway Conference Association's alphabetical list of railway stations in India. As a result of this order when abbreviation 'GX' was appended to any railway station it would *inter alia* mean that the station was not open for outward booking of coal, shale, lignite, patent fuel, soft coke and hard coke in wagon-loads. This course of conduct by the Central Government was assailed as violative of Art. 14 and Art. 19(1)(*g*), Constitution of India. When a few coal merchants by a group of writ petitions under Art. 32, Constitution of India alleged that they had been denied the use of railways for transport of coal from various coal fields and wayside stations to their destination by certain orders of the railways and as contended it was illegal and unconstitutional. But the Supreme Court upheld the vires of the action by the Central Government.[2] Dealing with the Preferential Traffic Schedules the Supreme Court dealt with different priorities and analysing priority 'C' which gave the movement of coal to sponsored dealers priority, the court observed "priority 'C' (*iii*) which deals with coal provides for transport of coal from collieries to various parts in India. It was subjected to varying constructions. In order to comply with the pre-conditions for eligibility under priority 'C', a list of sponsoring authortiy authorised to sponsor coal movements is drawn up and is set out in Annexure 'B' to the Preferential Traffic Schedule. There general conditions are further subject to Notes A to E.

1 *Director of Railway Movement* v *Akashwani Glass Works* AIR 1985 All 314.
2 *Vikilad Coal* v *Union of India* AIR 1984 SC 95; (1984)1 SCC 619; (1984)1 SCR 657.

In *Vikilad Coal's* case (*ibid*) the Supreme Court permitted the preferential traffic system on the basis of priority 'C' and one of the main conditions of priority 'C' was that booking of coal must be from the collieries. But in cases of areas having coal fields or having excess quantity of coal available for use in other parts of the country but having no railway stations in the collieries it will not be possible to supply coal to those places in Punjab and North where coal is required. This would be contrary to the system of equitable and reasonable readjustment of rights between the different sectors, upon the whole basis of which the decision rested in *Vikilad's* case unless the nominated stations, stations nominated by the Railways are treated as 'railway stations' in collieries in the spirit of *Vikilad's* case. The nominated stations are to be treated as 'railway stations' in collieries.[3]

Coal rejects answer Entry GX in Alphabetic List of Railway Stations in India introduced by Order NOTCR/1510/71 dt. 1.4.1972. Washery is a coal preparation plant in which cleaning process is carried out by wet methods. After washing the coal in the washery the high grades of coal with less ash contents are taken out for use in steel plants, foundry and other manufacturing plants where constant high temperature is required to be maintained and the left out materials are known as washery sinks, middlings and rejects with little burning capacity and sold for use where high grade of heat is not required. Thus the washery sinks, middlings and rejects being different forms of coal are coal within the Entry GX and as such the prohibition of booking of coal from wayside railway stations in Entry GX applies to them.[4]

4 Delegations of power Where the power to issue the rationalisation order in respect of the transport of goods, is vested only in the Central Government, the same cannot be delegated to the Railway Board or any other authority.[5]

5 Claim for differential amount of freight A consignor of special goods was required by railway to carry them by rationalised route, which was a longer route but the said goods were actually carried over a shorter route. The consignor claimed the differential amount due to freight paid by him for longer route. Such claim would fall under s. 72 of the Contract Act 1872.[6] But where freight for carriage of goods is charged for shortest

3 *Bansal & Co.* v *Union of India* AIR 1986 SC 452; (1986)1 SCC 556; (1986)1 Car Civ Cas 720; *B.G. Yadav* v *Union of India* AIR 1986 Del 353.
4 *B.G. Yadav* v *Union of India* (supra).
5 *Gujarat Ambuja Cement Ltd.* v *Union of India* AIR 1994 Guj 104; (1993)2 Guj LR 1460.
6 *Union of India* v *Steel Authority of India Ltd.* AIR 1997 Ori 77.

route by promise, the railway is estopped from rationalising the longest route on the ground that the shortest route is an uncontrolled section with punitive signalling arrangement.[7]

6 Power of rationalisation The power of rationalisation of the longest route is to be exercised as a temporary measure only in exceptional circumstances and cannot be invoked for increasing revenue and in the absence of such circumstances, the order is to be deemed to be one made with intent to charge enhanced freight.[8]

72. Maximum carrying capacity for wagons and trucks. (1) The gross weight of every wagon or truck bearing on the axles when the wagon or truck is loaded to its maximum carrying capacity shall not exceed such limit as may be fixed by the Central Government for the class of axle under the wagon or truck.

(2) Subject to the limit fixed under sub-section (1), every railway administration shall determine the normal carrying capacity for every wagon or truck in its possession and shall exhibit in words and figures the normal carrying capacity so determined in a conspicuous manner on the outside of every such wagon or truck.

(3) Every person owning a wagon or truck which passes over a railway shall determine and exhibit the normal carrying capacity for the wagon or truck in the manner specified in sub-section (2).

(4) Notwithstanding anything contained in sub-section (2) or sub-section (3), where a railway administration considers it necessary or expedient so to do in respect of any wagon or truck carrying any specified class of goods or any class of wagons or trucks of any specified type, it may vary the normal carrying capacity for such wagon or truck or such class of wagons or trucks and subject to such conditions as it may think fit to impose, determine for the wagon or truck or class of wagons or trucks such carrying capacity as may be specified in the notification and it shall not be necessary to exhibit the words and figures representing the carrying capacity so determined on the outside of such wagon or truck or such class of wagons or trucks.

1 Corresponding provision This section corresponds to s. 53 of the old Act.

2 Maximum carrying capacity Gross weight and maximum carrying capacity are laid down by the Commissioner of Railway Safety on behalf of the Government of India while the normal carrying capacity is marked on the wagon by the railway administration, but always below the limits prescribed in s. 53(1) of the old Act (corresponding to s. 72 of the Railways Act 1989).[9]

7 *Gujarat Ambuja Cement Ltd.* v *Union of India* AIR 1994 Guj 104; (1993)2 Guj LR 1460.

8 *Gujarat Ambuja Cement Ltd.* v *Union of India* (supra).

9 *J.C. Textile Mills* v *Chief Comml. Suptdt., N.R.* 1998 AIR SCW 1804; 1998 All LJ 1314; AIR 1998 SC 1959.

3 Meaning of term—"permissible carrying capacity" The words "permissible carrying capacity" occurring in r. 161A of the Indian Railways Conference Association Rules and s. 73 of the new Act refer to average carrying capacity mentioned in s. 53(1) of the old Act (corresponding to s. 72 of the Railways Act 1989) and the permissible carrying capacity cannot exceed the upper limit prescribed under s. 53(1) of the old Act.[10]

4 Penalty Penalty for loading wagons in excess of permissible capacity is not inconsistent between r. 161A of the IRCA Rules and ss. 53 and 54 of the old Act (corresponding to ss. 72 and 62 of the Railways Act 1989).[11]

73. Punitive charge for overloading a wagon. Where a person loads goods in a wagon beyond its permissible carrying capacity as exhibited under sub-section (2) or sub-section (3), or notified under sub-section (4) of section 72, a railway administration may, in addition to the freight and other charges, recover from the consignor, the consignee or the endorsee, as the case may be, charges by way of penalty at such rates, as may be prescribed, before the delivery of the goods:

Provided that it shall be lawful for the railway administration to unload the goods loaded beyond the capacity of the wagon, if detected at the forwarding station or at any place before the destination station and to recover the cost of such unloading and any charge for the detention of any wagon on this account.

1 Levy of penalty The Railway authorities can levy penalty after re-weighment of the consignment under proviso to s. 73 read with s. 87(2) of the Act only after issuing show cause to the person from whom the penalty is sought to be recovered and after affording him reasonable opportunity of placing his case before the competent authority.[12] The Railway is entitled to recover penalty for overloading from consignee both under the new Act and old Act.[13]

2 Weighment of goods en route and recovery of penalty for overloading No notice is required to be given to the consignor, the consignee or the endorsee before making any weighment of a wagon for determining as to whether the wagon has been loaded beyond its permissible carrying capacity for the purpose of levying punitive charges for overloading of wagon. There is no provision in the Act that weighment of goods en route is to be made in the presence of a party.[14]

10 *J.C. Textile Mills* v *Chief Comml. Suptdt., N.R.* 1998 AIR SCW 1804; 1998 All LJ 1314; AIR 1998 SC 1959.

11 *Straw Products Ltd.* v *Union of India* AIR 1995 Raj 193; see *Ballarpur Industries Ltd.* v *Union of India* (1989)93 CWN 949.

12 *Union of India* v *Salt Marketing Centre* (1996)1 CWLJ 702 (Gau).

13 *J.C. Textile Mills* v *Chief Council Suptdt., N.R.* 1998 AIR SCW 1804; 1998 All LJ 1314; AIR 1998 SC 1959.

14 *Raghu Forwarding Agency* v *Union of India* AIR 2000 Gau 27.

3 Recovery of penalty from consignee for overloading Under the new Act of 1989 as well as under the old Act of 1890 the railway can recover the penalty for overloading of wagons even from the consignee. Section 73 of the Railways Act 1989 clearly stated that the penal charges can be collected from the consignor, consignee or endorsee, as the case may be. Under s. 74 of the Railways Act 1989 once the railway receipt is delivered to the consignee, not only the rights of the consignor but also the liabilities of the consignor pass on to the consignee. Thus the word "liability" in s. 74 includes the liability of the consignee to pay the penal charges under s. 73 for overloading of the wagon. Rule 161A of the Indian Railways Conference Association Rules providing for penalty for overloading of coal is not excluded by rr. 6 and 29 of the Eastern Railway Coal Tariff Part I. Penal charges for overloading of wagon can be recovered from the consignee even under s. 83 of the new Act. Thus, s. 73 of the new Act and r. 161A are not violative of Art. 14 of the Constitution.[15]

4 Overloading of wagon Railway administration is empowered to check weight of wagon at any point of time before delivery of goods.[16] When there is overloading of wagons, levy of punitive charges is imposed. But if the order is passed without assigning reasons, such order having civil consequences, is bad in law. In absence of reasons no foundation can be laid by aggrieved party and only argument can be advanced in this regard that the order is based upon non-application of mind. Thus, such non-speaking order is liable to be set aside.[17]

5 Presumption of negligence When there is a loss or destruction of consignment, presumption of negligence of railway administration arises and it is for the administration to rebut such presumption by contrary evidence.[18]

6 Levy of punitive charges The Railways have the power to decide about the charges to be borne by the consigners for transportation of the goods and punitive charges are also part of the prescribed charges.[16] Punitive charges were imposed on the ground that the consignor failed to establish weight of consignment en route at two stations or at destination station. Weighment of consignment was done by the Railways at one station without representative of the consignor. Opportunity of weighment was

15 *J.C. Textiles Mills* v *Chief Coml. Supt., N.R.* AIR 1998 SC 1959; 1998 All LJ 1314; 1998 AIR SCW 1804.

16 *S. Goenka Lime & Chemicals Ltd.* v *Union of India* AIR 2016 MP 70.

17 *Century Textile & Industries Ltd.* v *Union of India* AIR 2007 NOC 1277 (All); see *Union of India* v *Agarwala & Co.* AIR 2008 NOC 1396 (Cal). (No punitive charge can be levied unless goods are re-weighed in presence of parties); see also *Union of India* v *Bajranglal* AIR 2008 NOC 1608 (Cal). (Refund of overcharge amount, improper).

18 *Union of India* v *Orissa Cement Ltd.* AIR 2007 NOC 1328 (Ori).

denied to the consignor. Thus, levy of punitive charges by the Railways was held to be improper.[19]

7 Overloading wagon involves no breach of civil obligation Railway is a service provider and service provider when charges for the service rendered, they are within their rights to get the charges since service provider charges for the service rendered, it cannot be said that there is any delinquency ingrained in the levy that is penalty or charges which the railway would ask the consignor to pay for overloading and therefore, it involves no breach of civil obligation and that being the position, the charges have been demanded by the Railways for the service rendered and overloading it cannot be considered to be one which is beyond its competency under s. 73 of the Railways Act 1989 and other provisions of the said Act. The charges were for the services rendered and not for the penalties for breach of any act which has the colour of civil obligation. Therefore, observance of principles of natural justice is not necessary.[20]

8 Section 73 of Railways Act vis-a-vis r. 3 of Railway (Punitive charges for Overloading of Wagon) Rules 2005 Section 73 empowers the Railway Administration to collect penalty charges at prescribed rate and r. 3 states that the person becomes liable to pay such rates for entire weights of commodities loaded beyond permissible carrying capacity for the distance to be travelled by train, irrespective of the detection of overloading. When overloading of wagons resulted in damage of coaches, engines and rails, the cascading effect may be more than the amount prescribed as penalty. The fact that overloading is detected en route cannot be the ground to levy penalty from the point of detection.[21]

74. Passing of property in the goods covered by railway receipt. **The property in the consignment covered by a railway receipt shall pass to the consignee or the endorsee, as the case may be, on the delivery of such railway receipt to him and he shall have all the rights and liabilities of the consignor.**

Scope Properly set out in consignment covered by railway receipt as defined in s. 2(33) read with s. 65 of the Act passes to the consignee or the endorsee, as the case may be, on transfer of such railway receipt to him and the transferee shall have all rights and liabilities of the consignor.

75. Section 74 not to affect right of stoppage in transit or claims for freight. **Nothing contained in section 74 shall prejudice or affect—**

(*a*) any right of the consignor for stoppage of goods in transit as an unpaid vendor [as defined under the Sale of Goods Act, 1930 (3 of 1930)] on his written request to the railway administration;

19 *Rameshwar Das* v *Union of India* AIR 2015 NOC 498 (Cal).

20 *Action Committee for Resolving the Problems of Gujarat Salt Manufactures* v *Union of India* AIR 2010 NOC 556 (Guj) relying on *J.C. Textile Mills* v *Chief Commercial Superintendent, N.R.* AIR 1998 SC 1959.

21 *S. Goenka Lime & Chemicals Ltd.* v *Union of India* AIR 2016 MP 70.

> (*b*) any right of the railway to claim freight from the consignor; or
>
> (*c*) any liability of the consignee or the endorsee, referred to in that section by reason of his being such consignee or endorsee.

1 Scope Section 75 curves out the rights and liabilities shifted under the railway receipt under s. 74 of the Act. The railway administration reserves its rights under s. 75 of the Act in respect of the following reliefs: (*i*) any right of the consignor for stoppage of goods in transit as an unpaid seller under the Sale of Goods Act, (*ii*) any right of railway to claim freight from the consignor, (*iii*) any liability of the consignee or the endorsee.

2 Refund of excess amount Excess amount was charged owing to mistake committed by railway officials in ascertaining distance travelled by consignment from booking station to destination station. Railway administration having realised the excess amount from the consignor even after transfer of railway receipt cannot refuse to refund excess amount of what it was entitled to. Claim for refund though made after consignments were delivered to consignee, amount was realised from consignor prior to delivery of consignment. The consignor is thus entitled to claim refund of excess amount realized even after delivery of consignment to consignee.[1]

> **76. Surrender of railway receipt.** The railway administration shall deliver the consignment under a railway receipt on the surrender of such railway receipt:
>
> Provided that in case the railway receipt is not forthcoming, the consignment may be delivered to the person, entitled in the opinion of the railway administration to receive the goods, in such manner as may be prescribed.

1 Scope The holder of railway receipt is entitled to get delivery of consignment from a railway administration on surrender of railway receipt. But where a railway receipt is lost, destroyed or not forthcoming, a railway administration may deliver the consignment to such person as may be prescribed.

2 Claim for compensation for unauthorized delivery of consignment without original railway receipts Railways ought to deliver goods only on production of railway receipts. Goods were directed to be delivered only on production of original railway receipts by the consignee. But consignments were delivered to unauthorized person without obtaining original railway receipts on the basis of Indemnity Bond/Note. Though railway authority was aware that original railway receipts were lying with the Bank, even then it accepted inadmissible indemnity bond/note. Such act of railway administration caused loss to the consignor/claimant. There was also no order obtained from the Divisional Commercial Superintendent while delivering goods on indemnity bond instead of railway receipts. Consignment was delivered in violation of ss. 151 and 152 of the Indian

1 *Jaypee Rewa Cement* v *Union of India* AIR 2012 Gau 178.

Contract Act 1872. Phonogram and letter were sent to the railways instructing by the consignor not to delivers goods without production of original railway receipts. Thus, breach of such instruction gives rise to cause of action against the Railways and as such no notice under s. 106 of the Railways Act 1989 was not necessary. The Railway Claims Tribunal has jurisdiction to adjudicate the claim. Section 15 of the Railway Claims Tribunal Act 1987 expressly bars civil court to entertain any claim for compensation against the railways. Thus, the railways were liable to pay compensation to the claimants for the loss caused to it.[2]

77. Power of railway administration to deliver goods or sale proceeds thereof in certain cases. Where no railway receipt is forthcoming and any consignment or the sale proceeds of any consignment are claimed by two or more persons, the railway administration may withhold delivery of such consignment or sale proceeds, as the case may be, and shall deliver such consignment or sale proceeds in such manner as may be prescribed.

1 **Corresponding provision** This section corresponds to s. 57 of the old Act.

2 **Scope** Section 77 empowers the railway administration to withhold delivery of consignment or sale proceeds under the following circumstances: (*i*) the railway receipt is not produced; (*ii*) there are claims on the consignment by two or more persons. The railway administration can, however, determine the dispute in accordance with the prescribed manner.

3 **Indemnity** If the railway authorities deliver the goods on production of the receipt, they are protected. When the receipt is not produced, law does not protect the railway from the consequences of delivery to a wrong person. This section enables the railway to protect itself by withholding delivery, until the person entitled in its opinion to receive them has given an indemnity to its satisfaction against the claims of any other person with respect to the goods.[3]

Where the railway authorities delivered the goods to consignee, contrary to the directions of the consignor, taking an indemnity bond, the railway was held to be liable for the price of the goods to the consignor. This section was of no avail to the railway to escape liability.[4] Where any rule provides for the forwarding of such indemnity bond to the Divisional Superintendent, it is the duty of the station-master to do so. Demurrage must cease to run from the date of delivery of the bond.[5]

4 **Delivery on indemnity bond and liability of surety** In deserving cases the station master is empowered on being satisfied about the identity of the claimant to release and deliver the consignment from the destination station to the claimant—owner of the goods. The relevant rule namely

2 *Union of India* v *Halasidhanth Sahakari Sakhar Karkhana Ltd., Nipani* AIR 2011 Gau 78.

3 *Gopalan* v *Union of India* AIR 1959 AP 331.

4 *Mussadi Lal* v *Union of India* AIR 1964 Punj 20; 65 Punj LR 1107.

5 *Durga Prosad* v *Union of India* AIR 1958 Pat 558.

r. 149 of the General Rules framed under the Indian Railways Act stands as follows—

> "Rules 149. *Delivery of goods when railway receipt is lost.* (1) When a railway receipt has been lost, mislaid or is for other reasons not forthcoming, the railway reserves the right to demand an Indemnity Note before giving delivery of animals or goods therein concerned.
>
> * * * *
>
> (7) In the case of goods sent value payable or goods consigned by the sender to 'self' when the railway receipts have been lost, delivery may be granted only when the person claiming the consignment produces a stamped Indemnity Note, signed by the sender and counter-signed by the Station Master of the forwarding station. The name stamp of the forwarding station must be impressed on the Note immediately below the signature of the Station Master. This Note must be endorsed by the sender in favour of the person to whom the consignment is to be delivered.
>
> (8) *It is further incumbent on the person claiming delivery to execute a second stamped Indemnity note signed by him* along with a surety and two witnesses to the satisfaction of the Station Master at the destination station before delivery can be effected".

It is clear from sub-rule (8) of r. 149 that it is incumbent upon the railway authority to obtain a second indemnity note, executed by the person claiming delivery along with a surety and two witnesses to the satisfaction of the station master before any delivery could be effected. This second indemnity note is in addition to the first indemnity note signed by the sender and countersigned by the station master of the forwarding station, where the railway receipt is said to have been lost or mislaid or is not forthcoming for one reason or the other.

When there is no such second stamped indemnity bond or any such bond not signed by the surety, he is not bound, although under s. 128 Contract Act, the liability of surety is co-extensive with the principal debtor.[6]

5 Delivery of different goods There was a booking of 507 pieces of sized timber weighing 100 quintals by the respondent with the railway. At the time of delivery goods were found to be different consequent the respondent refused to accept the delivery of the goods and claimed damages. Factum of booking was proved by the respondent by fitting railway receipt and export permit. In the circumstances the award of compensation at 70% of price claimed by the respondent along with interest was proper.[7]

78. Power to measure, weigh, etc. Notwithstanding anything contained in the railway receipt, the railway administration may, before the delivery of the consignment, have the right to—

(*i*) re-measure, re-weigh or re-classify any consignment;

6 *Union of India* v *N. Jugadeswararao* AIR 1981 AP 215; 1981 Andh LT 379.

7 *Union of India* v *Santosh Kumar Mund* AIR 2001 Ori 3.

(*ii*) re-calculate the freight and other charges; and

(*iii*) correct any other error or collect any amount that may have been omitted to be charged.

1 Scope Section 78 empowers the railway administration to exercise any of the following rights before delivery of consignment: (*i*) re-measure, re-weigh or re-classify; (*ii*) re-calculate the freight and other charges; (*iii*) correct any other error or collect any deficit charges.

2 Re-weighment of consignment en route Railway administration has power to re-weigh consignment en route without notice to or in absence of consignor, consignee or endorsee under s. 78 of the Railways Act 1989. But under the first proviso to s. 79 of the said Act, an element of discretion does not rest with the railway servant concerned to re-weigh goods which are booked at owner's risk, the consequence will be that when omission to exercise the discretion is challenged, the railways must be in a position to satisfy the court that in the facts and circumstances of the case, the railway servant concerned could not have exercised his discretion to reweight the consignment.[8] Railways allowed re-weighment of wagons in question at weigh-bridge maintained by public sector undertaking in presence of both sides. Results of such re-weighment are binding upon railways in absence of proof that such re-wieghment was faulty or defective.[9]

79. Weighment of consignment on request of the consignee or endorsee. A railway administration may, on the request made by the consignee or endorsee, allow weighment of the consignment subject to such conditions and on payment of such charges as may be prescribed and the demurrage charges if any:

Provided that except in cases where a railway servant authorised in this behalf considers it necessary so to do, no weighment shall be allowed of goods booked at owner's risk rate or goods which are perishable and are likely to lose weight in transit:

Provided further that no request for weighment of consignment in wagon-load or train-load shall be allowed if the weighment is not feasible due to congestion in the yard or such other circumstances as may be prescribed.

1 Scope A railway administration is under obligation to allow weighment of consignment on request of the consignee or endorsee on such conditions and payment as may be prescribed.

2 Demand for re-weighment of consignment Demand for re-weighment of consignment was made by consignee in presence of representatives of parties and it was refused by railway authorities. If consignee disputes excess weight, railway authorities cannot deny the right of consignee to have the said consignment weighed in his presence. Refusal by railway

8 *Nirmal Traders* v *Union of India* AIR 2003 Gau 122; see *Jyoti Enterprises* v *Union of India* AIR 2003 Jhar 48.

9 *Raghu Forwarding Agency* v *Union of India* AIR 2006 Gau 13.

authorities is violative of the principles of natural justice. Consequently, the demand for under charge made by railway authorities is improper.[10]

3 Demand for additional freight The railways may demand additional freight consequent upon conducting a re-weighment under s. 78 in absence of representation on behalf of person entitled to the consignment despite rejecting request for further weighment under s. 79 on cogent grounds.[11]

4 Penalty for overloading of wagon Consignee was not aware of railways claim of overloading prior to consignments being released. In fact claims were raised several weeks subsequent to delivery of consignments. Even if railway authorities was to impose penalty, it cannot be levied unless goods are re-weighed in presence of representatives of parties concerned. Consignee was not afforded chance to exercise such right conferred on them under s. 79 of the Railways Act 1989. Hence railways are in violation of the provision of law. Claim for penalty was held to be not sustainable.[12]

> **80. Liability of railway administration for wrong delivery.** Where a railway administration delivers the consignment to the person who produces the railway receipt, it shall not be responsible for any wrong delivery on the ground that such person is not entitled thereto or that the endorsement on the railway receipt is forged or otherwise defective.

1 Corresponding provision This section corresponds to s. 76B of the old Act.

2 Delivery of consignment against indemnity bond A suit was instituted by the consignor against the railway administration for delivery of goods to the consignee on executing indemnity bond contrary to the consignor's instructions. The railway was highly negligent in making the delivery.[13]

3 Misdelivery of goods Under the old law the railway administration as a bailee was to take proper steps to prevent misdelivery on forged railway receipts. Even if it were to be held that the administration will not be liable in the clear counterfeit, a forgery which cannot be detected by the use of reasonable diligence and ordinary prudence, the facts must be such as to lead to the conclusion that it was impossible for the railway employees at the destination to detect and prevent the practice of such fraud. Again it is for the bailee to take proper care and the duty of recovering the goods from the wrongdoer and restoring them to the lawful owner clearly lies on the railway.[14] If the misdelivery was caused by negligence in not comparing the entries in the railway receipt with those in Delivery Books, the railway was held to be liable. Where the railway authorities delivered the goods to a person in whose favour the railway receipt was not endorsed,

10 *Pradip Kumar Shah* v *Union of India* AIR 2013 Cal 132.
11 *Union of India* v *Biswanath Agarwal* AIR 2015 Cal 225 (FB).
12 *Union of India* v *Ultra Tech Cement Ltd.* AIR 2011 Cal 216.
13 *Mussadi Lal* v *Union of India* AIR 1964 Punj 20.
14 *Bhairuddin* v *Union of India* AIR 1957 Cal 573.

the railway administration cannot escape its liability.[15] The railway administration shall not be liable for misdelivery of the goods or animals if it has delivered the same in good faith to the person who produces the original railway receipt duly endorsed.

This section makes the position of the railway clear. The railway administration cannot be held responsible for misdelivery if it has delivered the animals or goods in good faith to a person who produces the original railway receipt. The duty of proving good faith is on the railway and if it succeeds in doing so, the real owner shall not be permitted to contend that the person taking delivery was not legally entitled to such animals or goods or that the endorsement on the railway receipt was forged or otherwise defective.

4 Instructions for preventing delivery of goods against forged railway receipt
In view of s. 76B (s. 80 of the Railways Act 1989) the railway is protected when delivery of goods and animals booked for carriage by railway is effected against an original railway receipt in good faith. For invoking the protection railway is to prove first, the fact that the receipt against which railway gave delivery was a genuine original railway receipt and secondly, the railway acted in good faith. Railway have issued positive instructions to prevent delivery against forged railway receipt. Needless to say that when delivery is effected through forged railway receipt s. 76B of the old Act (corresponding s. 80 of the Railways Act 1989) cannot be invoked. The instruction is reiterated in a Madras case as follows:[16]

> "When delivery of a valuable consignment (i.e. consignment exceeding approximately ₹1,000 in value) is demanded by a person not known to the station staff, delivery should not be given until the Railway Receipt is compared with the through Invoice. If the through Invoice is not available, the station staff should request the party to get himself identified by someone known to the station staff. If he refuses to do this, delivery should be given only after the Station Master is satisfied of the *bona fides* of the person asking for the delivery. If necessary, an urgent telegram may be sent to the sending station to get the booking particulars confirmed before delivery is effected.
>
> The Station Master should be careful in delivering the consignments which are not of a nature normally received at his station.
>
> If the railway receipt is lost, delivery of parcels or goods should be granted to the consignee on execution of an Indemnity Note provided the Station Master is satisfied that the person claiming the consignment is really the consignee. In all cases where the Station Master is not satisfied that the person claiming the consignment is really the consignee the matter

15 *Union of India* v *Ramji Lal* AIR 1965 All 184.
16 *Union of India* v *Joseph Textiles* AIR 1985 Mad 360 (366); (1985)1 Mad LJ 274; 1984 TLNJ 345.

should be referred to the Divisional Commercial Superintendent for orders. In no case delivery be given by the Station Master, if it is demanded by a person not known to the Station Master. Similarly no delivery on Indemnity Note should be given for such consignments which are of nature not normally received at the station until all invoiced particulars are properly verified and party's identity established.

It should be ensured that all important documents like railway receipts etc. should be kept in the personal custody of a responsible official of the station nominated for this purpose; and

Delivery on Indemnity Note should not be granted without prior permission of the Divisional Commercial Superintendent in cases—

(*a*) where consignments claimed by a person other than the invoiced consignee or by a person when the column of consignee on the way bill is erroneously left blank by the booking station;

(*b*) consignments through booked from abroad;

(*c*) consignments obtained by more than one person; and

(*d*) consignment booked to sender when the sender is not personally known at the destination station.

Railway receipt books on receipt from Forms Depot should be very carefully checked for any missing/defective foils. Any loss of Railway Receipt books/foils should be immediately reported to the concerned authorities.

Instructions also exist [*vide* para 1813 of Commercial Manual (Vol. II)] regarding maintenance of the Inward Invoice Index Register at the stations. Unless the staff concerned at the stations/goods sheds maintain them correctly and promptly, it may not help the R.P.F./G.R.P./C.I.D. taking preventive and detecting action in cases of delivery of goods on forged Railway/ Receipts.

It is also imperative that the Station Master/Goods Clerks/Commercial Inspectors/Accounts Inspectors who came to know of the deliveries, if any, on forged Railway Receipts should, without loss of any time report to the local Government Railway Police concerned.

The failure to follow this instruction cannot but amount to utter carelessness on the part of the Railways."

5 Liability of different railways Where goods were delivered to one railway, the other railways through which the goods travelled would also be deemed to have contracted with the person delivering the goods for their carriage.[17] The existence of a contract alone, however, is not sufficient to fasten the liability, although all the railways will be deemed to have entered into the contract. Once the liability has been fixed the railway cannot argue that it had not entered into contract with the persons who made the consignment.

17 *Union of India* v *Shamsuddin* AIR 1958 Pat 575.

81. Open delivery of consignments. Where the consignment arrives in a damaged condition or shows signs of having been tampered with and the consignee or the endorsee demands open delivery, the railway administration shall give open delivery in such manner as may be prescribed.

Open delivery of consignment When the consignment arrives in a damaged condition or shows to have been tampered with, the consignee or the endorsee may insist on the railway administration to give open delivery of goods according to the prescribed manner.

82. Partial delivery of consignments. (1) The consignee or endorsee shall, as soon as the consignment or part thereof is ready for delivery, take delivery of such consignment or part thereof notwithstanding that such consignment or part thereof is damaged.

(2) In the case of partial delivery under sub-section (1), the railway administration shall furnish a partial delivery certificate, in such form as may be prescribed.

(3) If the consignee or endorsee refuses to take delivery under sub-section (1), the consignment or part thereof shall be subject to wharfage charges beyond the time allowed for removal.

Scope Section 82 empowers railway administration to deliver part of the consignment which is ready for delivery. If the consignee or endorsee refuses to take partial delivery of consignment, he will be liable to wharfage charges.

83. Lien for freight or any other sum due. (1) If the consignor, the consignee or the endorsee fails to pay on demand any freight or other charges due from him in respect of any consignment, the railway administration may detain such consignment or part thereof or, if such consignment is delivered, it may detain any other consignment of such person which is in, or thereafter comes into its possession.

(2) The railway administration may, if the consignment detained under sub-section (1) is—

(*a*) perishable in nature, sell at once; or

(*b*) not perishable in nature, sell, by public auction,

such consignment or part thereof, as may be necessary to realise a sum equal to the freight or other charges:

Provided that where a railway administration for reasons to be recorded in writing is of the opinion that it is not expedient to hold the auction, such consignment or part thereof may be sold in such manner as may be prescribed.

(3) The railway administration shall give a notice of not less than seven days of the public auction under clause (*b*) of sub-section (2) in one or more local newspapers or where there are no such newspapers in such manner as may be prescribed.

(4) The railway administration may, out of the sale proceeds received under sub-section (2), retain a sum equal to the freight and other charges including expenses for the sale due to it and the surplus of such proceeds and the part of the consignment, if any, shall be rendered to the person entitled thereto.

1 Corresponding provision This section corresponds to s. 55 of the old Act.

2 Liability for freight Section 55 of the old Act (corresponding to s. 83 of the Railways Act 1989) details the provision when on demand the consignee of goods fails to pay the freight or other charges in respect of goods or animals carried by railway. First, the railway has the power to detain the said goods or animals, secondly, if the said goods or animals are removed without due freight or other rates being paid, the railway may detain any other goods or animals of the person liable to pay freight etc., which subsequently may come into possession of the railway.

Sub-section (2) of s. 55 of the old Act details the procedure for sale by public auction of the goods or animals detained and of offsetting the charges and expenses for the goods or animals detained or later sold.

The aforesaid remedy apart, on railway administration is also competent to sue for recovery of freights and other charges. The existence of the remedy detailed in sub-secs. (1) to (4) of s. 55 of the old Act does not exclude the common law remedy of civil suit by the railway.[18] In this connection it is apposite to refer to the following Rules:

Rule 1820 of the Indian Railway Commercial Manual (Vol. II) reads as under—

> "1820. *Recovery of railway dues before delivery of goods.* Before delivery of goods, it should be seen that the railway dues and other charges have been paid. Wharfage and demurrage charges should be levied under tariff rules and recovered, from the consignees before the removal of goods from railway premises. Similarly, all undercharges noticed as a result of check of invoices, weighment of goods etc. should be recovered from consignees before delivery of goods. As regards overcharges claimed at the time of delivery, the procedure indicated in Chapter XXI should be followed."

Similar provision is contained in Rule 10 of the Goods Tariff General Rules (Part I), which is as under—

> "10. *Payment of Charges.* Except in the case of dangerous and other goods specially provided for in this Tariff or in Exception Lists for which prepayment of freight is compulsory, all charges must be paid either when goods are presented for despatch or at the time of delivery, and all goods are subject to lien not only for the freight, wharfage, demurrage and handling charges on the particular goods, but also for any general balance which may be due to the railway by the owner or consignor or consignee of such goods. If the

18 For the Constitutional validity of the onerous method of distraint and sale see the discussions under the caption."Liability for freight and other charges; alternative remedy by suit; validity of coercive mode", under this s. 52.

money in respect of goods which are detained, be not paid, they may be sold by auction, in the case of perishable goods at once and in the case of other goods, on the expiration of 15 days' notice of the intended auction and the proceeds applied in liquidation or reduction of the amount due and expenses."

The consignor is primarily liable for freight. The consignee is liable only if acting as agent of consignor to the knowledge of Railway. Third party is not liable unless there is express or implied contract between Railway and such third party.[19]

3 Lien The term "lien" comes from Latin term *"ligament"* meaning "binding". Its lexical meaning is "right to retain". The word "lien" is now variously described and used under different contexts such as "contractual lien", "equitable lien", "specific lien", "general lien" etc.[20] Lien can be defined as a legal right or interest that a creditor has in another's property, lasting usually until a debt or duty that it secures is satisfied.[21] A lien is a charge imposed upon specific property by which it is made security for the performance of an act. In its most extensive signification it is a charge upon property for the payment or discharge of a debt or duty. It differs from an estate in, or title to, the property, as it may be discharged at any time by payment of the sum for which the lien attaches. It differs from a mortgage in the fact that the mortgage is made and the property delivered, or otherwise, for the express purpose of security; while the lien attaches as identical to the main purpose of bailment.

In this work *Carriage by Railway,*[1] Disney says: "Every carrier has one very important security for the payment of his charges that is his right to retain possession of the goods until he is paid. The right is called in law a 'lien' and, like other carriers, a railway company possesses this carrier's lien. This lien is merely a passive right to retain the goods, to refuse to give them up till the money is received." A lien in respect of carriage is a right to hold the goods which have been carried in respect of the carriage of the particular parcel of goods. To stop them at the commencement of the journey and hold them for a debt is entirely contrary to the nature of a lien.[2] It is a right to retain the goods. If goods are sold without any legal sanction, railway will be guilty of conversion.[3]

Section 55 of the old Act (corresponding to s. 83 of the Railways Act 1989) provides that the lien accrues on the happening of two things. Firstly, there should be a liability in respect of charges payable to the railway and secondly, a demand for such payment by the railway. Until these two things happen, particularly the demand, there would accrue no lien.[4]

19 *Adoni Fertilisers Manufacturers* v *Union of India* AIR 1977 AP 74; (1976)2 APLJ (HC) 227; (1976)2 Andh WR 345.

20 *Triveni Shankar Saxena* v *State of UP* AIR 1992 SC 496.

21 Black's *Law Dictionary,* 10th Ed., 2014.

1 8th Ed., pp. 90,100.

2 *Wiltshire Iron Co.* v *G.W. Railway* [1871] LR 6 QB 776.

3 *Mulliner* v *Florence* [1878]3 QBD 484.

4 *Dehri Rohtas Light Railway Co. Ltd.* v *Godhar Colliery Co.* AIR 1965 Pat 49.

4 Tariff rates—applicability A contract of carriage emerges only after the goods are loaded and a receipt for the same has been issued. Till that time there is but an offer to take the goods subject to wagons being available. While they are on the railway premises the railway acts as mere bailee but not as carrier. Hence the tariff rates existing on that date when the goods are loaded and the railway receipt is prepared and not those existing on the date when the goods are accepted for consignment are applicable in such a case.[5]

5 Right to sell The right to sell does not arise in the absence of a demand for payment of a fixed sum. Therefore a notice to the effect that if they did not hear anything in the matter of taking delivery of the goods consigned, the notice should be treated as one issued under ss. 55 and 56 of the (old) Indian Railways Act is not a sufficient compliance with the provisions and a sale of goods by the railway under such circumstances is invalid. There should also be a proclamation of the proposed sale in local newspapers as required under sub-sec. (2).[6] The railway has no right under s. 55(1) of the old Act to sell the goods consigned for failure to pay demurrage etc., where it has made no demand for payment of a fixed sum even if the consignee had refused delivery for pre-assessment of damage and if there is no publication in newspaper as required under sub-sec. (2) of the intended auction the sale will be vitiated.[7]

6 Mode of publishing notice For mode of publishing notices of auction sales in places where there are no local newspapers in Bombay, *see Bombay Government Gazette,* 1885, Part I, p. 1320.

7 Right of remeasurement Where the right of "remeasurement, re-weighment, reclassification and recalculation of the rates" is reserved by the Railways Co. in the railway receipt, the railway has the right to re-classify and recalculate rates and charge as an additional sum of money.[8]

8 Refusal to allow remeasurement If under the contract of carriage, the Railway Co. were entitled to have the goods re-weighed and the finding is that they did re-weigh and demand—(as they were entitled to do under s. 55)—the freight due on the weight so calculated by them (which was in excess of that noted at the place of booking), the mere fact that the Railway Co. refused to comply with the request of the plaintiffs to have the goods re-weighed in their presence does not amount to a refusal to deliver and does not render the Railway Co. liable in damages for non-delivery.[9]

5 *Kabra & Co.* v *Union of India* AIR 1958 MP 294.
6 *Union of India* v *Hukumchand* AIR 1970 MP 55; 1969 MPLJ 737.
7 *Niranjanlal* v *Union of India* AIR 1973 All 303; 1972 All WR (HC) 318.
8 *Secretary of State* v *Harbans Prasad* AIR 1929 All 848. But see *Secretary of State* v *D.P. Agashe* AIR 1933 Nag 135; see also *Chhogalal* v *Secretary of State* 29 NLR 333; AIR 1933 Nag 261.
9 *B.N. Railway Co.* v *Ravan* 139 IC 802; 55 CLJ 603; AIR 1932 Cal 877.

9 "Local"—meaning of The word "local" in s. 55(2) means papers of place where the sale is to be held, and the provision is intended to give notice of the sale to persons of the locality who are likely to attend the purchases.[10] "Local newspaper" means a newspaper which is issued from the locality and not a newspaper which may be read at the place.[11] Where the formalities prescribed by the Act for conducting sale of goods detained are not observed, the Railway Co. would be liable in tort.[12]

10 Right to recover undercharges Under s. 55(5) of the (old) Indian Railways Act, a railway administration may recover by a suit the sums for which it can detain goods under s. 55(1) of the old Act. A railway administration is therefore entitled to recover by suit undercharges in respect of consignments even after all the goods have been delivered over to the consignee.[13]

In *G.I.P. Railway* v *Firm Radhey Mal Manni Lal*[14] the respondents consigned goods in nine bags to Salamatpur from a railway station at Cawnpore. When the goods arrived at Salamatpur, it was found that two of the packages sent were not the same as had been consigned at Cawnpore. The person who wanted to take delivery on behalf of the consignees proposed that seven of the bags should be handed over to him and the two remaining bags, which did not belong to the consignment, should be left there. The station master did not agree to this arrangement. Later on, higher railway officials intimated agreement to this arrangement. Even then the station master at Salamatpore would not agree that the seven bags admitted to be a part of the consignment should be removed. Thereafter, there was some correspondence and the suit was brought. It was held (1) that s. 55 of the (old) Indian Railway Act applied to ordinary cases and not where the plaintiffs at the request of the railway company themselves wanted to remove the goods but were not allowed to do so; (2) that the railway company retained the goods at their own risk and the plaintiffs were entitled to recover the market value of the goods consigned and were not bound to accept such price as was fetched by the sale of the goods held at the instance of the railway administration.

In *Bengal & N.W. Ry.* v *Matru Ram,*[15] where out of seven wagon-loads of salt consigned by plaintiff through the defendant railway company four got damaged through wet and the plaintiff having refused to take delivery, the salt was sold at auction by the company within six months of its arrival

10 *Secretary of State* v *Simla Footware Co.* AIR 1935 All 601.

11 *Secretary of State* v *Harnarain* 53 All 596; I31 IC 683; 1931 ALJ 335; AIR 1931 All 337.

12 *Sunderji* v *Secretary of State* 151 IC 995; AIR 1934 Pat 507.

13 *Krishna Nayak & Sons* v *South Indian Railway Co. Ltd.* (1942)2 MLJ 348; AIR 1942 Mad 627.

14 23 ALJ 398; AIR 1925 All 656.

15 25 ALJ 159.

and without presenting a proper bill for wharfage to the plaintiff, s. 55 of the (old) Indian Railways Act did not apply, that the auction amounted to illegal conversion and that the plaintiff was entitled to damages.

Though a station master is an agent of the railway, and it is within his authority to agree to carry passengers at certain rates, if he agrees to a wrong rate, it is not binding on the company. Rule 23 of the Coaching Tariff Rules is a clear notice to the passengers that the Railway Company will have a right to correct any charges that may have been incorrectly made and to recover undercharges, from whatever causes arising. So where a station master gave a wrong rate and subsequently at the time of the issue of the tickets demanded the proper rate, and it was paid by the passenger, the latter could not recover the excess which he was forced to pay.[16] But the railway administration cannot claim wharfage charge for the period subsequent to the expiry of the period of notice for removal of goods.[17] But under the old s. 77(4) the owner of the animals or goods is liable for demurrage or wharfage for so long as the animals or goods are not unloaded. But where the railway re-classified the goods and refused to deliver the same without payment of additional charges unjustifiably demanded, the railway is liable for wrongful detention.[18]

11 Perishable goods Section 55(1) of the old Act lays down that railway can detain goods and animals when on demand the freights and other charges are not paid. Sub-section (2) of s. 55 provides that railway can realise the charges by public auction preceded by notice. But no notice is needed, as goes sub-sec. (2), when the goods are of perishable nature and is likely to be offensive. Perishable goods are those which decay and lose their value, if not consumed soon—e.g. fish, fruit or the like.

It is apposite to refer to r. 7(*e*) of the Rules framed under s. 47(1)(*f*) of the (old) Railways Act. It runs as follows:

> "(*e*) perishable article unclaimed or not taken delivery of, will be disposed of by auction at owner's risk and expenses by the station master of the station at which they may be left after the expiry of 24 hours or earlier, *if they are or likely to become offensive.*"

The words under *italics* are important. Unless there is found by the court to the effect that the goods were such which were likely to become offensive the provisions of r. 7(*e*) would not apply and the railway has no power to sell the same by auction.[19] A consignment of potatoes reached the destination on 10.2.1963. The consignor having been known to the

16 *Bhagwati Prasad* v *B.B. & C.I. Railway* ILR (1940) All 212.
17 *Probhu Narayan* v *Union of India* AIR 1961 Pat 119.
18 *Governor-General of India in Council* v *Radhey Lal* AIR 1956 All 149.
19 *T.B. Muhamed* v *Union of India* AIR 1966 Ker 97; 1965 Ker LJ 1085; 1966 Ker LT 80; ILR (1966)1 Ker 404; *Union of India* v *Sobhraj Bhag Chand* AIR 1980 All 163 (165).

railway, a telegram was sent to the consignor to take delivery within 15 days. Immediately the consignor replied that he would be coming to take delivery. But the potatoes were auctioned on 13.2.1963. There is no finding that it was or was likely to be offensive in nature. The railway acted negligently in not waiting for the consignor and in disposing of the potatoes before expiry of 15 days from transmission of telegram. The railway was held liable for damages.[20]

If a Railway Company sells perishable goods by public auction after trying to find out the address of the consignor and the consignee and also waiting for sometime to see if anybody turned up to take delivery of them, it is protected under s. 56 of the Indian Railways Act 1890 and there is no breach of the rules made under s. 47 of the (old) Act.[1]

12 Limitation for suit Where the Railway Company has sold the goods in exercise of the powers conferred by s. 56 of the Indian Railways Act 1890, a suit by the consignor to recover the surplus sale proceeds from the Railway Company was governed by Art. 62 and not Art. 31 of the (old) Limitation Act 1908. Such a suit is entirely different from a suit for compensation for non-delivery of the goods.[2] In Limitation Act 1963, Art. 24 has taken place of old Art. 62.

13 Notice A notice under s. 55 is not invalid merely because the sum claimable is not specified in the notice. It is obvious that the sum may increase from day to day when it is claimable on account of demurrage.[3] A notice is not effective unless it specifies the time and place of the proposed public auction, the nature of the goods intended to be sold and all other particulars necessary to enable the members of the public appreciate what is intended to be sold at the public auction.[4] A notice which does not give these particulars is not a notice of the intended sale.[5]

The power conferred on the railway administration by s. 55 of the (old) Act is in its capacity as a bailee acting as a carrier of goods. A bailee selling the goods in violation of the provisions of ss. 55 and 56 of the (old) Act will no doubt be guilty of wrongful conversion. In the appeal, the sale held under s. 55 was found by the courts below to be not valid. Even then the failure to deliver the goods in consequences of such wrongful conversion will result in the loss of goods within the meaning of s. 77 of the (old) Act.[6]

20 *Union of India* v *Sobhraj Bhag Chand* AIR 1980 All 163.
1 *Jugeshwar* v *M. & S.M. Ry.* 26 Pat 516; AIR 1948 Pat 378.
2 *Tarachand* v *M.& S.M. Railway* AIR 1921 Mad 362; 44 Mad 823; 41 MLJ 205.
3 *Firm Bhola Ram* v *E.I. Railway Co.* AIR 1926 Lah 651.
4 *Secretary of State* v *Sunderji Shivji & Co.* AIR 1938 PC 12; 65 IA 21; 42 CWN 225; 17 Pat 58; 40 Bom LR 258; (1938)1 MLJ 83.
5 *Sunderji Shivji & Co.* v *Secretary of State* AIR 1934 Pat 507; 13 Pat 752.
6 *Sree Sai Baba Textiles* v *Union of India* AIR 1966 Ker 199; 1966 Ker LJ 309; ILR (1966)1 Ker 428; 1966 Ker LT 318.

14 Public auction Public auction means a public sale at which each bidder offers an increase upon the price offered by the preceding bidder, the article being sold to the highest bidder. This involves the auction being held in public, all members of the public having a right to attend, and a valuable element being the compensation between the persons who are openly bidding for the article. Where the railway company did not observe the rules, the sale cannot be held to be a public auction and it cannot rely on the protection given by the Act.[7] If no notice was published in local newspapers the sale was not a valid sale and the railway was guilty of conversion.[8] The railway administration is not at liberty to sell the goods without notice merely because the goods are likely to get deteriorated. In case of perishables a sale without notice might be justified if the right to sell has accrued. Any sale in contravention of the provision of law is invalid.[9] Upon such sale the railway administration is entitled to deduct the freight and demurrage charges.[10]

15 Liability for freight and other charges—alternative remedy by suit—validity of coercive mode It may be found from s. 55 of the old Act that it creates a lien in favour of railway administration over the goods and animals carried but in respect of which charges and freights therefor have not been paid on demand. Thus when freights and other charges are not paid on demand due to the goods and animals carried to destination the railway is authorised to detain the said goods and animals or to detain any other goods or animals of the defaulter subsequently coming into possession of the railway administration. And in the alternative the railway administration also can sue the defaulter in ordinary civil court. The railway administration can pursue either of the remedies for recovery of the charges, freights due. It is not that after unsuccessfully proceeding under sub-sec. (1) the railway can switch to sub-sec. (5). Railway can resort to either of the modes. The choice as to which process it would resort to has been left entirely with the railway administration. The statute lays down no guideline as to when the remedy of civil suit would be pursued or where the railway administration would pursue the more onerous process of distraint and sale. The authorities may pick and choose some defaulters for suit and may pursue the process of distraint and sale against others. An element of arbitrariness may percolate the choice. Arbitrariness is an antithesis of equality. From a positivistic point of view equality and arbitrariness are sworn enemies, one belongs to the Rule of law and other to the whim and caprice of an absolute monarch. Where an

7 *Secretary of State* v *Sunderji Shivji & Co.* AIR 1938 PC 12; 65 IA 21; 17 Pat 58; 42 CWN 225.

8 *Niranjanlal* v *Union of India* AIR 1973 All 303; 1972 All WR (HC) 318.

9 *G.P. Venkataraman* v *Eastern Railway* AIR 1958 Mad 231; ILR (1958) Mad 342; (1958)1 MLJ 175.

10 *Dominion of India* v *Adam Haji* AIR 1953 Mad 217; ILR (1953) Mad 916.

act is arbitrary, it is implicit in it that it is unequal both according to political logic and constitutional law and is therefore violative of Art. 14, Constitution of India.[11]

It is apposite to recall that under ss. 235 to 247 (distraint and sale) of the (old) Calcutta Municipal Act 1951 (since repealed) Calcutta Corporation was empowered to recover the amount due towards tax and rates from a defaulter by detaining and then by sale of any movable property found on the holding in default. Section 251, of the (old) Calcutta Municipal Act provided that instead of the remedy of distraint and sale, the corporation could sue the defaulter for realisation of dues in civil court. The Corporation thus was empowered to pick and choose amongst the defaulters as to which remedy the corporation would follow. A full Bench of Calcutta High Court observed that as between the defaulters who can be proceeded against by way of suit and defaulters who can be proceeded against in other modes, the statute has made no classification and it has been clearly left to the discretion of municipal authorities whether a particular defaulter would be proceeded against in one way or other. In the matter selection or classification no principle or policy can be spelt out from the relevant statute. The presence of these two alternative modes for recovery of arrears of consolidated rates without any indication of any principle to guide the discretion of the Commissioner as to the circumstances under which one of the two alternative modes are to be applied makes the more onerous procedure void.[12]

It may be recalled that as held by the Supreme Court Railway Board and as a matter of that railway administration answers the definition of State within the meaning of Art. 12 of the Constitution.[13] Singling out a news weekly and banning its sale on Railway Platform was held violative of Art. 14, Constitution of India, it being discriminatory.[13]

In this perspective it is a question not free from difficulty, whether s. 55 of the (old) Railways Act that permits the railway administration to single out defaulters in payment of freights and other charges for being proceeded against honourably by a suit where the alleged defaulters would have an opportunity to defend their action, whereas to detain the goods and animals of others for alleged default in freights and charges can survive the attack based on Art. 14, Constitution of India.

16 Wharfage Petitioner booked certain consignments and approached the railway authorities in time for delivery of goods. The railway authorities

11 *E.P. Royappa* v *State of TN* AIR 1974 SC 555 (583); (1974)2 SCR 348; (1974)4 SCC 3; *A.L. Kalra* v *Project Equipment Corporation* AIR 1984 SC 1361 (1367); (1984)3 SCC 316; (1984)3 SCR 646.

12 *S.M. Nawab Arif* v *Corporation of Calcutta* 64 CWN 1.

13 *Railway Board* v *Observer Publication* AIR 1972 SC 1792; (1972)1 SCWR 696; (1972)2 SCC 266.

detained goods of the petitioner on their own in purported exercise of their lien and refused to deliver them on the ground of non-clearance of wharfage dues in respect of earlier consignment. It has been held to be improper exercise of power of lien by the railway authority.[14]

84. Unclaimed consignment. (1) If any person fails to take delivery of—

(*a*) any consignment; or

(*b*) the consignment released from detention made under sub-section (1) of section 83; or

(*c*) any remaining part of the consignment under sub-section (2) of section 83,

such consignment shall be treated as unclaimed.

(2) The railway administration may,—

(*a*) in the case of an unclaimed consignment which is perishable in nature, sell such consignment in the manner provided in clause (*a*) of sub-section (2) of section 83; or

(*b*) in the case of an unclaimed consignment which is not perishable in nature, cause a notice to be served upon the consignee if his name and address are known, and upon the consignor if the name and address of the consignee are not known, requiring him to remove the goods within a period of seven days from the receipt thereof and if such notice cannot be served or there is a failure to comply with the requisition in the notice, sell such consignment in the manner provided in clause (*b*) of sub-section (2) of section 83.

(3) The railway administration shall, out of the sale proceeds received under sub-section (2), retain a sum equal to the freight and other charges including expenses for the sale due to it and the surplus, if any, of such sale proceeds shall be rendered to the person entitled thereto.

1 Corresponding provision This section corresponds to s. 56 of the old Act.

2 Unclaimed goods—procedure Section 56 of the old Act (corresponding to s. 84 of the Railways Act 1989) contemplates a situation where the animals and goods have come into possession of the railway and the apparent owner of the goods or animals does not claim the same. Two possibilities are open. First, the owner of the goods or animals may be known. Secondly, it may be unknown. If known, the person concerned is to be served by a notice to remove the same. If the railway administration does not know the person concerned or having received the notice the apparent owner of the goods or animals defaults in removing them, or the notice cannot be served on him, the railway administration is empowered to sell those goods or animals in public auction and appropriate the sale proceeds in payment of freights and charges.

14 *Anurag Ferro Products Pvt. Ltd.* v *Union of India* AIR 2008 NOC 265 (Ori).

Section 56 of the old Act is to be read in conjunction with s. 77 of the (old) Railways Act. If the goods and animals are brought by carriage, liability of the railway would remain for seven days after the transit. So, it is not prudent on the part of the Railway to sell the goods brought by carriage to sell them by public auction on the ground of its not being claimed, within seven days after the termination of transit, except when it is a perishable goods.

3 Liability of consignor or consignee In order to ascertain whether the consignor or the consignee is liable to pay the amount of freight and demurrage, it is necessary to find out who were the contracting parties and what was the nature of the contract between them. The consignor is primarily liable for the payment of the freight and this is to be implied from the fact that he had made over the goods to the carrier for the purpose of being carried to the destination. Where a consignee gives intimation that he will not take delivery of the goods it is the duty of the railway to unload the wagons and to sell the goods by public auction, without delay and in the facts of the case the railway was held to be entitled to demurrage for detention of wagons for one month and not for 202 days.[15] Following this Supreme Court decision it has been held that while the consignor as the party entering into the contract with the railway is primarily liable for freight, the consignee is liable if the consignor, to the knowledge of the carrier acted as the agent of the consignee. The consignee is liable if there is an express contract between the consignee and the carrier.[16] This liability of the consignor may be independent of the question of ownership of the goods. The consignee is ordinarily not a party to the contract of carriage; as such he is not liable to pay the freight or demurrage. But where it is shown that the consignor acted to the knowledge of the carrier as agent only, the person on whose behalf he acted as agent is in reality the principal and liable to pay.[17]

4 Notice Notice must be given to safeguard the position of the railway when it seeks to sell the goods as 'not claimed'. In other cases failure to issue notice does not entail any liability as the railway is not under any obligation to give notice.[18] For a sale under s. 56 of the Indian Railways

15 *Kuchwar Limestone Co.* v *Dehri Rohtas Light Railway Co. Ltd.* AIR 1969 SC 193; (1969)1 SCR 359; (1969)1 SCJ 340; 1969 All LJ 323; 1969 MPWR 262; 1969 BLJR 315.

16 *Adoni Fertilisers Manufacturers* v *Union of India* AIR 1977 AP 74; (1976)2 APLJ 227; (1976)2 Andh WR 345.

17 *Dehri Rohtas Light Railway Co. Ltd* v *East Keshalpur Colliery* AIR 1963 Pat 46; 1962 BLJR 968.

18 *Panna Lal* v *E.I. Railway* AIR 1952 All 880; (1952) ALJ 657.

Act 1890 (corresponds to s. 84 of the Railways Act 1989), a notice of 14 days is sufficient.[19]

The object of a public notice of auction under s. 55 of the Indian Railways Act 1890 (corresponds to s. 83 of the Railways Act 1989) and the provision that the notice is to be inserted in local newspapers is an indication that it was the intention of the legislature that the local public shall be informed of a particular auction in order that persons may be attracted to bid at the auction. In order to attract bidders to the auction, the notice should contain adequate materials so that possible bidders may be informed of the class of the goods and the time and place where the sale is to be held. A notice that does not state when the sale would take place or the nature of the goods or the places at which they would be sold or the condition of the goods or indeed any particulars which would be calculated to attract purchasers to the sale is not "notice of the intended sale" as prescribed by s. 55[1] of the Indian Railways Act 1890 (corresponds to s. 83 of the Railways Act 1989).

The Railway Company received several consignments and delivered the same to the consignee at certain rates. It appeared, however, that, owing to a mistake in calculation, a lower rate of freight had been levied and on discovery of the same by the Railway auditor, the undercharge was sought to be recovered from the consignor and consignee. The suit was held to be time-barred as against the consignee. The consignors were justified in believing that the rate charged was correct and in acting on such a belief, and that under the particular circumstances, the Railway Company had by their conduct deprived themselves of any right to obtain redress as against the consignors.[2] Where a Railway Company quotes rates for carriage of goods from a certain station on the line of that company to another junction station on that line for traffic to a station on the foreign line, the rate so quoted is for carriage of goods from the station of despatch to the junction station and does not include the rate chargeable from the junction station to the station of destination on the foreign line.[3]

5 "Public auction" The words "public auction" in ss. 55 and 56 of the old Act (corresponding to ss. 83 and 84 of the Railways Act 1989 respectively) must bear the meaning which is ordinarily given to them in the English language. The words mean a public sale at which each bidder offers an increase upon the price offered by the proceeding bidder, the article put up being sold to the highest bidder. This involves the auction being held in public, all members of the public having a right to attend, and

19 *Secretary of State* v *Simla Footwear* AIR 1935 All 601; 57 All 843.
1 *Sunderji* v *Secretary of State* AIR 1934 Pat 507; 151 IC 995.
2 *Shahdara Saharanpur Light Railway* v *Protap Singh* AIR 1931 Lah 511; 131 IC 749; 32 PLR 397.
3 *Secretary of State* v *Nand Kishore* AIR 1932 Nag 180.

a valuable element being the competition between the persons who are openly bidding for the subject matter of the sale. This is of importance not only to the Railway Company but also to the owner of the goods, the competition being calculated to produce the highest price. Where notice of the intended sale of coal was given by Railway Company by proclamation and notice on the board at the station and some offers were sent to the station master which were forwarded by him to the superior officer who directed him to accept the offer which was in fact the highest. There was no public auction in the ordinary meaning of the words; there was no sale in public, there was no opportunity for competitive bidding, in fact, what was done bore no resemblance to a public auction. The Railway Company did not sell the coal in the manner prescribed by the sections, and therefore could not rely on the protection given by the (old) Railways Act.[4]

6 Suit to recover surplus sale proceeds—limitation Article 24 of the Limitation Act 1963, governs a suit to recover surplus proceeds of sale held by the Railway Company, under s. 56 of the old Act as the proceeds are received for plaintiff's use.[5]

7 Sale of unclaimed consignment Though there is no specific provision for the necessity to furnish the date of sale, yet it is imperative that notice of sale or auction should contain the date of auction so that the aggrieved party may secure a competitive purchaser.[6]

85. Disposal of perishable consignments in certain circumstances. (1) Where by reason of any flood, land-slip, breach of any lines of rails, collision between trains, derailment of, or other accident to a train or any other cause, traffic on any route is interrupted and there is no likelihood of early resumption of such traffic, nor is there any other reasonable route whereby traffic of perishable consignment may be diverted to prevent, loss or deterioration of, or damage to, such consignment, the railway administration may sell them in the manner provided in clause (*a*) of sub-section (2) of section 83.

(2) The railway administration shall, out of the sale proceeds received under sub-section (1), retain a sum equal to the freight and other charges including expenses for the sale due to it and the surplus, if any, of such sale proceeds, shall be rendered to the person entitled thereto.

1 Corresponding provision This section corresponds to s. 56A of the old Act.

2 Disposal of perishable goods—accidental cause delaying arrival at destination Section 56A of the old Act (corresponding to s. 85 of the Railways Act

4 *Secretary of State* v *Sunderji Shivji & Co.* AIR 1938 PC 12; 65 IA 21; 47 LW 78; 66 CLJ 476; 40 Bom LR 285; 42 CWN 225; (1938)1 MLJ 83 (PC).
5 *Ramesam* v *Madras & Southern Mahratta Ry. Co.* 41 MLJ 205; 44 Mad 823.
6 *Ramakrishna Steel Industries Ltd.* v *Union of India* AIR 2001 Mad 227.

1989) makes special provision for disposal of perishable goods carried by railway. For application of the section the following should be present:

(*a*) the railway must be carrying perishable goods;

(*b*) there must occur either of the following eventualities, namely, flood, landslide, breach of line of rails, collision between trains, or other accident to the train or *other causes;*

(*c*) that because of the occurrence of either of the eventualities above said or more than one such eventuality early resumption of traffic is not possible;

(*d*) there is no other alternative route whereby traffic of perishable goods may be sent to destination to prevent decay to perishable goods;

then the railway administration is entitled to sell the perishable goods by public auction.

To invoke the provision the goods must be perishable goods. Perishable goods means those goods which decay and lose their value, if not consumed soon.[7]

In regard to perishable goods the law is that the Railway Company are agents to carry and not to sell. Circumstances must exist to give the Railway Company a right to sell which is necessary in the interests of the owner. These conditions do not arise if the Railway Company can communicate with the owner and get his instructions in the matter. The carrier must give the owner an opportunity of deciding how he will deal with the goods. To justify a sale by a Railway Company they must show that it was impossible to communicate with the owner and receive instructions from him. If they show that, the sale would be regarded as the only course open to them.[8]

3 Causes for disposal of perishable goods—ejusdem generis rule It may be found that to invoke the provision of s. 56A, there should be no likelihood of early resumption of traffic, nor there should be an alternative route, to divert the traffic of perishable goods to destination owing to causes detailed in s. 56A(1) of the (old) Act. The first set of causes envisage an act of God namely, flood, landslide, second set contemplates an accidental cause namely, breach line in rail, collision etc. The enumeration of categorical causes has been followed by the general cause namely 'any other cause'. Here, it is submitted the doctrine of *ejusdem generis* rule should apply. The doctrine is that when particular words forming part of the same class

7 Mitra's *Legal and Commercial Dictionary,* 6th Ed., 2006.

8 *Union of India* v *Satyananda Rout* AIR 1963 Ori 17. See also notes under s. 55. Also see *Union of India* v *Sobhraj Bhag Chand* AIR 1980 All 163.

or same category are followed by general words, then the general words must be construed in the context of particular words.[8]

86. Sales under sections 83 to 85 not to affect the right to suit. Notwithstanding anything contained in this Chapter, the right of sale under sections 83 to 85 shall be without prejudice to the right of the railway administration to recover by suit, any freight, charge, amount or other expenses due to it.

Corresponding provision This section corresponds to s. 55(5) of the old Act.

87. Power to make rules in respect of matters in this Chapter. (1) The Central Government may, by notification, make rules to carry out the purposes of this Chapter.

(2) In particular, and without prejudice to the generality of the foregoing power, such rules may provide for all or any of the following matters, namely:—

(*a*) goods in respect of which no forwarding note shall be executed under proviso to sub-section (1) of section 64;

(*b*) dangerous and offensive goods for the purposes of sub-section (1) of section 67;

(*c*) infectious or contagious diseases for the purposes of section 68;

(*d*) rates of penalty charges under section 73;

(*e*) the manner in which the consignment may be delivered without a railway receipt under section 76;

(*f*) the manner of delivery of consignment or the sale proceeds to the person entitled thereto under section 77;

(*g*) the conditions subject to which and charges payable for allowing weighment and circumstances for not allowing weighment of consignment in wagon-load or train-load under section 79;

(*h*) the manner of giving open delivery under section 81;

(*i*) the form of partial delivery certificate under sub-section (2) of section 82;

(*j*) the manner of sale of consignment or part thereof under the proviso to sub-section (2) of section 83;

(*k*) the manner in which a notice under sub-section (3) of section 83 may be given;

(*l*) generally, for regulating the carriage of goods by the railways.

8 Maxwell on *Interpretation of Statutes*, 12th Ed., p. 229; *Sureswar Dutta* v *State of West Bengal* (1979)1 Cal LJ 569; *D. Mallaiah* v *Govt. of AP* (1986)1 Andh LT 253.

(3) Any rule made under this section may provide that a contravention thereof shall be punishable with fine which may extend to one hundred and fifty rupees.

(4) Every railway administration shall keep at each station a copy of the rules for the time being in force under this section, and shall allow any person to refer to it free of charge.

1 Corresponding provision This section corresponds to s. 56E of the old Act.

2 Power of Central Government to make rules The Central Government is empowered under s. 87 of the Act to make rules in respect of subject matters in ss. 64(1), 67(1), 68, 73, 76, 77, 79, 81, 82(2), 83(2), 83(3) and other matters regulating the carriage of goods by the railway under Chapter IX of the Railways Act 1989 after a notification in the Official Gazette.

CHAPTER X
Special Provisions as to Goods Booked to Notified Stations

88. Definitions. In this Chapter, unless the context otherwise requires,—

(*a*) "essential commodity" means an essential commodity as defined in clause (*a*) of section 2 of the Essential Commodities Act, 1955 (10 of 1955);

(*b*) "notified station" means a station declared to be a notified station under section 89;

(*c*) "State Government", in relation to a notified station, means the Government of the State in which such station is situated, or where such station is situated, in a Union territory, the administrator of that Union territory appointed under Article 239 of the Constitution.

1 Corresponding provision This section corresponds to s. 56B(1) of the old Act.

2 Meaning of terms

(a) *Essential commodity.* The term "essential commodity" is defined in s. 2(*a*) of the Essential Commodities Act 1955 to mean ten classes of commodities and also any other class of commodity which the Central Government may, by notification, declare to be an essential commodity for the purposes of the said Act.

(b) *Notified station.* The term "notified station" is defined in s. 88(*b*) of the Act to mean a railway station as covered by the provisions of s. 89 of the Act.

(c) *State Government.* This term "State Government" has been defined in s. 88(*c*) of the Act in relation to a "notified station" as defined in s. 88(*b*) read with s. 89 of the Act.

89. Power to declare notified stations. (1) The Central Government may, if it is satisfied that it is necessary that goods entrusted for carriage by train intended solely for the carriage of goods to any railway station should be removed without delay from such railway station, declare, by notification, such railway station to be a notified station for such period as may be specified in the notification:

Provided that before declaring any railway station to be a notified station under this sub-section, the Central Government shall have regard to all or any of the following factors, namely:

(*a*) the volume of traffic and the storage space available at such railway station;

(*b*) the nature and quantities of goods generally booked to such railway station;

(*c*) the scope for causing scarcity of such goods by not removing them for long periods from such railway station and the hardship which such scarcity may cause to the community;

(*d*) the number of wagons likely to be held up at such railway station if goods are not removed therefrom quickly and the need for quick movement and availability of such wagons;

(*e*) such other factors (being relevant from the point of view of the interest of the general public) as may be prescribed:

Provided further that the period specified in any notification issued under this sub-section in respect of any railway station shall not exceed six months in the first instance, but such period may, by notification, be extended from time to time by a period not exceeding six months on each occasion.

(2) If any person entrusting any goods to a railway administration to be carried to a notified station makes an application in such form and manner as may be prescribed and specifies therein the address of the person to whom intimation by registered post of the arrival of the goods at the notified station shall be given and pays the postage charges required for giving such intimation, the railway administration shall, as soon as may be after the arrival of the goods at the notified station, send such intimation accordingly.

(3) There shall be exhibited at a conspicuous place at each notified station a statement in the prescribed form setting out the description of the goods which by reason of the fact that they have not been removed from the station within a period of seven days from the termination of transit thereof are liable to be sold, in accordance with the provision of sub-section (1) of section 90, by public auction and the dates on which they would be so sold:

Provided that different statements may be so exhibited in respect of goods proposed to be sold on different dates.

(4) If the goods specified in any statement to be exhibited under sub-section (3) include essential commodities, the railway servant preparing the statement shall, as soon as may be after the preparation of such statement, forward a copy thereof to—

(*a*) the representative of the Central Government, nominated by that Government in this behalf;

(*b*) the representative of the State Government, nominated by that Government in this behalf; and

(*c*) the District Magistrate within the local limits of whose jurisdiction the railway station is situated.

1 Corresponding provision This section corresponds to s. 56B(2) of the old Act.

2 Rotational allotment of railway wagons System of rotational allotment of railway wagons to different stations to carry goods and subsequent modification of the said system by the railway authorities is a policy decision which cannot be interfered with under writ jurisdiction.[1]

90. Disposal of unremoved goods at notified stations. (1) If any goods entrusted for carriage to any notified station by a train intended solely for the carriage of goods are not, removed from such station by a person entitled to do so within a period of seven days after the termination of transit thereof at such station, the railway administration may, subject to the provisions of sub-section (2), sell such goods by public auction and apart from exhibiting, in accordance with the provisions of sub-section (3) of section 89, a statement containing a description of such goods, it shall not be necessary to give any notice of such public auction, but the date on which such auction may be held under this sub-section may be notified in one or more local newspapers, or where there are no such newspapers, in such manner as may be prescribed:

Provided that if at any time before the sale of such goods under this sub-section, the person entitled thereto pays the freight and other charges and the expenses due in respect thereof to the railway administration, he shall be allowed to remove such goods.

(2) If any goods which may be sold by public auction under sub-section (1) at a notified station, being essential commodities, are required by the Central Government or the State Government for its own use or if the Central Government or such State Government considers that it is necessary for securing the availability of all or any such essential commodities at fair prices so to do, it may, by order in writing, direct the railway servant incharge of such auction to transfer such goods to it or to such agency, co-operative society or other person (being an agency, co-operative society or other person subject to the control of the

1 *Rice Millers Assocn.* v *General Manager, S.C. Rly* AIR 2000 AP 121.

Government) engaged in the business of selling such essential commodities as may be specified in the direction.

(3) Every direction issued under sub-section (2) in respect of any essential commodity shall be binding on the railway servant to whom it is issued and the railway administration and it shall be a sufficient defence against any claim by the person entitled to the goods that such essential commodities have been transferred in compliance with such direction:

Provided that—

(*a*) such direction shall not be binding on such railway servant or the railway administration—

(*i*) if it has not been received by the railway servant sufficiently in time to enable him to prevent the sale of the essential commodities to which it relates; or

(*ii*) if before the time appointed for such sale, the person entitled to such goods pays the freight and other charges and the expenses due in respect thereof and claims that he be allowed to remove the goods; or

(*iii*) if the price payable for such goods (as estimated by the Central Government or, as the case may be, the State Government) is not credited to the railway administration in the prescribed manner and the railway administration is not indemnified against any additional amount which it may become liable to pay towards the price by reason of the price not having been computed in accordance with the provisions of sub-section (4);

(*b*) where directions are issued in respect of the same goods both by the Central Government and the State Government, the directions received earlier shall prevail.

(4) The price payable for any essential commodity transferred in compliance with a direction issued under sub-section (2) shall be the price calculated in accordance with the provisions of sub-section (3) of section 3 of the Essential Commodities Act, 1955 (10 of 1955):

Provided that—

(*a*) in the case of any essential commodity being a food-stuff in respect whereof a notification issued under sub-section (3A) of section 3 of the Essential Commodities Act, 1955 (10 of 1955), is in force in the locality in which the notified station is situated, the price payable shall be calculated in accordance with the provisions of clauses (*iii*) and (*iv*) of that sub-section;

(*b*) in the case of an essential commodity being any grade or variety of foodgrains, edible oil-seeds or edible oils in respect whereof no notification issued under sub-section (3A) of section 3 of the Essential Commodities Act, 1955 (10 of 1955), is in force in the locality in which the notified station is situated, the price payable shall be calculated in accordance with the provisions of sub-section (3B) of that section;

(*c*) in the case of an essential commodity being any kind of sugar in respect whereof no notification issued under sub-section (3A) of section 3 of the Essential Commodities Act, 1955 (10 of 1955), is in force in the locality in which the notified station is situated, the price payable shall, if such sugar has been booked by the producer to himself, be calculated in accordance with the provisions of sub-section (3C) of that section.

Explanation. For the purposes of this clause, the expressions "producer" and "sugar" shall have the meanings assigned to these expressions in the *Explanation* to sub-section (3C) of section 3, and clause (*e*) of section 2 of the Essential Commodities Act, 1955 (10 of 1955), respectively.

Corresponding provision This section corresponds to s. 56C of the old Act.

91. Price to be paid to person entitled after deducting dues. (1) Out of the proceeds of any sale of goods under sub-section (1) of section 90 or the price payable therefor under sub-section (4) of that section, the railway administration may retain a sum equal to the freight and other charges due in respect of such goods and the expenses incurred in respect of the goods and the auction thereof and render the surplus, if any, to the person entitled thereto.

(2) Notwithstanding anything contained in sub-section (1), the railway administration may recover by suit any such freight or charge or expenses referred to therein or balance thereof.

(3) Any goods sold under sub-section (1) of section 90 or transferred in compliance with the directions issued under sub-section (2) of that section shall vest in the buyer or the transferee free from all encumbrances but subject to a priority being given for the sum which may be retained by a railway administration under sub-section (1), the person in whose favour such encumbrance subsists may have a claim in respect of such encumbrance against the surplus, if any, referred to in that sub-section.

Corresponding provision This section corresponds to s. 56D of the old Act.

92. Power to make rules in respect of matters in this Chapter. (1) The Central Government may, by notification, make rules to carry out the purposes of this Chapter.

(2) In particular, and without prejudice to the generality of the foregoing power, such rules may provide for all or any of the following matters, namely:—

(*a*) the factors to which the Central Government shall have regard under clause (*e*) of the first proviso to sub-section (1) of section 89;

(*b*) the form and manner in which an application may be made under sub-section (2) of section 89;

(*c*) the form in which a statement is required to be exhibited under sub-section (3) of section 89;

(*d*) the manner in which the dates of public auctions may be notified under sub-section (1) of section 90;

(*e*) the manner of crediting to the railway administration the price of goods referred to in sub-clause (*iii*) of clause (*a*) of the proviso to sub-section (3) of section 90.

1 Corresponding provision This section corresponds to s. 56E(1) and (2) of the old Act.

2 Scope Section 92 empowers the Central Government to make rule by notification published in the Official Gazette in respect of matters stated in first proviso (*e*) to s. 89(1), ss. 89(2), 89(3), 90(1) and 90(3)(*a*)(*iii*) under Chapter X of the Act.

CHAPTER XI

Responsibilities of Railway Administrations as Carriers

93. General responsibility of a railway administration as carrier of goods. Save as otherwise provided in this Act, a railway administration shall be responsible for the loss, destruction, damage or deterioration in transit, or non-delivery of any consignment, arising from any cause except the following namely:—

(*a*) act of God;

(*b*) act of war;

(*c*) act of public enemies;

(*d*) arrest, restraint or seizure under legal process;

(*e*) orders or restrictions imposed by the Central Government or a State Government or by an officer or authority subordinate to the Central Government or a State Government authorised by it in this behalf;

(*f*) act or omission or negligence of the consignor or the consignee or the endorsee or the agent or servant of the consignor or the consignee or the endorsee;

(*g*) natural deterioration or wastage in bulk or weight due to inherent defect, quality or vice of the goods;

(*h*) latent defects;

(*i*) fire, explosion or any unforeseen risk:

Provided that even where such loss, destruction, damage, deterioration or non-delivery is proved to have arisen from any one or more of the aforesaid causes, the railway administration shall not be relieved of its responsibility for the loss, destruction, damage, deterioration or non-delivery unless the railway administration further proves that it has used reasonable foresight and care in the carriage of the goods.

1 Corresponding provision This section corresponds to s. 73 of the old Act.

2 History of legislation as to liability of Railway Company The first legislation on the subject is that contained in Act XVIII of 1854, s. 11 of which was as follows: "The liability of such Railway Company for loss or injury to any articles or goods to be carried by them other than those specially provided for by this Act shall not be deemed or construed to be limited or otherwise affected by any public notice given, or any private contract made by them; but such Railway Company shall be answerable for such loss or injury when it shall have been caused by gross negligence or misconduct on the part of their agents or servants". This continued to be the case until the passing of the Carriers Act 1855. In 1867, it was decided in the case of *E.I.R.* v *Jordon*[1] by a Division Bench of the Calcutta High Court (PEACOCK, CJ. and MACPHERSON, J.) that Railway Companies in India were common carriers, and liable as such, that is to say, as insurers of goods delivered to them. Then came the Railways Act of 1879. Section 2 of that Act contained the following provisions: "Nothing in the Carriers Act 1865, shall apply to carriers by railway". Consequently, the Act of 1879 repealed all the provisions of the Carriers Act which relate exclusively to carriers by railway and confined the operation of the remaining provisions to carriers other than carrier by railway, so that by the repeal of the Carriers Act as related to railways and of the whole of the Railways Act of 1854, the liability of carriers by railway as it stood before the Acts of 1854 and 1865 were restored. It follows that after the passing of the Act of 1879 the liability of carriers in India, including carriers by railway, was not limited to a liability for negligence, but was a liability as insurers of the goods delivered to them. The Indian Railways Act of 1890 substituted the obligation as a bailee for the obligation of an insurer of such goods, which prior to the passing of that Act was the liability imposed upon them under the Common Law.

The Indian Railways (Amendment) Act 1961, has brought about a change in the basic responsibility of a railway which was that of bailee to that of a common carrier although at the same time extensive provisions have been made in the said Amending Act of 1961, to relieve the railway administration of its basic liability as a common carrier.

In pursuance of the provisions of the repealed s. 72(2), the Central Government approved certain forms of agreements which are known as Risk Notes. Each of the Risk Notes dealt with particular circumstances and defined the liability of the railway concerned in such circumstances. The consignor was to execute one or more of such Risk Notes at the time of delivery of the goods to the railway administration. This system remained in force until by Act 56 of 1949, sub-sec. (2) of old s. 72 was repealed and the Risk Notes approved under that sub-section became out of use. By that Act ss. 73, 74A, 74B and 74C were incorporated in the Railways Act

1 4 BLR OC 97.

which began to serve the purpose of the Risk Notes. The above sections have now been repealed by Act 39 of 1961 and new sections have been substituted in their places. The Risk Notes forms and corresponding sections of the old Act and the new Act are given below—

Risk Notes	*Sections of Act 56 of 1949*	*Sections of Act 39 of 1961*
Form A	74A & 74E	77C & 76D
Form B	74C	74
Form C	74B & 74E	75A & 76D
Form D & G	74C	74
Form E	73	77A
Form H & Z	74C	74
Form X & Y	75	77B

3 Liability of railways under English law and under the old Indian Railways Act—difference of The extent of the liability of railways for carriage of goods differs in India from that under the law in England in certain respects. Under English law the railway is a common carrier. Under English law a common carrier is responsible for the safety of the goods entrusted to him in all events except for act of God or the King's enemies. That high degree of liability is imposed on a common carrier in England under the common law and is independent of any contractual liability. The cause of action will be at common law for breach of duty. It is not necessary for the owner of the goods to prove any contract. In such high degree of liability the common carrier will be liable for loss of the goods carried even though the loss be due to action of other persons over whom he has no control and even where they are stolen from him even though taken by force.[2]

In India until the Indian Railways (Amendment) Act 1961 came into force, the general liability of a railway administration, subject to certain provisions in the Act, was that of a bailee under ss. 151, 152 and 161 of the Indian Contract Act 1872. Under the repealed s. 72(3) neither the common law of England nor the provisions of the Carriers Act 1865, regarding the responsibility of common carriers applied to a railway administration. The Act of 1961 changed the basic responsibility of a railway which was that of a bailee to that of a common carrier. But at the same time extensive provisions have been made to relieve the railway administration of its basic liability as a common carrier.

2 *Gobbs* v *Bernard* [1703]2 Lord Raymond 909; *Forward* v *Pittard* [1785]1 Teron Rep 27 (34).

4 Basic responsibility of the railway (prior to 1st January 1962) Before 1st January1962 on which day the Amending Act 39 of 1961 came into force the basic responsibility of the railway was laid down in ss. 72 and 74C. According to the now repealed s. 72, the railway was liable as a bailee. Against under s. 74C if the goods or animals were delivered to the railway for carriage at owner's risk rate, the railway administration shall not be responsible, except upon proof that the loss, destruction, deterioration or damage was due to negligence or misconduct on the part of the railway administration or of any of its servants. This basic responsibility of the railway was subjected to certain exceptions in certain circumstances which were enumerated in the other sections now repealed.

5 Basic responsibility of the railway (after 1st January1962) The Amending Act 39 of 1961 has changed the character of the basic responsibility of a railway which was that of a bailee to that of a common carrier. Section 73 of the old Act (corresponding to s. 93 of the Railways Act 1989) lays down the general responsibility of a railway for loss, destruction etc., of animals or goods and the subsequent sections are enacted for the purpose of either altering or varying the same in particular circumstances or as exceptions thereto. Thus the high degree of the liability of a common carrier has been diluted which to some extent relieves the railway administration of its basic liability as a common carrier.

Act 39 of 1961 seeks to lay down the basic responsibility of the railway with reference to three periods of time during which the goods may be in the possession of the railway—

(1) Up to the termination of transit, *i.e.* up to the free time allowed for termination of transit, *i.e.* up to the free time allowed for unloading from the railway wagons without payment of demurrage.

(2) Within a period of 30 days (since the amendment by Act 71 of 1972 this period has been changed to 7 days) after the termination of transit, and

(3) After 30 days after the termination of transit (by Act 71 of 1972 this period has been changed to 7 days).

Section 73 of the old Act lays down that the railway shall be liable for loss etc. caused in the course of transit except in circumstances enumerated in cls. (*a*) to (*i*) in which cases the railway administration shall be relieved of its responsibility for the loss etc. if the railway administration can prove that it has used reasonable foresight and care in the carriage of the animals of goods.

But the position will be different if the goods are sent at owner's risk rate. Under s. 74 of the old Act where the goods are tendered for carriage at owner's risk rate the railway shall not be held responsible for loss etc. in transit, except upon proof that such loss etc. was due to negligence or misconduct on the part of the railway administration or any of its servants. Thus up to the period of the termination of transit, the liability of the railway for goods carried at owner's risk rate remains the same, *i.e.* that of a bailee as under the old law. While in regard to goods carried at railway's risk rate the liability of the railway has been changed from that of a bailee under the old law to that of a common carrier more or less.

Section 77 of the old Act deals with the responsibility of the railway administration for loss etc. of goods (not animals) caused during the period of seven days after the termination of transit and thereafter. For loss etc. caused during the period of seven days after termination of transit, the liability of the railway would be that of a bailee. But during the same period for loss etc. of goods carried at owner's risk rate, the railway would be liable only on proof of negligence or misconduct. So that for loss etc. of goods carried at railway's risk rate caused during this period of seven days, the liability of the railway is considerably less as compared with the period of transit. But the extent of liability of the railway for goods carried at owner's risk rate remains the same.

For loss etc. of goods caused after the expiry seven days after the termination of transit, it has been expressly provided in s. 77(2) of the old Act that the railway administration shall not be held liable in any case. It appears that these provisions have been made for more free movement of goods traffic and for avoidance of congestion in the goods yard.

6 Responsibility of railway administration for animals and goods in transit Except when the eventuality answers any or more of the causes enumerated in cls. (*a*) to (*i*) of s. 73 of the old Act, the responsibility of the railway as carrier is absolute. The point to be noticed is that s. 73 of the old Act has changed the character of the liability of the Railways from that of a bailee under old s. 72 to that of an insurer. In order to be absolved from such absolute responsibility the railway administration will have to prove that the loss etc. have arisen from any of the causes in cls. (*a*) to (*i*) of s. 73 of the old Act. The responsibility of the railway administration under s. 73 of the old Act is for loss etc. that occurred in transit, *i.e.* up to free time allowed under the rules for unloading from the railway wagons without payment of demurrage.

The liability of the railway arises if the goods are delivered to the railway for carriage. The railway administration cannot be held liable for the act of its servants in issuing a railway receipt without delivery of the goods for carriage by the consignor to the railway administration. Whenever there is a dispute as to the fact of actual delivery to the railway administration the same has to be determined on the evidence adduced in the case, since it is the fact of actual delivery and not the circumstance of issue or non-issue or railway receipts which provides the starting point of the responsibility of the railway administration. The value of the railway receipt is merely that of a document of title and not similar to that of a negotiable instrument. If it is shown that no real contract of carriage resulted, notwithstanding the issue of the railway receipt, on account of want of delivery of goods by the consignor to the railway administration for carriage by rail, the right to claim return of the goods does not arise, since there has been, in effect, no such contract of carriage created.[3]

If the railway wants to invoke immunity because of the cause of loss, destruction, damage etc. coming under the purview of any of the clauses, to wit cls. (*a*) to (*i*) of s. 73 of the old Act, then in view of the proviso to s. 73 of the old Act, the immunity can be claimed only by further proving that reasonable foresight and care had been used. The burden, therefore, is squarely on the railway administration to come under the umbrella of protection of immunity.[4]

7 Pre-1961 responsibility of railway as bailee Before Act 39 of 1961 came into force, sub-sec. (1) of s. 72 (old) made the railway administration liable as bailees under ss. 151, 152 and 161 of the Indian Contract Act 1872. The primary question in all cases having regard to old s. 72 of the Railways Act read with ss. 151 and 152 of the Indian Contract Act 1872 obviously was, has the railway company taken as much care of the goods as a man of ordinary prudence would under similar circumstances take of his own goods of the same description—in bulk, quality and value.

The railway administration as bailee was ordinarily liable to make good the loss suffered by the bailor unless it could be shown by the railway that it took such care as a person of ordinary prudence would under similar circumstances take of his own goods of the same bulk, quality or value. It was however, open to the railway administration by agreement with the consignor to limit its responsibility, as a bailee, provided the agreement under Risk Note A, *i.e.* owner's risk was executed in the manner prescribed by s. 72(2) (old) of the Railways Act. In a case Risk Note A by the consignor was exhibited and the railway was absolved from the liability despite short delivery at the destination.[5]

3 *Radheshyam Agarwala* v *Union of India* AIR 1980 MP 90; 1979 MPLJ 793.
4 *Union of India* v *Orissa Textile Mills* AIR 1979 Ori 165; (1979)48 Cut LT 245.
5 *Jeetmal Ram Gopal* v *Union of India* (1972)4 SCC 162.

Where goods were stolen while in transit due to raid by organised and large-scale operations by thieves, the railway was not guilty of any neglect specially when the record did not justify the inference that the administration failed to discharge its duties as bailee, and was hence bound to make good the loss.[6] The liability as bailee continued during the free time allowed.[7] Where the railway protection police specially deputed to protect goods in transit took no steps for protection of the goods, the railway was held to be liable.[8]

The responsibility of the railway as a bailee continued until terminated in accordance with ss. 55 and 56 of the (old) Indian Railways Act.[9]

8 Burden of proof The railway administration is liable for loss, destruction, damage, deterioration or non-delivery in transit of goods and animals delivered to it unless the railway administration can prove that the loss etc. occurred due to any of the causes enumerated in cls. (*a*) to (*i*) of s. 73 of the old Act. A combined reading of the principal provision along with the proviso makes it clear that even in cases where loss etc. is proved to have arisen from any of the causes enumerated in cls. (*a*) to (*i*), the administration will remain liable until it has proved that it has used reasonable foresight and care. Section 73 of the old Act has changed the character of the liability of the railways from that of a bailee to an insurer. A combined reading of the principal provision along with the proviso makes it clear that even in cases where loss etc. is proved to have arisen from any of the causes enumerated in cls. (*a*) to (*i*), the railway will be held liable unless it proves that it had used reasonable foresight and care. In short the character of liability of the railway is that of an insurer.[10] So long as there is a failure to use reasonable care and foresight on the part of the railway, the railways cannot escape their liability by pointing out that loss etc. was a result of causes enumerated in cls. (*a*) to (*i*) of s. 73 of the old Act. What is reasonable care and foresight is a question of fact to be decided in each case on its particular circumstances on the basis of evidence produced by the railway.[11]

On the question of duration of the burden s. 77(1) of the old Act shows that the railway administration has to deal with the goods put in its care as a bailee and has no responsibility for any loss, destruction, deterioration

6 *Kanakaiya Chetty* v *Union of India* AIR 1963 Mad 394; ILR (1963) Mad 1175; (1964)2 Mad LJ 329; 76 Mad LW 331.
7 *Gobind Sharma* v *Union of India* AIR 1965 All 480.
8 *Union of India* v *Udho Ram* AIR 1963 SC 422; 1963 SCR 39; (1963)2 SCR 702. Also see *Jugal Kishore* v *Union of India* AIR 1965 Pat 196.
9 *Union of India* v *West Punjab Factories Ltd.* AIR 1966 SC 395; (1966)1 SCJ 350; 1966 SCD 988; (1966)1 SCWR 246.
10 *Punjab National Bank* v *Beniprasad* AIR 1981 MP 95; 1981 MPLJ 380.
11 *T.M. Veerappa* v *Union of India* AIR 1972 Mys 164; (1972)1 Mys LJ 96; *K.R. Rajamanickam* v *Union of India* AIR 1974 Mad 375; 87 Mad LW 245.

or non-delivery, if it arises after the expiry of seven days after the termination of the transit.

The railways however can claim protection only in a case where loss occurs after the expiry of the period of seven days from the termination of transit. The onus is on the railways to show that no loss, destruction, deterioration or damage had taken place not only during the period of transit, but also during the subsequent period of transit, but till seven days after the termination of transit.[12]

In cases prior to Amending Act 39 of 1961 to the old Act came into force the railway administration was held liable for the loss, destruction etc., if it happened by its default or negligence. The burden of proof as to negligence ultimately rested with the plaintiff. He was to satisfy the court that the defendant was negligent but the duty of showing how the consignment was dealt with during transit lay on the railway administration as a matter within its special knowledge. If the defendant did not adduce all the evidence at its command, the plaintiff might in proper cases ask the court to make a presumption under *illustration* (*g*) of s. 114, Indian Evidence Act 1872, that the evidence which had been withheld would have gone against the defendant.[13] Loss or damage to the goods entrusted to a bailee is *prima facie* evidence of negligence on its part and it lies on the railway administration to disprove negligence. Where the goods were lost by an accidental fire over which the railway had no control and the railway administration took all possible steps to extinguish the fire, the railway administration cannot be held liable.[14]

Except in cases covered by old s. 74A, the primary onus of a bailee to show that he has taken reasonable care of the goods is on the railway.[15] Even under the new provision the law is the same. As held by MATHEW, J. (minority) in *Union of India* v *Sri Saroda Mills,*[16] it is not for the plaintiff in the first instance to prove when the goods consigned were destroyed or damage occurred (here the defence case was that the consignment was involved in a fire-accident). The burden is on the railway administration to show how the goods were dealt with and if that has not been done, the court is entitled to presume negligence on the part of the administration. The majority view did not differ from this view, but expressed a different opinion on another point. See also Note *Burden of proof* under s. 98.

12 *Raman & Co.* v *Union of India* AIR 1985 Mad 37 (38-40); (1984)97 Mad LW 320; 1984 TLNJ 307.

13 *Indian Trade and General Insurance* v *Union of India* AIR 1957 Cal 190; 98 CLJ 106.

14 *Union of India* v *Bhagwan Sah* AIR 1957 Pat 325; *Fushraj Thanmull* v *Union of India* AIR 1960 Cal 458.

15 *M.K. Manickam Chettiar* v *Union of India* (1959)2 MLJ 365; 72 Mad LW 464; *Union of India* v *S.S. Works* AIR 1976 SC 1414; (1976)3 SCC 32; (1976)3 SCR 614.

16 (1972)2 SCC 877; AIR 1973 SC 281; (1973)2 SCR 464.

9 Res ipsa loquitur and proof of liability of railway Derailment of train causing non-delivery of goods on whole or part to the consignee may itself speak for the negligence on the part of railway without requiring any further proof of negligence on the part of the railway, by the plaintiff. In such an eventuality the doctrine *res ipsa loquitur* applies.[17]

The words *res ipsa loquitur* means the thing speaks for itself. This maxim means only that in certain cases one fact raises a *prima facie* presumption of another fact unless and until the contrary is proved; thus where a ship under way collides with a ship at anchor, that is *prima facie* evidence of negligence on the part of the ship which is in motion.[18]

The general purport of the words *res ipsa loquitur* is that accident "speaks for itself" or tells its own story. There are cases in which the accident speaks for itself so that it is sufficient for the plaintiff to prove the accident and nothing more. It will then be for the defendant to establish that the accident happened due to some other cause than his own negligence. Once this doctrine is found to be applicable, the burden of proof would shift on the defendant.[19]

It is respectfully submitted if collision between two trains result in non-delivery of goods the negligence on the part of railway would be apparent and unless rebutted the presumption of negligence on the part of the railway would be concluded and the railway would be liable.

Res ipsa loquitur is not a principle of substantive law. It is a rule of evidence, an expression which it is convenient to apply to those circumstances in which a plaintiff is deemed to have discharged his task of establishing want of care on the part of the defendant without having to prove any specific negligence or omission by the defendant. The general rule is that it is for the plaintiff to prove negligence, and not for defendant to disprove it. In some cases it causes considerable hardship to the plaintiff, because, if may be that the true cause of the accident lies only with the defendant. The plaintiff can prove the accident; but he cannot prove how it happened so as to show its origin in the negligence of the defendant. This hardship is avoided to a considerable extent by the principle of *res ipsa loquitur*. When all the facts are known, there is no room for application of the maxim; in such a case the only question for consideration is whether an inference of negligence is practically certain or practically impossible. But when all the facts are not known, the maxim helps the plaintiff to discharge the onus which lies upon him, of proving negligence. If the accident is proved in such a way that *prima facie* it could not have happened without negligence in the part of the defendant then it is for the

17 *Khedul Oil Cake Industries* v *Union of India* AIR 1988 Del 88; (1987)33 Del LT 297.
18 Jowitt's *Dictionary of English Law*, p. 1557.
19 *Cholan Roadways Ltd.* v *G. Thirugnonasambandan* (2005)3 SCC 241.

defendant to explain how the accident could have happened without negligence.[20]

When the defendant railway after unloading the consignment kept the same on station platform, it was destroyed by some fire accident. The evidence adduced showed that the railway authorities did not take even the elementary precaution to protect it from such accident. The principle *res ipsa loquitur* applied and the railway was held liable for the loss. The absence of reasonable foresight and care by the railway administration being patent on the face of circumstances.[21]

10 Forwarding note Under present s. 72 of the old Act, a consignor delivering to a railway administration any animal or goods to be carried by railway shall execute a forwarding note in such form as prescribed by the railway administration and approved by the Central Government. At present three different forms of forwarding notes have been approved by the Central Government—(1) forwarding note for general merchandise, (2) forwarding note for dangerous goods and (3) forwarding note for animals or articles enumerated in the Second Schedule of the Indian Railways Act other than dangerous goods. If the goods are not accepted by the railway for any reason and the consignor so desires, the railway is to issue a certificate to that effect. If the railway accepts the goods it grants a receipt therefor. But it is not true that the responsibility of the railway starts with the grant of the receipt. The railway administration really accepts the goods on the date on which the weights of the consignment are noted on the forwarding note and liability begins from that time.[22] The forwarding note and the railway receipt together constitute documents which evidence as well as contain the terms and conditions of the contract between the parties.[1]

11 Act of God A railway administration shall not be liable for loss etc. of animals or goods if the same has been caused by act of God as laid down in cl. (*a*) to s. 73 of the old Act (corresponding to s. 93(*a*) of the Railways Act 1989). The expression "Act of God" means an event which happens independently of human action, such as death from natural causes, storm, earthquake etc. which no human foresight or skill could reasonably be expected to anticipate.[2] Act of God is an overwhelming, unpreventable event caused exclusively by forces of nature, such as an earthquake, flood or tornado.[3] So railway administration, is not liable for any accident as to

20 *Associated Cotton Traders* v *Union of India* (1977)2 Mad LJ 335; 90 Mad LW 438.
21 *Associated Cotton Traders* v *Union of India* (supra).
22 *Union of India* v *Hamirmull Champalal* AIR 1959 Cal 400; *Dhanaraj Agarwala* v *Union of India* AIR 1958 Assam 5.
1 *Commissioners for the Port of Calcutta* v *General Trading Corporation Ltd.* AIR 1960 Cal 290; 68 CWN 410.
2 Jowitt's *Dictionary of English Law*.
3 Black's *Law Dictionary*, 10th Ed., 2014.

which it can show that it is due to natural causes directly and exclusively without human intervention, and that it could not have been prevented by any amount of foresight and care reasonably to be expected from its officers.[4] As already stated the liability of railway has been changed since 1962 from that of a bailor to an insurer. In the law of insurance, the insurer is usually by express provision, but also by implication, not liable to indemnify the insured against an act of God and the same rule applies to a common carrier.

12 Reasonable foresight and care A railway is not absolved from all liabilities if the loss etc. have been caused for reasons other than those enumerated in cls. (*a*) to (*i*) of s. 73 of the old Act (corresponding to s. 93(*a*) to (*i*) of the Railways Act 1989). In order to avail itself of the benefit of the section, the railway administration is required to prove that it has used reasonable foresight and care in the carriage of the animals or goods. If the railway fails to prove that, it shall be held responsible for the loss etc. due to causes enumerated in cls. (*a*) to (*i*) of s. 73 of the old Act. What is reasonable foresight and care is however, a question of fact to be decided on the facts and circumstances of each particular case.[5] The words 'foresight and care' are of wide amplitude and should not be understood to apply to the carriage of the goods only. In the case of non-delivery of the goods due to seizure by legal process, the railway authorities are to intimate the factum of seizure of goods to the consignor/consignee within a reasonable time. Failure to do so postulates want of reasonable foresight and care.[6]

13 Loss by fire Section 73 of the old Act itself indicates that loss by fire is one of the things in respect of which the railway is protected provided it proves that it has used reasonable foresight and care in the carriage of goods. A fire may occur due to numerous causes and where fire is extensive it may not be possible to ascertain the cause of fire; but mere inability or impossibility to ascertain the cause of fire cannot be attributed to negligence or want of care on the part of railway.[7] Certain bales of cotton duly consigned were kept in the open on the platform at the destination station and the goods were not cleared for some days. Fire broke out and destroyed another stock of bales lying adjacent. Fire Brigade was called. The Station Master and the Fire Officer thought that the fire had been completely extinguished. But after a day or two, the plaintiff's bales lying nearby were also destroyed by fire. The reason was that in all probability the fire was due to sparks from the bales burnt earlier. The court found that all that could possibly have been done had not been done.

4 *Province of Madras* v *Machado* AIR 1955 Mad 519; (1955)2 MLJ 240.
5 *K.R. Rajamanickan* v *Union of India* AIR 1974 Mad 375; 87 Mad LW 245; *T.M. Verappa* v *Union of India* AIR 1972 Mys 164; (1972)1 Mys LJ 96.
6 *Union of India* v *Gajanand Oil Mill* (1984)2 Andh WR 269.
7 *Union of India* v *Haji S. Umbichi Koya* AIR 1973 Ker 83; ILR (1972)2 Ker 588.

The fire still inside the bowels were not put out and the railway was held to be negligent.[8]

14 Short delivery—railway's liability where there was no evidence to prove actual weight Where there was no evidence to prove actual weight of the goods (groundnut oil) loaded in tank wagon weighment of which could not be taken by the railway for want of facility and the loading was done at the despatching station by the consignor himself under L/U condition, the railway administration was not liable for the short delivery detected at the destination. From the mere mention of a particular weight of the consignment on the railway receipt and forwarding note which carried such endorsement only for calculating the freight charge, no admission on the part of the railway as to correctness of the weight loaded could be made out to fix liability.[9] Merely because it was found leaky at the destination in the absence of proof that defective or leaky wagon was supplied to the consignor at the despatching station, no inference as to negligence of the railway and/or misconduct of its employees could be drawn to arrive at the liability of the railway.

15 Non-delivery or failure to deliver Under old s. 72 the railways were liable for loss, destruction and deterioration of animals or goods; failure to deliver did not furnish a cause of action on which a suit might lie against the railway administration distinct from a cause of action for loss or destruction.[10] Under s. 73 of the old Act (corresponds to s. 93 of the Railways Act 1989), the railway administration has been specifically made responsible for non-delivery.

16 Pilferage—loss of goods—short delivery—plea of defective packing Loss of goods by pilferage, that is by stealing goods in small quantities is different from loss by damage, deterioration, leakage or wastage of goods. When goods are consigned at railway risk and there is shortage in delivery on account of pilferage in transit the case comes within the general responsibility of the railway administration under s. 73 of the old Act (corresponding to s. 93 of the Railways Act 1989) and the onus lies upon the railway to prove that the railway had taken reasonable care even if the goods were proved to have been defectively packed by consignor; in such cases s. 77C of the old Act (s. 77C of the old Act corresponds to s. 98 of the Railways Act 1989) has no application because s. 77C of the old Act (s. 77C of the old Act corresponds to s. 98 of the Railways Act 1989) was obviously intended to cover cases of damage, deterioration, leakage or wastage of goods due to defective or improper packing.[11]

8 *Union of India* v *Balaji Trading Corporation* (1977)1 Mad LJ 110.
9 *Union of India* v *Chotelal Shewnath Rai* AIR 1973 Pat 244.
10 *Governor-General-in-Council* v *Musaddi Lal* AIR 1961 SC 725; (1961)1 SCJ 597; (1961)3 SCR 647.
11 *T.M. Verappa* v *Union of India* AIR 1972 Mys 164; (1972)1 Mys LJ 96.

17 Loss of part of consignment or short delivery—plea of wrong entry in railway receipt In case the railway booked certain goods for transit, and issued a railway receipt mentioning the extent of the goods so booked, it is for the railway to ensure that the goods were delivered back at the place of destination. They cannot take shelter under their own negligence, if any, in case railway receipts are recklessly issued, giving description and extent of goods without checking and ensuring that they are accordingly so. Of course, it is another matter that the goods are brought in packed condition, and the railways have no opportunity to open the packages and verify the contents. In that case, it would appear that the railways may be entitled to challenge the contents of the goods actually brought in sealed packages.

Thus a consignment of sugar booked at railway risk arrived at destination short of weight. The plea that the weight of the consignment as recorded in the railway receipt was wrong was not entertained and the suit was decreed.[12]

18 Loss The expression "loss" has not been defined in the Act. According to the dictionary meaning, "loss" means an undesirable outcome of a risk or the disappearance or diminution of value, usually in an unexpected or relatively unpredictable way.[13] The expression "loss" means "the fact of losing." The statute does not specify the manner or the circumstances in which the loss should be occasioned. The fact that an article has been lost by misappropriation or by theft or by misdelivery does not alter the fact that it has been lost.[14]

Under s. 72 of the old Act prior to the Indian Railways (Amendment) Act 1961 the liability of the railway was for loss, destruction or deterioration of animals and goods. 'Non-delivery' was not a ground which furnished cause of action on which a suit might lie against the railway administration. Under s. 73 of the old Act the railway administration has been made responsible specifically for 'non-delivery' also. In cases governed by that s. 72 of the old Act, there was much controversy on the point whether the cases of non-delivery and misdelivery would be covered by the term 'loss'. The position may be summarised as follows:

(A) One set of judicial decisions held that "loss" of the goods means loss of the goods by the railway and does not mean pecuniary or monetary loss to the consignee or the owner "and every case of misdelivery or non-delivery may not amount to loss". PAGE, J. held in the case of *E.I. Railway* v *Jogpat Singh*[15] that 'loss' means loss of goods by the railway and does not mean pecuniary or other loss suffered by the owner of goods through being wrongfully deprived of the possession, use or enjoyment thereof but

12 *Mohan Lal* v *Union of India* AIR 1985 Del 209.

13 Black's *Law Dictionary,* 10th Ed., 2014.

14 *Babloo Ram Hari Chand* v *S.M. Railway Co. Ltd.* 19 Bom 159; *Seetha Rama* v *S.I. Railway Ltd.* AIR 1936 Mad 491; 163 IC 840.

15 51 Cal 615; 28 CWN 1001; AIR 1924 Cal 725.

means loss of the goods by railway while in transit and such loss occurs whenever the railway involuntarily or through inadvertence loses possession of the goods and for the time being is unable to trace them and as non-delivery or misdelivery may be due to loss or due to other causes. The term "loss" did not include every case of non-delivery, misdelivery and detention and action or the ground of non-delivery and misdelivery for damages must be based either on contract or tort and this finds support also in the cases of *Secretary of State* v *Jiwan*,[16] and *Railway* v *Kishan Lal.*[17] Patna High Court attributed the same meaning to the term 'loss' as in the above two decisions of Allahabad High Court in *E.I. Railway* v *Kali Charan Ram Prasad*,[18] by the Chief Court of Punjab in *Changa Mal's* case[19] in Bombay High Court by KAJIJI, J. in *G.I.P. Railway* v *Ramchandra Jagannath.*[20] On appeal, *see*, 43 Bom 386; 21 Bom LR 6; and in Lahore High Court by ABDUL RAOOF, J. in *Hill Sawyers & Co.* v *Secretary of State.*[21] In each of the last two cases, however, a Division Bench held that 'loss' means loss to the owner or consignor of the goods.

CHATTERJEE, J. in the case of *G.A. Jolli* v *Dominion of India*[1] in dealing with the meaning of the word "loss" observed as follows: "There is some conflict of judicial opinion on the meaning of the word 'loss'. Some High Courts have taken the view that 'loss' means loss to the owner and non-delivery or misdelivery is 'loss' to the consignor or owner. Calcutta High Court has taken a contrary view and has consistently held that the word 'loss' means loss of goods by the railway and does not mean pecuniary or monetary loss to the consignor or the owner. In some cases it has been held that non-delivery or wrong delivery may amount to 'loss' and there may be a 'loss' although it is due to wilful neglect of the railway administration. Relying on the judgment of PAGE, J. in the case of *E.I. Railway Co.* v *Jogpat Singh*[2] the court held that there is no justification for the contention of the railway that it can successfully plead 'loss' when the goods are identifiable and available ... The judgment of PAGE, J. has been followed in *Gopiram Behariram* v *Agents, E.I. Railway*,[3] *G.I.P. Railway Co. Ltd.* v *Jes Raj Patwari*,[4] *Haji Tilloi Mahammad Umar Buksh* v *B.N. Railway Co. Ltd.*[5] *Secretary of State for India in Council* v

16 45 All 380; 21 ALJ 220; AIR 1923 All 426.
17 AIR 1923 All 605; 45 All 530; 21 ALJ 438.
18 AIR 1922 Pat 106.
19 6 PB 1897.
20 20 Bom LR 591.
21 AIR 1921 Lah 1 (FB); 61 IC 926.
1 AIR 1949 Cal 380.
2 51 Cal 615; AIR 1924 Cal 725.
3 30 CWN 209; AIR 1926 Cal 612.
4 32 CWN 76; 65 Cal 132; AIR 1928 Cal 65.
5 57 Cal 73; AIR 1929 Cal 700.

Surjyamall Haribaksh,[6] *B.N. Railway Co. Ltd.* v *Nibaran Chandra Bahar*,[7] *G.I.P. Railway Co.* v *Gopiram Gouri Shankar*.[8]

(B) On the contrary, in some other decision it was held that "loss" means loss to the owner or consignor of the goods and goods which are not delivered or misdelivered are "lost" within the meaning of the term as used in Risk Note (B) and in ss. 72 and 80 of the Indian Railways Act 1890 Division Bench decisions in *G.I.P. Railway* v *Ramchandra Jagannath*.[9]

(C) MULLICK and BUCKNIL, JJ. in *G.I.P. Railway* v *Jitan Ram*,[10] held "that if the loss to the owner was meant then there was no necessity for any reference to liability for destruction of the goods."

In the case of *M. & S.M. Railway Co.* v *Subba Rao*,[11] the court was unable to accept the view that the term "loss" in the Risk Note (B) includes "destruction, deterioration or damage" and held that "if goods entrusted to the care of the company ceases to have any resemblance to the goods of the description which they undertook to carry, it seems to us that the company should be held to have lost the goods".

(D) RANKIN, CJ. (as he then was) in *G.I.P. Railway Co. Ltd.* v *Jesraj Patwari*,[12] observed that as the word "loss" is used there may be a "loss" although it is caused by theft of the servants of the railway administration or its agents and there may be a loss although it is due to wilful neglect of the railway administration itself.

(E) Some later decisions held that the word 'loss' in old s. 77 must include loss arising from whatever cause. It includes a claim on the footing of non-delivery, negligence, wrongful detention or conversion on the part of the railway administration.[13] The meaning of the word "loss" as used in s. 73 of the old Act should be the same as in s. 78B of the old Act. Non-delivery of a portion of the consignment due to the fact that the railway involuntarily or through inadvertence lost possession of the goods and was unable to trace them amounts to loss.[14] The word "loss" can never mean loss to the owner. It means that the goods have disappeared in the course of transit and neither the railway nor the consignor nor the consignee

6 61 Cal 599; AIR 1934 Cal 783.
7 50 CWN 86; AIR 1946 Cal 235.
8 7 Pat 192; AIR 1928 Pat 270.
9 43 Bom 386; 21 Bom LR 6; *Hill Sawyers & Co.* v *Secretary of State* 2 Lah 133; 61 IC 926; *G.I.P. Railway* v *Jitan Ram* AIR 1923 Pat 285.
10 AIR 1923 Pat 285.
11 43 Mad 617; 38 MLJ 360.
12 55 Cal 132; 32 CWN 76.
13 *Martab Ali* v *Union of India* AIR 1954 Bom 297; 56 Bom LR 150.
14 *Union of India* v *Meghraj* AIR 1958 Cal 434.

are or is in a position to trace them.[15] No distinction can be made of a loss being to the railway or loss to the owner. Loss means that the goods are lost by the railway since they are not forthcoming and therefore they have no control over the goods, the resultant loss occurring to the owner. But if the court on evidence comes to the conclusion that there is any wilful withholding of the goods by the railway, then it cannot be said to have been lost.[16]

19 In transit The expression means during the time the goods are accepted for carriage by railway up to the expiry of the free time granted for taking delivery of the same.

20 Destruction In *G.I.P. Railway Co.* v *Jitan Ram Nirmal Ram*,[17] MULLICK, J. observed as follows: "Destruction must always be included in loss and the draftsman of the risk note has merely availed himself of the device of first stating the generality and then without prejudice thereto reciting the particulars. The word "destruction" is surplusage but it does not alter the sense. In my opinion, therefore, the risk note will apply not only when the goods have been lost by the bailee in the sense that he cannot trace them but also when they are lost to the owner because the bailee fails to deliver them to him in breach of his contract for any reason whatsoever, and I cannot admit that by merely suing for compensation for non-delivery the plaintiff can take the case out of the risk note."

21 Destruction by health authorities—liability of the railways Oil was consigned under Risk Note 2 from Kanpur to Calcutta. After the goods reached Calcutta safely, it was seized by Health Authorities and destroyed as adulterated under High Court orders. The railway was not responsible for non-delivery and is not liable for damages. The plea that failure to give notice has resulted in prejudice to the consignor is untenable when the consignor was aware of the seizure and was also a party to the proceedings and such a plea cannot be taken for the first time in appeal under Art. 136 of the Constitution of India as it involves a mixed question of law and facts.[18]

22 Deterioration The interpretation to be put on the word "deterioration" has been the subject of some controversy in various High Courts in India and even in the same High Court. In the case of *Madras Railway Co.* v *Govinda Ram*,[19] decided so long ago as 1898, SUBRAHMANIA AYYAR and

15 *Union of India* v *Shah Vastimull Harakchand* AIR 1959 Mys 13; ILR (1958) Mys 481.

16 *Ardhanari Chettiar* v *Union of India* AIR 1956 Mad 483; ILR (1957) Mad 195; (1956)2 MLJ 6; 69 Mad LW 375.

17 AIR 1923 Pat 285.

18 *Juggilal Kamalapat Oil Mills* v *Union of India* AIR 1976 SC 227; (1976)1 SCC 893.

19 21 Mad 172.

BENSON, JJ. interpreted the word "deterioration" as used in s. 72 of the Indian Railways Act prior to the Amendment Act 1961, in the following terms: "Clearly therefore in the case before us if the plaintiff had alleged and proved that, owing to the loss of the special opportunity for sale of which he wished to take advantage, the cloth had fallen in value compared to what he could have got for it, had he been able to dispose of it at K as he intended, the plaintiff would have been entitled to a finding that there was a "deterioration" within the meaning of s. 72." A similar question came up before a Division Bench of the Punjab Chief Court in *I.G.N. & Railway Co.* v *Haricharan Das*[20] where the learned Judges observed that they saw no reason for doubting that "deterioration" included decrease in market value consequent on detention. This interpretation of the word "deterioration" has been affirmed by MUKERJI, J. in *Bhagwan Das* v *B.N. Railway.*[1] Later in *G.I.P. Railway Co.* v *Jugal Kishore*[2] a Division Bench of Allahabad High Court consisting of SULAIMAN, CJ. and KENDALL, J. has decided after consideration of the authorities on the point that the word "deterioration" in the risk note is wide enough to include depreciation in value on account of fall in the price of the goods despatched. Depreciation in value of the goods on account of a fall in the price of goods is deterioration.[3]

In *E.I. Railway Co.* v *Diana Mal Gulab Singh*[4] a Division Bench of Lahore High Court after full discussion of the question arrived at the following conclusion: "The 'deterioration' of a thing, whether it be in quality or in value, implies in ordinary parlance a change for the worse in the thing itself. If a thing is worthless than it was before only because the market rate has gone down, it would be correct to say that it has depreciated in value, but not that it has deteriorated." The interpretation given was not accepted by DIN MOHAMMAD, J. in *Secretary of State* v *Khan Chand Ram Lal*[5] and the learned Judge expressed his view as follows: "With all due deference, I feel inclined to follow the interpretation put on the word by the Madras High Court as well as by the Punjab Chief Court and affirmed and re-affirmed by the Allahabad High Court and to hold that the words "deterioration from any cause whatever" include depreciation in value on account of detention or delay in delivery." But BHIDE, J. did not concur with DIN MOHAMMAD, J., in the interpretation put by him on the word "deterioration" in that case. According to BHIDE, J. the word "deterioration" as used in the Risk Note H does not cover depreciation of value due to fall in the market price.

20 111 PR 1912; 15 IC 12.
1 AIR 1920 All 507; 51 All 805.
2 52 All 238; AIR 1930 All 132.
3 *Kishanlal* v *Union of India* AIR 1960 MP 289; *Union of India* v *Sheobux Satyanarayan* AIR 1963 Ori 68; ILR (1962) Cut 690.
4 5 Lah 523; AIR 1925 Lah 255; 85 IC 404.
5 AIR 1925 Lah 492.

The Supreme Court has preferred to adopt the view of Lahore High Court[6] and held that the words used in s. 76 of the old Act, namely, "loss, destruction, damages or deterioration" must be read as *ejusdem generis* so as to indicate actual and physical loss or change in the goods, as distinguished from depreciation in its value according to market price. That being so, it is clear that the word "deterioration" used in s. 76 of the old Act refers to the physical and actual deterioration of the goods.[7]

23 General responsibility of railways—seizure of goods by legal process In a case goods were loaded for transport in violation of a levy order by Government. The goods were seized. The consignor sued the railway for damages. Section 73 of the (old) Railways Act deals with the general responsibility of a railway administration as a carrier of animals and goods. A railway administration is charged with responsibility, thereunder for the loss, destruction, damage, deterioration or non-delivery, in transit of animals or goods delivered to the administration to be carried by railway. The liability ceases to exist in nine categories of cases. One such category is where the loss, destruction, damages, deterioration or non-delivery of the goods is due to seizure of the goods under legal process. In a case one *J* was both consignor and consignee of the goods booked from Sindi railway station to Mirzapur. But at Sindi railway station the police seized the goods on the footing that these were stolen property; *J* was prosecuted on a charge under ss. 379/411, IPC. *J* later was acquitted 1½ years after. Under order of the court, the goods were released in favour of *J*. But the plaintiff on the footing that he was an indorsee of the railway receipt, sued the railway as also *J*. In such circumstances railway cannot be held liable.[8]

A consignment of mustard oil was booked from Kanpur to Calcutta and the consignment arrived at Calcutta on 4th September 1949. The consignor wrote to the railway authority at Kanpur so that the consignment could be rebooked from Kanpur to Calcutta on 6th September 1949. But on that very date Food Inspector under s. 419, Calcutta Municipal Act 1923 seized the entire consignment on the footing that it was adulterated and destroyed. The seizure being under the legal process, the railway administration was held not answerable for the loss. This decision further held that the request for reconsignment should have been made to railway authority, Calcutta and that too with the original railway receipt accompanying the request. Since this was not done, there was no question of rebooking.[9]

6 AIR 1925 Lah 255.
7 *Union of India* v *S.S.H. Syndicate* AIR 1976 SC 879; (1976)3 SCR 504; (1976)3 SCC 108; (1976)1 SCJ 361.
8 *Luxmi Dutt Roopchand* v *Union of India* AIR 1975 SC 760; (1975)1 SCC 341.
9 *Juggilal Kamalapat Oil Mills* v *Union of India* AIR 1976 SC 227; (1976)1 SCC 893. [See also the heading Destruction of health authorities—liability of the railways in this section].

The railway administration claiming exemption, must however prove that it has used reasonable foresight and care in the carriage of the animals or goods. The words "foresight and care" are of wide amplitude and should not be understood to apply to the carriage of the goods only. In the case of non-delivery of the goods due to seizure of the same under legal process the "care" to be exhibited by the railway administration takes within its ambit an obligation to intimate the factum of seizure of goods to the consignor/consignee within a reasonable time from the date of seizure so as to enable him to pursue his lawful remedies to recover the goods from the concerned authority that seized the goods under legal process. In that case, the appellant railway did not send any intimation whatsoever appraising the consignor/consignee of the fact of seizure of the goods. Therefore, the railway cannot escape the liability for non-delivery of the goods.[10]

24 Delay in transhipping causing damage to perishable goods—compensation Under the old law when a consignment containing perishable goods was damaged or deteriorated due to delayed transhipment, the liability of the railway company was governed by ss. 151 and 152 of the Indian Contract Act 1872 if no risk note was executed. The company was bound to take as much care of the goods as a man of ordinary prudence would take of his own goods under similar conditions. A consignor of perishable articles prove in order to recover damages for their deterioration not only that there was delay in transhipping the articles due to want of good care on the part of the railway servants but also that those damages were due to such delay.[11] Where a wagon of perishable goods was detached and detained without necessity, the court might well presume that the delay was the cause of the deterioration of the goods.[12] Now, if the consignment containing perishable goods is damaged by reason of delay in transit, the railway would be responsible unless the cause is attributable to any of the causes enumerated in cls. (*a*) to (*i*) of s. 73 of the old Act. Even if the consignment is booked at owner's risk rate, delay itself would prove *ipso facto* negligence or misconduct on the part of the railway and accordingly the railway would be liable for damages.

25 Deterioration of goods due to overcarriage Railway company is not protected by either the Risk Note A or B and is liable for damages when there is overcarriage of goods, the overcarriage being not within the terms of the contract embodied in risk notes, beyond the station of destination involving a delay of three days resulting in deterioration of the goods consigned.[13]

10 *Union of India* v *Gajanand Oil & Dal Mill* (1984)2 Andh WR 269.
11 *Bengal & N.W. Railway Co. Ltd.* v *Sobrati Miya* AIR 1944 Cal 50; ILR (1943)1 Cal 397.
12 *Union of India* v *Ganesh Chandra* AIR 1959 Cal 337; 63 CWN 343.
13 *B.B. & C.I. Railway* v *Ganu Daji* AIR 1929 Bom 421.

26 Loss of whole consignment When goods in the custody of the railway become rotten and destroyed under the orders of the railway authorities, it must be held that the owners had suffered "loss of a whole consignment" within the meaning of that phrase used in Risk Note B or H.[14]

In cases where goods consigned by railways are only deteriorated and not absolutely lost, the consignee is bound to take delivery of the goods and then claim damages for the deterioration. Where the consignee not only refuses to take delivery of the goods, but also prevents the railway company from selling them, he is not entitled to claim damages on the basis of actual loss.[15] Where, owing to the consignee's failure to take delivery, no evidence exists regarding the amount and extent of damage, he cannot recover any compensation.

27 Difference—if any—in meaning of loss, destruction In the case of *Ardhanari* v *Union of India*,[16] KRISHNASWAMI NAYUDU, J. has said as to the meaning of the words "loss, destruction or deterioration" in s. 75 of the (old) Indian Railways Act: "There is no reason way the words "loss, destruction and deterioration" in s. 75 of the (old) Railways Act, should be given a different meaning from that given to them in the other sections of Chapter VII of the Railways Act. Goods may deteriorate by any negligence on the part of the company and deterioration may to a certain extent depend upon the nature of the goods. In the case of deterioration of goods, the goods are not lost, but the railway company is not in a position to deliver them in the same condition in which they have received them from the consignor. In case of destruction, destruction of goods may occur by fire, when the entire goods may disappear or part of them may be burnt by fire and the remaining may be available or there may be destruction by flood or by other act of God and in such cases the railway company would not be in a position to produce the goods since they completely or partly disappeared by reason of the destruction. In the case of loss, the railway company is not in a position to have control over the goods; that means, the goods are not forthcoming and the railway company is therefore unable to deliver the same. The loss must necessarily occur after the goods are put in charge of the railway company by the consignor delivering them to the railway authorities and it does not matter at what stage the goods are not forthcoming".

28 Delivery of goods to railway company—commencement of responsibility The question as to when certain goods will be deemed to have been delivered in a particular case to the railway company is really a question of fact to be decided with reference to the special circumstances of each case.

14 *Jagannath* v *Secretary of State* AIR 1926 Lah 614; *M. & S. Railway* v *Mattai Subba Rao* 43 Mad 617; 28 MLJ 360; *E.I. Railway Co.* v *Md. Shah* AIR 1927 Lah 854.

15 *Lakhiram* v *Secretary of State* AIR 1934 Cal 834.

16 AIR 1956 Mad 483.

And where it is shown that the consignor has done all that is possible for him to put the goods in the possession of the railway company and that there is nothing left for him to be done in that connection and there is clear evidence, direct or circumstantial, that the railway company has accepted the custody of the goods, the liability of the railway as a bailee will begin to operate. Where goods are delivered to a railway company for carriage under a risk-note and are so accepted, the responsibility of the railway company for each parcel of goods accrues forthwith on the delivery of the goods and the acceptance of such delivery and accordingly the risk-note attaches to them immediately on such delivery and acceptance and before their actual despatch when they are lying on the platform awaiting transport, though no receipt might have been given for such goods and though the goods had not been loaded in wagons for transport.[17] See also "Forwarding note", *ante*.

In the case of *Ram Chandra Natha* v *G.I.P. Railway Co.*[18] HEATON, J. made the following observation:

> "A delivery to be carried by the railway means something more than a mere depositing of goods on the railway premises: it means some sort of acceptance by the railway, a taking as well as a giving. What that taking occurs is a matter which depends on the course of business and the fact of each particular case; but it certainly may be completed before the railway receipt is granted."

Certain goods had been taken to the railway station and there a forwarding note being filled in, the consignor had the goods duly entered in the railway register by the registering clerk. It was then found in that case that nothing further remained to be done by the consignor except to obtain a formal receipt for the goods from the railway company and in these circumstances the goods were held to have been delivered to the railway company even though the latter denied responsibility for the custody of the goods on the ground that no formal receipt had been issued by them.

Certain goods had been actually handed over by the plaintiff's servant to the railway officials and accepted by the latter though no receipt was actually granted by them. The liability of the railway company would accrue from the time when the goods had been accepted and was not dependent upon the granting or withholding of the receipt for the goods on behalf of the railway company by the officials who had accepted the goods.[19]

17 *Ardeshir Bhicaji* v *Agent, G.I.P. Railway Co.* AIR 1929 PC 24; 55 IA 67; 32 CWN 544; 52 Bom 169; 30 Bom LR 275; 26 ALJ 546; *Union of India* v *Hamirmull* AIR 1959 Cal 400.

18 AIR 1923 All 499; 45 All 235.

19 *Sohan Pal, Munna Lal* v *E.I. Railway Co.* AIR 1922 All 9; 44 All 218 (FB).

When the goods were found to have been placed in the goods yard, registered in the company's books, weighed and marked by the railway company and it was further found that the consignment notes in respect of the goods had been received by the goods clerk, but he had not yet issued a receipt in respect of those goods. In these circumstances it was held that the goods should be deemed to have been delivered to the railway company.[20]

Certain goods had been delivered to the station master to be booked, but he being unable to book on account of stoppage of booking, kept the goods on the railway premises without definitely directing the plaintiff to remove the goods or telling him in unmistakable terms that the goods were being kept at his own risk, though at the same time not definitely accepting the goods at the railway risk. In these circumstances it was held that the conduct of the station master in retaining the goods in the railway shed afforded satisfactory evidence that he had accepted the bailment of the goods on behalf of the railway company.[1]

A consignment containing 84 bales of cotton was taken by the consignor's agent to the railway station for despatch to another station. The consignment was tendered to the station master, but no wagon being immediately available for the purpose of despatch, the consignment with the consent and permission of the station master, who was the authorised agent of the railway administration, was deposited in the station premises and stacked on the down platform pending the availability of a suitable wagon. No forwarding note was tendered by the consignor's agent, nor any receipt given to him by the railway administration. Within three days of the deposit of the goods in the station yard the goods were destroyed by fire by a spark from the engine. It was held that having regard to all the circumstances of the case, the goods must be taken to have been delivered to be carried within the meaning of s. 72 of the (old) Indian Railways Act and that therefore the railway administration was liable to the consignor for the loss incurred by the destruction of the bales by fire.[2]

In the case of *Mariappa* v *Governor-General of India*,[3] MACK, J., observed: "Whether there has or there has not been delivery to the railway administration is an inference of fact from the circumstances of each case. If the consignor was specifically refused permission to keep his goods in the goods shed overnight and direct to remove them by the officials responsible, it may be possible to hold that the goods would lie there entirely at the consignor's risk without any contract of bailment. But in

20 *Narsing Girji Mfg. Co.* v *G.I.P. Railway* 21 Bom LR 406; 51 IC 309.

1 *Munna Lal* v *E.I. Railway Co.* AIR 1923 All 71.

2 *Governor-General of India* v *Jubilee Mills Ltd.* AIR 1953 Bom 46; 54 Bom LR 652.

3 AIR 1950 Mad 700.

cases where to the knowledge of the goods shed officials or with their permission specific goods lie in a goods shed, deposited there before the shed is locked up for the night, the railway company cannot, as it appears to me, avoid the responsibilities of bailees. It must be remembered that the consignor in such a case is afforded no facilities for watching his goods at night."

29 Non-delivery The expression has not been defined in the Act. Even when it is a case of wilful delivery to a person not entitled to the goods, it was held to be non-delivery.[4] In *Uttam Singh* v *Union of India*[5] wherein the railway servant himself committed theft, it was held that it would amount to 'non-delivery.'

In a case a consignor left the goods in the goods shed in the absence of any railway servant and there was sufficient evidence in the case to hold that it was the practice of merchants and traders to bring their goods and place them in the goods shed at their own risk, this being permitted by the railway company solely for the convenience of the traders. The goods had neither been marked nor weighed and all that had happened was that the consignment notes had been made over to the maker who used also to discharge the duties of the Goods Clerk when the latter was busy otherwise. The goods had not been put in the possession of the railway company and the mere acceptance of the consignment notes was not equivalent to the acceptance of the goods by the railway company.[6]

In a case certain goods had been brought to the railway station and a forwarding note had been presented to the loading clerk who marked a number on them. The clerk told the consignor to come the next day for the receipt and have the goods marked. In the meantime the goods were deposited in a tin shed where it was the custom to leave goods in similar circumstances in the custody of the owners. In these circumstances the learned Judges who decided the case took the view that on the evidence that was before them, they were unable to find that anything had been done by the plaintiff which would amount to putting the goods in question in the possession of the railway company or to any person authorised on behalf of the railway.[7]

In the case of *Laxmi Narain Brahma Narain* v *Governor-General-in-Council*[8] the question was whether the passing of the goods through the gate and issuing by the gate-keeper of a forwarding not duly signed by

4 *Union of India* v *Joseph Textiles* AIR 1985 Mad 360 (371); (1985)1 Mad LJ 274; 1984 TLNJ 345.

5 AIR 1971 Del 79.

6 *Hardayal* v *B. & N.W. Railway Co.* AIR 1929 Pat 296.

7 *Lachmi Narain* v *B.B. & C.I. Railway Co.* AIR 1923 All 449.

8 AIR 1950 East Punj 87.

him to the consignor amounts to delivery to the railway or the consignor has to do something more and has to tender the goods to some other person or has to do some other act in order to make the delivery effective to impose in the railway the liability for any loss if it takes place. In deciding the point KAPUR, J. observed: "According to s. 72, Indian Railways Act, the liability for loss etc., of a railway administration is the same as that of a bailee under ss. 152 and 161, Indian Contract Act 1872, but before a liability can arise against the railway it is necessary to find out at what time their liability commences and for this purpose I would refer to Paragraph 23 at page 17 of the 4th vol. of Halsbury's *Laws of England, Hailsham*, 2nd Ed., which says:

> "The duties and liability of a carrier do not begin until he has accepted the goods for carriage. He may accept them either personally, or by his agent or servant with authority to accept them, or he may impliedly accept them as where he permits goods to be placed by another in the usual place for carriage. In my opinion, the rule which will apply to this case is found in *Hardayal Ram Dass Ray* v *B.N.W. Railway*,[9] where it was found as a fact that the bags had neither been marked nor weighed and all that had happened was that the consignment notes had been made over to the marker who used also to discharge the duties of the goods clerk when the latter was busy otherwise. In these circumstances, it was held that the goods had not been put in possession of the railway company and that the mere acceptance of the consignment notes was not equivalent to acceptance of the goods by the railway. In the case that I have to decide the evidence only shows that goods were allowed to pass into the railway premises. There is no reliable evidence to show that goods were as a matter of fact with the permission, express or implied, put at any place in the goods shed or there was an express delivery of the goods to the railway by being made over to a person authorised or deposited at a place reserved for or usually used for this purpose ...... In the present case, I find that beyond the fact that the gate clerk of the railway signed the forwarding note and allowed the goods to pass into the railway premises, nothing has been proved to establish the "passing from the physical custody" of the plaintiff's agent to "the physical custody" of the railway or its agent nor was there any implied acceptance of goods nor anything done which would bring it within the rule mentioned in Halsbury's *Laws of England* mentioned above. And the stage was never reached where the liability (in case of "loss") of the carrier commence."

30 Delayed delivery of goods The plaintiff was entitled under a railway receipt to take delivery of the goods on 19th August 1931, when he presented the railway receipt. He was also entitled to take delivery of the consignment according to the description thereof given in the railway receipt. The railway officials, however, offered to deliver goods bearing a different number. The plaintiff's suspicions were roused and he claimed open inspection of the consignment which was allowed on 1st September.

9 AIR 1929 Pat 296; 8 Pat 808.

In the meanwhile prices of goods contained in the consignment went down. The plaintiff sued the railway administration for damages. Thus, the plaintiff was entitled to damages and that the plaintiff was justified in not accepting the goods, except after an examination in order to satisfy himself whether they contained the goods he had ordered.[10]

Where by some mistake of the railway official the parcel of the books which ought to have reached Lucknow in two days and which was proved to have been despatched on 19th July 1930, did not reach Lucknow till 26th August 1930, and even then intimation of the arrival of the parcel was not given to the plaintiff till 17th September 1930, when so far as the plaintiff was concerned, the value of the books contained in the parcel had sunk to zero, the plaintiff was justified in declining to pay demurrage and take delivery of the parcel, and the decree awarding damages to the extent of the price of the goods with interest was upheld.[11] In the absence of a guarantee by the railway that the goods would reach on any particular date, and of notice by the consignor at the time of consignment that the goods were required in connection with a certain festival the consignor was not entitled to special damages but that he was entitled to ordinary damages for the non-delivery of goods within reasonable time.[12]

Where the goods in question were consigned from Tarighat near Gazipore on the E.I. Railway to Manbhum on 26th January 1922, and the goods were not lost or destroyed but the railway company took five months to convey them and they did not reach their destination until 25th June 1922, the damages suffered by the consignor owing to such unreasonable delay during transit entitled the consignor to sue the company in such case.[13] In *E.I. Railway* v *Firm Inderman Tulshi Ram*[14] the railway was held to be responsible for delay in the delivery of goods at the proper time. In *B.N.W. Railway* v *Firm Munna Lal*[15] the railway was held liable for unreasonable delay in transmission of goods which it could not explain. Where the railway receipt showed that goods were booked to be carried from Bhilai to Pune which was on the Wagpur route but the railway diverted the goods to a different route and took the goods to Aurangabad which did not fall on the route to Pune, the railway is guilty of gross negligence and liable in damages.[16]

The detention of the goods by the railway company was in order to prevent any possible theft and it was done by railway servants in the

10 *Secretary of State* v *Madhuri Das* AIR 1933 All 477.
11 *Secretary of State* v *School Book Depot* AIR 1933 Oudh 399.
12 *Fazal Ilahi* v *E.I. Railway Co.* AIR 1922 All 323.
13 *E.I. Railway Co.* v *Firm Gopi Krishna Kashi Prasad* AIR 1924 All 8.
14 AIR 1922 All 63.
15 AIR 1924 All 760.
16 *Union of India* v *S.S.H. Syndicate* AIR 1976 SC 879; (1976)3 SCR 504; (1976)1 SCJ 361; (1976)3 SCC 108.

discharge of their duty to prevent theft. It was found that a wire had been cut and they suspected that a theft had taken place or that theft might take place unless proper steps were taken, and they removed the wagons to the proper shed and properly sealed the wagons again. The railway company was not responsible for the delay caused by such detention.[17] In the case of *Raigarh Jute Mills Ltd.* v *Commissioners for the Port of Calcutta*[18] GENTLE, J. observed as follows:

> "Transit of goods on railways more particularly during the war period is subject to delay and goods handed to a railway in one bulk are frequently delivered by instalments spread over a considerable period. In such delivery it cannot be said that the railway is in default of its obligations by failing to deliver the whole at one and the same time. When one consignment is loaded in several wagons, they do not always reach the destination at the same time but often one wagon travels quicker and its contents are delivered before the others arrive. When that occurs, if a suit were immediately instituted after arrival of one of several wagons, for the balance, it would be met with a plea that a reasonable time for delivery had not expired and the action was premature."

The plaintiff delivered to the defendants railway company a consignment of cherries to be carried by passenger train or other similar service upon the terms that, in consideration of being charged a lower rate than the defendants' ordinary rate for the carriage of fruit, he would relieve the defendants from all liabilities for delay except upon proof that such delay arose from wilful misconduct on the part of the defendants servants. The cherries were duly despatched by passenger train, but in the course of the journey they were transferred to a goods train, with the result that they were delayed and because deteriorated as a consequence. The defendants were liable and they were not entitled to the advantage of the conditions of the consignment note relieving them from liability except upon proof of wilful misconduct.[19]

31 Delayed delivery of consignment Oranges when booked were green and in good condition, but delay in delivery of consignment had caused deterioration and decay of consignment. The fact that the consignor failed to prove that acid coming out of oranges caused the damages would not disentitle him to claim damages with interest.[20]

32 Delay in delivery due to strike In calculating what is a reasonable time within which goods which have been entrusted to a railway company for carriage must be delivered, regard must be had to all the circumstances existing at the time and these include the existence of a strike on the part

17 *M. & S.M. Railway* v *Haji Latif* AIR 1935 Cal 809.
18 AIR 1947 Cal 98.
19 *Gunyon* v *South Eastern & Chatham Railway* 84 LJKB 1212; [1915]2 KB 370.
20 *Rajinder Singh Brothers & Co.* v *Union of India* AIR 2003 Del 99.

of the railway company's own servants, provided it is not established that such strike has been brought about by any default on the part of the railway company.[1]

33 Damage by fire Where a consignment of jute despatched by railway under railway risk was damaged by fire and in a suit for damages against the railway, the defendant contended that the first was purely accidental but did not produce all the evidence it should have done and it was also found that the wagon containing the jute was taken along a longer route. In such circumstances the court must draw presumption which the court is permitted to do under *illustration* (*g*) of s. 114 of the Indian Evidence Act 1872 and come to the conclusion that the defendant was negligent in dealing with the goods. In case of damage by fire the onus of proving the value of the goods and the extent of damage caused to the goods is on the plaintiff.[2]

34 Liability of railway after arrival of goods The liability of a railway as a carrier to the consignee after the arrival of the goods is not the same as that of a warehouseman or a bailee for hire, and therefore, where a consignee refuses to take delivery of goods which have not become valueless on the ground that they are damaged, and the railway sells the goods by auction the consignee is entitled only to the price fetched at the auction sale minus any demurrage due to the railway company. In such a case the proper remedy of the consignee is to take delivery of the damaged goods and claim damages from the railway company.[3] The liability of the railway company as bailee commences from the period when the goods are delivered to them to the period when the goods are ready for delivery. The liability of the railway company is limited to the period of transit or carriage of the goods with the addition of a reasonable period of time for loading the goods and a reasonable period of time which is to be given to the consignee to take delivery. There is nothing in the (old) Indian Railways Act or in any other law in India which would impose the liability of a bailee upon a railway company for any period beyond this time.

In the case of *Lalji Raja* v *Governor-General of India*[4] the firm of Gainsingh Ganeshdas booked a consignment of 419 bags of rapeseed from Tandilanwala Railway Station in the United Provinces to Bankura. The railway receipt had been endorsed by the consignor to the plaintiff and it was in the custody of the Imperial Bank of India. There was a dispute going on between the consignor, Gainsingh Ganeshdas and the plaintiff as

1 *Hick* v *Raymond* 62 LJKB 98.

2 *Indian Trade and General Insurance Co. Ltd.* v *Union of India* AIR 1957 Cal 190.

3 *Secretary of State* v *Firm Harkishan Das Kuramal* AIR 1926 Lah 575. See also *B.N.W. Railway* v *Mulchand* 42 All 655; *Sri Gangaji Cotton Mills* v *E.I. Railway* AIR 1922 All 514.

4 54 CWN 902.

a result of which the railway receipt could not be made over to the plaintiff on 13th or 14th of June 1943. The plaintiff, therefore, could not take delivery of the goods before 22nd of June 1943. The plaintiff then brought a suit claiming damages on the allegation that the rapeseed was left on the platform without any cover and that it was damaged by rain water on the 13th and 14th June and also on subsequent days. The railway company was not liable as bailee to any damage caused after 14th June, since twenty-four hours (from 13th June, the date of arrival) would be reasonable time for the consignee to take delivery but the latter failed without reasonable cause.

In the case of *Jagannath Marwari* v *East India Railway Co.*[5] a Division Bench of Calcutta High Court took the same view and it was said: "The position then would seem to be that the suit must fail either for failure to comply with the provisions of s. 77 of the Indian Railways Act or because the goods were at the plaintiff's risk by reason of their failure to take delivery." The same view has been taken also by Allahabad High Court in the case of *Bengal & North-Western Railway* v *Mul Chand.*[6] In the case of *Vidya Sagar* v *Governor-General-in-Council, New Delhi,*[7] the same view was expressed by Achhru Ram, J. as follows: It is not the business of the railway administration to work as warehouseman or a bailee for hire. Its proper function is that of a public carrier that it is held responsible as a bailee. The duty as a carrier is discharged on the arrival of the goods at their destination and it is not for the railway administration to keep the goods as a warehouseman or a bailee for hire. The consignee, on the other hand, is expected to take delivery within a time fixed by the rules and if he neglects to do so, the railway administration can claim demurrage and not hire. That being so, its liability to the consignee after the arrival of the goods is not the same as that of a warehouseman or a bailee for hire. A contrary view was expressed in *Yusuf & Ismail Co.* v *Governor-General-in-Council,*[8] but that view was disapproved in *Lalji Raja & Sons* v *Governor-General-in Council.*[9]

In the case of *Union of India* v *Serajuddin,*[10] one consignment of four cases of cigarettes was booked at railway risk and another consignment of cigarettes was booked at owner's risk. The consignee, although he was

5 AIR 1918 Cal 221; 22 CWN 902.
6 AIR 1920 All 280; 42 All 655.
7 AIR 1949 Lah 166. See also *Secretary of State* v *Harkishan Das* 7 Lah 370.
8 AIR 1948 Nag 65.
9 54 CWN 902.
10 AIR 1953 Pat 206.

not entitled to claim open delivery, did ask for it and the railway company granted the request of the consignee. Thereupon it was found that 760 cigarettes were short. In both the cases, the plaintiff refused to take delivery on the ground that the contents were rotten and unfit for human consumption. The plaintiffs instituted a suit for damages charging the railway administration with pilferage, gross negligence and misconduct in regard to the goods. SINHA, J., in delivering the judgment observed: "In the present case, there is no doubt that the plaintiff had refused to take delivery when the goods arrived and although they were to entitled to open delivery, the plaintiff did ask for it and the railway company granted the request, and when the railway officer came to deliver the goods, it was found that most of the packages containing the cigarettes were badly damaged. If the goods had been kept properly in a protected place, no damage would have been caused to the goods. If after the railway company, as a bailee, had taken all possible care to protect the goods and the goods had been damaged by the default of the consignee in taking delivery of those goods Mr. Ghosh would have been right in suggesting that the consignee was not entitled to damages."

The liability of a railway administration as a bailee does not extend beyond a reasonable period of time for loading the goods and reasonable period of time (namely 24 hours) for taking delivery.[11] Even though the responsibility of the railway as a carrier may come to an end within a reasonable time after the goods have reached the destination station, its responsibility as a warehouseman continues, that responsibility being also the same as that of a bailee. The responsibility as a warehouseman can only come to an end in the manner provided in ss. 55 and 56 of the (old) Indian Railways Act and the rules framed as to disposal of the goods.[12]

35 Refusal to take delivery A consignee cannot insist on weighing and endorsement of shortage and to refuse to take delivery if the railway refuses to weigh and make the endorsement. He should take delivery of the consignment as it is after giving notice to the delivering officer as to the condition and then sue the railway administration for damages.[13]

In *Union of India* v *Mohan Rai*,[14] the goods booked at Auwa Railway Station on 18th November 1965 were initially contained in wagon No. 26811, when they were booked by the plaintiff at Auwa Railway Station but then while on transit, a part of the goods was transhipped at

11 *Sarjug Prosad* v *Union of India* AIR 1960 Pat 571.

12 *Union of India* v *W.P. Factories* AIR 1966 SC 395; (1966)1 SCR 580.

13 *Martin & Co.* v *Seth Deokinandan* AIR 1959 MP 276; *Union of India* v *Mohan Rai* AIR 1983 Raj 200; 1983 WLN 258; 1983 Raj LW 541; *Motilal* v *Union of India* (1985)2 Cur Civ Cas 186.

14 AIR 1983 Raj 200.

Mehsana Railway Station to wagon No. 5594 in order to avoid or eliminate chances of an accident occurring on account of logs of wood projecting outside the wagon. Both the wagons reached the destination station on 23rd November 1965. But as there were no identification marks, in respect of the goods contained in wagon No. 5594, they were sent back to Mehsana where after on an enquiry it was found that those goods formed part of the plaintiff's consignment and were originally contained in wagon No. 26811, the said goods were again sent back to the destination Railway Station on 30th January 1966. The plaintiff had refused to take delivery of the part of the consignment that was contained in wagon No. 26811 on the ground that it weighed only 62½ quintals being only a part of the total consignment and the station master of the destination station was refusing to issue short Certificate. The station master at the destination, having no means to verify as to whether 62.50 qtls. of firewood contained in wagon No. 26811 represented the entire goods consigned under the aforesaid railway receipt or merely constituted a part of the consigned goods, in such circumstances, it was not possible for the Station Master to issue a short delivery certificate, unless the consignee produced positive proof about the quantity of firewood booked in the consignment. As the plaintiff was at fault in not taking the delivery of the goods forming part of the consignment, contained in wagon No. 26811, when the same was offered to him or his representative and further the plaintiff's failure to take delivery of the entire consignment of firewood contained in both the wagons even upon receiving an intimation dated 21st January 1966, the plaintiff has no right to claim damages.

The plaintiff booked hardcoke from Pathardini station for delivery to him as consignee at Aligarh to be carried in a wagon which was well covered and revetted and sealed. When the consignment reached Aligarh, the original seal and rivett were missing and only a negligible quantity of coal was found on the wagon. He declined to take delivery unless the consignment was reweighed. Reweighment having been refused, he sued the railway for damages.[15]

It is proper to quote r. 118 of the Goods Tariff Rules which stands as follows:

> 118. *Reweighment of consignment at destination.* Railway do not undertake to weigh consignment at destination stations as a matter of course. Such weighment at destination station can only be considered in exceptional cases when the condition of consignment or package warrants this.

In *Motilal* v *Union of India*[16] this Rule was held reasonable and refusal to take delivery was held fatal.

15 *Motilal* v *Union of India* (1985)2 Cur Civ Cas 186.
16 (1985)2 Cur Civ Cas 186.

Thus a consignor or a consignee of goods is not justified in refusing to take delivery from the railway on the ground that the quality of the consignment was bad or that there was a shortage in the consignment at the time of the delivery. He can sue for damages in such cases.[17] Although the consignee cannot ordinarily refuse to accept delivery, even if the goods are damaged, he is not bound to accept delivery after he has filed a suit for damages for non-delivery.[18]

36 Consignee—right to pre-delivery damage assessment It has been held in *Niranjanlal* v *Union of India*,[19] that neither Goods Tariff No. 31 nor the Act contains provision for consignee to ask for damage assessment before taking delivery. He must take delivery within reasonable time in the condition in which they are found after giving notice to the authorities showing damage to or shortage of the goods. In *Gopinath* v *Union of India*,[1] upon on examination of the relevant provisions and case laws bearing on the question it was held that it is not open to a consignor or consignee to refuse to take delivery and to insist on re-weighment and 'open delivery' even if it is indicated that there has been pilferage or a part of the consignment had been lost or damaged in transit. The railway administration was not bound to grant 'open delivery' unless there was something in the contract itself.

The effect of refusal to take open delivery or assessment delivery is that the plaintiff would not be entitled to claim damages for the loss which might have been caused to the goods for the period after the same had been offered to the plaintiff by the railway administration, and that the defendant in that case might also be liable for wharfage or damage under the relevant statutory rules. However, the fact that the plaintiff was not justified in asking for 'open delivery' could not absolve the railway administration from the liability which might already have arisen if it is found that the consignment was damaged or lost as a result of negligence or misconduct of the railway administration while the goods were in transit or prior to the offer made by the railway administration to the plaintiff-respondent.[2]

17 *Dehri Rohtas Light Railway* v *East Keshalpur Colliery* AIR 1963 Pat 46; 1962 BLJR 968.

18 *Union of India* v *Damodardas Narayandas* AIR 1958 Bom 238; 60 Bom LR 103. Also see *Yusaf & Ismail & Co.* v *Governor-General* AIR 1948 Nag 65; *The Bengal Coal Supplying Firm* v *Union of India* 70 Bom LR 254; ILR (1969) Bom 32; *Union of India* v *Hukamchand* AIR 1970 MP 55; 1969 MPLJ 737.

19 AIR 1973 All 303; 1972 All WR (HC) 318.

1 AIR 1978 All 79; 1978 All WC 71; 1978 ACJ 262.

2 *Nizamuddin* v *Union of India* AIR 1981 All 444.

37 Open delivery There is no provision in the Railways Act or the Rules authorising the consignee to claim open delivery or assessment of damages before delivering the goods. In *Union of India* v *Gyani Ram*,[3] *Manbhardayal & Co.* v *Union of India*,[4] *Union of India* v *Jutharam*,[5] and *Union of India* v *Hukam Chand*,[6] the consignor/consignee cannot claim open delivery or assessment of damage before delivery, as of right. If the consignee does not take delivery of goods alleged to have been damaged in transit or before delivery is given, he does so at his own risk and the railway administration would be justified in disposing of the goods by public auction, after due notice to the consignee, in accordance with the provisions of s. 56(1) of the (old) Railways Act.

A consignee is not entitled to demand open delivery from the railway administration.[7] The railway administration is not bound to give open delivery and it is not liable for loss on account of fall in market price due to delay in obtaining open delivery.[8]

38 Consignee—right to pre-delivery—inspection and re-weighment of goods on railway premises Although in *Manbhardayal & Co.* v *Union of India*,[9] it was held that a consignee can demand re-weighment of the goods when he has reason to suspect damage or shortage of the goods; in a majority of cases it has been held that a consignee has no right to demand that the goods shall be opened and inspected on the railway premises before he can be called upon to take delivery. There is no provision of law or any statutory rule which obliges a railway company to make or to allow to be made in its delivery register any note alleging that goods are in a damaged condition. A consignee cannot refuse to take delivery because the railway company refuses to make an entry in their books. The consignee cannot insist upon an entry. If he has any complaint he is entitled to make his representation to the company in any other way.[10]

3 AIR 1967 Pat 32.

4 AIR 1967 Pat 412.

5 AIR 1968 Pat 35.

6 AIR 1970 MP 55; 1969 MPLJ 737; *Union of India* v *Ram Prasad* AIR 1982 Raj 253; 1982 Raj LW 213; 1982 WLN 88; 1982 Raj LR 533.

7 *Union of India* v *Sarajuddin* AIR 1953 Pat 206; *Union of India* v *Jutharam* AIR 1968 Pat 35.

8 *Governor-General in Council* v *Badri Das* AIR 1951 All 720. But see AIR 1963 AP 415.

9 AIR 1927 Nag 77.

10 *Sri Gangaji Mills Co.* v *E.I. Railway Co.* AIR 1922 All 514; 44 All 763; 20 ALJ 761; *Secretary of State* v *Sham Lal Deoki Nandan* AIR 1922 Lah 448; 67 IC 312; *Firm of Chaitsingh Shewaising* v *Secretary of State* AIR 1926 Sind 102; 91 IC 437.

In the case of *Dominion of India* v *Netai Chandra*,[11] GUHA, J. observed: "It seems to me that the principle of law deducible from the above cases has been correctly summarised in the case of *Surajmal Marwari* v *Agent, Bengal Nagpur Railway*.[12] I may quote the following passage from the judgment in that case: "With regard to the question of refusal to take delivery before reweighment it is settled that a railway company is not bound by law either to reweigh goods or to certify shortage at the time of delivery." A further passage from that judgment may also be usefully quoted: "It is clear that if the plaintiffs were dissatisfied either with the amount of freight charged or the condition of the goods when they arrived they should have taken delivery and pay the charges demanded and then have been able to take states to obtain any refund which was proved due to them." The cases to which reference has been made before lend support to this view of the Patna case. Special reference may in this connection be made to the case of *Janaki Das* v *Bengal Nagpur Railway*,[13] specially to the observations of JENKINS, CJ. at page 358 of the report, left-hand observations column. It seems to be clear from all these cases that the railway administration is under no obligation to reweigh and that if the consignee refuses to accept delivery he does so at his own risk. The Lower Appellate Court has not referred to any of these cases nor was this aspect of the question examined. The learned appellate judge purported to follow the rulings reported in the case of *Messrs Kishan Lal Matrund* v *B.B. & C.I. Railway Co.*[14] and *Secretary of State* v *Madhuri Das Narain Das*.[15] So far as the case reported in AIR 1938 All 477 is concerned it is to be noticed that in this case the consignee did not accept delivery without satisfying himself about the identity of the goods. That particular feature is absent in the present case ... As regards the other case, viz., AIR 1938 All 561, the facts are also different though no doubt in that case, as in our present case, there was diversion of the goods by a different route. In AIR 1938 All 561 it was held on the facts of that case. That the diversion of the route and the transfer of goods from a small to a bigger wagon constituted a breach of a necessarily implied term of contract between the parties and the railway company could not claim any exemption under Risk Note Forms A and B."

39 Right of remeasurement—re-weighment—reclassification and recalculation for rates—terminals and other charges Clause 6 of the forwarding note is in the following terms: "That the Railway Administration has the right of measurement, re-weighment, reclassification, and recalculation of rates terminal and other charges at the place of destination and of

11 56 CWN 217.
12 58 IC 200.
13 16 CWN 356.
14 AIR 1938 All 561.
15 AIR 1933 All 477.

collecting before delivery of goods any amount that may have been remitted or undercharged."

In the case of *Dominion of India* v *Virjee Doya & Co.*[16] it was contended that condition 6 appearing on the back of the forwarding note is not a part of the contract. DAS, J. (HARRIES, CJ. concurring) observed in the judgment as follows: "It appears that on the face of the forwarding note it is stated that the goods are carried subject to the conditions on the back of the forwarding note. It cannot be suggested that the freight which is mentioned in the forwarding note and the rate which has been charged therein form the sole term of the contract. We must regard all the terms contained in the forwarding note as forming the basis of the contract and one of the terms is that that contained in condition 6." Some cases[17] were noticed and discussed by DAS, J. in his judgment.

It was held that where a wrong rate was charged through mistake and it was later discovered that the rates actually charged for the goods carried were less than those charged, the railway administration can very well claim to charge at the station of destination at the higher and correct rate under cl. 6 of the forwarding note.

In *Firm Balmukund Harikishan* v *Union of India*,[18] one of the questions was whether the railway authorities were entitled to recover what they contended to be the appropriate charges recoverable under the provisions of Goods Tariff. The court referred to *Firm Ladhuram* v *N.W. Railway*,[19] *Chunnilal* v *Nizam's Guaranteed State Railway Co. Ltd.*[1] and *Joint Family Business of Ram Chandra Srinivas* v *S.S.L. Railway*,[2] and observed that it follows from the aforesaid decision that "where a clerk at the despatching station issues a railway receipt incorporating a condition that the goods would be carried at owner's risk thereby charging lower rates, it will not be open to charge at higher rates on the basis that the goods were chargeable on railway risk as that is the only rate according to Goods Tariff Rules and that condition No. 6 of the railway receipt and the terms of Rule No. 15 of Goods Tariff Rules, Part I, Chapter I which entitle the railway company to reclassify, remeasure and recalculate the rates cannot have the effect of altering the basis of the contract". On the other hand

16 AIR 1952 Cal 70; 55 CWN 758.

17 *Chunni Lal* v *Nizam's Guaranteed State Railway Co. Ltd.* 29 All 228; *Secretary of State* v *Harbans Prasad* AIR 1944 Mad 444; 52 All 81; *Dawood Rowther* v *South Indian Railway Co. Ltd.* AIR 1929 All 848; ILR (1945) Mad 174; *Firm Ramnath Laddhu Ram* v *North Western Railway* AIR 1926 Lah 631.

18 AIR 1955 Madh B 181.

19 AIR 1926 Lah 631; 7 Lah 412.

1 29 All 228 (FB); 1907 All WN 21.

2 AIR 1953 Hyd 274; ILR (1953) Hyd 451.

there are cases which take a contrary view.[3] "The reasoning adopted in these cases is that the contract of carriage entered into on behalf of the railway by the clerk of the railway is subject to Goods Tariff Rules and he has no authority to contract outside the terms of the tariff. Term No. made good at the destination. In AIR 1952 Cal 70, it is further held that the charges demanded in a case such as this can be included within the phrase "other charges" as used in Rule No. 15 of the Rules aforesaid. This case expressly referred to the cases of 29 All 288 (FB) and AIR 1926 Lah 631 (*supra*) and refused to follow them." AIR 1952 Cal 70 (*supra*) was followed since according to the court, it "lays down the correct law".

In *Union of India* v *Mahadeo Dal Mills*,[4] it was held: "The language of r. 115 of the Goods Tariff Rules (Part I), does not authorise the railway administration to alter the basis of six moreover printed at the back of a railway receipt is a notice to the consignor that the railway authority has reserved the right of remeasuring, reclassifying and recalculating rates and therefore where there is undercharge owing to mistake on the part of he clerk at the despatching station it can always be the charge. For instance, if the railway accepts for transport a certain quantity of goods, which is less than a wagon load, and does actually carry it in a full wagon and the rest of the space goes empty, it cannot call upon the consignor or the consignee at the destination station to pay for the empty space as well".

A person entitled to take delivery of the goods is not entitled to demand that the goods should be weighed or examined and loss enforced before he takes delivery or refuse to take delivery. Ordinarily it is his duty to take delivery of the consignment as it is, after giving notice to the officer giving delivery as to its condition. He can then sue the railway for damage, loss or deterioration, if any.[5]

40 Measure of damages The railway is liable for the price of goods at the place of destination on the date on which they reach the place.[6] Where the plaintiff claims not only the price of goods but also profits he would have earned by their sale, the profits should be determined with reference to the price prevailing at the destination on the date of the receipt of the goods. But where the plaintiff does not claim any profits, he can get only the cost price of the goods.[7] In the absence of evidence as to prevailing

3 *Dawood Rowther* v *S.I. Railway Co. Ltd.* AIR 1944 Mad 447; AIR 1952 Cal 70; ILR (1953)1 Cal 45.

4 1978 AWC 537 (All); (1978)4 ALR 719; *Dominion of India* v *Virjee Doya & Co.* AIR 1952 Cal 70; 55 CWN 758.

5 *Bengal Coal Supplying Firm* v *Union of India* ILR (1969) Bom 32; 70 Bom LR 254; *Dominion of India* v *Netai Chandra Haldar* 56 CWN 217.

6 *Dominion of India* v *Rupchand* AIR 1953 Nag 169; ILR (1953) Nag 314.

7 *Union of India* v *Asharfi Devi* AIR 1957 MP 114; 1957 Jab LJ 550.

market rate at the time the goods ought to have been delivered, the plaintiff is not entitled to the profits. He is only entitled to the cost price of goods and interest *pendente lite* and future.[8] In the absence of evidence as to prevailing market rate at the time the goods ought to be delivered in case of non-delivery, the plaintiff is entitled to the cost price plus freight charges paid by the plaintiff (here interest was not claimed).[9] Where a consignment of goods despatched by rail is damaged and a suit is brought against the railway for damages, the onus of proving the value of the goods booked, the actual loss and the extent of damages is on the plaintiff. A damage certificate states only the fact that the damages had, in fact, been caused to the goods but it does not amount to an acknowledgment of fact that the damage was caused by negligence or misconduct on the part of the railway administration.[10] The expenses incurred by the plaintiff in tracing the goods and in keeping his factory closed as a result of non-delivery are remote damages and cannot be recovered.[11]

41 Loss due to fall in market price Delay in delivery of goods by the railway may entail damage to the consignor or the consignee due to fall in market price. While impressing that s. 73 of the (old) Railways Act converting liability of the railway administration from that of a carrier to that of an insurer, has imposed heavier responsibility on the railway administration, the Supreme Court observed: "It is well settled that the liability of an ordinary carrier even in the English common law does not extend to a damage which is indirect or remote. Loss of profit or loss of a particular market has been held by a number of decisions to be a remote damage and can be awarded only if it is proved that the party which is guilty of committing the breach was aware or had knowledge that such a loss would be caused. Section 78(*d*) (old), however, seeks to bar the remedy of this kind of damage".[12]

In a Kerala case[13] the goods booked at Jogbani on 10th July 1975 reached destination on 18th November 1975. The High Court distinguishing the Supreme Court case[14] on the ground that there was no claim for damages based on fall of price allowed the claim of damages due to fall in market price. Reliance was placed on *Union of India* v *Madan*

8 *Bihar Agents Ltd.* v *Union of India* AIR 1960 Pat 111.
9 *New Swadeshi Sugar Mills* v *Union of India* AIR 1981 All 268; 1981 All WC 430.
10 *Union of India* v *Madon Mohon* AIR 1981 Ori 9; (1980)50 Cut LT 29.
11 *Union of India* v *Panipat Woollen and General Mills Co. Ltd.* AIR 1967 Punj 497.
12 *Union of India* v *Steel Stock Holders* AIR 1976 SC 879; (1976)1 SCJ 361; (1976)3 SCR 504; (1976)3 SCC 108.
13 *Union of India* v *P.K. Parameswaran Pillai* AIR 1986 Ker 199; 1985 Ker LJ 879; 1986 Ker LT 43; (1986)1 Cur CC 833; ILR (1986)1 Ker 662.
14 *Union of India* v *Steel Stock Holders* AIR 1976 SC 879; (1976)3 SCC 108; (1976)3 SCR 504.

Lal,[15] where the court held that the bar of a claim for damages "for loss of particular market" in cl. (*d*) of s. 78 of the Indian Railways Act (old) does not relate to a claim for damages on the ground of fall in market price. If the plaintiff had got delivery of the goods consigned in due time, he would have succeeded in selling them at a higher price; in other words, the goods were more valuable at the time when they ought to have been delivered, but deteriorated in value due to fall, in the market price on the date on which the goods were actually delivered. The learned Judge accordingly held: "that being so, I think an owner of the goods is entitled to claim damages from the railway administration for late delivery based upon the deterioration in their value due to the fall in market price. Ordinarily, it will be difficult to visualise cases where, on account of late delivery an owner of goods will be entitled to claim damages on any other basis".

It is firmly settled that the difference between the price paid and the price prevalent at the place of destination is not remote damages and can be recovered.[16] Contract price may be taken to be the correct basis for compensation.[17] It is well-settled that it is the market price at the time the damage occurred which is the measure of damages to be awarded.[18]

The measure of damages is the market value of the goods at the place and time at which they should have been delivered, less the amount which would have been spent to get them at the place of delivery. A person claiming damages will, therefore, have to lead evidence to prove the market value of the goods at the place of delivery. If the freight has not been paid, that must be deducted; but if the freight has already been paid, nothing falls to be deducted from the market value.[19]

In a case the plaintiff claimed damages on account of delay in delivery of goods. A consignment of certain goods was booked for carriage by railway administration to be delivered to the plaintiff. The railway administration took time much in excess of the ordinary and usual time in the delivery of the goods. The delay was not explained by the railway administration. The railway administration did not adduce any evidence to disprove the charge of negligence and misconduct. There was a fall in price of the goods in question during that period or the period between the due date of delivery and the actual date of delivery. While awarding damages for breach of contract, a plaintiff must be placed in the same

15 AIR 1968 Pat 94.

16 *Dominion of India* v *B.L. Butt* AIR 1957 Pat 328; ILR 36 Pat 495; *Union of India* v *P.K. Parameswaran Pillai* AIR 1986 Ker 199; 1985 Ker LJ 879; 1986 Ker LT 43; (1986)1 Cur CC 833; ILR (1986)1 Ker 662.

17 *Union of India* v *S.S. Works* AIR 1976 SC 1414; (1976)3 SCC 32; (1976)3 SCR 614.

18 *Union of India* v *W.P. Factories Ltd.* AIR 1966 SC 395; (1966)1 SCR 580.

19 *Bala Prasad* v *Union of India* AIR 1965 Pat 408.

position as he would have been, if the contract had been performed in proper time. In the case of delayed delivery of goods sent by railway, the measure of such damages, in order for indemnity to consignee, should be stated to show the difference between the market price at the respective date of due and actual delivery of the goods consigned.[20]

42 Interest on claims against railway Section 76 of the (old) Indian Railways Act provides that railway administration is liable for loss, destruction, damage or deterioration of animals or goods occasioned by delay or detention in their carriage. Section 78 of the (old) Indian Railways Act, *inter alia* provides that railway administration is not liable for any indirect or consequential loss or for loss of particular market. Interest on the amount of damage up to the date of suit cannot be allowed but interest *pendente lite* and future interest can be given.[21] No interest can be awarded for the period before the suit (*anti litem*) on the amount of damages decreed. Legal position with respect to this is well settled. See *B.N. Railway Co. Ltd.* v *Ruttonji Ramji*.[22] That decision of the Judicial Committee was relied upon by the Supreme Court in *Thawardas Pherumal* v *Union of India*.[23] The same view was expressed in *Union of India* v *A.L. Rallia Ram*.[24] In the absence of any usage or contract, express or implied, or of any provision of law to justify the award of interest, it is not possible to award interest, by way of damages.[1] Railway is liable for loss suffered by the owner due to fall in market price on account of delay in delivery.[2]

The plaintiff booked a consignment on 15th December 1961 at Bhilai for carriage to Poona but the consignment which had been diverted to Aurangabad reached Poona more than seven months after on 21st July 1962. The plaintiff alleged that the delay in the delivery was due to gross negligence of the defendant railway. As the defendant had committed an inordinate delay in delivering the goods, it was liable to pay damages to the plaintiff for the loss occurred to him because of the amount of money deposited in the Bank being locked up for more than six months.[3]

20 *Union of India* v *Matilal Agarwalla* 79 CWN 419.
21 *Union of India* v *Panipat Woollen* AIR 1967 Punj 497.
22 AIR 1938 PC 67; 65 IA 66.
23 AIR 1955 SC 468; (1955)2 SCR 48; 1955 SCJ 445.
24 AIR 1963 SC 1685; (1964)3 SCR 164.
1 *Union of India* v *Watkins Mayor & Co.* AIR 1966 SC 275; *Union of India* v *West Punjab Factories Ltd.* (1966)1 SCR 580; (1966)1 SCJ 350; (1966)1 SCWR 246; 1966 SCD 988; (1966)2 Andh LT 269; AIR 1966 SC 395.
2 *Union of India* v *Madanlal Kejriwal* AIR 1968 Pat 94.
3 *Union of India* v *Steel Stock Holders Syndicate* AIR 1976 SC 879; (1976)3 SCR 504; (1976)1 SCJ 361; (1976)3 SCC 108.

In case of short delivery of goods by the railways the plaintiff is entitled to "loss" as contemplated under s. 76 of the (old) Act of 1890 and is not entitled to claim anything more than that in view of the provisions of s. 78 of the old Act. The loss is the actual value of the goods lost, and the value has to be the market value of the goods on the date of loss. Therefore, in the suit against the railways to recover the loss the plaintiff is not entitled to include the freight charges and departmental fees in the value of the goods lost. He can claim the loss on account of his capital being locked up from the date of filing the claim up to the date of the suit.[4]

43 Negligence—Union Government when not liable for damages The consignor 'A' consigned the goods for carriage by railway. The R.R. was consigned to self. The goods were seized by Railway Police who prosecuted the consignor under s. 379/411, IPC. He was, however, acquitted and the goods were returned to him as he was both consignor and consignee. In the meantime 'B' claimed the price of goods from the railway administration. 'B' was directed to approach the Criminal Court for release of the consignment. But 'B' did not take any step nor did he claim to be an endorsee of the R.R. In a civil suit no negligence or breach of duty on railway's part was proved. 'B' got a decree against 'A' and court held that 'B' was not entitled to any damage against Union of India.[5]

44 Right of suit Ordinarily the consignor or the consignee or the person in whose favour the railway receipt has been endorsed may sue for damages against the railway. But where there is no railway receipt, it is a case of bailment in favour of the railway administration and the owner of the goods may sue the railway administration.[6] The right of action to recover compensation for loss or damage to the goods ordinarily rests on the consignor. Where the goods lost or damaged in transit are the subject matter of a contract of sale, the owner of the goods may, in the absence of a contract to the contrary, sue the railway administration. Therefore a consignment who is in possession of a railway receipt duly endorsed by the consignor may maintain an action for compensation for loss of the goods covered thereby, but he can do so not because he is the consignee but because he is the owner of the goods. A consignor may sue for compensation for loss relying upon the breach of contract of consignment. An owner of goods covered by a railway receipt may sue for compensation relying upon him title and the loss of goods by misconduct of the railway administration. But a bare consignee who is not a party to the contract of

4 *Union of India* v *Visweswaraya Iron & Steel* AIR 1987 Kant 161; ILR (1986) Kant 2961.

5 *Firm Luxmi Dutt Roop Chand* v *Union of India* AIR 1975 SC 760; (1975)1 SCC 341; 77 PLR 647.

6 *Dhanaraj* v *Union of India* AIR 1958 Assam 5.

consignment and who is not the owner of the goods cannot maintain a suit for compensation for loss or damage to the goods. He has no cause of action *ex contractu* or *ex delicto.*[7] When the goods are lost in transit, the consignor can sue not the consingee.[8]

When the consignee filed the suit for compensation and stated in his replication that he was a consignee for consideration and being a commission agent had interest in the goods despatched and explained this in his statement and the consignor did not challenge the title of the consignee, the consignee can maintain a suit for compensation.[9] Again a consignor is entitled to sue where the consignee is his commission agent as the ownership of the goods is with the consignor.[10] A consignee who is not the owner of the goods but to whom the goods were consigned for the purpose of sale on commission basis is entitled to maintain a suit for damage for loss of goods in transit.[11] This case was severely criticised by a Division Bench of Calcutta High Court where A.K. MUKHERJEA, J. observed: "Though considering that it is a Full Bench decision which is entitled to the utmost respect, I must say that the whole decision is full of observations and arguments which cannot be supported either by precedent or authority or on general principles". The court held "where the action is founded on contract, the right to maintain an action on the contract belongs to the person who entered into the contract".[12] Relying on this observation it is held in a Calcutta case that although a railway receipt is endorsed in favour of a consignee, consignor has right to sue (here it was of non-delivery) the question whether the plaintiff is or is not the owner of the goods being irrelevant.[13]

Mere endorsement or delivery of railway receipt does not transfer the contract contained in or evidenced by the railway receipt to the transferee. An endorsee of a railway receipt cannot sue the railway on the contract of carriage not being a party to the contract even if the property in the goods covered by the R/R has been transferred to the endorsee. In such a case, the endorsee, as the owner of the goods, can sue the railway in his own name for conversion or negligence only.[14] A mere endorsee, whether

7 *Chhangamal* v *Dominion of India* AIR 1957 Bom 276; *Devi Charan Sri Chand* v *Union of India* AIR 1982 All 396; 1982 All CJ 305; 1982 All WC 473; *Shah Nemji Chitarmal* v *Union of India* AIR 1983 NOC 152 (Raj); 1983 Raj LW 301; 1982 WLN (UC) 441.

8 *Union of India* v *Shankar Stores* AIR 1974 Ori 85; 39 Cut LT 1043.

9 *Bhai Meher Singh* v *Union of India* AIR 1979 Del 158; 1979 Rajdhani LR 145.

10 *Thakur Prasad* v *Union of India* AIR 1960 Pat 419.

11 *Dominion of India* v *Gaya Prasad* AIR 1956 All 338 (FB).

12 *Commissioner, Port of Calcutta* v *General Trading Corporation* AIR 1964 Cal 290 (315).

13 *Traders Syndicate* v *Union of India* AIR 1983 Cal 337.

14 *Commissioners of Port of Calcutta* v *General Trading Corporation* AIR 1964 Cal 290.

he is the consignee or someone else, only has the right to receive delivery of the goods but has no right to bring an action on the contract of carriage.[15] In *Union of India* v *Dayabhai*.[16] RAJU, J. differed from the Full Bench decision[17] and a Division Bench of Gujarat High Court refused to follow Allahabad Full Bench case in *Ibrahim* v *Union of India*.[18] But a consignee who has endorsed the railway receipt to a third person cannot sue unless he proves that even after endorsement he retained the property in the goods to himself.[19] In this case *Shamji Bhanji* v *N.W. Railway*[20] was relied on and *Sree Ram Krishna Mills* v *G.G. in Council*[21] was distinguished.

An assignee of a railway receipt is entitled to bring and maintain a suit on the strength of the endorsement made in his favour.[22] The endorsement of the railway receipt without more conveys the title to the goods consigned and the endorsee has the right to sue.[1] A Division Bench of Calcutta High Court did not agree with the decision in this case in *Commissioners, Port of Calcutta* v *General Trading Corporation*.[2] See also Notes under s. 100 where the matter has been discussed in details.

45 Right to sue by non-owner consignor—goods when damaged or deteriorated because of delay or detention It has been explained that when goods are booked for carriage by railway there arises a contract between the consignor on the one hand and the railway. So, when the goods are lost, destroyed or deteriorated or not delivered, the consignor has *locus standi* to sue basing the cause of action on breach of contract.

When the goods booked at owner's risk are damaged or deteriorated or lost or destroyed by reason of delay or detention in transit, it may be found that it is for the railway to prove absence of negligence or of misconduct. But, the words employed in s. 76 of the old Act would show that before the railway is called upon to show absence of negligence or of misconduct, there must be proof by owner that the loss, destruction, deterioration etc. has been caused by reason of delay or detention. The words "proved by the owner to have been caused by delay or detention" in s. 76 of the old Act are material. Relying upon these words it was contended in a case that non-owner consignor has no *locus standi* to sue

15 *Union of India* v *West Punjab Factories Ltd.* AIR 1966 SC 395; see also AIR 1965 SC 195; AIR 1973 Cal 74.
16 AIR 1962 Guj 266.
17 *Dominion of India* v *Gaya Prosad* AIR 1956 All 338 (FB).
18 AIR 1966 Guj 6; 65 Guj LR 897.
19 *Bihariji Mills Ltd.* v *Union of India* AIR 1960 Pat 257.
20 AIR 1947 Bom 169.
21 AIR 1945 Pat 387.
22 *Martin & Co.* v *Deokinandan* AIR 1959 MP 276.
1 *Md. Shafique* v *Union of India* AIR 1963 Cal 339; 67 CWN 279.
2 AIR 1964 Cal 290 (319, 322).

for damages when delay or detention has entitled the damage or deterioration etc. Repelling the contention and pinpointing the distinction between the right of a party to contract to file a suit for breach of contract and the right of an owner of the goods to bring an action for damage caused to or loss of his goods independently of any contract entered into in between the consignor carrier, the High Court held for breach of contract, the right of consignor to sue is always there. When a consignor is not the owner of the goods consigned the owner of the goods also may sue for compensation basing his claim on title, for the loss of goods or damage caused to them by misconduct on the part of railway employee. However in such a case the cause of action will be *ex delicto.*[3]

46 Right to sue when goods insured When an owner of goods or animals before despatching the goods or animals insure them, usually the insurance company is subrogated to the rights of assured. But cause of action of the owner due to loss, destruction, deterioration or non-delivery of goods and animals does not perish on giving the letter of subrogation. But decree in favour of assured operates as a bar to the institution of any suit by the insurance company. The owner-plaintiff becomes answerable and accountable to the insurance company for the moneys recovered in the suit to the extent the insurance company had paid the plaintiff. The insurance company did not enforce its claim by virtue of subrogation. It was held that the insured has right to sue.[4]

When the insured goods was sent by consignor, the insurance agreement provided that the insurer would stand subrogated to rights and remedies available to sender. The goods were damaged during transit due to negligence of the railway. The claim was settled by the insurer. The insurer can sue and he can avail of the benefit of notice under s. 76B of the old Act sent by the consignor.[5]

Where the consignor sued the railway for compensation for damages to the machinery and it is found that the plaintiff had received part of damages from insurance company which had insured the machinery, it cannot be submitted that the plaintiff after receiving a part of the compensation from the insurance company could not claim that amount from the railway company. The position of the insurance company in the circumstances is that of an indemnifier. The railway company continues

3 *Union of India* v *Tolaram Hariram* AIR 1980 Guj 172.

4 *Union of India* v *Sri Saroda Mills* (1972)2 SCC 877; AIR 1973 SC 281; (1973)2 SCR 464 affirming *Sri Saroda Mills* v *Union of India* AIR 1966 Mad 381; 79 Mad LW 237; (1966)2 Mad LJ 16; 1966 Mad WN 196.

5 *Union of India* v *Orissa Textile Mills* AIR 1979 Ori 165; (1979)48 Cut LT 245.

to be primarily liable for the damages sustained by the plaintiff and it not being a party to the contract of indemnity cannot be absolved of its liability to pay the damages to consignor merely because the consignor had already recovered the money from the insurance company under a contract of insurance. In such a case the consignor will receive the compensation for damage suffered by him in trust for the insurance company. After the consignor receives the amount from the railway company, he will have to make it over to the insurance company to the extent to which it had already indemnified him.[6]

In *Indian Trade and General Insurance Co.* v *Union of India*[7] G.K. MITTER, J. observed: "I think that the plaintiff cannot call the provisions of s. 135A (Transfer of Property Act 1882) to his aid. The plaintiff is not suing on the policy and, therefore, whether or not the policy was assigned has not got to be considered. Sub-section (1) of s. 135A of the Transfer of Property Act 1882, has no application. Sub-section (2) also, to my mind, does not apply as there was no total loss either of the whole of the goods or any apportionable part thereof. ... In my view, sub-sec. (3) would be the proper statutory provision applicable to this case. The insurer before me has paid for a partial loss and he, therefore, acquires no title to the subject-matter, but is subrogated to all rights and remedies of the insured person as from the time of the casualty causing the loss. MITTER, J. also relied on LORD HOBHOUSE'S observations in *King* v *Victoria Insurance Co. Ltd.*[8] "Subrogation by act of law would not give the insurer the right to sue in a court of law in his own name", and said: "The principle has been followed in India in the case of *K.V.P. Marakkayyar & Sons* v *Banians & Co.*[9] In my opinion, the deed of subrogation gave the plaintiff nothing more than what he would have under s. 135A, sub-sec. (3) of the T.P. Act 1882. The words used in the said document are "subrogated to all our rights and remedies." I cannot hold that there was any assignment of the subject-matter of insurance in this case by the document (of subrogation). The plaintiff had become subrogated to the rights of Sarawgi Trading Co. in respect of the said goods. But this did not entitled the plaintiff to file a suit in its own name." As insurer who has paid for loss of goods can maintain a suit in its own name for reimbursement of the amount paid to the insured for the loss.[10]

Where assignment was made of all rights, title and interest, the assignment was not an assignment of a mere right to sue for damages,

6 *Union of India* v *Deoria Sugar Mills* AIR 1979 All 200; 1980 ACJ 140; 1980 TAC 332.
7 AIR 1957 Cal 190; 98 CLJ 106.
8 [1896] AC 250 at 256.
9 AIR 1926 Mad 544; ILR 49 Mad 156.
10 *Alliance Assurance Co.* v *Union of India* (1958)62 CWN 539; (1958)1 CLJ 58.

and as such it is not hit by s. 6(*e*) of the Transfer of Property Act 1882.[11] In this case the following observations were made in respect of the legal aspects of an assignment made by the assured in favour of the insurance company BACHAWAT, J. said: "The plaintiff insurer having paid the claim for shortage arising under the policy has, by way of subrogation, an equitable right to all the claims of the assured against the carrier in respect of the shortage. The contract of insurance against loss is a contract of indemnity. On payment of the amount of loss the insurer as indemnifier has an equitable right of subrogation to the claims of the assured against the carrier. But his equity does not give the insurer the right to sue the third party in his own name; see *K.V.P. Marakkayyar and Sons* v *Banians & Co.*[12] In the absence of an assignment, the insurer, who is subrogated to the rights of the assured, can only sue in the name of the assured. But there can be no doubt that if after receiving payment from the insurer the assured obtained damages from the carrier, the court would treat the assured as a trustee for the insurer to the extent of the payment received. And if it were necessary for the insurer to sue the carrier in the name of the assured, the court would have compelled the assured to permit the use of his name on the usual terms. The true position, therefore, is that after receiving payment of their claims under the insurance policy, the assured defendant No. 2 was a bare trustee of all their rights of action against the railway administration concerned. Those rights of action were thenceforth held by the defendant No. 2 for the benefit of the plaintiff. In these circumstances it cannot be said that the subsequent assignment of the right to sue is hit by s. 6(*e*) of the Transfer of Property Act. Such an assignment enables the assignee to sue in his own name and to enforce the claim which was already held for his benefit by the assignor."[13] The plaintiff insurance company would have *locus standi* to maintain the suit in its own name be it considered to be one under sub-sec. (2) or (3) of s. 135A, Transfer of Property Act 1882. Operation on this aspect of the law as expressed.[14] Where the claim of the plaintiff against a railway administration is satisfied by the insurance company which was subrogated to the claim of the plaintiff, though appropriately the suit should be

11 *Union of India* v *Alliance Assurance Co. Ltd.* (1962)66 CWN 419; 1962 CLJ 140.
12 AIR 1926 Mad 544 (550); ILR 49 Mad 156 (174).
13 AIR 1964 Cal 31; 66 CWN 419; 1962 CLJ 140.
14 *Indian Trade and General Insurance Co.* v *Union of India* AIR 1957 Cal 190; relying *inter alia* on *King* v *Victoria Insurance Company Ltd.* [1896] AC 250 was not followed *Alliance Assurance Co.* v *Union of India* (1958)62 CWN 539 was approved *Union of India* v *The Great American Insurance Co. Ltd.* AIR 1971 Cal 491; 75 CWN 563; ILR (1971)1 Cal 614; 1971 ACJ 291. This case was relied on in *G.M. Roadway Co.* v *Fort Gloster Industries Ltd.* AIR 1971 Cal 494; 76 CWN 17.

brought by the insurance company, the suit by the plaintiff himself is not barred by s. 135 of the Transfer of Property Act 1882.[15]

47 Special responsibility Section 73 of the old Act (corresponding to s. 93 of the Railways Act 1989) lays down the general responsibility of the railway administration as a carrier of goods for the loss, destruction, damage, deterioration or non-delivery in transit. This is specifically made subject to other provisions in the Act as is clear from the expression 'save as otherwise provided in this Act' with which s. 73 of the old Act opens. Section 77B of the old Act whittles down the general responsibility of the railway administration as a carrier with respect to articles of specific value.[16] To attract the section or in other words to confer immunity on railway in respect of liability for loss etc., the following must co-exist, namely (*a*) the article delivered to railway for carriage must answer any of the items in second schedule, (*b*) the articles are contained in a parcel or packet or when it answers sub-sec. (4) of the s. 77B of the old Act may not be contained in a parcel or packet, (*c*) value of such article in the parcel or packet exceeds ₹500, then the railway administration shall not be liable for any loss, destruction, deterioration, damage of the parcel unless (1) the value is declared by the consignor and (2) if so required by the railway paid or engaged to pay in writing a percentage on the value so declared by way of compensation for the increased risk.

The consignor delivered to the railway for carriage silver bars of value above ₹500. The article answered the second schedule and by reason of sub-sec. (4) required no packing or parcelling. The consignor despite asked by the booking clerk concerned neither paid or engaged to pay in writing, the percentage of value declared. The silver bar was not delivered. It was held the railway is protected.[17] When goods consigned was terylene cloth that answers item No. 16 of the second schedule, the value of the article having not been declared during booking, the railway was held not responsible for short delivery.[18]

This section does not apply where the claim for compensation is below the sum mentioned in this section. Where the claim exceeds the sum and the case falls under this section, the plaintiff cannot get a decree up to that sum.[19] Unless both the conditions, namely, declaration of value and

15 *Sri Sarada Mills Ltd.* v *Union of India* AIR 1966 Mad 381; 79 Mad LW 237; (1966)2 Mad LJ 16; 1966 Mad WN 196.

16 *Union of India* v *Kailash Chandra Jain* AIR 1985 All 21; 1984 All CJ 640; (1985)11 All LR 72; 1985 ACJ 153.

17 *Ibid.*

18 *Deepchand Kherajmal* v *Union of India* AIR 1979 Mad 88; (1978)2 Mad LJ 184; 1979 ACJ 75; 1978 TAC 132.

19 *Governor-General in Council* v *Basanta Kumar* 54 CWN 39; *Krishna Charan* v *Governor-General in Council* AIR 1950 Cal 100.

payment or engagement to pay a percentage are complied with, the railway administration shall not be responsible for loss of the goods of the nature described in this section. It is immaterial how the loss has been caused.[20]

In order to attract the operation of this section the railway must prove that the consignment was lost or destroyed or deteriorated.[1]

48 Benefit for non-delivery Under the present law the railway may get the benefit of this section by proof of damage of the parcel or package as also to non-delivery, failure to deliver being a specie of loss.[2] In support of the proposition that s. 77B of the old Act also attracts non-delivery, the High Court relied on a Supreme Court case[3] where it is observed "failure to delivery is the consequence of loss or destruction of goods; it does not furnish a cause of action on which a suit may lie against the railway administration, distinct from a cause of action for loss or destruction. By the use of the expression, 'loss, destruction or deterioration', what is contemplated is loss or destruction or deterioration of the goods and the consequent loss to the owner thereof".

According to another view s. 77B of the old Act has no application to a case of non-delivery of goods consigned. In one case, Madras High Court observed: "After the amendment of the Railways Act in 1961, non-delivery has been made an independent cause of action, distinct and different from the cause of action based upon the loss of the goods. Non-delivery may be consequence of loss or destruction or it may be a consequence of other cause. Therefore, when the Legislature has used the five expression, namely, loss, destruction, deterioration, damage and non-delivery separately, each one of the expression must be given an appropriate meaning so as to give full effect to the intention of the legislature. Whether the omission to include the expression 'non-delivery' in s. 77B of the old Act was intentional or accidental, the result is that the compensation for non-delivery is not comprehended by s. 77B of the old Act and when that ground is not found in s. 77B of the old Act it is not open to a court to supply the omission by any process of interpretation. Therefore, where a plaintiff of non-delivery, since he is not likely to know the exact cause of non-delivery, it may be open, in appropriate cases, to the railway administration to put forward a defence on the basis of s. 77B of the old Act by proving that since the goods were lost or destroyed, they could not

20 *Banarsi Stores* v *Union of India* AIR 1953 All 318; ILR (1954)1 All 76; *Bhukhandas D. Chevli & Co.* v *Union of India* AIR 1963 Guj 150.

1 *Union of India* v *D.N. Mondal* 63 CWN 253; *Union of India* v *Paul Scientific and Chemical Corporation* AIR 1972 All 192; 1971 All WR (HC) 652; 1971 All LJ 1160.

2 *Union of India* v *Kailash Chandra Jain* AIR 1985 All 21; 1984 All CJ 640; (1985)11 All LR 72; 1985 All CJ 153.

3 *Governor-General in Council* v *Musaddilal* AIR 1961 SC 725; (1961)3 SCR 647; (1961)1 SCJ 597.

be given delivery of and therefore that section would apply. But where it is not proved that the articles in question had been lost or destroyed non-delivery of the articles must be the result of causes other than loss or destruction and s. 77B of the old Act cannot afford any protection to the railway administration against the claim for compensation".[4]

In a case, the High Court observed: "The bar contained in s. 77B of the old Act is absolute, but it does not deal with non-delivery. Sections 77 and 77A of the old Act specifically mention loss, destruction, damage, deterioration or non-delivery as the ground occasioning the claim for damages. Curiously enough, in s. 77B of the old Act non-delivery is not mentioned, namely, loss, destruction, damage or deterioration. When the legislature has consistently used above-mentioned five specific categories, it must be deemed to have done with a purpose. It must not have thought of including loss arising out of non-delivery as included in the genus 'Loss'. Were it so, the term 'non-delivery' would not have been used in those earlier provisions. It is, therefore, evident that the term "non-delivery", according to the legislature is something distinct from loss.[5]

A consignment of silver bars was booked by the plaintiff under Risk Note 'X' after declaring the contents and value thereof but without paying any special rates for the goods to be insured under s. 75 of the old Act. The plaintiff brought a suit for compensation for non-delivery alleging wrongful deprivation of conversion. A condition in the Risk Note provided that the railway was exempted from liability if the consignment was not booked under special rate. The railway in the written statement stated that the loss was due to misconduct of railway employees by delivery to a third party without production of railway receipt. The court held that loss contemplated by the Risk Note and s. 75 of the old Act is loss to the railway and the railway administration cannot rely upon the provision in the Risk Note exempting the liability if the consignment was not booked under special rate. The railway administration having failed to discharge the onus of loss the plaintiff's claim is for damages for non-delivery. Even if consignment was not booked under special rate, if the railway fails to prove that the goods were lost, destroyed or deteriorated, the plaintiff will be entitled to get damages for non-delivery.[6]

49 Value of parcel or package If a number of packages are booked in an entire wagon, what is material is the value of each consignment and not

4 *Union of India* v *Jetmull Sukanraj* AIR 1972 Mad 134; (1971)2 Mad LJ 257; 84 Mad LW 719.

5 *Union of India* v *K. Mansukhram & Sons* (1979)20 Guj LR 333.

6 *Surajnath Prasad Kedarnath* v *Union of India* AIR 1975 Cal 203.

the value of the entire consignment. If value of individual package does not exceed five hundred rupees, s. 77B of the old Act is not attracted.[7]

50 Parcel or package The word 'parcel' is defined in s. 2(27) of this Act. Parcel is a small package or bundle.[8] According to *Webster's Dictionary,* the meaning of parcel is: "a number or quantity of things wrapped up together, a bundle, package, packet" and also "a collection of articles, as of merchandise put up in lots for sale." The meaning of package is: "a bundle made up for transportation, a packet, a bale, parcel" and also "that in which anything is packed, a box, case, barrel, crate, etc., in which goods are packed; a container." Glass bangles made into garlands by tying together a number of them with a string would be a parcel or package.[9] When a silver bar is transported, it cannot be said that it was contained in a parcel or package and the railway cannot claim the protection of this section.[10] The value of each parcel or package must be declared.[11]

51 Articles mentioned in Second Schedule of the old Act Gold and silver contents in medicines made *bona fide* for the purpose of a doctor are not gold and silver as understood in general parlance and therefore do not fall under cl. (*a*) of Schedule II of the old Act.[12] Sweepings and gathering of goldsmith's shop from which gold is separated by miaris were held not to fall within cl. (*a*).[13] Fountain pens with gold nibs do not fall within cl. (*a*).[14]

Wax pearls do not come within cl. (*d*) or cl. (*k*) of Schedule II of old Act.[15] Account books are included in the term 'writing' in cl. (*i*).[16] Shawls mean only Kashmiri shwals.[17] "Lohis" of very low value are not shawl.[18] A radio set falls under the Second Schedule.[19].

7 *Lakshmi Bangle Stores* v *Union of India* AIR 1975 AP 235; 1974 Andh LT 282; (1975)1 Andh WR 1.
8 Black's *Law Dictionary,* 10th Ed., 2014.
9 *Mahesh Glass Works* v *Governor-General in Council* AIR 1950 All 543; 1950 ALJ 625.
10 *Kaluram Sitaram* v *Dominion of India* ILR (1953) Bom 1301; AIR 1954 Bom 50.
11 *Sorabji* v *B.N. Railway* 15 Pat 394; AIR 1936 Pat 393; *Governor-General in Council* v *Sakhalchand* (1954)2 MLJ 677; 67 Mad LW 807.
12 *Narendra Nath* v *E.I. Railway Co.* AIR 1925 Cal 115; 51 Cal 929.
13 *Alla Ditta* v *Secretary of State* AIR 1928 Lah 102.
14 *Dominion of India* v *Eversharp Agency* AIR 1955 Bom 98; AIR 1959 Mys 43; ILR (1954) Bom 1202.
15 *Kedar Nath, Raj Narain* v *E.I. Railway Co.* (1923) ILR 45 All 453.
16 *Ramchandra* v *G.I.P. Railway* 20 Bom LR 591.
17 *East Indian Railway Co.* v *Dayabhai* (1922)24 Bom LR 416; 67 Ind Cas 852; AIR 1922 Bom 416; *Sarat* v *Secy. of State* 39 Cal 1029; *Union of India* v *Jagatpal* AIR 1960 Pat 340. But see *G.I. Railway Co.* v *Chella Ram* AIR 1921 Mad 510.
18 *Government of Mysore* v *Kapurchand & Bros.* AIR 1953 Mys 16.
19 *Governor-General in Council* v *Spare Bros.* ILR (1947) Nag 169; AIR 1947 Nag 128.

52 Delay in transit The plaintiff consignee despatched 275 bags of wheat under the railway receipt. There was a delay of 95 days in transit. Damage certificate was issued by officer of railway department showing that there was a deterioration in quality of wheat due to delay. The plaintiff is entitled to claim damages.[20]

53 Compensation for damage of goods in transit Goods were consigned in old bags for transit bags were not damaged at the time of packing. There was delay in delivery of the goods on the part of the railway. Damage due to inherent defect of the goods was not established. Loss occurred due to negligence of the railway. The Tribunal apportioned the liability of the consignor to the extent of 25% for loss. It was held to be not justified and consequently the order of apportionment was set aside and the railway was held liable.[21]

54 Loss of goods in transit In a suit for recovery of money for loss of goods in transit against the railway administration there were concurrent findings by two courts that the goods were lost because of negligence of employees of the railways. Thus, the plaintiff is entitled to the cost of goods lost.[22]

55 Damages for non-delivery of goods by railways In compliance with directions by the plaintiffs, a partnership firm, third party booked goods with railways which failed to deliver goods to the plaintiffs. Thus, the plaintiffs claimed damages. Though the claim by the plaintiffs against the railways did not arise out of a contract between them, yet the railways could not avoid the liability for loss. The dismissal of the plaintiffs' suit on the ground that the plaintiffs failed to prove that they are a registered partnership firm was held to be improper. Non-mentioning of provision of s. 106 of the Railways Act 1989 regarding notice would be no consequence.[23]

56 Liability of railway for loss or damage of consignment Consignment was received in rotten condition, damaged by water. Nothing was on record to show that goods were handed over to Railways in damaged condition. Railways have not taken proper monsoon precaution by providing gunny strips in good crevices and no reasonable care and foresight were exercised in carrying the consignment. The Railways were held liable to pay compensation.[24]

20 *Sujanmal* v *Union of India* AIR 2001 MP 247.

21 *Jugal Kishore Naresh Kumar* v *Union of India* (2001)3 Civ LJ 715 (Mad).

22 *Union of India* v *Kessi Chand Manak Chand* AIR 2006 Raj 263; see *Pawan Oil Industries* v *Union of India* AIR 2006 Bom 109 (damage in transit of goods by railway); *Rajen Hukumchand Jain* v *Union of India* AIR 2006 Bom 129; *Union of India* v *Indian Iron & Steel Co. Ltd.* AIR 2007 NOC 2380 (Del).

23 *Bharat Kumar* v *Union of India* AIR 2005 Raj 124.

24 *Union of India* v *Bharat General & Textile Industries Ltd.* AIR 2010 NOC 453 (Del).

57 Shortage of consignment—responsibility of railways Loading was done on claimant's site and seals were put on top and bottom of tanker wagons by staff of claimant. But dip measurement was taken jointly by staff of claimant and railways and thus transit risk was of railways. Section 94 of the Railways Act 1989 is not applicable as both the seals were found broken showing negligence of railways. Railways are responsible to pay compensation to claimants.[24]

94. Goods to be loaded or delivered at a siding not belonging to a railway administration. (1) Where goods are required to be loaded at a siding not belonging to a railway administration for carriage by railway, the railway administration shall not be responsible for any loss, destruction, damage or deterioration of such goods from whatever cause arising, until the wagon containing the goods has been placed at the specified point of interchange of wagons between the siding and the railway administration and a railway servant authorised in this behalf has been informed in writing accordingly by the owner of the siding.

(2) Where any consignment is required to be delivered by a railway administration at a siding not belonging to a railway administration, the railway administration shall not be responsible for any loss, destruction, damage or deterioration or non-delivery of such consignment from whatever cause arising after the wagon containing the consignment has been placed at the specified point of interchange of wagons between the railway and the siding and the owner of the siding has been informed in writing accordingly by a railway servant authorised in this behalf.

1 Corresponding law This section corresponds to s. 76C of the old Act.

2 Absolving liability of railway administration The railway administration is absolved for any loss, damage or non-delivery of goods if goods are delivered at a siding which does not belong to the railway administration, or when the wagon containing the goods has been placed where the wagons are exchanged between the railway administration and the owner of the siding who has been informed in writing that the wagon was so placed.[1]

3 Onus of proof In a suit for damages for loss of goods against the railway administration, onus of proof lies on the plaintiff to establish actual loading of goods.[2]

4 Liability of railway when goods delivered at siding Section 76C of the old Railways Act (corresponding to s. 94 of the Railways Act 1989) absolves the railway administration for loss, damage or non-delivery of goods at a

24 *Union of India* v *Indian Oil Corporation, New Delhi* AIR 2013 All 144.
1 *Orient Paper Mills Ltd.* v *Union of India* AIR 1984 Ori 156.
2 *Ibid.*

siding whatever be the reason for such an occurrence provided two conditions are fulfilled:

(*a*) the goods are to be delivered at a siding which does not belong to the railway administration; and

(*b*) the wagon containing the goods has been placed at the place where the wagons are exchanged between railway administration and the owner of the siding, who has been informed in writing that the wagon has been so placed.

Where the wagon had been placed on the consignee's siding at the point of interchange and information had been given about it but an employee of the consignee who had signed in the relevant register as the representative of the consignee giving the date and time of making over the wagon for unloading was not examined. To prove whether at the time the wagon was placed at the siding of the consignee there had been any damage to the seal or that the wagon was empty, justifiably an adverse inference can be drawn against the consignee for non-examination of such person. Thus there was lack of evidence from the consignee, that there had no seal and label in the wagon, when placed at the private siding and as such the railway administration cannot be held responsible for any shortage.[3]

95. Delay or detention in transit. **A railway administration shall not be responsible for the loss, destruction, damage or deterioration of any consignment proved by the owner to have been caused by the delay or detention in their carriage if the railway administration proves that the delay or detention arose for reasons beyond its control or without negligence or misconduct on its part or on the part of any of its servants.**

1 Corresponding law This section corresponds to s. 76 of the old Act.

2 Scope The liability of a railway under this section would not arise unless the plaintiff proves that such loss was caused by delay in transit. When it is proved then the railway administration has to prove that the delay or detention arose without negligence on the part of the railway or its servant.[4] This section is not restricted to cases where goods or animals are booked at railway risk rate.[5] This section applies to cases of delay and detention only. When the owner of goods proves delay, then it is for the railway administration to prove that the delay or detention was without negligence on its part. When the owner does not prove delay, then he has to prove negligence or misconduct as required by s. 97 of the Act.[6]

3 *Orient Paper Mills Ltd.* v *Union of India* AIR 1984 Ori 156.
4 *A.R. Ahmed & Co.* v *Union of India* AIR 1972 Mad 454; 85 Mad LW 413.
5 *Ibid.*
6 *Union of India* v *Shankarlal* AIR 1972 MP 201; 1972 MPWR 444; 1972 MPLJ 843; *Union of India* v *Mamehand Agarwalla* AIR 1967 Cal 133.

3 No presumption When at the delivery station goods are found damaged, there is no presumption that the damage was caused due to negligence or misconduct of the railway administration or of its servants.[7] Besides, the damage certificate issued by the railway administration does not amount to acknowledgment of the fact that it was caused by negligence or misconduct of railway authority.[7]

4 Goods sent by route contrary to agreement When goods are carried by a route not agreed upon, and the loss or damage occurs during transshipment of goods the plaintiff is entitled to get damages.[8]

5 Misconduct and negligence—distinguished If a thing is not done within a reasonable time, the delay or detention is either deliberate or due to carelessness. In the former case it is misconduct and in the latter case it is negligence. In other words, delay or detention is *per se* indicative of misconduct or negligence.[9]

6 Quantum of loss for short delivery In a suit for the recovery of loss against the railway for short delivery of consignment the plaintiff is not entitled to include the freight charged and departmental fees in the value of the goods lost. But he can claim the loss on account of his capital being locked up from the date of filing of the claim upto the date of the suit. He would be entitled to interest at the rate of 12% on the value of the goods lost. He will also be entitled to interest from the date of the suit till the date of realisation.[10] Where awarding damage for breach of contract a plaintiff must be placed in the same position as he would have been of the contract had been performed in proper fine.[11]

7 Meaning of words "loss, destruction, damage or deterioration" The words "loss, destruction, damage or deterioration" used in s. 76 of the old Act must be read as *ejusdem generis* so as to indicate the actual and physical loss or charge in the goods contemplated by that section. In this view of the matter it is clear that the word "deterioration" used in that section referred to the physical and actual deterioration of the goods.[12]

8 Burden of proof The burden of proof that deterioration was not caused due to misconduct or negligence of the railway servant is on the railway administration and failure to prove it relieves the consignee of the burden to prove under s. 97 of the present Act.[13] The burden of proof that the

7 (1972)1 Cut WR 1005.
8 *Sahu Vanaspati* v *Union of India* AIR 1966 All 333; ILR (1965)2 All 127.
9 *Union of India* v *Shankarlal* AIR 1972 MP 201; 1972 MPWR 444; 1972 MPLJ 843.
10 *Union of India* v *Visveswaraya Iron & Steel Ltd.* AIR 1987 Kant 161.
11 *Union of India* v *Matilal Agarwalla* (1975)1 CLJ 212; 79 CWN 419.
12 *Union of India* v *Steel Stock Holders* AIR 1976 SC 879; (1976)3 SCC 108; (1976)3 SCR 504.
13 *Union of India* v *Ram Prasad* AIR 1982 Raj 253; 1982 WLN 88; 1982 Raj LW 213; 1982 Raj LR 533.

goods had reached the destination intact, that is in the same condition in which they were handed over to the railway is upon the railways.[14]

9 Competency of a person to sue Section 76 of the old Act (corresponding to s. 95 of the Railways Act 1989) does not provide for the competency or otherwise of a person to sue for damages in the circumstances mentioned therein. If a consignor can sue under s. 74(3) of the old Act (corresponding to s. 97 of the new Act), there is no reason why he cannot sue in a case contemplated under s. 76 of the old Act.[15]

10 Open delivery and claim of damages Insistence on open delivery does not take away the right to claim damages.[16]

11 Misdespatch of consignment Where the railway is negligent in misdespatching the consignment and goods were damaged before termination of the transit, the case would fall within s. 76 and not s. 77 of the old Act (corresponding to ss. 95 and 99 of the Railway Act 1989 respectively).[17]

12 Background of s. 95 of the Act Under the law in vague before the incorporation of the s. 76 of the old Act, the railway administration was bound to carry the goods under ordinary circumstances within a reasonable time. The reasonable time for delivery of goods depends on the facts and circumstances of each case. If there was unreasonable delay but there was sufficient cause for such delay, the railway was not liable. But if such delay was due to misconduct on the part of the railway, the court might presume that the delay was the cause of the deterioration of the goods and award damages.[18] Where the consignment was misdespatched from Bareilly to New Delhi and detained there for sufficiently long time, the railway was responsible for damage under s. 76 of the old Act.[19]

Under the present section the railway administration is liable for the loss etc. of the goods caused by delay or detention in their carriage. But the railway may avoid the liability by proving that such delay or detention was not due to any negligence or misconduct on the part of the railway administration or of any of its servants. The burden of proof of absence of negligence or misconduct is on the railway and on failure to discharge the burden the railway would be held liable for the loss, destruction, damage or deterioration of animals or goods.

13 Section 95 if controlled by s. 97 It may be found from s. 95 that if damage or deterioration etc. is proved to have been caused by reason of delay or

14 *Union of India* v *Jagdish Oil Mills* (1992)2 Civ LJ 81.
15 *Union of India* v *Tolaram Hariram* AIR 1980 Guj 172.
16 *Nizamuddin* v *Union of India* AIR 1981 All 444.
17 *Niranjan* v *Union of India* AIR 1973 All 303; 1972 All WR (HC) 318.
18 *Union of India* v *Ganesh Chandra* AIR 1959 Cal 337; 63 CWN 343.
19 *Niranjanlal* v *Union of India* AIR 1973 All 303; 1972 All WR (HC) 318.

detention of animals or goods in their carriage the railway is not absolved from the responsibility unless the railway administration proves that the delay or detention arose without negligence or misconduct on their part. But at the sametime s. 97 which postulates carriage at owner's risk provides that railway administration is absolved from any responsibility for any loss or destruction, damage or deterioration etc. *from whatever cause arising* except upon proof that such loss, destruction, damage, deterioration etc. was due to negligence or misconduct by the railway.

In the context of ss. 76 and 74(3) of the old Act in *Union of India* v *Manchand Agarwalla*[20] it was held: "When goods are delivered for carriage at the owner's risk there is no general responsibility for damage or deterioration of quality of goods under s. 73 and, therefore, s. 76 will not come into operation. The operation of s. 76 is controlled by s. 73 and as s. 73 is excluded by s. 74, s. 74 would apply in such a case rather than s. 76". It was further observed: "Therefore, except with regard to cases included in exception (provided in s. 73 of the Act) there is the general responsibility on the railway for loss, destruction, damage, deterioration arising from any cause. After s. 73, different causes for damage are considered under ss. 75A, 76, 76A, 76B and 76C. Section 75A refers to cases where goods are carried by open vehicles. Section 75 considers the cases where responsibility arises for delay or detention. Section 76A relates to destruction or deterioration because of goods being carried on a deviated route. Hence, s. 76 is one of the sections which deal with the causes for destruction, damage or deterioration of the goods. Therefore, s. 76 really deals with one particular case of deterioration when there is a general responsibility under s. 73. But when there is no general responsibility under s. 73, s. 76 will not come into operation. Therefore, the operation of s. 76 is controlled by s. 73 and as s. 73 is excluded by s. 74, s. 74 would apply rather than s. 76."

In *Union of India* v *Shankarlal*[1] expressing a contrary view observed that s. 74 of the old Act does not exclude the operation of s. 76 of the old Act in case where the goods or animals are booked at owner's risk.

Madras High Court in *A. Rafeeq Ahmed* v *Union of India*[2] agreeing with Calcutta view observed that "since s. 76 deals specially and expressly with delay and detention in the carriage of the goods, it could be said that whenever an owner of the goods comes to court and claims damage on the basis of loss etc. on account of delay or detention in transit, it is only s. 76 which would apply and not s. 74(3)".

20 AIR 1967 Cal 133.
1 AIR 1972 MP 201; 1972 MPWR 444; 1972 MPLJ 843.
2 AIR 1972 Mad 454; 85 Mad LW 413.

The High Court in *Hundraj* v *Union of India,*[3] dissented from the Calcutta decision (supra) and followed the M.P. decision (*supra*), the Division Bench holding that "s. 76 is not controlled by s. 73 and the operation of s. 76 is not controlled by s. 74(3) ...."

The High Court in *Union of India* v *Sita Ram Sah*[4] referred to accept the proposition that s. 76 (of the old Act) stands independent of s. 74 (of the old Act) and would apply *Fortiori* to all cases of deterioration etc. irrespective of the nature of booking of the consignment, *i.e.* 'railway risk' or 'owner's risk', where it is on account of delay in delivery of the consignment the High Court proceeded to observe that if that view is taken, then the restriction contemplated under s. 74(3) (of the old Act) to the effect that the railway administration should not be responsible for loss, destruction, damage, deterioration or non-delivery, in transit, *from whatever cause,* would become redundant. For, deterioration of goods on account of delay is one cause for deterioration. A wagon of onion booked at owner's risk rate reached late resulting in 60% deterioration. But it was due to chinese aggression which led to heavy military movement resulting in goods trains being detained. Thus, s. 74(3) of the old Act applies and as the plaintiff failed to prove negligence or misconduct on the part of the railway administration, the suit failed.

14 Delay in carriage tests As to the question as to what is 'delay in carriage of goods or animal', in the context in which the word is used in s. 76 of the (old) Act (corresponding to s. 95 of the Railways Act 1989), it may be taken as meaning 'loss of time in excess of the time which may be normally or usually taken in carriage of such goods in such circumstances'. The law presumes that when the railway undertakes to carry the goods with all these materials before it, the goods must reach the destination station without deterioration, if the same is carried in normal or usual time. Any time spent in excess of that, is termed as 'delay' and if such delay results in deterioration of goods, the railway is bound to show that the delay was caused without negligence or misconduct on its part.[5]

A reasonable time is certainly not necessarily always the actual time for the consignment to reach the destination. In fact sometimes the consignment might reach the destination earlier and sometimes later.[6]

The normal and usual time is alone the relevant criterion or test to be taken into consideration for finding out the *prima facie* reasonable time which would be taken in transit of the goods for raising the necessary

3 (1978)19 Guj LR 34.
4 AIR 1980 Pat 93; 1979 BBCJ (HC) 800; 1980 BLJR 1; 1980 BLJ 22.
5 *Hundraj Chhangomal* v *Union of India* (1978)19 Guj LR 34.
6 *Union of India* v *Bhagwan Raut* AIR 1969 Ori 100; 35 Cut LT 196.

statutory presumption under s. 76. The time wasted in the transit of the goods which could have been saved by exercise of reasonable foresight and care on the part of the railway administration is the delay or detention in carriage and if it results in damage to the goods, the railway has to prove that it was caused without misconduct or negligence on its part of any of its servants, for ultimately rebutting the statutory provision, therefore, the goods were really delivered within reasonable time in the circumstances of the case. The *prima facie* reasonable time is to be found out on the relevant test of only the normal or ordinary transit period and in doing so, the court has to take into consideration, particularly, the nature of the goods carried. If nature of the goods is perishable or highly perishable, higher degree of foresight and care is expected of the railway administration and, therefore, the goods should have been delivered in the present case latest within a period of six or seven days from the date of the booking, and if there was failure to do so, on the resulting deterioration being established the *prima facie* case of neglect or misconduct was established, and the evidential burden to rebut the same shifted to the railway.[7]

96. Traffic passing over railways in India and railways in foreign countries. **Where in the course of carriage of any consignment from a place in India to a place outside India or from a place outside India to a place in India or from one place outside India to another place outside India or from one place in India to another place in India over any territory outside India, it is carried over the railways of any railway administration in India, the railway administration shall not be responsible under any of the provisions of this Chapter for the loss, destruction, damage or deterioration of the goods, from whatever cause arising, unless it is proved by the owner of the goods that such loss, destruction, damage or deterioration arose over the railway of the railway administration.**

1 Corresponding provision This section corresponds to s. 76E of the old Act.

2 Carriage of goods by Indian Railway via foreign country A suit was filed against railway administration for damage to and short delivery of goods which were carried by railway via Pakistan. Absence of pleadings to show that Indian Railway acted as a bailee in such carriage of goods, the suit would fail.[8] Where the railway administration receiving goods for carriage over foreign railway is liable for loss, even though the loss did not occur on their railway.[9]

7 *Hundraj Chhangomal* v *Union of India* (1978)19 Guj LR 34.
8 *Union of India* v *Kewal Prakash* AIR 1977 Del 146.
9 *B. & N.W. Rly* v *Haji Mutsaddi* 7 ALJ 833. This was approved in *Union of India* v *Brijlal* AIR 1969 SC 817.

3 Foreign and Indian Railways Where the goods are to be carried over Indian and foreign railways, the Indian Railways can be made liable only if it is proved by the owner of the goods or animals that the loss, destruction, damage or deterioration was caused during the transit over the railway administration which is sued. The object of this section is to protect the Indian railway administration for loss etc. caused during transit over railways in other countries. Section 76E of the old Act (corresponding to s. 96 of the new Act) is a special provision for fixing responsibility of Indian Railways in case of traffic passing over a Railway in India and a Railway in foreign countries. Thus, in case of damage to goods booked from any station (here Peshwar) in Pakistan to any station in India (here Delhi) this section would apply. And if the plaintiff fails to show that the loss arose on the railway administration in India, and also does not plead any bailment, the plaintiff would not be entitled to any relief. The Fundamental and subsidiary Rules regarding interchanging to traffic between India and Pakistan cannot be availed of since these Rules have not been framed under the provisions of the Indian Railways Act, but framed in pursuance of a treaty between India and Pakistan.[10]

4 Liability of India and Pakistan under the Indian Independence (Rights, Property and Liabilities) Order 1947 In the case of *Krishna Ranjan Basu Ray* v *Union of India represented by Eastern Railway*,[11] the suit was brought on the allegation that the plaintiff booked a consignment of torchlights and batteries with the Bengal and Assam Railway on 16th November 1946, and that these were not delivered. The suit was brought in Barisal Court against the Governor-General in Council as represented by the Bengal and Assam Railway and it was decreed. That decree was hit by the provision of the Indian Independence Pakistan Courts Act (Act IX of 1952) and thereupon the plaintiff brought a fresh suit against the Union of India in the Court of Small Cause at Sealdah. The question was raised that in view of the provisions of s. 8 of the Indian Independence (Rights, Property and Liabilities) Order 1947, the Government of Pakistan is wholly responsible for any liability that may arise for breach of the contract and that the Government of India has no liability. When goods booked with a railway, the purpose of the contract as used in paragraph 8 of the Indian Independence (Rights, Property and Liabilities) Order 1947, was the carriage of goods and where the destination was some point in Pakistan, the purpose was the 'purpose' of Pakistan. Where on the contrary the carriage was to a point which remained in the Indian Dominion, it would be a "purpose" of the Dominion of India. The profit-earning motive of either party to the contract is not the criterion by which "purpose" within the meaning of s. 8 is to be judged.

10 *Union of India* v *Kewal Parkash* AIR 1977 Del 146.
11 59 CWN 99.

The provisions of paragraph 8(1) of Indian Independence (Rights, Property and Liabilities) Order 1947, apply as such to a contract which has remained unbroken on the appointed day, *i.e.* the 15th day of August 1947, as to a contract entered into on a date earlier than the 15th day of August 1947, and broken before that day. The case of *Union of India* v *Loke Nath Saha*[12] decided by ROXBURGH, J. was not followed by DAS GUPTA and DEBABRATA MOOKERJEE, JJ. in *Krishna Ranjan Basu Ray* v *Union of India.*[13]

In *Assam Supplies Ltd.* v *Union of India*[14] THADANI, CJ. observed: "The question remains as to the liability of the Union of India. It is not disputed that the contract was for the carriage of goods over more than one railway, the railway which would have delivered the consignment was the Assam Railway in the Union of India. The liability of a railway as a carrier is governed by s. 72, Indian Railways Act 1890. In other words, the liability of the Union of India is the same as liability of a bailee under the Indian Contract Act 1872 in the absence of any risk note. It is an admitted position in this case that no risk note was executed in respect of the carriage of the goods. As a bailee the Union of India had to discharge the duties which are prescribed by the Indian Contract Act 1872. After the Union of India had discharged its duties as a bailee, the question of negligence or misconduct might have arisen but until the Union of India had led evidence that it had discharged its duties as a bailee the question of misconduct or negligence did not arise ... It was contended by the learned advocates for the respondents that the Union of India cannot be held liable for the acts and omissions of the North-Western Railway. The short answer to the contention is that the position in regard to contracts which were made before the appointed day and which were not exclusive for the purpose of the Dominion of Pakistan, are to be deemed to have been made on behalf of the Dominion of India and the rights and liabilities arising out of such contracts which fall within the purview of cl. (*b*) of s. 8(1) of the Indian Independence (Rights, Property and Liabilities) Order 1947, shall be the rights and liabilities of the Dominion of India. How those rights and liabilities are to be proved is not a matter for our consideration. If the rights and liabilities arising out of a contract statutorily involve certain duties which had to be performed under the Indian Contract Act read with s. 72, Indian Railways Act 1890, by the Union of India, then in the absence of evidence led by the Union of India that those duties were discharged, we think the position is that the Dominion of India would be liable for the breach of contract without going into the question of misconduct or negligence."

12 55 CWN 195.
13 59 CWN 99.
14 AIR 1952 Assam 88.

In *Chhatumull Chowthmull* v *Union of India*[15] on 22nd August 1951, the petitioner delivered 125 bales of four maunds of jute per bale to the station master, on a railway in East Pakistan, for carriage to Cossipore Road Station on the Eastern Railway in the Union of India. The goods were carried by the Pakistan Railway to the border, and the goods were received by the Eastern Railway from the Pakistan Railway. DAS GUPTA, J. who delivered the judgment, observed: "From these circumstances, the proper conclusion, in my opinion, is not that the Pakistan Railway as a principal made a contract with the Eastern Railway but that it made the contract with the Eastern Railway as an agent of the consignor of the goods to Cossipore Road Station and delivery to the consignee. The plaintiff as the principal can, therefore, enforce the contract."

Where goods were booked from a Pakistan Railway to a station in the Indian Union, s. 80 of the Indian Railways Act 1890 (corresponds to s. 107 of the Railways Act 1989) does not apply. Nor the principles that the receiving railway was the agent of the forwarding railway or that each railway acted as the agent of the other apply, in the absence of treaty arrangements between the two States. But if the forwarding railway took the goods in their custody, it could not be denied that their responsibility in regard to the said goods would be that of a bailee.[16]

97. Goods carried at owner's risk rate. Notwithstanding anything contained in section 93, a railway administration shall not be responsible for any loss, destruction, damage, deterioration or non-delivery in transit, of any consignment carried at owner's risk rate, from whatever cause arising, except upon proof, that such loss, destruction, damage, deterioration or non-delivery was due to negligence or misconduct on its part or on the part of any of its servants:

Provided that—

(*a*) where the whole of such consignment or the whole of any package forming part of such consignment is not delivered to the consignee or the endorsee and such non-delivery is not proved by the railway administration to have been due to fire or to any accident to the train; or

(*b*) where in respect of any such consignment or of any package forming part of such consignment which had been so covered or protected that the covering or protection was not readily removable by hand, it is pointed out to the railway administration on or before delivery that any part of that consignment or package had been pilfered in transit,

the railway administration shall be bound to disclose to the consignor, the consignee or the endorsee how the consignment or the package was dealt with throughout the time it was in its possession or control, but if negligence or misconduct on the part of the railway administration or of any of its servants

15 59 CWN 504.

16 *Union of India* v *Amar Singh* AIR 1960 SC 233; (1960)2 SCR 75; 1960 SCJ 543.

cannot be fairly inferred from such disclosure, the burden of proving such negligence or misconduct shall lie on the consignor, the consignee or the endorsee.

1 Corresponding provision This section corresponds to ss. 76F and 74(3) of the old Act.

2 Applicability The provisions of this section will be attracted where the whole of the consignment of goods carried at owner's risk is not delivered to the consignee or the whole of any package forming part of a consignment carried at owner's risk is not delivered to the consignee. It is not applicable in case of short delivery.[17]

3 Duty of disclosure The obligation on the railway administration is two fold, namely (*a*) non-delivery of consignment, and (*b*) package being pilfered. This section does not apply to a case of refusal to take delivery of goods as they were in a rotten condition.

Clearly one object of the provision is to obviate, if possible, the necessity for litigation. As to the extent of the disclosure, it is confined to the period during which the consignment was within the possession or control of the railway administration; it does not relate, for instance, to the period after the goods have been theftuously removed from the premises. On the other hand it does envisage a precise statement how the consignment was dealt with by the administration or its servants. The character of what is requisite may vary according to the circumstances of different cases, but if the consignor is not satisfied that the disclosure has been adequate, the dispute must be judicially decided. As to the accuracy or truth of the information given, if the consignor is doubtful or unsatisfied and considers that these should be established by evidence, the railway administration should submit their evidence first at the trial.[18]

In case the railway administration does not produce such evidence, an adverse presumption would be drawn against them under *illustration* (*g*) of s. 114 of the Indian Evidence Act 1872. The presumption would be stronger where the plaintiff calls upon the railway administration to adduce certain evidence.[19] The obligation to lead evidence as to how the railway dealt with the consignment is implicit in the duty of disclosure imposed by this section. The administration should adduce its evidence first at the trial, and it is only when negligence or misconduct cannot fairly be inferred from such evidence that the burden of proof of negligence or misconduct shifts to the plaintiff.[20]

17 *Tirthmal* v *Union of India* AIR 1976 Pat 169; ILR (1975)54 Pat 240; 1976 Pat LJR 158.

18 *Surat Cotton Spinning and Weaving Mills* v *Secretary of State for India in Council* AIR 1937 PC 152; 64 IA 176; 41 CWN 837 relied upon *Union of India* v *Mahadeo Lal Prabhudayal* AIR 1965 SC 1755; (1965)3 SCR 145.

19 *Union of India* v *Delhi Cloth and General Mills Co. Ltd.* AIR 1964 Punj 147.

20 *Union of India* v *Brijlal Purshottamdas* AIR 1969 SC 817; (1969)2 SCJ 203; (1969)1 SCR 910.

For failure to produce and prove documents relating to transit particulars though asked for by the plaintiff, an inference could be legitimately made that, if produced, they would have gone against the railway.[1]

4 Burden of proof of negligence or misconduct In the event of owner's risk rate goods in entirety or in part is not delivered, the railway is to disclose how the consignment was dealt with. If such disclosure coupled with evidence in support thereof *prima facie* shows that the railway is not negligent, the burden shifts to the plaintiff. Where the railway administration fails to disclose as to how they dealt with the consignment, booked at owner's risk rate which was found empty at the destination, during the entire period the goods were in its possession, the burden of proof does not shift to the consignor or the plaintiff.[2] But where on disclosure made by the railway injury or loss cannot be inferred, then the burden shifts on the consignor under s. 76F of the (old) Act.[3]

Once the plaintiffs succeed in proving that the goods in question were damaged or deteriorated as a result of delay or detention in carriage, the burden shifts on the railway administration to prove that delay or detention arose without negligence or misconduct on its part or of any of its servants.[4]

Where the administration leads no evidence to prove that the loss or destruction, etc. was not due to their misconduct or negligence, s. 76 relieves the plaintiff of his burden under s. 74(3). If the consignee proves that the destruction, damage or deterioration was caused by delay or detention in transit, then the burden shifts on the railway authorities to prove that the delay or detention arose without negligence, or misconduct on the part of the administration or any of its servants. Where the owner does not prove delay or detention, he has to prove the misconduct or negligence of the railway as required by s. 74(3) of the old Act.[5]

Where both parties have adduced all available evidence, it is well settled that the burden of proof assumes little or no importance.[6]

5 General responsibility of railway vis-a-vis liability on owner's risk rate When the goods are carried at owner's risk rate in case of loss, destruction,

1 *Hundraj* v *Union of India* (1978)19 Guj LR 34 following *State of Punjab* v *Modern Cultivators* AIR 1965 SC 17; (1964)8 SCR 273; (1964)2 SCJ 796 which in turn followed AIR 1917 PC 6 (*Murugesum Pillai's* case).

2 *Union of India* v *Batchu Subba Rao* AIR 1977 AP 289; (1976)2 APLJ 363; (1977)1 Andh WR 110; 1977 Andh LT 70.

3 *Union of India* v *Batchu Subba Rao* (1977)1 Andh WR 110; 1977 Andh LT 70.

4 *Hundraj* v *Union of India* (1978)19 Guj LR 34.

5 *Union of India* v *Shankarlal* AIR 1972 MP 201; 1972 MPWR 444; 1972 MPLJ 843.

6 *Union of India* v *Eastern Match Co.* AIR 1964 AP 172.

damage, deterioration or non-delivery, the owner could by the application of s. 74(3) of the old Act (corresponding to s. 97 of the Railways Act 1989), succeed only by proving that it was due to negligence or misconduct on the part of the railway administration or of any of its servants that such loss, destruction, damage, deterioration or non-delivery in transit had occurred. The burden to prove negligence or misconduct on the part of the railway administration is on the owner: no burden is cast on the railway administration, to prove that the delay or detention resulting in loss, destruction, damage, deterioration or non-delivery is without negligence or misconduct on its part.[7]

Explaining the difference in scope of various provisions a Gujarat case held that the railway is a common carrier with foresight. It is expected to carry the goods, or animals of the consignor with the care with which a man of prudence would carry his own goods or animals. Such carrier knowing the perishable nature of the goods is bound to carry the goods without unavoidable delay so that the goods may not be damaged or deteriorated due to delay or detention in transit. It does not restrict its scope to particular class of goods or animals or to goods or animals carried at particular risk rate. In the language in which it is framed it applies to all cases of liability of the railway for compensation where the goods are damaged or deteriorates as a result of the delay or detention in transit irrespective of the rate at which the goods are carried by the railway thereby meaning including the goods carried at owner's risk rate. Therefore, it is quite clear that provision of s. 76 of the old Act is not governed either by s. 73 or by s. 74 of the (old) Act.[8]

6 Owner's risk rate Where the railway administration has prescribed two different tariff rates for carriage of animals or goods, namely the ordinary tariff rate or the railway risk rate and the special reduced rate or the owner's risk rate, it shall be presumed, unless the consignor or his agent has agreed in writing to pay the railway risk rate, that such animals or goods have been tendered for carriage by the railway at the owner's risk rate. Where the consignor has agreed in writing to pay the railway administration is to issue a certificate to the consignor to that effect. The liability of the railway administration when the animals or goods are carried or are tendered for carriage at the owner's risk rate. The railway administration shall not be held liable for loss, destruction, damage, deterioration or non-delivery of such animals or goods except upon proof that such loss, etc., was due to negligence or misconduct on the part of the railway or its servants and the principle "*generalibus specialia derogant* (things special derogate from general)" has to be applied remembering that in contradiction to the general provisions contained in s. 73 of old Act.

7 *Union of India* v *Universal Traders Corporation* AIR 1983 Ker 173; 1983 Ker LT 146; 1983 ACJ 319.

8 *Hundraj Chhangomal & Co.* v *Union of India* (1978)19 Guj LR 34.

In view of s. 73 of the old Act the general responsibility of the railway is similar to that of a common carrier, s. 74 of the old Act restricts the liability of the railway administration when the goods are not carried at railway risk rate but at owner's risk rate. Then, in view of s. 74(3) of the old Act (corresponding to s. 97 of the new Act) the railway administration shall not be responsible for any loss, destruction, damage, deterioration or non-delivery of the goods or animals from whatever cause arising, except upon proof that such loss, destruction, damage, deterioration or non-delivery was due to negligence or misconduct, which also includes delay or detention, on the part of the railway administration or of any of its servants. Thus, when the goods are carried at the owner's risk rate, the liability of the railway administration will not be absolute as that of an insurer but will be as that of a bailee.[9]

The railway must plead and prove that it was quoting two rates before they could resort to s. 74 of the old Act.[10] Where no certificate under s. 74(2) of the old Act was taken, sub-sec. (3) of s. 74 of the old Act applies.[11] Oral evidence that goods were sent at railway risk rate is inadmissible.[12]

7 Burden of proof Where the goods are tendered for carriage at the owner's risk rate, it is erroneous to hold that the loss or damage of goods is *prima facie* proof of negligence on the part of the railway administration.[13] Under this section there must be some distinction between damage to the goods by some external agency and damage sustained because of some inherent defect or weakness in the goods themselves.[14] The railway administration would be liable for the loss, damage, etc., only where it is found by the court that such loss, damage etc., was caused by negligence or misconduct on the part of the railway. The burden of proof of negligence or misconduct on the part of the railway is on the person claiming damages. Where the consignor did not allege that the short-delivery was due to negligence or misconduct, s. 74 of the old Act has no application and the railway administration is not liable to compensation.[15]

Where there was delay in transit, the delay was *prima facie* proof of misconduct or negligence and the court entitled to draw an adverse presumption under *illustration* (*g*) of s. 114 of the Indian Evidence Act and it was for the railway to explain the delay.[16] If the railway administration fails to make the disclosure or to disclose further particulars

9 *Union of India* v *Tolaram Hariram* AIR 1980 Guj 173 (177-178).
10 *Union of India* v *Sadhu Ram* AIR 1967 Pat 425.
11 *Union of India* v *Rajasthan Supplying Agencies* AIR 1968 AP 327.
12 *Union of India* v *Ram Kumar Agarwala* AIR 1967 Pat 447.
13 *Sarjug Prasad* v *Union of India* AIR 1960 Pat 571.
14 *Union of India* v *Oudh Sugar Mills* AIR 1961 Bom 130; 63 Bom LR 44.
15 *Tirthmal* v *Union of India* AIR 1976 Pat 169; ILR (1975)54 Pat 240; 1976 Pat LJR 158.
16 *Union of India* v *B. Prahlad & Co.* AIR 1976 Del 236; ILR (1976)1 Del 436; 1976 Rajdhani LR 278.

called for by the plaintiff then the court may draw an adverse presumption against the railway. If the plaintiff is not satisfied with the disclosure made, he can call upon the railway administration to adduce evidence in support of the disclosure made. If any material evidence is withheld, the railway may expose itself to the presumption under *illustration* (*g*) of s. 114 of the Indian Evidence Act 1872. If the railway administration makes the disclosure and produces evidence in support thereof and negligence or misconduct may fairly be inferred from such disclosure or evidence, the plaintiff is relieved from the burden of proving negligence or misconduct. But if no such inference can be drawn from the evidence disclosed, the plaintiff must discharge the burden of proving negligence or misconduct.[17]

In view of s. 74(3) of the (old) Indian Railways Act, except upon proof that the damage or deterioration was due to negligence or misconduct on the part of the railway administration, the administration cannot be held responsible for such damage or deterioration. Therefore, the plaintiffs have necessarily to prove that such damage or deterioration is due to negligence or misconduct on the part of the railway administration. But the railway administration should place all the necessary evidence regarding the movement of the goods, because that is exclusively within its knowledge, and therefore when the administration does not place all the necessary evidence to explain the delay it is not unreasonable to infer that there has been negligence on its part in the transport of goods. Here, such deterioration to goods was not due to delay in transshipment.[18]

When the plaintiff sued railway for damages to goods, the certificate issued at the time of delivery showing that part of tobacco consigned was wet and damaged. The railway in defence led no evidence. Negligence or misconduct on the part of the railway was held proved.[19]

Where the disclosure made is nothing but an apology for disclosure, it cannot be urged that the obligation of the railway administration has been discharged simply because no demand for further particulars has been made.[20]

8 Defective wagon Tobacco leaves sent by wagon without taking necessary precaution and water entered in large quantity was held to be a case of grave negligence amounting to misconduct.[1] Dry chillies were despatched by loading them in a leaky wagon in cloudy weather. The wagon was not examined by wagon examiner who are specially skilled in examination of

17 *Governor-General in Council* v *Thakursi Dass* AIR 1948 Pat 45; *G.A. Jolli* v *Dominion of India* AIR 1949 Cal 380; *Union of India* v *Munagala Krishnayya* AIR 1960 AP 495.

18 *Union of India* v *C.A. Akhtar* (1976)1 Mad LJ 153; 89 Mad LW 519.

19 *Union of India* v *Gangaram Bhagwandas* AIR 1977 MP 215; 1977 Jab LJ 763; 1977 MPLJ 318.

20 *Mahadeo Lal* v *Union of India* AIR 1959 Pat 202; ILR 37 Pat 1034.

1 *Moolji Sicka* v *Dominion of India* (1955)59 CWN 976.

the condition of wagons. In such circumstances the railway administration and its servants were liable for negligence. Absence of statutory rule for examination of wagons does not absolve the railway administration.[2]

9 Goods or animals at owner's risk—damage—need of pleading railway's negligence or misconduct When goods or animals are consigned at owner's risk rate, and reach destination station damaged, deteriorated or short, and burden is upon the plaintiff to prove negligence or misconduct on the part of the railway. To have the opportunity to prove the misconduct, the plaintiff is to plead the negligence or misconduct of the railways. For, unless the basis thereof is laid in the pleading, no amount of evidence in its support is receivable by court. So, it follows that in such a case failure to plead negligence or misconduct of the railways is fatal for the plaintiff.[3]

10 Negligence is to be established by circumstances or by positive proof Slack coal was delivered short and the plaintiff pleaded negligence of the employees of the railway administration but could not produce any specific evidence. Negligence like any other fact has to be established either by circumstances or by positive proof and the plaintiff cannot succeed by letting in general type of evidence.[4] The consigned goods were kept at booked station for four days. After the goods reached the destination station it was not delivered. Telegram was sent to the plaintiff to take delivery within fifteen days but on the very next day the goods on the footing that these are unclaimed property was auction sold. The railway not having waited for the time given in its telegram, and without even waiting, for a reply to its telegram, having auctioned hastily it is guilty of misconduct and of inordinate delay. As no notice of sale also was given to the plaintiff, the sale is wholly illegal. That itself is sufficient to establish railway's misconduct.[5]

11 Object of the section Section 97 of the Act imposes statutory obligation upon the railway administration to disclose to the consignor of goods how the consignment was dealt with when it was in its control. The object of this provision is to enable the consignor to point out to the railway administration that the fact disclosed by it raises a fair inference of negligence or misconduct on the part of the railway or its servants. Construing s. 74D of the old Act, the Supreme Court in *Union of India* v

2 *Piramal Banwarilal* v *Union of India* AIR 1974 Cal 107.
3 *Tribunal* v *Union of India* AIR 1976 Pat 169; ILR (1975) Pat 240; 1976 Pat LJR 158.
4 *Maharashtra State Electricity Board* v *Union of India* AIR 1973 Bom 44; 1972 Mah LJ 865; ILR (1973) Bom 843.
5 *Union of India* v *Sobhraj Bhag Chand* AIR 1980 All 163.

Brijlal Purshottam[6] followed by *E.I.D. Parry Ltd.* v *South Central Railway*[7] held that the contemplated disclosure must be in the form of a precise statement of how the consignment was dealt with by the administration followed by evidence at the trial in proof of that statement. Although the section does not expressly provide that the administration is bound, if necessary, to lead evidence as to how it dealt with the consignment before the consignor is called upon to prove misconduct or negligence but this obligation is implicit in the duty of disclosure imposed by the section. It is only when negligence or misconduct cannot be fairly inferred from such evidence that the burden of proving the negligence or misconduct shifts to the consignor.[8]

Section 74(3) of the old Act carves an exception to the general rule when the goods or animals are booked at owner's risk rate. The difference in application between s. 74(3) and s. 76 of the old Act is this: in the case of goods delivered for carriage at owner's risk rate, governed by s. 74(3) of the old Act, it is for the owner to prove positively that the loss, destruction, damage, deterioration or non-delivery was due to negligence or misconduct on the part of the railway administration or of any of its servants: whereas in the case covered by s. 76 of the old Act if the owner proves that due to delay or detention in the carriage of goods, loss, destruction, damage, deterioration or non-delivery of goods had occurred, for the railway administration to escape liability arising out of the general responsibilities stated in s. 73 of the old Act it is to be proved that the delay or detention arose without negligence or misconduct on the part of the railway administration or of any of its servants.

12 Non-delivery of entire consignment Pleading as to how consignment was dealt with after it was received through forwarding note taking endorsement of railway authorities with respect to even condition of bag was absent. Fact that consignment was received by railway was proved. Railway authorities were liable to make the loss of goods. Claim for higher price for consignment could not be granted, since rate was calculated as per evidence. The claimant was also entitled to simple interest at the rate of 6% per annum from the date of filing of the suit till the date of payment of the decreetal amount.[9]

6 AIR 1969 SC 817; (1969)2 SCJ 203.

7 (1977)2 Andh WR 227.

8 *Union of India* v *Brijlal Purshottam* AIR 1969 SC 817; (1969)2 SCJ 203; *Union of India* v *Rameshwar Prosad* AIR 1983 MP 59 (63); 1983 Jab LJ 197; 1983 MPLJ 165; 1983 Cur Civ J (MP) 138.

9 *Union of India* v *Mahindra Sah* AIR 2012 Pat 71.

98. Goods in defective condition or defectively packed. (1) Notwithstanding anything contained in the foregoing provisions of this Chapter, when any goods entrusted to a railway administration for carriage—

(*a*) are in a defective condition as a consequence of which they are liable to damage, deterioration, leakage or wastage; or

(*b*) are either defectively packed or not packed in such manner as may be prescribed and as a result of such defective or improper packing are liable to damage, deterioration, leakage or wastage;

and the fact of such condition or defective or improper packing has been recorded by the consignor or his agent in the forwarding note, the railway administration shall not be responsible for any damage, deterioration, leakage or wastage or for the condition in which such goods are available for delivery at destination:

Provided that the railway administration shall be responsible for any such damage, deterioration, leakage or wastage or for the condition in which such goods are available for delivery at destination if negligence or misconduct on the part of the railway administration or of any of its servants is proved.

(2) When any goods entrusted to a railway administration for carriage are found on arrival at the destination station to have been damaged or to have suffered deterioration, leakage or wastage, the railway administration shall not be responsible for the damage, deterioration, leakage or wastage of the goods on proof by railway administration,—

(*a*) that the goods were, at the time of entrustment to the railway administration, in a defective condition, or were at that time either defectively packed or not packed in such manner as may be prescribed and as a result of which were liable to damage, deterioration, leakage or wastage; and

(*b*) that such defective condition or defective or improper packing was not brought to the notice of the railway administration or any of its servants at the time of entrustment of the goods to the railway administration for carriage by railway:

Provided that the railway administration shall be responsible for any such damage, deterioration, leakage or wastage if negligence or misconduct on the part of the railway administration or of any of its servants is proved.

1. **Corresponding provision** This section corresponds to s. 77C of the old Act.

2 **Liability of a railway administration for goods in defective condition or defectively packed** Section 77C of the old Act (corresponding to s. 98 of the new Act) contemplates a case of damage to or deterioration, leakage or wastage of the goods, resulting in some monetary damage to the plaintiff. When there is a shortage in the quantity of goods or there is a loss of complete package, s. 77C of the (old) Act has no application.[10]

10 *National Coal Development Corpn.* v *Union of India* (1976)1 Cut WR 169.

Section 73 of the old Act prescribes the general liability of the railway administration and this section is in the nature of an exception.[11] When oil tins were consigned from Alleppy to Kanpur involving transshipment from boat to railway wagons at Cochin. Since the carriage involved transshipment packing condition p/3 of the General Rules required that the tins should be given over packing by wooden cases. This Rule was not complied with. The evidence showed that upto loading at wagon at Cochin there was no damage. But the consignment arrived at destination station damaged and oil leaked. Such damage occurred at any place from Cochin to Kanpur, and it cannot be attributed to the packing condition. The loading into wagons at Cochin was done by railway. The goods were damaged in transit while in custody of carrier and dunnage was insufficient, which raises a presumption of negligence on part of carrier. And it was the duty of the railway to give sufficient dunnage as provided in Rule 1519 of the Railway Commercial Manual. The railway was found negligent and was held responsible for the damage.[12]

3 Need of getting defective condition of packing recorded in forwarding note If the goods are in defective condition as a consequence of which they are liable to damage, deterioration or wastage, it is the duty of the booking clerk to get such condition recorded by the sender or his agent in the forwarding note. Unless the same is got recorded, the railway administration is not entitled to say that at the time of booking of the goods they were in a defective condition as a consequence of which they were liable to deterioration. In view of the provisions of the Act, presumption arises that the goods were not in such defective condition when they were booked and, therefore, it is not open to the railway administration to say that the deterioration was the result of the defective condition of the goods when they were booked.[13]

4 Need of proof of forwarding note to show condition of packing There is no question of burden to prove on the plaintiff nor s. 77C of the old Act can be invoked when the forwarding note is not proved. The consignment five tins of oil were found empty and twenty tins were found leaking. Oil was lost during transit and delivered short. The defendant railway administration took the plea that the consignment was defectively packed and the packing condition was duly noted in the forwarding note. The defendant however did not produce the original Forwarding Note,

11 *Kesrimal Ratanlal Sarada Co.* v *Union of India* AIR 1968 MP 199; 1968 Jab LJ 540.

12 *Babu Oil & Flour Mills* v *Union of India* AIR 1980 Ker 90; 1980 Ker LT 116.

13 *Hundraj Chhangomal & Co.* v *Union of India* (1978)19 Guj LR 34.

nor any copy authenticated by any certificate by an officer having custody of the records stating that it is a true copy of original Forwarding Note, was produced. The plain copy of Forwarding Note was excluded from consideration.[14]

Patna High Court too did not allow invocation of s. 77C of the old Railways Act when the Forwarding Note was not produced, nor any explanation was offered for its non-production.[15]

5 Burden of proof This section deals with the case of goods being found on arrival at destination to have been damaged or to have suffered deterioration, leakage or wastage. This section does not apply to cases where goods are consigned at railway risk and the loss or shortage has resulted from pilferage.[16] Loss of pipes cannot be covered by the word 'leakage' in s. 77C(1)(*a*) of the old Act.[17] In such cases of damage, deterioration, leakage or wastage, contemplated under this section the provision of this section shall apply notwithstanding anything contained in foregoing sections. The liability of the railway in such cases depends on the fact as to whether such goods were, at the time when they were delivered to the railway administration, in a defective condition or were defectively packed or were packed in a manner not in accordance with any order by the Central Government. If such condition of the goods or such defective or improper packing is proved the railway administration shall not be held responsible for any damage, deterioration, leakage or wastage or for the condition of goods except upon proof of negligence or misconduct on the part of the railway administration or of its servants. But if damage is caused to perishable goods like fruit due to delay due to non-availability of wagon space or locomotive, train connection or handling personnel, it is no excuse against the loss of fruit value to say that coaching tariff prescribed basket containers were not used for packing the fruit where the loss was occasioned by delay and not by type of packing.[18]

In a situation contemplated by s. 77C(1) of the old Act the consignor of the goods in order to make a claim against the railway administration for negligence of leakage has to discharge the burden by showing that the leakage or damage was entirely due to the railway administration or its servants.[19]

14 *Union of India* v *Rameshwar Prasad* AIR 1983 MP 59; 1983 Jab LJ 197; 1983 MPLJ 165; 1983 Cur Civ J (MP) 138.
15 *Bihar State Co-operative Marketing* v *Union of India* AIR 1978 Pat 213; 1978 BLJR 177; 1978 ACJ 364.
16 *T.M. Veerappa* v *Union of India* AIR 1972 Mys 164; (1972)1 Mys LJ 96.
17 *Union of India* v *Khandelwal Bros.* AIR 1975 Mad 389; 88 Mad LW 543.
18 *Gokalchand Srichand* v *Union of India* AIR 1972 All 330.
19 *Meenambika Trading Co.* v *Union of India* (1983)2 Mad LJ 508.

There was a concurrent finding of courts below that the consignment was not packed in accordance with the prescribed rules on the subject. Thus, burden of proof lies on the plaintiff to show that loss could not have been occasioned as a consequence of defective packing. Since the plaintiff led no evidence to show that the railway or its servants had negligently dealt with the consignment or that they were guilty of misconduct, the railway was absolved from liabilities.[20]

When at the instance of plaintiff the court directed the railway to produce its records showing how the consignment was handled by the railway or its servants throughout its transit, the railway failed to comply with the direction; the suppression of such material on the vital issue gave rise to an adverse inference of negligence against the railway. In the circumstances the plaintiff was entitled to the damages claimed.[1]

Not only the fact of defective or improper packing should be recorded in the forwarding note but it has to be further recorded that as a consequence of such defective or improper packing the goods are liable to damage, deterioration, leakage or wastage.[2]

The burden is on the consignor when defective condition of booking is recorded, to prove that loss was due to misconduct or negligence on the part of the railway.[3] According to the railways, for fragile goods like earthenware, etc., P-17 packing condition for outer packing as laid down under r. 120 of the Goods Tariff General Rules framed as proved under s. 77C(4) of the old Act would apply and to comply with that condition the goods must be packed in wooden cases. The packing condition P-17 applies even to full wagon load; but when fragile goods defectively packed is loaded on a wagon and the railways omit to affix caution label, the railways are not absolved from liability for damage to the goods.[4]

The railway had, apart from proving defective packing, to prove further the fact that at the time the consignment was booked the railway authorities had no notice of the defective packing. No such evidence had been adduced. The responsibility was of the railway to check up as to in which condition the goods had been entrusted to it for consignment. The forwarding note

20 *Union of India* v *Firm Chittarmal Ram Dayal* AIR 1979 All 294; 1979 All WC 358.

1 *Chabildas Manickdas* v *Union of India* AIR 1980 AP 78.

2 *Union of India* v *Laduram Fakirchand* AIR 1974 Cal 207; 77 CWN 383.

3 *Kesarimal Ratanlal Sarda & Co.* v *Union of India* AIR 1968 MP 199; 1968 Jab LJ 540.

4 *Union of India* v *Chhabildas Manickdas* AIR 1978 AP 262; (1978)1 Andh LT 219; 1978 ACJ 271.

which could have shown whether the package was defective or not had not been produced by the railway and no explanation had been given for its non-production. No witness was examined on behalf of the railway to prove that the shortage was due to the negligence and carelessness of the consignor. Therefore, the railway was responsible for damage.[5]

6 Misconduct—meaning and expanse Misconduct means a dereliction of duty or unlawful, dishonest or improper behaviour, specially by someone in a position of authority or trust.[6] In *B.N. Railway Co.* v *Moolji Sicka & Co.*[7] the word "misconduct" was defined as denoting any unbusiness-like conduct and including negligence or want of proper care which a bailee is to take under s. 152 of the Contract Act. In *Secretary of State* v *Allah Ditta,*[8] the word "misconduct" was used in a sense which carried an imputation of some degree of moral obliquity, while in a later part of the judgment HILTON, J. remarked as follows: "If duties are intentionally shirked because there is a disinclination to perform them, an inference justified by the facts here found, that is, I think, misconduct whatever meaning of the word is chosen". In *B.B. & C.J. Railway Co. Ltd.* v *Rajnagar Spinning, Weaving and Manufacturing Co. Ltd.*,[9] it was remarked that the word "misconduct" in the Risk Note suggested that a railway servant had been guilty of doing something which was inconsistent with the conduct required of him by the rules of the company. Also see *Ramkrishna Ramnath* v *Union of India.*[10] In *B.N. Railway Co.* v *Dhanji Shah Pestonji,*[11] MUKHERJI, J. observed that culpable negligence or gross negligence as distinguished from ordinary negligence may amount to misconduct. He defined negligence as the omission to do something which a reasonable man, guided upon those considerations, which ordinarily regulate the conduct of human affairs, would do, or, doing something which a prudent and reasonable man would not do.

In *B.N. Railway Co.* v *Moolji Sicka & Co.*,[12] MITTER, J. held misconduct established in a case wherein contravention of the standing order of the railway company to the effect that goods liable to damage should be loaded well away from the door to minimise the risk of damage from rain

5 *Bihar State Co-operative Marketing* v *Union of India* AIR 1978 Pat 213; 1978 BLJR 177; AIR 1973 Pat 244 was dissented from 1968 BLJR 22 was followed.
6 Black's *Law Dictionary,* 10th Ed., 2014.
7 AIR 1930 Cal 815; 129 IC 769.
8 AIR 1930 Lah 120; 120 IC 286.
9 AIR 1930 Bom 129; 54 Bom 105; 124 IC 229.
10 AIR 1960 Bom 344.
11 AIR 1930 Cal 298; 57 Cal 634; 124 IC 332.
12 AIR 1932 Cal 70.

water leaking through the flap door and door crevices, the servants of the railway company had packed a wagon fully. In *M. & S.M. Railway Co.* v *Sundarjee Kalidas,*[13] GUHA, J. observed that "to establish misconduct on the part of the railway administration's servants, it must be shown that the servants were actually responsible for the guilt or wrongful act, where knowledge on the part of the railway administration or of their servants that one was likely to cause injury is not sufficient." The learned Judge added that misconduct was not necessarily established by proving even culpable negligence. It was something opposed to accident or negligence and was the intentional doing of something which the doer knew to be wrong or which he did recklessly not caring what the result would be.

In *Roshan Umar Karim & Co.* v *M. & S.M. Railway Co. Ltd.,*[14] the view of GUHA, J. being based on English decisions was not sound and should not be adopted in the interpretation of the word 'misconduct' in the Risk Note, Form A. Because English decisions put emphasis on 'wilful' which would mean that even culpable negligence or gross negligence would not be misconduct. In *Secretary of State* v *Meah Raj*[15] a Division Bench of Lahore High Court held misconduct established in a case where goods were delivered in contravention of the express and definite instructions of the sender. In *Secretary of State* v *Madhuri Das Narain Das,*[16] NIAMATULLA, J. observed that want of proper care and caution might amount to misconduct within the meaning of Risk Note, Form "B". In *Jamunadas* v *E.I.R. Co.,*[17] JAWALA PRASAD, J. defined misconduct as a failure to do what was required of a person to be done.

In *Ardeshir Bhicaji Tamboli* v *Agent, G.I.P. Railway Co.,*[18] Their Lordships of the Judicial Committee of the Privy Council approved what MADGAVKAR, J. had said in the High Court in regard to the question of 'willful neglect' reproduced below:

> "The remaining question is whether any willful neglect ...... was proved. It appears upon the evidence that the means of extinguishing fire were not as they ought to be in the case of a large cotton exporting station such as Amalner. One hydrant was certainly not working and the water was not at sufficient pressure. Probably, on the whole, this was neglect, but not, I think, willful neglect within the meaning of Risk Note Form H. So that the company should be made liable merely on this account."

13 AIR 1933 Cal 742; 60 Cal 996.
14 AIR 1936 Mad 58; 59 Mad 789.
15 AIR 1935 Lah 425; 144 IC 404.
16 55 All 625; AIR 1933 All 477.
17 AIR 1933 Pat 630; 148 IC 396.
18 AIR 1929 PC 24.

Their Lordships of the Privy Council observed: "In support of this view reference may be made to the cases of *R.* v *Downes,*[19] and *R.* v *Senior,*[20] in the latter of which cases Lord Russel interpreted the expression "willful neglect" as meaning that the act is done deliberately and not by accident or inadvertence, but so that the mind of the person who does the act goes with it. In the present case there was ample evidence of neglect, but no evidence or finding of willful neglect."

Misconduct has been held to be something more serious than mere neglect. The only other term which is convertibly employed for it is willful neglect. "Willful neglect" has been defined in *R.* v *Downes,*[19] and *R.* v *Senior,*[20] referred to in 9 PLT 171 at p. 175, to mean and support that the "act" must have been done deliberately and intentionally and not by accident or inadvertence, but so that the mind of the person who does the act goes with it.[21] Where, in a suit against the railway administration for damages for non-delivery of jute loaded in a wagon non-delivery being alleged as due to the misconduct of the defendants' servants, the defendants alleged destruction of the jute by fire, the withholding by the defendants of all contemporaneous documents and oral evidence as to their dealing with the jute during the whole time it was in their possession or control and the absence of satisfactory evidence establishing that it was that wagon which was on fire and its contents wholly destroyed, bring *illustration* (*g*) of s. 114 of the Indian Evidence Act 1872 which must be kept in mind by a railway administration, into operation and it is fair to presume and infer that if all available evidence had been produced it would have shown that the non-delivery of the plaintiff's jute was occasioned by the misconduct of the defendants' servants.[1]

The B.N.W. Railway Company took charge of a consignment of *ata* bags booked at Cawnpore for Motihari on 22nd August 1941, in a sound condition under a clear receipt loaded in a wagon which was examined and found fit to run and whose flap doors had been securely closed and sealed. The wagon reached Dighwara railway station on 26th August 1941, where the train was detained until 6th September 1941 as there was sinkage of railway line owing to heavy incessant rains. The wagon reached Motihari station on 7th September 1941. The seals and rivets of the wagon were found intact; but sixty bags of *ata* were found damaged

19 [1875]1 QB 25.
20 [1899]1 QB 283.
21 *Governor-General in Council* v *Lachmi Narain* AIR 1947 Pat 459.
1 *Raigarh Jute Mills Ltd.* v *Commissioners for the Port of Calcutta* AIR 1947 Cal 98.

by wet. In a claim for damages the misconduct had to be proved by the plaintiff and cannot be inferred.[2]

Misconduct is something more than mere negligence. It is the intentional doing of something which the doer knows to be wrong or which he does recklessly not caring what the result may be.[3] Misconduct implies some degree of *mens rea* on the part of the person concerned or at any rate a very grave degree of negligence or serious failure to carry out instructions or comply with regulations.[4]

Failure by the railway administration to provide rain-proof wagons during monsoon is misconduct.[5] The railway administration is guilty of misconduct if it does not provide proper type of wagons for the carriage of goods and cause unnecessary delay in transit.[6] If the railway is unable to provide locomotives for hauling of goods, it cannot be said to be a cause beyond the control of the railway and the railway should be held to be guilty of misconduct or negligence.[7]

Where the plaintiff's agents were daily in touch with the railway servants but they were not informed about the arrival of the goods and consequently there was delay in taking delivery of the consignment, there was misconduct on the part of the railway servants.[8] But delay on the part of the railway to carry goods which is unreasonable is not misconduct.[9] If, however, the delay is caused due to not following the advice of the despatching station, the railway should be held to be guilty of misconduct.[10]

7 Negligence—meaning and expanse Negligence is a specific tort and in any given circumstances is the failure to exercise that care which the circumstances demand. What amounts to negligence depends on the facts of each particular case, and the categories of negligence are never closed. It may consist in omitting to do something which ought to be done or in doing something which ought to be done either in a different manner or not at all. The degree of care required in the particular case depends on the accompanying circumstances and may vary according to the amount of risk to be encountered.[11]

2 *Governor-General in Council* v *Motilal* AIR 1945 Pat 159.
3 *Dominion of India* v *Ado Shaw* AIR 1957 Pat 219; *Rasabati Bewa* v *Union of India* ILR (1961) Cut 32; AIR 1961 Ori 113.
4 *Gordhan Das* v *Governor-General in Council* AIR 1957 Punj 196; 58 Punj LR 230.
5 *Ramkrishna* v *Union of India* AIR 1960 Bom 344; ILR (1960) Mah 507; 62 Bom LR 445.
6 *Dominion of India* v *Rupchand* AIR 1953 Nag 169; ILR (1953) Nag 314.
7 *Union of India* v *S. Bagchi* AIR 1957 All 259; ILR (1957)1 All 450.
8 *Union of India* v *Asharfi Devi* AIR 1957 MP 114; 1957 Jab LJ 550.
9 *Sheikh Makbul* v *Union of India* AIR 1960 Ori 146.
10 *Union of India* v *Ganesh Chandra Das* AIR 1959 Cal 337; 63 CWN 343.
11 *Central Asbestes Co. Ltd.* v *Dodd* [1973] AC 518.

Dictionary meaning of 'negligence' is the failure to exercise the standard of care that a reasonably prudent person would have exercised in a similar situation, or any conduct that falls below the legal standard established to protect others against unreasonable risk of harm, except for conduct that is intentionally, wantonly or willfully disregardful of others rights.[12]

Negligence is breach of duty caused by omission to do something which a prudent and reasonable man would not do. Negligence means either subjectively a careless state of mind, or objectively careless conduct. It is not an absolute term but is a relative one; it is rather a comparative term. Negligence is strictly nonfeasance and not malfeasance. It is omission to do what the law requires or failure to do anything in a manner prescribed by law.[13]

The authority for this latter proposition is the House of Lords decision in *Glasgow Corporation* v *Muir,*[14] where LORD MACMILLAN said:

> "My Lords, the degree of safety of others which the law requires human beings to observe in the conduct of their affairs varies according to the circumstances. There is no absolute standard, but it may be said generally that the degree of care required varies directly with the risk involved. Those who engage in operations inherently dangerous must take precautions which are not required of persons engaged in the ordinary routine of daily life ......"

In *Daborn* v *Bath Tramways Limited,*[15] ASQUITH, J. observed:

> "In determining whether a party is negligent, the standard of reasonable care is that which is reasonably to be demanded in the circumstances. A relevant circumstance to take into account may be the importance of the end to be served by behaving in this way or in that. As has often been pointed out, if all the trains in this country were restricted to a speed of 5 miles an hour, there would be fewer accidents, but our national life would be intolerably slowed down. The purpose to be served, if sufficiently important, justifies the assumption of abnormal risk."

In *Mahon* v *Osborne,*[16] it was observed:

> "Common practice by persons habitually engaged in a particular operation is strong evidence of what is reasonable care in the performance of that operation."

In *Vancouver General Hospital* v *McDavid,*[17] a defendant charged with negligence can clear himself if he shows that he has acted in accordance with general and approved practice.

12 Black's *Law Dictionary,* 10th Ed., 2014.
13 *Malay Kumar Ganguly* v *Dr. Sukumar Mukherjee* (2009)9 SCC 221.
14 [1943] AC 448.
15 [1946]2 All ER 338.
16 [1939]2 KB 14.
17 [1934]152 LT 56.

In *Hamzah D. 494* v *Wan Hanafi Bin Wan Ali*[18] it was held that where the railway had issued written notices warning travellers not to travel on steps, etc., the steps taken by the railway were adequate even though the defendant-respondent while attempting to get down from the running train was injured.

The accident took place while the deceased was trying to walk across the lines. Struck by the right side of the bumper of the engine, he fell on the gangway between two quod lines and died on the spot. His widow brought a suit claiming ₹15,000 as damages for the death of her husband. A.C. GUPTA, J. of Calcutta High Court (as His Lordship then was) said: "The principles governing a case like this are not in doubt. On the principle that a person cannot derive advantage from his own wrong, a trespasser sustaining injury cannot recover damages if he had himself courted the accident, though the accident may have been partly due to the negligence of the owner of the land or his servants or agents. The rule, however, is subject to the qualification that an act done in willful or wanton disregard of the personal safety even of a trespasser is not permissible." His Lordship relied on the decision of the House of Lords in *Guard Trunk Railway Co. of Calcutta,*[19] wherein the rule was stated as follows:

> "The railway company was undoubtedly under a duty to the plaintiff not wilfully to injure him: they were not entitled, unnecessarily and knowingly, unexpected to increase the normal risk by deliberately placing dangers in his way, but to say that they were liable to a trespasser for the negligence of their servants is to place them under a duty to him of the same character as that which they undertake to those whom they carry for reward ...... The general rule, therefore, is that a man trespasses at his own risk ...... Again, even if he be a trespasser, a question may arise as to whether or not the injury was due to some willful act of the owner of the land involving something worse than the absence of reasonable care."

The House of Lords in that case emphasised the distinction between willful or reckless disregard of ordinary humanity and a mere absence of reasonable care. His Lordship also referred to the decision of Bombay High Court in *Ismail* v *B.B.C.J. Railway,*[20] which, following the same principle, held a railway company is not liable for damages to a trespasser for a mere error of judgment even if it amounts to negligence on the part of its servants, and that the company will be liable only if the servant acts in willful disregard of the safety of the trespasser.[21] The exact meaning

18 1976 ACJ 17.
19 [1911] AC 361.
20 AIR 1932 Bom 452.
21 *Mokshada Sundari Ghosh* v *Union of India* 1972 ACJ 1 (Cal). Also see *B.N. Railway Company Ltd.* v *Taraprasad Maity* AIR 1928 Cal 504 and *Cherubin Gregory* v *State of Bihar* AIR 1964 SC 205; (1964)4 SCR 199; (1964)1 SCJ 417.

of the word "misconduct" was not resolved by the Supreme Court in *Shiva Nath* v *Union of India.*[22]

When negligence is breach of duty to take care imposed by law, it may be called 'statutory negligence', and when it is breach of duty to take care arising out of circumstances of a particular case, it may be termed 'actionable negligence'.[1]

"Negligence", said Baron Alderson, "is the omission to do something which a reasonable man, guided upon those considerations which ordinarily regulate the conduct of human affairs would do or doing something which a prudent man would not do."[2] The said definition, therefore, assumes a duty to take care and it also assumes that the degree of the said care is to be measured by the standard of a reasonable man. So, negligence is a breach of duty to take care resulting in damage to one whether in person or property. The said duty to take care may be imposed by statute or it may arise due to relation in which one may stand to another, *i.e.* when the person or property of one is in such proximity to the person or property of another that if due care is not taken damages may be caused by one to the other.

Where the delivery memo and the railway receipt could not be connected and there was delay in delivery of the consignment, the railway was held to be liable for the loss due to the negligence of the railway company.[3] Where a consignment was delivered to a person not authorised to take them, the railway is guilty of negligence.[4] Where the clerk without comparing the entries in the Delivery Book with the railway receipt gives delivery of the goods to the person producing the railway receipt, the misdelivery of the goods was held to be the direct result of the negligence.[5] Where a consignment was overcarried but it was not re-booked to the proper station, the railway was held to be liable for the loss.[6] Keeping a parcel of sarees on the veranda of station without entrusting it to any person is negligence.[7] Failure to keep the goods under lock and key is

22 AIR 1965 SC 1666.

1 *Union of India* v *Hindustan Lever Ltd.* AIR 1975 P&H 259.

2 *Prafulla Kumar Rout* v *State of Orissa* 1995 CrLJ 1277 (Ori); *Blythe* v *Birmingham Water Works* [1856]11 Ex 781; 4 WR 294; 25 LJ Ex 212.

3 *Milapchand Hiralal* v *Union of India* AIR 1959 Assam 183; ILR (1957) Assam 199.

4 *Kaluram Sitaram* v *Dominion of India* AIR 1954 Bom 50; ILR (1953) Bom 1301; 55 Bom LR 595.

5 *Mohammad Ekram* v *Union of India* AIR 1959 Pat 337; ILR 37 Pat 1355.

6 *Rajendra Prasad* v *Governor-General in Council* AIR 1955 Pat 138.

7 *Union of India* v *Shantilal Nanchand* AIR 1957 MP 192; 1957 Jab LJ 873.

negligence.[8] Failure to affix caution label to wagon carrying fragile goods is negligence.[9]

The consignment booked by railway reached the destination short. A witness for the plaintiff proved proper packing and loading at starting station. Further, the invoice under which the goods were booked was proved. The short certificate too was produced. The railway did not examine any witness not produced any document. Negligence on the part of the railway was held proved.[10]

8 Negligence and misconduct—difference between In a Calcutta case[11] GENTLE, J. discussed at length the difference between negligence and misconduct as follows:

> "Negligence and misconduct are both wrong. Is there any difference in degree between an act which is negligence and an act which is misconduct? Negligence is the failure to take that care which an ordinary prudent man would take in the circumstances and is the omission to do something which such man would do, or in doing something which he would not do. Misconduct is not easy to define. In the *Oxford Dictionary* it is said to be bad management, mismanagement, malfeasance and culpable neglect of an official in regard to his office........."

The opinions expressed in the several decisions are not in accord. In *B.N. Railway Co.* v *Moolji Sicka & Co.*,[12] the meaning was considered of the word "misconduct" in a Risk Note containing the same or similar language as in Risk Note "B". SUHRAWARDY, J. with whom PATTERSON, J. agreed, observed at pp. 139-140 as follows:

> "I am inclined to hold that the word 'misconduct' as used in the new Risk Note 'B' is wide enough to include wrongful commission or omission intentional or unintentional, any act which it wrongfully did or wrongfully neglected to do or, to put it in another way, did what he should not have done and did not do what he should have done." Later he said: "In my judgment the word 'misconduct' denotes any unbusinesslike conduct and includes negligence or want of proper care which a bailee is to take under s. 152, Indian Contract Act 1872" VENKATARAMANA, J. agreed with this view in *Roshan Umar Karim & Co.* v *M. & S.M. Railway.*[13]

In this view there would seem to be no difference in degree between negligence and misconduct and that these words are co-relative and bear

8 *Union of India* v *Bikanir Textiles* AIR 1961 Raj 211.
9 *Union of India* v *Chabildas Manikdas & Bros.* AIR 1978 AP 262; (1978)1 Andh LT 219; 1978 TAC 361; 1978 ACJ 271.
10 *Union of India* v *Khetwat Oil Mills* AIR 1988 Ori 233; (1988)1 Ori LR 288; (1988)22 Reports 101.
11 *Ralliaram* v *Governor-General* AIR 1946 Cal 249; 48 CWN 554; (1944)2 Cal 487.
12 35 CWN 133.
13 AIR 1936 Mad 508; 59 Mad 789.

the same meaning. In *Manilal* v *B.N. Railway Co. Ltd.*[14] MITTER, J. expressed the opinion that misconduct is something more than negligence. In *M. & S.M. Railway Co.* v *Sunderjee Kalidas*[15] an exhaustive review of the authorities was made and GUHA, J. at p. 285, expressed the opinion that misconduct is not necessarily established by proving even culpable negligence, it is the intentional doing of something which the doer knows to be wrong or which he does recklessly not caring what the result may be. BARTLEY and GUHA, JJ. concurred with this view and adopted this definition in *Banwarilal Jagannath* v *B.B. & C.I. Railway.*[16] In *B.N. Railway Co.* v *Haji Latif,*[17] JACK, J. observes at p. 412 that negligence in his view would not always be tantamount to misconduct, which is the view held in *Lewis* v *G.W. Railway Co.*[18] in which it was said that misconduct is something opposed to accident or negligence.

"In my opinion for an act to amount to misconduct there must be a greater degree of wrong than is required for negligence. Misconduct is something in the nature of improper behaviour and is not merely either wrongful commission or wrongful omission. An act of misconduct can well be, and in most cases probably is, negligence; but a negligent act is not by itself misconduct. It seems to me that misconduct is the genus and negligence a species of the genus." The view of SUHRAWARDY, J. (*supra*) was dissented from in this case. See also *Jnanendra Kumar* v *Union of India.*[19]

9 Contributory negligence Negligence on part of the injured party through failure to take precautions against an accident is contributory negligence.[20] The question of contributory negligence does not depend upon any breach of duty between the plaintiff and the negligent defendant; it depends entirely on whether the plaintiff could reasonably have avoided the consequence of the defendant's negligence. Where the plaintiff has not done anything which a person exercising reasonable care would not have done, he cannot be held guilty of contributory negligence.[21]

'Contributory negligence' is an expression which implies that the person, who has suffered damage, is also guilty of some negligence and has contributed towards the damage. In such a case, the court has power to apportion the loss between the parties, who can be held guilty of negligence by act or omission on their part, as it deems just and equitable.[1]

'Composite negligence' would arise when negligent acts of omission of two or more persons have caused damage to a third person. In such a case,

14 39 CWN 114.
15 57 CLJ 281.
16 61 CLJ 256.
17 AIR 1937 Cal 410.
18 [1877]3 QBD 195.
19 AIR 1957 Pat 147.
20 Mitra's *Legal and Commercial Dictionary,* 6th Ed., 2006.
21 *Jeet Kumari* v *Chittagong Engr. & Electric Supply Co.* AIR 1947 Cal 195; 51 CWN 419.
1 *Union of India* v *Hindustan Lever Ltd.* AIR 1975 P&H 259.

the said third person does not contribute to the mishap or to the damage, and as such he is entitled to sue all or any one of the negligent persons for damages. It is no concern of his whether there is any duty of contribution or indemnity between the negligent persons.[2]

In the case of 'statutory negligence', the same having arisen out of breach of statutory obligation, neither the defence of 'contributory negligence' nor that of 'composite negligence', is open or available to the wrong-doer.[3]

A defence based on contributory negligence proceeds on the assumption that the person raising the defence was himself negligent and that negligence would not afford a cause of action to the plaintiff, either because of its remoteness to the accident or because the plaintiff, who had the last opportunity to avoid the accident, did not do so, or that he did not act with reasonable care and prudence and that this negligence of the claimant was the direct cause of the accident but for which the accident would not have taken place.[4]

10 Finding of negligence—examination in second appeal As to scope of second appeal to High Court, CPC (Am.) Act 1976 has brought about a shift in the position of law. Under the present s.100, CPC a second appeal lies only on a substantial question of law. The tests for ascertaining what can be said to be a substantial question of law have been laid down in *Mahindra* v *Mahindra*[5] and *Budhwanti* v *Gulab Chandra Prasad.*[6] The question whether certain facts constitute negligence is a question of law.[7]

In *Akhil Chandra Saha* v *I.G.N. Railway Co.,*[8] a Division Bench of Calcutta High Court held that if the contention is that there is no evidence of negligence, the question is one of law for the Judge to decide, but the question as to whether the evidence is sufficient to justify the inference of negligence is one of fact. In the case of *Nafar Chandra Pal Chowdhury* v *Shukur Sheikh,*[9] Their Lordships of the Judicial Committee made the following observation: "Questions of law and of fact are sometimes difficult to disentangle; the proper legal effect of a proved fact is essentially

2 *Union of India* v *Hindustan Lever Ltd.* AIR 1975 P&H 259 relying on *Manjula Devi* v *Manjushree Raha* 1968 ACJ 1 (MP); *K.V. Narasappa* v *Kamalamma* AIR 1968 Mys 345; 1969 ACJ 127.
3 *Bailey* v *Geddes* [1938]1 KB 156; *Caswell* v *Powell Duffryn Associated Collieries Ltd.* [1940] AC 152.
4 *Swarnalata Barua* v *Union of India* AIR 1963 Assam 117.
5 AIR 1979 SC 788; (1979)2 SCC 529; 49 Comp Cas 419.
6 AIR 1987 SC 1484; (1987)2 SCC 153; (1987)2 SCR 534. [For an elaborate discussion on the point *see* Saha on *Court of Civil Procedure*, 3rd Ed., pp. 288-289].
7 *Safdar Hossein* v *Union of India* AIR 1978 All 53; (1977)3 All LR 631; (1978)1 Serv LR 118.
8 AIR 1916 Cal 647; 21 CLJ 565.
9 AIR 1918 PC 92; 46 Cal 189.

a question of law; so also the question of admissibility of evidence, and the question of whether any evidence has been offered on one side or the other; but the question whether the fact has been proved when evidence for and against has been admitted is necessarily a pure question of fact." In another Privy Council case,[10] Their Lordships held that the court's decision must stand final as to facts; but the soundness of conclusions may involve matter of law and may be questioned by a court of second appeal.

In *Maung Kyaing* v *P.L.T.A.A. Chetyyar Firm*,[11] BAGULEY, J. observed as follows: "There is no such thing as 'legal negligence', and 'negligence' is, I think, nowhere defined. Whether certain facts constitute negligence is a deduction from those facts, and, although I am bound by the finding of fact by the lower Appellate Court, I am not bound by its deductions from those facts. On this point I would refer to *Durga Chowdhurani* v *Jewahir Singh Chowdhri*[12] and *Ramgopal* v *Shamskhaton*.[13] In *S. Ananda Rao* v *Venkatadra Appa Rao*[14] it has been held that gross negligence is a mixed question of law and fact. In *Phulchand Khandelwal* v *Governor-General for India in Council*,[15] it has been held that, where in a suit for damages against a railway company for non-delivery of goods owing to negligence, evidence has been led as to how the goods were kept in the custody of the railway company and from this evidence a conclusion has been drawn by the lower court that there was no negligence, the question is not purely one of fact and it can be examined in second appeal to find out whether the conclusion of the lower court is right.

11 Neglect and willful neglect 'Neglect' means the omission of proper attention to a person or thing, whether inadvertent, negligent or willful. And 'willful neglect' is the intentional or reckless failure to carry out a legal duty.[16] "Neglect" means the omission to perform a duty and implies that a man does something which ought either to be done in a different manner or not at all, or that he omits to do something which ought to be done. "Willful neglect" goes far beyond this and implies that the defendant knew that he should do a particular act and that he deliberately abstained from doing it. There may be cases where neglect may be deliberate and yet not willful, as for instance, when the act is not that of a free agent.[17] Willful neglect means and imports that the act must have been done deliberately and intentionally and not by accident or inadvertence.[18]

According to ASHWORTH, J. as expressed in *Sheo Narain* v *E.I. Railway*,[19] "the expression 'willful neglect' means failure to take such precautions as

10 *Ramgopal* v *Shamskhaton* 19 IA 228; 20 Cal 93.
11 AIR 1929 Rang 17; 116 IC 470.
12 17 IA 112; 18 Cal 23.
13 19 IA 228; 20 Cal 93.
14 AIR 1925 Mad 258.
15 AIR 1949 Pat 110.
16 Black's *Law Dictionary*, 10th Ed., 2014.
17 *E.I. Railway Co.* v *Sukhdeo Das Gobardhan* AIR 1924 Pat 25.
18 *Governor-General in Council* v *Lachmi Narain* AIR 1947 Pat 459.
19 AIR 1928 All 103; 50 All 246.

a prudent man would in respect of his own goods take to provide against such loss or theft as he would contemplate as not merely possible but as likely." The expression 'willful neglect' means that the act was done deliberately and intentionally and not by accident or inadvertence so that the mind of the person who does the act goes with it. The mere fact that the wagons are locked on one side only and on the other side seals were used does not justify an inference that there was willful neglect. Where the guard found the seals on the wagons broken at one station and had them resealed at the next station, the omission to reseal them earlier did not amount to willful neglect if in fact goods had been lost before the discovery of the seals having broken.[20] In *Badridas* v *Secretary of State,*[21] SHADI LAL, CJ. observed as follows: "It cannot be affirmed that the locking of a wagon is always an adequate safeguard against theft, especially when it is remembered that the railway administration owns thousands of wagons and it is impracticable to have a different lock for each wagon. If a standard lock is used it would not be difficult for thieves to make keys fitting it."

The question of willful neglect is one to be determined in the light of the circumstances of each case. It cannot be laid down as a hard and fast rule that the mere fact that the wagon was sealed and not locked constitutes willful neglect within the meaning of Risk Note B. Some of the package of sugar consigned to a railway company under two risk notes in Form B were lost. The wagons in which the bags were loaded had no lock on it but a tin shackle had been put on it which could be broken by an instrument. There had been many thefts on the line and it was found that theft did not take place on the running train. Thus, there was legal evidence to support finding a willful neglect.[1]

As an abstract proposition, it is impossible to lay down that a mere failure to secure wagons always amounts to willful neglect, or that the mere sealing of the wagon necessarily excludes willful neglect. Every case must depend on its circumstances. The absence of any device to shut out thieves is a circumstance which the court is entitled to take into account. It is for the courts which have to find facts to hold whether the absence of precautions under the circumstances of that particular case amounted in their opinion to willful neglect on the part of the railway administration. The frequency of thefts that had taken place, and the steps or absence of steps to prevent them, are matters which can be legitimately taken into consideration.[2]

A consignment was placed in a road-van attached to a mixed train. The doors of the van were closed with bolts or cotter pins but were neither

20 *Durga* v *Secretary of State* AIR 1930 Pat 283.
21 AIR 1931 Lah 267.
1 *Secretary of State* v *Nand Ram* AIR 1929 All 749.
2 *Brindaban* v *G.I.P. Railway Co.* AIR 1926 All 394; 48 All 766.

locked nor sealed. When the train reached an intermediate station at about 10 p.m., one of the station staffs called out that the door of the road-van was open and on examination two bundles of cotton yarn belonging to two consignments were found missing. It was urged on behalf of the railway company that the road-van is not locked but its doors are secured with bolts because goods have to be loaded and unloaded at intermediate stations and that the guard on duty is required to examine the bolts at every intermediate station. If such a practice prevails it is not consistent with the security which the railway company is bound to provide for the goods entrusted to its custody for transit and that in the circumstances above mentioned, willful neglect may be inferred from the fact that the steps taken to secure the goods against loss by the theft were inadequate.[3]

The plaintiff was the consignee of 26 bags which were loaded at Kidderpore Station and were despatched to Cawnpore. The wagon admittedly arrived at Cawnpore and the seals on the wagon were found intact. As the railway company had many other wagons to unload, this wagon was put on a siding and remained there for two days when it was reported that the seals on one side of the wagon were broken. When the contents were checked it was discovered that six bags were missing. The plaintiff instituted the suit to recover damages for the loss of the bags. It was found on evidence that the yard where the wagon was kept was a very large one and that its wall on the jungle side was broken at several places at the time when the goods were stolen. Though ordinarily the neglect or theft has to be proved by the plaintiff in this case, it has been sufficiently proved and therefore the railway is liable.[4]

When a train was in motion and the guard observed that goods were dropping down from the wagons but he did not stop or try to stop the train but allowed the train to run on, there was willful neglect on his part and consequently the railway company was liable.[5] Where it is established that wagon containing consignments were despatched from a certain station but did never reach their destination, and the railway company refused to vouchsafe any sort of explanation as to the non-delivery, the only conclusion which the court can reasonably form is that the loss has been due to their willful neglect.[6]

99. Responsibility of a railway administration after termination of transit. (1) A railway administration shall be responsible as a bailee under sections 151, 152 and 161 of the Indian Contract Act, 1872 (9 of 1872), for the loss, destruction,

3 *Rohilkhand & K. Railway* v *Brij Raj* AIR 1923 Oudh 212; 72 IC 428.
4 *E.I. Railway Co.* v *Sri Ram Mahadeo* AIR 1924 All 177; 46 All 125.
5 *Kashi Ram* v *E.I. Railway Co.* AIR 1927 Pat 9; 6 Pat 168.
6 *E.I. Railway Co.* v *Ali Raza* AIR 1927 Oudh 355; 104 IC 728.

damage, deterioration or non-delivery of any consignment up to a period of seven days after the termination of transit:

Provided that where the consignment is at owner's risk rate, the railway administration shall not be responsible as a bailee of such loss, destruction, damage, deterioration or non-delivery except on proof of negligence or misconduct on the part of the railway administration or of any of its servants.

(2) The railway administration shall not be responsible in any case for the loss, destruction, damage, deterioration or non-delivery of any consignment arising after the expiry of a period of seven days after the termination of transit.

(3) Notwithstanding anything contained in the foregoing provisions of this section, a railway administration shall not be responsible for the loss, destruction, damage, deterioration or non-delivery of perishable goods, animals, explosives and such dangerous or other goods as may be prescribed, after the termination of transit.

(4) Nothing in the foregoing provisions of this section shall affect the liability of any person to pay any demurrage or wharfage, as the case may be, for so long as the consignment is not unloaded from the railway wagons or removed from the railway premises.

1 Corresponding provision This section corresponds to s. 77 of the old Act.

2 Liability after termination of transit The liability of the railway administration for loss, etc., of animals and goods during the period from the delivery of the goods to it up to the termination of transit is laid down in ss. 93 and 97 of the Act and also in other sections. The words "in transit" have been used to indicate the responsibility of the railway in respect of the period up to the termination of transit. On a reading of various sections in Chapter VII, it appears that "transit" and "carriage" have been used synonymously and for giving full effect to legislative object for enacting provision in s. 77(5) of the old Act the said words should be construed to mean the same thing.[7]

The liability of the railways is that of a bailee as defined in the Contract Act and is not that of a common carrier, though they may be common carriers as regards goods which they profess to carry or actually carry for persons, including live animals and passengers' personal luggage. Sub-section (2) of s. 77 of the old Act shows that the railway administration shall not be responsible for any loss, destruction, deterioration or non-delivery, if it arises after the expiry of seven days after the termination of the transit.[8]

The consigned goods reached *S* station on 14th January 1968 and unloaded there to be kept in Railway Store House. The plaintiffs

7 *Union of India* v *Haji S. Umbichi* AIR 1973 Ker 83; ILR (1972)2 Ker 588.

8 *Raman* v *Union of India* AIR 1985 Mad 37; (1984)97 Mad LW 320; 1984 TNLJ 307; 1984 ACJ 637; (1985)1 ACC 138.

approached for delivery on 22nd May 1968 for the first time. But when they went to Railway Store House, the goods were found missing. The railway was not held liable at all. In such a case s. 56 of Indian Railways Act 1890 (corresponds to s. 84 of the Railways Act 1989) is not available. Section 56 of the old Act applies only when the goods are available to the railway at any length of time after the arrival at the destination.[9]

When the goods that arrived at the destination station, it was unloaded by the coolies of the consignee company and were kept on the railway platform for long. The consignee company as a matter of fact used the platform as warehouse. The company posted watchmen and also covered the bales of cotton constituting the consigned goods by tarpaulin. The bales caught fire after thirteen days of unloading. Then under old unamended s. 77, the railway was liable for loss etc. upto the time of 30 days from the date of termination of transit. It is not clear from the reported judgment whether the consignment was booked at owner's risk rate or at railway risk rate, but as the railway was found to have taken all due care, the railway was held not responsible for the loss.[10]

It is not the law that the railway administration is burdened with two years of liability one as a bailee for seven days and the other as a mere custodian of goods after the period of seven days.[11] It is the law that the railway administration cannot be held responsible as a bailee or a warehouseman for such destruction, damage or deterioration or non-delivery of goods arising after the expiry of the period of seven days after termination of transit. In such case, railway is protected under s. 77(2) of the old Act.[12]

There was absolutely no evidence when the loss occurred although admitted loss occurred somewhere. The onus is on the railway to show that no loss, destruction, deterioration or damage had taken place not only during the period of transit, but also during the subsequent period of transit, but seven days after the termination of transit. When the railway fails to discharge the onus, the railway cannot escape its liability through s. 77(2) of the (old) Railways Act.[13]

9 *M. Veerabhadra Rao* v *Union of India* AIR 1984 AP 328; (1983)2 APLJ (HC) 327.

10 *Union of India* v *U.I.F. & G. Insurance Co.* AIR 1981 Mad 162; 94 Mad LW 7; ILR (1981)1 Mad 233; (1981)2 Mad LJ 128.

11 *Lloyed Bitumen Products* v *Union of India* (1980)2 Mad LJ 363.

12 *Union of India, Eastern Railway* v *Joseph Textile* AIR 1985 Mad 360; 1984 TNLJ 345; (1985)1 Mad LJ 274.

13 *Raman* v *Union of India* AIR 1985 Mad 37; (1984)97 Mad LW 320; 1984 TNLJ 307; 1984 ACJ 637; (1985)1 ACC 138.

A consignment was booked by the plaintiff who was the consignee himself. The goods however were delivered on an indemnity bond to defendant No. 2 on 28th February 1970 and 6th March 1970 on the ground that original railway receipt had been lost. In view of s. 77(2) of the (old) Act, railway is absolved from the liability of loss etc. occurring after the expiry of seven days after termination of transit. If railway wanted to take advantage of s. 77 of the (old) Act, it was obligatory on it to have pleaded as to what was the free period allowed when the goods had actually delivered. Since the railway in that case failed to plead those facts, the court held that loss to the plaintiff occurred during the transit. The suit was decreed.[14]

A careful reading of s. 77(3) of the (old) Act will show that the railway administration will not be liable for any damage caused to the goods after the termination of the transit. Therefore, in order to escape liability, the railway administration is duty bound to prove that the destruction or damage was caused after the termination of the transit period.[15]

> **100. Responsibility as carrier of luggage.** **A railway administration shall not be responsible for the loss, destruction, damage, deterioration or non-delivery of any luggage unless a railway servant has booked the luggage and given a receipt therefor and in the case of luggage which is carried by the passenger in his charge, unless it is also proved that the loss, destruction, damage or deterioration was due to the negligence or misconduct on its part or on the part of any of its servants.**

1 Corresponding provisions in the old Act This section corresponding to s. 75 of the old Act.

2 Responsibility of railway as carrier of luggage The railway administration is not as carrier of luggage is dependent on issue of receipt by a railway servant against booking of the luggage and is confined to the proof of loss, destruction, damage or deterioration which is carried by the passenger in his charge.

3 What is "Luggage" In *Macrow* v *Great Eastern Railway*,[16] COCKBURN, CJ. said: "We hold the true rule to be that whatever the passenger takes with him for his personal use and convenience according to the habits or wants of the particular necessities or to the ultimate purpose of the journey,

14 *Punjab National Bank* v *Beniprosad* AIR 1981 MP 95; 1981 MPLJ 380.

15 *Union of India* v *West Punjab Factories Ltd.* AIR 1966 SC 395; (1966)1 SCR 580 distinguished *Union of India* v *Urvasi Enterprises* AIR 1979 NOC 43 (AP).

16 [1871] LR 6 QB 612.

must be considered as personal luggage. This would include not only all articles of apparel, whether for use or ornament ...... but also gum-case and fishing apparatus of the sportsman, the easel of the artist on a sketching tour, or the books of the student, and other articles of an analogous character, the use of which is personal to the traveller and the taking of which has arisen from the fact of his journeying".

4 Carrier's liability as to luggage The section, as it reads, makes it clear that the company is liable only for property entrusted to it, being booked by a railway servant and a receipt being given for it. It will be going beyond the section to hold the company liable for the personal luggage of a passenger which has not been so booked and which is taken by the passenger with him at his own risk. The word "unless" in the (old) section clearly indicates that the liability is not imposed on the company without what is required by the section. Where a passenger had some currency notes about him at the time of the accident, the loss of such notes could not be the cause of action against the railway as the loss of the notes was only a remote and not an immediate result of the accident.[17] Under the present section a passenger can recover damages for loss etc. of luggages carried by him in his charge only on proof that the same was booked and receipt obtained therefor as also on proof that the loss etc. was due to negligence or misconduct on the part of the railway administration or of any of its servants. But if the goods were not carried by the passenger in his charge but was in charge of the railway administration, the liability of the latter will be determined under s. 73 of the old Act.

The railway administration cannot avoid the liability where the goods had been booked by an adult upon a passenger-half-ticket obtained on misrepresentation as to age of the passenger.[18]

5 Parcel way bill and railway receipt—distinction If a consignment is booked as a parcel or parcels, then a parcel way bill is issued in which case the consignment is carried by a passenger by a parcel train not by a goods train; whereas if the consignment is booked as "goods" then railway receipt is issued and the goods would be carried by a goods train.[19]

6 Railway receipt—effect of endorsement A railway receipt answers a "document of title to goods" as defined in the Sale of Goods Act. As to the

17 *Secretary of State* v *Gokal Chand* AIR 1925 Lah 636; 6 Lah 451; 90 IC 1026.
18 *Union of India* v *Benode Kumar* AIR 1962 Cal 48; 65 CWN 727E.
19 *Union of India* v *Tolaram Hariram* AIR 1980 Guj 172 (174).

effect of endorsement of railway receipt, the following lines from the Privy Council decision[1] may be pertinent:

> 'The railway receipt, though a document of title, was in form merely an authority to take delivery of the goods, and the possession of such document contained no representation that the holder had any implied authority or right to dispose of the goods. It was, at the best, an ambiguous document. Its possession no more conveyed a representation that the merchants were entitled to dispose of the property than the actual possession of the goods themselves would have conveyed any such representation. It is not like a negotiable instrument; the possession of the railway receipt is no more significant for this purpose than the possession of the goods would have been'.

Calcutta High Court further pointed out: "Clearly enough his Lordship (LORD WRIGHT) holds that a mere possession of a railway receipt would not confer title on the possessor. It must be remembered, however, that their Lordships of the Privy Council were not dealing with the case of endorsement of a railway receipt. In fact, the case before their Lordships was that the railway receipt did not bear any endorsement. All that their Lordships said in this case was that no inference as to title can be drawn from the mere possession of a railway receipt".[2] In *Hari Mohon Dutta* v *Dominion of India,*[3] MITTER, J. of the Calcutta High Court, after referring to the said observations of the Privy Council said: "It would follow, therefore, that an endorsement on the railway receipt by itself is not enough to constitute the endorsee the owner of the goods. The cases *Bhabani Prosad Lahiri* v *Rai Radhica Bhusan Ray Bahadur,*[4] and *Kalooram Agarwala* v *Jonishatalal Chakravarty,*[5] dealt with assignment by endorsement of negotiable instruments. In each case, the endorsement conveyed to the endorsee the right, title and interest under the document concerned. A railway receipt is not in the same position, although by trade usage it might assume some of attributes of a negotiable instrument. In my view, therefore, mere endorsement of a railway receipt either by the consignor or by the consignee does not convey the property in the goods to the endorsee".

In *Commissioners for the Port of Calcutta* v *General Trading Corporation,*[6] A.K. MUKHERJEA, J. after an exhaustive review of

1 *Mercantile Bank of India* v *Central Bank of India Ltd.* AIR 1938 PC 52; 65 IA 75.
2 *Commissioners, Port of Calcutta* v *General Trading Corporation* AIR 1964 Cal 290.
3 AIR 1954 Cal 59; 57 CWN 167.
4 40 CWN 1349.
5 40 CWN 161; AIR 1936 Cal 349.
6 AIR 1964 Cal 290.

the important case laws on the subject laid down the following propositions:

(*i*) (*a*) Where the action is founded on contract, the right to maintain an action on the contract belongs to the person who entered into the contract.

(*b*) Where, however, the consignor acts as an agent of the consignee and the contract is actually entered into on behalf of the consignee, the consignee may sue in his own name.

(*c*) Thus, if the property in the goods passed to the consignee at the time of the delivery of the goods to the railway (as indeed it often can happen under s. 23 of the Indian Sale of Goods Act 1930), the consignee would be deemed to be the person who had entered into the contract of carriage with the property in the goods had passed to the consignee. In such a case, the consignee is the proper party to sue.

(*d*) It would be open nonetheless to the consignor to make a special contract with the railway company whereby the railway company would, even though the property in the goods had passed to the consignee at the time of the consignment, remain liable to the consignor.

(*ii*) Subsequent dealings with the railway receipt after the goods have been consigned would have no effect on the incidents of contract as between the consignor and the railway company. They would have a bearing on the right and liabilities of the consignor and the consignee *inter se*.

(*iii*) (*a*) The owner of the goods, however, is entitled as such to sue for the loss or non-delivery of or injury to the goods.

(*b*) Ordinarily the consignee is presumed to be the owner of the goods. Such presumption is, however, rebuttable. (Accepted in AIR 1960 SC 395).

(*c*) Where the consignor has parted with his title to and ownership of the goods, the consignor cannot maintain an action against the carrier on the basis of such ownership.

(*d*) Where, however, the property has not passed out of the consignor, the consignor must sue in his own name as, for instance, in the case of goods sent for sale on approval (at page 303 of the Report).

These principles are valid as much in India as they are in England and that "in most of the Indian cases on the subject, however, we find that the question of the rights of the consignor or the consignee to maintain an action against the railways for non-delivery or loss of goods is mixed up with the question of the rights of an endorsee to maintain such an action."

In *Bhai Mehar Singh Kishan Singh* v *Union of India*,[7] JAIN, J. observed (at page 195): "In a decision of this court reported in *Union of India* v *B. Prahlad & Co.*[8] AWADH BEHARI, J. had, after careful consideration of the Supreme Court decision[9] and several other cases, laid down that a consignee can, if he is a commission agent, institute a suit for compensation against the railways if he is able to show that the goods represented by the railway receipt had been transferred to him or sufficient interest therein had been created on his favour. That is, if I may say so, because, to borrow VISCOUNT SIMON, LC. in Luxor[10] "contract with commission agents do not follow a single pattern and the primary necessity in each instance is to ascertain with precision what are the express terms of the particular contract under discussion". There is, however, a contrary decision of this court delivered by ANAND, J. on 8th April 1976, and reported in *Union of India* v *Jashan Mal & Co.*[11] The Learned Judge appears to have taken a view that a commission agent had no right or property in the goods which may justify an action for damages against the railways, because what he has is a bare right to receive the goods and sell them on behalf of the principal. MISHRA, J. in *Union of India* v *Gopal Dass Ramesh Chand*[12] noticed both the decisions and observed that there is no real conflict between the two decisions as the question in each case was answered on the facts and circumstances disclosed. He held that a commission agent is not by nature an employee or agent and it is consistent with its position to deal with the goods as principal to principal and acquire the property in the goods as well as realise the commission ... I find it easy to state that in case of loss or damage to the goods, the person who suffers the loss will have a cause of action to sue. Therefore, the general rule is that the owner of the goods is the proper person to sue for damage. *Vide* Halsbury's *Laws of England*, Hailsham Ed., vol. 5, para 452. This proposition is supported by s. 74 of the Indian Railways Act, relating to owner's risk rate, ss. 76 and 76E thereof placing the burden on the owner to prove the damage in case of delay or detention or in case of carriage over foreign railways ...... It is a matter of evidence as to who is the owner of the goods where they are in transit".

7 AIR 1979 Del 158; 1979 Rajdhani LR 145.
8 AIR 1976 Del 236; ILR (1976)1 Del 436.
9 *Union of India* v *West Punjab Factories* AIR 1966 SC 395; (1966)1 SCR 580.
10 *Eostborne Ltd.* v *Cooper* [1941] AC 108.
11 AIR 1976 Del 335; 1976 Rajdhani LR 298.
12 ILR (1976)2 Del 508.

In *Union of India* v *West Punjab Factories*[13] the Supreme Court of India observed as follows: "Ordinarily, it is the consignor who can sue if there is damage to the consignment, for the contract of carriage is between the consignor and the railway administration. Where the property in the goods carried has passed from the consignor to someone else, that other person may be able to sue. Whether in such a case the consignor can also sue does not arise on the facts in the present case and as to that we say nothing. The argument on behalf of the appellant is that the railway receipt is a document of title to goods [*see* s. 2(4) of the Indian Sale of Goods Act, No. 3 of 1930], and as such it is the consignee who has title to the goods where the consignor and the consignee are different. It is true that a railway receipt is a document of title to goods covered by it, but from that alone it does not follow, where the consignor and the consignee are different, that the consignee is necessarily the owner of the goods and the consignor in such circumstances can never be the owner of the goods. The mere fact that the consignee is different from the consignor does not necessarily pass title to the goods from the consignor to the consignee, and the question whether title to the goods has passed to the consignee will have to be decided on other evidence. It is quite possible for the consignor to retain title in the goods himself while the consignment is booked in the name of another person. Take a simple case where a consignment is booked by the owner and the consignee is the owner's servant, the intention being that the servant will take delivery at the place of destination. It cannot therefore, be accepted simply because a consignee in a railway receipt is different from the consignor that the consignee must be held to be the owner of the goods and he alone can sue and not the consignor. As we have said already, ordinarily, the consignor is the person who has contracted with the railway for the carriage of goods and he can sue; and it is only where title to the goods has passed that the consignee may be able to sue. Whether title to goods has passed from the consignor to the consignee will depend upon the facts of each case" (at pp. 396, 398-99).

In *Union of India* v *West Punjab Factories Ltd.*[14] the Supreme Court analysed the provisions of the Contract Act 1872 and the Indian Sale of Goods Act 1930 and took the view that the owner had absolute right of pledge and the pledgee had sufficient interest in goods and can sue the carrier for non-delivery of the goods. The Supreme Court gave railway receipt a symbol of goods itself. Relying on this Supreme Court case, a Delhi case *Lal Chand Madhab Das* v *Union of India*[15] held that if pledgee can be held entitled to sue the railway, consignee for consideration certainly can sue for damages.

13 AIR 1966 SC 395; (1966)1 SCR 580; (1966)1 SCJ 350.
14 AIR 1966 SC 395; (1966)1 SCR 580.
15 AIR 1986 Del 29; (1985)9 Del Rep J 317.

7 Luggage deposited in cloak-room—liability of railway as warehouseman The question whether the railway company receiving passenger's luggage in the cloak-room becomes responsible to the owner of the luggage deposited as a carrier or as a warehouseman only was discussed in the case of *H.K. Ray* v *Governor-General of India in Council representing the E.I. Railway*,[16] where it was held that railway is otherwise a carrier and is so in relation to the owner of the luggage does not make it a carrier as the luggage left in a cloak-room, either in fact or in the contemplation of Art. 30 of the Limitation Act 1963. The luggage which a passenger brings to a cloak-room for deposit is, at that time, luggage under his personal control and although the party which provides the convenience of a temporary custody is his carrier, it is not so in relation to the transaction of the deposit. The contract is not a contract of carriage and a passenger who deposits his luggage in the cloak-room of an intermediate station, cannot ask for its delivery to him when he reaches the end of his journey. Article 30, of the Limitation Act 1963 again speaks of a suit against a carrier for losing or injuring goods and clearly contemplates a case where the person sued has lost or injured the goods as and in the capacity of a carrier. It does not cover a person, following the profession of a carrier, who accepted certain goods from a passenger for mere custody at a particular place and lost or injured them, not in carrying out a contract of carriage, but through negligence in the discharge of his duties as a custodian. It hardly needs be pointed out that a person, holding a certain professional capacity, cannot be regarded as bearing that capacity in all his dealings. If a railway sells food and refreshments to its passengers in a dining-car, it cannot be said that it does so as a carrier, except perhaps when provision of meals is part of the contract of carriage.

8 Short certificate—endorsement "without prejudice"—effect The certificate issued by the railways to the consignee during delivery stating that it is without prejudice means only this that it is without prejudice to railways liability. If the liability is once established, the court is not precluded from looking into the certificate as evidence of measure of damages for the damage caused to the goods by the negligence of the railways.[17]

101. Responsibility as a carrier of animals. A railway administration shall not be responsible for any loss or destruction of, or injuries to, any animal carried by railway arising from freight or restiveness of the animal or from overloading of wagons by the consignor.

1 Corresponding provision in the old Act This section corresponds to s. 77A of the old Act.

16 AIR 1949 Cal 591.

17 *Union of India* v *B. Prahlad & Co.* AIR 1976 Del 236; (1976)12 R 1 Del 436; 1976 Rajdhani LR 278.

2 Scope The railway administration has no responsibility as a carrier of animals for any loss or destruction of or injuries to any such animal which may arise from fright or restiveness of the animal or from overloading of wagon by the consignor.

3 Value of animals Risk Note Form E is used when animals of the kind specified in s. 73 of the Indian Railways Act 1890 (corresponds to s. 93 of the Railways Act 1989) are booked. The person on whose behalf this Risk Note is executed is bound by his declaration of value made herein in respect of the animals booked. The omission to declare the value has the effect that the railway company cannot be held responsible for the value higher than at rates specified in s. 73 of the old Act.[18] The word "value" has been interpreted to mean intrinsic value at the time the thing is delivered.[19] It does not mean market value.[20]

102. Exoneration from liability in certain cases. Notwithstanding anything contained in the foregoing provisions of this Chapter, a railway administration shall not be responsible for the loss, destruction, damage, deterioration or non-delivery of any consignment,—

(*a*) when such loss, destruction, damage, deterioration or non-delivery is due to the fact that a materially false description of the consignment is given in the statement delivered under sub-section (1) of section 66; or

(*b*) where a fraud has been practised by the consignor or the consignee or the endorsee or by an agent of the consignor, consignee or the endorsee; or

(*c*) where it is proved by the railway administration to have been caused by, or to have arisen from—

(*i*) improper loading or unloading by the consignor or the consignee or the endorsee or by an agent of the consignor, consignee or the endorsee;

(*ii*) riot, civil commotion, strike, lock-out, stoppage or restraint of labour from whatever cause arising whether partial or general; or

(*d*) for any indirect or consequential loss or damage or for loss of particular market.

1 Corresponding provisions in the old Act This section corresponds to s. 78 of the old Act.

2 Applicability of the section Two conditions are necessary before the railway administration can be protected from loss. In the first place, the description must be found to be materially false and to have been delivered under

18 *M.J. Arraton* v *E.I. Railway Co.* AIR 1917 All 172.
19 *Storessiger* v *S.E. Railway Co.* [1854]3 E&B 149.
20 *G.I.P. Railway* v *Ramchandra* 43 Bom 386; 21 Bom LR 6.

sub-sec. (1) of s. 66 of the 1989 Act. This section imposes no obligation on a consignor of goods to deliver an account containing a description of every article in the box. All that the section contemplates is a description of such general nature as may be sufficient to determine the correct freight chargeable. When he has himself valued the contents of a box, he cannot claim from the railway anything in excess of that valuation on the ground that the box really contained things of greater value.[21] The provisions of s. 78 of the (old) Act could apply where the declaration given for the purposes of s. 58 of the (old) Act (corresponding to s. 66 of the new Act) was false, in so far as it represented the value of the consignment and in so far as it represented the basis of the calculation of percentage payable by way of compensation for increased risk.[22] It relieves the railway from responsibility for loss, etc., where fraud has been practised on the railway or where such loss, etc., have arisen from improper loading or unloading or from riot, civil commotion, strike etc. The railway should not also be held responsible for loss of particular market. The railway is also relieved of the liability for indirect or consequential damages which means remote damages. *See* s. 73 of the Indian Contract Act 1872.

3 Non-delivery due to wrong mention of destination station in forwarding note Section 97 operates *inter alia,* when animals or goods despatched at owner's risk rate is not delivered at the destination. It may so happen that by slip of pen a wrong name as the destination station has been referred to in the forwarding note. It may be a patent error e.g. when no such station exists on the Indian Railways. In that event it is unlikely that railway authority would accept the consignment for booking. At any rate then s. 102 can be invoked and the railways stand absolved from all liability. In a case the plaintiff misdescribed the destination of the goods sent by railways as "BHAINSA" instead of "BHAISA O/A". "BHAINSA" is a station on the North Eastern Railway, while "BHAISA O/A" is in Nizamabad of AP. The goods having not reached either BHAISA O/A or BHAINSA the plaintiff who booked it owner's risk sued the railway for damages. The claim was allowed in appeal. Thus, unless the goods reached "BHAINSA" (wrongly named station), the question to redirect the goods does not come in. The defendant railway failed to allege and prove that the goods even crossed its zone or jurisdiction. So, the railway authority cannot disown their liability for the goods they carried and they are liable to make good the loss suffered by the plaintiff.[1]

4 Damages caused to consignment Railway receipt depicts that goods were loaded by consignor directly from truck to wagon. Wagon was chosen by him. Loading was also done in absence of railway officials. There had

21 *Chunilal* v *Governor-General in Council* AIR 1949 Mad 754; (1949)1 MLJ 538.
22 *Sorabji* v *B.N. Railway Co.* AIR 1936 Pat 393; 15 Pat 394.
1 *E.I.D. Parry (India) Ltd.* v *South Central Railway* (1977)2 Andh WR 227.

been no shortage of consignment as clear from inspection note. There could be no claim on account of short delivery. There was no proof that goods were fit for human consumption at the loading point. Thus, it cannot be concluded that damage was caused in transit.[2]

103. Extent of monetary liability in respect of any consignment. (1) Where any consignment is entrusted to a railway administration for carriage by railway and the value of such consignment has not been declared as required under sub-section (2) by the consignor, the amount of liability of the railway administration for the loss, destruction, damage, deterioration or non-delivery of the consignment shall in no case exceed such amount calculated with reference to the weight of the consignment as may be prescribed, and where such consignment consists of an animal, the liability shall not exceed such amount as may be prescribed.

(2) Notwithstanding anything contained in sub-section (1), where the consignor declares the value of any consignment at the time of its entrustment to a railway administration for carriage by railway, and pays such percentage charge as may be prescribed on so much of the value of such consignment as is in excess of the liability of the railway administration as calculated or specified, as the case may be, under sub-section (1), the liability of the railway administration for the loss, destruction, damage, deterioration or non-delivery of such consignment shall not exceed the value so declared.

(3) The Central Government may, from time to time, by notification, direct that such goods as may be specified in the notification shall not be accepted for carriage by railway unless the value of such goods is declared and percentage charge is paid as required under sub-section (2).

1 Extent of monetary liability for loss of goods There was a claim for compensation and damages for loss of goods in a consignment. Party sought to file documents such as letters issued by the Government of India and other authorities. Matter requires to be redetermined by permitting parties to produce evidence and prove the documents. The High Court remitted the matter to the trial court.[3]

2 Monetary liability of railway Luggages were handed over to railway for safe custody as there was no space to keep cartons inside passenger compartment. Railway is legally liable for missing of the cartons and to pay compensation for such loss. Cartons containing valuable goods were taken by the railway staff. Railway cannot avoid to pay the full compensation.[4]

104. Extent of liability in respect of goods carried in open wagon. Where any goods, which, under ordinary circumstances, would be carried in covered wagon

2 *Suresh Kumar Agarwal* v *Union of India* AIR 2010 Cal 90.
3 *Union of India* v *Dharmaraju Patro* 1998 AIHC 2944 (Ori).
4 *Dr. Guru Prasad Chhoteray* v *Union of India* AIR 2009 NOC 249 (Ori).

and would be liable to damage, if carried otherwise, are with the consent of the consignor, recorded in the forwarding note, carried in open wagon, the responsibility of railway administration for destruction, damage or deterioration which may arise only by reason of the goods being so carried, shall be one-half of the amount of liability for such destruction, damage or deterioration determined under this Chapter.

1 Corresponding provision in the old Act This section corresponds to s. 75A of the old Act.

2 Liability of the railway for carriage of goods in open vehicles Under Risk Note C, the railway did not enjoy any absolute immunity from liability when goods were carried in open vehicles at the request of the sender. The exemption from liability must relate to damage which arose from the goods being carried in an open truck. The Risk Note C exempted the railway from loss caused by its servants' negligence or misconduct but to a limited extent, namely, loss which may arise by reason of the consignment being carried in the open wagon.[5] The exemption granted to the railway administration from any liability for the destruction, deterioration and damage to goods when Risk Note C is executed is absolute and no question relating to the misconduct of the railway employees can at all be relevant in such a case.[6]

This section however does not grant immunity to the railway in case of loss of the goods.[7] Section 75A of the old Act (corresponding to s. 104 of the new Act) is attracted when the goods under the ordinary circumstances should be carried in covered vehicle or vessels for their being liable to damage if carried in open vehicle or vessels. The goods were sent by the railway, on covered wagon not being available, in open wagon covered by tarpaulin. The railways had offered to send it as such covered by tarpaulin and the consignor agreed. It is not a case of plaintiff's agreeing to despatching of the goods in open vehicle. And if by reason of defect in tarpaulin water percolates inside the goods and cause damage to it, the railway is not absolved from the liability.[8]

105. Right of railway administration to check contents of certain consignment or luggage. **Where the value has been declared under s. 103 in respect of any consignment a railway administration may make it a condition of carrying such consignment that a railway servant authorised by it in this behalf has been satisfied by examination or otherwise that the consignment tendered for carriage contain the articles declared.**

5 *Ralliaram* v *Governor-General in Council* AIR 1946 Cal 249; ILR (1944)2 Cal 487; 48 CWN 554.

6 *North Eastern Railway* v *Ram Lal* AIR 1960 Pat 489.

7 *Jiwanji Esmailjee* v *Union of India* ILR (1959) Bom 819; 61 Bom LR 682.

8 *Sadi Ram* v *Union of India* AIR 1982 All 246; 1982 All CJ 218; 1982 ACJ 442.

Right of railway administration to check or reweigh the consignment or luggage Section 105 empowers the railway administration to check contents of consignment or luggage through an authorised servant if there is any doubt as to the value declared under s. 103 of the Act. But when goods are weighed in route by the railway without any information to the consignor/consignee, this is not justified. The consignor/consignee can claim reweightment of goods at the station of destination in case of doubt of reweightment. Moreso, when railway administration has levied penalty on the basis of reweightment in route the right of consignor/consignee cannot be ignored.[9]

106. Notice of claim for compensation and refund of overcharge. (1) A person shall not be entitled to claim compensation against a railway administration for the loss, destruction, damage, deterioration or non-delivery of goods carried by railway, unless a notice thereof is served by him or on his behalf—

(*a*) to the railway administration to which the goods are entrusted for carriage; or

(*b*) to the railway administration on whose railway the destination station lies, or the loss, destruction, damage or deterioration occurs,

within a period of six months from the date of entrustment of the goods.

(2) Any information demanded or enquiry made in writing from, or any complaint made in writing to, any of the railway administrations mentioned in sub-section (1) by or on behalf of the person within the said period of six months regarding the non-delivery or delayed delivery of the goods with particulars sufficient to identify the goods shall, for the purpose of this section, be deemed to be a notice of claim for compensation.

(3) A person shall not be entitled to a refund of an overcharge in respect of goods carried by railway unless a notice therefor has been served by him or on his behalf to the railway administration to which the overcharge has been paid within six months from the date of such payment or the date of delivery of such goods at the destination station, whichever is later.

1 Corresponding provision in the old Act This section corresponds to s. 78B of the old Act.

2 Scope Section 106 of the Act provides a precondition that no claim for compensation and refund of overchange can be made against a railway administration without serving a notice in writing by the claimant within six months from the date of entrustment of the goods.

3 Notice of claim under s. 78B of the old Act Section 78B of the Indian Railways Act 1890 (corresponds to s. 106 of Railways Act 1989) contemplate a notice of claim in writing to be served. The effect of s. 78B and s. 140

9 *Salf Marketing Centre, Gwahati* v *Union of India* AIR 1996 Gau 36.

(both of the Act of 1890) is to bar plaintiff's claim unless he can show that he has complied with the requirements of law as regards notice of claim.[10]

The object of service of notice is obviously to enable the railway administration to make an enquiry and investigate as to whether the loss, destruction or deterioration or non-delivery was due to the plaintiff's laches or due to willful neglect of the company or its servants or due to the theft or robbery committed by the servants of the company.

The notice must satisfy the requirements of s. 78B of the Railways Act 1890. A mere letter by a consignee to the railway company stating that the goods had not arrived and asking that enquiries might be made cannot be regarded as a notice satisfying the requirements of s. 77 which was supplemented by old s. 78B when no claim for compensation was made in that letter.[11] But a letter stating that a part of a consignment had not reached the destination and requesting the General Manager to make a search for the goods is a sufficient notice.[12]

Under the proviso to present s. 78B of the (old) Act an enquiry made or information demanded or a complaint made in writing should be deemed to be a notice. If there is an admission by the railway company of the loss of goods, then the admission dispenses with the enquiry into the validity or invalidity of the notice of claim made by the plaintiff, since s. 77 is only intended to give an opportunity to the railway company to make satisfactory investigation.[13]

This proviso was pressed into service where a claim was addressed to Divisional Traffic Superintendent. It was however forwarded to the Commercial Superintendent who acted upon it. He deputed an officer to assess the damage. This claim letter was held to be sufficient compliance with old s. 78B, Railways Act.[14] The Karnataka case[15] is a case indeed under the old s. 77, Railways Act, but there too a letter demanding open delivery of the goods followed by inspection jointly made by Insurance Co., the plaintiff and railway followed by a report etc. were held to be a sufficient compliance with s. 77 (old) of the Railways Act. There a transformer reached the destination station severely damaged, the damage being externally visible. A letter of demand for open delivery was sent to all concerned including the Chief Commercial Supdt. with

10 *Mahadeva* v *S.I. Railway Co.* 45 Mad 135.

11 *Salem Dayalbagh Stores Ltd.* v *Governor-General in Council* AIR 1947 Mad 362; (1947)1 MLJ 152.

12 *Jetmull Bhojraj* v *Darjeeling Himalayan Railway* AIR 1962 SC 1879; (1963)2 SCR 832.

13 *Govindlal* v *Governor-General in Council* AIR 1947 Nag 369.

14 *Union Northern Railway* v *Firm Anis Khan* AIR 1981 All 18.

15 *State of Karnataka* v *Union of India* AIR 1982 Kant 292; (1982)2 Kant LJ 32.

a special note that the claim for damage may be accepted and that actual damages would be intimated after taking actual delivery. It was followed by a joint inspection by the representatives of plaintiff (State Government), the Railway and the Insurance Co. They gave a report that correspondence would amount to a notice under s. 77 of the (old) Railways Act.[16]

4 Short delivery and loss of goods—distinction between There is a real distinction between a suit against the railway administration based on short delivery of goods and a suit against the railway administration based on loss of the goods.[17] In *Janeshwar Lal* v *Dominion of India*,[18] HARMAN SINGH, J. in pointing out the distinction between a case of short delivery and a case of loss observed as follows: "In deciding issue the trial court seems to think that a suit for compensation for short delivery of the goods is a suit for compensation for the loss of the goods. This is not so for there is a real distinction between a suit against the railway administration based on 'short delivery of goods' and a suit against the railway administration based on 'loss of the goods'. That this is so is apparent from the fact that short delivery may be due to the loss of the goods or may be due to detention, misdelivery, conversion, or wrongful sale of goods by the railway administration. Clearly, 'loss' and 'short delivery' are not interchangeable terms. Section 72 of the (old) Act deals only with the responsibility arising from loss, destruction or deterioration of goods delivered to the administration for carriage and does not deal with the responsibility for short delivery where short delivery is not due to the loss of the goods ...... Indeed, the distinction between 'short delivery' and 'loss' receives statutory recognition in Arts. 30 and 31 of Schedule I to the Limitation Act 1963. Article 30 provides that limitation for a suit starts from when the loss or injury occurs, while Art. 31 provides limitation *inter alia* for a suit against a carrier for compensation for non-delivery starting from the date when the goods are to be delivered. Article 31 was added in the Limitation Act in the year 1877 but notwithstanding the addition of Art. 31 to the Limitation Act in 1890, it was not considered necessary to add the words "non-delivery, misdelivery or detention to ss. 72 and 77 of the (old) Act".

5 Old ss. 77 and 140—object of notice Section 77 of the (old) Indian Railways Act 1890, is obviously a limitation section, while s. 140 of the (old) Act is merely an enabling section. The object of the notice on the manager is simply to give an opportunity to the railway administration to inquire immediately into the complaint. Section 77 of the (old) Act deals with the

16 *State of Karnataka* v *Union of India* (supra).

17 This is also true in respect of an application for claim before Railway Claims Tribunal.

18 AIR 1951 Punj 383.

conditions under, or cases in, which refund or compensation may be claimed from the railway; s. 140 of the old Act lays down the provisions as to the railway officer to whom the claim should be preferred and also the manner of serving the notice upon such railway officer. In enacting s. 77 of the (old) Act the intention of the legislature must have been to afford only a protection to the railway administration against fraud and not to provide a means for depriving the consignors of their legitimate claim for compensation. A notice should therefore be liberally construed.[19]

If the plaintiff wants to succeed, notice under this section must be served in accordance with s. 140 of the old Act. If he does not serve the notice his claim will fail in a court of law.[20]

6 Notice on which railway In view of s. 78B of the (old) Act when delivery of goods is made to one railway for transshipment and the goods are transshipped through the line of that railway and another, and while in transit through the latter the goods are lost, it is open to the owner to sue either of the railways for damages. But under s. 77 of the (old) Act, it was not enough if the notice of claim is given to that railway to which goods were delivered and such notice must be given within the prescribed time to the railway whom the plaintiff wishes to hold liable. It was incumbent on the plaintiff to serve notice on all the railways.[1]

Under (old) s. 77, the position was that notice was to be served on all the railways over which the goods were carried and notice to one railway administration could not avail a party for the claim against another railway company. A new proviso to s. 78B has been added under which an inquiry made, or an information demanded or a complaint made in writing should be deemed to be a notice. The proviso has done away with the strictness of the formality in order that just claims are not defeated on the ground of technicality.

In a case the destination station situated on S.S. Light Railway. Notice on that railway alone was held a sufficient compliance with s. 78B of the old Act. It was held the General Managers of the Railways where the consignment was booked or the consignment travelled, need not be served with notice. Requirement of service of notice does not form a part of a contract between the railway on one hand and consignor or consignee of the goods.[2]

7 Notice by whom to be given Under the old s. 77 as also s. 78B read with s. 140 of the (old) Act, it is not absolutely necessary that a person who puts

19 *Jetmull* v *Darjeeling Himalayan Railway* AIR 1962 SC 1879; 1963 SCD 509; (1963)2 SCR 832; (1963)1 SCJ 505.

20 *Surendra Nath* v *Governor-General in Council* AIR 1952 Cal 340.

1 *Jetmull Bhojraj* v *D.H. Railway* AIR 1962 SC 1879 (1885); (1963)2 SCR 832; *State of WB* v *Union of India* (1986)2 CHN 75 (79).

2 *Ram Prakash Gupta* v *Union of India* AIR 1977 All 482; (1977)3 All LR 435.

forward a claim against the railway should himself give notice to the Manager or Agent of the railway; but if he elects to take the risk of giving the notice to any person other than the Manager or the Agent, it is necessary for him to show that the notice was delivered on his behalf to the proper person, that is to say, to the Manager or the Agent, as the case may be, within six months.[3]

Notice can be sent by the plaintiff himself or by some one on his behalf. Then the mere omission to state that the notice is being issued on behalf of the plaintiff is not material.[4]

8 Notice—contents of Section 78B of the old Act merely requires that a demand for compensation must be made and does not enact that the money value of the claim must be stated in the notice of demand.[5]

9 Defects in the notice Failure to state correctly the name of the railway station from where the consignment was booked is a fatal defect.[6] But mention of a wrong place of destination, where all other particulars were correctly given, does not invalidate the notice.[7]

10 Notice if necessary in case of short delivery or non-delivery There was a conflict of decisions on the point as to whether in case of non-delivery of goods notice under (old) s. 77 of the Indian Railways Act 1890, is necessary. Because of the later decisions of the Supreme Court holding that a notice is necessary in cases of short delivery or non-delivery the controversy has been set at rest. In case of non-delivery the cause of action is the same as in loss and notice under s. 78B (then s. 77) was mandatory.[8] Section 78B of the (old) Act has inserted the word non-delivery. So, there is no speck of doubt that in case of non-delivery too, notice under s. 78B of the old Act (corresponding to s. 106 of the new Act) is mandatory.[9] The service of notice is a *sine qua non* for instituting a suit against a carrier.[10] However, the older conflicting decisions are summarised below:

In *Mutsaddilal* v *Governor-General in Council*,[11] it has been held that where non-delivery is due to "loss, destruction or deterioration" of

3 *Firm of Birdi Chand* v *Secretary of State and B.B. & C.I. Railway* AIR 1925 Sind 62; 78 IC 735.
4 *Union of India* v *Punjab State Co-operative Supply* AIR 1984 Punj 41.
5 *Firm of Sheonath Joinarain* v *G.I.P. Railway Co.* AIR 1926 Nag 405.
6 *Union of India* v *Nageshwar Prasad* AIR 1964 Pat 373; *Chaturbhai Bhailabhai* v *Union of India* AIR 1961 Pat 334; 1961 Pat LR 26.
7 *Bisanchand Lalchand* v *Union of India* AIR 1961 MP 220.
8 *Union of India* v *Mahadeolal* AIR 1965 SC 1755; 1966 All LJ 74; 1966 BLJR 91; (1965)3 SCR 145.
9 *Bhola Ram and Sons* v *Union of India* 1977 All WC 106.
10 *The Jullundur Ex-Servicemen Motor Transport Co-operative Society Ltd.* v *The General Assurnace Society Ltd.* (1978)80 Punj LR 415.
11 AIR 1952 All 897.

the goods, then a notice under s. 77 of the Indian Railways Act 1890 is required, but where non-delivery is due to any other cause, e.g. conversion, detention, misconduct, misdelivery, wrongful delivery, capricious acts, etc., then a notice under s. 77 is not necessary. A similar view was taken in *Governor-General in Council* v *Mahabir Ram*[12] and also in *Ram Narain* v *Dominion of India*.[13] The High Court in *Haridas Banmalidass* v *M. & S.M. Railway*,[14] took a similar view. LORD WILLIAM, J. of Calcutta High Court in the case of *Shamsul Huq* v *Secretary of State*,[15] held on the same line that "section 77 refers only to loss, destruction or deterioration of goods and it has nothing whatsoever to do either with detention or conversion" and PAGE, J. of Calcutta High Court in *E.I. Railway* v *Jogpat Singh*[16] held that non-delivery of goods may be due to loss or various other causes and because the goods have not been delivered it cannot be said that they have been lost. See also *Gobinda Chandra* v *Union of India*,[17] *Makhanlal Harnarain* v *Union of India*.[18]

But a contrary view was taken in some cases. DESAI, J. in *Martab Ali* v *Union of India*,[19] held that the word 'loss' in s. 77 of the 1890 Act is applicable to the case of non-delivery as well as to cases of negligence and wrongful detention or conversion on the part of the railway administration. Again, where the plaintiff's case in the plaint is that the goods have been lost due to the negligence on the part of the servants of the defendant company, the case must be treated as one of loss even though the plaintiff may have framed the suit as for non-delivery.[20]

The controversy has been resolved by the decision of the Supreme Court in *Governor-General in Council* v *Musaddilal*.[1] Notice under s. 77 (of 1890 Act) is necessary in case of non-delivery or short delivery whether it is due to "loss, destruction or deterioration" or it is due to negligence or even wrongful act of the railway administration. The Supreme Court observed: "Section 77 is enacted with a view to enable the railway administration to make enquiries and, if possible, to recover the goods and

12 AIR 1952 All 891; ILR (1953)1 All 64.
13 AIR 1953 All 460.
14 41 Mad 871.
15 AIR 1930 Cal 312.
16 AIR 1924 Cal 725; 28 CWN 1001; 51 Cal 615.
17 AIR 1960 Cal 571.
18 AIR 1960 Pat 150.
19 AIR 1954 Bom 297; 56 Bom LR 150.
20 *Dominion of India* v *Hazarilal* AIR 1949 Pat 410 (FB).
1 AIR 1961 SC 725; (1961)3 SCR 647; (1961)1 SCJ 597.

to deliver them to the consignee and to prevent stale claims. It imposes a restriction on the enforcement of liability declared by s. 72. The liability declared by s. 72 is for loss, destruction or deterioration. Failure to deliver is the consequence of loss or destruction of goods; it does not furnish a cause of action on which a suit may lie against the railway administration distinct from a cause of action for loss or destruction. By the use of the expression 'loss, destruction or deterioration', what is contemplated is loss or destruction or deterioration of the goods and the consequent loss to the owner thereof. If because of negligence or inadvertence or even wrongful act on the part of the employees of the railway administration goods entrusted for carriage are lost, destroyed or deteriorated, the railway administration is guilty of failing to take the degree of care which is prescribed by s. 72 of the Railways Act.

"But because the Indian Limitation Act 1963, provides different points of time from which the period of limitation is to run, it is not possible to infer that the claim covered by either article is not for compensation for loss, destruction or deterioration of the goods. We are unable to project the provisions of Arts. 30 and 31 of the Limitation Act upon ss. 72 and 77 of the Railways Act 1890 and to hold that a suit for compensation for loss because of non-delivery of goods does not fall within s. 77. The view expressed to the contrary in the Allahabad High Court in *Governor-General in Council* v *Mahabir Ram*,[2] and by the Patna High Court in *Jais Ram Ramrakha Das* v *G.I.P. Railway*[3] is in our judgment erroneous."

Thus the Supreme Court has in very clear terms wiped out any difference between cases or loss, destruction or deterioration and short delivery or non-delivery due to other causes such as negligence or even wrongful acts of the railway administration. The position has been reaffirmed by the Supreme Court in *Union of India* v *Mahadeolal Prabhu Dayal*.[4]

11 Manner of service of notice Section 77 of the 1890 Act requires service of notice in the manner laid down in s. 140 of the old Act. But the protection can be waived.[5]

12 Notice on whom Notice under s. 78B can be served upon the General Manager or the Chief Commercial Superintendent of the concerned railway (*vide* discussion under s. 140).

13 Recovery of freight twice realised—notice—if necessary Where freight in respect of goods consigned by a railway company is prepared by the consignor before they are booked, but owing to the non-receipt of the

2 AIR 1952 All 891; ILR (1953)1 All 64.
3 AIR 1929 Pat 100; ILR 8 Pat 545.
4 AIR 1965 SC 1755; (1965)3 SCR 145.
5 *S.I. Co-operative Stores* v *Union of India* 60 CWN 985.

railway receipt, the consignee is made to pay the freight at destination, the consignee being ignorant of the prepayment of freight by the consignor, a suit by the consignee for recovery of the freight paid by him by mistake is not barred by reason of failure to give a notice under s. 77 of the Indian Railways Act 1890. The amount sought to be recovered is not in the nature of an overcharge within the meaning of s. 77 of the 1890 Act, and hence no notice under that section is necessary.[6]

14 Notice as to refund of overcharge There is nothing in s. 77 or s. 140 which makes it imperative on the plaintiff to mention in the plaint that refund had been demanded from the railway administration in the manner required by law. If the fact is denied by the defendant but appears from the evidence, the plaintiff's suit is not liable to be dismissed. Where in a suit for refund of overcharge realised by the railway company, the plaint recited that a notice under s. 80, Code of Civil Procedure had been given to the Manager of the railway within six months of the delivery of the goods and more than two months before the institution of the suit, there was substantial compliance with the requirements of ss. 77 and 140 and the suit could not be dismissed on that ground.[7]

'Demurrage' and 'wharfage' charges are clearly terminal charges and though it is true that they are charges in respect of the period subsequent to the completion of the transit, all the same, they are incidental to the business of the railway administration as a carrier. These charges are, therefore, not unrelated to the business of a carrier carried on by the railway administration. The railway also makes these charges because there is delay in unloading the wagon or removing the goods from the platform. These are clearly charges in respect of the goods carried by railway as much as freight and other charges. If, therefore, there is any overcharge made by the railway administration in respect of demurrage and wharfage charges, a claim for its refund would clearly come within the scope and ambit of s. 77. It would be a claim for refund of an overcharge in respect of goods carried by railway within the meaning of s. 77 (renumbered as s. 78B) of the Indian Railways Act 1890. The plaintiffs or claimants before Claims Tribunal, therefore, is or not entitled to maintain a suit claim in the absence of a requisite notice to the railway administration under s. 77.[8]

'Overcharge' is not a term of art. It is an ordinary word of the English language which, according to its plain natural sense, means any charge in excess of that prescribed or permitted by law. To be an overcharge, a sum of money must partake of the same character as the charge itself or must

6 *Kaluram* v *B.N. Railway Co.* 13 Cut LT 60.

7 *Mela Ram* v *Secretary of State for India* AIR 1932 All 381; 1932 ALJ 405; 137 IC 205.

8 *Shah Raichand Amulakh* v *Union of India* 12 Guj LR 93.

be of the same genus or class as a charge: it cannot be any other kind of money such as money recovered where nothing is due. Overcharge is simply a charge in excess of that which is due according to law.[9]

Where the plaintiff claims that the railway administration had collected certain charges illegally, arbitrarily and unreasonably, they cannot be termed 'overcharge' so as to attract the provisions of s. 78B of the Act.[10]

15 Claim for refund of overcharges Goods were booked for carriage by longer route and freight was also charged for longer route only. But in fact goods were carried by shorter route. The claim was for refund of money and not for refund of overcharges. Thus no statutory notice is necessary.[11]

16 Railway claim—need of notice under s. 80, Code of Civil Procedure Notice under s. 80, Code of Civil Procedure is mandatory unless leave under s. 80(2) is given by the court for any suit against the Government. Section 80(1)(*b*), Code of Civil Procedure reads that notice in respect of a railway claim is to be served on the General Manager of the concerned railway. But the word "suit" in s. 80 is very material. In making a claim against the Union of India in respect of compensation for loss, destruction to goods or animals or for recovery of excess fare or freight paid, in view of s. 16, Railways Claims Tribunal Act an application is to be made. Such an application cannot be equated to plaint and proceeding a suit because in s. 78A of the old Railways Act the Legislature very consciously substituted the word "suit" by the words "application before the Claims Tribunal". Further, in view of s. 18, the Claims Tribunal is not bound to follow the procedure laid down in the Code of Civil Procedure. In this perspective it seems that application for railway claim before the Claims Tribunal need not be preceded by a notice under s. 80, Code of Civil Procedure.

But the position of law earlier was different and that position of law must prevail till the declaration of appointed date by the Central Government for enforcement of the Railway Claims Tribunal Act. A suit for any claim against railway being essentially a suit against the Union Government, notice under s. 80 was mandatory. In suits against State-owned railways, a previous notice of suit was required to be given to the General Manager of the railway concerned containing the particulars specified in s. 80 of the Code of Civil Procedure. A notice under s. 77, the Indian Railways Act 1890, did not dispense with the necessity of a notice under s. 80, Code of Civil Procedure.[12]

17 Combined notice under s. 77, the Railways Act 1890 and s. 80, Code of Civil Procedure In the case of a State railway, it is open to a party to give

9 *Shah Raichand Amulakh* v *Union of India* 12 Guj LR 93.

10 *Union of India* v *Mansukhlal Jethalal* AIR 1975 Guj 116.

11 *Union of India* v *Steel Authority* AIR 1997 Ori 77.

12 *Shaik Elahi* v *E.I. Railway* AIR 1931 Pat 326; 10 Pat 466; *Secretary of State* v *Fazaluddin* AIR 1933 All 53; *N.W. Railway* v *Dwarkaram* AIR 1931 Pat 393; *Vellayyaram Chettiar* v *Government of the Province of Madras* AIR 1947 PC 197.

a combined notice which would satisfy all the requirements of s. 77, the Indian Railways Act 1890 and s. 80, Code of Civil Procedure 1908. But if a party does not do that, he must give a notice under s. 77 within six months in order to enable him to claim compensation for loss of goods and he must also give a notice under s. 80, Code of Civil Procedure, in order to enable him to file a suit against the Central Government.[13] One composite notice under this section and s. 80, Code of Civil Procedure 1908, to a General Manager of one of the Government railways over which through traffic passed will be sufficient.[14]

In *Dharamsi Liladhar Vora* v *Union of India*,[15] ROXBURGH, J. observed as follows: "The only question then that remains is whether it is essential that notices under s. 77 of the Railways Act 1890 and s. 80 of the Code of Civil Procedure 1908, must be written on separate pieces of paper, and must be specially labelled with their descriptions. I do not think that this is essential. The Full Bench (referring to the Full Bench of the Calcutta Court of Small Causes) has disposed of the argument by saying that the purposes of the two sections are quite different. The main difference between the two sections, of course, is that, under s. 77 of the Indian Railways Act 1890 the party is barred from ever becoming able to recover the claim unless notice is given to the railway within a certain period of the occurrence in connection with which the claim is made, whereas the service of notice under s. 80 fixes a period of two months within which no suit on the claim mentioned in the notice can be brought. If the notice given is within the limits of time taken from either end it may well comply therefore in this respect with the purposes both of s. 77 of the Railways Act and s. 80 of the Code of Civil Procedure. The notice under s. 80 must, of course, be a notice indicating that a suit will be brought. The cause of action is to be stated. It may be, in some cases, that a notice under s. 77 could not, by any reading of its contents, be said to comply with the requirements of s. 80 ...... That one paper may serve the purpose of both the sections in certain circumstances has been held in the case of *Radha Shyam Basak* v *Secretary of State for India*,[16] though in that case it was held that the notice served as a notice under s. 80 could be treated as a notice under s. 77 of the Railways Act 1890.

As a result of the amendment to s. 80 of the Code of Civil Procedure, it so happens that notices under each of the sections are required to be served on or delivered to, in the case of claims in respect of loss on a State railway, the same person, namely, the General Manager of the railway. Hence, if the contents of the paper giving notice fulfil the requirements of both sections as is the case here, and are correctly delivered, I consider that due notice has been given thereby under both the sections."

13 *G.I.P. Railway* v *Sreeramulu* AIR 1928 Mad 599.
14 *Sugandha Bhandar* v *Union of India* 68 Bom LR 877; 1966 Mah LJ 555.
15 AIR 1952 Cal 439; 55 CWN 65.
16 44 Cal 16.

A notice under s. 80 of the Code of Civil Procedure given by the consignor can be construed as a notice also under s. 77, the Indian Railways Act 1890 when it fulfils the requirements of the latter section.[17] The same view was taken in *Union of India* v *Lakshmi Narain*.[18] In *Moolji Bhai Maneklal* v *Dominion of India*,[19] HIDAYATULLAH, J. observed: "No good reason has been shown why, after the amendment, two separate notices should be sent. It is possible to give a single notice complying with the conditions of both the sections. It is possible to give a notice of claim and also of a suit. Such a combined notice will have to be given before six months and the plaintiff will have to wait for two months." A combined notice under s. 77, the Indian Railways Act 1890 and s. 80 of the Code of Civil Procedure is not bad.[20]

18 Waiver of notice The requirement of notice under s. 77 of the 1890 Act may be waived.[1] Where the Chief Commercial Superintendent in reply to the notice under s. 77 of the 1890 Act refused to entertain the claim on the ground that there was no negligence or misconduct on the part of the railway or its servants but did not dispute the validity of the notice, there has been waiver.[2] Where the railway administration contested the suit on the footing that it was a case of non-delivery and not of loss and the defence failed, the railway administration cannot claim that the suit should be dismissed for want of notice under s. 77 of the 1890 Act.[3] When a defective notice is addressed to a proper officer and when such officer instead of ignoring the defective notice enters into correspondence, makes enquires, the defect in the notice stands waived.[4]

19 Time-limit for sending notice As to whether a notice under s. 77 of the 1890 Act should reach the railway administration within six months or whether it will suffice if it is preferred or sent within six months there is no uniformity of decisions among the High Courts of India. In *Secretary of State* v *Imperial Metal Works*[5] it was held that it is not sufficient if the notice is posted within limitation. The High Court in *Ram Gopal Marwari* v *B.N.W. Railway Co.*[6] has held that it is sufficient if the notice is posted within the period of limitation. The reason for holding that it is sufficient if the notice is posted within limitation given by the learned Judge in the Patna case seems to be sound.

17 *Union of India* v *Gangaji Kalyanji* AIR 1957 MP 222.
18 AIR 1954 Pat 424.
19 AIR 1952 Nag 22.
20 *Chaturbhai Bhailabhai Patel* v *Union of India* AIR 1961 Pat 334; 1961 Pat LR 26.
1 *Radhamadhab Kundu* v *Union of India* 61 CWN 433.
2 *South Indian Co-operative Stores* v *Union of India* AIR 1957 Cal 17; 60 CWN 985.
3 *Mahadeo Lal* v *Union of India* AIR 1959 Pat 202; ILR 37 Pat 1034.
4 *State of WB* v *Union of India* (1986)2 CHN 75 (80).
5 AIR 1926 All 214.
6 AIR 1927 Pat 241.

The notice should be given six months from the date of delivery of the goods for carriage by the railway and not within six months from the date of the delivery to the consignee.[7] A time-barred notice is of no avail.[8] The words "carriage by railway" qualify the word "delivery" and not the word "goods". The period of six months should be counted from the date of consignment of the goods to the railway for carriage.[9] Section 78B of the (old) Act does not speak about the knowledge of the person. A consignor has to claim delivery within six months of the date of consignment and if delivery within six months is not given, he would be entitled to claim compensation for non-delivery of goods and will be under the obligation to give notice. He cannot wait indefinitely. The time begins to run from the date of delivery of the goods for carriage by railway and the consignor or the consignee has to give notice within six months of the date of delivery. If he does not give such a notice the claim will be time barred.[10]

In *Amarchand* v *Union of India*,[11] SARJOO PROSAD, CJ. said: "I have my own doubts as to whether this period of six months should be calculated from the date on which the goods were delivered to the consignee or to his representative or from the date on which the goods were originally consigned to the railway. The words 'for carriage by railway' may be read as qualifying the term 'goods' only, and not the date of delivery of the goods. It seems to me reasonable to hold that the period of limitation should be counted from the day when the goods were to be delivered or delivered to the consignee or his representative and not from the date when the goods were originally consigned."

The Assam case has been dissented from in *O. & T. Railway* v *Mrs. Karamchand*;[12] *Union of India* v *M. Pullappa*;[13] *Union of India* v *Shah Vastimull*[14] and *Union of India* v *K.T. Rizvi*.[15]

20 Service by post Where the notice has been posted on the last day of the period of six months and it could not have reached the addressee in the ordinary course of post on the same day, the claim must be held not to have been preferred or served within the prescribed period.[16]

7 *Union of India* v *Ramdas Amritlal Pali* ILR (1964)14 Raj 254.
8 *Tashil Co-operative Agricultural Association Ltd.* v *Union of India* AIR 1968 MP 185; 1968 Jab LJ 855.
9 *Union of India* v *Lakshmi Textiles* AIR 1968 Ker 23; ILR (1966)2 Ker 662; 1967 Ker LJ 76; 1967 Ker LT 111; *Union of India* v *K.T. Rizvi* AIR 1985 Bom 84; 1984 Mah LJ 1011; (1985)1 Civ LJ 312.
10 *Bhola Ram* v *Union of India* 1977 All WC 106.
11 AIR 1955 Assam 221.
12 AIR 1955 All 234.
13 AIR 1958 AP 475.
14 AIR 1959 Mys 13; ILR (1958) Mys 481.
15 AIR 1985 Bom 84; 1984 Mah LJ 1011; (1985)1 Civ LJ 312.
16 *Union of India* v *Lakshmi Textiles* AIR 1968 Ker 23; ILR (1966)2 Ker 662; 1976 Ker LJ 76; 1967 Ker LT 111.

Claim to refund or compensation has not only to be posted within six months but must also reach the hands of the railway administration within the said period of six months. Mere posting of the notice on the last day of limitation is not sufficient, but it must be posted so that it must reach the railway administration in the ordinary course of six months.[17]

21 Loss of goods A party claiming compensation for loss of goods sought to file documents in support of the claim. The matter was remitted to produce evidence and prove documents.[18]

22 Limitation for suit Demand made by claimants for taking open delivery of goods after preparation of statutory report by railway authorities within statutory period regarding claim of compensation was not barred by limitation.[19] Where the claim of excess freight charges was denied on the ground of limitation, the plea of the claimant that it should be granted to him as limitation starts running from the date of discovery of such mistake by operation of s. 17(1)(*c*) of the Limitation Act 1963 would not be sustainable as the provisions of the Limitation Act have no application to the Railway Claims Tribunal.[20]

23 Claim for refund of freight Section 106 of the new Act would be attracted for a claim for refund of overcharge at an inflated rate. No writ under Art. 226 of the Constitution would lie in respect of such claim except resort to the Railway Claims Tribunal.[21]

24 Delivery of goods to wrong person on bogus railway receipt The oral and documentary evidence show that the railways were negligent in delivering goods to a wrong person on the basis of bogus railway receipt. Thus, the consignor and insurance company are entitled to claim loss with interest and costs for negligence and failure to take proper care and caution.[22]

25 "Overcharge" meaning of In s. 78B of the Indian Railways Act 1890 the expression "overcharge" was not defined. To be an overcharge a sum of money must partake of the same character as the charge itself or most be of the same genus or class as a charge. It cannot be any other kind of money such as money recovered where nothing is due. Overcharge is simply a charge in excess of that which is due according to law.[23]

17 *Union of India* v *Amin Chand Payarelal* AIR 1974 Punj 190; 1974 Cur LJ 1; 76 Punj LR 10; *Union of India* v *Bansidhar Premsukh* AIR 1976 All 491; 1976 All WC 330.
18 *Union of India* v *Dharmaraju Patro* 1998 AIHC 2944 (Ori).
19 *Union of India* v *India Cements Ltd.* 1996 AIHC 3047 (Ker).
20 *Birla Cement Works* v *G.M., Western Rly.* AIR 1995 SC 1111; 1995 AIR SCW 1140; (1995)2 SCC 493; JT 1995(2) SC 59.
21 *Rajasthan State Electricity Board* v *Union of India* AIR 2001 Bom 310.
22 *Union of India* v *Shree Emporium* AIR 2002 Mad 48.
23 *Union of India* v *West Coast Paper Mills Ltd.* (2004)3 SCC 458.

26 Notice to issue certificate of damage Lemon is perishable commodity. The consignment of lemon did not reach the destination within the time. In such case inference can be drawn that the said consignment is either lost or damaged. Notice was issued by the claimant under ss. 106 and 192 of the Railways Act 1989, but no reply was given thereto. Thus, it is improper to dismiss the claim petition for not filing along with the petition damage/deficiency/non-delivery certificate. The notice itself may be considered as damage certificate.[24]

27 Refund of deposited undercharged amount The Tribunal passed an order without recording reasons for refund of the amount deposited towards under charges. Such an order is improper.[1]

28 Burden of proof for short delivery There was shortage of rice bran oil by 1.295 MT at the time of delivery. Shortage-cum-damage certificate was issued by railways. Railways had not chosen to enter into witness-box, nor had it disapproved the said certificate. It can be said that the burden had been duly discharged by the claimant and it is entitled to damages for short delivery.[2]

29 Settlement of time barred refund cases Circular was issued in the year 2010 taking away power conferred on railway administration to consider time barred claims. The said circular was made effective from a retrospective date. Right was accrued in favour of the petitioner for consideration of time barred claim for refund of overcharge. The General Manager would be under an obligation to consider such time-barred claim of the petitioner for refund of overcharge.[3]

> **107. Applications for compensation for loss, etc., of goods.** An application for compensation for loss, destruction, damage, deterioration or non-delivery of goods shall be filed against the railway administration on whom a notice under section 106 has been served.

1 Corresponding provision in the old Act Section 107 of the new Act corresponds to s. 80 of the old Act.

2 Scope An application for compensation for loss, destruction, damage, deterioration or non-delivery of a consignment is to be filed against that railway administration on whom notice under s. 106 has been addressed. Section 107 categorically fixes the defendant to be claimed against.

24 *Mahendra Kumar* v *Union of India* AIR 2008 NOC 2417 (MP).
1 *Union of India* v *Rashtriya Ispat Nigam Ltd.* AIR 2008 NOC 1609 (P&H).
2 *Union of India* v *Sri Venkatarama Oil Industries Ltd.* AIR 2007 NOC 2260 (AP); see *Tata Iron & Steel Co. Ltd.* v *Union of India* AIR 2008 NOC 537 (AP).
3 *Maihar Cement* v *Union of India* AIR 2012 MP 104.

First, if the passenger is or the goods or animals are booked from one Railway Station to another on the same railway administration, the claim should be against that railway administration.

Secondly, if the passenger concerned purchased tickets or obtains pass from one station for journey to another of different railway administrations, then claim for loss of life or for personal injury may be made against either the railway administration from which the ticket was purchased or pass obtained or the railway administration of the destination station or against the railway administration within whose jurisdiction the loss of life or injury occurred.

Thirdly, if the animals or goods are booked from one station to another of different railway administration then claim for loss, destruction, deterioration, or non-delivery may be made against the railway administration of the booking station or of the destination station or of the station where such loss, destruction etc. occurred.

A consignment of steel goods was booked at a station of Eastern Railway to carriage to a station on North East Frontier Railway. A part of the consignment was not delivered. The consignor sued only the N.E.F. Rly., omitting to implead the Eastern Railway. The suit in view of the amended s. 80 of the (old) Act was tenable.[4]

This section applies only to cases of through booked traffic involving two or more railway administrations in India. It does not apply where the receiving railway is situated in a foreign country and the forwarding railway in the Indian territory. In the absence of any treaty arrangement between such foreign State and India, the principles that the receiving railway was the agent of the forwarding railway or that both the railways constituted a partnership and each acted as the agent of the other do not apply.[5]

In the absence of any special provision relating to places of suing for suits for compensation both in respect of through-booked-traffic and traffic carried over one single railway system, the general provisions relating to places of suing contained in s. 20 of the Code of Civil Procedure or in s. 18 of the Presidency Small Cause Courts Act 1882, as the case might be, used to apply also to suits for compensation against the railways. Thus, before the insertion of substituted s. 80 of the Indian Railways Act 1890 a suit for compensation against the railway administration could be instituted in a court within whose jurisdiction the cause of action, wholly, or in part, arose.[6]

4 *Barakar Engineering* v *Union of India* AIR 1982 Pat 140; 1982 BLJR 355; 1982 BBCJ (HC) 423; 1982 BLT (Rep) 227.

5 *Union of India* v *Amar Singh* AIR 1960 SC 233; (1960)2 SCR 75; 1960 SCJ 543. This case was followed in *Jetmull Bhojraj* v *D.H. Railway Co. Ltd.* (1963)2 SCR 832; AIR 1962 SC 1879 (*infra*).

6 *Union of India* v *Ratan Lall Aduka* AIR 1987 Cal 311; (1987)2 CLJ 1; (1987)2 CHN 95 (FB).

If the consignor wanted to sue a railway administration other than the one which booked the consignment, it was for him to establish that the damage had occurred on its system. But where the consignor received the consignment in a damaged condition, the burden would shift to the delivering railway administration to show that the damage had not occurred on its railway. The burden would be discharged by showing that the consignment was already damaged before it was received by that railway.[7]

Where the place of loss can be traced precisely that company alone, over whose railway the loss occurred, will be liable for the goods; but where the place of loss is not known or cannot be located, both the forwarding company and the delivering company should be sued and the company requiring to be exonerated from the liability must prove that the loss did not occur on its railway. Indeed, the section gives an option to sue either the forwarding company or the delivering company, but there is no logic to contend that where the place of loss cannot be located the impleading of both the companies will be bad for the defect of parties.[8] But under s. 80 of the (old) Act no suit will lie against a railway company to whom the goods were not entrusted unless it is shown that the loss occurred while the goods were in their possession.[9] The actual decision in this case was reversed on another point.[10]

In a case,[11] SINHA and DAS, JJ. after reviewing previous case laws with reference to s. 80 of the (old) Railways Act, have observed: "The brief review of the Indian case law on the subject demonstrates the fact that there is a wide divergence of judicial opinion on the question of the exact relationship between the consignor and the receiving railway and the other railway system over which the goods may have to be carried in order to reach their destination. Hence it may be said that the legislature intervened in the year 1890, and laid down a specific rule of law governing the liabilities of the different railway administrations as regards compensation for loss, etc., caused to the owner of the goods carried over those several railway systems. Section 80, therefore, being a specific provision in this behalf must be given effect to, irrespective of any other considerations based on the doctrine of agency or of partnership which may lead to conflicting results. When the legislature has intervened to

7 *Jetmull* v *Darjeeling Himalayan Railway* AIR 1962 SC 1879; (1963)2 SCR 832.

8 *G.I.P. Railway Co.* v *Jugal Kishore* AIR 1930 All 132; 52 All 238.

9 *B.N. Railway Co.* v *Balabux* AIR 1939 Cal 377; *Agents, G.I.P. Railway & E.I. Railway* v *Karaylal* AIR 1917 Nag 119; *Sri Gangaji Cotton Mills Co. Ltd.* v *E.I. Railway Co.* AIR 1922 All 514; 44 All 763; *Darbari Mal* v *Secretary of State* AIR 1926 Lah 116; 6 Lah 499; *G.I.P. Railway* v *Sham Manohar* 34 All 422; *E.I. Railway Co.* v *Nopechand* AIR 1914 Cal 623; 19 CLJ 434; see also *D.H. Railway* v *Jetmull Bhopraj* 60 CWN 683; AIR 1956 Cal 390.

10 *Jetmull Bhojraj* v *D.H. Railway Co. Ltd.* AIR 1962 SC 1879; (1963)2 SCR 832. See *Union of India* v *Brijlal Purshottamdas* AIR 1969 SC 817; (1969)2 SCJ 203.

11 *Governor-General of India in Council* v *Sukhdeo Ram* AIR 1949 Pat 329.

make the position absolutely clear, it is not safe to appeal to certain doctrines of law of general application." Their Lordships have held that s. 80 of old Act gives the plaintiff the choice of claiming his remedy either against the railway administration to which the goods are consigned or against the railway administration on which the loss occurs. The remedy is alternative and not cumulative, and where the goods are consigned to a railway for delivery at a railway station on another railway and the suit for damages for short delivery is brought against the Governor-General representing the latter railway where, however, the loss does not take place the latter cannot be made liable for the loss on the theory of agency or partnership.[12]

The liability under this section is statutory and this section overrides all agreements purporting to limit the liability of an administration with respect to through-booked traffic. In the case of goods booked through over the railway of two or more railway, a suit for compensation for loss of goods can be brought against the administration to which the goods were booked by the consignor. The suit can be brought against the other administrations only if the loss occurred on their railways.[13]

3 Suit for compensation against railway-forum As to the forum of trial concerning claims against railway for personal injury to a passenger, loss, destruction and deterioration or non-delivery of goods or animals delivered to a railway for carriage and for recovery of excess fare or freight paid to railway, the Railway Claims Tribunal Act 1987 has brought about a major change. That Act, however, would be enforced on such date as appointed by the Central Government. Since such appointed date, the forum for trial of claim-cases against the railway is the Claims Tribunal defined in s. 2(*e*) of the Act and not a civil court. Such Railway Claims Tribunal are to be established by the Central Government under s. 3, Railway Claims Tribunal Act 1987.

Section 13(1), Railway Claims Tribunal Act runs as follows:

> 13. *Jurisdiction, powers and authority of Claims Tribunal.* (1) The Claims Tribunal shall exercise, on and from the appointed day, all such jurisdiction,

12 The following earlier cases were reviewed, namely, *Arjun Das Gulab Rai Firm* v *E.I. Railway Co.* AIR 1924 Pat 811; *Jamunadas* v *E.I. Railway Co.* AIR 1933 Pat 630; *Gujendra Mohan* v *E.B. Railway Co.* 18 WR 145; *Kalu Ram* v *Madras Railway Co.* 3 Mad 240; *Narang Rai* v *R.S.N. Co.* 34 Cal 419; 11 CWN 1071; *Chunni Lal* v *The Nizam's Guaranteed State Railway Co.* 29 All 228; 4 ALJ 80 (FB); *Dekhari Tea Co. Ltd.* v *A.B. Railway Co.* 47 Cal 6; AIR 1920 Cal 758; *Koka Mal* v *G.I.P. Railway Co.* 11 ALJ 775; 21 IC 428; *G.I.P. Railway* v *Sham Monohar* 34 All 422; *Sri Gangaji Cotton Mills Co.* v *E.I. Railway Co.* 44 All 763; AIR 1922 All 514; *Railway* v *Jugal Kishore* 52 All 238; AIR 1930 All 132; *S.I. Railway Co.* v *Nanjiah Narayanaswami* AIR 1934 Mad 652; 151 IC 774; *S.I. Railway Co.* v *Krishnaswami* AIR 1935 Mad 878; 164 IC 903; *Palanichami* v *Governor-General in Council* AIR 1946 Mad 133; 224 IC 436; *M. & S.M. Railway* v *P.C. Nagiah & Co.* AIR 1946 Mad 227; 225 IC 481.

13 *Union of India* v *Brijlal Purushottamdas* AIR 1969 SC 817; (1969)2 SCJ 203.

powers and authority as were exercisable immediately before that day by any Civil Court or a Claims Commissioner appointed under the provisions of the Railways Act—

(*a*) relating to the responsibility of the railway administrations as carriers under Chapter VII of the Railways Act in respect of claims for—

(*i*) compensation for loss, destruction, damage deterioration or non-delivery of animals or goods entrusted to a railway administration for carriage by railway;

(*ii*) compensation payable under section 82A of the Railways Act or the rules made thereunder; and

(*b*) in respect of the claims for refund of fares or part thereof or for refund of any freight paid in respect of animals or goods entrusted to a railway administration to be carried by railway.

Once the appointed date as aforesaid is declared, the operation of s. 18(1), Railway Claims Tribunal Act is retrospective. For, all pending suits and claims before the Claims Commissioner consequent to an accident to trains would stand transferred to Claims Tribunal. Section 24, Railway Claims Tribunal Act stands as follows:

24. *Transfer of pending cases.* Every suit, claim or other legal proceeding (other than an appeal) pending before any court, Claims Commissioner or other authority immediately before the appointed day, being a suit, claim or proceeding the cause of action whereon it is based is such that it would have been, if it had arisen after the appointed day, within the jurisdiction of the Claims Tribunal, shall stand transferred on that day to the Claims Tribunal.

(2) Where any suit, claim or other legal proceeding stands transferred from any court, Claims Commissioner or other authority to the Claims Tribunal under sub-section (1)—

(*a*) the court, Claims Commissioner or other authority shall, as soon as may be after such transfer, forward the records of such suit, claim or other legal proceeding to the Claims Tribunal;

(*b*) the Claims Tribunal may, on receipt of such records, proceed to deal with such suit, claim or other legal proceeding, so far as may be, in the same manner as an application, from the stage which was reached before such transfer or from any earlier stage or *de novo* as the Claims Tribunal may deem fit.

It is also apposite to mention that the Claims Tribunal is not bound to follow the procedures laid down in Code of Civil Procedure (*vide* s. 18) although a proceeding before the Claims Tribunal is a judicial proceeding (*vide* s. 25). Two other material provisions are ss. 15 and 28.

Section 15 provides that on and from the appointed date, no court or authority shall exercise any jurisdiction or power or authority in relation to matters referred to in s. 13(1). Section 28 provides for overriding effect of the Railway Claims Tribunal Act 1987.

The Railway Claims Tribunal Act 1987 has repealed s. 80, Railways Act and substituted a new section in its place as above. In the perspective of such changes on the declaration of the appointed date by the Central Government the question of interaction between s. 20 of the Code of Civil Procedure is not material.

But old s. 80, Railways Act holds the field till the declaration by the Central Government of the appointed date. Therefore the interaction between s. 80 (repealed) of the Railways Act and s. 20, Code of Civil Procedure may not be altogether irrelevant.

Section 20, Code of Civil Procedure is a general provision as to forum of civil suit. And in view of s. 20, Code of Civil Procedure a suit of civil nature can be instituted in the court having jurisdiction over the place where the defendant resides, or carries on business or cause of action in whole or in part arises. In the *Explanation* to s. 20, Code of Civil Procedure it has been provided that a corporation shall be deemed to carry on business at its sole or principal office in India, or in respect of any cause of action arising at any place where it has also a subordinate office, at such place.

Section 80 of the (old) Railways Act purports to deal with the subject of places for instituting particular class of suits which was previously covered by s. 20, Code of Civil Procedure which is a general enactment. Two provisions namely s. 20, Code of Civil Procedure and repealed s. 80 of the (old) Railways Act cover the same field, *i.e.* territorial jurisdiction. When repealed s. 80 of the (old) Railways Act as amended by Act 39 of 1961 was introduced, s. 20, Code of Civil Procedure was already in existence. Mentioning for the first time in s. 80 of the (old) Railways Act of the places where suits for compensation might be instituted was itself 'introductive of a new law implying a negative'. When the same subject of territorial jurisdiction has been dealt with in the subsequent legislation, *i.e.* the then s. 80 of the (old) Railways Act, the prior law (s. 20, Code of Civil Procedure) on the same subject were not intended to subsist. In other words the then s. 80 of the (old) Railways Act by requiring some thing special to be done repealed by necessary implication the former general statute relating to territorial jurisdiction of courts in so far as the suits for compensation against the railways were concerned. Thus, s. 20, Code of Civil Procedure shall have no application for determination of the forum of a suit for compensation envisaged in s. 80 of the (old) Railways Act. The second part of the then s. 80 of the (old) Railways Act would determine the forum.[14]

In the decision of *Bengal Coal Co.* v *Union of India*,[15] which has been overruled by the Full Bench a consignment of goods were booked at Burnpur to be carried at China Kuri by South Eastern Rly. and the plaintiff filed a suit for compensation for short delivery of the goods at

14 *Union of India* v *Ratan Lal Aduka* AIR 1987 Cal 311; (1987)2 CLJ 1; (1987)2 CHN 95 (FB) overruling *Bengal Coal* v *Union of India* (1979)2 CLJ 363.

15 (1979)2 CLJ 363.

Alipore. M.M. DUTTA, J. (as his Lordship of the Supreme Court then was) and SHARMA, J. held that Union of India owning South Eastern Rly. carries on such business of railway at Garden Reach, a place within the jurisdiction of Alipore and therefore in view of s. 20, Code of Civil Procedure, Alipore Court had territorial jurisdiction to decide the suit. Being unable to subscribe to the view that s. 80 of the (old) Railways Act being a special provision would override s. 20, Code of Civil Procedure in so far as the suit is for compensation envisaged in the first part of s. 20, Code of Civil Procedure is concerned, DUTTA, J. observed that it is clear that in addition to the forum where the suit can be instituted in other forums under s. 80 of the (old) Railways Act; s. 20, Railways Act is not inconsistent or repugnant to the provisions of s. 80 and there would be no difficulty for the two provisions to exist simultaneously. DUTTA, J. drew sustenance for his theory from a case of Assam and Nagaland.[16] The wrong determination of DUTTA, J. in *Bengal Coal's* case (*ibid*) was followed by a single Judge in a case.[17]

In *Bengal Coal Company's* case (*ibid*) the Division Bench had no opportunity to notice the most leading judgment on the point rendered in *Union of India* v *C.R. Prabhanna*[18] nor DUTT AND SHARMA, JJ. in *Bengal Coal's* case (*ibid*) could notice an earlier three-member Bench judgment of Calcutta High Court itself laying down that s. 20(*c*), Code of Civil Procedure would not apply to a suit covered by s. 80, Railways Act,[19] as none appeared for the respondent Union of India in *Bengal Coal's* case and the judgment was rendered *ex parte*.

From this stand point the decision in *Bengal Coal Company's* case was a judgment by *non sum informatus*[20] and also a judgment *per incuriam*[21] and the learned Judges (ANIL KR. SEN and S.N. SANNYAL, JJ.) who referred the question to Full Bench that led to the decision[1] could have ignored the determination of *Bengal Coal Co.* It is not known, however, if the most leading judgment on the point rendered by High Court also escaped the attention of the referring Judges.

Be that as it may the view that s. 80 of the (old) Railways Act being a special provision would override the general provision enacted in

16 *Assam Coal Storage* v *Union of India* [wrongly described by the Division Bench of Calcutta or misprinted as *Ratna Kanta Dutta* v *Secretary to the Govt. of Assam*] AIR 1971 Assam 69; Assam LR (1970) Assam 202.

17 *Traders Syndicate* v *Union of India* AIR 1981 Cal 223.

18 AIR 1977 Kant 132; ILR (1977)1 Kant 543; (1977)1 Kant LJ 247.

19 *Oghadmal Chowdhury* v *Union of India* 1974 CLJ 420.

20 Judgment by *non sum informatus* means a judgment rendered on defendant's default.

21 Judgments *per incuriam* are judgments rendered in ignorance or forgetfulness of the existence of an earlier binding decision or statute which is not brought to the attention of the court. A judgment *per incuriam* is not binding—*Mamleswar* v *Kanhaiyalal* AIR 1975 SC 907; (1975)2 SCC 232; (1975)1 SCWR 405.

1 *Union of India* v *Ratan Lall Aduka* (ibid).

s. 20, Railways Act was pinpointed in a Karnataka case.[2] There the goods had been despatched from Wadi Bunder Railway Station, Bombay, to Bangalore City Railway Station, but the suit came to be filed before the Munsiff, Tumkur. This was done on the footing that the railway receipt had been negotiated through the State Bank of Mysore, Tumkur and payment had been made by the plaintiffs at that place. Thus it was contended that part of the cause of action had arisen at Tumkur and jurisdiction was sought to be conferred on the Munsiff, Tumkur, by placing reliance on the provision contained in s. 20(*c*) of the Code of Civil Procedure. It was contended before the High Court that the court of the Munsiff at Tumkur had no territorial jurisdiction to entertain the suit in view of the special provisions contained in the then s. 80 of the Railways Act as substituted by the Railways (Amendment) Act 1961 (39 of 1961).

Accepting the contention, the High Court observed "that Parliament when it enacted the new s. 80 intended to specify the courts before whom alone suits under s. 80 of the Railways Act could be filed. It should be remembered that s. 20 of the Code of Civil Procedure was in existence even at the time when s. 80 was substituted in the year 1961. If Parliament intended that s. 20 of the Code of Civil Procedure should continue to be applicable, then there was no need for specifying in s. 80 the courts which could entertain the suits referred to therein as they would also fall within the category of courts specified in s. 20 of the Code of Civil Procedure. While interpreting statutory provisions we should bear in mind that no legislature would ordinarily indulge in superfluity."

Relying on this Karnataka decision, a Bombay case[3] held that the special provision in s. 80, Railways Act should override the general provision of s. 20, Code of Civil Procedure. There the goods consigned at Lucknow for carriage to Lalitpur arrived at destination in damaged condition. The suit was filed at Bombay, namely at Head Quarters of Central Railway, on the strength of s. 20, Code of Civil Procedure. But the court held that Bombay Court had no jurisdiction. The suit could have been filed either in Lucknow or Lalitpur or at place of damage. The view that the second part of s. 80, Railways Act provides the forum where a suit for compensation envisaged in the first part of s. 80, Railways Act can be filed and that this special provisions overrides the general provision contained in s. 20, Code of Civil Procedure was followed by Delhi High Court in an earlier decision. The High Court observed: Section 80 of the Railways Act specifies the places where suits have to be instituted against the railways. The conflict here is between the special provision and the general provision. It is well settled that special overrides the general, and to such a situation the well known maxim '*generalia specialibus non derogant*' applies. The rule that

2 *Union of India* v *C.R. Prabhanna* AIR 1977 Kant 132; ILR (1977)1 Kant 545; (1977)1 Kant LJ 247.

3 *Union of India* v *Indian Hume Pipe* AIR 1981 Bom 414; 1981 Mah LJ 752.

general provisions should yield to specific provisions is not an arbitrary principle made by lawyers and Judges but springs from the common understanding of men and women that when the same person gives the directions one covering a large number of matters in general and another to only some of them his intention is that these latter directions should prevail as regards those while as regards all the rest the earlier direction should have effect.[4]

In *Bengal Coal Company* v *Union of India*[5] DUTT, J. relied upon the Assam and Nagaland case.[6] There a consignment of Union was booked at Lasanlogal Railway Station for carriage and delivery at Tinsukia Railway Station on the North-East Frontier Railway. The goods were delivered in a damaged condition by the railway at the time of delivery. Consequently, a suit was filed by the plaintiff in the court of the subordinate Judge of Gauhati. The jurisdiction of Gauhati Court was sought to be sustained by the plaintiff on the ground that the defendant carried on business at a place within the jurisdiction of that court. On the other hand, the railway contended that s. 80 of the Railways Act being special provision on the point impliedly repealed s. 20 of the Code of Civil Procedure GOSWAMI, CJ. observed thus (at p. 71):

> "The precise point that arises for consideration in this appeal is whether, after the amendment of s. 80, it is permissible to add any other place of suing outside the limits of s. 80 even though it may be permissible under s. 20, Code of Civil Procedure. In other words, has s. 80 impliedly repealed s. 20, Code of Civil Procedure or, could these two sections co-exist without any inconvenience or difficulty? It will be noticed that when the Legislature sought to amend s. 80, it must be assumed that it had s. 20 before it, which was the earlier section in the field on the subject. If so, in absence of any express provision to the contrary, or in absence of a clear implication in the provision, it is not possible to hold that s. 20, Code of Civil Procedure has been impliedly repealed by s. 80. When it is a question of place of suing, both the sections can co-exist and there is no repugnancy or inconsistency in the two sections standing together."

This Assam case was discussed and dissented from in the Karnataka case.[7]

Another single Judge in *South Eastern Railway* v *Govindlal Gopikisan*[8] following *C.R. Prabhanna* v *Union of India*[9] held: while s. 20, Code of Civil Procedure is a general provision for institution of suits of a civil nature in courts, in s. 80 of the Railways Act 1890 there is a special provision in regard to institution of suits for enforcing the liability of the

4 *New India Assurance* v *Union of India* AIR 1981 Del 135; 1981 Rajdhani LR 207; (1981)20 DLT 68.

5 (1979)2 CLJ 363.

6 *Assam Cold Storage* v *Union of India* AIR 1971 Assam 69; Assam LR (1970) Assam 202.

7 *Union of India* v *C.R. Prabhanna* AIR 1977 Kant 132; ILR (1977)1 Kant 543.

8 AIR 1984 Bom 223; 1984 Mah LJ 443; (1984)2 ACC 183.

9 AIR 1977 Kant 132.

railways as carriers and, therefore, it would seem that the special provisions of s. 80 of the Railways Act 1890 would override the general provision of s. 20 of the Code of Civil Procedure. Therefore, a suit for compensation as contemplated in the first part of s. 80, Railways Act has to be instituted as against the railway administration under the provisions of s. 80 of the Railways Act 1890 at either the place where the goods were delivered for carriage to the railways or in the court having jurisdiction where the goods were to be delivered and were in fact not delivered and short delivered or at any other place in between where the plaintiffs could allege the loss, destruction or damage to the goods consigned occurred.

Section 80 of the (old) Railways Act though it uses the expression 'may' has the effect of mandatory direction. A suitor is permitted by that section to file a suit for compensation against any one of the railway administrations (1) which receives the goods in transit; (2) which ultimately delivered the goods; and (3) the railway during the transit upon which damages to the good actually occurred. There is no other category of railway which can be sued. If it is the intention of the Act that because the Union of India owns all the railways a suit can be laid against the Union of India without anything more, s. 80 of the (old) Act would for the most part be rendered nugatory.[10] Where there is loss in transit of goods consigned at Madurai to a place on the North Eastern Railway, a suit for damages against the Union of India represented by the General Manager, North Eastern Railway, would obviously be in terms of s. 80 of the (old) Railways Act and it should be instituted at the place where the court has jurisdiction over the railway. The court will therefore have no jurisdiction to entertain such a suit. There was no scope for the question whether s. 80 of the (old) Railways Act overrides s. 20, Code of Civil Procedure to be raised. For, the suit was well within the penumbra of s. 80 of the (old) Railways Act. But the question categorically cropped up in a Madras Division Bench case and dissenting from the views stated earlier the Madras Division Bench[11] discussing elaborately the principles of implied repeal held s. 80 of the (old) Railways Act does not repeal s. 20, Code of Civil Procedure in so far as suits for compensation envisaged by the first part of s. 80 of the (old) Railways Act is concerned. Thus, s. 80 of the (old) Act does not exclude the operation of s. 20, Code of Civil Procedure and cl. 12, Letters Patent in so far as suits against the Railways for compensation are concerned. Section 80 of the (old) Act enables the plaintiff to file a suit for compensation against the railway for loss or damage to goods in the court having jurisdiction over the place (1) where goods were delivered for carriage; (2) where destination station lies; (3) where loss or damage to goods occurred. Under s. 20, Code of Civil Procedure and cl. 12, Letters Patent the plaintiff can file the suit in the court having jurisdiction

10 *Union of India* v *Swaminatha Mudaliar* (1970)1 Mad LJ 272; 82 Mad LW 647.

11 *Hindustan Machine Tools* v *Union of India* AIR 1985 Mad 130; (1984)17 Mad LW 432; 1985 ACJ 324.

over the place where (1) the cause of action arises, and (2) the defendant resides or carries on business. Thus, for suits based on cause of action in s. 80 of the (old) Act specifies the forums where suits for compensation against the railway could be instituted. But for suits based on the person of the defendant s. 80 of the (old) Act says nothing. Therefore, s. 80 of the (old) Act cannot be called a complete Code in respect of the institution of suits against the railway for compensation. When the Legislature amended s. 80 in 1961 it had the earlier s. 20, Code of Civil Procedure and cl. 12, Letters Patent before it. There is no express term in the language of s. 80 repealing s. 20, Code of Civil Procedure and cl. 12, Letters Patent and as regards place of suing both s. 80 on the one hand and s. 20, Code of Civil Procedure and cl. 12, Letters Patent on the other, can co-exist without any inconsistency. Therefore, s. 20, Code of Civil Procedure and cl. 12, Letters Patent cannot be said to have been impliedly repealed by the new amended s. 80. From the mere fact that s. 80 provides for certain courts in which the plaintiff can institute suit against the railway for compensation, it cannot be assumed that s. 80 ousted the jurisdiction of the civil courts to entertain suit for compensation under s. 20, Code of Civil Procedure and cl. 12, Letters Patent. Moreover, the use of the word 'may' in the expression "a suit for compensation may be instituted in a court having jurisdiction......" in s. 80 of the (old) Act only gives a discretion to enable the plaintiff to file a suit in the courts mentioned in s. 80 of the (old) Act and does not take away the right of the plaintiff to file a suit in accordance with the provisions of s. 20, Code of Civil Procedure and cl. 12, Letters Patent. This High Court overruled a contrary single Judge decision,[12] which held that s. 80 of the (old) Railways Act provides for a complete and self-contained Code regarding the courts before which the suit referred to in that section can be instituted. Section 20, Code of Civil Procedure had been in existence at the time when s. 80 of the (old) Railways Act was substituted by Act 39 of 1961 and even so, Parliament thought fit to provide for the institution of suits claiming compensation against railway only before certain courts under the circumstances set out in s. 80 of the (old) Railways Act. If it had been intended that s. 20, Code of Civil Procedure should continue to be applicable even with reference to the institution of suit claiming compensation against railways, there was no need for specifying and enumerating in s. 80 such courts before which alone suits claiming compensation and referred to in s. 80 of the (old) Act could be filed. Hence, s. 20, Code of Civil Procedure and s. 80 of the (old) Railways Act cannot co-exist and be given effect to for the purpose of institution of suits claiming compensation against railways.

Subject to what has been discussed above, when cause of action arises within the jurisdiction of different railways, suit can be instituted in any court where the headquarters of a railway is situate.

12 *Annamalai Chettiar* v *Union of India* AIR 1982 NOC 86 (Mad); (1981)2 Mad LJ 91; 94 Mad LW 447.

Thus, there is a sharp divergence of view between Assam and Madras High Courts on the one hand and other High Courts including Calcutta, Delhi, Bombay, Karnataka on the other.

4 Suit for compensation against railway—suit against Union Government Section 80 of the (old) Railways Act (corresponding to s. 107 of the new Act) broadly indicates that suit for compensation for loss of life of, or personal injury to a passenger or for loss, destruction, damage, deterioration or non-delivery of animals and goods are to be instituted against the Railway Administration. There is a distinction between the owner of the railway namely the Union of India, and the authority which actually runs the railway and to whom duties have been assigned for this purpose by the Railways Act. The manager of the railways is such an authority. When, however, liability is sought to be fastened on the railway administration and a suit is brought against it on that account, the suit would have to be brought against the Union of India because it is the Union who owns the railway and who would have the funds to satisfy the claim in case a decree is awarded in such a suit.[13]

5 Suit by State Government against railway for compensation In suit against railway, the defendant is Union of India. But then, Art. 131, Constitution of India whether would apply or not is a pertinent question. Article 131 reads as follows:

> 131. *Original jurisdiction of the Supreme Court*. Subject to the provisions of this Constitution, the Supreme Court shall, to the exclusion of any other court, have original jurisdiction in any dispute—
>
> (*a*) between the Government of India and one or more States; or
>
> (*b*) between the Government of India and any State or States on one side and one or more other States on the other; or
>
> (*c*) between two or more States.

After reviewing the earlier Supreme Court cases[14] the court however held that a suit for recovery of compensation against Union of India arising out of a railway claim does not attract Art. 131, Constitution of India. Nor the forum of such suit is Supreme Court. Such a suit is triable in ordinary civil court. Article 131, Constitution of India is attracted only when a dispute raised between or amongst the States and the Union in the context of the constitutional relationship that exists between them and the powers, rights, duties, immunities, liabilities, disabilities etc.

13 *State of Kerala* v *General Manager, Southern Railway* (1976)4 SCC 265; AIR 1976 SC 2538; 1976 BBCJ (SC) 114; 1976 UJ (SC) 750.

14 *State of Rajasthan* v *Union of India* (1978)1 SCR 1; AIR 1977 SC 1361 and *State of Karnataka* v *Union of India* AIR 1978 SC 68; (1978)2 SCR 1.

flowing therefrom. Any dispute which may arise between a State in the capacity of an employer in a factory, a manufacturer of goods subject to excise duty, a holder of a permit to run a stage carriage, a trader or businessman carrying on business not incidental to the ordinary functions of Government, a consumer of Railway Services etc. like any other private party on the one hand and the Union of India on the other cannot be construed as a dispute arising between the State and the Union in discharge of their respective executive powers attracting Art. 131, Constitution of India.[15]

To attract Art. 131 of the Constitution, the legal right which is the subject matter of dispute must arise in the context of the Constitution and the Federalism.[16] Relying on this decision it was held that suit for compensation for non-delivery of goods by State Government against the Union of India need not be filed in Supreme Court as envisaged in Art. 131, Constitution of India. Ordinary civil court can take cognizance of such a suit.[17]

But when the suit was filed by the State Government of Kerala for compensation for non-delivery or short delivery, the Supreme Court held such a suit can be filed only in the Supreme Court.[18]

6 Pucca adatiya It is well established that the pucca adatiya has no authority to pledge the credit of the up-country constituent to the Bombay merchant and there is no privity of contract as between the up-country constituent and the merchant. The pucca adatiya is entitled to substitute his own goods towards the contract made for the principal and buy the principal's goods on his personal account. In other words, the pucca adatiya is not the agent of his constituent but he is acting as a purchaser as regards his constituent and not as a disinterested middleman to bring two principals together. The legal position has been explained in *Bhagwandas Narotamdas* v *Kanji Deoji*,[19] and affirmed by the Judicial Committee of the Privy Council in *Bhagwandas Parasram* v *Burjorji Ruttonji Bomanji*,[1] *Shivanarayan* v *Madras*.[2] A commission agent or a "*pucca adatiya*" cannot institute a suit against railway administration unless he can show that the goods represented by railway receipt have been transferred to him or any interest therein has been created in his favour.[3]

15 *Union of India* v *State of Rajasthan* (1984)4 SCC 238; AIR 1984 SC 1675.
16 *State of Bihar* v *Union of India* AIR 1970 SC 1446; (1970)2 SCR 522; (1970)2 SCJ 717.
17 *State of WB* v *Union of India* (1986)2 CHN 75.
18 *State of Kerala* v *General Manager, Southern Railway* AIR 1976 SC 2538; (1976)4 SCC 265; 1976 UJ (SC) 75.
19 ILR (1906)30 Bom 205.
1 AIR 1917 PC 101; 45 IA 29.
2 AIR 1967 SC 986; (1967)1 SCR 138; (1967)1 SCJ 825.
3 *Union of India* v *B. Prahlad & Co.* AIR 1976 Del 236; ILR (1976)1 Del 436.

7 Cause of action and jurisdiction of court The Railway Claims Tribunal in view of s. 80 of the (old) Act as substituted by s. 33, Railway Claims Tribunal Act has exclusive jurisdiction to try a claim concerning railway, civil court can exercise jurisdiction for the limited time till the appointed date. In determining the question of jurisdiction of a court to entertain suit for compensation for loss, destruction, deterioration, non-delivery or short delivery of the goods, or for refund of overcharges against the railway, the facts constituting the cause of action are to be taken into consideration. The question whether the service of a notice under (old) s. 77 of the Indian Railways Act 1890, constitutes any part of the cause of action, which has been fully considered in *Bansi* v *Governor-General of India in Council*,[4] where it has been held that the service of a notice of claim under s. 77 is not a part of cause of action for a suit against the railway administration within s. 18(*a*) of the Presidency Small Cause Courts Act 1887 and consequently service of such a notice on a place within the jurisdiction of Calcutta Small Cause Court cannot give the court jurisdiction to try the suit. This decision expressly overruled *Golab Rai* v *Secretary of State*;[5] *Dominion of India* v *Jagdish Prosad Pannalal*[6] and *Dominion of India* v *Gopal Chandra Tapadar*,[7] and, therefore, the decision of SINHA, J. in *Dunlop Rubber Co. (India) Ltd.* v *Governor-General*,[8] is no longer a good law. Similarly, notice under s. 80 does not give rise to a cause of action.[9] Sending of a notice constitute no part of cause of action. So, the place from which the notice is issued or posted does not give the court of that place jurisdiction.[10]

Then comes the question whether the court has jurisdiction to entertain a suit against the Government where the cause of action has arisen wholly outside the ordinary original jurisdiction of that court on the sole ground that the Government resides or carries on business or personally works for gain within the local limits of that court. In *Rodricks* v *Secretary of State*,[11] Sir Lawrence Jenkins observed: "The court has no jurisdiction to entertain a suit against the Secretary of State where the cause of action has arisen wholly outside the ordinary original jurisdiction of that court on the sole ground that the Secretary of State dwelt or carried on business or personally worked for gain within the limits of that court." Sir Lawrence Jenkins followed an earlier decision of Calcutta High Court reported in

4 AIR 1952 Cal 35; 56 CWN 83; 89 CLJ 1 (FB).
5 ILR (1941)2 Cal 160.
6 AIR 1949 Cal 622; 84 CLJ 175.
7 AIR 1951 Cal 37; 55 CWN 113.
8 ILR (1950)2 Cal 551.
9 *Commissioner of Income Tax* v *M. Ramlingam* (1979)2 Mad LJ 327.
10 *Niranjan Agarwala* v *Union of India* AIR 1960 Cal 391; 64 CWN 502; *Union of India* v *Kedar Prasad* AIR 1970 Pat 212.
11 40 Cal 308; 21 IC 1.

Doya Narain Tewari v *Secretary of State*.[12] The above two decisions were followed in *Govindarajulu* v *Secretary of State*[13] where it was pointed out that the word "resides" must be taken to refer to natural persons and not to legal entities; and further, the word "business" is a commercial business and not a business of the State or the Government and as such the Secretary of State cannot be said to carry on business in running the administration of the railways. The decision in *Rodricks* v *Secretary of State*[14] was also followed in *Dominion of India* v *R.C.K.C. Nath & Co.*[15] and *Calcutta Motor Cycle Co.* v *Union of India*.[16]

There is one decision by LORD WILLIAMS, J., in *Golab Rai* v *Secretary of State*,[17] where his Lordship took the view that carriage by railway is a business within the meaning of cl. 12, Letters Patent, and is carried on by the Government of India. But this view was not accepted as correct in *Dominion of India* v *Gopal Chandra Tapadar*,[18] *Bata Shoe Co.* v *Union of India*,[19] *Azizuddin* v *Union of India*.[20]

Next comes the question whether notice under s. 80 of the Code of Civil Procedure is part of the cause of action for the purpose of jurisdiction. In *Raj Kumar Shaw* v *Dominion of India*[1] BACHAWAT, J., held that notice under s. 80, Code of Civil Procedure 1908, is part of the cause of action for the purpose of jurisdiction. That such notice is part of the cause of action was decided by SINHA, J., in *Dunlop Rubber Co. (India) Ltd.* v *Governor-General in Council*[2] and was so held in *Dominion of India* v *Jagdish Prasad Pannalal*.[3] His Lordship felt that these cases were binding on him. BACHAWAT, J., distinguished the case of *Nilima Sarkar* v *Governor-General in Council*.[4] The phrase 'cause of action' as used in Art. 10 of the Indian Independence (Rights, Property and Liabilities) Order 1947, does not include a notice under s. 80, Code of Civil Procedure. But the court expressly stated that it was unnecessary in that case to decide whether for the purpose of jurisdiction notice under s. 80, Code of Civil Procedure, might be regarded as a part of the cause of action.

12 14 Cal 256.
13 AIR 1927 Mad 689; 50 Mad 449.
14 40 Cal 308; 21 IC 1.
15 AIR 1950 Cal 207.
16 AIR 1953 Cal 1; 90 CLJ 25.
17 ILR (1941)2 Cal 160.
18 AIR 1951 Cal 37; 55 CWN 113.
19 AIR 1954 Bom 129; ILR (1953) Bom 1157.
20 AIR 1955 Mad 345; ILR (1955) Mad 912.
1 AIR 1953 Cal 235; 90 CLJ 295.
2 ILR (1950)2 Cal 551.
3 AIR 1949 Cal 622; 84 CLJ 175.
4 86 CLJ 98.

In *Bansi* v *Governor-General in Council*,[5] it was held that notice under s. 77 of the Railways Act 1890, is no part of the cause of action for the purpose of jurisdiction, which was distinguishable. The ground for that decision was that notice under s. 77 of the Indian Railways Act 1890, is not a condition precedent to the institution of the suit because that notice could be given even during the pendency of the suit. Notice under s. 80, Code of Civil Procedure 1908, is a condition precedent to the institution of the suit.

In *Dominion of India* v *Jagdish Prasad Pannalal*,[6] a question had arisen as to whether notices under s. 77 of the Indian Railways Act 1890 and s. 80 of the Code were a part of the cause of action under s. 18 of the Small Cause Courts Act. HARRIS, CJ. (at p. 179 of CLJ and at p. 624 of AIR) held that part of the cause of action against the Governor-General is the service of notice under s. 77 of the Railways Act and s. 80 of the Code. In other words, it is an authority for the proposition that the service of notice can be a part of the plaintiff's cause of action for jurisdiction of courts.

In *Dunlop*[7] (supra), SINHA, J.'s reasons were that according to the meaning of the phrase 'cause of action' given by RANKIN, CJ. in ILR 58 Cal 539; AIR 1931 Cal 659, the plaintiff was obliged to prove as a fact that notice was given in compliance with the provision of s. 80 of the Code and, therefore, the notice was a part of the cause of action. But it should be noticed that almost immediately following the *Dunlop* decision, S.B. SINGH, J. sitting with HARRIS, CJ. in *Nilima Sarkar* v *Governor-General in Council*,[8] agreed with the following observations of the learned Chief Justice: "It seems to me that for the purposes of bringing a suit the notice under s. 80 of the Code of Civil Procedure is not part of the cause of action. Section 80 expressly provides that the cause of action must be stated in the notice. If the delivery of the notice was part of the cause of action, then how could the whole cause of action be stated in the notice because it would have to be stated before the notice was sent." It follows that SINHA, J. must have resiled from his earlier view.

In *Niranjan Agarwala* v *Union of India*,[9] P.B. MUKHARJI, J. (as he then was) observed: "It may be said that in *Nilima Sarkar's* case, the point was not finally decided but, as will appear from the observations quoted above, a very definite opinion was expressed. Although earlier in the judgment, HARRIS, CJ. had expressed the wish that he would prefer to reserve his opinion on this point, yet subsequently in the judgment he expressed himself in no unequivocal terms that s. 80 was not a part of the cause of

5 AIR 1952 Cal 35 (FB); 56 CWN 83 (FB).
6 AIR 1949 Cal 622; 84 CLJ 175.
7 ILR (1950)2 Cal 551.
8 86 CLJ 98.
9 AIR 1960 Cal 396; 64 CWN 502.

action and gave some reasons for it which will be clear from the observations quoted above."

The same learned Judge in *Calcutta Motor Cycle Co.* v *Union of India*,[10] said: Then against the decision in *Jagdish Prasad Pannalal's* case has been criticised by HARRIS, CJ. himself in his subsequent judgments, first in an appeal from the Original Side in *Nilima Sarkar* v *Governor-General in Council*,[11] and then again in the Full Bench case in *Bansi* v *Governor-General in Council*.[12] There the reference was made on two points distinctly. The first point was whether notice under s. 77, the Indian Railways Act 1890, was a part of the cause of action ...... The leading judgment in the Full Bench was delivered by DAS, J., BANERJEE, J. agreeing. HARRIS, CJ. also agreed but added these few words: "I desire to add that I am satisfied that the view taken in the case of *Dominion of India* v *Jagdish Prasad Pannalal*,[13] a decision to which I was a party, is erroneous."

Referring to the observations of HARRIS, CJ. in *Nilima Sarkar's* case (supra) on the point of s. 80, Code of Civil Procedure quoted above, A.N. RAY, J. (as he then was) said in *Jaharlal Pagalia* v *Union of India*.[14] "This observation of HARRIS, CJ. with regard to s. 80, in my view is a clear authority for the proposition that the cause of action is complete before the notice under s. 80 can go. As I read the decision whether the cause of action is one for the purpose of jurisdiction of the court or the cause of action is one in relation to the basis of the claim in suit or the cause of action is one with regard to Art. 10 of the Indian Independence Order, a notice under s. 80 has to be delivered stating the cause of action. Therefore, the cause of action in suits which require notice under s. 80 cannot be extended to include any fact after the cause of action has been stated in the notice to be delivered. If anything has not been stated in the notice it will not form part of the cause of action."

The same learned Judge referred to *Bansi's* case (supra) thus: "In the case of *Bansi*, the court considered the question whether service of notice under s. 77 of the Railways Act was a part of the cause of action. Their Lordships held that service of notice under s. 77 of the (old) Act was not a part of the cause of action inasmuch as service of such a notice was not a condition precedent to the right to institute a suit. G.N. DAS, J. looked at the question from the point of view of the plea of absence as well as waiver of notice under s. 80 to decide whether the notice under s. 77 of the (old) Railways Act was not a part of the cause of action. Their Lordships further held that a notice under s. 77 of the Indian Railways Act 1890, was not a part of the cause of action because it might be waived by the defendant in the suit and not prior to the institution of the suit.

10 AIR 1953 Cal 1; 90 CLJ 25.
11 86 CLJ 98.
12 56 CWN 83.
13 84 CLJ 175; AIR 1949 Cal 622.
14 AIR 1959 Cal 273.

Furthermore, the absence of notice was a plea to be raised in the written statement and therefore the notice could not be regarded as part of the cause of action. Similar observations apply *proprio vigore* to a notice under s. 80 of the Code of Civil Procedure. A notice under s. 80 can be waived in the suit and the absence of a notice under s. 80 can be a plea taken in the written statement. Therefore, the notice under s. 80 cannot be a part of the cause of action. In the case of *Bansi* v *Governor-General in Council*, HARRIS, CJ. expressly observed that the Bench decision in *Jagdish Prasad Pannalal*[15] was erroneous. It is true that the decision in *Bansi's* case was one which related to s. 77 of the (old) Railways Act, but the observations of HARRIS, CJ. to my mind, make it clear that His Lordship held that the earlier decision was wrong in this respect, that neither the notice nor the service thereof was a part of the cause of action."

In *Nalini Ranjan Guha* v *Union of India*,[16] BACHAWAT, J. held that the issue and posting of the notice under s. 80 of the Code are pieces of evidence necessary for proving the service of the notice but are not part of the cause of action. The service of the notice is a part of the cause of action. He disagreed with the view expressed by SINHA, J. in ILR (1950)2 Cal 551 and also distinguished the case of *Engineering Supplies Ltd.* v *Dhandhania & Co.*,[17] on which S.B. SINHA, J. had relied on the ground that the latter was based on the law of contract and founded on offer and acceptance and consequently the place of offer was a part of the cause of action on the contract. In other words, BACHAWAT, J. therefore, refused to extend the principle of the decision in the *Engineering Supplies Company's* case to the case of a notice under s. 80 of the Code of Civil Procedure 1908.

H.K. BOSE, J. (as he then was), in *Hindusthan Housing and Land Development Trust Ltd.* v *State of West Bengal*,[18] followed the view taken in *Nalini Ranjan Guha's* case (supra).

In *Anath Bandhu Dev* v *Dominion of India*,[19] P.B. MUKHARJI, J. (as he then was), said: "But the place of the issue of notice under s. 80 is not important or relevant. To apply the notion of jurisdiction in respect of contracts formed by correspondence where both the places from where letters are sent and where they are received are relevant to the notice under s. 80 of the Code of Civil Procedure is to compare the incomparable. If s. 80 of the Code of Civil Procedure is a part of the cause of action, although it itself is required to state the cause of action and it requires only that the plaint shall state that such notice has been delivered or left,

15 AIR 1949 Cal 622; 84 CLJ 175.
16 93 CLJ 373.
17 AIR 1931 Cal 659; ILR 58 Cal 539.
18 59 CLJ 405 at p. 417.
19 AIR 1955 Cal 626; 97 CLJ 9.

then the place of receipt of that notice and not the place of its issue determines part of the cause of action and there is the express emphasis in the language of that section on the place of the receipt of the notice." Since the cause of action was required to be stated in the notice under s. 80, the cause of action must have been complete prior to the issue or delivery of the notice.

In *Jaharlal Pagalia's* case (supra), the above-mentioned cases were duly noticed and in the ultimate analysis, A.N. RAY, J. (as he then was), held that the observations made in the Full Bench decision in *Bansi's* case "apply *proprio vigore* to a notice under s. 80 of the Code of Civil Procedure".

In *Niranjan Agarwala* v *Union of India*,[20] P.B. MUKHARJI, J. (as he then was), referred to the previous decisions. He also referred to the decision of *Bata Shoe Co. Ltd.* v *Union of India*[21] and *Azizuddin & Co.* v *Union of India*.[1] His Lordship held that the notice under s. 80 of the Code of Civil Procedure did not furnish any cause of action.

In *Bata Shoe* case (*supra*), GAJENDRAGADKAR, J. (as he then was), said: "A statutory notice required by the provision of the Railways Act as well as the Civil Procedure Code is no doubt an essential preliminary step for the valid institution of a suit; but that would not make such a notice a part of the cause of action for the suit itself. If it is borne in mind that such a notice is required to state among other facts the cause of action on which the proposed suit would be based and the relief intended to be claimed, it would be clear that the notice follows the cause of action and it merely paves the way for the institution of the suit itself. That is why it is an essential preliminary step and no more." (*See* p. 132 of the Report). This view was followed in *Azizuddin's* case (*supra*).

In *I.S.P. Trading Co.* v *Union of India*,[2] it was held following *Commissioners for the Port of Calcutta* v *General Trading Corporation*[3] that negotiation of railway receipt is part of the cause of action.

In *Hari Mohan Dutta* v *Dominion of India*,[4] a question arose as to whether an endorsement of a railway receipt is a part of the cause of action. Mere endorsement of a railway receipt either by the consignor or by the consignee would not convey the property in the goods to the endorsee. If, however, there was an endorsement of a railway receipt for valuable consideration and property passes to the endorsee, and if such a transaction

20 AIR 1960 Cal 391; 64 CWN 502.
21 AIR 1954 Bom 129; ILR (1953) Bom 1157.
1 AIR 1955 Mad 345; ILR (1955) Mad 912.
2 AIR 1960 Cal 74.
3 AIR 1964 Cal 290.
4 AIR 1954 Cal 59; 57 CWN 167.

takes place within the ordinary original jurisdiction of Calcutta High Court, then a part of the plaintiff's cause of action must inevitably arise within the said jurisdiction. Such a transaction must not only be regarded as part of the plaintiff's cause of action but an essential part, inasmuch as without it the plaintiff would not be entitled to maintain the suit. In *Ganpatrai Sagarmull* v *Union of India*[5] it was observed with reference to this case that the decision "seems to proceed on the basis that endorsement of a railway receipt for valuable consideration would necessarily result in the property in the goods passing to the endorsee".

Section 80 of the (old) Act in no way affects the jurisdiction of the High Court when the cause of action partly arises within the original jurisdiction of the High Court and leave is obtained under cl. 12 of the Letters Patent.[6] Under cl. 12 of the Letters Patent, the High Court is empowered to try and determine suits of every description, in all cases, if the cause of action shall have arisen in part within the local limits of the ordinary original jurisdiction of the High Court in case the leave of the court has been obtained first. The only limitation imposed in this clause is that the High Court shall not have original jurisdiction in cases falling within the jurisdiction of the Small Cause Courts Act. The language of cl. 12 is not the language of s. 4 of the Code of Civil Procedure. Therefore, even if it be held that cl. 12 of the Letters Patent affects the special jurisdiction conferred by s. 80 of the Indian Railways Act 1890, in the absence of any inherent limiting clause as in s. 4 of the Code of Civil Procedure 1908, s. 80 of the Indian Railways Act 1890 should not be construed as to take away the jurisdiction of the court to try such suits.[7]

In *Hari Mohon Dutta* v *Dominion of India*,[8] MITTER, J. had distinguished the decisions in *Bhabani Prosad Lahiri* v *Rai Radhica Bhusan Roy*[9] and *Kalooram Agarwala* v *Jonishta Lal Chakrabarty*[10] on the ground that they dealt with assignments by endorsement of negotiable instruments whereas a railway receipt was not in the same position. But in *Alliance Assurance Co.* v *Union of India*,[11] the above cases were referred to and followed, P.B. MUKHARJI, J. (as he then was) observing that reference was

5 AIR 1975 Cal 265.

6 AIR 1966 SC 893; (1969)3 SCC 694; AIR 1966 SC 1718; AIR 1964 SC 1268; AIR 1964 SC 322 relied on.

7 *Ganpatrai Sagarmull* v *Union of India* AIR 1975 Cal 265.

8 AIR 1954 Cal 59; 57 CWN 167.

9 40 CWN 1349.

10 40 CWN 161.

11 AIR 1959 Cal 563; 63 CWN 806.

made to the "well-known trilogy of cases[12] decided by PANCKRIDGE, J. which supported the proposition that assignment is a part of the cause of action and that the place where the assignment takes place gives the court of that place jurisdiction to entertain the suit on the basis of that assignment. The court of appeal in *Bhabani Prosad Lahiri* v *Rai Radhica Bhusan Roy*[13] came to the conclusion that in a suit by the assignee of a promissory note, the making of an endorsement which effects the assignment, is not only a part of the cause of action but is the most essential part thereof. On the basis of this authority and especially the last decision of the Court of Appeal I must find in favour of the jurisdiction of this court to entertain this suit."

It was contended that the aforesaid decisions related to negotiable instruments and the doctrine of negotiability should not be applied to a railway receipt which lacked that quality. But the learned Judge rejected the contention and observed: "The railway receipts by themselves would not give jurisdiction. But the point is that the railway receipts are themselves documents of title and can be negotiated and transferred. By the assignment or letter of subrogation ...... these railway receipts or the claims thereunder were transferred or negotiated in favour of the plaintiff insurance company. The letter of subrogation or assignment shows that the insurance company is subrogated to all the rights of the consignor. In other words, the railway receipts stand transferred in favour of the insurance company. In that view of the matter even the doctrine of negotiability can be invoked ...... to grant jurisdiction to this court. The transfer of those railway receipts and the rights thereunder were made by the subrogation and assignment which took place within the jurisdiction of this court."

An earlier decision by the same learned Judge in *Alliance Assurance Co.* v *Union of India and Goodyear Tyre*[14] holding that the assignment and the transfer in that case was good, valid and enforceable on a policy of this nature, was referred to and followed. But in *Fushraj Thanmull* v *Union of India*,[15] A.N. RAY, J. (as he then was) doubted the proposition laid down in AIR 1959 Cal 563 (*supra*) and his Lordship stated that on the facts of that particular case, MUKHARJI, J. took the view that it would furnish a cause of action. The question in *Fushraj Thanmull* (supra) was whether the handing over of the railway receipt by the consignor to the consignee is a part of the cause of action of the plaintiff. His Lordship referred to the decision in *Shamji Bhanji & Co.* v *N.W. Railway Ltd.*,[16]

12 *Kalooram Agarwala* v *Jonishta Lal Chakrabarty* AIR 1936 Cal 349; 40 CWN 161; *Daulatram Rawatmull* v *Maharajilal* AIR 1936 Cal 219; 40 CWN 164 and *Harnathrai Binjraj* v *Sew Prosad Singh* AIR 1936 Cal 230; 40 CWN 165.

13 40 CWN 1349.

14 AIR 1959 Cal 563; 63 CWN 806.

15 AIR 1960 Cal 458.

16 AIR 1947 Bom 169; 48 Bom LR 698.

wherein the character of a railway receipt was discussed. After referring to the judgment of BHAGWATI, J. in that case, his Lordship observed:

> "It thus appears that the rights, if any, on transfer of the documents of title are between the endorser and the endorsee of the receipt. The transfer of a document of title operates only as a token or authority to take possession and not as a transfer of possession and as between the immediate parties there is nothing to modify the common law rule. If the railway receipt is endorsed by the consignor to the consignee for valuable consideration such endorsement might form part of the endorsee's cause of action."

In *S. Ramarao* v *Union of India*,[17] SRINIVASACHARI, J. said:

> "...... Railway receipts are not treated as negotiable instruments. I may, with advantage, also refer to question in Halsbury's *Laws of England* at page 143, vol. 29, para 179, dealing with railway receipts and bills of lading: 'Such documents although they may purport to be, or may commonly be treated as, transferable are not negotiable instruments, unless there be a trade usage to that effect.' Therefore, I am not sure if the observations of the learned Judge in *Alliance Assurance Co.* v *Union of India*[18] to say that the principle relating to the endorsement of a negotiable instrument as furnishing a cause of action, could be applied also to railway receipts endorsed in favour of third parties. The right that the endorsee gets on transfer or assignment of the railway receipt is only a right to take possession of the goods."

A suit for compensation for the breach of a contract must be brought either in the court within the jurisdiction of which the goods were booked for carriage by railway or in the court within whose jurisdiction the loss thereof took place. This is precisely the position prior to enforcement of the Railway Claims Tribunal Act 1987.

8 "Deterioration"—meaning of "Deterioration" in s. 80 of the old Act (corresponding to s. 107 of the new Act) includes decrease in market value consequent on detention.[19] It would also include the depreciation in value of the animals due to negligence of the railway in giving food or water during the delay in transit.[20]

9 Suit against Private Railway Company In the case of a Private Railway Company, a suit for damages in respect of loss, etc., must be filed against the company itself.[1]

10 Suit for refund of Overcharge Where goods are carried over two railways and the transferee railway overcharges the goods, a suit to refund does not lie against the transferring railway.[2]

17 AIR 1961 AP 282.
18 AIR 1959 Cal 563.
19 *I.G.N. & Railway Co. Ltd.* v *Harcharan* 15 IC 12.
20 *Alday* v *G.W. Railway Co.* [1864]5 B&S 903; 11 LT 267.
1 *I.G.S.N. Railway Co. Ltd.* v *Lal Mohan* 43 Cal 441; 22 CLJ 241.
2 *Sheo Dayal* v *G.P. Railway Co.* AIR 1926 All 698; 49 All 236; 25 ALJ 89.

11 Suit against Government or State In a case where the railway is administered by a Government or State, a suit under s. 80, Indian Railways Act, can be brought against the Government or the State concerned. In the Full Bench case of the Assam High Court,[3] SARJOO PRASAD, CJ. who delivered the judgment (RAM LABHAYA AND DEKA, JJ. agreeing) observed: "The section (s. 80) evidently contemplates that for the loss, destruction or deterioration of goods, a suit may be brought against the railway administration to which the goods were consigned or, alternatively, against the railway administration on which the loss occurred. The words, "railway administration" have not been defined in the section itself and, therefore, one has to look beyond the four corners of the section to find out what this expression means. It must be, however, conceded that these railway administrations, namely, the railway administration to which the goods were consigned, or the railway administration on which the loss occurred, are treated as different units and separate and distinct entities. But this is only so with the object of ascertaining the liability of the administration or administrations concerned as the goods may travel over various railways. The distinction acquires special significance where these railway administrations are owned by different bodies, and not by the same owner. "Railway administration" has been defined in s. 3(6) of the Act. It says "railway administration" or "administration in the case of a railway administered by the Government or a State" means the manager of the railway administered by the Government or State. Therefore in a case where the railway is administered by a Government or State, a suit under s. 80 of the Act can be brought against the Government or the State concerned. Thus, where the railway administration to which the goods were consigned and the railway on which the loss occurred were both owned by the same Government or State, it follows from the language of s. 3(6) that a suit can be brought against the State or Government which owns both the railways. But the plaint must, on the face of it, state the cause of action as to how and in what capacity the State is sought to be made liable whether as owner of the railway to which the goods were consigned or as owner of the railway on which the loss occurred, or both. If these facts are not stated in the plaint, then there is no cause of action against the Government or the State which owns the railway administration concerned, and the mere fact that the Government or the State is impleaded as a party defendant to the suit will not give a cause of action to the plaintiff where, on the recitals in the plaint itself, none exists. I do not see anything in the section to prevent the party from suing the Government or the State as owner of a particular railway, because in that case the Government or the State is the 'railway administration' and adequately represents the railway which it administers. I do not see any reason why if all the necessary facts are there in the plaint and it is shown how the

3 *Chandra Mohan* v *Union of India* AIR 1953 Assam 193.

Government concerned has been made a party to the suit, it should be still insisted upon that the 'railway administration', as such, should be made a party to the suit. It is, on the face of it, a tautological fallacy, because a Government or a State, on the terms of the definition itself, is the railway administration and, as such, liable to be sued within the meaning of s. 80, Railways Act."

It has been held in *Dominion of India* v *Firm Museram Kishunprasad*[4] that merely suing the Governor-General as representing the entire State-owned railways (at least before the Indian Independence Act was passed) is not a proper form of suit because that would render s. 80 of the old Act otiose and meaningless. It is not sufficient to implead the Union of India; it is necessary to implead one or more of the railway administration.[5]

Each railway administration is a separate entity and a different legal person capable of suing and being sued independently. Notice against one railway administration of the claim of the plaintiff is not therefore sufficient compliance of the provisions of old s. 77 to constitute a notice against the other railway administration.[6]

Where a suit was brought for damages on account of short delivery of goods consigned with the Eastern Railway and there was no proof that Eastern Railway had handed over the entire consignment to the Western Railway, the Western Railway could not be held liable. The mere fact of payment of freight charges to the Western Railway would not be enough to raise any presumption against it.[7]

12 Compensation for damage to consignment When there is damage to compensation and assessment of damages is made by two independent surveyors, the original reports of the surveyors are to be placed on record. Typed copies of the reports cannot be relied upon in absence of evidence of assessors. But if order awarding damages is made in accordance with the assessment of the Railway Official, that is proper.[8]

13 Limitation Not the civil court but a Railway Claims Tribunal is now the forum for recovery of compensation or damages when any goods or animal entrusted to the railway for carriage through railway is lost, destroyed, non-delivered or damaged. Similarly not the Claims Commissioner but Railway Claims Tribunal is the forum for application for compensation pursuant to an accident to railway:

The Railway Claims Tribunal Act, s. 15 has prescribed a specific period of limitation for preferring application for recovery of damages or

4 AIR 1950 Nag 85.
5 *Central India Chemicals* v *Union of India* AIR 1962 MP 301.
6 *Fagumani* v *Dominion of India* AIR 1956 Ori 29.
7 *Chandulal* v *Union of India* AIR 1956 Ajmer 1.
8 *Lakshmi Chand Textiles* v *Union of India* AIR 2005 Del 2.

compensation for such loss, destruction etc. Section 17 also provides a specific period of limitation when compensation pursuant to an accident to a train is claimed. Section 17, Railway Claims Tribunal Act stands as under:

> 17. *Limitation*. (1) The Claims Tribunal shall not admit an application for any claim—
>
> (*a*) under sub-clause (*i*) of clause (*a*) of sub-section (1) of section 13 unless the application is made within three years from the date on which the goods in question were entrusted to the railway administration for carriage by railway;
>
> (*b*) under sub-clause (*ii*) of clause (*a*) of sub-section (1) or, as the case may be, sub-section (1A) of section 13 unless the application is made within one year of occurrence of the accident;
>
> (*c*) under clause (*b*) of sub-section (1) of section 13 unless the application is made within three years from the date on which the fare or freight is paid to the railway administration:
>
> Provided that no application for any claim referred to in sub-clause (*i*) of clause (*a*) of sub-section (1) of section 13 shall be preferred to the Claims Tribunal until the expiration of three months next after the date on which the intimation of the claim has been preferred under section 78B of the Railways Act.
>
> (2) Notwithstanding anything contained in sub-section (1), an application may be entertained after the period specified in sub-section (1) if the applicant satisfied the Claims Tribunal that he had sufficient cause for not making the application within such period.

Therefore, when the application before the Claims Tribunal is for compensation for loss, destruction, damage, deterioration or non-delivery of animals or goods entrusted to a railway administration for carriage by railway, limitation starts from the date when the goods in question or animals in question were entrusted to the railway administration for carriage by railway. And the period of limitation is three years from such date. When the application is for refund of fares or part thereof or for refund of freight paid in respect of animals or goods entrusted to a railway administration to be carried by railway, the starting point of limitation is the date on which the fare or freight is paid to the railway administration. And the limitation is three years.

When the claim is for compensation consequent on an accident to a train, the starting point is the date of the occurrence of the accident and the limitation is only one year.

This clearly supersedes Arts. 10 and 11 of Limitation Act 1963 which stand as follows. But Arts. 10 and 11 would apply so long the Central Government does not fix the appointed date for enforcement of the Railway Claims Tribunal Act 1987.

Section 23, Railway Claims Tribunal Act 1987 projects the High Court as the forum for appeal against an adjudication by Claims Tribunal except one made on consent and except an interlocutory order. The limitation is ninety days from the date of order appealed from.

Sub-section (2) of s. 17, Railway Claims Tribunal Act provides that notwithstanding anything in sub-sec. (1) of s. 17, Claims Tribunal may permit a claimant to present an application claiming damages or compensation in a railway claim beyond the period of limitation if the Claims Tribunal is satisfied that there is sufficient cause for such delay: This corresponds to s. 5, Limitation Act. So whether s. 5, Limitation Act does or does not apply to a railway claim before the Railway Claims Tribunal is academic.

Articles 10 and 11 of the Limitation Act 1963:

Description of suit	*Period of limitation*	*Time from which period begins to run*
10. Against a carrier for compensation for losing or injuring goods.	Three years.	When the loss or injury occurs.
11. Against a carrier for compensation for non-delivery of, or delay in delivering, goods.	Three years.	When the goods ought to be delivered.

14 Applicability of Limitation Act to Claims Tribunal The scope of Limitation Act 1963 has been considerably enlarged so as to include generally all court proceedings. The insertion of a definition of "applicant" as including a "petition" and the inclusion of "petitioner" in the definition of "applicant" in s. 2 and the applicability of ss. 5 to 12 to special laws unless otherwise excluded specifically or by necessary implication are indicative of such enlargement. The Act of 1908 governed suits appeal and certain applications. The present Limitation Act 1963 applies to suits and other legal proceedings and for purpose connected therewith.[9] The Limitation Act thus is applicable in respect of applications or petitions under any Special Act, if such applications are filed in court. As a matter of fact Limitation Act applies to all court proceedings only.[10]

But, Railway Claims Tribunal is not a court. The proceedings before such Tribunal is to be deemed to be judicial proceedings within the meaning

9 U.N. Mitra on *Limitation and Prescription*, 8th Ed., p. 13; see also *Ram Kumar Kajaria* v *Ohandra Engineers* 76 CWN 426.

10 *Kerala State Electricity Board* v *T.P. Kunhaliamma* AIR 1977 SC 282; (1976)4 SCC 634; (1977)1 SCR 996.

of ss. 193, 219, 228 of the Indian Penal Code (*vide* s. 25, Railway Claims Tribunal Act). But, nowhere a Railway Claims Tribunal has been described in the Act as a court. It is therefore submitted that Limitation Act does not apply to a proceeding under the Railway Claims Tribunal Act before the Tribunal. This presumably led the Legislature to enact s. 17(2), Railway Claims Tribunal Act which section is in *pari matria* with s. 5, Limitation Act 1963. The Legislature has added s. 17(2) not as an abundant caution but because the Legislature was very much aware that the provisions of Limitation Act 1963 do not apply to a proceeding before the Railway Claims Tribunal.

15 Applicability of Articles of Limitation Act to suits The Railway Claims Tribunal Act is to come into force on the date appointed for the purpose. Till that date ordinary civil court is competent to decide a railway claim. The scope of Arts. 10 and 11, Limitation Act 1963 from this point of view is pertinent.

Article 10 is applicable to a case where there is loss in the contents of the units of a consignment, while Art. 11 is applicable where it is a case of loss of units of articles.[11] Article 10 is applicable where there was delivery of goods but in a damaged condition.[12] In either case notice under s. 80, Code of Civil Procedure is required to be served. And this period of notice is liable to be excluded. So suit filed within three years and two months from the date when the goods ought to have been delivered (it was a case of total non-delivery), is a suit within time.[13] The onus to prove the date of loss or injury is on the railway concerned and in the absence of satisfactory evidence on its part on the point the date of delivery to the party should be taken as the date of loss or injury,[14] Limitation starts when the railway loses or injures the goods and not when loss occurs to the plaintiff for some other fault of the railway.[15]

A case of misdelivery falls within Art. 11.[16] A suit for non-delivery of a part of the goods is governed by Art. 11.[17] Where the consignment was not delivered at all, old Art. 31 was applicable.[18]

16 Starting point of limitation under Art. 11 The expression "when goods ought to be delivered" only means the reasonable time taken (in the absence of any express or implied contract as to time for delivery) in the carriage of goods to the place of destination. What is reasonable time must

11 *Union of India* v *Madhusudan Sahu* AIR 1964 Ori 198; ILR (1964) Cut 606.
12 *Sivdutt Rai* v *Union of India* AIR 1960 AP 406; ILR (1958) AP 849.
13 *Khedul Oil Cake* v *Union of India* AIR 1988 Del 88; (1987)32 Del LT 297.
14 *Union of India* v *Gujarat Trading Co.* AIR 1955 Cal 448; 59 CWN 278.
15 *Oudh & Trihut Railway* v *Karam Chand* AIR 1958 All 234.
16 *Abdulrahiman* v *Abdulkandar* AIR 1962 Ker 56.
17 *Gajadhar Shaw* v *Union of India* AIR 1959 Cal 21; ILR (1956)1 Cal 394.
18 *Union of India* v *Jagatpal* AIR 1960 Pat 340.

depend upon the circumstances of each case. The correspondence can only be taken into account to determine what would be the reasonable time and not to show that by the subsequent conduct of the railway in tracing the goods the reasonable time was extended,[19] upholding the Full Bench decision in *Dominion of India* v *Aminchand Bhola Nath.*[20] Where a portion of the goods has been delivered, limitation starts from that date (*ibid*). Where the carrier agreed to deliver by a certain date, limitation starts from that date. Where no time is fixed for delivery and where after the non-delivery correspondence took place between the consignor and the railway in course of which the latter goes on promising enquiries and never denying any liability, limitation does not begin to run till the correspondence ends either fruitlessly or till the railway states its inability to deliver or finally repudiates the claim.[21]

But see *Union of India* v *Banarashilal Agarwalla*[1] holding that the starting point of limitation for a suit for compensation for non-delivery of goods entrusted to a public carrier is, where there is an agreed date of delivery, the date so agreed and where there is no such date the date after the lapse of a reasonable time for delivery. The starting point is not the date of final refusal after correspondence by the carrier for claim for compensation. The expression "when the goods ought to be delivered" means the point of time when the railway undertakes to deliver the goods or the date when the railway informs the consignee that it would be delivered or when the railway communicates to the consignee its inability to deliver the goods or a reasonable date that may be fixed on a consideration of events subsequent to the handing over of the consignment to the railway for carriage.[2]

108. Person entitled to claim compensation. (1) If a railway administration pays compensation for the loss, destruction, damage, deterioration or non-delivery of goods entrusted to it for carriage, to the consignee or the endorsee producing the railway receipt, the railway administration shall be deemed to have discharged its liability and no application before the Claims Tribunal or any other legal proceeding shall lie against the railway administration on the ground that the consignee or the endorsee was not legally entitled to receive such compensation.

(2) Nothing in sub-section (1) shall affect the right of any person having any interest in the goods to enforce the same against the consignee or the endorsee receiving compensation under that sub-section.

Locus standi of person to claim compensation Compensation for loss of goods or damage to the consignment is payable to the consignee or endorsee producing the railway receipt by the railway administration.

19 *Bootamal* v *Union of India* AIR 1962 SC 1716; (1963)1 SCR 70.
20 AIR 1957 Punj 49.
21 *R.K. Kanodia* v *Union of India* AIR 1959 Cal 701; 63 CWN 757.
1 AIR 1975 Cal 417.
2 *Lalchand Chowdhury* v *Union of India* AIR 1960 Cal 270.

109. Railway administration against which application for compensation for personal injury is to be filed. An application before the Claims Tribunal for compensation for the loss of life or personal injury to a passenger, may be instituted against,—

(*a*) the railway administration from which the passenger obtained his pass or purchased his ticket, or

(*b*) the railway administration on whose railway the destination station lies or the loss or personal injury occurred.

1 Corresponding provisions in the old Act This section corresponds to s. 80 of the old Act.

2 Scope Claim under s. 109 of the new Act for personal injury falls within the jurisdiction of Railway Claims Tribunal. The application for such claim for compensation is to be made against (*i*) the railway administration from which the passenger obtained his pass or purchased his ticket; or (*ii*) the railway administration on whose railway the destination station lies or the loss or personal injury occurred. Section 80 of the old Act corresponding to s. 109 of the new Act is a complete, self-contained and exhaustive Code in regard to the place of suing regarding a suit for compensation for personal injuries against railway administration constituting a special law for such suit excluding, by necessary implication, the operation of provisions of s. 20 of the Code of Civil Procedure and s. 18 of the Presidency Small Causes Court Act. The use of the expression "may be instituted" in s. 80 of the old Act is equivalent to "shall be instituted".[3]

110. Burden of proof. In an application before the Claims Tribunal for compensation for loss, destruction, damage, deterioration or non-delivery of any goods, the burden of proving—

(*a*) the monetary loss actually sustained; or

(*b*) where the value has been declared under sub-section (2) of section 103 in respect of any consignment that the value so declared is its true value,

shall lie on the person claiming compensation, but subject to the other provisions contained in this Act, it shall not be necessary for him to prove how the loss, destruction, damage, deterioration or non-delivery was caused.

1 Corresponding provisions in the old Act This section corresponds to s. 78A of the old Act.

2 Scope This section deals with burden of proof for compensation or monetary loss, damage or non-delivery of any goods to the claimant before the Railway Claims Tribunal lies on the claimant.

3 *Union of India* v *Ratan Lall Adukia* AIR 1987 Cal 311 (FB); (1987)2 CLJ 1; (1987)2 CHN 95 affirmed in *Ratanlal* v *Union of India* AIR 1990 SC 104; (1989)3 SCC 537; (1989)3 SCR 583; JT 1989(3) SC 148.

3 Burden of proof In the case of *Secretary of State for India in Council* v *Ramdhan Das Dwarka Das*,[4] the learned Judges in dealing with the burden of proof observed as follows: "As regards burden of proof, the three classes of suits have to be kept apart from each other: one, dependent entirely upon ss. 151 and 152 of the Indian Contract Act 1872; another in which s. 9 of the Carriers Act 1865 has to be borne in mind; and the third, within which category the present suits fall, in which not only ss. 151 and 152 of the Indian Contract Act 1872 but s. 76 of the Indian Railways Act 1890 have to be applied. So far as the class of suits last mentioned is concerned, SCOTT, CJ. in the case of *Lakhi Chand* v *G.I.P. Railway*[5] observed that s. 76 of the Indian Railways Act 1890, is not by any means the same in terms as s. 9 of the Carriers Act 1865 and it should not be read as increasing the onus of proof laid upon a bailee by s. 151 of the Indian Contract Act 1872. The learned Chief Justice was inclined to take the view that the section may have been enacted to make it clear that a suit against a railway company was to be regarded as an action for breach of contract and not an action in case. BATCHELOR, J. and ROBERTSON, J. in the same case seem to have been inclined to the view that s. 76 of the Indian Railways Act 1890, by taking away from the plaintiff the burden of proving how the loss, destruction or deterioration was caused, has recognised the principle that loss, destruction or deterioration itself is *prima facie* evidence that due care was not taken, because the goods were in defendant's sole possession and he ought to be able to account for the loss, destruction or deterioration. In the view taken by the learned Judges, this presumption or inference of negligence may be rebutted or repelled on behalf of the railway administration. The foundation of this presumption was explained in the case of *Phipps* v *New Claridge's Hotels Ltd.*[6] in which it was said that where goods are given into the sole custody of a person and accepted by him as bailee and they are lost while in his custody, the onus lies on him to show circumstances negativing negligence on his apart ...... In a large number of cases it has been held by Indian courts that loss or damage of goods entrusted to a bailee is *prima facie* evidence of negligence and the burden of proof to disprove negligence lies on a railway administration in the absence of special contract to the contrary."

In a case coming under ss. 72 and 76 of the Indian Railways Act 1890, two questions are: first, what is the degree of care that the railway

4 37 CWN 1109 (1111).
5 37 Bom 1.
6 22 TLR 49.

administration has taken with regard to all consignments generally which may be similarly placed, and second, what care has it taken with regard to the particular consignment? Each of the two questions, again, has two branches, one with reference to the duty of taking all reasonable precautions to obviate the risk of loss, and the other with reference to the duty of taking all proper measures for the protection of goods when such risk has already occurred.

In a suit for damages for short delivery, etc., of goods, the burden of proving the amount of loss, is upon the plaintiff and in the absence of any proof adduced by the plaintiff, the court cannot grant a decree for the amount which was accepted by the assessing Inspector of Railways without prejudice at the time of granting delivery.[7] But see *Union of India* v *Haji Latif*,[8] to the contrary. The burden of proof is on the railway to show that as much care as required was taken by them. Non-production of such materials will justify raising adverse presumption against them.[9]

4 Burden of proof under new section Where a consignment of goods despatched by rail is damaged and a suit is brought against the railway for damages, the onus of proving the value of the goods booked, the actual loss and the extent of damage is on the plaintiff. A Damage Certificate state only the fact that the damages had, in fact, been caused to the goods but it does not amount to an acknowledgment of fact that the damage was caused by negligence or misconduct on the part of the railway administration.[10]

5 Short delivery of goods The burden of proof to establish the fact that shortage of delivery of goods took place lies on the claimant himself. To discharge the said burden, the claimant submitted applications before the Railway Claims Tribunal on various dates praying for discovery of documents alleged to be in custody of railway authorities. Order sheet showed that such applications received any consideration of the Tribunal. The Tribunal held that railway authorities failed to produce documents and as such allowed the claim applications. The Tribunal did not construe provisions of ss. 110 and 65 of the Railways Act 1989 as to burden of proof in claim cases. The order of the Tribunal was, therefore, liable to be set aside.[11]

7 *Union of India* v *Shew Bux* AIR 1965 Cal 636.

8 AIR 1961 MP 190.

9 *Union of India* v *Munnalal Pasari* AIR 1971 MP 131; 1970 MPLJ 758; 1970 MPWR 983.

10 *Union of India* v *Madan Mohan* AIR 1981 Ori 9; (1980)50 Cut LT 29.

11 *Union of India* v *P.P. Enterprise* AIR 2014 Gau 99.

6 Compensation claimed for short delivery of goods Claimant must prove actual entrustment and loading of consignment in its quantity and nature of consignment as well as its value. Claimant failed to establish actual quantity of goods that were loaded. Merely because of the fact that R.R. contained weight on which basis the Railways had charged freight, quantity of shortfall cannot be ascertained by merely taking weight and measure of quantity which had been received at destination. Dismissal of claim was held to be proper.[12]

111. Extent of liability of railway administration in respect of accidents at sea. (1) When a railway administration contracts to carry passengers or goods partly by railway and partly by sea, a condition exempting the railway administration from responsibility for any loss of life, personal injury or loss of or damage to goods which may happen during the carriage by sea from act of God, public enemies, fire, accidents from machinery, boilers and steam and all and every other dangers and accidents of the seas, rivers and navigation of whatever nature and kind shall, without being expressed, be deemed to be part of the contract, and, subject to that condition, the railway administration shall, irrespective of the nationality or ownership of the ship used for the carriage by sea, be responsible for any loss of life, personal injury or loss of or damage to goods which may happen during the carriage by sea, to the extent to which it would be responsible under the Merchant Shipping Act 1958 (44 of 1958), if the ships were registered under that Act and the railway administration were owner of the ship and not to any greater extent.

(2) The burden of proving that any such loss, injury or damage as is mentioned in sub-section (1) happened during the carriage by sea shall lie on the railway administration.

1 Corresponding provisions in the old Act This section corresponds to s. 82 of the old Act.

2 Scope Section 111 of the Act deals with the extent of liability of railway administration in respect of accidents at sea where a railway administration contracts to carry passengers or goods partly by railway and partly by sea.

3 Proof The case *Davey* v *L. & S.W. Railway Co.*,[13] laying down the law on the point where the plaintiff claimed damages from a railway company for negligence says: "In such an action as this, the burden of proof lies entirely upon the plaintiff. There are two things for him to establish, one affirmative, the other negative. It is for the plaintiff to show that the accident which happened to him was caused by a negligent act of the defendants, or of those for whose negligent acts the defendants are liable,

12 *Indian Oil Corporation Ltd.* v *Union of India* AIR 2010 Raj 28 relying on *Hari Sao* v *State of Bihar* AIR 1970 SC 843.

13 [1884]12 QBD 70; 53 LJQB 58; 49 LT 739.

and that the accident was produced as between him and the defendants solely by the defendants' negligence in this sense that he himself was not guilty of any negligence which contributed to the accident, so that the accident was the result of the joint negligence of the plaintiff and of the defendants then the plaintiff cannot recover, it being understood that, if the defendants' servants could by reasonable care have avoided injuring the plaintiff, although he was negligent, then the negligence of the plaintiff would not contribute to the accident."

112. Power to make rules in respect of matters in this Chapter. (1) The Central Government may, by notification, make rules to carry out the purposes of this Chapter.

(2) In particular, and without prejudice to the generality of the foregoing power, such rules may provide for all or any of the following matters, namely:—

(*a*) the manner of packing of goods entrusted to a railway administration under clause (*b*) of sub-section (1) of section 98;

(*b*) the goods for the purposes of sub-section (3) of section 99; and

(*c*) the maximum amount payable by the railway administration for the loss, destruction, damage, deterioration or non-delivery of any consignment under sub-section (1) of section 103.

CHAPTER XII
Accidents

113. Notice of railway accident. (1) Where, in the course of working a railway,—

(*a*) any accident attended with loss of any human life, or with grievous hurt, as defined in the Indian Penal Code (45 of 1860), or with such serious injury to property as may be prescribed; or

(*b*) any collision between trains of which one is a train carrying passengers; or

(*c*) the derailment of any train carrying passengers, or of any part of such train; or

(*d*) any accident of a description usually attended with loss of human life or with such grievous hurt as aforesaid or with serious injury to property; or

(*e*) any accident of any other description which the Central Government may notify in this behalf in the Official Gazette,

occurs, the station master of the station nearest to the place at which the accident occurs or where there is no station master, the railway servant in charge of the section of the railway on which the accident occurs, shall, without delay, give notice of the accident to the District Magistrate and Superintendent of Police, within whose jurisdiction the accident occurs, the officer in charge of the police station within the local limits of which the accident occurs and to such other Magistrate or police officer as may be appointed in this behalf by the Central Government.

(2) The railway administration within whose jurisdiction the accident occurs, as also the railway administration to whom the train involved in the accident belongs, shall without delay, give notice of the accident to the State Government and the Commissioner having jurisdiction over the place of the accident.

1 Corresponding old provisions in the Act This section corresponds to s. 83 of the old Act.

2 Meaning of words

(a) "*Accident*". Ordinarily, it means a mishap or an untoward event.[1]

"Accident" connotes something unexpected and not attributable to person concerned.[2] The "accident" envisaged by the first part of s. 82A(1) of the Railways Act 1890 is an accident to "the train" or "a part of the train" and not an accident to a passenger. An accident is an occurrence or an event which is unforeseen and startling, happening of which is not inherent in the normal course of events and is not ordinarily expected to happen or to occur. An event or occurrence the happening of which is ordinarily expected in the normal course by almost everyone undertaking a railway journey cannot be called an "accident."[3]

(b) "*Loss*". It means an invasion of a legally protected interested vested in another person.[4]

3 Railway accident report—admissibility Section 83 of the (old) Railways Act (corresponding to s. 113 of the new Act) provides that if there is any accident attended with loss of human life or grievous hurt or with serious injury to property, notice shall be given to various persons. Section 84 of the (old) Railways Act confers power on the Central Government to make Rules for several purposes including the purpose of prescribing the duties of railway servants, police officers, inspectors or Magistrates on the occurrence of an accident. The Central Government authorised the Railway Board to make Rules in pursuance of s. 84 of the (old) Railways Act. Rule 18 of the Railway Board Rules provides that whenever an accident has occurred in the course of working of a railway, the agent or manager shall cause an enquiry to be promptly made by a committee or railway officers (to be called a joint enquiry) for the thorough investigation of the causes which led to the accident. This enquiry report is admissible in evidence without any proof under ss. 5, 7 and 9, Evidence Act. The Supreme Court endorsed the view of the High Court that the report is admissible under ss. 5, 7 and 9, Evidence Act. And significantly observed that

1 *Bal Shakti* v *New Manekchowk Mills Co.* AIR 1961 Guj 34.

2 *LIC* v *Hira Lal* (2011)14 SCC 445.

3 *Union of India* v *Sunil Kumar Ghosh* AIR 1984 SC 1737.

4 *Consumer Unity and Trust Society* v *Chairmen and Managing Director* (1995)2 SCC 150; JT 1995(2) SC 51.

High Court did not go into the question whether it is admissible under s. 35, Evidence Act.[5]

4 Railway accident Railway authorities failed to conduct any enquiry as per ss. 114 and 115 of the Railways Act 1989. Adverse inference can be drawn against railways for non-production of the enquiry report as per s. 113 of the said Act. There was negligence on the part of the railway administration for not taking precautionary measures at a time when train was due to pass through level crossing. Thus, accident happened due to negligence of railway authorities. According to r. 3 of the Railway Accident and Untoward Incidents (Compensation) Rules 1990, railway accident happened due to negligence for not taking sufficient safeguards at the level crossing as a result of which there were deaths of three children and 85% disability of a person. The High Court, therefore, awarded compensation of ₹3.50 lakh to each one of the petitioners whose child died and ₹5.00 lakh to the injured claimant with interest @ 7% per annum on the compensation amount from the date of the claim till realisation.[6]

> **114. Inquiry by Commissioner.** (1) On the receipt of a notice under section 113 of the occurrence of an accident to a train carrying passengers resulting in loss of human life or grievous hurt causing total or partial disablement of permanent nature to a passenger or serious damage to railway property, the Commissioner shall, as soon as may be, notify the railway administration in whose jurisdiction the accident occurred of his intention to hold an inquiry into the causes that led to the accident and shall at the same time fix and communicate the date, time and place of inquiry:
>
> Provided that it shall be open to the Commissioner to hold an inquiry into any other accident which, in his opinion, requires the holding of such an inquiry.
>
> (2) If for any reason, the Commissioner is not able to hold an inquiry as soon as may be after the occurrence of the accident, he shall notify the railway administration accordingly.

Scope The Commissioner of Railway Safety on receipt of any railway accident under s. 113 of the 1989 Act shall immediately notify the railway administration in whose jurisdiction the accident occurred of his intention to make an inquiry into the causes of the accident. The said notice shall specify the time, date and place of such inquiry. But if for any reason the Commissioner is not in an position to hold the inquiry immediately after the receipt of notice under s. 113 of the Act, they shall notify the same to the railway administration concerned.

5 *Union of India* v *Sagauli Sugar* AIR 1976 SC 1414; 1976 UJ (SC) 328; (1976)3 SCC 32; (1976)2 APLJ 28; (1976)3 SCR 614; ILR (1976) Kant 1185.

6 *Guri Behera* v *D.R.M., East Coast Railway, Khurda* AIR 2012 Ori 62.

115. Inquiry by railway administration. Where no inquiry is held by the Commissioner under sub-section (1) of section 114 or where the Commissioner has informed the railway administration under sub-section (2) of that section that he is not able to hold an inquiry, the railway administration within whose jurisdiction the accident occurs, shall cause an inquiry to be made in accordance with the prescribed procedure.

Inquiry by railway administration If no inquiry is held by the Commissioner of Railway Safety under s. 114 of the Act, it is the bounden duty of the concerned railway administration within whose jurisdiction the accident occurred to cause an inquiry by himself in accordance with the prescribed procedure.

116. Powers of Commissioner in relation to inquiries. (1) For the purpose of conducting an inquiry under this Chapter into the causes of any accident on a railway, the Commissioner shall, in addition to the powers specified in section 7, have the powers as are vested in a civil court while trying a suit under the Code of Civil Procedure, 1908 (5 of 1908), in respect of the following matters, namely:

(*a*) summoning and enforcing the attendance of persons and examining them on oath;

(*b*) requiring the discovery and production of documents;

(*c*) receiving evidence on affidavits;

(*d*) requisitioning any public record or copies thereof from any court or office;

(*e*) any other matter which may be prescribed.

(2) The Commissioner while conducting an inquiry under this Chapter shall be deemed to be a Civil Court for the purposes of section 195 and Chapter XXVI of the Code of Criminal Procedure, 1973 (2 of 1974).

Powers of the Commissioner relating to inquiries The Commissioner of Railway Safety while conducting an inquiry into the causes of accident shall, in addition to the powers vested in him under s. 7 of the Act, have the powers of a civil court under the Code of Civil Procedure in respect of the following matters: (*a*) Summoning and enforcing the attendance of a witness on oath; (*b*) Requiring the discovery and production of any document; (*c*) Receiving evidence on affidavit; (*d*) Requisitioning any public record or copies thereof from any court or office; (*e*) Any other prescribed matter.

The Commissioner in such inquiry shall be deemed to be a civil court for the purposes of s. 195 of the Code of Criminal Procedure 1973.

117. Statement made before Commissioner. No statement made by a person in the course of giving evidence in an inquiry before the Commissioner shall subject him to, or be used against him in, any civil or criminal proceeding, except a prosecution for giving false evidence by such statement:

Provided that the statement is—

(*a*) made in reply to a question which is required by the Commissioner to answer; or

(*b*) relevant to the subject-matter of the inquiry.

118. Procedure, etc. Any railway administration or the Commissioner conducting an inquiry under this Chapter may send notice of the inquiry to such persons, follow such procedure, and prepare the report in such manner as may be prescribed.

119. No inquiry, investigation, etc., to be made if the Commission of Inquiry is appointed. Notwithstanding anything contained in the foregoing provisions of this Chapter, where a Commission of Inquiry is appointed under the Commissions of Inquiry Act, 1952 (3 of 1952), to inquire into an accident, any inquiry, investigation or other proceeding pending in relation to that accident shall not be proceeded with, and all records or other documents relating to such inquiry shall be forwarded to such authority as may be specified by the Central Government in this behalf.

Appointment of Commission of Inquiry In case of appointment of Commission of Inquiry under the Commissions of Inquiry Act 1952 to inquire into an accident, the inquiry by the Commissioner of Railway Safety shall not be proceeded with.

120. Inquiry into accident not covered by section 113. Where any accident of the nature not specified in section 113 occurs in the course of working a railway, the railway administration within whose jurisdiction the accident occurs, may cause such inquiry to be made into the causes of the accident, as may be prescribed.

1 Power of railway administration Even if an accident is not covered by s. 113 of the Act, the railway administration within whose jurisdiction it occurred may hold an inquiry into the causes of the accident.

2 Claim by legal representative Where there was death of a passenger by falling from train the legal representative of only *bona fide* passenger with valid ticket for journey is entitled to compensation.[7]

121. Returns. Every railway administration shall send to the Central Government, a return of accidents occurring on its railway, whether attended with injury to any person or not, in such form and manner and at such intervals as may be prescribed.

Corresponding provision in the old Act This section corresponds to s. 85 of the old Act.

7 *Union of India* v *Smt. Kaushalya Devi* (2002)1 Civ LJ 695 (Pat).

122. Power to make rules in respect of matters in this Chapter. (1) The Central Government may, by notification, make rules to carry out the purposes of this Chapter.

(2) In particular, and without prejudice to the generality of the foregoing power, such rules may provide for all or any of the following matters, namely:

(*a*) the injury to property which shall be considered serious under clause (*a*) of sub-section (1) of section 113;

(*b*) the forms of notice of accidents to be given under section 113 and the particulars of the accident such notices shall contain;

(*c*) the manner of sending the notices of accidents, including the class of accidents to be sent immediately after the accident;

(*d*) the duties of the Commissioner, railway administration, railway servants, police officers and Magistrates on the occurrence of an accident;

(*e*) the persons to whom notices in respect of any inquiry under this Chapter are to be sent, the procedure to be followed in such inquiry and the manner in which a report of such inquiry shall be prepared;

(*f*) the nature of inquiry to be made by a railway administration into the causes of an accident under section 120;

(*g*) the form and manner of sending a return of accidents by a railway administration under section 121.

Corresponding provisions in the old Act This section corresponds to s. 84 of the old Act.

CHAPTER XIII
Liability of Railway Administration for Death and Injury to Passengers due to Accidents

123. Definitions. In this Chapter, unless the context otherwise requires,—

(*a*) "accident" means an accident of the nature described in section 124;

(*b*) "dependant" means any of the following relatives of a deceased passenger, namely:

(*i*) the wife, husband, son and daughter, and in case the deceased passenger is unmarried or is a minor, his parent;

(*ii*) the parent, minor brother or unmarried sister, widowed sister, widowed daughter-in-law and a minor child of a pre-deceased son, if dependant wholly or partly on the deceased passenger;

(*iii*) a minor child of a pre-deceased daughter, if wholly dependant on the deceased passenger;

(*iv*) the paternal grant parent wholly dependant on the deceased passenger.

[1][(c) "untoward incident" means—

(1) (*i*) the commission of a terrorist act within the meaning of sub-section (1) of section 3 of the Terrorist and Disruptive Activities (Prevention) Act, 1987 (28 of 1987); or

(*ii*) the making of a violent attack or the commission of robbery or dacoity; or

(*iii*) the indulging in rioting, shoot out or arson,

by any person in or on any train carrying passengers, or in a waiting hall, cloak room or reservation or booking office or on any platform or in any other place within the precincts of a railway station; or

(2) the accidental falling of any passenger from a train carrying passengers].

1 Scope Derailment of a goods train is not covered for the purposes of s. 123 of the Act. The definitions given in this section relate to death and injury to passengers due to railway accident. Accident means an accident of the nature described in s. 124 of the Act.

2 Untoward incident The term "untoward incident" has been defined in s. 123(*c*) of the Act. It includes accidental falling of any passenger from train carrying passengers.[2] Death of a railway passenger due to strangulation by another passenger while travelling in train amounts to "untoward incident" as defined in s. 123(*c*) of the Act. Thus, the claimants of the victim are entitled to compensation.[3] There was a claim for compensation for death due to untoward incident. Evidence should show that the guard and motorman failed to stop train in spite of ringing of alarm. It amounted to complete dereliction of duty resulting in loss of life of the deceased. Liability was thus due to fault of railway official. The husband of the deceased was awarded compensation.[4]

The deceased received injuries by falling from train. There was no evidence that the deceased committed suicide or that he died of his own criminal act or he was in a state of intoxication. Thus, the railway administration was liable to pay compensation.[5]

Deceased while travelling in passenger train had fallen from train and died when train was in motion. Evidence of witness and investigating

1 *Inserted* by Act 28 of 1994, s. 2. (w.e.f. 1.8.1994).

2 *V. Vijayasankar* v *Union of India* 1995 AIHC 6309 (Ker).

3 *Union of India* v *Aleykutty Devasia* AIR 1997 Ker 321.

4 *P.A. Narayanan* v *Union of India* AIR 1998 SC 1659; (1998)3 SCC 67; JT 1998(1) SC 749.

5 *Union of India* v *Smt. Deomani Devi* AIR 2007 All 178. See *Karri Nagamani* v *Union of India* AIR 2007 AP 241; *Union of India* v *Nakka Lalitha* AIR 2007 NOC 1710 (AP); *Union of India* v *Shaik Prasad Basha* AIR 2007 NOC 166 (AP) (Accident resulting in amputation of both legs); *Rama Shankar Sharma* v *Union of India* AIR 2008 Del 87 (amputation of right leg); *Union of India* v *Sanjoy Bahera* AIR 2009 NOC 875 (Ori).

officer clearly established that deceased had boarded train in question. Deceased was a *bona fide* passenger when he slipped from train. Factum of deceased being *bona fide* passenger cannot be doubted on ground that no luggage was found on his dead body. Railway authority would be liable to pay compensation to the claimants. Under s. 13 of the Railway Claims Tribunal Act 1987, the claimants were also awarded interest at the rate of 6% per annum on the amount of compensation.[6]

Death of passenger occurred due to violent attack or commission of robbery or dacoity. It is not necessary that death should be of several persons. Provision of s. 123(*c*)(1) of the Railways Act 1989 will come into play even if death is of a single person. Fact that the deceased had travelled from one station to another and died of attack by robbers on railway station was established. Refusal to grant compensation on ground that the deceased was the only person who died was held to be not proper.[7]

3 Claim for compensation as dependent Claimant filed an application before the Railway Claims Tribunal due to death of her minor brothers in a railway accident. The case of the claimant does not come under cl. (*i*) or cl. (*iii*) or (*iv*) of s. 123(*b*) of the Railways Act 1989. The claimant cannot be considered as dependent on minor brothers. Thus, the claim of the claimant is not maintainable in connection with death of minor brothers.[8]

4 Daughter, whether dependent Section 123(*b*) of the Railways Act 1989 defines "dependent". Daughter comes within, the definition of "dependent" irrespective of the fact whether she is married or unmarried. Thus, accident claim preferred by married daughters is maintainable. Further, she is not required to prove that she was dependent on her deceased father.[9]

5 Quantum of compensation Railway Accident Rules prior to amendment provided for grant of ₹2,00,000 as compensation in respect of one person's death, but by amendment on 1st November 1997 the said amount was increased to ₹4,00,000 irrespective of earning capacity of the deceased. This amount was distributed among the parents and children of the deceased. But the parents were required to show that they were dependents on the deceased.[10]

6 "Violent attack" The expression "violent attack" being an ingredient of untoward incident should not be construed narrowly. In certain cases

6 *Mummidi Durga* v *Union of India* AIR 2011 NOC 1 (AP).
7 *Sunita* v *Union of India* AIR 2015 NOC 686 (Del).
8 *Union of India* v *Kumari Diptee* AIR 2000 P&H 105.
9 *Union of India* v *N. Kantabai* AIR 2004 AP 228.
10 *Saraswati Das* v *Union of India* AIR 2003 Gau 11; see *Sudhira Mondal* v *Union of India* AIR 2004 Cal 270.

injuries are suffered by the train passengers on account of throwing of stones by the strangers or even by the persons in the precincts of the railway station could hardly be excluded from being called as "untoward incidents" within the meaning the said expression unless the railway administration is able to establish that throwing of stones was either provoked by the passengers themselves.[11]

7 Untoward incident—bona fide passenger Passenger fell down from the running train who was travelling with valid ticket. Claimants in support of their plea filed the train ticket. Specific evidence was also given by passenger travelling with the deceased that he had purchased two tickets and boarded the train along with the deceased. Absence of any evidence by the Railways to disprove the claimants' assertion that the deceased accidentally fell from the train as *bona fide* passenger. The Railways were held liable to pay compensation.[12]

Ticket held by the deceased was not valid for concerned train. He would nevertheless be termed as *bona fide* passenger. Legal heirs of the deceased were held to be entitled to claim compensation under the Railways Act 1989.[13]

Deceased was run over by fast train coming from other side while he was lying on railway track having been thrown out of crowded train due to sudden jerk of train. No evidence led by railway authority to discharge the burden that the deceased was travelling without ticket. Presumption would arise that the deceased was a *bona fide* passenger. Thus, the railway authority was liable to pay compensation.[14]

Inquest report and final report of police showed that the deceased, passenger in Electric Motor Unit, slipped and fell down due to jerk and died due to head injuries. The said reports would be enough to discharge the burden of proof cast on the claimants. On failure of the authority to prove contrary thereto the deceased was rightly held to be *bona fide* passenger. Thus, the Railways were liable to pay compensation.[15]

8 Untoward incident—proof Actual falling of passenger need not be outside train. Passenger can be hit by stone pelted by miscreants from outside who falls within the train. The wording of s. 123(*c*) of the Railways Act 1989 does not require that he should necessarily fall outside the train.[16]

11 *Sanjay Sampatrao Gaikwad* v *Union of India* AIR 2005 Bom 409; see *Lakhi Barna* v *Union of India* AIR 2008 Cal 59.

12 *Makar Gochhi* v *Union of India* AIR 2014 NOC 119 (Ori).

13 *Parisa Anjali* v *Union of India* AIR 2010 AP 67.

14 *Union of India* v *Smt. Sarla* AIR 2010 NOC 1006 (P&H).

15 *Union of India* v *A. Logambal* AIR 2014 Mad 72.

16 *Sahadeo Sindhu Sanas* v *Union of India* AIR 2010 Bom 67 relying on *Union of India* v *Prabhakaran Vijaya Kumar* 2008 AIR SCW 4165.

9 Untoward incident—when not Deceased died because of his own negligence. The deceased was hit by pole resulting in instant death while he was leaning outside the coach. Travelling on step of footboard of any carriage is criminal negligence. Thus, Railway cannot be held to be liable for criminal negligence of the deceased.[17]

DRM's report as well as post mortem report established that the deceased was run over by train while he was crossing railway line. Death was not said to be on account of falling from a running train. Deceased died of his own criminal act or negligence. It could not be said to be an untoward incident. No explanation of witness regarding purchase of ticket was also not found to be cogent one indicating that the deceased was a *bona fide* passenger. Thus, the claim petition was dismissed.[18]

124. Extent of liability. When in the course of working a railway, an accident occurs, being either a collision between trains of which one is a train carrying passengers or the derailment of or other accident to a train or any part of a train carrying passengers, then whether or not there has been any wrongful act, neglect or default on the part of the railway administration such as would entitle a passenger who has been injured or has suffered a loss to maintain an action and recover damages in respect thereof, the railway administration shall, notwithstanding anything contained in any other law, be liable to pay compensation to such extent as may be prescribed and to that extent only for loss occasioned by the death of a passenger dying as a result of such accident, and for personal injury and loss, destruction, damage or deterioration of goods owned by the passenger and accompanying him in his compartment or on the train, sustained as a result of such accident.

Explanation.—For the purposes of this section "passenger" includes a railway servant on duty.

1 Corresponding provisions in the old Act This section corresponds to s. 82A of the old Act.

2 Nature of accident described in s. 124 Accident occurs (*a*) in course of working in a railway, (*b*) due to (*i*) a collision between trains, one of which is carrying passenger, or (*ii*) the derailment of, or (*iii*) other accident to a train or a part of the train carrying passengers, (*c*) a passenger is injured or has suffered loss. Involvement of a train carrying passengers is an essential ingredient of 'accident' as described in s. 124 read with s. 123(*a*) of the Act.

3 Liability of railway administration If death of any railway passenger "occurs due to untoward incident"[19] or complete dereliction of duty on the

17 *Sukhdev Kamlani* v *Union of India* AIR 2011 Del 206.
18 *Mamta* v *Union of India* AIR 2011 Del 118.
19 *Union of India* v *Aleykutty Devasia* AIR 1997 Ker 321.

part of a railway servant[20] compensation is payable to the "dependant" of the victim as defined in s. 123(*b*) of the Act. The liability of railway administration under s. 124 is absolute. It is liable to pay compensation irrespective of the fact whether death is caused by wrongful act, neglect or default on the part of the railway administration or its servants. The factum of derailment itself would give rise to presumption of negligence on the part of the railway administration though the normal rule is that it is for the claimant to prove negligence when the claim is not founded on no fault liability. Mere fact of derailment or any railway accident would, *prima facie*, constitute the negligence on the part of the railway administration. An accident was caused to a railway employee who made a claim under the Workmen's Compensation Act and the Railway deposited certain amount to meet the obligation arising out of that Act. The amount was disbursed to the claimant. Subsequently an application for compensation before the Railway Tribunal was made. Such claim application was not barred. It could not be said that the claimant filed two application for the same cause of action. The amount received earlier could be deducted.[21] The question whether a railway servant on duty at the time of the accident is a passenger has been clarified by the *Explanation* to s. 124 of the new Act and interest is payable on the amount of compensation.[1] In a claim petition arising out of accident a passenger of train fell out of the boggie of the train and died on being caught between the platform and the running train, the claim petition is not cognizable by the Tribunal as the "accident" in question was not an "accident" within the meaning of s. 82A of the old Act.[2]

In 1942, the Dacca Mail met with an accident at Joya Rampur in Bengal. On that occasion, the Bengal Government urged the Government of India the possibility of paying compensation through the medium of insurance scheme. This question was considered by the Government of India. The Government thought that making it compulsory to implement the insurance scheme in such a matter was not free from difficulty, specially for the poor class of people. The Government of India, thereafter, proposed by means of a Bill, which was presented by the Law Minister on 22nd September 1942. Dealing with the requirement of obtaining insurance, the Law Minister felt that some sort of compensation should be paid to the dependants, but making of a provision to obtain an insurance was not possible. To meet the situation, he observed: "The only possible method, therefore, appears to be to take each ticket carry some insurance. We do

20 *P.A. Narayanan* v *Union of India* AIR 1998 SC 1659; (1998)3 SCC 67; JT 1998(1) SC 749.
21 1995 Lab IC 2000 (Kant).
1 *Savitri Roy* v *Union of India* AIR 1994 All 239.
2 *Ratnakar Tanbaji* v *Union of India* AIR 1994 Bom 132.

not want to propose that there should be an additional charge for this purpose, one reason being that, with a very large number of passengers that we carry any insurance scheme would involve the levy of so small a charge which we could possibly make, namely, one pie, would result in sum very much in excess of what we have been paying out in compensation in the past. It is, therefore, proposed that railway revenues shall carry the liability involved".[3] Thus existing fault liability has been turned to "fault or no fault" liability.[4]

4 Applicability The ingredients for invoking the provision of s. 124 of the Act are the following—

(1) The machinery of the section is set in motion only provided there is an *'accident'*.

(2) The accident must be 'to' the 'train' or 'part of the train' carrying passengers.

(3) The *accident* to the train carrying passengers may be due to:

(*a*) collision of two trains one of which is the train carrying passengers; or

(*b*) *derailment* of such train; or

(*c*) other *accident* 'to' such a train.

(4) In case any passenger travelling by such train dies, or sustains any injury to his person or property, as a result of or on account of such accident to the train or a part of the train carrying passengers, compensation *to the extent* provided in the section will become payable.

(5) Such compensation will be payable regardless of whether or not the accident to the train carrying passengers is due to negligence or fault on the part of the railway administration. This provision as no application and cannot refer to an accident to a passenger "whilst" on a passenger train even if the said train is not at all involved in any accident. The philosophy of s. 82A of the old Act (corresponding to s. 124 of the new Act) is to turn an existing 'fault' liability into a 'fault or no fault' liability. Why? Because a carrier who transports passengers as a part of his business, when he charges fare, impliedly guarantees to carry him with safety in so far as such safety is within his power. It is within his power to transport the passenger *without an accident to the train*, for such an accident is not something which is ordinarily or in the

3 *Sundri* v *Union of India* AIR 1984 All 277; 1984 All WC 438; 1984 All CJ 383; (1984)10 All LR 344; (1984)1 ACC 211; 1984 ACJ 614 (FB).

4 *Union of India* v *Sunil Kumar* AIR 1984 SC 1737; (1984)4 SCC 246; 1984 All WC 991.

normal course of events inherent in the running of a train. And presumably in order to be 'fair' to the passengers who pay the 'fare' for a safe (safe from accident to the train) journey, the legislature, with an eye on social welfare, has provided for compensation by a summary proceeding and has made the liability fault-free.[5]

5 Accident to train is essential To attract s. 124, there must be an accident to the train. What is provided is compensation for death or injury caused or loss sustained on account of accident '*to*' the train. What is '*not*' provided is compensation for death of the passenger 'whilst' travelling or injury sustained by a passenger 'whilst' travelling on the train, say, by reason of his own act, defaults or misfortune, which has no nexus with the '*accident to the train*'. In other words, what the section does is to turn a liability which was '*contingent on fault*' into an 'absolute' liability. What, however, it *does not* do, is to provide a free 'insurance cover' to the person and property of a passenger so that compensation can be claimed for the accidental death of or injury to the passenger and/or loss or damage to his property even when there has been no 'accident' to the train carrying such a passenger. So, if a passenger falls from a train when the boggie in which he is travelling is being shunted, he cannot claim any compensation under the section.[6]

6 Forum for deciding a claim consequent to accident to train The forum for deciding a claim consequent to a railway accident is not Claims Commissioner but Railway Claims Tribunal with effect from the date appointed by the Central Government for enforcement of the Railway Claims Tribunal Act 1987 (*vide* s. 13(1)(*a*)(*ii*), Railway Claims Tribunal Act).

The jurisdiction of Claims Commissioner has been ousted retrospectively the moment the appointed date is declared (*vide* s. 15, Railway Claims Tribunal Act). All claims pursuant to and consequent upon an accident to train on the appointed date shall stand transferred to the Claims Tribunal (*vide* s. 24, Railway Claims Tribunal Act).

Union of India, however, might move the High Court under Art. 226 of the Constitution of India alleging that compensation granted to a victim or his heirs is on wrong principle.[7]

The Railway Claims Tribunal Act has entrusted the task of deciding about compensation consequent to accident in trains to Railway Claims

5 *Union of India* v *Sunil Kumar* AIR 1984 SC 1737; (1984)4 SCC 246; 1984 All WC 991.

6 *Union of India* v *Sunil Kumar* (supra).

7 *Union of India* v *Ad hoc Claims Commissioner* AIR 1977 Cal 393; 81 CWN 649; (1977)1 CLJ 456.

Tribunal exclusively. A civil suit is patently barred. For s. 15, Railway Claims Tribunal Act provides that no court or other authority with effect from the appointed date shall be entitled to exercise jurisdiction in the matter. This is an instance of express bar envisaged in s. 9, Code of Civil Procedure. But any one aggrieved by the order of Claims Tribunal may appeal to the High Court within 90 days from the date of order appealed against. No appeal lies against an interlocutory order or consent-order (*vide* s. 23, Railway Claims Tribunal Act).

Tribunal has no jurisdiction to order for deposit of amount of compensation in fixed deposit in case where the claimant is major.[8]

7 Bona fide passengership—essential Section 124 on more places than one has used the expression passenger who is entitled to recover, damages in the event of personal injury in a train-accident, to him or when he is dead due to the accident compensation to his heirs. The word 'passenger' has not been defined in the Act, but the consideration of the legislative history and the scheme of the Act warrant the view that only the dependants of a *bona fide* passenger are entitled to get compensation in the event of death occurring in an accident. Section 124 does not entitle the dependant of a trespasser to get the benefit of the provision. For being a passenger within the meaning of the Act, he must be a person travelling with a ticket, pass or permission of the railway authority.[9]

Compensation can be claimed only in respect of a person who was a *bona fide* passenger. Any body having no ticket, valid pass or travel document cannot be held to be a *bona fide* passenger, burden of proof lies on claimant.[10]

Section 82A of the old Act applies only when the death is of a passenger travelling by train and meeting with an accident. But when somebody other than a passenger is killed in the accident that section has no application.[11] Where the deceased had not bought a ticket but paid the fare to the ticket examiner who had authority to receive the fare on behalf of the railway administration and issue a receipt therefor, the deceased was a *bona fide* passenger and not a trespasser.[12]

A person, who was travelling in a train without a proper pass, ticket or permission, is not a passenger within the meaning of s. 82A of the (old)

8 *Rameshwar Lal* v *Union of India* AIR 2010 NOC 1008 (P&H) relying on *H.S. Ahammed Hussain* v *Irfan Ahammed* AIR 2002 SC 2483.

9 *Sundri* v *Union of India* AIR 1984 All 277; 1984 All WC 438; 1984 All CJ 383; (1984)10 All LR 344.

10 *Yoshada Devi* v *Union of India* AIR 1979 All 287; 1979 All WC 568; ILR (1979)2 All 537; *Sudha Srivastava* v *Claims Commissioner* AIR 1985 All 52; 1985 All LJ 66; 1985 ACJ 404.

11 *Union of India* v *Lalman Badri Prasad* AIR 1954 Vindhay Pradesh 17.

12 *Rajammal* v *Union of India* (1970)2 MLJ 497.

Railways Act.[13] The railway administration is not liable to pay compensation for injuries to a person who was travelling by goods train without a ticket.[14] Where the deceased having purchased a ticket was waiting on a stationary jetty to board a steamer owned and operated by a railway administration and the steamer dashed against the jetty causing death, the deceased would not be deemed to be a passenger nor the jetty a part of the steamer. But the steamer should be deemed to be a railway within the meaning of s. 82A of the old Act.[15]

8 Loss of currency notes—power to award compensation The railway accident is the immediate cause for payment of compensation under s. 82A of the old Act irrespective of whether the accident is or is not due to neglect or wilful act on the part of the railway. Hence if it is found that the loss of money or currency notes is due to a railway accident, compensation is payable.[16]

9 Partial disablement The person who suffers from temporary disablement is entitled to some compensation under the provisions of s. 82A, Indian Railways Act 1890. The basis on which the compensation is to be fixed is not the same on which damages are allowed under the common law of any wrongful act, neglect or default on the part of the railway administration. The only safe criterion for fixing the amount of compensation payable will be on the basis of loss of earning capacity. Neither s. 82A of the old Act nor any of the rules indicates that medical expenses reasonably incurred by the injured person have to be taken into consideration.[17]

10 Compensation more than once. Where a person has recovered compensation under s. 82A of the old Act, he or, in case of his death, his heirs cannot claim compensation over again in respect of the same accident under any other law. Section 82H of the old Act clearly provides that.[18]

11 Compensation for injury or death caused by accident The basic principle on which calculations as to damages should ordinarily be made in cases of injury or death caused by a railway accident is that laid down by Lord Blackburn in *Livingstone* v *Rawyards Coal Co.*,[19] which is said to be as follows: "Where any injury is to be compensated by damages, in settling the sum of money given for reparation or damages you should as nearly as possible get at that sum of money which would put the party who has

13 *Ramchandra Prasad* v *Union of India* AIR 1959 Pat 316.
14 *Union of India* v *Harbans Kaur* AIR 1957 Punj 164; 59 Punj LR 189.
15 *Mohamad Khaliluddin* v *Union of India* AIR 1962 Pat 109.
16 *Union of India* v *B.K. Ojha* AIR 1972 All 266; 1972 All WR (HC) 168; 1972 All LJ 311.
17 *Suresh Chandra* v *E.I.R.* AIR 1954 Pat 507.
18 *Zaibunisa* v *Divisional Superintendent* AIR 1965 Mys 306; (1965)1 Mys LJ 215.
19 [1880]5 AC 25; 42 LT 334.

been injured, or who has suffered, in the same position as he would have been if he had not sustained the wrong for which he is now getting the compensation or reparation".

Under the Fatal Accidents Act 1855 damages may be claimed under two heads. In s. 1A of the Act, a right has been given to ask for damages proportionate to the loss resulting from such death to the parties claiming such damages. This is the first head of damages, that is, it is reparation for the loss caused to the beneficiaries mentioned in the Act. There is a second head of claim which is mentioned in s. 2 of the Fatal Accidents Act 1855:

> "Provided that, in any such action or suit, the executor, administrator or representative of the deceased may insert a claim for and recover any pecuniary loss to the estate of the deceased occasioned by such wrongful act, neglect or default, which sum, when recovered, shall be deemed part of the assets of the estate of the deceased".
>
> [But the above mentioned provision has been repealed by Act of 1871.]

Unless there is a specific claim under the second head, the court will confine itself to the first head of loss to the beneficiaries themselves.[20] The provision in s. 86 of the old Act that the authority may order that a victim may be examined by qualified medical practitioner is not an essential condition for determining compensation and absence of such examination will not render any determination of compensation for a railway accident nugatory. The section is not mandatory but merely directory.[1]

12 Accident of a bus hired by railway A combined reading of s. 124 and s. 2(31)(*e*) of the new Act makes it clear that if an accident of a bus hired by the railway authority takes place, it would be, for the purpose of compensation, termed as a railway accident. The doctrine of remoteness is not applicable in view of the definition of the word "railway".[2]

13 Compensation for untoward incident The injured person purchased a valid season ticket and was actually in possession of the same and while attempting to board the train carrying passengers fell from the train and was seriously injured. The claimant is entitled to compensation. The High Court declined to interfere with the award of the Tribunal.[3]

14 Claim for accidental death The deceased fell down from train and was crushed between train and platform while travelling as a passenger in the second class railway compartment. The finding of the Tribunal was that

20 *Jeet Kumari* v *Chittagong E. & E. Supply Co.* AIR 1947 Cal 195; 51 CWN 419.
1 *Union of India* v *Ad hoc Claims Commissioner* AIR 1977 Cal 393; 81 CWN 649; (1981)1 CLJ 456.
2 *Nridhaniya Devi* v *Union of India* AIR 2000 Gau 4.
3 *Union of India* v *Uggina Srinivasa Rao* AIR 2001 AP 360.

it was a case of accidental fall. Thus, the award of compensation by the Tribunal cannot be interfered with in appeal.[4]

15 Compensation for injuries The provisions under s. 124 of the Railways Act 1989 and rr. 3 and 4 of the Railway Accidents (Compensation) Rules 1990 are like a contract of insurance in the widest sense of the term. They are beneficial provisions for providing monetary help in the event of a passenger suffering injuries in an accident or giving compensation to the dependents of the deceased in the event of an accident taking place. The relief under these provisions is an alternative remedy apart from what he can claim under the law of torts or any other law inforce.[5]

[6]**124A. Compensation on account of untoward incident.** When in the course of working a railway an untoward incident occurs, then whether or not there has been any wrongful act, neglect or default on the part of the railway administration such as would entitle a passenger who has been injured or the dependant of a passenger who has been killed to maintain an action and recover damages in respect thereof, the railway administration shall, notwithstanding anything contained in any other law, be liable to pay compensation to such extent as may be prescribed and to that extent only for loss occasioned by the death of, or injury to, a passenger as a result of such untoward incident:

Provided that no compensation shall be payable under this section by the railway administration if the passenger dies or suffers injury due to—

(*a*) suicide or attempted suicide by him;

(*b*) self-inflicted injury;

(*c*) his own criminal act;

(*d*) any act committed by him in a state of intoxication or insanity;

(*e*) any natural case or disease or medical or surgical treatment unless such treatment becomes necessary due to injury caused by the said untoward incident.

Explanation.—For the purposes of this section, "passenger" includes—

(*i*) a railway servant on duty; and

(*ii*) a person who has purchased a valid ticket for travelling by a train carrying passengers, on any date or a valid platform ticket and becomes a victim of an untoward incident.

1 Compensation for untoward incident Making a violent attack or the commission of robbery or dacoity would amount to an untoward incident and if the victim dies of such incident, the claimant would be entitled to compensation under s. 124A of the Act.[7] If a passenger falls from a train

4 *General Manager, South Central Rly.* v *K. Narayana Rao* AIR 2000 AP 53.
5 *L. Sridhar* v *Union of India* AIR 2000 Kant 344.
6 *Inserted* by Act 28 of 1994, s. 3 (w.e.f. 1.8.1994).
7 *Union of India* v *Aleykutty Devasia* AIR 1997 Ker 321.

in stationary state which resulted in a complete damage to spinal cord, he is entitled to compensation.[8] Where an accident occurred at the time the deceased was getting down from compartment with child in her hand and the compartment stopped short of platform and no warning or signal was given before the train started and nor was the level of platform raised after converting the rail to broad gauge, the accident was due to negligence on the part of the railway servant and not contributory negligence on the part of the deceased.[9]

Where Railways discharged their statutory liabilities by installing warning board on both sides of level crossings and the deceased having ignored the said warning fell and being the victim of incident he died due to multiple injuries, such an incident cannot be said to be railway accident and/or untoward incident within the meaning of the Railways Act 1989 and the Railway Claims Tribunal Act 1987. The deceased was not a passenger so as to claim compensation. Section 124A of the Railways Act 1989 debars compensation even to a passenger as defined in s. 2(29) of the said Act if a passenger dies or suffers injury due to incident mentioned in the said section. Section 161 of the Railways Act 1989 debars negligence in crossing an unmanned level crossing. Therefore, the claim for compensation under the Act was not maintainable.[10]

Person possessing valid ticket is a *bona fide* passenger. The intendment of legislation is not to extend benefits of compensation under the Railways Act 1989 to each and every victim irrespective of whether he possesses a valid ticket or not to travel by train. Section 2(29) of the Act clearly postulates that a passenger is one who possesses valid ticket to travel by train. The concept of *bona fide* passenger is emanated from this provision.[11]

Deceased fell down from train while throwing banana skin from door which was open. Standing near the open door and travelling in another coach in the same train and not in particular seat of reserved coach are not criminal acts so as to absolve the Railways from liability to pay compensation to the lawful claimants. Acts of the deceased do not come within any of categories in cls. (*a*) to (*e*) of proviso to s. 124A of the Railways Act 1989. Death was caused due to untoward incident. Deceased travelling on valid ticket was a *bona fide* passenger. The claimants who are parents of the deceased are, therefore, entitled to compensation.[12]

The claimant was engaged as Mazdoor under the Nagaland Mazdoor Co-operative Society Ltd. Railway Administration engaged contractor for

8 *V. Vijayasankar* v *Union of India* 1995 AIHC 6309.

9 *Ulahannan Rajan* v *Union of India* AIR 1992 Ker 230.

10 *Smt. Ranjana Bala Chanda* v *Assistant Registrar, Railway Claims Tribunal* AIR 2012 Gau 73.

11 *Gatten Rajya Laxmi* v *Union of India* AIR 2011 NOC 293 (AP).

12 *Varkey* v *Union of India* AIR 2011 Ker 62.

handling parcel under whom the claimant was engaged. The said society duly authorised the claimant to render services and earn wages in railway station. In course of discharging his duty he sustained injury on his leg resulting in imputation. Claim for compensation by the claimant is maintainable under s. 124A of the Railways Act 1989.[13]

Deceased was a *bona fide* passenger. He fell down from train on account of heavy rush of passengers and sudden jerk of train. The claim application under s. 16 of the Railway Claims Tribunal Act 1987 was filed before the Tribunal by the dependants of the deceased. But the Tribunal dismissed the said claim application. No evidence was produced by the Railway administration to establish that the deceased tried to get down negligently from a running train. In cross-examination of eyewitness of incident nothing was brought out by railway authorities to discredit said witnesses. Falling down of the deceased was said to be clearly accidental. Thus, the claimants were entitled to receive compensation with interest.[14]

2 Transfer of pending cases before civil courts Section 124A of the Railways Act 1989 is to be read in conjunction with ss. 13 and 24 of the Railway Claims Tribunal Act 1987 so as to find out as to whether an untoward accident look place after commencement of s. 124A of the Railways Act as amended in 1994. The award made by the Railway Claims Tribunal cannot be interfered with the ground of lack of jurisdiction.[15]

3 Untoward incident The deceased, a military personnel, had fallen down from train and died. There was no proof that he was travelling without ticket or that he had intention to commit suicide. Incident was held to be an untoward incident and as such the order awarding compensation by the Railway Claims Tribunal was proper.[16]

The claimant was a *bona fide* passenger holding Monthly Seasonal Ticket (MST). On the fateful day he by mistake entered a compartment reserved for army personnel. It was alleged that the claimant was thrown out by army personnel and in consequence thereof he suffered grievous injuries. The claimant suffered injuries because of untoward incident as per s. 124A of the Railways Act 1989. The claimant was entitled to ₹2,00,000 as compensation along with interest @ 10% p.a. from the date of the petition till actual payment.[17]

4 Compensation for accidental fall from train on the basis of amended rules The right of the injured to claim compensation as well as the liability of the railway administration are both reposed in s. 124A of the Railways

13 *Haree Narajan Gupta* v *Union of India* AIR 2011 NOC 55 (Gau).
14 *Harvinder Kaur* v *Union of India* AIR 2011 Del 115.
15 *Union of India* v *Mulko Bai* AIR 2002 MP 22.
16 *Union of India* v *Ishna Kanhar* AIR 2000 Ori 147; (2001)1 Civ LJ 848.
17 *Ashutosh Dwivedi* v *Union of India* AIR 2009 NOC 1710 (All).

Act 1989. The right is to maintain an action and recover the damages. The liability is to pay "compensation to such extent as may be prescribed." The collocation of the words "as may be prescribed" in s. 124A is to be understood to mean "as may be prescribed from time to time". The relevance of the date of untoward incident is that the right to claim compensation from the railway administration by the injured on that date. The statute did not fix the amount of compensation, but left it to be determined by the Central Government from time to time by means of rules. Hence the time of ordering payment is more important to determine as to what is the extent of the compensation which is prescribed by the rules to be disbursed to the claimant. When a claimant goes before the Railway Claims Tribunal claiming compensation, the determination of the amount should be as on the date of such determination. The Railway Accident Compensation Rules 1990 after amendment with effect from 1st November 1997 have raised the quantum of compensation. Though the accident occurred on 3rd September 1996, the victim cannot be deprived of the increased compensation amount as revised with effect from 1st November 1997 with interest thereon.[18]

5 Additional compensation The additional compensation is claimable on the happening of a subsequent event, namely the death of the person who was injured in the accident. It is in the nature of a second cause of action. Quantum has to be assessed on the basis of Rule which is in force at the time of the death. A reference is to given to the provisions of the Railways Act 1989 which provided for interim relief by the railway administration. Thus, the non-obstante clause in ss. 124 and 124A would exclude the provisions of s. 5 of the General Clauses Act 1897. Sections 124 and 124A would clearly show that it is not the provisions of the General Clauses Act that have been excluded, but reference is to the provisions of other statutes like the Fatal Accidents Act 1855, Workmen's Compensation Act 1923 etc. Apart from the above, it can be seen that the Amendment Rules of 1997 to the Untoward Incident (Compensation) Rules 1990 provided that they would come into force on 1st November 1997.[19]

6 Compensation for robbery as untoward incident A combined reading of s. 123 and s. 124A of the Railways Act 1989 is that the intention of the Legislature was to compensate a person who suffers the loss/injury/death while travelling in train or even in the precincts of railways under licence after obtaining required tickets. The railway has got its own separate police force called Railway Protection Force. When offence is committed on the precincts of railways, such offence can be tried by Railway Magistrate duty appointed in this respect. The railway is bound to see or make all arrangements of protection of the passengers for their safety till their

18 *Rathi Menon* v *Union of India* AIR 2001 SC 1333; (2001)2 Civ LJ 724 (SC).
19 *Union of India* v *M. Thakaraj* AIR 2000 Ker 91.

destination. If a passenger is attacked and robbed of his valuable and such incident is tried by the Railway Claims Tribunal or by a court of competent jurisdiction, such passenger on submitting sufficient proof can maintain a claim against the railway as because such incident would fall within the definition of untoward incident. Section 124A of the Railways Act 1989 mentions the word "injury" which includes not only bodily injury but also any type of violence, minor or major, or hurt or threat which ultimately results in robbing the passenger, particularly when the robbery can be caused under the fear of instant death or hurt as defined in s. 390 of the Indian Penal Code. It is not at all essential that the passenger must also physically bleed before being robbed and only then application for compensation is maintainable.[20]

7 Claim for compensation for death due to untoward incident There is no dispute that under the new Act there is a statutory liability of the railway administration for death and/or injury of a passenger due to any untoward incident while travelling in train. Besides, it is a breach of common law duty of reasonable case which lies upon all carriers including the railways. The standard of case is high and strict. Where there is a complete dereliction of duty of railway officials which resulted in a precious life been taken away rendering the guarantee under Art. 21 of the Constitution illusory. The deceased was robbed and assaulted while travelling in a local train. The guard and motorman failed to stop the train in spite of ringing of alarm. Thus, the husband of the deceased was awarded compensation of rupees two lakhs.[21]

8 Railway Accidents and Untoward Incidents (Compensation) Rules 1990 as amended in 1997 The question arose in *N. Parmeswaran Pillai* v *Union of India*[22] as to whether enhanced rate of compensation according to the amended Rules of 1997 which came into force on 1st November 1997 would be payable to an accidental death occurred prior to the commencement date of the amended Rules. The Railway Claims Tribunal must consider what the Rules prescribed at the time of making the order for payment of the compensation. In this connection reference was also made to *Rathi Menon* v *Union of India.*[23]

9 Bona fide passenger A deceased while boarding a train fell down, because the train moved immediately without giving any whistle. Person who accompanied the deceased while travelling stated on affidavit that the deceased purchased the ticket. No evidence was produced by the railway

20 *Union of India* v *Kamlesh Goyal* AIR 2001 Raj 102.
21 *P.A. Narayanan* v *Union of India* AIR 1998 SC 1659; (1998)3 SCC 67; JT 1998(1) SC 749.
22 (2002)4 SCC 306.
23 (2001)3 SCC 714.

administration to rebut the said statement. Thus, the deceased was a *bona fide* passenger. The claimants of the deceased were entitled to compensation of ₹2 lakhs.[24]

Mere non-production of ticket cannot be ground to draw adverse inference that the person who got injured and succumbed to death was travelling without a valid journey ticket and that he was not a *bona fide* passenger. Normal presumption is that a passenger in a railway holds a valid ticket. Burden is heavily upon the railway to prove that the deceased attempted such journey without purchasing a ticket.[25]

10 Scope of s. 124A and s. 123(c) The words used in s. 124A of the Railways Act 1989 or in the Amendment Act of 1994 do not indicate that the Parliament intended to apply the section with retrospective, effect. Therefore cl. (*c*) of s. 123 and s. 124A inserted by the Amending Act of 1994 cannot legitimately be pressed in service for testing the question of liability of the railways on the date of incident which occurred on 14th July 1992 when such definition of untoward incident was not in the statute book.[1]

11 Burden of proof regard unauthorised traveller After the Amendment Act 28 of 1994 in order to claim compensation, the burden is not cast on the claimants to prove negligence, wrongful act or default on the part of the railway administration. But the burden is now on the railways to prove that the deceased is not a *bona fide* passenger with a valid ticket and the nature of death falls within any of the exceptions to s. 124 of the Railways Act 1989.[2]

Burden of proof that the deceased was a ticketless traveller or not a *bona fide* passenger is on the railway administration.[3]

Burden of proving that a person travelling in railway has a valid ticket is on him. But such principle is not applicable to a case of a dead person who had been proved to have died in course of railway travel and whose body was taken in custody of railway police. In such a case it is the duty of the railway authority to first give evidence that he was without a valid ticket. On such evidence being given, the onus shifts upon the claimants to prove that he was a *bona fide* passenger having a valid ticket.[4]

24 *Devkabai* v *Union of India* AIR 2006 MP 201.
25 *Union of India* v *Leelamma* AIR 2009 Ker 134.
1 *Union of India* v *Satish Patidar* AIR 2003 MP 205.
2 *Union of India* v *Baburao Koddekar,* AIR 2003 AP 23; see *Dasari Laxmi* v *Union of India* AIR 2003 AP 56; *Sugan Chand* v *Union of India* AIR 2003 Del 455 (non-production post-mortem report of the deceased was not material when accident was admitted by the respondent); *Union of India v Murti Devi* AIR 2004 Del 216; *Leelavathamma* v *Union of India* AIR 2004 Kant 215; *G.M.S.E.Rly.* v *K.N. Rao* AIR 2004 AP 442; *Bhagwani Giri* v *Union of India* AIR 2005 Raj 54.
3 *Gabinda Pradhan* v *Union of India* AIR 2009 NOC 302 (Ori).
4 *Asharani Das* v *Union of India* AIR 2009 Cal 205.

12 Entry into train from off-side of platform Immediately after boarding the train from the off-side of the platform, that is from non-platform side, the train began to move with a jerk due to which the deceased fell down. It cannot be said that there was negligence on the part of the deceased. The railway has failed to provide clear passage to board train as wooden logs were kept due to which way was obstructed. There was no evidence in rebuttal to prove that it was a self-inflicted injury adduced by railways. Thus, the railways cannot escape liability to make payment of compensation.[5] Jolt of train is not usual one. Deceased falling down from train because of sudden jerk of train is an untoward incident.[6]

13 Passengers thrown out of train When passengers thrown out of train by anti-social elements resulting in their death, compensation for untoward incidents is to be decided by Railway Tribunal and none else.[7]

14 Licensed porter A licensed porter is not an employee under the railways. Fact that licensed porters are entitled to free travel in the railways and medical facilities does not make them employees. But a licensed porter is entitled to compensation on account of death caused in an untoward incident under s. 124A of the Railways Act 1989. Under the *Explanation* to s. 124A, a passenger is given a wide meaning to cover even a person who holds a platform ticket. A licensed porter is entitled to work in the railway premises, by virtue of his licence which partakes the character of a platform ticket. When a passenger and even a platform ticket holder is entitled to compensation for injury and death in an untoward incident, there is no reason why a licensed porter cannot be given the benefit, because denial of such benefit will amount to violation of equality clause contained under Art. 14 of the Constitution of India.[8]

15 Damage/Compensation for tort In *Sumatidevi M. Dhanwatey* v *Union of India*,[9] the appellant was travelling by 1st class air-conditioned berth from Nagpur to Bombay by Howrah-Bombay Mail. She was carrying her luggage which included valuable ornaments she was assaulted by some unauthorised passengers who also took away her valuable ornaments by force. They also assaulted other *bona fide* passengers and molested women passengers. The appellant pulled the chain and approached the railway authorities for protection but without any assistance. On reaching Bombay she lodged a complaint with the police about the incident and them approached the Consumer Disputes Redrassal Commission, Maharashtra

5 *Ramesh Kusaria* v *Union of India* AIR 2007 MP 106; see *Union of India* v *Hari Narayana Gupta* AIR 2007 Raj 38; *Inderjit Singh* v *Union of India* AIR 2007 Raj 144; *Union of India* v *Hari Mangaraj* AIR 2007 NOC 2010 (Ori); *Union of India* v *Pullaswamy* AIR 2008 NOC 536 (AP); *K.V. Thomas* v *Union of India* AIR 2008 Ker 153 (negligence of claimant would not disentitle compensation).

6 *Union of India* v *M'Siva Parvati* AIR 2008 AP 145.

7 *Union of India* v *Ashok Shankar Sarkale* AIR 2006 Bom 198.

8 *Philomina* v *Indian Railways* AIR 2007 Ker 210.

9 (2004)6 SCC 113.

claiming compensation of ₹9,32,256. The State Commission awarded a sum of ₹1,41,756 as compensation against which the Railway Administration preferred an appeal before the National Consumer Disputes Redressal Commission which set aside the order of the State Commission. The appellant preferred an appeal against the said impugned order to the Supreme Court. The Railway Administration contended that in view of ss. 100 and 103 of the Railways Act 1989 such complaint was not maintainable. But in view of the facts and under s. 124A of the Railways Act 1989, the Railway Administration cannot escape the liability. Besides, the Railway Administration did not raise the plea of maintainability of the complaint or jurisdictional question before the State Commission and as such under s. 3 of the Consumer Protection Act 1986 the complaint could be entertained by the State Commission.

16 Interest on compensation Compensation is payable for railway accident and untoward incident. Payment of compensation relates to the date of accident. If cannot be said that the amount is determined only from the date of the award and interest can be directed to be paid only from the date of the award. Interest is payable from the date of application at such rate at the discretion of the Tribunal. While awarding interest tribunal can consider. The bank rate preventing at that time.[10] Compensation of ₹4 lakhs has been enhanced from ₹2 lakhs after amendment. The court of appeal has power to enhance the amount of award to ₹4 lakhs from ₹2 lakhs which was awarded by the Tribunal, since there was no cross-objection under Or. 41, r. 22, Code of Civil Procedure is preferred.[11]

17 Claim of interest fastened on date of determine of compensation There being no specific provision in the Railways Act 1989 providing for award of interest and the entire enquiry being summary in nature, unaffected by the remedies provided under other laws and the provisions of Code of Civil Procedure cannot squarely be made applicable, which includes s. 34. Hence award of interest cannot be claimed as a matter of right unless the statute specifically provides it or provided for under the specific terms of contract. The Tribunal is at its discretion to take into consideration facts and circumstances of each case for award of interest, but not as a right. Thus, liability towards interest can be fastened only on date of determination of compensation, but not from the date of filing of application before tribunal.[12]

10 *Union of India* v *Smt. Brigeet Chacko* AIR 2007 Ker 268; see *Prasant Kumar Choudhury* v *Union of India* AIR 2007 Ori 33; *Union of India* v *Shamim* AIR 2008 Raj 99 (Claim Tribunal has power to grant interest under ss. 18(3)(*i*), 13 of the 1987 Act and s. 34 of the Code of Civil Procedure) *Abdul Kareem* v *Union of India* AIR 2009 Ker 24.

11 *Union of India* v *Ram Bachan Singh* AIR 2007 MP 232; see also *V. Gurulakshmi* v *Union of India* AIR 2007 Mad 280.

12 *Union of India* v *Kanduru Venkata Reddy* AIR 2008 AP 211 relying on *Rathi Menon* v *Union of India* AIR 2001 SC 1333; but see *Abdul Kareem* v *Union of India* AIR 2009 Ker 24 (interest payable from date of application).

18 Expressions "untoward incident" and accidental falling of any passenger from a train carrying passengers In *Union of India* v *Prabhakaran Vijay Kumar*[13] a lady while trying to enter a train fell down on the railway track and was runover by the train and died. Her legal representatives filed a claim petition before the Railway Claims Tribunal which held that it was not an "untoward incident" within the meaning of the said expression in s. 123(*c*) of the Railways Act 1989. In the appeal it was held that the case fell within the expression "accidental falling of a passenger from a train carrying passengers" which was an "untoward incident". Therefore the High Court awarded compensation of Rupees two lakhs with interest @ 12% from the date of the petition till the date of the payment. Against that order the appellant preferred an appeal to the Supreme Court which held that: (*a*) There is no legal difference whether the deceased was actually inside the train when she fall down or whether she was only trying to get into the train when she fell down. In either case it amounted to an "accidental falling of a passenger from a train carrying passenger". Hence, it was an "untoward incident" as defined in s. 123(*c*) of the Railways Act 1989. (*b*) If a restricted meaning of the expression "accidental falling of a passenger" as used in s. 123(*c*) of the Railways Act 1989 is adopted, then a large number of *bona fide* passengers would be deprived of compensation. (*c*) The accident in the instant case was clearly covered by s. 124A of the Railways Act 1989 and not its proviso. Section 124A lays down strict liability or no fault liability in case of railway accident. Hence if a case comes within the purview of s. 124A, it is wholly irrelevant as to who was at fault. (*d*) The appeal was dismissed.

In *Usha Rani* v *Union of India,*[14] a passenger travelling with valid ticket falling from train and dying amounts to untoward incident. His dependants' are entitled to compensation under s. 124A of the Railway Act 1989. In *Rakesh Saini* v *Union of India,*[15] a passenger, aged 27 years was working in a technical post drawing a salary of ₹3,300 p.m. and died in train accident. Under r. 3(2) of the Railway Accidents and Untoward Incident (Compensation) Rules 1990 his dependants, are entitled to compensation. The quantum of compensation will be arrived at by deducting $^1/_3$rd of his income and applying multiplier 18 which world come to ₹4,75,200. Three dependants of the deceased were entitled to receive amounts in equal shares with interest @ 6% p.a.[16]

13 (2008)9 SCC 527.

14 AIR 2004 P&H 148; *Union of India* v *K. Parvathamma* AIR 2005 AP 106; *Union of India* v *Vidyawati* AIR 2008 All 124; *Union of India* v *Nalini Parida* AIR 2009 Ori 56.

15 AIR 2004 Del 107.

16 *R. Geetha* v *Union of India* AIR 2005 Ker 33; *Sakhia Naik* v *Union of India* AIR 2005 Ori 169.

19 Liability to pay compensation Injuries were sustained due to untoward incident as alleged by the claimant. But the railway authority proved that the claimant sustained injuries on account of quarrel between him and other persons. The injured was not a *bona fide* passenger having no valid railway ticket. Thus, the railway authority was not liable to pay compensation.[17]

Deceased was not a *bona fide* passenger as no ticket was found from goods or her person. Death occurred on account of her own criminal negligence and self-inflicted injuries. Liability of railways is strict liability even if there is negligence of the deceased. But once there is criminal negligence or self-inflicted injuries, compensation cannot be awarded. Thus, railways are not liable to pay compensation.[18]

Passenger fell down from a running train while travelling on valid ticket. Fact that he was standing at open doors of compartment of running train might be negligent act or even rash act. But certainly it is not a criminal act. Negligence of passenger does not have effect on liability of railways. Claimant is entitled to compensation with interest.[19]

20 Entitlement of compensation Petition was filed by dependant-father of the deceased. Death of the father happened during the pendency of the petition. Brothers of the deceased claimed compensation as legal representatives of the father. Though they were not dependants of the deceased, their claim as legal representatives of the deceased would be maintainable. Order awarding compensation to the brothers of the deceased was held to be proper.[20]

It has been proved from uncontroverted evidence that the victim was a *bona fide* passenger on the day of the accident with a valid general class ticket and that his dead body having been also found from the railway track at the relevant time and removed by the railway authority. Under these circumstances of the case it must be presumed that he died due to the fall from the train. Once the court found that it is a clear case of untoward incident within the meaning of s. 124A of the Railways Act 1989 and the claimant is entitled to get ₹4 lakhs as provided in the Schedule to the Railway Accidents and Untoward (Incidents) Compensation Rules 1990 and the railway authority is directed to pay a sum of ₹4 lakhs to the claimant with interest at the rate of 8% p.a. from the date of filing such application till actual payment.[1]

17 *Sohan Lal* v *Union of India* AIR 2010 NOC 361 (Del).
18 *Shahajad* v *Union of India* AIR 2014 Del 41 relying on *Jameela* v *Union of India* AIR 2010 SC 3705.
19 *Jameela* v *Union of India* AIR 2010 SC 3705.
20 *Union of India* v *Phoolsaye* AIR 2010 NOC 1007 (P&H).
1 *Bandana Mondal* v *Union of India* AIR 2010 NOC 564 (Cal).

The deceased was having valid ticket and reservation in sleeper coach. He got down at railway station and again tried to board in the train but due to jerk and jolt he fell down and sustained injuries leading to his death. The impugned order was by the Railway Claims Tribunal rejecting compensation claim on the ground that the deceased himself was responsible for his death and his case comes within the exception (*b*) of s. 124A of the Railways Act 1989. The order of the Tribunal was set aside.[2]

21 Accidental death of passenger Deceased was thrown out of moving train on account of sudden jerk. Railway authorities though claimed it as self inflicted injury, but failed to lead any oral or documentary evidence to prove the same. "Untoward incident" defined in s. 123(*c*)(2) of the Railways Act 1989 also includes incidental falling of passenger from a train carrying passengers. The Railways Act 1989 being a beneficial piece of legislation should receive liberal and wider interpretation. Thus, the railway authorities were held liable to pay compensation.[3]

22 Platform ticket holder, whether passenger Definition under s. 2(29) of the Railways Act 1989 makes it clear that in order to consider a person travelling in train as a passenger, he must possess a valid pass or ticket and a person who merely holds a valid platform ticket is not entitled to travel in train as a passenger. Reading of s. 123(*c*)(2) of the said Act makes it clear that if a person travelling as a passenger in a train accidently falls from a train carrying passengers, such an act would come within expression "untoward incident". Although s. 124A of the said Act in *Explanation* mentions that for purposes of s. 124A, a person who had a valid platform ticket is also included within the meaning of "passenger", but the *Explanation* (*ii*) makes it clear that "passenger" includes a person who has purchased valid ticket for travelling a train carrying passenger. Thus, accident of the deceased holding platform ticket cannot be termed as "untoward incident" and the claimant is not entitled to compensation.[4]

23 Self-inflicted injury or untoward incident Passenger attempted to board moving train from off side; his act was highly careless and imprudent. Injury suffered by him would be termed as self-inflicted injury and not as untoward incident. Thus, the claimant would not be entitled to any compensation from the railway authority in view of the proviso (*b*) to s. 124A of the Railways Act 1989.[5]

24 Denial of compensation The plea of the railway authority was that the alleged claim was for a self-inflicted injury. But no evidence was on record

2 *Pinki Devi* v *Union of India* AIR 2014 Jhar 88 relying on *Union of India* v *Prabhakaran Vijaya Kumar* AIR 2009 SC (Supp) 383.

3 *Mahaboob Sah* v *Union of India* AIR 2011 Kar 8 relying on *Union of India* v *Prabhakaran Vijaya Kumar* (2008)9 SCC 527.

4 *Puttamani* v *Union of India* AIR 2010 Kar 109.

5 *Joseph P.T.* v *Union of India* AIR 2014 Ker 12.

to prove that the deceased was alighting from a moving train. Constable on duty on platform stated that he evacuated the deceased from beneath the train from open line side of railway track and had admitted him to casualty ward. Doctor also had given opinion that injuries were ante mortem in nature and was caused in railway accident. In absence of any positive evidence that the deceased was himself negligent, order awarding compensation would be proper.[6]

125. Application for compensation. (1) An application for compensation under section 124 [7][or section 124A] may be made to the Claims Tribunal—

(*a*) by the person who has sustained the injury or suffered any loss, or

(*b*) by any agent duly authorised by such person in this behalf, or

(*c*) where such person is a minor, by his guardian, or

(*d*) where death has resulted from the accident, [7][or the untoward incident] by any dependant of the deceased or where such a dependant is a minor, by his guardian.

(2) Every application by a dependant for compensation under this section shall be for the benefit of every other dependant.

1 Corresponding provision in the old Act This section corresponds to s. 82C of the old Act.

2 Application by person for compensation and the forum of application The persons competent to make applications are (*i*) the person who has sustained injury or suffered any loss; (*ii*) A duty authorised agent of an aggrieved person; (*iii*) Guardian of an aggrieved minor; (*iv*) Any dependant of the victim. The competent forum for making compensation is the Railway Claims Tribunal.

Claimants made application under the Workmen's Compensation Act 1923 but they were held to be not dependants within the meaning of s. 2(*d*) of that Act. Subsequently, there was amendment in the Act making the application maintainable. Even then the application was not maintainable as because the amendment was not made with retrospective effect.[8]

3 Accident to train—persons entitled to claim compensation Section 125 of the Act lays down who are the persons entitled to compensation in the event of an accident to train. First, the *bona fide* passenger who has sustained an injury in the accident is so entitled. An agent of such adult passenger can also claim. When the injured *bona fide* passenger is a minor, his guardian also can claim. But if the *bona fide* passenger dies in

6 *Union of India* v *Smt. Reeta* AIR 2010 NOC 1009 (P&H).
7 *Inserted* by Act 28 of 1994, s. 4 (w.e.f. 1.8.1994).
8 *Sarat Chandra Nanda* v *Union of India* AIR 1997 MP 70.

an accident, none other than the person or persons dependant on the deceased can claim compensation, the definition of dependant in s. 2(*d*), Workmen's Compensation Act being adopted by the Railways Act.

Thus when an qualified engineer but at the relevant time jobless met with death in a train accident, his parents who were not dependant on him cannot recover compensation.[9] A minor son of a deceased, however is entitled to compensation in view of the provisions of the Workmen's Compensation Act, although the minor son may not be dependant upon the deceased.[10]

4 "Dependant"—meaning of When the deceased person is an adult individual, and a *bona fide* passenger, cl. (*d*) of s. 82C of the old Act provides that only a person dependant on the deceased has *locus standi* to claim compensation. For meaning of the word dependant, the Railways Act has adopted the definition of the term as used in the Workmen's Compensation Act, according to the Workmen's Compensation Act 1923, "dependant" means any of the following relatives of a deceased workman, namely (*i*) a widow, minor legitimate son and unmarried legitimate daughter, or a widowed mother; and (*ii*) if wholly or in part dependant on the earnings of the workman at the time of his death, a widower, a parent other than a widowed mother, a minor illegitimate son, an unmarried illegitimate daughter, a daughter legitimate or illegitimate if married and a minor or if widowed, a minor brother, an unmarried or widowed sister, a widowed daughter-in-law, a minor child of a deceased son, a minor child of a deceased daughter where no parent of the child is alive, or where no parent of the workman is alive, a paternal grandparent.

Where a son cannot be said to be minor, the mere fact that on account of some infirmity he was maintained by his deceased father does not given him the right to be regarded as a dependant within the meaning of the Workmen's Compensation Act.[11] A minor adopted son is a dependant.[12] But an adopted daughter is not a dependant.[13] A widowed mother includes an adoptive widowed mother for the purposes of s. 2(1)(*d*) of the Workmen's Compensation Act.[14] A widowed stepmother is not a dependant.[15]

9 *G.N. Bhandary* v *Railway Administration, New Delhi* AIR 1983 All 150; 1983 All CJ 37; 1983 ACJ 596.

10 *Union of India* v *Vinod Prakash Singh* AIR 1982 All 68; 1981 All WC 707; 1982 ACJ 137.

11 *In the matter of compensation for the life of Karim Dad* 125 IC 637; AIR 1930 Lah 657.

12 In re, *Devi Ditta* 12 Lah 50; AIR 1931 Lah 661.

13 *In the matter of Jamadar Munsh Ram* 12 Lah 658; AIR 1931 Lah 399.

14 *Addl. Dy. Commissioner* v *Laxmibhai* AIR 1945 Nag 238.

15 *Manada* v *Bengal Bone Mill* AIR 1940 Cal 285; *Dirji* v *Goalin* AIR 1942 Pat 33; 21 Pat 173.

5 Limitation for application for compensation An application for compensation under s. 82C of the old Act shall be made within one year of the date of the accident. The Claims Tribunal may on sufficient cause shown allow any application to be made at any time after one year of the occurrence. What constitutes sufficient *cause* cannot be laid down by hard and fast rules. The discretion should be exercised in each particular case on its own facts with a view to secure furtherance of justice. There may be cases where unavoidable circumstances would prevent an application to be made within one year of the occurrence of the accident, and in such cases the Claims Tribunal may entertain the application for compensation made beyond the time prescribed in s. 17(1)(*b*), Railway Claims Tribunal Act. The provision for condonation of delay is laid down in s. 17(2), Railway Claims Tribunal Act 1987.

6 Claim petition for death due to untoward incident All relevant documents were brought on record by the claimant. The claim could not be thrown out if the documents produced were not marked as exhibits by the Tribunal. Documents ought to have been marked as exhibits by the Tribunal in absence of any objection to the documents. No evidence was adduced by the Railway authorities to deny claim including the claim that the deceased was not a *bona fide* passenger. Dismissal of claim by the tribunal was not proper. The claimant was entitled to a sum of ₹4,00,000 as prescribed in Part-I under the Schedule of the Railway Accidents and Untoward Incidents (Compensation) Rules 1990 with simple interest at the rate of 6% per annum from the date of filing of the claim application till payment.[16]

7 Liability of railway authorities to pay compensation for untoward incident Legal heirs/representatives of deceased passenger are not dependents for the purpose of s. 123(*b*) of the Railways Act 1989. Sections 124, 124A of the said Act do not specifically say who will be entitled to claim compensation. Liability of railways is declared, but the beneficiary is not expressly specified. Expression "person who has ..... suffered any loss" appearing in cl. (*a*) of s. 125(1) of the said Act includes the legal heirs/legal representatives of such deceased person who sustained the injury. The purpose of "non-obstante" clause in ss. 124, 124A of the said Act is only to clarify that this payment by the railways will not affect other claims, if any available under other laws. Such non-obstante clause cannot obviously lead to the conclusion that other provisions of relevant laws shall not be applicable. There would be no abatement or extinction of claims of dependent on his death after filing of the application for claim of compensation owing to the death of the victim. Expression "dependent" in the context must certainly be held to refer to those who represent the estate of a deceased dependent whose death has occurred subsequent to the vesting of the right. Right under s. 124A of the said Act is heritable.

16 *Munni Kuwar* v *Union of India* AIR 2012 Pat 92.

Order passed by the Railway Claims Tribunal has all the incidents of decree of civil court. Decree in favour of the claimant awarding compensation prior to the death of the claimant can be executed by the legal heirs of the claimant.[17]

126. Interim relief by railway administration. (1) Where a person who has made an application for compensation under section 125 desires to be paid interim relief, he may apply to the railway administration for payment of interim relief along with a copy of the application made under that section.

(2) Where, on the receipt of an application made under sub-section (1) and after making such inquiry as it may deem fit, the railway administration is satisfied that circumstances exist which require relief to be afforded to the applicant immediately, it may, pending determination by the Claims Tribunal of the actual amount of compensation payable under section 124 or section 124A pay to any person who has sustained the injury or suffered any loss, or where death has resulted from the accident, to any dependant of the deceased, such sum as it considers reasonable for affording such relief, so however, that the sum paid shall not exceed the amount of compensation payable at such rates as may be prescribed.

(3) The railway administration shall, as soon as may be, after making an order regarding payment of interim relief under sub-section (2), send a copy thereof to the Claims Tribunal.

(4) Any sum paid by the railway administration under sub-section (2) shall be taken into account by the Claims Tribunal while determining the amount of compensation payable.

127. Determination of compensation in respect of any injury or loss of goods. (1) Subject to such rules as may be made, the rates of compensation payable in respect of any injury shall be determined by the Claims Tribunal.

(2) The compensation payable in respect of any loss of goods shall be such as the Claims Tribunal may, having regard to the circumstances of the case, determine to be reasonable.

128. Saving as to certain rights. (1) The right of any person to claim compensation under section 124 or section 124A shall not affect the right of any such person to recover compensation payable under the Workmen's Compensation Act, 1923 (8 of 1923), or any other law for the time being in force; but no person shall be entitled to claim compensation more than once in respect of the same accident.

(2) Nothing in sub-section (1) shall affect the right of any person to claim compensation payable under any contract or scheme providing for payment of compensation for death or personal injury or for damage to property or any sum payable under any policy of insurance.

17 *Krishnakumar G.* v *Union of India* AIR 2011 Ker 166.

1 Corresponding provision in the old Act This section corresponds to s. 82H of the old Act.

2 Successive claims for compensation Section 82H of the old Act did not forbid successive claims for compensation under the same Act but to prohibit claims for compensation in respect of the same accident under more than one law in force. Thus, once a person has recovered compensation under s. 82A of the old Act, he or his heirs cannot claim compensation once again in respect of the same accident under the Workmen's Compensation Act or any other law.[18]

3 Determination of interest by tribunal In view of the provisions of the Interest Act 1978 read with the definition of "court" as defined in s. 2(*a*) of the Interest Act read with s. 34 of the Code of Civil Procedure it is clear that the court can grant interest. As the Railway Tribunal is coming under the definition of "Court" it can award interest on the compensation payable to the claimant. It is the discretion of the tribunal to award compensation with *pendente lite* and further interest.[19]

129. Power to make rules in respect of matters in this Chapter. (1) The Central Government may, by notification, make rules to carry out the purposes of this Chapter.

(2) In particular, and without prejudice to the generality of the foregoing power, such rules may provide for all or any of the following matters, namely:

(*a*) the compensation payable for death;

(*b*) the nature of the injuries for which compensation shall be paid and the amount of such compensation.

1 Corresponding provision in the old Act This section corresponds to s. 82J of the old Act.

2 Compensation outside scheduled injury Claimant passenger sustained internal injury of ear due to accident leading to partial deafness and the injury does not fall in a schedule. Compensation was paid on the basis of medical evidence in the interest of justice.[20]

3 Computation of compensation by prevailing rules During the pendency of the claim petition for compensation, the Railway Accidents Claims Rules 1989 were replaced by new Rules of 1990. The Tribunal is to be guided by new Rules irrespective of date of accident or commencement of new Rules.

18 *Zaibunnisa (Smt.)* v *Divl. Supdt. S.R.* AIR 1965 Mys 306.

19 *Union of India* v *Nalini Parida* AIR 2009 Ori 56; *Ramahari Behera* v *Union of India* AIR 2009 NOC 878 (Ori); *Union of India* v *Trilochan Nayak* AIR 2009 Ori 91.

20 *K.P. Shammughan* v *Union of India* AIR 2000 Ker 237.

Thus, grant of ₹20,000 for pelvis injury falling under Item No. 32 of 1990 Rules is not improper.[21]

Chapter XIV
Regulation of Hours of Work and Period of Rest

130. Definitions. In this Chapter, unless the context otherwise requires,—

(*a*) the employment of a railway servant is said to be "continuous" except when it is excluded or has been declared to be essentially intermittent or intensive;

(*b*) the employment of a railway servant is said to be "essentially intermittent" when it has been declared to be so by the prescribed authority on the ground that the daily hours of duty of the railway servant normally include periods of inaction aggregating to fifty percent. or more (including at least one such period of not less than one hour or two such periods of not less than half an hour each) in a tour of twelve hours duty (on the average over seventy-two consecutive hours), during which the railway servant may be on duty, but is not called upon to display either physical activity or sustained attention;

(*c*) the employment of a railway servant is said to be "excluded" if he belongs to any one of the following categories, namely:

(*i*) railway servants employed in a managerial or confidential capacity;

(*ii*) armed guards or other personnel subject to discipline similar to that of any of the armed police forces;

(*iii*) staff of the railway schools imparting technical training or academic education;

(*iv*) such staff as may be specified as supervisory under the rules;

(*v*) such other categories of staff as may be prescribed;

(*d*) the employment of a railway servant is said to be "intensive" when it has been declared to be so by the prescribed authority on the ground that it is of a strenuous nature involving continued concentration or hard manual labour with little or no period of relaxation.

1 Corresponding provision in the old Act This section corresponds to s. 71A of the old Act.

2 Definitions Section 130 defines four terms namely, "continuous", "essentially intermittent", "excluded" from employment of railway servant, and "intensive" for the purpose of Chapter XIV of the Railways Act 1989.

The term "essentially intermittent" as used in s. 71A of the old Act relating to a post could be declared as such by the authority empowered in that behalf. Such declaration could not be challenged in summary proceedings under the Payment of Wages Act 1936.[1] The term "essentially

21 *Union of India* v *Deenal* AIR 2000 Mad 360.

1 *Aroora Ram Kapur* v *Supdt. Lahore* AIR 1947 Lah 379.

intermittent" was also used in s. 71A of the old Act. Merely because a booking clerk was roastered to longer hours of work, the same would not justify a change of classification from "essentially intermittent" to continuous. But the classification of railway servant cannot be of permanent nature and the same is liable to vary according to fluctuation in the quantum of work. Such classification is liable to be reviewed as and when found necessary.

131. Chapter not to apply to certain railway servants. Nothing in this Chapter shall apply to any railway servant to whom the Factories Act, 1948 (63 of 1948) or the Mines Act, 1952 (35 of 1952) or the Railway Protection Force Act, 1957 (23 of 1957) or the Merchant Shipping Act, 1958 (44 of 1958), applies.

1 Corresponding provision in the old Act This section corresponds to s. 71B cf the old Act.

2 Scope A railway servant shall not be governed by the provision of Chapter XIV of the Act if the provisions of (*i*) the Factories Act 1948; (*ii*) the Mines Act 1952; (*iii*) Railway Protection Force Act 1957; or (*iv*) Merchant Shipping Act 1958 are applicable to him.

132. Limitation of hours of work. (1) A railway servant whose employment is essentially intermittent shall not be employed for more than seventy-five hours in any week.

(2) A railway servant whose employment is continuous shall not be employed for more than fifty-four hours a week on an average in a two weekly period of fourteen days.

(3) A railway servant whose employment is intensive shall not be employed for more than forty-five hours a week on an average in a two weekly period of fourteen days.

(4) Subject to such rules as may be prescribed, temporary exemptions of railway servants from the provisions of sub-section (1) or sub-section (2) or sub-section (3) may be made by the prescribed authority if it is of opinion that such temporary exemptions are necessary to avoid serious interference with the ordinary working of the railway or in cases of accident, actual or threatened, or when urgent work is required to be done to the railway or to rolling stock or in any emergency which could not have been foreseen or prevented, or in other cases of exceptional pressure of work:

Provided that where such exemption results in the increase of hours of employment of a railway servant referred to in any of the sub-sections, he shall be paid overtime at not less than two times his ordinary rate of pay for the excess hours of work.

Corresponding provision in the old Act This section corresponds to s. 71C of the old Act.

133. Grant of periodical rest. (1) Subject to the provisions of this section, a railway servant—

(*a*) whose employment is intensive or continuous shall, for every week commencing on a Sunday, be granted a rest of not less than thirty consecutive hours;

(*b*) whose employment is essentially intermittent shall, for every week commencing on a Sunday, be granted a rest of not less than twenty-four consecutive hours including a full night.

(2) Notwithstanding anything contained in sub-section (1),—

(*i*) any locomotive or traffic running staff shall be granted, each month, a rest of at least four periods of not less than thirty consecutive hours each or at least five periods of not less than twenty-two consecutive hours each, including a full night;

(*ii*) the Central Government may, by rules, specify the railway servants to whom periods of rest on scales less than those laid down under sub-section (1) may be granted and the periods thereof.

(3) Subject to such rules as may be made in this behalf, if the prescribed authority is of the opinion that such circumstances as are referred to in sub-section (4) of section 132 are present, it may exempt any railway servant from the provisions of sub-section (1) or clause (*i*) of sub-section (2):

Provided that a railway servant so exempted shall, in such circumstances as may be prescribed, be granted compensatory periods of rest for the periods he has foregone.

Corresponding provision in the old Act This section corresponds to s. 71D of the old Act.

134. Railway servant to remain on duty. Nothing in this Chapter or the rules made thereunder shall, where due provision has been made for the relief of a railway servant, authorise him to leave his duty until he has been relieved.

Corresponding provision in the old Act This section corresponds to s. 71F of the old Act.

135. Supervisors of railway labour. (1) Subject to such rules as may be made in this behalf, the Central Government may appoint supervisors of railway labour.

(2) The duties of supervisors of railway labour shall be—

(*i*) to inspect railways in order to determine whether the provisions of this Chapter or of the rules made thereunder are duly observed; and

(*ii*) to perform such other functions as may be prescribed.

(3) A supervisor of railway labour shall be deemed to be a Commissioner for the purposes of sections 7 and 9.

Corresponding provision in the old Act This section corresponds to s. 71G of the old Act.

136. Power to make rules in respect of matters in this Chapter. (1) The Central Government may, by notification, make rules to carry out the purposes of this Chapter.

(2) In particular, and without prejudice to the generality of the foregoing power, such rules may provide for all or any of the following matters, namely:

(*a*) the authorities who may declare the employment of any railway servant essentially intermittent or intensive;

(*b*) the appeals against any such declaration and the manner in which, and the conditions subject to which any such appeal may be filed and heard;

(*c*) the categories of staff that may be specified under sub-clauses (*iv*) and (*v*) of clause (*c*) of section 130;

(*d*) the authorities by whom exemptions under sub-section (4) of section 132 or sub-section (3) of section 133 may be made;

(*e*) the delegation of power by the authorities referred to in clause (*d*);

(*f*) the railway servants to whom clause (*ii*) of sub-section (2) of section 133 apply and the periods of rest to be granted to them;

(*g*) the appointment of supervisors of railway labour and their functions.

1 Corresponding provision in the old Act This section corresponds to s. 71E of the old Act.

2 Rules The Central Government is empowered to make rules in respect of certain matters in this chapter. The Ticket Collector having worked beyond eight hours daily is entitled to overtime allowance.[2]

CHAPTER XV
Penalties and Offences

137. Fraudulently travelling or attempting to travel without proper pass or ticket. (1) If any person, with intent to defraud a railway administration,—

(*a*) enters or remains in any carriage on a railway or travels in a train in contravention of section 55, or

(*b*) uses or attempts to use a single pass or a single ticket which has already been used on a previous journey, or in the case of a return ticket, a half thereof which has already been so used,

he shall be punishable with imprisonment for a term which may extend to six months, or with fine which may extend to one thousand rupees, or with both:

Provided that in the absence of special and adequate reasons to the contrary to be mentioned in the judgment of the court, such punishment shall not be less than a fine of five hundred rupees.

2 *Anantakumar* v *Union of India* 1989 Lab IC 1878 (Cal).

(2) The person referred to in sub-section (1) shall also be liable to pay the excess charge mentioned in sub-section (3) in addition to the ordinary single fare for the distance which he has travelled, or where there is any doubt as to the station from which he started, the ordinary single fare from the station from which the train originally started, or if the tickets of passengers travelling in the train have been examined since the original starting of the train, the ordinary single fare from the place where the tickets were so examined or, in case of their having been examined more than once, were last examined.

(3) the excess charge referred to in sub-section (2) shall be a sum equal to the ordinary single fare referred to in that sub-section or [1][two hundred and fifty rupees], whichever is more.

(4) Notwithstanding anything contained in section 65 of the Indian Penal Code (45 of 1860), the court convicting an offender may direct that the person in default of payment of any fine inflicted by the court shall suffer imprisonment for a term which may extend to six months.

1 Corresponding provision in the old Act This section corresponds to s. 112 of the old Act.

2 Fraudulent intention Mere travelling without a pass or ticket is not punishable unless it can be inferred from the circumstances that any person travelled with intent to defraud the railway administration.[2]

Illustration (*b*) to s. 106 of the Evidence Act 1872, has obvious reference to a very special type of case, namely, to offences under ss. 112 and 113 of the old Railways Act (corresponding to ss. 137 and 138 of the new Act).[3]

3 Forcible removal of passengers There is no provision in the Railways Act for ejecting passengers except in certain circumstances, such as are specified in s. 120 of the old Act (corresponding to s. 145 of the new Act). Section 122 of the old Railways Act (corresponding to s. 147 of the new Act) which authorises a railway servant to eject, under certain circumstances, any person unlawfully entering upon a railway has no application to the case of passengers.

It follows, therefore, that when a person travels without a ticket, he cannot be evicted forcibly from the railway carriage.[4] In *Butler* v *Man Sh. & Lin, Railway Co.*[5] LORD ESHER, MR, held that no one had any right to lay hands forcibly on a passenger in the absence of some legal authority

1 *Substituted* by Act 56 of 2003, s. 3 for "fifty rupees."

2 *Sudhir Chandra Gupta* v *State of Assam* AIR 1965 Assam 38; ILR (1964)16 Assam 196.

3 *Sambhu Nath Mehra* v *State of Ajmer* AIR 1956 SC 404; 1956 SCR 199; 1956 SCJ 429.

4 *Md. Hosain* v *Farlya* 44 C 179; 18 CrLJ 647; 40 IC 295; *Radhakissen* v *Emperor* AIR 1923 Lah 70; 68 IC 846; 23 CrLJ 622.

5 [1888]21 QBD 207.

to do so. Section 68 of the (old) Railways Act prohibits against travelling in a railway carriage without proper pass or ticket. But, if a person with intent to defraud so travels in contravention of the provisions of s. 68 of the old Act, he is liable to a conviction under s. 112 of the old Act. If he so travels without any intent to defraud he may be proceeded against under s. 113 of the old Act (corresponding to s. 138 of the new Act), and he may be arrested only under circumstances specified in s. 132 of the old Act.

Section 112 of the old Act does not penalise mere ticketless travelling but what it penalises is ticketless travelling with an intent to defraud a railway administration.[6]

4 Summary trial Summary trial of a Government servant, who might lose his job in case of conviction, is not desirable.[7]

138. Levy of excess charge and fare for travelling without proper pass or ticket or beyond authorised distance. (1) If any passenger,—

(*a*) being in or having alighted from a train, fails or refuses to present for examination or to deliver up his pass or ticket immediately on a demand being made therefor under section 54, or

(*b*) travels in a train in contravention of the provisions of section 55,

he shall be liable to pay, on the demand of any railway servant authorised in this behalf, the excess charge mentioned in sub-section (3) in addition to the ordinary single fare for the distance which he has travelled or, where there is any doubt as to the station from which he started, the ordinary single fare from the station from which the train originally started, or, if the tickets of passengers travelling in the train have been examined since the original starting of the train, the ordinary single fare from the place where the tickets were so examined or in the case of their having been examined more than once, were last examined.

(2) If any passenger,—

(*a*) travels or attempts to travel in or on a carriage, or by a train, of a higher class than that for which he has obtained a pass or purchased a ticket; or

(*b*) travels in or on a carriage beyond the place authorised by his pass or ticket,

he shall be liable to pay, on the demand of any railway servant authorised in this behalf, any difference between the fare paid by him and the fare payable in respect of the journey he has made and the excess charge referred to in sub-section (3).

6 *Sukhdeo Singh* v *State* 1950 ALJ 529; AIR 1951 All 410; *Narain* v *Rex* AIR 1950 All 441; 51 CrLJ 1174.

7 *Ram Lochan* v *State* 1978 All Cr R 76.

(3) The excess charge shall be a sum equal to the amount payable under sub-section (1) or sub-section (2), as the case may be, or [8][two hundred and fifty rupees], whichever is more:

Provided that if the passenger has with him a certificate granted under sub-section (2) of section 55, no excess charge shall be payable.

(4) If any passenger liable to pay the excess charge and the fare mentioned in sub-section (1), or the excess charge and any difference of fare mentioned in sub-section (2), fails or refuses to pay the same on a demand being made therefor under one or other of these sub-sections, as the case may be, any railway servant authorised by the railway administration in this behalf may apply to any Metropolitan Magistrate or a Judicial Magistrate of the first or second class, as the case may be, for the recovery of the sum payable as if it were a fine, and the Magistrate if satisfied that the sum is payable shall order it to be so recovered, and may order that the person liable for the payment shall in default of payment suffer imprisonment of either description for a term which may extend to one month but not less than ten days.

(5) Any sum recovered under sub-section (4) shall, as and when it is recovered, be paid to the railway administration.

1 Corresponding provision in the old Act This section corresponds to s. 113 of the old Act.

2 Scope The High Court held in *Governor-General in Council* v *Roop Chand*[9] that as there is right to imprison in default under s. 113 of the old Act the proceedings under s. 113(4) of the old Act is criminal. But Allahabad High Court has taken a contrary view and held that s. 113 of the old Act does not speak of any offence, it merely creates statutory liability for payment of penalty and provides for the mode of enforcement of that liability,[10] that s. 113 of the old Act provides a procedure for recovery of railway dues and does not define any offence and the procedure provided by s. 113 of the old Act is set in motion by an application and not by a complaint.[11]

3 Improper ticket Where a half ticket has been purchased by an adult person, the contract is voidable at the option of the railway administration. The provision for realisation of excess charge is one for validating the improper ticket. But the booking of luggage on the strength of such improper half ticket is not a void contract.[12]

139. Power to remove persons. Any person failing or refusing to pay the fare and the excess charge referred to in section 138 may be removed by any railway

8 *Substituted* by Act 56 of 2003, s. 3 for "fifty rupees".
9 AIR 1949 Nag 330.
10 *Narain* v *Rex* AIR 1950 All 441; 51 CrLJ 1174.
11 *Sukhdeo Singh* v *State* AIR 1951 All 410; 1950 ALJ 529.
12 *Union of India* v *Benode Kumar* AIR 1962 Cal 48.

servant authorised in this behalf who may call to his aid any other person to effect such removal:

Provided that nothing in this section shall be deemed to preclude a person removed from a carriage of a higher class from continuing his journey in a carriage of a class for which he holds a pass or ticket:

Provided further that a woman or a child if unaccompanied by a male passenger, shall not be so removed except either at the station from where she or he commences her or his journey or at a junction or terminal station or station at the headquarters of a civil district and such removal shall be made only during the day.

1 Corresponding provision in the old Act This section corresponds to s. 113A of the old Act.

2 Scope Section 139 merely deals with a situation created by an accident or a mishap where a passenger who was supplied with a ticket and was travelling lawfully has not, at a particular time, the ticket with him. It is clear from the section that what is demanded and recovered from a passenger—leaving aside the excess charge—is a single railway fare for the distance the passenger has travelled. This is not recovered as a penalty or a fine and not even as an excess charge. It is recovered as a fare because the passenger has not at the time the evidence of his having paid the fare for the journey. Rather than obliging the railway administration to enquire if the passenger has committed a fraud or not, and then in the case of fraud to seek out the passenger and to recover fare from him, the legislature empowered the railway administration to recover the fare leaving it to the passenger to prove his *bona fides* and to put forward his claim for refund on that ground. Section 139 no doubt places the passenger under obligation to pay the fare for the time being, but it does not take away his right to claim a refund and does not create any right in the railway administration to retain fare realised twice for a single journey. In fact, it may be said that the statutory obligation created by the section in the matter of payment of fare is temporary, *i.e.* so long as the passenger has not satisfied the railway administration that he had paid the fare and secured a ticket.[13] Section 113 of the old Act does not apply to offenders against justice, but ordinarily to innocent persons, who may find themselves in the wrong by mere accident. It imputes no criminal intention or offence to person to be dealt with thereunder.[14]

Section 139 requires that passengers must have in their possession immediately available throughout the journey the tickets which entitle them to travel. There is no room in the phraseology of the provision for a loose interpretation of its terms, since it has been obviously framed to prevent the enormous inconvenience and trouble which would otherwise

13 *Narendra Nath* v *Governor-General in Council* AIR 1948 Nag 106.
14 *Laxmichand* v *Dominion of India* AIR 1955 Nag 265.

arise in the matter of checking and collecting tickets from passengers by the railway. Where the excess fare is realised from the passenger, the mere fact that he is willing to produce the tickets later does not entitle him to a refund.

140. Security for good behaviour in certain cases. (1) When a court convicting a person of an offence under section 137 or section 138 finds that he has been habitually committing or attempting to commit that offence and the court is of the opinion that it is necessary or desirable to require that person to execute a bond for good behaviour, such court may, at the time of passing the sentence on the person, order him to execute a bond with or without sureties, for such amount and for such period not exceeding three years as it deems fit.

(2) An order under sub-section (1) may also be made by an appellate court or by the High Court when exercising its powers of revision.

Corresponding provision in the old Act This section corresponds to s. 113B of the old Act.

141. Needlessly interfering with means of communication in a train. If any passenger or any other person, without reasonable and sufficient cause, makes use of, or interferes with, any means provided by a railway administration in a train for communication between passengers and the railway servant in charge of the train, he shall be punishable with imprisonment for a term which may extend to one year, or with fine which may extend to one thousand rupees, or with both:

Provided that, in the absence of special and adequate reasons to the contrary to be mentioned in the judgment of the court, where a passenger, without reasonable and sufficient cause, makes use of the alarm chain provided by a railway administration, such punishment shall not be less than—

(*a*) a fine of five hundred rupees, in the case of conviction for the first offence; and

(*b*) imprisonment for three months in case of conviction for the second or subsequent offence.

1 Corresponding provision in the old Act This section corresponds to s. 108 of the old Act.

2 Scope Section 141 provides protection for personal safety of passengers and with that object in view has laid down for punishment for needlessly interfering with the means of communication in a train.

3 Meaning of expression "reasonable and sufficient cause" The expression "reasonable and sufficient cause" used in the section is a question of fact to be determined according to circumstances of each case.[15] In deciding whether there was just and reasonable cause, the tests applied are:

15 *G.S. Sahay* v *Emperor* AIR 1936 Pat 499.

(*i*) whether risk to passenger was very great as compared with risk of danger, loss and discomfort, to other passengers, (*ii*) whether necessity or occasion for pulling the chain arises from fault of railway administration, (*iii*) the importance of line and train.[16] The following circumstances were held to be considered as just and reasonable cause: (*a*) Pulling chain for enforcing right to have the compartment vacated to bring down number of passengers within maximum limit.[17] (*b*) Pulling alarm signal to recover valuable evidence book (e.g. account books) in suit thrown out by adversary.[18] Passenger standing near door losing his thali and gold kautha by their dropping down.[19] The following facts were not held to be just and reasonable cause: (*a*) The fact that the accused left his coat containing valuables.[20] (*b*) Any additional reason for pulling chain which is not just and reasonable.[1]

No arrest can be made for the offence of pulling chain without sufficient and reasonable cause. In such a case if the driver and the guard assaults the passenger concerned, the railway company cannot be proceeded against for torts of its servants as because such steps by them fell outside the scope of their employment.[2] Where an accused was charged for pulling the chain for the purpose of stopping the train and in the FIR it was also stated that at the same time a constable brought another person for stopping the train from the other side of the coach, both the persons where held to be liable for the offence under s. 141 of the Act. What is a reasonable or probable cause depends on the facts and circumstances of each case. Even, if a passenger is himself responsible for the accident due to his negligence, he can pull the alarm chain.[3]

142. Penalty for transfer of tickets. (1) If any person not being a railway servant or an agent authorised in this behalf—

(*a*) sells or attempts to sell any ticket or any half of a return ticket; or

(*b*) parts or attempts to part with the possession of a return ticket against which reservation of a seat or berth has been made or any half of a return ticket or a season ticket,

in order to enable any other person to travel therewith, he shall be punishable with imprisonment for a term which may extend to three months, or with fine

16 *Asharfilal* v *King Emperor* AIR 1927 All 647; 25 ALJ 975.
17 *Ishwar Das* v *King Emperor* AIR 1922 Pat 8.
18 *Shiblal* v *Hukum Chand* AIR 1927 Lah 476.
19 *G.S. Sahay* v *Emperor* AIR 1936 Pat 499.
20 *Emperor* v *Kaikobar Sorabji* AIR 1926 Bom 288.
1 *Popatlal* v *Emperor* AIR 1930 Bom 160; 32 Bom LR 111.
2 *Girjashankar* v *B.B. & C.I. Rly.* AIR 1918 Bom 129.
3 *G.S. Sahay* v *Emperor* AIR 1936 Pat 499. Also see *Emperor* v *Kaikobar* AIR 1926 Bom 288; *Popatlal Bhaichand Shah* v *Emperor* AIR 1930 Bom 160; *Asharfilal* v *King Emperor* AIR 1927 All 647; 25 ALJ 975; *Arjun Das* v *The Crown* AIR 1927 Lah 476.

which may extend to five hundred rupees, or with both, and shall also forfeit the ticket which he sells or attempts to sell or parts or attempts to part.

(2) If any person purchases any ticket referred to in clause (*a*) of sub-section (1) or obtains the possession of any ticket referred to in clause (*b*) of that sub-section from any person other than a railway servant or an agent authorised in this behalf, he shall be punishable with imprisonment for a term which may extend to three months and with fine which may extend to five hundred rupees and if the purchaser or holder of any ticket aforesaid travels or attempts to travel therewith, he shall forfeit the ticket which he so purchased or obtained and shall be deemed to be travelling without a proper ticket and shall be liable to be dealt with under section 138:

Provided that in the absence of special and adequate reasons to the contrary to be mentioned in the judgment of the court, the punishment under sub-section (1) or sub-section (2) shall not be less than a fine of two hundred and fifty rupees.

1 Corresponding provision in the old Act This section corresponds to s. 114 of the old Act.

2 Applicability of the section This section applies to both purchasers and transferees of tickets and not to transferors alone. Offences under this section when detected should be punished and not to be allowed to go scot free even if the offender has no previous conviction.[4] Under this section the prosecution is required to prove that the accused had purchased ticket in the name of another and allowed some other person to travel therewith.

Section 66 of the old Act postulates that there may exist railway servant or recognised agent, authorised by railway administration who can supply tickets on receipt of due fare to a passenger desirous of travelling by a train. Section 66 of the old Act in effect creates a right in a passenger to have ticket either from the aforesaid railway servant or an agent authorised by railway in this behalf to have a ticket on payment of due fare. An agent eligible to sell tickets to a passenger has been authorised so to do by appointment of Railways Tourist Agent Rules 1980. In this backdrop s. 114A of the old Act makes any one not being one authorised to sell ticket, who sells ticket to passengers by way of business liable to punishment. It is not hit by Art. 14 of the Constitution and is constitutionally valid.[5]

143. Penalty for unauthorised carrying on of business of procuring and supplying of railway tickets. (1) If any person, not being a railway servant or an agent authorised in this behalf,—

(*a*) carries on the business of procuring and supplying tickets for travel on a railway or from reserved accommodation for journey in a train; or

4 *Emperor* v *Kodumal* AIR 1935 Sind 90.

5 *Inder Mal Jain* v *Union of India* AIR 1984 SC 415; 1984 UJ (SC) 855; (1984)1 SCC 361; 1984 Cur Civ LJ (SC) 518.

(*b*) purchases or sells or attempts to purchase or sell tickets with a view to carrying on any such business either by himself or by any other person,

he shall be punishable with imprisonment for a term which may extend to three years or with fine which may extend to ten thousand rupees, or with both, and shall also forfeit the tickets which he so procures, supplies, purchases, sells or attempts to purchase or sell:

Provided that in the absence of special and adequate reasons to the contrary to be mentioned in the judgment of the court, such punishment shall not be less than imprisonment for a term of one month or a fine of five thousand rupees.

(2) Whoever abets any offence punishable under this section shall, whether or not such offence is committed, be punishable with the same punishment as is provided for the offence.

1 Corresponding provision in the old Act This section corresponds to s. 114A of the old Act.

2 Constitutional validity of the section Section 114A of the old Act was held to be not *ultra vires* the provisions of Art. 19(1)(*g*) of the Constitution.[6]

144. Prohibition on hawking, etc., and begging. (1) If any person canvasses for any custom or hawks or exposes for sale any article whatsoever in any railway carriage or upon any part of a railway, except under and in accordance with the terms and conditions of a licence granted by the railway administration in this behalf, he shall be punishable with imprisonment for a term which may extend to one year, or with fine which may extend to two thousand rupees, or with both:

Provided that, in the absence of special and adequate reasons to the contrary to be mentioned in the judgment of the court, such punishment shall not be less than a fine of one thousand rupees.

(2) If any person begs in any railway carriage or upon a railway station, he shall be liable for punishment as provided under sub-section (1).

(3) Any person referred to in sub-section (1) or sub-section (2) may be removed from the railway carriage or any part of the railway or railway station, as the case may be, by any railway servant authorised in this behalf or by any other person whom such railway servant may call to his aid.

1 Corresponding provision in the old Act This section corresponds to s. 120A of the old Act.

2 Applicability of the section Section 144 has no application with regard to tickets. Where two accused were advancing and collecting money from the members of the staff on the pay, they could not be held liable for indulging in any act of canvassing in absence of any evidence to that effect.

6 *Inder Mal Jain* v *Union of India* AIR 1984 SC 415; (1984)1 SCC 361; 1984 UJ (SC) 855.

3 Enhancement of licence fee Vendors being licensees, cannot continue the business if they are aggrieved by enhancement of fees. Licence can be terminated at any time. If decision to enhance licence fee is a policy decision, then court cannot interfere with it.[7]

145. Drunkenness or nuisance. If any person in any railway carriage or upon any part of a railway—

(*a*) is in a state of intoxication; or

(*b*) commits any nuisance or act of indecency or uses abusive or obscene language; or

(*c*) wilfully or without excuse interferes with any amenity provided by the railway administration so as to affect the comfortable travel of any passenger,

he may be removed from the railway by any railway servant and shall, in addition to the forfeiture of his pass or ticket, be punishable with imprisonment which may extend to six months and with fine which may extend to five hundred rupees:

Provided that in the absence of special and adequate reasons to the contrary to be mentioned in the judgment of the court, such punishment shall not be less than—

(*a*) a fine of one hundred rupees in the case of conviction for the first offence; and

(*b*) imprisonment of one month and a fine of two hundred and fifty rupees, in the case of conviction for second or subsequent offence.

1 Corresponding provision in the old Act This section corresponds to s. 120 of the old Act.

2 Applicability of the section This section is applicable when a person in any railway carriage or upon any part of railway (*a*) is in a state of intoxication or (*b*) commits any nuisance or act of indecency or uses abusive or obsence language, or (*c*) wilfully or without excuse interferes with any amenity provided by the railway administration.

Where two incidents were reported against the accused one inside the railway station and the other committed outside the railway station, conviction of the accused under s. 145 of the Act by the Magistrate on the basis of the incident committed outside the railway station would be improper. The word "person" used in s. 120 of the old Act corresponding to s. 145 of the new Act includes employee of railway and as such it applies to railway servants.[8]

7 *Budh Singh & Sons* v *Union of India* AIR 2004 All 428.

8 *Appeal Swamy* v *Emperor* AIR 1934 Pat 52; 35 CrLJ 205; see *Dinanath* v *Emperor* AIR 1946 Nag 150; 47 CrLJ 397.

3 Meaning of "person" The provisions of s. 120 of the old Act are wide enough to make any individual including a railway servant liable thereunder.[9] In other cases it has been held that this section is not applicable to the acts of a railway servant.[10]

The word "person" includes a railway employee who was not on duty when the offence was committed by him.[11]

4 State of intoxication The expression "state of intoxication" suggests a condition more grave and more extreme than that which is suggested by such words as "drunk" or "under the influence of drink". The distinction should be clearly kept in mind. A person may be under the influence of liquor and yet not in a state of intoxication. If as a result of taking liquor a person's physical and mental faculties were appreciable and materially impaired in the conduct of his ordinary affairs or acts of daily life, he must be held to be in a state of intoxication.[12]

5 Nuisance Nuisance ordinarily is that which annoys or hurts or that which is offensive. Beating a person on a railway platform is bound to cause annoyance to other persons who happen to be there at the time.[13]

6 Abusive language Section 120(*b*) of the old Act penalises the use of abusive language.[14]

7 Using the delivery shed as a market place for selling fish A person who persists in selling fish in the delivery shed of railway, which is not meant to be a market, and obstructs the business for which the shed is prepared is guilty of nuisance within s. 120(*b*) of the old Act.[15] A conviction under s. 120(*b*) is not sustainable when the particular words used are not in evidence. The mere statement of witnesses that words of abuse were used

9 *A.F. Cuffley* v *M.M. Ibrahim* AIR 1919 Mad 971; 19 CrLJ 313; *Appeal Swamy* v *Emperor* AIR 1934 Pat 52; 35 CrLJ 205; *Dinanath* v *Emperor* AIR 1946 Nag 150; 47 CrLJ 397; *Gajadhar* v *Emperor* AIR 1946 Nag 200; *Durga Prasad* v *State* AIR 1962 Raj 92; In re *Venkataswami* AIR 1950 Mad 406.

10 *Mulchand* v *Emperor* AIR 1929 Sind 249; *Gurunath Shankar* v *Emperor* AIR 1937 Bom 357; 38 CrLJ 962; *Lalit* v *State* AIR 1957 All 636; 1957 CrLJ 1041 followed AIR 1919 Mad 971; AIR 1934 Pat 52; AIR 1946 Nag 150 but dissented from AIR 1929 Sind 249; AIR 1937 Bom 357; *Durga Prasad* v *State* AIR 1962 Raj 92 relied on AIR 1919 Mad 971; AIR 1934 Pat 52; AIR 1946 Nag 150 and 200 and AIR 1957 All 636. It dissented from AIR 1937 Bom 357; AIR 1929 Sind 249; AIR 1960 All 721; *Hazara Singh* v *State* AIR 1963 Punj 362 dissented from the Madras decisions in AIR 1919 Mad 971; AIR 1950 Mad 406; AIR 1934 Pat 52; AIR 1946 Nag 200. If relied on AIR 1937 Bom 357; AIR 1929 Sind 249; AIR 1960 All 721.

11 *Kinkar Roy* v *State* AIR 1965 Cal 635; (1965)2 CrLJ 741.

12 *Hari Charan Tanti* v *State* AIR 1968 Ori 31; ILR (1967) Cut 663; 1968 CrLJ 210.

13 *Durga Prasad* v *State* AIR 1962 Raj 92; ILR (1961)11 Raj 959.

14 *Dinanath* v *Emperor* AIR 1946 Nag 150; 1946 NLJ 78; *Durga Prasad* v *State* ILR (1961)11 Raj 959; AIR 1962 Raj 92; AIR 1937 Bom 357 (*Gurunath* v *Emperor*) and AIR 1960 All 721 (*Viswanath* v *State*) dissented from.

15 *Deoki* v *King-Emperor* 25 CWN 603; 22 CrLJ 604.

is not sufficient to support a conviction.[16] Conviction can be sustained although the exact words used are not proved.

146. Obstructing railway servant in his duties. If any person wilfully obstructs or prevents any railway servant in the discharge of his duties, he shall be punishable with imprisonment for a term which may extend to six months, or with fine which may extend to one thousand rupees, or with both.

1 Corresponding provision in the old Act This section corresponds to s. 121 of the old Act.

2 Scope and applicability Section 146 of the Act deals with punishment for destructing railway servant in his duties. A person can be convicted for wilfully obstructing or impeding or impeding a railway servant in the discharge of his duties. But before such conviction can be had it must be shown that the obstruction or resistance was offered to him in discharge of his duties as authorised by law.[17] Threat or violence can amount to obstructing a public servant in discharge of his duty, if the attitude of the person holding out threats indicated that violence would be used if public servant persisted performance of his duty. Thus, where a pointsman having grudge against guard threatened him with scythe in hand, it was held to be obstruction of the guard in discharge of his duties.[18] Where the proceedings against the accused for pushing a Ticket collector when the latter asked for ticket in a trifling incident remained pending for a long time, the accused had also suffered from mental agony, the High Court. Thought it fit to quash the proceedings.[19]

3 Refusal to show ticket Refusal by a passenger alighting from a train to show his ticket when demanded by a railway servant is an offence. After evidence has been recorded by a mobile Magistrate, he should question the accused with regard to the circumstances that appear against him. Otherwise the whole proceedings will be vitiated.[1]

4 Refusal to pay excess fare Refusal to pay excess fare cannot possibly amount to obstructing or impeding a railway servant in the discharge of his duty within the meaning of s. 121 of the old Act.[2]

5 Essentials for conviction Before a person can be convicted of wilfully obstructing or impeding a railway servant in the discharge of his duties,

16 *Budha Singh* v *King-Empereor* 6 Lah 459; AIR 1925 Lah 151. But see contra: *Raja Ram* v *Emperor* (1936) ALJ 82; 160 IC 1088.
17 *Radha Kissan* v *Emperor* AIR 1923 Lah 71; 68 IC 846.
18 *Shyamlal* v *State* AIR 1963 SC 1511; (1964)2 SCR 61; (1964)1 SCJ 377.
19 *Krishna Kumar Gupta* v *State of West Bengal* (1987)1 Crimes 409 (Cal).
1 *G.G. Jaganathan,* in re AIR 1958 Mad 333; (1958)1 MLJ 242.
2 *Polarao* v *Emp.* 1933 MWN 874.

it must be shown that the obstruction or resistance was offered to such railway servant in the discharge of his duties as authorised by law.[3] Where a person without sufficient and reasonable cause pulls the emergency chain, he renders himself liable for prosecution under s. 108 of the old Act only, and not under s. 121 of the old Act for preventing the running of the train and thus obstructing or impeding a railway servant in the discharge of his duty.[4] Abuse of insult does not necessarily constitute obstruction or impediment to a railway servant in the discharge of his duty.[5]

147. Trespass and refusal to desist from trespass. (1) If any person enters upon or into any part of a railway without lawful authority, or having lawfully entered upon or into such part misuses such property or refuses to leave, he shall be punishable with imprisonment for a term which may extend to six months, or with fine which may extend to one thousand rupees, or with both:

Provided that in the absence of special and adequate reasons to the contrary to be mentioned in the judgment of the court, such punishment shall not be less than a fine of five hundred rupees.

(2) Any person referred to in sub-section (1) may be removed from the railway by any railway servant or by any other person whom such railway servant may call to his aid.

1 Corresponding provision in the old Act This section corresponds to s. 122 of the old Act.

2 Scope and applicability This section provides for punishment for trespass and useful of the person to desist for trespass. Unlawful entry was the essence of offence under s. 122 of the old Act (corresponding to s. 147 of the new Act).[6] The word "passenger" had not been defined in this old Act. But s. 2(29) of the present Act has defined the word "passenger." Offence under s. 147 of the Act is to be considered in the light of the definition of s. 2(29) of the Act. Whether a person is a passenger or a stranger.[7]

3 Object of section Two things are necessary to bring a man under that section: (1) that the place of entry must be "railway" as defined in s. 3(4) of the Act, and (2) the entry should have been unlawful in the inception.[8] The most important words in s. 122 are the words 'unlawfully enters' for

3 *Jowanda* v *Crown* AIR 1925 Lah 650; 91 IC 33; 6 Lah 467; 27 CrLJ 1.

4 43 Bom 103 followed *Popatlal Bhaichand Shah* v *Emperor* 32 Bom LR 111; AIR 1930 Bom 160.

5 *Radha Kissen* v *Emperor* 68 IC 846; 23 CrLJ 622; AIR 1923 Lah 71.

6 *Durrell* v *Kumud Kanta Chakraborty* AIR 1919 Cal 718.

7 *Sundri* v *Union of India* AIR 1984 All 277 (FB); 1984 All CJ 383; (1984)10 All LR 344.

8 *Emperor* v *Lodai* 25 ALJ 710; 28 CrLJ 648; AIR 1927 All 646.

unless and until a person has made an unlawfully entry upon the railway premises he cannot be brought within this penal provision. The word "unlawful" means "contrary to the law laid down in the statute." If the railway made a general rule under the Act that nobody should enter upon railway platform except passengers with tickets, any other persons entering upon the platform might be guilty of unlawful entry. But where no such rule exists, and where the station master leaves the platform gate open, those who enter upon the platform can hardly be considered to be other than licensees. A person who enters in this manner may be quite lawfully ordered to leave the railway premises, but as he has not entered unlawfully he can never be brought within the mischief of s. 122. See also *In the matter of Baroda Kanto Pramanick.*[9]

4 Eviction of unauthorised occupant A licensee occupying licensed premises after termination of licence can be evicted by the railway authority by taking resort to s. 147 of the Railways Act 1989. Use of reasonable amount of "force" is permissible under s. 147 of the said Act.[10]

> **148. Penalty for making a false statement in an application for compensation.** If in any application for compensation under section 125, any person makes a statement which is false or which he knows or believes to be false or does not believe to be true, he shall be punishable with imprisonment for a term which may extend to three years, or with fine, or with both.

1 Corresponding provision in the old Act This section corresponds to s. 82C(3) of the old Act.

2 Scope This section provides for punishment for making false statement in an application for compensation under s. 125 of the Act before the Railway Claims Tribunal.

> **149. Making a false claim for compensation.** If any person requiring compensation from a railway administration for loss, destruction, damage, deterioration or non-delivery of any consignment makes a claim which is false or which he knows or believes to be false or does not believe to be true, he shall be punishable with imprisonment for a term which may extend to three years, or with fine, or with both.

Scope This section provides that if a person makes a false claim for compensation to a railway administration on account of loss, destruction, damage, deterioration or non-delivery of any consignment, he may be punished with imprisonment for a term not exceeding three years or with a fine or with both.

9 1 CWN 74.

10 *Dhurjati Prosad Das* v *Union of India* AIR 2014 NOC 200 (Cal).

150. Maliciously wrecking or attempting to wreck a train. (1) Subject to the provisions of sub-section (2), if any person unlawfully,—

(*a*) puts or throws upon or across any railways, any wood, stone or other matter or thing; or

(*b*) takes up, removes, loosens or displaces any rail, sleeper or other matter or things belonging to any railway; or

(*c*) turns, moves, unlocks or diverts any points or other machinery belonging to any railway; or

(*d*) makes or shows, or hides or removes, any signal or light upon or near to any railway; or

(*e*) does or causes to be done or attempts to do any other act or thing in relation to any railway,

with intent or with knowledge that he is likely to endanger the safety of any person travelling on or being upon the railway, he shall be punishable with imprisonment for life, or with rigorous imprisonment for a term which may extend to ten years.

Provided that in the absence of special and adequate reasons to the contrary to be mentioned in the judgment of the court, where a person is punishable with rigorous imprisonment, such imprisonment shall not be less than—

(*a*) three years, in the case of a conviction for the first offence; and

(*b*) seven years, in the case of conviction for the second or subsequent offence.

(2) If any person unlawfully does any act or thing referred to in any of the clauses of sub-section (1)—

(*a*) with intent to cause the death of any person and the doing of such act or thing causes the death of any person; or

(*b*) with knowledge that such act or thing is so imminently dangerous that it must in all probability cause the death of any person or such bodily injury to any person as is likely to cause the death of such person,

he shall be punishable with death or imprisonment for life.

1 Corresponding provision in the old Act This section corresponds to s. 126 of the old Act.

2 Scope Where a person maliciously wrecks or attempts to wreck a train, he is liable for punishment. A person who is charged with having placed stones on railway line, with an intention of mischief, he is liable for punishment under this section. Where a person unlocked and turned the turn-label at a railway station with knowledge that he is thereby endangering safety of a person travelling on railway, the said person was guilty of an offence under this section of the Act, lying on rails in order to prevent movements of trains is not an offence under this section.[11] An offence under this section does not fall within the meaning of the term "offence" as used in s. 149 of the Indian Penal Code 1860.[12] Where a person is prosecuted under s. 130 of the old Act read with s. 126(*a*) of that Act, the offence is not triable exclusively by a Court of Session, a Magistrate has jurisdiction to try it and to try it summarily.[13] There is nothing in this section which can be said to create any vicarious liability or make a person who receives a railway property after an offence under this section has been committed by removal of such property by another person guilty of an offence punishable under this section.[14]

151. Damage to or destruction of certain railway properties. (1) If any person, with intent to cause, or knowing that he is likely to cause damage or destruction to any property of a railway referred to in sub-section (2), causes by fire, explosive substance or otherwise, damage to such property or destruction of such property, he shall be punishable with imprisonment for a term which may extend to five years, or with fine, or with both.

(2) The properties of a railway referred to in sub-section (1) are railway track, bridges, station buildings and installations, carriages or wagons, locomotives, signalling, telecommunications, electric traction and block equipments and such other properties as the Central Government being of the opinion that damage thereto or destruction thereof is likely to endanger the operation of a railway, may, by notification, specify.

1 Corresponding provision in the old Act This section corresponds to s. 126A of the old Act.

2 Scope Section 151 is attracted where a person (*i*) with interest the cause or knowingly to cause damage or destruction (*ii*) to any railway property, (*iii*) sets fire or uses explosive substance or any other thing else, he shall be punishable with imprisonment for a term not exceeding five years or with fine or with both.

152. Maliciously hurting or attempting to hurt persons travelling by railway. If any person unlawfully throws or causes to fall or strike at, against, into or upon any rolling stock forming part of a train, any wood, stone or other matter or thing with intent, or with knowledge that he is likely to endanger the safety of any person being in or upon such rolling stock or in or upon any other rolling stock forming part of the same train, he shall be punishable with imprisonment for life, or with imprisonment for a term which may extend to ten years.

1 Corresponding provision in the old Act This section corresponds to s. 127 of the old Act.

11 *Mukundlal Sircar* v *Emperor* 1930 MWN 1264.
12 In re, *Puvanur Athamn* AIR 1925 Mad 239.
13 *Emperor* v *Dhodya* AIR 1919 Bom 173; 20 Civ LJ 699.
14 *Hari* v *State* 1976 All Civ Cas 276.

2 Scope and applicability Section 152 provides for punishment if a person maliciously hurts or attempts to hurt a person travelling by railway. Persons gathering together with the object of obstructing trains and throwing stones at trains are liable to be convicted under this section.[15] But boys of tender age throwing stones at a train would not be punished under this section.[16]

> **153. Endangering safety of persons travelling by railway by wilful act or omission.** If any person by any unlawful act or by any wilful omission or neglect, endangers or causes to be endangered the safety of any person travelling on or being upon any railway, or obstructs or causes to be obstructed or attempts to obstruct any rolling stock upon any railway, he shall be punishable with imprisonment for a term which may extend to five years.

1 Corresponding provision in the old Act This section corresponds to s. 128 of the old Act.

2 Scope Where an unlawful act is wilfully done, rashness cannot be predicted. Boys aged 14 years placed on iron mile post across rails at dusk with the result that had it not been discovered a train might have been derailed. Thus the acts of the boys are wilful and not "rash or negligent."[17] In every case where a travelling train is actually diverted to a wrong line on which there was another train, safety of persons in two trains is endangered. It is not enough if it is merely that an act or omission is likely to endanger the safety of any person. Whether the act is rash and negligent and might have resulted in endangering the safety of any person is a question of fact. The offence of lying on rails cannot be said to endanger the safety of passengers and comes under s. 128 and not under s. 126 of the old Act which correspond to s. 153 and s. 150 respectively of the present Act.[18] Proper conviction for such an act may come under s. 120B of the Indian Penal Code. A person who stops a train reversal times by pulling an alarm chain and thereafter obstructs the train by sitting in front of the engine is guilty under this section. But in assessing sentence the fact that he made the protect in the interest of the public should be considered.[19] Protest for overcrowding and refusing to add additional carriages also come within the purview of this section. A conviction under this section read with s. 149 of the Indian Penal Code is illegal. Persons gathering to obstruct a railway line and throwing stones at trains cannot all the convicted except those who actually committed the offence. The principle of constructive liability cannot be applied to such a case.[20]

15 *Vasudeva Mudaliar* v *Emperor* AIR 1929 Mad 880.
16 *Emperor* v *Wati Muhammad* AIR 1936 Sind 185.
17 *Queen Empress* v *Shivappa* 1889 Rat Un Cr C 458.
18 *Mukundlal Sircar* v *Emperor* 1930 Mad WN 1264.
19 *Emperor* v *Ramchander* AIR 1931 Oudh 85; 32 CrLJ 547.
20 *Vasudeva Mudaliar* v *Emperor* AIR 1929 Mad 880.

154. Endangering safety of persons travelling by railway by rash or negligent act or omission. If any person in a rash and negligent manner does any act, or omits to do what he is legally bound to do, and the act or omission is likely to endanger the safety of any person travelling or being upon any railway, he shall be punishable with imprisonment for a term which may extend to one year, or with fine, or with both.

1 Corresponding provision in the old Act This section corresponds to s. 129 of the old Act.

2 Applicability Coolie on a moving train was trying to haul himself into the train and fell down and injured a guard who was not under duty to prevent persons from getting into the train while it is in motion.

155. Entering into a compartment reserved or resisting entry into a compartment not reserved. (1) If any passenger—

(*a*) having entered a compartment wherein no berth or seat has been reserved by a railway administration for his use, or

(*b*) having unauthorisedly occupied a berth or seat reserved by a railway administration for the use of another passenger,

refuses to leave it when required to do so by any railway servant authorised in this behalf, such railway servant may remove him or cause him to be removed, with the aid of any other person, from the compartment, berth or seat, as the case may be, and he shall also be punishable with fine which may extend to five hundred rupees.

(2) If any passenger resists the lawful entry of another passenger into a compartment not reserved for the use of the passenger resisting, he shall be punishable with fine which may extend to two hundred rupees.

1 Corresponding provision in the old Act This section corresponds to s. 109 of the old Act.

2 Scope Section 155 of the Act provides for punishment of an offence when a passenger enters into a compartment where no berth or seat has been reserved for him or where he unauthorisedly occupied a berth or seat reserved for the use of another passenger. The railway authority has power to reserve a compartment for passengers of a particular class.

3 Meaning of word "passenger" Section 2(29) of the Act defines "passenger" which means a person travelling with a valid pass or ticket. Under the old Act there was no definition of the word "passenger". The word "passenger" under the old Act included a possible passenger who was to join at any later station[1] and a class of passenger.[2]

1 *Kamaran* v *Emperor* 1922 MWN 34; ILR 45 Mad 215.
2 *Bhupendra Nath Dutt* v *Emperor* AIR 1924 Cal 687; ILR 51 Cal 168.

4 Power to resist entry Sub-section (2) recognises by implication the rights of a passenger to resist the entry of another passenger (*i*) into a reserved compartment reserved for his use, (*ii*) or into a compartment which already contains the maximum number of passengers. (*See* ss. 63 and 102).

If a person objects to the coming in of more passengers (though the compartment does not contain the maximum number of passengers) and stands against the door he commits an offence falling under s. 109(2) and s. 120(*c*) and is liable to removal not only from the carriage, but also from the railway by any railway servant.[3]

> **156. Travelling on roof, step or engine of a train.** If any passenger or any other person, after being warned by a railway servant to desist, persists in travelling on the roof, step or footboard of any carriage or on an engine, or in any other part of a train not intended for the use of passengers, he shall be punishable with imprisonment for a term which may extend to three months, or with fine which may extend to five hundred rupees, or with both and may be removed from the railway by any railway servant.

1 Corresponding provision in the old Act This section corresponds to s. 118(3) of the old Act.

2 Applicability This section is applicable to a passenger or a non-passenger who travels on roof, step or footboard or on an engine in spite of warning by a railway servant to desist from such travelling and in such case that person is liable to punishment with imprisonment for a term not exceeding three months or with fine to the extent of five hundred rupees or with both.

3 Non-passenger—if liable A licensed sweetmeat seller sold some sweets to a passenger. Before the price could be recovered from the passenger the train started. The sweetmeat seller got up on the foot-board of the compartment in which the passenger was sitting to recover his price. In spite of the police warning he did not get down before the train ran the whole length of the platform and then jumped off. The sweetmeat seller was prosecuted for standing on the foot-board against the railway rule. He was not liable to be convicted.[4] But a friend who went to see a friend off was intentionally standing on foot-board of the carriage after it had begun to move. It was held to be a trespassing passenger, though he had purchased no ticket.[5] A passenger entered into ice vendor's compartment though warned. He refused to leave it in spite of asking. Thus, he committed the offence under s. 118 of the (old) Railways Act.[6]

3 *Harisarup* v *Emperor* 26 PR 1910; 11 CrLJ 451; 200 PLR 1910; 51 PWR 1910.
4 *Ladhu* v *Emperor* 15 Bom LR 996; 14 CrLJ 654.
5 *Nur Muhammad* v *King-Emperor* 31 PR 1905; *Emperor* v *Bulaki* 5 NLR 151.
6 *Durga Prosad* v *Emperor* AIR 1936 All 439; 37 CrLJ 388; 161 IC 17.

157. Altering or defacing pass or ticket. If any passenger wilfully alters or defaces his pass or ticket so as to render the date, number or any material portion thereof illegible, he shall be punishable with imprisonment for a term which may extend to three months, or with fine which may extend to five hundred rupees, or with both.

1 Corresponding provision in the old Act This section corresponds to s. 116 of the old Act.

2 Applicability This section deals with an offence for altering or defacing a pass or ticket.

158. Penalty for contravention of any of the provisions of Chapter XIV. Any person under whose authority any railway servant is employed in contravention of any of the provisions of Chapter XIV or of the rules made thereunder shall be punishable with fine which may extend to five hundred rupees.

1 Corresponding provision in the old Act This section corresponds to s. 71H of the old Act.

2 Scope This section provides for penalty for contravention of any of the provisions contained in Chapter XIV of the Act.

159. Disobedience of drivers or conductors of vehicles to directions of railway servant, etc. If any driver or conductor of any vehicle while upon the premises of a railway disobeys the reasonable directions of any railway servant or police officer, he shall be punishable with imprisonment for a term which may extend to one month, or with fine which may extend to five hundred rupees, or with both.

1 Corresponding provision in the old Act This section corresponds to s. 123 of the old Act.

2 Applicability This section applies to a driver or conductor of a vehicle for disobeying the directions of a railway servant or police officer.

160. Opening or breaking a level crossing gate. (1) If any person, other than a railway servant or a person authorised in this behalf, opens any gate or chain or barrier set up on either side of a level crossing which is closed to road traffic, he shall be punishable with imprisonment for a term which may extend to three years.

(2) If any person breaks any gate or chain or barrier set up on either side of a level crossing which is closed to road traffic, he shall be punishable with imprisonment for a term which may extend to five years.

Scope and applicability of the section This section provides for punishment of an offence when a person other than a railway servant opens or breaks a level crossing gate. In case of the level crossing over a public carriage road, the railway administration must employ persons to open and shut the gates chains or bars and these must be kept constantly closed against roads on both sides of the railway except when horses, cattle or vehicles are crossing and must be closed again as soon as such traffic has passed. Failure of railway administration to provide any warning of approaching trains amounts to negligence on its part.[7] Since s. 160 is a penal provision, mere knowledge or a reasonable belief about the approaching of any train or engine is sufficient warning to the public not to cross the level crossing.

When gates are open and no warning is given, the public are permitted to cross the level-crossing and pass through the land belonging to the railway within the level-crossing and to that extent they fall within the category of "licensees", during such periods. But, the moment the public come to know of the approaching train or engine, by whatever source, e.g. ringing of gongs, the warning by gate-man, or burning of red lights they are expressly prohibited under s. 124 from crossing the level crossing and in such contingencies they fall under the category of trespassers to whom the duty of the occupier (railway) to invite or licensee does not arise.[8]

161. Negligently crossing unmanned level crossing. If any person driving or leading a vehicle is negligent in crossing an unmanned level crossing, he shall be punishable with imprisonment which may extend to one year.

Explanation. For the purposes of this section, "negligence" in relation to any person driving or leading a vehicle in crossing an unmanned level crossing means the crossing of such level crossing by such person—

(*a*) without stopping or caring to stop the vehicle near such level crossing to observe whether any approaching rolling stock is in sight, or

(*b*) even while an approaching rolling stock is in sight.

1 Applicability of the section This section applies to a person who negligently crosses an unmanned level crossing.

2 Meaning of the word "negligence" Negligence in common parlance means and implies failure to exercise due care expected of a reasonable prudent person. It is a breach of duty and negligence in law ranges from inadvertence to shameful disregard of safety of others.[9]

162. Entering carriage or other place reserved for females. If a male person knowing or having reason to believe that a carriage, compartment, berth or seat in a train or room or other place is reserved by a railway administration for the exclusive use of females, without lawful excuse,—

(*a*) enters such carriage, compartment, room or other place, or having entered such carriage, compartment, room or place, remains therein; or

7 *Yatayat Nigam* v *Union of India* AIR 1983 Raj 17; 1982 Raj LR 484.
8 *V. Krishappa Naidu* v *Union of India* AIR 1976 Mad 95; (1975)2 Mad LJ 353.
9 *M.S. Grewal* v *Deep Chand Sood* AIR 2001 SC 3660.

(b) occupies any such berth or seat having been required by any railway servant to vacate it,

he shall, in addition to being liable to forfeiture of his pass or ticket, be punishable with fine which may extend to five hundred rupees and may also be removed by any railway servant.

1 Corresponding provision in the old Act This section corresponds to s. 119 of the old Act.

2 Entering into lady's compartment A person who entered into a lady's compartment for assisting his wife was interfered with by railway police constable. On altercation, he was convicted under s. 332, IPC. On revision it was held that (*i*) the legislature deliberately refrained from allowing railway police constables to interfere in such matters until called upon by railway authorities; and (*ii*) provisions of s. 119 of the old Act were overlooked while considering the case and the accused had lawful excuse to enter the compartment.[10]

163. Giving false account of goods. If any person required to furnish an account of goods under section 66, gives an account which is materially false, he and, if he is not the owner of the goods, the owner also shall, without prejudice to his liability to pay any freight or other charge under any provision of this Act, be punishable with fine which may extend to five hundred rupees for every quintal or part thereof of such goods.

1 Corresponding provision in the old Act This section corresponds to s. 106 of the old Act.

2 Applicability of the section There can be no offence or giving false account of goods unless the false description is given when a request by the railway to describe the goods has been made. The court imposing fine cannot decide the amount of other charges due to the railways. It should return goods to accused subject to other charges due to railway.[11] Where a consignor does not give any wrong description of the goods nor of the weightment more, the consignor does not commit any offence as the weighing part is done by the railway.

3 Meaning of words The words "and the fine shall be in addition to the rate or other charges" as used in s. 106 of the old Act mean that the consignor on payment of fine cannot be said to have been absolved from liability to pay charge to railway and no more. The charges are to be recovered by railway in due course of law and not through the agency of criminal court as fine.[12]

10 *Chhajju Mal* v *Emperor* 76 Punj LR 1903.
11 *State of Punjab* v *Chunni Lal Vohara* AIR 1968 Punj 294; 1968 CrLJ 970.
12 *State of Punjab* v *Chunni Lal Vohara* (supra).

4 Master's liability for wrongful acts of servants "The general rule is that the master is answerable for every such wrong of the servant or agent as is committed in the course of the service and for the master's benefit, though no express command or privity of the master be proved. That principle is acted upon everyday in running down cases. It has also been applied to direct trespass to goods, as in the case of holding the owners of ships liable for the acts of masters abroad, improperly selling the cargo. It has been held applicable to actions of false imprisonments in case where officers of railway companies, entrusted with the execution of bye-laws relating to imprisonment, and intending to act in the course of their duty, improperly imprisoned persons who are supposed to come within the terms of the bye-laws. In all these cases it may be said that the master has not authorised the Act. It is true, he has not authorised the particular act, but he has put the agent in his place to do that class of acts, and he must be answerable for the manner in which the agent has conducted himself in doing the business which it was the act of his master to place him in."[13]

5 Order by the Magistrate Where a consignor is fined under this section, the Magistrate should order the return of goods to the accused on payment of any charge of the railway. It is beyond the jurisdiction of the Magistrate to ascertain the charge of the railway.[14]

164. Unlawfully bringing dangerous goods on a railway. If any person, in contravention of section 67, takes with him any dangerous goods or entrusts such goods for carriage to the railway administration, he shall be punishable with imprisonment for a term which may extend to three years, or with fine which may extend to one thousand rupees or with both and shall also be liable for any loss, injury or damage which may be caused by reason of bringing such goods on the railway.

1 Corresponding provision in the old Act This section corresponds to s. 107 of the old Act.

2 Scope and applicability This section deals with an offence for unlawfully bringing dangerous goods on a railway in contravention to s. 67 of the Act. A person who gives a false declaration in respect of fire works consigned, is liable to punishment under this section. In case the packages are exploded causing death to one coolie and injury to another, the consignor is liable to be convicted under ss. 340A and 338, IPC.

13 Per WILLES, J. in *Barwick* v *English Joint Stock Bank* [1867] LR 2 Ex 259 (265-68).

14 *State of Punjab* v *Chunni Lal Vohara* ILR (1968)1 Punj 619; AIR 1968 Punj 294; 1968 CrLJ 970.

165. Unlawfully bringing offensive goods on a railway. If any person, in contravention of section 67, takes with him any offensive goods or entrusts such goods for carriage to the railway administration, he shall be punishable with fine which may extend to five hundred rupees and shall also be liable for any loss, injury or damage which may be caused by reason of bringing such goods on the railway.

1 Corresponding provision in the old Act This section also corresponds to s. 107 of the old Act.

2 Scope This section provides for punishment of an offence if a person unlawfully brings offensive goods on a railway in contravention of s. 67 of the Act.

166. Defacing public notices. If any person without lawful authority—

(*a*) pulls down or wilfully damages any board or document set up or posted by the order of a railway administration on a railway or any rolling stock; or

(*b*) obliterates or alters any letters or figures upon any such board or document or upon any rolling stock,

he shall be punishable with imprisonment for a term which may extend to one month, or with fine which may extend to five hundred rupees, or with both.

1 Corresponding provision in the old Act This section corresponds to s. 111 of the old Act.

2 Scope Section 166 of the Act deals with an offence for defacing public notice by any person without lawful authority.

167. Smoking. (1) No person in any compartment of a train shall, if objected to by any other passenger in that compartment, smoke therein.

(2) Notwithstanding anything contained in sub-section (1), a railway administration may prohibit smoking in any train or part of a train.

(3) Whosoever contravenes the provisions of sub-section (1) or sub-section (2) shall be punishable with fine which may extend to one hundred rupees.

1 Corresponding provision in the old Act This section corresponds to s. 110 of the old Act.

2 Applicability of the section The Magistrate can take cognizance of the offence under this section on police report even though it is non-cognizable.[15] This section is applicable to railway servants also.

15 *Triloki Nath Sinha* v *State* AIR 1962 Raj 94.

3 Meaning of words

(a) *"Fellow passengers"*. The words "fellow passengers" used in s. 110 of the old Act does not make any difference because railway servant is also a passenger in compartment if he happens to be travelling therein.[16]

(b) *"Compartment"*. "Compartment" used in s. 110 of the old Act indicates that the quality of complete separation should be attributed to the compartment.[17]

4 Smoking by a railway servant A railway servant travelling on duty in a train is a passenger and he comes within the meaning of the term "person" used in the section.[18] Unless the ingredients of the section are fulfilled no one can be prosecuted.[19]

168. Provision with respect to commission of offence by the children of acts endangering safety of person travelling on railway. (1) If a person under the age of twelve years is guilty of any of the offences under sections 150 to 154, the court convicting him may require the father or guardian of such person to execute, within such time as the court may fix, a bond for such amount and for such period as the court may direct for the good conduct of such person.

(2) The amount of the bond, if forfeited, shall be recoverable by the court as if it were a fine imposed by itself.

(3) If a father or guardian fails to execute a bond under sub-section (1) within the time fixed by the court, he shall be punishable with fine which may extend to fifty rupees.

1 Corresponding provision in the old Act This section corresponds to s. 130 of the old Act.

2 Scope Under s. 130 of the old Act corresponding to s. 168 of the present Act enacts an offence which is distinct from offences under ss. 126 to 129 of the old Act. A minor who is entitled to benefit of s. 82 or s. 83, IPC does not commit an offence when he is guilty of any of the acts or omissions referred to in ss. 126 to 129 of the old Railways Act. It is s. 180 of the old Act which by excluding the operation of the exceptions, creates the offence.[20] Where boys of eight and five years were throwing stones at a railway train, they committed offence under s. 130 of the old Act.[1] Offence under s. 127 of the old Act read with s. 130 of the old Act is triable only by a Court of Session or by a Magistrate invested with special powers

16 *Ibid.*
17 *Dadabhoy,* in re (1900)24 Bom 293 (SB).
18 *Triloki Nath Sinha* v *State* AIR 1962 Raj 94.
19 *Sudhir Chandra* v *State* AIR 1965 Assam 38; ILR (1964)16 Ass 196.
20 *Emperor* v *Dhodya* AIR 1919 Bom 173.
1 *Emperor* v *Wati Mohamed* AIR 1936 Sind 185.

under s. 30 of the (old) Code of Criminal Procedure. Offence punishable under s. 130 of the old Act read with s. 126(*a*) of the old Act not exclusively triable by a Court of Session but could be tried by a competent Magistrate.[2] In view of s. 29B of the (old) Code of Criminal Procedure an offence under s. 130 of the (old) Railways Act could be tried only by a District Magistrate.[3]

169. Levy of penalty on non-Government railway. If a non-Government railway fails to comply with, any requisition made, decision or direction given, by the Central Government, under any of the provisions of this Act, or otherwise contravenes any of the provisions of this Act; it shall be open to the Central Government, by order, to levy a penalty not exceeding two hundred and fifty rupees and a further penalty not exceeding one hundred and fifty rupees for every day during which the contravention continues:

Provided that no such penalty shall be levied except after giving a reasonable opportunity to the non-Government railway to make such representation as it deems fit.

170. Recovery of penalty. Any penalty imposed by the Central Government under section 169, shall be recoverable by a suit in the District Court having jurisdiction in the place where the head office of the non-Government railway is situated.

1 Corresponding provision in the old Act Section 170 corresponds to s. 97 of the old Act.

2 Scope This section deals with recovery of penalty imposed by the Central Government under s. 169 of the Act. The procedure is to file a suit in the District Court having jurisdiction over the head office of the non-Government railway.

171. Section 169 or 170 not to preclude Central Government from taking any other action. Nothing in section 169 or 170 shall preclude the Central Government from resorting to any other action to compel a non-Government railway to discharge any obligation imposed upon it by or under this Act.

172. Penalty for intoxication. If any railway servant is in a state of intoxication while on duty, he shall be punishable with fine which may extend to five hundred rupees and when the performance of any duty in such state is likely to endanger the safety of any person travelling on or being upon a railway, such railway servant shall be punishable with imprisonment for a term which may extend to one year, or with fine, or with both.

1 Corresponding provision in the old Act Section 172 corresponds to s. 100 of the old Act.

2 *Emperor* v *Dhodya* AIR 1919 Bom 173.
3 *Emperor* v *Mt. Jannat* AIR 1928 Lah 909.

2 Applicability of the section Section 172 provides for penalty of a railway servant who is in a state of intoxication while on duty. Drunkenness of a guard while on duty is offence. Members of railway police force even though appointed by police authorities are in the pay roll of railway and therefore owe it a duty. Hence where a constable was found asleep while on duty, he was liable for conviction under the old provisions of railway law.[4] Where a Magistrate proceeded against an accused under the first part of s. 100 of the old Act and the accused was convicted under the second part without adopting the procedure for trial of warrant case, it was held that the conviction was illegal.[5] A railway servant is not punishable under s. 100 of the old Act (corresponding to s. 172 of the present Act) if he is not on duty and as such he will not be held liable under this section if he is guilty of any other offences under the Act.

173. Abandoning train, etc., without authority. If any railway servant, when on duty, is entrusted with any responsibility connected with the running of a train, or of any other rolling stock from one station or place to another station or place, and he abandons his duty before reaching such station or place without authority or without properly handing over such train or rolling stock to another authorised railway servant, he shall be punishable with imprisonment for a term which may extend to two years, or with fine which may extend to one thousand rupees, or with both.

1 Corresponding provision in the old Act This section corresponds to s. 100A of the old Act.

2 Scope Section 173 deals with an offence when a railway servant who is on duty abandon his duty or the train without any authority.

174. Obstructing running of train, etc. If any railway servant (whether on duty or otherwise) or any other person obstructs or causes to be obstructed or attempts to obstruct any train or other rolling stock upon a railway—

(*a*) by squatting or picketing or during any *Rail roko* agitation or *bandh*; or

(*b*) by keeping without authority any rolling stock on the railway; or

(*c*) by tampering with, disconnecting or interfering in any other manner with its hose pipe or tampering with signal gear or otherwise,

he shall be punishable with imprisonment for a term which may extend to two years, or with fine which may extend to two thousand rupees, or with both.

1 Corresponding provision in the old Act This section corresponds to s. 100B of the old Act.

4 *Reg.* v *Sayad Hazi* 1867 Rat Un Cr C 51.
5 *Trousdel,* in re (1909)5 Mad LT 204.

2 Applicability of the section Section 174 of the Act applies to both railway servant and any other person who obstructs or causes to obstruct a train by any of the following means: (*a*) squatting or picketing during any *rail roko* agitation or *bandh*; (*b*) keeping without authority any rolling stock on the railway; (*c*) tampering with, disconnecting or interfering in any other manner with its hose pipe or tampering with signal gear or otherwise. Punishment for such an offence is imprisonment for a term not exceeding two years or fine to the extent of two thousand rupees or both.

175. Endangering the safety of persons. If any railway servant, when on duty, endangers the safety of any person—

(*a*) by disobeying any rule made under this Act; or

(*b*) by disobeying any instruction, direction or order under this Act or the rules made thereunder; or

(*c*) by any rash or negligent act or omission,

he shall be punishable with imprisonment for a term which may extend to two years, or with fine which may extend to one thousand rupees, or with both.

1 Corresponding provision in the old Act This section corresponds to s. 101 of the old Act.

2 Disobedience of a Rule To render a person liable to conviction under s. 101 of the old Act, it must be proved that the safety of a person was actually endangered in point of fact. Where a station master allows a goods train to run over the loop line on receiving a signal from the pointsman, when in fact one of the points was not properly set, with the result that there was a collision and certain persons on the goods train sustained injuries, the station master is not guilty of an offence under s. 101 of the old Act, although he committed a breach of the rules in allowing the train to run on to the loop line when the main line was clear. Before he can be held guilty of an offence under that section, it must be proved that he endangered human life by failure to comply with the rules and regulations of the railway company.[6]

Before a person can be convicted under the section, the prosecution must prove that a general rule had been disobeyed and that by reason of such disobedience the safety of any person was endangered. Actual harm need not be caused but a possibility of harm being caused would be sufficient.[7] It is no defence that the accused carried out the orders of his superior.[8] In case of collision between two trains at the station for the prosecution of station master for negligence the correct approach to impute negligence on the part of the station master is to see whether the signals were lowered at that crucial moment.[9] What is meant is that a breach of the rule must

6 *Bhagwan Das* v *Emperor* AIR 1936 All 745; 1936 ALJ 951.
7 *M. Pandurangam* v *State* 1961 MLJ 498; (1961)2 Andh WR 80.
8 *State* v *Kanhaiyalal* ILR (1959)9 Raj 589.
9 *Awadh Behari Sharma* v *State of Madhya Pradesh* AIR 1956 SC 738.

be of a character which endangers the safety of persons. Indeed, that is the *sine qua non* as mentioned in s. 101 of the old Act itself.[10]

Rule 37(2) of the Subsidiary Rules of Western Railway requires that the assistant station master must keep the key in his personal custody. Therefore in whatever manner the pointsman gets the key the station master must be held negligent and must be held to have disobeyed the rules, unless it is found that there is any force or fraud used against him.[11] Where an engine driver, in driving the engine backwards, disobeys a red signal and also takes the engine beyond the authorised point which results in collision with a goods train, he is guilty of endangering his own safety and the safety of the crew of other train and acting in rash and negligent manner.[12]

3 Some illustrative cases

(*a*) Station master under duty was required to send porter to set and lock points which he omitted to do. Similarly, engine driver by breaking rules proceeded with the train without stopping when he found no porter at the point, the accused station master was held guilty in omitting to send a porter.[13]

(*b*) Where the danger was not proximate result of act or omission of the accused, he cannot be liable under this section.[14]

(*c*) A station master left a lock open and handed over the charge to assistant station master who did not know that the lock was unlocked. Thus, he cannot be held under s. 101 of the old Act.[15]

(*d*) Breach of rule of railway company without evidence that it endangered safety of passengers is not sufficient for conviction.[16]

(*e*) Where a person is charged for disobedience of one rule, he cannot be convicted for non-complying with a different rule.[17]

10 *Ramchandra Govinda* v *State* AIR 1962 Bom 41.

11 *State of Madhya Pradesh* v *Ranjit Kumar Chatterjee* AIR 1959 MP 284; 1959 CrLJ 983.

12 *A.V. Raju* v *State of Orissa* AIR 1974 SC 1350; (1974)3 SCC 666; 1974 UJ (SC) 142; 1974 SCC (Cri) 196.

13 *Bishan Sarup* v *Emperor* AIR 1925 Lah 423.

14 *Bhagwan Das* v *Emperor* AIR 1936 All 745; 38 CrLJ 227.

15 *Gouri Dayal Dube* v *Emperor* AIR 1935 All 121; 36 CrLJ 630.

16 *Parbhu Dayal* v *Emperor* AIR 1924 Oudh 250.

17 *Parasram Kundraj* v *Emperor* AIR 1933 Sindh 225.

(*f*) In a prosecution under s. 101 of the old Act of a station master in connection with collusion at his station, the crucial issue to impute negligence on the part of the station master was whether when the collusion occurred, signals had been found lowered. This issue is to be determined not on mere balance of oral evidence, but on broader consideration and clean probabilities as oral evidence may be honestly discrepant.[18]

(*g*) A person who actually carried out the repairs, he can be liable under this section not only for negligently doing the repair work but also he has breached the rules endangering public safety.[1]

(*h*) There was a collision in between two signals occurring in the driver's ignorance of first signal after crossing it and following only second signal proves his rash and negligent driving.[2]

(*i*) When an accident occurred due to collision of two railways, a departmental enquiry was initiated against the driver for substantially the same charges which were framed against him in a criminal case in which he was acquitted. But in the departmental enquiry he was ordered to be removed. Such order was improper.[3]

(*j*) It is the duty of the driver to ascertain terms of message for assistance sent to him by guard. His omission to do so would make him liable under the old s. 101(*c*) where it endangers safety of any person.[4]

(*k*) Where a train is stopped outside distant signal, omission of a guard to place detonators to protect train is disobedience of working instruction and it is punishable under s. 101 of the old Act.

(*l*) Engine driver is not bound to stop train merely because wayfarer shout to him.[5]

(*m*) Contributory negligence on the part of some one else cannot be regarded as valid defence to charge under s. 101 of the old Act.[6]

176. Obstructing level crossing. If any railway servant unnecessarily—

(*a*) allows any rolling stock to stand across a place where the railway crosses a public road on the level; or

18 *Awadh Behari* v *State of MP* AIR 1956 SC 738; 1956 CrLJ 1372.
1 *Ramchandra Govinda* v *State* AIR 1962 Bom 41.
2 *Namadevan* v *State of Madras* 1972 CrLJ 1414.
3 *R.J. Divekar* v *Union of India* 1984 Lab IC 1752.
4 *Local Govt.* v *Khairat Ali* AIR 1920 Nag 18; 21 CrLJ 204.
5 *D'Cruz* v *Emperor* AIR 1933 Pat 94; 34 CrLJ 576.
6 *Ram Raj Kahar* v *State* AIR 1955 NUC 5910 (Cal).

(*b*) keeps a level crossing closed against the public,

he shall be punishable with fine which may extend to one hundred rupees.

1 Corresponding provision in the old Act This section corresponds to s. 104 of the old Act.

2 Scope Section 176 of the Act deals with an offence for obstructing level-crossing by any railway servant unnecessarily.

177. False returns. If any railway servant required to furnish a return by or under this Act, signs and furnishes a return which is false in any material particular or which he knows or believes to be false, or does not believe to be true, he shall be punishable with imprisonment which may extend to one year, or with fine which may extend to five hundred rupees, or with both.

1 Corresponding provision in the old Act This section corresponds to s. 105 of the old Act.

2 Scope This section provides for punishment of an offence committed by a railway servant in submitting false returns.

178. Making a false report by a railway servant. If any railway servant who is required by a railway administration to inquire into a claim for loss, destruction, damage, deterioration or non-delivery of any consignment makes a report which is false or which he knows or believes to be false or does not believe to be true, he shall be punishable with imprisonment for a term which may extend to two years, or with fine which may extend to one thousand rupees, or with both.

Scope This section provides that a railway servant who is required to submit a report under this Act makes a false report and in such a case he is liable to punishment with imprisonment for a term not exceeding two years or with fine which may extend to one thousand rupees or with both.

[7][179. Arrest for offences under certain sections. (1) If any person commits any offence mentioned in sections 150 to 152, he may be arrested without warrant

7 *Substituted* by the Act 51 of 2003, s. 3, for s. 179 (w.e.f. 1.7.2004). Provisions of original section 179 prior to substitution are reproduced below:

"*179. Arrest for offences under certain sections.* (1) If a person commits any offence mentioned in sections 137, 141 to 147, 150 to 157, 160 to 162, 164, 166, 168 and 172 to 175, he may be arrested without warrant or other written authority by any railway servant or police officer not below the rank of a head constable.

(2) The railway servant or the police officer may call to his aid any other person to effect the arrest under sub-section (1).

(3) Any person so arrested under this section shall be produced before the nearest Magistrate within a period of twenty-four hours of such arrest excluding the time necessary for the journey from the place of arrest to the court of the Magistrate."

or other written authority by any railway servant or police officer not below the rank of a head constable.

(2) If any person commits any offence mentioned in sections 137 to 139, 141 to 147, 153 to 157, 159 to 167 and 172 to 176, he may be arrested, without warrant or other written authority, by the officer authorised by a notified order of the Central Government.

(3) The Railway servant or the police officer or the officer authorised, as the case may be, may call to his aid any other person to effect the arrest under sub-section (1) or sub-section (2), as the case may be.

(4) Any person so arrested under this section shall be produced before the nearest Magistrate within a period of twenty-four hours of such arrest excluding the time necessary for the journey from the place of arrest to the court of the Magistrate.]

1 Commentaries All the officers of and above the rank of Assistant Sub-Inspector in the Railway Protection Force are notified to be the "officer authorised" for the purposes of the Act [*vide* S.O. 593(E) dt. 17th May, 2004].

2 Corresponding provision in the old Act This section corresponds to s. 131 of the old Act.

3 Applicability Where the complainant railway servant has no reason to believe that the accused would abscond, he has no right to arrest the accused under this section.

4 Meaning of the word "person" The word "person" used in s. 131 of the old Act includes a railway servant to whom ss. 100 and 101 of the old Act were applicable.

180. Arrest of persons likely to abscond, etc. (1) If any person who commits any offence under this Act, other than an offence mentioned in [8][sub-section (2) of section 179], or is liable to pay any excess charge or other sum demanded under section 138, fails or refuses to give his name and address or there is reason to believe that the name and address given by him are fictitious or that he will abscond, [8][the officer authorised] may arrest him without warrant or written authority.

(2) [8][The officer authorised] may call to his aid any other person to effect the arrest under sub-section (1).

(3) Any person arrested under this section shall be produced before the nearest Magistrate within a period of twenty-four hours of such arrest excluding the time necessary for the journey from the place of arrest to the court of the Magistrate unless he is released earlier on giving bail or if his true name and

8 *Substituted* by Act 51 of 2003 (w.e.f. 01.07.2004).

address are ascertained on executing a bond without sureties for his appearance before the Magistrate having jurisdiction to try him for the offence.

(4) The provisions of Chapter XXIII of the Code of Criminal Procedure, 1973 (2 of 1974), shall so far as may be, apply to the giving of bail and the execution of bonds under this section.

1 Corresponding provision in the old Act This section corresponds to s. 132 of the old Act.

2 Detention—when legal Under s. 132 of the old Act detention is legal not only where there is refusal to give name and address but also where though the name and address are given the servants of the company have reason to believe them to be incorrect. Thus there may be a case where the arrest is legal though the name and address given ultimately prove to be correct. At the same time when name and address are as a matter of fact given the passenger can be arrested only where there is material for believing that the same is incorrect. Here belief is not sufficient and the passenger cannot be arrested at the mere caprice of the railway servant or the police officer. The belief must be based on reason but whether the reason is sufficient to justify the belief is a matter within the discretion of the person arresting.

3 Illustrative cases

(*a*) In case of trespass as well as travelling without ticket it must be shown that there was reason to believe that the person to be arrested would abscond or that his name and address were unknown or that he refused to give his name and address or that there was reason to believe that the name or address given was incorrect in order to arrest without warrant. It must also be shown that he refused to pay the sum charged.[9]

(*b*) Under this section it is not necessary that both name and address should be believed to be incorrect but either the name or the address.[10]

(*c*) An accused cannot be acquitted merely on the ground that there was no complaint by railway authority.[11]

[12][**180A. Inquiry by officer authorised to ascertain commission of offence.** For ascertaining facts and circumstances of a case, the officer authorised may make an inquiry into the commission of an offence mentioned in sub-section (2) of section 179 and may file a complaint in the competent court if the offence is found to have been committed.

9 *S.A. Hamid* v *Sudhirmohan Ghosh* AIR 1929 Cal 730.

10 *Motiram* v *Emperor* AIR 1941 Sind 117.

11 *Public Prosecutor* v *Moturru* AIR 1940 Mad 268.

12 *Inserted* by Act 51 of 2003, s. 5 (w.e.f. 01.07.2004).

180B. Powers of officer authorised to inquire. While making an inquiry, the officer authorised shall have power to,—

(*i*) summon, and enforce the attendance of any person and record his statement;

(*ii*) require the discovery and production of any document;

(*iii*) requisition any public record or copy thereof from any office, authority or person;

(*iv*) enter and search any premises or person and seize any property or document which may be relevant to the subject-matter of the inquiry.

180C. Disposal of persons arrested. Every person arrested for an offence punishable under sub-section (2) of section 179 shall, if the arrest was made by a person other than the officer authorised, be forwarded, without delay, to such officer.

180D. Inquiry how to be made against arrested person. (1) When any person is arrested by the officer authorised for an offence punishable under this Act, such officer shall proceed to inquire into the charge against such person.

(2) For this purpose, the officer authorised may exercise the same powers and shall be subject to the same provisions as the officer in charge of a police station may exercise and is subject to the provisions of the Code of Criminal Procedure, 1973 (2 of 1974), when investigating a cognizable case:

Provided that—

(*a*) if the officer authorised is of the opinion that there is sufficient evidence or reasonable ground of suspicion against the accused person, he shall either admit him to bail to appear before a Magistrate having jurisdiction in the case, or forward him in custody to such Magistrate;

(*b*) if it appears to the officer authorised that there is no sufficient evidence or reasonable ground of suspicion against the accused person, he shall release the accused person on his executing a bond, with or without sureties as the officer authorised may direct, to appear, if and when so required, before the Magistrate having jurisdiction.

180E. Search, seizure and arrest how to be made. All searches, seizures and arrests made under this Act shall be carried out in accordance with the provisions of the Code of Criminal Procedure, 1973 (2 of 1974), relating respectively to searches and arrests made under that Code.

180F. Cognizance by Court on a complaint made by officer authorised. No court shall take cognizance of an offence mentioned in sub-section (2) of section 179 except on a complaint made by the officer authorised.

180G. Punishment for certain offences in relation to inquiry. Whoever intentionally insults or causes any interruption in the inquiry proceedings or

deliberately makes a false statement before the inquiring officer shall be punished with simple imprisonment for a term which may extend to six months, or with fine which may extend to one thousand rupees, or with both].

181. Magistrate having jurisdiction under the Act. Notwithstanding anything contained in the Code of Criminal Procedure, 1973 (2 of 1974), no court inferior to that of a Metropolitan Magistrate or a Judicial Magistrate of the first class shall try an offence under this Act.

1 Corresponding provision in the old Act This section corresponds to s. 133 of the old Act.

2 Competence of Magistrate Section 133 of the old Act cannot be invoked to invest a second class Magistrate with jurisdiction to try an offence falling under that section in spite of the fact that Schedule II, Code of Criminal Procedure (old) does not give him that power.[13] Similarly, a Magistrate of third class has no jurisdiction to try an offence under s. 133 of the old Act. Offences under the old Railways Act punishable with fine not exceeding twenty rupees cannot be tried by a Magistrate inferior to first class Magistrate.

182. Place of trial. (1) Any person committing an offence under this Act or any rule made thereunder shall be triable for such offence in any place in which he may be or which the State Government may notify in this behalf, as well as in any other place in which he is liable to be tried under any law for the time being in force.

(2) Every notification under sub-section (1) shall be published in the Official Gazette, and a copy thereof shall be exhibited for the information of the public in some conspicuous place at such railway stations as the State Government may direct.

1 Corresponding provision in the old Act This section corresponds to s. 134 of the old Act.

2 Place of trial This section lays down the conditions for invoking jurisdiction for any offence committed under this Act or any rule made thereunder. If a person is accused of an offence committed whilst a journey or voyage was going on, he might be tried if any of that part of journey or voyage during which the offence the offence of which the accused was alleged to have committed is within the local limits of the court's jurisdiction. Even where cases are to be tried by the Special Magistrate while he was on the line, yet this would be no justification for refusing a proper trial as because the accused wanted to produce evidence to show that it was not his intention to defraud the railway.[14]

13 *Emperor* v *Wati Mahommad* AIR 1936 Sind 185.

14 *Abdul Waquar* v *State* AIR 1954 All 12; 1953 CrLJ 1855.

CHAPTER XVI
Miscellaneous

183. Power to provide other transport services. (1) A railway administration may, for the purpose of facilitating the carriage of passengers or goods or to provide integrated service for such carriage, provide any other mode of transport.

(2) Notwithstanding anything contained in any other law for the time being in force, the provisions of this Act shall apply to the carriage of passengers or goods by the mode of transport referred to in sub-section (1).

Scope Section 183 of the Act empowers a railway administration to provide other transport services for the purpose of facilitating the carriage of passengers or goods.

184. Taxation on railways by local authorities. (1) Notwithstanding anything to the contrary contained in any other law, a railway administration shall not be liable to pay any tax in aid of the funds of any local authority unless the Central Government, by notification, declares the railway administration to be liable to pay the tax specified in such notification.

(2) While a notification of the Central Government under sub-section (1) is in force, the railway administration shall be liable to pay to the local authority either the tax specified in the notification or, in lieu thereof, such sum, if any, as an officer appointed in this behalf by the Central Government may, having regard to all the circumstances of the case, from time to time, determine to be fair and reasonable.

(3) The Central Government may at any time revoke or vary a notification issued under sub-section (1).

(4) Nothing in this section shall be construed to prevent any railway administration from entering into a contract with any local authority for the supply of water or light, or for the scavenging of railway premises, or for any other service which the local authority may be rendering or be prepared to render to the railway administration.

1 Corresponding provision in the old Act This section corresponds to s. 135 of the old Act.

2 Scope This section debars a local authority to tax a railway in absence of any notification by the Central Government in this regard. Section 135 of the old Act which corresponds to s. 184 of the present Act was saved under Art. 285(1) and not by Art. 285(2) of the Constitution of India.[1]

1 *Union of India* v *Purna Municipal Council* AIR 1992 SC 1597; 1991 Supp (1) SCR 183; (1992)1 SCC 100.

3 Liability of railways to taxation Where a notification has been issued under this section authorising a local authority to levy certain tax, all properties existing before or after the notification shall be liable to such taxation as are specified in the notification.[2] In order to attract the provision of s. 135 of the old Act not only there must be a notification of the Central Government under sub-sec. (1) of s. 135 of the old Act but there must be a liability upon the railway administration to pay a tax by virtue of the notification. It is only where the railway administration is made *prima facie* liable to pay a tax to a local authority that it can approach the appropriate authority for determining the quantum of such liability.[3]

Baktiapur Bihar Light Railway is a tramway constructed under the special Act, Bengal Tramways Act 1883. The railway is liable to pay municipal tax and no Central Government notification is necessary for the purpose.[4] It is submitted that in view of the decision of the Supreme Court in *S.S.L. Railway Co.* v *Saharanpur Municipality*[5] the Patna decision is no longer good law.

By virtue of the notification under s. 135(1) of the old Act making the G.I.P. Railway liable to municipal tax on buildings and lands makes the railway liable to consolidated tax imposed by the municipality and the railway cannot get exemption by distinguishing tax on "buildings and land" and "consolidated tax".[6]

4 Liability to taxation by local authority—levy of octroi duty Section 135 of the (old) Railways Act specifically deals with railway property which could be subjected to levy of taxes in aid of the funds of the local authority. Under that section unless the railway administration is expressly declared as being liable to pay a tax, that tax cannot be levied on the railway administration. This declaration has to be made by a notification issued by the Central Government. Now Notification dated 29th November 1907, which is issued in exercise of power under s. 135 (old), enables the local authority to impose all such taxes in respect of property of the railway administration which could be imposed by that local authority in aid of its funds. This provision has, however, a close nexus with Art. 285, Constitution of India. It reads as under:

> "(1) The property of the Union shall, save in so far as Parliament may by law otherwise provide, be exempt from all taxes imposed by a State or by any authority within a State.

2 *Governor-General of India in Council* v *Corporation of Calcutta* AIR 1948 Cal 116; *Dominion of India* v *Motihari Municipality* AIR 1954 Pat 568; *Union of India* v *Sahibganj Municipality* AIR 1966 Pat 223.

3 *Municipal Corporation of Greater Bombay* v *Akbar S. Sarela* AIR 1960 Bom 141.

4 *General Manager, B.B. Light Railway* v *Municipal Commissioner of Bihar* AIR 1968 Pat 59.

5 AIR 1967 SC 1747; (1967)3 SCR 243.

6 *Union of India* v *Lonavala Borough Municipality* AIR 1971 SC 211; (1970)3 SCR 920; (1970)1 SCC 641.

(2) Nothing in clause (1) shall, until Parliament by law otherwise provides, prevent any authority within a State from levying any tax on any property of the Union to which such property was immediately before the commencement of this Constitution liable or treated as liable, so long as that tax continues to be levied in that State".

Article 285 of the Constitution is thus in two parts. Sub-Art. (1) provides for exemption of the property of the Union from all taxes imposed by a State or by any authority within a State which will include a local authority like a Municipal Council. This exemption can, however, be taken away by a law made by the Parliament. The latter part of Art. 285 was intended to save the taxes which were being levied on the property of the Union at the commencement of the Constitution by any authority within a State so long as the tax continued to be levied in that State. Thus, where a property of the Union was, immediately before the commencement of the Constitution, liable to tax or treated as liable to tax levied by a local authority, that tax could continue to be levied in view of the express provisions in Art. 285(2). Such property could not be exempted from taxation only by a law made by the Parliament. The provisions of Art. 285 will, therefore, make it clear that the property of the Union of India could not be subjected to tax by a local authority unless the condition in sub-Art. (2) was satisfied.

Section 3, Railways (Local Authorities' Taxation) Act 1941 enables the local authority to levy a tax in aid of its funds in respect of property vested in the Central Government, being a property of a railway, only if the Central Government issues a notification declaring the railway administration to be so liable. Therefore, after coming into force of Part III of the Government of India Act 1935, before the railway property can be taxed, a notification under s. 3 of the 1941 Act has to be issued by the Central Government. Section 4 only empowers the Central Government to revoke or modify a notification issued under s. 135 of the (old) Railways Act. The consequence of revocation is that the liability to pay tax to any local authority under that notification ceases. The position, as it appears, is that the notification of 1907 was revoked in October 1953. Therefore, even assuming that the notification of 1907 empowered the local authority to levy octroi duty, that liability ceased in terms of s. 4 of the 1941 Act with effect from 3rd October 1953 and no recovery of octroi duty could have been made thereafter.[7]

5 Demand of service charges by municipalities from railways Article 285(1) of the Constitution of India provides for exemption in respect of the property of the Union from all taxes imposed by a State or by any authority within a State and as such a Municipal Corporation cannot impose taxes

7 *Union of India* v *Bhusawal Municipal Council* AIR 1982 Bom 512; (1981)83 Bom LR 452.

on the property of the Union unless law made by Parliament provides otherwise. Section 184(1) of the Railways Act 1989 lays down that it is only by way of notification in the Official Gazette that the railway administration can be declared to be liable to pay the taxes. Therefore, the recovery of property taxes or service charges in lieu of such taxes under the demand notices and orders issued for coercive recovery of the municipal taxes is *ultra vires* the powers of the Municipal Corporation.[8]

6 Some illustrative cases relating to exemption from taxation on railway

(*a*) Land belonging to administration of G.I.P. Railway subject to charge by for Municipal taxes and s. 135 of the old Act has no application to such cases.[9]

(*b*) Under s. 135 of the old Act unless the railway administration is expressly declared as being liable to pay a tax, that tax cannot be levied on the railway administration.[10]

(*c*) The tax was imposed by the (old) Railways Act but by the Calcutta Municipal Act 1923. If no tax were payable under the latter Act, a mere notification by the Governor-General could not impose any such liability.[11]

(*d*) Specific notification imposing liability for a particular tax is necessary to make the railway administration liable. Previous notification make the administration liable for other taxes is not sufficient.[12]

(*e*) In absence of notification the railway administration is not liable in respect of licence fee payable for warehouse under the Bengal Act 1 of 1893 which is a tax in aid of the fund of a local authority.[13]

(*f*) Once a sum has been fixed as payable for tax by an officer acting under s. 135(2) of the old Act, that amount cannot be varied for the period for which it is fixed. But the officer can vary it for subsequent period where the exigencies require such variation.[14]

(*g*) In order to attract s. 135(2) of the old Act not only must there be a notification of the Central Government under s. 135(1) of the old Act, but there must be a liability upon railway administration to pay a tax by virtue of the notification. It is only where railway administration is made *prima facie* liable to pay a tax to a local

8 *Union of India* v *Rajkot Municipal Corporation* AIR 2003 Guj 87; (2002)3 GLR 904; see also *Union of India* v *State of Orissa* AIR 2007 NOC 1813 (Ori) (Entry tax, payable by railway).

9 *Secretary of State* v *Municipal Corpn. Bombay* AIR 1935 Bom 352.

10 *Union of India* v *Bhasawal Municipal Council* AIR 1982 Bom 512; (1981)83 Bom LR 452.

11 *Corporation of Calcutta* v *B&D Rly. Co. Ltd.* AIR 1940 Cal 531.

12 *Municipal Council* v *M. & S.M. Rly. Co.* AIR 1929 Mad 746.

13 *R.E. Marriott* v *Municipality of Howrah* AIR 1941 Cal 319.

14 *Municipal Council Bezwada* v *M. & S.M. Rly Co. Ltd.* AIR 1944 Mad 355.

authority that it can approach appropriate authority for determining the quantum of such liability.[15]

(*h*) The Municipal Board cannot claim in its own right to enhance an amount of tax payable by railway administration and make a demand and on failure of the railway administration to meet the demand to issue a distress warrant or thereon to cut-off the water supply.[16]

(*i*) The use of the term "scavenging tax" in the notification issued under s. 135 of the old Act must be taken to import a reference to a scavenging tax as given in the Berar Municipal Law. So long as the notification has not been superseded, tax can be collected from the railway concerned under s. 135 of the old Act.[17]

(*j*) Government notification exempted application of s. 135(1) of the old Act to the B.B. Light Railway and as such it was liable to pay Municipal tax.[18]

185. Taxation on railways for advertisement. (1) Notwithstanding anything to the contrary contained in any other law, a railway administration shall not be liable to pay any tax to any local authority in respect of any advertisement made on any part of the railway unless the Central Government, by notification, declares the railway administration to be liable to pay the tax specified in such notification.

(2) The Central Government may at any time revoke or vary a notification issued under sub-section (1).

Scope Section 185 exempts railway from any liability to pay tax to any local authority for any advertisement made on any part of the railway except any notification by the Central Government in this regard.

186. Protection of action taken in good faith. No suit, prosecution or other legal proceeding shall lie against the Central Government, any railway administration, a railway servant or any other person for anything which is in good faith done or intended to be done in pursuance of this Act or any rules or orders made thereunder.

Scope Section 186 protects the Central Government, any railway administration or a railway servant to be liable under any suit or to be prosecuted in any criminal case for any action taken by any of them in good faith.

15 *Municipal Corpn.* v *A.S. Sarela* AIR 1960 Bom 141.
16 *Municipal Board of Kanpur* v *Dominion of India* AIR 1954 All 56.
17 *G.-G.-in-Council* v *Murtizapur Municipality* AIR 1953 Nag 297.
18 *General Manager, B.B. Light Rly.* v *Municipal Commrs., Bihar* AIR 1968 Pat 59.

187. Restriction on execution against railway property. (1) No rolling stock, machinery, plant, tools, fittings, materials or effects used or provided by a railway administration for the purpose of traffic on its railway, or of its stations or workshops, shall be liable to be taken in execution of any decree or order of any court or of any local authority or person having by law the power to attach or distrain property or otherwise to cause property to be taken in execution, without the previous sanction of the Central Government.

(2) Nothing in sub-section (1) shall be construed to affect the authority of any court to attach the earnings of a railway in execution of a decree or order.

1 Corresponding provision in the old Act This section corresponds to s. 136 of the old Act.

2 Scope and applicability Section 187 bars execution of a decree or order of any court or any other competent authority against railway property. The Health Centre of the Northern Railway does not fall within the purview of s. 136 of the old Act. Thus when the Union of India failed to pay compensation money for the acquisition of land under the Land Acquisition Act 1894, the claimants were entitled to attach the Health Centre of Railway in execution proceedings.

188. Railway servants to be public servants for the purposes of Chapter IX and section 409 of the Indian Penal Code. (1) Any railway servant, who is not a public servant within the meaning of section 21 of the Indian Penal Code (45 of 1860), shall be deemed to be a public servant for the purposes of Chapter IX and section 409 of that Code.

(2) In the definition of "legal remuneration" in section 161 of the Indian Penal Code (45 of 1860), the word "Government" shall, for the purposes of sub-section (1), be deemed to include any employer of a railway servant as such.

1 Corresponding provision in the old Act This section corresponds to s. 137 of the old Act.

2 Public servants The amendments in 1955 mean that those railway servants who were not public servants as defined in s. 21 of the Indian Penal Code shall also be deemed to be public servants for the purpose of Chapter IX of the Code. The amendment of sub-sec. (1) was not intended to affect the position of railway servants in the State owned railway who had been already public servants. It was intended to apply to the servants of such railways as were not affected by the State taking over the railways but remained under the control of private agencies. Such persons would be public servants only for the purpose of s. 409 and all the sections of Chapter IX of the Indian Penal Code.[19] A guard is a public servant and the court is not competent to take cognizance of the offence under ss. 342

19 In re, *Dorairaj* (1964)2 MLJ 477.

and 500 of the Indian Penal Code in the absence of requisite sanction under s. 197, CrPC.[20]

189. Railway servants not to engage in trade. A railway servant shall not—

(*a*) purchase or bid for, either in person or by an agent, in his own name or in that of another, or jointly or in shares with others, any property put to auction under section 83 or section 84 or section 85 or section 90; or

(*b*) in contravention of any direction of the railway administration in this behalf, engage in trade.

1 Corresponding provision in the old Act This section corresponds to s. 137(3) of the old Act.

2 Scope Section 189 of the Act restrains a railway servant to carry on any trade or business in relation to any railway property either directly or indirectly.

190. Procedure for delivery to railway administration of property detained by a railway servant. If a railway servant is discharged from service or is suspended, or dies or absconds or absents himself, and he or his wife or widow or any member of his family or his representative refuses or neglects, after notice in writing for that purpose, to deliver up to the railway administration or to a person appointed by the railway administration, in this behalf, any station, office or other building with its appurtenances, or any books, papers, keys, equipment or other matters, belonging to the railway administration and in the possession or custody of such railway servant at the occurrence of any such event as aforesaid, any Metropolitan Magistrate or Judicial Magistrate of the first class may, on application made by or on behalf of the railway administration, order any police officer, with proper assistance, to enter upon the station, office or other building and remove any person found therein and take possession thereof, or to take possession of the books, papers or other matters, and to deliver the same to the railway administration or to a person appointed by the railway administration in that behalf.

1 Corresponding provision in the old Act This section corresponds to s. 138 of the old Act.

2 Discharge of railway servant It may be found from the opening lines of s. 138 of the old Act that it envisages a railway servant who is discharged, suspended from his office or dies or absconds or absents himself. In connection with the question it retirement of a railway servant amounts to his discharge, the High Court held: the word 'discharge' embraces all types of termination of contract. It is well settled that the relationship of master and servant is created by a bilateral act. The contract of service is continuing in nature and

20 *Krishna Lal* v *Ajit Singh* 68 Punj LR 386.

the obligation under the said contract is terminable by following certain modes, or by operation of statutes. Retirement or even resignations are well recognised modes of terminating the contract of employment, since the object of these modes of termination is the same, *i.e.* the person concerned is relived of the charge or of the office. Therefore, the word 'discharge' in the context will embrace in its fold the fact of termination of contract, including the contract of employment. It postulates some act by the parties, or otherwise, which brings the contract of employment to an end.[21]

Bombay High Court followed a Calcutta case[1] which held that the word "discharge" occurring in s. 138 of the (old) Indian Railways Act is generally wide enough to include in it "discharge on retirement" so that even if a railway servant has been relieved of his office on retirement, he will come within the mischief of the section.

3 Railway servants who are—summary eviction invocable against Section 138 of the old Act envisages a railway servant discharged, suspended etc. A railway servant means any person employed by a railway administration in connection with the service of a railway. In view of s. 148(2) of the old Act a person fulfilling a contract with the railway administration too answers the item "railway servant".

Thus a railway stall-holder under agreement with the railway administration under which the railway administration reserves extensive power of directing and regulating the stall-holder's work, is a railway servant as defined under s. 3(7) read with s. 148 of the Railways Act 1890, against whom action can be taken under s. 138 of the old Act for summary delivery of railway property.[2]

In *Union of India* v *B.N. Prasad*,[3] the Supreme Court of India speaking through M. FAZAL ALI, J., observed: "In our opinion, a close perusal of this section clearly reveals that the provision has widest amplitude and takes within its fold not only a railway servant but even a contractor who is engaged for performing services to the railway and the termination of his contract by the railway amounts to his discharge as mentioned in s. 138 of the old Act. As the provision is in the public interest meant to avoid inconvenience and expense for the travelling public and gear up the efficiency of the railway administration, it must be construed liberally, broadly and meaningfully so as to advance the object sought to be achieved by the Railways Act. Furthermore, the section only requires that an application should be made by or on behalf of the railway administration.

21 *Arjun Babloo Tukaral* v *G.V. Javalkar* AIR 1981 Bom 72; 1980 Bom CR 863; 1980 Cr LR (Mah) 490; 1981 Mah LJ 525; (1981)2 Kant LR 181.

1 *Divisional Supdt. of E. Rly.* v *Suresh Chandra* AIR 1957 Cal 97; 1957 CrLJ 175.

2 *N. Awatrai* v *Union of India* (1971)2 SCJ 636; (1971)1 SCR 650; (1971)23 FLJ 17; 1971 CrLJ (N) 10.

3 AIR 1978 SC 411; (1978)2 SCC 462.

The section does not require that any particular person holding a particular post should be authorised to file a complaint. In *Union of India* v *B.N. Prasad*,[4] the respondent was a contractor who was to supply food in the railway refreshment room. After the term of his agreement expired he refused to vacate the station. That led the Deputy Commercial Superintendent to invoke s. 138 of the old Act. Two points were settled by the Supreme Court. First, that in the particular case Deputy Commercial Superintendent could invoke s. 138 of the old Railways Act because any one on behalf of the Railway can press into service s. 138 of the old Act, and that it is not necessary that any one holding a particular post can invoke it. Secondly, even a contractor who is engaged to perform service to the railway can be brought under the pale of s. 138 of the old Railways Act. Termination of his contract by the railway amounts to his discharge as mentioned in s. 138 of the old Railways Act. The matter was considered by the Supreme Court in *N. Awatrai Chainani* v *Union of India*[5] where the court pointed out, while relying on decisions of Lahore and Calcutta High Courts that a Railways contractor was a railway servant and an order of eviction could be passed against him. The court relied on the definition of the railway servant as contained in s. 3(7) read with s. 142(2) of the old Act. The court approved of the decision in *S.L. Kapoor* v *Emperor*[6] and *R.L. Majumdar* v *Alfred Earnest Young*,[7] which had taken the view that even a contractor is a railway servant within the meaning of s. 132 of the old Act. However, in view of the contract, he was not governed by Art. 311.

4 Person competent to invoke the provision Section 138 of the old Act requires that an application should be made by or on behalf of the railway administration. The section does not require that any particular person holding a particular post should be authorised to file a complaint.[8]

It does not lay down that any person holding a particular authority or post should be authorised to file or continue as a complainant.[9]

5 Public Premises (Eviction of Unauthorised Occupants) Act 1971—impact The provision of the Public Premises (Eviction of Unauthorised Occupants) Act 1971 is deemed to have been given retrospective effect since 16th September 1958, except to some of its provisions. The provisions of that

4 AIR 1978 SC 411; (1978)2 SCR 397; 1978 CrLJ 494; (1978)1 SCWR 166; 1978 All Cr C 35; 1978 Cr LR (SC) 42; 1978 SCC (Cri) 245; (1978)2 SCC 462.

5 (1971)1 SCR 650; (1970)2 SCC 321.

6 AIR 1937 Lah 547.

7 AIR 1959 Cal 64.

8 *Union of India* v *B.N. Prasad* AIR 1978 SC 411; (1978)2 SCR 397; 1978 CrLJ 494; (1978)1 SCWR 166; (1978)1 SCJ 363; 1978 Mad LJ (Cri) 245; 1978 Pat LJR 355; 1978 All Cr C 35.

9 *Arjun Babloo Tukaral* v *G.V. Javalkar* AIR 1981 Bom 72; 1980 Bom CR 863; 1980 Cr LR (Mah) 490; 1981 Mah LJ 525; (1981)2 Kant LR 181.

Act are somewhat parallel to the provisions in s. 138 of the old Railways Act. In *Arjun Babloo Tukaral* v *G.V. Javalkar*[10] after an analysis of both the provisions it was held that the provisions of Act of 1971 is a general provision. Whereas those in s. 138 of the old Act is a special provision invocable only when the concerned person is a railway servant. Invocation of special procedure is unexceptionable.

The provisions of s. 138 of the old Railways Act is not without guidelines and is not hit by Art. 14, Constitution of India.

6 Summary eviction of railway personnel and railway contractor—vires Section 138 of the old Act contemplates a summary procedure for eviction of a railway servant as also a railway contractor etc. A railway contractor whose term of agreement has come to an end or whose agreement has been terminated too can be brought under the purview of s. 138 of the old Act. Any railway officer on behalf of railway administration can invoke the summary procedure for eviction.[11]

The summary procedure contemplated in s. 138 of the old Act consists of (*a*) giving a notice to the alleged unauthorised occupant a notice requiring him to vacate the station, dwelling house, office or other building, etc. belonging to the railway, (*b*) in the event of the notice not being complied with, the railway officer (any one on behalf of the railway) is to apply to any Presidency Magistrate or Magistrate of the first class, (*c*) the Magistrate may order eviction through any police officer. It is noticeable that there is no provision of giving the alleged unauthorised occupant any opportunity to be heard before Magisterial order of eviction. It has already been said that any railway officer on behalf of the railway administration may apply to the Magistrate.

A railway contractor who earns a livelihood through the job thus may be dispossessed and deprived of his livelihood through such summary process. In view of the settled law that life as contemplated in Art. 21, Constitution of India includes livelihood, the statutory validity of this provision is seriously in doubt.

It is better to start with the landmark decision of the Supreme Court in *Maneka Gandhi* v *Union of India*,[12] where a seven-member-Bench of the Supreme Court held that concept of reasonableness must be projected in the procedure contemplated by Art. 21, Constitution of India.. That article reads that no person shall be deprived of his life or personal liberty except according to the procedure established by law.

10 AIR 1981 Bom 72; 1980 Bom LR 863; 1981 Mah LJ 525; 1980 Cr LR (Mah) 490.
11 *Union of India* v *B.N. Prasad* AIR 1978 SC 411; (1978)1 SCC 462; (1978)2 SCR 397.
12 AIR 1978 SC 597; (1978)2 SCR 621; (1978)1 SCC 248.

Bhagawati, J. in *Maneka Gandhi's* case said that the principles of reasonableness which legally and philosophically is an essential element of equality or non-arbitrariness pervades Art. 14 like a brooding omnipresence and the procedure contemplated by Art. 21 must answer the test of reasonableness in order to be in conformity with Art. 24, Constitution. As explained in *Bachan Singh* v *State of Punjab*,[13] where the question of *vires* of death penalty as an alternative punishment for murder was on the anvil, the Supreme Court explaining the aforesaid proposition observed that Art. 21 in the context of interpretation put to it in *Maneka* is "No person shall be deprived of his life or personal liberty except according to fair, reasonable and just procedure established valid law".

As held in *A.K. Roy* v *Union of India*,[14] the word "established" is used in Art. 21 to denote that the procedure prescribed by law must be defined with certainty in order that those who are deprived of their life or liberty must know the precise extent of their deprivation.

So, if now the expression "life" in Art. 21 includes livelihood, in the context of *Maneka*, *Bachan Singh* and *A.K. Roy* Art. 21 should be read as no person shall be deprived of his life including livelihood or personal liberty except according to fair, reasonable and just procedure defined with certainty and established by valid law. Now the question is does life in Art. 21, Constitution include livelihood? If so, what kind of livelihood does it envisage; can the vocation of a railway contractor answer the concept of "life" in Art. 21, Constitution of India.

The Supreme Court in *Olga Tellis* v *Bombay Municipal Corporation*[15] has although answered the first question in the affirmative and reiterated the answer in *K. Chandran* v *State of TN*,[16] yet the question may be probed into with reference to a few earlier Supreme Court cases.

In Re, *Sant Ram*,[17] in the context of Supreme Court Rules framed under Art. 145 of the Constitution prohibiting acceptance of engagements by a lawyer through a tout it is held that "life" does not include livelihood and, therefore, Art. 21 is not available in a challenge to the said Rule by a tout.

In the context of policy of nationalisation of the life insurance business under the Life Insurance Corporation Act 1956, this point arose in the case of *A.V. Nachane* v *Union of India*.[18] It was held: "The challenge based

13 AIR 1980 SC 898; 1980 CrLJ 636; (1980)2 SCC 684.
14 AIR 1982 SC 710; 1982 CrLJ 340; (1982)1 SCC 271; (1982)2 SCR 272.
15 AIR 1986 SC 180; (1985)3 Bom CR 434; (1985)3 SCC 545.
16 AIR 1986 SC 204; (1985)3 SCC 536; 1985 Supp (2) SCR 100.
17 AIR 1960 SC 932; (1960)3 SCR 499; (1961)1 SCJ 98.
18 AIR 1982 SC 1126; (1982)2 SCR 246; (1982)1 SCC 205.

on Art. 19(1)(*g*) and Art. 21 does not appear to have any substance. Apart from anything else, a claim based on the 1974 settlements is certainly not a fundamental right that could be enforced through this court. As regards Art. 21, the first premises of the argument that the word "life" in Article includes livelihood was considered and rejected in *In re Sant Ram*".[19]

In the case of *Begulla Bapi Raju* v *State of Andhra Pradesh*,[20] question arose in the context of the Andhra Pradesh Land Reforms (Ceiling on Agricultural Holdings) Act 1973. Section 3(1) of the said Act defines 'family unit' which includes even a separated minor son. The said definition was challenger *inter alia* on the ground of violation of Art. 21. Following the case of *Sant Ram* (supra) as affirmed by the case of *Nachane* (supra) it was held that the word 'life' in Art. 21 does not include livelihood.

In *Maneka Gandhi* v *Union of India*,[1] in the context of the Passports Act 1967 it is held that 'life' is not restricted to mere physical existence but includes right to livelihood with all its relevant facets. This view is reiterated in *Francis Coralie Mullin* v *Administrator, UTA Delhi*,[2] in the context of detenue's right to confer with legal adviser under COFEPOSA 1974. In *Peoples Union for Democratic Rights* v *Union of India*,[3] in the context of complaint of non-observance of the Contract Labour (Regulation and Abolition) Act 1970 and the Inter-State Migrant Workmen (Regulation of Employment & Conditions of Service) Act 1979 it was held that the complaint related to violation of Art. 21. The case of *Board of Trustees of the Bombay Port* v *Dilip Kumar Raghavendranath Nadkarni*[4] deals with the question of fairness of a departmental inquiry where permission sought by a delinquent to be represented through a lawyer was rejected even though the employer was represented by a legally trained representative. In that context it is held that "life" in Art. 21 of the Constitution includes livelihood.

In *State of Maharashtra* v *Chandrabhan Tale*[5] second proviso to r. 151(1)(*ii*)(*b*) of the Bombay Service Rules 1959 providing for nominal subsistence allowance of Re 1 per month to a suspended Government servant upon his conviction during pendency of appeal and prohibition against any other engagement was struck down being *ultra vires* Art. 21. The case of *Bandhua Mukti Morcha* v *Union of India*,[6] deals with the

19 (1960)3 SCR 499; AIR 1960 SC 932; (1961)1 SCJ 98.
20 AIR 1983 SC 1073; (1984)1 SCC 66; (1983)3 SCR 701.
1 AIR 1978 SC 597; (1978)2 SCR 621; (1978)1 SCC 248.
2 AIR 1981 SC 1582; 1981 CrLJ 1309; (1981)3 SCC 608.
3 AIR 1982 SC 1473; (1982)3 SCC 235; (1983)1 SCR 456.
4 AIR 1983 SC 109; (1983)1 SCC 124; (1983)1 SCR 828.
5 (1983)3 SCC 387; AIR 1983 SC 803; (1983)3 SCR 337.
6 AIR 1984 SC 802; (1984)3 SCC 161; (1984)2 SCR 67.

rights of bonded labourers under Art. 21 in the context of Directive Principles. The following observations in that decision are significant:

> "It is the fundamental right of everyone in this country, assured under the interpretation given to Art. 21 by this court in *Francis Mullin's* case, to live with human dignity, free from exploitation. This right to live with human dignity enshrined in Art. 21 derives its life breath from the Directive Principles of State Policy and particularly cls. (*e*) and (*f*) of Art. 39 and Arts. 41 and 42 at the least, therefore, it must include protection of the health and strength of workers, men and women and of the tender age of children against abuse, opportunities and facilities for children to develop in a healthy manner and in conditions of freedom and dignity, educational facilities just and humane conditions of work and maternity relief".

In the context of rights of certain pavement and slum dwellers, Art. 21 was passed into service in the case of *Olga Tellis* v *Bombay Municipal Corporation*.[7] In this decision the court held in no uncertain voice that life in Art. 21 includes livelihood. *Sant Ram*, Re,[8] which too was a decision by five-member-Bench of the Supreme Court, was noticed in *Olga Tellis* v *Bombay Municipal Corporation*,[9] but was not followed distinguishing it on facts on the ground that it was a claim of a tour to carry a nefarious activity.

All the aforesaid decisions pertaining the question if life includes livelihood were cited and discussed in a Bombay case.[10] Bombay High Court preferred to follow *Olga Tellis* observing at page 206 of the report 'settled legal position' is that if there is conflict between decisions rendered by Benches of equal strength the later prevails.

This is really the Bombay view;[11] but Bombay High Court in a later case held otherwise.[12] There Bombay High Court followed the case of *Indo Swiss* v *Umrao*.[13] In case of direct conflict between two Supreme Court decisions of co-equal Bench, the court is to follow the decision which states the law more accurately whether it is earlier or later.[14]

7 AIR 1986 SC 180; (1985)3 Bom CR 434; (1985)3 SCC 545.

8 AIR 1960 SC 932; (1960)3 SCR 499; (1961)1 SCJ 98.

9 AIR 1986 SC 180; 1985 Supp (2) SCR 51; (1985)3 SCC 545.

10 *Rashtriya Mill Mazdoor Sangh* v *State of Maharashtra* (1988)1 Bom CR 188.

11 *Narinder Singh* v *State of Maharashtra* 1981 CrLJ 772 (Bom).

12 *Special L.A. Officer* v *Greater Bombay Municipal Corpn.* AIR 1988 Bom 9; (1988)2 Bom CR 588; 1988 Mah LR 583.

13 AIR 1981 Punj 213 (FB); 1981 Punj LJ 189; (1981)83 Punj LR 335.

14 *Union of India* v *Ashok* AIR 1983 Sik 19.

It is needless to probe into this academic question any further because in *Olga Tellis* (ibid), *Sant Ram* (ibid) was referred to and distinguished. The proposition now can be summed up as follows: Right to carry a livelihood by a nefarious activity is not but right to carry on an innocent livelihood is protected by Art. 21, Constitution. And no person shall be deprived of such livelihood except according to fair, reasonable and just procedure defined with certainty and established by valid law.

Coming back to the original query if s. 138 authorising any railway officer to deprive a railway contractor of his livelihood in hit by Art. 21, Constitution of India, the question may be posed who is to judge if the contract has come to an end? Can any railway officer with no forensic knowledge or background settle the question? Magistrate can do so, but there is no provision of his giving any hearing. The principles of natural justice, *nemo debet esse judex in propria causa sua* (none can be a judge of his own cause) and *audi alteram partem* (none can be condemned unheard) s. 138 of the old Railways Act permits to be violated. The notice which is to precede railway officer's invocation of s. 138 of the old Act is not one asking the railway contractor or stall holder to show cause. It is not one by a judge tampered with democratic spirit or forensic compassion. Rather, it smacks of a command of an absolute monarch. It is doubtful if the procedure is reasonable. Consequently the statutory validity of the provision is seriously in doubt.

7 Unauthorised detention of railway property by railway servant—no mesne profit Where a railway employee after his retirement unauthorisedly retains the possession of railway property, claim of *mesne profit* under s. 138 of the Railways Act 1890 (corresponding to s. 190 of the Railways Act 1989) for the period during which the possession of railway property unauthorisedly retained is impermissible. But the railway administration may resort to other alternative remedy available to it under the law.[15]

> **191. Proof of entries in records and documents.** Entries made in the records or other documents of a railway administration shall be admitted in evidence in all proceedings by or against the railway administration, and all such entries may be proved either by the production of the records or other documents of the railway administration containing such entries or by the production of a copy of the entries certified by the officer having custody of the records or other documents under his signature and stating that it is a true copy of the original entries and that such original entries are contained in the records or other documents of the railway administration in his possession.

1 Corresponding provision in the old Act This section corresponds to s. 139 of the old Act.

15 *S.K. Sarma* v *Mahesh Kumar Verma* (2002)7 SCC 505.

2 Proof of entries This section dispenses with the production of the original records or other documents of the railway administration. A copy of such record or document duly certified by the proper person would be accepted in a court of law without production of the original and without formal proof. Section 139 does not provide that the contents of certified copies of the railway records tendered in evidence thereunder would be presumed by the court to be correct unless there is evidence to the contrary.[16] Before a copy can be tendered and accepted as a proof of such entries, a certificate by the officer having custody of the records or other documents under his signature and stating that it is a true copy of the original entries and that such original entries are contained in the records or other documents of the railway administration in his possession, has to be appended to that copy. When this has not been done, the copy remains inadmissible in evidence.[17]

192. Service of notice, etc., on railway administration. Any notice or other documents required or authorised by this Act to be served on a railway administration may be served, in the case of a Zonal Railway, on the General Manager or any of the railway servant authorised by the General Manager, and in the case of any other railway, on the owner or lessee of the railway or the person working the railway under an agreement.

(*a*) by delivering it to him; or

(*b*) by leaving at his office; or

(*c*) by registered post to his office address.

1 Corresponding provision in the old Act This section corresponds to s. 140 of the old Act.

2 Service of notice on whom to be made Before Act 39 of 1961 came into force, notices were to be served upon the Manager or Agent of the railway or railways concerned. A longdrawn controversy arose as to whether a notice under the old Act served upon the Chief Commercial Manager or Superintendent should be regarded as good service.[18] In this case the Supreme Court observed: "In the light of s. 3(6) there would be sufficient compliance with s. 77 if the notice was served on the Manager of the State-owned railway, s. 140 only provides for the manner of service of notice". The notice under s. 77 of the old Act was served on the Chief Commercial Manager (Claims and Refunds) of the erstwhile Bengal and Assam Railway which did not have any officer of the designation of

16 *I.S.P. Trading Co.* v *Union of India* AIR 1973 Cal 74.

17 *Union of India* v *Rameshwar Prasad* AIR 1983 MP 59 (63); 1983 Jab LJ 197; 1983 MPLJ 165.

18 *Radhamadhab Kundu* v *Union of India* 61 CWN 433; *Niranjan Lall* v *Union of India* AIR 1969 SC 23; (1968)2 SCJ 723; (1968)3 SCR 415; (1968)2 SCWR 905; 1969 SCD 291; (1969)1 SCA 62.

a manager though there was an officer known as General Manager having overall charge of many departments of that railway administration. It was found that the Chief Commercial Manager (Claims and Refunds) was equal in status to the Manager. On these facts the Supreme Court found that the service of notice on Chief Commercial Manager (Claims and Refunds) is a sufficient compliance with s. 140 read with s. 3(6) of the old Railways Act. This decision was distinguished by Allahabad case.[19] Where notice was served on the Chief Commercial Superintendent, although both the railways, *i.e.* the railways of booking and railways of destination, had General Managers who were superior in rank to Chief Commercial Superintendent. So, notice on Chief Commercial Superintendent was held invalid.

As pointed out in an Orissa case[20] the Allahabad decision[21] was rendered for a cause of action that arose prior to the amendment of s. 140 of the old Railways Act by the Indian Railways (Am.) Act 1961 with effect from 1st January 1962 and change of law has neutralised the ratio of *Ram Padarath's* case (supra). This Orissa decision[1] after reviewing a large number of decisions held that notice under s. 78B of the old Railways Act upon Chief Commercial Superintendent is valid. The Orissa case in coming to the conclusion further pressed into service the phraseology of s. 140 of the old Act as amended. It observed that railway administration as envisaged on s. 78B of the old Act would mean the General Manager of the Railway on whom notice under s. 78B of the old Act should be served. But s. 140 of the old Railways Act provides the manner of service of notice on the railway administration. According to it, any notice or other document required or authorised by the Act to be served on a railway administration may be served, in the case of railway administered by the Government on the Manager or the Chief Commercial Superintendent by forwarding it by post in a prepaid letter addressed to the Manager or the Chief Commercial Superintendent and registered under the Indian Post Office Act. It is thus immensely clear that notice under s. 78B of the old Act can be served either on the General Manager or on the Chief Commercial Superintendent of the railway concerned.

The controversy has been set at rest by the amending Act 39 of 1961 which provides that notice may be served upon the Chief Commercial Superintendent also.

Under the present law even though there is no delegation by the General Manager or the Chief Commercial Superintendent of their right to receive notice, authorisation by the Ministry of Railways to any other

19 *Ram Padarath* v *Union of India* AIR 1974 All 465.
20 *Union of India* v *Khetwat Oil Mills* AIR 1988 Ori 233; (1988)1 Ori LR 288.
21 *Ram Padarath* v *Union of India* AIR 1974 All 465.
1 *Union of India* v *Khetwat Oil Mills* AIR 1988 Ori 233; (1988)1 Ori LR 288.

officer is sufficient. A notice to an officer so authorised satisfies the requirements of the statute.[2]

Notice must be served if the plaintiff wants to succeed. If he does not serve the notice his claim will fail.[3] Section 77 read with ss. 80 and 140 of the old Act treats each railway administration as separate entity and notice of claim should be served on each.[4]

3 Mode of service This section prescribes the mode of service of notices and other documents on the railway administrations. Clauses (*a*) and (*b*) relate to the service of a notice or other document through a messenger of the sender of the notice or document and cl. (*c*) through the agency of postal department. Clause (*c*) has two ingredients. First, the notice/document should be enclosed in a prepaid envelope and secondly, it should be registered. This section deals with the presumption in case the notice/document is sent by post. It, *inter alia,* provides that a notice/document would be deemed to be served if it was sent by post under registered cover and addressed properly. When notice is issued under certificate of posting and too when is not properly addressed, the presumption of s. 142 of the old Act does not arise.[5]

Section 140 of the old Act refers not only to notices but to documents which have to be served on the Company and when a claim is made under s. 77 of the old Act, it is a claim in writing to be preferred to the railway administration which involves the service of the document on the Company.[6] If a person wishing to serve such a notice chooses to send otherwise than by a registered letter addressed to the Agent at his office it is for him to prove that the letter was received and that its contents came to the knowledge of the Agent. If he sends a registered letter addressed to the Agent, it is only necessary for him to prove that he forwarded it in this manner. It is unnecessary for him to prove that the Agent received it. But, if he prefers to send the letter by unregistered post it is for him to prove that it was received and the contents became known to the Agent. If he establishes this, it appears to be immaterial whether the letter be or be not addressed to the Agent.[7]

4 Some illustrative cases

(*a*) A statutory notice required by the Act as well as the Code of Civil Procedure is no doubt an essentially preliminary step for valid institution of suit, but that would not make such a notice a part of cause of action for the suit itself.[8]

2 *Brooke Bond India (Private) Ltd.* v *Union of India* AIR 1960 Cal 39.
3 *Surendra Nath* v *Governor-General in Council* AIR 1952 Cal 340.
4 *Kondapalli Virraju* v *General Manager, South-Eastern Railway* AIR 1959 AP 594.
5 *Union of India* v *Punjab State Co-op. Supply* AIR 1984 P&H 41.
6 *E.I. Railway Co.* v *Sowa Lall* 10 Pat LT 24; 112 IC 616.
7 *Mahabir Prasad* v *Secretary of State* 98 IC 742.
8 *Bata Shoe Co.* v *Union of India* AIR 1954 Bom 129.

(*b*) Section 140 of the old Act is exhaustive of the class of persons on whom notice may be served.[9]

(*c*) The object of notice on the manager is simply to give an opportunity to the railway administration to enquire immediately into the complaint. The claim may be preferred to subordinate officers also who are authorised to entertain it.[10]

(*d*) Service of notice on the Chief Commercial Manager (Claims and Refunds) was held to be sufficient.[11]

(*e*) The provisions of s. 140 of the old Act are in consonance with the view that each railway administration is treated as having a separate existence and therefore it should be informed of any claim which an aggrieved person proposes to make within the time prescribed.[12]

(*f*) Section 140 of the old Act does not say that notice or document may be served only in the manner specified therein. It is not exhaustive of the modes in which service can be effected.[13]

(*g*) The manager of the railway means the person who is in the management of the entire railway. It does not mean the manager of any particular department. Service of notice on the Chief Transportation Manager instead of the General Manager is not, therefore, a compliance with the mandatory provisions of ss. 77 and 140 of the old Act.[14]

(*h*) Where the Chief Commercial Manager is authorised by the Manager to receive claim under s. 77 of the old Act, claim sent to the Chief Commercial Manager by registered post was held to be sufficient service.[15]

(*i*) A notice under s, 77 of the old Act cannot be served on a subordinate officer like the Chief Commercial Superintendent where there is a Manager or General Manager, in view of s. 140 of the old Act.[16]

(*j*) Notice to the Traffic Superintendent does not amount to proper notice under s. 77 of the old Act in view of s. 140 of the old Act under which notice is to be sent to the Manager.[17]

9 *B. & N.W. Rly.* v *Special Manager, Court of Wards, Balrampur* AIR 1925 Oudh 419.

10 *Amarchand* v *Union of India* AIR 1955 Assam 221.

11 *Niranjan Lall* v *Union of India* AIR 1969 SC 23; (1968)3 SCR 415.

12 *Kondapalli Virraju* v *Southern Rly.* AIR 1959 AP 595.

13 *Ramco Textiles* v *Union of India* AIR 1960 Ker 257.

14 *Surendra Nath* v *G.-G.-in Council* AIR 1952 Cal 341.

15 *Radha Madhab* v *Union of India* 61 CWN 433.

16 *Ram Padarath* v *Union of India* AIR 1974 All 465; see also *Union of India* v *H.N. Sugar Mills* AIR 1968 Pat 146; ILR 46 Pat 987; 1968 BLJR 674.

17 *State of WB* v *Union of India* AIR 1987 Cal 226; (1987)91 CWN 376; (1986)2 CHN 75.

(*k*) Service of notice of claim for refund or Refunds Officer is legal.[18]

(*l*) The requirements of s. 77 of the old Act read with s. 140 of the old Act are satisfied by serving a notice within the prescribed period on the Chief Commercial Manager or any other subordinate officer of a railway owned by Government provided it is established as a fact that terms of contract between the parties has held out a particular official as competent to deal with claims on receipt of notice to him.[19]

(*m*) Where notice under s. 78B of the old Act was forwarded by post and certificate of posting and was not properly addressed, no presumption of service under s. 140, cl. (*c*) of the old Act could arise.[20]

(*n*) Where notice is sent by ordinary post presumption under s. 142 of the old Act may arise about the receipt of the letter at the other end.[1]

(*o*) Giving of notice to railway is an act which is covered by cl. (*c*) of s. 140 of the old Act as it permits forwarding of notice by post in a prepaid letter. There appears, therefore, no reason to hold that plaintiff cannot take the advantage of s. 10 of the General Clauses Act.[2]

(*p*) Proper service of notice is not a question of law but of fact.[3]

(*q*) Notice, though inaccurate in mentioniong execution of decree of subrogation, gave full particulars, it was held that the notice was sufficient.[4]

(*r*) Mere posting of notice on the last day of limitation is not sufficient. It must be posted as to reach the addressee within the specified in the normal course.[5]

193. Service of notice, etc., by railway administration. Unless otherwise provided in this Act or the rules framed thereunder, any notice or other document

18 *Brooke Bond India Ltd.* v *Union of India* AIR 1969 Cal 39.

19 *Governor-General-in-Council* v *Gouri Shankar Mills Ltd.* AIR 1949 Pat 347; 28 Pat 178 (FB).

20 *Union of India* v *Punjab State Co-op. S&M Fedn. Ltd.* AIR 1984 P&H 41.

1 *Union of India* v *Kalinga Textiles* AIR 1969 Bom 401; 1968 Mah LJ 797; 71 Bom LR 214; ILR (1969) Bom 864.

2 *Union of India* v *Asharfi Devi* AIR 1957 MP 114.

3 *Chatturbhug* v *Secy. of State* AIR 1927 All 215.

4 *Union of India* v *Alliance Assurance Co.* AIR 1967 Cal 47.

5 *Union of India* v *Firm B.P. Dass* AIR 1976 All 491; 1976 All WC 330; see *Khandelwal Ferro Alloys Ltd.* v *Union of India* AIR 1999 Bom 50; *Union of India* v *Amin Chand Payarelal* AIR 1974 P&H 190; 1974 Cur LJ 1; 76 Punj LR 10.

required or authorised by this Act to be served on any person by a railway administration may be served—

(*a*) by delivering it to the person; or

(*b*) by leaving it at the usual or last known place of abode of the person; or

(*c*) by registered post addressed to the person at his usual or last known place of abode.

1 Corresponding provision in the old Act This section corresponds to s. 141 of the old Act.

2 Scope Section 193 of the present Act relates to service of notice by a railway administration on any person either of the following manners: (*i*) by delivering it to the person; (*ii*) by leaving it at the usual or last known place of abode of the person; (*iii*) by registered post addressed to the person at his usual or last known place of abode. Section 141 of the old Act governs the manner of service of claims or notice under s. 56(1) of the old Act.[6]

194. Presumption where notice is served by post. Where a notice or other document is served by post, it shall be deemed to have been served at the time when the letter containing it would be delivered in the ordinary course of post, and in proving such service, it shall be sufficient to prove that the letter containing the notice or other document was properly addressed and registered.

1 Corresponding provision in the old Act This section corresponds to s. 142 of the old Act.

2 Notice by registered post—properly addressed—presumption Analogous to s. 27 of the General Clauses Act, s. 142 of the old Railways Act lays down that if a notice is sent by registered post and is addressed correctly, a presumption of law arises that it has been served at the time when the letters are delivered in the ordinary course. When both s. 27, General Clauses Act and *illustration* (*e*) of s. 114, Evidence Act embody a presumption of fact, s. 142 of the old Railways Act embodies a presumption of law, rather a conclusive proof, The words "shall be deemed" in s. 142 of the old Act show that in every case where the notice or other document has been sent by registered post in correct address, the court is bound to raise the conclusion. By a legal fiction the notice or other documents sent by registered post in correct address, is treated to have been served. It is a conclusive proof.

For raising the conclusion the examination of serving peon is not necessary. A case on s. 27, General Clauses Act read with *illustration* (*e*) of s. 114 of the Evidence Act lays down that denial of service by the addressee may shift the burden and then the plaintiff is to prove service by some other evidence.[7] The ratio of this decision is not applicable to a case

6 *Union of India* v *Lakshmi Textiles* AIR 1968 Ker 23; 1967 KLT 111.

7 *Puwada Venkatasewara Rao* v *C.V. Raman* AIR 1976 SC 869; (1976)3 SCR 551; 1976 Raj LR 631; (1976)1 SCJ 372; (1976)1 APLJ (SC) 37; (1976)2 SCC 409.

of a notice sent under s. 194 of the Railways Act 1989 because of the words "shall be deemed" occurring in s. 194 of the Act.

195. Representation of railway administration. (1) A railway administration may, by order in writing, authorise any railway servant or other person to act for, or represent it, as the case may be, in any proceeding before any civil, criminal or other court.

(2) A person authorised by a railway administration to conduct prosecutions on its behalf shall, notwithstanding anything in section 302 of the Code of Criminal Procedure, 1973 (2 of 1974), be entitled to conduct such prosecutions without the permission of the Magistrate.

1 Corresponding provision in the old Act This section corresponds to s. 145 of the old Act.

2 Some illustrative cases

(*a*) Where special power of attorney was executed in favour of *X* under s. 145 of the old Act by the General Manager East Indian Rly., it was wide enough to authorise to represent, act, plead and do all necessary things in the suit against that railway administration and *X* had actually acted and pleaded in trial court. *X* was the authorised agent of that railway and therefore notice of appeal arising out of that suit could in law be effectively served on *X*.[8]

(*b*) Section 145(2) of the old Act contemplates only private prosecution undertaken by the railway administration for offences under the old Act. It only entitles a person authorised by the agent to conduct the prosecution without permission of the Magistrate under s. 495, CrPC (old). But where the prosecution is in the hands of Public Prosecutor the pleader instructed by the agent or person authorised by him shall have to act under the directions of the Public Prosecutor.[9]

3 Signing of Memo of Appeals Even, if the authority to file an appeal is given to three persons under s. 145 of the old Act, the signing of the memorandum of appeal by one of them is quite enough and the presentation by him is proper. If the other two sign the memorandum after the appeal is filed, it is a mere technical irregularity and cannot be taken as fatal to the filing of the appeal.[10]

196. Power to exempt railway from Act. (1) The Central Government may, by notification, exempt any railway from all or any of the provisions of this Act.

(2) Every notification issued under sub-section (1) shall be laid as soon as may be after it is issued before each House of Parliament.

8 *Union of India* v *Abdul Razak* AIR 1956 Pat 511.

9 *B.N. Rly. Co. Ltd.* v *Shaikh Makbul* AIR 1925 Pat 755.

10 *P.C. Verma and Sons* v *Governor-General in Council* AIR 1950 East Punjab 160.

Corresponding provision in the old Act This section corresponds to s. 147 of the old Act.

197. Matters supplemental to the definitions of "railway" and "railway servant". (1) For the purposes of sections 67, 113, 121, 123, 147, 151 to 154, 160, 164, 166, 168, 170, 171, 173 to 176, 179, 180, 182, 184, 185, 187 to 190, 192, 193, 195 and of this section, the word "railway" whether it occurs alone or as a prefix to another word, has reference to a railway or portion of a railway under construction and to a railway or portion of a railway not used for the public carriage of passengers, animals or goods as well as to a railway falling within the definition of that word in clause (31) of section 2.

(2) For the purposes of sections 7, 24, 113, 146, 172 to 176 and 188 to 190, the expression "railway servant" includes a person employed under a railway in connection with the service thereof by a person fulfilling a contract with the railway administration.

1 **Corresponding provision in the old Act** This section corresponds to s. 148 of the old Act.

2 **Penalty for overloading—vires** On wagons being allotted to persons indenting them, sometimes loading is made by the consignor's own labour force. But each wagon has marked carrying capacity and the minimum weight for the charge of freight of coal is specified. Overloading is not permitted by the railway administration, because the overloaded wagon is a potential danger to the safety of a running train. The Ministry of Railways have, therefore, issued strict instructions to railway employees to ensure that wagons are not allowed to be overloaded. The railway administration has amended r. 161A, Goods Tariff Part I to impose heavy penalty on the person overloading, the wagon. So far as the loading of goods on the wagon it is the rule that the wagons after having been loaded with coal under the supervision of the railway staff must be weighted on the weigh-bridges, in case the weigh-bridge is not provided at the forwarding station, the same may be weighed at the first weigh-bridge station and in case the wagon is found to be overloaded, the excessive load should be off-loaded and the wagons despatched to the destination station. Since imposition of penalty does not entail total ban on transportation, the r. 161A does not foul Art. 19(1)(*g*) of the Constitution of India.[11]

3 **Railway Parcel porters on contract labour** In *National Federation of Railway Porters, Vendors and Bearers* v *Union of India*[12] the Supreme Court gave the following directions to the respondents, Union of India and

11 *Darshan Kumar* v *Union of India* AIR 1988 J&K 28; (1988)21 Reports 55; 1987 Kash LJ 684.

12 AIR 1995 SC 1617; 1995(2) SLR 709; 1995 Supp (3) SCC 152.

the Railway Administration for absorption on regular and permanent basis the Railway Parcel Porters on contract labours basis:

(1) The said respondents having control over the railway over the railway stations where the writ petitioners are working as Railway Parcel Porters on contract labour should be absorbed permanently as Railway Parcel Porters of those stations subject to the number of basis available to them on a perennial basis.

(2) When the writ petitioners are appointed on permanent basis, they shall be entitled to get from the dates of their absorption the minimum scale of pay or wages and other service benefits.

(3) only those Railway Parcel Porters of the writ petitioners would be absorbed who have not completed the superannuation age of 58 years.

(4) The writ petitioners who are not found medically fit for employment need not be absorbed on permanent basis.

(5) The writ petitioners may be engaged in any other suitable manual work.

(6) The writ petitioners who have worked for a longer periods as contract labour shall be preferred to those who have put in shorter period of work.

(7) The report of the Assistant Labour Commissioner shall be the basis in deciding the period of work done.

(8) The course of implementation is to be covered within six months from the date of the order.

4 Appointment to the post of General Manager The post of General Manager is to be filled up by selection on merit from amongst very senior and suitable administrative grade officers. The scheme for filling up posts of General Managers and equivalents was notified and it was further amended. It is proper that actual appointment is made at least within three months from the date of accrual of vacancy.[13]

5 "Re-employed" meaning of Considering the object of r. 21(*ii*) of the Railway Services (Pension) Rules 1993 the wider meaning has been ascribed to the expression "re-employed" which finds place in r. 21(*ii*) of the Rules. Thus, this expression would include first regular appointment in the service.[14]

6 Qualifying service for pension Under the Railway Servant (Pass) Rules 1986 the service which is counted for the retirement of a railway servant is service on the railway alone. Thus, services rendered elsewhere other than railway would not be counted to qualify for pension.[15]

13 *Union of India* v *B.S. Agarwal* AIR 1998 SC 1537; 1998(1) SCT 581; (1997)8 SCC 89.

14 *Union of India* v *Rekha Majhi* 2000(2) SCT 676; 2000(2) SLR 642.

15 *Union of India* v *(Dr.) Baliar Singh* 1998(1) SCT 317.

7 Railway Services (Pension) Rules, 1993, rr. 70, 49 Section 2(*e*) of the Payment of Gratuity Act 1972 takes out from the purview of the said Act a person who holds *inter alia* post under the Central Government and whose terms and conditions of service are governed by an Act or Rules providing for payment of gratuity. The Railway Services (Pension) Rules, 1993 provide for payment of gratuity under r. 70 to railway servants. Rule 49 of the said Rules provides for the manner in which emoluments of such employee should be calculated. "Pay" in those Rules means the pay in the revised scales.[16]

8 Calculation of pension in compulsory premature retirement In *R.P. Kapur* v *Union of India*,[17] it has been held that the plea of the appellant who was under suspension before his compulsory premature retirement that his pension be calculated on the basis of subsistence allowance fixed as per the revised pay scales is permissible under the Railway Service (Pension) Rules 1993, suspension allowance is an emolument.

9 Dearness relief on family pension as well as on salary on re-employment In *Union of India* v *Rekha Majhi*,[18] it has been held that the dearness relief on family pension is not allowed to a re-employed employee to draw dearness relief on salary as well as on the family pension.

10 Family pension The deceased worked as "substitute" continuously for a period of more than six months and consequently he acquired rights and privileges admissible to temporary railway servants. Thus, his widow was entitled to family pension.[19]

11 Compassionate appointment Deceased, a technical-1 in railway, died while in service. The petitioner, being the second wife of the deceased was not entitled for compassionate appointment. The respondent authority is justified in refusing the request to consider her claim for compassionate appointment. However, the petitioner, being the nominee of the deceased is entitled to receive the amount due under PF, GIS and DCRG benefits.[20]

> **198. General power to make rules.** **Without prejudice to any power to make rules contained elsewhere in this Act, the Central Government may make rules generally to carry out the purposes of this Act.**

1 Corresponding provision in the old Act This section corresponds to s. 143 of the old Act.

16 *Union of India* v *Manik Lal Banerjee* (2006)9 SCC 643.
17 AIR 1999 SC 3589.
18 AIR 2000 SC 1562.
19 *Prabhavati Devi* v *Union of India* AIR 1996 SC 752; (1996)7 SCC 27. But see *Union of India* v *Rabia Bikaner* AIR 1997 SC 2843 (Widow of casual labourer in Railway Establishment who died after putting six months service and obtained status of temporary workman without being appointed to a temporary post after screening was not entitled to family pension under 1964 Family Pension Scheme for Railway employees).
20 *Samadhanam* v *Divisional Railway Manager (P)/SC Office* 2009 Lab IC (NOC) 758 (AP).

2 Railway servant and railway A tea-stall contractor at a railway station, and not his servant can be regarded as a railway servant within the meaning of ss. 138 and 148(2) of the old Railways Act.[1]

A railway contractor running a refreshment room under the authority of railway administration is a railway servant. A complaint filed by the Deputy Chief Commercial Superintendent is legal.[2]

3 Enhancement of licence fee for catering Enhancement of licence fee to 12% of an annual sales turnover in view of circular issued by the Director (Catering) Railway Board was held to be not exhorbitant in view of price-rises.[3]

4 Hoardings—grant of renewal of licence "It is the settled law that grant of renewal is a fresh grant though it breathes life into the operation of the previous lease or licence granted as per existing appropriate provisions of the Act, rules or orders or acts *intra vires* or as per the law in operation as on the date of renewal. The right to get renewal of a permit under the Act is not a vested right but privilege subject to fulfilment of the conditions precedent enumerated under the Act."[4] Relying on this decision it has been held in *T.N. Outdoor Advertising Association* v *Union of India*[5] that imposition of condition for renewal of licence for hoarding taking in view the safety of passengers and free movement of goods traffic is not unreasonable or contrary to the provisions of Art. 19(1)(*a*) of the Constitution of India.

5 Transport of Animals Rules, 1978—At what stage certificate to be furnished The required certificate under r. 96 of the Transport of Animals Rules 1978 clearly provides that in absence of the required certificate, the carrier shall refuse to accept the consignment for transport, hence the question of loading animals first does not arise. Thus it cannot be said or inferred that the required certificate is to be furnished after loading of the animals in the wagons.[6]

6 Railway catering contract Termination of petitioner's contract on ground of failure to pay licence fees was made. Petitioner has not been able to demonstrate that the Catering Policy of 2010 is arbitrary or contrary to any statutory provision or irrational. Thus, the order of cancellation of contract was held to be proper.[7]

199. Rules to be laid before Parliament. **Every rule made under this Act shall be laid, as soon as may be after it is made, before each House of Parliament, while it is in session, for a total period of thirty days which may be comprised**

1 *Ratanlal Mazumdar* v *Alfred Earnest Young* AIR 1959 Cal 64.
2 *Union of India* v *B.N. Prasad* AIR 1978 SC 411; (1978)2 SCR 397; (1978)2 SCC 462.
3 *M.T. & Sons* v *Union of India* AIR 2001 MP 214.
4 *Gajraj Singh* v *State Transport Appellate Tribunal* AIR 1997 SC 412.
5 AIR 2003 Mad 340.
6 *Union of India* v *Vijay Prakash Goel* (2004)11 SCC 343.
7 *Devendra Kumar Ray* v *Union of India* AIR 2015 NOC 688 (Jhar).

in one session or in two or more successive sessions, and if, before the expiry of the session immediately following the session or the successive sessions aforesaid, both Houses agree in making any modification in the rule or both Houses agree that the rule should not be made, the rule shall thereafter have effect only in such modified form or be of no effect, as the case may be; so, however, that any such modification or annulment shall be without prejudice to the validity of anything previously done under that rule.

Loss of railway ticket There was an enquiry against ticket collector for recovery of amount of loss. When it is satisfactorily established that railway servant has sold tickets and thereby caused losses to railways, he is liable for the deficiency or loss of railway ticket. But where no case is made out for department to recover the price of the lost ticket, recovery from the salary of the ticket collector is illegal.[8]

200. Repeal and saving. (1) The Indian Railways Act, 1890 (9 of 1890), is hereby repealed.

(2) Notwithstanding the repeal of the Indian Railways Act, 1890 (9 of 1890) (hereinafter referred to as the repealed Act)—

(*a*) anything done or any action taken or purported to have been done or taken (including any rule, notification, inspection, order or notice made or issued, or any appointment or declaration made or any licence, permission, authorisation or exemption granted or any document or instrument executed or any direction given or any proceedings taken or any penalty or fine imposed) under the repealed act shall, in so far as it is not inconsistent with the provisions of this Act, be deemed to have been done or taken under the corresponding provisions of this Act;

(*b*) any complaint made to the Railway Rates Tribunal under sub-section (1) of section 41 of the repealed Act but not disposed of before the commencement of this Act and any complaint that may be made to the said Tribunal against any act or omission of a railway administration under the repealed Act, shall be heard and decided by the Tribunal constituted under this Act in accordance with the provisions of Chapter VII of this Act.

(3) The mention of particular matters in sub-section (2) shall not be held to prejudice or affect the general application of section 6 of the General Clauses Act, 1897 (10 of 1897), with regard to the effect of repeal.

[9][**Repeal and savings** (1) The Railway (Amendment) Ordinance, 2008 (Order 2 of 2008) is hereby repealed. (2) Notwithstanding such repeal, anything done or any action taken under the principal Act, as amended by the said Ordinance, shall be deemed to have been done or taken under the corresponding provisions of the principal Act, as amended by this Act.]

8 *Civil Commercial Manager, 5 Rly.* v *K. Vijaykumar* AIR 2006 Kant 41.

9 *Vide* Act No. 11 of 2008 (w.e.f. 31.01.2008), s. 4.

APPENDICES

APPENDIX 1

The Railway Claims Tribunal Act, 1987

(Act No. 54 of 1987)

An Act to provide for establishment of a Railway Claims Tribunal for inquiring into and determining claims against a railway administration for loss, destruction, damage, deterioration or non-delivery of animals or goods entrusted to it to be carried by railway or for the refund of fares or freight or for compensation for death or injury to passengers occurring as a result of railway accidents [1][or untoward incidents] and for matters connected therewith or incidental thereto.

Objects of the Act The claimants for compensation for death, injury, loss or damage to the goods in transit were previously decided by the railway administration or by suits in the courts. As the litigation in the courts or before the Claims Commissioner was very protracted, it was decided to set up a specialised Tribunal for speedy adjudication of claims. The Claims Tribunal with Benches in different parts of India and with judicial and technical members is intended to provide much relief to the passengers who become victims or injured in rail accidents and also to those whose goods are lost or damaged in transit. The Claims Tribunal would also expeditiously settle all disputes regarding refund of fares and freight charges. The Act provides *inter alia* (*a*) the jurisdiction powers and authority of the Claims Tribunal; (*b*) the procedure to be followed by the Claims Tribunal; (*c*) the exclusion of jurisdiction of civil courts; (*d*) transfer of all pending proceedings before any civil court or other authority to the Claims Tribunal.[2]

1 *Inserted* by Act 28 of 1994, s. 7.

2 *See* Statement of Objects and Reasons Gaz. of India, 23-11-1987, pt. II, s. 2, Ext. p. 13 and Preamble to the Act.

BE it enacted by Parliament in the Thirty-eighth Year of the Republic of India as follows:

CHAPTER I

PRELIMINARY

1. Short title, extent and commencement. (1) This Act may be called the Railway Claims Tribunal Act, 1987.

(2) It extends to the whole of India.

(3) It shall come into force on such date as the Central Government may, by notification, appoint.

2. Definitions. In this Act, unless the context otherwise requires,—

(*a*) "application" means an application made under section 16;

(*b*) "appointed day" means the date with effect from which the Claims Tribunal is established under section 3;

(*c*) "Bench" means a Bench of the Claims Tribunal;

(*d*) "Chairman" means the Chairman of the Claims Tribunal;

(*e*) "Claims Tribunal" means the Railway Claims Tribunal established under section 3;

(*f*) "Judicial Member" means a Member of the Claims Tribunal appointed as such under this Act, and includes the Chairman or Vice-Chairman who possesses any of the qualifications specified in sub-section (3) of section 5;

(*g*) "Member" means a Member (whether Judicial or Technical) of the Claims Tribunal, and includes the Chairman and Vice-Chairman;

(*h*) "notification" means a notification published in the Official *Gazette*;

(*i*) "prescribed" means prescribed by rules;

(*j*) "Railways Act" means the Indian Railways Act, 1890 (9 of 1890);

(*k*) "rules" means rules made under this Act;

(*l*) "Technical Member" means a Member of the Claims Tribunal who is not a Judicial Member, and includes the Chairman or a Vice-Chairman who possesses any of the qualifications specified in sub-section (4) of section 5;

(*m*) "Vice-Chairman" means a Vice-Chairman of the Claims Tribunal.

Explanation. References to the Vice-Chairman in this Act shall be construed as references to each of the Vice-Chairman;

[3][(*n*) "untoward incident" shall have the meaning assigned to it in clause (*c*) of section 123 of the Railways Act, 1989 (24 of 1989)];

(*o*) words and expressions used and not defined in this Act but defined in the Railways Act or the rules made thereunder shall have the meanings respectively assigned to them in that Act or the said rules.

3 *Inserted* by Act 28 of 1994, s. 8.

CHAPTER II

ESTABLISHMENT OF RAILWAY CLAIMS TRIBUNAL AND BENCHES THEREOF

3. Establishment of Railway Claims Tribunal. The Central Government shall, by notification, establish a Claims Tribunal, to be known as the Railway Claims Tribunal, to exercise the jurisdiction, powers and authority conferred on it by or under this Act.

Order of tribunal not revisable by High Court under s. 115, Code of Civil Procedure The Motor Accident Claims Tribunal, the Railway Claims Tribunal and the Education Appellate Tribunal were established under the respective statutes. They are not courts subordinate to the High Court for the purpose of s. 115, Code of Civil Procedure. "Court" as referred to in sub-sec. (1) of s. 115, Code of Civil Procedure is a regular court as contemplated in ss. 3 and 9, Code of Civil Procedure. Jurisdiction which has been taken away from the civil court and has been conferred upon the Tribunal is exercised in the capacity of Tribunal and not in the capacity of a civil court. Thus, it has been held that because of exclusion of jurisdiction of ordinary civil court by separate enactment, order passed by such a tribunal will not be amenable to revisional jurisdiction under s. 115, Code of Civil Procedure.[4]

4. Composition of Claims Tribunal and Benches thereof. (1) The Claims Tribunal shall consist of a Chairman, four Vice-Chairmen and such number of Judicial Members and Technical Members as the Central Government may deem fit and, subject to the other provisions of this Act, the jurisdiction, powers and authority of the Claims Tribunal may be exercised by Benches thereof.

(2) Subject to the other provisions of this Act, a Bench shall consist of one Judicial Member and one Technical Member.

(3) Notwithstanding anything contained in sub-section (1), the Chairman—

(*a*) may, in addition to discharging the functions of the Judicial Member or the Technical Member of the Bench to which he is appointed, discharge the functions of the Judicial Member or, as the case may be, the Technical Member, of any other Bench;

(*b*) may transfer a Vice-Chairman or other Member from one Bench to another Bench;

(*c*) may authorise the Vice-Chairman or the Judicial Member or the Technical Member appointed to one Bench to discharge also the functions of the Vice-Chairman or, as the case may be, the Judicial Member or the Technical Member of another Bench.

(4) Notwithstanding anything contained in the foregoing provisions of this section, it shall be competent for the Chairman or any other Member authorised by the Chairman in this behalf to function as a Bench consisting of a single Member and exercise the jurisdiction, powers and authority of the Claims Tribunal

4 *Union of India* v *Mysore Paper Mills Ltd.* AIR 2004 Kant 1 (FB). See also *Jolly Steel Industries Pvt. Ltd.* v *Union of India* 2003 ACJ 1423 (Jurisdiction of civil court to adjudicate claim is ousted).

in respect of such classes of cases or such matters pertaining to such classes of cases as the Chairman may, by general or special order, specify:

Provided that if at any stage of the hearing of any such case or matter, it appears to the Chairman or such Member that the case or matter is of such a nature that it ought to be heard by a Bench consisting of two Members, the case or matter may be transferred by the Chairman or, as the case may be, referred to him for transfer, to such Bench as the Chairman may deem fit.

(5) Subject to the other provisions of this Act, the Benches shall sit at such places as the Central Government may, by notification, specify.

5. Qualifications for appointment as Chairman, Vice-Chairman or other Member. (1) A person shall not be qualified for appointment as the Chairman unless he—

(*a*) is, or has been, a Judge of a High Court; or

(*b*) has, for at least two years, held the office of a Vice-Chairman.

(2) A person shall not be qualified for appointment as the Vice-Chairman unless he—

(*a*) is, or has been, or is qualified to be, a Judge of a High Court; or

(*b*) has been a member of the Indian Legal Service and has held a post in Grade I of that service or any higher post for at least five years; or

(*c*) has, for at least five years, held a civil judicial post carrying a scale of pay which is not less than that of a Joint Secretary to the Government of India; or

(*d*) has, for at least five years, held a post under a railway administration carrying a scale of pay which is not less than that of a Joint Secretary to the Government of India and has adequate knowledge of rules and procedure of, and experience in, claims and commercial matters relating to railways; or

(*e*) has, for a period of not less than three years, held office as a Judicial Member or a Technical Member.

(3) A person shall not be qualified for appointment as a Judicial Member unless he—

(*a*) is, or has been, or is qualified to be, a Judge of a High Court; or

(*b*) has been a Member of the Indian Legal Service and has held a post in Grade I of that service for at least three years; or

(*c*) has, for at least three years, held a civil judicial post carrying a scale of pay which is not less than that of a Joint Secretary to the Government of India.

(4) A person shall not be qualified for appointment as a Technical Member unless he has, for at least three years, held a post under a railway administration carrying a scale of pay which is not less than that of a Joint Secretary to the Government of India and has adequate knowledge of rules and procedure of, and experience in, claims and commercial matters relating to railways.

(5) Subject to the provisions of sub-section (6), the Chairman, Vice-Chairman and every other Member shall be appointed by the President.

(6) No appointment of a person as the Chairman shall be made except after consultation with the Chief Justice of India.

6. Vice-Chairman to act as Chairman or to discharge his functions in certain circumstances. (1) In the event of the occurrence of any vacancy in the office of the Chairman by reason of his death, resignation or otherwise, such one of the Vice-Chairman as the Central Government may, by notification, authorise in this behalf, shall act as the Chairman until the date on which a new Chairman, appointed in accordance with the provisions of this Act to fill such vacancy, enters upon his office.

(2) When the Chairman is unable to discharge his functions owing to absence, illness or any other cause, such one of the Vice-Chairman as the Central Government may, by notification, authorise in this behalf, shall discharge the functions of the Chairman until the date on which the Chairman resumes his duties.

7. Term of office. The Chairman, Vice-Chairman or other Member shall hold office as such for a term of five years from the date on which he enters upon his office or until he attains,—

(*a*) in the case of the Chairman, the age of sixty-five years; and

(*b*) in the case of the Vice-Chairman or any other Member, the age of sixty-two years,

whichever is earlier.

8. Resignation and removal. (1) The Chairman, Vice-Chairman or other Member may, by notice in writing under his hand addressed to the President, resign his office:

Provided that the Chairman, Vice-Chairman or other Member shall, unless he is permitted by the President to relinquish his office sooner, continue to hold office until the expiry of three months from the date of receipt of such notice or until a person duly appointed as his successor enters upon his office or until the expiry of his term of office, whichever is the earliest.

(2) The Chairman, Vice-Chairman or any other Member shall not be removed from his office except by an order made by the President on the ground of proved misbehaviour or incapacity after an inquiry made by a Judge of the Supreme Court in which such Chairman, Vice-Chairman or other Member had been informed of the charges against him and given a reasonable opportunity of being heard in respect of those charges.

(3) The Central Government may, by rules, regulate the procedure for the investigation of misbehaviour or incapacity of the Chairman, Vice-Chairman or other Member referred to in sub-section (2).

9. Salaries and allowances and other terms and conditions of service of Chairman, Vice-Chairman and other Members. The salaries and allowances payable to, and the other terms and conditions of service (including pension, gratuity and other retirement benefits) of, the Chairman, Vice-Chairman and other Members shall be such as may be prescribed:

Provided that neither the salary and allowances nor the other terms and conditions of service of the Chairman, Vice-Chairman or other Member shall be varied to his disadvantage after his appointment.

10. Provision as to the holding of offices by Chairman, Vice-Chairman etc., on ceasing to be such Chairman or Vice-Chairman, etc. On ceasing to hold office—

(*a*) the Chairman of the Claims Tribunal shall be ineligible for further employment either under the Government of India or under the Government of a State;

(*b*) a Vice-Chairman shall, subject to the other provisions of this Act, be eligible for appointment as the Chairman of the Claims Tribunal, or as the Chairman, Vice-Chairman or member of any other Tribunal established under any law for the time being in force, but not for any other employment either under the Government of India or under the Government of a State;

(*c*) a Member (other than the Chairman or Vice-Chairman) shall, subject to the other provisions of this Act, be eligible for appointment as the Chairman or Vice-Chairman or as the Chairman, Vice-Chairman or member of any other Tribunal established under any law for the time being in force, but not for any other employment either under the Government of India or under the Government of a State;

(*d*) the Chairman, Vice-Chairman or other Member shall not appear, act or plead before the Claims Tribunal.

Explanation. For the purposes of this section, employment under the Government of India or under the Government of a State includes employment under any local or other authority within the territory of India or under the control of the Government of India or under any corporation or society owned or controlled by the Government.

11. Financial and administrative powers of Chairman. The Chairman shall exercise such financial and administrative powers over the Benches as may be vested in him under the rules:

Provided that the Chairman shall have authority to delegate such of his financial and administrative powers as he may think fit to the Vice-Chairman or any other officer of the Claims Tribunal, subject to the condition that the Vice-Chairman or such officer shall, while exercising such delegated powers, continue to act under the direction, control and supervision of the Chairman.

12. Staff of Claims Tribunal. (1) The Central Government shall determine the nature and categories of the officers and other employees required to assist the Claims Tribunal in the discharge of its functions and provide the Claims Tribunal with such officers and other employees as it may think fit.

(2) The officers and other employees of the Claims Tribunal shall discharge their functions under the general superintendence of the Chairman.

(3) The salaries and allowances and conditions of service of the officers and other employees of the Claims Tribunal shall be such as may be prescribed.

CHAPTER III

JURISDICTION, POWERS AND AUTHORITY OF CLAIMS TRIBUNAL

13. Jurisdiction, powers and authority of Claims Tribunal. (1) The Claims Tribunal shall exercise, on and from the appointed day, all such jurisdiction, powers and authority as were exercisable immediately before that day by any civil court or a Claims Commissioner appointed under the provisions of the Railways Act,—

(*a*) relating to the responsibility of the railway administrations as carriers under Chapter VII of the Railways Act in respect of claims for—

(*i*) compensation for loss, destruction, damage, deterioration or non-delivery of animals or goods entrusted to a railway administration for carriage by railway;

(*ii*) compensation payable under section 82A of the Railways Act or the rules made thereunder; and

(*b*) in respect of the claims for refund of fares or part thereof or for refund of any freight paid in respect of animals or goods entrusted to a railway administration to be carried by railway.

[5][(1A) The Claims Tribunal shall also exercise, on and from the date of commencement of the provisions of section 124A of the Railways Act, 1989 (24 of 1989), all such jurisdiction, powers and authority as were exercisable immediately before that date by any civil court in respect of claims for compensation now payable by the railway administration under section 124A of the said Act or the rules made thereunder].

(2) The provisions of the [6][Railways Act, 1989 (24 of 1989)] and the rules made thereunder shall, so far as may be, be applicable to the inquiring into or determining, any claims by the Claims Tribunal under this Act.

Jurisdiction The jurisdiction of the Claims Tribunal cannot be enlarged by regarding s. 33 in s. 13 of the Act. When the provisions of s. 13 are clear, plain and unambiguous, s. 33 cannot be read with s. 13, because the object and scope of s. 33 are different from those of s. 13 of the Act.[7] The jurisdiction of civil court is not totally barred, but is barred only in respect of matters specifically enumerated in s. 13(1) of the Act.[8] Under s. 13 of the Railway Claims Tribunal Act, the Tribunal has jurisdiction to deal with all categories of compensation payable under s. 82A of the old Act.[9]

Claim arose out of damage caused to consignment of the claimant due to carelessness and negligence on the part of the Railway administration. Consignment in question was booked with company to carry goods. Agreement was entered into between the claimant and the company which clearly stated that the company though was non-Government Railway, it was working with the Railways under the agreement. The company was, therefore, included in the definition of "Railway administration" as contained in s. 2(32) of the Railways Act 1989. Thus, the Railway Claims Tribunal has jurisdiction to decide the claim petition.[10]

Grant of interest The grant of interest on an award may be made by application of the principles of s. 34 of the Code of Civil Procedure though s. 34, Code of Civil Procedure has not been expressly made applicable to proceedings before Claims Commissioner.[11] Tribunal must award compensation and interest thereon in view of power conferred upon it. It is incumbent on the Tribunal to exercise power of civil court in awarding compensation since it pertains to substantive right of the claimant.[12]

Interest has to be paid on amount awarded as compensation by the Tribunal at the rate of 6% per annum from the date of the presentation

5 *Inserted* by Act 28 of 1994, s. 9.
6 *Substituted.* by Act 28 of 1994, s. 9, for "Railway Act".
7 *Ratnakar Tanbaji Itankar* v *Union of India* AIR 1994 Bom 132.
8 *Ibid.*
9 *Union of India* v *Nanda* AIR 1999 Kant 335.
10 *Manglam Cement Ltd.* v *Union of India* AIR 2014 NOC 126 (Raj).
11 *Union of India* v *Laxmipati* AIR 1995 MP 90.
12 *D.B. Avalakki* v *Union of India* AIR 2000 Kant 269.

of the claim petition till the date of the award and thereafter at the rate of 9% per annum till the date of realisation.[13]

Claim for compensation The civil court has no jurisdiction to claim compensation against railways for loss on account of non-delivery of goods in view of the provisions of the 1987 Act.[14] Where a person fell from a stationary railway train and sustained injuries, he can claim compensation from railway and Claims Tribunal has jurisdiction to entertain the claim.[15]

The claim petition arose out of an accident in which the passenger fell out of a bogie of the train and died. It was held that the petition was not cognisable by the Tribunal under s. 82A of the old Act.[16]

"Other accidents to a train" Where there was a sudden fall of a heavy iron grider loosely fixed for electrification work on the claimant while he was boarding a train and received grievous injuries, the incident is covered by "other accident to a train" and not by the word "mishap" to the passenger.[17]

Short delivery In determining the damages for short delivery of rice the Tribunal fixed the price at a lower rate than the one claimed by the claimant without assigning any reasons. Such act of the Tribunal is arbitrary.[18]

Maintainability of writ petition on ground of alternative remedy In *Rajasthan State Electricity Board* v *Union of India*,[19] it has been held by the Supreme Court that availability of alternative remedy is not an absolute bar for granting relief in exercise of power under Art. 226 of the Constitution particularly when there is no disputed question of facts. Thus, the alternative remedy under s. 13 of the Railway Claims Tribunal Act 1987 is no bar to exercise power by the High Court under Art. 226 of the Constitution of India.

Limitation, claim for refund of over charges Railway Board issued a circular correcting tariff order and immediately thereafter consignor sought refund of excess freight and over charges under s. 13 of the Railway Claims Tribunals Act 1987. The claim was not barred by limitation under s. 17(1)(*e*) of the 1987 Act as limitation starts from date of correction order.[20]

Jurisdiction of Consumer Forum Claim for loss or misplacement of consignment by Railways was made before the Consumer Forum. It was

13 *Mulpuri Kamala Kumari* v *Union of India* AIR 2010 NOC 460 (AP).
14 *MP State Co-op. Marketing Federation Ltd.* v *Union of India* AIR 1998 MP 143.
15 *V. Vijayasankar* v *Union of India* 1995 AIHC 6309 (Ker).
16 *Ratnakar Tanbaji Itankar* v *Union of India* AIR 1994 Bom 132.
17 *D. Srinivasa* v *Union of India* AIR 1995 Kant 223.
18 *Hanuman Prasad Sarma* v *Union of India* AIR 2004 Gau 26. See *Assam State Co-operative Marketing & Consumers' Federation Ltd.* v *Union of India* AIR 2004 Gau 69 (assessment of market value of goods short delivered by Tribunal as per its own discretion is illegal).
19 (2008)5 SCC 632.
20 *Union of India* v *Rashtriya Ispat Nigam Ltd.* (*Steel Plant*) AIR 2005 AP 184 relying on *Jethmull Bhojraj* v *D.H. Railway Co. Ltd.* AIR 1962 SC 1879.

held that only the Railway Claims Tribunal has jurisdiction to entertain such claim. The Forum Constituted under the Consumer Protection Act 1986 would have no jurisdiction to entertain claims particularly in view of the fact that the Railway Claims Tribunal Act 1987 was enacted subsequent to the Consumer Protection Act 1986.[1]

Claim for refund of excess of freight charged Appellants booked bamboo cuts for transportation by Railways. Railways charged freight taking distance between two stations as 1769 kms. But goods were transported through shorter route covering distance of 1510 kms. only. Freight was charged under provision of "station to station rate". As per rules Railway administration was obliged to carry goods by shortest route at charges by cheapest route. Thus, Railways were not to make undue profit by charging freight on basis of longer route in name of "station to station rate" and then carrying goods by shorter route. The appellants were, therefore, entitled to refund to excess freight charged.[2]

14. Distribution of business amongst Benches. (1) Where any Benches are constituted, the Central Government may, from time to time, by notification, make provisions as to the distribution of the business of the Claims Tribunal amongst the Benches and specify the matters which may be dealt with by each Bench.

(2) If any question arises as to whether any matter falls within the purview of the business allocated to a Bench, the decision of the Chairman shall be final.

Explanation. For the removal of doubts, it is hereby declared that the expression "matters" includes an application under section 20.

Powers of Chairman of Tribunal Distribution of business amongst Benches and raising jurisdiction of the claim of ₹2 lakhs to a single member Bench are forming part of the functions of the Chairman of the Tribunal. Thus, order issued by the Chairman under s. 4(4) of the Railways Claims Tribunal Act 1987 and/or confirming jurisdiction and/or authorising single member Bench to exercise jurisdiction of Claims Tribunal up to pecuniary jurisdiction of ₹2 lakhs is not in any way in conflict with s. 13 of the said Act of 1987.[3]

15. Bar of jurisdiction. On and from the appointed day, no court or other authority shall have, or be entitled to, exercise any jurisdiction, powers or authority in relation to the matters referred to in [4][sub-sections (1) and (1A)] of section 13.

Scope By virtue of the express provision contained in s. 15 of the 1987 Act the jurisdiction of the civil court or any other authority is barred only in regard to the matters specified in s. 13(1) of the said Act so far as other matters are concerned not covered by s. 13(1) of the said Act, the civil court will have jurisdiction to entertain a civil suit.[5]

1 *Union of India* v *State Commissioner Consumer Protection, UP Lucknow* AIR 2012 NOC 6 (All) relying on *General Manager, Telecom* v *M. Krishnan* AIR 2010 SC 90.
2 *Kalpataru Agro Forest Enterprise* v *Union of India* AIR 2013 Gau 30.
3 *Union of India* v *Ganpat L Kachhava* AIR 2006 Guj 181.
4 *Substituted* by Act 28 of 1994, s. 10.
5 *Ratnakar Tanbaji Itnakar* v *Union of India* AIR 1994 Bom 132.

CHAPTER IV

PROCEDURE

16. Application to Claims Tribunal. (1) A person seeking any relief in respect of the matters referred to in sub-section (1) [6][or sub-section (1A)] of section 13 may make an application to the Claims Tribunal.

(2) Every application under sub-section (1) shall be in such form and be accompanied by such documents or other evidence and by such fee in respect of the filing of such application and by such other fees for the service or execution of processes as may be prescribed:

Provided that no such fee shall be payable in respect of an application under sub-clause (*ii*) of clause (*a*) of sub-section (1) [7][or, as the case may be, sub-section (1A)] of section 13.

Railway Claim—Claim against delivery to third party of consignment addressed by consignee claimant to self The Supreme Court in *Shree Shyam Agency* v *Union of India*[8] has held that after going through the Railways Act 1989 and the Railway Claims Tribunal Act 1987 as well as the Railways (Manner of Delivery of Consignments and Sale Proceeds in absence of Railway Receipt) Rules 1990 and the statutory forms what the Tribunal has to inquire into and determine is the claim against the Railway administration, that is whether the Railway Administration is at fault in discharging its responsibility under the Railways Act, Rules and Regulations and not the *inter se* disputes between the claimant and third parties.

"Untoward incident"—Application before Tribunal Death was due to electrocution by coming in contact with electric pole erected on platform. Death of the deceased would come under definition of "untoward incident" even though technically deceased did not meet his death due to accident falling from train carrying passenger.[9]

Necessary party to claim Claim against delivery of consignment to third party is made consignee-claimant addressed to self. Party claiming to be purchaser of goods in question and claiming to have paid price to the claimant need not be impleaded.[10]

17. Limitation. (1) The Claims Tribunal shall not admit an application for any claim—

(*a*) under sub-clause (*i*) of clause (*a*) of sub-section (1) of section 13 unless the application is made within three years from the date on which the goods in question were entrusted to the railway administration for carriage by railway;

(*b*) under sub-clause (*ii*) of clause (*a*) of sub-section (1) [11][or, as the case may be, sub-section (1A)] of section 13 unless the application is made within one year of occurrence of the accident;

6 *Inserted* by Act 28 of 1994, s. 11.
7 *Inserted* by Act 28 of 1994, s. 11.
8 AIR 2013 SC 267.
9 *Manorama Nath* v *Union of India* AIR 2012 Ori 104.
10 *Shree Shyam Agency* v *Union of India* AIR 2013 SC 267.
11 *Inserted* by Act 28 of 1994, s. 12.

(c) under clause (b) of sub-section (1) of section 13 unless the application is made within three years from the date on which the fare or freight is paid to the railway administration:

Provided that no application for any claim referred to in sub-clause (i) of clause (a) of sub-section (1) of section 13 shall be preferred to the Claims Tribunal until the expiration of three months next after the date on which the intimation of the claim has been preferred under section 78B of the Railways Act.

(2) Notwithstanding anything contained in sub-section (1), an application may be entertained after the period specified in sub-section (1) if the applicant satisfies the Claims Tribunal that he had sufficient cause for not making the application within such period.

Limitation The Claims Tribunal is competent to entertain an application under s. 124A of the Railways Act 1989 within one year of the occurrence of the untoward incident. It can also entertain the application under s. 124A of the 1989 Act beyond one year if it is satisfied that the applicant had sufficient cause for not making the application within such period.

Where the Tribunal had jurisdiction to entertain an application even after the period specified in s. 17(1) of the Railways Claims Tribunal Act 1987, but where these is no right of the claimant, the question of limitation to enforce that right cannot arise.[12]

Absence of any specific provisions in the Railway Claims Tribunal Act 1987 excluding the applicability of the Limitation Act 1963, the Limitation Act 1963 would be applicable to appeal preferred under s. 23 of the Railway Claims Tribunal Act 1987. Thus, the Claims Tribunal would have jurisdiction to condone the delay in filing appeal.[13]

Condonation of delay 30 days time is fixed under the Railway Claims Tribunal (Procedure) Rules. Rule 18 of the Railway Claims Tribunal (Procedure) Rules prescribes the said period of 30 days within which an application for setting an order for dismissing the application for default is to be filed. Tribunal which has all the trappings of a court can condone delay on sufficient reasons. This is applicable to the Railways Claims Tribunal in setting aside an order of dismissal for the application under s. 18(3) of the Railway Claims Tribunal Act 1987.[14]

Only requirement of law under s. 17(2) of the Railway Claims Tribunal Act 1987 is to show "sufficient cause" to the satisfaction of the Tribunal for delay. Separate application for condonation of delay is not required. This provision is not to be confused with s. 5 of the Limitation Act or with Or. 41, r. 3A of the Code of Civil Procedure. Where grounds shown to explain delay were vague and baseless and the appellant was all along careless and callous to claim relief, delay cannot be condoned.[15]

18. Procedure and powers of Claims Tribunal. (1) The Claims Tribunal shall not be bound by the procedure laid down by the Code of Civil Procedure, 1908 (5 of 1908),

12 *Union of India* v *Satish Patidar* AIR 2003 MP 205.
13 *Union of India* v *Ashok Kumar Saboo* AIR 2014 Ori 46.
14 *K.K. Pushpakaran* v *Union of India* AIR 2008 Ker 107.
15 *Hulash Chand Choraraia* v *Union of India* AIR 2003 Gau 151.

but shall be guided by the principles of natural justice and, subject to the other provisions of this Act and of any rules, the Claims Tribunal shall have powers to regulate its own procedure including the fixing of places and times of its enquiry.

(2) The Claims Tribunal shall decide every application as expeditiously as possible and ordinarily every application shall be decided on a perusal of documents, written representations and affidavits and after hearing such oral arguments as may be advanced.

(3) The Claims Tribunal shall have, for the purposes of discharging its functions under this Act, the same powers as are vested in a civil court under the Code of Civil Procedure, 1908 (5 of 1908), while trying a suit, in respect of the following matters, namely:

(*a*) summoning and enforcing the attendance of any person and examining him on oath;

(*b*) requiring the discovery and production of documents;

(*c*) receiving evidence on affidavits;

(*d*) subject to the provisions of sections 123 and 124 of the Indian Evidence Act, 1872 (1 of 1872), requisitioning any public record or document or copy of such record or document from any office;

(*e*) issuing commissions for the examination of witnesses or documents;

(*f*) reviewing its decisions;

(*g*) dismissing an application for default or deciding it *ex parte*;

(*h*) setting aside any order of dismissal of any application for default or any order passed by it *ex parte*;

(*i*) any other matter which may be prescribed.

Applicability of Civil Procedure Code Although the 1987 Act and the Rules made thereunder do not specifically provide for the application of Or. 33, Code of Civil Procedure, there is nothing in the Act or the Rules which preclude the Tribunal from following that procedure if the ends of justice so requires. When an indigent person approaches the Tribunal for compensation for the wrong done to him, the Tribunal cannot refuse to exercise jurisdiction merely on the ground that he does not have the means to pay the fee.[16] For assessment of lawyer's fee for a claim of ₹1 crore 32 lakhs, the Tribunal can take recourse to C.O. (Civil), Vol. 1 in absence of specific guideline provided in the 1987 Act or rules made thereunder.[1]

Proper procedure—not followed The claim petition was filed before the Railway Claims Tribunal written statement was also filed; issues were framed. But parties were not called to adduce evidence. The Tribunal on hearing the arguments of the parties awarded compensation. It was held that the Tribunal did not comply with the procedure and acted contrary to s. 18 of the Act of 1987 and r. 21 of the Railway Claims Tribunal (Procedure) Rules 1989 and as such the order of the Tribunal was set

16 *A.A. Haja Muniuddin* v *Indian Railways* AIR 1993 SC 361; (1992)4 SCC 736; JT 1992 (Supp) SC 642.

1 *Union of India* v *Steel Authority of India Ltd.* AIR 1997 Ori 77.

aside and the matter was remanded for fresh disposal in accordance with the law.[2]

Liability to pay interest Where claim proceedings are delayed due to responsibility of the railway authorities, the claimant is entitled to interest for the period before expiry of 60 days' time for making payment from the date of the award.[3]

Accident claim The Tribunal has to frame issues and thereafter is to afford opportunity to the parties to adduce evidence. It is not proper to frame issues and to answer them in the judgment itself.[4]

Power of Tribunal to review its own decision In *Kalpataru Agroforest Enterprises* v *Union of India*[5] the Supreme Court has held that from perusal of sub-sec. (1) of s. 18 of the Railway Claims Tribunal Act it will be clear that in deciding the claims the Tribunal is not bound by the procedure laid down in Code of Civil Procedure but it shall be guided by the principles of natural justice and subject to other provisions of the Act and the Rules framed thereunder. Sub-section (3) however provides that in respect certain matters enumerated in cls. (*a*) to (*i*) the Tribunal shall have the same powers as are vested in civil court under Code of Civil Procedure. Clause (*f*) refers to reviewing of its own decision. From a combined reading of s. 114 and r. 1 of Or. 47, Code of Civil Procedure it is clear that the decree or order from which an appeal is allowed, but from which no appeal is preferred, can be reviewed. Section 23 of the 1987 provides for appeal. Admittedly no appeal was filed, consequently the review petition is maintainable before the Tribunal. Rule 32 of the Railway Claims Tribunal (Procedure) Rules 1989 restricts the scope of power of review vested under s. 18(3)(*f*) of the Act. Rule 32 runs counter to s. 18(3)(*f*) of the Act. Thus r. 32 is repugnant to the statutory provisions.

Rule 32 of Railway Claims Tribunal (Procedure) Rules 1989 repugnant to s. 18(3)(f) of Railway Claims Tribunal Act 1987 Rule 32 of the Railway Claims Tribunal (Procedure) Rules 1989 restricts the scope of power of review vested under s. 18(3)(*f*) of the Railway Claims Tribunal Act 1987 to non-appealable orders only and leaves out from its ambit orders which are appealable under s. 23 of the Act though such orders could be reviewed in view of s. 114 and r. 1 of Or. 47, Code of Civil Procedure. Thus r. 32 runs counter to s. 18(3)(*f*) of the Act and is certainly bad and in no case can it be allowed to override the specific provision of the Act.[6]

Procedure for adjudication of claim petition The Railway Claims Tribunal shall first frame issues of facts and law. When there are issues of facts, the Tribunal shall proceed to take depositions relating to them and record its findings on both the issues of facts and law. But where a petition is dismissed without framing any issue and recording findings of the Tribunal, the order of dismissal is bad in law.[7]

2 *Union of India* v *Bharat Petroleum Corpn. Ltd.* (2001)1 Civ LJ 839 (Ori).
3 *Union of India* v *Indian Iron & Steel Co. Ltd.* AIR 2000 P&H 33.
4 *Union of India* v *N. Trinath Reddy* AIR 2000 Ori 184.
5 AIR 2002 SC 1402.
6 *Kalpataru Agroforest Enterprises* v *Union of India* AIR 2002 SC 1402.
7 *Nirupama Sethi* v *Union of India* AIR 2003 Ori 10.

No succession certificate necessary An amount awarded as compensation to individual is not treated as debts or security. Thus, no succession certificate can be issued in relation to amount awarded as compensation to deceased claimant. Order of court directing claimants to produce succession certificate to withdraw the amount is not proper.[8]

19. Right to legal representation and presenting officers. (1) A person making an application to the Claims Tribunal may either appear in person or take the assistance of a legal practitioner of his choice to present his case before the Claims Tribunal.

(2) A railway administration may authorise one or more legal practitioners or any of its officers to act as presenting officers and every person so authorised by it may present its case with respect to any application before the Claims Tribunal.

Withdrawal of deposit against railway accident Petitioner, father of the deceased, had *bona fide* filed an application for permission to withdrawn the deposit for railway accident. Such application was dismissed. It was held that the dismissal of such application without considering the *bona fide* of the petitioner was improper.[9]

20. Power of Chairman to transfer cases from one Bench to another. On the application of any of the parties and after notice to the parties, and after hearing such of them as he may desire to be heard, or on his own motion without such notice, the Chairman may transfer any case pending before one Bench, for disposal, to any other Bench.

21. Decision to be by majority. If the Members of a Bench differ in opinion on any point, they shall state the point or points on which they differ, and make a reference to the Chairman who shall either hear the point or points himself or refer the case for hearing on such point or points by one or more of the other Members and such point or points shall be decided according to the opinion of the majority of the Members who have heard the case, including those who first heard it.

22. Execution of orders of Claims Tribunal. (1) An order made by the Claims Tribunal under this Act shall be executable by the Claims Tribunal as a decree of civil court, and, for this purpose, the Claims Tribunal shall have all the powers of a civil court.

(2) Notwithstanding anything contained in sub-section (1), the Claims Tribunal may transmit any order made by it to a civil court having local jurisdiction and such civil court shall execute the order as if it were a decree made by that court.

CHAPTER V

APPEALS

23. Appeals. (1) Save as provided in sub-section (2) and notwithstanding anything contained in the Code of Civil Procedure, 1908 (5 of 1908) or in any other law, an appeal shall lie from every order, not being an interlocutory order, of the Claims Tribunal, to the High Court having jurisdiction over the place where the Bench is located.

8 *Chitrapu Chinabapanaiah* v *Union of India* AIR 2004 AP 413.
9 *G. Nazeer Ahmad* v *Union of India* AIR 2003 NOC 414 (AP).

(2) No appeal shall lie from an order passed by the Claims Tribunal with the consent of the parties.

(3) Every appeal under this section shall be preferred within a period of ninety days from the date of the order appealed against.

Appeal The Claims Tribunal rejected a petition for claim of compensation for falling from stationary railway train on the ground of lack of jurisdiction. Subsequently amendment was made conferring jurisdiction in Tribunal. Considering the pitiable condition of the claimant the High Court in appeal awarded compensation instead of remitting the case to the Tribunal.[10] The decision on the question of limitation amounts to final adjudication of a right of the parties. Thus, an appeal is maintainable against such order which is not an interlocutory order.[11]

Award of compensation for untoward incident Materials on record show that there was an untoward incident resulting in death of the passenger having valid ticket. Plea of suicide by the said passenger was based on hearsay evidence.[12]

Compensation for shortage of consignment The consignee alleged that there was shortage of consignment, but failed to adduce evidence to establish the quantity of goods actually booked at forwarding station. The order awarding compensation was set aside. The matter was remanded for fresh hearing in the interest of justice.[13]

Where there is a case for compensation for short delivery of goods, the assessment of market value by the Tribunal as per its own discretion is illegal.[14]

Appeal arising out of Old Act 1890 Although the provision of appeal before the High Court in the (old) Railways Act 1890 against the order of the Claim Commissioner was repealed by giving jurisdiction of the Claim Commissioner to the Tribunal with effect from 8th November 1989 by the Railways Claims Tribunal Act 1987, yet the forum of appeal against the order of the Tribunal remained with the High Court as before by virtue of s. 23 of the Act of 1987. Thus, such appeal does not require hearing under Or. 41, r. 11 of the Code of Civil Procedure.[15]

CHAPTER VI
MISCELLANEOUS

24. Transfer of pending cases. (1) Every suit, claim or other legal proceeding (other than an appeal) pending before any court, Claims Commissioner or other authority

10 *V. Vijayasankar* v *Union of India* 1995 AIHC 6309 (Ker).
11 *Union of India* v *India Cement Ltd.* 1996 AIHC 3047 (Ker).
12 *General Manager, South Eastern Rly.* v *Deptymayee Jena* AIR 2000 Ori 138.
13 *Union of India* v *Steel Authority of India, Bhubaneswar* AIR 2000 Ori 27.
14 *Assam State Co-op Mftg. and Consumer's Federation Ltd.* v *Union of India* AIR 2004 Gau 69.
15 *Union of India* v *Santi Ranjan Dutta* AIR 2008 Cal 106.

immediately before the appointed day, [16][or, as the case may be, the date of commencement of the provisions of sub-section (1A) of section 13] being a suit, claim or proceeding the cause of action whereon it is based is such that it would have been, if it had arisen after the appointed day, [16][or, as the case may be, the date of commencement of the provisions of sub-section (1A) of section 13] within the jurisdiction of the Claims Tribunal, shall stand transferred on [17][that day or, as the case may be, date] to the Claims Tribunal.

(2) Where any suit, claim or other legal proceeding stands transferred from any court, Claims Commissioner or other authority to the Claims Tribunal under sub-section (1),—

(*a*) the court, Claims Commissioner or other authority shall, as soon as may be after such transfer, forward the records of such suit, claim or other legal proceeding to the Claims Tribunal;

(*b*) the Claims Tribunal may, on receipt of such records, proceed to deal with such suit, claim or other legal proceeding, so far as may be, in the same manner as an application, from the stage which was reached before such transfer or from any earlier stage or *de novo* as the Claims Tribunal may deem fit.

Transfer of pending cases When s. 13(1A) is read with s. 24 of the 1987 Act, it is clear that Parliament has transplanted the civil court jurisdiction regarding all claims set out in s. 13(1) of the Act with Claims Tribunal from date the Railway (Amendment) Act 28 of 1994 came into force.[18] Where the Railway Claims Tribunal has exclusive power and jurisdiction to decide a claim for recovery of damages with effect from 8th November 1989, any order passed by the District Judge subsequent to that date is without jurisdiction.[19]

25. Proceedings before Claims Tribunal to be judicial proceedings. All proceedings before the Claims Tribunal shall be deemed to be judicial proceedings within the meaning of sections 193, 219 and 228 of the Indian Penal Code, 1860 (45 of 1860).

26. Members and staff of Claims Tribunal to be public servants. The Chairman, Vice-Chairman and other Members and the officers and other employees of the Claims Tribunal shall be deemed to be public servants within the meaning of section 21 of the Indian Penal Code, 1860 (45 of 1860).

27. Protection of action taken in good faith. No suit, prosecution or other legal proceeding shall lie against the Central Government or against the Chairman, Vice-Chairman or other Member, or any other person authorised by the Chairman, Vice-Chairman or other Member for anything which is in good faith done or intended to be done in pursuance of this Act or any rule or order made thereunder.

28. Act to have overriding effect. The provisions of this Act shall have effect notwithstanding anything inconsistent therewith contained in any other law for the time being in force or in any instrument having effect by virtue of any law other than this Act.

16 *Inserted* by Act 28 of 1994, s. 13.
17 *Substituted* by Act 28 of 1994, s. 13, for "that day".
18 *V. Vijayasankar* v *Union of India* 1995 AIHC 6309 (Ker).
19 *PCI* v *General Manager, Northern Rly.* AIR 1998 Bom 233.

29. Power to remove difficulties. (1) If any difficulty arises in giving effect to provisions of this Act, the Central Government may, by order published in the Official Gazette, make such provisions, not inconsistent with the provisions of this Act, as appear to it to be necessary or expedient for removing the difficulty:

Provided that no such order shall be made after the expiry of a period of three years from the appointed day.

(2) Every order made under this section shall, as soon as may be after it is made, be laid before each House of Parliament.

30. Power to make rules. (1) The Central Government may, by notification, make rules to carry out the provisions of this Act.

(2) Without prejudice to the generality of the foregoing powers, such rules may provide for all or any of the following matters, namely:

(*a*) the procedure under sub-section (3) of section 8 for the investigation of misbehaviour or incapacity of the Chairman, Vice-Chairman or other Member;

(*b*) salaries and allowances payable to, and the other terms and conditions of service (including pension, gratuity and other retirement benefits) of, the Chairman, Vice-Chairman and other Members under section 9;

(*c*) the financial and administrative powers which the Chairman may exercise over the Benches under section 11;

(*d*) the salaries and allowances and conditions of service of officers and other employees of the Claims Tribunal under sub-section (3) of section 12;

(*e*) the form of application, the documents and other evidence to be accompanied with such application and fee in respect of filing of such application and fee for the service or execution of processes under sub-section (2) of section 66;

(*f*) the rules subject to which the Claims Tribunal shall have powers to regulate its own procedure under sub-section (1) of section 18 and the additional matters in which the Claims Tribunal may exercise powers of civil court under clause (*i*) of sub-section (3) of that section;

(*g*) any other matter which is required to be, or may be, prescribed.

(3) Every rule made under this Act shall be laid, as soon as may be after it is made, before each House of Parliament, while it is in session, for a total period of thirty days which may be comprised in one session or in two or more successive sessions, and if, before the expiry of the session immediately following the session or the successive sessions aforesaid, both Houses agree in making any modification in the rule or both Houses agree that the rule should not be made, the rule shall thereafter have effect only in such modified form or be of no effect, as the case may be; so, however, that any such modification or annulment shall be without prejudice to the validity of anything previously done under that rule.

Assessment of lawyer's fee Under r. 29 of the Railway Claims Tribunal (Procedure) Rules 1989 the Claims Tribunal may assess the lawyer's fee at ₹1 lakh 33 thousand for a claim of ₹1 crore 32 lakhs.[20]

20 *Union of India* v *Steel Authority of India Ltd.* AIR 1997 Ori 77.

[21][30A. **Power to make rules retrospectively.** The power to make rules under clause (*b*) of sub-section (2) of section 30 shall include the power to make such rules or any of them retrospectively from a date not earlier than the date on which this Act received the assent of the President, but no such retrospective effect shall be given to any such rule so as to prejudicially affect the interests of any person to whom such rule may be applicable].

Amendment Section 30A has been inserted by the Railway Claims Tribunal (Amendment) Act 1998 (Act No. 4 of 1999).

CHAPTER VII

AMENDMENTS TO THE RAILWAYS ACT

31. Amendment of section 3. In section 3 of the Railways Act, after clause (18), the following clause shall be inserted, namely:

"(19) 'Claims Tribunal' means the Railway Claims Tribunal established under section 3 of the Railway Claims Tribunal Act, 1987."

32. Amendment of section 78A. In section 78A of the Railways Act, for the word "suit", the words "application before the Claims Tribunal" shall be substituted.

33. Substitution of new section for section 80. For section 80 of the Railways Act, the following section shall be substituted, namely:

"80. *Application for compensation.* An application to the Claims Tribunal for compensation for loss of the life of, or personal injury to, a passenger or for loss, destruction, damage, deterioration or non-delivery of animals or goods may be made,—

(*a*) if the passenger was, or the animals or goods were, booked from one station to another on the railway of the same railway administration, against that railway administration;

(*b*) if the passenger was, or the animals or goods were, booked through over the railway of two or more railway administrations, against the railway administration from which the passenger obtained his pass or purchased his ticket or to which the animals or goods were delivered for carriage, as the case may be, or against the railway administration on whose railway the destination station lies, or the loss, injury, destruction, damage or deterioration occurred."

No enlargement of jurisdiction of Claims Tribunal The jurisdiction of Claims Tribunal cannot be enlarged by reading s. 33 in s. 13 of the 1987 Act.[22]

34. Omission of sections 82B, 82D and 82F. Sections 82B, 82D and 82F of the Railways Act shall be *omitted*.

35. Amendment of section 82C. In section 82C of the Railways Act,—

(*a*) in sub-section (1), for the words "Claims Commissioner", the words "Claims Tribunal" shall be substituted;

(*b*) sub-section (2) and the *Explanation* thereto shall be *omitted*.

21 *Inserted* by Act 4 of 1999, sec. 2.

22 *Ratnakar Tanbaji Itankar* v *Union of India* AIR 1994 Bom 132.

36. Amendment of sections 82E, 82G and 82HH. In sections 82E, 82G and 82HH of the Railways Act, for the words "Claims Commissioner", wherever they occur, the words "Claims Tribunal" shall be substituted.

37. Amendment of section 82-I. In section 82-I of the Railways Act, for the words, figures and letters "sections 82A to 82HH", the words, figures and letters "sections 82A, 82C, 82E and 82G to 82HH" shall be substituted.

38. Amendment of section 82J. In section 82J of the Railways Act,—

(*a*) in sub-section (1), for the words, figures and letters "sections 82A to 82H inclusive", the words, figures and letters "sections 82A, 82C, 82E, 82G and 82H" shall be substituted;

(*b*) in sub-section (2), clause (*i*) and clauses (*iv*) to (*vi*) shall be *omitted*.

APPENDIX 2

The Railway Claims Tribunal (Procedure) Rules, 1989

G.S.R. 842(E), dated 19th September 1989 In exercise of the powers conferred by clauses (*c*), (*e*), (*f*) and (*g*) of sub-section (2) of section 30 of the Railway Claims Tribunal Act, 1987 (54 of 1987), the Central Government hereby makes the following rules, namely:

1. Short title and commencement. (1) These rules may be called the Railway Claims Tribunal (Procedure) Rules, 1989.

(2) They shall come into force on the 'appointed day' within the meaning of clause (*b*) of section (2) of the Act.

2. Definitions. In these rules, unless the context otherwise requires:

(*a*) "Act" means the Railway Claims Tribunal Act, 1987 (54 of 1987);

(*b*) "accident" means an accident of the nature described in section 82A of the Indian Railway Act, 1890 (9 of 1890);

(*c*) "applicant" means a person making an application to the Tribunal under section 16 of the Act;

(*d*) "Form" means a form appended to these rules;

(*e*) "legal practitioner" shall have the meaning assigned to it under clause (*i*) of section 2 of the Advocates Act, 1961 (25 of 1961);

(*f*) "legal representative" means a person who in law represents the estate of deceased;

(*g*) "Registrar" means the person who is for the time being discharging the functions of the Registrar of the Tribunal and includes an Additional and Assistant Registrar.

(*h*) "Registry" means the Registry of any Bench of the Tribunal;

(*i*) "Schedule" means a schedule to these rules;

(*j*) "Section" means a section of the Act;

(*k*) "Transferred application" means a suit, claim or other legal proceeding which has been transferred to the Tribunal under section 24 of the Act;

(*l*) "Tribunal" means the Railway Claims Tribunal established under section 3 of the Act;

(*m*) Words and expressions used and not defined in these rules but defined in the Act shall have the meanings respectively assigned to them in that Act.

3. Territorial jurisdiction of Benches. [1][(1) The number of Benches, the Headquarters of each Bench and the territorial jurisdiction of every such Bench shall be as specified in Schedule I and Schedule I(A)].

(2) If an application is received by a Bench which does not have territorial jurisdiction to deal with the matter, the Registrar of the Bench shall return the application to the applicant.

(3) Notwithstanding anything contained in sub-rule (2) the applicant may apply to the Chairman and the Chairman may thereupon for reasons to be recorded in writing direct a Bench other than the Bench before which an application has been filed to hear such application and issue such orders as may be necessary for the transfer of the application.

4. Language of the Claims Tribunal. (1) The pleadings before the Claims Tribunal may, at the option of the respective parties, be either in English or in Hindi.

(2) All orders and judgments of the Claims Tribunal may, at the option of the Claims Tribunal, be either in Hindi or in English.

5. Procedure for filing applications. (1) An application to the Tribunal shall be presented in Form I or Form II or Form III as the case may be either by the applicant in person or by an agent or by his duly authorised legal practitioner [1][in the office of the Registrar or the Additional Registrar, or the Assistant Registrar, as the case may be].

(2) An application referred to in sub-rule (1) may also be sent by registered post [2][in the office of the Registrar or the Additional Registrar, or the Assistant Registrar, as the case may be] of the Bench concerned.

[3][(2A) An application sent by post under sub-rule (2) shall be deemed to have been presented to the Registrar on the day on which it is received in the Tribunal].

(3) The application under sub-rule (1) or sub-rule (2) shall be presented in triplicate.

(4) Where the number of respondents is more than one, as many extra copies of the application as there are respondents, together with unused file size envelopes, bearing the full address of such respondents, shall be furnished by the applicant.

(5) The applicant may attach to and present with his application a receipt slip in Form IV which shall be signed by the Registrar or the office receiving the application on behalf of the Registrar in acknowledgment.

(6) Every application including any miscellaneous application, shall be typed legibly in double space on one side on thick paper of good quality.

6. Application fees for cases other than compensation for death or injury to passengers. (1) Every application made under sub-section (1) of section 16 for seeking relief

1 *Substituted* by G.S.R. 167(E), dt. 29.2.2000 (w.e.f. 29.2.2000).

2 *Substituted* by the Railway Claims Tribunal (Procedure) Amendment Rules, 2002, *vide* G.S.R. 787(E) (w.e.f. 2.12.2002).

3 *Inserted* by the Railway Claims Tribunal (Procedure) Amendment Rules, 2002, *vide* G.S.R. 787(E) (w.e.f. 2.12.2002).

in respect of matters, other than claim of compensation for death or injuries to passengers, shall be accompanied by a fee as specified in Schedule II.

(2) The amount of the fee as referred to in sub-rule (1) shall be payable by crossed demand draft on a nationalised bank drawn in favour of the Registrar of the concerned Bench or remitted through a crossed Indian Postal Order and drawn in favour of the Registrar of the concerned Bench.

7. Documents to accompany the application. (1) Every application for compensation in respect of loss, destruction, damage, deterioration or non-delivery of animals or goods or in respect of refund of fare or freight shall be accompanied by the following documents, namely:

(*a*) copy of the railway receipt/parcel way bill/luggage ticket;

(*b*) original sale invoice (Bijak), if any;

(*c*) copy of order or letter, if any, of the railway administration deciding the claim of the party;

(*d*) copy of the original certificate issued by the railway administration regarding loss, deterioration or damage to the goods, at the time of granting open delivery or assessment delivery;

[4][(*e*) copy of notice under section 106 of the Railways Act, 1989];

(*f*) copies of any other relevant document in possession of the applicant.

[5][(2) The documents referred to in sub-rule (1) may be attested by a legal practitioner or by a Gazetted Officer of the Central Government or a State Government.

(3) An application filed under sub-rule (1) of rule 5 by a legal practitioner shall be accompanied by a *Vakalatnama* and that by an agent shall be accompanied by a document authorizing him to act as such.

(4) When any document accompanying an application or reply appears to be defaced, torn, or in any way damaged or otherwise its condition or appearance requires special notice, a mention regarding its condition and appearance shall be made by the party producing the same in the index of such application or reply, as the case may be, and the same shall be verified by the Registrar].

[6][**8. Place of filing application for compensation in accident or untoward incident claim.** An application for compensation payable under section 124 and 124A of the Railways Act, 1989 may be filed before the Bench having territorial jurisdiction over the place from which the passenger obtains or purchases his pass or ticket or where the accident or untoward incident occurs or where the place of destination station lies or where the claimant normally resides].

9. Place of filing application for compensation for loss, damage, destruction, deterioration or non-delivery of goods or animals. An application for compensation referred to in

4 *Substituted* by the Railway Claims Tribunal (Procedure) Amendment Rules, 2002, *vide* G.S.R. 787(E) (w.e.f. 2.12.2002).

5 *Inserted* by the Railway Claims Tribunal (Procedure) Amendment Rules, 2002, *vide* G.S.R. 787(E) (w.e.f. 2.12.2002).

6 *Substituted* by the Railway Claims Tribunal (Procedure) Amendment Rules, 2002, *vide* G.S.R. 787(E) (w.e.f. 2.12.2002).

sub-clause (*i*) of clause (*a*) of sub-section (1) of section 13 of the Act may be filed before the Bench having territorial jurisdiction over the place where—

(*a*) the goods or animals were delivered for carriage; or

(*b*) where the destination station lies; or

(*c*) the loss, destruction, damage or deterioration of goods or animals occurred.

10. Place of filing application for refund of fare and freight. An application in respect of a claim for refund of fare or freight referred to in clause (*b*) of sub-section (1) of section 13 of the Act may be filed before the Bench having territorial jurisdiction over the place at which such fare or freight was paid of the place where the destination station lies.

[7][**10A.** Every application made under rule 9 or 10 shall be accompanied with a fee of ten rupees for each respondent for the service or execution of process].

11. Scrutiny of applications. (1) The Registrar, or the officer authorised by him, shall endorse on every application, the date on which it is presented or received through post under Rule 5, and sign the endorsement.

(2) If, on scrutiny, the application is found to be in order, it shall be registered and given a serial number.

[8][(3) If on scrutiny an application, is found defective and defect noticed is formal in nature, the Registrar may allow the applicant to rectify the same in his presence, and if the defect is not formal in nature, the Registrar may allow the applicant to rectify defect in a week's time, which may be extended in appropriate cases on the written request of the applicant].

(4) If the applicant fails to rectify the defect within the time allowed under sub-rule (3), the Registrar may, by order and for reasons to be recorded in writing, decline to register the application and inform the applicant accordingly.

(5) An appeal against the order passed under sub-rule (4) may be preferred by the person aggrieved within fifteen days from the date of such order to any Member and such appeal shall be dealt with and disposed of in Chamber by the Member whose decision thereon shall be final.

[9][**11A. Maintenance of Cash Register.** (1) All payments received by way of Indian Postal Orders or demand drafts or in cash by the Registrar shall be entered immediately by the Registration Clerk on their receipt side in a Cash Register maintained in Form VI.

(2) On every last working day of the week, the payments received during the week by way of Indian Postal Orders or demand drafts shall be transmitted by the Registration Clerk to the official incharge of the cash section, who after scrutiny and verification shall acknowledge the receipt of all moneys in the Cash Register.

7 *Inserted* by the Railway Claims Tribunal (Procedure) Amendment Rules, 2002, *vide* G.S.R. 787(E) (w.e.f. 2.12.2002).

8 *Substituted* by G.S.R. 513(E), dt. 9.7.2001 (w.e.f. 9.7.2001).

9 *Inserted* by the Railway Claims Tribunal (Procedure) Amendment Rules, 2002, *vide* G.S.R. 787(E) (w.e.f. 2.12.2002).

(3) The payments received in cash shall be transmitted by the Registration Clerk to the official-in-charge of the cash section on each day, who after verification shall acknowledge the receipt of all moneys in the Cash Register.

(4) The official incharge of the cash section shall deposit all payments received by way of Indian Postal Order or demand draft or cash in the Bank account of the Tribunal].

12. Notice to opposite party. (1) The Tribunal shall issue [10][notice in Form VII] to the respondent to show cause against the application on a date of hearing to be specified therein. Such [10][notice in Form VII] shall be accompanied by a copy of the application.

(2) If the respondent does not appear on the date specified in the [10][notice in Form VII] or appears and admits claim, the Claims Tribunal shall forthwith proceed to dispose of the application.

(3) If the respondent contests the claim it may file a reply along with copies of such documents on which it relies on or before the date of hearing and such reply and copies of documents shall form part of the record.

13. Service of notices and processes issued by the Tribunal. (1) Any notice or process to be issued by the Tribunal may be served in any one of the following modes as may be directed by the Bench:

(*a*) by hand delivery through a process server;

(*b*) by registered post with acknowledgment due;

(*c*) service by the party himself.

(2) Where a notice issued by the Tribunal is served by the party himself by 'hand delivery', he shall file with the Registry the acknowledgment, together with an affidavit of service.

(3) Notwithstanding anything contained in sub-rule (1), the Tribunal may, taking into account the number of respondents and their places of residence or work and other circumstances, direct that notice of the application shall be served upon the respondents in any other manner, including any manner of substituted service, as it appears on the Tribunal just and convenient.

[11][(4) A notice or process may also be served on the legal practitioner representing the applicant or the respondent, as the case may be, in any proceeding or on any person authorized to accept a notice or a process, and such service on the legal practitioner or on the authorized person shall be deemed to be proper service."

(5) Where the Tribunal directs a service under sub-rule (3), such amount of charges, as may be determined by the Tribunal from time to time, but not exceeding the actual charges incurred in effecting the service, shall be deposited in the Tribunal].

14. Filing of Affidavit. (1) The Tribunal may direct the parties to give evidence, if any, by affidavit.

10 *Substituted* by the Railway Claims Tribunal (Procedure) Amendment Rules, 2002, *vide* G.S.R. 787(E) (w.e.f. 2.12.2002).

11 *Inserted* by the Railway Claims Tribunal (Procedure) Amendment Rules, 2002, *vide* G.S.R. 787(E) (w.e.f. 2.12.2002).

(2) Notwithstanding anything contained in sub-rule (1), where the Tribunal considers it necessary for just decision of the case, it may order cross-examination of any deponent.

[12][(3) Every affidavit to be filed before the Tribunal shall be in Form VIII].

15. Filing of reply and other documents by the respondents. (1) Each respondent may file his reply to the application and copies of the documents on or before the date of hearing.

(2) In reply filed under sub-rule (1), the respondent shall specifically admit, deny or explain the facts stated by the applicant in his application and state such additional facts as may be found necessary in his reply.

[13][(3) When the respondent admits the facts stated in the application, the Tribunal may make order in this regard].

[14][**15A. Filing of Rejoinder.** The applicant intending to file rejoinder to the written reply filed by the respondent may do so with the permission of the Tribunal.

15B. Admissions and denial of documents. The Tribunal may, before framing issues ascertain from parties or their authorized representatives whether they admit or deny documents accompanying the application or reply, if any, and shall record such admission and denial.

15C. Marking of Documents. The documents filed by the applicant shall be marked as 'A' series and the documents filed by the respondent shall be marked as 'R' series and the Tribunal exhibits shall be marked as 'C' series].

16. Summary dismissal of application. The Tribunal, may, after considering the application, summarily dismiss the application, if for reasons to be recorded, the Tribunal is of opinion that there are not sufficient grounds for proceeding therewith.

17. Hearing of applications. The Tribunal shall notify to the parties the date and place of hearing of the application in such manner as the Chairman may, by general or special order, direct.

[15][**17A. Oath to the witness.** The Court Master or the Commissioner, as the case may be, shall administer the following oath to a witness:—

"I do swear in the name of God that what I shall state shall be truth and nothing but the truth].

18. Action on application for applicant's default. (1) Where on the date fixed for hearing of the application or on any other date to which such hearing may be adjourned, the applicant does not appear when the application is called for hearing, the Tribunal may, in its discretion, either dismiss the application for default or hear and decide it on merit.

12 *Inserted* by the Railway Claims Tribunal (Procedure) Amendment Rules, 2002, *vide* G.S.R. 787(E) (w.e.f. 2.12.2002).

13 *Inserted* by the Railway Claims Tribunal (Procedure) Amendment Rules, 2002, *vide* G.S.R. 787(E) (w.e.f. 2.12.2002).

14 *Inserted* by the Railway Claims Tribunal (Procedure) Amendment Rules, 2002, *vide* G.S.R. 787(E) (w.e.f. 2.12.2002).

15 *Inserted* by the Railway Claims Tribunal (Procedure) Amendment Rules, 2002, *vide* G.S.R. 787(E) (w.e.f. 2.12.2002).

(2) Where an application has been dismissed for default and the applicant files an application within thirty days from the date of dismissal and satisfies the Tribunal that there was sufficient cause for his non-appearance when the application was called for hearing, the Tribunal shall make an order setting aside the order dismissing the application and restore the same:

Provided, however, where the case was disposed of on merits the decision shall not be reopened except by way of review.

19. Ex parte hearing and disposal of applications. (1) Where on the date fixed for hearing the application or on any other date to which such hearing may be adjourned, the applicant appears and the respondent does not appear when the application is called for hearing, the Tribunal may, in its discretion adjourn the hearing or hear and decide the application *ex parte*.

(2) Where an application has been heard *ex parte* against a respondent or respondents, such respondent or respondents may apply to the Tribunal for an order to set it aside and if such respondent or respondents satisfy the Tribunal that the notice was not duly served, or that he or they were prevented by any sufficient cause from appearing when the application was called for hearing, the Tribunal may make an order setting aside the *ex parte* hearing as against him or them upon such terms as it thinks fit, and shall appoint a day for proceeding with the application:

Provided that where the *ex parte* hearing of the application is of such nature that it cannot be set aside as against one respondent only, it may be set aside as against all or any of the other respondents also.

20. Procedure and powers of Tribunal. The Tribunal shall have for the purposes of discharging its functions under this Act, the same powers as are vested in a civil court under the Code of Civil Procedure, 1908, while trying a suit, in respect of the following matters, namely:

(*a*) summoning and enforcing the attendance of any person and examining him on oath;

(*b*) requiring the discovery and production of documents;

(*c*) receiving evidence on affidavits;

(*d*) subject to the provisions of sections 123 and 124 of the Indian Evidence Act, 1872, requisitioning any public record or document or copy of such record or document from any office;

(*e*) issuing commissions for the examination of witness or documents;

(*f*) reviewing its decisions;

(*g*) dismissing an application for default or *ex parte*;

(*h*) setting aside any order of dismissal of any application for default or any order passed by it *ex parte*.

21. Framing and determination of issue. (1) After considering the reply, the Tribunal shall ascertain upon what material propositions of fact or of law the parties are at variance and shall thereupon proceed to frame and record the issues upon which the right decision of the case appear to it to depend.

(2) In recording the issues, the Tribunal shall distinguish between those issues which in its opinion concern points of facts and those which concern points of law.

(3) After framing the issues, the Tribunal shall proceed to record evidence thereon which each party may desire to produce.

Adjudication procedure Tribunal has to frame first issues both of facts and law and has to proceed to record evidence on issues of fact and then record its findings on the said issues. Rejection of claim by ignoring such procedure is not proper.[16]

[17][**22. Summoning of witnesses and method of recording evidence.** (1) If an application is presented by any party to the proceedings for summoning of witnesses, the Tribunal shall issue summons for the appearance of such witnesses with recording the reasons for doing so, unless it considers that his appearance is not necessary for the just decision of the case.

(2) The Tribunal shall make a brief memorandum of the substance of the evidence of every witness as the examination of the witness proceeds and such memorandum shall form part of the record:

Provided that if the Tribunal is prevented from making such memorandum, it shall record the reasons of its inability to do so and shall cause such memorandum to be made in writing from its dictation and shall sign the same, and such memorandum shall form part of the record.

[18][(3) Where summons are issued by the Tribunal under sub-rule (1) to any witness to give evidence or to produce any document, the person so summoned shall be entitled to such travelling and daily allowance sufficient to defray the travelling and other expenses, as may be determined by the Registrar].

[19][**22A. Documents not to form part of records.** Unless duly permitted by the Tribunal, the following documents shall not form part of the records of the case.

(*a*) written statement filed after the expiry of time granted for the purpose;

(*b*) rejoinder filed without leave of the Tribunal or after the expiry of time granted;

(*c*) additional pleading filed without leave of the Tribunal or filed after expiry of time granted; and

(*d*) documents not tendered into evidence].

23. Power to issue commission. Any Bench of the Tribunal may issue a commission for the examination on interrogatories or otherwise of any person [20][***] who is unable to attend the Tribunal for any justifiable reason.

24. Procedure in connected cases. (1) Where two or more applications pending before a Tribunal arise out of the same facts and any issue involved is common to two or more such applications, such applications may, so far as the evidence bearing on such issue is concerned, be heard simultaneously.

16 *Nirupoma Sethi* v *Union of India* AIR 2003 Ori 10.

17 *Substituted* by G.S.R. 384(E), dt. 22.10.2003 (w.r.e.f. 9.7.2001).

18 *Inserted* by the Railway Claims Tribunal (Procedure) Amendment Rules, 2002, *vide* G.S.R. 787(E) (w.e.f. 2.12.2002).

19 *Inserted* by the Railway Claims Tribunal (Procedure) Amendment Rules, 2002, *vide* G.S.R. 787(E) (w.e.f. 2.12.2002).

20 *Omitted* by the Railway Claims Tribunal (Procedure) Amendment Rules, 2002, *vide* G.S.R. 787(E) (w.e.f. 2.12.2002).

(2) Where action is taken under sub-rule (1), the evidence bearing on the common issue or issues shall be recorded on the record of one application the Tribunal shall certify under its hand on the records of any such other application, the extent to which evidence so recorded applies to such other case and the fact that the parties to such other case had the opportunity of being present, and, if they were present of cross-examining the witnesses.

25. Calendar of transferred cases. Each Bench shall draw up a calendar for the hearing of transferred cases in such manner as the Chairman may, by general or special order direct and, hear and decide the cases according to the calendar.

26. Substitution of legal representatives. (1) In the case of death of a party during the pendency of the proceedings before Tribunal, the legal representatives of the deceased party may apply within ninety days of the date of such death for being brought on record.

(2) Where no application is received from the legal representatives within the period specified in sub-rule (1), the proceedings shall abate:

Provided that for good and sufficient reasons shown, the Tribunal may allow substitution of the legal representatives of the deceased.

27. Assessors. (1) In an enquiry into a claim, the tribunal may call in the aid of assessors, not exceeding two in number, who possess any technical or special knowledge with respect to any matter before the Tribunal for the purpose of assisting the Tribunal.

(2) An assessor shall perform such functions as the Tribunal may direct.

(3) The remuneration, if any, to be paid to an assessor shall in every case be determined by the Tribunal and be paid by it.

28. Adjournment of hearing. If the Tribunal finds that an application cannot be disposed of at one hearing it shall record the reasons which necessitate the adjournment and also inform the parties present of the date of adjourned hearing.

[21][Provided that no such adjournment shall be granted more than three times to a party during the proceedings before the Tribunal:

Provided further that all the documents shall be filed by the parties along with pleadings and no adjournment shall be granted for filing documents at a later stage except in circumstances which are beyond the control of the concerned party].

29. Costs. The claims Tribunal may, in its discretion, pass such orders in respect of costs incidental to any proceedings before it, as it may deem fit.

30. Decision of the Tribunal. The Tribunal shall decide every application as expeditiously as possible on perusal of documents, affidavits and other evidence, if any, and after hearing such oral arguments as may be advanced.

21 *Inserted* by the Railway Claims Tribunal (Procedure) Amendment Rules, 2002, *vide* G.S.R. 787(E) (w.e.f. 2.12.2002).

31. Order to be passed and signed. [22]["(1) The Tribunal, after hearing the applicant and respondent, shall pass an order either at once, or as soon as thereafter, as may be practicable, but not later than twenty-one days from the date of conclusion of the arguments; and where it is unable so to do, it shall record its reasons for such inability"].

(2) An order made by the Tribunal shall be executable by the Tribunal as a decree of a civil court and the provisions of the Code of Civil Procedure, 1908, so far as may be, shall apply as they apply in respect of decree of a civil court.

(3) Every order of the Tribunal shall be in writing and shall be signed by the Member or Members constituting the Bench, which pronounced the order.

[23]**[31A. Execution of order.** An order of the Tribunal may be executed by the Bench which pass it if the respondent is within the territorial jurisdiction of the said Bench or by any other Bench or court to which it is sent for execution, when the respondent is having his office within the territorial jurisdiction of such Bench or court, as the case may be.

31B. Application for execution. For execution the holder of an order shall make an application to the Tribunal in Form IX.

31C. Issue of process of execution. (1) On receipt of an application under rule 31B, the Tribunal shall issue a process for execution of its order in Form X.

(2) The Tribunal shall consider objection, if any, raised by the respondent and make such order as it may deem fit and shall issue attachment or recovery warrant in Forms XI and XII, as the case may be].

32. Review of decision. (1) Any person considering himself aggrieved by any order of the Tribunal from which no appeal is allowed [24][or from which appeal is allowed, but has not been preferred] and who on account of some mistake or error apparent on the face of the record, or for any other sufficient reason, desires to obtain a review of the order made against him, may apply for review of a final order not being an interlocutory order, to the Tribunal.

[25](2) Where it appears to the Tribunal that there is not sufficient ground for a review, it shall reject the application and its reasons for so doing.

22 *Substituted* by the Railway Claims Tribunal (Procedure) Amendment Rules 2005, *vide* G.S.R. 173(E), Gazette of India, Ext. Pt. II s. 3(*i*), dt. 16.3.2005 (w.e.f. 16.3.2005). *Former sub-rule as inserted* by the Railway Claims Tribunal (Procedure) Amendment Rules, 2002, *vide* G.S.R. 787(E) (w.e.f. 2.12.2002) [(1) The Tribunal, after hearing the applicant and respondent, shall make and pronounce an order either at once or as soon as thereafter as may be practicable but not later than twenty-one days from the final hearing].

23 *Inserted* by the Railway Claims Tribunal (Procedure) Amendment Rules, 2002, *vide* G.S.R. 787(E) (w.e.f. 2.12.2002).

24 *Inserted* by the Railway Claims Tribunal (Procedure) Amendment Rules, 2002, *vide* G.S.R. 787(E) (w.e.f. 2.12.2002).

25 *Substituted* by the Railway Claims Tribunal (Procedure) Amendment Rules, 2005, published in Gazette of India Extra Pt II, s. 3(*i*) dt. 16.3.2005 (w.e.f. 16.3.2005).

(3) Where the Tribunal is of the opinion that the application for review should be granted, it shall grant the same:

Provided that no such application shall be granted without previous notice to the opposite party to enable him to appear and be heard in support of the order, a review of which is applied for.

Penal Charges for excess of weight The Tribunal passed order condoning penal charges. A review petition was made which was rejected. It was held that an appeal against original judgment and order was maintainable. The scope of review under s. 114 read with Or. 47, r. 1, Code of Civil Procedure as well as under r. 32 of the Railway Claims Tribunal (Procedure) Rules 1987 is very limited. The scope of review and that of appeal are completely different. The appellate jurisdiction is wide and in the first appeal the court can go into the question of fact even.[26]

33. Publication of orders. Any order of the Tribunal deemed by it to be fit for publication in any authoritative report or other media may be released for such publication on such terms and conditions as the Chairman or Vice-Chairman or Member concerned may specify by general or special order.

34. Certified copy of the order and inspection of record. (1) If the applicant or the respondent to any proceeding requires a copy of any order passed by the Tribunal, the same shall be supplied to him on payment of rupees ten per order. [1][In the normal course of time within seven working days from the receipt of an application for the said purpose and on payment of rupees twenty on urgent basis within three working days from the receipt of an application for the said purpose].

(2) The parties to any case or their Counsel may be allowed to inspect the record of the case on making an application in writing to the Registrar and payment of rupees ten per inspection.

[2][(3) Notwithstanding anything contained in sub-rule (1), in compensation cases relating to accident and untoward incidents, one copy of the order made by the Tribunal shall be sent within three working days by the Registrar to both the parties free of cost with an endorsement thereon Free copy].

35. Orders or directions by the Tribunal. The Tribunal may pass such orders or give such directions as may be necessary or expedient to give effect to its orders or to prevent abuse of its process or to secure the ends of justice.

36. Registration of legal practitioner's clerks. (1) No clerk employed by a legal practitioner shall act as such before the Tribunal or be permitted to have access to the records and obtain copies of the orders of a Bench of the Tribunal in which the legal practitioner ordinarily practises, unless his name is entered in the Register of Clerks maintained by the said Bench. Such clerk shall be known as a "Registered Clerk".

26 *Union of India* v *Harinagar Sugar Mills Ltd.* AIR 2008 Gau 161.

1 *Added* by the Railway Claims Tribunal (Procedure) Amendment Rules, 2002, *vide* G.S.R. 787(E) (w.e.f. 2.12.2002).

2 *Inserted* by the Railway Claims Tribunal (Procedure) Amendment Rules, 2002, *vide* G.S.R. 787(E) (w.e.f. 2.12.2002).

(2) A legal practitioner desirous of registering his clerk shall make an application to the Registrar in Form V. On such application being allowed by the Registrar, his name shall be entered in the Register of Clerks.

[3][(3) An Identity Card shall be issued in Form XIII to a Registered Clerk of the legal practitioner on payment of a fee of rupees fifteen by way of Indian Postal Order or demand draft drawn in favour of the Registrar].

37. Powers, functions and duties of the Registrar. (1) The Registrar shall have the custody of the records of the Tribunal and shall exercise such other functions as are assigned to him under these rules or from time to time by the Chairman or the Vice-Chairman or the Member.

(2) Without prejudice to the foregoing sub-rule (1), the Registrar shall have the following powers and duties, subject to the general or special order of the Chairman, Vice-Chairman or Member, namely:

(*i*) to receive all applications and other documents including transferred applications under sub-rule (3) of Rule 3;

(*ii*) to decide all questions arising out of the scrutiny of the applications before they are registered in accordance with Rule 11;

(*iii*) to require any application presented to the Tribunal to be amended for compliance with any provision of the Act or the rules;

(*iv*) subject to the direction of the respective Benches, to fix the date of hearings and to issue notices therefor;

(*v*) to direct any formal amendment of records;

(*vi*) to order grant of copies of documents to parties to the proceedings;

(*vii*) to grant leave to inspect the records of the Tribunal;

(*viii*) to dispose of all matters relating to the service of notices or other processes, applications for the issue of fresh notices and for extending the time for filing such applications and to grant time not exceeding [4][thirty] days for filing a reply or rejoinder, if any, and to place the matter before the Bench for appropriate orders after the expiry of the aforesaid period;

(*ix*) to requisition or transfer any records of such suit, claim or other legal proceeding as are transferred to the Claims Tribunal from any court, Claims Commissioner or other authority under clause (*a*) of sub-section (2) of section 24 of the Act.

(*x*) to receive and dispose of applications for substitution, except where the substitution would involve setting aside an order of abatement;

(*xi*) to receive and dispose of applications by parties for return of documents.

[5][(*xii*) to supply to the Central Government the information in Form XIV;

3 *Inserted* by the Railway Claims Tribunal (Procedure) Amendment Rules, 2002, *vide* G.S.R. 787(E) (w.e.f. 2.12.2002).

4 *Substituted* by the Railway Claims Tribunal (Procedure) Amendment Rules, 2002, *vide* G.S.R. 787(E) (w.e.f. 2.12.2002).

5 *Inserted* by the Railway Claims Tribunal (Procedure) Amendment Rules, 2002, *vide* G.S.R. 787(E) (w.e.f. 2.12.2002).

(*xiii*) to dismiss the application for default in case the applicant or his legal practitioner does not appear before him on the date fixed for hearing of the case;

(*xiv*) to dismiss the application in case the applicant fails to serve the opposite party with the notice; and

(*xv*) to restore the application, if he is satisfied that there are sufficient reasons for non-appearance or for not serving the opposite party].

(3) The official seal shall be kept in the custody of the Registrar.

(4) Subject to any general or special direction by the Chairman, the seal of the Tribunal shall not be affixed to any order, summons or other process save under the authority in writing of the Registrar.

(5) The seal of the Tribunal shall not be affixed to any certified copy issued by the Tribunal save under the authority in writing of the Registrar.

(6) The Registrar of each Bench shall make out, every month a brief summary of the important decisions given by that Bench during the previous month and send it to the Registrar of the Principal Bench who shall after suitable editing, circulate it to all the Benches of the Tribunal in the country and to all Chief Claims Officers of Zonal Railways of their information.

38. Working hours of the Tribunal. Except on Saturdays, Sundays and other public holidays, the office of the Tribunal shall, subject to any order made by the Chairman, remain open from 9-30 a.m. to 6-00 p.m.

39. Sitting hours of the Tribunal. The sitting hours of the Tribunal shall ordinarily be from 10.30 a.m. to 1.30 p.m. and 2.30 p.m. to 4.30 p.m. subject to any general or special order made by the Chairman or by Vice-Chairman or Member concerned with the prior approval of the Chairman.

40. Seal and emblem. The official seal and the emblem of the Tribunal shall be such as the Central Government specify.

41. [6][***]

[7][**42. Headquarters of the Tribunal.** The Tribunal shall have its Headquarters at Delhi and have four administrative zones with their Headquarters as mentioned in Schedule I and Schedule I(A) to sub-rule (1) of rule 3.

(2) The presiding officers and administrative head of administrative zones shall exercise such administrative powers as delegated by chairman and will act under directions, control and supervision of chairman].

43. Preservation of record. All necessary documents and records relating to applications dealt with by the Tribunal shall be kept in a record room and shall be preserved for a period of three years after the passing of the final order.

44. Inherent powers of the Tribunal. Nothing in these rules shall be deemed to limit or otherwise affect the inherent powers of the Tribunal to make such orders as may be necessary for the end of justice or to prevent abuse of the process of the Tribunal.

6 Rule 41 *omitted* by G.S.R. 719(E), dated 15.10.1999 (w.e.f. 26.10.1999).

7 *Substituted* by G.S.R. 167(E), dated 29.2.2000 (w.e.f. 29.2.2000).

[8][**45. Monthly progress report of Tribunal.** The Tribunal shall furnish every month to the Central Government in Form XIV, the information with regard to institution, disposal and pendency of claims cases, accident cases and other information relating to the functioning of the Tribunal and its Benches.

46. Maintenance of order sheets. The Registrar shall attach to every application an order sheet in duplicate in Form XV.

47. Maintenance of Court Diary. The Court Master shall maintain a court diary in Form XVI for recording the proceedings of the Tribunal for each working day with respect to all applications listed in the daily cause list.

48. Preparation and publication of daily cause list. The Court Master shall on each working day prepare for the next working day, the cause list in Form XVII and fix a copy of the same on the Notice Board of the Tribunal.

49. Retention, preservation and destruction of records. (1) The Record Keeper shall be responsible for the records consigned to the Record Room. He shall scrutinize the records received by him within three days and prepare an index.

(2) If on scrutiny, any deficiency is found in the records, the Record Keeper shall return the records back to the concerned Branch or Section.

(3) On the expiry of the period for preservation of the records prescribed under rule 43, the Registrar shall weed out the record].

FORM I

[*See* Rule 5 of the Railway Claims
Tribunal (Procedure) Rules, 1989]

Application under section 16 of the Act in respect of claims for compensation for loss; destruction, damage, deterioration or non-delivery of animals or goods

PART I

Title of the case:

PART II

Index

Sl. No.	*Description of documents attached*	*Page No.*
1.	Application	
2.		
3.		
4.		
5.		
6.		

Signature of the Applicant

8 *Inserted* by the Railway Claims Tribunal (Procedure) Amendment Rules, 2002, *vide* G.S.R. 787(E) (w.e.f. 2.12.2002).

FOR USE IN TRIBUNAL'S OFFICE

Date of filing

or

Date of Receipt by post

Registration No.

Signature for Registrar

PART III

In The Railway Claims Tribunal

.... Bench

Between

A.B.

Applicant

And

C.D.

Respondent

1. Particulars of the applicant:

   Name and address:

2. Particulars of the respondent/respondents;

3. Value of Claim and details of application fee—

   (*i*) Value of claims

   (*ii*) Details of application fee:

4. (*i*) Name and address of the Bank on which the draft is drawn;

   (*ii*) Demand Draft No. and the Branch at which payable.

or

   (*i*) Number of Indian Postal Order(s)

   (*ii*) Name of issuing Post Office

   (*iii*) Date of issue of Postal Order(s)

   (*iv*) Post Office at which payable.

5. Full Booking particulars of the consignment—

Date of booking	*Railway Receipt or Parcel Way Bill*	*Station*		*Description of Consignment*	*Value of Consignment*	*Any other particulars*
		From	*To*			
1	2	3		4	5	6

6. Date on which notice served on the Railway Administration under section 78B of Indian Railways Act, 1890

   (Attach proof)

7. (*i*) Facts of the case:

   (Give here a concise statement of facts in a chronological order, each paragraph containing as nearly as possible, a separate issue, fact or otherwise).

   (*ii*) (*a*) Nature of relief sought; and

   (*b*) Grounds of relief.

8. Matters not previously filed or pending with any other court.

   (State whether the applicant had previously filed any claim, writ petition or suit regarding the matter in respect of which the present application has been made).

   In case the applicants had previously filed any claims, application, writ petition or suit, indicate the stage at which it is pending, and if decided, attach a certified copy of the order.

9. Jurisdiction of the Bench (indicate the facts on the basis of which the Bench to which application is made, has the jurisdiction).

10. List of enclosures:

    1. ....
    2. ....
    3. ....
    4. ....
    5. ....
    6. ....

Verification

I, ... (Name of the application) S/o, D/o, W/o, ... age .... resident of .... do hereby verify that the contents of paragraphs .... to .... are true to my personal knowledge, and paragraphs .... to .... are believed to be true to the best of my knowledge or the legal advice given to me, and that I have not suppressed any material fact.

Date:

Place:

Signature of the applicant

Full Address:

To

The Registrar,

Railway Claims Tribunal

....

....

FORM II

[*See* Rule 5 of the Railway Claims Tribunal (Procedure) Rules, 1989]

Application under section 16 of the Act in respect of claims for compensation arising out of accident to a train.

PART I

Title of the case:

PART II

Index

Sl. No.	*Description of documents attached*	*Page No.*
1.		
2.		
3.		
4.		
5.		
6.		

Signature of the Applicant

FOR USE IN TRIBUNAL'S OFFICE

Date of filing

or

Date of Receipt by post

Registration No.

Signature for Registrar

PART III

(*See* rule 5)

Application for compensation under section 16 of the Act in respect of claim for compensation for death, injury, etc., in a train accident

To

The Railway Claims Tribunal

....

....

I, ..., son/daughter/wife/widow of .... residing at .... having been injured [9][in accident to train or untoward incident] hereby apply for the grant of compensation for the injury sustained.

I, ..., son/daughter/wife/widow of .... residing at .... hereby apply as dependent for the grant of compensation

9 *Substituted* by G.S.R. 270(E), dated 8.7.1996.

on account of the death/injury sustained by Shri/Kumari/Shrimati .... son/daughter/wife/widow of Shri/Shrimati .... who died/was injured [10][in accident to train or untoward incident] referred to hereunder.

Necessary particulars in respect of the deceased/injured in the accident [10][or untoward incident] are given below:

1. Name and father's name of the person injured/dead (husband's name in the case of married woman or widow).
2. Full address of the person injured/dead.
3. Age of the person injured/dead.
4. Occupation of the person injured/dead.
5. Name and address of the employer of the deceased, if any.
6. (*a*) Brief particulars of the accident indicating the date and place of accident and the name of the train involved—

   [11][(*b*) Brief particulars of the untoward incident indicating the date and place of the untoward incident].
7. Class of travel, and [10][tickets/pass/platform ticket number], to the extent known ....
8. Nature of injuries sustained along with medical certificate.
9. Name and address of the Medical Officer/Practitioner, if any, who attended on the injured/dead and period of treatment ....
10. Disability for work, if any, caused.
11. Details of the loss of any luggage on account of the accident [12][to the train] ....
12. Has any claim been lodged with any other authority? If so, particulars thereof ....
13. Name and permanent address of the applicant ....

[13]13A. (*i*) Bank Account Number of the claimant ....

(*ii*) Name of the Bank and Branch ....

(*iii*) Type of Account ....

14. Local address of the applicant, if any ....
15. Relationship with the deceased/injured ....
16. Amount of compensation claimed ....
17. Where the application is not made within one year of the occurrence of the accident, [12][to the train or untoward incident] the grounds thereof ....
18. Any other information or documentary evidence that may be necessary or helpful in the disposal of the claim ....
19. Mention the documents, if any, filed along with application.

10 *Substituted* by G.S.R. 270(E), dated 8.7.1996.
11 *Inserted* by G.S.R. 270(E), dated 8.7.1996.
12 *Substituted* by G.S.R. 270(E), dated 8.7.1996.
13 *Inserted* by G.S.R. 96(E), dated 22.2.2010.

I, ... solemnly declare that ....

(*a*) the particulars given above are true and correct to the best of my knowledge and

(*b*) I have not claimed or obtained any compensation in relation to the [14][injury/death/loss of luggage] which is the subject-matter of this application.

Date ....

Place ....

Signature or left thumb-impression of the applicant

Name of witness and his address in case Left Thumb Impression is put by applicant.

Verification

I, ... (Name of the applicant) S/o, D/o, W/o, ... age .... resident of .... do hereby verify that the contents of paragraphs .... to .... are true to my personal knowledge, and paragraphs .... to .... are believed to be true to the best of my knowledge or the legal advice given to me, and that I have not suppressed any material fact.

Date:

Place:

Signature of the applicant

Full address

To

The Registrar,

Railway Claims Tribunal

....

FORM III

[*See* Rule 5 of the Railway Claims Tribunal (Procedure) Rules, 1989]

Application under section 16 of the Act in respect of claims for refund of freight or part thereof or for refund of any freight paid in respect of animals or goods entrusted to a railway administration to be carried by railway.

PART I

Title of the case

PART II

Index

Sl. No.	*Description of documents attached*	*Page No.*
1.		
2.		
3.		
4.		
5.		
6.		

Signature of the Applicant

14 *Substituted* by G.S.R. 270(E), dated 8.7.1996.

For use in Tribunal's Office
Date of filing
or
Date of Receipt by post
Registration No.
Signature for Registrar

PART III

In the railway claims tribunal

.... Bench

Between

A.B.

Applicant

And

C.D. Respondent

1. Particulars of the applicant:
   Name and address:
2. Particulars of the respondent/respondents
3. Value of claim and details of application fee—
   (*i*) Value of claims
   (*ii*) Details of Application Fee
4. Particulars of Bank Draft/Postal Order in respect of Application Fee:
   (*i*) Name and address of the Bank on which the Draft is drawn;
   (*ii*) Demand Draft No. and the Branch at which payable

   or

   (*i*) Number of Indian Postal Order(s)
   (*ii*) Name of issuing Post Office
   (*iii*) Date of issue of Postal Order(s)
   (*iv*) Post Office at which payable.
5. Full Particulars of payment of fare/freight.
   (*i*) Claim for refund of freight.

Date of Booking	*Railway Receipt or Parcel Way Bill*	*Station* *From* *To*	*Description of consignment*
1	2	3	4

Freight paid	*Amount Refund of Claims*	*Money Receipt / Credit Note or other payment particulars*
5	6	7

(*ii*) Claim for refund of fare.

Date of journey	*Train No.*	*Class of travel*	*Class actually travelled*
1	2	3	4

Ticket or Ticket Deposit Receipt / Excess Fare Ticket etc., Guards or Conductors, Certificate	*Fair Paid Rs.*	*Refund Claimed Rs.*
5	6	7

6. Date on which notice served on the Railway Administration under section 78B of Indian Railways Act, 1890 (in respect of claims for refund of freight)—attach proof.

7. (*i*) Facts of the case:

   (Give here a concise statement of facts in a chronological order, each paragraph containing as nearly as possible, a separate issue, fact or otherwise).

   (*ii*) (*a*) Nature of relief sought; and

   (*b*) Grounds of relief.

8. Matters not previously filed or pending with any other court.

   (State whether the applicant had previously filed any claim, writ petition or suit regarding the matter in respect of which the present application has been made).

   In case the applicants had previously filed any claims, application, writ petition or suit, indicate the stage at which it is pending, and if decided, attach a certified copy of the Order.

9. Jurisdiction of the Bench (indicate the facts on the basis of which the Bench to which application is made, has the jurisdiction).

10. List of enclosures:

1.
2.
3.
4.
5.

Verification

I, ... (Name of the applicant) S/o, D/o, W/o, ... age .... resident of .... do hereby verify that the contents of paragraphs .... to .... are true to my personal knowledge, and paragraphs .... to .... are believed to be true to the best of my knowledge or the legal advice given to me, and that I have not suppressed any material fact.

Date: Signature of the applicant

Place: Full Address:

To
The Registrar,
Railway Claims Tribunal
.... Bench
....

FORM IV

[*See* sub-rule (5) of Rule 5 of the Railway Claims Tribunal (Procedure) Rules, 1989]

Receipt Slip No. ....

Received an application filed before the .... Bench of the Railway Claims Tribunal on .... by Shri/Kumari/Smt. ....

For the Registrar of the
.... Bench of the
Railway Claims Tribunal

Date ....
Seal ....

FORM V

[*See* Rule 36]

Application for the registration of a clerk

1. Name of legal practitioner on whose behalf the clerk is to be registered.
2. Particulars of the Clerk to be registered:

(*i*) Full Name:
(in capital)

(*ii*) Father's name:

(*iii*) Age and Date of Birth:

(*iv*) Place of Birth:

(*v*) Nationality:

(*vi*) Educational qualifications:

(*vii*) Particulars of previous employment, if any.

Attested passport size photograph to be pasted

I, ... (Clerk above named) do hereby affirm that the particulars relating to me given above are true.

Signature of Clerk

3. Whether the legal practitioner has a Clerk already registered in his employment and whether the Clerk sought to be registered is in lieu of or in addition to the Clerk already registered.
4. Whether the Clerk sought to be registered or is already registered as a Clerk of any other legal practitioner and if so, the name of such practitioner.

I, ... (legal practitioner) certify that the particulars given above are true to the best of my information and belief and that I am not aware of any fact which would render unsuitable the registration of the said .... (name) as a Clerk. Further, I enclose Postal Order for ₹5.00 being the cost of Identity Card along with 2 passport size photographs of the applicant duly attested by me.

Signature of the Legal Practitioner

Date: Full Address:

To
The Registrar,
Railway Claims Tribunal,
....
.... Bench

[15]FORM VI

[*See* Rule 11A]

Form of Cash Register

Sr. No.	*Case number*	*Indian postal order or demand draft number*	*Amount of Indian postal order or demand draft*	*Amount received in cash*	*Date of receipt*	*Signature of Receipt Clerk*	*Date of remittance to Cash Section*	*Signature of Cash Section*
1	2	3	4	5	6	7	8	9

FORM VII

[*See* Rule 12]

Notice to the Opposite Party

O.A. No. ....

....

Applicant(s)

Versus

Union of India through General Manager
.... Railway
.... Respondent(s)

To

....

....

Whereas the above noted applicant has filed an application claiming compensation against you and the said application has been listed for hearing in this Tribunal on .... at 10.30 a.m.

You are hereby summoned to appear in this Tribunal in person or through a legal practitioner duly authorised, who is able to answer all material questions relating to the application, and you are hereby further directed to file on that day a reply in your defence and to produce all documents in your possession or power upon which you base your defence.

Take notice that, in default of your appearance on the day mentioned above, the application will be heard and determined in your absence.

Given under my hand and seal of the Tribunal, this .... day of ....

Registrar

15 *Inserted* by the Railway Claims Tribunal (Procedure) Amendment Rules, 2002, *vide* G.S.R. 787(E) (w.e.f. 2.12.2002).

FORM VIII

[*See* Rule 14]

Form of Affidavit

Before the Railway Claims Tribunal .... Bench

Original Application No. ....

Title ....

Affidavit of .... son of/daughter of/wife of .... aged .... years .... occupation .... resident of ....

I, the above named do hereby solemnly affirm and declare as under:

(State all relevant facts of first person in paragraphs numbered consecutively).

Place:
Date:

Deponent

Verification

I ....(the above named) further declare that para No. .... to .... are true and correct to my personal knowledge and para No. .... to .... are true and correct on the basis of information derived from available records and para No. .... to .... are believed to be true on the legal advice received from my legal practitioner. No part of it is false and nothing relevant has been concealed therein.

Place:

Date:

Deponent

NOTES: 1. Affidavit shall be affirmed before a Judicial Officer; or a Magistrate; or Registrar, or Additional Registrar, or Assistant Registrar of the Tribunal; or a Notary; or Oath Commissioner or an Advocate.

2. The attestor shall make an endorsement on the documents annexed in the affidavit under his signatures.

FORM IX

[*See* Rule 31B]

Application for Execution of Order

PART I

Title ....

PART II

Sr. No.	*Description of document attached*	*Page No.*
1.		
2.		
3.		
4.		

Signature of applicant

For use in Registrar office
Date of filing ....
or
Date of receipt by post ....
Signature of Registrar

PART III

Before the Railway Claims Tribunal .... Bench
Execution application of ....
in
Original application No. ....

.... Applicant(s)

Versus

.... Respondent(s)

1. Particulars of applicant(s).
2. Particulars of respondent(s).
3. Date of pronouncement of order.
4. Whether any appeal preferred against the order or not ....
5. Orders, if any passed in appeal ....
6. Payment/adjustment made, if any.
7. Review application, if any, filed and result thereof.
8. Previous execution, if any, filed.
9. Amount and interest allowed by the Tribunal.
10. Amount and interest due upon the order or other relief granted thereby.
11. Costs, if any, awarded by order.
12. Against which zonal railway administration to be executed.
13. Mode in which the assistance of the Tribunal is required.
14. List of enclosures.

Applicant

Verification

I ...., do hereby declare that the contents of paragraph Nos. 1 to 14 of the application are true and correct to the best of my knowledge and brief.

Signed at .... this .... day of ....

Applicant

FORM X

[*See* Rule 31C]

Notice to Respondent about the Date Fixed for Hearing in Execution Application

Execution Application No. .... in

Original Application No. ....

.... Applicant(s)

Versus

Union of India through General Manager

....

Railway .... Respondent(s)

To

....

....

....

Whereas the applicant mentioned above has made an application to this Tribunal for execution of orders passed in Original Application/Transferred Application No. .... on the allegations that the said order has not been complied with so far. You are hereby directed to appear before the Tribunal either in person or through a legal practitioner duly appointed for the purpose on .... day of .... at .... to show cause why execution should not be granted.

Take notice that in default of your appearance on the date fixed the execution application will be heard and decided *ex parte*.

Given under by hand and seal this .... day of ....

Seal

Registrar

FORM XI

[*See* Rule 31C]

Warrant of Attachment of Movable Property in Execution of Order of the Tribunal

Execution Application No. .... in

Original Application No. ....

.... Applicant(s)

Versus

Union of India through General Manager

.... Railway

.... Respondent(s)

To
Bailiff of Court ....
....
....

Whereas General Manager .... Railway .... was ordered by this Tribunal vide orders dated .... in O.A. No. ...., to pay to the applicant the sum of ₹ .... as detailed hereunder and whereas the said sum of ₹ .... has not been paid.

Detail of Awarded amount

Principal	....
Interest	....
Costs	....
Costs of execution	....
Farther interest	....
Total	....

These are to command you to attach the movable property of the said .... as set forth in the Schedule hereunto annexed and unless the said .... shall pay to you through Cheque the said sum of ₹ .... together with ₹ ...., the costs of this attachment, to hold the same until further orders from this Tribunal.

You are further commanded to return this warrant on or before .... day of .... with an endorsement certifying the day on which and the manner in which it has been executed or why it has not been executed.

Given under my hand and seal this .... day of ....

Registrar

FORM XII

[*See* Rule 31C]

Warrant to Recover Payment in Execution of an Order

Execution Application No. .... in case No. ....
Original Application No. ....

.... Applicant(s)

Versus

Union of India through General Manager
.... Railway
.... Respondent(s)

To

.... Bank

....

....

Whereas General Manager .... Railway .... was ordered by this Tribunal *vide* orders dated .... in case No. ...., to pay to the applicant the sum of ₹ .... as detailed hereunder and whereas the said sum of ₹ .... has not been paid.

Detail of Awarded amount

Principal	....
Interest	....
Costs	....
Costs of execution	....
Farther interest	....
Total	....

You are hereby directed to seize the said account of respondent maintained in your branch to the extent of ₹ .... and further to remit the said amount of ₹ .... through Cheque to this Tribunal to satisfy the orders.

You are further commanded to return this warrant on or before .... day of .... with an endorsement certifying the day on which and manner in which it has been executed or why it has not been executed.

Given under my hand and seal this .... day of ....

Registrar

FORM XIII

[*See* Rule 36]

Identity Card. No. ....

Shri ....

S/o/ D/o/ W/o Shri ....

.... Applicant

Address .... has been registered as a clerk of Shri .... legal practitioner, Address ....

Photograph of the applicant

Identity Card is valid upto ....

Specimen signature of the Registered Clerk ....

Specimen signature of the legal practitioner ....

Seal of the Tribunal

Dated: Registrar

FORM XIV

[*See* Rule 37]

PART I

Institution and disposal of
Total Cases of the Tribunal during the month of ....

Bench	*Opening Balance*			*Receipts*		
	Original Application	*Transferred Application*	*Total*	*Original Application*	*Transferred Application*	*Total*

Disposal			*Closing Balance*		
Original Application	*Transferred Application*	*Total*	*Original Application*	*Transferred Application*	*Total*

PART II

Institution and disposal of
Railway Accident Cases for the month of ....

Bench	*Opening Balance*			*Receipts*		
	Original Application	*Transferred Application*	*Total*	*Original Application*	*Transferred Application*	*Total*

Disposal			*Closing Balance*		
Original Application	*Transferred Application*	*Total*	*Original Application*	*Transferred Application*	*Total*

PART III

Institution and disposal of
Untoward Incidents Cases for the month of ....

Bench	*Opening Balance*			*Receipts*		
	Original Application	*Transferred Application*	*Total*	*Original Application*	*Transferred Application*	*Total*

Disposal			*Closing Balance*		
Original Application	*Transferred Application*	*Total*	*Original Application*	*Transferred Application*	*Total*

FORM XV
[*See* Rule 46]

Order Sheet

Nature of application .... Number .... Year ....
.... *Versus* ....

Date	*Proceedings of the Bench*	*Notes of Registrar*

FORM XVI
[*See* Rule 47]

Railway Claims Tribunal .... Bench

Sr. No.	*Application number*	*Names of the parties*	*Name of Applicants legal practitioner*	*Name of respondents legal practitioner*	*Purpose for hearing*	*Previous date of hearing*	*Next date of hearing*	*Remarks*

FORM XVII
[*See* Rule 48]

Cause list of Railway Claims Tribunal .... Bench number .... of dated ....

Sl. No.	*Application number*	*Names of the applicant*	*Name of the respondent*	*Applicant's legal practitioner*	*Respondent's legal Practitioner*	*Purpose of hearing*	*Remarks*
1	2	3	4	5	6	7	8

[16]SCHEDULE I
(*See* Rule 3)

Sl. No	*Headquarters of the Bench of the Railway Claims Tribunal*	*Territorial jurisdiction of the Bench*
(1)	(2)	(3)
1.	Ahmedabad	Gujarat, Union Territory of Diu.
2.	Bangalore	Karnataka.
3.	Bhopal	Madhya Pradesh and Chattisgarh.
4.	Bhubaneswar	Orissa.

16 *Substituted* by the Railway Claims Tribunal (Procedure) Amendment Rules, 2002, *vide* G.S.R. 787(E) (w.e.f. 2.12.2002).

SCHEDULE I—*continued*

Sl. No	*Headquarters of the Bench of the Railway Claims Tribunal*	*Territorial jurisdiction of the Bench*
(1)	(2)	(3)
5.	Bombay	(*i*) Districts of Bombay, Thane, Raigad, Pune, Nasik, Ahmednagar, Satara, Ratnagiri, Sindhudurg, Kolhapur, Sangli, Solapur, Dhule, Aurangabad, Beed of Maharashtra. (*ii*) Union Territories of Dadra and Nagar Haveli. (*iii*) Goa.
6.	Nagpur	All districts of Maharashtra except those included in item (*i*) of column (3) against serial number 5.
7.	Chandigarh	Punjab, Haryana, Himachal Pradesh, Jammu and Kashmir and Union Territory of Chandigarh.
[17]8.	Calcutta (2)	West Bengal, Union Territory of Andaman and Nicobar Islands.
9.	Guwahati	Assam, Sikkim, Mizoram, Arunachal Pradesh, Tripura, Manipur, Meghalaya, Nagaland.
10.	Ernakulam	Kerala, Union Territory of Lakshadweep.
11.	Gorakhpur	[18][Districts of Gorakhpur, Deoria, Azamgarh Mau, Basti, Sidharthnagar, Robertsganj, Jaunpur, Faizabad, Gonda, Varanasi, Maharaj Ganj, Kushinagar, Sant Kabir Nagar, Chanduli, Sant Ravi Das Nagar, Balrampur and Ambedkar Nagar of Uttar Pradesh].
12.	Ghaziabad	[19][Districts of Agra, Bulandshahr, Moradabad, Bijnore, Mathura, Ghaziabad, Meerut, Aligarh, and Saharanpur Jyoitiba Phule Nagar (Amroha), Baghpat, Etah, Firozabad, Gautam Budh Nagar (Noida), Maha Maya Nagar (Hathras), Muzaffar Nagar, Rampur, Pilibhit and Mainpuri of the State of Uttar Pradesh and Districts of Haridwar and Dehradum of the State of Uttaranchal].
12A.	Lucknow	[20][All Districts of Uttar Pradesh and Uttaranchal except those included in column (3) against serial numbers 11 and 12].

17 *Substituted* by G.S.R. 498(E), dated 23.8.2006 (w.e.f. 1.10.2006).
18 *Substituted* by G.S.R. 283(E), dated 11.4.2007 (w.e.f. 11.4.2007).
19 *Substituted* by G.S.R. 66(E), dated 15.2.2006 (w.e.f. 16.2.2006).
20 *Substituted* by G.S.R. 384(E), dated 22.10.2003 (w.e.f. 1.11.2003).

SCHEDULE I—*continued*

Sl. No	*Headquarters of the Bench of the Railway Claims Tribunal*	*Territorial jurisdiction of the Bench*
(1)	(2)	(3)
13.	Jaipur	Rajasthan.
14.	New Delhi (2)	Union Territory of Delhi.
[21][15.	Patna	Bihar.
15A	Ranchi	Jharkhand].
16.	[22][Chennai]	Tamil Nadu and Union Territory of Pondicherry.
[23][17.	Secunderabad	Andhra Pradesh and Telangana].

[24]SCHEDULE I(A)

[*See* Rule 3(1)]

Sl. No.	*Zone*	*Administrative Head*	*Headquarter*	*Benches*
(1)	(2)	(3)	(4)	(5)
1.	North Zone	Vice-Chairman (Technical)	Delhi	Delhi, Chandigarh, Ghaziabad, Gorakhpur, Lucknow,
2.	East Zone	Vice-Chairman (Technical)	Calcutta	Calcutta, Bhubaneshwar, Guwahati, Patna
3.	South Zone	Vice-Chairman (Judicial)	Chennai	Chennai, Bangalore, Ernakulam, Secundrabad
4.	West Zone	Vice-Chairman (Judicial)	Mumbai	Mumbai, Ahmedabad, Bhopal, Jaipur, Nagpur.

NOTE. Whenever the Chairman Railway Claims Tribunal happens to be from Technical side, North Zonal Headquarter at Delhi Shall be presided by Vice-Chairman (Judicial) and *vice-versa*].

21 *Substituted* by G.S.R. 498(E), dated 23.8.2006 (w.e.f. 1.10.2006).
22 *Substituted* by G.S.R. 283(E), dated 11.4.2007 (w.e.f. 11.4.2007).
23 *Substituted* by G.S.R. 711(E), dated 17.9.2015 (w.e.f. 17.9.2015).
24 *Substituted* by G.S.R. 167(E), dated 29.2.2000 (w.e.f. 29.2.2000).

[25][SCHEDULE II

APPLICATION FEE

(*See* Rule 6)

Every application under sub-section (1) of section 14 of the Railway Claims Tribunal Act, 1987 shall be accompanied by fee in respect of filing of such application at the following rates:

		Application fee payable
1	2	3
(*i*)	Where the value of claim exceeds rupees 1 but does not exceed rupees 100.	Rupees 10.00.
(*ii*)	Where the value of the claim exceeds rupees 100 but does not exceed rupees 500.	Rupees 10.00 plus 9 per cent on the amount exceeding rupees 100.
(*iii*)	Where the value of the claim exceeds rupees 500 but does not exceed rupees 1,000.	Rupees 46 plus 8 per cent on the amount exceeding rupees 500.
(*iv*)	Where the value of the claim exceeds rupees 1,000 but does not exceed rupees 5,000.	Rupees 86 plus 7 per cent on the amount exceeding rupees 1,000.
(*v*)	Where the value of claim exceeds rupees 5,000 but does not exceed rupees 20,000.	Rupees 366 plus 6 per cent on the amount exceeding rupees 5,000.
(*vi*)	Where the value of claim exceeds rupees 20,000 but does not exceed rupees 30,000.	Rupees 1,266 plus 5 per cent on the amount exceeding rupees 20,000.
(*vii*)	Where the value of claim exceeds rupees 30,000 but does not exceed rupees 40,000.	Rupees 1,766 plus 4 per cent on the amount exceeding rupees 30,000.
(*viii*)	Where the value of claim exceeds rupees 40,000 but does not exceed rupees 50,000.	Rupees 2,166 plus 3 per cent on the amount exceeding rupees 40,000.
(*ix*)	Where the value of claim exceeds rupees 50,000.	Rupees 2,466 plus 1 per cent on the amount exceeding rupees 50,000 upto rupees one lakh.
(*x*)	Where the value of claim exceeds rupees one lakh.	Rupees 2,966 plus one half per cent on the amount exceeding rupees one lakh.

25 *Substituted* by the Railway Claims Tribunal (Procedure) Amendment Rules, 2002, vide G.S.R. 787(E) (w.e.f. 2.12.2002).

APPENDIX 3

The Railway Property (Unlawful Possession) Act, 1966

(Act No. 29 of 1966)

An Act to consolidate and amend the law relating to unlawful possession of railway property.

Objects of the Act With the increase in quantum of goods traffic on the railways the incidence of theft and pilferage has been increasing every year. This is evident from the fact that the claims were ₹29 millions in 1953-54 and ₹42 millions in 1963-64. Thus, there was an amendment in the Indian Railways Act in 1961. There was also the Railway Stores (Unlawful Possession) Act 1955 which was applicable as offence to unlawful possession of Railway Property owned by the railway and not to offence relating to goods and parcels entrusted to railway for transport. Such offences were tried under the Code of Criminal Procedure 1898. The jurisdiction of State Police being restricted to State boundary only, it became difficult for the police to make a thorough and fruitful investigation into offences relating to railway working. The Railway Protection Force are not also well equipped with requisite powers of investigation and prosecution. It was, therefore proposed to replace the Railway Stores (Unlawful Possession) Act 1955 and to deal with powers of investigation and prosecution of offences relating to railway property, the Railway Property (Unlawful Possession) Act 1966 was passed. This Act is intended to consolidate and amend the law relating to unlawful possession of railway property.[1]

Be it enacted by Parliament in the Seventeenth Year of the Republic of India as follows:

1. Short title, extent and commencement. (1) This Act may be called the Railway Property (Unlawful Possession) Act, 1966.

(2) It extends to the whole of India.

1 *See* Statement of Objects and Reasons Gazette of India, dated 1-8-1966, Pt. II, s. 2, Ext. p. 422 and Preamble to the Act.

(3) It shall come into force on such date as the Central Government may, by notification in the Official Gazette, appoint.

2. Definitions. In this Act, unless the context otherwise requires,—

(*a*) "force" means the Railway Protection Force constituted under section 3 of the Railway Protection Force Act, 1957;

(*b*) "member of the Force" means a person appointed to the Force, other than a superior officer;

(*c*) "officer of the Force" means an officer of and above the rank of Assistant Sub-Inspector appointed to the Force and includes a superior officer;

(*d*) "railway property" includes any goods, money or valuable security or animal, belonging to, or in the charge or possession of, a railway administration;

(*e*) "superior officer" means any of the officers appointed under section 4 of the Railway Protection Force Act, 1957, and includes any other officer appointed by the Central Government as a superior officer of the Force;

(*f*) words and expressions used but not defined in this Act and defined in the Indian Railways Act, 1890, shall have the meanings respectively assigned to them under that Act.

Member of the Force In absence of officer-in-charge Head Rakshak is competent to register a case at an out post.[2]

Officer of the Force A Sub-Inspector of Railway Protection Force is an officer. He is not, however, an officer-in-charge of police station under s. 173, CrPC.[3] Assistant Sub-Inspectors, Railway Protection Force is an officer of the Force.[4]

Railway property Mere possession of articles manufactured by a private concern for the use of railway administration cannot be regarded as railway property as defined in s. 2(*d*) of the 1966 Act.[5] The meaning of "railway property" as defined in s. 2(*d*) of the 1966 Act is wider than "railway stores" as defined in the repealed 1956 Act. Under the new Act mere unlawful possession is an offence. No proof that the material is for use in construction or maintenance of the railway is necessary.[6] Railway property includes property not only owned by railway in its charge or possession.[7] Goods in transit are railway property.[8] Plates in railway stores in serviceable condition are railway property.[9] Where dynamo belts were not manufactured by the railways but were purchased by the railways under an agreement from private manufacturers, the dynamo belts were not railway properties.[10]

2 *State of Rajasthan* v *Jagdish* 1983 CrLJ (NOC) 100 (Raj).
3 *State of Gujarat* v *Abdul Rehman* 1972 CrLJ 1101.
4 *State of Rajasthan* v *Jagdish* 1983 CrLJ (NOC) 100 (Raj).
5 *Umarkhan* v *State* 1973 CrLJ 1706.
6 *State of UP* v *Ram Dass* 1976 CrLJ 1401.
7 *Birbal* v *State* 1980 CrLJ (NOC) 96 (All).
8 *Bishambhar* v *State of Bihar* 1979 CrLJ (NOC) 197 (Pat).
9 *Gopal Thakur* v *State of Bihar* 1975 CrLJ 122 (Pat).
10 *State of UP* v *Suresh* 1996 CrLJ 3970.

[11]**3. Penalty for theft, dishonest misappropriation or unlawful possession of railway property.** [12]Whoever commits theft, or dishonesty misappropriates or is found, or is proved to have been, in possession of any railway property reasonably suspected of having been stolen or unlawful obtained shall, unless he proves that the railway property came into his possession lawfully, be punishable—

(*a*) for the first offence, with imprisonment for a term which may extend to five years, or with fine, or with both and in the absence of special and adequate reasons to be mentioned in the judgment of the court, such imprisonment shall not be less than one year and such fine shall not be less than one thousand rupees;

(*b*) for the second or a subsequent offence, with imprisonment for a term which may extend to five years and also with fine and in the absence of special and adequate reasons to be mentioned in the judgment of the court, such imprisonment shall not be less than two years and such fine shall not be less than two thousand rupees.

[13]*Explanation*. For the purposes of this section "theft" and "dishonest misappropriation" shall have the same meanings as assigned to them respectively in section 378 and section 403 of the Indian Penal Code.

Scope The essential requirements of s. 3 are that (*i*) the property in question should be railway property; (*ii*) it should be reasonably suspected of having been stolen or unlawfully obtained, and (*iii*) it should be found or proved the accused was or had been in possession of that property.[14] In proceedings under s. 3 of the (old) Railways Act, the provisions of s. 20(3) of the Railway Protection Force Act can be invalid.[15] Where a Rakshak in Railway Protection Force was found in possession of railway property and was awarded sentence of three months, simple imprisonment, order of dismissal from service passed against him on the basis of such conviction would not be illegal.[16] An accused committing offence under this Act can be given benefit under s. 95, IPC.[17] State and its functionaries are not allowed to move the court in revision against an order passed in proceedings relating to offences punishable under this Act.[18] The fact that no report of theft from the railway yard was made is not a ground for holding that the accused came into possession of the articles by lawful means.[19] No proof but reasonable suspicion that property recovered from the accused having been stolen or unlawfully obtained by him is sufficient.[20]

Constitutional validity of s. 3 Section 3 of the 1966 Act is not hit by Art. 14 of the Constitution as no discrimination is made between two persons

11 *Substituted* by Act 25 of 2012.
12 *Substituted* by Act 25 of 2012.
13 *Inserted* by Act 25 of 2012.
14 *State of Maharashtra* v *V.T. Umale* AIR 1979 SC 1825; (1980)1 SCR 190; (1979)4 SCC 23.
15 *Parmjit* v *Dhaneshwar Sah* 1976 CrLJ 1131.
16 *Umesh Prasad Singh* v *Union of India* 1997 Lab IC 2498.
17 *State of MP* v *Mahadeo* 1972 CrLJ 1097.
18 *State of West Bengal* v *Rupa Shaw* (1995)1 CHN 83.
19 *The Public Prosecutor* v *Shaik Galob* 1975 CrLJ 952.
20 *Mahabook Batcha* v *State* 1992 CrLJ 3050 (Mad).

found in unlawful possession of railway property.[21] A case under s. 3(*a*) of the Act was taken cognizance of by the Magistrate on a complaint by Sub-Inspector, Railway Protection Force and not on a police report under s. 173, CrPC. The inquiry by the Assistant Sub-Inspector is not investigation under CrPC. The Act is a special Act creating offence and prescribing special procedure for inquiry and prosecution. Thus, Art. 14 of the Constitution is not attracted.[22]

Railway property Finding that property belongs to railway and it is recovered from the possession of some unauthorised person is sufficient to sustain conviction.[23] Where there is a theft of railway property which is recovered from the accused, the inference as to ownership of such property can be drawn not merely from the possession thereof but also from the circumstances of possession. The accused can be convicted under s. 3 of the Act.[1] There should be clear proof of the fact that article in question is a railway property before the accused could be convicted under s. 3 of the Act.[2] Where there is no specific marking on seized articles although the accused admitted possession and purchase from an unidentified person, no knowledge can be imputed to accused that at the time of purchase he knew that it was railways property.[3] Where it was proved that the dynamo belt recovered from the accused was not manufactured by the railway authorities but it was purchased from private manufacturer and it was not proved by the prosecution that after having obtained the belt from private manufacturer it was fitted in a railway coach from where it was stolen. It was held that the acquittal of the accused was rightly recorded as two ingredients of s. 3 were missing, namely that dynamo belt was not proved to be railway property and that it was not proved to be stolen.[4] Absence of documentary evidence that recovered articles belonged to railways, probability is that the said articles are disposed articles of 60 years old. Thus, the accused is entitled to be acquitted by giving benefit of doubt.[5] Where the accused was found in possession of articles belonging to the railway which were never condemned or auctioned or were available in open market and where the accused confessed to the railway authority that he was a regular thief pilfering railway articles from the yard, the accused is liable to be convicted.[6] Non-production of one bag containing coal seized in court does not prove fatal for prosecution and consequently conviction is to be sustained.[7] Cement is common goods. By itself it cannot be said to be rail property. However, it can be proved to be railway property by proving other similar goods of similar make in possession and

21 *Kallu Ram* v *State of UP* 1975 CrLJ 160.
22 *R. Muthu* v *Assistant Sub-Inspector, RPF, Erose* 1983 CrLJ 1309.
23 *Ramshrishta Singh* v *State of Bihar* 1976 CrLJ 38.
1 *Ganesh* v *State* 1981 CrLJ 812.
2 *State by Public Prosecutor* v *Veerapillai* 1986 CrLJ 1132.
3 *State by Sub-Inspector* v *Subramanta Pillai* 1995 CrLJ 1600 (Mad).
4 *State of UP* v *Suresh* 1996 CrLJ 3970. See also *Ram Narain* v *State of UP* 1978 CrLJ (NOC) 218.
5 *Abdul Rashid* v *State of UP* 1991 CrLJ 3065.
6 *State* v *K. Subramaniam* 1986 CrLJ 1055.
7 *Sekh Gunny* v *State* 1989 CrLJ 1622 (Ori).

proving that there was shortage of one.[8] "Possession" in s. 3 may involve consciousness or knowledge of the existence of the article. It is physical *de facto* possession including a precarious one.[9] Possession includes not only actual possession but also "constructive possession."

Possession of railway contractor of railway property Stock of cement was found in the possession of railway contractor for completion of particular railway work. Thus, such possession cannot be said to be unlawful. It was, therefore, held that such possession would come within the purview of s. 3 of the Act.[10]

Procedure Offences under the 1966 Act are not cognizable.[11] Police instead of Railway Protection Force has power to investigate.[12] Investigation made by officer of Railway Protection Force into an offence of unlawful possession of railway property under s. 3 of the Act is not investigation under s. 161, CrPC and therefore the provisions of s. 173, CrPC do not apply and the accused is not entitled to copies of the statements of prosecution witnesses recorded during the enquiry by the Officer of the Railway Protection Force.[13] In view of the nature of the provisions of the Railway Property (Unlawful Possession) Act 1966 cases instituted thereunder are not on a police report but on a complaint attracting the provisions of s. 252 onwards of the CrPC 1898 making it ultimately unnecessary on the part of the prosecution to conform to the provisions of s. 173(4) of the said old Code and serve copies of documents and statements as enjoined therein upon the accused.[14] In respect of a prosecution instituted on a complaint by the RPF officer under s. 3(*a*) of the 1966 Act, the accused is not entitled to the benefit of s. 173(4), CrPC. However, in the interest of fair trial such copies should if so required be made available to the counsel of the accused.[15] The landlord of a shop from which the railway stolen property was recovered with the help of the landlord in absence of the tenant owner of the shop cannot be summoned and proceeded against without any reason assigned for the same. It was held that the trial court exercised its jurisdiction illegally.[16]

Anticipatory bail The offence under s. 3 of the 1966 Act is an offence punishable with imprisonment of five years, it is a non-bailable offence. Therefore, in case there is apprehension of arrest under s. 3 of the said Act, provisions of s. 438, CrPC will be applicable.[17] Persons apprehending arrest for offence under s. 3 of the 1966 Act are not precluded from seeking anticipatory bail under s. 438, CrPC.[18]

8 *State* v *Lajarus Bahal* 1992 CrLJ 152 (Ori).
9 *Bishambar* v *State of Bihar* 1979 CrLJ (NOC) 197.
10 *Ramu* v *Inspector, R.P.F. Post South Central Rly. Chittoor* 2002 CrLJ 3222 (AP).
11 *State of UP* v *Bhura* 1985 CrLJ 536.
12 *Mahabir Prasad* v *State of Bihar* 1975 CrLJ 1951.
13 *Behari Lal* v *State* 1978 CrLJ 247 (All).
14 *State* v *D. Surya Rao* AIR 1969 Cal 594; 1969 CrLJ 1480.
15 *Balukrishan* v *State of Maharashtra* 1975 CrLJ 1891; see *Bishambhar* v *State of Bihar* 1979 CrLJ (NOC) 197.
16 *Nabi Khan* v *State* 1984 CrLJ (NOC) 86 (Ori).
17 *Ganesh Chandra Saini* v *State* 1987 CrLJ 931.
18 *Ashraf* alias *Lal* v *Inspector of Police, RPF, Harihar* 1995 CrLJ 182.

Detention under MISA There was detention of the accused under the MISA for unlawful possession of railway property. According to the District Magistrate witnesses were afraid to depose against the detenue for fear of their lives. It was held that the case could not be dropped for the above reason, but the accused could not be detained under the MISA.[19]

Charge The accused was charged of stealing railway property which were not found in his possession. There were allegations and proofs that they had been in his possession. Thus, charge framed under s. 3 of the 1966 Act was held to be justified.[20]

Onus of proof Mere unlawful possession of the property of any railway administration is not an offence. The prosecution must prove that the articles were being actually used or were intended to be used in the construction, operation or maintenance of a railway.[21] Prosecution must prove beyond reasonable doubt that the property in possession of the accused is railway property for shifting of burden of proof on the accused embodied in s. 3 of the 1966 Act.[22] Where there is no material to hold that the property alleged to be in unlawful possession of the accused, was owned by or belonging to railway nor is there any material to hold that the property was entrusted to the railway for carriage or as carrier, conviction under s. 3 cannot be sustained.[23] The resumption of guilt under s. 3 cannot be rebutted till the accused proves that he obtained that property lawfully. The burden of proof on the accused in such a case can be discharged by him only by positive proof and not by merely offering a reasonable or probable explanation.[1]

Theft of railway property AC bearing plates and permanent way materials were recovered from godowns of accused persons. Onus is on the accused to prove that he came into lawful possession of such railway property. Such onus is not discharged by the accused persons. Plea of the accused that non-production of expert witness for cross-examination was serious enough to disprove the nature of the property as railway property was not tenable. The accused were liable to be convicted.[2]

No proof of theft of railway property Where the accused persons were alleged to have stolen railway property as railway employees, it is incumbent on the railway authority to prove the theft and also the accused as the railway employees. In absence of any such proof the conviction of the accused under s. 3(*a*) of the Act is not proper.[3]

Appreciation of evidence The order of RPF making inquiry in respect of an offence under s. 3 of the 1966 Act is not a "police officer" within the

19 *Srilal Shaw* v *State of West Bengal* AIR 1975 SC 393; 1975 CrLJ 423; (1975)2 SCR 913.
20 *State of Maharashtra* v *Vishwanath* AIR 1979 SC 1825; 1979 CrLJ 1193; (1980)1 SCR 190.
21 In re, *Muthusamy Odayar* 1972 CrLJ 795.
22 In re, *B. Mohan* 1987 CrLJ 1390; 1987 Mad LW (Cri) 202.
23 *Nishit Ranjan Bhatra* v *State of Assam* 1982 CrLJ 2253.
1 *State of UP* v *Bansraj Singh* 1974 CrLJ 1240.
2 *A.N. Pandey* v *Gopal Das* 2015 CrLJ (NOC) 223 (Cal).
3 *Sahdeo Ram* v *State of Bihar* 2002 CrLJ 1090 (Pat).

meaning of s. 25 of the Evidence Act and therefore any confessional or incriminating statement recorded by him in the course of inquiry under the 1966 Act cannot be excluded from evidence under the said section.[4] Alleged confession before the RPF officer at the inquiry which was denied was not sufficient to sustain conviction.[5] Recovered railway property was accessible to all. Contents of *panchanama* did not corroborate with other evidence. Confessional statement made in Marathi but was recorded in Hindi. There were material contradictions in evidence of recording officer. Offence was not established beyond reasonable doubt and as such the acquittal of the accused was confirmed.[6] Where from the seizure list it was not clear from whose possession each of the materials was seized, the proceedings under s. 3 of the 1966 Act is not maintainable.[7] Conviction of a railway servant under s. 3 of the Act can be based on circumstantial evidence.[8] Concurrent finding that the property is railway property and seized from possession of the accused persons. Confessional statement of the accused person was not obtained under duress conviction of the accused persons were proper[9] seized articles were recovered from the alleged lands of the accused. Witnesses to seizure turned hostile. Thus, the acquittal of the accused not perverse,[10] railway property was alleged to be found in the possession of the accused. No independent witness to support seized nor to support prosecution case. Accused was entitled to the benefit of doubt.[11]

Sentence Since theft of railway property has become much common, the sentence of one year cannot be said to be severe.[12] Clause (*a*) of s. 3 of the 1966 Act does not make it obligatory on the court to pass the sentence of imprisonment and also to impose fine. Awarding of any one of the sentences is permissible.[13] The marked difference between s. 3(*a*) and s. 3(*b*) of the 1966 Act is that the former gives discretion to the court either to impose imprisonment or fine or both, but in the latter case the court is obliged if the offence is proved to impose both imprisonment and fine.[14] Where the occurrence had taken place about eight years back a long lapse of time would be the circumstances justifying a lenient view.[15] Offence relating to railway property and "Railway" being covered by the Union List in Schedule VII of the constitution, State Government has no power to remit sentence.[16]

4 *Bal Kishan* v *State of Maharashtra* AIR 1981 SC 379; 1980 CrLJ 1424.
5 *State of Orissa* v *Kapildeo* 1983 CrLJ (NOC) 188 (Ori).
6 *Atar Singh* v *State* 1977 CrLJ 1464 (All).
7 *Gour Mohan Chowdhury* v *State of West Bengal* 1995 CrLJ 1214.
8 *Tara Chand* v *State* 1973 CrLJ 1098.
9 *Dayanidhi* v *State* 1995 CrLJ 1331.
10 *State* v *Radhakrishnan* 1993 CrLJ 1457.
11 *Gopal Behera* v *State of Orissa* 1995 CrLJ 3962 (Ori).
12 *Ramshrishta Singh* v *State of Bihar* 1976 CrLJ 38.
13 *State of UP* v *Bans Raj Singh* 1974 CrLJ 1240. See *Abdul Rashid* v *State of UP* 1991 CrLJ 3065.
14 *Public Prosecutor A.D. Hoghlourt* v *Patnana* 1995 CrLJ 1410.
15 *Mahaboob Batcha* v *State*1992 CrLJ 3050.
16 *Mahaboob Batcha* v *State* (supra).

Modification of sentence The petitioner was caught red handed for theft of railway property. The petitioner was sentenced of one year rigorous imprisonment by the trial court after lapse of more than eleven years in trial. The sentence was modified on appeal to the term of three months rigorous imprisonment with fine of ₹1,000.[17]

Release on probation It is open to the court while trying a person and convicting him of an offence under s. 3 of the 1966 Act to release him under s. 4(1) of the Probation of the Offenders Act with minimum sentence of imprisonment and fine.[18] Accused aged 45 years was convicted under s. 3 of the 1966 Act. He cannot be given the benefit of s. 3 of UP First Offenders, Probation Act.[19]

Theft railway property A truck was found to be loaded with cast iron Grade I. Accused was present near the truck. On being asked to unload stolen iron he got it unloaded through his labourers. The plea of the accused that he was only a labourer. It was held that the accused was in unlawful possession of cast iron Grade I. Thus, conviction under s. 3 of the Railway Property (Unlawful Possession) Act 1966 was justified.[20]

[21]**4. Punishment for abetment, conspiracy or connivance at offences.** [22]Whoever abets or conspires in the commission of an offence punishable under this Act, or any owner or occupier of land or building, or any agent of such owner or occupier incharge of the management of that land or building, who wilfully connives at an offence against the provisions of this Act, shall be punishable with imprisonment for a term which may extend to five years, or with fine, or with both.

[23]*Explanation.* For the purposes of this section, the words "abet" and "conspire" shall have the same meanings as assigned to them respectively in sections 107 and 120A of the Indian Penal Code (45 of 1860).

Scope Section 4 deals with punishment for connivance at offences. Where many employees of the railways and other personnel were accused in the case on the premise that during the enquiry their complicity was radiantly revealing inasmuch as they conspired together to permit or assist the unlawful removal of the railway property and for this purpose it appeared that a number of witnesses have been cited and were to be produced to establish the guilt of the applicants, the High Court declined to quash the first information report and the inquiry report under its inherent powers.

5. Offences under the Act not to be cognizable. Notwithstanding anything contained in the Code of Criminal Procedure, 1898, an offence under this Act, shall not be cognizable.

Non-cognizable offence Assistant Sub-Inspector, Railway Protection Force is an officer of the Force. He is fully competent to investigate an offence

17 *Hemanta Kumar Parida* v *State of Orissa* 2003 CrLJ 2206 (Ori).
18 *State* v *Rathinavelu* 1973 CrLJ 354.
19 *Behari Lal* v *State* 1978 CrLJ 247.
20 *Om Prakash* v *State of UP* AIR 2008 SC 1112.
21 *Inserted* by Act 25 of 2012.
22 *Substituted* by Act 25 of 2012.
23 *Inserted* by Act 25 of 2012.

under s. 3(*a*) of the 1966 Act and file a complaint before the Magistrate. He is not a police officer and therefore s. 155(2), CrPC is not applicable. Though the offence is non-cognizable, he can investigate without prior approval of the Magistrate.[24] The offences under the 1966 Act are not cognizable and therefore the report filed by the Sub-Inspector of Police would be deemed to a complaint by the public servant within the meaning of s. 378(5) of the Code of Criminal Procedure.[25]

6. Power to arrest without warrant. Any superior officer or member of the Force may, without an order from a Magistrate and without a warrant, arrest any person who has been concerned in an offence punishable under this Act or against whom a reasonable suspicion exists of his having been so concerned.

Scope Section 6 of the 1966 Act empowers any superior officer or member of the Force to arrest any person who is involved in an offence under this Act without warrant. Thus, where the Head Rakshak arrested the accused and seized the property from him and forwarded the accused to Sub-Inspector of Police who instituted the inquiry, acquittal of the accused on the ground that inquiry was conducted by the Head Rakshak is illegal.[26]

7. Disposal of persons arrested. Every person arrested for an offence punishable under this Act shall, if the arrest was made by a person other than an officer of the Force, be forwarded without delay to the nearest officer of the Force.

Scope Section 7 of the Act provides the procedure for disposal of persons arrested. This section comes into operation only after arrest of the accused person and it has no application to situation which arose prior to the arrest for which s. 468, CrPC makes a provision.

8. [1][Inquiry how to be made]. (1) [1][When an officer of the Force receives information about the commission of an offence punishable under this Act, or when any person is arrested] by an officer of the Force for an offence punishable under this Act or is forwarded to him under section 7, he shall proceed to inquire into the charge against such person.

(2) For this purpose the officer of the Force may exercise the same powers and shall be subject to the same provisions as the officer in charge of a police station may exercise and is subject to under the Code of Criminal Procedure, 1898, when investigating a cognizable case:

Provided that—

(*a*) if the officer of the Force is of opinion that there is sufficient evidence or reasonable ground of suspicion against the accused person, he shall either admit him to bail to appear before a Magistrate having jurisdiction in the case, or forward him in custody to such Magistrate;

(*b*) if it appears to the officer of the Force that there is no sufficient evidence or reasonable ground of suspicion against the accused person, he shall release the accused person, on his executing a bond, with or without sureties as the officer of the Force may direct, to appear, if and

24 *R. Muthu* v *Assistant Sub-Inspector, RPF, Erode* 1983 CrLJ 1309 (Mad).
25 *State of UP* v *Bhura* 1985 CrLJ 536.
26 *State* v *Sankaran* 1983 CrLJ (NOC) 208.
1 *Substituted* by Act 25 of 2012.

when so required before the Magistrate having jurisdiction, and shall make a full report of all the particulars of the case to his official superior.

Inquiry against arrested person An Officer of a Railway Protection Force is entitled to make search, investigate a case and thereafter file a complaint. A Sub-Inspector of Railway Protection Force is an "officer" within the meaning of s. 2(*c*) of the 1966 Act. He is, however, not an officer in charge of police station as envisaged by s. 173, CrPC but the court could take cognizance of the offence on receipt of report from him.[2] The inquiry in a case[3] was conducted by an officer of the Railway Protection Force under s. 8(1) of the 1966 Act cannot be deemed to be an investigation for the purpose of s. 162, CrPC. Hence statements made during the inquiry under s. 8(1) of the 1966 Act are not on par with statement made during the course of investigation. It cannot be said that in taking signatures of the witnesses on the statements made by them, the inquiry officer had committed flagrant violation of s. 162, CrPC. Similarly, confession or incriminating statement made to an officer of RPF in course of inquiry cannot be excluded from evidence under s. 25 of the Evidence Act.[4] A Magistrate taking cognizance of a compliant for an offence under s. 3(*a*) of the 1966 Act on the report of an officer of the Railway Protection Force does not do so on a report under s. 173, CrPC and hence sanction for trial from Magistrate is not necessasry.[5] The Railway Magistrate is entitled to exercise powers of a Magistrate under the Code of Criminal Procedure by virtue of s. 8(2) of the Railway Property (Unlawful Possession) Act 1966. Thus, he can grant police custody to accused under s. 167(2), CrPC.[6] An officer of RPF making an inquiry under the Act is not a police officer and if any person suspected by him makes any incriminating statement before him if no formal complaint is launched in court, such person cannot avail of Art. 20(3) of the Constitution as he cannot at that stage during inquiry be considered as a "person accused of an offence".[7]

Sections 8, 3, 5 Under proviso to s. 8(2) of the Railway Property (Unlawful Possession) Act 1966 three situations are envisaged. Two of them relate to cl. (*a*) of the proviso. If the officer of the force is of the opinion that there is sufficient evidence or reasonable ground of suspicion against the accused person he shall: (*a*) either admit him to bail to appear before a Magistrate having jurisdiction in the case; or (*b*) forward him in custody of such Magistrate. It deals nowhere with the right of the accused to get bail. The third category is contemplated by cl. (*b*) of the proviso. This category deals with a case where there is absence of sufficient evidence or reasonable ground of suspicion. In such a case the officer concerned has the power to release the accused person on his execution of bonds. Thus, it is not

2 *State of Gujarat* v *Abdul Rehman* 1972 CrLJ 1101.
3 *State of UP* v *Dwega Prasad* AIR 1974 SC 2136; (1975)1 SCR 881; 1974 CrLJ 1465; see *State of UP* v *Vyas Tewari* AIR 1981 SC 635; 1981 CrLJ 38; 1980 CrLJ (SC) 653.
4 *State of Kerala* v *M. Ramadasan* 1989 CrLJ (NOC) 110.
5 *R. Muthu* v *Assistant Sub-Inspector, RPF, Erode* 1983 CrLJ 1309 (Mad).
6 *State of Maharashtra* v *Gendalal* 1975 CrLJ 815 (Bom).
7 *Balkishan* v *State of Maharashtra* AIR 1981 SC 379; (1981)1 SCR 175; 1980 CrLJ 1424.

justified to hold that all the offences under the said Act are bailable. Such view is contrary to the provisions contained in s. 8 of the Act.[8]

9. Power to summon persons to give evidence and produce documents. (1) An officer of the Force shall have power to summon any person whose attendance he considers necessary either to give evidence or to produce a document, or any other thing in any inquiry which such officer in making for any of the purposes of this Act.

(2) A summons to produce documents or other things may be for the production of certain specified documents or things or for the production of all documents or things of a certain description in the possession or under the control of the person summoned.

(3) All persons, so summoned, shall be bound to attend either in person or by an authorised agent as such officer may direct; and all persons so summoned shall be bound to state the truth upon any subject respecting which they are examined or make statements and to produce such documents and other things as may be required:

Provided that the exemptions under sections 132 and 133 of the Code of Civil Procedure, 1908 (5 of 1908), shall be applicable to requisitions for attendance under this section.

(4) Every such inquiry as aforesaid, shall be deemed to be a "judicial proceeding" within the meaning of sections 193 and 228 of the Indian Penal Code (45 of 1860).

Scope Section 9 of the 1966 Act confers powers on an officer of the Force to summon any person to give evidence and produce documents. An officer of Railway Police Force making inquiry in respect of an offence under s. 3 of the 1966 Act is not a police officer within s. 25 of the Evidence Act. In order to bring him within the purview of a "police officer" for the purpose of s. 25 of the Evidence Act, it is not enough to show that he exercises some or even many of the powers of a Police Officer conducting an investigation under the Criminal Procedure Code.[9] Statements of persons recorded under this section are not public documents within the meaning of s. 74 of the Evidence Act.[10] Such statements can be used for corroboration or for cross-examination.[11]

Section 9 of the 1966 Act and Art. 20(3) of the Constitution Section 9 of the 1966 Act is not hit by Art. 20(3) of the Constitution. Until a complaint is filed by an officer of RPF before a Magistrate, there is no formal accusation which is the condition precedent for application of Art. 20(3) of the Constitution.[12] In cases under the 1966 Act unless a complaint by an officer of RPF is filed in court under s. 199(1)(*a*), CrPC, the concerned person who is directed to be present and give statement under s. 9 of the 1966 Act cannot be considered to be "a person accused of an offence" within the meaning of Art. 20(3) of the Constitution and he cannot claim

8 *Union of India* v *State of Assam* (2004)7 SCC 474.
9 *Balkishan* v *State of Maharashtra* AIR 1981 SC 379; 1980 CrLJ 1424.
10 *Babulal* v *State* 1977 CrLJ 2008.
11 *Ibid*.
12 *Balkishan* v *State of Maharashtra* 1975 CrLJ 1891.

protection under Art. 20(3) of the Constitution when the enquiry is being conducted under s. 9 of the 1966 Act.[13]

10. Issue of search warrant. (1) If an officer of the Force has reason to believe that any place is used for the deposit or sale of railway property which has been stolen or unlawfully obtained, he shall make an application to the Magistrate, having jurisdiction over the area in which that place is situate, for issue of a search warrant.

(2) The Magistrate to whom an application is made under sub-section (1), may, after such inquiry as he thinks necessary, by his warrant, authorise any officer of the Force—

(*a*) to enter with such assistance as may be required, such place;

(*b*) to search the same in the manner specified in the warrant;

(*c*) to take possession of any railway property therein found which he reasonably suspects to be stolen or unlawfully obtained; and

(*d*) to convey such railway property before a Magistrate, or to guard the same on the spot until the offender is taken before a Magistrate, or otherwise to dispose thereof in some place of safety.

Scope An officer of RPF can issue a search warrant if he believes that a place is being used for the deposit or sale of railway property. A Magistrate having no jurisdiction issued a search warrant. Search and seizure on the basis of such warrant cannot be made valid by invoking s. 94 or s. 460, CrPC.[14]

11. Searches and arrests how to be made. All searches and arrests made under this Act shall be carried out in accordance with the provisions of the Code of Criminal Procedure, 1898, relating respectively to searches and arrests made under that Code.

Procedure for search and arrest Mere fact that the witnesses to seizure were not local persons will not make the search and seizure illegal.[15] A person was searched in a railway workshop and brass parts were found in his pant pocket. Mere fact that panchas were railway servants or that they had acted as panchas on a previous occasion was not sufficient to reject their evidence.[16]

12. Officers required to assist. All officers of Government and all village officers are hereby empowered and required to assist the superior officers and members of the Force in the enforcement of this Act.

13. Power of courts to order forfeiture of vehicles, etc. Any court trying an offence punishable under this Act may order the forfeiture to Government of any property in respect of which the Court is satisfied that an offence under this Act has been committed and may also order the forfeiture of any receptacles, packages or coverings in which such property is contained, and the animals, vehicles, or other conveyances, used in carrying the property.

13 *B.C. Saxena* v *State* 1983 CrLJ 1432.
14 *Sakti Steel Traders* v *Ashoke Chakraborty* 1993 CrLJ 969.
15 *Ramshrishta Singh* v *State of Bihar* 1976 CrLJ 38.
16 *Enas Elish Sutari* v *State of Maharashtra* 1976 CrLJ 1859.

14. Act to override other laws. The provisions of this Act shall have effect notwithstanding anything inconsistent therewith contained in any other law for the time being in force.

Scope There is no inconsistency between s. 14 of this Act and s. 95 of the Indian Penal Code.[17] There is nothing inconsistent in s. 190, CrPC as contemplated by s. 14 of this Act regard mode of taking cognizance of an offence by a court. Though the Assistant Sub-Inspector of the Railway Police Force is not competent to file a report or complaint yet it can be treated as an irregularity under s. 537, CrPC.[18]

15. Construction of references to laws not in force in Jammu and Kashmir. Any reference in this Act to a law which is not in force in the State of Jammu and Kashmir shall, in relation to that State, be construed as a reference to the corresponding law, if any, in force in that State.

16. Repeal and savings. (1) The Railway Stores (Unlawful Possession) Act 1955 (51 of 1955), is hereby repealed.

(2) Nothing contained in this Act shall apply to offences punishable under the Act, hereby repealed and such offences may be investigated and tried as if this Act had not been passed.

(3) The mention of particular matters in sub-section (2) shall not be held to prejudice or affect the general application of section 6 of the General Clauses Act, 1897 (10 of 1897), with regard to the effect of repeals.

17 *State of MP* v *Mahadeo* 1972 CrLJ 1097.
18 *State of UP* v *Ram Charan* 1974 CrLJ 1247.

APPENDIX 4

The Railway Protection Force Act, 1957

(Act No. 23 of 1957)

Objects of the Act The Watch and Ward Department functioning on the railways had no defined status and power to protect the railway property and goods entrusted to railways for transport. The railway had thus to suffer heavy losses on account of theft and pilferage for which huge claim for compensation was preferred by the claimants against the railway authorities. The Act is intended to redesignate the watch and ward staff as the Railway Protection Force so as to achieve quick and effective results. The Railway Protection Force is mainly charged with the responsibility for overall maintenance of law and order in railway premises.[1] The Act is to provide for constitution and regulation of an armed force of the Union for better protection and security of railway property and also to deal with matters connected therewith.[2]

Railway Protection Force (Amendment) Act (60 of 1985) This amendment was brought with a view to achieving the following objectives: (*a*) to declare the Railway Protection Force as an Armed Force of the Union with the consequential changes in the nomenclature of different ranks; (*b*) to confer additional powers on the members of the Force, such as to arrest without warrant, to restrain misbehavious on the part of the members of the Force; to effectively intervene for prevention of imminent danger to the life of a person concerned, etc.; (*c*) to restrict on the right to form association by the Forces, etc.[3]

An Act to provide for the constitution and regulation of an armed force of the Union for the better protection and security of railway property and for matters connected therewith.

1 *See* Statement of Objects and Reasons Gazette of India 1956, Ext., pt. II, s. 2, p. 1028.
2 Preamble to the Act 23 of 1957.
3 *See* Statement of Objects and Reasons to the Bill, published in Gazette of India, dt. 22-8-1985, Pt. II, s. 2, Ext. p. 90 (No. 48).

Be it enacted by Parliament in the Eighth Year of the Republic of India as follows:

1. Short title, extent and commencement. (1) This Act may be called the Railway Protection Force Act, 1957.

(2) It extends to the whole of India.

(3) It shall come into force on such date as the Central Government may, by notification in the *Official Gazette*, appoint.

2. Definitions. (1) In this Act, unless the context otherwise requires,—

(*a*) "Force" means the Railway Protection Force constituted under section 3;

(*b*) "Director-General" means the Director-General of the Force appointed under sub-section (1) of section 4;

(*ba*) "enrolled member of the Force" means any subordinate officer, under officer or any other member of the Force of a rank lower than that of under officer;

(*bb*) "Force custody" means the arrest or confinement of a member of the Force in accordance with rules made under this Act;

(*c*) "member of the Force" means a person appointed to the Force under this Act;

[4][(*ca*) "passenger" shall have the meaning assigned to it in the Railways Act, 1989 (24 of 1989);

(*cb*) "passenger area" shall include railway platform, train, yard and such other area as is frequently visited by passengers;]

(*d*) "prescribed" means prescribed by rules made under this Act;

(*e*) "railway property" includes any goods, money or valuable security, or animal, belonging to, or in the charge or possession of, a railway administration;

(*ea*) "subordinate officer" means a person appointed to the Force as an Inspector, a Sub-Inspector or an Assistant Sub-Inspector;

(*f*) "superior officer" means any of the officers appointed under section 4 and includes any other officer appointed by the Central Government as a superior officer of the Force;

(*fa*) "under officer" means a person appointed to the Force as a Head Constable or Naik;

(*g*) words and expressions used but not defined in this Act and defined in the Indian Railways Act, 1890 (9 of 1890), shall have the meaning respectively assigned to them under that Act.

(2) Any reference in this Act to a law which is not in force in any area shall, in relation to that area, be construed as a reference to the corresponding law, if any, in force in that area.

Clerical staff Clerical staff under the railway administration does not fall within categories of Railway Protection Force.[5]

4 *Inserted* by Act 52 of 2003, s. 3 (w.e.f. 1.7.2004).
5 *H.K. Bose* v *Union of India* (1985)89 CWN 1167.

3. Constitution of the Force. (1) There shall be constituted and maintained by the Central Government an armed force of the Union to be called the Railway Protection Force for the better protection and security of railway property.

(2) The Force shall be constituted in such manner, shall consist of such number of superior officers, subordinate officers, under officers and other enrolled members of the Force and shall receive such pay and other remuneration, as may prescribed.

Railway Protection Force as armed force of the Union The Railway Protection Force is the armed force of the Union to which the Administration Tribunal Act 1985 has no application.[6]

4. Appointment and powers of superior officers. (1) The Central Government may appoint a person to be the Director-General of the Force and may appoint other persons to be Inspectors-General, Additional Inspectors-General, Deputy Inspectors-General, Assistant Inspectors-General, Senior Commandants, Commandants or Assistant Commandants of the Force.

(2) The Director-General and every other superior officer so appointed shall possess and exercise such powers and authority over the members of the Force under their respective commands as is provided by or under this Act.

Assistant Security Officer Superior officer includes Assistant Security Officer and as such he is competent to hold enquiry against Sub-Inspector of Force.[7]

5. *Omitted* by Act 60 of 1985, s. 6.

6. Appointment of members of the Force. The appointment of enrolled members of the Force shall rest with the Inspector-General, Additional Inspector-General or Deputy Inspector-General who shall exercise that power in accordance with rules made under this Act:

Provided that the power of appointment under this section may also be exercised by other superior officer as the Inspector-General, Additional Inspector-General or Deputy Inspector-General concerned may, by order specify in this behalf.

Power to appoint The powers of the Security Officer and the Assistant Security Officer to make appointments under Sch. 1 may be exercised by them only when the power to do so is delegated by the Chief Security Officer under the proviso to s. 6.[8] Provisions require that the Chief Security Officer is to delegate the Powers to the Security Officer and the Security Officer.[9] The Chief Security Officer will have overall control in the matter of appointment that is to be exercised in accordance with rules, along with other members and the order of dismissal passed by the appointing authority is not *ultra vires* under the provision of the Act.[10] Where appointments of head Rakshaks were made by the Asst. Security Officers

6 *Shivkumar* v *Union of India* 1987 Lab IC 746.
7 *Ramniwas* v *Union of India* 1983 Lab IC 828 (Gau).
8 *Brij Narain Singh* v *Union of India* 1979 Lab IC (NOC) 151.
9 *Bhimrao* v *Chief Security Officer Western Railway* 1991 Lab IC 404; (1991)1 Bom CR 483.
10 *Union of India* v *Rajendra Singh* AIR 1993 SC 205; 1993 Supp (2) SCC 176; 1992 Lab IC 2435; 1992(5) SLR 857.

and their removals were made by Security Officer, there was no violation of Art. 311 of the Constitution.[11]

7. Certificates to members of the Force. (1) Every member of the Force shall receive on his appointment a certificate in the form specified in the Schedule, under the seal of the Inspector-General, Additional Inspector-General or Deputy Inspector-General or such other superior officer as the Inspector-General, Additional Inspector-General or Deputy Inspector-General may specify in this behalf, by virtue of which the person holding such certificate shall be vested with the powers of a member of the Force.

(2) Such certificate shall cease to have effect whenever the person named in it ceases for any reason to be a member of the Force.

Scope The whole purpose of granting a certificate under s. 7 of the Act is to vest the members of the Force concerned with powers of the Force. The certificate cannot be said to be the railway property. Unless a certificate under s. 7 of this Act is issued, a direct recruitee cannot exercise the powers of a member of the Force.

8. Superintendence and administration of the Force. (1) The superintendence of the Force shall vest in the Central Government, and subject thereto and to the provisions of this Act and of any rules made thereunder, the command, supervision and administration of the Force shall vest in the Director-General.

(2) Subject to the provisions of sub-section (1), the administration of the Force, within such local limits in relation to a railway as may be prescribed shall be carried on by an Inspector-General, an Additional Inspector-General or a Deputy Inspector-General in accordance with the provisions of this Act and of any rules made thereunder and they shall, subject to any direction that may be given by the Central Government or the Director-General in this behalf discharge his functions under the general supervision of the General Manager of the Railway.

9. Dismissal removal, etc. of members of the Force. (1) Subject to the provisions of Article 311 of the Constitution and to such rules as the Central Government may make under this Act, any superior officer may—

(*i*) dismiss, suspend or reduce in rank any enrolled member of the Force whom he shall think remiss or negligent in the discharge of his duty, or unfit for the same; or

(*ii*) award anyone or more of the following punishments to any enrolled member of the Force who discharges his duty in a careless or negligent manner, or who, by any act of his own renders himself unfit for the discharge thereof, namely—

(*a*) fine to any amount not exceeding seven days' pay or reduction in pay scale;

(*b*) confinement to quarters for a period not exceeding fourteen days with or without punishment, drill, extra guard, fatigue or other duty;

(*c*) removal from any office of distinction or deprivation of any special emolument.

11 *Union of India* v *Babban Singh* 1982 Lab IC 89. See *Dayashankar* v *Union of India* 1992 Lab IC 866.

(2) Any enrolled member of the Force aggrieved by an order made under sub-section (1) may, within thirty days from the date on which the order is communicated to him, prefer an appeal against the order to such authority as may be prescribed:

Provided that the prescribed authority may entertain the appeal after the expiry of the said period of thirty days if it is satisfied that the appellant was prevented by sufficient cause from filing the appeal in time.

(3) In disposing of the appeal, the prescribed authority shall follow such procedure as may be prescribed:

Provided that no order imposing an enhanced penalty under sub-section (2) shall be made unless a reasonable opportunity of being heard has been given to the person affected by such order.

Scope An appointment was made by the Chief Security Officer and the order of the appointee for compulsory retirement was passed by the Security Officer. It was held that the order was passed without jurisdiction.[12] The order of removal of Rakshak by the Senior Security Officer is not valid as he is not authorised to do so under s. 6 of the Act.[13] The dismissal, removal etc. of the members of the force are subject to Art. 311 of the Constitution and such other rules as the Central Government may frame under this Act.[14] Thus, where the dismissal of an employee by the Asst. Security Officer who is also the appointing authority is not violative of Art. 311 of the Constitution.[15] Where the order of removal from service was passed without holding any enquiry on the ground that it was not reasonably practicable to hold disciplinary enquiry under normal rules without disclosing the reasons, the order of dismissal was held invalid.[16] Where a member of RPF was removed for using improper language against a superior officer, the penalty awarded was held to be not commensurate with the quit established.[17] A RPF was dismissed on the basis of an *ex parte* enquiry conducted by an officer who is biased against the delinquent, there is a violation of the principle of natural justice.[18] Where in case of removal from service and enquiry is dispensed with on the grounds of humiliation to witnesses, the same does not constitute justification for dispensing with enquiry.[19] Where in a disciplinary enquiry the defence counsel failed to appeal and the delinquent did not request for another defence counsel but conducted the defence himself the disciplinary proceeding were not vitiated as illegal and opposed to the principles of natural justice.[20] Where r. 153(8), Railway Protection Force Rules permits

12 *Sher Bahadur Singh* v *Union of India* 1977 Lab IC 1562.

13 *Dayashankar* v *Union of India* 1992 Lab IC 866.

14 *Union of India* v *Rajendra Singh* AIR 1993 SC 205; 1993 Supp (2) SCC 176; 1992 Lab IC 2435; 1992(5) SLR 857.

15 *Union of India* v *Rajendra Singh* (supra).

16 *Kamal* v *Union of India* (1994)2 CLJ 133.

17 *Union of India* v *Ramji Singh* 1994 Lab IC 817.

18 *Chandra Kamal* v *Union of India* 1988 Lab IC 1076.

19 *Chief Security Officer* v *Singasan Rabi Das* AIR 1991 SC 1043; (1991)1 SCC 729; 1991(2) SLR 140; 1991 Lab IC 1318.

20 *Ved Pal Singh* v *Union of India* 1987 Lab IC 1553.

assistance of "friend" and not a legal practitioner to participate in disciplinary proceedings. Rule however deprives friend to cross examine witnesses and address enquiry officer. The rule is not violative of Arts. 14, 16, 21 and 311 of the Constitution as the delinquent was not deprived of such rights.[21] The grounds for dispensing with disciplinary enquiry are that if the witnesses are asked to appear at a confronted enquiry they would suffer personal humiliation and their family members may become targets or acts of violence. These grounds were held insufficient for dispensing with enquiry.[22] Where the revising authority reduces punishment of removal to compulsory retirement, the retirement would take effect from the date of the removal.[1]

Dispensation of enquiry In *Sahadeo Singh* v *Union of India*[2] the delinquents were charged for their involvement in theft of rice bags from goods train in collusion with certain miscreants and other officials. The disciplinary authority decided to dispense with the inquiry in exercise of power under r. 47 of the Railway Protection Force Rules, 1959. Three internal enquiries were conducted by the officials of the Railway Protection Force and on perusal of those reports it showed that no one was willing to give statement in writing or give evidence apprehending danger to their life. Thus, it was held that the disciplinary authority rightly came to the conclusion that it would be impracticable for the Railways to hold any fair enquiry. From the preliminary reports it was clear that the delinquents were involved in the theft of rice bags from goods train. The instant case was distinguished from *Chief Security Officer* v *Singasan*[3] and *Jaswant Singh* v *State,*[4] where the facts were otherwise.

Punishment for misconduct Normally, the punishment imposed by the disciplinary authority should not be disturbed by the High Court unless the punishment imposed is grossly or shockingly disproportionate after examining the relevant factors including the nature of charges proved against the delinquent, the part conduct, penalty imposed earlier etc. Merely because it is fell that the punishment imposed was extremely severe, is not enough to disturb or modify the punishment imposed on a delinquent. The court has to record reasons as to the disproportionality of the punishment of removal or dismissal from service. It is not in every case of removal or dismissal from service the High Court can modify such punishment by saying that it is shocking disproportionate. Alternatively, the High Court or Tribunal cannot remit the case to the disciplinary authority for reconsideration on the quantum of punishment on the ground that the punishment imposed is shockingly disproportionate.[5]

10. Officers and members of the Force to be deemed to be railway servants. The Director-General and every member of the Force shall, for all purposes be regarded as

21 *Om Prakash* v *Union of India* 1995 Lab IC 1981 (Raj).
22 *Ainul Haque* v *Union of India* 1995 Lab IC 2164 (Cal).
1 *Udai Pratap Singh* v *Rly. Protection Spl. Force, Trichhnapalli* 1992 Lab IC 2121.
2 AIR 2003 SC 1568.
3 1991 AIR SCW 295.
4 AIR 1991 SC 385.
5 *Director-General, R.P.F.* v *Ch. Sai Babu* AIR 2003 SC 1437.

railway servants within the meaning of the Indian Railways Act, 1890 (9 of 1890),[6] other than Chapter VIA thereof, and shall be entitled to exercise the powers conferred on railway servants by or under that Act.

Scope A person in the employment of railway working as Assistant Security Officer of Railway Protection Force on the date of the accident was a workman within s. 10 of this Act. Railway Protection Force Officers are not "Police Officers" within the meaning of s. 25 of the Evidence Act.[7] Though the members of Railway Protection Force have been categorised as railway servants as per s. 10 of this Act, yet they are a category apart from the other railway servants in the sense that they are creatures of the Railway Protection Force.[8] Under the provisions the members of RPF are deemed to be railway servants and under s. 3 of this Act they are treated as members of armed force of the Union and the Administrative Tribunal Act will not apply to them.[9]

[10][**11. Duties of members of Force.** It shall be the duty of every superior officer and member of the Force—

(*a*) promptly to execute all orders lawfully issued to him by his superior authority;

(*b*) to protect and safeguard railway property, passenger area and passengers;

(*c*) to remove any obstruction in the movement of railway property or passenger area; and

(*d*) to do any other act conducive to the better protection and security of railway property, passenger area and passengers].

Scope Section 11 of the Act prescribes the duties of every superior officer and member of the Force. One of the most important duties is to protect and safeguard railway property.

12. Power to arrest without warrant. Any member of the Force may, without an order from a Magistrate and without a warrant, arrest—

(*i*) any person who voluntarily causes hurt to, or attempts voluntarily to cause hurt to, or wrongfully restrains or attempts wrongfully to restrain, or assaults, threatens to assault, or uses, or threatens or attempts to use, criminal force to him or any other member of the Force in the execution of his duty as such member, or with intent to prevent or to deter him from discharging his duty as such member, or in consequence of anything done or attempted to be done by him in the lawful discharge of his duty as such member; or

(*ii*) any person who has been concerned in, or against whom a reasonable suspicion exists of his having been concerned in, or who is found taking precautions to conceal his presence under circumstances which afford reason to believe that he is taking such precautions with a view to committing a cognizable offence which relates to railway property, passenger area and passengers; or

6 Now the Railways Act 1989 (24 of 1989).
7 *Balukishan A. Devidayal* v *State of Maharashtra* 1975 CrLJ 1891.
8 *Om Prakash* v *Union of India* 1995 Lab IC 1981 (Raj).
9 *Chandra Kamal* v *Union of India* 1988 Lab IC 1076 (Gau).
10 *Substituted* by Act 52 of 2003, s. 4, for s. 11 (w.e.f. 1.7.2004).

(*iii*) any person found taking precautions to conceal his presence within the railway limits under circumstances which afford reason to believe that he is taking such precautions with a view to committing theft of, or damage to, railway property, passenger area and passengers; or

(*iv*) any person who commits or attempts to commit a cognizable offence which involves or which is likely to involve imminent danger to the life of any person engaged in carrying on any work relating to [11][railway property, passenger area and passengers].

Power to arrest by Railway Protection Force The statements and confessions made to a member of RPF during course of enquiry would be admissible against person and are not hit by s. 25 of the Evidence Act.[12] Power to arrest under s. 12 of the 1957 Act is not confined to railway premises only.[13]

13. Power to search without warrant. (1) Whenever any member of the Force, not below the rank of a Senior Rakshak, has reason to believe that any such offence as is referred to in section 12 has been or is being committed and that a search warrant cannot be obtained without affording the offender an opportunity of escaping or of concealing evidence of the offence, he may detain him and search his person and belongings forthwith and, if he thinks proper, arrest any person whom he has reason to believe to have committed the offence.

(2) The provisions of the Code of Criminal Procedure, 1973 (2 of 1974), relating to searches under that Code shall, so far as may be, apply to searches under this section.

Power to search Search conducted in the course of administrative duties of those in charge of workshop, viz., keeping a watch on the employees who leave the workshop gate concealing any of the properties of the workshop on their person, do not attract the procedure prescribed under s. 13(2) of the Act and the rules framed under s. 21 of the Act.[14] Section 13 confers power on a member of the Force not below the rank of a senior Rakshak to search without warrant any person who is suspected to have committed an offence as is referred to in s. 12 of this Act.

14. Procedure to be followed after arrest. Any member of the Force making an arrest under this Act, shall, without unnecessary delay, make over the person so arrested [15][to a police officer together with a detailed report of the circumstances leading to the arrest of such person], or, in the absence of a police officer, take such person or cause him to be taken to the nearest police station.

Scope Section 14 requires that any member of the RPF making an arrest under this Act must make over the person so arrested to a Police Officer, or take him to the nearest Police Station as they have not all the powers of Police Officer under the CrPC.

15. Officers and members of the Force to be considered always on duty and liable to be employed in any part of the railways. (1) Every member of the Force shall, for the

11 *Substituted* by Act 52 of 2003, s. 5, for "railway property" (w.e.f. 1.7.2004).
12 *Balukishan A. Devidayal* v *State of Maharashtra* 1975 CrLJ 1891; 77 Bom LR 295.
13 *Parimjit Singh Bedi* v *Dhaneshwar Sah* 1976 CrLJ 1131.
14 *K. Dakshinamoorthy* v *Dist. Signal Telecom. Engn*. AIR 1969 Mad 201; (1968)2 Mad LJ 191; 1968 Mad LJ (Cri) 497.
15 *Substituted* by Act 52 of 2003, s. 5, for "to a police officer" (w.e.f. 1.7.2004).

purposes of this Act, be considered to be always on duty, and shall, at any time, be liable to be employed at any place within India.

(2) No member of the Force shall engage himself in any employment or office other than his duties under this Act.

Employment in a railway "Employment in a Railway" means employment in a railway owned by the State throughout India. It does not mean employment only in zonal railway.[16] Permanent and temporary transfers are both included within the ambit of s. 15 of the Act. Transfer made in exercise of the powers conferred by the Act and rules and regulations made thereunder is not invalid merely because it affects the seniority or the promotional chances of a member of the Force.[17] Where Inspector Grade II (Fire) in Railway Protection Force working in one division for a period exceeding seven years was transferred to another division by the Chief Security Officer, it is not illegal.[18] Regulation 14 dealing with transfer of employees is in conformity with r. 32 of the Railway Protection Force Rules 1959 framed under s. 21(1) of this Act and as such is not *ultra vires* the Act.[19]

15A. Restrictions respecting right to form association, etc. (1) No member of the Force shall, without the previous sanction in writing of the Central Government or of the prescribed authority,—

(*a*) be a member of, or be associated in any way with, any trade union, labour union, political association or with any class of trade unions, labour unions or political associations; or

(*b*) be a member of, or be associated in any way with, any other society, institution, association or organisation that is not recognised as part of the Force or is not of a purely social, recreational or religious nature; or

(*c*) communicate with the press or publish or cause to be published any book, letter or other document except where such communication or publication is in the *bona fide* discharge of his duties or is of a purely literary, artistic or scientific character or is of a prescribed nature.

Explanation. If any question arises as to whether any society, institution, association or organisation is of a purely social, recreational or religious nature under clause (*b*) of this sub-section, the decision of the Central Government thereon shall be final.

(2) No member of the Force shall, participate in, or address, any meeting or take part in any demonstration organised by any body of persons for any political purposes or for such other purposes as may be prescribed.

16. Responsibilities of members of the Force during suspension. A member of the Force shall not, by reason of his suspension from office, cease to be a member of the Force; and he shall, during that period, be subject to the same responsibilities, discipline and penalties to which he would have been subject, if he were on duty.

16A. Surrender of certificate, arms, etc. by persons ceasing to be members of the Force. (1) Every person who for any reason ceases to be a member of the Force, shall

16 *Guruprasad* v *Railway Board* 1974 Lab IC 616; 77 CWN 249.

17 *Mathura Prasad* v *Inspector General, Rly. Protection Force, New Delhi* 1974 Lab IC 1177.

18 *P. Dutta* v *Union of India* 1983 Lab IC 1648; 87 CWN 990.

19 *Guruprasad* v *Railway Board* 1974 Lab IC 616; 77 CWN 249.

forthwith surrender to any superior officer empowered to receive the same, his certificate of appointment, the arms, accoutrements, clothing and other articles which have been furnished to him for the performance of his duties as a member of the Force.

(2) Any person who wilfully neglects or refuses to surrender his certificate of appointment, the arms, accoutrements, clothing and other articles furnished to him, as required by sub-section (1), shall, on conviction, be punished with the imprisonment for a term which may extend to one month, or with fine which may extend to two hundred rupees, or with both.

(3) Nothing in this section shall be deemed to apply to any article which, under the orders of the Director-General, has become the property of the person to whom the same was furnished.

17. Penalties for neglect of duty, etc. (1) Without prejudice to the provisions contained in section 9, every enrolled member of the Force who shall be guilty of any violation of duty or wilful breach or neglect of any rule or lawful order made by a superior officer, or who shall withdraw from duties of his office without permission, or who, being absent on leave, fails, without reasonable cause, to report himself for duty on the expiration of the leave, or who engages himself without authority for any employment other than his duty as an enrolled member of the Force, or who shall be guilty of cowardice may be taken into Force custody and shall, on conviction, be punished with imprisonment which may extend to one year.

(2) Notwithstanding anything contained in the Code of Criminal Procedure, 1973 (2 of 1974) an offence punishable under this section shall be cognizable, and non-bailable.

(3) Notwithstanding anything contained in the Code of Criminal Procedure, 1973 (2 of 1974) the Central Government may invest Assistant Inspector-General, Senior Commandant or Commandant with the powers of a Magistrate of any class for the purpose of inquiring into or trying any offence committed by an enrolled member of the Force and punishable under this Act, or any offence committed by an enrolled member of the Force against the person or property of another member of the Force:

Provided that—

(*i*) when the offender is on leave or absent from duty; or

(*ii*) when the offence is not connected with the offender's duties as an enrolled member of the Force; or

(*iii*) when it is a petty offence even if connected with the offender's duties as an enrolled member of the Force; or

(*iv*) when, for reasons to be recorded in writing, it is not practicable for the Commandant invested with the powers of a Magistrate to inquire into or to try the offence,

the offence may, if the prescribed authority within the limits of whose jurisdiction the offence has been committed so requires, be inquired into or tried by an ordinary criminal court having jurisdiction in the matter.

(4) Nothing contained in this section shall be construed to prevent any enrolled member of the Force from being prosecuted under any other law for any offence made punishable by that law, or for being liable under any such law to any

other or higher penalty or punishment than is provided for such offence by this section:

Provided that no person shall be punished twice for the same offence.

Scope Section 17 deals with penalties for neglect of duty or wilful violation of a lawful order made by a superior officer. Where the employee refuses to vacate quarters in spite of orders, such misconduct would have serious consequences on the discipline in force and the punishment of compulsory retirement would not be disproportionate to charges levelled against the employee. But if an employee is dismissed for absence from duty without any reasonable excuse and without affording him any opportunity of hearing, the order is liable to be quashed.

18. Application of Act 22 of 1922 to members of the Force. The Police (Incitement to Disaffection) Act, 1922 shall apply to members of the Force as it applies to members of a police force.

Scope Section 18 is applicable to the Police (Incitement to Disaffection) Act 1922. But that does not make the Railway Protection Force Officers while exercising powers under the Railway Property (Unlawful Possession) Act 1966 as Police Officers.[20]

19. Certain Acts not to apply to members of the Force. Nothing contained in the Payment of Wages Act, 1936 (4 of 1936), or the Industrial Disputes Act, 1947 (4 of 1947), or the Factories Act, 1948 (63 of 1948), or any corresponding law relating to investigation and settlement of industrial dispute in force in a State shall apply to members of the Force.

20. Protection of acts of members of the Force. (1) In any suit or proceeding against any member of the Force for any act done by him in the discharge of his duties, it shall be lawful for him to plead that such act was done by him under the order of a competent authority.

(2) Any such plea may be proved by the production of the order directing the act, and if it is so proved, the member of the Force shall thereupon be discharged from any liability in respect of the act so done by him, notwithstanding any defect in the jurisdiction of the authority which issued such order.

(3) Notwithstanding anything contained in any other law for the time being in force, any legal proceeding, whether civil or criminal, which may lawfully be brought against any member of the Force for anything done or intended to be done under the powers conferred by, or in pursuance of, any provisions of this Act or the rules thereunder shall be commenced within three months after the act complained of shall have been committed and not otherwise; and notice in writing of such proceeding and of the cause thereof shall be given to the person concerned and his superior officer at least one month before the commencement of such proceeding.

Protection under the Act An Assistant Traffic Superintendent was prosecuted on the allegation of assaulting a ticket collector without following the procedure laid down in s. 20(3) of the Act. It was held that the prosecution was not valid. Where it is *prima facie* established that the accused hurted filthy abuses to complainant and used a *danda* blows causing injuries to

20 *Balukishan A. Devidayal* v *State of Maharashtra* 1975 CrLJ 1891; 77 Bom LR 295.

him and also threatened him to kill, the provisions of s. 20(3) of the Act cannot be pressed into service at the discharge stage, because without recording evidence in the case, it could not be held that the impugned acts were done by the accused while discharging his official duty.[21]

21. Power to make rules. (1) The Central Government may, by notification in the official Gazette, make rules for carrying out the purposes of this Act.

(2) In particular, and without prejudice to the generality of the foregoing powers, such rules may provided for—

(*a*) regulating the classes and grades and the pay and remuneration of and members of the Force and their conditions of service in the Force;

(*b*) regulating the powers and duties of members of the Force authorised to exercise any functions by or under this Act;

(*c*) fixing the period of service for members of the Force;

(*d*) prescribing the description and quantity of arms, accoutrements, clothing and other necessary articles to be furnished to the members of the Force;

(*e*) prescribing the places of residence of the member of Force;

(*f*) institution, management and regulation of any fund for any purpose connected with the administration of the Force;

(*g*) regulating the punishments and prescribing authorities to whom appeal shall be preferred from orders of punishment, or remission of fines, or other punishments and the procedure to be followed for the disposal of such appeals;

(*h*) regulating matters with respect to Force custody under this Act, including the procedure to be followed for taking persons into such custody;

(*i*) regulating matters with respect to disposal of cases relating to offences under this Act and specifying the places in which persons convicted under this Act may be confined;

(*j*) any other matter which has to be, or may be, imposed, or in respect of which rules are required to be made under this Act.

(3) Every rule made under this Act shall be laid as soon as may be after it is made, before each House of Parliament, while it is in session, for a total period of thirty days which may be comprised in one session or in two or more successive sessions, and if, before the expiry of the session immediately following the session or the successive sessions aforesaid, both Houses agree in making any modification in the rule or both Houses agree that the rule should not be made, the rule shall thereafter have effect only in such modified form or be of no effect, as the case may be; so, however, that any such modification or annulment shall be without prejudice to the validity of anything previously done under that rule.

Rule making power of Central Government Under s. 21 of the Act the Central Government may make rule for carrying out the purposes contemplated under this Act.[22] The procedure prescribed under r. 18 framed under s. 21

21 *Syed Azar Ahmad* v *State of Rajasthan* 1997 CrLJ 1822.

22 *Union of India* v *Rajendra Singh* AIR 1993 SC 205; 1993 Supp (2) SCC 176; 1992(5) SLR 857; 1992 Lab IC 2435.

of the Act is not applicable to searches conducted in the course of administrative duties of the Railway Protection Force.[1] No rule or regulation abridging or curtailing the obligation of the members of the RPF to serve anywhere and in any part of the railways can be framed.[2] The laying requirement of the rule before each House of Parliament is not mandatory but directory.[3] The Chief Security Officer is empowered under r. 25 to transfer an Inspector Grade II (Fire) from one division to another division.[4] Where in a disciplinary proceeding, the defence counsel engaged by the employee did not appear and no request for another defence counsel was made the termination order is not violated on the ground of violation of r. 44(5).[5] Where an order is passed to dispense with the enquiry under r. 47 of the Railway Protection Force Rules 1959, the same is subject to judicial review.[6] Where a Rakshak is involved in theft in a railway wagon and was implicated in a secret CBI report, the dispensation of enquiry cannot be held to be illegal.[7]

But if a delinquent employee is removed from service without holding any disciplinary proceedings, he has the right in the appeal to show that the charges are not true.[8] Where the reasons are assigned to dispense with enquiry that witnesses would suffer personal humiliation and their members might be the targets of violence, these are totally insufficient reasons.[9] Where delinquent employee was inflicted with two charges and was absolved from the second charge, the appellate authority must apply its mind to question the quantum of punishment.[10] Power under Rules to place a member under suspension must not be exercised mechanically but according to guideline as provided in r. 135.[11] Where a Head Constable has failed to prevent thefts, he can be held guilty of negligence by reason of the fact that unmanageable burden has been placed upon him.[12] Rules provide that the delinquent should submit a list of witnesses with gists of their evidence and also to file written statements within ten days, these provisions are not violative of the principles of natural justice.[13]

THE SCHEDULE

[*See* section 7]

A.B., has been appointed a member of the Railway Protection Force under the Railway Protection Force Act, 1957, and is vested with the powers, functions and privileges of a member of the Force.

1 *K. Dakshinamoorthy* v *Dist. Signal Telecom. Engn.* AIR 1969 Mad 201; (1968)2 Mad LJ 191; 1968 Mad LJ (Cri) 497.
2 *Guruprasad* v *Railway Board* 1974 Lab IC 616; 77 CWN 249.
3 *Mathura Prasad* v *Inspector General, Rly. Protection Force, New Delhi* 1974 Lab IC 1177.
4 *P. Dutta* v *Union of India* 1983 Lab IC 1648; 87 CWN 990.
5 *Ved Pal Singh* v *Union of India* 1987 Lab IC 1553.
6 *Bhagirath Mai* v *Union of India* 1990 Lab IC 47.
7 *Raj Kishore* v *Union of India* 1988 Lab IC 1391.
8 *Kailash Narain Rai* v *Union of India* 1989 Lab IC 2039.
9 *Ainul Haque* v *Union of India* 1995 Lab IC 2164.
10 1996 Lab IC 1423.
11 *Keshari Prasad* v *Union of India* 1995 Lab IC 1835.
12 *Dhirendra Nath Kundu* v *Union of India* 1994 Lab IC 718.
13 *Om Prakash* v *Union of India* 1995 Lab IC 1981 (Raj).

APPENDIX 5

The Railway Protection Force Rules, 1987

G.S.R. 951 (E), dated 3rd December, 1987[1] In exercise of the powers conferred by section 21 of the Railway Protection Force Act, 1957 (23 of 1957), the Central Government hereby makes the following rules, namely:

CHAPTER I
PRELIMINARY

1. Short title and commencement. (1) These rules may be called the Railway Protection Force Rules, 1987.

(2) They shall come into force on the date of their publication in the official Gazette.

(3) These rules shall apply to all persons who are subject to the Act:

Provided that the provisions of rules 83 to 86 shall not apply to superior officers and other enrolled members of the Force appointed on deputation and officers appointed on contract who shall continue to be governed by their own rules and the terms of deputation or, as the case may be, by the conditions of their contract.

2. Definitions. In these rules, unless the context otherwise requires,—

(*a*) "*Act*" means the Railway Protection Force Act, 1957 (23 of 1957);

(*b*) "*accoutrements*" means personal articles of equipment and trappings, as approved by the Director-General, from time to time, which are issued to members of the Force for their use;

(*c*) "*battalion*" means a unit of the Force constituted as a battalion by the Director-General;

(*d*) "*Chief Security Commissioner*" means an officer, not below the rank of Deputy Inspector General, who is the head of the Force in a zonal railway or a superior officer so appointed in the headquarters of the Director-General or in any other formation of the Force;

1 Published in Gazette of India, (Extra), Part II, section 3(*i*), dated 3.1.1987 (w.e.f. 3.12.1987), pp. 74-159.

(*e*) *"close arrest"* means confinement of any enrolled member of the Force within the Force or the detachment of the Force or a post quarter-guard, building or tent under charges of a guard;

(*f*) *"court of inquiry"* means a Court presided over by any member of the Force not below the rank of an Inspector and constituted to investigate into any disciplinary matter or any other matter specified in rule 265;

(*g*) *"detachment"* in relation to the Force, includes detachment of any part of the Force required or ordered to proceed on duty away from the headquarters;

(*h*) *"Directives"* means directions issued by the Director General under rule 28;

(*i*) *"division"* means a portion of the railway declared to be a division for security purposes by the Central Government or the Director-General;

(*j*) *"Divisional Security Commissioner"* means an officer, not below the rank of a Commandant, who is the head of the Force in a division or in a railway establishment at any other place connected with the railways;

(*k*) *"extant Railway Rules"* means the rules contained in the Indian Railway General Code, Indian Railway Establishment Code, Indian Railway Establishment Manual, Indian Railway Code for accoutrement, Indian Railway Code for Accounts Department, Indian Railway Code for the Engineering Department and includes any rules made under the Indian Railways Act, 1890 for railway servants;

(*l*) *"open arrest"* means confinement of any enrolled member of the Force, within the precincts of any barracks, lines or camp for the time being occupied by any detachment of the Force;

(*m*) *"Post"* means any unit or place declared generally or specially by the Chief Security Commissioner to be a post and includes any railway area specified by the Chief Security Commissioner in this behalf;

(*n*) *"railway establishment"* means any unit of the railways (other than zonal railway) which is engaged in research, development, designing, construction or production of rolling stock, its parts or other equipment used on a railway;

(*o*) *"RPF Staff Council"* means the Staff Council of the Force constituted in accordance with rule 111(3);

(*p*) *"section"* means a section of the Act;

(*q*) *"Schedule"* means a Schedule annexed to these rules;

(*r*) *"Security Court"* means a court of an officer invested with the powers of a Magistrate under rule 30;

(*s*) *"superior officer"* means any of the officer appointed to the Force under section 41;

(*t*) *"zonal railway"* means a portion of the railway declared as zonal railway by the Central Government by notification in the Official Gazette;

(*u*) all other words and expressions used herein but not defined, and defined in the Act or the Indian Railways Act, 1890 shall have the meanings assigned to them in the Act or the Indian Railways Act, 1890.

CHAPTER II

ORGANISATION AND STRUCTURE OF THE FORCE

3. Organisational set up at the headquarters of the Director-General. The command, supervision and administration of the Force is vested in the Director-General, who shall be assisted by such superior officers at his headquarters as may be appointed for the purpose.

4. Office and designation of superior officers and enrolled members of the Force. The superior officers and enrolled members of the Force holding office as specified in column 2 of Schedule I shall also be known by designations as specified in column 3, of that Schedule.

5. Other superior officers. The Central Government may, having regard to the provisions of sub-section (2) of section 15, appoint any other officer by notification in the official Gazette to be the superior officer of the Force defining his rank, designation, powers and responsibilities.

6. Superior officers and enrolled members of the Force at the headquarters of the Director-General. (1) The officers appointed under rule 3 shall discharge such duties and supervise the functioning of such other branches as provided in these rules as may be assigned to them by the Director-General from time to time.

(2) All officers appointed under rule 3 may have under them a number of other superior officers and enrolled members of the Force as may be appointed from time to time, and shall exercise such powers over them as are prescribed under these rules and are exercisable by their counter parts of equivalent rank and designation in the zonal railways.

7. Railway Protection Special Force. (1) The Force shall have a specially trained unit called the Railway Protection Special Force to be raised as a reserve Force on the battalion pattern.

(2) The number of battalions as also their strength and composition shall be such as may be determined by the Director-General.

(3) Each battalion shall function as a division and shall have at its head an officer not below the rank of Commandant who shall be known as Commanding Officer.

(4) A Commanding Officer shall be assisted by such number of other superior officers and enrolled members of the Force as may be appointed from time to time.

(5) Enrolled members of the Force who constitute the Railway Protection Special Force shall form a separate cadre for the purposes of fixation of seniority.

[2](6) Battalions will have trained wireless personnel like Armorers. These posts will be ex-cadre. The number of posts will be as decided from time to time. These post will be governed by the Directives issued in this regard by D.G./R.P.F. from time to time.

8. Central Crime Bureau. (1) A Central Crime Bureau consisting of such number of superior officers and enrolled members of the Force as may be determined by the Director-General shall be maintained at his headquarters.

2 *Inserted* by G.S.R. 313, dated 25.8.2004 (w.e.f. 18.9.2004).

(2) The Central Crime Bureau shall consist of Central Detective Wing, a Central Records Wing and shall perform such duties, maintain such records, compile and submit such reports and returns as may be directed by the Director-General.

9. Breeding-cum-training Centre for police dogs. (1) For better prevention and detection of crime, a breeding-cum-training centre for 'police dogs' shall be maintained under the charge of such officer as may be appointed by the Director-General.

(2) This centre shall undertake breeding of pups and their training as 'police dogs' and shall undertake such other duties as may be specified by the Director-General.

10. Central Weapons Store. There shall be a Central Weapons Store under the immediate command and control of such superior officer as may be appointed by the Director-General for procurement and supply of arms, ammunition and ordnance stores.

11. Arms workshop. (1) There shall be such number of arms workshops, each under the charge of an officer not below the rank of an Inspector, as may be set up for carrying out repair, phosphating of the arms held by the Force and such other functions as may be specified by the Director-General.

(2) Notwithstanding anything contained in sub-rule (1), the administrative and technical control of the arms workshops shall also vest in such superior officer as may be appointed by the Director-General.

12. Arms inspection teams. There shall be such number of arms inspection teams as may be constituted by the Director General for carrying out periodical inspection of the arms held by the Force in all its units.

13. Training institutions. (1) *Railway Protection Force Academy.* There shall be a Railway Protection Force Academy under the charge of a Principal, not below the rank of Deputy Inspector General, for providing initial, inservice, special and other advanced professional and technical training courses to the members of the Force.

(2) The said Academy shall have such number of qualified instructors in various disciplines as may be appointed by the Director-General from time to time.

(3) The Director-General may declare the Principal of the Academy or any other superior officer to be the officer-in-charge (training) for the Force and that officer shall exercise general supervision on behalf of Director General over all the training institutions of the Force, formulate training curricula and syllabi, arrange publication of training material and maintain close liaison with sister training institutions of other disciplines.

(4) *Zonal training institute.* Each zonal railway shall have a training institute for the Force under the charge of a superior officer for providing initial, induction, inservice and other refresher and promotional courses and to cater to the training needs of enrolled members of the Force of that zone or who may be specially sent for the purpose.

14. Organisational set up on zonal railway. (1) For purposes of the Act, a unit of the Force shall be distributed over each zonal railway including railway establishments and other railway areas served by that zonal railway.

(2) The head of the Security Department in each zonal railway shall be a Chief Security Commissioner and the entire unit of the Force posted on that railway (including railway establishments located on that railway) shall be under his command, supervision and administration.

(3) A Chief Security Commissioner shall be assisted at his headquarters (hereinafter referred to as the Security Commissariat) by such number of superior officers and enrolled members of the Force as may be appointed from time to time to look after the work of administration including personnel matters, crime and special intelligence, fire, [3][* * *], stores, reserve companies, training and claims prevention.

15. Organisational set up in the division. (1) The Force on each zonal railway shall be further distributed over divisions and railway establishments.

(2) Each division or railway establishment shall be headed by a Divisional Security Commissioner, who shall be assisted by such number of other superior officers and enrolled members of Force as may be appointed from time to time.

(3) For operational purposes, a division may be divided into sub-divisions each under the charge of a superior officer.

(4) A division or sub-division shall consist of one or more static posts and mobile companies organised in the manner specified in sub-rules (2) and (3) of rule 17.

(5) Each post or a company shall be under the charge of an officer not below the rank of an Inspector who may be assisted by such number of enrolled members of the Force as may be determined from time to time by the Chief Security Commissioner.

(6) A static post or a mobile company may have one or more outposts or detachments attached to it, each headed by an officer not below the rank of Sub-Inspector and comprising of such number of other enrolled members of the Force as may be determined by the Chief Security Commissioner.

(7) A Fire Station shall be headed by any officer not below the rank of a Sub-Inspector and shall consist of such number of other enrolled members of the Force as may be appointed from time to time for fire fighting and fire prevention.

16. Branches of the Force on a zonal railway. [4][(1) Force deployed on each zonal railway shall consist of an Executive branch.]

(2) [4][Executive branch] shall consist of such number of superior officers and other enrolled members of the Force as may be determined by the Chief Security Commissioner with the approval of the Director-General.

[5][* * *]

3 The word "prosecution" *omitted* by G.S.R. 719(E), dated 31.10.2013 (w.e.f. 31.10.2013).
4 *Substituted* by G.S.R. 719(E), dated 31.10.2013 (w.e.f. 31.10.2013).
5 *Omitted* by G.S.R. 719(E), dated 31.10.2013 (w.e.f. 31.10.2013).

17. Executive branch. (1) *The Executive Branch consists of five wings, namely:*

(*i*) Static Wing,

(*ii*) Mobile Wing,

(*iii*) Crime Wing,

(*iv*) Special Wing, and

(*v*) Stores Wing.

(2) The Static Wing shall be organised on a post pattern comprising of such number of enrolled members of the Force as may be needed for ensuring better protection and security of railway property and combating crimes against it.

(3) The Mobile Wing organised on such company pattern as may be decided by the Chief Security Commissioner concerned, shall primarily perform the duties other than those required to be performed by the static wing under sub-rule (2), especially those having inter-post ramifications.

(4) Crime Wing shall function as a specialised squad for collection and collation of information pertaining to criminals prying on railway property, detection of crime, inquiries into difficult cases having wider ramifications, arrest of criminals and their prosecution. The Chief Security Commissioner may attach some enrolled members of the Force working in this. Wing of his Security Commissariat as also the Dog Squad and handlers to each division. Control over such staff shall be shared functionally between the division and the Security Commissariat as may be ordered by the Chief Security Commissioner.

(5) The Chief Security Commissioner may deploy enrolled members of the Force working in Special Wing of his Security Commissariat in the divisions for collection of intelligence affecting the security and functioning of the railways. All the members of the branch shall function directly under the control of the Chief Security Commissioner through the immediate supervision and control of a superior officer incharge of Special Wing at his Commissariat. Intelligence requiring immediate attention and action of the part of the division shall be passed on directly to the Divisional Security Commissioner by the unit deployed in that division.

(6) The Stores Wing shall look after and cater to the requirements of Force for uniform, accoutrements, arms, ammunition, equipment and other stores items. This Wing shall also arrange for condemnation of unserviceable articles and their disposal. The Chief Security Commissioner may attach some enrolled members of the Force working in this Wing to each division who may work under the control of the Divisional Security Commissioner.

18. [6][* * *]

19. [7][* * *]

20. Security Control Room. (1) A Security Control Room shall be set up at the headquarters of the Director General, Chief Security Commissioner and of the Divisional Security Commissioner.

(2) It shall function round the clock and be manned by such members of the Force as may be appointed to it from time to time.

6 Rule 18, *omitted* by G.S.R. 719(E), dated 31.10.2013 (w.e.f. 31.10.2013).

7 Rule 19, *omitted* by G.S.R. 245(E), dated 5.7.2004 (w.e.f. 24.7.2004).

(3) All information necessary for exercising constant vigil on the incidence and pattern of crime and the areas endemic to such crime or for any other purposes shall be promptly collected by the Security Control Room and swiftly disseminated to the authorities specified on this behalf by the respective functionaries listed in sub-rule (1) above.

(4) In particular, any occurrence—

(*a*) which is a 'Special Report' or 'Special Occurrence' case as defined in rules 229 and 230 or which is unusual or of striking nature either in itself or because of its *modus operandi*;

(*b*) which involves destruction of or damage to railway property or of overhead traction or is a case of mischief by fire within railway premises;

(*c*) which is a case of suspected sabotage or tampering with track or in any other manner has affected the movement of railway property or the security and functioning of the railways;

(*d*) in which a member of the Force of a railway employee on duty has been assaulted or arrested or has opened fire;

(*e*) in which railway property exceeding the value, to be fixed by the Director-General, has been recovered or in which any other important case has been detected;

(*f*) which is likely to provoke reprisal from commuters and others;

(*g*) which is likely to arouse interest of or criticism from railway users; and

(*h*) which otherwise appears important to the Security Control Room, shall invariably be reported.

CHAPTER III

DIRECTION AND CONTROL

21. Superintendence of the Force. The superintendence of the Force shall vest in the Central Government and it may issue such directions relating to administration of the Act and these rules, as it may think necessary.

22. Command, supervision etc., at the Union level. (1) Subject to the provision of rule 21, the command, supervision and administration of the Force at the Union level shall vest in the Director General who shall be responsible for the efficient functioning and management of the Force in accordance with the provision of the Act and these rules.

(2) Being the head of the Force, the Director General shall take all possible steps for the coordinated and integrated growth of infrastructural facilities for the development and well being of the Force.

(3) The Director-General shall scrutinize the various proposals in the budget estimates of the Force, as submitted by the General Managers of the railways to the Central Government, and make his own assessment and recommendations in respect of allotment of funds and issue such directions in this behalf to Chief Security Commissioner concerned as he may consider necessary.

(4) The Director-General shall advise the Central Government in all matters relating to the service conditions of the members of the Force and exercise of disciplinary control over them.

(5) All references relating to the Force from the zonal railways, railway establishments etc, to the Central Government shall be received and be processed through the Director General and all orders of the Central Government in connection with the Force shall also be issued through him.

(6) It shall be under directions of the Director-General that the administration of the Force on the zonal railways and any other railway establishment shall be carried out by the Chief Security Commissioner and he shall be their principal controller or chief co-ordinator.

23. Command, supervision, etc., at the zonal railway level. (1) Subject to any directions issued by the Central Government or the Director General, the administration of the Force in zonal railway shall be carried out by the Chief Security Commissioner who shall discharge his functions in relation to the other departments of the zonal railway under the general supervision of the General Manager of such railway:

Provided that the powers of general supervision of the General Manager shall not extend to giving any directions to any member of the Force with regard to professional conduct of criminal cases or the exercise of any legal powers conferred on such member by any law for the time being in force.

(2) The Chief Security Commissioner shall be the head of the Security Department in the zonal railway administration and shall have irrespective of his rank and pay, the status, financial and administrative powers and privileges of a head of the department of the highest grade on the zonal railway.

(3) The Chief Security Commissioner shall maintain the Force under his command in a state of high efficiency, training, discipline and morale and shall take all such steps as he may consider necessary, from time to time, including inspections, supervision of cases, examination of records, calling for reports and issuing of necessary instructions to the superior officers and enrolled members of the Force under his command.

(4) The Chief Security Commissioner shall ensure that all instructions and directions issued by the Director-General in accordance with the provisions of the Act and rules are followed and complied with by all superior officers and enrolled members under his command.

24. Command. (1) An officer of the Force appointed to command shall have the power of command over all officers, irrespective of their seniority, placed under his command.

(2) In the contingency of an officer being unable to exercise the command, due to any reason, the command shall—

(*a*) devolve on the second-in-command, if one has been so appointed;

(*b*) if no second-in-command has been appointed, it shall devolve on the officer who may be appointed to command by the immediate superior of the officer unable to exercise command; and

(*c*) if no such officer has been so appointed, the command shall devolve on the senior-most officer of the Force present.

CHAPTER IV

POWERS AND RESPONSIBILITIES

25. General Powers and responsibilities of superior officers. The superior officers of the Force shall exercise such administrative and disciplinary powers over the members of the Force placed under their command as are specified in Schedules II to IV and such other powers as are conferred on railway servants of equivalent rank by any rules relating to such servants and discharge such responsibilities as are specified in these rules or may be specified in any directions issued by the Central Government or the Director-General in this behalf.

26. Responsibilities of the Director General connected with the security of the railways. (1) The Director-General shall—

(*a*) be responsible for providing better protection and security to railway property;

(*b*) advise the Central Government, the State Governments and zonal railway administration on all matters connected with railway security and handle all references concerning Police including railway police received from State Government or other Ministries of the Central Government;

(*c*) guide the Chief Security Commissioners in the protection and security of railway property and in combating crime against it;

(*d*) compile a monthly review on the performance of the Force in regard to its statutory duties and functions; and

(*e*) do all such other acts as may be necessary or incidental to the discharge of his duties under the Act and the rules.

(2) The Director-General may take all such steps as he considers necessary for effectively discharging his responsibilities referred to in sub-rule (1) including steps by way of tour and inspections, supervision of cases, examination of records, calling for reports and issuing of instructions and directions and holding periodical conferences and co-ordination meetings with the superior officers of Police including railway police and Civil Military administration and of the Force.

27. Administrative powers of the Director General. (1) *General.* The Director General shall—

(*a*) exercise all executive and administrative powers in relation to the Force and its deployment;

(*b*) arrange recruitment of Assistant Commandants and Sub-Inspectors against such posts in the Force which are reserved for being filled up by direct recruitment;

(*c*) order posting, transfer including inter-zonal railway transfers and training of all superior officers and enrolled members of the Force;

(*d*) select superior officers and enrolled members of the Force for specialised or advanced courses;

(*e*) compile on an all India basis, a seniority list of all Inspectors and superior officers and maintain it up-to-date at his headquarters;

(*f*) act as the appellate authority against the order of a Chief Security Commissioner;

(*g*) correspond with the State Government and other Ministries of the Government of India for securing deputation of officers for appointment as superior officers of the Force.

(2) *Powers to constitute Departmental Committees.* The Director-General may,—

(*a*) constitute such Departmental Committees as may be necessary for efficient functioning of the Force and performance of its duties;

(*b*) constitute the Departmental Promotion Committee, preferably in the beginning of each year, for selection to the rank of Assistant Commandant and above and maintain an up-to-date gradation list and dossiers of confidential reports of the officers;

(*c*) nominate the members of the Selection Board constituted under rule 49(1) for selecting direct recruits for the posts of sub-Inspectors; and

(*d*) nominate the members of the Selection Committee to select Sub-Inspectors for promotion to the rank of Inspectors on all zonal railways.

(3) *Powers to appoint Central Examination Committee.* (*a*) The Director-General shall appoint a Central Examination Committee as and when required, under the chairmanship of one of the Chief Security Commissioners, to conduct the final examination of Sub-Inspector cadets and of officers of higher rank undergoing training at any institution.

(*b*) It shall be after his approval that the final examination results of such courses shall be declared.

28. Powers of the Director General to issue "Directives". The Director-General may, from time to time, issue such directions, in the form of Directives, relating to the enforcement and furtherance of the provisions of the Act and these rules, as he may think necessary and the superior officers and enrolled members of the Force shall be governed by such "Directives" in the performance and discharge of their duties.

29. Powers of other superior officers to issue orders. The Chief Security Commissioner at the headquarters of the Director-General or on the zonal railway, the Divisional Security Commissioners and the Commanding Officer of the battalion may, in conformity with the provisions of the Act, the rules, the Directives and instructions of his superior officers, issue general or special orders to other superior officers and enrolled members of the Force under their command.

30. Magisterial powers. (1) All officers of the rank of Assistant Inspector General, Senior Commandant and Commandant of the Force, irrespective of their designation by virtue of their postings, who have rendered service for a period of not less than seven years as superior officers or combined service for a total period of not less than seven years as officers holding equivalent ranks in any Police service and as superior officers, shall exercise the powers of a—

(*a*) Metropolitan Magistrate in relation to a metropolitan area;

(*b*) Judicial Magistrate of the First Class in relation to any area outside a metropolitan area.

With respect to all or any of the matters specified in Part I of Schedule V;

(*c*) Chief Judicial Magistrate or, as the case may be, Chief Metropolitan Magistrate with respect to all or any of the matters specified in Part II of Schedule V.

for the purposes of sub-section (3) of section 17:

Provided that the exercise of powers by the aforesaid officers with respect to any matter specified in Schedule V shall be without prejudice to the exercise of any powers by such officers as Metropolitan Magistrate, Judicial Magistrate of the First Class, Chief Judicial Magistrate or Chief Metropolitan Magistrate under the Code of Criminal Procedure, 1973 for the matters mentioned in sub-section (3) of section 17.

31. Superior officers to exercise all those powers which can be exercised by their subordinates. (1) For the purposes of sub-section (2) of section 4, a superior officer may exercise any such power or perform any such duty as is assigned by the Act, the rules or by a lawful order to any member subordinate to him.

(2) In case, any duty is imposed on such subordinate, a superior officer may aid, supplement, supersede or prevent action of such subordinate by his own action or that of any person lawfully acting under his command or authority whenever the same shall appear necessary or expedient for giving a more complete or convenient effect to the law or for avoiding any infringement thereof.

32. Powers and functions of superior officers at the headquarters of the Director-General.
1 *Chief Security Commissioner (Administration).* (1) The Chief Security Commissioner in charge of administration shall assist the Director General in looking after all the matters connected with the administration of the Force and shall attend to such other duties as may be entrusted to him by the Director-General.

(2) He may have under him one or more other superior officers to look after the following branches or such other branch as may be created by the Director-General:—

(*i*) Administration including recruitment, deputation, induction, training, placement, transfer, promotion, pay and allowances, budget, discipline, legal matters and data processing.

(*ii*) Planning and Development including manpower planning, career planning, appraisal of performance, job requirements, personnel's record and manuals, follow up action on inspection notes and publicity.

(*iii*) Welfare and Service including grievances, employee relations, housing, education, sports, medical, provident fund, pension and other retirement and post-retirement benefits, welfare scheme, funds, canteen and messes.

(3) The Chief Security Commissioner in charge of administration shall be the *ex officio* Member Secretary of the Railway Protection Force Staff Council constituted under sub-rule (3) of rule III.

2 *Chief Security Commissioner (Railway Security).* (1) The Chief Security Commissioner incharge of the railway security shall assist the Director-General in providing better protection and security to railway property and collection, collation and dissemination of crime and special intelligence affecting the security and functioning of the railways.

(2) He shall—

(*i*) deal with logistics and transport for the Force, procurement and distribution of clothing, stores, fire prevention measures on railways;

(*ii*) assist his counterparts over the zonal railways in prevention and detection of crime and shall compile the monthly reviews on the performance of the Force in regard to its statutory duties and functions;

(*iii*) deal with all matters concerning the Police including the railway police as well as matters relating to security of railway referred to Director-General of the State Governments or any other organisation;

(*iv*) attend to such other duties as may be assigned to him by the Director-General.

(3) He may have under him a number of other superior officers and enrolled members of the Force as may be appointed from time to time to look after the railway security.

3 *Chief Security Commissioner (Railway Protection Special Force).* (1) The Chief Security Commissioner in-charge of the Railway Protection Special Force shall be responsible:—

(*i*) to the Director-General for efficiently maintaining the Railway Protection Special Force;

(*ii*) to ensure that a uniform standard of refresher training is imparted to all enrolled members of the Force in different battalions of the Force; and

(*iii*) for procuring arms and ammunition for use by the Force and to exercise technical supervision over the arms workshops constituted under rule 11.

(2) He shall undertake such other duties and discharge such other functions as may be assigned to him by the Director-General.

(3) He may have under him a number of other superior officers and enrolled members of the Force as may be appointed from time to time to look after the Railway Protection Special Force.

4 *Other superior officers at the headquarters of the Director-General.* All other superior officers posted at the headquarters of the Director-General shall look after branches or attend to such work as may be assigned to them by the Director-General or by their respective Chief Security Commissioners.

33. Powers and responsibilities of Commanding Officers of Railway Protection Special Force battalion. (1) The Commanding Officer of a battalion be responsible for—

(*a*) the internal administration, economy, efficiency, morale, discipline, training and welfare of the members of the Force placed under his command;

(*b*) safety and security of arms and ammunition and for ensuring its proper maintenance, repairs and cleaning thereof;

(*c*) correct and proper maintenance of clothing, uniform and other stores of the battalion; and

(*d*) making a physical check of all inventories at least once a year.

(2) When at headquarters, he shall attend morning parade and hold orderly rooms atleast once a week and meet his men, as stipulated in rule 109, once a month.

(3) He shall exercise powers as laid down in Schedule II to Schedule IV and under the extant Railway Rules and be guided by such instructions as may be

issued to him from time to time and submit such returns and reports as may be prescribed by Chief Security Commissioner in charge of Railway Protection Special Force or the Director-General.

34. Powers and responsibilities of other officers of the Railway Protection Special Force. (1) The powers and responsibilities of other superior officers of the Railway Protection Special Force shall be such as may be specified in the Directives.

35. Powers and responsibilities of the Chief Security Commissioner of the zonal railway. (1) The Chief Security Commissioner shall be the head of the Security Organisation of the zonal railway assigned to him and shall exercise such powers as are prescribed for the Heads of Departments under the extant Railway Rules.

(2) Subject to the provisions contained in the Act, rules and the Directives, he shall exercise administrative, executive and operational control over all members of the Force placed under his command.

(3) He shall deal with—

(*i*) all establishment and welfare matters pertaining to the Force and shall keep the Force at a high pitch of efficiency particularly through effective personal and financial management and inspection of branches under his control;

(*ii*) all matters referred by the Police including railway police or any other agency to the zonal railway concerning railway security.

(4) He shall responsible for providing in his jurisdiction better protection and security to railway property and deal with all matters connected therewith and to perform *inter alia* the following functions:

(*i*) to arrange collection and dissemination of crime and special intelligence affecting the security and functioning of the railways, maintenance of statistics, records and files relating thereto;

(*ii*) to devise ways and means for deducting incidents of theft, pilferages, losses and shortages of booked consignments leading to claims for compensation and for combating crimes affecting railway property including railway revenue;

(*iii*) to arrange thorough enquiries into cases of thefts of railway property or goods in transit or into cases of loss of railway revenue arising from misappropriation, evasion of wharfage and demurrage, cheating, etc.;

(*iv*) to maintain close liaison, on behalf of the railways, with the State Police including the railway police as well as the civil administration by holding meetings and conferences with his counterparts for ensuring better protection and security to the railway property;

(*v*) to advise the General Manager on all matters relating to the better protection and security of railway property, fire prevention measures and security of existing railway installations, such as workshops, stores, sheds, tracks, yards, etc. and of the new assets which the zonal railway may be planning to acquire or build; and

(*vi*) to watch and monitor the progress, of disciplinary action recommended by the Security Department against the delinquent railway servants.

36. Powers and responsibilities of Additional or Deputy Chief Security Commissioner. (1) The Additional or the Deputy Chief Security Commissioner as may be posted as Deputy Head of the Security Organisation of the zonal railway, shall exercise all such financial, administrative and disciplinary powers as are delegated to him under these rules or through Directives or as provided for railway servants of corresponding rank under the extant Railway Rules.

(2) He shall—

(*a*) represent the Chief Security Commissioner concerned at all official meetings in his absence or when especially deputed for the purpose;

(*b*) assist the Chief Security Commissioner concerned in discharge of his functions pertaining to protection and security of railway property and to combat crime against it, prosecution of criminals, maintenance of statistics, collection of crime intelligence—its collation and dissemination—enforcement of fire prevention measures, liaison with other railway departments etc; and

(*c*) perform the following other functions:

(*i*) review the cases of losses, thefts, pilferages, shortages and misappropriation of railway property with a view to bringing down their incidence;

(*ii*) watch and study the trends of claims arising under clause (*c*)(*i*) and initiate appropriate measures for their prevention in conjunction with Claims Organisation as well as with his counterparts on the other zonal railways;

(*iii*) scrutinize special report cases of crime and other important cases under the Railway Property (Unlawful Possession) Act, 1966 coming to Commissariat and issue instructions as considered necessary; and

(*iv*) organise and attend meetings and conferences with Police including railway police and other civil departments as directed by Chief Security Commissioner concerned to ensure better protection of railway property and take followup action on the decisions taken therein.

(3) He shall also—

(*i*) look after the logistics, transport, procurement and distribution of arms, ammunition, clothing, stores, etc.;

(*ii*) ensure prompt and correct replies to all questions received from Parliament, Estimates Committee, Public Accounts Committee etc., pertaining to his zonal railway;

(*iii*) be the incharge of the Zonal Security Control Room and shall monitor and take appropriate action on messages received by it;

(*iv*) carry out inspections of the offices and units of the Force in the zonal railway as may be entrusted to him by the Chief Security Commissioner concerned and suggest ways and means for their better functioning; and

(*v*) conduct such enquiries and attend to such other duties as may be entrusted to him by Chief Security Commissioner concerned.

37. Powers and responsibilities of Staff Officer or Personal Assistant. (1) The Staff Officer or Personal Assistant shall assist the Chief Security Commissioner concerned in the discharge of the following functions:

(*a*) *Administration.*—Including recruitments, deputation, training, placement, transfer, promotion, pay and allowances, budget, discipline, legal matters and data processing, reserve companies, band etc.;

(*b*) *Planning and development.*—Including manpower planning, career planning, appraisal of performance, job requirement, personnel's record and manuals, follow up action on inspection notes and publicity;

(*c*) *Welfare and Service.*—Including grievances, employee relations, housing education, sports, medical, provident fund, pension and other retirement and post retirement benefits, welfare schemes, funds, canteen and messes.

(2) He shall also be responsible for—

(*a*) organising periodical meetings required to be convened at the headquarter level;

(*b*) maintaining liaison with other departments of the railway at headquarters; and

(*c*) organising ceremonial parades, VIP visits and other matters of like nature.

(3) He shall exercise the same administrative and disciplinary powers, in respect of ministerial staff posted at the Security Commissariat as prescribed for his counterparts under these rules and/or under the extant Railway Rules and shall discharge such other duties as may be entrusted to him by the Chief Security Commissioner concerned.

38. Powers and responsibilities of other superior officers posted in Security Commissariat. The responsibilities of other superior officers posted in-charge of crime special intelligence, [8][* * *] and fire service etc., shall be such as may be specified through Directives or by the orders of the Chief-Security Commissioner concerned.

39. Powers and responsibilities of the Divisional Security Commissioner. (1) The Divisional Security Commissioner shall be directly responsible to the Chief Security Commissioner concerned for better protection, security the smooth movement of railway property as well as for efficient administration of the Force in his jurisdiction and shall deal with all establishment matters concerning the enrolled members of the Force placed under his control.

(2) He shall exercise such powers in respect of establishment and other matters as are given in Schedules II to IV and under the extant Railway Rules.

(3) The Divisional Security Commissioner shall devise ways and means for providing better protection and security to railway property in his division and matters connected therewith and shall carry out such directions as may be given to him on the subject by the Chief Security Commissioner concerned or on his behalf by any other superior officer of the Force.

(4) He shall keep in close touch with the superior officer posted in the division, Post Commanders and Company Commanders for ensuring effective co-ordination

8 The word "prosecution" *omitted* by G.S.R. 719(E), dated 31.9.2013 (w.e.f. 31.10.2013).

amongst them and to aid, advise or direct their activities for providing better protection and security to railway property.

(5) He shall inspect, as frequently as possible and in any case not less than once a year, the work of his Assistant Security Commissioners, all Railway Protection Force Posts, Companies important Posts, detachments, etc., coming in his jurisdiction and take such action as may lie within his competence or issue such directions as considered necessary to remedy existing defects or to streamline the working.

(6) His other functions shall include—

(*a*) attending parades and kit inspections at important stations and holding monthly meetings with superior officers, Post Commanders and Company Commanders of his division to review the crime situation;

(*b*) ensuring effective and result-oriented deployment of Force placed under his command;

(*c*) studying all basic security arrangements against thefts, pilferages and other crimes against railway property and suggesting such improvements to the authorities concerned as may be called for;

(*d*) ensuring correct accountal of crime, thorough and prompt enquiries for recovery of stolen railway property and prosecution of offenders and receivers;

(*e*) liaison with his counterparts in the Police including railway police, civil administration and other railway departments for taking effective measures for better protection and security of railway property and matters connected therewith;

(*f*) keeping watch over claims preferred and paid on account of theft, pilferages, losses and shortages of booked consignment and taking preventive measures in co-operation with his counterpart in the Claims Prevention Office to arrest the upward trend in incidents leading to such claims noticed anywhere in his jurisdiction;

(*g*) submitting to his superior officers such reports and returns as may be called for including reports on subversive and other objectionable activities affecting the security and functioning of the railway noticed anywhere in his division; and

(*h*) ensuring full compliance by all concerned under his command of all directions and instructions issued by the Director-General or the Chief Security Commissioner concerned under the Act and these rules.

40. Powers and responsibilities of other superior and subordinate officers of the division. The powers and responsibilities of other superior and subordinate officers posted to assist the Divisional Security Commissioner shall be such as may be specified in the Directives.

41. General powers and functions of enrolled members of the Force. (1) The primary functions of enrolled members of the Force shall be:—

(*a*) to protect and safeguard railway property and to combat crime against it;

(*b*) to do any other act conducive to better protection and security of railway property;

(*c*) to remove any obstruction in the movement of railway property; and (*d*) to perform other functions of an armed force of the Union and to exercise powers of a railway servant as conferred by or under the Indian Railways Act, 1890.

(2) The other functions of enrolled members of the Force shall be—

(*i*) to identify the situations that have potentials for the commission of crime against the railway property either static or in transit or mobile and take remedial measures or suggest improvement in basic security arrangements of faulty procedures where necessary, to the railway administration;

(*ii*) to reduce the opportunities of thefts, pilferages, misappropriation, trades, etc., against railway property and leakage of railway revenue through surprise preventive checks or other appropriate measures, like detailing of patrols in vulnerable sectors, posting of guards and pickets as black spots, escorting of affected trains, keeping open or unobtrusive watch at workshops, stores, goods-sheds, depots, parcel officers, yards and other such places and at any station or enroute the destination of railway property;

(*iii*) to aid co-operate and co-ordinate the measures of other railway agencies or the Police or other authorities in implementing other appropriate measures for ensuring prevention of crime against the railway property and providing for its better security;

(*iv*) to interpose at any time or place for preventing any attempt to steal, misuse, damage or temper with the railway property or to convert it into private use without lawful authority and to initiate action against offenders;

(*v*) to register and take up enquiries under Railway Property (Unlawful Possession) Act, 1966, apprehend the offenders and participate in subsequent legal proceedings connected therewith;

(*vi*) to register or to promptly pass on reports for registration to the local Police of all cognizable offences against the railway property, conduct enquiries and collect evidence for localising the crime or which is otherwise considered necessary and render such other assistance as may be possible in investigation of such cases;

(*vii*) to obtain intelligence relating to the commission of or intention to commit any offence specified in clauses (*i*), (*ii*), (*iii*), (*iv*), (*v*), (*vi*), (*vii*), (*viii*), (*ix*) of sub-section (1) of section 39 of the Code of Criminal Procedure, 1973 on the railways and to lay such information and to take such other steps consistent with law and with the orders of his superiors as shall be best calculated to bring offenders to justice and to prevent the commission of cognizable and, within his view of non-cognizable offences;

(*viii*) to collect intelligence about subversive and other objectionable activities affecting the security and functioning of the railways as well as about the activities of criminals and suspect prying on railway property;

(*ix*) to study all cases of suspected sabotage or tampering with track or obstruction to movement of railway property with a view to suggesting preventive measures to railway administration and the Police;

(*x*) subject to rule 42, to assist the railway administration during strikes and lockouts as well as the Police during mob violence or civil disturbances or for maintenance of law and order and control of railway crime or when deputed anywhere in India in aid to civil power;

(*xi*) to assist the commercial and other department of the railway during raids on ticketless travellers, alarm chain pullers, unauthorised hawkers and on those indulging in, hose pipe disconnections or infringing other provisions of the Indian Railways Act, 1890;

(*xii*) to aid any other member of the Force called upon by such other member or in the case of need in the discharge of the duty of such other member, in such ways as would be lawful and reasonable on the part of the member thus aided;

(*xiii*) to use his best endeavours to prevent any loss or damage by fire to railway property;

(*xiv*) to record and study all cases of fire incidents involving railway property and suggest preventive measures and to operate and maintain fire fighting equipment at railway stations installations, etc.

(*xv*) to guard cash offices of railway and escort their pay clerks;

(*xvi*) to take prompt measures to procure necessary medical help for any wounded or sick person under arrest or in custody;

(*xvii*) to arrange for the proper sentence and shelter to every person who is under arrest or in custody;

(*xviii*) to undertake any other security duty assigned to the Force by or with the concurrence of railway administration for the execution of which necessary resources have been provided and approval of the Director General or the Chief Security Commissioner, as the case may be, obtained; and

(*xix*) to promptly obey and execute all orders lawfully issued to him by any superior officer of the Force and to discharge such other duties as are imposed upon him by any law for the time being in force or cast on him by any railway rule.

42. Restriction on deployment of Force. (1) Notwithstanding anything contained in this Chapter, no member of the Force shall be called upon to carry out any functions relating to law and order (except when detailed under Chapter XVI) or to attend to problems which are purely of an administrative nature requiring certain standard of discipline to be maintained by the railway servants or users of the railways:

Provided that the Force may be deployed to combat mob violence against the safety and security of railway property where there is delay in arrival of the police or the Magistrate.

(2) Without prejudice to rule 41(2)(*x*), the Force may make adequate arrangements during strike and lock-outs for ensuring protection and security of railway property and provide protection to the loyal workers and for maintenance of law and order with the assistance of local Police or otherwise.

(3) Except for reasons to be recorded in writing, no member of the Force shall be deployed in railway colonies:—

(*a*) for rounding up and removal of stray cattle, hawkers, beggars, anti-social elements and such other duties;

(*b*) for regulating the crowd for ensuring law and order in the sale of controlled commodities by railway co-operative societies;

(*c*) to perform traffic duties; to control the crowd and to regulate vehicular traffic;

(*d*) to collect toll taxes; or

(*e*) to guard the schools and colleges run by the railway administration;

Provided that the Force may be deployed in any railway colony for guarding vital installations like sub-stations, pump houses, etc.

[9][(4) Whenever the Force is called upon to help remove encroachments and unauthorised occupations either on railway stations or in the railway premises, it shall be the duty of the Force to render such help as is necessary, to the authority seeking help subject to the following restrictions:

(*a*) the Force shall not be called upon to help evict railway employees from railway quarters or trade union from railway buildings. Nor shall the Force be called upon to help evict any Government or semi-Government agency from railway quarters, railway stations, railway buildings or railway premises;

(*b*) the requisition or help shall be made in writing to the Post Commander by Railway Officer not below the rank of an Assistant Officer;

(*c*) the Post Commander, while rendering assistance to the Railway Officer requisitioning assistance, shall follow such procedure as may be prescribed by the Directives.]

(5) No member of the Force shall be deployed for serving order of dismissal or removal from service or suspension on any railway servant or to verify the antecedents or character of any employee.

(6) No member of the Force shall be called upon to remove any posters which seem objectionable to the railway administration but if any other railway servant is commissioned to remove such posters, the Force shall provide protection to him.

43. Procedure on arrest. For the purposes of section 14, while handing over a person arrested under section 12 to the Police Officer or at the nearest Police Station, a brief note giving the time, date and reasons of arrest shall also be furnished and a record of the same kept at the Post.

44. Search. For purposes of section 13 of the Act, if any railway property reasonably suspected of having been stolen or unlawfully obtained is found during any search of a person or his belongings that person shall be arrested and dealt with under the provisions of the Railway Property (Unlawful Possession) Act, 1966 or sent to

9 *Substituted* by G.S.R. 756(E), dated 2.11.1999 (w.e.f. 5.11.1999).

the Police along with the property thus recovered as the circumstances of the case may warrant.

CHAPTER V

RECRUITMENT, TRAINING AND CAREER PLANNING

45. Recruitment. (1) Direct recruitment to the Force shall be made at the level of Constables, Sub-Inspectors and Assistant Commandants and all other posts shall be filled in by promotion or through a limited departmental competition from amongst the eligible enrolled members of the Force or by taking personnel on deputation in accordance with these rules.

(2) The Chief Security Commissioner concerned shall work out each year the number of vacancies in each rank and shall take steps to fill them up in accordance with these rules.

(3) The procedure for filling up these posts and other matters not specially provided for in these rules shall be such as may be specified in the Directives.

46. Ineligibility. No person—

(*a*) who is not a citizen of India, or

(*b*) who has entered into or contracted a marriage with a person having a spouse living, or

(*c*) who having a spouse living, has entered into or contracted a marriage with any person,

shall be eligible for appointment as member of the Force.

47. Enlistment of standards. *Physical standards.* The minimum physical standard for enlistment as an enrolled member of the Force (including ancillary staff specified in Schedule I) shall be as under:—

(*a*) Height—165 cms.

(*b*) Chest : Unexpanded—80 cms.

Expanded—85 cms.

[10][* * *]

[Provided] that for persons who have not attained the age of 20 years, a relaxation of 2.5 cms. in height and 5 cms. in chest measurements may be allowed if the Divisional Medical Officer certifies that the person concerned is likely to attain the minimum prescribed standard on attaining the maximum age applicable in the case:

Provide further that the Director-General may prescribe separate physical standard for female candidates for direct recruitment.

48. Age and educational qualifications. (1) A candidate for the post of Sub-Inspector by direct recruitment,—

(*i*) must be above 20 years but below 25 years of age on the date of notification of recruitment, and

(*ii*) must possess a Bachelor's degree or equivalent from a recognised University.

[11][* * *]

10 First proviso *omitted* by G.S.R. 574, dated 7.11.1994 (w.e.f. 19.11.1994).

11 *Omitted* by G.S.R. 719(E), dated 31.10.2013 (w.e.f. 31.10.2013).

(2) A candidate for the post of Constable; by direct recruitment,—

(*i*) must be above the age of 18 years but below the age of 25 years on the date of notification of recruitment, and

(*ii*) must have passed High School Examination or its equivalent from a recognised Board or University:

Provided that the upper age limit for posts to be filed by direct recruitment may be relaxed for candidates belonging to the Scheduled Castes or Scheduled Tribes and other special categories of persons in accordance with orders issued by the Central Government from time to time in this regard.

Provided further that proficiency in games, sports and athletics, music, membership of National Cadet Corps and other organisations or institutions as may be approved by the Director-General shall be given due weightage as additional qualifications:

Provided further that preference may be given to the children of the members of the Force who, while facing criminals or in action during civil strife, violent demonstration or during any other active or operational duty, are killed or became disabled or invalidated out of service in case such children are otherwise eligible and suitable for the post.

[12][**49. Procedure of recruitment.** (1) Selection for direct recruitment to the posts of Sub-Inspectors shall be made by a departmental committee of four persons holding the post of Inspector General or Additional Inspector General, Deputy Inspector General of Railway Protection Force or Railway Protection Special Force who shall be nominated by the Director-General and where such selection includes the selection for reserved posts for the Scheduled Castes/Scheduled Tribes or the Backward Classes, one Officer holding any of the said posts and belonging to the Scheduled Castes or the Scheduled Tribes or the Backward Classes, as the case may be, shall also be nominated by the Director-General to be a member in such committee.

(2) Selection for direct recruitment to the posts of Constables shall be made by a departmental committee of four persons holding the post of Commandant or Senior Commandant nominated by the Inspector General/Deputy Inspector General of the Zonal Railway or Railway Protection Special Force and where such selection includes the selection for reserved posts for the Scheduled Castes/Scheduled Tribes or the Backward Classes, one officer holding any of the said posts and belonging to the Scheduled Castes/Scheduled Tribes or the Backward Classes, as the case may be, shall also be nominated by the Inspector General Deputy Inspector General to be a member in such committee.

(3) Places for holding selections shall be so fixed as to attract best talents from various regions or States, as the case may be, and need not be restricted merely to the applicants sponsored by the employment exchange or other such Government agencies.

(4) Procedure of selection shall be so evolved as to—

(*a*) reduce the chances of impersonation;

(*b*) eliminate at the initial stage all such candidates who are unfit for consideration; and

12 *Substituted* by G.S.R.*114, dated 14.6.2007 (w.e.f. 23.6.2007).

Final selection shall be based on uniform standards of tests for which guidelines shall be prescribed by the Director-General.]

50. Appointment in special cases. The Central Government may, for reasons to be recorded in writing, provide for appointments being made otherwise than as prescribed in this Chapter to give effect to special claims or to meet any special case or situation.

51. Medical examination. (1) No candidate who is not certified by the Divisional Medical Officer to be in good mental and bodily health of prescribed standard and free from any physical deformity or defect likely to interfere with the efficient performance of his duties in the Railway Protection Force shall be called in for training or appointed to the Force.

(2) Candidates who use spectacles or have knock-knee or flat-foot shall not be eligible for appointment to the Force [13][* * *].

52. Verification. (1) As soon as a recruit is selected but before he is formally appointed to the Force, his character and antecedents shall be got verified in accordance with the procedure prescribed by the Central Government from time to time.

(2) Where after verification, a recruit is not found suitable for the Force, he shall not be appointed as a member of the Force.

53. Execution of agreement, etc.—Every person shall—

(*a*) at the time of his joining the initial training course, execute an agreement in the form specified in Schedule VI, and

(*b*) on appointment as a member of the Force, make solemn affirmation in the form specified in Schedule VII and also receive a certificate of appointment in the form specified in the Schedule of the Act.

54. Cadre of superior officers of the Force. (1) The cadre of superior officers of the Force shall be named by—

(*a*) direct recruits through the Civil Services Examination conducted by the Union Public Service Commission;

(*b*) promotees from lower ranks of the Force;

(*c*) deputationists from Indian Police Service and other State Police Services;

(*d*) occasional admission of other qualified persons on the recommendation of the Union Public Service Commission, who would enter laterally as considered necessary from time to time.

(2) The strength of the cadre and its composition shall be such as may be determined by the Central Government from time to time.

55. Recruitment and promotion of superior officers. (1) Subject to these rules, recruitment of superior officers and promotion to the rank of Assistant Commandants and from one rank of superior officer to the other rank of superior officers shall be made in accordance with the Railway Protection Force (Group 'A' and 'B' Posts) Recruitment Rules, 1981, as amended from time to time.

13 *Omitted* by G.S.R. 719(E), dated 31.10.2013 (w.e.f. 31.10.2013).

(2) Confirmation and regularisation in each rank shall be made on all India availability of the posts in that rank.

56. Appointment to the Force. All appointments to the Force,—

(*a*) in respect of Group 'A' shall be made by the Central Government; and

(*b*) in respect of enrolled members shall be made by the authorities as specified in Schedule II.

57. Probation. (1) Every member on appointment to the Force either by direct recruitment or by promotion shall be on probation for a period of two years:

Provided that the controlling authority may extend the period of probation in accordance with the instructions or orders issued by the Central Government from time to time in this regard:

Provided further that any decision for extension of a probationary period shall be taken immediately after the expiry of the probationary period and communicated in writing to the concerned member of the Force together with the reasons for so doing within a period of two months from the expiry of the probationary period.

(2) On successful completion of the period of probation or any extension thereof, a member of the Force shall be retained in his appointment on regular basis and be confirmed in due course against the available substantive vacancy.

(3) If, during the period of probation of any extension thereof, as the case may be, the appointment authority is of the opinion that the member of the Force is not fit for permanent appointment, the appointing authority may terminate the services of a direct recruit or revert the member of the Force to the post held by him prior to such appointment:

Provided that in case of termination of service a probationer shall be given a notice of one month to that effect or pay in lieu thereof:

Provided further that a notice or pay in lieu thereof shall not be required where the termination of service results as a consequence of the failure of the probationer to pass the initial training course or a repeat course, if any.

(4) During the period of probation or any extension thereof, a member of the Force may be required by the appointing authority to undergo such courses of training and instructions and to pass such examinations and tests as may be specified by it for satisfactory completion of the probation.

58. Refund of cost of training. A person appointed as a member of the Force shall ordinarily serve for a period of three years. In the event of such person resigning from service, he shall refund the cost of training as determined by the appointing authority or three months' pay whichever is less.

TRAINING

59. Initial training of direct recruits. (1) Every person on entering service as direct recruit in any rank shall undergo an initial training course for the efficient performance of his duties.

(2) Officers coming on deputation to the Force for field postings shall undergo an orientation course as may be specified by the Director-General from time to time.

(3) Deputationists of subordinate ranks may undergo the orientation course at the Railway Protection Force Academy or in any other Zonal Training Institute of the Force as may be specified by the Chief Security Commissioner concerned.

60. Standard of training and syllabus. (1) The Director-General shall specify the standard of training and syllabus for different ranks as well as for refresher, orientation, promotional, special and other in-service courses and fix the duration of training for such courses.

(2) The ancillary staff specified in Schedule I may only be given a short training in discipline, wearing of uniform, rudiments of drill including saluting, etc.

61. Syllabus for basic training. The syllabus for basic training for all direct recruits shall be such as may be specified by the Director-General and shall *inter alia* include the following matters, in addition to practical training, namely:

(*a*) *Out-door*—

(*i*) correct wearing of uniform, *i.e.* clothing and accoutrements;

(*ii*) ceremonial drill and guard mounting;

(*iii*) squad, platoon and company drill and extended order movements;

(*iv*) weapon training including field craft, tear-gas smoke, riot drill and handling of explosives;

(*v*) physical training; and

(*vi*) self-defence, karate, swimming and leadership.

(*b*) *In-door*—

(*i*) Organisation of the railways, the Railway Protection Force and their working;

(*ii*) establishment and accounts matters and procedure of Railway Protection Force;

(*iii*) general duties of Railway Protection Force including prevention and investigation of crimes connected with Railway property and prosecution of offenders;

(*iv*) law with special emphasis on criminal law, Indian Railways Act, 1890, Railway Protection Force Act, 1957, Railway Protection Force Rules, Directive and Railway Property (Unlawful Possession) Act, 1966;

(*v*) psychology, criminology and scientific aids to investigation including finger prints;

(*vi*) first aid and fire fighting;

(*vii*) scriptory work at the Posts and Company headquarters;

(*viii*) intelligence course and security work including security of prisoners;

(*ix*) insurgency against mass transportation and measures to combat it;

(*x*) working of the transportation, commercial, mechanical, electrical, signal and telecommunication and other allied departments of railway and liaison with them;

(*xi*) liaison with Police (including railway police) and other agencies when detailed in aid to Civil Power;

(*xii*) dealing with weaker sections, *e.g.* women, juveniles, lunatics, including their search, arrest, questioning, etc.;

(*xiii*) codes of conduct and behaviour of Railway Protection Force personnel;

(*xiv*) disaster management and public relation work in order to help create better image of Railway Protection Force; and

(*xv*) any other matter which may be considered desirable to be introduced by the Director-General.

62. Special courses. The Chief Security Commissioner concerned may, at any time, depute any member of the Force to undergo a course of training or instructions having a bearing on the Railway Protection Force work conducted by the Central Government or the State Government or by any training establishment or the Railway Protection Force or army institution or Directorate of Co-ordination (Police Wireless) or railway training institution or any other institution:

Provided that in the case of superior officer, the Chief Security Commissioner concerned shall obtain prior permission of the Director-General.

63. Regulation of training period. (1) Subject to sub-rule (2), the period of training including in-service courses shall be treated as duty for all purposes.

(2) During the period of training, the recruits shall be paid stipend or pay and allowances as may be specified from time to time.

64. Promotion courses. (1) Enrolled members of the Force on being regularly selected for promotion to the rank of [14][* * *], Head Constable, Assistant Sub-Inspector and Sub-Inspector shall undergo a special course (hereinafter referred to as promotion course) at any training institution of the Force a duration which may be fixed by the Director-General:

Provided that the promotion course of promotee Sub-Inspectors (Fire) eligible for admission to the National Fire Service College, Nagpur shall be at the said College.

(2) Passing of per-promotional course shall be essential for regular promotion which will take effect from the date on which such enrolled member of the Force reports for duty against a clear vacancy after passing the said course.

65. Examination on conclusion of course at any training institution of the Force. (1) At the conclusion of each course at any training institution of the Force, the final examination shall be conducted by a Board of Examiners which shall be nominated by—

(*a*) the Director-General in case training courses for Sub-Inspectors and above, and

(*b*) the Chief Security Commissioner concerned in case of training courses for other members of the Force.

(2) *Pass marks.* In order to pass the examination, the candidates would be required to obtain a minimum of 50 per cent marks in each subject and 60 per cent marks in the aggregate.

14 Certain words *omitted* by G.S.R. 229, dated 15.7.1999 (w.e.f. 24.7.1999).

[15][(3) *Second attempt.*—Any candidate who fails the examination shall be allowed a second attempt to appear for that subject or course in such manner as may be specified by the Director-General or the Chief Security Commissioner concerned, without any stipend or any other remuneration:

Provided that candidates belonging to the Scheduled Castes/Scheduled Tribes categories shall be given a second attempt with stipend or remuneration and a third attempt without any stipend or any other remuneration.]

(4) On failure in the [15][second] attempt or, where the candidate is eligible for the [15][third] attempt, on failure in the [15][third] attempt, the candidate shall be discharged from service without notice or reverted to his substantive rank.

(5) *Approval of results.*—The Board of Examiners on conclusion of examination of each course, shall submit the proceedings and result of the examination to the authority which constituted the Board for approval.

(6) The authority on receipt of proceeding and result may approve or for reasons to be recorded in writing, pass such other orders as it may deem fit in the circumstances of the case.

66. Refresher courses. (1) Members of the Force while in service may be required to undergo such refresher courses, for such durations and at such places as may be determined by the Director-General.

(2) A roster in respect of members of the Force who are required to attend in-service training or special training shall be prepared and maintained at the Security Commissariat of the Chief Security Commissioner concerned for strict compliance and order shall be issued to the concerned members of the Force well in advance.

(3) The release of members of the Force for training shall under no circumstances be deferred except in exceptional circumstances and when such postponement has been made, it shall not be deferred further beyond the immediate next course.

(4) A member deputed for training shall, so long as possible, be posted back to the place from where he has proceeded on training if he is otherwise not due for transfer or promotion.

67. Disciplinary control. (1) The staff and trainees at any training institution of the Force, shall, so long as they are at such institution or undergoing practical training at some other place, be under disciplinary control of the Principal of that training institution.

(2) A direct recruit selected for being appointed as enrolled member, till such time he is not formally appointed to the Force, is liable to be discharged at any stage if the Chief Security Commissioner for reasons to be recorded in writing, deems it fit so to do in interest of the Force.

PROMOTION AND CAREER PLANNING

68. Cadre review. A cadre review of all branches of the Force shall be undertaken once in five years or earlier as decided by the Central Government.

15 *Substituted* by G.S.R. 556(E), dated 16.8.2013 (w.e.f. 19.8.2013).

69. Basis of promotion. (1) Promotion of member of the Force upto rank of Commandant shall be made on the basis of merit having due regard to seniority.

(2) Promotion to ranks higher than that of the Commandant shall be made on the basis of merit only.

70. Procedure for promotion of enrolled members of the Force. (1) The age limit, length of service and other matters relating to promotions and procedures for determining the seniority on appointment or on promotion shall be in accordance with these rules or where no provision has been made herein for these matters be in accordance with the Directives.

(2) A panel shall be drawn up preferably each year by the Departmental Promotion Committee for each specified category of posts which are required to be filled on the basis of promotion.

(3) The number of candidates called for selection under rule 71 shall, ordinarily, be three times the number required to be empanelled and their names shall be notified thirty days in advance of the date fixed for holding selection.

Provided that the name of any enrolled member who has continuously failed to qualify in three attempts shall not be taken into consideration for three subsequent selection for that rank, while calling the candidates for selection as specified above:

Provided further that a candidate whose work and conduct has been assessed as below average or whose integrity has been found to be doubtful in two or more years out of the five years preceding the selection shall not be empanelled.

(4) The size of a panel drawn up in accordance with sub-rule (3) shall ordinarily be such as shall provide for all existing vacancies and vacancies anticipated within the next twelve months from the date on which the Departmental Promotion Committee is constituted plus ten per cent of such total and limited to percentage, if any, specified in Schedule IV against that category.

(5) Nomination of members of the Departmental Promotion Committee for holding selections to various ranks mentioned in column (1) of the Table below shall be made by the superior officers mentioned against that rank, in column (2) of the said Table:

TABLE

(1)	(2)
(*i*) [16][* * *], Head Constable and Asstt, Sub-Inspector	Deputy Chief Security Commissioner.
(*ii*) Sub-Inspector	Chief Security Commissioner.
(*iii*) Inspector	Director General.

16 *Omitted* by G.S.R. 229, dated 15.7.1999 (w.e.f. 24.7.1999).

(6) The composition of Departmental Promotion Committee shall be as under:

(1)	(2)
[17][(*i*)] [18][Promotion from Constable to Head Constable]	Three Assistant Security Commissioners.
[19][(*ii*)] Promotion from Head Constable to Assistant Sub-Inspector	Two Security Commissioners and one Assistant Security Commissioner.
[20][(*iii*)] Promotion from Assistant Sub-Inspector to Sub-Inspector	Three Security Commissioners.
[20][(*iv*)] Promotion from Sub-Inspector to Inspector	Three Chief Security Commissioners.

(7) (1) All panels drawn up by the Departmental Promotion Committee shall be submitted for appropriate authority who nominated the said Committee.

(2) If the said authority does not accept the recommendations of the said Committee, it shall record the reasons for the same and the matter shall be referred to the next higher authority, which may, for reasons to be recorded in writing pass such orders as are considered appropriate.

(8) A panel drawn up in accordance with this rule shall remain operative for a period of one year from the date of its approval or till it is exhausted, whichever is earlier.

71. Guidelines for Departmental Promotion Committee for holding selection under rule 70. (1) Allocation of marks for written examination and practical test shall be as follows, namely:—

	Maximum marks		*Qualifying marks*
(*a*) Written Examination	40	60	36
(*b*) Practical test including IT, PT and Riot Drill	20		

(2) Candidates qualifying in the above test shall be subjected to a *viva voce* test for which marks may be awarded having regard to factors specified in the Directives, and the maximum marks shall be as follows, namely:—

	Maximum marks
(*a*) Personality, comprehension, oral expression, temperament and response, social consciousness	20
(*b*) Record of service	20

17 Entry (*ii*) renumbered as entry (*i*) by G.S.R. 229, dated 15.7.1999 (w.e.f. 24.7.1999).
18 *Substituted* by G.S.R. 229, dated 15.7.1999 (w.e.f. 24.7.1999).
19 Entry (*iii*) renumbered as entry (*ii*) by G.S.R. 229, dated 15.7.1999 (w.e.f. 24.7.1999).
20 Entries (*iv*) and (*v*) renumbered as entries (*iii*) and (*iv*) by G.S.R. 229, dated 15.7.1999 (w.e.f. 24.7.1999).

(3) A panel shall be drawn from amongst the candidates securing sixty percent or more marks in the order of their respective seniority in the rank:

Provided that candidates obtaining eighty percent marks in the aggregate or more shall be declared as "outstanding" and shall take higher position by fifty percent of successful candidates above him in order of seniority.

(4) Qualifying marks for candidates belonging to the Scheduled Castes and Scheduled Tribes shall be thirty marks under sub-rule (1) and fifty percent under sub-rule (3).

72. Guidelines for holding limited departmental competition. (1) Applications from eligible candidates for appearing in the limited departmental competition to the ranks of Head Constable and Assistant Sub-Inspector shall be invited thirty days in advance of the proposed date of holding the said competition.

(2) The procedure for holding the said competition shall be the same as provided in rules 70 and 71 except sub-rule (3) of the said rules.

(3) A panel shall be drawn from amongst the candidates securing sixty percent marks or more in the order of merit.

73. [21][* * *]

74. Promotion to short-term vacancies. (1) Promotion to short-term vacancies may be made on an officiating basis if the exigencies of service so require.

(2) Such promotion may be made from amongst persons who are on the panel or if there is no candidate on the panel then on the basis of seniority subject to rejection of unfit.

75. Special provision for ancillary staff. (1) Ancillary staff, as specified in Schedule I, shall form part of the enrolled members of the Force.

(2) Notwithstanding anything contained in sub-rule 48(2)(*ii*) and in rule 49, a candidate who, in the opinion of the appointing authority, is otherwise qualified and proficient in his trade or skill may be enlisted as a Constable for that trade or skill.

(3) Notwithstanding anything contained in rules 7 and 16, for purpose of promotion and advancement in career, the ancillary staff shall form a separate cadre for each trade or skill on the zonal railway or, as the case may, on the Railway Protection Special Force and shall be promoted to the next higher rank of their category on the basis of seniority to rejection of unfit.

76. Deputation of officers to the Force. Notwithstanding anything contained in this Chapter, with a view to ensuring highest professional standard and closest liaison with Police including railway police recruitment may be made by taking personnel

21 Rule 73 *omitted* by G.S.R. 229, dated 15.7.1999 (w.e.f. 24.7.1999).

on deputation from the police on such terms and conditions as may be specified by the Central Government from time to time. The period of deputation of Police Officers shall not normally be less than four years or more than seven years.

Provided that the deputation of officers to the posts of the Inspectors shall be limited to fifteen per cent unless the concerned Chief Security Commissioner is of the opinion that Sub-Inspectors who fulfil the conditions of eligibility for promotion to the posts of Inspectors are not available or if such candidates are available they are not of proved merit and ability.

77. Deputation of members of the Force to other departments. (1) No member of the Force shall directly approach any other department for deputation.

(2) With the prior approval of the Director-General or the concerned Chief Security Commissioner, as the case may be, members of the Force may be allowed to proceed on deputation in public interest to other departments of the railways or to other Government departments on such terms and conditions as may be offered by the borrowing department.

CHAPTER VI

PAY, REMUNERATION AND DURATION OF SERVICE

78. Pay and allowances. (1) The pay of superior officers and enrolled members of the Force shall be as follows or as may be prescribed by the Central Government from time to time:—

Superior Officers	
Rank	*Scale of Pay*
Director General	₹7600 (fixed)
Inspector General	₹5900-200-6700
Additional Inspector General	As may prescribed
Deputy Inspector General	₹5100-150-5400-150-6150 ₹5400 in 18th year or later
Senior Commandant Commandant	₹4100-125-4850-150-5300
Assistant Inspector General	₹3000-100-3500-125-4500
Deputy Commandant	As may be prescribed
Assistant Commandant	₹2200-75-2800-EB-100-4000

Provided that whenever the posts of Deputy Inspector General and Assistant Inspector General (in selection grade or otherwise) are held by IPS officers, these posts shall carry a special pay of ₹400 each subject to the condition that the pay plus special pay shall not exceed the maximum of the scale of pay of the post to which the special pay is attached.

Enrolled members of the Force	
[1][Inspector	₹6500-200-10,500]
Sub-Inspector	₹1400-40-1800-EB-50-2300
Assistant Sub-Inspector	₹1320-30-1560-EB-40-2040
Head Constable	₹975-25-1150-EB-30-1660
[2][* * *]	
Constable	₹825-15-900-EB-20-1200
Driver Grade I	₹1320-30-1560-EB-40-2040
Driver Grade II	₹1200-30-1440-EB-30-1800
Driver Grade III	₹950-20-1150-EB-25-1500
Fire Extinguisher (Gr. I)	₹1320-30-1560-EB-40-2040
Fitters, Hose Repairer	
Fitter/Mechanic, (Gr. II)	₹1200-30-1440-EB-30-1800
Fire Extinguisher (Gr. III)	₹950-20-1150-EB-25-1500
Painter	
Tailor Pump (Gr. I)	₹1320-30-1560-EB-40-2040
Operator (State Unit) (Gr. II)	₹1200-30-1440-EB-30-1900
Tailor	
Pump operator-cum (Gr. III)	₹950-20-1150-EB-25-1500
Driver (Mobile Unit)	

ANCILLARY STAFF

[3][* * *]

(2) The fixation of pay shall be done in accordance with extant Railway Rules as they apply for such fixation in relation to other organised services of the railways.

(3) The superior officers and enrolled members of the Force shall also be eligible, in accordance with the orders of the Central Government in this behalf to special pay and allowances as are or may be admissible to a railway servant of corresponding rank or grade and to any concession as may be sanctioned to the holder of any particular or technical post in the Force.

(4) The Principal and other members of the Force deployed on instructional duties at the Railway Protection Force Academy and other zonal training institutes shall be paid a monthly instructions allowance or special pay at the rate as admissible to their counterparts in the corresponding training institution of the railways.

1 *Substituted* by G.S.R. 14, dated 24.1.2007 (w.e.f. 27.1.2007).
2 *Omitted* by G.S.R. 229, dated 15.7.1999 (w.e.f. 24.7.1999).
3 *Omitted* by G.S.R. 803(E), dated 31.10.2008.

79. Special allowances and perquisites. To enable the Force to efficiently discharge its functions of—

(*a*) protection and safeguarding of railway property and to combat crime against it;

(*b*) 'railway servants' within the meaning of the Indian Railways Act, 1890; and

(*c*) an armed force of the Union;

The Central Government may also provide for payment of such other special allowances and perquisites as it considers appropriate.

80. Provident fund, gratuity, pension, medical facilities, passes etc. (1) In matters relating to—

(*i*) Provident fund,

(*ii*) Gratuity,

(*iii*) Pension,

(*iv*) Medical facilities,

(*v*) Pass and Privilege Ticket Orders,

(*vi*) Educational assistance.

(*vii*) Travelling and transfer allowances, and

(*viii*) Other financial matters,

Superior officers and enrolled members of the Force shall be governed by the provisions of these rules or where no specific provisions has been made in these rules then by the extant Railway Rules in the same manner as officers holding the corresponding ranks or grades in the railway are governed by the Railway Rules:

Provided that the extant Railway Rules relating to the aforesaid matters may be modified by the Central Government from time to time in their application to the members of the Force.

(2) A Provident Fund Account book shall be governed to each member of the Force in which deductions made by the Pay Drawing Authority shall be periodically entered and authenticated.

81. Deduction from pay and allowances. (1) Without prejudice to any other action that may be taken against any delinquent member, it shall be lawful for the superior officers under whom an enrolled member may be serving to order deduction of the following from his pay and allowances after giving such member an opportunity to show cause—

(*a*) any sum required by way of compensation as may be fixed for any loss, damage or destruction caused by him to—

(*i*) the railways or to any of its buildings or property; or

(*ii*) any fund of the Force;

(*b*) any sum required to make good the pay and allowances of any person subject to this Act, which he has lawfully taken on any authority letter and unlawfully retained or unlawfully refused to pay the same;

(*c*) pay and allowances for every day of absence either on discretion or without leave and for every day of imprisonment awarded by a criminal court or a Security Court;

(*d*) any sum required to be paid as fine imposed by a criminal court or Security Court or by an authorised officer in an Orderly Room.

(2) The amount so realised under clause (*a*)(*ii*) of sub-rule (1) shall be credited to the relevant fund of the Force.

(3) *Limit of deductions.*—The total deduction from the pay and allowances of a member made under sub-rule (1) except clause (*c*) thereof or whether he is being dismissed, removed or retired from service, shall not exceed in any one month one-half of his pay and allowances for that month.

(4) *Remission of deductions.*—Any authority superior to the one ordering any deduction under this rule shall be competent to remit, for reasons to be recorded in writing, the whole or any part of the said deductions on appeal made to him.

82. Duration of appointment. (1) Superior officers and enrolled members of the Force may be appointed either permanently or temporarily for specified periods or in an officiating capacity or on tenure basis or on deputation for a period as may be specified by the appointing authority.

83. Circumstances under which an enrolled member of the Force may resign. (1) Resignation of any enrolled member may be accepted by the officer empowered to appoint him.

(2) An enrolled member who intends to resign from service shall give to the appointing authority a three months notice in writing to that effect and shall not be permitted to withdraw himself from duty before formal acceptance of the resignation:

Provided that the appointing authority may at its discretion permit an enrolled member of the Force to withdraw himself from duty on his crediting to the Government three months' pay in lieu of notice.

(3) No enrolled member whose resignation has been accepted by the appointing authority shall be permitted to withdraw from duty until he has fully discharged all debts due from him to the Government or to any Railway Protection Force fund and has surrendered his certificate of appointment, arms accoutrements, uniform and all other Government property in his possession and has also rendered a complete account of all Government money and property for which he is responsible.

84. Retirement on grounds of unsuitability. (1) Whenever a Security Commissioner or an officer of a higher rank is of the opinion that a member of the Force (being an armed force of the Union), is unfit to be retained in service because of a steep fall in his competence, efficiency, effectiveness or otherwise and where action under Chapter XII is not feasible, he may recommend to the Chief Security Commissioner concerned that the member be retired from service:

Provided that where the Chief Security Commissioner has formed such opinion in relation to a superior officer of which he is not the appointing authority, he may submit the case to the Director- General for obtaining the orders of the appointing authority.

(2) The said Chief Security Commissioner or, as the case may be, the said appointing authority may, on receipt of such recommendations and after giving

the member of the Force an opportunity to explain his case, pass such order as he or it may deem fit:

Provided that whenever the Chief Security Commissioner or the Central Government, as the case may be, is of opinion that it will not be in the interest of the security of the State to give an opportunity to the member of the Force to explain his case, he or it may pass orders as aforesaid without giving such an opportunity.

85. Retirement on ground of physical and mental unfitness. (1) While in service, all members of the Force shall remain in good mental and bodily health in accordance with the medical category as may be prescribed in the Directives. The Director-General may also prescribe the periodicity for medical examination of each class and rank of the members of the Force while in service.

(2) Whenever an appointing authority, on receipt of a report or otherwise, considers that a member of the Force has become unfit to perform his duties as a member of the Force because of his physical or mental conditions, it may order that the member be examined by a Medical Board.

(3) Where the Medical Board considers the member to be unfit for service, the appointing authority shall communicate to the said member the findings of the Medical Board and call upon him to submit any representation as he may think proper within fifteen days of the date of receipt of such communication.

(4) The appointing authority, on receipt of the representation, may pass such orders as it deems fit:

Provided that the case of a member of the Force who fails in the vision test or otherwise becomes physically incapable of performing the duties of the post which he occupies but is capable of performing other duties or the case of a member of the Force who is completely incapacitated for further service in the Force may be regulated in accordance with the extant Railway Rules.

86. Retirement on superannuation. Superior officers and enrolled members of the Force shall retire from the service on attaning the age of superannuation in accordance with the provisions of the extant Railway Rules.

CHAPTER VII

DISTRIBUTION AND TRANSFER OF MEMBER OF THE FORCE

87. Distribution. The enrolled members of the Force shall ordinarily be employed throughout service on the zonal railway or the Railway Protection Special Force to which they are distributed on first appointment under these rules and shall have no claim as of right for transfer to another zonal railway or to the Railway Protection Special Force formations and *vice versa.*

88. Assistant Commandants. (1) Directly recruited Assistant Commandants shall be distributed among the zonal railways and the Railway Protection Special Force in such manner as may be considered necessary by the appointing authority in public interest.

(2) All other Assistant Commandants promoted from the ranks shall continue to retain their lien on the parent zonal railway or on the Railway Protection Special Force.

89. Enrolled members. (1) *Sub-Inspectors.* On successful completion of initial training, direct recruits shall be distributed amongst the zonal railways and Railway Protection Special Force in such manner as may be considered necessary by the appointing authority in public interest.

(2) *Constables.* On successful completion of initial training, direct recruits shall be distributed for enrolment amongst the division, production units and Railway Protection Special Force battalions in such manner as may be considered necessary by Chief Security Commissioner concerned in public interest.

TRANSFERS

90. General. Transfer of members of the Force may be ordered from one place to any other place in India in the exigencies of service or for administrative reasons or to avoid local entanglements of such members or for any such other consideration.

91. Inter-zonal transfers. (1) *Superior officers of the Force.* The Director-General on the recommendations of the Chief Security Commissioner concerned or otherwise may transfer any superior officer from one zonal railway to another zonal railway or from Railway Protection Special Force to a zonal railway or *vice versa* in the interest of administration of the force.

(2) *Enrolled members of the Force.* All inter-zonal railway transfers of the enrolled members of the Force shall be ordered by the Chief Security Commissioner concerned after obtaining the concurrence of the Director-General.

92. Periodical transfers. (1) *Transfer of superior officers within the zonal railway.* Transfer of superior officers within the zonal railway may be made by the concerned Chief Security Commissioner with the concurrence of the Director-General.

Provided that nothing contained in this sub-rule shall restrict the power of the Director-General to order transfer of any superior officer *suo motu* within a zonal railway.

(2) *Transfer of enrolled members of the Force.* Transfer of enrolled members of the Force may be ordered by the Chief Security Commissioner concerned and other officers specified in Schedule II.

93. General principles for effecting periodical transfers. (1) In the interest of continuity of command, discipline and accountability, the Director-General may prescribe a tenure of posting for various ranks in various places.

(2) Ordinarily, no member of the Force shall be transferred from one station to another unless he has been at that station for the normal prescribed tenure nor he shall be allowed to remain at that station for more than one year thereafter without the specific approval of the Chief Security Commissioner concerned in respect of enrolled members of the Force and of the Director General in respect of superior officers:

Provided that the members of the Force posted to bad climate areas or out of the way places may be transferred after they have served in such area or place for about two years.

(3) No one shall ordinarily be so posted that his home town falls within 100 kms. of railhead of his posting nor to a place where he holds or acquires immovable property nor he be posted back in the same capacity unless it is considered essential in public interest.

(4) Members of the Force who have been transferred out of a particular place or division on complaint of corruption or misconduct shall not be posted back to that post or place or division even if they so request.

(5) Members of the Force who have got adverse entries or enjoy poor reputation shall not be posted to sensitive posts till they get good entries for three consecutive years.

(6) Any member of the Force temporarily transferred to any place shall not be allowed to continue at that place for more than four months without the specific approval of the Chief Security Commissioner concerned and such member shall not again be temporarily posted to the same place without an interval of two years.

(7) Where a member of the Force before completion of the normal tenure at a particular place, wishes to get himself transferred to another place so that his children may have continuity of education at the new station for next few years, such members may be allowed transfer, before completion of normal tenure, after taking into account the interest of administration.

(8) Requests from members of the Force for mutual transfers within the division or from one division to the other shall be decided on merits keeping in view the general policy regarding transfer and postings and as far as possible, such requests shall be considered only during the time of periodical transfers.

(9) Any member of the Force facing departmental proceedings and who is due for periodical transfer on completion of normal tenure may not ordinarily be transferred unless such transfer is in public interest or where such transfer is in the interest of expeditious finalisation of disciplinary proceedings.

(10) If a member of the Force under order of transfer applies for leave, it shall not be granted to him without prior permission of the transferring authority:

Provided that where a transferred member is hospitalised as an indoor patient or in such other serious cases, he may be allowed leave under intimation to the transferring authority:

Provided further that the provisions contained in sub-rules (2) and (3) shall not apply to members of the Force, who are going to their last posting before superannuation.

CHAPTER VIII

INTERNAL MANAGEMENT AND CONDITIONS OR SERVICE SENIORITY

94. Seniority in initial grade. (1) *Inter se* seniority among the incumbents of posts in rank shall be determined on the basis of continuous regular appointment in that rank after completion of initial and practical training, if any, and the grant of pay higher than initial pay shall not confer any special right to seniority.

(2) When in exigencies of service, the training period of enrolled members of the Force who are direct recruits is curtailed or extended, the date of joining the post (hereafter in this Chapter referred to as working post) in case of such direct recruits shall be the date when they would normally have come to the working post after completion of prescribed period of training.

95. Seniority of Superior Officers. (1) In a particular rank—

(*i*) a Superior Officer appointed in a substantive capacity shall be senior to an officer appointed in an officiating capacity;

(*ii*) seniority of Superior Officers appointed to any post in a substantive capacity shall be determined in accordance with the date of appointment to that post in a substantive capacity and where two or more officers are appointed to a post in a substantive capacity on the same date, their seniority shall be determined in accordance with their order of selection for appointment to that post;

(*iii*) seniority of officers appointed to any post in an officiating capacity shall be determined in accordance with the order of selection for appointment to that post;

(*iv*) officers appointed on promotion as Assistant Commandant against the quota of vacancies reserved for them shall be placed below or above a particular batch of direct recruits accordingly as their dates for increments in time scale are earlier or later than the earliest date on which any one of the direct recruits in a particular batch joined service.

(2) Subject to the provisions of sub-rule (1), *inter se* seniority amongst officers holding the same rank shall be as follows, namely—

(*i*) seniority of officers promoted on the same day shall be determined in the order in which they are selected for promotion to that rank;

(*ii*) seniority of direct recruits shall be the same as determined by the Union Public Service Commission;

(*iii*) seniority of re-employed officers in a particular rank shall be determined from the date of re-employment in that rank;

(*iv*) within a particular rank, an officer on deputation shall maintain his seniority as between himself and other officers of his service on deputation;

(*v*) seniority between an officer on deputation and other officer shall be determined from the date of regular continuous appointment in that rank; and

(*vi*) seniority of officers recruited under sub-rule (1)(*d*) of rule 54 shall be governed by their date of appointment to the grade.

96. Seniority of directly recruited candidates. The seniority of candidates directly recruited shall be determined as under—

(*i*) Candidates who are sent for initial training to a training school shall rank in seniority in the relevant grade, in the order of merit obtained at the examination held at the end of training of period before being posted against working posts and those who pass examination in the second attempt shall rank junior to those who passed in the first attempt but shall rank senior to those who pass in the next or subsequent batches and where candidates secure equal marks, the seniority shall be determined by the date of birth, the elder candidate being senior;

(*ii*) In the case of candidates who are not required to undergo any training, the seniority shall be determined on the basis of their order of selection;

(*iii*) When two or more candidates are of equal merit at one and the same examination or selection, their relative seniority shall be determined by the date of birth—the elder candidate being the senior;

(*iv*) When a candidate whose seniority has been fixed under the above rules cannot join duty within three months from the receipt of order of appointment, his seniority among the candidates selected at the same examination or selection shall be reckoned from a date to be determined by the appointing authority;

(*v*) Candidates selected for appointment at an earlier selection shall be senior to those selected later irrespective of the date of joining;

(*vi*) Relative seniority of employees in an intermediate rank belonging to different seniority units appearing for a selection in higher rank shall be determined by the total length of continuous service in the same or equivalent rank irrespective of the date of confirmation of an employee. Only non-fortuitous service is to be taken into account for the purpose;

(*vii*) When a quota has been prescribed for direct recruitment of special categories of persons or class of persons, such seniority shall continue to be assigned under normal rules and such quota shall have no relevance. Shortfall in quota for any category of one year may be filled next year but in such cases benefit of seniority shall not be given retrospectively.

97. Seniority of departmental promotees. The seniority of promotees shall be determined according to the position assigned to them in the select panel by the Departmental Promotion Committee. Those who fail to qualify in the initial or pre-promotion training course and qualify in the second attempt shall be placed below all those who had qualified in the first attempt in order of their names on the select panel.

98. Inter se seniority of direct recruits and promotees. (1) *Inter se* seniority in posts of enrolled members of the Force filled up partly by direct recruitment and partly by promotion shall be so determined as not to disturb the *inter se* seniority of direct recruits and promotees. Criterion for determination of such seniority shall be the date of promotion in the case of promotees and the date of joining the working posts as referred to in sub-rule (2) of Rule 94 in the case of direct recruits. When the dates of entry into a grade of a promoted enrolled member of the Force and a direct recruit are the same, they shall be given alternative positions starting with promotees *e.g.* I—Promotee, II—Direct recruits, III—Promotee, IV—Direct recruit and so on. This rule shall apply to recruitments both in initial intermediate grades.

(2) In combined seniority list of candidates qualifying in the second attempt, the promotees shall maintain their seniority according to the panel position and direct recruits according to merit position and they shall be placed in the seniority list alternatively as provided in sub-rule (1).

(3) *Inter se* seniority of enrolled members especially promoted without their appearing for the normal selection and without undergoing prescribed initial or pre-promotion training for such ranks shall be determined in order of seniority in their previous ranks. While fixing their seniority *vis-a-vis* directly recruited enrolled members and promotees, such especially promoted enrolled members shall be placed below all of them including those who passed initial or pre-promotion training at the second attempt.

99. Determination of seniority on inter-zonal transfer. (1) *When transfer ordered in interest of administration.* Seniority of an enrolled member of the Force on transfer from one zone to another or to the Railway Protection Special Force and *vice versa* made in the interest of administration shall be regulated by the date of appointment to the grade or rank as the case may be, where the date of appointment of the transferred member of the Force is the same as that of another member of the Force already serving on that zonal Railway or Railway Protection Special Force, the relative seniority shall be determined on the basis of the date of birth—the elder being the senior.

(2) *Transfer on own request or on mutual exchange.* Seniority of an enrolled member of the Force transferred on his own request or on mutual exchange from one zonal railway to another or to the Railway Protection Special Force and *vice versa* shall be fixed below that of all existing confirmed and officiating enrolled members of the Force in the relevant rank of that railway or Railway Protection Special Force irrespective of the date of confirmation or length of officiating service of the transferred member of the Force.

100. Effect of reduction in rank, grade or pay on seniority. (1) Reduction in a scale of pay as distinct from reduction from a higher rank or grade, shall not affect the position of a member of the Force on the seniority list.

(2) In the case of reduction to a lower rank or to a lower scale of pay—

(*i*) if a member of the Force is punished with reduction to a lower scale of pay for a specified period his seniority and pay shall be restored as soon as the period of punishment is over;

(*ii*) if the member of the Force is punished with reduction to a lower rank or grade for a specified period, he shall be re-promoted automatically to the rank or grade from which he was reduced. The seniority of such member of the Force shall be fixed at a position in the higher rank or grade at which it would have been but for his reduction;

(*iii*) if the member of the Force has been punished by way of reduction from a higher rank or grade to a lower rank or grade, his seniority in the lower rank or grade shall be fixed with reference to his position to which he would have been entitled but for his promotion to the higher rank or grade from which he was reduced.

101. Miscellaneous provision governing seniority. All other cases of seniority, not specifically covered in the above provisions, shall be decided—

(*a*) in the case of superior officers by the Central Government;

(*b*) in the case of enrolled members of the Force by the appointing authority;

in accordance with the Directives or on the advice of the Director-General.

102. Representation against assignment of seniority. A member of the Force may represent to the appointing authority about his seniority position within a period of one year from the date of publication of the seniority list.

LEAVE

103. Quantum of leave. Superior officers and enrolled members of the Force shall be governed by the leave rules applicable to railway servants of corresponding rank. Those who are on deputation to the Force shall be governed by the leave rules applicable to them as if they were not on deputation to the Force or by the terms of their appointment.

104. General condition governing grant of leave. (1) The powers of superior officers and subordinate officers of the Force in respect of grant of leave shall be as specified in Schedule II.

(2) Leave of every description may be sanctioned, refused or revoked subject to exigencies of public service.

(3) No member of the Force shall leave his station even on holidays without the specific permission of authority empowered to grant him casual leave.

(4) A member of the Force before proceeding on leave shall record his leave address in office at which orders of recall or other communication will reach him with certainty.

(5) *Leave Certificate.* A leave certificate in the prescribed form shall be issued to every enrolled member of the Force proceeding on leave, other than casual leave and such certificate shall be presented by the member personally on his rejoining from leave to the officer-in-charge of the place at which be rejoins, who shall endorse on the certificate the hour and date of rejoining and forward the same to the office where his leave account is maintained.

(6) *Recall from leave.* The members of the Force on leave may be,—

(*i*) recalled at any time by the authority empowered to sanction their leave;

(*ii*) directed to report for duty either at their headquarters or to proceed direct to the place at which their services are required:

Provided that on being recalled, the members of the Force shall be entitled to duty passes and travelling allowance as on tour by the shortest route.

(7) *Return to duty from leave.* No member of the Force who has been granted leave on medical certificate can resume duty without first producing medical certificate of fitness. The authority competent to sanction leave may require a similar certificate in the case of any member of the Force who has been granted leave for reasons of his health even though such leave was not actually granted on medical grounds.

Removed from service without leave of absence. There is prohibition on any member of the Force to leave station even on holidays without specific permission of the authority empowering to grant casual leave. There modalities have been enumerated in Rule 104 of the R.P.F. Rules 1959, which clearly being out of the essence of discipline. Absence from duty without proper intimation is indicated to be a grave offence warranting removal from service. Therefore more making an application for leave by the delinquent cannot be construed to be of any consequence in the background of the strict requirement of giving proper intimation. Therefore, the order by the authorities that the delinquent was guilty of the offence of absence from duty without proper intimation cannot be said to be illegal.[4]

4 *Mithilesh Singh* v *Union of India* AIR 2003 SC 1724.

105. Restriction on grant of leave. (1) Whenever mobilisation of the Force under rule 241 is likely or is in force or a member of the Force is detailed or is likely to be detailed for training of any type, leave of any kind including casual leave shall not ordinarily be sanctioned except on emergent and compassionate grounds by an officer not below the rank of the Divisional Security Commissioner.

(2) Leave shall not be granted to a member of the Force whose conduct is under inquiry except when it is required for hospitalisation purpose or in extreme emergent cases.

(3) Similarly leave shall not be granted to a member of the Force who is under orders of transfer unless he is admitted in a hospital as an indoor patient:

Provided that if such member has been taken on a sick list by a railway doctor as an outdoor patient in situation not stipulated in rule 272, such member shall report the matter forthwith to his controlling authority and shall not leave his headquarters without obtaining prior sanction of that authority.

106. Performance appraisal. (1) *General.* The performance appraisal system shall be as follows, namely—

(*i*) a continuous performance appraisal which will be correctional and developmental in its impact; and

(*ii*) the annual performance appraisal which will be for organisational purposes including those connected with training, confirmation, placement and promotion.

(2) The said appraisal system shall apply to all ranks.

(3) For the purposes of continuous performance appraisal, every subordinate and superior officer shall maintain a running record (hereafter in this Chapter referred to as Critical Incidents Records) for each of his subordinates especially entrusted to him by the controlling authority for the purpose. He will record therein from month to month specific instances of good and bad work, coming to his notice, of his subordinates besides making a quarterly rating of their overall performance.

(4) Every subordinate and superior officer referred to in sub-rule (3) shall hold, as far as may be possible, a quarterly counselling session for the members of the Force for whom he is maintaining the Critical Incidents Records. A record of such counselling shall also be maintained. The counselling will be aimed at encouragement of a positive behaviour of the member concerned or for correcting his behaviour in the light of the quarterly rating. All officers of the Force during their periodical inspections may also record their assessment in the Critical Incidents Record and, if necessary, suitably counsel the member concerned.

107. Annual performance appraisal. (1) Annual performance appraisal by any reporting superior officer for writing the confidential report mentioned in rule 108 may not be carried out without having conducted atleast one inspection of the work of the subordinate unless the subordinate is one with whom such superior officer is interacting frequently or has been maintaining for him the Critical Incidents record mentioned in sub-rule (3) of rule 106 or has actually scrutinised such record.

(2) For the purposes of sub-rule (1), the proximity between the appraisee and his reporting superior officer shall be maintained at all levels. Such an appraisal shall be made by superior officer only so as to ensure that the appraisal is

professional, objective and presents the truest possible picture of the appraisee with regard to all facts of his work.

108. Confidential reports. (1) *Confidential reports in respect of Constables and under officers.* Confidential reports in respect of Constables and under officers shall be recorded in individual book form to be known as "Character and Service Rule", the format of which shall be prescribed by the Director-General. The said report shall be recorded during inspection or visit to the post where the member of the Force is or was posted and after taking stock of the work claimed to have been done by concerned member of the Force, if he is present during such inspection or visit, and the views of his controlling officer or as may have been recorded in the Critical Incidents Record.

(2) *Confidential reports of subordinate officers.* The formats for writing of confidential reports in respect of subordinate officers shall be prescribed by the Director General having regard to the specific nature of duties for each job and based on a detailed job evaluation. The format should reflect the essential requirements of professional competence, performance, personality and managerial attributes.

(3) *Confidential reports of superior officers.* (*i*) The formats for writing annual confidential reports in respect of superior officer shall be as prescribed for officers of corresponding ranks of the Indian Police Service under the All India Services (Confidential Roll) Rules, 1970, whether the superior officer has been holding the post substantively or in an officiating capacity.

(*ii*) When any superior officer is transferred, similar report for a broken period, if any, shall also be recorded by his superior officer.

(*iii*) When the reporting superior officer vacates his post on account of transfer, leave, etc., and is not likely to return to the post during the year or if he vacates his post on account of retirement, he shall before making over charge of his post to his successor, record his assessment of performance of all superior officers who have served under him for a period of three months or more.

(*iv*) The number of copies of confidential reports to be prepared in respect of each category of superior officers and the authorities to whom it should be sent for record shall be such as may be specified through the Directives.

(4) The overall rating shall be given as outstanding, very good, good, average or below average.

(5) Specific comments shall be made about the integrity of the officer reported upon so far as they relate to performance of his official duties or its consequential effect, if any, on the organisational strength and weakness of the Force under his command.

(6) The accepting authority shall communicate to the officer reported upon within thirty days of acceptance of a report of any adverse remarks recorded of in confidential report and certify so in that report.

(7) The officer reported upon shall submit the representation within thirty days of receipt of such communication to the said authority who may take into account the circumstances of the case and if it so deems fit interview the member and expunge or drop the remarks, if called for. The decision of the accepting

authority shall be final in such cases and shall also be communicated to the officer reported upon.

REDRESSAL OF GRIEVANCES

109. Redressal of individual grievances. (1) For redressal of individual grievances concerning non payment of salary. T.A., D.A., issue of kit passes, grant of leave and advances, allotment of family quarters, transfers, posting, *etc.*, of member of the Force, the superior officers shall avail themselves of every opportunity during their tours and inspections to hold meetings provided under sub-rule (2) and listen to such grievances and take appropriate remedial measures within their powers.

(2) The officer-in-charge of the Post or Company shall also hold such meetings atleast once a month. During the meetings, he shall disseminate to the enrolled members of the Force information on all important matters affecting them and enable them to ventilate their legitimate grievances, difficulties and their reaction to current affairs to him in the presence of all ranks. He shall refer to higher authorities all such cases where he cannot redress the grievances at his level and monitor the progress under intimation to the enrolled member concerned.

(3) The officer-in-charge of the Post or Company shall maintain a "Meeting Minutes Book" in which the proceedings of each meeting held by all level of officers shall be recorded together with final action taken on each point.

(4) The superior officers shall inspect this book during their inspections of the posts and their inspection notes shall include comments on this aspect also.

110. Representation against wrong. (1) Any member of the Force who deems himself wronged by any superior officer or other officer of the Force may represent within thirty days of the act complained against to the officer under whose command or orders he is serving:

Provided that each complaint shall be accompanied by a certificate as under from the aggrieved member of the Force:

> "I undertake that any false statement or false accusation made by me in the complaint shall render me liable for disciplinary action under Chapters XI and XII of the Railway Protection Force Rules, 1987."

(2) When the officer complained against is the officer to whom any representation should, under sub-rule (1) be preferred, the aggrieved member may represent to such officer's next superior officer.

(3) Every officer receiving any such representation shall make or cause to be made as complete an investigation into it as may be possible for giving full relief to the complainant or where necessary refer the representations to the higher authority for redressal:

Provided that if on enquiry the matter alleged against any such officer turns out to be false, vexatious or malicious, deterrent disciplinary action shall be taken against the complainant.

(4) Except as otherwise provided in sub-rule (1), no action shall be taken on any complaint—anonymous or pseudonymous—received against any superior officer or other officer of the Force in respect of any matter covered by that sub-rule.

[5][**111. Redressal of collective grievances through departmental channel.** The superior officers of the Force shall personally assess the collective grievances of the members of the Force posted under them and submit their recommendations to the Chief Security Commissioner concerned or the Director-General as the case may be. These officers in turn, shall keep the General Manager of the Railway or the Central Government fully posted about the nature of major grievances and highlight the need for issuing suitable orders for their redressal].

112. [6][* * *]

113. Redressal of grievances through outside influence. (1) Members of the Force are forbidden to approach officials of other departments, members of the Legislatures or private persons for support in pressing individual claims or obtaining redressal of their grievances. All members of the Force are similarly forbidden to approach members of Legislatures with a view to having their individual grievances made the subject of interpolation in the Legislatures.

114. Redressal of grievances through litigation. Any member of the Force seeking redressal of his individual grievances arising out of his employment or conditions of service shall first avail himself of all remedies available to him under these rules as to redressal of grievances before taking the issue to a Court of Justice. No permission from the department shall, however, be necessary if a member wants to agitate the matter before a Court of Justice.

RESTRICTIONS ON FUNDAMENTAL RIGHTS

115. Grant of sanction under section 15-A. The authority for purposes of granting sanction under sub-section (1) of section 15-A shall be the Chief Security Commissioner for his zonal railway and the Director General for the entire Force.

116. Political and non-military activities. (1) No person subject to the Act and these rules shall attend, address, or take part in any meeting or demonstration held for a political partly or for any political purposes or join or subscribe in the aid of any political association or movement.

(2) No person subject to the Act and these rules shall issue an address to electors or in any other manner publicity announce himself or allow himself to be publicly announced as a candidate or as a prospective candidate for election to Parliament, the Legislature of a State or a local authority, or any other public body or act as a member of a candidate's election committee or in way actively promote or prosecute the interests of any such candidate.

117. Other conditions of service. In all other matters not prescribed in these rules, all members of the Force, irrespective of their ranks shall be governed by the provisions contained in the extant Railway Rules as applicable to railway servants of corresponding grades:

Provided that the Central Government may by notification in the official Gazette, modify the extant Railway Rules in their application to members of the Force on the above matters where that Government is of the opinion that it is necessary so to do in the interest of the Force, being an armed force of the Union.

5 *Substituted* by G.S.R. 312(E), dated 13.5.2004 (w.e.f. 13.5.2004).

6 Rule 112 *omitted* by G.S.R. 312(E), dated 13.5.2004 (w.e.f. 13.5.2004).

CHAPTER IX

ENCAMPMENT AND ACCOMMODATION

118. Residential accommodation. (1) Members of the Force shall be classified as "essential" for the purpose of allotment of residential accommodation as they are required to live as near to the place of their duty as possible for the proper discharge of their duty.

(2) Enrolled members of the Force with less than three years' service or who are unmarried shall normally be allotted barrack accommodation which shall be rent free.

(3) Enrolled members of the Force, who have either been accommodated in barracks or given family accommodation or who have been offered any such accommodation but wish to stay outside under their private arrangements, shall obtain written permission from their superior officers.

(4) Enrolled members of the Force accommodated in barracks but keeping their families away from them in other towns shall be entitled to payment of house rent allowance as may be admissible to them under the extant Railway Rules.

119. Location of barrack and other accommodation. (1) The location of barrack or residential accommodation for the enrolled members of the Force shall, preferably, be provided in a separate cluster(s) away from those of other railway employees.

(2) The barracks shall be of approved pattern with built-in space for recreation purposes besides having adequate open space for use as parade and play ground.

(3) The enrolled members of the Force living in barracks shall be provided with steel cots, mattresses, kit boxes and lockers. Wherever twenty or more persons are accommodated in a barrack, cooking utensils for the mess and one cook and one *kahar* for every twenty members shall be provided.

(4) The scale of ancillary staff at Company headquarters and training institutions shall be such as may be specified by Directives.

(5) Adequate built-in-space for office, quarter-records, armour, malkhana, lock-ups, *etc.*, on the standardised pattern shall also be provided.

120. Maintenance and vacation of residential accommodation. (1) If any residential accommodation is allotted to a member of the Force, he shall reside therein subject to such conditions and terms as may be specified by the Chief Security Commissioner concerned and shall be responsible for maintaining it in a good state.

(2) It shall be a condition of his service that he shall vacate the accommodation on his ceasing to be a member of the Force or on his transfer from that place or whenever an officer not below the rank of Security Commissioner, for reasons to be recorded in writing, finds it necessary and expedient for him to do so.

(3) If any enrolled member of the Force who is required under sub-rule (2) to vacate any premises fails to do so, such superior officer may after giving him an opportunity of being heard, direct any officer subordinate to him, with such assistance as may be necessary, to enter upon and open the premises and remove therefrom any person found therein and to take possession of the premises and deliver the same to any person specified in the order.

CHAPTER X

UNIFORM AND EQUIPMENT

121. General instructions. (1) The Director-General may, by order, specify from time to time dress and pattern of various types of dresses for members of the Force.

(2) The badges of rank of all members of the Force holding their appointments on a regular basis shall be as specified in Scheme VIII.

Provided that the appointing authority while promoting a member of the Force under rule 74 may, looking to the nature and duration of the appointment, allow him to wear the uniform and badges of the rank of that higher appointment.

(3) All officers are forbidden to introduce or sanction for experimental or other purposes, any unauthorised deviation from the specified pattern of dress, clothing, equipment and badges.

122. Uniform and plain clothes. (1) All members of the force shall be in possession of uniform and shall invariably wear it as hereinafter provided except when specially deployed on plain clothes work.

(2) Mufti shall be worn when off duty.

(3) No superior officer or enrolled member of the Force shall appear at any time dressed partly in uniform and partly in plain clothes, while on duty.

123. Uniform when to be worn. (1) All superior officers and enrolled members of the Force shall wear uniform when attending parades, orderly rooms, courts of justice, official funerals or while inspecting guards or when an inspecting officer is present in office and on all other occasions when required to do so. Official uniform or any of its items shall not be worn when off duty.

Provided that there may not be any objection to its use in departmental cultural shows.

(2) No member of the Force shall turn up for duty unless properly dressed nor he shall smoke nor chew 'paan' in the open when on duty in uniform.

(3) All superior Officers and enrolled members of the Force shall wear with all types of uniform engraved name tabs above the right breast pocket in a manner that the lower edge of the tab shall be just above the top seam of the pocket flap. Name tab shall be of the size of 8.23×0.16 cms. of formica or similar material suitable for engraving. Letter shall be squat type upto fourteen in number.

(4) No unauthorised ornaments or emblem, sign or mark shall be worn with the uniform.

(5) Watch chains, trinkets, fountain pens, etc., shall not be worn with uniform so as to be visible. The wearing of signet ring is, however, permitted.

(6) Sun-glasses shall not be worn with uniform, except under medical advice, on the following occasions:

(*i*) on ceremonial parades or while on VIP duty; and

(*ii*) when on quarter guard duty or inspecting a guard or attending a parade.

124. Growth and dressing of the hair. (1) *Non-Sikh personnel—*

The hair of the head shall be kept short. The chin and underlip shall be shaved daily unless permission to grow the same is taken in writing for a specified period. Whiskers and mustaches. if worn, shall be of moderate length.

(2) *Sikh personnel.* Sikh personnel shall dress up their hair and beard properly. "Thathas" shall not be used over beard when in uniform.

(3) In the case of women serving in the Force, hair shall be neatly kept and make up, if used, shall be inconspicuous. Highly coloured nail varnish shall not be used.

125. Scale of uniform. (1) All enrolled members of the Force, including trainees, shall be furnished free of charge a set of uniform (*i.e.* clothing and other necessary articles) of such description and in such quantity and composition as may be specified by the Director General from time to time.

(2) The enrolled members of the Force, employed in the Crime Wing and the special Wing, including plain clothes staff in divisions, shall be granted an outfit allowance at the rates sanctioned by the Central Government from time to time.

(3) In the case of enrolled members of the Force posted in the wings mentioned in sub-rule (2), the uniform shall not be withdrawn and they shall be entitled to the aforesaid out-fit allowance in addition, for the duration of the period they work in such wings.

(4) Superior officers of the Force shall provide themselves with all articles of uniform and accountrements of the specified pattern for which they shall be paid out fit allowance as prescribed by the Central Government from time to time.

(5) All enrolled members of the Force serving at locations at an altitude of 1000 metres above sea level or more shall be entitled to an extra issue of woolen garments.

(6) The particulars stations at which such extra clothing shall be admissible will be notified by the Chief Security Commissioner concerned in zonal railways and by the Deputy Inspector General, Railway Protection Special Force in the case of members serving in Railway Protection Special Force battalions, through specific orders and such extra clothing shall be replaced on expiry of its period of serviceability as specified by the Director-General.

(7) An enrolled member of the Force on ceasing to be posted at a station for which extra issue of clothing is authorised, shall deposit the same in the stores of the Railway Protection Force or the Railway Protection Special Force concerned.

126. Replacement of uniform. (1) The life of each item of uniform shall be as specified by the Director-General through the Directives.

(2) Periodical inspections of kit issued to each enrolled member of the Force shall be held by the Divisional Security Commissioner or the Assistant Security Commissioners and articles which are no longer fit for use may be condemned and sent to the stores for replacement.

(3) If life of any article has not expired, proportionate cost (listed) shall be deducted from the enrolled member concerned, provided that no deduction may be made, if the article has been rendered unserviceable owing to fair wear and tear or has been lost through no fault of the members concerned, and the amount realised shall be credited to Government.

127. Arms and accoutrements. (1) The members of the Force to whom arms and accoutrements are issued or given or who are required to keep them under their charge shall be personally responsible for their safe custody and upkeep while in their charge and possession.

(2) The Director-General may issue orders relating to the procedure for safe custody, maintenance, storage, inspection of arms, etc.

(3) Enrolled members of the Force shall not be permitted to take arms while going on leave. Accountrements shall be deposited while proceeding on leave, other than casual leave, for more than thirty days.

128. Disposal of uniform due to transfer. All enrolled members of the Force when transferred shall take with them their uniform except the articles distinguishing particular divisions or branches or the battalions of the Railway Protection Special Force as the case may be. The latter shall be deposited in the stores of the division or battalion concerned and re-issued to other members for the unspent period of serviceability.

129. Disposal of uniform due to dismissal, discharge etc. (1) All articles of clothing and equipment issued to enrolled member of the Force shall be withdrawn from him when—

(*a*) he is placed under suspension;

(*b*) he is served with order of discharge;

(*c*) he is removed or dismissed from service; and

(*d*) his resignation is accepted.

(2) Articles of uniform withdrawn from an enrolled member of the Force placed under suspension shall be kept in safe custody by the Company Commander or Post Commander concerned for a period of four months. If within this period of fou. months the member is reinstated in service, his uniform shall be restored to him.

(3) If the enrolled member continue under suspension beyond a period of four months, the uniform withdrawn from him shall be transferred to the stores of the division or branch or battalion concerned and shall be restored to him at the time of his reinstatement in service.

130. Resuming of uniform articles on ceasing to be enrolled member of the Force. (1) When an enrolled member of the Force ceases to belong to Force, his kit shall be examined and serviceable articles brought on the resumed stock and subsequently re-issued. When any such resumed article is re-issued, its authorised life period shall include the period for which such article has remained issued earlier.

Provided that the kit of a person, who was suffering from contagious disease such as T.B., etc. shall be destroyed by burning in the presence of a superior officer after obtaining the orders of the Divisional Security Commissioner or the Commanding Officer in each case:

Provided further that items of uniform shall not be withdrawn in the case of death of enrolled member while a service.

131. Retention of articles of uniform on retirement. An enrolled member of the Force on his retirement or on superannuation shall be allowed to retain the uniform items to be worn only on ceremonial occasions or at the time of formally calling upon superior officers of Armed Forces and Central or State Police Organisations. The facility of wearing the uniform on the abovementioned occasions may be withdrawn at an time in the public interest under the orders of the Chief Security Commissioner concerned.

CHAPTER XI

DISCIPLINE AND CONDUCT

132. Rules governing discipline. (1) Save as otherwise provided in these rules, the Railway Servants (Discipline and Appeal) Rules, 1968 as amended from time to time shall, so far as may be, apply to superior officers subject to the modifications that—

(*a*) in sub-rule (1) of rule 3 of the said rules, clause (*b*) shall be *omitted;*

(*b*) references to "General Manager", whereever they occur in the said rules, shall be substituted by references to "Director General, Railway Protection Force."

(2) The enrolled members of the Force shall, in such matters, be governed by the rules in this Chapter and Chapter XII;

Provided that a recruit trainee, unless he has been formally enrolled as a member of the Force, shall not be governed by these rules.

133. Suspension. The enrolled members of the Force who may be placed under suspension and the authorities by whom they may be so placed, shall be as specified in Schedule III.

Provided that in exceptional circumstances, an Assistant Security Commissioner may place a Sub-Inspector under suspension and an Inspector may place any member of and below the rank of under officers under suspension.

Provided further that where any action is taken under the foregoing proviso, the authority suspending an enrolled member of the Force shall forthwith report to the authority competent to place such enrolled member under suspension, the circumstances under which the order was made and obtain his approval and where approval is not granted, the suspension order shall become void and inoperative *ab-initio.*

Explanation. For the purposes of this rule, where an enrolled member of the Force is officiating in a higher post, he shall be placed under suspension only by the authority competent to place an enrolled member of the Force holding such officiating rank under suspension.

134. Any superior officer or an enrolled member of the Force may be placed under suspension—

(*a*) where a disciplinary proceeding against him is contemplated or is pending, or

(*b*) where a preliminary inquiry into allegation made has revealed a *prima facie* case justifying criminal or departmental proceedings which are likely to lead to his conviction or dismissal, removal or compulsory retirement from service; or

(*c*) where a case against him in respect of any criminal offence is under investigation, inquiry or trial, or

(*d*) where his continuance in office will prejudice investigation, any inquiry or trial; or

(*e*) where his continuance in office is likely to seriously subvert discipline in the office in which he is working;

(*f*) where his continuance in office appears to be against the wider public interest; or (*g*) where he is suspected to have engaged himself in activities prejudicial to the interest of the security of the State.

135. Public interest shall be the guiding factor in deciding, whether or not a member of the Force, including when he is on leave, should be placed under suspension:

Provided before taking a decision or suspension the competent authority may consider whether the purpose would be served if the member is transferred from his post or sanctioned leave:

Provided further that charge on which a member has been placed under suspension shall be furnished to him within a period of thirty days from the date of suspension after which the incumbent shall be deemed to have been reinstated if no such charge is made available to him:

Provided further that the above provision of thirty days shall not apply to cases where a member has been placed under suspension on grounds that he has engaged himself in activities prejudicial to the interest and security of the State or a criminal case involving moral turpitude is pending against him.

136. (1) A member of the Force shall be deemed to have been placed under suspension by an order of the competent authority—

(*a*) with effect from the date of his detention, if he is detained in custody, whether on a criminal charge or otherwise, for a period exceeding forty-eight hours; or

(*b*) with effect from the date of his conviction, if, in the event of a conviction for an offence he is sentenced to a term of imprisonment exceeding forty-eight hours and is not dismissed or removed or compulsorily retired from service under Rule 162 consequent to such conviction.

Explanation. The period of forty-eight hours referred to in clause (*b*) shall be computed from the commencement of the imprisonment after the conviction.

(2) Notwithstanding anything contained in sub-rule (1), in cases where a detention or conviction results from an act committed by a member of the Force while acting or purporting to act in the discharge of his official duty, decision in each case shall be taken on merit.

137. Where a penalty of dismissal, removal or compulsory retirement from service imposed upon a member of the Force under suspension, is set aside in appeal or revision and the case is remitted for further inquiry or action or with any other directions, the order of his suspension shall be deemed to have continued in force on and from the date of the original order of dismissal, removal or compulsory retirement and shall remain in force until further orders.

138. Where a penalty of dismissal, removal or compulsory retirement from service imposed upon a member of the Force is set aside or declared or rendered void in consequence or by a decision of a Court and the disciplinary authority on consideration of the circumstances of the case, decides to hold a further inquiry against him on the allegations on which the punishment of dismissal, removal or compulsory retirement was originally imposed, the member of the Force shall be deemed to have been placed under suspension by the competent authority from the date of the original order of dismissal, removal or compulsory retirement and shall continue to remain under suspension until further orders:

Provided that no such further inquiry shall be ordered unless it is intended to meet a situation where the Court has passed an order purely on technical grounds without going into the merit of the case.

139. (1) Notwithstanding anything contained in rule 135 where member of the Force is suspended (whether in connection with any disciplinary proceedings or otherwise) and any other disciplinary proceedings, commenced against him during the continuation of that suspension, the authority competent to place him under suspension may, for reasons to be recorded in writing direct that the member of the Force shall continue to be under suspension until the termination of all or any of such proceedings.

(2) An order of suspension made or deemed to have been made may, at any time, be modified or revoked by the authority which made the order or is deemed to have made the order or by any authority to which that authority is subordinate.

140. The order and the period of suspension shall be recorded in the character roll and service book of the member of the Force concerned.

141. A member of the Force, under suspension or deemed to have been placed under suspension, shall draw subsistence allowance and other allowance in accordance with extant Railway Rules.

142. When a member is reinstated after suspension, the period of suspension shall be regularised in accordance with the extant Railway Rules.

143. Responsibilities of the member of the Force during suspension. (1) A member of the Force shall not, by reason of his suspension, cease to be a member of the Force during the period of his suspension. The powers vested in him as such member shall be in abeyance but he shall be subject to the same responsibilities and discipline and penalties to which he would have been subject if he were on duty.

(2) Every member of the Force shall during the period of his suspension stay at his headquarters or at such place which may be specified by the disciplinary authority and shall present himself daily for attendance to the authority nominated by the disciplinary authority:

Provided that the disciplinary authority may, for special reasons, grant permission in writing to the member to leave the station for a specified period and on revocation of such suspension the period of such absence shall be regularised as kind of leave due in case the period of suspension is treated as period spent on duty.

(3) An enrolled member of the Force under suspension shall deposit his arms and accountrements with the Quarter Master or such officer as may be specified by the disciplinary authority.

(4) A member of the Force under suspension shall not wear his uniform nor on any such duty which might entail exercise of his power as a member of the Force nor shall be issued arms and ammunition.

(5) A member of the Force under suspension shall be allowed reasonable facilities for the preparation of his defence in connection with the charges levelled against him.

144. Retirement while under suspension. (1) The right of voluntary retirement for a member of the Force under suspension, shall be subject to prior approval of the appointing authority.

(2) A member of the Force, under suspension, may not be retired on attainment of the age of superannuation. The appointing authority shall decide such cases in accordance with the provisions of the extant Railway Rules.

145. Rule governing conduct. The Railway Services (Conduct) Rules, 1966 as amended from time to time shall, so far as may be, apply to all members of the Force as they apply to Railway servants.

146. Code of behaviour for members of his Force. (1) All members of the Force, irrespective of their ranks, shall submit themselves to the requirement of the following Code of behaviour, both on and off duty. It shall be incumbent upon all members of the Force to respect the Code of behaviour and of an attitude of complete discipline and maintain to it. Any breach of these provisions on the part of any member of the Force shall constitute misconduct and shall be punishable under the Railway Servants (Discipline and Appeal) Rules, 1968 as applied to superior officers or, as the case may be, under section 9 or section 17.

(2) *Neglect of duty.* No member of the Force without good and sufficient cause shall—

(*i*) neglect or omit to attend to or fail to carry out with due promptitude and diligence anything which is his duty as a member of the Force to attend to or carry out; or

(*ii*) fail to work his beat in accordance with orders or leave the place of duty to which he has been ordered or having left his place of duty for a *bona fide* purpose fail to return thereto without undue delay; or

(*iii*) be absent without leave or be late for any duty; or

(*iv*) fail properly to account for, or to make a prompt and true return of any money or property received by him in the course of his duty.

(3) *Disobedience of orders.* No member of the Force shall—

(*i*) disobey or omit or neglect to promptly carry out any lawful orders, written or otherwise, or

(*ii*) contravene any provision of the Act, these rules or Directives containing restriction on the private lives of the members of the Force or requiring him to notify the Chief Security Commissioner concerned that he, or a relation included in his family, has business interest in his jurisdiction within the meaning of these rules and Directives.

(4) *Discreditable conduct.* No member of the Force shall act in any manner prejudicial to discipline or conduct himself in such a manner which is reasonably likely to bring discredit to the reputation of the Force.

(5) *Misconduct towards a member of the Force.* No member of the Force shall—

(*a*) conduct himself towards another member of the Force in oppressive or abusive manner; or

(*b*) assault or misbehave with such member.

(6) *Falsehood or prefabrication.* No member of the Force shall—

(*i*) knowingly or through neglect make any false, misleading or inaccurate oral or written statement or entry in any record or document made, kept or required for the purpose of Force; or

(*ii*) either wilfully and without proper authority or through lack of due care destroy or mutilate any record or document made, kept or required for the purpose of the Force; or

(*iii*) without good and sufficient cause alter or erase or add to any entry in such a record or documents; or

(*iv*) knowingly or through neglect make any false, misleading or inaccurate statement in connection with his appointment to the Force.

(7) *Corrupt or improper, practice.* No member of the Force shall—

(*i*) in his capacity as such member and without the written consent of the Chief Security Commissioner concerned directly or indirectly solicit or accept any gratuity, present or subscription; or

(*ii*) place himself under a pecuniary obligation to any person in such a manner as might affect the proper discharge of his duties as such member; or

(*iii*) improperly use or attempt so to use, his position as such member for his personal gain.

(8) *Abuse of authority.* No member of the Force shall—

(*a*) without good and sufficient cause make an arrest; or

(*b*) use any unnecessary violence towards any undertrial prisoners or other persons with whom he comes into contact in the execution of his duty.

147. Offences relatable to duties of enrolled members. Commission of any of the following act or acts by enrolled members of the Force—

(*i*) violation of any duty;

(*ii*) wilful breach or neglect of any provisions, of this Act or any rule or of Directives or of any other lawful orders which he is bound to observe or obey;

(*iii*) disobeying lawful command of superior officers;

(*iv*) withdrawing from duty of his office without permission;

(*v*) quitting his guard, picket, party or patrol without being duly relieved or without leave;

(*vi*) absenting himself without proper intimation to his controlling authority or without sufficient cause overstaying leave granted to him or falling without reasonable cause to report himself for duty on the expiry of such leave;

(*vii*) engaging himself without authority for any employment other than his duty as an enrolled member of the Force;

(*viii*) being guilty of cowardice;

(*ix*) being in a state intoxication while on duty or after having been altered for any duty;

(*x*) malingering or feigning or voluntarily causing hurt or infirmity to himself or intentionally delaying his cure or aggravating his disease or infirmity with the intention to render himself unfit for any duty or for the service;

(*xi*) resisting his lawful arrest or being under arrest or in confinement leaving his arrest or confinement before he is set at liberty by lawful authority;

(*xii*) assaulting or otherwise ill-treating any enrolled member of the Force subordinate to him in rank or position;

(*xiii*) being grossly insubordinate or insolvent to his higher officer or using or attempting to use criminal force against his colleague or higher officer whether on or off duty, knowing or having reason to believe him to be such;

(*xiv*) designedly or through neglect injuring or losing or fraudulently disposing of or unlawfully lending his arms, clothes, tools, equipments, ammunition or accountrements or any such articles entrusted to him or belonging to any other member of the Force;

(*xv*) taking part in procession, *gherao,* demonstration, shouting slogans or resorting to pamphleteering or otherwise indulging in any intimidating or coercive acts or *dharna,* hunger strike for forcing under duress or threats any supervisory authority to concede anything or striking work;

(*xvi*) being guilty of using insulting or threatening language in the case of Security Court or causing any interruption or disturbance in the proceedings of such Court;

(*xvii*) offering unwarrantable personal violence to any person in custody;

(*xviii*) entering or searching without lawful authority or reasonable cause any building or place;

(*xix*) seizing vexatiously and unnecessarily the property of any person;

(*xx*) detaining, searching or arresting any person vexatiously and without reasonable suspicion or cause;

(*xxi*) holding out any threat, inducement or promise not warranted by law; or

(*xxii*) aiding or abetting or attempting to commit any of the offences under this Act or these rules or doing any act towards the commission of such offence;

shall render him liable for punishment under section 9 or section 17 or both.

CHAPTER XII

DISCIPLINARY AND PENAL PUNISHMENTS

148. Description of punishments. (1) Any of the following punishments may, for good and sufficient reasons and as hereinafter provided, be imposed on an enrolled member of the Force.

(2) *Major punishments.* (*a*) Dismissal from service (which shall ordinarily be a disqualification for future employment under the Government);

(*b*) Removal from service (which shall not be a disqualification for future employment under the Government);

(*c*) Compulsory retirement from service;

(*d*) Reduction in rank or grade.

(3) *Minor punishments.* (*a*) Reduction to a lower stage in the existing scale of pay;

(*b*) Withholding of next increment with or without corresponding postponement of subsequent increments;

(*c*) Withholding of promotion for a specified period;

(*d*) Removal from any office of distinction or deprivation of any special emoluments;

(*e*) Censure.

(4) *Petty punishments.* (*a*) Fine to any amount not exceeding seven days' pay;

(*b*) Confinement to quarter-guard for a period not exceeding fourteen days with or without punishment drill, extra guard duty, fatigue duty or any other punitive duty;

(*c*) Reprimand.

(5) *Explanation.* The following shall not amount to a punishment within the meaning of this rule, namely:—

(*a*) withholding of increment of an enrolled member of the Force for failure to pass a departmental examination in accordance with the rules or orders governing class or grade or rank or post or as per the terms of his appointment;

(*b*) stoppage of an enrolled member of the Force at the efficiency bar in the existing scale of pay on the ground of his unfitness to cross the bar;

(*c*) non-promotion of an enrolled member of the Force, whether in a substantive or officiating capacity, due to his failure to pass the pre-promotion course, to a rank or grade to which he is eligible or has been empanelled;

(*d*) reversion of an enrolled member of the Force officiating in a higher rank or a grade to a lower rank or grade on the ground that he is considered to be unsuitable for such higher rank or grade on any administrative grounds not connected with his conduct;

(*e*) reversion of an enrolled member of the Force appointed on probation to his permanent rank, grade or post, during or at the end of the period of probation in accordance with the terms of his appointment or the rules and orders governing probation;

(*f*) repatriation of an enrolled member of the Force to his parent cadre or department;

(*g*) retirement of a member of the Force under rules 84 and 85 an grounds of unsuitability or physical and mental unfitness respectively;

(*h*) suspension of enrolled members of the Force under rule 134;

(*i*) termination of services of an enrolled member of the Force—

(1) appointed on probation, during the period of probation or any extension thereof in accordance with the provisions of sub-rule (3) of rule 57 or;

(2) reduction or withholding of the maximum pension admissible under the Pension Rules for a specified period.

149. Other minor punishments. (1) Enrolled members of the Force, being railway servant shall also be subject to the following minor punishments—

(*a*) withholding of the privileges of passes or Privilege Ticket Orders or both for a specified period;

(*b*) reduction or withholding of the maximum pension admissible under the Pension Rules for a specified period.

150. Effect of departmental punishment on prosecution. Any punishment specified in rules 148 and 149 which has been imposed on an enrolled member of the Force shall not affect his liability to prosecution and punishment under this Act or under any other law for the time being in force.

151. Disciplinary Authority. (1) The disciplinary authority in respect of any enrolled member of the Force for the purpose of imposing any particular punishment or the passing of any disciplinary order shall be the authority specified in this behalf in Schedule III in whose administrative control the member is serving and shall include any authority superior to such authority.

(2) The disciplinary authority, in the case of an enrolled member of the Force officiating in a higher rank, shall be determined with reference to the officiating post held by him at the time of taking action.

152. Authority to institute proceedings. (1) The appointing authority or any authority otherwise empowered by general or special order, may—

(*a*) institute disciplinary proceedings against any enrolled member; or

(*b*) direct a disciplinary authority to institute disciplinary proceedings against any enrolled member of the Force on whom the disciplinary authority is competent to impose, under these rules, any of the punishments specified in rules 148 and 149.

(2) A disciplinary authority, competent under these rules to impose any of the minor punishments may institute disciplinary proceedings for the imposition of any of the major punishments notwithstanding that such disciplinary authority is not competent, under these rules, to impose any of the latter punishment.

153. Procedure for imposing major punishments. (1) Without prejudice to the provisions of the Public Servants Inquiries Act, 1850, no order of dismissal, removal, compulsory retirement or reduction in rank shall be passed on any enrolled member of the Force (save as mentioned in rule 161) without holding an inquiry, as far as may be in the manner provided hereinafter, in which he has been informed in writing of the grounds on which it is proposed to take action and has been afforded a reasonable opportunity of defending himself.

(2) (*i*) Whenever the disciplinary authority is of the opinion that there are grounds for inquiring into the truth of any imputation of misconduct or misbehaviour against an enrolled member of the Force, it may itself inquire into or appoint an Inquiry Officer higher in rank to the enrolled member charged but not below the rank of Inspector, or institute a Court of Inquiry to inquire into the truth thereof.

(*ii*) Where the disciplinary authority itself holds the inquiry, any reference to the Inquiry Officer in these rules shall be construed as a reference to the disciplinary authority.

(3) On receipt of complaint or otherwise, the disciplinary authority on going through the facts alleged or brought out shall decide whether it is a case for major or minor punishment. No attempt shall be made to convert cases punishable under section 16A or section 17 into disciplinary cases nor divert cases in respect of which major punishments are imposable to the category of cases where minor or petty punishments are impossible.

(4) Where it is proposed to hold an inquiry against an enrolled member of the Force under this rule, the disciplinary authority may order that the enrolled member shall not be transferred to any other place nor given leave without its written permission till the conclusion of the disciplinary proceedings, and the disciplinary authority shall draw up or cause to be drawn up—

(*a*) the substance of the imputations of misconduct or misbehaviour into definite and distinct articles of charge;

(*b*) a statement of the imputations of misconduct or misbehaviour in support of each article of charge which shall contain,—

(*i*) a statement of all relevant facts including any admission or confession made by the enrolled member of the Force; and

(*ii*) a list of documents by which and a list of witnesses by whom the articles of charge are proposed to be sustained.

(5) The disciplinary authority shall deliver or cause to be delivered to the delinquent member, at least seventy-two hours before the commencement of the inquiry, a copy of the articles of charge the statement of imputations of misconduct or misbehaviour and a list of documents and witnesses by which each article of charge is proposed to be sustained and fix a date when the inquiry is to commence; subsequent dates being fixed by the Inquiry Officer.

(6) Where the enrolled member charged has absconded or where it is not possible to serve the documents on him in person or where he deliberately evades service, the procedure laid down in sections 62, 64, 65 and 69 of the Code of Criminal Procedure, 1973 shall be adopted by the Inquiry Officer for service of such documents and the same shall be deemed to be a conclusive proof of service.

(7) For securing the presence of private prosecution witnesses, the Inquiry Officer may allow free travel passes according to their status in accordance with extant Railway Rules.

(8) The enrolled member charged shall not be allowed to bring in a legal practitioner at the proceedings but he may be allowed to take the assistance of any other member of the Force (hereinafter referred to as "friend") where in the opinion of the Inquiry Officer may, at the request of the party charged, put his defence properly. Such "friend" must be a serving member of the Force of or below the rank of Sub-Inspector for the time being posted in the same division or the battalion where the proceedings are pending and not acting as a "friend" in any other proceedings pending anywhere. Such "friend" shall, however, not be allowed to address the Inquiry Officer nor to cross-examine the witnesses.

(9) If the enrolled member charged fails to turn up on the day fixed for the start of inquiry and no reasonable excuse is offered for not being present on the fixed time and day, the Inquiry Officer may commence the inquiry *ex parte*.

(10) At the commencement of the inquiry, the party charged shall be asked to enter a plea of "guilty" or "not guilty" after which evidence necessary to establish the charge shall be let in. The evidence shall be material to the charge and may either be oral or documentary. If oral—

(*a*) it shall be direct;

(*b*) it shall be recorded by the Inquiry Officer in the presence of the party charged; and

the party charged shall be allowed to cross-examine the witnesses.

(11) If the witnesses are Government officers of a rank superior to the party charged, the Inquiry Officer may, at the request of the party charged, put the questions to such officer.

(12) If the evidence shall be recorded, in the presence of the party charged, by the Inquiry Officer himself or on his dictation by a scribe. Cross-examination by the party charged or the fact of his declining to cross-examine the witness, as the case may be, shall also be recorded. The statement of each witness shall be read over to him and explained, if necessary, in the language of the witness, whose signature shall be obtained as a token of his having understood the contents. Statement shall also be signed by the Inquiry Officer and the party charged. Copy of each statement shall be given to the party charged who shall acknowledge receipt on the statement of witness itself. The Inquiry Officer shall recorded a certificate of having road over the statement to the witness in the presence of the party charged.

(13) Documentary exhibits, if any, are to be numbered while being presented by the concerned witness and reference of the number shall be noted in the statement of the witness. Such documents may be admitted in evidence as exhibits without being formally proved unless the party charged does not admit the genuineness of such a document and wishes to cross-examine the witness who is purported to have signed it. Copies of the exhibits may be given to the party charged on demand except in the case of voluminous documents, where the party charged may be allowed to inspect the same in the presence of Inquiry Officer and take notes.

(14) Unless specifically mentioned in these rules, the provisions of the Code of Criminal Procedure, 1973 and the Indian Evidence Act, 1872 shall apply to the departmental proceedings under these rules.

(15) The party charged shall then be examined and his statement recorded by the Inquiry Officer. If the party charged has pleaded guilty and does not challenge the evidence on record, the proceedings shall be closed for orders. If he pleads "not guilty", he shall be required to file within 10 days a written statement together with a list of such witnesses as he may wish to produce in his defence and giving therein a gist of evidence that each witness is expected to give. If he declines to file a written statement, he shall again be examined by the Inquiry Officer on the expiry of the period allowed and his statement, if any, recorded.

(16) If the party charged refuses to produce any witnesses or to produce any evidence in his defence, the proceedings shall be closed for orders. If he produce any evidence, the Inquiry Officer shall proceed to record the evidence. If the Inquiry Officer considers that the evidence of any witness or any document which the party charged wants to produce in his defence is not material to the issues involved in the case, he may refuse to call such witness or to allow such document to be produced in evidence, but in all such cases he must briefly record his reasons for considering the evidence inadmissible. When all relevant evidence has been brought on record, the proceedings shall be closed for orders after recording the statement, if any, of the party charged and obtaining any clarification, if necessary, from him.

(17) Under no circumstances additional prosecution witnesses shall be examined after the defence has been let in unless supplementary defence witnesses have been allowed on that ground. However, if at any stage during the inquiry, it appears to the Inquiry Officer that examination of any witness who has not been

produced by either party so far or recall of any witness who has already been examined is essential in the interest of justice or to clear any doubt, he may summon him for the purpose and examine him as a witness of the Inquiry Officer after recording his reasons for doing so. Such a witness may also be cross-examined by the party charged, if desired.

(18) Whenever any Inquiry Officer after having heard and recorded the whole or any part of the evidence in an inquiry, ceases to exercise jurisdiction therein and is succeeded by another Inquiry Officer who has and exercises such jurisdiction, the Inquiry Officer so succeeding may act on the evidence so recorded by his predecessor, or partly recorded by his predecessor, and partly recorded by him or himself record it afresh as he deems expedient.

(19) At the conclusion of the inquiry, the Inquiry Officer shall prepare a report of the inquiry recording his findings on each of the charges with reasons therefor. The findings must be of "guilty" or "not guilty" and no room shall be allowed for "benefit of doubt" or personal surmises. A charge shall be deemed to have been proved if after considering the evidence before him, the Inquiry Officer believes the ingredients constituting the charge to exist or considers their existence so probable that a prudent man ought, under the circumstances of the particular case, to act upon the supposition that they exist.

(20) If in the opinion of the Inquiry Officer, the proceedings of the inquiry establish charges different from those originally framed, he may record his findings on such charges:

Provided that findings on such charges shall not be recorded unless the party charged has admitted the facts constituting them and has had an opportunity of defending himself against them.

Departmental enquiry. Generally in domestic/departmental enquiry, the person accused of misconduct has to conduct his own case. If there is some rule which permits the accused person to be represented by some one else, then he can claim to be represented in an enquiry. There is no vested or absolute right in any charge sheeted employee to representation either through a counsel or through other person unless the statute or rules or standing orders provide for such a right. Moreover, the right to representation even if granted by rules, it is a restricted or controlled right. Refusal to grant representation through an agent does not violate the principles of natural justice. Rule 153(8) of the Railway Protection Force Rules, 1987 provides a restricted right. Thus, the said rule 153(8) as not unconstitutional.[7]

154. Action on the Inquiry Report. (1) If the disciplinary authority having regard to its own findings where it is itself the Inquiry Officer or having regard to its decision on all or any of the findings of the Inquiry Officer, is of the opinion that the punishment warranted as such as is within its competence, that authority may act on the evidence on record. However, in a case where it is of the opinion that further examination of any of the witnesses is necessary in the interest of justice, it may recall the witness, examine him and allow the party charged to cross-examine him. After that, it may impose on the party charged such punishment as is within its competence according to these rules.

7 *Railway Protection Force* v *K. Raghuram Babu* (2008)4 SCC 406; AIR 2008 SC 1958.

(2) While communicating the order imposing the punishment, a copy of the findings of the Inquiry Officer shall also be given to the party charged.

(3) Where such disciplinary authority is of the opinion that the punishment warranted is such, as is not within its competence, that authority shall forward the records of the inquiry to be appropriate disciplinary authority who shall act in the manner as hereinafter provided.

(4) The disciplinary authority, if it is not itself the Inquiry Officer may, for reasons to be recorded, remit the case to the Inquiry Officer for further inquiry and report. The Inquiry Officer shall thereupon proceed to hold further inquiry according to the provisions of rule 153 and submit to the disciplinary authority the complete records of such inquiry along with his report.

(5) The disciplinary authority shall, if it disagrees with the findings of the Inquiry Officer on any article of charge, record its reasons for such disagreement and record its own findings on such charges, if the evidence on record is sufficient for the purpose.

(6) If the disciplinary authority having regard to its findings on all or any of the articles of charge is of the opinion that any of the minor punishments should be imposed on the party charged, it shall, notwithstanding anything contained in rule 158, make an order imposing such punishment.

(7) If the disciplinary authority, having regard to its findings on all or any of the articles of charge and on the basis of evidence on record, is of the opinion that any of the major punishments should be imposed on the party charged, it shall make an order imposing such punishment and it shall not be necessary to give to the party charged, any opportunity of making representation on the punishment proposed to be imposed.

155. Determination of punishment. In determining the punishment, the character, previous bad record and punishment of party charged shall not be taken into consideration unless in a case where they are made subject matter of a specific charge in the proceeding itself. Offences connoting moral turpitude shall be carefully distinguished from smaller lapses of conduct. It is essential that the punishment shall be inflicted keeping in view the nature of duties executed from the member of the Force and the misconduct by him.

156. Imposing of punishment of dismissal, etc. Before coming to any lower punishment, the disciplinary authority with a view to ensuring the maintenance of integrity in the Force shall consider the award of punishment of dismissal or removal from services to any member of the Force in the following cases, namely—

(*a*) *Dismissal.*—(*i*) conviction by a Criminal Court;

(*ii*) serious misconduct or indulging in committing or attempting or abetting an offence against railway property;

(*iii*) discreditable conduct affecting the image and reputation of the Force.

(*iv*) neglect of duty resulting in or likely to result in loss to the railway or danger to the lives of persons using the railways;

(*v*) insolvency or habitual indebtedness; and

(*vi*) obtaining employment of his antecedents which would ordinarily have debarred him from such employment.

(*b*) *Removal from service*—(*i*) Any of the misconduct for which he may be dismissed under clause (*a*) above;

(*ii*) repeated minor misconducts;

(*iii*) absence from duty without proper intimation or overstay beyond sanctioned leave without sufficient cause.

157. Reduction in the rank, grade or in the scale of pay. (1) No enrolled member of the Force shall be reduced to a rank lower than that to which he was first appointed to the service nor shall he be reduced permanently in the sense that he shall never be eligible for repromotion however meritorious his subsequent service may be.

(2) When reduction to a lower rank, grade or a lower stage in the scale of pay is ordered, the order shall also specify—

(*i*) the date from which it will take effect and the period (in terms of years and months) for which the punishment shall be operative;

(*ii*) the stage in the scale of pay (in terms of rupees) to which the enrolled member of the Force is reduced; and

(*iii*) the extent (in terms of years and months), if any, to which the punishment referred to at (*i*) above shall be with or without cumulative effect.

Provided that when the punishment of reduction to a lower stage in the scale of pay is imposed during the currency of reduction in rank, the disciplinary authority shall clearly indicate in the punishment order whether the two punishments shall run concurrently or the subsequent punishment shall be implemented after the expiry of the first punishment.

(3) *Withholding of increments.* In the case of withholding of increment as a punishment, the order shall state the period for which the increment is to be withheld and whether it shall have the effect of postponing further increments.

158. Procedure for imposing minor punishments. (1) The disciplinary authority may impose any of the minor punishments provided in sub-rule (3) of rule 148 and in rule 149 after—

(*a*) informing the enrolled member of the Force charged in writing of the proposal to take action against him and of imputations of misconduct or misbehaviour on the basis of which action is proposed to be taken and giving him a reasonable opportunity of making such representation within a period of 10 days from the date of communication as he may wish to make against the proposal;

(*b*) taking the representation, if any, submitted by the party charged under clause (*a*) into consideration and recording a finding on each imputation of misconduct or misbehaviour.

(2) Notwithstanding anything contained in clause (*a*) of sub-rule (1), if it is proposed, after considering the representation, if any, made by the party charged under the said clause (*a*) to withhold increments of pay and such withholding of increments is likely to affect adversely the amount of pension payable to the party charged or to withhold increments of pay for a period exceeding three years or to withhold increments of pay with cumulative effect for any period or to reduce him by more than three stages in his scale of pay, an inquiry shall be held, as far as

possible, in the manner laid down in rule 153 before making any order imposing on the party charged any such punishment.

159. Departmental Proceedings File. Every departmental proceedings file shall contain documents in the following order with an index sheet:

(*i*) Order sheet,

(*ii*) Preliminary papers,

(*iii*) Charges,

(*iv*) Statement of Prosecution witnesses,

(*v*) Prosecution exhibits,

(*vi*) Defence statement of "guilty" or "not guilty,"

(*vii*) Statement of defence witnesses,

(*viii*) Written statement of defence, if any,

(*ix*) Findings of the Inquiry Officer,

(*x*) Order of the Disciplinary Authority,

(*xi*) Appeal and Order.

160. Procedure for imposing petty punishment. (1) Petty breaches of discipline and petty cases of misconduct by the enrolled members of the Force shall, as far as possible, be inquired into and disposed of in Orderly Room by an officer authorised to award petty punishment under Schedule III to any such enrolled member of the Force who is for the time being subject to his authority. Inquiries in the Orderly Room shall be held, as far as possible, at least once a week on a fixed day.

(2) If the offence calls for more severe punishment than the officer dealing with it is authorised to inflict, he shall:

(*i*) if at headquarters, have the delinquent member brought before the Assistant Security Commissioner or the Divisional Security Commissioner concerned as the case may be;

(*ii*) if away from the headquarters, forward the record with his recommendations to the Assistant Security Commissioner or the Divisional Security Commissioner concerned, as the case may be, for orders and further action.

(3) Proceedings of such inquiries shall be recorded in the Orderly Room Register.

(4) Punishment awarded in Orderly Room may be carried out in Reserve Lines, Training Institutes or Posts, as may be specified by the officer awarding the punishment.

(5) Fatigue duty and any other duty shall, however, be awarded only to Constables and Naiks and may consist of any one or more of the following duties, namely:—

(*a*) pitching and tending of tents and their mending;

(*b*) tending of gardens, farms, ponds, etc., of the Force;

(*c*) cutting of grass and mowing of lawns;

(*d*) clearing of jungles and cutting of wood;

(*e*) cleaning and marking of parade ground;

(*f*) cleaning and dusting of arms, equipment, stores, mess, class rooms and barracks; and or

(*g*) repairing of huts, butts and similar other works in the Reserve Lines, Post, etc.

161. Special procedure in certain cases. Notwithstanding anything contained anywhere in these rules—

(*i*) where any punishment is imposed on an enrolled member of the Force on the ground of conduct which has led to his conviction on a criminal charge; or

(*ii*) where the authority competent to impose the punishment is satisfied for reasons to be recorded by it in writing that it is not reasonable practicable to hold an inquiry in the manner provided in these rules;

(*iii*) where the President is satisfied that in the interest of Security of State and the maintenance of integrity in the Force, it is not expedient to hold any inquiry in the manner provided in these rules;

the authority competent to impose the punishment may consider the circumstances of the case and make such others thereof as it deems fit.

162. Procedure to be followed in case of conviction by a Criminal Court. (1) The Divisional Security Commissioner or the Commanding Officer shall go through the record of every case brought against an enrolled member of the Force in the Court, and shall take departmental cognizance of every criminal case in which an enrolled member of the Force is convicted or acquitted or discharged (except when the case is false) and record on appropriate order.

(2) *Effect of imprisonment.* Every enrolled member of the Force punished with imprisonment or released on probation after conviction for an offence implying moral turpitude, such as theft, perjury, rape, or with imprisonment exceeding one month for any other offence or for any matter specified in section 17 shall be proceeded against for dismissal, and shall ordinarily be dismissed from service.

(3) *Effect of fine.* When an enrolled member of the Force is sentenced to fine by a Criminal Court, disciplinary authority may examine the circumstances of the case and, if necessary in the interest of the Force, draw up proceedings for dismissal.

(4) *Form of charge in such cases.* (1) The charge in proceedings under sub-rules (2) and (3) shall be that the accused has been convicted, imprisoned or fined, as the case may be, for the offence concerned.

(2) Without prejudice to the right of the accused on final acquittal, such proceedings shall be taken up as soon as the first trial Court has passed orders of conviction and disposed of immediately in order to avoid the wasteful expenditure involved in allowing the enrolled member of the Force to remain under suspension.

(5) *Proceedings in case of discharge.* When an enrolled member of the Force is prosecuted before a Court but discharged for insufficiency of evidence or on any technical ground or by giving him the benefit of doubt, the disciplinary authority shall examine the possibility of instituting departmental proceedings after an objective consideration of all the facts and circumstances of the case and may take such action as deemed appropriate.

163. Procedure when two or more enrolled members are involved. Where two or more enrolled members of the Force including those on deputation to the Force are involved in any case, the disciplinary authority may make an order directing that the disciplinary action against two or all of them may be taken in a common proceeding.

164. Provision regarding enrolled member of the Force whose services are lent to other departments of Central or State Governments, etc. (1) Where the services of an enrolled member of the Force are lent to any other Ministry or Department of the Central Government or to a State Government or an authority subordinate thereto (hereinafter in this rule referred to as "the borrowing authority"), of the borrowing authority shall have the powers of the authority competent to place such member under suspension and of the disciplinary authority for the purpose of conducting disciplinary proceedings against him.

Provided that the borrowing authority shall forthwith inform the authority which lent the services of the enrolled member (hereafter in this rule referred to as "lending authority") of the circumstances leading to the orders of his suspension or the commencement of the disciplinary proceedings, as the case may be.

(2) In the light of the findings in the disciplinary proceedings conducted against the enrolled member of the Force—

(*i*) if the borrowing authority is of the opinion that any of the minor punishments should be imposed on such member, it may, after consultation with the lending authority, make such orders in the case as it deems necessary:

Provided that in the event of a difference of opinion between the borrowing authority and the lending authority, such member shall be repatriated; and

(*ii*) if the borrowing authority is of the opinion that any of the major punishments should be imposed as such member, it shall replace his services at the disposal of lending authority and transmit to it the proceedings of the inquiry and thereupon the lending authority may, if it is the disciplinary authority, pass such orders thereon as it may deem necessary or if it is not the disciplinary authority, submit the case to the disciplinary authority which shall pass such orders on the case as it may deem necessary:

Provided that before passing such orders, the disciplinary authority shall comply with the provisions of sub-rules (4) and (6) of rule 154:

Provided further that the disciplinary authority may make an order under this clause on the record of the inquiry transmitted it by the borrowing authority or after holding such further inquiry as it may deem necessary, as far as may be, in accordance with rule 153.

165. Provision regarding enrolled members of the Force on deputation. (1) Where the services of any person is borrowed for appointment as an enrolled member of the Force on deputation, the authority which appointed him as an enrolled member of the Force (hereinafter in this rule referred to as "borrowing authority") shall have the powers of the authority which lent the services of such person (hereinafter in this rule referred to as the "lending authority") for the purpose of placing him under suspension or for conducting disciplinary proceedings against him:

Provided that where an order suspending such person is made or disciplinary proceedings commenced against such person, the borrowing authority shall forthwith from the lending authority of the circumstances leading to the order of suspension or as the case may be, the commencement of the disciplinary proceedings against him.

(2) In the light of the findings in the disciplinary proceedings conducted against such person—

(*i*) if the borrowing authority is of the opinion that any of the minor punishments specified in the rules by which such person is governed should be imposed on him, it may after consultation with the lending authority, pass such orders in the case as it deems necessary, in accordance with the said rules.

Provided that in the event of a difference of opinion between the borrowing authority and lending authority, the services of such person shall be replaced at the disposal of the lending authority; or

(*ii*) if the borrowing authority is of the opinion that any of the major punishments specified in the rules by which such person is governed should be imposed on him, it shall replace his services at the disposal of the lending authority and transmit to it the proceedings of inquiry and thereupon the lending authority may pass such orders as it may deem necessary.

166. Entry of punishment in service roll. Any punishment imposed on an enrolled member of the Force shall be entered in the service roll of such enrolled member.

PENAL PUNISHMENTS

167. Penal punishments. Penal punishment on the enrolled members of the Force shall be imposed either by the ordinary Criminal Courts in accordance with the provisions of the Code of Criminal Procedure, 1973 or by the Security Court under the Act, in accordance with the provisions hereinafter contained.

168. Composition and constitution of Security Court. (1) The Assistant Inspector General, the Senior Commandant or the Commandant referred to in rule 30 (hereinafter referred to as the Presiding Officer) shall constitute a Security Court.

(2) The proceedings may be attended by two other members of the Force as observers who shall not be required to take oath or make affirmation.[8][* * *]

(3) The Presiding Officer and the said observers shall be in their prescribed uniform during the trial.

169. Powers of Security Court. (1) The Security Court may try any enrolled member subject to the Act and these rules.

(2) Any trial by a Security Court under these rules shall be deemed to be a judicial proceeding within the meaning of sections 193 and 228 of the Indian Penal Code, 1860 and the Security Court shall be deemed to be a Court within the meaning of sections 345 and 346 of the Code of Criminal Procedure, 1973.

8 *Omitted* by G.S.R. 719(E), dated 31.10.2013 (w.e.f. 31.10.2013).

(3) The findings and sentence of the Security Court shall not be required to be confirmed and may be carried out forthwith.

(4) A petition against an order of the Security Court may be made to be Chief Security Commissioner, who may dispose of the same, as provided in rule 210.

170. Investigation of charges. (1) On receipt of information or otherwise that an enrolled member of the Force has committed an offence under the Act or the rules made thereunder, the Security Commissioner or the Commanding Officer of a unit shall assemble a Court of Inquiry referred to in rule 265 or commission any other member of the Force for conducting the investigation.

(2) On receipt of the report, the Security Commissioner or the Commanding Officer may dismiss a charge brought against an enrolled member of the Force if, in his opinion, the evidence does not show that an offence under the Act has been committed, and may do so, if, in his discretion, he is satisfied that the charge ought not to be proceeded with.

(3) Where such an officer is of the opinion that the charge ought to be taken cognizance of, he shall, without unnecessary delay, decide whether the case be dealt—

(*a*) under the provisions of section 9; or

(*b*) by Security Court; or

(*c*) by an ordinary Criminal Court;

and take further action accordingly.

Provided that where the offence has been reported to the local police or otherwise registered by them and they after investigation have sent the accused enrolled member of the Force for trial before the ordinary Criminal Court, the Security Commissioner or Commanding Officer may, with the prior permission of the Chief Security Commissioner, call for such a case from such Court for trial by a Security Court under these rules:

Provided further that an accused may not be claimed for trial by a Security Court where the offence is committed by him alongwith any other person not subject to the Act.

171. Converting the Security Court. In all cases, where it is decided to try the accused enrolled member of the Force by the Security Court, the Security Commissioner or the Commanding Officer shall move the Chief Security Commissioner concerned who may, on being satisfied, convene the Security Court:

Provided that where a Security Commissioner or Commanding Officer is of the opinion that it is necessary to take immediate action and such prior approval cannot be obtained without detriment to discipline, he may convene the Security Court pending approval of the Chief Security Commissioner.

172. Choice of jurisdiction between the Security Court and the Criminal Court. Subject to the provisions or the proviso to sub-section (3) of section 17, where an offence is committed by the accused enrolled member of the Force—

(*a*) in the course of performance of his duty as such member; or

(*b*) in relation to property belonging to the Government or the Force or a person subject to the Act; or

(*c*) against a person subject to the Act, he shall be tried by a Security Court.

173. Prescribed authority for purposes of proviso to sub-section (3) of section 17. For the purposes of the proviso to sub-section (3) of section 17, the authority who may require enquiry into, or trial of, an offence by an ordinary Criminal Court shall be the Security Commissioner or the Commandant, as the case may be, within the limits of whose jurisdiction the offence has been committed.

174. Period of limitation for trial. No trial under these provisions shall commence:

(*a*) after the expiration of a period of 12 months from the date of such offence; or

(*b*) if a person has ceased to be an enrolled member.

175. Force custody. (1) Where a Security Commissioner or Commanding officer is of opinion that any enrolled member of the Force has committed an offence and should be tried by the Security Court, it shall be lawful for him, with the prior approval of the Chief Security Commissioner, to order the enrolled member of the Force to be taken into Force custody and kept either in close arrest or open arrest as he may deem fit from time to time depending on the gravity of the charge and the attending circumstances:

Provided that no enrolled member of the Force shall be detained in Force custody for a period of more than eight days without a Security Court for his trial having been convened or without a punishment having been awarded to him under section 9:

Provided further that where further detention is considered essential, such officer shall seek, written approval of the Chief Security Commissioner, who may sanction further detention for a specific period, which he may extend from time to time by not more than eight days subject to a total period of detention for two months.

(2) In each division or battalion, there shall be one or more places of confinement, as may be considered necessary by the Chief Security Commissioner, where arrested enrolled members of the Force shall be confined under this Act. Such places shall be under the supervision of the Divisional Security Commissioner or Commanding Officer of the unit, who shall be responsible for their upkeep.

(3) If any enrolled member of the Force in Force custody escapes or is rescued, the member of the Force from whose custody he escaped or was rescued should report the escape or rescue to his officer-in-charge and may immediately pursue and arrest such enrolled member in any place in India.

176. Framing of charges. (1) A charge-sheet shall contain the whole issue or issues to be tried by a Security Court at one time.

(2) A charge means an accusation contained in a charge-sheet that an enrolled member of the Force has been guilty of an offence.

(3) A charge-sheet may contain one charge or several charges.

177. Contents of charge. (1) Each charge shall state one offence only and in no case shall an offence be described in the alternative in the same charge.

(2) Each charge shall be divided into two parts—

(*a*) statement of offences, and

(*b*) statement of particulars of the act, neglect or omission constituting the offence.

(3) The particulars shall state such circumstances respecting the alleged offence as will enable the accused to know what act, neglect or omission is intended to be proved against him as constituting the offence.

(4) The particulars in one charge may be included wholly or partly by a reference to the particulars in another charge, and in that case so much of the latter particulars as are so referred to shall be deemed to form part of the first mentioned charge as well as of the other charge.

(5) Where it is intended to prove any facts in respect of which any deduction from pay and allowances can be awarded as a consequence of the offence charged, the particulars shall state those facts and the sum of the loss or damage it is intended to recover.

178. Signature on charge-sheet. The charge-sheet shall be signed by the Security Commissioner or the Commanding Officer under whose administrative control the enrolled member of the Force may be serving for the time being and shall contain the place and date of holding such trial.

179. Construction of charge-sheet. In the construction of a charge-sheet or charge, there shall be presumed in favour of supporting the charge, every proposition which may reasonably be presumed to be impliedly included though not expressed therein.

180. Warning to accused for trial. (1) The accused before he is arraigned shall be informed by any member of the Force of every charge for which he is to be tried and also that on his giving the names in writing of witnesses whom he desires to call in his defence twenty four hours before the trial, reasonable steps will be taken for procuring their attendance and those steps shall be taken accordingly.

(2) The interval between his being so informed and his arraignment shall not be less than ninety six hours or where the accused person is on active service if shall not be less than seventy two hours.

(3) The member of the Force at the time of so informing the accused shall give him a copy of the charge-sheet and shall, if necessary, read and explain to him the charges brought against him. If the accused desires to have it in a language which he understands, a translation thereof shall also be given to him.

(4) The accused shall also be furnished a copy of the relevant record or abstract of evidence collected against him and a notice of any additional evidence which the prosecution intends to adduce.

(5) The concerned member of the Force shall, if the accused so desires, give him the name of the Presiding Officer and also the names of other two members of the Force who will be attending as observers.

181. Joint trial of several accused persons. (1) Any number of accused persons may be charged jointly and tried together for an offence averred to have been committed by them collectively.

(2) Any number of accused persons, although not charged jointly, may be tried together for an offence averred to have been committed by one or more of them and to have abetted by the other or others.

(3) Where the accused are so charged under sub-rule (1) or are to be tried together under sub-rule (2), any one case or more of them at the same time be charged with and tried for any other offence averred to have been committed

individually or collectively, provided that, all the said offences are based on the same facts or form or are part of a series of offences of the same or similar character.

(4) In the cases mentioned above, notice of the intention to try the accused persons together shall be given to each of the accused at the time of his being informed of the charge, and any accused person may claim, either by notice to the authority convening the Security Court, or, when arraigned before the Security Court, by notice to that Court, that he or some other accused be tried separately on one or more of the charges included in the charge-sheet, on the ground that the evidence of one or more of the other accused persons proposed to be tried together with him will be material to his defence, or that otherwise he would be prejudiced in his defence.

(5) The authority convening the Security Court, if satisfied that the evidence will be material or that the accused may be prejudiced in his defence as aforesaid and if the nature of the charge admits of this, shall allow the claim, and such accused person, or, as the case may be, the other accused person or persons whose separate trial has been claimed, shall be tried separately.

182. Preparation of defence by the accused. An accused who has been remanded for trial, shall be afforded reasonable opportunity for preparing his defence and shall be allowed proper communication with his 'friend' who can be another enrolled member of the Force a legal practitioner. A person so assisting him may advise him on all points and suggest the question to be put to witness but shall not examine or cross-examine witnesses or address the Security Court:

Provided that in a case instituted on the charge-sheet of the Police where a Public Prosecutor appears for presenting the case, the 'friend' of the accused shall also be allowed similar facility to examine and cross-examine the witness or address the Security Court.

183. Attendance of witness. The provisions of section 69 of the Code of Criminal Procedure, 1973 shall apply for procuring the attendance of witness.

184. Commencement of proceedings. The Presiding Officer holding the trial, shall record, or cause to be recorded all the proceedings of the Security Court in English or in Hindi language, get the signature of the witnesses on their statements and may give a copy of the proceedings to the delinquent enrolled member (hereinafter referred to as the accused), free of charge, on demand.

185. Recording of evidence. (1) The provisions contained in the Indian Evidence Act, 1872 (excepting sections 25 and 26) shall apply to the Security Court unless they are repugnant to the express provisions of these rules.

(2) All evidence taken in the course of trial shall be on oath or affirmation and taken in the presence of the accused.

(3) All evidence shall be taken down in a narrative form, as nearly as possible in words used, but in any case where the Presiding Officer considers it material, the question and answer shall be taken down verbatim.

(4) All evidence so taken down shall be signed by the Presiding Officer and the witnesses and shall form part of the judicial record.

(5) If the witness gives evidence in a language other than Hindi or English, it may be, if practicable taken down in that language. If it is not practicable to

do so, a true translation in Hindi or in English of the evidence shall be prepared and kept on record.

(6) The statement of a witness taken down as stated above, shall be read over and if necessary be corrected. When a witness denies the correctness of the same, the Presiding Officer instead of correcting the evidence, may make a memorandum of objection made by such witness and shall record such remarks as he thinks necessary.

186. Evidence when translated. (1) When any evidence is given in a language which the Presiding Officer or the accused does not understand, the evidence shall be translated for the Presiding Officer or the accused in a language which the Presiding Officer or the accused understands.

(2) The Presiding Officer shall for this purpose either appoint an interpreter or shall himself act as interpreter after taking the oath or affirmation specified in rule 188(1).

(3) When documents are produced for the purpose of formal proof, it shall be in the discretion of the Presiding Officer to cause as much to be interpreted as appears necessary to him.

187. Commencement of trial. When the Presiding Officer, the interpreter, if any, and the members of the Force, if any, who may attend as observers are assembled the accused shall be brought before the Security Court and oath or affirmation specified in rule 188 shall be taken by the persons mentioned therein.

188. Oath or affirmation of Presiding Officer and Interpreter. (1) The Presiding Officer shall take oath or make affirmation in any one of the forms given in Schedule IX or in such other form to the same purport which would, according to the religion or otherwise, be blinding on the conscience of the Presiding Officer.

(2) The Presiding Officer or any other person empowered by him in his behalf, shall administer to the interpreter (if any) an oath or affirmation in any of the forms given in Schedule IX or in such other form to the same purport as the Presiding Officer considers to be according to the religion or otherwise blinding on the conscience of the person who is to act as interpreter.

189. Oath or affirmation of Presiding Officer to try several accused persons. (1) The Presiding Officer shall take oath or make affirmation at one time to try any number of accused persons then present before it, whether those persons are to be tried collectively or separately.

(2) In the case of several accused to be tried separately, the Presiding Officer when talking oath or making affirmation, shall proceed with one case postponing the other cases and taking them afterwards in succession.

(3) Where several accused persons are tried separately upon charges arising out of the same transaction, the Presiding Officer may, if he considers it to be desirable in the interest of justice, postpone consideration of any sentence to awarded to any one or more such accused persons until the trials of all such accused persons have been completed.

190. Arraignment of accused. (1) After the Presiding Officer and interpretation, if any, have taken oath or made affirmation as mentioned in rule 188, the accused shall be arraigned on the charges against him.

(2) The charges on which the accused is arraigned shall be read and, if necessary, translated to him and explained and he shall be required to plead separately to each charge.

191. Objection to jurisdiction. If a plea to the general jurisdiction of the Security Court or a plea in bar of trial is offered by the accused, the Security Court shall dispose of such plea before proceeding further.

192. Amendment of charge. (1) At any time during the trial or when objected to by the accused, if it appears to the Security Court that there is mistake in the description of the accused in the charge-sheet, it shall amend the charge-sheet so as to correct that mistake.

(2) If during the course of trial, it appears to the Security Court at any time before it has begun to examine the witness, that in the interest of justice any addition, or omission from or alteration in, the charge is required, it may amend such charge and may, after the due notice to the accused and with the sanction of the Chief Security Commissioner who conveyed the Court for trial, proceed with the trial on such amended charge.

193. Adjournments. (1) The proceedings of the trial shall be held as expeditiously as possible and in particular when the examination of witnesses has once begun the same shall be continued from day to day until all the witnesses in attendance have been examined, unless it appears to the Security Court that an adjournment is necessary for the end of justice or that such continuance is impracticable.

(2) If the Security Court after taking cognizance of an offence or commencement of trial, find necessary or advisable to postpone the commencement of or adjourn any inquiry or trial, it may from time to time, for reasons to be recorded, postpone or adjourn the same on such terms as it may thinks fit for such time as it considers reasonable, and may by a warrant remand the accused if in custody:

Provided that when witnesses are in attendance, no adjournment or postponement shall be granted without examining them except for special reasons to be recorded in writing.

194. Procedure of trial by Security Court. (1) Where the accused is brought before the Security Court, the particulars of charge-sheet already served upon him under rule 180 shall be stated to him and he shall be asked whether he pleads guilty or has any defence to make.

(2) If the accused admits the accusation and pleads guilty, the Security Court shall record the plea of the accused, as nearly as possible in words used by him, and may in its discretion convict the accused and pass a sentence on him accordingly:

Provided that before convicting the accused, the Security Court shall read the record or abstract of evidence and annex it to the proceedings, or if there is no such record or abstract, the Security Court shall take and record sufficient evidence to enable it to determine the sentence, and also to enable the authority, to whom the accused may petition, to know all the circumstances connected with the offence.

(3) If the accused refuses to plead or does not plead intelligibly either one way or the other, a plea of "no guilty" shall be recorded on each charge.

(4) Upon the record of plea of "guilty", if there are other charge(s) in the same charge-sheet to which the accused pleads "not guilty", the trial shall be proceed with respect to that charge for which he pleads "not guilty". After recording the findings on it, the Security Court shall proceed with the charge or charges where plea of "guilty" has been entered.

(5) If there are alternative charges, the Security Court may either proceed with respect to all the charges as if the accused had not pleaded "guilty" to any charge or may, instead of trying him, record a finding of "guilty" upon any one of the alternative charges to which he had pleaded "guilty" and finding of "not guilty" upon all the other alternative charges which precede such charges.

195. Withdrawal of plea of "not guilty." The accused may, if he thinks fit at any time during the trial, withdraw his plea of "not guilty" and plead "guilty" and in such case, the Security Court shall record a plea and finding of "guilty" and shall, so far as necessary, proceed in the manner provided in rule 194.

196. Procedure on plea of "not guilty." (1) After the plea of "not guilty" to any charge is recorded, the evidence for the prosecution shall be taken.

(2) For the said purpose, the Security Court shall fix a date for the examination of witnesses and shall also issue summons to witnesses directing them to attend or produce any document or any other thing on the fixed date.

(3) On the date so fixed, the Security Court shall proceed to take all such evidence as may be provided in support of the prosecution. In recording the evidence, the Security Court shall strictly adhere to the admissibility and relevancy of evidence as provided in the Indian Evidence Act, 1872 as applied for the purposes of these rule by rule 185(1).

(4) Every witness shall be subject to examination-in-chief in the first instance on behalf of the prosecution, then cross-examined by the accused and then re-examined by the prosecution to explain the matters which might have arisen in the course of cross-examination. Cross-examination of a witness may, in the discretion of Security Court, be deferred until any other witness or witnesses have been examined. The Security Court may also recall any witness for further cross-examination.

(5) At the close of the evidence for the prosecution, the accused shall be asked if he has anything to say in his defence. After the accused has entered upon his defence, the Security Court may, on his application, issue process for compelling the attendance of any witness including witness to character for the purpose of examination, or cross-examination or production of any document or other thing unless the Security Court considers, for reasons to be recorded, that such application be refused. Similarly, the Security Court may not issue process to compel the attendance of a witness for the purpose of cross-examination if it feels that the accused, before he entered on his defence, had already cross-examined the witness or had the opportunity to cross-examine such witness.

197. Witnesses in reply to defence. The Security Court may, if it thinks it necessary in the interest of justice, recall any witness in reply to the defence.

198. Charges in different charge-sheet. When the charges at a trial by Security Court are contained in different charge-sheets, the accused shall be tried on each charge-sheet separately upto and including the stage of finding.

199. Clearing the Court. (1) The Presiding Officer holding the trial may clear the Security Court to consider the evidence or for any other purpose connected with the trial.

(2) Subject to the provisions of sub-rule (1), all other proceedings of the Security Court including inspection of any place shall be open Court and in the presence of the accused.

200. Verdict. The Security Court shall after the evidence for prosecution and defence has been heard, give its opinion as to whether the accused is guilty or not guilty of the charge or charges.

201. Findings. (1) The finding on every charge upon which the accused is arraigned shall be recorded and except as otherwise provided in these rules such finding shall be of "guilty" or of "not guilty".

(2) When the Security Court is of the opinion as regards any charge that the facts proved do not disclose the offence charged or any offence of which he might under the Act legally be found guilty on the charge as laid, the Security Court shall find the accused "not guilty" of that charge.

(3) The Security Court shall not find the accused guilty on more than one of two or more charges laid in the alternative, even if conviction upon one charge necessarily connotes guilt upon the alternative charge or charges.

202. Procedure on acquittal. When the finding on each of the charges in charge-sheet is "not guilty" the Security Court shall date and sign the proceedings and the findings shall be announced in open Court and the accused shall be released, if in Force custody in respect of those charges.

203. Sentence. The Security Court shall award one sentence in respect of all offences committed in one transaction and on which accused is found guilty.

Provided that the Security Court shall take into consideration while awarding the sentence, the general character, age, service, and any recognized acts of gallantry, or distinguished conduct of the accused and previous convictions of the accused either by a Security Court or a Criminal Court, any previous punishment awarded to him after a departmental proceedings, the length he has been in arrest or in confinement on any previous sentence, and any decoration, on reward, of which he may be in possession or to which he may be entitled.

Provided further that the Security Court, where it is also the appointing authority of the accused, may also pass suitable orders under section 9 read with sub-rule (2) of rule 162 and rule 207. In other cases, the Security Court shall order, the proceedings to be sent to the appointing authority for taking suitable action under that section.

204. Authentication of proceeding. The Presiding Officer shall affix his signature and the date to the finding and such signature shall be deemed to authenticate the whole of the proceedings.

205. Promulgation of sentence. The sentence of a Security Court shall be promulgated in the manner prevalent in the Force at the earliest opportunity after it has been pronounced and shall subject to the provisions of the Act be carried out without delay after promulgation.

206. Transmission of proceedings of Security Court. (1) The proceedings of every Security Court including the report of the Court of Inquiry referred to in rule 265 shall, without delay, be forwarded to the Chief Security Commissioner within whose command the trial was held for his information.

[9][* * *]

207. Execution of sentence. (1) Subject to the provision of rule 162(2) every person sentenced under this Act to imprisonment may be dismissed from the Force and shall further be liable to forfeiture of any medals and decorations received by him.

(2) Every such person shall, if he is so dismissed, imprisoned in the civil prison, but if he is not so dismissed from the Force, he may be confined in the quarter-guard or such other places as the Chief Security Commissioner may consider suitable.

208. Warrants. (1) Warrants for:—

(*a*) committing a person to civil prison to undergo imprisonments;

(*b*) continued detention of a prisoner or getting him back into Force custody on a commutation of sentence by the Petitioner Authority;

(*c*) discharge of a prisoner when he is pardoned or his trial is set aside or the unexpired portion of the sentence is remitted,

shall be in Form A, Form B or as the case may be, Form C, specified in Schedule X.

(2) Such warrants shall be signed by the Presiding Officer or by the Chief Security Commissioner concerned.

209. Sentence of dismissal. Sentence of dismissal shall take effect from the date of promulgation of such sentence or from any subsequent date as may be specified at the time of promulgation by the appointing authority.

210. Petition. (1) Every accused convicted by the Security Court shall be allowed to put in one petition against the sentence to the Chief Security Commissioner.

(2) Such a petition shall be made within thirty days (excluding the time taken in procuring the copy) from the date of promulgation of the sentence:

Provided that the Chief Security Commissioner may entertain a petition after the expiry of the said period of thirty days if he is satisfied that the petitioner was prevented by sufficient cause from filing the petition in time.

(3) The Chief Security Commissioner, while disposing off such petition shall consider the correctness, legality or propriety of the proceedings and of the sentence awarded by the Security Court and pass suitable orders including fresh trial by another Security Court.

(4) The Chief Security Commissioner may annul the proceedings of any Security Court at any stage on the ground that they are not being carried on in accordance with provisions of the Act and the rules or that they are likely to result in miscarriage of the justice and may pass such orders as he deems fit.

9 *Omitted* by G.S.R. 719(E), dated 31.10.2013 (w.e.f. 31.10.2013).

CHAPTER XIII

APPEAL AND REVISION

211. Appeals against order of suspension. An enrolled member of the Force may appeal against an order of suspension to the authority to which the authority which made or is deemed to have made the order is immediately subordinate.

212. Appeal against orders imposing punishments. (1) An enrolled member may appeal against an order imposing upon him any of the punishments specified in rules 148 and 149 to the authority immediately superior to the authority imposing the punishment:

Provided that there shall be no appeal against the judgment of the Security Court or against an order of discharge of a recruit trainee who has not been formally enrolled as a member of the Force:

Provided further that appeals against the orders of a Chief Security Commissioner or the Deputy Inspector General, Railway Protection Special Force, shall lie to the Director General and against the orders of the Director General to the Central Government.

(2) There shall be no second appeal. But when the appellate authority imposes a punishment higher than the one appealed against, an appeal shall lie to the authority next superior to the appellate authority only if the punishment imposed by the appellate authority is higher than what was within the competence of the authority which imposed the original punishment.

213. Form and contents of appeal. (1) Every enrolled member of the Force submitting an appeal shall do so separately and in his own name. An appeal forwarded through or counter-signed by a legal practitioner or a defence counsel on a 'friend' shall not be entertained and the same shall be returned to the appellant with the direction to submit it directly and under his signature.

(2) The appeal shall be addressed to the authority to whom the appeal lies, shall contain all material statements and arguments on which the appellant relies, shall not contain any disrespectful or improper language, or irrelevant allegations and shall be complete in itself.

214. Submission of appeals. Every appeal, whether the appellant is still in the Force or not, shall be submitted to the authority which made the order appealed against:

Provided that if such authority is not the head of the office under whom the appellant may be serving, or if he is not in service, the head of the office under whom he was last serving, or is not subordinate to the head of such office, the appeal shall be submitted to the head of such office who shall forward it forthwith to the said authority.

215. Withholding of appeals. (1) The authority which made the order appealed against may withhold the appeal if:

(*a*) it is an appeal which made the order from which no appeal lies; or

(*b*) it does not comply with any of the provisions of rule 213; or

(*c*) it is not submitted with the period specified in sub-section (2) of section 9 and no cause is shown for the delay; or

(*d*) it is a second appeal where original appeal has already been decided by the competent authority:

Provided that an appeal withheld on the ground that it does not comply with the provisions of rule 213 shall be returned to the appellant and, if re-submitted within thirty days of such communication, after compliance with the said provisions, shall not be withheld.

(2) Where an appeal is withheld, the appellant shall be informed of the fact within thirty days together with brief reasons therefore. The appellant may, thereafter submit the appeal to the appellate authority concerned within thirty days of the date of communication of the order withholding the appeal.

(3) A quarterly statement of all appeals, withheld with brief reasons in respect of each appeal shall be furnished by the withholding authority to its superior authority.

216. Transmission of appeals. (1) The authority which made the order appealed against shall, without any avoidable delay, transmit to the appellate authority every appeal which is not withheld under rule 215 together with the following particulars and records;

(*a*) brief history of the case;

(*b*) para wise comments on the appeal;

(*c*) disciplinary case file in original, with all its connected papers;

(*d*) service book;

(*e*) confidential rolls folder, if maintained.

(2) The authority to which the appeal lies may direct transmission to it of any appeal withheld under rule 215 and thereupon such appeal shall be transmitted to that authority together with the comments of the authority withholding the appeal and the relevant records.

217. Consideration of appeals. (1) While considering the appeal, the appellate authority may, on request, grant personal hearing to the aggrieved enrolled member of the Force in case it considers it in the interest of administration and justice.

(2) In the case of an appeal against an order of suspension, the appellate authority shall consider whether, in the light of the provisions of rules 134 and 135 and having regard to the circumstances of the case, the order of suspension is justified or not and confirm or revoke the order accordingly.

(3) In the case of an appeal against an order imposing any of the punishments specified in rule 148 or 149 or enhancing any penalty imposed under the said rules the appellate authority shall consider:—

(*a*) whether the procedure prescribed in these rules has been complied with, and if not, whether such non-compliance has resulted in violation of any constitutional provisions or in miscarriage of justice;

(*b*) whether the findings are warranted and based on evidence on record; and

(*c*) whether the punishment or the enhanced punishment imposed is adequate or inadequate or severe and pass speaking orders for—

(*i*) setting aside, confirming, reducing or enhancing the punishment, or

(*ii*) remitting the case to the authority which imposed or enhanced the punishment or to any other authority with such directions as it may deem fit in the circumstances of the case:

Provided that—

(*i*) no order imposing an enhanced punishment shall be passed unless the appellant is given an opportunity of making any representation which he may wish to make against such enhanced punishment; and

(*ii*) if the enhanced punishment, which the appellate authority proposes to impose, is one of the punishments specified in clauses (*a*) to (*d*) of rule 148(2) and an inquiry under rule 153 has not already been held in the case, the appellate authority shall, subject to the provisions of rule 153 itself hold such inquiry or direct that such inquiry be held and thereafter on a consideration of the proceedings of such inquiry pass such orders as it may deem fit.

218. Implementation of orders in appeal. The authority which made the order appealed against shall give effect to the orders passed by the appellate authority.

219. Revision. (1) An enrolled member of the Force whose appeal has been rejected by a competent authority may prefer an application for revision to the next superior authority. The powers of revision may be exercised only when,—

(*a*) in consequence of some material irregularity, there has been injustice or miscarriage of justice; or

(*b*) fresh evidence is disclosed which could not be produced or was not available at the time of passing of the impugned order.

(2) The procedure prescribed for consideration of appeals under rule 217 shall, so far as may be, apply to application for revision.

(3) The superior authority while passing orders on the application for revision may at its discretion enhance punishments:

Provided that before enhancing the punishment, the aggrieved member shall be given an opportunity to show cause why his punishment should not be enhanced:

Provided further that subject to the provisions of sub-rule (2) of rule 212, an order enhancing the punishment shall be treated as an original order for the purpose of appeal, except when such an order has been passed by the Central Government in which case no further appeal shall lie. Where such order has been passed by the Chief Security Commissioner, appeal shall lie to the Director General and in the case of such order by the Director-General, the appeal shall lie to the Central Government.

(4) Any authority superior to the authority making the original order may, on its own motion, or otherwise, call for the records of any inquiry and revise any order made under these rules and may—

(*a*) confirm, modify or set aside the order; or

(*b*) confirm, enhance, reduce or set aside the punishment imposed by the order, or impose any punishment where no punishment has been imposed; or

(*c*) remit the case to the authority which made the order or to any other authority directing such authority to make such further inquiry as it may consider proper in the circumstances of the case; or

(*d*) pass such other orders as it may deem fit:

Provided that no action under this sub-rule shall be initiated after the expiry of one year from the date of the order aforesaid:

Provided further that no proceeding for revision shall be commenced until after—

(*i*) the expiry of the period for making an appeal specified in sub-section (2) of section 9; or

(*ii*) the disposal of the appeal, where any such appeal has been preferred;

Provided further that in a case in which it is proposed to enhance punishment further, the aggrieved member shall be given an opportunity to show cause either orally or in writing as to why his punishment should not be enhanced.

220. Time-limit for disposal of appeal or revision. (1) Every appeal or application for revision submitted by an enrolled member of the Force shall, as far as possible be disposed off within a period of three months from the date of its receipt by the authority competent to decide it.

(2) When more than one enrolled member in the same case are awarded punishment against which an appeal lies, all appeals should be forwarded together. If any one of such members does not wish to appeal, the fact shall be noted.

CHAPTER XIV

INVESTIGATION AND PROSECUTION

221. General. (1) Every Post Commander shall enter or cause to be entered, reports of all special occurrence on railways and all crimes against railway property in such records and registers and in such manner as are specified in these rules, or as may be specified by the Directives.

(2) The Post Commander shall—

(*a*) convey a gist of each such report in writing to higher authorities in such form as may be specified by Directives;

(*b*) in case of crime against railway property make or cause to be made without any delay all possible efforts to detect the case, recover stolen railway property, arrest the offenders and put them up for trial before a court; and

(*c*) enter the records as specified in these rules or Directives the day-to-day progress made in the inquiry into the matter and shall submit without avoidable delay continuation report at the close of the day to such superior officers as may be specified by Directives.

(3) Where the Post Commander is empowered to take action for any crime against railway property, he shall lodge a report at the Police Station having jurisdiction.

(4) *Expunction of crime.* After registration of a case of an offence against railway property, if as a result of inquiry, it is found that no such offence actually took place, the Post Commander after obtaining orders from the Divisional Security Commissioner, shall expunge the case from his records and inform the Police Station where such case may have been registered. In Special Report cases, sanction of the Chief Security Commissioner shall be required for expunging the cases.

222. Registration of crime. (1) All cases of crime affecting railway property shall be entered at the Post where the crime is first detected either in the "Localised Crime Register" or in the "Unlocalised Crime Register" as the case may be

"Localised" crimes are those crimes where the actual place of theft or pilferages of mis-appropriation, etc., of railway property namely, booked consignment and railway material, is known or is *prima facie* apparent from the inspection of the scene to have taken place within the jurisdiction of the Post concerned while the "unlocalised" crimes are those crimes where the actual place of crime cannot be immediately known or cannot be thus ascertained.

(2) In both the registers, the crime shall be entered in chronological order and numbered seriatim.

(3) In case the "unlocalised" crime after inquiry appears to have taken place within the jurisdiction of the Post, the same shall be transferred to the "Localised Crime Register" of the Post on the day on which this localisation takes place and given the next serial number. The same shall be expunged from the "Unlocalised Crimes Register."

(4) At the end of each month, a summary shall be prepared in the "Unlocalised Crime Register" indicating the number of cases transferred to—

(*a*) Localised Crime Register;

(*b*) Other Posts of the same division;

(*c*) Other divisions;

(*d*) Other zonal railways; and

(*e*) Pending inquiry for localisation.

(5) For the "Localised Crime Register", two summaries shall be prepared—one shall be causewise and the other commodity-wise. The causewise summary shall have its sub-headings as—

(*a*) Running Train Thefts;

(*b*) Yard Thefts;

(*c*) Goods Shed, Parcel godowns, and Platform Thefts;

(*d*) Pilferages;

(*e*) Thefts of fittings from rolling stock;

(*f*) Thefts of Railway Material including coal (except theft of fittings from rolling stock);

(*g*) Miscellaneous.

Each summary may have further sub-classifications as may be prescribed through the Directives.

(6) The list of the commodities for which summary may be prepared shall be specified by the concerned Chief Security Commissioner keeping in view the commodities generally affected in that zonal railway.

223. Seizures and recoveries of railway property. (1) All seizures or recoveries of railway property shall be entered in *Malkhana* Register and an entry to this effect made in the concerned Crime Register after its classification as—

(*a*) pertaining to cases in which theft or shortage memo has been issued or received; and

(*b*) where no such memo has been issued or received.

In respect of the first category, whenever any property is recovered or criminals are taken into custody, relevant entries shall be made in the "Localised Crime

Register" against the particular crime already registered. Such a seizure shall not be reflected separately in the RP (UP) Act Register though such seizures shall invariably be taken into account for compilation of statistics in respect of action under the Railway (Unlawful Possession) Act, 1966.

(2) In all other cases, where the seized property cannot be linked to the railway property for which theft or shortage memo has been issued or received shall be entered in the Railway Property (Unlawful Possession) Act Register maintained for this purpose and dealt with further.

(3) In cases where the property recovered is partly connected to theft or shortages and partly is seized as having been unlawfully obtained, then such a haul shall be split into two for purposes of registration. But if the criminal happens to be one and the same person, then his name shall be entered in the register in which bulk of the property recovered or seized is reflected and a cross-reference made in the Railway Property (Unlawful Possession) Act Register.

(4) Any railway property recovered by the police shall also be reflected in the records of the Post along with the particulars of the criminal(s) for purposes of accounting.

224. Procedure for dealing with shortages. (1) *Shortages from resealed wagons.* (*a*) All such shortages which are discovered either at unloading or repacking or transshipment or at destination station from resealed wagons shall be entered in the "Unlocalised Crime Register" of the Post unless the same appears to have taken place within the jurisdiction of the Post when it should be entered in the "Localised Crime Register."

(*b*) After preliminary inquiry, the case may be transferred as per procedure given in rule 226 to the Post in whose jurisdiction the crime is suspected to have taken place or the last resealing station in case the wagon was resealed at more than one station en route.

(2) *Shortage from seal intact wagons.* (*a*) *Full package shortages.* All cases of full package shortages shall be entered in a separate register and report sent to the loading station. Subsequently, if the consignment is received, a remark to that effect shall be made in the register and the case expunged. If the consignment is not received within thirty days, the Post concerned to whom the case has been transferred shall register the case in separate Register and make enquiries accordingly. This procedure shall apply *mutatis mutandis* to wagons which are loaded at transshipment points.

(*b*) *Partial shortages.* All cases of partial shortages from seal intact wagons, in which criminal interference is suspected, shall be registered at the unloading point in "Unlocalised Crime Register" and transferred to the Post concerned in which the loading stations fall, who shall not it in the "Localised Crime Register" for further action.

(3) *Shortages from open wagons or body panel cut or door crevices.* Cases of shortages from open wagons or body panel cut or door crevices, etc., shall be registered in the "Unlocalised Crime Register" of the Post at the point of unloading or transshipment or re-packing or destination where these are reported in the first instance if on inquiry, it is proved that the occurrence took place in the jurisdiction of another Post, through which the train or wagon passed, the case shall be transferred to that Post for registration in the "Localised Crime Register."

(4) *Shortages reported from the brakevans*—

(*a*) Sealed vans. All cases of shortages from the Seal Intact Vans shall be dealt with as per procedure laid down for seal intact wagons.

(*b*) Shortages from the charges of Assistant Guard in-charge of the brakevan: All such shortages shall be registered and proceeded as in the case of shortages from resealed wagons.

225. Nature of action to be taken where the wagons are resealed during transit. (1) In all cases of resealing of wagons, the Post Commander shall conduct or institute immediate enquiries to ascertain whether criminal interference be taken place with the wagon or not.

(2) If so and in case the criminal interference appears to have taken place within his jurisdiction, he shall immediately take measures or cause the means to be taken to recover the stolen property.

(3) In case, the criminal interference appears to have taken place outside his jurisdiction, he shall send the communication to his concerned counterpart by the quickest possible means who shall take action as above. In either case, an intimation shall also be sent to the destination station. The above procedure shall also apply to cases where the wagon already possesses one or more re-seals.

226. Transfer of cases. (1) Whenever a case is registered in an "Unlocalised Crime Register", the Post Commander concerned shall make or shall cause to be made inquiries upto the place where the criminal interference *prima facie* appears to have taken place and transfer the case to the Post having jurisdiction:

Provided that depending on the nature and value of the property lost, the Director General may extend or limit the extent of the place to which such inquiries be made before transferring the case.

(2) *From one Post to another Post in the same division.* If on inquiry, the Post Commander of a Post where the case has been registered, comes to the conclusion that criminal interference took place in another Post of the same division, the Post Commander shall immediately inform the officer-in-charge of that Post and transfer the case to him under intimation to his Divisional Security Commissioner. The Post Commander to whom the case, has been thus transferred shall register it in the "Localised Crime Register" and intimate the crime number to the Post concerned which has transferred the case for record.

(3) *Cases to be transferred to other division*—

(*a*) In the case pertains to the adjoining division of the same zonal railway, the Post Commander shall intimate the facts of the case and send all papers to the Post concerned of the division under intimation to his Divisional Security Commander. If the Post is not of adjoining division, then the papers shall be routed through his Divisional Security Commissioner but an intimation shall also be given by quickest possible means by the Post Commander to his counterpart for taking immediate action, if any. The Post Commander to whom the case has been referred shall register the case in the "Localised Crime Register."

(*b*) At the end of the month, the Divisional Security Commissioner shall send details of such cases to his Chief Security Commissioner for information and follow up action.

(4) Cases to be transferred to other zonal railways:

(*a*) If the case pertains to another zonal railway, the papers shall be sent by the Post Commander to his Divisional Security Commissioner who in turn shall pass them to his Chief Security Commissioner. However, an intimation shall also be sent by the quickest possible means by the Post Commander to the concerned Post Commander of that railway for taking action, if any.

(*b*) At the end of the month, each Chief Security Commissioner shall send a consolidated statement of such transferred cases to the Chief Secretary Commissioner (Railway Security) in the office of the Director-General for information and follow up action.

227. Reconciliation of transferred cases. (1) A Post Commander, to whom the case has been transferred, shall at one register the case.

(2) In case after inquiry, a Post Commander finds that the claim did not occur in his jurisdiction, he shall report full facts to his Divisional Security Commissioner whose decision pertaining to such disputed cases of his division shall be final. The decision of the Chief Security Commissioner in any inter-divisional disputed case of his zonal railway and of the Director-General in an inter-zonal disputed case shall be final.

(3) During January, April, July and October of each year, each Divisional Security Commissioner, Zonal Chief Security Commissioner and the Chief Security Commissioner (Railway Security) shall convene a meeting of the respective officers dealing with crime statistics to reconcile the figures of transferred cases, involving loss of railway property exceeding a value to be specified by the Director-General.

228. Investigation or inquiry into important cases of crime involving railway property. Inquiry or investigation into important cases of crime involving railway property or those having inter-post, inter-divisional or inter-zonal ramifications may be entrusted to the personnel of the Central Crime Bureau, Crime Wings of the Security Commissariat or the division respectively by the Director-General, Chief Security Commissioner or the Divisional Security Commissioner, as the case may be.

229. Special Reports. In cases of thefts registered at the Post involving loss of booked consignments or railway material exceeding the value to be fixed by the Director-General from time to time, the Divisional Security Commissioner shall submit special report addressed to the Director-General with copy to the Chief Security Commissioner and to concerned officers as may be specified through the Directives.

230. Special Occurrences. Wherever an occurrence takes place on railways under any of the following categories, the Divisional Security Commissioner concerned shall submit a special occurrence report addressed to the Director-General with copy to the Chief Security Commissioner and to other officers as may be specified through the Directives—

(*a*) dacoity;

(*b*) robbery;

(*c*) murder;

(*d*) fire incidents involving loss of railway property of a value to be fixed by the Director-General or explosion involving loss of life or damage to railway property;

(*e*) tampering with track, sabotage and serious accidents;

(*f*) serious cases of hooliganism and rowdyism within railway premises and prolonged holding up of trains due to agitations dharnas, etc.;

(*g*) cases in which a railway employee or a member of the Force on duty has been assaulted or arrested or has opened fire;

(*h*) theft of arms ammunitions and explosives;

(*i*) any other case which in the opinion of the Chief Security Commissioner is fit to be classified as such.

231. Prosecution of cases and disposal of seized or recovered property.

10[* * *]

(2) The Public Prosecutor or the Assistant Public Prosecutor as may be detailed for the purpose shall represent the railways on all matters connected with that case.

(3) *Custody and disposal of seized or recovered property.* The custody and disposal of seized or recovered property shall be in accordance with the provisions contained in the Police Regulations of the State in which a Post is located. The Chief Security Commissioner shall issue detailed instructions on the subject on that basis and in conformity with these rules.

232. Monthly Crime Review. (1) A monthly Crime Review giving a factual picture of the working of the Force in regard to its statutory duties and functions shall be prepared by the Divisional Security Commissioner and submitted to the concerned Chief Security Commissioner so as to reach him 7th of the month following the month to which it relates.

(2) The Chief Security Commissioner shall prepare a similar review for his zonal railway and shall submit it to the Director-General so as to reach him by the 15th of the month following the month to which it relates.

(3) The Monthly Crime Reviews shall be prepared in accordance with the instructions issued by the Director-General from time to time.

CHAPTER XV

REWARDS AND AWARDS

233. Power to grant monetary rewards. Monetary rewards may be granted out of the sanctioned grants to the enrolled members including direct recruits of the force, non-gazetted government servants including members of State Police and the railway servants and members of the public in accordance with the provisions hereinafter contained.

234. Eligibility for monetary rewards. (1) *Monetary rewards may be granted to the enrolled members of the Force for:* (*a*) doing outstanding work requiring special courage, skill or initiative, such as—

(*i*) the arrest of a criminal; or

10 *Omitted* by G.S.R. 719(E), dated 31.10.2013 (w.e.f. 31.10.2013).

(*ii*) securing information leading to the detection of crime or matters connected therewith; or

(*iii*) making exceptionally good inquiries; or

(*iv*) an encounter with a criminal in connection with protection and security of the railway property.

(*b*) doing work requiring prompt, honest and intelligent observance of and obedience to orders so as to be of material assistance in the protection and security of railway property.

(*c*) doing extra hard work in connection with the protection and security of railway property or in connection with a big operation against hostile or lawless elements.

(*d*) smartness, marksmanship, diligence, praiseworthy attention to the railway users or for any other purpose which is calculated to promote the efficiency of the Force:

Provided that 'general good work' or efficient discharge of ordinary duties shall not be a ground for grant of monetary rewards nor monetary rewards be granted on request.

(2) Monetary rewards may be granted to the non-gazetted government servants including members of the State Police and other railway servants and the members of the public as an incentive for assisting the Force—

(*a*) in the detection of any serious case; or

(*b*) in the apprehension of an offender; or

(*c*) in resisting a criminal or an anti-social element; or

(*d*) for any other purpose, which is for better protection and security of the railway property.

(3) Monetary rewards in the form of books of articles of value to be fixed through the Directives for each prize may also be granted to enrolled members (including direct recruits) of the Force for proficiency during training for every batch of trainees who pass out of the training college or training centre, as specified below:

I. Prize—for all-round efficiency;

II. Prize—for all-round proficiency in indoor subjects;

III. Prize—for proficiency in parade, musketry and sport;

Provided that it shall be permissible to grant III prize to a trainee who has also been granted first prize and or the second prize.

235. Authorities competent to grant monetary rewards. (1) The powers of various superior officers to grant monetary rewards under rule 234 shall be as specified in Schedule II.

(2) A monetary reward under rule 234 shall be granted by an officer competent to grant the same if he is of opinion, for reasons to be recorded in writing, that the person fulfils the requirements in this behalf.

(3) The order granting such monetary reward shall indicate the reasons therefor and the provision of the sub-rule under which it is granted.

(4) The procedure for payment of rewards to the recipients shall be such as may be specified by Directive.

236. Monetary rewards offered by the General Manager. (1) A superior officer of the Force may permit enrolled number of the Force to accept monetary reward offered by the General Manager or by any other authority in case he is of the opinion that it falls within the purview of rule 234.

237. Awards of decorations and medals. (1) All members of the Force, irrespective of their ranks shall also be eligible to all such awards, decorations and medals to which members of other armed force of the Union and personnel of the State Police are entitled.

(2) The conditions of eligibility and the order of precedence of wearing of such medals and decorations shall be such as may be determined by the President from time to time.

(3) The members of the Force shall also be eligible to receive other medals and decorations as railway servants.

238. Award of Director-General's commendation letter and insignia. (1) The Director-General may issue commendation letters to such members of the Force who may have done exceedingly well in the performance of their duties in operations as well as during peace time. Such commendation letters may be issued for—

(*a*) any conspicuous achievement during operation;

(*b*) doing any commendable work in natural calamities;

(*c*) any outstanding achievement in sports at international level;

(*d*) effecting any innovation which may bring significant improvement in the working of the Force;

(*c*) maintaining clean and good record of service for 25 years;

(*f*) accident free driving and good record for a continuous period of 20 years;

(*g*) processing of difficult cases;

(*h*) any other conspicuous and outstanding work which may be considered of a commendable nature; and

awarded on the eve of the anniversary day of the Force.

[11](2) [Such awarded shall wear an insignia—a silver elliptical disc—on the flap of the pocket and below the medal or ribbon plate on his uniform.]

239. Entry of rewards and rewards in service records. Rewards, or awards whether in cash or in the form of decorations, medals and commendations shall be duly entered in the Character and Service Roll of the member concerned and shall always be taken into consideration in any question affecting his placement and promotion.

CHAPTER XVI

AID TO CIVIL POWER

240. The Central Government or the Director-General or the Chief Security Commissioner or any other officer acting on their behalf may order any member of the Force to proceed to any place in India for duty in aid to civil power or for any other purpose.

11 *Substituted* by G.S.R. 366, dated 30.9.2005 (w.e.f. 15.10.2005).

241. Formation of Mobilisation Detachments. (1) Whenever such an eventuality arises, the Chief Security Commissioner may order mobilisation with his zonal railway. On such order, Mobilisation Detachments shall be formed by withdrawing preferable young and healthy members, from desired ranks of the Force from the Posts and other units. As far as may be possible, each section of 10 men shall be provided with a Naib-Subedar. Platoons shall be permanently numbered and shall correspond to the groups of Posts or Companies from which they are drawn and shall take positions according to that numbering whenever the Force is mobilised.

(2) *Senior officer to command.* Subject to rule 24, whenever a Mobilisation Detachment is raised or deputed, the senior most officer of the Force present in that detachment shall take command and shall be responsible for the proper supervision, discipline, conduct and control of the members under his command.

(3) It shall be duty of the Detachment Commander to:—

(*a*) carry out all instructions regarding training kit inspection, maintenance of arms and ammunitions and other stores etc., issued from time to time by the headquarters;

(*b*) ensure that no article of stores issued from the headquarters is loaned out or given to any other organisation without the express sanction of the headquarters; and

(*c*) ensure that all stores of the Force shall be used only for Government duties.

242. Deployment at a destination station. (1) On arrival at destination station, the Detachment Commander shall report to the accredited officer of the State Government under whose general report and directions he is required to work.

(2) The Detachment Commander shall maintain a close contact with the local authorities and carry out to the best of his ability their requests in regard to mutual co-operation and the maintenance of law and order.

(3) Under no circumstances shall the Force interfere with the internal administration of the State and shall limit its operation within the role assigned by the State authorities. Ordinarily, the Force shall not undertake any of the normal routine duties of the State Police without the approval of the Chief Security Commissioner, who in doubtful cases, may refer the matter to the Director-General for orders.

243. Dispersal of Unlawful Assembly. (1) *Deputation of Magistrate.* When the Detachment Commander is of opinion that the use of force or opposition to the Mobilisation detachment is probable or when a detachment is deputed for a protective duty during a strike or insurgency or any other uprising, he may move that a Magistrate be deputed with it.

(2) *Action in the absence of Magistrate.* Whenever the public security and peace shall be manifestly endangered by an unlawful assembly or any human obstruction the movement of railway property shall have to be removed and no Executive Magistrate can be communicated with without jeopardising the situation further, any superior officer of the Force may disperse such an unlawful assembly or remove the obstruction by force and may arrest and confine any person constituting that unlawful assembly or obstruction.

Provided that before using force, the superior officer of the Force shall command the unlawful assembly or person constituting the obstruction to disperse and give a warning that if they do not disperse, they shall be dispersed by force.

(3) *Use of Force.*—If upon being so commanded, any such assembly does not disperse or if without being so commanded the assembly conducts itself in such a manner as to show determination not to disperse, such officer shall proceed to disperse such an assembly by force:

Provided that care shall be taken to use minimum force which is necessary to disperse the assembly or to protect the life and property and secure safety of the contingent of the Force.

(4) *Opening of Fire.* Fire shall only be opened under instructions from an Executive Magistrate or when acting in his own discretion such officer deems it absolutely necessary to do so for the protection of life and property.

(5) *Responsibility of Executive Magistrate.* If the Executive Magistrate is present, the responsibility for using force against, or opening fire on, unlawful assembly shall rest with him and he alone shall direct the Detachment Commander (in writing if possible) to use force or open fire. When the Executive Magistrate has to directed the Detachment Commander, such Magistrate shall not fetter the discretion of the Detachment Commander in making his dispositions.

(6) *Responsibilities of Detachment Commander:*

(*a*) Actual order to fire shall invariably be given by—

(*i*) Detachment Commander or under his special instructions by any junior officer; or

(*iii*) an officer-in-command of a party further detached from the main body;

(*b*) Order to cease fire shall be given by the Detachment Commander or such other officer-in-command as soon as the mob shows disposition to retire or disperse. The Executive Magistrate, if present, shall also have the powers to order fire to cease.

(7) *Action after the dispersal of the mob.* When an unlawful assembly has been dispersed, first aid shall be rendered to the wounded who shall then be sent to the nearest hospital for treatment. Thereafter, the Executive Magistrate or officer-in-command shall draw up an accurate report of all that transpired, noting the rounds served out and expended and all the details. The officer-in-command shall then transmit copies of the report by the quickest means to the officer-in-charge of the nearest Police Station as well as to such other officers as may be specified by the Directives.

244. Limitations to inquiry. No inquiry by a State Government shall be ordered, without consultation with the Central Government, into any action taken by an officer of the Force in pursuance of duty in aid to civil power.

245. Expenditure incurred in providing aid to Civil Power. All expenditure incurred in providing aid to civil power shall be borne and recoverable from the State Government concerned unless such expenditure is waived fully or partly by the Central Government. Such claims shall be preferred by the Chief Security Commissioner in consultation with Financial Adviser-cum-Chief Accounts Officer concerned in whose jurisdiction Mobilisation Detachment was deployed.

246. Procedure when Force opens fire in exercise of the right of defence of person or property. (1) Whenever the Force uses fire arms in exercise of right of defence of person or property, a Court of Inquiry referred to in rule 265 shall invariably be ordered by the Chief Security Commissioner.

(2) Soon after the Force has opened fire, the senior-most member present on the occasion shall—

(*a*) immediately send an intimation to the nearest Police Station and arrange to cordon off the area so that the scene is preserved intact. He shall, however, render first aid to the injured and arrange to send them to the nearest hospital, if necessary;

(*b*) cause the empty cartridge cases to be picked up and checked with the number of rounds served out;

(*c*) draw up a concise but accurate report of the occurrence giving out minute details of all the relevant facts;

(*d*) send copies of such concise report by quickest means to the District Magistrate, the Superintendent of Police of the District concerned besides sending them to his Chief Security Commissioner and the Divisional Security Commissioner.

CHAPTER XVII

PLAINTS AND PROTECTION

247. Plaints. Every member of the Force against whom any criminal prosecution or a civil suit is instituted shall at once inform the Chief Security Commissioner, or as the case may be, his controlling officer.

248. Public complaints against the misconduct of the members of the Force. (1) Whenever a complaint against the misconduct of any member of the Force is received from the members of the public or where such complaint is received through a Court wherein civil or criminal proceedings against a member of the Force have been instituted otherwise, and controlling officer of such member of the Force is of the opinion that allegations are verifiable or otherwise an inquiry is called for, he may proceed to inquire himself into the complaint against a member of the Force specified in column (1) of the table below or depute any other officer as specified in the corresponding entry in column (2) of the said table:—

TABLE

Members of the Force against whom complaints received	Inquiry Officer
(1)	(2)
Constables/ [12][***]/ Head Constables	Of and above the rank of Inspector.
Sub-Inspector/Assistant Sub-Inspector	Of and above the rank of Assistant Commandant.
Inspector/Assistant Security Commissioner or above	Of and above the rank of Chief Security Commissioner or the Additional or the Deputy Chief Security Commissioner, if so authorised by him.

12 The word "Naik" *omitted* by G.S.R. 229, dated 15.7.1999 (w.e.f. 24.7.1999).

(2) *Complaint cells.* There shall be separate complaint cells at the headquarters each of the Director General, Chief Security Commissioner, the Divisional Security Commissioner and the Commanding Officer for handing, monitoring and ensuring the expeditious disposal of such complaints.

(3) *Manner of conducting inquiries.* While conducting inquiries, the Inquiry Officer shall so far as may be possible, proceed as under—

(*i*) complaint shall be heard in detail and every effort shall be made by the Inquiry Officer himself to ascertain the truth by examining such of the witnesses as he may deem necessary, without insisting on the complainant himself to secure the presence of witnesses;

(*ii*) important witnesses shall as far as possible be examined in the presence of the complainant so that he has the satisfaction of what they depose;

(*iii*) throughout the conduct of inquiry, the Inquiry Officer shall scrupulously avoid doing anything which might create a doubt in the mind of the complainant about objectivity and impartiality of the inquiry;

(*iv*) the inquiry shall, as far as practicable be conducted at an appropriate public building or place in or near the complainant's place of residence.

(4) The report of the Inquiry Officer may be treated as classified where the controlling officer for reasons to be recorded in writing so directs.

249. Prosecution by a public servant. (1) *Proceedings initiated by Government.* The Central Government shall not give any assistance to a member of the Force for his defence in any proceeding, civil or criminal, instituted against him by the State in respect of matters arising out of or connected with his official duties or his official position. However, reasonable costs of defence shall be paid to him in the event of his acquittal and where it is shown that his conduct throughout was free from blame and that the member acted or purported to have acted in good faith in discharge of his official duties. If, though acquitted of the offence charged, his conduct does not appear to be free from blame, he shall receive only such portion, if any, of the costs incurred by him, as the Chief Security Commissioner may deem fit.

(2) To enable the member of the Force to meet the expenses of his defence, the Chief Security Commissioner may sanction at his discretion, an interest free advance of an amount to the extent of three months' substantive pay of the member, after obtaining from the member, a bond in the form given in Schedule XI. The amount so advanced shall be subjected to adjustment subsequently against the amount, if any, to be reimbursed to the member under sub-rule (1).

250. Prosecution by private person. (1) A member of the Force shall always be defended in a civil suit or a criminal complaint instituted by a private person when it appears to the Chief Security Commissioner concerned that he had acted or purported to have acted in good faith in discharge of his official duties. The member thus being defended shall be deemed to be defending himself as on duty.

(2) In all other cases arising out of employment where the Chief Security Commissioner declines to defend, the member concerned may take such measures, as he considers necessary, at his own expenses, but the reasonable costs of defence shall be paid to him in the event of his acquittal and where it is shown that his conduct throughout had been free from all blame. If, though acquitted of

the offence charged, his conduct does not appear to be free from blame, reimbursement of cost shall be allowed in the manner prescribed under sub-rule (1) of rule 249.

(3) In either case, the member of the Force may be allowed a monetary advance as prescribed under sub-rule (2) of rule 249.

251. Procedure for undertaking defence. Whenever the cost of defence of the member of the Force is sanctioned to be borne by the railway administration, it shall be left to the member concerned whether to engage a Government Pleader, a Public Prosecutor or a private legal practitioner of his choice.

Provided that if a private legal practitioner is engaged, the scale of fees to be reimbursed to the member by the Railway Administration shall be limited to the amount fixed by the Chief Security Commissioner in consultation with the Law Officer of the zonal railway.

252. Refund of cost to Railways. If the member of the Force succeeds in the legal proceedings, and is awarded costs or damages or compensation by the Court, the member shall refund the amount to the extent of expenditure incurred by the railway administration.

253. Proceedings initiated by a member of the Force to vindicate his official conduct. If member of the Force is allowed to vindicate his conduct in a Court of law when specific allegations are made in the press or otherwise against him as an individual member of the Force, the Railway administration shall defray reasonable costs of his defence subject to the provision of rule 249 provided that the member concerned is fully and honourably discharged of allegation made against him.

(2) The Chief Security Commissioner may sanction advance as provided under sub-rule (2) of rule 249.

(3) A member shall not be entitled to receive any reimbursement of the cost or expenditure if he resorts to such litigation of his own and without the sanction of the Chief Security Commissioner.

254. Cost of filing appeal, etc. Where the Railway administration has undertaken the defence of a member of the Force, but the decision of the first Court is against him, the question whether an appeal should be filed at the cost of Railway administration or whether the damages awarded to the plaintiff or the fine imposed on the member should be paid by the railway administration, shall be decided by the Chief Security Commissioner either on the application of the member concerned who should move his immediate Superior Officer in the matter or on the recommendation of his Superior Officer.

PROTECTION

255. Protection being an armed force of the Union. In any suit or proceeding against any member of Railway Protection Force, being an armed force of the Union, he shall in addition to the provisions of section 20, be eligible for protection under—

(*a*) Sections 45, 132 and 197 of the Code of Criminal Procedure, 1973;

(*b*) the Judicial Officer's Protection Act, 1850 in so far as the members discharging magisterial powers and functions under section 17 are concerned.

256. Protection where a member of the Force has opened fire. Wherever a member of the Force has opened fire in pursuance of his statutory duties of providing better protection and security to railway property and for matters connected therewith or in exercise of the right of defence of person or property resulting in such or injury to the other party, the result of the magisterial or judicial inquiry instituted in this behalf shall be awaited. A member of the Force shall ordinarily be prosecuted and/or disciplinary proceedings instituted against him only when he is adversely commented upon in that inquiry or when the Court of Inquiry instituted under rule 265 finds his conduct suspicious.

CHAPTER XVIII

LIASION

257. Liasion with civil administration of the State. The Railway Protection Force shall act as a bridge between the railway administration and State's civil administration and Police (including railway police) for providing better protection and security to railway property and for matters connected therewith.

258. Liasion with Police. (1) *General.* Whenever any person arrested under section 12 is handed over, or any property recovered under section 13 is given, to the Police, or any other report relating to an offence is lodged with them, an acknowledgement shall be taken by the concerned member of the Force along with a true copy of the report recorded in the First Information Book. The Post Commander shall subsequently monitor the progress.

(2) Whenever approached by the police (including railway police) to keep unobtrusive watch at places within railway premises to detect crime against railway property or to cause the arrest of culprits or recovery of property involved in an offence, the Post Commander or Company Commander may depute the available men to assist such Police after recording a report in the Daily Diary.

259. Periodical meeting with Police. (1) Every Post Commander shall hold regular monthly meeting with the officer-in-charge of the Railway Police Station in his jurisdiction to—

(*a*) review the crime situation;

(*b*) exchange information useful and necessary for better control, prevention and detection of crime affecting railway property; and

(*c*) maintain law and order in railway trains and railway premises.

(2) The Post Commander shall also attend the monthly crime meeting of the Superintendent of Police of the district in which his Post is situated and exchange information about:

(*i*) criminals operating on the railways;

(*ii*) activities of receivers of stolen railway property;

(*iii*) absconders and wanted persons and progress achieved in their arrests during the previous month;

(*iv*) action being taken or proposed to be taken at vulnerable or black spots and the co-operation or assistance required by the Force from the District Police in this regard.

(3) The Assistant Security Commissioner shall hold co-ordination meetings with the concerned Sub-Divisional Police Officer of the Railway Police once in two months and its minutes shall be submitted to the Divisional Security Commissioner.

(4) The Divisional Security Commissioner shall hold co-ordination meetings with the Superintendent Railway Police and Superintendent of Police of the district falling in his jurisdiction once in three months for ensuring better co-operation and co-ordination between the Force, the Railway Police and the District Police. These meetings shall also be the forum for exchange of information and intelligence about crime, criminals and other matters relating to maintenance of law and order on railways and crime affecting the security and movement of railway property.

(5) The Chief Security Commissioner with a view to maintaining close liaison with the State Police authorities—

(*a*) shall hold periodical meetings and conferences with his counterparts in State Police including railway police and the civil administration for discussing all matters affecting railway security;

(*b*) avail himself of every opportunity to exchange information relating to crime on the railways with his counterparts; and

(*c*) exchange crime reviews with the State and the Railway Police.

(6) Any differences which may arise between the Force and the Railway Police shall be promptly and judiciously dealt with by superior officers of both the Force and a joint inquiry, if necessary, be held to resolve the matter.

260. Liaison with other railway departments. (1) In the performance of their statutory duties, all members of the Force shall maintain close contact and co-ordination with officers of other departments of the Railways.

(2) The Chief Security Commissioner, in consultation with the heads of other departments, shall issue orders for such joint action by officers and men of the other departments and members of the Force as may be conducive to the better protection and security of railway property.

(3) All such differences as may arise between the members of the Force and other railway servants shall be promptly and judiciously dealt with by an officer superior in rank to the member of the Force concerned, and, if deemed necessary by such superior officer, a joint inquiry may be held to resolve the matter.

(4) All complaints of recriminatory nature shall be disposed of departmentally and in no case recourse to legal action be taken without first obtaining permission from the Chief Security Commissioner or the Director-General as the case may be.

261. Miscellaneous. Detailed procedure for holding such periodical meetings and conferences at different levels, recording of minutes and their distribution for reviewing results obtained through joint efforts of the Force and other departments as well as for devising such methods as are considered necessary and proper to bring forth further improvements shall be specified through the Directives.

CHAPTER XIX

SPECIAL WELFARE MEASURES

262. Institution and regulation of welfare funds and schemes. (1) The Central Government or the Director-General may looking to the onerous and arduous nature of duties of the members of the Force, create any special fund or launch any special welfare measure or insurance scheme or any other scheme or a co-operative society and provide for finding of such measures on a continuing basis or on any other basis.

(2) *Such special measures may include.* (*a*) Providing for adequate living accommodation for the personnel and their families;

(*b*) provision of recreational facilities in the shape of indoor and outdoor games and equipping recreational rooms with radio and television;

(*c*) provision of libraries both static and mobile;

(*d*) provision of canteens and departmentally run grocery and allied stores;

(*e*) providing spare time employment for the members of the families to augment incomes;

(*f*) financial assistance to the families and dependents and to those who are disabled due to the rigours of service;

(*g*) rehabilitation of those who retire or are medically invalidated for active service;

(*h*) provision of vocational training for the handicapped;

(*i*) provision of schools with or without boarding facilities.

(*j*) sponsoring and running of correspondence courses for the personnel both in academic and technical fields;

(*k*) arranging subsidised technical and vocational training for the wards of the personnel and providing employment opportunities for them;

(*l*) encouraging group insurance and savings schemes;

(*m*) establishment of family welfare centres, creches and maternity centres;

(*n*) establishment of hospitals and dispensaries; and

(*o*) to alleviate distress arising from terminal and prolonged illness like tuberculosis, paralysis, cancer, etc.

(3) Whenever such scheme is launched or a special fund is constituted for the purposes of any of the measures specified in sub-rule (2), it shall be lawful for any member of the Force to participate in planning of such welfare measures, suggesting fresh schemes to meet their needs, make contributions or collect subscriptions from the beneficiaries for the purpose and to manage, operate and to administer such a scheme or a fund:

Provided that for ensuring adequate utilisation of any such fund for genuine welfare needs, its management shall be vested in a committee primarily comprising of beneficiaries;

Provided further that adequate arrangements shall be made for regular audit of the fund by a committee comprising of members from different ranks of the Force.

263. Co-operative housing society. (1) It shall be lawful for the members of the Force to set-up co-operative housing societies in any area or district and to secure financial assistance from public financial institutions.

(2) The Central Government or the Director-General may provide the services of expert personnel to such societies to meet their objectives.

264. Messes and canteens. (1) The Central Government may run messes and canteens for the benefit of the members of the Force where articles shall be sold at no profit basis.

(2) Wherever such messes and canteens provided with suitable buildings on hire or otherwise shall be preferred and financial and other paraphernalia provided for the purpose.

(3) The Director-General may prescribe the registers to be maintained and the manner in which the supervision is to be effected on such messes and canteens.

CHAPTER XX

MISCELLANEOUS

265. Court of Inquiry. (1) *When to be held.* A Court of Inquiry may be held to investigate into any offence alleged to have been committed by any enrolled member of the Force or into any disciplinary matter or any other matter of importance relating to the Force.

(2) A Court of Inquiry shall invariably be held in cases of—

(*a*) unnatural deaths of person subject to the Act or of other persons within the Force Lines. At the same time, an immediate report shall be sent through the messenger to the officer-in-charge of the police station within whose jurisdiction such unnatural death has taken place;

(*b*) each and every case of opening of free by members of the Force, whether operational or accidental;

(*c*) injuries sustained by persons subject to the Act which are likely to cause full or partial disability. The Court of Inquiry shall in such cases determine whether such injuries were attributable to exigencies of service or not;

(*d*) financial irregularities, losses, thefts and misappropriation of property, whether of public or Force, including arms and ammunitions;

(*e*) case in which any pet animal of the Force is lost, strayed or dies from or is destroyed on account of an incurable injury, in circumstances not arising out of operational conditions;

(*f*) loss of secret documents and any other material of secret or above security classification. Such a Court of Inquiry shall be ordered by an officer or authority superior to the person having lost the document or material on his charge;

(*g*) damage to person or property of an individual, in respect of which there is likely to be a claim against the Railways or the Force; and

(*h*) accident of motor vehicles of the Force.

(3) *Composition.* A Court of Inquiry shall consist of an officer as presiding Officer, not below the rank of Inspector and at least two other members of appropriate ranks. Persons not subject to the Act may be appointed as members

when the Court is to investigate matters of a specialised nature and member of the Force with specialist qualifications are not available to be the members.

(4) *Assembly.* A Court of Inquiry may be assembled by order of an Assistant Security Commissioner or any officer or authority superior to him.

(5) *Assembly order.* The order assembling the Court of Inquiry shall state the composition of the Court, the time and place for its assembly and clearly state the matters which the Court will investigate. It will also provide for the administrative requirements of such Court.

(6) *Procedure of Court of Inquiry.* (*a*) The proceedings of Court of Inquiry shall generally not be open to public. Only such persons may attend the proceedings as are permitted by the Court to do so.

(*b*) The evidence of all witnesses shall be taken on oath or affirmation.

(*c*) Evidence given by witnesses shall be recorded in narrative form unless the Court considers that any questions and answers may be recorded as such.

(*d*) The Court may be take into consideration any documents even though they are not formally proved.

(*e*) The Court may ask witnesses any questions and in any form, which it considers necessary to elicit the truth and may take into consideration any available evidence.

(*f*) No counsel or legal practitioner shall be permitted to appear before a Court of Inquiry in that capacity.

(*g*) The provisions of section 69 of the Code of Criminal Procedure, 1973, shall apply for procuring the attendance of witnesses before the Court of Inquiry.

(*h*) Before giving an opinion against any person subject to the Act, the Court may afford that person a reasonable opportunity of being heard.

(*i*) The records of Court of Inquiry shall be admissible in evidence in any subsequent proceedings:

Provided that the answers given by a witness to any question asked before the Court shall not be admissible against such a witness on any charge at any subsequent occasion except a charge of giving false evidence before such Court.

(7) *Time limit for completion of Inquiry.* Every inquiry shall be completed as expeditiously as possible and in any case within a period of three weeks from the date of assembly of the Court of Inquiry, unless for reasons to be recorded by the Presiding Officer, it is not possible to do so due to circumstances beyond his control.

(8) *Action on the proceedings of a Court of Inquiry.* The proceedings of a Court of Inquiry shall be submitted by the Presiding Officer to the officer or be submitted by the Presiding Officer to the officer or authority who ordered the Court of Inquiry. Such officer or authority on receiving the proceedings may either pass final orders on the proceedings himself, if he is empowered to do so, or refer them to a superior authority.

(9) *Copies of Court of Inquiry proceedings.* A person subject to the Act against whom the Court of Inquiry has given an opinion or who is being tried by a

Security Court on a charge relating to matters investigated by the Court of Inquiry, shall be entitled to copies of the proceedings of the Court of Inquiry unless the Chief Security Commissioner or the Director-General orders otherwise in public interest.

266. Inspection of offices and units of the Force. (1) The inspection of the Post and other subordinate units by various officers of the hierarchy shall be so rationalised as to reduce to the minimum the load of scriptory work in these formations.

(2) Detailed periodical inspections shall be made by one officer only who shall be a rank superior to the incumbent holding charge of that unit. Officers in higher levels shall primarily confine their attention to such aspects with a view to—

(*a*) having an overall view of the functioning of the inspected unit and to check that the orders and instructions issued from time to time are being duly observed;

(*b*) studying whether the existing basic security arrangements against thefts or pilferages of railway property, leakage of railway revenue, fire hazards etc., are adequate and acquainting themselves with the crime positions of their charge;

(*c*) ensuring that various records kept at the unit are being correctly and neatly maintained and that the full advantage is being taken by the staff of the collated information in crime prevention and control;

(*d*) seeing that clothing, equipments, furniture service and residential buildings are in good order and properly maintained;

(*e*) developing personal contact with members and to acquaint themselves with difficulties being faced by them in the field, assess the state of morale of the unit personnel and work out the nature of administrative assistance required from the headquarters in improving the overall effectivity of the units; and

(*f*) having an idea of the quality of supervision being effected by the supervisory officers and to suggest improvements where considered necessary.

267. Scriptory at the field units. (1) A Standing Committee comprising among others of Post Commanders or Company Commanders shall be formed in every Security Commissariat for examining once in three years whether—

(*a*) some of the returns can be altered or lumped together or even discontinued; and

(*b*) for standardising and updating the *pro forma* for collection of data,

with a view to reducing the load of repetitive and purposeless scriptory work in the field formations.

(2) A small statistical cell under the direct charge of Additional or the Deputy Chief Security Commissioner shall be constituted at the Security Commissariat to compile information from the material already available there, for answering questions raised in Parliament or State Legislatures. Reference to the subordinate units in the field may only be made when the required information is not available at the Security Commissariat.

268. Records and Registers. The records and registers to be maintained in the office of superior officers, Posts, Companies out-posts, detachments and other units and the performance therefore shall be such as specified by the Director-General from time to time.

269. Guards of Honour. (1) Guard of Honour shall be detailed to—

(*i*) attend the arrival and departure by railway train of the President, Vice-President, Prime Minister and the Governor of a State; and

(*ii*) for the Independence and Republic Day celebrations or other ceremonial functions of national importance.

(2) Guard of Honour shall not be detailed for the reception of any other dignitary without the express orders of the Director-General:

Provided that no Guard of Honour shall be supplied after 'Retreat' or before 'Reveille':

Provided further that all other instructions or orders issued by Central Government in the Ministry of Home Affairs to other armed forces of the Union regarding detailing of ceremonial and security guards shall also apply *mutatis mutandis* to ceremonial guards to be provided by the Force.

(3) *Compliments where not entitled.* An officer below the rank of the Chief Security Commissioner is not entitled to the compliment of the bugle sounding the salute or the drum beating a ruffle when a guard "present arms" to him. Similarly, an officer not in uniforms is not entitled to the compliments of guard turning out except on occasions specified in sub-rule (1).

270. Static guards. (1) Static guards consisting of 1 head constable and 3 constables or as may be necessary, shall be detailed for guarding the unit magazine, stores, Lines etc., as per-requirements. The area of duty for a particular guard, the duties of the Guard Commander and sentry shall be clearly exhibited in the Guard Room.

(2) Special guards shall be provided for the officers of the rank of and above the Chief Security Commissioner or Deputy Inspector General of Railway Protection Special Force and at places where the officers are camping (residence).

(3) The colour of the Force shall be hoisted at the residence of the Chief Security Commissioner and other higher officers of the Force. In case of others, their standard shall be hoisted. In operational areas, the Security Commissioner do away with hoisting of the colour if conditions so require after obtaining permission of the Chief Security Commissioner.

(4) When the officer for whom the guard is provided is present and if any officer junior to him passes by the side of the VIP guard, the guard shall not turn out but the sentry shall come to attention.

271. Security aids. (1) An enrolled member of the Force attached with any officer for purposes of sub-rule (3) shall be called security aide.

(2) *Entitlement.* Entitlement of assistance of security aide shall be determined by the Director-General not by the rank of the officer but by the actual need for such assistance with reference to the nature of duties and responsibilities of the officer;

(3) Entitlement of assistance to each officer shall be worked out by keeping the following duties of the security aide in view—

(*i*) to attend to petitioners, complainants and other visitors who come to see the officer;

(*ii*) to attend to telephone calls, particularly during the officer's absence, and furnish helpful replies to enable the caller to speak some other appropriate functionary for action;

(*iii*) to pass on messages on telephone to subordinate officers;

(*iv*) to accompany the officer on his field work and be present with him to afford security and assistance in dealing with any situation;

(*v*) to carry message and files from the officer to the local staff stationed nearby.

(*vi*) to assist the officer in keeping his uniform and arms in a neat and smart condition;

(*vii*) to maintain the officer's reception room and office premises in a neat and tidy condition for receiving visitors and transacting official business:

Provided the duties mentioned at (*i*) to (*iv*) may also be performed by other ranks while the rest may be entrusted to ancillary staff.

272. Members of the Force on sick list. [13][(1) No member of the Force shall be taken on sick list by any Railway Medical Officer unless such member comes with a written reference known as 'Sick Memo' from his controlling officer and also gives declaration in triplicate as per the *pro forma* at Annexure 'A'.

The Controlling Officer shall issue "Sick Memo" to the member of the Force on demand, whether such member is on duty or on leave at the Head Quarters. While issuing such memo, the Controlling Officer shall mention on it, if the member is required/detailed for Special duty, under transfer orders, facing DAR action and avoiding to attend departmental enquiry or is habitual of reporting sick, etc. In case such member is taken on sick list by Railway Medical Officer, the member shall intimate within 48 hours his Controlling Officer about his being taken on sick list and submit the Railway Medical Certificate to him.

The Railway Medical Officer taking the staff on sick list shall send one copy of the declaration as indicated in this rule to the Controlling Officer of the member, the second copy of the declaration will be kept by him for his record and the third copy will be handed over to the member of the Force alongwith Railway Medical Certificate and the member of the Force will submit the same to his Controlling Officer alongwith Railway Medical Certificate:

Provided that the member who due to emergency is not able to take "Sick Memo" from his Controlling Officer, may directly report to Railway Medical Officer for treatment. The member will have to inform the Railway Medical Officer immediately, if he wants to report sick and give the declaration as per Annexure 'A' in triplicate. In case the member is taken on sick list as outdoor patient, it shall be obligatory for the member to get a 'Sick Memo' from his Controlling Officer and submit the same to the Railway Medical Officer. If the member is taken on sick list as indoor patient, the Railway Medical Officer shall intimate the Controlling officer by sending him the copy of the declaration and the Controlling officer will issue 'Sick Memo' on receipt of the declaration from the Railway Medical Officer. The sick certificate in any case will be issued on

13 *Substituted* by G.S.R. 45(E), dated 29th January, 1997 (w.e.f. 30.1.1997).

receipt of sick memo from the Controlling officer or other equivalent or higher sources:

Provided further that a member who is on leave or on duty, away from his Head quarters, may take 'Sick Memo' from the nearest incharge Railway Protection Force post/out post or from Station Master/Assistant Station Master, if no Railway Protection Force post/out post is located nearby. The incharge Railway Protection Force post/out post or Station Master/Assistant Station Master issuing a 'Sick Memo' as mentioned above shall intimate the Controlling Officer of the member immediately. In case the member is taken on sick list as out-door patient, he will immediately intimate his Controlling Officer about this fact. The attending Railway Medical Officer shall examine the member with a view to find out, if the member is fit to travel up to his Head quarters, if so, he will issue fit to travel certificate.

Provided further that a member found to be habitually reporting sick frequently on occasion on his deployment to special duty or on refusal on leave may be sent for special medical examination by competent authority to ascertain as to the genuineness of the illness.]

[14][* * *]

[15][(3) Wherever there are more than one doctor in the hospital/Health Unit Outdoor Patient Department in the department of Railway Protection Force, the issuance of Railway Medical Certificate shall be dealt with only by one authorised doctor to be nominated by the incharge of Hospital/Divisional Incharge."]

[16][* * *]

[17][(5) Ordinarily, no Railway Medical Certificate shall be issued for more than 7 days at a time unless a member is admitted in the hospital as an indoor patient. Similarly, after discharge from the hospital a member shall not be kept on sick list for more than 14 days at a time:

Provided that in certain circumstances if the Medical Officer concerned is of the opinion that the patient will have to be kept as an outdoor patient Department case for domiciliary treatment for a longer period, the same may be done but a detailed report will have to be sent about such patient to the Chief Medical Superintendent/Medical Superintendent incharge of the division endorsing a copy of the same to the Controlling Officer of the patient.]

(6) A member who has been issued Railway Medical Certificate shall be examined regularly during the period of sickness by the Railway Medical Officers.

(7) Whenever any Sick Certificate or Extension Certificate is issued by the Railway Medical Officer, the duration of sick leave recommended shall invariably be mentioned therein along with date.

(8) Whenever any Sick Certificate, Extension Certificate or Fit Certificate is issued by the Railway Medical Officer, he shall invariably obtain the signature of the member concerned on the Certificate before handing it to him.

14 *Omitted* by G.S.R. 45(E), dated 29th January, 1997 (w.e.f. 30.1.1997).
15 *Substituted* by G.S.R. 45(E), dated 29th January, 1997 (w.e.f. 30.1.1997).
16 Subs-rule (4) *omited* by G.S.R. 45(E), dated 29.1.1997 (w.e.f. 30.1.1997).
17 *Substituted* by G.S.R. 45(E), dated 29.1.1997 (w.e.f. 30.1.1997).

(9) A member of the Force on sick list shall not leave his place of treatment without the written approval of the leave sanctioning authority except for such exercise as may be prescribed and notified in the order by the Railway Medical Officer.

[18][(10) To matters not covered under foregoing rules, extant provisions of Railway Rules/Indian Railway Medical Manual shall apply.]

ANNEXURE-A

Declaration to be given by the member of the force at the time of reporting sick

I am not feeling well, I may please be issued a Medical Certificate w.e.f. .... I shall bring the sick memo/I have brought sick memo from my authorised Departmental Officer/Superior, *i.e.* .... (Mention designation, Headquarter/State of Departmental Officer/Superior where intimation of sickness is required to be sent).

I declare that: (strike out whichever is not applicable).

(*i*) I am/I am not under order of transfer, temporary/Emergency duty or under DAR action.

(*ii*) That I am on sanctioned casual leave/Leave on average pay w.e.f. .... to ....

(*iii*) I was not a sick list/declared fit by any railway/Private Doctor immediately prior to this date.

or

I was on sick list with .... and have been given fit/transfer certificate on ....

Signature/LTI of the Employee

Name ....

Rank and Number ....

Place of Posting: ....

Divn. Railway: ....

273. Benefits on account of risk of 'office'. If in the discharge of his duty or as a consequent of anything done by him in the discharge of his duty or on account of the special risks of his office, a member of the Force is permanently or temporarily disabled or his condition is aggravated, he shall be governed by the Central Civil Service (Extraordinary Pension) Rules as amended from time to time.

274. Discharge certificate. A person ceasing to be a member of the Force shall surrender to his immediate superior, his certificate of appointment and thereafter he shall be issued a Discharge Certificate as specified in Schedule XII.

275. Re-enlistment. A member of the Force, who has ceased to be a member of the Force as a result of resignation or removal from service and whose previous service had been assessed as good and who is medically fit may be re-enlisted, with the sanction of the Chief Security Commissioner within a period of two years

18 *Added* by G.S.R. 45(E), dated 29.1.1997 (w.e.f. 30.1.1997).

of his ceasing to be a member of the Force. Such re-enlistment shall be treated as fresh appointment.

276. Ministerial Staff. (1) In view of the strictly confidential and technical nature of work which the ministerial staff shall be required to handle, the Force may have a ministerial cadre of its own, though in the initial stages persons may be taken on deputation also. The ranks of the cadre shall be.

(*a*) Superintendents.

(*b*) Assistants.

(*c*) Stenographers.

(*d*) Senior Clerks.

(*e*) Clerk-cum-Typists.

(2) The method of recruitment and other conditions of service relating to the said posts shall be in accordance with the rules and procedure laid down in the Railway Establishment Code.

(3) The ministerial cadre presently posted with the Security Department shall be subject to the control of the Chief Security Commissioner who shall be their head of the department.

277. Powers of Central Government to absorb in the Force any officer on deputation. Nothing contained in these rules shall be deemed to affect the right of the Central Government to absorb in the Force; for reasons to be recorded in writing and in exceptional circumstances, any officer on deputation to the Force, where in the opinion of the Central Government such officer has given a creditable account of himself in the post or posts held by him for a minimum period of three years, if such deputationist officer has a minimum of three years service left for his attaining the normal age of retirement prescribed for the post held by him.

278. Railway Protection Force Band. (1) A band shall be maintained on each zonal railway and in each Railway Protection Special Force battalion shall consist of such number of members of the Force as may be determined by the Chief Security Commissioner.

(2) The bandsmen shall be drawn from the regular cadre of the Force and shall play the band in addition to their normal duties till separate provision is made for the purpose.

(3) The aims and objects for raising the band shall be:

(*i*) to facilitate the training of the members of the Force;

(*ii*) to function as the official band in all ceremonial occasions like Independence Day, Republic Day and other such important functions; and

(*iii*) to provide entertainment in the field of staff welfare.

(4) The band may be permitted to play at private functions on payment of charge as may be determined by the Chief Security Commissioner.

279. Relation with Press. Subject to the restrictions specified in section 15-A, the Divisional Security Commissioners and officers of higher rank are permitted to give to the press statistical and other relevant details concerning crime against railway property and obstruction to its movement as well as details concerning all other important and sensational cases under investigation or inquiry with the

Force and shall endorse a copy of such communique to the Public Relations Department of the Railway:

Provided that nothing contained herein shall authorise any officer to divulge the details of—

(*i*) any operation to be undertaken by the Force;

(*ii*) the intelligence on the basis of which such operation is being or was planned;

(*iii*) privacy of any individual; and

(*iv*) the judicial requirements of any case.

CHAPTER XXI

REPEAL AND SAVINGS

280. Repeal and Savings. (1) The Railway Protection Force Rules, 1959 and the Railway Protection Force Regulation, 1966 are hereby repealed.

(2) Nothwithstanding such repeal anything done or any action taken under the provisions of the said rules or regulations shall in so far as such thing or action is not inconsistent with the provisions of these rules, be deemed to have been done or taken under the provisions of these rules as if these rules were in force when such thing was done or such action was taken and shall continue to be in force accordingly until superseded by anything done or any action taken under these rules.

SCHEDULE I

OFFICE AND DESIGNATION

[*See* rule 4]

Sl. No.	*Office*	*Designation*
1	2	3
	I. SUPERIOR OFFICERS	
1.	Director General	Director General
2.	Inspector General	Chief Security Commissioner.
3.	Additional Inspector General	Chief Security Commissioner.
4.	Deputy Inspector General/RPF (which posted as zonal RPF Chief)	Chief Security Commissioner.
5.	Deputy Inspector General/RPSF (when posted as Head of RPSF)	Chief Security Commissioner/ RPSF.
6.	Deputy Inspector General/Principal Railway Protection Force Academy	Principal Railway Protection Force Academy.
7.	Deputy Inspector General.	Additional Chief Security Commissioner.
8.	Assistant Inspector General	Assistant to Director General.

SCHEDULE I—*continued*

1	2	3
9.	Senior Commandant (when posted as second-in-command at zonal railway headquarters)	Deputy Chief Security Commissioner.
10.	Senior Commandant (when posted as head of a security division)	Divisional Security Commissioner.
11.	Senior Commandant	Senior Security Commissioner.
12.	Assistant Inspector General	Assistant Inspector General.
13.	Commandant (when posted as head of a security division)	Divisional Security Commissioner.
14.	Commandant/RPF	Security Commissioner.
15.	Commandant/RPSF	Commanding Officer.
16.	Commandant-cum-Staff Officer to Inspector General/Additional Inspector General.	Staff Officer.
17.	Commandant (Small Arms)	Commanding Officer (Small Arms)
18.	Deputy Commandant	Deputy Security Commissioner.
19.	Assistant Commandant-cum-Personal Assistant to Deputy Inspector General/RPF	Personal Assistant.
20.	Assistant Commandant	Assistant Security Commissioner
21.	Assistant Commandant/RPSF	Assistant Commandant.
22.	Assistant Commandant (Adjutant).	Adjutant.
23.	Assistant Commandant (Principal, Training School)	Assistant Security Commissioner (Principal, Zonal Training Institute).
	II. SUBORDINATE OFFICERS	
24.	Inspector (Post)	Post Commander.
25.	Inspector (Mobile Wing)	Company Commander.
26.	[19][* * *]	
27.	Inspector (H. qrs.)	Divisional Inspector.
28.	Inspector (Stores)	Quarter Master.
29.	Inspector (Fire)	Fire Inspector.
30.	Inspector (Crime Wing)	Crime Inspector.
31.	Inspector (Special Wing)	Special Inspector.
32.	Sub-Inspector	Subedar.
33.	Sub-Inspector (Mobile Wing)	Assistant Company Commander.

19 *Omitted* by G.S.R. 719(E), dated 31.10.2013 (w.e.f. 31.10.2013).

SCHEDULE I—*continued*

1	2	3
34.	[20][* * *]	
35.	Sub-Inspector (Fire)	Fire Station Officer.
36.	Sub-Inspector (Reader)	Crime Reader
37.	Assistant Sub-Inspector	Naib Subedar
38.	Driver Grade I	Sergeant Driver.
	III. UNDER OFFICERS	
39.	Head Constable	Havildar.
40.	Driver Grade II	Head Driver.
41.	[21][* * *]	
42.	Driver Grade III	Naik Driver.
	IV. OTHER MEMBERS OF THE FORCE	
43.	Constable	Constable.
44.	Constable (Fire)	Fireman.
	V. ANCILLARY STAFF (ENROLLED MEMBERS)	
45.	Head Constable (Kahar)	Head Cook.
46.	Head Constable (Tailor)	Head Tailor.
47.	Head Constable (Barber)	Head Barber.
48.	Head Constable (Mali)	Head Mali.
49.	Head Constable (Dhobi)	Head Dhobi.
50.	Head Constable (Safaiwala)	Head Safaiwala.
51.	Head Constable (Cobbler)	Head Cobbler.
52.	Naik (Kahar)	Cook.
53.	Naik (Tailor)	Naik Tailor.
54.	Naik (Barber)	Naik Barber.
55.	Naik (Mali)	Naik Mali.
56.	Naik (Dhobi)	Naik Dhobi.
57.	Naik (Safaiwala)	Naik Safaiwala.
58.	Naik (Cobbler)	Naik Cobbler.
59.	Constable (Kahar)	Kahar
60.	Constable (Tailor)	Tailor
61.	Constable (Barber)	Barber
62.	Constable (Mali)	Mali

20 *Omitted* by G.S.R. 719(E), dated 31.10.2013 (w.e.f. 31.10.2013).
21 *Omitted* by G.S.R. 229, dated 15.7.1999 (w.e.f. 24.7.1999).

SCHEDULE I—*continued*

1	2	3
63.	Constable (Dhobi)	Dhobi
64.	Constable (Safaiwala)	Safaiwala
65.	Constable (Cobbler)	Cobbler
66.	Constable (Motor cleaner)	Motor Cleaner

[SCHEDULES II to IV not printed here for reference *see* Gazette]

SCHEDULE V

JUDICIAL POWERS OF SECURITY COURT

[*See* rule 30]

Part I

Sl. No.	*Powers*	*Section of Code of Criminal Procedure,* 1973
1	2	3
1.	Power to arrest or direct arrest of and commit to custody a person committing an offence in his presence.	Section 44(1).
2.	Power to arrest or direct the arrest in his presence of any person for whose arrest he is competent at the time and in the circumstances to issue a warrant.	Section 44(2).
3.	Power to forward warrant for execution outside jurisdiction.	Section 78.
4.	Power to issue proclamation for person absconding.	Section 82.
5.	Power to order attachment of property of person absconding and scrutiny of claims or objections to attachment.	Sections 83 and 84
6.	Power to release, sale and restoration of attached property	Section 85
7.	Power to issue search warrant	Section 93
8.	Power to issue search warrants in relation to places suspected to contain stolen property, forged documents, etc.	Section 94
9.	Power to issue search warrants for discovery of persons wrongly confined	Section 97

SCHEDULE V—*continued*

Sl. No.	*Powers*	*Section of Code of Criminal Procedure,* 1973
1	2	3
10.	Power to dispose of things found in search beyond jurisdiction	Section 101
11.	Power to record confessions and statements	Section 164
12.	Power to authorise detention when investigation cannot be completed within twenty-four hours	Section 167
13.	Power to take cognizance of offences upon complaint, police report or upon his own knowledge	Section 190(1)
14.	Powers to postpone issue of process	Section 202
15.	Power to stop proceedings in certain cases	Section 258
16.	Power to require attendance of prisoners	Section 267
17.	Power to examine witnesses on commission	Section 287
18.	Power to allow affidavit to be sworn or affirmed before him	Section 297
19.	Power to tender pardons to accomplices	Section 306
20.	Power to make local inspection	Section 310
21.	Power to make order for release on probation of good conduct or after admonition	Section 360
22.	Power to recover penalty on forfeited bond	Section 446
23.	Power to require fresh security	Section 447
24.	Power to pass orders for custody and disposal of property pending trial in certain cases	Section 451
25.	Power for disposal of property at the conclusion of trial	Section 452
26.	Power to dispose off property seized of recovered under the Act	Section 457
27.	Power to sell perishable property	Section 459

SCHEDULE V—*continued*

Part II

Sl. No.	*Powers*	*Section of Code of Criminal Procedure,* 1973
1	2	3
1.	Power to require the postal or telegraph authority to cause search to be made and to detain any document, parcel or thing	Section 92
2.	Power to make over cases after taking cognizance for inquiry or trial to another Magistrate	Section 192

SCHEDULE VI

FORM OF AGREEMENT

[*See* rule 53(*a*)]

To:

The President of India

In consideration of the President of India having agreed to appoint me as ...... in the Railway Protection Force, I .... son/daughter of ....

(*i*) Serve in the Railway Protection Force for a period of not less than three years with effect from the date of my appointment in the Force.

(*ii*) carry out all duties and functions entrusted to me and all lawful orders given to me by members of the Force superior to me in rank;

(*iii*) refund all the cost of training imparted to me in the Force or a sum equal to three months pay and allowance whichever is less in the event of tendering my resignation from the Force for any reason or reasons whatsoever during the aforesaid period of three years; and if after three years I desire to resign, I shall submit my request in writing and will not withdraw from my duties until I am duly relieved.

(2) I understand and agree that my services can be terminated by:

(*i*) the Chief Security Commissioner without giving me any notice under sub-rule (2) of rule 67 or under the second proviso to sub-rule (3) of rule 57;

(*a*) at any time during the period of my initial training; or

(*b*) on my failure to pass the final examination of initial training course; and

(*ii*) the appointing authority under sub-rule (3) of rule 57 during the period of my probation or any extension thereof on issue of notice of one month's or the tender of one months pay and allowances in lieu of such notice.

Note. The term "pay and allowances", used in Clause (*iii*) of Para I and Clause (*ii*) of Para (2) mean the usual pay and allowances paid to me immediately prior to the date of my resignation or termination from service.

Witness	Signature of the recruit.
Signature	Designation
Designation	Date
Date	Place
Place.	

ACCEPTED

For and on behalf of the President of India
(Signature of the Accepting Authority)

SEAL ....

SCHEDULE VII

FORM OF AFFIRMATION OF ALLEGIANCE

[*See* rule 53(*b*)]

I .... son/daughter of .... do solemnly affirm that I will be faithful and bear true allegiance to India and to the Constitution of India as by law established and that I will carry out the duties of my office with loyally, honestly and with impartiality.

Date .... Place	Signature of the enrolled member of the Force.
Date	Signature and designation of the Superior Officer (in whose presence the affirmation is made).

SCHEDULE VIII

BADGES OF RANKS

[*See* rule 121]

Sl. No.	*Rank*	*Badges of rank*
1	2	3
1.	Director General	Crossed sword and baton and the State Emblem to be worn in a manner that the point of sword is to the front.
2.	Inspector General & Addl. Inspector General	Crossed sword and baton; and one Star to be worn in a manner that the point of swords is to the front.

SCHEDULE VIII—*continued*

Sl. No.	*Rank*	*Badges of rank*
1	2	3
3.	Dy. Inspector General	The State Emblem and three Stars to be worn in a triangle.
4.	(*i*) Senior Commandant	
	(*ii*) Commandants who have put in 15 years of service	The State Emblem and two Stars.
5.	Asstt. Inspector General / Commandant.	The State Emblem and one Star.
6.	Deputy Commandant	The State Emblem.
7.	Asstt. Commandant with more than 5 years service or Asstt. Commandant in independent charge of a division	Three Stars.
8.	Asstt. Commandant with less than 5 years but above 2 years service	Two Stars.
9.	Asstt. Commandant with less than 2 years service or on probation	One Star.
10.	Inspector	Three 5-pointed Stars of yellow metal with a navy blue silken bar one cm. in width.
11.	Sub-Inspector	Two 5-pointed Stars of yellow metal with a navy blue silken bar one cm. in width.
12.	Asstt. Sub-Inspector	One 5-pointed Star of yellow metal with a navy blue silken bar one cm. in width.
13.	Head Constable	Chevrons white cloth 3 stripes to be worn on the right upper arm and entering between the elbow and shoulder joints.
14.	Naik	Chevrons white cotton 2 stripes to be worn on the right upper arm and entering between the elbow and the shoulder joints.

Note. 1. The Stars worn by superior officers shall be of white metal/silver 5 pointed (Star of India).

2. Assistant Commandant and Adjutant in the Railway Protection Special Force shall be entitled to wear 3 Stars and 2 Stars respectively irrespective of their length of service unless they are entitled to higher badges by virtue of their length of service.

3. Officers wearing the State Emblem and two Stars and officers wearing the State Emblem and three Stars shall wear gorget patches of dark blue woolen

material with a central silver stripe; and officers of higher rank shall wear similar gorget patches with a silver oak-leaf pattern central stripe.

4. Officers of and above the entitlement of State Emblem and two Stars shall wear a dark blue band of woolen material to be placed between the two lower wealts with silver embroidered Railway Protection Force crest on their peak caps with chain strap of brown leather. The above shall be worn on Pagri by entitled officers.

5. The term "service" for the purpose of badges of rank shall mean the length of non-fortuitous service rendered as a superior officer in Group 'A'.

6. The navy blue silken bar shall be stitched to the material of the shirt by the subordinate officers. Similarly, chevron shall be stitched to the material of the shirt, jersey and, as the case may be, overcoat by under officers.

7. Superior officers on deputation from the Indian Police Service or the State Police Services shall wear the uniform and badge of the rank held by them before their deputation or of such higher ranks to which they may be appointed by the Central Government.

SCHEDULE IX

FORM OF OATH FOR COURT

[*See* rule 188]

I .... do swear in the name of Almighty God that I will well and truly try the accused (or accused persons) before the Security Court according to the evidence, and that I will duly administer justice according to the Railway Protection Force Act, 1957 and RPF Rules, 1987 made thereunder without partiality, favour or affection and to the best of my understanding of the law and the tradition of the Force.

FORM OF AFFIRMATION FOR COURT

[*See* rule 188]

I .... solemnly, sincerely and truly declare and affirm that I will well and truly, try the accused (or accused persons) before the Security Court according to the evidence and that I will truly administer justice according to the Railway Protection Force Act, 1987, and RPF Rules, 1987 made thereunder without partiality favour or affection and to the best of my understanding of the law and the tradition of the Force.

FORM OF OATH FOR INTERPRETER

[*See* rule 188]

I .... do swear in the name of Almighty God that I will well and truly interpret and explain all questions put to, and evidence given by, witnesses and translate correctly and accurately all documents given to me for translation as I shall be required to do touching the matter before this Security Court.

FORM OF AFFIRMATION FOR INTERPRETER

[*See* rule 188]

I .... solemnly affirm that I will well and truly declare and affirm that I will well truly interpret and explain all questions put to and evidence given by, witnesses and translate correctly and accurately all documents given to me for translation as I shall be required to do touching the matters before this Security Court.

SCHEDULE X

FORM 'A'

WARRANT OF COMMITMENT ON A SENTENCE OF IMPRISONMENT

[*See* rule 208]

To

The Superintendent

.... Prison

(Give address)

WHEREAS at a Security Court presided over by Shri .... held at........... on the .... day of .... 20, ... Name of the accused .... staff No. .... rank .... Unit .... having .... as his identification mark was duly convicted of .... (state the offence) under section 17 of the Railway Protection Force Act, 1957 read with rule 147 of Railway Protection Force Rules, 1987.

AND WHEREAS the said Security Court on the .... day of .... 20, ... passed the following sentence upon the said (Name ....) that is to say ....

(Sentence to be entered in full but without signature)

This is to authorise and require you to receive the said prisoner (Name .... into your custody in the said Jail together with the warrant, and thereby carry the aforesaid sentence of imprisonment into execution according to law. The sentence has effect from the .... (give the date on which the original sentence was signed).

The prisoner shall be entitled to all remissions/benefits by the State/Central Government from time to time by special or a general order and also benefit of set off in terms of section 428 of Code of Criminal Procedure, 1973.

Given under my hand and seal at .... on this .... day of .... 20........... .

SEAL OF THE SECURITY COURT

....

(Signature of Authorised Officer)

FORM 'B'

WARRANT AFTER A COMMUTATION OF A SENTENCE

[*See* rule 208]

To

The Superintendent

.... Prison

....

(Give address)

WHEREAS at a Security Court presided over by Shri .... held at .... on the .... day of .... 20 .... (No............... Rank .... Name .... Unit ....) was duly convicted for .... (state the offence) .... under section 17 of the Railway Protection Force Act, 1957 read with rule 147 of the Railway Protection Force Rules, 1987.

AND WHEREAS the said Security Court on the .... day of .... 20 ...., passed the following sentence upon the said (Name ....) that is to say .... (sentence to be entered in full but without signature) and thereupon committed to your custody; and whereas by order of the Petitionary Authority (a duplicate copy of which is hereto annexed), the punishment adjudged by the said sentence has been commuted to the punishment of ....

THIS is to authorise and require you to *send back the said .... (Prison's name) for Force custody / *safely to keep the said .... (Prison's name) in your custody in the said Jail and thereby carry into execution the punishment of imprisonment under the said order according to law.

Date, this .... day of .... 20 ....

(Signature of Authorised Officer)

*Delete whichever is inapplicable.

FORM 'C'

WARRANT WHEN A PRISONER IS PARDONED OR HIS TRIAL IS SET ASIDE OR WHEN THE UNEXPIRED PORTION OF THE SENTENCE IS REMITTED

[*See* rule 208]

To

The Superintendent

....

.... Prison

....

(Give address)

WHEREAS (No. .... Rank .... Name .... of the .... Unit ....) is confined in the .... prison under a warrant issued by the Security Court presided over by Shri .... in pursuance of a sentence of .... passed upon him by said Security Court held at .... on .... and whereas the Petitionary Authority has in exercise of powers conferred upon him by rules 206 and 210 of the Railway Protection Force Rules, 1987 passed the following order regarding the aforesaid sentence that is to say ....

This is to require and authorise you to forthwith discharge the said (Name) .... from your custody unless he is liable to be detained for some other cause, and for your so discharging him this shall be your sufficient warrant.

Given under my hand at .... this the .... day of .... 20 ....

SEAL ....

(Signature of Authorised Officer)

SCHEDULE XI

FORM OF BOND FOR TAKING ADVANCE

[*See* rule 249]

By the bond, I .... having taken an advance of ₹ .... (Rupees .... only) from the President of India (hereinafter called the "Government") promise to pay to the Government the said sum of ₹ .... in .... equal monthly instalments of ₹ .... payable by the 10th of every month commencing from ....

2. And I agree that in case I cease to be in Government service for any reason whatsoever, the entire balance of the amount shall become at once due and payable and that in case I fail to pay by the same before the date of expiry of six months from the date on which the payment of last instalment under this bond would have become due but for my ceasing to be in Government service, whichever date is earlier the Government without prejudice to any other right to which it shall be entitled under any law for the time being in force, shall recover the entire balance of the amount from me.

Dated this .... day of .... 20.

Signature of the Member
of the Force

Witnesses:

....

....

....

SCHEDULE XII

FORM OF DISCHARGE CERTIFICATE

[*See* rule 244]

.... Railway/RPSF Bn.

1. No .... Rank ....

2. Name ....
3. Father's name ....
4. Postal address ....
5. Date of birth ....
6. Identification marks (if any) ....
7. Period of service from ....
8. Certificate of appointment surrendered on ....
9. Post held immediately prior to ceasing to be a member of the Force
....
10. Bench of the Force in which employed ....
11. Division or battalion ....
12. Last pay drawn ....
13. Grounds for termination/ceasing to be a member of the Force ....
14. Conduct and character at the time of his leaving the Force ....
15. Signature of the member discharged from service ....

OFFICIAL SEAL

....

(Signature and designation of Superior Officer)

Station ....

Dated ....

APPENDIX 6

The Indian Railway Board Act, 1905

(Act No. 4 of 1905)

An Act to provide for investing the Railway Board with certain powers or functions under the Indian Railways Act, 1890 [1](9 of 1890).

WHEREAS a Railway Board has been constituted for controlling the administration of railways in India and it is expedient to provide for investing such Board with certain powers or functions under the Indian Railways Act, 1890 [1](9 of 1890). It is hereby enacted as follows:

1. Short title and construction. (1) This Act may be called the Indian Railway Board Act, 1905; and

(2) It shall be read with, and taken as part of, the Indian Railways Act, 1890 [1](9 of 1890).

2. Investment of Railway Board with powers under Indian Railways Act, 1890 [1](9 of 1890). The Central Government may, by notification in the *Official Gazette*, invest the Railway Board, either absolutely or subject to conditions,—

(*a*) with all or any of the powers or functions of the Central Government under the Indian Railways Act, 1890 [1](9 of 1890), with respect to all or any railways, and

(*b*) with the power of the officer referred to in section 47 of the said Act to make general rules for railways administered by the Government.

Powers of Railway Board Section 2 of the 1905 Act empowers the Central Government to invest the Railway Board with all or any of its powers and functions under the Railways Act.[2] Thus, any notification issued by the Railway Board would be the notification of the Central Government itself.[3]

1 Since revised as the Railways Act, 1989.
2 *Vide* Notification No. S.O. 731(E), dated 4.7.2002.
3 *Puttu Lal* v *N.E. Railway* AIR 1960 All 438.

Powers of the Central Government which are invested to the Railway Board shall continue even after the repeal of the Railways Act 1890. Such vesting of power is allocation of power and not delegation of power. Thus, where the Railway Board empowers the General Manager to frame subsidiary rules relating to formation and functions of the Staff Council, it is valid.[4]

Status of Railway Board The Railway Board is an entity separate from the Central Government. The powers of the Railway Board are derived by way of delegation either absolutely or subject to conditions imposed by notification issued by the Central Government.[5]

3. Mode of signifying communications from the Railway Board. Any notice, determination, direction, requisition, appointment, expression of opinion, approval or sanction, to be given or signified on the part of the Railway Board, for any of the purposes of, or in relation to any powers, or functions with which it may be invested by notification under section 2, shall be sufficient and binding if in writing signed by the Secretary to the Railway Board, or by any other person authorized by the said Railway Board to act in its behalf in respect of the matters to which such authorization may relate; and the said Railway Board shall not in any case be bound in respect of any of the matters aforesaid unless by some writing signed in manner aforesaid.

Mode of communication Communication of reversion orders signed by Dy. Chief Personnel Officer was held to be bad.[6]

4. Cessation of Railway Board on establishment of Federal Railway Authority. Rep. by the A.O. 1948.

4 *P. Purusothaman* v *I.C.F. Staff Council* 1994 Lab IC 2220.

5 *K.N. Shukla* v *Navnit Lal Manilal Bhat* AIR 1967 SC 1331; (1967)2 SCR 290; 1967 CrLJ 1200.

6 *Amar Nath* v *N.F. Railway* 1969 Lab IC 1192.

APPENDIX 7

The Railway Accidents and Untoward Incidents (Compensation) Rules, 1990

G.S.R. 552(E), dated 7th June 1990[1] In exercise of the powers conferred by section 129 of the Railways Act, 1989 (24 of 1989) read with s. 22 of the General Clauses Act, 1897 (10 of 1897) and in supersession of the Railway Accidents (Compensation) Rules, 1989 except in respect of things done or omitted to be done before such supersession, the Central Government hereby makes the following rules, namely:

PRELIMINARY

1. Short title and commencement. (1) These rules may be called the [2][Railway Accidents and Untoward Incidents (Compensation) Rules, 1990].

(2) They shall come into force on the date of commencement of the Act.

2. Definitions. [3][(1)] In these rules, unless the context otherwise requires—

(*a*) "*accident*" means an accident of the nature described in section 124 of the Act;

(*b*) "*Act*" means the Railways Act, 1989 (24 of 1989);

(*c*) "*Claims Tribunal*" means the Railway Claims Tribunal established under section 3 of the Railway Claims Tribunal Act, 1987 (54 of 1987);

(*d*) "*Schedule*" means the schedule to these rules; and

(*e*) [3]["*Untoward incident*" means an incident defined in clause (*c*) of section 123 of the Act].

[3][(2) The words used and not defined in these rules but defined in the Act shall have the meanings respectively assigned to them in that Act].

1 Published in *Gazette of India,* (Extraordinary), Part II, s. 3(*i*), dated 7th June 1990.
2 *Substituted* by G.S.R. 592(E), dated 21st July 1994 (w.e.f. 1.8.1994).
3 *Inserted* by G.S.R. 592(E), dated 21st July 1994 (w.e.f. 1.8.1994).

Negligence by railway authorities—Compensation Passengers were hit by running train when they were boarding another train. There was total failure of electricity at railway station at the material point of time. The deceased along with other passengers were compelled to cross railway track meant for incoming train to board train standing on outgoing track. Negligence on the part of the railways in not providing proper platform as well as over-bridge cannot be overlooked. There was so evidence to show any contributory negligence on the part of the deceased. Compensation was awarded to dependants of the deceased.[4]

CLAIMS FOR COMPENSATION

3. Amount of Compensation. (1) The amount of compensation payable in respect of death or injuries, shall be as specified in the Schedule.

(2) The amount of compensation payable for an injury not specified in Part II or Part III of the Schedule but which, in the opinion of the Claims Tribunal is such as to deprive a person of all capacity to do any work, shall be [5][rupees four lakhs].

(3) The amount of compensation payable in respect of any injury (other than an injury specified in the Schedule or referred to in sub-rule (2) resulting in pain and suffering, shall be such as the Claims Tribunal may after taking into consideration medical evidence, besides other circumstances of the case, determine to be reasonable:

Provided that if more than one injury is caused by the same accident, compensation shall be payable in respect of each such injury:

Provided further that the total compensation in respect of all such injuries shall not exceed [6][rupees eighty thousand].

(4) Where compensation has been paid for any injury which is less than the amount which would have been payable as compensation if the injured person had died and the person subsequently died as a result of the injury, a further compensation equal to the difference between the amount payable for death and the already paid shall become payable.

(5) Compensation for loss, destruction or deterioration of goods or animals shall be paid to such extent as the Claims Tribunal may, in all the circumstances of the case, determine to be reasonable.

4. Limit of Compensation. Notwithstanding anything contained in Rule 3, the total compensation payable under that rule shall in no case exceed [7][Rupees four lakhs] in respect of any one person.

4 *Rakesh Saini* v *Union of India* AIR 2004 Del 107.

5 *Substituted* by G.S.R. 620(E), dated 25th October 1997 (w.e.f. 1.11.1997), for "rupees two lakhs".

6 *Substituted* by G.S.R. 620(E), dated 25th October 1997 (w.e.f. 1.11.1997), for "rupees fourty thousand."

7 *Substituted* by G.S.R. 620(E), dated 25th October 1997 (w.e.f. 1.11.1997), for "rupees two lakhs."

[8]SCHEDULE

[*See* rule 3]

COMPENSATION PAYABLE FOR DEATH AND INJURIES

	Amount of Compensation (in rupees)
PART I	
For death	4,00,000
PART II	
(1) For loss of both hands or amputation at higher sites	4,00,000
(2) For loss of hand and a foot	4,00,000
(3) For double amputation through leg or thigh or amputation through leg or thigh on one side and loss of other foot	4,00,000
(4) For loss of sight to such an extent as to render the claimant unable to perform any work for which eye sight is essential	4,00,000
(5) For very severe facial disfigurement	4,00,000
(6) For absolute deafness	4,00,000
PART III	
(1) For amputation through shoulder joint	3,60,000
(2) For amputation below shoulder with stump less than 8" from tip of acromion	3,20,000
(3) For amputation from 8" from tip of acromion to less than 4½" below tip of olecranon	2,80,000
(4) For loss of a hand or the thumb and four fingers of one hand or amputation from 4½" below space tip of olecranon	2,40,000
(5) For loss of thumb	1,20,000
(6) For loss of thumb and its metacarpal bond	1,60,000
(7) For loss of four fingers of one hand	2,00,000
(8) For loss of three fingers of one hand	1,20,000
(9) For loss of two fingers of one hand	80,000
(10) For loss of terminal phalanx of thumb	80,000
(11) For amputation of both feet resulting in end bearing stumps	3,60,000
(12) For amputation through both feet proximal to the metatarso-phalangeal joint	3,20,000
(13) For loss of all toes of both feet through the metatarso-phalangeal joint	1,60,000

8 *Substituted* by G.S.R. 620(E), dated 25th October, 1997 (w.e.f. 1.11.1997).

	Amount of Compensation (in rupees)
(14) For loss of all toes of both feet proximal to the proximal interphalangeal joint	1,20,000
(15) For loss of all toes of both feet distal to the proximal interphalangeal joint	80,000
(16) For amputation at hip	3,60,000
(17) For amputation below hip with stump not exceeding 5" in length measured from tip of great trenchanter but not beyond middle thigh	3,20,000
(18) For amputation below hip with stump exceeding 5" in length measured from tip of great trenchanter but not beyond middle thigh	2,80,000
(19) For amputation below middle thigh to 3½" below knee	2,40,000
(20) For amputation below knee with stump exceeding 3½" but not exceeding 5"	2,00,000
(21) Fracture of Spine with paraplegia	2,00,000
(22) For amputation below knee with stump exceeding 5"	1,60,000
(23) For loss of one eye without complications the other being normal	1,60,000
(24) For amputation of one foot resulting in end-bearing	1,20,000
(25) For amputation through one foot proximal to the metatarso-phalangeal joint	1,20,000
(26) Fracture of Spine without paraplegia	1,20,000
(27) For loss of vision of one eye without complications of disfigurement of eye ball, the other being normal	1,20,000
(28) For loss of all toes of one foot through the metatarso-phalangeal joint	80,000
(29) Fracture of Hip-joint	80,000
(30) Fracture of Major Bone—Femur, Tibia of both limbs	80,000
(31) Fracture of Major Bone—Humerus, Radius of both limbs	60,000
(32) Fracture of Pelvis not involving joint	40,000
(33) Fracture of Major Bone—Femur, Tibia of one limb	40,000
(34) Fracture of Major Bone—Humerus, Radius and Ulna of One limb	32,000

Compensation for untoward accident Compensation was enhanced by notification dated 25th October 1997 by substituting words "Rupees four lakhs" for words "Rupees two lakhs". The said enhanced compensation goes back to earlier Notification. Accident took place in 1996. The claimant is entitled to get compensation of ₹4 lakhs as provided in Notification dated 25th October 1997.[9]

9 *Pramath Kumar Jena* v *Union of India* AIR 2012 Ori 32.

APPENDIX 8

The Railway Passengers (Manner of Investigation of Untoward Incidents) Rules, 2003

G.S.R. 646(E), dated 8th August 2003[1] In exercise of the powers conferred by section 129 of the Railways Act, 1989 (24 of 1989), read with section 22 of the General Clauses Act, 1897 (10 of 1897), the Central Government hereby makes the following rules, namely:

1. Short title and commencement. (1) These rules may be called the Railway Passengers (Manner of Investigation of Untoward Incidents) Rules, 2003.

(2) They shall come into force on the date of their publication in the Official Gazette.

2. Definitions. (1) In these rules, unless the context otherwise requires,—

(*a*) '*Act*' means the Railways Act, 1989 (24 of 1989);

(*b*) '*Claims Tribunal*' means Tribunal constituted under the Railway Claims Tribunal Act, 1987;

(*c*) '*diary*' means the station diary being maintained by the Station Superintendent for recording daily events happened at the station;

(*d*) '*Divisional Office*' means the divisional headquarter of the Zonal Railway;

(*e*) '*Divisional Railway Manager*' means the administrative in-charge of the force of the Divisional Office; [2][or the Additional Divisional Railway Manager nominated by him].

[3](*f*) '*Divisional Security Commissioner*' means an officer, not below the rank of a commandant, who is the head of the force of a Division or a Railway Establishment at any other place connected with the Railways;

1 Published in the *Gazette of India*, (Extraordinary), Part II, s. 3(*i*), dated 8th August 2003 (w.e.f. 8.8.2003).

2 *Added* by the Railway Passengers (Manner of Investigation of Untoward Incidents) Amendment Rules, 2007 published in *Gaz. of India*, Extra. Pt. II, s. 3(*i*), dt. 9.8.2007 (w.e.f. 9.8.2007).

3 *Substituted* by the Railway Passengers (Manner of Investigation of Untoward Incidents) Amendment Rules, 2007 (w.e.f. 9.8.2007).

(g) '*Force*' means the Railway Protection Force;

(h) '*Form*' means the Form appended to these rules;

(i) '*Inquest Report*' means the report prepared by the police containing details of incident;

(j) '*Jama Talashi*' means the report about the recovery of any belongings of the person affected by the untoward incident;

[4](ja) '*Officer of the Force*' means the authorised officer as defined in clause (c) of section 2 of the Railway Property (Unlawful Possession) Act, 1966 and cluase 26A of section 2 of the Railways Act, 1989;

(k) '*Police*' means a State Police;

(l) '*Station Superintendent*' includes Deputy Station Superintendent, Station Master and Assistant Station Master or other officer being incharge of the station;

[5](m) [*omitted*]

[5](n) [*omitted*]

(o) '*untoward incident*' means an incident defined under clause (c) of section 123 of the Act; and

(p) '*Zonal Railway*' means a zonal railway constituted under section 3 of the Act.

(2) The words and expressions used herein and not defined but defined in the Act shall have the meaning respectively assigned to them in the Act.

3. Report about untoward incident. Any railway servant, including guard and driver of the train, on coming to know of the occurrence of untoward incident, shall report the incident immediately to the nearest Station Superintendent.

[6][**4. Duties of Station Superintendent, Guard, Conductor and Train Ticket Examiner incharge of the train.** (1) If an untoward incident occurs at the station, the concerned Station Superintendent shall immediately arrange for medical assistance to the injured passengers and report such incident within twenty-four hours of the occurrence to the Divisional Security Commissioner in Form 1.

(2) If an untoward incident occurs in the mid-section, the Guard of the concerned train shall inform the Station Superintendent of the nearest station who shall perform the duties referred to in sub-rule (1).

(3) In case the Guard is injured in an untoward incident, the Conductor of the concerned train shall inform the Station Superintendent of the nearest station who shall perform the duties referred to in sub-rule (1).

4 *Added* by the Railway Passengers (Manner of Investigation of Untoward Incidents) Amendment Rules, 2007 published in *Gaz. of India*, Extra. Pt. II, s. 3(*i*), dt. 9.8.2007 (w.e.f. 9.8.2007).

5 Clauses (*m*) and (*n*), *omitted* by G.S.R. 540(*E*), dated 9.8.2007 (w.e.f. 9.8.2007).

6 *Substituted* by the R.P. (M. of I. of U.I.) Amendment Rules, 2007 (w.e.f. 9.8.2007). Old Rule—"4. *Duties of guard, driver and Train Ticket Examiner.* Any guard or driver or Train Ticket Examiner, who is on duty at the time of occurrence of untoward incident, shall,—

(*i*) immediately arrange for medical assistance to the injured passengers, and

(*ii*) report the occurrence of such incident to the Supervisor in Form 1."

(4) In case both the Guard and the Conductor are injured in an untoward incident, the Train Ticket Examiner incharge shall inform the Station Superintendent of the nearest station who shall perform the duties referred to in sub-rule (1).

(5) If an untoward incident occurs in mid-section, in the absence of officers mentioned in sub-rules (2), (3), and (4), the Station Superintendent, if it comes to his notice, shall perform the duties referred to in sub-rule (1).]

[7][**5. Duties of Supervisor.** On receipt of a report in Form I, the Supervisor shall forward the same to the Division Railway Manager.]

6. Duties of Station Superintendent. The Station Superintendent, on receipt of an information about the occurrence of an untoward incident under Rule 3, shall,—

(*i*) make necessary entries to this effect in the station diary;

(*ii*) arrange for medical assistance to the injured passengers;

(*iii*) make out a brief report in respect of spot of the untoward incident and forward copies thereof to the Divisional Office, Zonal Railways, police and [8][Divisional Security Commissioner] of the Force;

[9](*iv*) [*omitted*]

[9](*v*) [*omitted*]

7. Conducting of investigation and submission of report by the Force. (1) On receipt of information under rule 6, an Officer of the Force, [9][not below the rank of Inspector], shall carry out the investigation and shall,—

(*i*) obtain copies of the inquest report, post-mortem report and Jama Talashi report from the Police investigating the incident;

[8][(*ii*) obtain a copy of the report specified under clause (*iii*) of Rule 6;]

(*iii*) obtain information about the untoward incident in Form 2;

(*iv*) record statement of additional witnesses, if so required;

(*v*) collect any other evidence required by the circumstances of the case.

(2) The Officer of the Force, [8][shall complete the investigation within sixty days and] submit a report to the [8][authority] specified under sub-rule (2) of rule 10.

8. Conducting of investigation and submission of report by the Police. (1) The police on receipt of the report under clause (*iii*) of Rule 6, shall immediately initiate investigation and prepare inquest report or injury report in accordance with the procedure laid down in Criminal Procedure Code, 1973.

(2) After preparation of report, as mentioned in sub-rule (1), the police shall immediately give clearance certificate for movement of trains from the site of incident so that minimum delay is caused in restoration of train movement.

9. The injured and the next of kin of the deceased passenger may submit evidence and assist police and Force. The injured and the next of kin of the deceased passengers may submit all the relevant evidence before the police and assist the police and the force to complete the investigation.

7 *Omitted* by the R.P. (M. of I. of U.I.) Amendment Rules, 2007 (w.e.f. 9.8.2007).

8 *Substituted* by the R.P. (M. of I. of U.I.) Amendment Rules, 2007 (w.e.f. 9.8.2007).

9 *Omitted* by the R.P. (M. of I. of U.I.) Amendment Rules, 2007 (w.e.f. 9.8.2007).

10. Forwarding of investigation report by the police and the Force. (1) The police on completion of the investigation, shall forward the report thereof to the Magistrate, as required under the Criminal Procedure Code, 1973.

(2) The officer of the Force shall forward the report prepared under sub-rule (2) of rule 7 to [10][the Divisional Railway Manager and] Divisional Security Commissioner of the Force.

[11][(3) The Divisional Security Commissioner shall submit the report to Divisional Railway Manager within fifteen days of the receipt of report of investigation from officer of the force.]

11. Action on the report by the Divisional Railway Manager. (1) The Divisional Railway Manager, on receipt of the report, [10][mentioned in sub-rule (3) of rule 10 shall examine the same within fifteen days.]

(2) When, on examination, Divisional Railway Manager is satisfied that the investigation is complete, he shall pass an order accepting the said report.

(3) If the Divisional Railway Manager has reason to believe that some more inquiry is required in the matter, it shall refer the same back for investigation to the officer of the Force along with his observations for further investigation.

(4) On receipt of a reference under sub-rule (3), the officer of the Force shall investigate the matter further and submit the report immediately to the Divisional Railway Manager.

12. Communication of order. Final order passed on the report by the Divisional Railway Manager shall be communicated to the Station Superintendent who shall maintain the records and make necessary entries in the Station Diary to this effect.

[12][**13. Sending report to Claim Office.** (1) The investigation report along with acceptance of Divisional Railway Manager thereon shall be sent within fifteen days to the administrative in-charge of the Claim Office of the Zonal Railway where the incident has occurred.

(2) The administrative in-charge of Claim Office of the Zonal Railway who has received the notice of claim for that particular incident shall arrange to collect the report from the claim office of Railway where the incident has occurred and submit the same to the concerned Bench of the Railway Claims Tribunal along with the Written Statement.]

FORM I

[*See* rule 4]

REPORT OF UNTOWARD INCIDENT

1. Kilometer at which untoward incident occurred:
2. Name of Driver of the train with Headquarter:
3. Name of Guard of the train with Headquarter:

10 *Omitted* by the R.P. (M. of I. of U.I.) Amendment Rules, 2007 (w.e.f. 9.8.2007).
11 *Inserted* by the R.P. (M. of I. of U.I) Amendment Rules, 2007 (w.e.f. 9.8.2007).
12 *Substituted* by the R.P. (M. of I. of U.I.) Amendment Rules, 2007 (w.e.f. 9.8.2007).

4. Name of Train Ticket Examiner of train, if posted, with Headquarter:
5. Nature of the untoward incident:
   (*a*) accidental fall
   (*b*) bomb blast
   (*c*) rioting/shoot-out
   (*d*) others
6. Time of occurrence:
7. Position of human body in relation to track:
8. Whether medical help was given to the injured:
9. Whether train stopped or not:
10. Condition of doors and occupation of coach:

Date: Signature

Name and designation

FORM II

[*See* rule 7]

BRIEF PARTICULAR OF UNTOWARD INCIDENT

1. In case of death:
   (*a*) time and place the body was detected:
   (*b*) position of the body in relation to the tracks:
   (*c*) blood strains on ballast or engine, extent of the injuries and whether *prima facie* inflicted by a train or otherwise:
   (*d*) position of any clothing etc. found on or near the rails:
   (*e*) Name of information, his parentage and address:
2. In case of accidental falling or other untoward incidents:
   (*a*) kilometerage at which the passenger fell or person was knocked down:
   (*b*) was the incident noticed by the Guard/Driver/TTE and the train stopped or was the alarm chain pulled to stop the train:
   (*c*) was the train backed to the incident spot:
   (*d*) how the injured or dead person was dealt with:
3. In case the passenger falling out:
   (*a*) name, age, sex and address of the passenger, with the particulars of ticket, if any, held:
   (*b*) if child, also give the name and address of the guardian at the time, and his relationship to the child;
   (*c*) where was the person or child seated or standing at the time last seen by fellow passengers;
   (*d*) owning railway, painted number, compartment number, type description and position of the carriage from the engine;
   (*e*) condition of doors;

(*f*) officer of the Force on train;

(*g*) brief statement of the injured person containing cause of accident;

(*h*) name and signature of the passenger in whose presence the statement is recorded;

(*i*) in the case of a child, the name and signature of the guardian;

(*j*) statement of co-passengers;

(*k*) type of injuries sustained by the injured, *i.e.* temporary, permanent, partial or complete disablement;

Date:

Signature

Name and designation

APPENDIX 9

The Railway (Notices of and Inquiries into Accidents) Rules, 1998[1]

In exercise of the powers conferred by section 122 of the Railways Act, 1989 (24 of 1989), the Central Government hereby makes the following rules, namely:

1. Short title and commencement. (1) These rules may be called the Railway (Notices of and Inquiries into Accidents) Rules, 1998.

(2) They shall come into force on the date[2] of their publication in the Official Gazette.

2. Particulars to be given in the notices. The notices mentioned in section 113 of the Railways Act, 1989 (24 of 1989) (hereinafter referred to as the Act), shall contain the following particulars, namely—

(*i*) Kilometerage, or station, or both, at which the accident occurred;

(*ii*) time and date of the accident;

(*iii*) number and description of the train, or trains;

(*iv*) nature of the accident;

(*v*) number of people killed or injured, as far as is known;

(*vi*) cause of the accident, as far as is known; and

(*vii*) probable detention to traffic.

3. Responsibility for sending notices, to whom to be sent and mode thereof. Whenever any accident, as falls under section 113 of the Act (hereinafter referred to as "Reportable train accident") occurs in the course of working a railway, the Station Master nearest to the place at which the accident has occurred or, where there is no Station Master, the railway servant in charge of the section of the railway on which the accident has occurred or any other Station Master in charge of a section of a railway to whom the report of the accident is made, shall give notice of the

1 *Vide* G.S.R. 5, dated 21st December 1998, published in the *Gazette of India*, Pt. II, s. 3(*i*), dated 2nd January 1999.

2 2nd January 1999.

accident by telegraph to the Commissioner of Railway Safety, the District Magistrate and the District Superintendent of Police of the district in which the accident has occurred or such other Magistrate or police officer as may be appointed in this behalf by the State Government concerned and by telegraph, telephone or through special messenger or such other quick means as may be available, to the Superintendent of Railway Police and to the officer-in-charge of the police station within the local limits of which the accident has occurred.

Explanation. For the purpose of this rule, "Reportable Train accident" under section 113 of the Act also includes those usually attended with loss of human life (such as accidents to passenger trains involving collisions, derailments, train-wrecking, or attempted train-wrecking, cases of running over obstructions placed on the line, of passengers falling out of trains or of fires in trains), or grievous hurt as defined in the Indian Penal Code (hereinafter referred to as the grievous hurt), or serious damage to railway property of the value exceeding [3][Rupees two crore] which have not actually occurred but which by the nature of the accident might reasonably have been expected to occur; and also cases of landslides or of breach by rain or flood which cause the interruption of any important through-line of communication for at least 24 hours.

4. Mode of sending notices to the State Government. The notice of accidents, required under section 113 of the Act, to be sent without delay by the Railway Administration, shall be sent to the State Government—

(*a*) by telegram in the case of—

(*i*) accidents deemed, under the *Explanation* to rule 3, to be serious by reason of loss of human life;

(*ii*) accidents by reason of which the permanent way is likely to be blocked for more than twenty-four hours; and

(*iii*) train-wrecking or attempted train-wrecking; and

(*b*) by letter in all other cases.

5. Railway servants to report accidents. Every railway servant shall report, with as little delay as possible every accident occurring in the course of working the railway which may come to his notice and such report shall be made to the nearest Station Master, or, where there is no Station Master, to the railway servant in charge of the section of the railway on which the accident has occurred.

6. Station Master or railway servant in charge of the section to report accidents. The Station Master or the railway servant in charge of the section, shall report all accidents in accordance with the rules laid down by the Railway Administration concerned for the reporting of accidents.

[4][**6A. Responsibility of ensuring correct reporting of accidents.** The responsibility of ensuring correct reporting of accidents shall be of the Divisional Railway Manager (DRM) at Divisional Level and the General Manager (GM) at Zonal Level.]

7. Railway Administration to report serious accidents. (1) Whenever a serious accident, as defined in sub-rule (2) of rule 2 of the Statutory Investigation into Railway

3 *Substituted* by G.S.R. 526(E) dated 2nd August 2013 (w.e.f. 2.8.2013).

4 *Inserted* by the Railway (Notices of and Inquiries into Accidents) Amendment Rules 2001, published in the Gazette of India, Extr., Pt. II, s. 3(*i*), dated 22nd November 2001.

Accidents Rules, 1998, occurs, the railway administration concerned shall, as soon after the accident as possible, by telegram, supply to the Press such particulars as are mentioned in rule 2 and as are till then available, and by supplementary telegrams if necessary, immediately after further information is available. A copy shall be sent simultaneously by express telegram to the Railway Board, the Commissioner of Railway Safety of the circle concerned and the Chief Commissioner of Railway Safety. In addition, the Commissioner of Railway Safety shall be informed, telephonically, of any serious accident, by the control of the division in which the accident has occurred.

(2) For other purpose of sub-rule (1), an accident shall be a serious railway accident where—

(*i*) accident to a train carrying passengers which is attended with loss of life or with grievous hurt to a passenger or passengers in the train, or with serious damage to railway property of the value exceeding [5][rupees two crore] and any other accident which in the opinion of the Chief Commissioner of Railway Safety or Commissioner of Railway Safety requires the holding of an inquiry by the Commissioner of Railway Safety, shall be deemed to be a serious accident. A workmen's train or a ballast train carrying workmen or cattle special train or a tower wagon or such other train carrying workmen or cattle special, military special carrying authorised escorts or similar such train shall be treated as a passenger train;

(*ii*) an accident involving a train carrying passengers leads to loss of life or grievous injury to any railway servant irrespective of whether he was travelling in that passenger train or not, it shall come under the purview of inquiry by the Commission of Railway Safety and shall be treated as a serious railway accident.

Provided that—

(*a*) cases of trespassers run over and injured or killed through their own carelessness or of passengers injured or killed through their own carelessness, and

(*b*) cases involving persons being railway servants or holding valid passes/ tickets or otherwise who are killed or grievously injured while travelling outside the rolling-stock of a passenger train such as on footboard or roof or buffer but excluding the inside of vestibules between coaches, or run over at a level crossing or elsewhere on the Railway track by a passenger train, and

(*c*) collision, between a Road Vehicle and a passenger train at a Level Crossing where no passenger or Railway Servant is killed or grievously hurt shall not be treated as a Serious Railway Accident even if those travelling in the road vehicle are killed or grievously hurt shall not be treated as serious railway accident, unless the Chief Commissioner of Railway Safety or Commissioner of Railway Safety is of the opinion that the accident requires the holding of an inquiry by the Commissioner of Railway Safety.

5 *Substituted* by G.S.R. 526(E) dated 2nd August 2013 (w.e.f. 2.8.2013).

8. Facility for reaching the site of the accident. Whenever any accident has occurred in the course of working a railway, the Head of the Railway Administration concerned shall give all reasonable aid to the District Magistrate or the Magistrate appointed or deputed under rule 17 or to the Commission of Inquiry appointed under the Commissions of Inquiry Act, 1952 (60 of 1952), or any other authority to whom all or any of the provisions of the said Act have been made applicable, and to the Commissioner of Railway Safety, medical officers, the police and others concerned to enable them to reach the scene of the accident promptly and shall also assist those authorities in making inquires and in obtaining evidence as to the cause of the accident.

9. Medical aid to the persons grievously hurt in accidents. Whenever an accident, occurring in the course of working a railway, has been attended with grievous hurt, it shall be the duty of the Head of the Railway Administration concerned to afford medical aid to the sufferers, and to see that they are properly and carefully attended to till they are removed to their homes or handed over to the care of their relatives or friends. In any such case, or in any case in which any loss of human life or grievous hurt has occurred, the nearest available local Medical Officer shall be sent for if such Medical Officer is nearer at hand than the Railway Medical Officer.

10. Arranging attendance of railway servants at the place of judicial inquiries or inquiries conducted by Commissioner of Railway Safety or a Magistrate. When an inquiry under rule 2 of the Statutory Investigation into Railway Accidents Rules, 1998, or under rule 17 of these rules, or a judicial inquiry is being made, the Head of the Railway Administration concerned shall arrange for the attendance, as long as may be necessary, at the place of inquiry, of all railway servants whose evidence is likely to be required at such inquiry; and if the inquiry is to be held by the Commissioner of Railway Safety under rule 2 of the Statutory Investigation into Railway Accidents Rules, 1998 the Head of the Railway Administration concerned shall,—

(*a*) cause notice of the date, hour and place at which the inquiry will begin to be given to the officers mentioned in clauses (*a*) and (*c*) of sub-rule (1) of rule 14, and

(*b*) arrange for the attendance of the divisional officers, railway servants required as witness at the inquiry.

11. Action to be taken by Head of the Railway Administration on receipt of the report of Commissioner of Railway Safety. Whenever the Head of the Railway Administration concerned receives a copy of the report of the Commissioner of Railway Safety under rule 4 of the Statutory Investigation into Railway Accidents Rules, 1998, he shall at once acknowledge its receipt, and—

(*a*) submit his remarks, on the views expressed in the report, to the Chief Commissioner of Railway Safety with copy to the Commissioner of Railway Safety immediately on receipt of the report by the Railway Administration and if he is not able to submit his remarks immediately he shall in his acknowledgment of the report indicate his contention to submit his remarks later as early as possible;

(*b*) if the Head of the Railway Administration concerned agree with the views expressed in the report and considers the prosecution of any person or persons desirable, he shall immediately forward a statement of such persons to the District Magistrate of the district in which the accident occurred, or to such other officer as the State Government may appoint in this behalf and to the concerned police authorities;

(*c*) in case the District Magistrate or Police Authorities require copies of the report, it may be sent to them, and the confidentiality of the report should be made clear to the District Magistrate, Police Authorities, and the Police Authorities shall, as soon as possible, intimate the Head of the Railway Administration concerned about their decision regarding launching any prosecution.

12. Head of the Railway Administration to offer remarks on the suggestions made in the report of Commissioner of Railway Safety. Whenever the report of the Commissioner of Railway Safety points to the necessity for or suggests a change in any of the rules or in the system of working of the railway, the Head of the Railway Administration concerned shall, intimate the action which has been taken, or which it proposes to take, to prevent a recurrence of similar accidents, to the Chief Commissioner of Railway Safety with copy to the Commissioner of Railway Safety.

13. Joint inquiry when dispensed with. (1) Whenever a reportable train accident, such as is described in section 113 of the Act has occurred in the course of working a railway, the Head of the Railway Administration concerned shall cause an inquiry to be promptly made by a committee of railway officers (to be called a "joint inquiry") for a thorough investigation of the causes which led to the accident:

Provided that such an inquiry may be dispensed with,—

(*a*) if any inquiry is to be held by the Commissioner of Railway Safety under rule 2 of the Statutory Investigation into Railway Accidents Rules, 1998, or a Commission appointed under the Commissions of Inquiry Act, 1952 (60 of 1952) or any other authority appointed by the Central Government to which all or any of the provisions of the said Commission of Inquiry Act have been made applicable under rule 2 of the said Statutory Investigation into Railway Accidents Rules, or

(*b*) if there is no reasonable doubt as to the cause of the accident; or

(*c*) if any department of the railway administration concerned intimates that it accepts all responsibility in the matter.

(2) Where such inquiry is dispensed with under clause (*b*) or clause (*c*) of the proviso to sub-rule (1), it shall be the duty of the Head of the Department of the Railway Administration responsible for the accident to make such inquiry (to be called a "departmental inquiry") as he may consider necessary and, if his staff or the system or working is at fault, to adopt or suggest such measures as he may consider necessary for preventing a recurrence of similar accidents.

14. Notice of joint inquiry. (1) Whenever a joint inquiry is to be made, the Head of the Railway Administration concerned shall cause notice of the date and hour at which the inquiry will commence, to be given to the following officers, namely:

(*a*) the District Magistrate of the district in which the accident occurred, or such other officer as the State Government may appoint in this behalf, the Superintendent of the Railway Police and the District Superintendent of Police;

(*b*) the Commissioner of Railway Safety for the section of the railway on which the accident occurred; and

(*c*) the Head of the Railway Police having jurisdiction at the place where the accident occurred or, if there are no Railway Police, the officer-in-charge of the police station having jurisdiction at such place.

(2) The date and hour at which the inquiry will commence shall be fixed so as to give the officers mentioned in sub-rule (1) sufficient time to reach the place where the inquiry is to be held.

(3) When a joint inquiry is held into an accident after receipt of information about the inability of the Commissioner of Railway Safety to hold an inquiry, under sub-rule (5) of rule 2 of the Statutory Investigation into Railway Accidents Rules, 1998, the Head of the Railway Administration concerned shall issue a Press Note in this behalf inviting the public to tender evidence at the inquiry or send information relating to the accident to the Joint Inquiry Committee at an address specified in the Press Note.

15. Report of joint inquiry or departmental inquiry to be sent to the Head of the Railway Administration and the action to be taken thereon. (1) As soon as any joint inquiry or departmental inquiry has been completed, the President of the Committee of railway officers or the Head of the Department, as the case may be, shall send to the Head of the Railway Administration concerned a report containing *inter alia*,—

(*a*) brief description of the accident;

(*b*) description of the locality of the accident;

(*c*) detailed statement of the evidence taken;

(*d*) the conclusions arrived at together with a note of dissent, if any;

(*e*) reasons for conclusions arrived at;

(*f*) the nature and extent of the damage done;

(*g*) when necessary, a sketch illustrative of the accident;

(*h*) the number of railway servants killed or injured;

(*i*) the number of passengers killed or injured;

(*j*) an appendix containing extracts of the rules violated by the staff responsible for the accidents.

(2) The Head of the Railway Administration concerned shall forward, with his remarks as to the action that is intended to be taken in regard to the staff responsible for the accident or for the revision of the rules or the system of working, a copy of the report referred to in sub-rule (1),—

(*a*) to the Commissioner of Railway Safety for the section of the railway on which the accident occurred;

(*b*) if no inquiry or investigation has been made under rule 17 or if a joint or departmental inquiry has been held, first, to the District Magistrate or the officer appointed under clause (*a*) of sub-rule (1) of rule 14, and

(*c*) if any judicial inquiry is being made, to the Magistrate making such inquiry.

(3) The copy of the report aforesaid shall be accompanied,—

(*a*) in the case referred to in clause (*b*) of sub-rule (2), by a statement of the persons involved in the accident whose prosecution the Head of the Railway Administration concerned considers to be desirable;

(*b*) in the case referred to in clause (*c*) of sub-rule (2), by a copy of the evidence taken at the inquiry.

16. Reports of inquiries into accidents not covered by section 113 to be forwarded to Commissioner of Railway Safety. (1) Whenever any accident, not of the nature specified in section 113 of the Act, such as averted collisions, breaches of block rules or other technical accidents, occurs in the course of working a railway, the Railway Administration concerned may cause an inquiry, either a joint inquiry or a departmental inquiry, to be held into the accident.

(2) Where an inquiry is held as provided under sub-rule (1), the Head of the Railway Administration concerned shall forward a copy of the report of the inquiry to the Commissioner of Railway Safety for the section of the railway on which the accident occurred.

17. Magisterial inquiry. Whenever an accident, such as is described in section 113 of the Act, has occurred in the course of working a railway, the District Magistrate or any other Magistrate who may be appointed in this behalf by the State Government, may either,—

(*a*) himself make an inquiry into the causes which led to the accident; or

(*b*) depute a subordinate Magistrate, who if possible, should be a Magistrate of the first class, to make such an inquiry; or

(*c*) direct investigation into the causes which led to the accident, to be made by the police:

Provided that where, having regard to the nature of the accident, the Central Government has appointed a Commission of Inquiry to inquire into it under the Commission of Inquiry Act, 1952 (60 of 1952), or has appointed any other authority to inquire into it and for that purpose has made all or any of the provisions of the said Act applicable to that authority, a Magistrate or a police officer shall not make his inquiry or investigation under this rule and, where he has already commenced the inquiry or investigation, shall not proceed further with it; and such Magistrate or police officer shall hand over the evidence, records or other documents in his possession relating to the inquiry or investigation to such authority as may be specified by the Central Government in this behalf.

18. Notice of Magisterial inquiry. Whenever it is decided to make an inquiry under clause (*a*) or clause (*b*) of rule 17, the District Magistrate or other Magistrate appointed as aforesaid or the Magistrate deputed under clause (*b*) of rule 17, as the case may be, shall at once inform the Head of the Railway Administration concerned and the Divisional Railway Manager by telegraph, of the date and hour at which the inquiry will commence so as to enable the Railway Administration to summon the requisite expert evidence, and thereafter, he shall proceed to the scene of the accident and conduct the inquiry.

19. Judicial inquiry. A Magistrate, making an inquiry under rule 17, may summon any railway servant, and any other person whose presence he may think necessary, and after taking the evidence and completing the inquiry shall, if he considers that there are sufficient grounds for holding a judicial inquiry, take the requisite steps for bringing to trial any person whom he may consider to be criminally liable for the accident.

20. The result of magisterial inquiry to be communicated to the Head of the Railway Administration. The result of every inquiry or investigation made under rule 17 shall be communicated by the Magistrate who has held such inquiry or investigation, to the Head of the Railway Administration concerned and to the Commissioner of Railway Safety.

21. Procedure for summoning railway servants to assist the Magistrate holding judicial inquiry. (1) If in the course of any judicial inquiry into an accident occurring in the course of working a railway, the Magistrate holding such inquiry desires the assistance of the Commissioner of Railway Safety or Head of the Railway Administration concerned, he shall issue a requisition to the Chief Commissioner of Railway Safety or the Railway Board, for the presence of the Commissioner of Railway Safety or the Head of the Railway Administration, stating at the same time the nature of the assistance required, and if the assistance of any Railway Officer is required the Magistrate shall issue a requisition to the Head of the Railway Administration for his attendance in the court.

(2) The requisition referred to in sub-section (1) shall state the nature of the assistance required. In summoning railway officials, the Magistrate shall take care not to summon on the same day so large a number of the employees, especially of one class, as to cause inconvenience to the working of the railway. In the case of serious accidents the Magistrate may obtain reports from the Commissioner of Railway Safety and the Head of the Railway Administration concerned in regard to the accident, before finally concluding the judicial inquiry.

22. Communication of the decision of judicial inquiry to the Railway Administration, Commissioner of Railway Safety and the State Government. On the conclusion of the judicial inquiry the Magistrate shall send a copy of his decision to the Head of the Railway Administration concerned and to the Commissioner of Railway Safety, and shall, unless in any case he thinks it unnecessary to do so, report the result of the inquiry to the State Government.

23. Police investigation—when to be dispensed with—report on loss of life, grievous hurt, or damage to railway property. (1) The Railway Police may make an investigation into the causes which led to any accident occurring in the course of working a railway and shall do so whenever,—

(*a*) any such accident is attended with loss of human life or with grievous hurt, or with serious damage to railway property of the value exceeding [6][rupees two crore] or has *primâ facie* been due to any criminal act or omission; or

(*b*) the District Magistrate or the Magistrate appointed under rule 17 has given a direction under clause (*c*) of that rule:

Provided that where, having regard to the nature of the accident, the Central Government has appointed a Commission of Inquiry to inquire into it under the Commissions of Inquiry Act, 1952 (60 of 1952), or has appointed any other authority

6 *Substituted* by G.S.R. 526(E) dated 2nd August 2013 for "₹25,00,000" (w.e.f. 2.8.2013).

to inquire into it and for that purpose has made all or any of the provisions of the said Act applicable to that authority, or where a magisterial inquiry is being held under clause (*a*) or clause (*b*) of rule 17, the Railway Police shall not make an investigation under this rule, and, where they have already commenced their investigation shall not proceed further with it; and shall hand over the records or other documents in their possession relating to the investigation to such authority as may be specified by the Central Government in this behalf.

(2) The Railway Police shall report, with as little delay as possible to the nearest Station Master, or where there is no Station Master, to the railway servant in charge of the section of the railway, on which the accident has occurred, every accident which may come to their notice occurring in the course of working a railway attended with loss of human life, or with grievous hurt or with serious damage to railway property of the value exceeding [7][rupees two crore] or which has *prima facie* been due to any criminal act or omission.

24. Status of police officer investigating the accident. (1) Whenever an investigation is to be made by the Railway Police,—

(*a*) in a case in which an accident is attended with loss of human life or with grievous hurt, or with serious damage to railway property of the value exceeding [7][rupees two crore]; or

(*b*) in pursuance of a direction given under clause (*c*) of rule 17,

the investigation shall be conducted by the Head of the Railway Police of the area in which the accident has occurred, or if that officer is unable to conduct the investigation himself, by an officer to be deputed by him.

(2) The officer deputed under sub-rule (1) shall ordinarily be the senior officer available, and shall whenever possible be a Gazetted Officer, and shall in no case be of a rank lower than that of an inspector:

Provided that the investigation may be carried out by an officer-in-charge of a police station,—

(*i*) in a case such as is referred to in clause (*a*) of sub-rule (1), if no loss of life or grievous hurt has been caused to more persons than one or no damage to railway property of value exceeding [7][rupees two crore] has been caused or there is no reason to suspect that any servant of the railway has been guilty of neglect of any rule relating to the working of the railway;

(*ii*) in the case referred to in clause (*b*) of sub-rule (1), if the District Magistrate so directs.

25. Notice of police investigation. The officer who is to conduct an investigation in pursuance of rule 24 shall at once inform the Head of the Railway Administration concerned and the Divisional Railway Manager by telegraph of the date and hour at which the investigation will commence so that, if possible, the presence of a railway official may be arranged for to watch the proceedings and to aid the officer making the investigation, and, thereafter, he shall proceed without delay to the scene of the accident and conduct the investigation there; so, however, that the absence of a railway official shall not be allowed to delay the investigation which shall be conducted as soon as possible after the accident has taken place.

7 *Substituted* by G.S.R. 526(E) dated 2nd August 2013 for "₹25,00,000" (w.e.f. 2.8.2013).

26. Assistance by the District Police. (1) In every case to which rule 24 applies, immediate information shall be given by the Railway Police of the area to the District Police, who, if so, required, shall afford all necessary assistance and shall, if occasion arises, carry the investigation beyond the limits of the railway premises. But the Railway Police of the area shall primarily be responsible for carrying on the investigation within such limits.

(2) Subject to the provisions of these rules, the further prosecution of the case; on the conclusion of the police investigation, shall rest with the Railway Police.

27. Communication of the result of police investigation. The result of every police investigation shall be reported at once to the District Magistrate or other officer appointed in this behalf by the State Government to the Head of the Railway Administration concerned or other officer appointed by him, and to the Commissioner of Railway Safety.

28. District Police to discharge duties of Railway Police. Where there is no Railway Police in the area, the duties imposed by rules 23, 24 and 25 sub-rule (2) of rule 26, and rule 27 on the Railway Police of the area, or on the Head of such Railway Police, shall be discharged by the District Police or by the District Superintendent of Police, as the case may be.

29. Repeal and saving. (1) The Railway (Notices of and Inquiries into Accidents) Rules, 1973, are hereby repealed.

(2) Notwithstanding such repeal, anything done or any action taken under the rules hereby repealed shall be deemed to have been done or taken under the corresponding provisions of these rules.

APPENDIX 10

The Railway Servants (Discipline and Appeal) Rules, 1968

In exercise of the power conferred by the proviso to Article 309 of the Constitution, the President hereby makes the following rules, namely:

PART I

GENERAL

1. Short title and commencement. (1) These rules may be called the Railway Servants (Discipline and Appeal) Rules, 1968.

(2) They shall come into force on the 1st day of October 1968.

2. Definitions. (1) In these rules, unless the context otherwise requires,—

(*a*) 'Appointing authority' in relation to a railway servant means,—

(*i*) the authority empowered to make appointments to the service of which the railway servant is, for the time being, a member or to the grade of the service in which the railway servant is, for the time being, included, or

(*ii*) the authority empowered to make appointments to the post which the railway servant, for the time being holds, or

(*iii*) the authority which appointed the railway servant to such service, grade or post, as the case may be, or

(*iv*) where the railway servant having been a permanent member of any other service or having substantively held any other permanent post has been in continuous employment under the Ministry of Railways, the authority which appointed him to that service or to any grade in that service or to that post;

whichever authority is the highest authority;

(*b*) "Commission" means the Union Public Service Commission;

(*c*) 'Disciplinary authority' means,—

(*i*) in relation to the imposition of a penalty on a railway servant, the authority competent, under these rules, to impose on him that penalty,

(*ii*) in relation to rule 9 and clauses *(a)* and *(b)* of sub-rule (1) of rule 11 in the case of any gazetted railway servant, an authority competent to impose any of the penalties specified in rule 6,

(*iii*) in relation to rule 9 and in the case of any non-gazetted railway servant, an authority competent to impose any of the major penalties specified in rule 6,

(*iv*) in relation to clauses *(a)* and *(b)* of sub-rule (1) of rule 11, in the case of a non-gazetted railway servant, an authority competent to impose any of the penalties specified in rule 6;

(*d*) 'Head of the department' for the purpose of exercising the powers as appointing, disciplinary, appellate or revising authority, means the authority declared to be head of the department in terms of clause (21) of rule 103 of Volume I of the Indian Railway Establishment Code;

(*e*) 'Railway servant' means a railway servant as defined in clause (43) of rule 103 of Volume 1 of the Indian Railway Establishment Code and includes any such railway servant on foreign service or whose services are temporarily placed at the disposal of any other department of the Central Government or a State Government or a local or other authority;

(*f*) 'Service' means a service under the Ministry of Railways;

(*g*) 'Schedule' means a schedule appended to these rules.

(2) All other words and expressions used but not defined in these rules and defined in the Indian Railways Act, 1890 (9 of 1890) shall have the meanings respectively assigned to them under that Act.

3. Application. (1) These rules shall apply to every railway servant but shall not apply to—

(*a*) any member of the All India Services;

(*b*) any member of the Railway Protection Force as defined in the Railway Protection Force Act, 1957 (23 of 1957);

(*c*) any person in casual employment; and

(*d*) any person for whom special provision is made, in respect of matters covered by these rules by or under any law for the time being in force or by or under any agreement entered into by or with the previous approval of the President before or after the commencement of these rules, in regard to matters covered by such special provisions.

(2) Notwithstanding anything contained in sub-rule (1), the President may, by order, exclude any class of railway servants from the operation of all or any of these rules.

PART II
SUSPENSION

4. Authorities competent to place a railway servant under suspension. The classes of railway servants who may be placed under suspension and the authorities by whom they may be so placed, shall be specified in Schedules I, II & III:

Provided that, in exceptional circumstances, any authority specified in any of the Schedules may place any subordinate railway servant specified therein, under suspension:

Provided further that where any action is taken under the foregoing proviso, the authority concerned shall forthwith report to the authority competent to place such railway servant under suspension, the circumstances in which the order was made and obtain his approval.

Explanation. For the purposes of this rule, in respect of a railway servant officiating in a higher post, the competent authority shall be determined with reference to the officiating post held by such railway servant at the time of taking action.

5. Suspension. (1) A railway servant may be placed under suspension—

(*a*) where a disciplinary proceeding against him is contemplated or is pending; or

(*b*) where, in the opinion of the authority competent to place a railway servant under suspension, he has engaged himself in activities prejudicial to the interest of the security of the State; or

(*c*) where a case against him in respect of any criminal offence, is under investigation, inquiry or trial;

(2) A railway servant shall be deemed to have been placed under suspension by an order of the competent authority—

(*a*) with effect from the date of his detention, if he is detained in custody, whether on a criminal charge or otherwise, for a period exceeding forty-eight hours;

(*b*) with effect from the date of his conviction, if, in the event of a conviction for an offence, he is sentenced to a term of imprisonment exceeding forty-eight hours and is not forthwith dismissed or removed or compulsorily retired consequent to such conviction.

Explanation. The period of forty-eight hours referred to in clause (*b*) of this sub-rule, shall be computed from the commencement of the imprisonment after the conviction and for this purpose, intermittent periods of imprisonment, if any, shall be taken into account.

(3) Where a penalty of dismissal, removal or compulsory retirement from service imposed upon a railway servant under suspension is set aside in appeal or on review under these rules and the case is remitted for further inquiry or action or with any other directions, the order of his suspension shall be deemed to have continued in force on and from the date of the original order of dismissal, removal or compulsory retirement and shall remain in force until further orders.

(4) Where a penalty of dismissal, removal or compulsory retirement from service imposed upon a railway servant, is set aside or declared or rendered void in consequence of or by a decision of a court of law and the disciplinary authority

on consideration of the circumstances of the case, decides to hold a further inquiry against him on the allegations on which the penalty of dismissal, removal or compulsory retirement, was originally imposed, the railway servant shall be deemed to have been placed under suspension by the competent authority from the date of the original order of dismissal, removal or compulsory retirement and shall continue to remain under suspension until further orders:

Provided that no such further order shall be ordered unless it is intended to meet a situation where the court has passed an order purely on technical grounds without going into the merits of the case.

(5) (*a*) An order of suspension made or deemed to have been made under this rule, shall continue to remain in force until it is modified or revoked by the authority competent to do so.

(*b*) Where a railway servant is suspended or is deemed to have been suspended (whether in connection with any disciplinary proceeding or otherwise), and any other disciplinary proceeding is commenced against him during the continuance of that suspension, the authority competent to place him under suspension may, for reasons to be recorded by him in writing, direct that the railway servant shall continue to be under suspension until the termination of all or any of such proceedings.

(*c*) An order of suspension made or deemed to have been made under this rule, may, at any time, be modified or revoked by the authority which made or is deemed to have made the order or by any authority to which that authority is subordinate.

(6) Notwithstanding anything contained in sub-rule (5), an order of suspension made or deemed to have been made under sub-rule (1) or sub-rule (2) of this rule shall not be valid after a period of ninety days unless it is extended after review in the manner provided in sub-rule (7) of this rule, for a further period before expiry of ninety days.

(7) The review of an order of suspension shall be done by the authority which is competent to modify or revoke the suspension, on the recommendation of the review committee constituted for the purpose, and such competent authority shall pass orders either extending or revoking the suspension before expiry of ninety days from the date of order of suspension. Subsequent reviews shall be made before expiry of the extended period of suspension. Extension of suspension shall not be for a period exceeding one hundred and eighty days at a time.

PART III

PENALTIES AND DISCIPLINARY AUTHORITIES

6. Penalties. (1) The following penalties may, for good and sufficient reasons and as hereinafter provided, be imposed on a railway servant, namely—

Minor Penalties—

(*i*) Censure;

(*ii*) Withholding of his promotion for a specified period;

(*iii*) Recovery from his pay of the whole or part of any pecuniary loss caused by him to the Government or Railway Administration by negligence or breach of orders;

(*iii-a*) Withholding of the Privilege Passes or Privilege Ticket Orders or both;

(*iii-b*) Reduction to a lower stage in the time scale of pay by one stage for a period not exceeding three years, without cumulative effect and not adversely affecting his pension;

(*iv*) Withholding of increments of pay for a specified period with further directions as to whether on the expiry of such period this will or will not have the effect of postponing the future increments of his pay;

Major Penalties—

(*v*) Save as provided for in clause (*iii-b*) reduction to a lower stage in the time-scale of pay for a specified period, with further directions as to whether on the expiry of such period, the reduction will or will not have the effect of postponing the further increments of his pay;

(*vi*) Reduction to a lower time-scale of pay, grade, post or service, with or without further directions regarding conditions of restoration to the grade or post or service from which the railway servant was reduced and his seniority and pay on such restoration to that grade, post or service;

(*vii*) Compulsory retirement;

(*viii*) Removal from service which shall not be a disqualification for future employment under the Government or railway administration;

(*ix*) Dismissal from service which shall ordinarily be a disqualification for future employment under the Government or Railway Administration;

Provided that in cases of persons found guilty of any act or omission, which resulted or would have, ordinarily resulted in collisions of Railway trains, one of the penalties specified in clauses (*viii*) and (*ix*) shall, ordinarily, be imposed and in cases of passing railway signals at danger, one of the penalties specified in clauses (*v*) to (*ix*) shall, ordinarily, be imposed and where such penalty is not imposed, the reasons therefor shall be recorded in writing:

Provided further that in case of persons found guilty of possessing assets disproportionate to known sources of income or found guilty of having accepted or having obtained from any person any gratification, other than legal remuneration, as a motive or reward for doing or forbearing to do any official act, one of the penalties specified in clauses (*viii*) or (*ix*) shall ordinarily be imposed and where such penalty is not imposed, the reasons therefor shall be recorded in writing.

Explanation. The following shall not amount to a penalty within the meaning of this rule, namely—

(*i*) withholding of increments of pay of a railway servant for failure to pass any departmental examination in accordance with the rules or orders governing the service to which he belongs or post which he holds or the terms of his appointment;

(*ii*) stoppage of a railway servant at the efficiency bar in the time-scale of pay on the ground of his unfitness to cross the bar;

(*iii*) non-promotion of a railway servant, whether in a substantive or officiating capacity, after consideration of his case, to a service, grade or post for promotion to which he is eligible;

(*iv*) reversion of a railway servant officiating in a higher service, grade or post to a lower service, grade or post on the ground that he is considered to be unsuitable for such higher service, grade or post or on any administrative ground unconnected with his conduct;

(*v*) reversion of a railway servant, appointed on probation to any other service, grade or post, to his permanent service, grade or post during or at the end of the period of probation in accordance with the terms of his appointment or the rules and orders governing such probation;

(*vi*) replacement of the services of a railway servant, whose services had been borrowed from any other Ministry or Department of the Central Government or a State Government or an authority under the control of the Central Government or a State Government, at the disposal of the Government or the authority from which the services of such railway servant had been borrowed;

(*vii*) compulsory retirement of a railway servant in accordance with the provisions relating to his superannuation or retirement;

(*viii*) termination of the services—

(*a*) of a railway servant appointed on probation, during or at the end of the period of his probation, in accordance with the terms of his appointment or the rules and orders governing such probation; or

(*b*) of a temporary railway servant in accordance with rule 301 contained in Volume I of the Indian Railway Establishment Code; or

(*c*) of a railway servant employed under an agreement, in accordance with the terms of such agreement;

(*ix*) discharge of railway servants—

(*a*) for inefficiency due to failure to conform to the requisite standard of physical fitness;

(*b*) on reduction of establishment.

7. Disciplinary Authorities. (1) The President may impose any of the penalties specified in rule 6 on any railway servant.

(2) Without prejudice to the provisions of sub-rule (1), any of the penalties specified in rule 6 may be imposed on a railway servant by the authorities specified in Schedules I, II and III.

(3) The disciplinary authority in the case of a railway servant officiating in a higher post, shall be determined with reference to the officiating post held by him at the time of taking action.

8. Authority to institute proceedings. (1) The President or any other authority empowered by him by general or special order may—

(*a*) institute disciplinary proceedings against any railway servant;

(*b*) direct a disciplinary authority to institute disciplinary proceedings against any railway servant on whom that disciplinary authority is competent to impose, under these rules, any of the penalties specified in rule 6.

(2) A disciplinary authority competent under these rules to impose any of the penalties specified in clauses (*i*) to (*iv*) of rule 6 may, subject to the provisions of clause (*c*) of sub-rule (1) of rule 2, institute disciplinary proceedings against any railway servant for the imposition of any of the penalties specified in clauses (*v*) to (*ix*) of rule 6, notwithstanding that such disciplinary authority is not competent, under these rules, to impose any of the latter penalties.

PART IV

PROCEDURE FOR IMPOSING PENALTIES

9. Procedure for imposing major penalties. (1) No order imposing any of the penalties specified in clauses (*v*) to (*ix*) of rule 6 shall be made except after an inquiry held, as far as may be, in the manner provided in this rule and rule 10, or in the manner provided by the Public Servants (Inquiries) Act, 1850 (37 of 1850), where such inquiry is held under that Act.

(2) Whenever the disciplinary authority is of the opinion that there are grounds for inquiring into the truth of any imputation of misconduct or misbehavior against a railway servant, it may itself inquire into, or appoint under this rule or under the provisions of the Public Servants (Inquiries) Act, 1850, as the case may be, a Board of Inquiry or other authority to inquire into the truth thereof.

Provided that were there is a complaint of sexual harassment within the meaning of rule 3C of the Railway Services (Conduct) Rules, 1966, the Complaints Committee established for inquiring into such complaints, shall be deemed to be the inquiring authority appointed by the disciplinary authority for the purpose of these rules and the Complaints Committee shall hold, if separate procedure has not been prescribed for the Complaints Committee for holding the inquiry into the complaints of sexual harassment, the inquiry as far as practicable in accordance with the procedure laid down in these rules.

(3) Where a Board of inquiry is appointed under sub-rule (2) it shall consist of not less than two members, each of whom shall be higher in rank than the Railway servant against whom the inquiry is being held and none of whom shall be subordinate to the member or members as the ease may be, of such Board.

(4) Where the Board of inquiry consists of two or more than two members, the senior member shall be the Presiding Officer.

(5) Every decision of the Board of inquiry shall be passed by a majority of votes, and where there is an equality of votes on the findings, the findings of each member shall be incorporated in the report prepared under clause (*i*) of sub-rule (25).

Explanation. Where the disciplinary authority itself holds the inquiry, any reference in sub-rule (12) and in sub-rules (14) to (25), to the inquiring authority shall be construed as a reference to the disciplinary authority.

(6) Where it is proposed to hold an inquiry against a railway servant under this rule and rule 10, the disciplinary authority shall draw up or cause to be drawn up—

(*i*) the substance of imputations of misconduct or misbehaviour into definite and distinct articles of charge;

(*ii*) a statement of the imputations of misconduct or misbehaviour in support of each article of charge which shall contain—

(*a*) a statement of all relevant facts including any admission or confession made by the railway servant,

(*b*) a list of documents by which, and a list of witnesses by whom, the articles of charge are proposed to be sustained.

(7) The disciplinary authority shall deliver or cause to be delivered to the railway servant a copy of the articles of charge, the statement of the imputations of misconduct or misbehaviour and a list of documents and witnesses by which each article of charge is proposed to be sustained and shall require the railway servant to submit a written statement of his defence within ten days or such further time as the disciplinary authority may allow.

Note. If copies of documents have not been delivered to the railway servant along with the articles of charge and if he desires to inspect the same for the preparation of his defence, he may do so, within ten days from the date of receipt of the articles of charge to him and complete inspection within ten days thereafter and shall state whether he desires to be heard in person.

(8) The railway servant may, for the purpose of his defence, submit with the written statement of his defence, a list of witnesses to be examined on his behalf.

Note. If the railway servant applies in writing for the supply of copies of the statements of witnesses mentioned in the list referred to in sub-rule (6), the disciplinary authority shall furnish him with a copy of each of such statement as early as possible and in any case not later than three days before the commencement of the examination of the witnesses on behalf of the disciplinary authority.

(9) (*a*) (*i*) On receipt of the written statement of defence, the disciplinary authority shall consider the same and decide whether the inquiry should be proceeded with under this rule.

(*ii*) Where the disciplinary authority decides to proceed with the inquiry it may itself inquire into such of the articles of charge as are not admitted or appoint under sub-rule (2) a Board of inquiry or other authority for the purpose.

(*iii*) Where all the articles of charge have been admitted by the railway servant in his written statement of defence, the disciplinary authority shall record its findings on each charge, after taking such further evidence as it may think fit and shall act in the manner laid down in rule 10.

(*iv*) If the disciplinary authority, after consideration of the written statement of defence, is of opinion that the imposition of a major penalty is not necessary, it may drop the proceedings already initiated by it for the imposition of major penalty, without prejudice to its right to impose any of the minor penalties, not attracting the provisions of the sub-rule (2) of rule 11. Where the disciplinary authority so drops the proceedings but considers it appropriate to impose any of the minor penalties, not attracting the provisions of sub-rule (2) of Rule 11, it may make an order imposing such penalty and it will not be necessary to give the railway servant any further opportunity of making representation before the penalty is imposed.

(*b*) If no written statement of defence is submitted by the railway servant, the disciplinary authority may itself inquire into the articles of charge or may, if it considers necessary to do so, appoint, under sub-rule (2) an inquiring authority for the purpose also inform the servant of such appointment.

(*c*) Where the disciplinary authority itself inquires into an article of charge or appoints a Board of Inquiry or any other inquiring authority for holding an inquiry into such charge, it may, by an order in writing, appoint a railway or any other Government servant to be known as Presenting Officer to present on its behalf the railway case in support of the articles of charge.

(10) The disciplinary authority shall, where it is not the inquiring authority, forward the inquiring authority—

(*i*) a copy of the articles of charge and the statement of the imputations of misconduct or misbehaviour;

(*ii*) a copy of the written statement of defence, if any, submitted by the railway servant;

(*iii*) a copy of the statement of witnesses, if any, referred to in sub-rule (6);

(*iv*) evidence proving the delivery of the documents referred to in sub-rule (6) to the railway servant;

(*v*) A copy of the order appointing the 'Presenting Officer' if any; and

(*vi*) a copy of the list of witnesses, if any, furnished by the railway servant.

(11) The railway servant shall appear in person before the inquiring authority on such day and at such time within ten working days from the date of receipt by the inquiring authority of the order appointing him as such, as the inquiring authority may; by a notice in writing, specify in this behalf, or within such further time not exceeding ten days, as the inquiring authority may allow.

(12) The inquiring authority shall, if the railway servant fails to appear within the specified time, or refuses or omits to plead, require the Presenting Officer, if any, to produce the evidence by which he proposes to prove the articles of charge and shall adjourn the case to a later date not exceeding thirty days, after recording an order that the railway servant may for the purpose of preparing his defence, give a notice within ten days of the order or within such further time not exceeding ten days as the inquiring authority may allow for the discovery or production of any documents which are, in possession of Railway Administration but not mentioned in the list referred to in sub-rule (6).

Note. The railway servant shall indicate the relevance of the documents required by him to be discovered or produced by the Railway Administration.

(13)(*a*) The railway servant may present his case with the assistance of any other railway servant (including a railway servant on leave preparatory to retirement) working under the same Railway Administration, subject to whose jurisdiction and control he is working. He cannot engage a legal practitioner for the purpose, unless the Presenting Officer appointed by the disciplinary authority is a legal practitioner or the disciplinary authority having regard to the circumstances of the case, so permits. If the railway servant is employed in the office of the Railway Board, its attached office or subordinate office, he may present his case with the assistance of any other railway servant (including a railway servant on leave preparatory to retirement), employed in the office of the Railway Board, attached office or sub-ordinate office, as the case may be, in which he is working.

(*b*) The railway servant may also present his case with the assistance of a retired railway servant, subject to such conditions as may be specified by the President from time to time by general or special order in this behalf.

Note 1. A non-gazetted railway servant may take assistance of an official of a Railway Trade Union, recognised by the Railway Administration under which the railway servant is employed, to present his case before an inquiring authority but shall not engage a legal practitioner for the above purpose except in the circumstances brought out in clause (*a*). An official of a Railway Trade Union shall not be allowed to appear on behalf of an alleged delinquent railway official in connection with a disciplinary case pending against that official, to present his case favourably before an inquiring authority unless he has worked as such in a recognised Railway Trade Union for a period of at least one year continuously prior to his appearance before an inquiring authority for the above purpose and subject to the condition that he takes no fees.

Note 2. (*i*) Nomination of an assisting railway servant or an official of a recognised Railway Trade Union, who is a full time union worker, shall be made within twenty days from the date of appointment of the inquiring authority.

(*ii*) The nomination shall not be accepted if the person assisting has three pending disciplinary cases on hand in which he has to assist.

Provided that an official of a recognised Railway trade Union may assist in more than three pending disciplinary cases.

(14) After the nomination of the assisting railway servant or the official of a Railway Trade Union and other necessary steps preliminary to the inquiry, are completed, a date, ordinarily not exceeding one month from the date of appointment of the inquiring authority shall be fixed for the inquiry and railway servant informed accordingly.

(15) The inquiring authority shall, on receipt of the notice for discovery or production of documents, forward the same or copies thereof to the authority in whose custody or possession documents are kept with a requisition for the production of the documents by such date as may be specified in such requisition:

Provided that the inquiring authority may, for reasons to be recorded by it in writing, refuse to requisition such of the documents as are, in its opinion, not relevant to the case.

(16) On receipt of the requisition referred to in sub-rule (15), every authority having the custody or possession of the requisitioned documents shall produce the same before the inquiring authority by the specified time:

Provided that if the authority having the custody or possession of requisitioned documents is satisfied for reasons to be recorded by it in writing that the production of all or any of such documents would be against the public interest or security of the State, it shall inform the inquiring authority accordingly and the inquiring authority shall, on being so informed, communicate the information to the railway servant and withdraw the requisition made by it for the production or discovery of such documents.

(17) On the date fixed for the inquiry, the oral and documentary evidence by which the articles of charge are proposed to be proved, shall be produced by or on behalf of the disciplinary authority. The witnesses shall be examined by or on behalf of the Presenting Officer, if any, and may be cross-examined by or on behalf of the railway servant. The Presenting Officer, if any, shall be entitled to re-examine the witnesses on any points on which they have been cross-examined, but not on any new matter without the leave of the inquiring authority. The inquiring authority may also put such questions to the witnesses as it thinks fit.

(18) If it shall appear necessary before the close of the case on behalf of the disciplinary authority, the inquiring authority may, in its discretion, allow the Presenting Officer, if any, to produce evidence not included in the list given to the railway servant or may itself call for new evidence or recall and re-examine any witness and in such case the railway servant shall be entitled to have, if he demands it, a copy of the list of further evidence proposed to be produced and an adjournment of the inquiry for three clear days before the production of such new evidence, exclusive of the day of adjournment and the day to which the inquiry is adjourned. The inquiring authority shall give the railway servant an opportunity of inspecting such documents before they are taken on the record. The inquiring authority may also allow the railway servant to produce new evidence if it is of the opinion that the production of such evidence is necessary in the interest of justice.

Note. New evidence shall not be permitted or called for or any witness shall not be recalled to fill up any gap in the evidence. Such evidence shall be called for only when there is an inherent lacuna or defect in the evidence which has been produced originally.

(19) When the case for the disciplinary authority is closed, the railway servant shall be required to state his defence orally, or in writing as he may prefer. If the defence is made orally, it shall be recorded and the railway servant shall be required to sign the record. In either case a copy of the statement of defence shall be given to the Presenting Officer, if any.

(20) The evidence on behalf of the railway servant shall then be produced. The railway servant may examine himself in his own behalf, if he so prefers. The witnesses produced by the railway servant shall then be examined by or on behalf of him and shall be cross-examined by or on behalf of the Presenting Officer, if any. The railway servant shall be entitled to re-examine the witnesses on any point on which they have been cross-examined, but not on any new matter, without the leave of the inquiring authority. The inquiring authority may also put such questions to the witnesses as it thinks fit.

(21) The inquiring authority may, after the railway servant closes his case, and shall, if the railway servant has not examined himself, generally question him on the circumstances appearing against him in the evidence for the purpose of enabling the railway servant to explain any circumstances appearing in the evidence against him.

(22) The inquiring authority may, after the completion of the production of evidence, hear the Presenting Officer, if any, and the railway servant, or permit them to file written briefs of their respective cases, if they so desire.

(23) If the railway servant, to whom a copy of the articles of charge has been delivered, does not submit the written statement of defence on or before the date specified for the purpose or does not appear in person before the inquiring authority or otherwise fails or refuses to comply with the provisions of this rule, the inquiring authority may hold the inquiry *ex parte*.

(24) Whenever any inquiring authority, after having heard and recorded the whole or any part of the evidence in an inquiry ceases to exercise jurisdiction therein and is succeeded by another inquiring authority which has, and which exercises, such jurisdiction, the inquiring authority so succeeding may act on the

evidence so recorded by its predecessor or partly recorded by its predecessor and partly recorded by itself:

Provided that if the succeeding inquiring authority is of the opinion that further examination of any of the witnesses whose evidence has already been recorded is necessary in the interests of justice, it may recall, examine, cross-examine and re-examine any such witnesses as hereinbefore provided.

(25) (*i*) After the conclusion of the inquiry, a report shall be prepared and it shall contain—

(*a*) the articles of charge and the statement of the imputations of misconduct or misbehaviour;

(*b*) the defence of the railway servant in respect of each article of charge;

(*c*) an assessment of the evidence in respect of each article of charge; and

(*d*) the findings on each article of charge and the reasons therefor.

Explanation. If in the opinion of the inquiring authority the proceedings of the inquiry establish any article of charge different from the original articles of charge, it may record its findings on such article of charge:

Provided that the findings on such article of charge shall not be recorded unless the railway servant has, either admitted the facts on which such article of charge, is based, or has had a reasonable opportunity of defending himself against such article of charge.

(*ii*) The inquiring authority, where it is not itself the disciplinary authority, shall forward to the disciplinary authority the records of inquiry which shall include—

(*a*) the report prepared by it under clause (*i*);

(*b*) the written statement of defence if any, submitted by the railway servant;

(*c*) the oral and documentary evidence produced in the course of the inquiry;

(*d*) written briefs, if any, filed by the Presenting Officer, if any, or the railway servant or both during the course of the inquiry; and

(*e*) the orders, if any, made by the disciplinary authority and the inquiring authority in regard to the inquiry.

Departmental enquiry Though assumption can be drawn that paras 704 and 705 of the Railway Vigilence Manual being execution instructions do not create any legal right, yet it should be emphasized that total violation of guidelines together with other factors should be taken into consideration whether the Department has been able to prove the charges against the delinquent official. Where on evidence the doctrine of proportionality has not been satisfied, the Tribunal was within its domain to interfere. Doctrine of unreasonableness gives way to the doctrine proportionality. On certain aspects even judicial review of facts is permissible. The examination-in-chief was conducted by the enquiry officer himself. Why the presenting officer did not examine the witness is beyond comprehension. The questions asked do not comply with rule 9(21) of the Railway Servants (Discipline and Appeal) Rules, 1968.[1]

1 *Moni Shankar* v *Union of India* (2008)3 SCC 484.

Railway Establishment Code—Disciplinary Proceedings In a disciplinary proceeding charge was framed on the basis of raid conducted by Vigilence Department. In such proceeding it has been held that the Chief Vigilence Officer cannot be appointed as Inquiry Officer. Railway Establishment Code (Vol. I, Chapter 5, Para 3) provides the procedure for examination of witness. When the delinquent makes an application for examination of witnesses and for summoning a witness, the Inquiry Officer ought to consider such prayer of the delinquent. Refusal of such prayer by the Inquiry Officer amounts to unfairness in conducting the inquiry.[2]

10. Action on the inquiry report. (1) If the disciplinary authority—

(*a*) after considering the inquiry report, is of the opinion that further examination of any of the witnesses is necessary in the interests of justice, it may recall the said witness and examine, cross-examine and re-examine the witness;

(*b*) is not itself the inquiring authority may, for reasons to be recorded by it in writing, remit the case to the inquiring authority for further inquiry and report and the inquiring authority shall thereupon proceed to hold further inquiry according to the provisions of rule 9, as far as may be.

(2) The disciplinary authority—

(*a*) shall forward or cause to be forwarded a copy of the report of the inquiry, if any, held by the disciplinary authority or where the disciplinary authority is not the inquiring authority a copy of the report of the inquiring authority, its findings on further examination of witnesses, if any, held under sub-rule (1) (*a*) together with its own tentative reasons for disagreement, if any, with findings of the inquiring authority on any article of charge to the Railway Servant, who shall be required to submit, if he so desires, his written representation or submission to the disciplinary authority within fifteen days, irrespective of whether the report is favourable or not to the Railway Servant;

(*b*) shall consider the representation if any, submitted by the Railway Servant and record its findings before proceeding further in the matter as specified in sub-rules (3), (4) and (5).

(3) Where the disciplinary authority is of the opinion that the penalty warranted is such as is not within its competence, he shall forward the records of the inquiry to the appropriate disciplinary authority who shall act in the matter as provided in these rules.

(4) If the disciplinary authority having regard to its findings on all or any of the articles of charge, is of the opinion that any of the penalties specified in clauses (*i*) to (*iv*) of rule 6 should be imposed on the railway servant, it shall, notwithstanding anything contained in rule 11, make an order imposing such penalty:

Provided that in every case where it is necessary to consult the Commission, the record of the inquiry shall be forwarded by the disciplinary authority to the

2 *Union of India* v *Prakash Kumar Tandon* AIR 2009 SC 1375 relying on *M.V. Bijlani* v *Union of India* (2006)5 SCC 88; *S.L. Kapoor* v *Jagmohan* AIR 1981 SC 136.

Commission for its advice and such advice shall be taken into consideration before making any order imposing any penalty on the Railway Servant.

(5) If the disciplinary authority, having regard to its findings on all or any of the articles of charge and on the basis of the evidence adduced during the inquiry, is of the opinion that any of the penalties specified in clauses (*v*) to (*ix*) of rule 6 should be imposed on the railway servant, it shall make an order imposing such penalty and it shall not be necessary to give the railway servant any opportunity of making representation on the penalty proposed to be imposed:

Provided that in every case where it is necessary to consult the Commission, the record of the inquiry shall be forwarded by the disciplinary authority to the Commission for its advice and such advice shall be taken into consideration before making an order imposing any such penalty on the railway servant.

Departmental enquiry report Where the enquiry officer has, in his report, proceeded on surmises and conjectures, the disciplinary authority can disagree with the said finding, but it is required to record its reasons. Sub-rules (2) and (3) of rule 10 of the Railway Servants (Discipline and Appeal) Rules 1968 aim at achieving the same purpose. If sufficient materials are not available on record, a direction for holding a further enquiry may be issued in terms of sub-rule (2) of rule 10 so as to enable the department to lead further evidence before him. But for the order reasons are required to be recorded by the Disciplinary Authority. An opportunity of hearing to the delinquent railway servant is to be given. In the event the disciplinary authority comes to the conclusion that the inquiry officer has come to the conclusion on the basis of materials on record, he may disagree with the enquiry officer, but still then he is required to record reasons in terms of sub-rules (2) and (3) of rule 10 of the aforesaid Rules.[3]

11. Procedure for imposing minor penalties. (1) Subject to the provisions of sub-clause (*iv*) of clause (*a*) of sub-rule (9) of rule 9 and of sub-rule (4) of rule 10, no order imposing on a railway servant any of the penalties specified in clauses (*i*) to (*iv*) of rule 6 shall be made except after—

(*a*) informing the railway servant in writing of the proposal to take action against him and of the imputations of misconduct or misbehaviour on which it is proposed to be taken, and giving him a reasonable opportunity of making such representation as he may wish to make against the proposal;

(*b*) holding an inquiry in the manner laid down in sub-rules (6) to (25) of rule 9, in every case in which the disciplinary authority is of the opinion that such inquiry is necessary;

(*c*) taking the representation, if any, submitted by the railway servant under clause (*a*) and the record of inquiry, if any, held under clause (*b*) into consideration;

(*d*) recording a finding on each imputation of misconduct or misbehaviour; and

(*e*) consulting the Commission where such consultation is necessary.

3 *Mathura Prasad* v *Union of India* (2007)1 SCC 437.

(2) Notwithstanding anything contained in clause (*b*) of sub-rule (1), if in a case, it is proposed, after considering the representation, if any, made by the railway servant under clause (*a*) of that sub-rule to withhold increments of pay and such withholding of increments is likely to effect adversely the amount of pension or SC to PF payable to the railway servant or to withhold increments of pay for a period exceeding three years or to withhold increments of pay with cumulative effect for any period, an inquiry shall be held in the manner laid down in sub-rules (6) to (25) of rule 9, before making any order imposing on railway servant any such penalty.

(3) Deleted.

(4) The record of the proceedings in cases specified in sub-rules (1) and (2) shall include—

(*i*) a copy of the intimation to the railway servant for the proposal to take action against him;

(*ii*) a copy of the statement of imputations of misconduct or misbehaviour delivered to him;

(*iii*) his representation, if any;

(*iv*) the evidence produced during the inquiry, if any;

(*v*) the advice of the Commission, if any;

(*vi*) the findings on each imputation of misconduct or misbehaviour; and

(*vii*) the orders on the case together with the reasons therefor.

12. Communication of Orders. Orders made by the disciplinary authority shall be communicated to the railway servant who shall also be supplied with a copy of the report of the inquiry, if any, held by the disciplinary authority and a copy of its findings on each article of charge, or, where the disciplinary authority is not the inquiring authority, a copy of the report of the inquiring authority and a statement of the findings of the disciplinary authority together with brief reasons for its disagreement, if any, with findings of the inquiring authority (unless they have already been supplied to him) and also a copy of the advice, if any, given by the Commission and, where the disciplinary authority has not accepted the advice of Commission a brief statement of the reasons for such non-acceptance.

Dismissal for misappropriation of money In *M.L. Khalsa* v *Union of India*[4] the appellant misappropriated money by making false claim for honorarium payable to another employee. Charge against him was proved is enquiry proceedings under rules 12 and 10(3) of the Railway Servants (Discipline and Appeal) Rules 1968 affording all reasonable opportunities to him. It was held that the order of dismissal was proper. But the Supreme Court considering the lapse of time and long period of service rendered by the appellant, the order of reinstatement in service withholding two increments with cumulative effect and with consequential loss of seniority but without break in service for the purpose of pension was passed.

13. Common Proceedings. (1) Where two or more railway servants are concerned in any case, the President or any other authority competent to impose the penalty of dismissal from service on all such railway servants, may make an order directing that disciplinary action against all of them may be taken in a common proceedings.

4 1988 (Supp) SCC 436.

Note. If the authorities competent to impose the penalty of dismissal on such railway servants are different, an order for taking disciplinary action in a common proceeding may be made by the highest of such authorities with the consent of the others.

(2) Any such order shall specify—

(*i*) the authority which may function as the disciplinary authority for the purpose of such common proceedings;

(*ii*) the penalties specified in rule 6 which such disciplinary authority shall be competent to impose; provided that such authority shall not impose the penalties specified in clauses (*vii*) to (*ix*) of that rule if that authority is subordinate to the Appointing Authority; and

(*iii*) whether the procedure laid down in rule 9 and rule 10 or rule 11 shall be followed in the proceedings.

14. Special procedure in certain cases. Notwithstanding anything contained in rules 9 to 13—

(*i*) where any penalty is imposed on a railway servant on the ground of conduct which has led to his conviction on a criminal charge; or

(*ii*) where the disciplinary authority is satisfied, for reasons to be recorded by it in writing, that it is not reasonably practicable to hold an inquiry in the manner provided in these rules; or

(*iii*) where the President is satisfied that in the interest of the security of the State, it is not expedient to hold an inquiry in the manner provided in these rules;

the disciplinary authority may consider the circumstances of the case and make such orders thereon as it deems fit:

Provided that the railway servant may be given an opportunity of making representation on the penalty proposed to be imposed before any order is made in a case falling under clause (*i*) above:

Provided further that the Commission shall be consulted, where such consultation is necessary, before any orders are made in any case under this rule.

15. Provisions regarding railway servants lent to State Governments, etc. (1) Where the services of a railway servant are lent to any other Ministry or Department of the Central Government or to a State Government or an authority subordinate thereto or to a local or other authority (hereinafter in this rule referred to as "the borrowing authority") the borrowing authority shall have the powers of the authority competent to place the railway servant under suspension for the purpose of placing him under suspension and of the disciplinary authority for the purpose of conducting a disciplinary proceedings against him:

Provided that the borrowing authority shall forthwith inform the authority which lent the services of the railway servant (hereinafter in this rule referred to as "the lending authority") of the circumstances leading to the order of his suspension or the commencement of the disciplinary proceedings, as the case may be.

(2) In the light of the findings in the disciplinary proceedings conducted against the railway servant—

(*i*) if the borrowing authority is of the opinion that any of the penalties specified in clauses (*i*) to (*iv*) of rule 6 should be imposed on the railway servant, it may, after consultation with the lending authority, make such orders on the case as it deems necessary:

Provided that in the event of a difference of opinion between the borrowing authority and the lending authority, the services of the railway servant shall be replaced at the disposal of the lending authority;

(*ii*) if the borrowing authority is of the opinion that any of the penalties specified in clauses (*v*) to (*ix*) of rule 6 should be imposed on the railway servant, it shall replace his services at the disposal of the lending authority and transmit to it the proceedings of the inquiry and thereupon the lending authority may, if it is the disciplinary authority, pass such orders thereon as it may deem necessary, or, if it is not the disciplinary authority, submit the case to the disciplinary authority which shall pass such orders on the case as it may deem necessary:

Provided that before passing such orders, the disciplinary authority shall comply with the provisions of sub-rule (4) of rule 10.

Explanation. The disciplinary authority may make an order under this clause on the record of the inquiry transmitted to it by the borrowing authority, or after holding such further inquiry as it may deem necessary, as far as may be, in accordance with rule 9.

16. Provisions regarding officers borrowed from Central or State Government etc. (1) Where the services of a Government servant from any Ministry or Department of the Central Government other than the Ministry of Railways, or a State Government, or an authority subordinate thereto, or of a person from a local or other authority (hereinafter in this rule referred to as "the lending authority") are borrowed for appointment to a service or post under the Ministry of Railways, the authority which appointed him to that service or post (hereinafter in this rule referred to as "the borrowing authority") shall have the powers of the lending authority for the purpose of placing such Government servant or person under suspension or for conducting disciplinary proceedings against him:

Provided that where an order suspending such Government servant or person is made or a disciplinary proceeding is conducted against such Government servant or person, the borrowing authority shall forthwith inform the lending authority of the circumstances leading to the order of suspension or, as the case may be, the commencement of the disciplinary proceedings against such Government servant or person.

(2) In the light of the findings in the disciplinary proceeding conducted against such Government servant or person—

(*i*) if the borrowing authority is of the opinion that any of the minor penalties specified in the rules by which such Government servant or person is governed, should be imposed on him, it may, after consultation with the lending authority, pass such orders on the case as it deems necessary, in accordance with the said rules:

Provided that in the event of a difference of opinion between the borrowing authority and the lending authority, the services of such

Government servant or person shall be replaced at the disposal of the lending authority;

(*ii*) if the borrowing authority is of the opinion that any of the major penalties specified in the rules by which such Government servant or person is governed, should be imposed on him, it shall replace his services at the disposal of the lending authority and transmit to it the proceedings of the inquiry and thereupon the lending authority may pass such orders thereon as it may deem necessary.

PART V
APPEALS

17. Orders against which no appeal lies. Notwithstanding anything contained in this part, no appeal shall lie against—

(*i*) any order made by the President;

(*ii*) any order of an interlocutory nature or of the nature of step-in-aid of the final disposal of a disciplinary proceedings other than an order of suspension;

(*iii*) any order passed by an inquiring authority in the course of an inquiry under rule 9.

18. Orders against which appeal lies. Subject to the provisions of rule 17, a railway servant may prefer an appeal against all or any of the following orders, namely—

(*i*) an order of suspension made or deemed to have been made under rule 5;

(*ii*) an order imposing any of the penalties specified in rule 6 whether made by the disciplinary authority or by an appellate or revising authority;

(*iii*) an order enhancing any penalty imposed under rule 6;

(*iv*) an order which—

(*a*) denies or varies to his disadvantage his pay, allowances, pension. Provident Fund benefits, service gratuity or other conditions of service as regulated by rules or by agreement; or

(*b*) interprets to his disadvantage the provisions of any such rule or agreement;

(*v*) an order—

(*a*) stopping him at the efficiency bar in the time-scale of pay on the ground of his unfitness to cross the bar;

(*b*) reverting him while officiating in a higher service, grade or post to a lower service, grade or post, otherwise than as a penalty;

(*c*) reducing or withholding the pension or denying the maximum pension admissible to him under the rules, if he is a pensionable railway servant;

(*d*) reducing or withholding the Government Contribution to Provident Fund and Special Contribution to Provident Fund or Gratuity admissible to him under the State Railway Provident Fund Rules and Gratuity Rules, if he is a non-pensionable railway servant;

(*e*) determining the subsistence and other allowances to be paid to him for the period of suspension or for the period during which he is deemed to be under suspension or for any portion thereof;

(*f*) determining his pay and allowances—

(*i*) for the period of suspension; or

(*ii*) for the period from the date of his dismissal, removal or compulsory retirement from service to the date of his reinstatement;

(*g*) determining whether or not the period from the date of his suspension or from the date of his dismissal, removal or compulsory retirement to the date of his reinstatement shall be treated as a period spent on duty for any purpose.

Explanation. In this rule—

(*i*) the expression 'railway servant' includes a person who has ceased to be in railway service;

(*ii*) the expression 'pension' includes additional pension gratuity and any other retirement benefit.

19. Appellate Authorities. (1) A railway servant, including a person who has ceased to be in railway service, may prefer an appeal against all or any of the orders specified in rule 18 to the authority specified in this behalf either in the Schedules or, where no such authority is specified—

(*i*) where a penalty is imposed by a revising authority under rule 25, to the authority to which it is immediately subordinate;

(*ii*) where a penalty is enhanced, either in appeal or on revision, to the authority to which the authority making the order is immediately subordinate;

(*iii*) in the case of an appeal against an order specified in clause (*iv*) of rule 18, relating to a rule, to the authority which appointed the appellant or the authority which made the rule to which the order under appeal relates, whichever of them may be the higher authority, and in the case of an appeal relating to an agreement, to the authority which appointed the appellant;

(*iv*) in the case of an appeal against an order specified in clause (*v*) of rule 18—

(*a*) in respect of a railway servant on whom the penalty of dismissal from service can be imposed only by the President, to the President; and

(*b*) in respect of any other railway servant, to the authority to which the authority making the order is immediately subordinate.

(2) Notwithstanding anything contained in sub-rule (1)—

(*i*) an appeal against an order in a common proceeding held under rule 13, shall lie to the authority to which the authority functioning as the disciplinary authority for the purpose of that proceeding, is immediately subordinate;

(*ii*) where the person who made the order appealed against becomes, by virtue of his subsequent appointment or otherwise, the appellate authority in respect of such order, an appeal against such order shall lie to the authority to which such person is immediately subordinate:

Provided that in a case where the appellate authority is the Railway Board, the appeal shall be dealt with by any Member of the Railway Board, who has not made the order appealed against.

(3) A railway servant may prefer an appeal against an order imposing any of the penalties specified in rule 6 to the President, where no such appeal lies to him under sub-rule (1) or sub-rule (2), if such penalty is imposed by any authority other than the President, on such railway servant in respect of his activities connected with his work as an office bearer of an association, federation or union participating in the Joint Consultation and Compulsory Arbitration Scheme.

20. Period of limitation for appeals. No appeal preferred under this part, shall be entertained unless such appeal is preferred within a period of forty-five days from the date on which a copy of the order appealed against, is delivered to the appellant:

Provided that the appellate authority may entertain the appeal, after the expiry of the said period, if it is satisfied that the appellant had sufficient cause for not preferring the appeal in time.

21. Form and contents and submission of appeal. (1) Every person preferring an appeal shall do so separately and in his own name. An appeal forwarded through or countersigned by a legal practitioner or an assisting railway servant or a Railway Trade Union Official shall not be entertained but shall be returned with the direction to submit it under the signature of the appellant only.

(2) The appeal shall be presented to the authority to whom the appeal lies, a copy being forwarded by the appellant to the authority which made the order appealed against. It shall contain all material statements and arguments on which the appellant relies, shall not contain any disrespectful or improper language, and shall be complete in itself.

(3) The authority which made the order appealed against, shall, on receipt of a copy of the appeal, forward the same with its comments thereon together with the relevant records to the appellate authority without any avoidable delay and without waiting for any direction from the appellate authority.

22. Consideration of appeal. (1) In the case of an appeal against an order of suspension, the appellate authority shall consider whether in the light of the provisions of rule 5 and having regard to the circumstances of the case, the order of suspension is justified or not and confirm or revoke the order accordingly.

(2) In the case of an appeal against an order imposing any of the penalties specified in rule 6 or enhancing any penalty imposed under the said rule, the appellate authority shall consider—

(*a*) whether the procedure laid down in these rules has been complied with, and if not, whether such non-compliance has resulted in the violation of any provisions of the Constitution of India or in the failure of justice;

(*b*) whether the findings of the disciplinary authority are warranted by the evidence on the record; and (*c*) whether the penalty or the enhanced penalty imposed is adequate, inadequate or severe; and pass order—

(*i*) confirming, enhancing, reducing or setting aside the penalty; or

(*ii*) remitting the case to the authority which imposed or enhanced the penalty or to any other authority with such directions as it may deem fit in the circumstances of the case:

Provided that—

(*i*) the Commission shall be consulted in all cases where such consultation is necessary;

(*ii*) if the enhanced penalty which the appellate authority proposes to impose is one of the penalties specified in clauses (*v*) to *(ix)* of rule 6 and an inquiry under rule 9 has not already been held in the case, the appellate authority shall, subject to the provisions of rule 14, itself hold such inquiry or direct that such inquiry be held in accordance with the provisions of rule 9 and thereafter, on a consideration of the proceedings of such inquiry pass such orders as it may deem fit;

(*iii*) if the enhanced penalty which the appellate authority proposes to impose is one of the penalties specified in clauses (*v*) to (*ix*) of sub-rule (1) of rule 6 and an inquiry under rule 9 has already been held in the case, the appellate authority shall, make such orders as it may deem fit; and

(*iv*) subject to the provisions of rule 14, the appellate authority shall—

(*a*) where the enhanced penalty which the appellate authority proposes to impose, is the one specified in clause (*iv*) of rule 6 and falls within the scope of the provisions contained in sub-rule (2) of rule 11; and

(*b*) where an inquiry in the manner laid down in rule 9, has not already been held in the case, itself hold such inquiry or direct that such inquiry be held in accordance with the provisions of rule 9 and thereafter, on a consideration of the proceedings of such inquiry, pass such orders as it may deem fit; and

(*v*) no order imposing an enhanced penalty shall be made in any other case unless the appellant has been given a reasonable opportunity, as far as may be, in accordance with the provisions of rule 11 of making a representation against such enhanced penalty.

(3) In appeal against any other order specified in rule 18, the appellate authority shall consider all the circumstances of the case and make such orders as it may deem just and equitable.

23. Implementation of orders in appeal. The authority which made the order appealed against, shall give effect to the orders passed by the appellate authority.

24. Special provisions for non-gazetted staff. (1) Where the penalty of dismissal, removal, compulsory retirement, reduction or withholding of increment has been imposed, appellate authority may, at its discretion and if it considers it necessary, give the non-gazetted railway servant a personal hearing before disposing of the appeal. At this personal hearing the railway servant may be accompanied, if he so chooses, by another railway servant employed on the same railway administration; office of the Railway Board, its attached office or subordinate office, as the case may be, in which the appellant was or is working or an official (who is not a legal practitioner) of a Railway Trade Union recognised by the Railway Administration on which the appellant was or is employed.

(2) A Group 'C' Railway servant who has been dismissed, removed or compulsorily retired from service may, after his appeal to the appropriate appellate authority has been disposed of, and within 45 days thereafter, apply to the General Manager for a revision of the penalty imposed on him. In this application, he may, if he so chooses, request the General Manager to refer the case to the Railway Rates Tribunal for advice before the disposes of the revision petition. On receipt of such a request, the General Manager shall refer the case to the Chairman, Railway Rates Tribunal for advice sending all the relevant papers.

On receipt of the revision application by the General Manager, or on receipt of advice from the Railway Rates Tribunal, as the case may be, the General Manager shall dispose of the application in accordance with the procedure laid down in rule 25 and pass such orders as he may think fit:

Provided that the procedure mentioned in this sub-rule shall not apply in cases where the General Manager or the Railway Board are the Appellate Authority:

Provided further that where a revision application has been disposed of by the General Manager under this sub-rule, no further revision shall lie under rule 25.

(3) A Group 'D' Railway servant, who has been dismissed, removed or compulsorily retired from service may, after his appeal to the appropriate appellate authority has been disposed of and within 45 days thereafter, apply to the Divisional Railway Manager and where he is not under the control of any Divisional Railway Manager to the senior-most Administrative Grade Officer under whose control he may be working, for a revision of the penalty imposed on him. The Divisional Railway Manager or the senior-most Administrative Grade Officer, as the case may be, shall thereafter dispose of the revision application in accordance with the procedure laid down in rule 25 and pass such orders as he may think fit:

Provided that the procedure mentioned in this sub-rule shall not apply where the Divisional Railway Manager or the senior-most Administrative Grade Officer or any higher authority, as the case may be, is the appellate authority:

Provided further that where a revision application has been disposed of by the Divisional Railway Manager or the senior-most Administrative Grade Officer under this sub-rule, no further revision shall lie under rule 25.

PART VI
REVISION & REVIEW

25. Revision. (1) Notwithstanding anything contained in these rules,—

(*i*) the President, or

(*ii*) the Railway Board, or

(*iii*) the General Manager of a Railway Administration or an authority of that status in the case of a railway servant serving under his control, or

(*iv*) the appellate authority not below the rank of a Deputy Head of Department or a Divisional Railway Manager in cases where no appeal has been preferred, or

(*v*) any other authority not below the rank of a Deputy Head of Department in the case of a Railway Servant serving under his control—

may at any time, either on his or its own motion or otherwise, call for the records of any inquiry and revise any order made under these rules or under the rules repealed by rule 29, after consultation with the Commission, where such consultation is necessary, and may—

(*a*) confirm, modify or set aside the order; or

(*b*) confirm, reduce, enhance or set aside penalty imposed by the order, or impose any penalty where no penalty has been imposed; or

(*c*) remit the case to the authority which made the order or to any other authority directing such authority to make such further inquiry as it may consider proper in the circumstances of the case; or

(*d*) pass such other orders as it may deem fit:

Provided that—

(*a*) no order imposing or enhancing any penalty shall be made by made be any revising authority unless the railway servant concerned has been given a reasonable opportunity of making a representation against the penalty proposed;

(*b*) subject to the provisions of rule 14, where it is proposed to impose any of the penalties specific in clauses (*v*) to (*ix*) of rule 6 or the penalty specified in clause (*iv*) of rule 6 which falls within the scope of the provisions contained in sub-rule (2) of rule 11 or to enhance the penalty imposed by the order under revision to any of the penalties specified in this sub-clause, no such penalty shall be imposed except after following the procedure for inquiry in the manner laid down in rule 9, unless such inquiry has already been held, and also except after consultation with the Commission, where such consultation is necessary.

(2) No proceeding for revision shall be commenced until after—

(*i*) the expiry of period of limitation for an appeal; or

(*ii*) the disposal of the appeal, where any such appeal has been preferred:

Provided that the provisions of this sub-rule shall not apply to the revision of punishment in case of railway accidents.

(3) An application for revision shall be dealt with in the same manner as if it were an appeal under these rules.

(4) No power of revision shall be exercised under this rule—

(*i*) by the appellate or revising authority where it has already considered the appeal or the case and passed orders thereon; and (*ii*) by a revising authority unless it is higher than the appellate authority where an appeal has been preferred or where no appeal has been preferred and the time limit laid down for revision by the appellate authority, has expired:

Provided that nothing contained in clauses (*i*) and (*ii*) above, shall apply to revision by the President.

(5) No action under this rule shall be initiated by—

(*a*) an appellate authority other than the President; or

(*b*) the revising authorities mentioned in item (*v*) of sub-rule (1)—

after more than six months from the date of the order to be revised in cases where it is proposed to impose or enhance a penalty or modify the order to the detriment of the Railway servant; or more than one year after the date of the order to be revised in cases where it is proposed to reduce or cancel the penalty imposed or modify the order in favour of the Railway servant:

Provided that when revision is undertaken by the Railway Board or the General Manager of a Zonal Railway or an authority of the status of a General Manager in any other Railway Unit or Administration when they are higher than the appellate Authority, and by the President even when he is the appellate authority, this can be done without restriction of any time limit.

Explanation. For the purposes of this sub-rule the time limits for revision of cases shall be reckoned from the date of issue of the orders proposed to be revised. In cases where original order has been upheld by the appellate authority, the time limit shall be reckoned from the date of issue of the appellate orders.

25-A. Review. The President may at any time either on his own motion or otherwise review any order passed under these rules when any new material or evidence which could not be produced or was not available at the time of passing the order under review and which has the effect of changing the nature of the case has come or has been brought to his notice:

Provided that no order imposing or enhancing any penalty shall be made by the President unless the railway servant concerned has been given a reasonable opportunity of making a representation against the penalty proposed or where it is proposed to impose any of the major penalties specified in rule 6 or to enhance the minor penalty imposed by the order sought to be reviewed to any of the major penalties and if an enquiry under rule 9 has not already been held in the case, no such penalty shall be imposed except after inquiring in the manner laid down in rule 9, subject to the provisions of rule 14 and except after consultation with the Commission where such consultation is necessary.

PART VII

MISCELLANEOUS

26. Service of orders, notices etc. Every order, notice and other process made or issued under these rules, shall be served in person on the railway servant concerned or communicated to him by registered post.

26-A. Service of orders, notices etc. on behalf of the Railway Board or President. Any of the following officers in the Ministry of Railways shall be competent to sign on behalf of the Railway Board or President any notice, process, order, etc. made or issued under these rules:

(*i*) Secretary, Railway Board/Joint Secretary/Deputy Secretary.

(*ii*) Executive Director/Director/Joint Director.

27. Power to relax time limit and to condone delay. Save as otherwise expressly provided in these rules, the authority competent under these rules to make any order may, for good and sufficient reasons or if sufficient cause is shown, extend the time specified in these rules for anything required to be done under these rules or condone any delay.

28. Supply of copy of Commission's advice. Whenever the Commission is consulted as provided in these rules, a copy of the advice by the Commission and, where such advice has not been accepted, also a brief statement of the reasons for such non-acceptance, shall be furnished to the railway servant concerned along with a copy of the order passed in the case, by the authority making the order.

29. Repeal and saving. (1) The Discipline and Appeal Rules for Railway Servants, other than those employed in the Railway Protection Force, in force with effect from the 1st August, 1961 and any orders issued thereunder in so far as they are inconsistent with these rules are hereby repealed:

Provided that—

(*a*) such repeal shall not affect the previous operation of the said rules, or any order made, or anything done, or any action taken, thereunder; and

(*b*) any proceedings under the said rules, pending at the commencement of these rules, shall be continued and disposed of, as far as may be, in accordance with the provisions of these rules, as if such proceedings were proceedings under these rules;

(2) Nothing in these rules shall be construed as depriving any person to whom these rules apply, of any right of appeal which had accrued to him under the rules or orders in force before the commencement of these rules.

(3) An appeal pending at the commencement of these rules against an order made before such commencement, shall be considered and orders thereon shall be made, in accordance with these rules, as if such orders were made and the appeal were preferred under these rules.

(4) As from the commencement of these rules, any appeal or application for revision and/or review against any orders made before such commencement, shall be preferred or made under these rules, as if such orders were made under these rules:

Provided that nothing in these rules shall be construed as reducing any period of limitation for any appeal or revision and/or review provided by any rule in force before the commencement of these rules.

30. Removal of doubts. If any doubt arises as to the interpretation of any of the provisions of these rules, the matter shall be referred to the President through the Railway Board, and the President shall decide the same.

31. Right to submit petitions to the President. Nothing in these rules shall operate to deprive a railway servant from exercising his right of submitting a petition to the President in accordance with the instructions contained in Appendix II to the Indian Railway Establishment Code, Volume I.

32. Power of the General Manager to frame subsidiary rules. The General Manager may, in respect of non-gazetted Railway servant under his administrative control, make subsidiary rules not inconsistent with these rules or any rules made by the Railway Board for the purpose of giving effect to the provisions of these rules in so far as it is applicable to such railway servant.

SCHEDULE I

[*See* rule 4 and sub-rule (2) of rule 7]

Sl. No.	*Authority empowered to place a railway servant under suspension or to impose penalties*	*Class of Railway Servants over whom disciplinary powers can be exercised*	*Nature of penalties mentioned in rule 6 which the authorities specified in Column 2 are empowered to impose on Railway Servants mentioned in corresponding entries in Column 3 and powers of that authority to place them under suspension*	*Appellate Authority*
1	2	3	4	5

RAILWAY BOARD'S OFFICE

1	2	3	4	5
1	Secretary, Railway Board	All classes of non-gazetted railway servants including Group 'B' non-gazetted Ministerial Staff.	All penalties and suspension.	Railway Board
2	Joint Secretary, Railway Board	All classes of non-gazetted Railway servants including Group 'B' non-gazetted Ministerial Staff appointed up to 30th June, 1988.	Penalties specified in clauses (*i*) to (*vi*) and suspension.	Secretary, Railway Board
3	Joint Secretary, Railway Board	All classes of non-gazetted Railway servants including Group 'B' non-gazetted Ministerial Staff appointed on or after 1st July, 1988.	All penalties and suspension.	Secretary, Railway Board

1	2	3	4	5
4	Under Secretary, Railway Board	Staff with Grade Pay of up to and including ₹1650 appointed up to 30th June, 1988.	Penalties specified in clauses (*i*) to (*iv*) and suspension.	Joint Secretary, Railway Board.
5	Under Secretary Railway Board	Staff with Grade Pay of up to and including ₹1650 appointed on or after 1st July, 1988.	All Penalties and suspension.	Joint Secretary, Railway Board.

RESEARCH, DESIGNS AND STANDARDS ORGANISATION

1	2	3	4	5
1	Juniar Administrative Grade/ Selection Grade Officers or Senior Administrative Grade Officers or Higher Administrative Grade Officers or Additional Director General or Director General.	All classes of non-gazetted Railway Servants including Group 'B' non-Gazetted staff.	All penalties and suspension.	Next higher authority to whom the authority in column 2 is immediately subordinate.
2	Deputy Director and other Officers in Senior Scale or equivalent.	All staff with Grade Pay of up to and including ₹2800.	Penalties specified in clauses (*i*) to (*vi*) and suspension.	Next higher authority to whom the authority in column 2 is immediately subordinate.
3	Junior Scale or Group 'B' Officers (Gazetted)	All staff with Grade Pay of up to and including ₹1650.	Penalties specified in clauses (*i*) to (*vi*) and suspension.	Next higher authority to whom the authority in column 2 is immediately subordinate.
4	Junior Scale or Group 'B' Officers (Gazetted).	All staff with Grade Pay of up to and including ₹2400.	Penalties specified in clauses (*i*) to (*v*) and suspension.	Next higher authority to whom the authority in column 2 is immediately subordinate.

1	2	3	4	5
5	Senior Supervisors with Grade Pay of ₹4200 and above.	All staff with Grade pay of up to and including ₹2000.	Penalties specified in clauses (*i*), (*iii*), (*iii-a*) and (*iv*) (no such power can be exercised where inquiry under sub-rule (2) of rule 11 is required) and also suspension subject to report to Junior Scale or Group 'B' (Gazetted) Officer of the Respective branch within twenty four hours in the case of Group 'C' staff.	Next higher authority to whom the authority in column 2 is immediately subordinate.

RAILWAY STAFF COLLEGE, VADODARA

1	2	3	4	5
1	Director General, Higher Administrative Grade Officers, Senior Administrative Grade Officers, Junior Administrative Grade Officers	All classes of non-gazetted Railway Servants.	Full powers in respect of non-gazetted staff placed under their control (except that only Appointing Authority or above will impose penalties under clauses (*vii*), (*viii*) and (*ix*).)	Next higher authority to whom the authority in column 2 is immediately subordinate.
2	Senior Scale Officers	All classes of non-gazetted Railway Servants— (*a*) with Grade Pay of up to and including ₹2400. (*b*) for whom the officer concerned is the appointing authority.	(*a*) Panalties specified in clauses (*i*) to (*iv*) and suspension. (*b*) Penalties specified in clauses (*vii*) to (*ix*).	Next higher authority to whom the authority in column 2 is immediately subordinate.

1	2	3	4	5
3	Officers in Junior Scale or in Group 'B' (Gazetted)	All classes of non-gazetted Railway Servants— (a) with Grade Pay of up to and including ₹2000.	 (*a*) Penalties specified in clauses (*i*) to (*iv*) and suspension.	Next higher authority to whom the authority in column 2 is immediately subordinate.
		(*b*) for whom the Officer concerned is the appointing authority.	(*b*) Penalties specified in clauses (*vii*) to (*ix*).	

INDIAN RAILWAY'S INSTITUTE OF CIVIL ENGINEERING, PUNE INDIAN RAILWAYS' INSTITUTE OF ELECTRICAL ENGINEERING, NASIK, INDIAN RAILWAYS' INSTITUTE OF MECHANICAL & ELECTRICAL ENGINEERING, JAMALPUR, INDIAN RAILWAYS' INSTITUTE OF SIGNAL ENGINEERING AND TELECOMMUNICATION, SECUNDERABAD

1	2	3	4	5
1	Director, Senior Administrative Grade Officers (Other than Director), Junior Administrative Grade Officers.	All classes of non-gazetted Railway Servants.	Full powers in respect of non-gazetted staff placed under their control (except that only Appointing Authority or above will impose penalties under clauses (*vii*), (*viii*) and (*ix*)).	Next higher authority to whom the authority in column 2 is immediately subordinate.
2	Senior Scale Officers	All classes of non-gazetted Railway Servants— (*a*) with Grade Pay of up to and including ₹2400.	 (*a*) Penalties specified in clauses (*i*) to (*iv*) and suspension.	Next higher authority to whom the authority in column 2 is immediately subordinate.
		(*b*) for whom the officer concerned is the appointing authority.	(*b*) Penalties specified in clauses (*vii*) to (*ix*).	

1	2	3	4	5
3	Officers in Junior Scale or in Group 'B' (Gazetted).	All classes of non-gazetted Railway Servants— (*a*) with Grade Pay of up to and including ₹2000. (*b*) for whom Officer concerned is the appointing authority.	 (*a*) Penalties specified in clauses (*i*) to (*iv*) and suspension. (*b*) Penalties specified in clauses (*vii*) to (*ix*).	Next higher authority to whom the authority in column 2 is immediately subordinate.

RAILWAY RECRUITMENT BOARDS

1	2	3	4	5
1	Chairman	All classes of non-gazetted Railway Servants	All penalties and suspension	Railway Board

RAILWAY RATES TRIBUNAL

1	2	3	4	5
1	Chairman	All classes of non-gazetted Railway Servants	All penalties and suspension	Railway Board
2	Secretary	All classes of non-gazetted Railway Servants	Penalties specified in clauses (*i*) to (*iv*) and suspension	Chairman, Railway Rates Tribunal

RAILWAY LIAISON OFFICE

1	2	3	4	5
1	Joint Secretary, Railway Board	All classes of non-gazetted Railway Servants	All penalties and suspension	Railway Board

ALL OTHER OFFICES (NOT SHOWN ABOVE)

1	2	3	4	5
1	Head of Office	All classes of non-gazetted Railway Servants	All penalties and suspension	Railway Board

Note: (1) The Railway Board may impose any of the penalties specified in rule 6 on all non-gazetted Railway Servants employed in the offices mentioned in this Schedule and place them under suspension.

(2) The penalty of compulsory retirement or removal or dismissal from service shall be imposed only by the Appointing Authority or an authority of equivalent rank or a higher authority.

SCHEDULE II

[*See* rule 4 and sub-rule (2) of rule 7]

Schedule of Disciplinary powers and powers of suspension of different grades of Railway Officers and Senior Supervisors in respect of non-gazetted staff of Zonal Railways, Chittaranjan Locomotive Works, Diesel Locomotive Works, Integral Coach Factory, Rail Wheel Factory, Metro Railway (Kolkata), Diesel Loco Modernisation Works (Patiala), Rail Coach Factory (Kapurthala), Railway Electrification Projects and Metropolitan Transport Projects (Railways).

Sl. No.	*Authority empowered to place a railway servant under suspension or to impose penalties under rule 6*	*Class of Railway Servants over whom disciplinary powers can be exercised*	*Nature of penalties mentioned in rule 6 which the authority in column 2 is empowered to impose on Railway Servants mentioned in corresponding entries in column 3 and powers of that authority to place them under suspension*	*Appellate Authority*
1	2	3	4	5
1	Senior Supervisors incharge with Grade Pay of ₹4200 and above. (Described as Supervisors In-charge by the Railway Administration for this purpose)	All staff who are three grades (Grade Pay) below and lower than the Disciplinary Authority.	Penalties specified in clauses (*i*) to (*iv*) (no such power can be exercised where inquiry under sub-rule (2) of rule 11 is required) and suspension subject to report to Divisional Officer or Assistant Officer Incharge within twenty four hours in the case of Group 'C' staff.	Assistant Officers (Junior Scale and Group 'B') (Gazetted)

1	2	3	4	5
2	Assistant Officers (Junior Scale and Group 'B') (Gazetted)	All staff with Grade Pay of up to and including ₹2400.	Penalties specified in clauses (*i*) to (*v*) and suspension. Also penalty specified in clause (*vi*) on staff with Grade Pay of up to and including ₹1650 only.	Senior Scale Officers and Assistance Officers (Junior Scale and Group 'B' (Gazetted) holding independent charge.
3	Senior Scale Officers and Assistant Officers (Junior Scale and Group 'B' (Gazetted) holding independent charge)	All staff with Grade Pay of up to and including ₹2800.	Penalties specified in clauses (*i*) to (*vi*) and suspension.	Junior Administrative Grade Officers and Senior Scale Officers holding independent Charge or In-charge of a Department in the Division.
4	Junior Administrative Grade Officers and Senior Scale Officers holding independent Charge or In-charge of a Department in the Division	All classes of non-gazetted staff.	Penalties specified in clauses (*i*) to (*vi*) and suspension	Additional Divisional Railway Managers in relation to the Departments attached to them or Divisional Railway Managers.
5	Additional Divisional Railway Managers in relation to the Departments attached to them or Divisional Railway Managers.	All classes of non-gazetted staff.	Penalties specified in clauses (*i*) to (*vi*) and suspension.	Senior Administrative Grade Officers in the Zonal Railways' Head Quarters in Pay Band-4 with Grade Pay ₹10000 including Principal Heads of Departments in Pay Band-4 wih Grade Pay ₹12000.

1	2	3	4	5
6	Senior Administrative Grade Officers in the Zonal Railways' Head Quarters in Pay Band-4 with Grade Pay ₹10000 including Principal Heads of Departments in Pay Band-4 with Grade Pay ₹12000.	All classes of non-gazetted staff.	Penalties specified in clauses (*i*) to (*vi*) and suspension.	Additional General Managers in relation to Departments attached to them or Chief Administrative Officers or General Managers.
7	Additional General Managers in relation to Departments attached to them or Chief Administrative Officers or General Managers.	All classes of non-gazetted staff.	Penalties specified in clauses (*i*) to (*vi*) and suspension.	Railway Board.
8	Railway Board	All classes of non-gazetted staff.	Penalties specified in clauses (*i*) to (*vi*) and suspension	President

Note: (1) An Appointing authority or an authority of equivalent rank or any higher authority shall be competent to impose penalties specified in clauses (*vii*), (*viii*) and (*ix*) of rule 6.

(2) Where the post of appellate authority as shown in column 5 is vacant, then, in that case, the next higher authority shown in the row just below that authority shall be the appellate authority.

(3) The appointing authority or an authority of equivalent rank or any higher authority who is competent to impose the penalty of dismissal or removal or compulsory retirement from service, may also impose any lower penalty.

SCHEDULE III

[*See* rule 4 and sub-rule (2) of rule 7]

Item No.	*Class of Railway Servants*	*Authority empowered to place a Railway Servant under suspension or to impose penalty and its nature*	*Appellate Authority*
1	2	3	4
1.	Railway Servants Group 'A'	President—Full powers.	....
		Railway Board—Suspension and the penalties specified in clauses (*i*) to (*vi*) of rule 6.	President

Item No.	*Class of Railway Servants*	*Authority empowered to place a Railway Servant under suspension or to impose penalty and its nature*	*Appellate Authority*
1	2	3	4
		General Manager/Additional General Manager who has been ordered by the Competent Authority to look after the current duties of General Manager in the absence of a regularly posted General Manager, Director General/ RDSO, Principal/Railway Staff College, Chief Administrative Officers (having Independent charge of thier organisations)—Suspension and the penalties specified in clauses (*i*), (*iii*), (*iii-a*), (*iii-b*) and (*iv*) of rule 6 in the case of Officers upto and including Selection Grade Officers of Junior Administrative Grade.	President
		Principal Heads of Departments—Suspension and the penalties specified in clauses (*i*), (*iii*), (*iii-a*), (*iii-b*) and (*iv*) of rule 6 in the case of Officers in Junior Scale.	General Manager/ Additional General Manager who has been ordered by the Competent Authority to look after the current duties of General Manager in the absence of a regularly posted General Manager.
2.	Railway Servants Group 'B'	President—Full powers.	....
		Railway Board—Full Powers	President
		General Manager/Additional General Manager who has been ordered by the Competent Authority to look after the current duties of General Manager in the absence of a regularly posted General Manager, Director General/ RDSO, Principal/Railway Staff College, Chief Administrative Officers (having independent charge of their organisations)—Suspension and the penalties specified in clauses (*i*) to (*vi*) of rule 6.	Railway Board

Item No.	*Class of Railway Servants*	*Authority empowered to place a Railway Servant under suspension or to impose penalty and its nature*	*Appellate Authority*
1	2	3	4
		Secretary, Railway Board—Suspension and the penalties specified in clauses (*i*), (*iii*), (*iii-a*), (*iii-b*) and (*iv*) of rule 6 in the case of Group 'B' officers of the Railway Secretariat Service.	Railway Board
		Principal Heads of Departments—Suspension and the penalties specified in clauses (*i*), (*iii*), (*iii-a*), (*iii-b*) and (*iv*) of rule 6.	General Manager/ Additional General Manager who has been ordered by the the Competent Authority to look after the current duties of General Manager in the absence of a regularly posted General Manager.
3.	Railway Servants not classified either as Group 'A' or Group 'B' such as Temporary Assistant Officers.	President—Full powers.	....
		Railway Board — Full Powers	President
		General Manager/Additional General Manager who has been ordered by the Competent Authority to look after the current duties of General Manager in the absence of a regularly posted General Manager, Director General/ RDSO, Principal/Railway Staff College, Chief Administrative Officers (having independent charge of their organisations)—Suspension and the penalties specified in clauses (*i*), (*iii*), (*iii-a*), (*iii-b*) and (*iv*) of rule 6.	Railway Board
		Principal Heads of Departments—Suspension and the penalties specified in clauses (*i*), (*iii*), (*iii-a*), (*iii-b*) and (*iv*) of rule 6.	General Manager/ Additional General Manager who has been ordered by the Competent Authority to look after the current duties of General Manager in the absence of a regularly posted General Manager.

Note: (1) Disciplinary powers of Principal Heads of Departments under this Schedule shall also be exercised by the co-ordinating Heads of Departments or Heads of Departments in Senior Administrative Grade who are in independent charge, in their respective departments in the Production Units viz., Chittaranjan Lopcomotive Works, Chittaranjan, Diesel Components Works, Patiala, Diesel Locomotive Works, Varanasi, Integral Coach Factory, Perambur, Wheel and Axle Plant, Yelahanka (Bangalore) and Rail Coach Factory, Kapurthala and in new Zonal Railways viz., East Coast Railway, Bhubaneshwar, East Central Railway, Hajipur, North Central Railway, Allahabad, North Western Railway, Jaipur, South Western Railway, Hubli, West Central Railway, Jabalpur and South East Central Railway, Bilaspur in respect of officers in Junior Scale and Group 'B' who are under their administrative control.

Note: (2) Disciplinary powers of Principal Heads of Departments under this Schedule shall also be exercised by the Directors of Railway Training Institutes, namely, Director, Indian Railways Institute of Civil Engineering, Pune, Director, Indian Railways Institute of Electrical Engineering, Nasik, Director, Indian Railways Institute of Mechanical and Electrical Engineering, Jamalpur, Director Indian Railways Institute of Signal Engineering and Telecommunications, Secunderabad and Director, Indian Railways Centre for Advanced Maintenance Technology, Gwalior in respect of officers in Junior Scale and Group 'B' under their administrative control.

Note: (3) Disciplinary powers of Principal Heads of Departments under this Schedule shall also be exercised by Senior Executive Directors and Executive Directors who are in independent charge, in Research, Designs and Standards Organization; Coordinating Heads of Departments in Senior Administrative Grade or by the Heads of Departments in Senior Administrative Grade who are in independent charge, in Metro Railway, Kolkata, Central Organization for Railway Electrification, Allahabad, Central Organization for Modernisation of Workshops, New Delhi; and Chairmen of respective Railway Recruitment Boards, in respect of officers in Junior Scale and Group 'B' who are under their administrative control.

STANDARD

FORM No. 1

Standard Form of Order of Suspension Rule 5(1) of the RS (D&A) Rules, 1968.

No ....

Railway ....

Place of issue ....

Dated ....

ORDER

Whereas disciplinary proceeding against Shri	Whereas a case against Shri ....
....	
....	
(Name and designation of the Railway servant) is contemplated/ Pending	(Name and designation of the Railway servant) in respect of whom a criminal offence is under investigation inquiry trial.

Now, therefore, the undersigned (the authority competent to place the Railway servant under suspension in terms of the Schedules II and III appended to RS (D&A) Rules, 1968/an authority mentioned in proviso to [Rule 4 of the RS (D&A) Rules, 1968], in exercise of the powers conferred by Rule 4/proviso to Rule 4 of RS (D&A) Rules, 1968, hereby places the said Shri .... under suspension with immediate effect/with effect from ....

It is further ordered that during the period this order shall remain in force, the said Shri, ... shall not leave the headquarters without obtaining the previous permission of the competent authority.

Signature ....

Name ....

....

(Designation of the suspending authority)

Copy to:

Shri ....

(Name and designation of the suspended Railway servant)

Orders regarding subsistence allowance admissible to him during the period of suspension will issue separately.

FORM NO. 2

[Standard Form for Deeming Railway Servant under Suspension Rule 5(2) of RS (D&A) Rules, 1968]

No. ....

Railway ....

Place of issue ....

Dated ....

ORDER

Whereas case against Shri ....

(Name and designation of the Railway servant)

In respect of a criminal offence is under investigation.

And whereas the said Shri .... was detained in custody on .... for a period exceeding forty-eight hours.

Now, therefore the said Shri .... is deemed to have been suspended with effect from the date of detention, *i.e.* the .... in terms of Rule 5(2) of (D&A) Rules, 1968 and shall remain under suspension until further orders.

Signature ....

Name ....

....

(Designation of the suspending authority)

Copy to :

Shri ....

(Name and designation of the suspended Railway servant)

Orders regarding subsistence allowance admissible to him during the period of suspension will issue separately.

FORM NO. 3

[Standard Form of Certificate to be furnished by Suspended Official under Rule 2043(2) R-II (Rule 1342(2) 1987 ed.)]

I, ...

(Name of the Railway servant)

having been placed under suspension by Order No. .... dated .... while holding the post of .... do hereby certify that I have not been employed in any business, profession, or vocation for profit/ remuneration/salary.

Signature ....

Name of Railway servant ....

Address ....

....

FORM NO. 4

Standard Form of Order for Revocation of Suspension Order [Rule 5(5) (c) of RS (D&A) Rules, 1968]

No. ....

Railway ....

Place of issue ....

Dated ....

ORDER

Whereas the order placing Shri...

(Name and designation of the Railway servant.)

under suspension was made/was deemed to have been made by .... on ....

Now, therefore, the undersigned (the authority which made or is deemed to have made the order of suspension or any other authority to which that authority is subordinate) in exercise of the powers conferred by Clause (*c*) of sub-rule (5) of Rule 5 of the RS (D&A) Rule, 1968, hereby revokes the said order of suspension with immediate effect with effect from ....

Signature ....

Name ....

(Designation of the authority making this order)

Copy to:

Shri ....

(Name and designation of the suspended Railway servant)

Address...

....

FORM NO. 5

Standard Form of Charge-sheet
[Rule 9 of Railway Servants (Discipline and Appeal) Rules, 1968]

No. ....

(Name of Railway Administration)

....

(place of issue) .... Dated ....

MEMORANDUM

1. [1]The President/Railway Board/undersigned propose(s) to hold an inquiry against Shri .... under Rule 9 of Railway Servants (Discipline and Appeal) Rules, 1968. The substance of the imputations of misconduct and misbehaviour in respect of which the inquiry is proposed to be held is set out in the enclosed statement of articles of charge (Annexure I). A statement of the imputations of misconduct or misbehaviour in support of each article of charge is enclosed (Annexure II). A list of documents by which and a list of witnesses by whom, the articles of charge are proposed to be sustained are also enclosed (Annexures III & IV). [2]Further, copies of documents mentioned in the list of documents, as per Annexure III are enclosed.

2. [2]Shri .... is hereby informed and if he so desires, he can inspect and take extracts from the documents mentioned in the enclosed list of documents (Annexure III) at any time during office hours within ten days of receipt of this memorandum. For this purpose he should

1 Strike out whichever is not applicable.

2 To be *deleted* if copies are given/not given with the Memorandum as the case may be.

contact[3] .... immediately on receipt of this memorandum.

3. Shri .... is further informed that he may, if he so desires, take the assistance of another Railway servant/an official of Railway Trade Union (who satisfies the requirements of Rule 9(13) of the Railway Servants (Discipline and Appeal) Rules, 1968, and Note 1 and/or Note 2 thereunder as the case may be) for inspecting the documents and assisting him in presenting his case before the Inquiring Authority in the event of an oral inquiry being held. For this purpose, he should nominate one or more persons in order of preference. Before nominating the assisting Railway servant(s) or Railway Trade Union Official(s), Shri .... should obtain an undertaking from the nominee(s) that he (they) is (are) willing to assist him during the disciplinary proceedings. The undertaking should also contain the particulars of other case(s) if any, in which the nominee(s) had already undertaken to assist and the undertaking should be furnished to the undersigned/General Manager ....[4].......................... Railway alongwith the nomination.

4. Shri .... is hereby directed to submit to the undersigned (through General Manager .... Railway)[4] a written statement of his defence (which should reach the said General Manager)[4] within ten days of receipt of this Memorandum, if he does not require to inspect any documents for the preparation of his defence, and within ten days after completion of inspection of documents if he desires to inspect documents, and also:

(*a*) to state whether he wishes to be heard in person; and

(*b*) to furnish the names and addresses of the witnesses if any, whom he wishes to call in support of his defence.

5. Shri .... is informed that an inquiry will be held only in respect of those articles of charge as are not admitted. He should, therefore, specifically admit or/deny each article of charge.

6. Shri .... is further, informed that if he does not submit his written statement of defence within the period specified in para 2 or does not appear in person before the inquiring authority or otherwise fails or refuses to comply with the provisions of Rule 9 of the Railway Servants (Discipline and Appeal) Rules, 1968, or the orders/directions issued in pursuance of the said rule, the inquiring authority may hold the inquiry *ex parte.*

7. The attention of Shri .... is invited to Rule 20 of the Railway Servant (Conduct) Rules, 1966 under which no Railway servant shall bring or attempt to bring any political or other influence to bear upon any superior authority to further his interests in respect of matter pertaining to his service under the Government. If any representation is received on his behalf from another person in respect of any matter dealt within these proceedings, it will be presumed that Shri .... is aware of

3 Name of the authority. (This would imply that whenever a case is referred to the disciplinary authority by the Investigation Authority or any authority who arc in the custody of the listed documents or who would be arranging for inspection of the document or to enable that authority being mentioned in the draft memorandum).

4 To be retained wherever applicable President or the Railway Board is the competent authority.

such a representation and that it has been made at his instance and action will be taken against him for violation of Rule 20 of the Railway Services (Conduct) Rules, 1966.

8. The receipt of this Memorandum may be acknowledged.

[5][By order and in the name of the President]

(Signature)

Name and designation of competent authority.

Encls :

To

Shri .... (Designation)

.... (Place)

[6]Copy to Shri .... (name and designation of the lending authority) for information.

FORM NO. 6

Standard Form for Refusing Permission to inspect Document (Rule 9 (16) RS (D&A) Rules, 1968)

No. ....

Railway ....

Place of issue ....

Dated ....

ORDER

Shri ....

(Name and designation of the Railway servant)

.... has requested permission to inspect and take extracts from the records *specified below* for the purpose of preparing his defence in the inquiry pending against him in pursuant to Memorandum No. .... dated .... The undersigned has carefully considered the request and has decided to refuse such permission for the *reasons recorded* below against each item:

Description of records extracts	*Reasons for refusing inspection or taking*
1.	....
2.	....
3.	....

5 Where the President is the Disciplinary Authority.

6 To be used wherever applicable—Note to be *inserted* in the copy sent to the Railway servant.

4. ....

5. ....

Signature..
Name ....
(Designation of the Inquiry Authority)

FORM NO. 7

Standard Form of Order Relating to Appointment of Inquiry Officer/Board of Inquiry [Rule 9(2) of RS (D&A) Rules, 1968]

No. ....
Railway ....
Place of issue ....
Dated..

ORDER

Whereas an Inquiry under Rule 9 of the Railway Servants (Discipline and Appeal) Rules, 1968 is being held against Shri ....

(Name and designation of the Railway servant)

AND WHEREAS the undersigned considers that a Board of Inquiry/an Inquiry Officer should be appointed to inquire into the charge framed against him.

NOW, THEREFORE, the undersigned, in exercise of the powers conferred by sub-rule (2) of the said Rule, hereby appoints.

A Board of Inquiry consisting of:

Name of Member	*Designation*
1.	....
2.	....
3.	....

or

Shri ....

(Name and designation of the Inquiry Officer)

as Inquiry Officer to Inquire into the charges against the said Shri ....

Signature ....
Name ....
(Designation of the Disciplinary Authority)

Copy to :

Shri ....

(Name and designation of the Railway servant)

Copy to :

1. Shri ....

(Name and designation of the Member)

2. Shri ....

(Name and designation of the Member)

3. Shri ....

(Name and designation of the Member)

or

Shri ....

(Name and designation of the Inquiry Officer)

[7]FORM NO. 8

Form for appointment of Presenting Officer
[Sub-rule (9)(iv) (c) of Rule 9 of RS (D&A) Rules, 1968]

No. ....

Railway ....

Place of issue ....

Dated ....

ORDER

Whereas an inquiry under Rule 9 of the Railway Servants (Discipline and Appeal) Rules, 1968 is being held against Shri ....

And whereas the undersigned considers it necessary to appoint a person to present the case in support of the charges before the Inquiring Authority.

Now, therefore, the undersigned in exercise of the powers conferred by Sub-rule 9*(iv)*(*c*) of Rule 9 of the RS (D&A) Rules, 1968 hereby appoints Shri .... as Presenting Officer to present the case in support of the charges before the Inquiring Authority.

Shri .... is also authorised to appoint, during his temporary non-availability[7] any other CBI/Railway Official not below his rank for representing the case before the Inquiry Officer on his behalf and on

7 Word "nominate" replaced by appoint/appointment *vide* RBE 19/92, E(D&A) 91 RG 6-71 of 4.2.92] Standard Forms 9(*a*) to 9(*c*) circulated *vide* Board's No. E(D&A) 66 RG 6-7, dated 5.9.70 & 24.10.72 are cancelled. Hence not reproduced, [E(D&A) 80 RG 6-12, dated 31.7.80, NR 7626].

behalf of the disciplinary authority for examination, cross examination as well as the arguments etc.

Signature ....
Name ....
(Designation of the Disciplinary Authority)
Dated ....

Copy forwarded for information to:

Shri ....

(Name and designation of the Railway servant)

Signature ....
Name ....
(Designation)

No. ....

Copy forwarded for information to:

1. Shri ....

(Name and designation of the Inquiry Officer)

2. Shri ....

(Name and designation of the Presenting Officer ....

Signature ....
Name ....
(Designation)

FORM No. 10

Standard Form of Order for taking Disciplinary Action, in Common Proceedings [Rule 13 of RS (D&A) Rules, 1968]

No. ....
Railway ....
Place of issue. Dated ....

ORDER

Name of Railway servants

1. Shri ....
2. Shri ....
3. Shri ....
4. Shri ....
5. Shri ....

Whereas the Railway servants specified in the margin are jointly concerned in a disciplinary case.

[8]Now, therefore, in exercise of the powers conferred by sub-rules (1) and (2) of Rule 13 of Railway Servants (Discipline and Appeal) Rules, 1968, the undersigned hereby directs:

[9](1) Disciplinary action against all the said Railway servants shall be taken in the common proceedings.

[10](2) Shri..

(Name and designation of authority) shall function as the Disciplinary Authority for the purpose of the common proceeding and shall be competent to impose the following penalties:

....[11]

[12](3) that the procedure prescribed in Rule 9 and Rule 10/Rule 11 shall be followed in the said proceedings.

Signature ....
Name ....

[Designation of competent authority Rule 13(1)]

Copy to :

1. Shri ....

(Name and designation)

2. Shri ....

(Name and designation)

3. Shri ....

(Name and designation)

4. Shri ....

(Name and designation)

5. Shri ....

(Name and designation)

8 The authority competent to impose the penalty of dismissal from service on all such Railway servants or if they are different, highest of such authorities with the consent of others.

9 Score out the portion not applicable.

10 *See* Rule 13 (2)(*i*).

11 Here specify the penalties, see Rule 13 (2)(*ii*).

12 *See* Rule 13 (2)(*iii*).

FORM NO. 10-A

Standard Form for appointment of Enquiring Authority in common proceedings [Rule 13 of RS (D & A) Rules, 1968]

No. ....

(Name of Rly. Administration)

(Place of issue)............dt.........

ORDER

WHEREAS the Railway servants specified in the margin are jointly concerned in a disciplinary case.

WHEREAS common proceedings have been ordered against the said Railway servants in terms of Rule 13 of the Railway Servants (Discipline and Appeal) Rules, 1968 *vide* Order No .... dated ....
appointing .... (Name and Designation of the authority) to function as the disciplinary authority for the purpose of the common proceedings.

WHEREAS an inquiry in accordance with Rule 9 and Rule 10 or Rule 11 of the Railway Servants (Discipline and Appeal) Rules, 1968 is being held against the Railway servants specified in the margin.

AND WHEREAS the President/Railway Board/the undersigned considers that an Inquiring Officer should be appointed to inquire into the charges framed against the said Railway servants.

NOW THERFORE, the [13]President/Railway Board/the undersigned in exercise of the powers conferred by sub-rule 2 of Rule 9 of the Railway Servants (Discipline and Appeal) Rules, 1968 hereby appoint(s) Shri .... (Name and designation of the Inquiry Officer) as the Inquiry Authority to inquire into the charges framed against the said Railway servants.

[13]By order and in the name of President.

Disciplinary Authority/
'Authority competent to authenticate order in the name of the President/
Secretary, Railway Board.

To

1. .... The accused Rly. servants
2. Presenting Officer
3. Inquiring Authority with relevant documents.

[14]4. The C.V.C.

[Introduced vide Railway Board's letter No. E(D&A) 76 RG 6-57. dated 14.8.78]

[NR 7094); NF/DAC333. SC 145/78]

13 Delete where not applicable.

14 Note: to be used where applicable. Not to be *inserted* in the copy sent to the accused Railway servants.

FORM NO. 10-B

Standard form for appointment of Presenting Officer in common proceedings [Rule 13 of RS (D & A) Rules, 1968]

No ....

(Name of Rly. Administration)

(Place of issue) .... dt ....

ORDER

WHEREAS the Railway servants specified in the margin are jointly concerned in a disciplinary case.

WHEREAS common proceedings have been ordered against the said Railway servants in terms of Rule 13 of the Railway Servants (Discipline and Appeal) Rules, 1968 *vide* Order No .... dated .... appointing .... (Name and designation of the authority) to function as the disciplinary authority for the purpose of the common proceedings.

WHEREAS an inquiry in accordance with Rule 9 and Rule 10 or Rule 11 of the Railway Servants (Discipline and Appeal) Rules, 1968 is being held against the Railway servants specified in the margin.

AND WHEREAS the [15]President/Railway Board/the undersigned consider it necessary to appoint a Presenting Officer to present the case in support of the articles of charge against the said Railway servants before the Inquiry Authority.

NOW, THEREFORE, the [15]President/Railway Board/the undersigned in exercise of powers conferred by sub-rule 9(*c*) of the said Rule 9 of the Railway Servants (Discipline and Appeal) Rules, 1968 hereby appoint(s) Shri .... (Name and Designation of Presenting Officer to present the case in support of the articles of charges against said Railway servants before the Inquiring Authority.

Shri .... is also authorised to nominate during his temporary non-availability any other CBI/Railway official not below his rank for representing the case before the Inquiry Officer on his behalf and on behalf of the disciplinary authority for examination, cross-examination and re-examination as well as for argument etc.

[15]By order and in the name of the President.

Disciplinary Authority/
[15]Authority Competent to authenticate order
in the name of the President/ Secretary,
Railway Board

Copy to:

1. Accused Officer.
[16]2. Central Bureau of Investigation.
[16]3. Central Vigilance Commission.

15 Delete where not applicable.

16 Not to be used where inapplicable—not to be *inserted* in the copy sent to the accused Railway servants.

Note : *[SF 10 A and 10 B introduced by Bd. No. E(D&A) 76 RG 6-57, dated 14.8.78; (NF/DAC 333) NR 7094, SC 145/78)].*

4. Inquiry Authority.
5. Presenting Officer.

FORM NO. 11

Standard Form of Memorandum of Charge for Imposing Minor Penalties [Rule 11 of RS (D&A) Rules, 1968]

No. ....
Railway ....
Place of issue ....
Dated ....

MEMORANDUM

1. Shri ....

(Name, designation and office in which working)

is hereby informed that the undersigned proposes to take action against him under Rule 11 of the Railway Servants (Discipline and Appeal) Rules, 1968. A statement of the imputations of misconduct or misbehaviour on which action is proposed to be taken as mentioned above, is enclosed.

2. Shri .... is hereby given an opportunity to make such representation as he may wish to make against the proposal. The representation, if any, should be submitted to the undersigned so as to reach within ten days of receipt of this Memorandum.

3. If Shri .... fails to submit his representation within the period specified in para 2, it will be presumed that he has no representation to make and orders will be liable to be passed against Shri .... *ex parte.*

4. The receipt of this Memorandum should be acknowledged by Shri ....

Signature ....
Name ....
....
(Designation of the competent authority)

To
Shri ....

(Name, designation and office of the Railway servant)

FORM NO. 11(*b*)

Standard Form of Charge-sheet for Initiation of Minor Penalty Proceedings (In cases where Disciplinary Authority decides to hold the inquiry under Rule 11(1)(b)/11(2) of Railway Servants (Discipline and Appeal) Rules, 1968.

No. ....
(Name of Railway Administration) ....
(Place of Issue) .... Dated ....

MEMORANDUM

In continuation of Memorandum No .... dated .... issued to Shri .... under Rule 11 of the Railway Servants (Discipline and Appeal) Rules, 1968.

....

After careful consideration of the explanation given by Shri .... with reference to Memorandum No .... dated .... issued to him under Rule 11 of the Railway Servants (Discipline and Appeal) Rules, 1968 .... the [17]President/Railway Board/undersigned is/are of the opinion that it is necessary to hold an inquiry against Shri .... under Rule 11(1)(*b*)/Rule 11(2) of the Railway Servants (Discipline and Appeal) Rules, 1968. The substance of the imputations of misconduct or misbehaviour in respect of which the inquiry is proposed to be held is set out in the enclosed statement of articles of charge (Annexure I). A statement of the imputations of misconduct or misbehaviour in support of each article of charge, is enclosed (Annexure II): A list of documents by which, and a list of witnesses by whom the articles of charges, are proposed to be sustained, are also enclosed (Annexure III & IV). [18]Further copies of documents mentioned in the list of documents, as per Annexure III are enclosed.

2. Shri .... is hereby informed that if he so desires, he can inspect and take extracts from the documents mentioned in the enclosed list of documents (Annexure III) at any time during office hours within seven days of receipt of this memorandum. For this purpose he should contact[18] .... immediately on receipt of this Memorandum.

3. Shri .... is further informed that he may, if he so desires, take the assistance of any other Railway servant/an official of Railway Trade Union (who satisfies the requirements of Rule 9(13) of Railway Servants (Discipline and Appeal) Rules, 1968 and Note 1 and or Note 2 thereunder as the case may be), for inspecting the documents and assisting him in presenting his case before the Inquiring Authority in the event of an oral inquiry being held. For this purpose, he should nominate one or more persons in order of preference. Before nominating the assisting Railway servant(s) or Railway Trade Union Official(s) Shri .... should obtain an undertaking from the nominee(s) that he (they) is (are) willing to assist him during the disciplinary proceedings. The undertaking should also contain the particulars of other case(s), if any in which the nominee(s) had already undertaken to assist and the undertaking should be furnished to the undersigned/General Manager[19] Railway alongwith the nomination.

4. Shri .... is hereby directed to submit to the undersigned (through General Manager .... Railway)[19] written statement of defence (which should reach the said General Manager)[20] within ten days of receipt of this Memorandum, if he does not require to inspect any documents for

17 Delete where not applicable.

18 Name of authority having custody of documents.

19 To be retained wherever President or the Railway Board is the competent authority.

20 This time limit may be extended up to ten days at the discretion of the competent authority.

the preparation of his defence, and within ten days after completion of inspection of documents if he desires to inspect documents and also,

(*a*) to state whether he wishes to be heard in person; and

(*b*) to furnish the names and addresses of the witnesses if any, whom he wishes to call in support of his defence.

5. Shri .... is informed that an inquiry will be held only in respect of those articles of charge as are not admitted. He should, therefore, specifically admit or deny each article of charge.

6. Shri .... is further informed that if he does not submit his written statement of defence within the period specified in para 4 or does not appear in person before the inquiring authority or otherwise fails or refuses to comply with the provisions of Rules 9 and 11 of the Railway Servants (Discipline and Appeal) Rules, 1968 or the orders/directions issued in pursuance of the said rule, the inquiring authority may hold the inquiry *ex parte*.

7. The attention of Shri .... is invited to Rule 20 of the Railway Services (Conduct) Rules, 1966, under which no Railway servant shall bring or attempt to bring any political or other influence to bear upon any superior authority to further his interest in respect of matters pertaining to his service under the Government. If any representation is received on his behalf from another person in respect of any matter dealt within these proceedings, it will be presumed that Shri .... is aware of such a representation and that it has been made at his instance and action will be taken against him for violation of Rule 20 of the Railway Services (Conduct) Rules, 1966.

8. The receipt of this Memorandum may be acknowledged.

[21][By order and in the name of the President]

(Signature)

Encls:

Name and designation of competent authority

To

Shri ....

.... (Designation)

.... (Place etc.)

[22]Copy to Shri .... name and disignation of the lending authority for information.

21 Strike out whichever is not applicable.

22 To be used wherever applicable—*See* Rule 16(1) of the Railway Servants (Discipline and Appeal) Rules. 1968. —Not to be *inserted* in the copy sent to the Railway servant.

APPENDIX 11

The Railway Services (Conduct) Rules, 1966

1. Short title. (1) These rules may be called the Railway Services (Conduct) Rules, 1966.

(2) They shall come into force at once.

2. Definitions. In these rules, unless the context otherwise requires—

(*a*) 'Government' means, in relation to—

(*i*) gazetted officers holding posts in the Railway Board, the President;

(*ii*) other gazetted officers, the Railway Board;

(*iii*) non-gazetted officers in the Railway Board, the Secretary, Railway Board;

(*iv*) other non-gazetted officers in offices directly under the administrative control of the Railway Board, the Heads of the offices concerned; and

(*v*) other non-gazetted officers, the General Managers of the Railway administration concerned:

Provided that for purposes of sub-rules (2) and (3) of rule 5, sub-rule (1) of rule 8, sub-rule (1) of rule 10, rule 12, rule 14, sub-rules (1) and (3) of rule 15, sub-rule (3) of rule 16, sub-rule (1) of rule 19 and rule 21. 'Government' means the Railway Board in the case of all non-gazetted Railway Servants.

(*b*) "railway servant" means a railway servant as defined in rule 103(43)[1] of the Indian Railway Establishment Code.

Explanation. A railway servant whose services are placed at the disposal of a company, corporation, organisation or a local authority shall, for the purpose of these rules, be deemed to be a railway servant notwithstanding that his salary is drawn from sources other than the Consolidated Fund of India.

1 Railway servant means a person who is a member of a service or who holds a post under the administrative control of the Railway Board and includes a post in the Railway Board. Persons lent from a service or post which is not under the administrative control of the Railway Board to a Service or post which is under such administrative control do not come within the scope of this definition.

(*c*) "members of family" in relation to a railway servant includes,—

(*i*) the wife or husband, as the case may be, of the railway servant, whether residing with the railway servant or not but does not include a wife or husband, as the case may be, separated from a railway servant by a decree or order of a competent court;

(*ii*) son or daughter or step-son or step-daughter of the railway servant and wholly dependent on him, but does not include a child or step-child who is no longer in any way dependent on the railway servant or of whose custody the railway servant has been deprived by or under any law;

(*iii*) any other person related whether by blood or marriage to the railway servant or to the railway servant's wife or husband, and wholly dependent on the railway servant.

3. General. (1) Every railway servant shall at all times—

(*i*) maintain absolute integrity;

(*ii*) maintain devotion to duty; and

(*iii*) do nothing which is unbecoming of a railway or Government servant.

(2) (*i*) Every railway servant holding a supervisory post shall take all possible steps to ensure the integrity and devotion to duty of all railway servants for the time being under his control and authority;

(*ii*) no railway servant shall, in the performance of his official duties, or in the exercise of powers conferred on him, act otherwise than in his best judgment except when he is acting under the direction of his official superior.

(*iii*) The direction of the official superior shall ordinarily be in writing, and where the issue of oral direction becomes unavoidable, the official superior shall confirm it in writing immediately thereafter; and

(*iv*) A railway servant who has received oral direction from his official superior, shall seek confirmation of the same in writing as early as possible, whereupon it shall be the duty of the official superior to confirm the direction in writing.

Explanation I. A railway servant who habitually fails to perform the task assigned to him within the time set for the purpose and with the quality of performance expected of him shall be deemed to be lacking in devotion to duty within the meaning of clause (*ii*) of sub-rule (1).

Explanation II. Nothing in clause (*ii*) of sub-rule (2) shall be construed as empowering a railway servant to evade his responsibilities by seeking instructions from or approval of, a superior officer or authority when such instructions are not necessary under the scheme of distribution of powers and responsibilities.

3A. Promptness and Courtesy. No Railway servant shall—

(*a*) in the performance of his official duties, act in a discourteous manner;

(*b*) in his official dealings with the public or otherwise adopt dilatory tactics or willfully cause delays in disposal of the work assigned to him.

3B. Observance of Government's policies. Every railway servant shall, at all times—

(*i*) act in accordance with the Government's policies regarding age of marriage, preservation of environment, protection of wildlife and cultural heritage;

(*ii*) observe the Government's policies regarding prevention of crime against women.

3C. Prohibition of sexual harassment of working women.

(1) No railway servant shall indulge in any act of sexual harassment of any woman at her work place.

(2) Every railway servant who is incharge of a work place shall take appropriate steps to prevent sexual harassment to any woman at such work place.

Explanation. For the purpose of this rule, "sexual harassment" includes such unwelcome sexually determined behaviour, whether directly or otherwise, as:

(*a*) physical contact and advances;

(*b*) demand or request for sexual favours;

(*c*) sexually coloured remarks;

(*d*) showing any pornography; or

(*e*) any other unwelcome physical, verbal or non-verbal conduct of a sexual nature.

4. Employment of near relatives of railway servants in Company or Firm enjoying Government patronage. (1) No railway servant shall use his position or influence directly or indirectly to secure employment for any member of his family in any company or firm.

(2) (*i*) No Group A officer shall, except with the prior sanction of the Government permit his son, daughter or other dependent to accept employment in any company or firm with which he has official dealings or in any other company or firm having official dealings with the Government:

Provided that where the acceptance of the employment cannot await prior permission of the Government or is otherwise considered urgent, the employment may be accepted provisionally subject to the permission of the Government and the fact of such acceptance shall at once be reported to the Government.

(*ii*) A railway servant shall, as soon as he becomes aware of the acceptance by a member of his family of an employment in any company or firm, intimate such acceptance to the Government and shall also intimate whether he has or has had any official dealings with that company or firm:

Provided that no such intimation shall be necessary in the case of a Group "A" officer if he has already obtained the sanction of, or sent a report to the Government under clause (*i*).

(3) No railway servant shall in the discharge of his official duties deal with any matter or give or sanction any contract to any company or firm or any other person, if any member of his family is employed in that company or firm or under that person or if he or any member of his family is interested in such matter or contract in any other manner and the railway servant shall refer every such matter or contract to his official superior officer or authority and the matter or

contract shall thereafter be disposed of according to the instructions of such officer or authority.

5. Taking part in politics and elections. (1) No railway servant shall be a member of or be otherwise associated with, any political party or any organisation which takes part in politics nor shall he take part in, subscribe in aid of, or assist in any other manner, any political movement or activity.

(2) It shall be the duty of every railway servant to endeavour to prevent any member of his family from taking part in, subscribing in aid of or assisting in any other manner any movement or activity which is, or tends directly or indirectly to be, subversive of the Government as by laws established and where a railway servant is unable to prevent a member of his family from taking part in, or subscribing in aid of or assisting in any other manner, any such movement or activity, he shall make a report to that effect to the Government.

(3) If any question arises whether a party is a political party or whether any organisation takes part in politics or whether any movement or activity falls within the scope of sub-rule (2), the decision of the Government thereon shall be final.

(4) No railway servant shall canvass, otherwise interfere with, or use his influence in connection with or take part in, an election to any legislature or local authority:

Provided that—

(*i*) a railway servant qualified to vote at such election may exercise his right to vote, but where he does so, he shall give no indication of the manner in which he proposes to vote or has voted;

(*ii*) a railway servant shall not be deemed to have contravened the provisions of this sub-rule by reason only that he assists in the conduct of an election in the performance of a duty imposed on him by or under any law for the time being in force.

Explanation. The display by a railway servant on his person, vehicle or residence of any electoral symbol shall amount to using his influence in connection with an election within the meaning of this sub-rule.

6. Joining of associations or unions by railway servants. No railway servant shall join, or continue to be a member of an association or union the objects or activities of which are prejudicial to the interest of the sovereignty and integrity of India or public order or morality.

Note. It is not permissible for a gazetted railway servant to join any association of non-gazetted railway servant like a Railway Employees' Union. When a non-gazetted railway servant who is a member of a Railway Employees' Union is promoted to gazetted rank, either in officiating or permanent capacity he shall resign his membership of such Union. If, however, the officer concerned satisfies the General Manager of the Railway concerned that by such resignation he will lose financially or otherwise under any *beneficent* scheme organised by such Union such as death or accident insurance, he may be permitted to continue as an ordinary member, but not as office bearer or representative, of that Union. The responsibility for satisfying the General Manager in this respect will rest with the office concerned.

7. Demonstration. No railway servant shall engage himself or participate in any demonstration which is prejudicial to the interests of the sovereignty and integrity of India, the security of the State, friendly relations with foreign States, public order, decency or morality, or which involves contempt of court, defamation or incitement to an offence.

8. Connection with the Press or other media. (1) No railway servant shall, except with the previous sanction of the Government, own wholly or in part, or conduct or participate in the editing or management of, any newspaper or other periodical publication or electronic Media.

(2) Nothing in sub-rule (1) shall apply in case a railway servant in the *bona fide* discharge of his official duties publishes a book or participate in a public media.

(3) A railway servant publishing a book or participating in a public media shall, at all times, make it clear that the views expressed by him are his own and not that of Government.

9. Criticism of Government. No railway servant shall, in any radio broadcast, telecast through any electronic media or in any document published in his own name or anonymously, pseudonymously or in the name of any other person or in any communication to the press or in any public utterance, make any statement of fact or opinion—

(*i*) which has the effect of an adverse criticism of any current or recent policy or action of the Central Government or State Government;

(*ii*) which is capable of embarrassing the relations between the Central Government and the Government of any State; or

(*iii*) which is capable of embarrassing the relations between the Central Government and the Government of any foreign State:

Provided that nothing in this rule shall apply to any statement made or views expressed by a railway servant in his official capacity or in the due performance of the duties assigned to him.

10. Evidence before committee or any other authority. (1) Save as provided in sub-rule (3), no railway servant shall, except with the previous sanction of the Government, give evidence in connection with any enquiry conducted by any person, committee or authority.

(2) Where any sanction has been accorded under sub-rule (1), no railway servant shall in the course of giving such evidence criticise the policy or any action of the Central Government or of a State Government.

(3) Nothing in this rule shall apply to—

(*a*) evidence given at an enquiry before an authority appointed by the Government, Parliament or a State Legislature; or

(*b*) evidence given in any judicial inquiry; or

(*c*) evidence given at any departmental inquiry ordered by authorities subordinate to the Government.

11. Unauthorised communication of information. No railway servant, shall except in accordance with any general or special order of the Government or in the performance in good faith of the duties assigned to him communicate, directly or indirectly, any official document or any part thereof or information to any Government or railway servant or any other person to whom he is not authorised to communicate such documents or information.

Explanation. Quotation by a railway servant (in his representations to officials superior authorities or from any letter, circular of office memorandum, or from the notes on any file to which he is not authorised to have access or which he is not authorised to keep in his personal custody or for personal purposes) shall amount to unauthorised communication of information within the meaning of this rule.

12. Subscription. No railway servant, shall, except with the previous sanction of the Government or of the competent authority, ask for or accept contributions to or otherwise associate himself with the raising, of, any funds or other collections in cash or in kind in pursuance of any object whatsoever.

13. Gifts. (1) Save as otherwise provided in these rules, no railway servant shall accept, or permit any member of his family or (any other person acting on his behalf) to accept, any gift.

Explanation. The expression "gift" shall include free transport, boarding, lodging or other service or any other pecuniary advantage when provided by any person other than a near relative or personal friend having no official dealings with the railway servant.

Note: (1) A casual meal, lift or other social hospitality shall not be deemed to be a gift.

Note: (2) A railway servant shall avoid accepting lavish hospitality or frequent hospitality from any individual, industrial or commercial firms, organisations, etc. having official dealings with him.

(2) On occasions such as weddings, anniversaries, funerals or religious functions, when the making of gift is in conformity with the prevailing religious and social practice, a railway servant may accept gifts from his near relatives or from his personal friends having no official dealings with him, but shall make a report to the Government, if the value of such gifts exceeds—

(*i*) rupees *seven thousand* in the case of a railway servant holding any Group 'A' post;

(*ii*) rupees *four thousand* in the case of a railway servant holding any Group 'B' post;

(*iii*) rupees *two thousand* in the case of a railway servant holding any Group 'C' post;

(*iv*) rupees *one thousand* in the case of a railway servant holding any Group 'D' post.

(3) In any other case, a railway servant shall not accept any gift without the sanction of the Government if the value exceeds—

(*i*) rupees *one thousand five hundred* in the case of railway servants holding any Group 'A' or Group 'B' post; and

(*ii*) rupees *five hundred* in the case of railway servants holding any Group 'C' or Group 'D' post.

(4) Not withstanding anything contained in sub-rules (2) and (3), a railway servant, being a member of the Indian delegation or otherwise, may receive and retain gifts from foreign dignitaries if the market value of gifts received on one occasion does not exceed rupees one thousand. In all other cases, the acceptance and retention of such gifts shall be regulated by the instructions issued by the Government in this regard from time to time.

(5) A railway servant shall not accept any gifts from any foreign firm which is either contracting with the Government of India or is one with which the railway servant had, has or is likely to have official dealings. Acceptance of gifts by a railway servants from any other firm shall be subject to the provisions of sub-rule (3).

13A. Dowry. No Railway servant shall—

(*i*) give or take or abet the giving or taking of dowry; or

(*ii*) demand directly or indirectly, from the parents or guardian of a bride or bridegroom as the case may be, any dowry.

Explanations. For the purpose of this rule 'dowry' has the same meaning as in the Dowry Prohibition Act, 1961.

In this Act, 'dowry' means any property or valuable security given or agreed to be given either directly or indirectly—

(*a*) by one party to a marriage to the other party to marriage; or

(*b*) by the parents of either party to a marriage or by any other person, to either party to the marriage or to any other person;

at or before or after the marriage as consideration for the marriage of the said parties, but does not include dower or mahr in the cases of persons to whom the Muslim Personal Law [Shariat] applies.

Explanation I. Foı the removal of doubts, it is hereby declared that any presents made at the time of a marriage to either party to the marriage in the form of cash, ornaments, clothes or other articles shall not be deemed to be dowry within the meaning of this section, unless they are made as consideration for the marriage of the said parties.

Explanation II. The expression "Valuable security" has the same meaning as in section 30 of the Indian Penal Code.

14. Public demonstrations in honour of railway servants. No railway servant shall except with the previous sanction of the Government receive any complimentary or valedictory address or accept any testimonial or attend any meetings of entertainment held in his honour, or in the honour of any other Government servant:

Provided that nothing in this rule shall apply to—

(*i*) a farewell entertainment of a substantially private and informal character held in honour of a railway servant or any other Government servant on the occasion of his retirement or transfer or any person who has recently quit the service of any Government; or

(*ii*) the acceptance of simple and inexpensive entertainments arranged by public bodies or institutions.

Note. Exercise of pressure or influence of any sort on any railway servant to induce him to subscribe towards any farewell entertainment even if it is of a substantially private or informal character, and the collection of subscriptions from Group 'C' or Group 'D' employees under any circumstances for the entertainment of any railway or other Government servant not belonging to Group 'C' or Group 'D' is forbidden.

15. Private trade or employment. (1) Subject to the provisions of sub-rule (2), no railway servant shall, except with the previous sanction of the Government.

(*a*) engage directly or indirectly in any trade or business, or

(*b*) negotiate for, or undertake, any other employment, or

(*c*) hold an elective office, or canvas for a candidate or candidates for an elective office, in anybody, whether incorporated or not, or

(*d*) canvas in support of any business of insurance agency, commission agency, etc. owned or managed by any member of his family; or

(*e*) take part except in the discharge of his official duties, in the registration, promotion or management of any bank or other company registered or required to be registered, under the Companies Act, 1956 (1 of 1956) or any other law for the time being in force, or of any co-operative society for commercial purposes.

(*f*) Participate in or associate himself in any manner in the making of—

(*i*) a sponsored media (radio or television) programme; or

(*ii*) a media programme commissioned by government media but produced by a private agency; or

(*iii*) a privately produced media programme including video magazine;

Provided that no previous permission shall be necessary in case where the railway servant participates in a programme produced or commissioned by Government media in his official capacity.

(2) A railway servant may, without the previous sanction of the Government—

(*a*) undertake honorary work of a social or charitable nature; or

(*b*) undertake occasional work of a literary, artistic or scientific character; or

(*c*) participate in sports activities as an amateur; or

(*d*) take part in the registration, promotion or management [not involving the holding of an elective office] of a literary, scientific or charitable society or of a club or similar organisation the aims or objects of which relate to promotion of sports, cultural or recreational activities, registered under the Societies Registration Act, 1860 [21 of 1860], or any other law for the time being in force, or,

(*e*) take part in the registration, promotion or management (not involving the holding of an elective office) of a co-operative society substantially for the benefit of railway servants, registered under the Co-operative Societies Act, 1912 (2 of 1912), or any other law for the time being in force;

Provided that—

(*i*) he shall discontinue taking part in such activities, if so directed by the Government; and

(*ii*) in a case falling under clause (*d*) or clause (*e*) of this sub-rule, his official duties shall not suffer thereby and he shall, within a period of one month of his taking part in such activity, report to the Government giving details of the nature of his participation.

(3) Every railway servant shall report to the Government if any member of his family is engaged in a trade or business or owns or manages an insurance agency or commission agency.

(4) Unless otherwise provided by general or special orders of the Government no railway servant may accept any fee for any work done by him for any private or public body or any private person without the sanction of the prescribed authority.

Explanation. The term 'fee' used here shall have the meaning assigned to it in rule 103(18)—R.I.

15A. Subletting and vacation of Government accommodation.

(1) Save as otherwise provided in any other law for the time being in force, no railway servant shall sub-let, lease or otherwise allow occupation by any other person of Government accommodation which has been allotted to him.

(2) a railway servant shall, after the cancellation of his allotment of Government accommodation vacate the same within the time limit prescribed by the allotting authority.

16. Investment, lending and borrowing. (1) No railway servant shall speculate in any stock, share or other investment.

Provided that nothing in this sub-rule shall apply to occasional investments made through stock brokers or other persons duly authorised and licensed or who have obtained a certificate of registration under the relevant law.

Explanation. Frequent purchase or sale or both, of shares, securities or other investments shall be deemed to be speculation within the meaning of this sub-rule.

(2) No railway servant shall make, or permit any member of his family or any person acting on his behalf to make, any investment which is likely to embarrass or influence him in the discharge of his official duties. For this purpose, any purchase of shares out of the quotas reserved for Directors of Companies or their friends and associates shall be deemed to be an investment which is likely to embarrass the railway servant.

(3) If any question arises whether any transaction is of the nature referred to in sub-rule (1) or sub-rule (2) the decision of the Government thereon shall be final.

(4) (*i*) No railway servant shall, save in the ordinary course of business with a bank or a public limited company either himself or through any member of his family or any other person acting on his behalf—

(*a*) Lend or borrow or deposit money, as a principal or an agent, to or from or with, any person or firm or private limited company with whom he is likely to have official dealings or otherwise place himself under pecuniary obligation to such persons, or firm or private limited company;

(*b*) Lend money to any person at interest or in a manner whereby return in money or in kind is charged or paid:

Provided that a railway servant may give to, or accept from, a relative or a personal friend, a purely temporary loan of a small amount free of interest, or operate a credit account with a *bona fide* tradesman or make an advance or pay to his private employee.

Provided further that nothing in this sub-rule shall apply in respect of any transaction entered into by a railway servant with the previous sanction of the Government.

(*ii*) When a railway servant is appointed or transferred to a post of such nature as would involve him in the breach of any of the provisions of sub-rule (2) or sub-rule (4), he shall forthwith report the circumstances to the competent authority and shall thereafter act in accordance with such order as may be made by such authority.

17. Insolvency and habitual indebtedness. (1) A railway servant shall so manage his private affairs as to avoid habitual indebtedness or insolvency. A railway servant against whom any legal proceeding is instituted for the recovery of any debt due from him or for adjudging him as insolvent shall forthwith report the full facts of the legal proceedings to the Government.

Note. The burden of proving that the insolvency or indebtedness was the result of circumstances which, with the exercise of ordinary diligence, the railway servant could not have foreseen, or over which he had no control, and had not proceeded from extravagant or dissipated habits, shall be upon the railway servant.

(2) The following procedure shall be followed in the case of non-gazetted railway servant:

(*i*) The report required under sub-rule (1) above, shall be submitted by the railway servant to his immediate superior who should forward it through the normal channels to the authority competent to remove or dismiss the employee from service. Except where such authority requires guidance or clarification from a higher authority, it shall consider and pass appropriate orders thereon. A railway servant desiring to seek the benefit of the Insolvency Act shall apply to the Head of his Department, or to such authority as a Government may specify in this behalf, for permission to file a Schedule in a Court of Law. Same time, he shall explain in such form as the Government may prescribe in this behalf all the circumstances which led to his financial embarrassment. The said authority will then consider his case in the light of those circumstances. If the railway servant can prove that the indebtedness was the result of circumstances, which, with the exercise of ordinary diligence, he could not have foreseen or over which he had no control, and did not proceed from extravagant or dissipated habits and if as the result of investigation, the said authority considers that sufficient justification exists for the retention of the employee in service, he may permit him to have recourse to the court. Otherwise he should take steps either to dismiss or remove the employee from service as the circumstances of the case may warrant. If a railway servant asks for permission to seek the benefit of the Insolvency Act for a second time such permission may not be granted by an authority lower than the General Manager or Head of Office, who, if he decides to retain the employee in service, shall report the circumstances to the Railway Board for information. As the Railway Co-operative Credit Society is often a creditor in such a case and other railway servants are sureties for the debtor, the said authority will, in deciding whether or not the debtor, should be retained in railway service, consider the effect of his dismissal or removal on the railway and on his fellow employees.

(*ii*) A railway servant who seeks the assistance of the Insolvency Court without the previous permission of the competent authority shall render himself liable to removal from service.

(*iii*) A railway servant who is arrested for debt is liable for dismissal.

(*iv*) Steps will be taken from time to time by the Head of an Office to ascertain from pay sheets, etc. whether any railway servant under him are in a habitual state of indebtedness. If a moiety of the pay of a railway servant is being frequently attached for debit, has been continuously so attached for a period exceeding two years or is attached for a sum which under ordinary circumstances he could not repay within two years, such railway servant shall be considered liable for dismissal.

(*v*) Every case falling under (*iii*) or (*iv*) shall be considered in the light of the instructions contained in clause *(i)* above before it is finally decided whether or not the railway servant concerned should be dismissed or removed, but except in exceptional circumstances such railway servant should not be retained in service.

(3) A railway servant shall also report to the Government or to such authorities as may be specified in this behalf the facts when a portion of his salary is constantly being attached, has been continuously attached for a period exceeding two years or is attached for a sum which, in ordinary circumstances cannot be paid within a period of two years.

(4) When a moiety of a railway servant's salary is attached, the report by his superior officer to the Government competent authority should show what is the proportion of the debts to the salary; how for they detract from the debtor's efficiency as a railway servant, whether the debtor's position is irretrievable; and whether, in the circumstances of the case, it is desirable to retain him in the post occupied by him when the matter was brought to notice, or in any post under the Government.

18. Movable, immovable and valuable property. (1) Every railway servant shall on his first appointment to the railway service submit a return of his assets and liabilities, in such form as may be prescribed by the Government, giving full particulars regarding—

(*a*) the immovable property inherited by him or owned or acquired by him or held by him on lease or mortgage, either in his own name or in the name of any member of his family or the name of any other person;

(*b*) the shares, debentures and cash including bank deposits inherited by him or similarly owned, acquired or held by him;

(*c*) other movable property inherited by him or similarly owned, acquired or held by him;

(*d*) debts and other liabilities incurred by him directly or indirectly.

Note 1. Sub-rule (1) shall not ordinarily apply to Group 'D' railway servants, but the Government may in appropriate cases direct that it shall apply to any of such railway servants or any class of such railway servants.

Note 2. In every return, the value of items of movable property with less than ₹10,000 may be added and shown as a lumpsum. The values of articles of daily use such as clothing, utensils, crockery, books and the like, need not be included in such return.

Note 3. (1) (*i*) Where a railway servant already belonging to a service or holding a post is appointed to any other Government or Railway service or post, he shall not be required to submit a fresh return under this clause.

(*ii*) Every railway servant belonging to any service or holding any post included in Group A or Group B shall submit an annual return in such form as may be prescribed by the Government in this regard giving full particulars regarding immovable property inherited by him or owned by him or acquired by him or held by him on lease or mortgage either in his own name or in the name of any member of his family or in the name of any other person.

(2) No railway servant shall, except with the previous knowledge of the Government, acquire or dispose of any immovable property by lease, mortgage, purchase, sale, gift or otherwise either in his own name or in the name of any member of his family:

Provided that the previous sanction of the Government shall be obtained by the railway servant if any such transaction is with a person having official dealings with him.

(3) Where a railway servant enters into a transaction in respect of movable property either in his own name or in the name of a member of his family, he shall, within one month from the date of such transaction, report the same to the Government, if the value of such property exceeds ₹20,000 in the case of a railway servant holding any Group A or Group B post or a Temporary Gazetted Officer or ₹15,000 in the case of a railway servant holding any Group C or Group D post:

Provided that the previous sanction of the Government shall be obtained by the railway servant if any such transaction is with a person having official dealings with him.

Note 1. Purchase of items of movable property for giving presents at the time of marriage will be regulated by rule 18(3) above like any other transaction in movable property.

Note 2. The powers of a Government so fas as sub-rule (3) is concerned, may be exercised by—

(*i*) the General Manager and the Chairman, Railway Rates Tribunal, in respect of both gazetted and non-gazetted officers under their respective administrative control; and

(*ii*) Senior Deputy General Managers on Zonal Railways in respect of gazetted officers below the Senior Administrative Grade and non-gazetted officers subject to the condition that the powers hereby delegated are not further delegated by them to lower authorities so far as cases of gazetted officers are concerned.

(4) The Government or any authority empowered by it in this behalf may, at any time, by general or special order, require a railway servant to furnish, within a period specified in the order, a full and complete statement of such movable or immovable property held or acquired by him or on his behalf or by any member of his family as may be specified in the order. Such statement shall, if so required by the Government or by the authority so empowered, include the details of the means by which, or the source from which, such property was acquired.

(5) The Government may exempt any category of railway servants belonging to Group 'C' or Group 'D' from any of the provisions of this rule except sub-rule (4). No such exemption shall, however, be made without the concurrence of the Railway Board, who will consult the Ministry of Home Affairs.

Explanation I. For the purpose of this rule, the expression 'movable property' includes—

(*a*) jewellery, insurance policies the annual premium of which exceeds ₹10,000 or one sixth of the total annual emoluments received from Government whichever is less, shares, securities and debentures;

(*b*) All loans, whether secured or not, advanced or taken by the Government servant;

(*c*) Motor Cars, Motor Cycles, horses or any other means of conveyance; and

(*d*) Refrigerators, radios and radiograms and television sets.

Explanation II. For the purpose of this rule, "lease" means, except where it is obtained from, or granted to, a person having official dealings with the railway servant, a case of immovable property from year to year for any term exceeding one year or reserving a yearly rent.

18A. Restrictions in relation to acquisition and disposal of immovable property outside India and transaction with foreigners etc. Notwithstanding anything contained in sub-rule (2) of rule 18. No railway servant shall except with the previous sanction of the Government—

(*a*) Acquire, by purchase, mortgage, lease, gift or otherwise, either in his own name or in the name of any member of his family, any immovable property situated outside India;

(*b*) dispose of, by sale, mortgage, gift or otherwise, or grant any lease in respect of any immovable property situated outside India which was acquired or is held by him either in his own name or in the name of any member of his family;

(*c*) enter into any transaction with any foreigner, foreign Government, foreign organisation or concern—

(*i*) for the acquisition, by purchase, mortgage, lease, gift or otherwise, either in his own name or in the name of any member of his family, or any immovable property.

(*ii*) for the disposal of, by sale, mortgage, gift or otherwise, or the grant of any lease in respect of, any immovable property which was acquired or held by him either in his own name or in the name of any member of his family.

19. Vindication of acts and character of railway servants. (1) No railway servant shall, except with the previous sanction of the Government, have recourse to any court or to the press for the vindication of any official act which has been the subject matter of adverse criticism or an attack of a defamatory character.

Provided that if no such sanction is received by the railway servant within a period of three months from the date of receipt of his request by the Government, he shall be free to assume that the permission as sought for has been granted to him.

(2) Nothing in this rule shall be deemed to prohibit a railway servant from vindicating his private character or any act done by him in his private capacity and where any action for vindicating his private character or any act done by him in his private capacity is taken, the railway servant shall submit a report to the Government regarding such action.

20. Canvassing of non-official or other influence. No railway servant shall bring or attempt to bring any political or other influence to bear upon any superior authority to further his interests in respect of matters pertaining to his service under the Government.

21. Restrictions Regarding Marriage. (1) No railway servant shall enter into, or contract, a marriage with a person having a spouse living; and

(2) No railway servant, having a spouse living, shall enter into, or contract, a marriage with any person.

(3) A railway servant who has married or married a person other than of Indian Nationality shall forthwith intimate the fact to the Government.

Provided that the Government may permit a railway servant to enter into, or contract, any such marriage as is referred to in clause (1) or clause (2), if it is satisfied that—

(*a*) such marriage is permissible under the personal law applicable to such railway servant and the other party to the marriage; and

(*b*) there are other grounds for so doing.

22. Consumption of intoxicating drinks and drugs. (1) A railway servant shall—

(*a*) strictly abide by the law relating to intoxicating drinks or drugs during the course of his duties and shall also take due care that the performance of his duties at anytime is not affected in any way by the influence of such drink or drug.

(*b*) refrain from consuming any intoxicated drink or drug in a public place.

(2) A railway servant shall not—

(*a*) appear in a public place in a state of intoxication;

(*b*) use any intoxicating drink or drug to excess;

(*c*) if he belongs to the category of running staff (both loco and traffic) or is connected directly with train passing, have taken or used any intoxicating drinks or drugs within eight hours of the commencement of duty or take such drinks or drugs during the course of duty.

Explanation. For the purpose of this rule "Public place" means any place or premiss (including conveyance) to which public have, or permitted to have, access whether on payment or otherwise.

22A. Prohibition regarding employment of Children below 14 years of age. No railway servant shall employ to work and child below the age of 14 years.

23. Interpretation. The power of interpreting these rules is reserved to the President.

24. Delegation of powers. The Government may, by general or special order, direct that any power exercisable by it under these rules shall, subject to such conditions, if any, as may be specified in the order, be exercisable also by such officer or authority as may be specified in the order.

25. Repeal and Savings. The Railway Services (Conduct) Rules, 1966, contained in Appendix VI of the Indian Railway Establishment Code, Volume I, shall cease to be in force except as respects things done or omitted to be done.

26. Obligation to abide by all administrative instructions. Notwithstanding anything contained in these rules, a railway shall be governed by all the administrative instructions that may be issued from time to time in regard to the conduct of railway servants.

APPENDIX 12

The Railway Servants (Hours of Work and Period of Rest) Rules, 2005

G.S.R. 75, dated 28th February, 2005[1] In exercise of the powers conferred by section 136 of the Railways Act, 1989 (24 of 1989) the Central Government hereby makes the following rules, namely:

PART I

1. Short title, commencement and application. (1) These rules may be called the Railway Servants (Hours of Work and Period of Rest) Rules, 2005.

(2) They shall come into force on the date of their publication in the Official Gazette.

(3) They shall apply only to those railway servants to whom Chapter XIV of the Act applies.

2. Definitions. In these rules, unless the context otherwise requires,—

(*a*) 'Act' means the Railways Act, 1989 (24 of 1989);

(*b*) 'full-night' means the period between 10.00 p.m. and 6.00 a.m.;

(*c*) 'long-on' means a period of duty over either hours in the case of 'intensive' workers, over ten hours in the case of 'continuous' workers and over twelve hours in the case of 'essentially intermittent' workers;

(*d*) 'ordinary rate of pay' includes—

(*i*) pay as defined in Rule 1303 (F.R. 9) of the Indian Railway Establishment Code, Volume-II (1990 Edition) and includes element of running allowance to the extent of 30 per cent of basic pay in the case of running staff as defined in Rule 1507 of the aforesaid Code;

(*ii*) Dearness Allowance, Additional Dearness Allowance and Dearness Pay, if any; and

(*iii*) Compensatory (City) Allowance;

1 Published in the Gazette of India, Pl.-II, section 3(*i*), dated 5.3.2005 (w.e.f. 5.3.2005).

(*e*) 'Railway servants employed in confidential capacity' includes—

(*i*) Stenographers working either in a separate confidential cell or attached to the officers in Administrative offices;

(*ii*) Cypher operators;

(*iii*) Confidential Assistants and Personal Assistants; and

(*iv*) Any other railway servant who may be so specified by the Head of the Railway Administration to have been employed in confidential capacity;

(*f*) 'Regional Labour Commissioner' means an officer appointed as such by the Government of India in the Ministry of Labour by notification in the Official Gazette;

(*g*) 'Roadside station' means a station other than—

(*i*) an important junction station;

(*ii*) a station with marshalling yard;

(*iii*) an important terminal station;

(*iv*) a station from which trains are ordered as a regular measure; and

(*v*) a station where a separate goods office under a supervisory Goods Clerk, in the grade of Chief Goods Clerk or of higher rank sanctioned on the basis of workload in that Goods Office has been provided:

Provided that the Head of the Railway Administration or the authority to whom he may delegate this power, may draw up a list of roadside stations keeping in view the above definition;

(*h*) 'roster' means a document which shows the hours that a railway servant is expected to be on duty every day, the daily as well as weekly rest and break between spells of duty in a day besides other necessary particulars;

(*i*) 'running staff' means the staff who are defined to be so in Rule 1507 of Indian Railway Establishment Code, Volume II;

(*j*) "section" means a section of the Act;

(*k*) 'short off' means a period of rest which is—

(*i*) in the case of intensive workers—

(*A*) less than 12 hours in a roster of six hours duty; and

(*B*) less than 14 hours in a mixed roster of 6 and 8 hours duty;

(*ii*) in the case of continuous worker—less than 10 hours;

(*iii*) in the case of essentially intermittent workers—less than 8 hours;

(*l*) 'split duty' means duty in two or more spells with intervening breaks each of half or more hour necessitated by exigencies of work and when the employee is free to leave his place of duty. Intervals for rest and meals shall not be breaks for the purpose of split-duty;

(*m*) 'sustained attention' as used in sub-section (*b*), section 130 implies mental effort.

Explanation. A Pointsman waiting for the arrival of a train after setting points is required to give sustained attention. Similarly, a Station Master or an Assistant Station Master is generally required to pay sustained attention from the time he gives line clear to the Station in rear till the time the train arrives and again from the time the line clear is asked for to the time the Block Section ahead is cleared. Wherever circumstances justify a different treatment, the period involving sustained attention may be decided by the Controlling Authority. In case of any doubt, the decision of the Head of the Department shall be final;

(*n*) all other words and expressions used but not defined in these rules shall have the meanings respectively assigned to them in the Indian Railway Establishment Code or the Act.

PART II

CLASSIFICATION OF EMPLOYMENT AND HOURS OF WORK

3. Prescribed authority to classify the employment of railway servant. (1) The power to declare the employment of railway servants as 'intensive' or 'essentially intermittent' within the meaning of section 130 shall vest in the Head of the Railway Administration:

Provided that the Head of the Railway Administration may, in his discretion, delegate the power vested in him under this sub-rule to the Chief Personnel Officer:

Provided further that during the period of emergency such as flood, accident, the power vested in the competent authority can be exercised by an officer not below the rank of senior scale.

(2) A copy of every declaration made by the prescribed authority under sub-rule (1) shall, as soon as may be, sent to the Regional Labour Commissioner concerned and, in case xthe declaration is made by an officer other than the Head of the Railway Administration, to the Head of the Railway Administration or the Chief Personnel Officer, as the case may be.

4. Appeals against classification. (1) Any railway servant aggrieved by the declaration of classification made under rule 3 may, within ninety days from the date of such declaration, prefer an appeal to the Regional Labour Commissioner, who after scrutiny of relevant documents or if considered necessary, after a fresh job analysis, may order for a change in the classification.

(2) Any railway servant or Railway Administration aggrieved by a decision of the Regional Labour Commissioner may, before the expiry of ninety days from the date on which the decision of the Regional Labour Commissioner is communicated to him, prefer an appeal to the Secretary to the Government of India in the Ministry of Labour who will dispose it of after hearing the parties concerned.

5. Supervisory staff. (1) The Ministry of Labour shall, by order in writing, specify the railway servants or classes of railway servants who shall be treated as supervisory staff under sub-clause (*iv*) of clause (*c*) of section 130 on the ground that the railway servant holds a position of responsibility, is employed on duties mainly of a supervisory character and is, from the nature of his work and position, comparatively free to adjust his hours of duty or work during such hours:

Provided that the railway servants who on the date of publication of these rules are treated as supervisory staff under the rules shall continue to be treated as such until the orders specifying the railway servants or classes of railway servants as supervisory staff is issued under this sub-rule.

(2) A copy of every such order issued under sub-rule (1) shall be furnished to the Chief Labour Commissioner (Central), New Delhi.

6. Excluded staff. The following categories of staff of the Health and Medical Department shall be treated as 'excluded' under sub-clause (*v*) of clause (*c*) of section 130, namely—

(*a*) Matrons;

(*b*) Sisters-in-charge;

(*c*) Midwives who are not posted on regular shift duty in Railway Hospitals;

(*d*) Health Educators and District Extension Educators (Male and Female);

(*e*) Family Planning Field Workers (Male and Female);

(*f*) Lady Health Visitors;

(*g*) Auxiliary Nurses-cum-Midwives;

(*h*) Projectionists.

In addition to the above, the Ministry of Railways may, by order in writing, specify any other category of railway staff in any of the Departments of the Indian Railways who shall be treated as 'excluded' on the consideration that such staff are available on call.

7. Criteria for determining classification of railway servants. (1) *Continuous:* All employments of railway servants except those excluded from the purview of the Hours of Employment Regulations are assumed to be 'continuous'. Thereafter, on the basis of factual job analysis the employment may be classified either as 'intensive' or 'essentially intermittent', as the case may be.

(2) *Intensive:* The two important factors in declaring an employment as 'intensive' under clause (*d*) of section 130 of the Act are—

(*i*) strenuous nature of the work tending to cause mental or physical strain; and

(*ii*) continuous application to such work with little or no periods of relaxation.

Explanation I. The term 'continued concentration' in clause (*d*) of section 130 is intended to convey that the attention demanded of the railway servant concerned for a particular nature of job should be exclusive not to allow any other thought or idea to enter the mind and must be of such nature as to cause strain (physical or mental or both) upon the railway servant concerned as a result of continuous application to such work over certain period without reasonable periods of respite. Thus, having regard to the entire period of duty and nature of work, the prescribed authority shall, before declaring any employment as 'intensive', satisfy itself that the above factors are present in the job concerned. In other words, the prescribed authority shall consider whether the job is of such a character that it demands continued concentration without any reasonable periods of relaxation.

Explanation II. Factor (*ii*) should be considered to have been satisfied where the periods of rest, inaction or relaxation do not aggregate 6 hours or more in a cycle of 24 hours or one hour or more in a shift of 8 hours.

(3) *Essentially Intermittent:* The work of an employee is to be regarded as 'essentially intermittent' if his daily duty hours which should be assumed to be twelve hours per day include—

(*a*) one period of inaction of not less than one hour, or two such periods of not less than half an hour each, and

(*b*) various periods of inaction including the period of inaction specified in clause (*a*) aggregating 50 per cent or more, during which he is not generally called upon to display either physical activities or sustained attention.

Note. In assessing the workload of the 'essentially intermittent' classification in accordance with sub-section (*b*) of section 130, periods of inaction of less than 5 minutes shall be ignored.

8. Fixation of hours of work. The hours of work of a railway servant as per roster (hereinafter referred to as the rostered hours of work) may be continuous or may have short interval for rest, or breaks due to exigencies of service or deployment.

(1) Subject to the limit specified in section 132 and having regard to the requirements of the service and the nature of work, the Railway Administration shall fix the normal rostered hours of work for the various categories of railway servants in the manner indicated in these rules.

(2) The rostered hours of work of railway servants shall consist of—

(*i*) standard hours of duty;

(*ii*) additional hours as may be prescribed in the case of certain categories classified as essentially intermittent; and

(*iii*) time required to do preparatory or complementary work or both for those who are required to do such work.

(3) The standard hours of duty for different classes of employment of railway servants shall be as under—

(*a*) Intensive	...	42 hours a week;
(*b*) Continuous	...	48 hours a week; and
(*c*) Essentially intermittent	...	48 hours a week.

(4) (*a*) Railway servants having essentially intermittent class of employment shall be called upon to work as per rule 8(2)(*ii*) additional hours as indicated below—

(*i*) Gatemen 'C, Caretakers of Rest Houses and Reservoirs etc., Chowkidars and Saloon Attendants	24 additional hours per week
(*ii*) Railway servants posted to work in Essentially Intermittent employment at roadside stations and provided with residential quarters within 0.5 kms. from their place of duty	
(*iii*) Rest of employees posted to work in Essentially Intermitted class of employment	12 additional hours per week

(*b*) Such additional hours of work shall be reflected in the duty rosters of the railway servants concerned.

(5) The time required by various categories of staff to do preparatory or complementary work or both, which includes the work of handing over and taking over charge, must necessarily be carried out outside the limits laid down for general working of an establishment, branch or shift and shall be determined by means of job analysis of such work in respect of representative posts in respective categories.

(6) The time determined under sub-rule (5) shall be added to the standard hours of duty of the staff in all the various classifications subject to maximum limit prescribed below—

(*a*) when employment is intensive ... 3 hours a week;

(*b*) when employment is continuous ... 6 hours a week;

(*c*) when employment is essentially intermittent—

(*i*) Gatemen 'C', Caretakers of Rest Houses and Reservoirs, Chowkidars, Saloon Attendants and those posted at roadside stations and provided with residential quarters within 500 metres from their place of duty ... 3 hours a week;

(*ii*) Railway servants other than those mentioned in sub-clause (*i*) ... 4½ hours a week;

(7) The time required for preparatory or complementary work by the running staff shall be deemed to be 4 hours a week.

Notes: (*i*) Where the time assessed for doing preparatory or complementary work is under 15 minutes per day, the same shall not be treated as duty and shall not be exhibited in the roster;

(*ii*) In the case of employment of a 'continuous' nature, the time assessed for doing preparatory or complementary work between 15 minutes and less than 45 minutes per day should be treated as half an hour's work and such time between 45 minutes and one hour per day should be treated as one hour's work;

(*iii*) In the case of intensive and essentially intermittent categories of employment, such time assessed between 15 minutes and 30 minutes per day shall be treated as half an hour's work;

(*iv*) The time assessed for the work mentioned in Note (*iii*) shall be reflected in the duty rosters of the concerned railway servants;

(*v*) Total hours for preparatory or complementary work or both shall be so fixed to ensure that the overall duty hours do not exceed the limits prescribed for respective classification in section 132.

(8) Where railway servants are required to perform split-duty, such duty shall be subject to the following conditions, namely—

(*a*) The spells of duty shall not exceed three and the number of breaks shall be limited to two;

(*b*) In the case of an employment of 'continuous' nature, the railway servant whose place of residence is beyond 1.6 kilometres from the place of duty, seven hours of split-duty shall be treated as equivalent to eight-hours of normal duty.

(9) While preparing rosters, 'long on' or 'short off' shall, accordingly, be avoided.

(10) Where, in accordance with the provisions of sub-section (4) of section 132 or sub-section (3) of section 133 and in the circumstances mentioned therein, a railway servant is called upon by an order of temporary exemption made under rule 9 below by the competent authority to render duty beyond the hours of work fixed in accordance with the foregoing sub-rules or beyond the hours prescribed in sub-sections (1), (2) and (3) of section 132, it shall be the duty of the railway servant concerned to render such extra hours of duty.

9. Power to make temporary exemption. (1) Subject to the provisions of sub-section (4) of section 132 and of sub-section (3) of section 133, Head of a Railway Administration may by order in writing make temporary exemption of any railway servant or class or railway servants from the provisions of sub-sections (1), (2) and (3) of section 132 and sub-sections (1) and (2) of section 133.

(2) The Head of Railway Administration may by order in writing delegate his powers under sub-rule (1) to any officer subordinate to him and whom he may deem fit to exercise the powers.

(3) A copy of every order of delegation made under sub-rule (2) shall be sent to the Regional Labour Commissioner concerned.

10. Principle of averaging and payment of overtime allowance. (1) Where a railway servant is required to render extra hours of duty beyond the rostered hours fixed in accordance with rule 8 or beyond the limits specified for different classes of railway servant under section 132, he shall be paid overtime for such extra hours of work, subject to the principle of averaging as specified in sub-rule (2).

(2) Averaging shall be done by averaging of the hours of work over the averaging periods as specified in section 132 which has been adopted to provide a reasonable measure of elasticity as essential in railway working for certain classes of railway servants and it shall apply to—

(*i*) running staff;

(*ii*) operating staff;

(*iii*) shift workers; and

(*iv*) those other railway servants whose work is connected with the work of any of the categories of railway servants mentioned in clauses (*i*), (*ii*) and (*iii*).

Subject to the provisions contained in sub-section (4) of section 132, payment of overtime for excess hours of work shall be made as under—

(*i*) for the excess hours of work rendered by a railway servant between the limits of prescribed rostered hours of work and the hours prescribed in section 132, during the relevant averaging period, payment shall be made at 1½ times the ordinary rate of pay; and

(*ii*) for the excess hours of work rendered beyond the limits prescribed in section 132, payment shall be made at two times the ordinary rate of pay.

(4) The hourly rate of overtime shall be worked out on the basis of rostered hours over the relevant averaging period as under—

(*i*) Hourly rate of pay (For staff governed by Averaging Principle)	$\dfrac{\text{Period of averaging}}{\text{No. of rostered hours of work in the averaging period}}$	×	1/30 of monthly ordinary rate of pay
(*ii*) Hourly rate of pay (For those not governed by Averaging Principle)	$\dfrac{1}{\text{No. of daily rostered hours of work}}$	×	1/30 of monthly ordinary rate of pay

11. Register of extra hours of work. The particulars of all extra hours of work done by a railway servant beyond the prescribed rostered hours of duty shall be recorded in a register to be maintained in Form 'A' appended to these rules by the officer authorised in this behalf of the Head of the Railway Administration.

12. Periodical Rest. (1) Railway servant whose employment is Intensive or Continuous shall be granted, every week commencing on a Sunday, rest of not less than thirty consecutive hours and those whose employment is Essentially Intermittent, shall be granted rest of not less than twenty-four consecutive hours including a full night.

(2) No railway servant classified as Intensive, Continuous or Essentially Intermittent shall be called on duty unless one has had a rest of not less than 12, 10, 8 consecutive hours respectively after completion of the previous tour of duty. Such rest shall be given as far as possible through the employment of rest givers and the rest givers so provided shall be separate for Continuous and Essentially Intermittent categories.

(3) Locomotive or traffic running staff shall be granted, each month, a rest of at least five periods of not less than twenty-two consecutive hours each, or a rest of at least four periods of not less than thirty consecutive hours each including a full night. The hours of work for this purpose shall be calculated from "signing on" to "signing off".

(4) The locomotive and traffic running staff shall not normally be away from headquarters for more than three or four days at a stretch and the periodic rest for such staff shall be given at headquarters. Rest at headquarters shall always include a night in bed, and as far as possible be once in every ten days.

(5) Staff on duty in running trains, other than locomotive and traffic running staff such as Travelling Pay Clerks and Catering Staff attached to Restaurant Cars shall be given periodic rest on the scale and in the manner laid down for the locomotive and traffic running staff. Some portion of the periodic rest may, however, be given away from their headquarters having regard to their length of trips.

(6) The working hours and periodic rest of marine staff, other than those who are governed by the Factories Act shall be regulated in the same manner as those of running staff.

(7) In accordance with clause (*ii*) of sub-section (2) of section 133 of the Act, the Head of the Railway Administration may, with the prior approval of the Ministry of Railways, specify the categories of railway servants to whom the periods of rest on scales less than those laid down under sub-section (1) of the said section can be prescribed.

13. Compensatory periods of rest. No railway servant in respect of whom an exemption has been made under rule 9 shall be required to work for more than fourteen days without a period of rest and shall be provided with compensatory rest within this period.

PART III

AUTHORITIES TO ENSURE PROPER IMPLEMENTATION OF THE PROVISIONS OF CHAPTER XIV OF THE ACT AND THESE RULES

14. Appointment of Supervisors. The supervisors of Railway labour shall be appointed by the Ministry of Labour. The manner of their appointment and the educational qualifications etc. prescribed for the purpose will be as laid down by the Ministry of Labour from time to time.

15. Display of rules and notices. Every Railway Administration shall display in a conspicuous place—

(*a*) where the railway servants work, notices specifying the classification of employment of railway servants; the duration of their hours of employment, their period of rest and rosters; and

(*b*) in each station or other establishment a copy of Chapter XIV of the Act and these rules in English, Hindi and in local language.

16. Annual Return. Every Railway Administration shall send each financial year a return in Form 'B' appended to these rules, so as to reach the Regional Labour Commissioner not later than the 15th day of May following the end of the financial year to which it relates.

PART IV

RESIDUARY POWERS

17. Power to make modification in special cases. (1) Notwithstanding anything provided in these rules, where, in the interest of efficient working of the Railways, there are certain conditions of special nature necessitating an immediate modification of any conditions laid down under these rules to suit local conditions, such modifications which are not inconsistent with any provisions of Chapter XIV of the Act, may be effected with prior approval of the Ministry of Railways.

(2) A copy of each such modification shall be sent to the Regional Labour Commissioner concerned.

(3) If any railway servant is adversely affected by any such modification made under sub-rule (1), he may prefer an appeal before the expiry of 90 days from the date of effecting such modification to the Ministry of Railways whose decision thereon shall be final.

PART V

REPEAL AND SAVING

18. The Railway servants (Hours of Employment) Rules, 1961 and any orders issued thereunder insofar as they are inconsistent with these rules, are hereby repealed; provided that—

(1) such repeal shall not affect the previous operation of the said rules or any orders made or anything done or any action taken thereunder;

(2) nothing in these rules shall be construed as depriving any person to whom these rules apply, of any right of appeal which had accrued to him under the rules or orders in force before the commencement of these rules;

(3) an appeal pending at the commencement of these rules against an order made before such commencement shall be considered and orders thereon shall be made in accordance with these rules as if such orders were made and the appeals were preferred under these rules;

(4) as from the commencement of these rules any appeal or application for review against any orders made before such commencement, shall be preferred or made under these rules as if such orders were made under these rules.

FORM 'A'

[*See* Rule 11]

REGISTER OF EXTRA HOURS OF WORK—REGISTER PRESCRIBED UNDER RULE 11 OF RAILWAY SERVANTS (HOURS OF WORK AND PERIOD OF REST) RULES, 2004

Station:

Division

Sl. No.	*Month and date overtime worked*	*Name and Father's name*	*Designation*	*Classification Intensive Continuous Essentially Intermittent*
(1)	(2)	(3)	(4)	(5)

Rate of Pay	*Rostered hours From To*	*Actual hours From To*	*Extra Hours Worked*
(6)	(7)	(8)	(9)

Reason for working extra hours	*Compulsory rest granted Date From to*	*Number of hours for which over-time payable*	*Reasons for granting temporary exemption under sections 132(4) and 133*
(10)	(11)	(12)	(13)

Signature of subordinate in charge granting exemption under rules	*Amount of overtime paid and date of payment*	*Remarks*
(14)	(15)	(16)

FORM 'B'

[*See* Rule 16]

ANNUAL RETURN FOR THE YEAR ENDING 31ST MARCH ....

			Intensive		*Continuous*			
					Running Staff		*Other than Running Staff*	
Sl. No.	*Name of Railway*	*Total No. of railway servants employed*	*No.*	*Per cent*	*No.*	*Per cent*	*No.*	*Per cent*
(1)	(2)	(3)	(4)	(5)	(6)	(7)	(8)	(9)

Essentially Intermittent		*Supervisory*		*Excluded Employed in confidential capacity*		*Others*		
No.	*Per cent*	*No.*	*Per cent*	*No.*	*Per cent*	*No.*	*Per cent*	*Remarks*
(10)	(11)	(12)	(13)	(14)	(15)	(16)	(17)	(18)

Place: Signature of Head/In charge

Date: Railway Administration

To (Seal)

The Regional Labour Commissioner (Central)

APPENDIX 13

The Railways (Manner of Delivery of Consignments and Sale Proceeds in the Absence of Railway Receipt) Rules, 1990

G.S.R. 595(E), dt. 22nd June 1990 In exercise of the powers conferred by clauses (*e*) and (*f*) of sub-section (2) of section 87 of the Railways Act, 1989 (24 of 1989) read with section 22 of the General Clauses Act, 1897 (10 of 1897), the Central Government hereby makes the following rules, namely:

1. Short title and commencement. (1) These rules may be called the Railways (Manner of Delivery of Consignments and Sale Proceeds in the Absence of Railway Receipt) Rules, 1990.

(2) They shall come into force on the date of their commencement of the Act.

2. Definitions. In these rules, unless the context otherwise requires—

(*a*) 'Act' means the Railways Act, 1989 (24 of 1989);

(*b*) 'Consignee' means the person named as consignee in a railway receipt;

(*c*) 'Consignment' means goods entrusted to a railway administration for carriage;

(*d*) 'Consignments booked to self' means consignments booked by the consignor to self at the destination instead of to a 'consignee', by name.

(*e*) 'Form' means the Form annexed to these rules;

(*f*) 'Railway receipt' means the railway receipt issued under section 65 of the Act;

(*g*) 'Station Master' means a Railway employee by whatever name called, in overall charge of a Railway Station and includes any other railway employee authorised by the railway administration to grant delivery of goods;

(*h*) words and expressions used herein and not defined but defined in the Act shall have the meanings respectively assigned to them in the Act.

3. Delivery of consignments when the railway receipt is not forthcoming. (1) Where the railway receipt is not forthcoming, the consignment may be delivered to the person, who in the opinion of the railway administration is entitled to receive the goods and who shall receive the same on the execution of an Indemnity Note as specified in Form I:

Provided, however, that if the consignee is a Government official in his official capacity, such delivery may be made on unstamped Indemnity Note.

(2) Where the railway receipt is not forthcoming and the consignment is addressed by the sender to self, delivery shall not be made unless Indemnity Note, duly executed in Forms 1A and 1B are produced by the persons claiming delivery of the consignment.

(3) Where the railway receipt is not forthcoming and the consignment is not addressed to self by the sender, delivery may be made on the basis of an Indemnity Note duly executed in Form II in lieu of Form I subject to the following conditions, namely—

(*a*) The General Indemnity Note shall be executed on stamp paper of the appropriate value applicable to the State in which delivery is made;

(*b*) Consignment is booked to self shall not be granted delivery on the basis of General Indemnity Notes;

(*c*) Where delivery of a consignment is taken on the basis of a General Indemnity Note, the consignee should surrender the railway receipt within 10 days from the date of taking delivery of such consignment;

(*d*) Where the consignee has not produced the railway receipt within the time-limit specified under clause (*c*), a separate Indemnity Note in Form I should be executed by the consignee in respect of such consignment;

(*e*) If a consignee fails to surrender the original railway receipt or fails to execute a separate Indemnity Note in respect of any consignment taken delivery on the basis of the General Indemnity Note, Station Master may refuse to deliver further consignment on the basis of the General Indemnity Note furnished by the consignee;

(*f*) The Railway Administration shall have the right to demand the execution of a fresh General Indemnity Note on expiry of three years from the date on which it was executed.

(4) When the railway receipt is not forthcoming and the consignee is a State Government, delivery may be made at the discretion of the Railway Administration on the basis of General Indemnity Note specified in Form III.

(5) Where the railway receipt is not forthcoming and the consignee is a Ministry of Department of the Central Government, delivery may be made at the discretion of the Railway Administration on the basis of General Indemnity Note specified in Form IV.

4. Delivery of consignments when railway receipt is not forthcoming and the consignments or sale proceeds are claimed by two or more persons. When the railway receipt is not forthcoming and the goods in possession of the Railway Administration are claimed by two or more persons, the Railway Administration may withhold delivery of such goods unless an Indemnity Note, as specified in Form I, is executed by the person, to whom the goods are delivered or sale proceeds are paid.

5. Delivery of perishable articles when the railway receipt is not forthcoming. (1) Notwithstanding anything contained in these rules, where the consignment consists of perishable articles and the railway receipt is not forthcoming, such consignment may be delivered to the person who, in the opinion of the railway administration is entitled to receive such consignments, and such person shall take delivery subject to the following conditions, namely—

(*a*) if the invoice copy of the railway receipt is available at the time of taking delivery and the booking is to a named consignee who is claiming delivery, such person shall, before taking delivery execute an Indemnity Note specified in Form I; and

(*b*) (*i*) if the invoice copy of the railway receipt is not available at the time of taking delivery; or

(*ii*) if such invoice copy is available and the consignment is booked to 'Self'

such person shall, deposit an amount equivalent to the cost of consignment by way of security apart from freight and other charges before taking delivery of such consignment.

(2) If any amount has been deposited by way of security under clause (*b*) of sub-rule (1), such amount shall be refunded by the railway administration on production of the original railway receipt within six months from the date of taking such delivery.

(3) In the absence of original railway receipt refund may be granted on execution of an Indemnity Note in Form I or IA and IB, as the case may be, provided the invoice copy of the railway receipt is available and the particulars of consignment can be connected with reference to the invoice copy, within six months from the date of taking delivery.

FORM I

[*See* Rule 3(1)]

FORM OF INDEMNITY NOTE

.... Railway

INDEMNITY NOTE

**I/We hereby acknowledge to have received from the .... Railway valued at Rupees .... which was despatched to **my/our address from the .... Station of the .... Railway on or about the .... day of .... the railway receipt for which has been .... and **for myself, my heirs, executors and administrators/and for our Company/Firm, their assigns, and successors,

**I/We undertake in consideration of such delivery as aforesaid to hold.

*President of India, his agents and servants the .... railway administration, its agents and servants harmless and indemnified in respect of all claims to the said goods.

**I/We also undertake to pay on demand to the railway administration freight charges, undercharges, wharfage, and any other charges that may be subsequently found due in respect of this transaction.

And **I/We the undersigned, signing below the consignee of these goods certify that first signor is the *bona fide* owner of the goods: and that **I/We undertake the whole of the said liability equally with the consignee, and for this purpose **I/We affix **my/our signature hereto.

Signature of Witness	Signature of the Consignee ....
Father's name	**Father's name ....
Age	Age ....
Profession	Profession ....
Residence	Residence ....
	....
	Designation and Seal of the Co./Firm
	....
	Registered Office/Place of business
Signature of witness	Signature of Surety ....
Father's name	**Father's name ....
Age	Age ....
Profession	Profession ....
Residence	Residence ....
....	
....	
	Designation and Seal of the Co./Firm
	....
	Registered Office/Place of business
Executed in my presence	....
....	....
Station Stamp	Station Master
Date 20	

* To be struck out when the form is used on other than Government Railways.
To be struck out when the form is used on Government Railways.

** To be struck out when Indemnity Note is executed by or on behalf of a Company/Firm.

NOTE: This note is an agreement ranging under clause (*c*) of Article 5 of Schedule I of Indian Stamp Act 11 of 1899 and therefore, chargeable with stamp duty, irrespective of the value of the goods.

FORM I-A

[*See* Rule 3(2)]

FORM OF INDEMNITY NOTE

.... Railway

INDEMNITY NOTE

**I/We hereby acknowledge to have received from .... Railway .... valued at ₹ .... which was despatched by **me/us booked to self/as value payable, from the .... Station of the ....

Railway on or about the .... day of .... the railway receipt for which has been .... and **for myself, my heirs, executors and administrators/and for our Company/Firm, their assigns, and successors.

**I/We undertake in consideration of such delivery as aforesaid to hold.

*President of India, his agents and servants the .... railway administration, its agents and servants harmless and indemnified in respect of all claims to the said goods.

**I/We undertake to pay on demand to the railway administration freight charges, undercharges, wharfage, and any other charges that may be subsequently found due in respect of this transaction.

And **I/We the undersigned, signing below the consignor of these goods certify that first signor is the *bona fide* owner of the goods: and that **I/We undertake the whole of the said liability equally with the consignor, and for this purpose **I/We affix my/our signature hereto.

Signature of Witness	Signature of the Consignee ....
Father's name	**Father's name ....
Age	Age ....
Profession	Profession ....
Residence	Residence ....
	....
	Designation and Seal of the Co./Firm
	....
	Registered Office/Place of business
	....
Signature of witness	Signature of Surety ....
Father's name	**Father's name ....
Age	Age ....
Profession	Profession ....
Residence	Residence ....
....	....
	Designation and Seal of the Co./Firm
	....

Executed in my presence ....

....

....

Station Stamp	Station Master of forwarding Station
Date .... 20...........	

I hereby endorse this note in favour of .... whose address is .... whom I hereby authorise, to these delivery of the consignments booked by me as self/as value payable on my behalf.

Signature of Sender ....

Date .... 20 ....

---

* To be struck out when the form is used on other than Government Railways.
To be struck out when the form is used on Government Railways.

** To be struck out when Indemnity Note is executed by or on behalf of a Company/Firm.

NOTE: This note is an agreement ranging under clause (*c*) of Article 5 of Schedule I of Indian Stamp Act 11 of 1899 and, therefore, chargeable with stamp duty, irrespective of the value of the goods.

FORM I-B

[*See* Rule 3(2)]

FORM OF INDEMNITY NOTE

.... Railway

INDEMNITY NOTE

**I/We hereby acknowledge to have received from the .... Railway .... valued of ₹ .... which was despatched by .... from .... Station of the .... Railway on or about the .... day of .... and booked to self/as value payable, the Railway Receipt for which has been .... and **for myself, my heirs, executors and administrator/and for our Company/ Firm, their assigns, and successors.

**I/We undertake in consideration of such delivery as aforesaid to hold.

*President of India, his agents and servants the ....† railway administration, its agents and servants harmless and indemnified, its agents and servants harmless and indemnified in respect of all claims to the said goods.

**I/We also undertake to pay on demand to the railway administration freight charges, wharfage, and any other charges that may be subsequently found due in respect of this transaction.

**I enclose a copy of a stamped Indemnity Note executed by the consignor and counter signed by the Station Master of the Forwarding Station which has been duly endorsed by the consignor in my favour authorising me to take delivery of the consignments on his behalf.

**I/We the undersigned, signing below the person authorised by the consignor to take delivery of the goods. I hereby certify that the first signor is the *bona fide* owner of the goods and **I/We undertake the whole of the said liability equally with the signor and for this purpose **I/We affix our signatures hereby.

Signature of Witness	Signature of the Consignor ....
Father's name	**Father's name ....
Age	Age ....
Profession	Profession ....
Residence	Residence ....
	....

Designation and Seal of the Co./Firm

....

Registered Office/Place of Business

....

Executed in my presence

Station stamp

....

Signature of Surety ....

**Father's name ....

Age ....

Profession ....

Residence ....

....

Designation and Seal of the Co./Firm

....

Place of Business ....

....

Station Master ....

Date .... 20 ....

Signature of the person ....
authorised by the sender ....
to take delivery

---

† To be struck out when the form is used on other than Government Railways.

* To be struck out when the form is used on Government Railways.

** To be struck out when Indemnity Note is executed by or on behalf of a Company/Firm.

NOTE: This note is an agreement ranging under clause (*c*) of Article 5 of Schedule I of Indian Stamp Act 11 of 1899 and therefore, chargeable with stamp duty, irrespective of the value of the goods.

FORM II

[*See* Rule 3(3)]

GENERAL INDEMNITY NOTE

(*For use of other than Government Departments*)

In consideration of the President of India (hereinafter referred to as "the railway administration") agreeing to deliver from time to time to .... (hereinafter referred to as "the Principal Obligor") herein, or to his agent or servants who shall be duly accredited by letters of authority on such behalf signed by .... all and every description of goods and parcels consigned to the name of the Principal Obligor that arrive at .... and without production of the railway receipt while taking delivery of them, the Principal Obligor undertakes to hold the railway administration harmless and indemnified in respect of all claims to the goods and losses to the railway administration arising out of the aforesaid delivery.

And we (1) .... (2) .... (hereinafter called "the sureties") in consideration of the .... railway administration agreeing to deliver the goods to the Principal Obligor as aforesaid without production of the Railway Receipt while taking delivery, we (for ourselves and *on behalf of our heirs, successors, executors, legal representatives and assigns) agree to bind ourselves each and every one of us, to the railway administration in the terms set out hereinafter in these presents.

The Principal Obligor agrees and undertakes to surrender the original and proper railway receipts to the railway administration at .... in respect of the goods delivered to them as aforesaid as soon as they are available (if not lost).

In the event of their failure to surrender the original railway receipt within ten days of the delivery of any consignment, the Principal Obligor agrees and undertakes to execute a separate Indemnity Note along with two sureties approved by the railway administration agreeing to indemnity and hold the railway administration harmless and free from any liability in respect of the delivery of such consignment.

If there is delay in surrendering railway receipts or in executing a separate Indemnity Note, as provided for above, the railway administration reserves the right to stop deliveries on the strength of this General Indemnity Note.

The Principal Obligor and the sureties shall jointly and severally, at all times, keep the railway administration and their agents and servants indemnified and harmless against all claims and demands of whatsoever nature and all losses, expenses, damages, costs and charges incurred by the Railway Administration and their Agents and servants as referred to above in consequence of the delivery to the Principal Obligor or his Agents of such goods and parcels without the production of the Railway Receipt.

The liability of the sureties shall not be impaired or discharged by reason of time-being given or for any forbearance at or/omission of the Railway Administration whatever (whether with or without the consent of the sureties) nor shall be necessary to sue the Principal Obligor before suing the sureties.

The railway administration shall have the right to call upon the Principal Obligors to execute a fresh Indemnity Note with sureties approved by the railway administration on the expiry of 3 years from the date of the original execution of these presents and until such Indemnity as aforesaid is executed with approved sureties, this indemnity shall remain in force for effecting delivery of goods/ parcels without production of original railway receipt and for indemnification for loss, etc., to the railway administration in respect thereof.

Notwithstanding anything contained hereinabove, the Principal Obligor agrees that in respect of any goods consigned as aforesaid, the railway administration may demand production of banker's guarantee to its satisfaction and may on the Principal Obligor's failure to comply with such demand, decline to deliver the said goods to the Principal Obligor or his nominee.

Signed by the Principal Obligor ....

(within mentioned)

Signature of the Principal Obligor

In the presence of

1. ....

2. ....

(Signature of the Sureties)

Signed by the Surety (within mentioned) in the presence of — 1. .... 2.	Accepted on .... Designation of Officer for and on behalf of the President of India in the presence of 1. .... 2. ....

* Words in brackets to be struck out when the surety is a judicial person.

FORM III

[*See* Rule 3(4)]

GENERAL INDEMNITY NOTE

(*For use by State Governments*)

In consideration of the President of India (hereinafter referred to as "the railway administration") agreeing to deliver from time to time to .... (hereinafter referred to as "Governor of") herein, or to his Agents or servants who shall be duly accredited by letters of authority on such behalf signed by .... all and every description of goods and parcels consigned to the name of the Governor of .... that arrive at .... and without production of the Railway Receipt while taking delivery of them Governor of .... undertakes to hold the Railway Administration harmless and indemnified in respect of all claims to the goods and losses to the Railway Administration arising out of the aforesaid delivery.

The Governor of .... agrees and undertakes to surrender the original and proper Railway Receipts to the railway administration at .... in respect of the goods delivered to them as aforesaid as soon as they are available (if not lost).

The Governor of .... shall at all times, keep the railway administration and their Agents and servants indemnified and harmless against all claims and demands of whatsoever nature and all losses, expenses, damage costs and charges incurred by the railway administration and their Agents and servants as referred to above in consequence of the delivery to the Governor of .... or his Agents or servants of such goods and parcels without the production of the Railway Receipt.

Signature of the

....

for and on behalf of the

Governor of ....

Accepted on ....

Designation of Officer

for and on behalf of the

President of India

in the presence of—

....

FORM IV

[*See* Rule 3(5)]

GENERAL INDEMNITY NOTE

(*For use by Ministries or Departments of Central Government*)

In consideration of the .... Railway delivering from time to time all consignments belonging to .... that may arrive at .... specifically consigned to .... without production of the Railway Receipts or when such railway receipts are not properly endorsed to .... hereby agree to hold the .... Railway and all other Administrations working in connection herewith and also all other Transport Agents or carriers employed by them respectively over whose Railways or by or through whose Transport Agency or Agencies such goods may be carried and their respective Agents or servants harmless and indemnified in respect of all claims for goods so delivered and further agree to defray the cost of all suits of whatsoever nature brought against the .... Railway or such Railway Administration and Transport Agents or carriers as aforesaid or their respective Agents or servants for having delivered such goods without the production of the railway receipt Notes or in the absence of proper endorsement or endorsements on the same. The .... also undertakes to notify the Administration of the names of the Officers authorised to act for and on behalf of .... Government and take delivery of the consignments as aforesaid and also to notify the Administration of the charges occurring in the personnel from time to time.

Signature of ....

....

....

.... Government

Signature of witnesses

1. ....

2. ....

APPENDIX 14

The Railway Rates Tribunal (Procedure) Regulations, 1990

G.S.R. 600(E), dt. 26th June, 1990 In exercise of the powers conferred by sub-section (1) of section 48 of the Railways Act, 1989 (24 of 1989) and in supersession of the Railway Rates Tribunal Rules, 1959, read with section 22 of the General Clauses Act 1897, (10 of 1897) the Railway Rates Tribunal, with the previous approval of the Central Government, hereby makes the following regulations, namely:

1. Short title and commencement. These regulations may be called the Railway Rates Tribunal (Procedure) Regulations, 1990.

(2) They shall come into force on the date of commencement of the Act.

2. Definitions. In these Regulations, unless the context otherwise requires—

(*a*) 'Act' means the Railways Act, 1989 (24 of 1989);

(*b*) 'Appendix' means Appendix to these Regulations;

(*c*) 'Applicant' means the Railway Administration making application under section 45;

(*d*) 'Chairman' means Chairman of the Tribunal;

(*e*) 'Code' means the Code of Civil Procedure, 1908 (5 of 1908);

(*f*) 'complainant' means a person making a complaint under section 36;

(*g*) 'intervener' means any person allowed to intervene in a proceeding with the leave of the Tribunal;

(*h*) 'Member' means Member of the Tribunal;

(*i*) 'pleading' means a complaint under section 36, an application under section 45, the answer to any of these by the respondent, a reply to the answer wherever allowed or directed by the Tribunal and includes the grounds of support or objections, as the case may be, filed by an intervener;

(*j*) 'proceeding' means proceeding before the Tribunal;

(*k*) 'reference' means a reference to the Tribunal by the Central Government under section 39;

(l) 'representative' means any person duly authorised in writing and incudes a legal practitioner within the meaning of Advocates Act, 1961 (25 of 1961);

(m) 'respondent' means any person impleaded as a party in a complaint under section 36 or in an application under section 45;

(n) 'Secretary' means the person who for the time being is discharging the functions assigned under these Regulations and such other functions as may from time to time be directed by the Tribunal and includes an Assistant Secretary and any other officer appointed by the Tribunal to discharge the functions of the Secretary;

(o) 'section' means a section of the Act;

(p) 'Tribunal' means the Railway Rates Tribunal constituted by the Central Government under section 33;

(q) words and expressions used herein and not defined but defined in the Act, shall have the meanings respectively assigned to them in the Act;

(r) words and expressions used herein and not defined either in these Regulations or in the Act, shall have the meanings respectively assigned to them in the General Clauses Act, 1897 (10 of 1897);

3. Typographical specifications. All pleadings, affidavits and interlocutory applications and copies thereof presented to the Tribunal shall be typewritten, or printed fairly and legibly on substantial white foolscap folio paper, with a left hand margin at least 4 cm. wide and a right hand margin about 2.5 cm. wide, and separate sheets shall be stitched together. The type-script or printing shall be on one side only of the paper, and be divided into paragraphs numbered consecutively. Dates, sums and numbers shall be mentioned expressly in figures.

4. Appointment of representative. (1) A party to the proceeding may appoint, in writing any person as his representative to appear, act and be heard on all occasions before the Tribunal:

Provided that such appointment shall take effect only from the date on which the appointment order is filed with the Secretary:

Provided further that no Member of the Tribunal who has held office as such member shall be appointed as a representative.

(2) Any such appointment or terms of appointment of representative may be revoked or varied by the party appointing him by a declaration in writing:

Provided that such revocation or variation shall not take effect unless it is filed with the Secretary.

(3) The provisions of Order III of the First Schedule of the Code shall, in so far as may be, apply to the representatives.

5. Authentication of documents, appearance and acting. A document may be signed, appearance made or act done:

(a) in the case of a firm, by any of its partners;

(b) in the case of a body corporate, association or authority, by its Chairman, President, Managing Director, General Manager or Secretary, as the case may be;

(*c*) in the case of a railway administration, by the General Manager or the Chief Commercial Superintendent or any Head of the Department concerned of that railway administration; and

(*d*) in the case of the Central Government, by a Secretary or a Joint Secretary or a Deputy Secretary or an Under Secretary to that Government and in the case of Ministry of Railways (Railway Board) by the Secretary or the Joint Secretary or the Deputy Secretary or an Executive Director or a Director, Joint Director or Deputy Director in the Railway Board.

6. Verification. (1) Every pleading shall be verified at the foot by the party or by one of the parties to the pleading or by some other person proved to the satisfaction of the Tribunal to be acquainted with the facts of the case.

(2) The person verifying shall specify by reference to the numbered paragraphs of the pleading what he verifies on his own knowledge and what he verifies upon information received and believed to be true.

(3) The verification shall be signed by the person making it and shall state the date on which and the place at which it was signed.

(4) Where the verification is by some person other than the party, his name and address shall be given underneath his signature.

7. Presentation. Unless otherwise specially provided, all pleadings and documents, applications and communications intended for the Tribunal shall be presented to the Secretary at the Headquarters of the Tribunal or despatched to him by registered post acknowledgment due.

8. Time for presentation. (1) Pleadings and other documents, required or directed to be filed within a certain time, shall be filed at the Tribunal's office within that time.

(2) The date of receipt at the office of the Tribunal shall be taken as the date of filing.

9. Service of notice and summons. (1) Unless otherwise directed by the Tribunal or the Secretary, notices and summonses to the parties or witnesses as the case may be, shall be served by registered post acknowledgment due to the address furnished to the Tribunal.

(2) A notice to a party may also be served on the representative.

10. Initiation of proceeding. Every proceeding before the Tribunal shall be initiated by a complaint under section 36 or by an application under section 45 or by a reference under section 39.

11. Complaint. (1) A complaint under section 36 shall be addressed to the Tribunal and shall be in writing signed and verified. It shall set out the name, description and full address of the complainant and, if there is a representative for the complainant in the matter, his name and full address shall also be stated.

(2) The complaint shall contain a clear and concise statement of facts, the grounds of complaint, the relief or remedy which the complainant claims and, where a person other than a railway administration is sought to be impleaded as a respondent. It shall also set forth the grounds for impleading him.

12. Joinder of complainants. (1) Two or more persons having the same interest in the proceeding may join in a complaint, in which case all subsequent proceeding shall be in their joint names.

(2) Where there are more complainants than one, they shall nominate in the complaint either one of the complainants or his representatives as the person on whom any summons or notice may be served for and on behalf of all the complainants.

13. Respondent. (1) Where a complaint is made against a railway administration such railway administration shall be impleaded as the respondent.

(2) Where the complainant has reason to believe that any other person is likely to be materially affected by the relief he is seeking, such person shall also be impleaded as a respondent.

(3) The name, description and address of the respondent shall be given in the complaint and, where a railway administration of the Government railway is the respondent the provisions of section 79 of the Code shall apply.

14. Copies of complaint. Every complaint shall be accompanied with twice as many copies as there are parties and three additional copies for the use of the Tribunal.

15. Fee and deposit. With each complaint, the complainant shall pay a fee of ₹250 and provisionally deposit of ₹150 to meet the charges of the service of notices and other processes and cost of preparation of paper book.

16. Security and registration of complaint. (1) On receipt of a complaint, the Secretary shall mark on it the date of its receipt and initial it, and he shall thereafter endorse on it a report whether *prima facie* the complaint is or is not within the jurisdiction of the Tribunal.

(2) Where the Secretary endorses that the complaint is not within the jurisdiction of the Tribunal, he shall lay his report before the Tribunal for orders.

(3) Where a complaint is not in accordance with these regulations or is not accompanied with the necessary fee or deposit, and the complainant does not rectify the defect within the time allowed by the Secretary, the Secretary shall lay it, as soon as possible, before the Tribunal for orders.

(4) The Secretary shall give to the complaints filed, serial numbers according to the order in which they are received by him and enter them in a register specified in Form I of Appendix II.

17. Return of complaint. (1) Where the Tribunal is of the opinion that a complaint is *prima facie* beyond its jurisdiction, it shall direct the Secretary to return the complaint with an endorsement to that effect.

(2) If within 30 days of the receipt of such endorsement, the complainant makes an application to be heard on the question of jurisdiction, the Tribunal shall decide the question after hearing the complainant and such other party as it may consider proper.

(3) The fee paid by the complainant shall be refunded to him if the complaint is returned to him as a result of an order passed under sub-regulation (1).

18. Adding and striking out parties. (1) The Tribunal may, at any stage, either upon or without the report of the Secretary or the application of either party, and on such terms as may appear to the Tribunal to be just, order that the name of any party improperly joined, whether as complainant or respondent, be struck out or that the name of any person who ought to have been joined, whether as complainant or respondent, or who may be materially affected by the relief asked for, or whose presence before the Tribunal is considered proper or necessary for adjudication upon the questions involved in the complaint, be added:

(1) Provided however that no person shall be added as a complainant without his consent.

(2) No proceeding shall be defeated by reason merely of misjoinder or non-joinder of parties.

(3) When respondents are added, the complaint and the register shall be accordingly amended; and the complainant shall also file such number of additional copies of his complaint as is equal to twice the number of respondents added.

19. Service of notice of complaint. (1) A copy of the complaint shall be served on each respondent with the seal of the Tribunal and an endorsement by the Secretary requiring the respondent to file his answer to the complaint within 30 days from the date of service, and also stating that, in default of such answer being filed within the said period, the Tribunal may proceed to hear the complaint in his absence and also stating that in such a case, the respondent will not be heard except by leave of the Tribunal and subject to such terms as the Tribunal may deem fit to impose.

(2) In the case of railway administration, the copy may be served on the General Manager of the railway concerned.

(3) Where the Tribunal is of the opinion that it is necessary in the public interest so to do, a public notice shall also be published, at the cost of the complainant and in the manner ordered by the Secretary of the Tribunal, mentioning the filing of the complaint, names of the parties, brief description of its allegations and relief sought, and calling upon any person wishing to intervene in support of or opposition to the relief sought in the complaint to petition the Tribunal within 30 days of publication of the notice for leave to intervene.

(4) If it is considered that there are persons who are not on the record but have the same interest in the proceeding as the complainant or respondent, that fact should be mentioned in the public notice, any decision given by the Tribunal after such public notice shall apply to all such persons.

20. Withdrawal of complaint. (1) The complainant may at any stage after the institution of the complaint withdraw his complaint, and in that case the Tribunal may pass such orders, including orders as to costs, as it may deem fit.

(2) In the case of withdrawal of complaint before the answer is filed, the fee paid by the complainant shall be refunded.

21. Compromise of complaint. When any complaint is adjusted by a compromise between the parties, both of them shall immediately notify the Tribunal of the same, and the Tribunal shall, after such notice, if any, as it may consider necessary, pass suitable orders disposing of the complaint.

22. Answer. (1) The answer shall admit or deny specifically each allegation of fact contained in the complaint and not by a general denial of the grounds alleged by the complainant, and, unless denied specifically or by necessary implication, an allegation of fact in the complaint shall normally be taken as admitted by the respondent. The answer shall contain a clear and concise statement of the material facts on which the respondent relies and shall raise all grounds of defence.

(2) The answer shall be divided into paragraphs numbered consecutively and signed and duly verified and it shall set out the name, description and full address of the respondent and, if there be a representative acting for the respondent in the matter, his name and full address shall also be stated.

(3) Every answer shall be accompanied with twice as many copies as there are parties and three additional copies for the use of the Tribunal, and a sum of ₹150 shall also be deposited to meet the charges of service of notice and other processes and the cost of preparation of paper book.

23. Scrutiny and service of Answer. (1) On receipt of an answer, the Secretary shall mark on it the date of its receipt and initial it.

(2) If the answer is not in accordance with these regulations, or is not accompanied with the necessary deposit, and the respondent does not rectify the defect within the time allowed by the Secretary, the Secretary shall lay it as soon as possible before the Tribunal for orders.

(3) Copies of the answers received from the respondent shall be sealed and initialled by the Secretary and served on the complainant and on such other party as the Tribunal may order.

24. Subsequent pleading. No pleading subsequent to the answer shall be presented except by the leave of the Tribunal and upon such terms as the Tribunal may deem fit, but the Tribunal may at any time require from any of the parties a reply or additional reply together with twice as many copies thereof as there are parties and three additional copies for the use of the Tribunal and fix a time for presenting the same.

25. Amendment of pleading. The Tribunal may at any stage allow any pleading to be amended, or order any matter to be struck out which may tend to prejudice, embarrass or delay the fair hearing of the case, and all such amendments shall be made as may be necessary for the purpose of determining the real question at issue between the parties.

26. Production of documents. (1) Unless for good cause shown and on such terms as the Tribunal may deem fit, all documents in possession of a party on which he wishes to rely at the hearing shall be produced by him, along with the list thereof, on or before such date as may be fixed by the Tribunal for the purpose. He shall file at the same time, as many copies of the documents as there are parties and three additional copies for the use of the Tribunal.

(2) The Tribunal may, at any time, order the production by any party of such of the documents in his possession or power relating to the matter in question as it may deem fit.

27. Interrogatories and discovery. Any party to the proceeding may apply to the Tribunal for leave to deliver interrogatories in writing for examination of the opposite party, or for an order directing the opposite party to make a discovery of the documents in his possession, and in either case the provisions of Order XI of the First Schedule of the Code as far as may be shall apply and such applications may be rejected if they are so delayed as to necessitate an adjournment of the hearing of the case.

28. Inspection of documents. (1) Either party shall be entitled at any time to give notice to the other party, in whose pleadings or affidavits reference is made to any document, to produce such document for the inspection of the party giving such notice, and to permit him to take copies thereof and the party not complying with such notice shall not afterwards be at liberty to put any such document in evidence on his behalf, unless he satisfies the Tribunal that he had sufficient cause for not complying with such notice.

(2) All books, documents and other things produced before the Tribunal, whether voluntarily or on requisition, may be inspected by the parties:

Provided that Tribunal may in its discretion refuse publication of such parts of the books, documents or things produced as the parties may submit to be prejudicial to their interests to publish.

29. Framing of issues. (1) After the closure of the pleading and the filing of documents, the Tribunal shall call upon the parties or representatives to furnish the draft issues.

(2) The Tribunal shall thereupon frame the issues.

(3) Where the Tribunal is of the opinion that the issues cannot be correctly framed without the examination of some person not before it or without the inspection of some documents not produced, it may, subject to any law for the time being in force, compel the attendance of, or the production of any document, by any person.

30. Examination of parties before hearing. The Tribunal may, before the hearing of the complaint examine the parties or their representatives for the purpose of considering:

(*a*) the simplification, narrowing down or adjustment of matters in issue between the parties;

(*b*) the admission or denial by each party of the documents of the others;

(*c*) the limitation of the number of witnesses;

(*d*) the procedure at the hearing; and

(*e*) such other matters as may aid in the speedy disposal of the complaint.

31. Amendment of issues. At any time before giving its decision, the Tribunal may amend the issues or frame additional issues, as it thinks fit, or may be necessary, for determining the matters in dispute between the parties, and it may strike out any issue that appears to it to be wrongly framed.

32. Intervener. (1) On the public notice given under sub-regulation (3) of regulation 19 any person may within the time prescribed in the said sub-regulation petition the Tribunal for leave to intervene in support of or in opposition to the relief sought for in the complaint.

(2) A petition for leave to intervene must set forth the grounds of the proposed intervention, the position and interest of the petitioner in the proceeding, and whether the same is in support of or opposition to the relief sought.

(3) It shall be within the Tribunal's discretion to grant or reject such leave in the light of the provisions of sub-regulation (1) of regulation 18 relating to addition of parties.

(4) If leave is granted, the petitioner shall be impleaded as intervener and notified of the same, and, within 7 days of receipt of such notice, he shall file his pleading which shall conform to the provisions of sub-regulation (2) of regulation 11 or sub-regulation (1) of regulation 22 as the case may be. He shall also deposit at the same time ₹150 to meet the cost of service of notice, other processes and the cost of preparation of paper book and a sum of ₹250 if he intervenes in support of the complaint. He shall file twice as many copies of his pleadings as there are parties and three additional copies for the use of the Tribunal.

33. Date of hearing. After the settlement of the issues the Tribunal shall fix a day, time and place for the hearing of the complaint and communicate the same to the parties concerned.

34. Right of audience. (1) Any party to a proceeding before the Tribunal shall be entitled to be heard either in person or by his representative.

(2) The Tribunal may permit any person likely to be of assistance to address the Tribunal.

35. Local inquiry and report. In any proceeding in which the Tribunal deems a local inquiry to be requisite or proper, it may appoint any Railway Officer not below the rank of an Assistant Officer to hold a local inquiry after notice to the parties and to report thereon to the Tribunal. The receipt of the report may be communicated to the parties for filing their objections, if any after making an inspection of the report, within the time fixed, and the Tribunal shall dispose of these objections:

Provided that it may refuse to consider, any objections not filed within the said time. The report shall be treated as part of the evidence in the case. The provisions of Order XXVI of the First Schedule to the Code shall apply as far as may be, to such local inquiries and reports.

36. Commission. The Tribunal may at any stage of the proceeding issue a commission for examination of witnesses. The provisions of Order XXVI of the Code shall apply as far as may be to the commissions issued under this regulation.

37. Summons to witnesses. (1) A party who desires to summon a witness for appearance before the Tribunal or before a Commissioner appointed under regulation 36, shall at least 30 days before the date of hearing, produce a list of persons whose attendance is required, stating the full name, description and address of each person and whether he is required to give evidence as an expert or otherwise or to produce documents, and, in the last mentioned case, specifying the date, if any, and to description of the documents so as to identify them. He shall with such a list deposit the trial amount of the allowances to which the said persons are entitled for travelling and attendance before the Tribunal, calculated in accordance with the rules of the High Court of Judicature at Madras in its ordinary original civil jurisdiction.

(2) Whenever the Tribunal deems it necessary, it may, of its own motion, summon any person to give evidence, or to produce any document in his possession, and pass necessary orders as to the costs of summoning such person.

(3) Witnesses shall be served with summonses in accordance with sub-regulation (1) of regulation 9 requiring them to attend or to produce a document at the time and place fixed. If a witness so served fails to attend as required, his

attendance may be enforced by recourse to the provisions of Order XVI of the First Schedule to the Code.

38. Further evidence. The Tribunal may, at any stage of the hearing, call for further evidence on any issue from any party.

39. Preliminary questions of law. The Tribunal may, with consent of the parties to any proceedings, or on the application of any party, or of its own motion, order any point of law raised by the pleadings to be set down for hearing and to be disposed of at any time before the hearing of the complaint. If, in the opinion of the Tribunal, the decision on such point of law substantially disposes of the whole complaint, the Tribunal may make such order as may seem to it to be just and proper.

40. Hearing. (1) Every complaint shall be heard in open court at the time and place fixed by the Tribunal.

(2) The hearing shall proceed from day to day as far as in the judgment of the Tribunal may be practicable and convenient, and the same shall not be adjourned at the instance of a party except for reasons considered sufficient by the Tribunal and on such terms, including payment of costs, as the Tribunal may deem fit.

41. Default of appearance. If the complainant does not appear at the time and place appointed for hearing, the Tribunal may dismiss the complaint or, at its discretion, proceed with the hearing at the instance of an intervener supporting the complaint, and if the respondent does not likewise appear, it may hear and decide the complaint in his absence. If at any adjourned date of the hearing the parties or any of them do not appear, the Tribunal may dismiss the complaint or decide it '*ex parte*', as the case may be, or it may dispose of the case in their absence.

42. Re-hearing. (1) When a complaint is dismissed for default, but the complainant satisfies the Tribunal that there was sufficient cause for default, the order of dismissal may, after notice to the opposite party, where necessary, be set aside and complaint proceeded with upon such terms as to costs or otherwise as the Tribunal may deem fit.

(2) When an '*ex parte*' decision has been made, but the respondent satisfies the Tribunal that notice was not duly served on him, or that he was prevented by any sufficient cause from appearing at the hearing, the '*ex parte*' decision may be set aside and the case proceeded with upon such terms as to costs or otherwise as the Tribunal may deem fit.

(3) An application for setting aside an order of dismissal of complaint or an '*ex parte*' decision shall be made within 30 days of the dismissal of the complaint or the passing of the '*ex parte*' decision, as the case may be, unless the Tribunal condones the delay for adequate reasons.

43. Act 1 of 1872 to apply. The provisions of the Indian Evidence Act, 1872 (1 of 1872) shall as far as may be, apply to the proceedings:

Provided that the Tribunal may in its discretion, without prejudice to the rights of the parties relax any of its provisions, for securing the necessary evidence inexpensively and expeditiously.

44. Affidavit. (1) The evidence at the hearing of a complaint may be taken either by affidavit or *viva voce*, or partly by affidavit and partly by *viva voce*:

Provided that if either party intends to rely on any evidence by affidavit, he shall, at least 10 days before the hearing, deliver or send by registered post to the other party a copy of the affidavit intended to be used, failing which he shall not be allowed to use the same except by special leave of the Tribunal.

(2) Either party may, within 7 days after receipt of a copy of any affidavit intended to be so used, deliver or send, by registered post to the other party, a notice requiring the deponent to be produced at the hearing of the complaint for cross-examination, and unless the deponent is so produced, his affidavit shall not be used except by special leave of the Tribunal.

(3) The Tribunal may at any time for sufficient reason, order that any particular fact may be proved by affidavit, or that the affidavit of any witness may be read at the hearing on such conditions as the Tribunal deems reasonable:

Provided that where it appears to the Tribunal that either party *bona fide* desires the production of a witness for cross-examination and that such witness can be produced, an order shall not be made authorising the evidence of such witness to be given by affidavit.

(4) An affidavit shall be confined to such facts as the witness is able of his own knowledge to prove, except in interlocutory proceedings, in which statements as to his belief with the grounds thereof may be admitted.

(5) For the purpose of any affidavit to be sworn in any proceeding before the Tribunal, the Chairman may empower any official of the Tribunal to administer on oath to the deponent of the affidavit.

45. Oral evidence. (1) The oral evidence of a witness shall be taken down in the open court in English under the direction of the Tribunal and the typewritten copy shall be initialled by the Chairman or by any member of the Tribunal.

(2) When evidence is given by a witness in a language other than English, the Tribunal may appoint an interpreter who shall take oath or solemnly affirm that he will render the evidence into English correctly. The interpreter shall be paid such fees as may be directed by the Tribunal.

46. Judgments. (1) The Tribunal after hearing and considering the evidence and arguments shall, give its decision, either at once or as soon thereafter as may be practicable on some future day; and when the decision is to be pronounced on some future day, the Tribunal shall fix a day for that purpose, of which due notice shall be given to the parties or the representatives.

(2) The decision shall be signed by the Chairman and the Members of the Tribunal, and a copy of the operative part of the decision shall be made available to each party.

47. Costs. (1) The Tribunal may in its discretion order payment of costs of the proceedings by either party to any other, either in whole or in part. The fact that the Tribunal has no jurisdiction in respect of the proceedings shall be no bar to the exercise of such powers.

(2) The scale of fees admissible for the award of costs for and in connection with the proceeding before the Tribunal shall be as shown in the Appendix I.

(3) The bill of costs shall be prepared by the Secretary and attached to the decision of the Tribunal, and a copy thereof shall be sent to the parties. The bill of costs may be corrected by the Secretary or the Tribunal at the instance of any party, if it be necessary to do so.

48. Change in Personnel of Tribunal. Where the Tribunal is prevented by a change in its personnel from concluding any proceedings before it the succeeding reconstituted Tribunal may resume the same from the stage at which the previous Tribunal left it, and it may give a decision, or submit a report, written but not given or submitted by its predecessor, and correct the bill of costs relating to a decision given by its predecessor.

49. Rectification of errors. Clerical or arithmetical mistakes in any decision or order of the Tribunal, or errors arising therein from any accidental slip or omission, may at any time be corrected by the Tribunal either of its own motion or on the application of any of the parties.

50. The Tribunal may at any time. And on such terms as to costs or otherwise as it deems fit, amend any defect or error in any proceedings before it and all necessary amendments shall be made for the purpose of determining the real question at issue raised by or depending on such proceeding.

51. Interlocutory orders. The Tribunal may pass, vary or set aside, after hearing or '*ex parte*' such interlocutory orders, including temporary injunctions, as may be necessary.

52. Enlargement or abridgement of time. The Tribunal may enlarge or abridge the time-limit for doing any act or taking any proceeding upon such terms as the justice of the case may require:

Provided that the period prescribed for applying for setting aside an order of dismissal of complaint or an '*ex parte*' decision, shall not be abridged.

53. Computation of time. In all cases in which a particular number of days is prescribed by these regulations or in an order passed by the Secretary or the Tribunal, the same shall be reckoned exclusively of the first day and inclusively of the last day, and if the office of the Tribunal is closed on the last day, the time shall be reckoned exclusively of that day also. If on any day on which an act is required to be done by a party and the office is closed on that day, it may be done on the day on which the office next opens.

54. Application, under sections. These regulations shall as far as may be, apply to the disposal of cases where a railway administration is an applicant under section 45.

55. Reference. A reference to the Tribunal for inquiry and report shall be in the form of a letter addressed to the Secretary of the Tribunal and sent by registered post. The letter shall specify, *inter alia*—

(*a*) the details of the matter referred to the Tribunal for inquiry and report; and

(*b*) all information in the possession of the Central Government which that Government may think relevant to the matter before the Tribunal.

56. Public notification of inquiry. The Tribunal may, at any stage, publish a notification, either generally about the inquiry or about any of the proceedings in connection therewith, to enable the trades or trade associations or persons interested in the matter to submit their memoranda of recommendations or offer oral evidence at the inquiry.

57. Public inquiry. At the discretion of the Tribunal, a public inquiry may be held at a time and place announced by public notification.

58. Report of the inquiry. The report of the inquiry shall be submitted to the Central Government, and that Government may, if it thinks fit, release it to the public.

59. Commissions for inquiry. For purposes of inquiry, the Tribunal may issue such commissions and summon such witnesses as it may consider necessary.

60. Paper books. In every case relating to a complaint or an application there shall be prepared typed paper books of the pleadings, issues evidence recorded, documents admitted and such other parts of the record as may be specifically ordered to form part of the paper book. As many copies of such paper books shall be prepared as may be required for the Members of the Tribunal and the parties. Cost of preparation of paper books shall be charged at ₹1.75 per page in respect of such matters as may be typed in the office of the Tribunal.

61. Working hours of the Tribunal. Except on Saturdays, Sundays and other Public holidays and subject to any order made by the Chairman, the working hours of the Tribunal shall be from 10.30 a.m. to 1.30 p.m. and 2.15 p.m. to 4.30 p.m. and that of the office of the Tribunal shall be from 10.00 a.m. to 1.30 p.m. and 2.00 p.m. to 6.00 p.m.

62. Holidays and vacations. The Tribunal may observe the same holidays and vacations as that of the Madras High Court:

Provided that the office shall remain open during the vacation and transact its normal business:

Provided further that no extension of time shall be granted merely on the ground that the Tribunal was closed for vacation.

63. Return of documents. (1) Documents admitted in evidence may after the disposal of the proceedings be returned to the party concerned either by being delivered to him in person or sent to him by registered post acknowledgment due, or by parcel at his risk and cost:

Provided that a document admitted in evidence may be returned earlier if the party applying therefor, delivers to the Secretary a certified copy to be substituted for the original and undertakes to produce the original if required to do so.

(2) Where a document is returned to a party by its being delivered to him, a receipt shall be given by the person receiving it.

(3) Documents not admitted in evidence shall not form a part of the record and shall be returned to the parties respectively producing them in the manner provided in sub-regulation (1).

64. Certified copies of record. Unless specially ordered otherwise by the Tribunal, a party to a proceeding shall be entitled to have certified copies of any part of the record of the proceeding. Such certified copies shall be prepared in the office of the Tribunal and charged at the rate at which certified copies are charged in the Madras High Court.

65. Remittance. All monies to be paid to or deposited with the Tribunal shall be paid in cash at the office of the Tribunal or remitted by money order in favour of the Secretary, Railway Rates Tribunal, Madras or crossed postal order or crossed bank draft in favour of the Chief Cashier, Southern Railway, Madras.

66. Refund or recovery against deposit. After the conclusion of a case, the Secretary shall calculate the amount spent out of the deposit made by each party and either return to him the excess or recover from him the deficit, as the case may be.

67. Forms and registers. The notices to be served and registers and other records to be maintained in the Office of the Tribunal shall be as specified in Appendix II.

68. Rules of practice of Madras High Court. The rules of practice of the Madras High Court, in so far as they are not inconsistent with the Act and these regulations, may in the discretion of the Tribunal be followed.

69. Court seal. The seal of the Tribunal shall be kept in the custody of the Secretary.

APPENDIX I

[*See* Regulation 47(2)]

Scale of fees for award of costs in connection with proceedings before the Tribunal

	Rs.
For filing a complaint under section 36/an application under section 45 or for intervening in support of a complaint	250.00
For vakalatnama	5.00
For filing any other application	3.00
For service of notice summons	5.00 or the actual cost whichever is more
For service of interrogatories	5.00
For filing any affidavit made outside the Tribunal	5.00
For injunction petition	10.00
For making any affidavit before an Officer of the Tribunal/Court	5.00

APPENDIX II

FORM I

Register of Complaint for the year ....

[*See* Regulation 16(4)]

Sl. No.	*Date of complaint and its receipt*	*Date of registration*	*Date of complaint*	*Name of respondent*	*Subject matter*	*Name of intervener*
(1)	(2)	(3)	(4)	(5)	(6)	(7)

Date of Judgment	*Operative part of judgment*	*Date of communication of the operative part to parties*	*Writ to High Court, Appeal to Supreme Court or correction and result*	*Miscellaneous Application, if any*
(8)	(9)	(10)	(11)	(12)

FORM II

Register of Applications for the year ....

[*See* Regulation 16(4) and Regulation 54]

Sl. No.	*Date of application and its receipt*	*Date of registration*	*Name of applicant*	*Name of Respondent*	*Cross reference to original proceedings*	*Name of intervener*
(1)	(2)	(3)	(4)	(5)	(6)	(7)

Date of judgment	*Operative part of judgment*	*Date of communication of operative part to parties*	*Miscellaneous Application, if any*	*Remarks*
(8)	(9)	(10)	(11)	(12)

FORM III

Register of Miscellaneous/Interlocutory Applications for the year ....

[*See* Regulation 51]

Sl. No.	*Date of application and its receipt*	*Date of registration*	*Name of the applicant*	*Name of the respondent*	*Subject matter*	*Cross references to the original complaint / application*
(1)	(2)	(3)	(4)	(5)	(6)	(7)

Name of the intervener	*Date of the order*	*Nature of the order*	*Date of communication of the order to the parties*	*Remarks*
(8)	(9)	(10)	(11)	(12)

FORM IV

Register of References for the year ....

[*See* Regulation 55]

Sl. No.	*Particulars of reference and date of its receipt*	*Date of registration*	*Subject matter of reference*	*Date of Report of the Tribunal*	*Recommendation*	*Date of despatch of the Report*	*Remarks*
(1)	(2)	(3)	(4)	(5)	(6)	(7)	(8)

FORM V

[*See* Regulation 18]

Before the Railway Rates Tribunal at Madras

Complaint No. .... of 20 ....

.... Complainant

vs.

.... Respondent

To

Whereas .... has instituted the above complaint against .... for .... and whereas it appears proper or necessary that you should be added as a complainant in the said matter in order to enable the Tribunal to adjudicate upon and settle the question involved in the complaint.

Take notice that under Regulation 18 of the Railway Rates Tribunal Regulations, 1990, you are required on or before the .... day of .... 20........, to signify to this Tribunal whether you consent to be so added.

Given under my hand and the seal of the Tribunal, this .... day of .... 20........, at No. 3, Victoria Crescent Road, Madras 600 105.

Sd/-

Secretary

Railway Rates Tribunal

FORM VI

[*See* Regulation 19]

Before the Railway Rates Tribunal at Madras

Complaint/Application No. .... of 20 ......

.... Complainant/Applicant

vs.

.... Respondent

Under Regulation 19(1) of the Railway Rates Tribunal Regulations, 1990, you are hereby required within 30 days from the date of service upon you of the enclosed complaint/application to put in your answer to the same together with .... copies and to take notice that in default of such answer being put in within the said time, the Tribunal may proceed to hear the said complaint/ application in your absence.

Your answer and the copies thereof may be presented to me at my office at the headquarters or sent to me by Registered post. You should also make a provisional deposit of ₹150 to meet the charges of service of notice, etc. and preparation of paper book. The amount may be remitted either in cash/money order in favour of the Secretary, Railway Rates Tribunal, Madras or by means of crossed postal order or crossed bank draft in favour of the Chief Cashier, Southern Railway, Madras.

Given under my hand and the seal of the Tribunal, this .... day of .... 20......... at No. 3, Victoria Crescent Road, Madras 600 105.

Secretary

Railway Rates Tribunal

FORM VII

[*See* Regulation 19(3) & (4)]

Before the Railway Rates Tribunal at Madras

Complaint/Application No. .... of 20 ......

.... *Complainant / Applicant*

vs.

.... *Respondent*

Whereas the complainant/applicant above named has made a complaint/ application that ....

And, whereas, it is thought that there are numerous persons who are not on record but have the same interest in the proceedings as the complainant/applicant or respondent above named.

This public notice is, therefore, given under Sub-regulations (3) and (4) of Regulation 19 of the Railway Rates Tribunal Regulations, 1990, so that any person who so desires may petition the Tribunal within 30 days of the publication of this notice for leave to intervene in support of or opposition to the relief sought in the complaint/application or be added on the side of the complainant/applicant or the respondent, setting forth the grounds of the proposed intervention and the position and the interest of the petitioner in the proceeding, on the grounds for being added as a party in the said case.

Any decision given by the Tribunal after such public notice shall apply to all such persons.

Given under my hand and the seal of the Tribunal, this .... day of .... 20 .... at No. 3, Victoria Crescent Road, Madras 600 105.

Secretary,
Railway Rates Tribunal

FORM VIII

[*See* Regulation 29(2)]

Before the Railway Rates Tribunal at Madras

Complaint/Application No. .... of 20 ......

.... Complainant/Applicant

vs.

.... Respondent

To

.... Complainant/Applicant/Respondent/Intervener

Whereas the Tribunal has to frame issues in the above case.

Take Notice that you shall file the draft issues in the above complaint under Regulation 29(1) of the Railway Rates Tribunal Regulations, 1990, on or before .... day of .... 20 ....

And also take notice that the above complaint will come up for hearing and framing issues before the Tribunal, in accordance with sub-regulations (2) and (3) of regulation 29 of the Railway Rates Tribunal Regulations, 1990, sitting at .... on the .... day of .... 20.................. at .... o'clock in the .... noon.

If no appearance is made on your behalf by yourself or your representatives, the case will be heard and decided in your absence.

Given under my hand and the seal of the Tribunal, this .... day of .... 20........... at No. 3 Victoria Crescent Road, Madras 600 105.

Secretary
Railway Rates Tribunal

FORM IX

[*See* Regulation 32(4)]

Before the Railway Rates Tribunal at Madras

Complaint/Application No. .... of 20 ......

.... Complainant/Applicant

vs.

.... Respondent

To

.... Intervener

On your application, dated .... under Regulation 32(1) of the Railway Rates Tribunal Regulations, 1990, you have been granted leave by the Tribunal to intervene in the above complaint/application (in support of/in opposition) to the relief sought.

Under Regulation 32(4) of the said Regulation, you are hereby required within 7 days of the date of receipt of the enclosed complaint/application, to put in your statement of grounds in support of/in opposition to the relief sought, duly signed and verified, together with .... copies thereof, and to take notice that in default of such statement being put in within the said period, the Tribunal may proceed to hear the said complaint/application in your absence.

Further, you are hereby called upon to make along with your statement a provisional deposit of ₹150 with the Tribunal to meet the charges for the service of notice, etc., and cost of preparation of paper book, and, as your intervention is in support of the relief sought, also a fee of ₹250. The amount may be remitted either in cash/money order in favour of the Secretary, Railway Rates Tribunal, Madras or by means of crossed postal order or crossed bank draft in favour of the Chief Cashier, Southern Railway, Madras.

Given under my hand and the seal of the Tribunal, this .... day of .... 20...... at No. 3 Victoria Crescent Road, Madras 600 105.

Sd/-
Secretary
Railway Rates Tribunal
Madras

FORM X

[*See* Regulation 33]

Before the Railway Rates Tribunal at Madras

Complaint/Application No. .... of 20 ....

.... Complainant/Applicant

vs.

.... Respondent

To

.... Complainant/Applicant/Respondent/Intervener

Take notice that the above complaint/application will come up for hearing before the Tribunal sitting at .... on the .... day of .... 20................. at .... o'clock in the .... noon, on the issues as already settled in this case.

If no appearance is made on your behalf by yourself or your representative .... along with your witnesses, the case will be heard and decided in your absence.

Given under my hand and the seal of the Tribunal, this .... day of .... 20........... at No. 3 Victoria Crescent Road, Madras 600 105.

Secretary
Railway Rates Tribunal
Madras

FORM XI

[*See* Regulation 35]

Before the Railway Rates Tribunal at Madras

Complaint/Application No. .... of 20 ......

.... Complainant/Applicant

vs.

.... Respondent

To

The person appointed to hold the enquiry.

Whereas the Tribunal deems a local enquiry to be requisite in this case, you are hereby required to hold such enquiry under Regulation 35 of the Railway Rates Tribunal Regulations, 1990 after notifying the parties concerned for the report on or before .... day of .... 20 ....

Process to compel the attendance before you of any witness or for the production of any document whom or which you may desire to examine or inspect will be issued by this Tribunal on your application.

The Tribunal will order payment of your remuneration and expenses after it has received your report.

Given under my hand and the seal of the Tribunal, this .... day of .... 20 ...., at No. 3 Victoria Crescent Road, Madras 600 105.

Secretary
Railway Rates Tribunal
Madras

APPENDIX 15

The Railway Passengers (Cancellation of Ticket and Refund of Fare) Rules, 1998[1]

In exercise of the powers conferred by sub-section (1) read with clause (*b*) of sub-section (2) of section 60 of the Railways Act, 1989 (24 of 1989) and in supersession of the Railway Passengers (Cancellation of Tickets and Refund of Fares) Rules, 1990 except as respects things done or omitted to be done before such supersession, the Central Government hereby makes the following rules, namely:

1. Short title and commencement. (1) These rules may be called the Railway Passengers (Cancellation of Ticket and Refund of Fare) Rules, 1998.

(2) They shall come into force on the first day of October, 1998.

2. Definitions. In these rules, unless the context otherwise requires—

(*a*) "clerkage" means a charge levied by a railway administration for the clerical work rendered by it in the refund of fares;

(*b*) "destination station" means the station for which the ticket has been issued;

(*c*) "RAC ticket" means a ticket on which a seat has been reserved against requisition for a berth and a berth may be subsequently provided against cancellation, if any;

(*d*) "fare" includes basic fare, supplementary charge on super-fast train and reservation fee;

(*e*) "reserved ticket" means a journey ticket on which a berth or seat has been reserved;

(*f*) "reservation fee" means the charge, in addition to the fare, levied by the railway administration for the reservation of a berth or seat;

(*g*) "station" means a railway station and includes other reservation offices or booking office in the same city;

1 *Vide* G.S.R. 410(E), dated 24th July 1998, published in the *Gazette of India* (Extraordinary), Part II, section 3(*i*) dated 24th July 1998.

(*h*) "station master" means a railway employee, by whatever name called having overall charge of a railway station and includes any other railway employee authorised to grant refund of fare at a station;

(*i*) "ticket" means a single journey ticket or any of a return ticket but does not include season ticket, an Indrail Pass ticket, or a special ticket for a reserved carriage or a tourist car or saloon, or a special train;

[2][(*j*) "ARP" means advance reservation period upto which a reserved ticket can be booked for a future journey date;

(*k*) "confirmed ticket" means a ticket on which a seat or berth has been reserved;

(*l*) "TDR" means ticket deposit receipt issued to the passengers in lieu of the surrendered ticket, at the station where the ticket has been surrendered by the passenger;

(*m*) "Tatkal ticket" means a ticket with shorter advance reservation period, issued to meet the requirements of those passengers who have to travel at short notice;

(*n*) "waitlisted ticket" means a ticket on which no berth or seat has been allotted.]

3. Station Master to refund fares. (1) Subject to the other provisions of these rules, every refund of fare on unused unreserved ticket shall, when such ticket is presented for refund of fare to the Station Master of ticket issuing station be granted by such Station Master after verifying the genuineness of the ticket from the record of the station.

(2) Subject to the other provisions of these rules, every refund of fare on reserved tickets, RAC tickets and waitlisted ticket shall, when such tickets are presented for refund of fare to the Station Master of ticket issuing station, be granted within the time limits prescribed in these rules, by such Station Master after verifying the genuineness of the tickets through computer or from the record of the station:

Provided that—(*a*) in case tickets which were issued for travel from a station other than the ticket issuing station, refund of fare shall be admissible at,—

(*i*) the ticket issuing station, if the ticket is surrendered before the schedule departure of the train from the station from where the ticket is valid for travel; and

(*ii*) the journey commencing station, if the ticket is surrendered within the time limits prescribed in these rules, and

(*b*) refund of fare may also be granted and the Station Master of a station other than the ticket issuing station and journey commencing station subject to the conditions that,—

(*i*) the ticket is surrendered for refund of fare during working hours of the reservation office and before the preparation of reservation chart, of the concerned train, for the station from where the ticket is valid; and

(*ii*) the genuineness of the ticket and its particulars are verifiable at the refund granting station through computer or from record of the station.

2 *Inserted* by G.S.R. 362(E), dated 6.6.2013 (w.e.f. 1.7.2013).

[3][**4. Levy of clerkage.** Subject to the other provisions of these rules, Station Master shall levy a clerkage charge per passenger for cancellation of unreserved, wait-listed and RAC tickets, at the rate of rupees fifteen for second class (unreserved) and rupees thirty for second class (reserved) and other classes.]

[3][**5. Unused tickets on which no reservation has been made.** If a ticket on which no reservation of a seat or berth has been made is presented to the Station Master for cancellation, refund of fare shall be made on every such ticket after deducting the clerkage—

(*i*) the ticket is present for cancellation within three hours of issue of ticket;

(*ii*) in case of tickets issued in advance, the ticket is presented upto 24.00 hours of the day preceding the day of journey.]

[3][**6. Unused tickets on which reservation has been made.** (1) Subject to the provisions of these rules, if a ticket on which reservation of a seat or berth has been made is presented by the passenger or his agent to a Station Master for cancellation, refund of fare shall be made after deducting cancellation charge from the fare as follows:

(*a*) if the ticket is presented for cancellation more than forty eight hours in advance of the scheduled departure of the train, a minimum per passenger cancellation charge shall be deducted at the flat rate of rupees one hundred and twenty for air conditioned first class/executive class, rupees one hundred for air conditioned II tier/ first class, rupees ninety for air-conditioned III tier/ 3 economy/ air-conditioned chair car, rupees sixty for sleeper class and rupees thirty for second class;

(*b*) if the ticket is presented for cancellation between forty eight hours and upto six hours before the scheduled departure of the train, cancellation charge shall be 25 per cent of the fare subject to a minimum of the cancellation charge referred to in clause (*a*);

(*c*) if the ticket is presented for cancellation within six hours before the scheduled departure of the train and upto two hours after the actual departure of the train irrespective of distance, the cancellation charge shall be fifty per cent of the fare subject to a minimum of the cancellation charge referred to in clause (*a*); and

(*d*) the passenger may get the ticket cancelled from any Passenger Reservation System (PRS) counters or the designated current countries;

Provided that for night trains leaving between 21.00 hours and 06.00 hours (actual departure), refund shall be admissible at the station within first two hours after the opening of reservation office in case no current counters are available at the station originating the journey.

(2) No refund shall be granted on the reserved ticket if it is surrendered for cancellation after two hours of the actual departure of the train.

(3) In case, on a party ticket or a family ticket issued for travel of more than one person, some persons have confirmed reservation and others are on waiting list, full refund of fare, less clerkage, shall be admissible for confirmed passengers

3 *Substituted* by G.S.R. 362(E), dated 6.6.2013 (w.e.f. 1.7.2013).

also provided that the entire ticket is surrendered for cancellation within six hours before the scheduled departure of the train and up to two hours after actual departure of the train.]

[4][**7. Unused waitlisted or RAC tickets.** (1) If a waitlisted ticket or RAC ticket is presented for cancellation, refund of fare shall be made after deducting the clerkage in the following manner, namely—

(*i*) the ticket is presented for cancellation upto three hours after the actual departure of the train irrespective of the distance;

(*ii*) the passenger may get the tickets cancelled from any Passenger Reservation System (PRS) counters or the designated current counters;

(*iii*) no refund of fare shall be granted on RAC ticket or waitlisted ticket after three hours of the actual departure of the train.

(2) In case no current counters are available at the station originating the journey night trains leaving between 21.00 hours and 06.00 hours (actual departure), refund of fare shall be admissible at the station within first two hours after the opening of reservation office.

(3) In remote and hill areas as identified by the Zonal Railway with the prior approval of the General Manager and printed in the time table, for night trains leaving between 19.00 hours and 06.00 hours (actual departure) refund shall be admissible at the station within first two hours after the opening of reservation or booking office, in case there is no reservation counters or booking office or current counters available in that area.

(4) Where confirmed reservation has been provided to RAC or waitlisted ticket holder at any time upto the final preparation of reservation chart, such ticket shall be treated as a reserved ticket and cancellation charge shall be payable in accordance with rule 6.

7A. Cancellation of e-tickets. (1) The e-ticket may be booked and cancelled through internet and the refund of fare shall be credited to the customer's account after deducting the charges applicable.

(2) In case of a confirmed e-ticket, refund of fare shall be granted in accordance with rule 6.

(3) In case of RAC e-ticket, refund of fare shall be graned in accordance with rule 7.

(4) In case of the waitlisted e-ticket on which status of all the passengers is on waiting list even after preparation of reservation charts, names of all such passengers booked on that Passenger Name Record (PNR) shall be dropped from the reservation chart and refund of fare shall be credited to the customer's account after deducting the clerkage.

(5) In case on a party e-ticket or a family e-ticket issued for travel of more than one person, some persons have confirmed reservation and others are on the list of RAC and waiting list, then in case of passengers on RAC or waitlisted not travelling, a certificate has to be obtained from the ticket checking staff to that effect and refund of fare shall be processed on-line through TDR, indicating the details of the certificate issued by ticket checking staff.

4 *Substituted* by G.S.R. 362(E), dated 6.6.2013 (w.e.f. 1.7.2013).

(6) The on-line TDR shall be filed upto seventy two hours of actual arrival of the train at passenger's destination and the original certificate issued by the ticket checking staff is to be sent through post to Indian Railway Catering and Tourism Corporation (IRCTC).

(7) The fare shall be refunded by Indian Railway Catering and Tourism Corporation (IRCTC) to the customer's account after due verification.

(8) In case of e-tickets (confirmed or RAC), if the reservation charts have been prepared, online TDR is required to be filed for obtaining refund.

(9) No refund of fare shall be admissible on e-ticket having confirmed reservation in case the request for refund is filed online after two hours of the actual departure of the train.

(10) No refund of fare shall be admissible on RAC e-tickets in case the request for refund is filed online after three hours of the actual departure of the train.

7B. Refund on Tatkal tickets. (1) No refund of fare shall be admissible on confirmed Tatkal ticket.

(2) In case of Tatkal ticket on waitlist, refund of fare shall be granted in accordance with rule 7.

(3) In case on a party Tatkal ticket or a family tatkal ticket issued for travel for more than one person, some persons have confirmed reservation and others are on waiting list, full refund of fare, less clerkage, shall be admissible for confirmed passengers also provided that the entire tatkal ticket is surrendered for cancellation within six hours before the scheduled departure of the train or upto two hours of the actual departure of the train.]

[5][**8. Cancellation charges on multiple journey tickets.** When an unused ticket involving more than one journey is surrendered for cancellation, the entire ticket shall be treated as one single journey ticket and refund to fare of the entire ticket, irrespective of reservation status of different laps of journeys, shall be granted as per reservation status of first lap of journey, as under—

(*i*) if reservation status of first lap of journey is confirmed, refund shall be granted in accordance with rule 6; and

(*ii*) if reservation status of first lap of journey is RAC or waiting list, refund shall be granted in accordance with rule 7.

Explanation. The cancellation charges or clerkage shall be levied only once on the entire amount of ticket and not separately for each lap of journey.]

[6][**9. Postponement or preponement of journey on a reserved, RAC or waitlisted ticket.** (1) The postponement of journey on confirmed or RAC or waitlisted ticket shall be allowed in the same class and for the same destination or any higher class by the same train or by any other train for any subsequent days, subject to condition that,—

(*i*) the ticket is surrendered during the working hours of reservation office and at least forty eight hours before the scheduled departure of the train in which originally booked;

5 *Substituted* by G.S.R. 212(E), dated 1.1.2000 (w.e.f. 1.3.2000).

6 *Substituted* by G.S.R. 362(E), dated 6.6.2013 (w.e.f. 1.7.2013).

(*ii*) the confirmed or RAC or waitlisted accommodation is available in the train in which fresh reservation is required;

(*iii*) in case of confirmed ticket, fresh reservation fee for the class for which reservation is required, is paid; and

(*iv*) in case of RAC or waitlisted ticket, clerkage charge is paid.

(2) The preponement of journey on confirmed or RAC or waitlisted ticket shall be allowed in the same class and for the same destination or any higher class by the same train or by any other train for any earlier days, subject to condition that—

(*i*) the ticket is surrendered during the working hours of reservation office and at least forty eight hours before the scheduled departure of the train in which originally booked;

(*ii*) the confirmed or RAC or waitlisted accommodation is available in the train in which fresh reservation is required;

(*iii*) in case of confirmed tickets, fresh reservation fee for the class for which reservation is required, is paid; and

(*iv*) in case of RAC or waitlisted ticket, clerkage charge is paid.

(3) In case of difference in fares for originally booked journey and revised journey, the difference of fare shall be refunded or recovered, as the case may be, subject to the provisions of sub-rules (1) and (2).

(4) The postponement or preponement of journey under the sub- rule (1) or sub-rule (2) shall be allowed only once.

(5) The postponement or preponement of journey on normal train ticket other than/Tatkal ticket shall not be applicable against Tatkal Quota even on payment of Tatkal charges.]

10. Change of journey from lower class to higher class. (1) Charge of reservation shall be allowed on a reserved ticket of lower class for higher class on the same train and day or when reserved for a seat in a class for reservation of a berth in the same class on the same train and day, without levying any cancellation charges but on payment of fresh reservation fee for higher class/berth, provided that,—

(*i*) accommodation is available, and

(*ii*) the request for change is made,—

(*a*) either during the working hours of reservation office and up to six hours before the scheduled departure of the train, or

(*b*) during the course of journey in the train.

(2) The change referred to under sub-rule (1) shall be allowed only once.

(3) If the ticket on which change of reservation has been allowed under sub-rule (1) is cancelled, cancellation charge shall be payable as follows, namely,—

(*a*) cancellation charge as would have been due if the original reservation had been cancelled at the time when the change of reservation was allowed; and

(*b*) cancellation charge due in respect of the altered reservation as if the altered reservation is a fresh reservation.

[7][**11. Non-commencement or missing of journey due to late running of trains.** (1) No cancellation charges or clerkage shall be levied and full fare shall be refunded to all passengers holding reserved, RAC and waitlisted tickets, if the journey is not undertaken due to late running of the train by more than three hours of the scheduled departure of the train from the station commencing the journey subject to condition that—

(*i*) the ticket is surrendered up to the actual departure of the train;

(*ii*) in case of e-tickets, the TDR is filed online before the actual departure of the train for availing full refund.

(2) In case the ticket is cancelled or surrendered or if the request for refund of fare is filed online after the actual departure of the train, no refund of fare shall be admissible.

(3) Where a passenger holding a ticket, with or without reservation, misses connection for continued journey by another train at any junction station owing to late running of the train by which he had been travelling, the fare for travelled portion shall be retained and the balance amount of ticket shall be refunded as the fare for untravelled portion, without levying any cancellation charge or clerkage, if he surrenders the ticket for such refund within three hours of the actual arrival of the train by which he had travelled and the refund of fare shall be granted at the junction station.]

12. Cancellation of tickets where railway administration is unable to provide accommodation. Where a railway administration is unable to provide accommodation for any reason whatsoever to passengers holding reserved tickets, no cancellation charge shall be levied and full refund of fare shall be granted to them if such tickets are surrendered for refund within three hours from the actual departure of the train:

Provided that when the train is cancelled due to unforeseen circumstances such as accidents, breaches and floods, the ticket is surrendered within three days excluding the scheduled day of departure of the train.

13. Partially used tickets. (1) Except as provided in these rules, no refund shall be granted at a station on a ticket on which part of the journey has been undertaken.

(2) Where a passenger terminates the journey *en route,* a ticket deposit receipt shall be issued to the ticket holder by the Station Master of the station in lieu of surrender of the ticket and refund shall be admissible in terms of rule 21. In such cases, fare for the travelled portion shall be retained and the balance amount of the ticket shall be refundable as the fare for the untravelled journey.

14. Discontinuation of journey due to dislocation of train services. (1) When a train journey is dislocated *en route* due to unforeseen circumstances, such as accidents, breaches and floods, full fare for the entire booked journey without any deduction for the travelled portion and without levy of cancellation charge shall be refunded at the station at which the journey is terminated under the following circumstances,—

(*a*) when the railway is unable to carry the passenger to destination station within a reasonable time by arranging transshipment or diversion or otherwise; or

7 *Substituted* by G.S.R. 362 (E), dated 6.6.2013 (w.e.f. 1.7.2013).

(*b*) when the passenger is involved in a railway accident and/or injured in the accident and does not continue his journey; or

(2) Where the railway administration offers to carry the passenger to his destination station by any diverted route by arranging transshipment or otherwise, and the passenger is not willing to avail of such an alternative arrangement, fare for travelled portion shall be retained and the balance amount of ticket shall be refunded as the fare for untravelled portion, without levying any cancellation charges, at the station at which the journey has been terminated.

(3) Where the train journey is dislocated *en route* due to bands, agitations or rail *roko,* fare for travelled portion shall be retained and the balance amount of ticket shall be refunded as the fare for untravelling portion, without levying any cancellation charges.

(4) If the trains, which have separate all-inclusive fare structure on point to point basis, are terminated at a non-scheduled stoppage of the train and the passenger is not willing to avail of the alternative arrangement made by the railway administration to carry the passenger to his destination station, fare for the distance travelled shall be retained based on the per kilometre fare of ticket and the balance amount shall be refunded as the fare for untravelled portion of journey.

15. Refund of certain fare on failure to provide air-conditioning facility in air-conditioned coaches. (1) Where the air-conditioning facility could not be provided for a portion of journey, refund on tickets issued for air-conditioned coaches shall be granted for such portion on the following basis, namely,—

(*a*) if the ticket is for air-conditioned first class, the difference between the air-conditioned first class fare and first class fare;

(*b*) if the ticket is for air-conditioned sleeper/air-conditioned 3-tier sleeper class, the difference between air-conditioned sleeper/air-conditioned 3-tier sleeper class fare and sleeper class fare (Mail and Express);

(*c*) if the ticket is for air-conditioned chair car, the difference between air-conditioned chair car fare and second class fare (Mail and Express);

(*d*) if the ticket is for executive class, the difference between the notified executive class fare for the concerned section and the first class fare (Mail and Express) for the concerned distance of that section.

(2) The refund of difference of fare under sub-rule (1) shall be granted at the destination station on production of the ticket along with a certificate from the conductor or the guard or the travelling ticket examiner of the train giving particulars of the ticket, number of the coach and stations between which the air-conditioning facility was not provided, and is presented within twenty hours of arrival of the train.

16. When passengers are made to travel in lower class for want of accommodation. If the ticket holder of a higher class is made to travel in a lower class for want of accommodation in the class for which the ticket was issued, refund of the difference between the fare paid and the fare payable for the class in which it is actually used shall be granted at the destination station or at the originating station, as the case may be:

[8][Provided that refund shall be granted at the destination station on production of a certificate from the conductor or the guard or the travelling ticket examiner of the train certifying that the holder of the ticket had to travel in a lower class for want of accommodation in the class for which it was issued and the ticket, along with the above certificate, is presented within two days of the date of issue of the certificate (excluding the date of issue of the certificate).]

[9][**17. Lost, misplaced, torn or mutilated tickets.** (1) No refund of fare in respect of a lost or misplaced ticket shall be granted.

(2) Refund of fare shall be granted in respect of a torn or mutilated ticket if its genuineness and authenticity are verifiable on the basis of the particulars visible on the face of the ticket.

(3) If the reservation status of a lost, misplaced, torn or mutilated ticket, at the time of receipt of the application for issuance of a duplicate ticket for the purpose of undertaking journey, is confirmed or RAC and that the duplicate ticket is sought before preparation of reservation chart of the concerned train, the Station Master shall issue a duplicate ticket in lieu of the original ticket on payment of rupees fifty per passenger in case of second and sleeper class and rupees one hundred per passenger for other classes.

(4) If a duplicate ticket in lieu of a lost or misplaced reserved ticket is sought after preparation of reservation charge of the concerned train, it shall be issued on payment of a charge equivalent to fifty per cent of the total fare.

(5) No duplicate ticket shall be issued in respect of RAC tickets after preparation of reservation chart of the concerned train.

(6) If duplicate ticket in lieu of a torn or mutilated reserved or RAC ticket is sought after preparation of reservation chart of the concerned train, it shall be issued on payment of a charge equivalent to twenty five per cent of the total fare.

(7) A duplicate ticket in respect of a party coach ticket or a special train ticket shall be issued upto the time of departure of the train, on payment of a charge equivalent to ten per cent of the total fare.

(8) No refund of fare shall be granted in respect of charges paid under sub-rules (3), (4), (5) and (6) except in cases where the lost or misplaced ticket is traced after the issuance of a duplicate ticket and presented alongwith the duplicate ticket before departure of the train and in that case charges collected towards the issuance of duplicate ticket shall be refunded after deducting five per cent thereof subject to a minimum deduction of rupees twenty.

(9) In case the journey is not undertaken, the cancellation charges on the original ticket shall be determined as specified in these rules.

(10) If the passenger, who has paid excess charges in train on account of his reserved ticket or RAC ticket being lost, misplaced, torn or mutilated, makes an application to a railway administration for grant of refund of the charges paid in train, the Chief Commercial Manager (Refunds) of that railway administration

8 *Substituted* by G.S.R. 453(E), dated 1.8.2006 (w.e.f. 1.8.2006).
9 *Substituted* by G.S.R. 362(E), dated 6.6.2013 (w.e.f. 1.7.2013).

may, after making such inquiry as he may deem necessary grant refund of fare total charges realised in the train, after retaining the cancellation charges at fifty per cent of a single journey ticket fare per passenger provided that no one has taken refund earlier on the original ticket.]

18. Waitlisted passengers or concession and privilege ticket order tickets. When any person has purchased a ticket on any concessional order or privilege ticket order, and is waitlisted for reservation in any train, he shall be entitled to avail of the same ticket for reservation in any other train on the same date or any other date, without losing the benefit of concessional fare.

19. Unused portion of return tickets. (1) No refund shall be granted on the unused portion of the concessional return tickets.

(2) When a return ticket is issued without any concession, it shall be treated like two single journey tickets and the refund shall be granted accordingly.

20. Refund of fare on unused tickets and freight realised on luggage tickets in respect of luggage booked on the same ticket in case the journey is not undertaken. (1) Refund of freight on luggage shall be granted by the Station Master as under—

(*a*) Luggage is withdrawn at starting station	Luggage ticket shall be cancelled and freight already collected shall be refunded after recovery of wharfage charges, if any, and deduction of cancellation charge of rupees five per luggage ticket. Journey ticket shall be endorsed to the effect.
(*b*) Luggage already despatched from the starting station	Freight charges on weight admissible as free allowance, shall be collected and remarks to this effect endorsed on journey ticket.

(2) On production of journey ticket on which luggage has been booked, the fare shall be refunded only if bearing the endorsement referred to in sub-rule (1) on the unused ticket after deducting the cancellation charges or clerkage as per rules.

[10][**21. Application for refund of Passenger Reservation System (PRS) tickets in other circumstances.** For refund of fare under circumstances other than those specified in these rules or under circumstances like 'bandh' or agitations or floods, etc., the passengers could not reach the reservation counter or station or current counters for cancellation of tickets, in those cases, a TDR shall be issued to the passenger and the passenger may apply for refund of fare within ten days from the day of commencement of journey to the Chief Commercial Manager (Refunds) of the railway administration under whose jurisdiction the TDR issuing station, comes, enclosing the original TDR.

(2) In the circumstances specified in sub-rule (1), the TDR shall be issued only upto three days after the scheduled departure of the train.]

10 *Substituted* by G.S.R. 362 (E), dated 6.6.2013 (w.e.f. 1.7.2013).

Appendix 16

The Weighment of Consignments in Wagon-load or Train-load Rules, 1990

G.S.R. 615(E), dated 3rd July 1990 In exercise of the powers conferred by clause (*g*) of sub-section (2) of section 87 read with section 79 of the Railways Act, 1989 (24 of 1989) the Central Government hereby makes the following rules, namely:

1. Short title and commencement. (1) These rules may be called the Weighment of Consignments in Wagon-load or Train-load Rules, 1990.

(2) They shall come into force on the date of their publication in the Official Gazette.

2. Definitions. In these rules unless the context otherwise requires—

(*a*) "Act" means the Railways Act, 1989 (24 of 1989);

(*b*) "Schedule" means Schedule annexed to these rules;

(*c*) "Train-load consignment" means consignment carried at train-load rate as notified by the Central Government from time to time;

(*d*) "Wagon-load consignment" means consignment carried at wagon-load rate as notified by the Central Government from time to time;

(*e*) Words and expressions used and not defined in these rules but defined in the Act shall have meaning respectively assigned to them in the Act.

3. Weighment of Wagon-load or Train-load consignment. (1) The consignee or the endorsee of a wagon-load or a train-load consignment booked at railway risk rate may, if he has reason to believe that the wagon offered to him for delivery at destination does not contain the quantity of goods entrusted for carriage, make a request in writing to the Divisional Commercial Superintendent or any other railway servant authorised in this behalf for the weighment of such consignment at the destination station.

(2) Subject to the provisions of rule 4, any railway servant authorised in this behalf may allow request for weighment under sub-rule (1) on a railway weigh bridge on the payment of,—

(*i*) charges for weighment of wagons as specified in Schedule I;

(*ii*) additional charges, for haulage of a wagon irrespective of distance as specified in Schedule II, if due to non-availability of railway weigh bridge at the destination station,

the wagon has to be sent to another station for weighment:

Provided that if the wagon had to be sent to another station due to the weigh bridge at the destination station being out of order, no additional charges shall be levied for such haulage;

(*iii*) demurrage charges, if any.

4. Circumstances for disallowing weighment. Where a request has been made under rule 3, any railway servant authorised in this behalf may disallow such request if:

(*i*) The consignment is received in covered wagon, and the seals of the loading station are intact and there is not other evidence of the consignment having been tampered in transit;

(*ii*) the consignment had been received in open wagon and there is no sign of tampering of the original packing or other evidence of such consignment having been tampered in transit;

(*iii*) the consignment is of perishable nature and is likely to lose weight in transit;

(*iv*) in the opinion of such railway servant, the weighment is not feasible due to congestion in the yard.

5. Weighment without prejudice. Weighment done on request under rule 3 shall be without prejudice to the rights of the railway administration to disclaim liability under the Act or under any other law for the time being in force.

[1]SCHEDULE I

CHARGES FOR WEIGHMENT OF WAGONS AT THE DESTINATION

Description of wagon	*Haulage charges* *Rs.*
(*i*) (*a*) Per B.G. 8-Wheeled wagon	3,330.00
(*b*) Per B.G. 4-Wheeled wagon	1,330.00
(*ii*) (*a*) Per B.G. 8-Wheeled wagon	1,000.00
(*b*) Per B.G. 4-Wheeled wagon	500.00
(*iii*) (*a*) Per B.G. 8-Wheeled wagon	280.00

1 *Substituted* by G.S.R. 632(E), dated 8th September 1999 (w.e.f. 1.10.1999).

SCHEDULE II

Description of wagon	*Haulage charges* *Rs.*
(*i*) (*a*) Per B.G. 8-Wheeled wagon	3,330.00
(*b*) Per B.G. 4-Wheeled wagon	1,330.00
(*ii*) (*a*) Per B.G. 8-Wheeled wagon	1,000.00
(*b*) Per B.G. 4-Wheeled wagon	500.00
(*iii*) (*a*) Per B.G. 8-Wheeled wagon	280.00

APPENDIX 17

The Carriage of Passengers Suffering from Infectious or Contagious Diseases Rules, 1990

G.S.R. 556(E), dated 7th June 1990[1] In exercise of the powers conferred by clauses (*c*) and (*f*) of sub-section (2) of section 60 of the Railways Act, 1989 (24 of 1989), read with section 22 of the General Clauses Act, 1897 (10 of 1897), the Central Government hereby makes the following rules for carriage of passengers suffering from infectious or contagious disease, namely:

1. Short title. (1) These rules may be called the Carriage of Passengers Suffering from Infectious or Contagious Diseases Rules, 1990.

(2) They shall come into force on the date of commencement of the Railways Act, 1989 (24 of 1989).

2. Persons suffering from any infectious or contagious diseases. (1) A railway administration shall not carry, except in accordance with the conditions laid down in these rules, persons suffering from the following infectious or contagious diseases:

(*i*) Cererbro-Spinal meningitis.

(*ii*) Chicken-pox.

(*iii*) Cholera.

(*iv*) Diphtheria.

(*v*) [2][* * *]

(*vi*) Measles.

(*vii*) Mumps.

(*viii*) [3][* * *]

1 Published in *Gazette of India*, (Extraordinary), Part II, s. 3(*i*), dated 7th June 1990.
2 *Omitted* by G.S.R. 340(E), dated 17.6.1997 (w.e.f. 25.6.1997).
3 *Omitted* by G.S.R. 340(E), dated 17.6.1997 (w.e.f. 25.6.1997).

(*ix*) Scarlet fever.

(*x*) Thyhus fever.

(*xi*) Typhoid fever, and

(*xii*) Whooping cough.

(2) Nothing in sub-rule (1) shall apply in the case of closed (non-infective) leprosy patients carrying a certificate from a Registered Medical Practitioner certifying them to be non-infective and such a certificate shall be produced on demand inside railways premises by any railway servant.

(3) A person suffering from any of such diseases, as mentioned in sub-rule (1) of this rule, shall not enter or remain in any carriage on a railway or travel in a train without the permission of the Station Master or other railway servant in charge of the place where such person enters upon the railways.

(4) A railway servant giving such permission may, on the person suffering from the disease, agreeing to pay the usual number of fares for reserving a compartment, arrange for his separation from the other persons being or travelling upon the railway.

3. Detention of passengers attacked with any infectious or contagious diseases. When a passenger is detained at railway station by a Medical Officer, as a measure for prevention of the spread of infectious or contagious diseases referred to in sub-rule (1) of Rule 2 and when such a passenger is unable to continue the journey by the train for when the ticket is issued and the period of its availability in terms laid down for break of journey on route is exceeded, the Station Master on the authority of certificate from the Medical Officer, shall make the ticket available for the further journey by an endorsement on the back of the ticket as under:

"Available by No. .... Train .... (date/from ....) (Station)" and sign his name in full.

APPENDIX 18

The Disposal of Consignment Rules, 1990

G.S.R. 901(E), dated 12th November 1990[1] In exercise of the powers conferred by clauses (*j*) and (*k*) of sub-section (2) of section 87 of the Railways Act, 1989 (24 of 1989), the Central Government hereby makes the following rules, namely:

1. Short title and commencement. (1) These rules may be called the Disposal of Consignment Rules, 1990.

(2) They shall come into force on the date of their publication in the Official Gazette.

2. Manner of disposal of detained or unclaimed consignment. (1) If any consignment,—

(*a*) detained under section 83 of the Railways Act, 1989, or

(*b*) treated as unclaimed in respect of which notice under section 84 of the Railways Act, 1989 cannot be served or there is a failure to comply with the requisition in the said notice—

is not sold by public auction, the Divisional Commercial Superintendent may, on being of the opinion that is not expedient to held that the auction, record reasons therefor in writing and may direct the sale of consignment or part thereof by inviting offers.

(2) Offers for the purchase of consignment may be invited,—

(*a*) from the regular dealers of such goods as are in the consignment; or

(*b*) from such departments of the Central Government and of the State Government as appear likely to purchase such goods; or

(*c*) from the Government undertakings.

(3) The highest of the offers of price may be accepted by the Divisional Commercial Superintendent and the goods may be sold to the highest offerer.

1 Published in *Gazette of India*, (Extraordinary), Part II, s. 3(*i*), dated 12th November 1990.

(4) Where only one offer is received, the Divisional Commercial Superintendent may, keeping in view the condition and quality of the goods and the prevailing market rate, accept that offer if he considers such offer to be a fair price for the goods and the goods be sold to that offerer.

3. Notice for public auction. Where there is no local newspaper in which notice of the public auction can be published, such notice shall be displayed at a conspicuous place,—

(*a*) at the goods shed:

(*b*) at the parcel office;

(*c*) at the lost property office, if any; or

(*d*) at the premises where such auction is to be held.

APPENDIX 19

The Transport of Animals Rules, 1978[1]

In exercise of the powers conferred by clause (*h*) of sub-section (2) of section 38 of the Prevention of Cruelty to Animals Act, 1960 (59 of 1960); the Central Government hereby makes the following rules, the same having been previously published as required by the said section, namely:

CHAPTER I

1. Short title. These rules may be called the Transport of Animals Rules, 1978.

2. Definitions. In these rules unless the context otherwise requires—

(*a*) qualified veterinary surgeon means one who holds a diploma or a degree of a recognised veterinary college;

(*b*) "Schedule" means a schedule appended to these rules.

CHAPTER II

TRANSPORT OF DOGS AND CATS

3. Rules 4 to 14 shall apply to the transport of dogs and cats of all breeds whether by rail, road, inland waterway, sea or air.

4. (*a*) A valid health certificate by a qualified veterinary surgeon to the effect that the dogs and cats are in a fit condition to travel by a rail, road, inland waterway, sea or air and are not showing any sign of infectious or contagious disease including rabies, shall accompany each consignment and the certificate shall be in the form specified in Schedule A.

(*b*) In the absence of such a certificate, the carrier shall refuse to accept the consignment for transport.

5. No dog or cat in an advanced stage of pregnancy shall be transported.

1 *Vide* Government of India, Ministry of Agriculture and Irrigation (Department of Agriculture). Notification No. 18-6/70 LDI, dated 23rd March, 1978.

6. (*a*) Dogs or cats to be transported in the same container shall be of the same species and breed.

(*b*) Unweaned puppies or kittens shall not be transported with adult dogs or cats other than their dams.

(*c*) No female dog or cat in season (cestrus) shall be transported with any male.

7. (*a*) Any dog or cat reported to be vicious or exhibiting a vicious disposition shall be transported individually in a cage, muzzled and labelled to give warning to handlers.

(*b*) In extreme cases, the dogs or cats shall be administered with sedative drugs by a qualified veterinary surgeon.

8. (1) When dogs or cats are to be transported for long distances—

(*a*) they shall be fed and given water atleast two hours prior to their transport and shall not be packed for transport if they are hungry or thirsty;

(*b*) they should be exercised as late as possible before despatch;

(*c*) they shall be given adequate water for drinking every four hours in summer or every six hours during winter;

(*d*) they shall be fed once in twelve hours in the case of adult dogs or cats and they shall be fed once in four hours in the case of puppies and kittens in accordance with the instructions of the consignors, if any;

(*e*) adequate arrangements shall be made for their care and management during the journey.

(2) When the dogs or cats are to be transported by rail involving a journey of more than six hours, an attendant shall accompany the dogs or cats to supply them with food and water on the way and the attendant shall have access to the dogs or cats for this purpose at all stations and no dog or cat shall be exposed to the direct blast of air during such journey.

9. Where dogs or cats are to be transported for short distance by road in a public vehicle, the following precautions are to be taken, namely—

(*a*) they shall be put in a cage and the cage containing the dogs or cats shall not be put on the roof of the vehicle but shall be put inside the vehicle preferably near the end of the vehicle;

(*b*) the vehicle transporting the dogs or cats shall as far as possible maintain constant speed, avoiding sudden stops and reducing effects of shocks and jolts to the minimum;

(*c*) at least one attendant shall be present at all times during transit who shall ensure that proper transit conditions are observed and shall also replenish food and water whenever necessary.

10. Where dogs or cats are to be transported by air—

(*a*) The cages shall be properly cleaned and disinfected before the dogs or cats are put in the cages;

(*b*) sufficient paddy straw or saw dust or paper cuttings shall be provided for cats in the cages as resting materials;

(*c*) for international transport, the dogs or cats shall be kept in a pressurized compartment with regulated temperature.

11. The size and type of crates for transport of dogs and cats shall conform as clearly as may be to the size and type specified in Schedule B and Schedule C respectively.

12. All containers of dogs or cats shall be clearly labelled showing the names, address and telephone number (if any) of the consignor.

13. The consignee shall be informed about the train or transport arrival or flight number and its time of arrival in advance.

14. Consignment of dogs or cats to be transported by rail or road shall be booked by the next passenger or mail train or bus and should not be detained after accepting the consignment for booking.

CHAPTER III

TRANSPORT OF MONKEYS

15. Rules 16 to 23 shall apply to the transport of all types of monkeys from the trapping area to the nearest rail-head.

16. (*a*) A valid health certificate by a qualified veterinary surgeon to the effect that the monkeys are in a fit condition to travel from the trapping area to the nearest unit-head and are not showing any sign of infections or contagious disease shall accompany each consignment.

(*b*) In the absence of such a certificate, the carrier shall refuse to accept the consignment for transport.

(*c*) The certificate shall be in a form specified in Schedule D.

17. (1) Monkeys from one trapping area shall not be allowed to mix with monkeys from any other trapping area for preventing the dangers of crossinfection.

(2) The time in transit from trapping area to the nearest rail-head shall be as short as possible and factors causing stress to monkeys shall be reduced to the minimum.

(3) If the travel time is longer than six hours provision shall be made to feed and to give water to the monkeys en route.

(4) During transit, precautions shall be taken to protect the monkeys from extreme weather conditions and monkeys that die en route shall be removed at the earliest available opportunity.

18. Monkeys that are not completely weaned, that is, under 1.8 kilogram in weight, shall not be transported except when specifically permitted by the Central Government.

19. (*a*) Pregnant and nursing monkeys shall not be transported except when specifically permitted by the Central Government.

(*b*) Pregnant and nursing monkeys as well as monkeys weighing more than 5 kilograms shall be transported in compartmented cages.

20. All monkeys in the same cage shall be of the same species and of approximately the same weight and size.

21. Monkeys captured within their natural habitat shall be placed in new, sterilized or thoroughly cleaned cages and subsequent transfer, if any, shall also be new, disinfected of thoroughly cleaned cages.

22. Monkeys shall be transported from trapping area to the nearest rail-head by the fastest means of transport available and the monkeys should not be left unattended at any time during the journey.

23. (1) (*a*) Monkeys shall be transported in suitable wooden or bamboo cages so constructed as not to allow the escape of the monkeys but permit sufficient passage of air ventilation.

(*b*) No nails, metallic projections or sharp edges shall be exposed on the exterior or in the interior of the cages.

(*c*) Each cage shall be equipped with appropriate water and feed receptacles which are leak proof and capable of being cleaned and refilled during transit.

(2) The floor of the cages shall be made of bamboo reapers and the space between each reaper shall range between 20 mm and 30 mm.

(3) To facilitate carriage of these cages, provision may be made for rope loops at the four top ends.

(4) The weight of any one loaded cage shall not exceed 45 kilograms.

(5) The following two sizes of cages shall be used—

(*a*) 910 × 760 × 510 mm—to contain not more than twelve monkeys, weighing between 1.8 and 3.00 kilograms each or ten monkeys weighing between 3.1 and 5.0 kilograms each.

(*b*) 710 × 710 × 510 mm—to contain not more than ten monkeys weighing between 1.8 and 3.00 kilograms each or eight monkeys weighing between 3.1 and 5.00 kilograms each:

Provided that wooden cages as specified in Schedule F to these rules may also be used for carrying monkeys from the trapping area to the nearest rail-head.

(6) The construction details of two types of cages shall be given in Schedule E.

24. Rules 25 to 32 shall apply to transport of monkeys from a rail-head to another rail-head or from a rail-head to nearest airport.

25. (*a*) Loading and unloading shall be carried out quickly and efficiently.

(*b*) Cages shall be stored in such a manner that ventilation is adequate and the monkeys are not exposed to draught and direct heat or cold.

(*c*) Monkeys found dead shall be removed as quickly as possible for suitable disposal.

26. The transport cages shall be in accordance with specification given in rule 28.

27. (1) Due provision shall be made by the sender for a sufficient supply of food and water for the journey.

(2) In case the journey is over six hours an attendant shall accompany the monkeys to supply them food, water, and such other things, on route and he shall have access to the monkeys for feeding, giving water and attention at all stations en route.

(3) The food and water containers shall be checked atleast every six hours and refilled, if necessary.

(4) Monkeys shall not be disturbed during the night hours.

28. Not more than one cage shall be placed over the other and gunny packing shall be placed between two cages, when one is placed over the other.

29. Monkeys shall be brought to the airport sufficiently early.

30. Monkeys shall be provided with food and water immediately before loading on the aircraft.

31. (*a*) The cages shall be clearly labelled showing the name, address and telephone number (if any) of the consignor and the consignee in bold red letters.

(*b*) The consignee shall be informed about the train in which the consignment of monkeys is being sent and its arrival time in advance.

(*c*) The consignment of monkeys to be transported shall be booked by the next passenger or mail train and should not be detained after the consignment is accepted for booking.

32. (*a*) A valid health certificate by a qualified veterinary surgeon to the effect that the monkeys are in a fit condition to travel from the nearest rail-head to another rail-head or from a rail-head to the nearest airport and are not showing any signs of infectious or contagious disease shall accompany each consignment.

(*b*) In the absence of such a certificate, the carrier shall refuse to accept the consignment for transport.

(*c*) The certificate shall be in a form specified in Schedule D.

33. Rules 34 to 45 shall apply in relation to the transport of monkeys by air.

34. The time in transit shall be as short as possible and factors causing stress to monkeys shall be reduced to the minimum.

35. Monkeys that are not completely weaned, that is, under 1.8 kilograms in weight, shall not be transported except when specifically permitted by the Central Government.

36. Pregnant and nursing monkeys shall not be transported except when specifically permitted by the Central Government. Pregnant and nursing monkeys and monkeys weighing over 5 kilograms shall be transported in specially designed individual cages.

37. All monkeys in the same cage shall be of the same species and of approximately the same weight and size.

38. (1) In view of the danger of infection, only monkeys of the same species shall be transported in the same cabin or compartment of the aircraft.

(2) Apparently sick or disabled monkeys exhibiting external injuries or infested with parasites shall not be transported.

(3) Transport of other species of animals, birds, fish, food stuff or poisonous materials, such as pesticides and insecticides, in the same cabin or compartment shall not be permitted.

39. (1) At no time during transit shall the monkeys be left unattended when carried in a freighter aircraft.

(2) At least one attendant shall be present at all times when the aircraft is on the ground.

40. (1) Monkeys shall be transported in suitable wooden cages, so constructed as not to allow the escape of the monkeys and shall allow sufficient passage of air for ventilation; no nails, metallic projections or sharp edges shall be exposed in the interior or on the exterior of such cages. Each cage shall be equipped with water and food receptacles which shall be leak-proof and be capable of being cleaned and refilled during transit. A suitable absorbent material such as saw dust shall be kept in the dropping trays.

(2) The weight of any one loaded cage shall not exceed 45 kilograms in any case.

(3) The following two sizes of cages shall be used—

(*a*) 460 × 460 × 460 mm—to contain not more than ten monkeys weighing from 1.8 to 3.0 kilograms each or four monkeys weighing from 3.1 to 5.0 kilograms each; and

(*b*) 760 × 530 × 460 mm—to contain not more than ten monkeys weighing from 1.8 to 3.0 kilograms each or eight monkeys weighing from 3.1 to 5.0 kilograms each.

(4) The construction details of the two types of cages shall be as given in Schedule F.

(5) The construction details of the two types of cages used for the transport of pregnant and nursing monkeys shall be as given in Schedule G.

41. (*a*) The cages shall be clearly labelled showing the name, address and telephone number (if any) of the consignor and the consignee in bold red letters.

(*b*) The consignee shall be informed in advance about the flight number of the freighter aircraft in which the consignment of monkeys is being sent and its arrival time.

(*c*) The consignment of monkeys to be transported shall be booked by the next flight of the freighter aircraft and should not be detained after the consignment is accepted for booking.

42. (1) A valid health certificate by a qualified veterinary surgeon to the effect that the monkeys are fit to travel by air and are not showing any signs of infectious or contagious disease shall accompany each consignment of monkeys.

(2) In the absence of such a certificate, the carrier shall refuse to accept the consignment for shipment.

(3) The form of a certificate under sub-rule (1) be as given in Schedule D.

43. (1) The air shall be changed not less than twelve times per hour and draughts shall be avoided and there shall be no dead pockets of air.

(2) Except when the monkeys are being fed and given water, they shall travel in semi-darkness to make them quieter and less inclined to fight and thus given them better opportunities of resting.

44. The food and water containers shall be checked at every stop and refilled; if necessary, and a sufficient stock of food shall be available on the aircraft and at likely stopping places.

Note. About 85 grams of food per monkey is required daily. Suitable foods are dry cereal grains or gram. It is recommended that whole gram made into biscuits or wheat meal bread should be fed. A minimum of 140 ml. of water shall be allowed for each monkey per day.

45. An empty cage of the usual dimensions with its sides covered except 50 mm at the top to allow for ventilation shall be provided in the freighter aircraft for housing the monkeys which fall sick or are injured during the journey.

CHAPTER IV

TRANSPORT OF CATTLE

46. Rules 47 to 56 shall apply to the transport by rail or of cows, bulls, bullocks buffaloes, yaks and calves (hereinafter in these rules referred to as 'cattle').

47. (*a*) A valid certificate by a qualified veterinary surgeon to the effect that the cattle are in a fit condition to travel by rail or road and are not suffering from any infectious or contagious or parasitic diseases and that they have been vaccinated against rinderpest and any other infectious or contagious or parasitic diseases shall accompany each consignment.

(*b*) In the absence of such a certificate, the carrier shall refuse to accept the consignment for transport.

(*c*) The certificate shall be in the form specified in Schedule E.

48. Veterinary first and equipment shall accompany all batches of cattle.

49. (*a*) Each consignment shall bear a label showing in bold red letters the name, address and telephone number (if any) of the consignee, the number and types of cattle being transported and quantity of rations and food provided.

(*b*) The consignee shall be informed about the train or vehicle in which the consignment of cattle is being sent and its arrival time in advance.

(*c*) The consignment of cattle shall be booked by the next train or vehicle and shall not be detained after the consignment is accepted for booking.

50. The average space provided per cattle in railway wagon or vehicle shall not be less than two square metres.

51. (*a*) Suitable rope and platforms should be used for loading cattle from vehicles.

(*b*) In case of railway wagon the dropped door of the wagon may be used as a ramp when loading or unloading is done to the platform.

52. Cattle shall be loaded after they are properly fed and given water.

53. Cattle in advanced stage of pregnancy shall not be mixed with young cattle in order to avoid stampede during transportation.

54. (1) Watering arrangements on route shall be made and sufficient quantities of water shall be carried for emergency.

(2) Sufficient feed and fodder with adequate reserve shall be carried to last during the journey.

(3) Adequate ventilation shall be ensured.

55. When cattle is to be transported by rail—

(*a*) an ordinary goods wagon shall carry not more than ten adult cattle or fifteen calves on broad gauge, not more than six adult cattle or ten calves on metre gauge, or not more than four adult cattle or six calves on narrow gauge;

(*b*) every wagon carrying cattle shall have atleast one attendant;

(*c*) cattle shall be loaded parallel to the rails, facing each other;

(*d*) rations for padding, such as straw, shall be placed on the floor to avoid injury if a cattle lies down and this shall not be less than 6 cms. thick;

(*e*) rations for the journey shall be carried in the middle of the wagon;

(*f*) to provide adequate ventilation, upper door of one side of the wagon shall be kept open properly fixed and the upper door of the wagon shall have wire gauge closely welded mesh arrangements to prevent burning cinders from the engines entering the wagon and leading to fire outbreak;

(*g*) cattle wagons should be attached in the middle of the train;

(*h*) cooking shall not be allowed in the wagons nor hurricane lamps without chimneys;

(*i*) two breast bars shall be provided on each side of the wagon, one at height of 60 to 80 cm. and the other at 100 to 110 cm.;

(*j*) Cattle-in-milk shall be milked at least twice a day and the calves shall be given sufficient quantity of milk to drink;

(*k*) as far as possible, cattle may be moved during the nights only;

(*l*) during day time, if possible, they should be unloaded, fed, given water and rested and if in milk, milking shall be carried out.

56. When cattle are to be transported by goods vehicle the following precautions are to be taken, namely—

(*a*) specially fitted goods vehicles with a special type of tail board on padding around the sides should be used;

(*b*) ordinary goods vehicles shall be provided with anti-slipping material, such as coir matting or wooden board on the floor and the superstructure, if now, should be raised;

(*c*) no goods vehicle shall carry more than six cattle;

(*d*) each goods vehicle shall be provided with one attendant;

(*e*) while transporting the cattle, the goods vehicle shall not be loaded with any other merchandise; and

(*f*) to prevent cattle being frightened or injured, they should preferably face the engine.

CHAPTER V

TRANSPORT OF EQUINES

57. Rules 57 to 63 shall apply to the transport by rail, road or sea of horses, mules and donkeys (hereinafter in these rules referred to as 'equines').

58. (*a*) A valid certificate by a qualified veterinary surgeon to the effect that the equines are in a fit condition to travel by rail; road or sea and are not suffering from any infectious contagious disease or diseases shall accompany each consignment.

(*b*) In the absence of such a certificate, the carrier shall refuse to accept the consignment for transport.

(*c*) The certificate shall be in a form specified in Schedule I.

59. (*a*) Each consignment shall bear a lable showing in bold red letters the name, address and telephone number (if any) of the consignor and consignee, the number and type of equines being transported and quantity of rations and food provided.

(*b*) The consignee shall be informed in advance about the train or vehicle or ship in which the consignment of equines is being sent and its arrival time.

(*c*) The consignment of equines shall be booked by the next train or vehicle or ship and shall be accepted for booking.

60. (*a*) Pregnant and young equines shall not be mixed with other animals.

(*b*) Different species of equines shall be kept separately.

(*c*) Equines shall be loaded after being fed and given water adequately, watering arrangements shall be made en route and sufficient food carried to last during the journey.

(*d*) Veterinary first-aid equipment shall accompany all batches of equines.

(*e*) Adequate ventilation shall be ensured.

(*f*) Suitable ramps and platforms, improvised where not available, shall be used for loading and unloading equines.

61. For the transport of equines by rail, the following precautions shall be taken—

(*a*) equines shall be transported by passenger or mixed trains only;

(*b*) ordinary goods wagon when used for transportation shall carry not more then eight to ten horses or ten mules or ten donkeys on broad gauge and not more than six horses or eight donkeys on metre-gauge;

(*c*) in extreme hot water shall be sprinkled over the wagons containing equines by the railway authorities to bring down temperature. Ice slabs in specially made containers may be placed inside the wagon, if recommended by a qualified veterinary surgeon;

(*d*) every wagon shall have two attendants if the equines are more than two in number;

(*e*) equines shall be loaded parallel to the rails, facing each other;

(*f*) material for padding, such as paddy straw, shall be placed on the floor to avoid injury if an animal lies down and this shall not be less than 6 cm thick;

(*g*) to provide adequate ventilation, upper door of the side of the wagon shall be kept upon and properly fixed and the upper door of the wagon shall have wire gauge closely welded mesh arrangements to prevent burning cinders from the engines entering the wagon and leading to fire break out;

(*h*) two breast bars shall be provided on each side of the wagon, one at a height of 50 to 80 cm and the other at 110 cm.

62. For the transport of equines by goods-vehicles, the following precautions shall be taken, namely—

(*a*) specially fitted vehicles with a special type of tail-board and padding around the sides shall be used;

(*b*) ordinary goods vehicles shall be provided with anti slipping material on the floor and the superstructure, if low, should be raised;

(*c*) bamboo poles of at least 8 cm diameter between each animal and two stout batons at the back shall be provided to prevent the animal from falling;

(*d*) to prevent horses from being frightened or injured their heads should face left away from the passing traffic;

(*e*) each vehicle shall not carry more than four to six equines;

(*f*) each vehicle shall be provided with one attendant;

(*g*) these vehicles shall be driven at a speed not more than 35 kilometers per hour.

63. For the transport of equines by sea the following precautions shall be taken, namely—

(*a*) horses may normally be accommodated in single stalls and mules in pens, each pen holding four to five mules;

(*b*) ample ventilation shall be ensured by keeping portholes and providing permanent air trunks or electric blowers on all decks, and exhaust fans shall be installed to blow out foul air;

(*c*) all standings shall be artwart the ship with heads facing inwards;

(*d*) to avoid distress specially during hot weather, the ship may go under way immediately after embarking and disembarking shall be done as early as possible after enchoring;

(*e*) colts and fillies shall be kept on the exposed decks;

(*f*) a pharmacy and spare stalls for five per cent of equines shall be available;

(*g*) passage between two rows of pens shall not be less than 1.5 metres.

CHAPTER VI

TRANSPORT OF SHEEP AND GOATS

64. Rules 65 to 75 shall apply to the transport of sheep and goats by rail or road involving journeys of more than six hours.

65. (*a*) A valid health certificate by a qualified veterinary surgeon to the effect that the sheep and goats are in a fit condition to travel by rail or road and are not suffering from infectious or contagious or parasitic disease shall accompany each consignment.

(*b*) In the absence of such a certificate, the carrier shall refuse to accept the consignment for transport.

(*c*) The certificate shall be in a form specified in Schedule I.

66. (*a*) Each consignment shall bear a label showing in bold red letter the name, address and telephone number (if any) of the consignor and consignee, the number and type of sheep or goats being transported and quantity of rations and food provided.

(*b*) The consignee shall be informed in advance about the train or vehicle in which the consignment of sheep or goats are being sent and its arrival time.

(*c*) The consignment of sheep or goats shall be booked by the next train or vehicle and shall not be detained after the consignment is accepted for booking.

67. (*a*) First-aid equipment shall accompany the sheep or goats in transit.

(*b*) Suitable ramps shall be provided for loading and unloading the sheep or goats.

(*c*) In the case of a railway wagon, when the loading or unloading is done on the platform the dropped door of the wagon shall be used as a ramp.

68. Sheep and goats shall be transported separately; but if the lots are small special partition shall be provided to separate them.

69. Rams and male young stock shall not be mixed with female stock in the same compartment.

70. Sufficient food and fodder shall be carried to last during the journey and watering facility shall be provided at regular intervals.

71. Material for padding, such as straw, shall be placed on the floor to avoid injury if an animal lies down, and this shall be not less than 5 cm thick.

72. The animals shall not be fettered unless there is a risk of their jumping out and their legs shall not be tied down.

73. The space required for a goat shall be the same as that for a woolled sheep and the approximate space required for a sheep in a goods vehicle or a railway wagon shall be as under—

Approximate weight of animal in kilogram

	Space required in square metres	
	Woolled	*Shorn*
Not more than 20	0.18	3.16
More than 20 but not more than 25	0.20	0.18
More than 25 but not more than 30	0.23	0.22
More than 30	0.28	0.26

74. (*a*) No railway wagon shall accommodate more than the following number of the sheep or goats—

Broad gauge	Metre gauge		Narrow gauge	
(1)	(2)	(3)	(4)	(5)
Area of Wagon	*Area of Wagon*	*Area of Wagon*	*Area of Wagon*	
Less than	21.1	Less than	12.5	
21.1	Square Metres and above	12.5	Square Metres and above	
70	100	50	60	25

(*b*) Adequate ventilation shall be provided in every wagon. Upper door of one side of wagon shall be kept open and properly fixed and the upper door of the wagon shall have wire gauge closely welded mesh arrangements to prevent burning cinders from the engines entering the wagon and leading to fire breakout.

75. (1) Goods vehicles of capacity of 5 or 4.5 tons, which are generally used for transporting animals, shall carry not more than forty sheep or goats.

(2) In the case of large goods vehicles and wagons, partition shall be provided at every two or three metres across the width to prevent the crowding and trapping of sheep and goats.

(3) In the case of ewes, goats or lambs or kids under six weeks of age, separate panels shall be provided.

SCHEDULE A

[*See* rule 4]

PROFORMA FOR CERTIFICATE OF FITNESS TO TRAVEL DOGS/CATS

This Certificate should be completed and signed by a qualified Veterinary Surgeon.

Date and time of examination ....

Species of dogs/cats ....

Number of cages .... Number of dogs/cats ....

Sex .... Age ....

Breed and identification marks, if any ....

Transported from .... to .... via ....

I hereby certify that I have read rules 8 to 14 in Chapter II of the Transport of Animals Rules, 1978.

1. That, at the request of (consignor) .... I have examined the above mentioned dogs/cats in their travelling cages not more than 12 hours before their departure.

2. That each of the dogs/cats appeared to be in good health, free from signs of injury, contagious and infectious disease including rabies and in a fit condition to travel by rail/road/inland waterway/sea/air.

3. That the dogs/cats were adequately fed and watered for the purpose of the journey.

4. That the dogs/cats have been vaccinated.

(*a*) Type of vaccine/s:

(*b*) Date of vaccination/s:

Signed ....

Address ....

Date ....

Qualifications ....

SCHEDULE B

[*Sec* rule 11]

SIZE AND TYPE OF CRATE FOR TRANSPORT OF DOGS

The design of the cage mentioned in rule 11 in Chapter II of Transport of Animal Rules, 1978 shall be as per the design as printed on page 7 of IS: 4746-1968 published by the Indian Standards Institution.

All dimensions in Centimetres

By rail/road/inland waterways sea, by air

Length (L)	A × 1½	A + C + 10
Width (W)	A	D + 2 + 10
Height (H)	B + 15	B + 10

Length—Tip of nose to root of tail (A)

Width—Width across the shoulders (D)

Height—Tip of ears to toe while standing (B)

Elbow Size—Toe to tip of elbow (C)

Note. Cages, cartons or crates, used to transport dogs, shall be of such material which will not tear or crumble. They shall be well constructed, well ventilated and designed to protect the health of the dogs by giving them adequate space and safety. It is essential that wire mesh should be nose and paw proof; suitable material is a welded wire mesh of not less than 3 mm, with a spacing 12 × 12 mm. Expended metal and wire netting are unsuitable for this purpose. There should be no protruding nails or unprotected edges of wire. Dogs Kennels in rail coaches shall be so placed as to give protection to dogs from extreme of temperature and disturbance from birds and by giving them adequate space for health and safety.

SCHEDULE C

[*See* rule 11]

SIZE AND TYPE OF CRATE FOR TRANSPORT OF CATS

The design of the cage mentioned in rule 11 in Chapter II of Transport of Animals Rules, 1978 shall be as per the design as printed on page 8 of IS: 4746-1968 published by the Indian Standards Institution.

All dimensions in Centimetres

By rail/road/inland water way/sea by air

Length (L)	A × 2	A × 2
Width (W)	A	A
Height (H)	B + 15	B + 10

Length—Tip of nose to root of tail (A)

Width—Width across the shoulders (D)

Height—Tip of ears to toe while standing (B)

Elbow Size—Toe to tip of elbow (C)

Note. Cages, cartons or crates, used to transport cats, shall be of such material which will not tear or crumble. They shall be well constructed, well ventilated and designed to protect the health of the cats by giving them adequate space and safety. It is essential that wire mesh should be nose and paw proof; suitable material is a welded wire mesh of not less than 3 mm, with a spacing 12 × 12 mm. Expended metal and wire netting are unsuitable for this purpose. There should be no protruding nails or unprotected edges of wire. Cats Kennels in rail coaches shall be so placed as to give protection to cats from extremes of temperature and disturbance from birds and by giving them adequate space for health and safety.

SCHEDULE D

[*See* rules 16 and 32]

PROFORMA FOR CERTIFICATE OF FITNESS TO TRAVEL MONKEYS

This Certificate should be completed and signed by a qualified Veterinary Surgeon.

Date and time of examination ....

Species of Monkeys ....

Number of Cages ....

Number of Monkeys ....

Sex .... Age ....

Breed and identification marks, if any ....

Transported from .... to .... via ....

I hereby certify that I have read rules 15 to 45 in Chapter III of the Transport of Animals Rules, 1978.

1. That, at the request of (consignor) .... I examined the above mentioned monkeys in their travelling cages not more than 12 hours before their departure.

2. That each monkey appeared to be in a fit condition to travel from the trapping area to the nearest rail-head/from the nearest rail-head to another rail-head/from the rail-head to the nearest airport/by air and is not showing any signs of infectious or contagious diseases.

3. That no monkeys appeared to be under 6 months of age and that no animal appeared to be pregnant.

4. That the monkeys were adequately fed and watered for the purpose of the journey.

5. That the monkeys have been vaccinated.

(*a*) Type of vaccine/s:

(*b*) Date of vaccination/s:

Signed ....

Address ....

Date .... Qualifications ....

SCHEDULE E

[*See* rule 23(5)(*a*) and rule 23(6)]

SIZE AND TYPE OF CRATE FOR TRANSPORT OF MONKEYS FROM TRAPPING AREA TO NEAREST RAIL-HEAD

The construction detail of two types of cages mentioned in rule 22(5)(*a*) in Chapter III of the Transport of Animals Rules, 1978 shall be as per the dimensions and design as printed on page 5 of IS: 3699 (Part-I)—1966 published by Indian Standard Institution.

SCHEDULE F

[*See* rule 40(4)]

SIZE AND TYPE OF CRATE FOR TRANSPORT OF MONKEYS BY AIR

The construction detail of two types of cages mentioned in rule 40(3)(*a*) and (*b*) in Chapter III of the Transport of Animals Rules, 1978 shall be as per the dimensions and design as printed on page 6 of IS: 3059—1965 published by Indian Standard Institution.

SCHEDULE G

[*See* rule 40(5)]

SIZE AND TYPES OF CRATE FOR TRANSPORT BY AIR OF PREGNANT AND NURSING MONKEYS AND MONKEYS WEIGHING OVER 5 KG.

The construction details of the two type of cages mentioned in rule 40(5) in Chapter III of Transport of Animal Rules, 1978 shall be as per the dimensions and design as printed on page 7 of IS: 3059—1965 published by Indian Standard Institution.

SCHEDULE H

[*See* rule 47]

PROFORMA FOR CERTIFICATE OF FITNESS TO TRAVEL CATTLE

This Certificate should be completed and signed by a qualified Veterinary Surgeon.

Date and time of examination ....

Species of Cattle ....

Number of Trucks/Railway Wagons ....

Number of Cattle ....

Sex .... Age ....

Breed and identification marks, if any ....

Transported .... to .... via ....

I hereby certify that I have read rules 46 to 56 in Chapter IV of the Transport of Animals Rules, 1978.

1. That, at the request of (consignor) .... I examined the above mentioned cattle in the goods vehicle/railway wagons not more than 12 hours before their departure.

2. That each cattle appeared to be in a fit condition to travel by rail/road and is not showing any signs of infectious or contagious or parasitic disease and that it has been vaccinated against rinderpest and any other infectious or contagious or parasitic disease(s).

3. That the cattle were adequately fed and watered for the purpose of the journey.

4. That the cattle have been vaccinated.

(*a*) Type of vaccine:

(*b*) Date of vaccination:

Signed ....

Address ....

Date .... Qualifications ....

SCHEDULE I

[*See* rule 58]

PROFORMA FOR CERTIFICATE OF FITNESS TO TRAVEL EQUINES

This Certificate should be completed and signed by a qualified Veterinary Surgeon.

Date and time of examination ....

Species of Equines ....

Number of Equines ....

Sex .... Age ....

Breed and identification marks, if any ....

Transported from .... to .... via ....

I hereby certify that I have read rules 57 to 63 in Chapter V of the Transport of Animals Rules, 1978.

1. That, at the request of (consignor) .... I examined the above mentioned equines not more than 12 hours before their departure.

2. That each equine appeared to be in a fit condition to travel by rail/road/sea and is not showing any signs of infectious or contagious disease(s) and that it has been vaccinated against any infectious or contagious disease(s).

3. That the equines were adequately fed and watered for the purpose of the journey.

4. That the equines have been vaccinated.

(*a*) Type of vaccine(s):

(*b*) Date of vaccination:

Signed ....

Address ....

Date .... Qualifications ....

SCHEDULE J

[*See* rule 65]

PROFORMA FOR CERTIFICATE OF FITNESS TO TRAVEL SHEEP AND GOATS

This Certificate should be completed and signed by a qualified Veterinary Surgeon.

Date and time of examination ....

Species of Animals ....

Number of Animals ....

Sex .... Age ....

I hereby certify that I have read rules 64 to 75 in Chapter VI of the Transport of Animals Rules, 1978.

1. That, at the request of (consignor) .... I examined the above mentioned animals not more than 12 hours before their departure.

2. That each appeared to be a fit condition to travel by rail/road/sea and is not showing any signs of infectious or contagious or parasitic disease(s) and that it has been vaccinated against any infectious or contagious disease(s).

3. That the animals were adequately fed and watered for the purpose of the journey.

4. That the animals have been vaccinated.

(*a*) Type of vaccine(s):

(*b*) Date of vaccination:

Signed ....

Address ....

Date .... Qualifications ....

Index